American History through Literature
1820–1870

American History through Literature
1820–1870

VOLUME 1

ABOLITIONIST
WRITING
to
GOTHIC FICTION

JANET GABLER-HOVER & ROBERT SATTELMEYER
Editors in Chief

CHARLES SCRIBNER'S SONS
An imprint of Thomson Gale, a part of The Thomson Corporation

THOMSON
GALE

Detroit • New York • San Francisco • San Diego • New Haven, Conn. • Waterville, Maine • London • Munich

American History through Literature, 1820–1870

Janet Gabler-Hover and Robert Sattelmeyer, Editors in Chief

LIBRARY OF CONGRESS CATALOGING-IN-PUBLICATION DATA

American History through Literature, 1820–1870 / Janet Gabler-Hover and Robert Sattelmeyer, editors-in-chief.
    p. cm.
    Includes bibliographical references and index.
    ISBN 0-684-31460-6 (set hardcover : alk. paper) — ISBN 0-684-31461-4 (v. 1) — ISBN 0-684-31462-2 (v. 2) — ISBN 0-684-31463-0 (v. 3) — ISBN 0-684-31492-4 (e-book)
    1. American literature—19th century—Encyclopedias. 2. Literature and history—United States—History—19th century—Encyclopedias. 3. United States—History—19th century—Historiography—Encyclopedias. 4. History in literature—Encyclopedias. I. Gabler-Hover, Janet II. Sattelmeyer, Robert.
PS217 .H57A84 2005
810. 9'358'09034—dc22

2005023615

This title is also available as an e-book
ISBN 0-684-31492-4
And may be purchased with its companion set,
American History through Literature, 1870–1920
ISBN 0-684-31468-1 (6-vol. print set)
Contact your Thomson Gale sales representative for ordering information

Printed in the United States of America
10 9 8 7 6 5 4 3 2 1

Contents

ACKNOWLEDGMENTS xv

PREFACE xvii

Volume 1

A

Abolitionist Writing 1
Emily E. VanDette

Agrarianism 9
William Conlogue

"Ain't I a Woman?" 15
Margaret Washington

Amateurism and Self-Publishing 19
Ann Fabian

American English. 21
Elsa Nettels

Americans Abroad 27
Daniel Kilbride

"The American Scholar" 31
Robert Sattelmeyer

An Appeal in Favor of That Class
of Americans Called Africans 35
Carolyn L. Karcher

Architecture 40
W. Barksdale Maynard

Art 45
David C. Miller

The Atlantic Monthly 56
Ellery Sedgwick

Autobiography 61
William Pannapacker

The Autocrat of the Breakfast-Table 67
Peter Gibian

B

Bachelors and Spinsters. 73
Angelic Rodgers

Baltimore 77
Gregory Scott George

Banking, Finance, Panics, and Depressions . . 81
Larry Schweikart

Baptists 88
Everett C. Goodwin

"Bartleby, the Scrivener" 92
David Kuebrich

Battle-Pieces 98
Michael Berthold

"Benito Cereno" 101
Allan Moore Emery

The Bible 108
Paul C. Gutjahr

"The Big Bear of Arkansas" 114
Kevin J. Hayes

Biography. 116
Scott E. Casper

"The Birth-mark" 121
Cindy Weinstein

Blacks 126
Elizabeth J. West

Blake 131
Shelley R. Block

The Blithedale Romance 135
William E. Cain

The Bondwoman's Narrative 140
Dickson D. Bruce Jr.

Book and Periodical Illustration 144
Kevin E. O'Donnell

Book Publishing 148
Steven Fink

Borders 154
Robert E. Abrams

Boston 162
Ronald J. Zboray
Mary Saracino Zboray

C

California Gold Rush 171
Michael Kowalewski

Calvinism 175
Merit Kaschig

Canada 181
Damien-Claude Bélanger

Captivity Narratives 185
Lorrayne Carroll

Catholics 191
Ross Labrie

"The Celebrated Jumping Frog
of Calaveras County" 196
James S. Leonard

Charleston 201
Natalie Collins Trice

Cherokee Memorials 203
Daniel Heath Justice

Childhood 207
Nancy D. Chase

Children's and Adolescent Literature 214
Anne Scott MacLeod

Chinese 220
Nikolas Huot

Cincinnati 224
LeAnne Garner

Circuses and Spectacles 228
Gregory J. Renoff

The Civil War 232
John Stauffer

Classical Literature 243
Elżbieta Foeller-Pituch

Clotel 248
Janet Gabler-Hover

Colleges 253
Roger L. Geiger

Compromise of 1850 and Fugitive
Slave Law 258
Desirée Henderson

Concord, Massachusetts 262
Robert E. Burkholder

The Confessions of Nat Turner 268
David A. Davis

The Confidence-Man 272
Tom Quirk

Confidence Men 277
William E. Lenz

Courtship 281
Karen Tracey

Crime and Punishment 286
Carol Colatrella

Cross-Dressing 292
Mary Lamb Shelden

"Crossing Brooklyn Ferry" 296
Patricia Spence Rudden

Curricula 299
Lynée Lewis Gaillet

"The Custom-House" 306
Frederick Newberry

D

Death 311
Russ Castronovo

Declaration of Sentiments 316
Denise D. Knight

Democracy 320
Julie Prebel

Democracy in America 326
David K. Heckerl

The Dial 332
Daniel R. Vollaro

Dialect 336
Gavin Jones

Dime Novels 340
Paul J. Erickson

Domestic Fiction 343
Lisa M. Logan

Dred Scott v. Sandford 349
Paul Finkelman

E

Editors 355
Patricia Okker

Education 361
Donald H. Parkerson
Jo Ann Parkerson

English Literature 367
Paul Giles

Ethnology 374
Kelli M. Olson

Evangelicals 381
Candy Gunther Brown

"Experience". 386
Robert Milder

Exploration and Discovery 389
Bruce Greenfield

F

Factories 397
Judith A. Ranta

"The Fall of the House of Usher" 400
Kevin J. Hayes

Fashion 404
Patricia Okker

Female Authorship 409
Susan Coultrap-McQuin

Feminism 414
Nina Baym

Fireside Poets 420
Christoph Irmscher

Folklore 425
John A. Burrison

Foreign Conspiracy against the Liberties
of the United States 432
Nancy Lusignan Schultz

Foreigners 435
Bruce A. Harvey

Free Love 441
Louis J. Kern

Friendship 445
Kristin Boudreau

Fur Trade 450
Robert Sattelmeyer

G

The Gates Ajar 455
Carol Farley Kessler

German Scholarship 459
LaVern J. Rippley

Gettysburg Address 462
Desirée Henderson

Gift Books and Annuals 466
Lorinda B. Cohoon

Godey's Lady's Book 472
Patricia Okker

Gothic Fiction 475
Ellen Weinauer

Volume 2

H

Harpers Ferry 483
Joseph M. Petrulionis

Harper's New Monthly Magazine 486
Ronald J. Zboray
Mary Saracino Zboray

"Hawthorne and His Mosses" 490
Brenda Wineapple

Health and Medicine 493
Cynthia J. Davis

The Hidden Hand 500
Carole Policy

History 504
Eileen Ka-May Cheng

History of the Conquest of Mexico 511
Mark A. Peterson

Honor 516
Bertram Wyatt-Brown

Hope Leslie 521
Philip Gould

The House of the Seven Gables 526
Monika Elbert

Humor. 533
Ed Piacentino

I

Immigration 545
James M. Bergquist

The Impending Crisis of the South 551
Ronald G. Walters

Incidents in the Life of a Slave Girl 554
Lovalerie King

Indians 560
Louise Barnett

"An Indian's Looking-Glass for
the White Man" 565
Arnold Krupat

Indian Wars and Dispossession 568
Arnold Krupat

Individualism and Community 580
Robert Shulman

The Innocents Abroad 587
Louis J. Budd

Irish 591
Stacey Lee Donohue

J, K

Jews. 599
Joseph Alkana

Journals and Diaries 602
Ronald J. Zboray
Mary Saracino Zboray

Knickerbocker Writers. 607
Kent P. Ljungquist

L

Labor 611
Nick Bromell

Landscape Architecture 615
James J. Schramer

Leatherstocking Tales 622
Kay Seymour House

Leaves of Grass 629
M. Jimmie Killingsworth

"The Legend of Sleepy Hollow" 635
Judith Richardson

Leisure. 639
William Gleason

Letters 644
Ronald J. Zboray
Mary Saracino Zboray

Letters on the Equality of the Sexes . . . 648
Stephen Howard Browne

The Liberator. 651
Sandra Harbert Petrulionis

Life and Adventures of Joaquín Murieta . . . 655
Ronald L. Pitcock

Life in the Iron Mills 659
Jane E. Rose

Literacy 664
Ronald J. Zboray
Mary Saracino Zboray

Literary Criticism 668
James Emmett Ryan

Literary Marketplace 673
Richard F. Teichgraeber III

Literary Nationalism 679
Christopher Gair

Little Women. 683
Anne K. Phillips

Lowell Offering 688
Michael Newbury

Lyceums 691
Kent P. Ljungquist

Lyric Poetry 695
Susan Carol Hauser

M

Manhood 703
T. Walter Herbert

Manifest Destiny 710
Robert J. Scholnick

Maritime Commerce 714
R. D. Madison

Marriage 718
Dale M. Bauer

Mental Health 723
Philip W. Leon

Methodists 728
Merit Kaschig

Mexican-American War 732
Donald E. Pease

Miscegenation 737
Michael Householder

*Miss Ravenel's Conversion from Secession
to Loyalty* 743
Gary Scharnhorst

Moby-Dick. 746
Carolyn L. Karcher

The Morgesons 755
Sandra A. Zagarell

Mormons 759
Terryl Givens

Mourning. 761
Dana Luciano

Music 766
Deane L. Root

N

*Narrative of the Life of David Crockett
of the State of Tennessee* 773
Thomas E. Scruggs

Narrative of the Life of Frederick Douglass . . 777
William L. Andrews

Native American Literature 782
Desirée Henderson

Nature 788
Lance Newman

Nature 796
Gustaaf Van Cromphout

Nautical Literature 802
John Peck

A New Home—Who'll Follow? . . . 805
Sandra A. Zagarell

New Orleans 810
Shirley E. Thompson

New York 814
John Evelev

O

Oral Tradition 821
Charlene Avallone

Oratory 826
James Perrin Warren

The Oregon Trail 833
Wil Verhoeven

Orientalism 838
Malini Johar Schueller

Our Nig 842
Eric Gardner

"Out of the Cradle Endlessly Rocking" . . . 847
Mark Bauerlein

P, Q

Periodicals 851
Martin T. Buinicki

Philadelphia 859
Emma J. Lapsansky-Werner

Philosophy 863
William M. Morgan

"The Philosophy of Composition" . . . 868
Barbara Cantalupo

Photography 872
John Stauffer

Pictorial Weeklies 877
Lorinda B. Cohoon

"Plymouth Rock Oration" 881
Stephen Howard Browne

Poems of Emily Dickinson 883
Domhnall Mitchell

"The Poet" 891
Joseph M. Thomas

Political Parties 898
Dennis Berthold

Popular Poetry 902
Ingrid Satelmajer

Popular Science 908
Samuel Chase Coale

Pornography 914
Joseph W. Slade III

Presbyterians 917
Philip W. Leon

Proslavery Writing 921
John Patrick Daly

Protestantism 926
Roger Lundin

Psychology 931
Joseph Alkana

Publishers 936
Marcy J. Dinius

Puritanism 942
Mason I. Lowance Jr.

Quakers 947
Michael L. Birkel

Volume 3

R

"The Raven" 953
Scott Peeples

Reform 957
Gregory Eiselein

Religion 965
Terrie Dopp Aamodt

Religious Magazines 971
Mark Fackler
Eric Baker

"Resistance to Civil Government" 974
Richard J. Schneider

Revolutions of 1848 979
Daniel Kilbride

Rhetoric 984
Granville Ganter

"Rip Van Winkle" 989
Steven Blakemore

The Romance 994
Michael J. Davey

Romanticism 1000
David M. Robinson

Ruth Hall 1007
Joyce W. Warren

S

Same-Sex Love 1013
Michael Borgstrom

CONTENTS

San Francisco 1017
Harriet Rafter

Satire, Burlesque, and Parody 1022
Frank Palmeri

The Scarlet Letter 1028
Melissa McFarland Pennell

Science 1036
Laura Dassow Walls

"Self-Reliance" 1045
Wesley T. Mott

Seneca Falls Convention 1050
Amy Cummins

Sensational Fiction 1054
David S. Reynolds

Sentimentalism. 1059
Joyce W. Warren

Sex Education 1065
April Rose Haynes

Sexuality and the Body 1069
Bruce Burgett

Short Story 1075
Rebecca Berne

Slave Narratives 1081
Yolanda Pierce

Slave Rebellions 1087
Helen Lock

Slavery 1092
Elizabeth J. West

Sociology for the South. 1100
John M. Grammer

Some Adventures of Captain Simon Suggs . . 1102
Johanna Nicol Shields

The Song of Hiawatha 1106
Christoph Irmscher

"Song of Myself" 1112
Ed Folsom

Spanish Speakers and Early "Latino"
Expression 1118
Lázaro Lima

Spiritualism. 1123
Janet Gabler-Hover

Suffrage 1128
James R. Britton

Swallow Barn 1132
Kevin J. Hayes

T

Tall Tales 1135
Ed Piacentino

Taste 1140
David Anthony

Technology. 1146
Klaus Benesch

Temperance. 1152
Amanda Claybaugh

Theater 1158
Alan Ackerman

Tourism 1164
Jeffrey Alan Melton

Trail of Tears 1167
Jennifer M. Wing

Transcendentalism 1171
David M. Robinson

Travel Writing 1180
James J. Schramer

"The Two Offers" 1186
Farah Jasmine Griffin

Two Years before the Mast 1189
John Peck

Typee 1193
Patrick W. Bryant

U

Uncle Tom's Cabin 1199
Cindy Weinstein

Underground Railroad 1206
Amy E. Earhart

Unitarians 1211
Dean Grodzins

Urbanization 1214
Dana Brand

Utopian Communities 1219
Daniel R. Vollaro

W

Walden 1225
Robert Sattelmeyer

Walker's Appeal 1234
R. J. Ellis

Washington, D.C. 1238
Sarah Luria

"When Lilacs Last in the Dooryard
Bloom'd" 1242
James Perrin Warren

The Wide, Wide World 1246
Jana Lea Argersinger

Wilderness 1251
Michael G. Ziser

Woman in the Nineteenth Century 1258
Christina Zwarg

Y

Young America *1265*
  Cheryl D. Bohde

"Young Goodman Brown". *1270*
  Lawrence I. Berkove

CONTRIBUTOR BIOGRAPHIES 1275

THEMATIC OUTLINE OF CONTENTS 1289

LIST OF ENTRIES TO
COMPANION SET 1293

PRIMARY SOURCES FOR
FURTHER READING 1297

INDEX 1299

Acknowledgments

Acknowledgment is gratefully made to those publishers and individuals who have permitted the use of the following material in copyright. Every effort has been made to identify and secure permission to reprint copyrighted material.

Excerpts from Emily Dickinson, *The Poems of Emily Dickinson: Reading Edition.* Edited by Ralph W. Franklin. Cambridge, Mass.: The Belknap Press of Harvard University Press, 1999. Copyright © 1998, 1999 by the President and Fellows of Harvard College. Copyright © 1951, 1955, 1979, 1983 by the President and Fellows of Harvard College. All rights reserved. Reprinted by permission of the publishers and the Trustees of Amherst College. Excerpts from Emily Dickinson, *The Letters of Emily Dickinson.* Edited by Thomas H. Johnson and Theodora Ward. Cambridge, Mass.: The Belknap Press of Harvard University Press, 1958. Copyright © 1958, 1986 The President and Fellows of Harvard College; 1914, 1924, 1932 by Martha Dickinson Bianchi; 1952 by Alfred Leete Hampson; 1960 by Mary L. Hampson. All rights reserved. Reprinted by permission of the publishers.

Preface

The half-century between 1820 and 1870 saw the transformation of the United States from a small nation of fewer than ten million people largely hugging the eastern seaboard to a country of nearly forty million stretching from the Atlantic to the Pacific. It was crisscrossed with railroads and telegraph lines, neither of which had existed when the period began. The United States had been wrenched apart by slavery and then forcibly reunited by a civil war that cost more casualties than all other American wars combined until Vietnam. With the conquest of the West had come war with Mexico and the wholesale relocation and extirpation of native peoples.

The period also began with a British critic, Sydney Smith, sneering in 1820, "In the four quarters of the globe, who reads an American book?" But by 1870 a diverse and vibrant literary culture had produced writers who are still household names today, such as Washington Irving, James Fenimore Cooper, Edgar Allan Poe, Ralph Waldo Emerson, Henry David Thoreau, Emily Dickinson, Walt Whitman, Louisa May Alcott, and Harriet Beecher Stowe. Mark Twain and Henry James had already launched careers that would span the rest of the century. A genteel literary tradition boasted familiar names no longer widely read today, such as Henry Wadsworth Longfellow, James Russell Lowell, Oliver Wendell Holmes, and John Greenleaf Whittier. Women and African American writers like Susan Warner, Sarah Payson Willis Parton ("Fanny Fern"), Margaret Fuller, Lydia Maria Child, Caroline Kirkland, Frederick Douglass, William Wells Brown, and Harriet Jacobs, once neglected, now command the attention and respect of a growing number of scholars and readers. It is the aim of *American History through Literature, 1820–1870* to place the development of this vibrant literary culture in the tumultuous historical transformations of that half century.

The guiding principle of this encyclopedia is perhaps best expressed in a well-known observation by Henry James in his study of his precursor Nathaniel Hawthorne: "The moral is that the flower of art blooms only where the soil is deep, that it takes a great deal of history to produce a little literature, that it needs a complex social machinery to set a writer in motion." Although James did not regard the "soil" of nineteenth-century American society as particularly deep (he had a rather narrower view of what constitutes both society and culture than we do today), the essays in these volumes address what we now understand as the rich, complex, and reciprocal relations between the literature of the period and the historical conditions that prevailed in America during the period 1820 to 1870.

In the main, however, James was right that wherever and whenever literature flourishes it does so not merely through the splendid isolation of individual genius but in the context of social, cultural, economic, geographical, religious, linguistic, and philosophical (to name only the most obvious) conditions that confront the writer. The literature produced in turn helps to illuminate and bring to life those conditions. The whaling industry, for example, was an important engine of economic growth in early-nineteenth-century America, but the person who studies its impact in terms of economic activity alone will know less about its human possibilities—ranging from the degraded to the heroic—than one who has also read Herman Melville's *Moby-Dick*. Conversely, the person who reads that novel only as a literary classic misses the light it sheds on American culture at mid-century: not only on the economy and adventure of whaling itself but on a host of racial, scientific, and religious issues as well.

Perhaps it would be best not to try to distinguish history and literature too finely but rather to recall that there are reasons why, in many languages, including French, German, and Spanish—the languages closely connected with English—the words for "story" and "history" are the same. Each involves some grounding in historical circumstance and each involves some degree of imaginative shaping of experience. Even a literary work as imaginative and otherworldly as Poe's "The Fall of the House of Usher," for example, may owe its very subject matter to widespread anxieties about premature burial, and the story's lack of a concrete setting is directly traceable to the conventions of transatlantic reprinting practices and the lack of international copyright at the time. Conversely, while the California gold rush, for example, was a historically specific phenomenon, it also played a role in larger American foundation myths and generated a discrete literary subculture that give rise to memorable works by Mark Twain and others.

American History through Literature, 1820–1870 is meant to address several kinds of readers at once: the high school or college student who wishes to acquire introductory information about a certain subject; library patrons who, out of desire to fill in some gap in their understanding, wish to peruse these volumes without premeditated purpose; the teacher of American literature, American history, or American studies who may consult these volumes in order to enrich his or her classes; the researcher who wishes to read an authoritative analysis or overview of a given subject and to be directed to other reliable sources of pertinent information on the subject; and finally, the so-called common reader, who, out of simple curiosity perhaps, wishes to learn more about the cultural ethos of America as it is reflected in history and literature. For all of these kinds of readers the essays in these volumes may serve either as a cogent brief analysis of the topic or as a starting point for further research. Although the essays are authoritative and accurate, they are not neutral synopses. Each expresses the point of view and, indeed, the argument of the contributor. In the aggregate, they reflect the diverse theoretical perspectives of contemporary literary criticism and historiology.

These volumes contain 245 essays ranging from 1,500 to 6,000 words. Each entry contains a bibliography and cross-references to related items. There are also over 200 entry-related illustrations, most of them contemporary to the time period under discussion; numerous sidebars containing key passages of important texts; and several helpful tables and maps. Entries fit broadly into the following categories, but it should be noted that a familiar category of literary encyclopedias will not be found, namely biographical essays on individual authors. This information is widely available in many other places, and the focus of these volumes is on key texts and contexts rather than on the lives of particular authors.

Works. This category comprises texts thought of as both literary and nonliterary, a selective list of "touchstone" titles chosen because they open out in some complex and revelatory fashion to American history. Some titles were popular in their own time or are in ours. Some are regarded as literary "classics," some were benchmarks of popular taste, some were both, and some were neither but reflect some important aspect of the culture of the times. Our "canon" is therefore dynamic and heterogeneous. Some titles (e.g., the witty *The Autocrat of the Breakfast-Table,* by the distinguished physician Oliver Wendell Holmes) reveal the fashions and manners of the period but are little known today. Once a best-seller and deemed a literary classic, Susan Warner's *The Wide, Wide World* is historically invaluable for its depiction of the period's religious evangelicalism. But many readers find it equally compelling artistically, as Jana Argersinger explains in her essay on this novel. Other women's works of the time (e.g., the African American writer Harriet Jacobs's *Incidents in the Life of a Slave Girl* and Elizabeth Drew Stoddard's *The Morgesons*) constitute psychologically and politically complex responses against conventional historical roles for women. Lovalerie King argues for the political awareness—feminist and otherwise—present in *Incidents,* and Sandra A. Zagarell discusses the compelling psychological eccentricities of *The Morgesons,* which she reveals to be surprisingly typical at a time when women, and families, were expected to be conventional.

Some of history's most intricate and lyrical voices are installed in the present-day canon, although some of their works, like Walt Whitman's *Leaves of Grass* and Herman Melville's *Moby-Dick,* were not always universally popular. Beyond plot summary, the literary entries follow a format of contextualizing authors within their personal histories and broader historical times. Entries also point out a work's relationship to specific historical incidents (e.g., the impact of the Civil War on the fourth edition of *Leaves of Grass,* or the motivational force of the Fugitive Slave Law on the composition of William Wells Brown's *Clotel*). *Works* also includes several historical documents, such as the Supreme Court ruling *Dred Scott v. Sandford,* which is described by Paul Finkelman as both a historical incident and a rhetorical document, an example again of the merging aspects of history and literature in these volumes.

Ideas. These entries characterize the heart and soul of a nation in the process of imagining its identity and in some instances in the process of rationalizing political or cultural decisions of the period, such as the rush to move westward. Examples include Manifest Destiny, manhood, feminism, and honor. Contributors accepted the challenge to hybridize history and literature, combining socially engaged literary texts with the complexities of the nation's historical profile. People seeking literary titles not present in the short list of *Works* can search the encyclopedia's index to find an extensive number of literary texts discussed in other contexts and embedded within American social history.

Genre or Genres. These entries describe literary forms (e.g., the slave narrative, domestic novel, gothic fiction, romance) that can be found within this historical period and that are invariably political and value driven. Slave narratives, for example, arose from a compelling need to document the abuses of slavery, to argue for freedom for the slave, and to alter society's perception about slavery as a necessary institution. *Genres* also dictate a set of literary conventions either invented or improvised upon by authors who resist creative, political, or social constraints. Antagonistic authors set against the social hypocrisies of antebellum society often played against generic expectations to stage their protests (e.g., Michael J. Davey's "The Romance" essay describes how Herman Melville creates an imaginative space in *Moby-Dick* in which to warn against the potential evils of demagoguery in democracy).

Aesthetics. Essays in this category (e.g., "Art and Architecture," "Fireside Poets," "Sentimentalism") identify conscious movements that sought to define what art should be, whether emotional, beautiful, useful, philosophical, or a combination of these things. This period was an especially important time for aesthetics because art was considered the seedbed of moral culture. Accordingly, important aesthetic movements are defined and their proponents identified along with the possible causes and the impact of each movement on American culture.

Institutions or Events. The Civil War dominates this category as "the greatest transforming event in American culture," as John Stauffer puts it in his essay on the conflict. In the longest entry in this encyclopedia, Stauffer characterizes the political, legal, and literary events that converged to catalyze this massive fracture in American identity. Suffice it to say 1820–1870 was an event-filled period (examined here in such entries as "Indian Wars and Dispossession," "California Gold Rush," "Trail of Tears," and "Banking, Finance, Panics, and Depressions"), a leisure-obsessed period ("Circuses and Spectacles," "Theater"), and, perhaps consequently, a period in which institutions for education and reform ("Colleges," "Temperance," "Religion") came into their own. Contributors with a special expertise in these areas describe their inception, various manifestations, and cultural impact.

Places. These essays address real, idealized, or utilitarian places (from Boston and San Francisco to "Nature," "Factories," and "Utopian Communities"); the international scene that was becoming increasingly attractive to Americans ("Canada," "Americans Abroad"), and the fluctuating geography of American space ("Borders," "Agrarianism," "Exploration and Discovery"). Essays describe the origins and defining characteristics of each locale, including the commercial enterprises and literature and cultural institutions (e.g., the thriving German newspaper industry in Cincinnati) that are particular to each. One can also infer from many of these entries that place entails a negotiation in cultural identity that is often fractious and involves winners and losers.

Society, Values, Culture, and/or Ethnicity. The far-reaching treatment of miscegenation (or mixed race relations) by Michael Householder is a good example of the approach and context of the philosophically weighty essays that appear in this category. His essay describes the legal, philosophical, and experiential history of race relations in America with a continual interweaving of important literary voices/texts (e.g., Lydia Maria Child's *Hobomok* and James Fenimore Cooper's *The Last of the Mohicans*) that responded as well as contributed to ongoing discussions about race. Both in literature and law, in the pulpit and the lyceum and on the lecture circuit, slavery, labor laws, women's rights, immigrant rights, and American domestic imperialism were being bitterly contested. American history springs to life in such provocative entries as "Abolitionist Writing," "Ethnology" (theories of race), "Marriage," "Political Parties," "Pornography," and "Technology."

Publishing. This category of essays analyzes American print culture found in this period (e.g., book publishing, periodicals, journalism), the location of important publishing centers (Boston, Philadelphia), the period's technological innovations ("Book and Periodical Illustration"), important personages involved in the publishing industry ("Editors"), and notable periodicals (e.g., *Godey's Lady's Book, The Atlantic Monthly*). Patricia Okker's entry on *Godey's,* for example, explains its phenomenal success and its special contribution to female authorship in the form of its canny editor Sarah Josepha Hale and its recruitment of women to produce lithographic fashion plates.

Gratitude is in order to many people who helped make this project possible. Stephen Wasserstein imagined it and stayed with it through its complex evolution. We thank him for his passionate investment and continued feedback. Without its project manager, Alja Collar, these volumes would not have been possible. Her steadfast pursuit of quality and flawless editorial management made all the difference. We also wish to thank our editorial board (William L. Andrews, Louis J. Budd, Lawrence J. Buell, Susan K. Harris, Denise D. Knight, and William J. Scheick) for valuable guidance—especially Lawrence J. Buell for his many suggestions on contributors. Ron and Mary Zboray helped greatly with defining historical topics and suggesting able contributors. William L. Andrews did double duty by writing on Frederick Douglass's *Narrative of the Life of Frederick Douglass,* as did Denise D. Knight by writing on the Declaration of

Sentiments. Finally, we wish to thank our companion editors of the 1870–1920 volumes, Tom Quirk and Gary Scharnhorst, for their friendship and helpful counsel, with a special thanks to Gary for contributing our thematic outline. Jan Gabler-Hover wishes to thank her husband and many of her friends—you know who you are—for bearing with her. Robert Sattelmeyer wishes to thank Leigh Kirkland for support and toleration throughout. The coeditors also wish to acknowledge Jennifer Wing and Johanna Ignacy for research assistance and one another for mutual support and productive badgering.

Janet Gabler-Hover
Robert Sattelmeyer

ABOLITIONIST WRITING

The largest political agenda of the nineteenth century, the antislavery movement, typically brings to mind a single work of literature. After selling more than 300,000 copies in the United States in its first year, Harriet Beecher Stowe's (1811–1896) *Uncle Tom's Cabin* (1852) was later translated into more than twenty languages and sold an astounding 1.5 million copies worldwide. Reportedly greeted by Abraham Lincoln as "the little woman who wrote the book that made this great war" in an 1862 visit to the White House, Stowe immediately reached iconic status for her phenomenally successful and provoking depiction of the horrors of slavery. At the same time, though, that her abolitionist efforts would be celebrated around the world, more radical-minded antislavery activists would denounce the problematic implications of the novel—implications that would ultimately characterize Stowe's legacy throughout most of the twentieth century. Riddled with racist stereotypes that have come to define modern-day memories of the novel—the submissive "Uncle Tom" character being the most (in)famous—and aligning itself with the conservative "Colonization" mission that advocated shipping slaves off to Africa, *Uncle Tom's Cabin* provides a compelling representation of the complex and highly fraught abolitionist movement. Stowe's novel, which would become the most recognizable abolitionist title, emerged from an already well-established tradition of literary projects that sought to end slavery and it played a role in the negotiation of various political agendas within the movement itself.

ANTISLAVERY NEWSPAPERS

The success of Stowe's abolitionist novel depended upon the existence of antislavery newspapers, which came into being three decades before the novel's publication. Before it was published in book form, *Uncle Tom's Cabin* was initially serialized in 1851–1852, in the Washington, D.C., abolitionist weekly, *National Era,* then under the editorship of Gamaliel Bailey (1807–1859). In addition to serialized fiction, abolitionist newspapers also printed essays, letters, speeches, sermons, and editorials, as well as short fiction and poetry. Starting with the 1821 launching of *Genius of Universal Emancipation* by the Quaker publisher Benjamin Lundy (1789–1839), the number of abolitionist newspapers would grow to more than twenty over the next thirty years. The most prominent among these, *The Liberator,* was launched in 1831 by Lundy's estranged disciple, William Lloyd Garrison (1805–1879), who would become one of the movement's most recognized leaders.

Although the newspapers would eventually serve multiple and often competing political agendas, Garrison's editorial preface to the first issue of *The Liberator* announced a resounding mission statement for the abolitionist newspaper tradition. In it he declares, "On this subject I do not wish to think, or speak, or write, with moderation . . . urge me not to use moderation in a cause like the present . . . I will not equivocate—I will not excuse—I will not retreat a single inch—AND I WILL BE HEARD." *The Liberator,* which Garrison published in partnership with Isaac

1

Black antislavery newspapers

Title	City	Established
Freedom's Journal	New York	30 March 1827
Rights of All	New York	28 March 1828
Weekly Advocate	New York	January 1837
Colored American (formerly the Weekly Advocate)	New York	4 March 1837
Elevator	Albany	1842
National Watchman	Troy, New York	1842
Clarion		1842
People's Press	New York	1843
Mystery	Pittsburgh	1843
Genius of Freedom		1845
Ram's Horn	New York	1 January 1847
North Star	Rochester, New York	1 November 1847
Moral Reform Magazine	Philadelphia	1847
Impartial Citizen	Syracuse, New York	1848
Christian Herald	Philadelphia	1848
Colored Man's Journal	New York	1851
Alienated American	Cleveland	1852
Christian Recorder (formerly the Christian Herald)	Philadelphia	1852
Mirror of the Times	San Francisco	1855
Herald of Freedom		1855
Anglo African	New York	23 July 1859

SOURCE: *Dictionary of American Negro Biography* (New York: Norton, 1982), pp. 134–135, 538–539; *Negro Year Book* (Tuskegee, Ala.: Negro Year Book, 1913), p. 75; Penn, *The Afro-American Press and Its Editors* (1891; New York: Arno, 1969).

Knapp, had a direct impact on the careers of many of the most influential abolitionists, including Frederick Douglass (1818–1895), Wendell Phillips (1811–1884), Lydia Maria Child (1802–1880), and Thomas Wentworth Higginson (1823–1911). *The Liberator* also published literature from some of the nineteenth century's foremost literary voices, such as poet John Greenleaf Whittier (1807–1892), whose famous poem "The Branded Hand" (1845) pays homage to abolitionist sea captain Jonathan Walker, who was branded "ss" for "slave stealer": "Then lift that manly right hand, bold ploughman of the wave! / Its branded palm shall prophesy, 'Salvation to the Slave!'" (ll. 41–42).

While his newspaper would bring together an impressive list of emerging and veteran abolitionists, Garrison was by no means a representative of a unified, cohesive movement. Rather, as an unyielding and steadfast leader, he evoked dissent as much as he inspired followers. Having diverged himself from the leanings of Lundy and the American Colonization Society, in 1833 Garrison was a principal organizer of the American Anti-Slavery Society, a group that opposed colonization efforts and sought the immediate emancipation of slaves. A pacifist, Garrison urged

fellow abolitionists to abandon political activity in a government that upheld slavery. The Garrisonian faction's belief in moral suasion, rather than political activism, as the preferred means for abolishing slavery, together with the growing number of antislavery newspapers, led to a phenomenal proliferation of literature that attempted to expose the evils of slavery to slaveholders and Northerners, including slave narratives and sentimental fiction.

Nevertheless, Garrison's insistent opposition to political and militant efforts and his commitment to other human rights agendas, namely women's suffrage, led to divisiveness within the abolitionist movement. As a result, a growing number of people distanced themselves from the mainstream abolition movement, prioritizing antislavery as their single mission and advocating political activity to end slavery. Two such antislavery groups formed in 1840, the Liberty Party, a political organization committed to abolishing slavery, and the American and Foreign Anti-Slavery Society, a group which refused to admit women. Several antislavery newspapers sprang from the faction that splintered away from Garrisonian abolitionism, including the first African American–owned-and-operated newspaper published in the United States, John Brown Russwurm (1799–1851) and Samuel Eli Cornish's (c. 1795–1858) *Freedom's Journal* (1827–1829), as well as, among others, Frederick Douglass's *North Star* (later *Frederick Douglass' Paper*, 1847–1860), and Henry Highland Garnet's (1815–1882) *National Watchman* (1842–1843). Whichever faction they represented, the subversive nature of abolitionist newspapers presented a constant threat to their creators. Editors were frequently victims of violent attacks, and in 1837, Elijah Parish Lovejoy (1802–1837), editor of the *Alton Observer* (Illinois), was murdered while trying to protect his printing press from a proslavery mob. Despite the brutal opposition to their production and dissemination, though, abolitionist newspapers succeeded in cultivating audiences for voices and messages that might otherwise have gone unheard, particularly those of slave narratives.

SLAVE NARRATIVES

The most compelling force in the antislavery movement to emerge from, and eventually diverge from, the auspices of Garrison and *The Liberator* was Frederick Douglass. As a speaker for the Massachusetts Anti-Slavery Society, Douglass's abolitionist career began to follow the path of moral suasion, rather than political or militant activism. To that end, *Narrative*

The Branded Hand. Daguerreotype by Albert Southworth and Josiah Hawes, 1845, shows the branded palm of Captain Jonathan Walker, who attempted to help a groups of slaves escape to the British West Indies. The attempt failed, and Walker was apprehended and convicted. As part of his sentence, his palm was branded with "ss," for "slave stealer." He later became an abolitionist lecturer. © MASSACHUSETTS HISTORICAL SOCIETY, BOSTON, MA/BRIDGEMAN ART LIBRARY

of the Life of Frederick Douglass (1845) poignantly recounts the author's experiences in slavery, including his successful attempt to "steal" literacy from his oppressors, his reliance on and protection of fellow slaves, his fight with slave "breaker" Covey, and his eventual escape from slavery. Douglass's direct account of his life in slavery appeals to values that include the importance of family and religion, such as, for instance, when he regrets the lack of connection to his mother: "Never having enjoyed, to any considerable extent, her soothing presence, her tender and watchful care, I received the tidings of [my mother's] death with much the same emotions I should have probably felt at the death of a stranger" (p. 19). With a frank and straightforward delivery that contrasts with the sentimental abolitionist writing of the day, Douglass's *Narrative* records as valuable a memory of the experience of slavery in the United States as of the rhetoric of African American antislavery

discourse. As a reviewer for Garrison's *Liberator* (30 May 1845) reflected, "Its stirring incidents will fasten themselves on the eager minds of the youth of this country with hooks of steel. The politics of the land will stand abashed before it, while her more corrupt religion will wish to sink back into the hot womb which gave it birth" (p. 86).

Although his *Narrative* opened with conventional white-authored prefaces (one by Garrison and another by Wendell Phillips) that attested to the legitimacy and authenticity of the narrative, Douglass's reliance on white sponsorship would be short-lived. In 1847, just two years after the publication of his *Narrative,* Douglass began his own antislavery newspaper in Rochester, New York, the *North Star* (later changed to *Frederick Douglass' Paper*). Finally, Douglass completed his break from Garrison in 1851, when he announced to the American Anti-Slavery Society that he intended to urge *North Star* readers to use political and militant means to end slavery, an agenda in direct conflict with Garrison's insistent pacifism and opposition to political activity. In his later autobiographies, Douglass would remark upon the role Garrison played in the early period of his career, including, significantly, the white abolitionist's heavy-handed editing of his *Narrative*.

Douglass's efforts, and particularly his initial alliance with Garrisonian abolitionism, were joined in 1843 by William Wells Brown (c. 1814–1884), who also served as a lecturer for the American Anti-Slavery Society. He would eventually become the most prolific African American writer of the mid-nineteenth century, with such distinctions as first African American playwright and novelist, but Brown's career as an abolitionist writer is highlighted by the 1847 publication of his personal account of slavery, *Narrative of William W. Brown, a Fugitive Slave*. In addition to its memorable descriptions of his experiences as a slave in St. Louis, Missouri, Brown's *Narrative* contributes the earliest detailed and compelling representation of the Underground Railroad. Brown's account of the system that supported slaves in their flight north draws upon his own experiences escaping with the help of Wells Brown, a Quaker whose name he later adopted, as well as his own work as an Underground Railroad "conductor," facilitating the escape of other slaves on a Lake Erie steamboat.

While best known for his slave narrative, Brown also wrote what are believed to be the first African American–authored plays, *Experience; or, How to Give a Northern Man a Backbone* (1856) and *The Escape; or, A Leap For Freedom* (1858), as well a collection of his poems, *Anti-Slavery Harp* (1848), and several volumes of black American history. Also, in *Clotel; or, The President's Daughter: A Narrative of Slave Life in the United States* (1853), the first African American novel, Brown relates the story of Thomas Jefferson's relationship with his slave mistress Sally Hemings (1773–1835). Originally published in England, the novel eventually came to U.S. readers, but only after it had been significantly revised, with references to the president removed. Much like the evolution of Douglass's antislavery agenda, Brown began his career as a pacifist who boycotted political abolitionism in the 1840s, but his writings over the course of the following decade reflect his growing militancy and preference for political activism to end slavery.

Henry Bibb (1815–1854) was another African American writer who evolved into a radical antislavery figure, eventually becoming a member of the Liberty Party. *Narrative of the Life and Adventures of Henry Bibb, an American Slave* (1849) tells the hair-raising story of the author's repeated escapes from slavery, as he was recaptured and escaped several times. Bibb's *Narrative* also gained attention for being one of the rare representations of slavery in the Deep South (Louisiana), as well as for offering one of the earliest depictions of slave folklife, including "conjure" traditions. What makes this narrative distinct from other slave narratives is the central emphasis it places on the role of marriage and family in slavery, as the author recounts his terrifying expeditions to free his wife and child. An advocate of militant and political means to end slavery, Bibb eventually moved to Canada, where he began the first black newspaper in that country, the *Voice of the Fugitive*.

Because of the highly political subject matter and the practical need for endorsement by male-centered abolitionist societies, in addition to many other racial and gender biases, the slave-narrative tradition was dominated by the male perspective. Significantly, one of the few female-authored, full-length slave narratives offers a unique and graphic portrayal of the sexual exploitation of women in slavery. Published under the pen name Linda Brent, Harriet Jacobs's (c. 1813–1897) *Incidents in the Life of a Slave Girl* (1861) tells the extraordinary story of the writer's seven-year refuge in the seven-foot by nine-foot and merely three-foot-high garret of her grandmother's house, where she hid to avoid the sexual advances of her master, "Dr. Flint." While *Incidents* features the white sponsorship conventional of the genre, in the form of an introduction by Lydia Maria Child, it is Jacobs's own preface that asserts the unparalleled value of the firsthand perspective of slave narratives: "Only by experience can any one realize how deep, and dark, and foul is that pit of abominations" (p. 126). Even more significantly, Jacobs's preface also appeals directly to white women readers, a rhetorical strategy typical to sentimental abolitionist literature: "But I do earnestly desire to arouse the women of the North to a realizing sense of the condition of two millions of women at the South, still in bondage, suffering what I suffered, and most of them far worse" (p. 126). With its emphasis on family, sexuality, and female virtue, Jacobs's narrative belongs as much to the slave-narrative tradition as to the sentimentalist tradition it simultaneously adopts and subverts.

POLEMICAL ABOLITIONIST LITERATURE

Slave narratives have clear political and social agendas, as they seek to expose and record the evils of slavery, but some of the most compelling antislavery writing appeared in nonliterary genres, as well. While many abolitionists adopted several different genres (e.g.,

Broadside of "Our Countrymen in Chains," 1837. The American Anti-Slavery Society published this broadside with John Greenleaf Whittier's passionate poem printed beneath the seal of the Society for the Abolition of Slavery in England. THE LIBRARY OF CONGRESS

Garrison, Douglass, Brown, and Child all wrote in literary and nonliterary forms), several are known chiefly for their polemical writings. Before his mysterious death, David Walker (1785–1830) worked to circulate to African Americans in both the North and South his controversial *Walker's Appeal, in Four Articles, Together with a Preamble, to the Coloured Citizens of the World, but in Particular, and Very Expressly, to Those of the United States of America* (1829). Inciting its African American audience to overthrow the system of slavery, *Walker's Appeal* provoked many Southern states to enact stronger laws against teaching slaves to read. "If any are anxious to ascertain who I am," writes David Walker near the end of his *Appeal*, "know the world, that I am one of the oppressed, degraded and wretched sons of Africa, rendered so by the avaricious and unmerciful, among the whites" (p. 71). From that perspective, Walker's rebellious messages especially outraged white readers, even including some abolitionists. In a *Liberator* editorial in 1831, Garrison himself denounced Walker's incendiary *Appeal*, reminding his readers that he and his followers "do not preach rebellion—no, but submission and peace. . . . the possibility of a bloody insurrection at the south fills us with dismay."

African American antislavery activist Henry Highland Garnet's radical "Address to the Slaves of the United States of America" also appalled pacifists, including Douglass and Brown, at the National Convention of Colored Citizens in Buffalo, New York, in 1843. In his address, Garnet implores slaves to use any means necessary to revolt, and he encourages militant political activism among abolitionists. Comparing slave rebellion to the patriotic rebellion of the American Revolution to motivate his audience, Garnet insists that it is the blacks' moral and religious duty to end slavery: "Fellow men! patient sufferers! behold your dearest rights crushed to the earth! See your sons murdered, and your wives, mothers, and sisters doomed to prostitution. In the name of the merciful God, and by all that life is worth, let it no longer be a debatable question whether it is better to choose LIBERTY or DEATH!" (p. 409).

Many radical abolitionists opposed the inclusion of women's voices, mostly for fear that women's suffrage might overshadow the antislavery agenda, but abolitionist societies increasingly invited women's participation by mid-century. Although their messages were less likely to appear in published polemical forums, the voices of women were nevertheless present throughout the major episodes of the abolitionist movement. In an 1860 meeting of the Pennsylvania Anti-Slavery Society, for instance, Lucretia Mott (1793–1880), a Quaker, spoke about John Brown

(1800–1859), who led the infamous raid on the federal arsenal at Harpers Ferry with the intention of arming slaves for revolt. In her speech, Mott expressed her own interpretation of pacifism: "I have no idea, because I am a non-resistant, of submitting tamely to injustice inflicted either on me or on the slave. I will oppose it with all the moral powers with which I am endowed. I am no advocate of passivity. Quakerism, as I understand it, does not mean quietism."

By the time of Mott's speech in 1860 American audiences were gradually becoming more accustomed to hearing women's voices in public, but the propriety of women participating in political forums was still hotly debated only a few decades earlier, as illustrated by the famous exchanges between Angelina Emily Grimké (1805–1879) and Catharine Beecher (1800–1878). Along with her sister, Sarah Moore Grimké, Angelina Grimké was among the first women to speak in the abolitionist lecture circuits by the time her first piece of polemical literature, *Appeal to the Christian Women of the South,* was published by the American Anti-Slavery Society in 1836. In response to Grimké's public plea to fellow Southern women to join the abolitionist cause, Beecher (sister to Harriet Beecher Stowe) published *An Essay on Slavery and Abolitionism, with Reference to the Duty of American Females* (1837). In that publication, Beecher discourages Grimké, and American women readers in general, from engaging in public speech and political activism, reminding them of the expectation that women restrict their influence to the private sphere of the domestic circle, rather than extend it to the public, political sphere. "The peculiar qualifications," she insists, "which make it suitable for a man to be an Abolitionist are, an exemplary discharge of all the domestic duties; humility, meekness, delicacy, tact, and discretion, and these should especially be the distinctive traits of those who take the place of *leaders* in devising measures" (pp. 150–151). The following year, Grimké published a long-awaited response to Beecher's critique of her political activism, in *Letters to Catherine E. Beecher, in Reply to an Essay on Slavery and Abolitionism, Addressed to A. E. Grimké* (1838). In this lengthy series of letters that defend her own role as an abolitionist, Grimké also provides a fascinating representation of many of the biggest figures and personalities in the abolitionist movement, including Garrison, whom she defends against implications in Beecher's essay. Most significantly, though, her exchanges with Beecher compelled Grimké to develop an extensive defense of her position, which led her to articulate a more secular argument against slavery as well as a firmer assertion of women's political rights.

SENTIMENTALISM

The public debates between Beecher and Grimké between the years 1836 and 1838 made the controversy over women's role in abolitionism famous, but Lydia Maria Child's own experiences had already demonstrated the devastating effects of polemical publications on a woman author's career. A very successful and famous novelist in the 1820s, Child's popularity plummeted when she outraged her readers with the publication of her first abolitionist piece in 1833, *An Appeal in Favor of That Class of Americans Called Africans.* With chapters that delineated the "Brief History of Negro Slavery" and offered a "Comparative View of Slavery, in Different Ages and Nations," Child's *Appeal* presented a rational argument in favor of immediate abolition of slavery and, most radically at the time, full integration of African Americans into society. Child situated her *Appeal* in logical, rather than sentimental, reasoning, and the ruinous consequences of that decision on her career indicate the restrictions women writers faced. For the most part, after she was vilified for participating in a masculine tradition, Child shifted her political campaign into her sentimental fiction writing, a genre carved out by and, mostly, for women.

The Boston-based antislavery gift book series *The Liberty Bell,* which ran from 1839 to 1858, provided the ideal forum for Child's abolitionist fiction. Child's *Liberty Bell* stories exemplify the emotionally charged emphasis on slavery's devastation of family and home that would become conventional in abolitionist fiction. In the short story "Charity Bowery" (1839), for example, the title character, a former slave, tells the narrator the story of how she came to be separated from each of her sixteen children. In this illustration of slavery's desecration of the mother-child bond, Child portrays the slave mother's struggle to keep her children and her tearful memories of how she lost each of them, including one that was killed by his master. Two other *Liberty Bell* stories, "The Quadroons" (1842) and "Slavery's Pleasant Homes" (1843), both expose the incompatibility of the slavery institution with monogamous marriage, a critique that developed into a common element of abolitionist fiction.

Child's short fiction helped to establish some of the major literary tropes to emerge from abolitionist fiction, including, most notoriously, the "tragic mulatto" convention, which would turn into a permanent fixture in American literature, as writers across different perspectives and eras would adopt, adapt, revise, criticize, and respond to the trope in their own literature. Child and other nineteenth-century white fiction writers typically represented the tragic mulatto as a beautiful, nearly white woman, the offspring of a white slave holder and his black female slave. With often only one-eighth black ancestry (or, "octoroon") and tragically unaware of her own and her mother's racial background, the tragic mulatto character usually falls in love with a white man who eventually either dies or abandons her, remanding her to slavery. Over a century after the popularization of the tragic mulatto figure, the African American writer and literary scholar Sterling Brown points out that the white writers' "favorite character, the octoroon, wretched because of the 'single drop of midnight in her veins,' desires a white lover above all else, and must therefore go down to a tragic end" (p. 145).

Despite the popularity of Child's antislavery fiction, *Uncle Tom's Cabin* would become the most recognizable example of sentimental abolitionist fiction, even though Harriet Beecher Stowe had arrived relatively late to the abolitionist literature scene. In addition to her legendary and controversial novel, Stowe herself practiced the conventions of sentimental antislavery fiction in a few "sketches," or short stories. Like *Uncle Tom's Cabin,* Stowe wrote "The Two Altars; or, Two Pictures in One" (1851) in response to the Fugitive Slave Law of 1850, a federal law that prohibited the harboring or aiding of fugitive slaves anywhere in the country, making it harder than ever for a slave to escape to the North. In that short story, Stowe uses domestic settings and emotional family scenes to illustrate the discrepancies between the nation's founding principles and the enactment of a federal law protecting the system of slavery.

After her remarkable entrance into the abolitionist movement, Stowe wrote a second abolitionist novel, *Dred, A Tale of the Great Dismal Swamp* (1856), which, although very popular in the nineteenth century, was virtually erased from the twentieth-century memory of the writer and of abolitionist literature. Nevertheless, *Dred* has been recognized as Stowe's attempt to revise her own representations of race in *Uncle Tom's Cabin*—representations which even many of her contemporaries criticized. In *Dred,* Stowe creates a revolutionary, rather than submissive, African American title character, and she abandons the Colonization agenda that concluded her first abolitionist novel. Otherwise, this novel maintains the conventional sentimental emphasis on the threat slavery poses to the institutions of family and monogamous marriage. Significantly, *Dred* even extends that warning beyond the traditional portrayal of weak and impossible slave families to represent fragmented and dysfunctional slaveholding families, as well.

For the most part, the representations of race politics that came from white-authored abolitionist fiction would go uncontested until the latter part of the nineteenth century. An extraordinary exception is a text rediscovered by Henry Louis Gates Jr., Harriet E. Wilson's (1825–1900) *Our Nig; or, Sketches of a Free Black* (1859), which is the first novel published by an African American woman. Bringing together conventions from sentimental fiction and the slave narrative tradition, *Our Nig* tells the story of a mulatto girl, who, in a significant reversal of the "tragic mulatto" trope, is abandoned by her white mother after the death of her black father. Ironically, the circumstances of Wilson's single-known literary production would seem fitting in a sentimentalist novel, as her novel's candid preface explains that she has written it in order to make a living to support her only son, who, according to historical records, ended up dying from "fever" six months later. Hardly an abolitionist piece, *Our Nig* would surely have angered white abolitionists with its account of a free black indentured servant's struggle against Northern racism in antebellum America. Wilson's novel nevertheless plays an important role in the history of abolitionist writing because it serves as an important countertext to the representations and stereotypes that emerged from the abolitionist movement.

Another African American writer who adopted sentimentalist conventions in her antebellum writing, often vacillating between adherence to and subversion of those conventions, is Frances Ellen Watkins Harper (1825–1911). Harper was an abolitionist lecturer, poet, and fiction writer, and her literary productions in the 1850s reflect her keen awareness of the trends in sentimentalist antislavery literature. Poems such as "To Mrs. Harriet Beecher Stowe" (1854), "Eliza Harris" (1853), and "Eva's Farewell" (1854) respond directly to Stowe's representations in *Uncle Tom's Cabin*. Although twentieth-century critics would dismiss her for her poetry's apparent alignment with the white perspective, several poems published alongside of these examples, including "The Slave Mother" (1854), seem to resituate white-centered sentimentalist conventions in the context of African American authorship. Also, in several poems narrated by her "Aunt Chloe" character, Harper adds dimension to the "mammy" figure stereotyped in fiction and minstrelsy. Eventually, in her 1892 novel *Iola Leroy*, which she sets in the Reconstruction Era, Harper would rewrite the "tragic mulatto" trope made famous in white-authored sentimental fiction, endowing the typically disempowered figure with political agency and racial consciousness. Although her light-skinned heroine still corresponded in many ways to white-authored representations, Harper's rewriting of the most ubiquitous convention of sentimental abolitionist writing

would mark the beginning of more radical revisions by African American women writers, from Zora Neale Hurston to Toni Morrison, reflecting the far-reaching impact of abolitionist writing on the history of American literature.

See also An Appeal in Favor of That Class of Americans Called Africans; Compromise of 1850 and Fugitive Slave Law; *The Liberator;* Slave Narratives; Slave Rebellions; Slavery; *Walker's Appeal*

BIBLIOGRAPHY

Primary Works

Beecher, Catharine E. *An Essay on Slavery and Abolitionism, with Reference to the Duty of American Females.* Philadelphia: H. Perkins, 1837.

Douglass, Frederick. *Narrative of the Life of Frederick Douglass.* 1845. In *Narrative of the Life of Frederick Douglass and Incidents in the Life of a Slave Girl.* New York: Modern Library, 2004.

"Frederick Douglass." *The Lynn Pioneer,* reprinted in *The Liberator,* 30 May 1845.

Garnet, Henry Highland. "Address to the Slaves of the United States of America." In *The Black Abolitionist Papers,* vol. 3., *The United States, 1830–1846,* edited by C. Peter Ripley, pp. 403–412. Chapel Hill: University of North Carolina Press, 1991.

Garrison, William Lloyd. "Walker's Appeal." *The Liberator,* 8 January 1831.

Jacobs, Harriet. *Incidents in the Life of a Slave Girl.* 1861. In *Narrative of the Life of Frederick Douglass and Incidents in the Life of a Slave Girl.* New York: Modern Library, 2004.

Mott, Lucretia. *National Anti-Slavery Standard,* 3 November 1860.

Walker, David. *Walker's Appeal.* 1829. Introduction by Sean Wilentz. New York: Hill and Wang, 1995.

Whittier, John Greenleaf. *The Complete Poetical Works of John Greenleaf Whittier.* Edited by Horace E. Scudder. Boston and New York: Houghton Mifflin, 1894.

Secondary Works

Blassingame, John W., Mae G. Henderson, and Jessica M. Dunn, eds. *Antislavery Newspapers and Periodicals.* Vol. 3, *1836–1854.* Boston: G. K. Hall, 1981.

Bormann, Ernest G., ed. *Forerunners of Black Power: The Rhetoric of Abolition* Englewood Cliffs, N.J.: Prentice-Hall, 1971.

Boyd, Melba Joyce. *Discarded Legacy: Politics and Poetics in the Life of Frances E. W. Harper, 1825–1911.* Detroit: Wayne State University Press, 1994.

Brown, Sterling. *Negro Poetry and Drama, and The Negro in American Fiction.* 1937. With a new preface by Robert Bone. New York: Atheneum, 1969.

Goodman, Paul. *Of One Blood: Abolitionism and the Origins of Racial Equality.* Berkeley: University of California Press, 1998.

Jacobs, Donald M., ed. *Courage and Conscience: Black and White Abolitionists in Boston.* Bloomington: Published for the Boston Athenaeum by Indiana University Press, 1993.

McBride, Dwight A. *Impossible Witnesses: Truth, Abolitionism, and Slave Testimony.* New York: New York University Press, 2001.

Quarles, Benjamin. *Black Abolitionists.* 1969. New York: Da Capo Press, 1991.

Sánchez-Eppler, Karen. *Touching Liberty: Abolition, Feminism, and the Politics of the Body.* Berkeley: University of California Press, 1993.

Stauffer, John. *The Black Hearts of Men: Radical Abolitionists and the Transformation of Race.* Cambridge, Mass.: Harvard University Press, 2002.

Thomas, Helen. *Romanticism and Slave Narratives: Transatlantic Testimonies.* Cambridge, U.K., and New York: Cambridge University Press, 2000.

Tompkins, Jane. *Sensational Designs: The Cultural Work of American Fiction, 1790–1860.* New York: Oxford University Press, 1985.

Waldstreicher, David. *The Struggle against Slavery: A History in Documents.* Oxford and New York: Oxford University Press, 2001.

Yee, Shirley J. *Black Women Abolitionists: A Study in Activism, 1828–1860.* Knoxville: University of Tennessee Press, 1992.

Emily E. VanDette

AFRICAN AMERICANS

See Blacks; Slavery

AGRARIANISM

The word "agrarianism" comes from the Latin *lex agraria,* an ancient Roman law that called for the equal division of public lands. In eighteenth- and nineteenth-century England, the word identified any land reform movement that sought to redistribute cultivated lands equally. Such agitation was a response in part to the eighteenth-century English Enclosure Acts, which disrupted traditional agricultural practices. In the twentieth century the word shed this radical reform definition. In the early twenty-first century agrarianism points to a collection of political, philosophical, and literary ideas that together tend to describe farm life in ideal terms.

Agrarianism finds expression in the literary pastoral tradition, which stretches back to ancient Greek and Roman writers such as Theocritus and Virgil. The pastoral envisions the natural world as an escape from the complexities of urban life. In a rural landscape the character is restored by his interaction with nature, which then enables him to return to the city. In many accounts the pastoral also represents the human hope for the return of a golden age, the simple, happy life of long ago.

Borrowing from the French Physiocrats the idea that farming is the only truly productive enterprise, agrarianism claims that agriculture is the foundation of all other professions and is the only source of wealth. Philosophically agrarianism reflects the ideas of John Locke, who declared in his *Second Treatise of Civil Government* (1690) that those who work land are its rightful owners. His labor theory of value influenced the thinking of Thomas Jefferson, who in turn shaped the way many nineteenth-century American homesteaders understood ownership of their farms.

In the late eighteenth century and early nineteenth century, agrarianism felt the influence of the European Romantic movement. The British Romantic William Wordsworth, for example, chose to describe rural life in his poems because in country living the "essential passions of the heart find a better soil in which they can attain their maturity" (p. 596). Romantics focused attention on the individual and described nature as a spiritual force. As someone in constant contact with nature, the farmer was positioned to experience moments that transcend the mundane material world.

AGRARIANISM IN THE UNITED STATES

Central to agrarianism is private property. In *Letters from an American Farmer* (1782), J. Hector St. John de Crèvecoeur asks, "What is an American?" His answer is a freeholder, a farmer who owns his own land and enjoys an agrarian utopia. Providing for his family using what he has available to him from nature and from his own abilities, this farmer draws his social and political identity from laboring in the earth. "This formerly rude soil has been converted by my father into a pleasant farm, and in return, it has established all our rights; on it is founded our rank, our freedom, our

The Veteran in a New Field, **1865.** Winslow Homer celebrates agriculture as a means of restoring the well-being of the divided and still ailing nation. THE METROPOLITAN MUSEUM OF ART, NEW YORK/THE BRIDGEMAN ART LIBRARY

power as citizens, our importance as inhabitants of such a district" (p. 54). Crèvecoeur's independent freeholder represented an economic and social alternative to Europe's feudal relationships, crowded cities, and emerging factory systems.

Following the American Revolution, the availability of land and a relatively small U.S. population convinced Thomas Jefferson—and many others—that an enduring republic of family farms was a real possibility. In *Notes on the State of Virginia* (1787), Jefferson defines the yeoman as a self-sufficient man free from "the casualties and caprice of customers" and the machinations of manufacturers and land speculators (p. 217). Jefferson's farmer owns a small piece of land that he and his family work to provide for themselves food, clothing, and shelter. In exchange for manufactured items, he sells any surplus goods to the "mobs of great cities" in Europe (p. 217). A defender of the Republic, this ideal farmer seeks to preserve his family's presence on the land through several generations. He embodies the bedrock virtues of the new nation: frugality, hard work, charity toward others, and love of God. Though

Jefferson later modified his agrarian stance ("Letter to Benjamin Austin," p. 549), his original vision was in play in nineteenth-century American politics as a contrast to Alexander Hamilton's plan for a primarily commercial, manufacturing economy.

Agrarianism is woven into the fabric of much U.S. culture and literature in the period 1820–1870. American writers of the time came of age in a predominantly agricultural nation. Roughly 80 percent of people lived on farms in 1820, major cities were mainly confined to the East Coast, and the nation's industrialization had yet to take hold. By 1870, however, just over half of the people lived on farms, cities had sprouted across the West, railroads linked both coasts, and U.S. industrial production was rapidly expanding.

With the Industrial Revolution transforming social and economic relationships, Americans turned nostalgically to representations of simple rural life. For example, the popular songs "Home Sweet Home" (1823) and "The Old Oaken Bucket" (1826) romanticized country living. In the visual arts, the work of Jasper Cropsey and Asher Durand, who played major roles in the Hudson River school, were attracted to pastoral landscapes. The idealized rural scenes of Nathaniel Currier and James Merritt Ives dominated the mid-nineteenth-century popular art market. Jerome Thompson's *The Haymakers* (1859) is typical of idyllic farm scenes painted in the antebellum period. George Inness, perhaps the greatest nineteenth-century landscape painter, depicted in *Peace and Plenty* (1865) a tranquil harvest scene that offers a sense of healing for a nation wounded by civil war.

Like the farms in these paintings, most antebellum farms appeared to be noncapitalist and to operate on a subsistence basis. Neighborhood work exchanges and homemade goods were common, and farmers who raised their own food had little need to enter a cash market. Farm communities knew few class distinctions, and many men at least had the opportunity to move from farm laborer to farm owner. But as the French observer Alexis de Tocqueville writes in *Democracy in America* (1840), "Americans carry their businesslike qualities into agriculture, and their trading passions are displayed in that as in their other pursuits" (p. 157). In fact, throughout the period 1820–1870 farmers were evolving into small capitalists. Caught up in regional and national markets, they turned more and more to labor-saving machinery to cut costs, adopting, for example, Cyrus McCormick's mechanical reaper (1834) and John Deere's steel moldboard plow (1846). As time wore on, farm realities looked less and less like the static world of Jefferson's agrarian ideal.

NEW ENGLAND

Agriculture in New England grew increasingly commercial between 1820 and 1840. As internal improvements brought increased competition from western farmers, many New England farmers moved west to new lands or left farming altogether. Those who remained specialized in milk, cheese, fruits, and vegetables for cities such as Boston, which grew rapidly in the 1830s and 1840s due to the Industrial Revolution's demand for wage laborers.

New England's transcendentalists often had mixed feelings about farmers and farming. Advocating self-reliance and understanding nature as symbolic of the spiritual realm, transcendentalists saw the farmer in a unique place to perfect himself. But as much as it is an occupation that offers the individual access to the divine, farming is also a material activity that can lead to a sole focus on financial gain, something Tocqueville notes: "Equality of conditions not only ennobles the notion of labor, but raises the notion of labor as a source of profit" (p. 152).

The arc of Ralph Waldo Emerson's thinking illustrates the transcendentalists' ambivalence. Early in his career Emerson drew on Jeffersonian agrarianism. In his essay *Nature* (1836), for example, he notes that farm life puts one in constant touch with the natural world and, by extension, spirit: "What is a farm but a mute gospel?" (p. 42). In 1837, in his poem "Concord Hymn," he immortalizes farmers as defenders of the nation:

By the rude bridge that arched the flood,
Their flag to April's breeze unfurled,
Here once the embattled farmers stood
And fired the shot heard round the world.
(P. 158)

In his 1844 lecture "The Young American," Emerson calls the farmer self-sufficient and notes that the land possesses "tranquillizing, sanative influences" that "repair the errors of a scholastic and traditional education" (p. 366). In this essay he even touches the city-country divide: "Whatever events in progress shall go to disgust men with cities and infuse into them the passion for country life and country pleasures, will render a service to the whole face of this continent" (p. 369). Pointing out that the West is "intruding a new and continental element into the national mind,"

Emerson asserts, "How much better when the whole land is a garden, and the people have grown up in the bowers of a paradise" (p. 370).

In his 1858 address "Farming," however, Emerson wrestles with an agriculture that he knows is becoming ever more complex. At the outset he praises farmers in the conventional way, describing them as creators who possess "tranquility and innocence" (p. 137), but he soon defines them as akin to factory workers, as minders of a great machine (p. 142). Rather than communing with nature, farmers now manipulate it with advances in science and technology.

In *Walden* (1854), Henry David Thoreau describes his experiment in independence, self-sufficiency, and communion with the natural world. Critiquing commercial progress, Thoreau points to his farmer-neighbors, whose lives seldom embody the agrarian ideal, and asks: "Who made them serfs of the soil? Why should they eat their sixty acres, when man is condemned to eat only his peck of dirt?" (p. 5). In his "Bean-Field" chapter, in which he outlines his own agricultural labors, Thoreau condemns farmers for attending only to material wants. He notes that husbandry was once a "sacred art" that is now "pursued with irreverent haste and heedlessness by us, our object being to have large farms and large crops merely" (pp. 182–183). But then again, Thoreau acknowledges that his farmwork is primarily a literary labor, admitting that he "must work in fields if only for the sake of tropes and expression, to serve a parable-maker one day" (p. 179).

Nineteenth-century communitarian experiments such as Brook Farm also felt the influence of the agrarian ideal. Attempting to marry manual labor and intellectual work in an egalitarian setting, Brook Farm's founder, George Ripley, sought to "prepare a society of liberal, intelligent, and cultivated persons, whose relations with each other would permit a more simple and wholesome life, than can be led amidst the pressure of our competitive institutions" (quoted in Delano, p. 47). Emerson and Thoreau, however, distanced themselves from communitarian experiments such as Brook Farm, which sought reform by changing society, and asserted the individual's necessary task of reforming himself. Brook Farm attracted several important New England figures including, for a time, Nathaniel Hawthorne.

In his *The Blithedale Romance* (1852), which alludes to Brook Farm, Hawthorne contrasts Silas Foster, the practical farmer, with the Blithedale idealists, who, in returning to the land, seek to show "mankind the example of a life governed by other than the false and cruel principles on which human society has all along been based" (p. 449). Unfortunately class issues doom the Blithedale idyll before it truly begins. Hawthorne's narrator, Coverdale, reminds readers near the beginning of his narrative that several people participate in the farm's experiment "not by necessity, but choice" (p. 452). He soon realizes that the dream of marrying heavy labor and intellectual activity does not work in practice: "The yeoman and the scholar . . . are two distinct individuals, and can never be melted or welded into one substance" (p. 477). Blithedale's "beautiful scheme of a noble and unselfish life" collapses under the weight of sex and death, a fall into history that ends many gardens of bliss (p. 584).

Agrarianism often holds in high esteem physical labor rather than intellectual work. The virtuous farmer does real work, unlike greedy speculators and factory owners who sport in the city, a site of vice and venality. This tension over definitions of work reflects a political contrast between aristocratic Europe and the democratic United States, where everyone labors for his bread. The dignity of work finds expression in Walt Whitman's *Leaves of Grass* (1855) but is often imagined sentimentally, as in John Greenleaf Whittier's "The Huskers":

> Swung o'er the heaped-up harvest, from pitch-
> forks in the mow,
> Shone dimly down the lanterns on the pleasant
> scene below;
> The growing pile of husks behind, the golden
> ears before,
> And laughing eyes and busy hands and brown
> cheeks glimmering o'er.
>
> *(P. 311)*

Arguments over labor and land tend to dominate this period of American history. The political crises surrounding the Missouri Compromise (1820) and the Compromise of 1850 pitted North and South over the extension of slavery. Should farming based on slavery be allowed in new states and territories? Should all labor be free? The South sought slavery's extension; the North sought its confinement if not end. The resulting compromises maintained a balance of power between the regions, but a final resolution of the conflict was only postponed. As the Civil War approached, slavery became a serious threat to the North's free-labor ideology.

But no matter their location, farmers in the agrarian ideal were always white men. Women, blacks, and Native Americans were excluded. For example, after Andrew Jackson signed the Indian Removal Act (1830), Cherokees fought displacement from Georgia using the agrarian ideal. Asserting that they were not hunter-gatherers living on unimproved land, they pointed to their cultivated fields as evidence that they had rights to the land they occupied. Though Cherokee memorials to Congress, as Timothy Sweet notes, "appeal[ed] directly to white culture's idealization of the Jeffersonian middle landscape," their appeals were ineffective (p. 126). In 1838 the U.S. Army removed Cherokees from their homelands and forced them west along the infamous Trail of Tears. White farmers quickly appropriated Cherokee land.

THE SOUTH

Agrarianism as described above was not universally embraced across the United States. The South's plantation system challenged the Jeffersonian vision of a nation populated by small farmers. Defenders of slavery knew that the yeoman ideal was a menace to the South's economy. For example, the radical proslavery writer George Fitzhugh, in *Cannibals All! or, Slaves without Masters* (1857), defended an agriculture based on slavery and rejected capitalism as a destroyer of civilization.

Revising the agrarian ideal, southern writers replaced agrarianism's small family farm with an aristocratic plantation worked by docile slaves overseen by paternalistic masters. From the perspective of John Taylor, a Virginia planter and slaveholder, agriculture "secures health and vigor to both [mind and body]; and by combining a thorough knowledge of the real affairs of life, with a necessity for investigating the areana [*sic*] of nature, and the strongest invitations to the practice of morality, it becomes the best architect of a complete man" (p. 243). Unlike his neighbor Thomas Jefferson, however, Taylor felt few qualms about slavery. He asserts in his *Arator* essays (1814) that "liberality to slaves and working animals, is the fountain of [farmers'] profit" (p. 237).

The South's plantation system spawned its own literature, beginning notably with John Pendleton Kennedy's *Swallow Barn* (1832). In *The Hireling and the Slave* (1854) the poet and politician William John Grayson defends slavery, claiming, for example, that a slave sale is simply "a transfer of labor from one employer to another. . . . The sale of the slave is the form in which the laws secure the slave from this misery of the hireling—secure to him a certainty of employment and a certainty of subsistence" (p. viii). In *Woodcraft* (1854) the novelist William Gilmore Simms answers Harriet Beecher Stowe's *Uncle Tom's Cabin* (1852) by depicting harmonious relationships between a master and his slave. For example, near the close of the novel, when his master, Captain Porgy, attempts to free him, the slave, Tom, refuses: "Ef I doesn't b'long to *you, you* b'long to *me. . . . You* b'longs to *me* Tom, jes' as much as me Tom b'long to *you*; and you nebber guine git *you* free paper from me long as you lib" (p. 528).

But thousands of antebellum slave narratives challenged these conceptions of southern farm life, reminding readers of the brutality and dehumanization of slavery. The *Narrative of the Life of Frederick Douglass, an American Slave* (1845) depicts the slave breaker Covey as a farmer who sees no contradiction between his Sunday churchgoing and his whipping and breeding of slaves. Douglass describes farms not as places of repose and virtue but as sites of violence and moral degeneracy. Similarly the national and international best-selling novel *Uncle Tom's Cabin* attacks the southern plantation ideal in its portrayal of violence and slave sales.

After the Civil War, African Americans, like the Cherokees before them, sought inclusion in the agrarian ideal. One step in that direction, the Southern Homestead Act (1866), intended to create farms like those in the North by opening to ex-slaves southern federal public lands. But freedmen's hopes for homesteads went largely unrealized, and African Americans were soon absorbed by the sharecropping system that

In his autobiography Narrative of the Life of Frederick Douglass, an American Slave *(1845), Frederick Douglass refutes the antebellum southern agrarian ideal in describing the farmer Edward Covey:*

Mr. Covey was a poor man, a farm-renter. He rented the place upon which he lived, as also the hands with which he tilled it. Mr. Covey had acquired a very high reputation for breaking young slaves, and this reputation was of immense value to him. It enabled him to get his farm tilled with much less expense to himself than he could have had it done without such a reputation. Some slaveholders thought it not much loss to allow Mr. Covey to have their slaves one year, for the sake of the training to which they were subjected, without any other compensation. He could hire young help with great ease, in consequence of this reputation. Added to the natural good qualities of Mr. Covey, he was a professor of religion— a pious soul—a member and a class-leader in the Methodist church. All of this added weight to his reputation as a "nigger-breaker."

Douglass, *Narrative of the Life of Frederick Douglass,* pp. 721–722.

dominated much of southern farm life for the rest of the nineteenth century.

The Southern Homestead Act was based on the 1862 Homestead Act. Important in settling the West, the Homestead Act offered settlers 160 acres of land in return for five years of residence and improvements plus payment of a $10 registration fee. The act was backed by urban activists such as the *New York Tribune* editor Horace Greeley, author of *What I Know of Farming* (1870), who followed Locke and Jefferson in believing that anyone who worked a piece of ground ought to have title to it. Greeley hoped that the act would resettle on western homesteads unemployed urban workers. As Henry Nash Smith asserts, advocates of the act "sincerely believed that the yeoman depicted in the myth of the garden was an accurate representation of the common man" (p. 172).

How farmers defined themselves, however, has been a matter of historical debate, though they likely understood that the ideal world described by writers and politicians was just that, an ideal. And though most farmers saw themselves before the Civil War as self-sufficient freeholders, by 1870 at least many described themselves as businessmen rather than Jeffersonian yeomen. The years following the war witnessed an intensification of U.S. industrialization that drew most existing subsistence-farming communities into capital-intensive farming. Soon agriculture became more and more mechanized, and economic disillusion spread in rural areas, giving rise to the late-nineteenth-century Populist movement.

See also Labor; Nature; Transcendentalism; Urbanization

BIBLIOGRAPHY

Primary Works

Crèvecoeur, J. Hector St. John. *Letters from an American Farmer.* 1782. In *Letters from an American Farmer and Sketches of Eighteenth-Century America,* edited by Albert E. Stone, pp. 35–227. New York: Penguin, 1986.

Douglass, Frederick. *Narrative of the Life of Frederick Douglass, an American Slave.* 1845. In *The Norton Anthology of World Masterpieces: The Western Tradition,* 7th ed., vol. 2, edited by Sarah Lawall et al., pp. 696–753. New York: Norton, 1999.

Emerson, Ralph Waldo. "Concord Hymn." 1837. In *The Complete Works of Ralph Waldo Emerson,* vol. 9, *Poems,* edited by Edward Waldo Emerson, pp. 158–159. New York: AMS Press, 1968.

Emerson, Ralph Waldo. "Farming." 1858. In *The Complete Works of Ralph Waldo Emerson,* vol. 7, *Society and Solitude,* edited by Edward Waldo Emerson, pp. 135–154. New York: AMS Press, 1968.

Emerson, Ralph Waldo. *Nature.* 1837. In *The Complete Works of Ralph Waldo Emerson,* vol. 1, *Nature: Addresses and Lectures,* edited by Edward Waldo Emerson, pp. 1–77. New York: AMS Press, 1968.

Emerson, Ralph Waldo. "The Young American." 1844. In *The Complete Works of Ralph Waldo Emerson,* vol. 1, *Nature: Addresses and Lectures,* edited by Edward Waldo Emerson, pp. 361–395. New York: AMS Press, 1968.

Fitzhugh, George. *Cannibals All! or, Slaves without Masters.* 1857. Edited by C. Vann Woodward. Cambridge, Mass.: Harvard University Press, 1968.

Grayson, William J. *The Hireling and the Slave.* Charleston, S.C.: J. Russell, 1854.

Greeley, Horace. *What I Know of Farming.* 1870. New York: Arno Press, 1975.

Hawthorne, Nathaniel. *The Blithedale Romance.* 1852. In *The Complete Novels and Selected Tales of Nathaniel Hawthorne,* edited by Norman Holmes Pearson, pp. 439–585. New York: Modern Library, 1937.

Jefferson, Thomas. "Letter to Benjamin Austin, 9 January 1816." In *The Portable Thomas Jefferson,* edited by Merrill D. Peterson, pp. 547–550. New York: Penguin, 1987.

Jefferson, Thomas. *Notes on the State of Virginia.* 1787. In *The Portable Thomas Jefferson,* edited by Merrill D. Peterson, pp. 23–232. New York: Penguin, 1987.

Kennedy, John Pendleton. *Swallow Barn; or, A Sojourn in the Old Dominion.* 1832. Philadelphia: Lippincott, 1861.

Locke, John. *Of Civil Government: Second Treatise.* 1690. Introduction by Russell Kirk, pp. 547–550. South Bend, Ind.: Gateway Editions, 1955.

Simms, William Gilmore. *Woodcraft; or, Hawks about the Dovecote.* 1854. Edited by Charles S. Watson. New Haven, Conn.: New College and University Press, 1983.

Stowe, Harriet Beecher. *Uncle Tom's Cabin.* 1852. Edited by Ann Douglas. New York: Penguin, 1986.

Taylor, John. *Arator: Being a Series of Agricultural Essays, Practical and Political.* 1813. Georgetown, Columbia: J. M. Carter, 1814.

Thoreau, Henry David. *Walden.* 1854. In *The Writings of Henry David Thoreau,* vol. 2. New York: AMS Press, 1968.

Tocqueville, Alexis de. *Democracy in America.* 1840. Vol. 2. Edited by Phillips Bradley. New York: Vintage, 1990.

Whitman, Walt. *Leaves of Grass.* 1855. Edited by Gay Wilson Allen. New York: New American Library, 1980.

Whittier, John Greenleaf. "The Huskers." In *The Poetical Works of John Greenleaf Whittier,* vol. 3, pp. 308–314. Boston: Houghton Mifflin, 1904.

Wordsworth, William. "Preface to Lyrical Ballads." 1802. In *Romantic Poetry and Prose*, edited by Harold Bloom and Lionel Trilling, pp. 592–611. New York: Oxford University Press, 1973.

Secondary Works

Burns, Sarah. *Pastoral Inventions: Rural Life in Nineteenth-Century American Art and Culture.* Philadelphia: Temple University Press, 1989.

Delano, Sterling F. "Brook Farm." In *The American Renaissance in New England*, vol. 223 of *Dictionary of Literary Biography*, edited by Wesley T. Mott, pp. 46–51. Detroit: Gale, 2000.

Govan, Thomas P. "Agrarian and Agrarianism: A Study in the Use and Abuse of Words." *Journal of Southern History* 30, no. 1 (1964): 35–47.

Inge, M. Thomas, ed. *Agrarianism in American Literature.* New York: Odyssey Press, 1969.

Kulikoff, Allan. *The Agrarian Origins of American Capitalism.* Charlottesville: University Press of Virginia, 1992.

Marx, Leo. *The Machine in the Garden: Technology and the Pastoral Ideal in America.* London: Oxford University Press, 1964.

Montmarquet, James A. *The Idea of Agrarianism: From Hunter-Gatherer to Agrarian Radical in Western Culture.* Moscow: University of Idaho Press, 1989.

Smith, Henry Nash. *Virgin Land: The American West as Symbol and Myth.* 1950. Cambridge, Mass.: Harvard University Press, 1979.

Sweet, Timothy. *American Georgics: Economy and Environment in Early American Literature.* Philadelphia: University of Pennsylvania Press, 2002.

William Conlogue

"AIN'T I A WOMAN?"

Sojourner Truth (c. 1797–1883) made the speech associated with the refrain "Ain't I a woman?" in May 1851, in Akron, Ohio, where she gained fame for eloquently and powerfully bringing together the issues of women's rights and slavery. Although Sojourner Truth was already a popular preacher, abolitionist, and woman's rights spokesperson in the East, she was unknown to westerners outside of the abolitionist movement headed by William Lloyd Garrison (1805–1879). Her Akron speech and other lectures while touring in Ohio as part of Garrison's American Anti-Slavery Society made her as popular in the West as she was in the East.

EARLY LIFE

Sojourner Truth, whose given name was Isabella, was born in slavery in New York's Dutch-speaking Hudson River valley. As a child, Isabella was nurtured on her mother's African mysticism and learned rudimentary Christianity from the white mistresses in the household engaged in training their own children. Sold away at age twelve, she had three owners within a year: an Englishman who beat her for not speaking English; a kind but uneducated lower-class Dutch farmer; and finally a well-to-do farmer, John Dumont. At the Dumont farm she married another slave, Thomas, and had five children. She remained Dumont's slave from late 1810 to 1826, when she fled with her baby daughter to the home of an antislavery Dutch farmer, whose last name, Van Wagenen, she took as her own. She was freed after New York State passed an antislavery law in 1827. That year she also experienced a cathartic baptism of the spirit and accepted Christian conversion. Her profession of faith evolved into a belief that she had received a special calling from God, manifested in the miraculous retrieval of her young son Peter, who had been sold into southern slavery; she fought in court for Peter's successful release in the winter of 1828.

In 1828 Isabella also moved to New York City, where she joined the African Methodist Church, called Zion's. She soon gravitated toward the Perfectionists, a radical Methodist offshoot of Charles Grandison Finney's Great Western Revival. Although unable to read and write, Isabella quickly became well known and much respected among the Methodists. As a popular revival preacher, the influence of her speaking brought many converts to the Christian faith. She also worked among prostitutes and the poor and was briefly ensnarled in a notorious religious cult. During her fifteen years in New York City, Isabella continued honing her speaking skills and biblical knowledge. In June 1843 she had a spiritual revelation that she experienced as the voice of God, beckoning her into service as a sojourner for truth. Thus she changed her name and embarked on her life-long social justice mission.

A SOJOURNER FOR TRUTH

Traveling through Long Island, Connecticut, and western Massachusetts and preaching abolition all the way, the anointed Sojourner Truth worked just enough to "pay tribute to Caesar" (Gilbert, p. 82). She survived on the kindness of strangers and drew strength from her authority as God's messenger. A great favorite at camp meetings, revivals, and among reformers, this tall, commanding figure had a dignified

Sojourner Truth, photographed in 1864. THE LIBRARY OF CONGRESS

manner, a gift of prayer, and a remarkable talent for singing. Most of all, Sojourner's conversations, sermons, lessons of wisdom and faith, and her remarkable biblical interpretations deeply impressed her listeners.

In March 1844 Sojourner Truth settled in the utopian community known as the Northampton Association in western Massachusetts. In this haven of "isms" she met many reformers, including William Lloyd Garrison, president of the American Anti-Slavery Society; Abby Kelley Foster, the American Society's only female lecturer; Frederick Douglass, the American Society's only self-emancipated lecturer; and Olive Gilbert, a New England reformer to whom Sojourner would dictate her autobiographical *Narrative of Sojourner Truth: A Northern Slave* (1850). Sojourner Truth made her first recorded abolitionist speech in August 1844 in Northampton. The following May she was a featured speaker at the American Anti-Slavery national convention in New York City. Sojourner published her *Narrative* and

began a New England speaking tour in 1850, just as the notorious Fugitive Slave Law was passed, requiring citizens of free states to assist in the recovery of runaway bondpeople. In late October 1850 she was a featured speaker at the first National Woman's Rights Convention in Worcester, Massachusetts. Two significant issues at this meeting had not been part of the 1848 Seneca Falls Declaration of Sentiments, in which the participants of the New York State convention demanded a reevaluation of the social condition and legal rights of women. One was a specific resolution about wrongs inflicted upon enslaved women and the other was a demand for women's suffrage. In February 1851 Sojourner Truth joined the antislavery campaign through western New York with the British abolitionist and Member of Parliament George Thompson, Abby Kelley Foster, Stephen S. Foster, and Frederick Douglass. The tour culminated in meetings in Syracuse and Rochester, New York, where western abolitionists invited Sojourner to come and lecture in Ohio.

AIN'T I A WOMAN?

Antislavery and women's rights were generally unpopular causes in Ohio. The large majority of whites in the state were proslavery Methodists, Presbyterians, Congregationalists, Episcopalians, and Baptists. Some however, were members of the Free Soil Party, a newly formed coalition organized around nonextension of slavery, maintaining slavery where it existed, and excluding free blacks from the territories for the sake of the union. Ohio's small white liberal element included abolitionists, Underground Railroad workers, and radical women's rights activists. They were mainly Quakers, Moravians, German Pietists, Unitarians, Universalists, Shakers, and other dissenting sects living in northern Ohio, called the Western Reserve. Although Ohio's first constitution, in 1802, had abolished slavery, beginning in 1804 the state passed "Black Laws" that denied to blacks all civil and educational rights and prohibited black settlement without a $500 bond and a white patron. Bloody riots occurred in Cincinnati in 1829, 1836, and 1841, causing many blacks either to leave the state or to arm themselves. The state's minuscule progressive element made small gains: in 1848 some Black Laws, including denial of education, were repealed, and in 1850 Ohio women were the first to campaign for the vote, joining blacks in a bid for a universal suffrage amendment to the new state constitution. Their failure led to the convening of the 1850 national woman's convention in Worcester, followed by the 1851 regional meeting in Akron.

Sojourner Truth arrived in Ohio to lecture for the antislavery cause in May 1851, stopped in Cleveland, and spoke among the black population. Hearing of the women's convention, and deeply interested in women's rights, she went on to Akron. As the story goes, the convention president, Frances Gage, and the convention secretary, Hannah Cutler, entered the hotel lobby and saw a tall black woman walking back and forth, carrying a basket of books. Embarrassed by the presence of a black woman, the two white Free Soil antislavery women ignored Sojourner, walking right past her into the parlor. Truth followed them, introduced herself, and explained her abolitionist mission. Gage and Cutler each bought a copy of Sojourner Truth's *Narrative* and assumed that was the end of her business at the convention.

The convention participants and their cause were not well received in Akron. The women had access to only one church, the Universalist, and only one hotel in the city was willing to rent rooms to the delegates. The convention was also divided ideologically. The Michigan radical Emma Coe compared women's position to that of southern slaves. She was sarcastic and bitter in accusing men of twofold injustices toward women—depriving them of education, then calling them incapable imbeciles. Jane Swisshelm, the Free Soil editor of a Pittsburgh, Pennsylvania, newspaper, the *Saturday Visitor*, strongly objected to the stance represented by Coe. Swisshelm insisted that she did not want to relinquish her femininity. The disagreement among the women on the platform created disquiet within the audience of females while some male clergy interrupted them and shouted disapproval.

Sojourner Truth sat on the steps leading to the pulpit, fanning herself with her sunbonnet, watching everything and occasionally interjecting comments. As the three-way battle waxed heavy between moderate and radical women, and between the sexes, one clergyman told the women to go home to their husbands and children because Jesus and all of his apostles were men. From her position near the platform, Sojourner shouted that the men claim all for themselves. An Oberlin student, Sallie Holley, who had left school for three days to attend the woman's convention, later wrote that the biblical edict against women speaking in public was strongly upheld in Ohio by the large presence of clerics there—making Truth's alacrity at taking on the clerics all the more impressive. As the exchanges heated, Sojourner Truth asked to address the entire audience, and Frances Gage gave her the floor. Jane Swisshelm in the *Saturday Visitor* later criticized Gage's handling of the convention and ignoring of parliamentary rules, but the moment gave

rise to the opportunity for Truth to make her riveting speech, which became known by the refrain "Ain't I a woman?" (or "A'rn't I a woman?") and secured her legendary place in history.

VERSIONS OF TRUTH

History has two versions of "Ain't I a Woman?" both relatively succinct by contrast with the full oration given by Truth at the Akron convention. An account by Frances Gage was published twelve years after the fact, during the Civil War, as a correction to comments made by Harriet Beecher Stowe in her highly publicized but distorted recollection of meeting Truth in 1855, and Gage's version of the speech established the way in which Truth's words are remembered. Stowe, in her *Atlantic Monthly* article titled "Sojourner Truth: The Libyan Sibyl," presents Truth disparagingly, as an oversized, humorous African-born oddity, possessing naive religious faith and speaking in droll, thick, almost incomprehensible southern dialect. Stowe attributes Truth as saying at Akron, "Sisters, I a'n't clear what you'd be after. Ef women want any rights, more'n dey's got, why don't dey 'jes' *take 'em*, an' not be talkin' about it." The April 1863 publication of Stowe's article led Gage to publish her own recollection in the *National Anti-Slavery Standard* on 2 May 1863. In recounting Truth's words Gage liberally added rhetorical flourish, dialect, and the ringing refrain "And a'rn't I a woman?" But a report in the Salem, Ohio, *Anti-Slavery Bugle*, published on 21 June 1851—about three weeks after the Akron meeting—is certainly the most authentic. It does not have a refrain, does not express Truth in dialect, and states that she said "I am a woman's rights," reflecting a common phrase used by female reformers. Nevertheless, in comparing the two versions, only one definite factual falsehood exists: Gage attributes thirteen children to Sojourner Truth, something she obviously copied from Stowe's article. In general, the *Bugle* and Gage versions correspond in content and meaning.

Whatever the exact words of her presentation, Sojourner Truth memorably fused issues of color, slavery, work, and gender under the rubric of spirituality. She had done this on other occasions, including the 1850 national woman's convention. Although not in the *Bugle* account, contemporary sources support Gage's comment that Sojourner Truth said she never found a man willing to help her over mud puddles and bad roads—as a retort to Jane Swisshelm's insistence that such assistance was a woman's privilege. Sojourner's point was that black women were no less female even though not placed on a pedestal. Here she might easily have interjected the phrase "And a'rn't I a woman?" Both accounts emphasize labor in the same way, although Gage insists that Sojourner (uncharacteristically) "bared her right arm to the shoulder." Truth suggested that although her enslaved sisters worked like mules and were strong and hardy, they were still women. Both accounts address education, except that Gage, again copying Stowe, resorts to minstrelsy: "'Den dey talks 'bout dis ting in de head—what dis dey call it?' 'Intellect,' whispered some one near. 'Dat's it honey. What's dat got to do with women's rights or niggers' rights?'" This demeaning language was tailored for white nineteenth-century audience appeal. Yet Gage, like the *Bugle,* emphasizes Sojourner's main remark, which followed up Emma Coe's emphasis of unequal educational opportunity: If women's intellectual capacity held only a pint, and men's a quart, why could women not have their measure full?

The two accounts agree that the speech emphasized the spiritual role of women, one of Sojourner Truth's favorite topics. The *Bugle* notes that Truth called women the most steadfast followers of Jesus, and she used the example of Lazarus' sisters. Because they approached Christ with faith and love, Lazarus arose as Jesus wept. In both accounts, Sojourner Truth reminded the critical ministers and her conflicted sisters that Christ was born of a woman, through Immaculate Conception. Where, she challenged, was man's part?

By both accounts, Sojourner Truth skillfully rebuked the men in the audience for belittling the convention and its goals. Yet as an accomplished orator, Sojourner Truth did not leave even detractors on a sour note. Both accounts reveal her biblical olive branch. The ministers maintained that human depravity rested upon the sins of Eve. Since Eve was powerful enough to upset the world, said Sojourner Truth, the daughters of Eve deserve the opportunity to set it right side up again.

Frances Gage's account fizzles out apologetically, claiming she could not follow Sojourner through it all. She does recall long continuous cheering and some crying among the women. Resorting (as she had earlier in the same account) to the figure of Stowe's imaginary black Amazon, Gage concludes that Sojourner Truth took all the white women up into "her strong arms and carried us safely." The *Bugle* however, provides a finale befitting Sojourner Truth's manner of connecting race, slavery, and gender. Assertive women had men between a rock and a hard place. Beset by the bondpeople on one side and their own women on the other, white men,

said Truth, were in a "tight place," and surely caught between "a hawk and a buzzard."

The authors of the multivolume *History of Woman's Suffrage* (1881–1922) chose to use Frances Gage's version rather than the the report from the *Anti-Slavery Bugle.* History may never know if Sojourner Truth actually used the refrain "Ain't I a woman?" However, the account in the *Bugle* calls Truth's remarks "one of the most unique and interesting speeches of the Convention," asserting that it had a powerful effect on the audience. Truth's pointed aptness and originality were instrumental in getting the most radical resolutions through the convention over the objections of moderate women. Indeed, a number of contemporary newspapers commented on the impact and influence of the speech (although Jane Swisshelm's paper was not among them—she wrote only that a tall black woman was at the convention, selling books). Gage's recollection that Sojourner Truth's words became a profound inspiration for Ohio women is supported by the farewell Truth received when she left the state, nearly two years later: the women of Ashtabula County honored her departure with a gift of a huge silk banner labeled "Am I Not a Woman and a Sister?"

See also Abolitionist Writing; Blacks; Female Authorship; Feminism; Oral Tradition; Oratory; Slavery

BIBLIOGRAPHY
Primary Works
Anti-Slavery Bugle (Salem, Ohio), 21 June 1851, p. 160.

Cutler, Hanna Tracy. "Reminiscences." *Woman's Journal,* 19–26 September 1896.

Gage, Frances. "Sojourner Truth." *National Anti-Slavery Standard,* 2 May 1863.

Gilbert, Olive. *Narrative of Sojourner Truth: A Northern Slave.* 1850. Reprinted as *Narrative of Sojourner Truth: A Bondwoman of Olden Time.* Edited by Margaret Washington. New York: Vintage, 1993.

Holley, Sallie. *A Life for Liberty.* 1899. Reprinted as *A Life for Liberty: Anti-Slavery and Other Letters of Sallie Holley.* Edited by John W. Chadwick. New York: Negro Universities Press, 1969.

Stowe, Harriet Beecher. "Sojourner Truth: The Libyan Sibyl." *Atlantic Monthly,* April 1863, pp. 473–481.

Vale, Gilbert. *Fanaticism: Its Source and Influence, Illustrated by the Simple Narrative of Isabella, in the Case of Matthias, Mr. and Mrs. Folger, Mr. Pierson, Mr. Mills, Catherine, Isabella, &c. &c.* 2 vols. New York: G. Vale, 1835.

Secondary Works

David, Linda, and Erlene Stetson. *Glorying in Tribulation: The Lifework of Sojourner Truth.* East Lansing: Michigan State University Press, 1994.

Mabee, Carleton. *Sojourner Truth: Slave, Prophet, Legend.* New York: New York University Press, 1993.

Painter, Nell I. *Sojourner Truth: A Life, a Symbol.* New York: Norton, 1996.

Margaret Washington

AMATEURISM AND SELF-PUBLISHING

About halfway through *Moby-Dick* (1851), Ishmael pauses to describe a beggar on the London docks. A one-legged man holds up a picture "representing the tragic scene in which he lost his leg" (p. 312). Not everyone believes this beggar's story, but, says Ishmael, "the time of his justification has now come" (p. 312). It is not that his story is true, but rather that "his three whales are as good whales as were ever published in Wapping" (p. 312). In one sense this self-published artist is a perfect amateur—a man whose works of art would never be printed in the modest commercial establishments found in the dockside neighborhood of Wapping. But he is also a professional—an artist with commercial aspirations, trying to live by selling his works.

As this scene suggests, it was not always easy to separate the amateur from the professional in the literary worlds of the first half of the nineteenth century. According to the literary historian William Charvat, the figure of the professional author in the United States emerged in the 1820s and 1830s, when for the first time it became possible to imagine writing as a full-time occupation. Professional writing, Charvat suggested, "provides a living for the author, like any other job; . . . it is a main and prolonged, rather than intermittent or sporadic, resource for the writer; . . . it is produced with the hope of extended sale in the open market, like any article of commerce; and . . . it is written with reference to buyers' tastes and reading habits" (p. 3).

AMATEURS AND THE LITERARY MARKETPLACE

Charvat defined the professional author, but what did it mean to be an amateur author? Was an amateur a part-time author, a one-time author, a poor, incompetent, or unpaid author, or merely a gentleman whose wealth freed him from the need to sell his work? Was an amateur an aspiring professional author? Or was an amateur one who was outside an emerging literary establishment—a woman, an African American, a former slave, a Native American, or a working person with experience and a few ideas who found a friendly printer willing to set words in type? Some amateurs surely wrote because they loved the craft; other were self-published writers; and still others occupied the low ranks of a literary establishment.

Many who commented on amateur authorship in the early years of the nineteenth century viewed amateurism with the disdain of aspiring professionals. In the summer of 1845, an author calling himself "Mimin" described for readers of *United States Magazine and Democratic Review* "the various divisions and subdivisions into which the trade of authorship is divided." "We recognize two classes," he wrote, "authors by profession, and amateur writers: those who regard study and composition as the business of their lives, and those who look upon them merely as incidental occupations." Amateurs, Mimin argued, plagued professionals, distorting the literary marketplace by selling their works on the cheap. The flood of cheap works undermined the value of good literature and, worse, stalled the development of a national culture sure to grow when all readers read great art. "An amateur in almost every walk is regarded as much inferior to the working member of the craft," he concluded (pp. 62–63).

Mimin's description makes clear that by the mid-1840s, those calling themselves amateurs were neither above nor outside the market. As magazine publishing expanded in the 1840s and 1850s, editors picked up cheap materials both from foreign periodicals and from homegrown amateurs. Proprietors took advantage of the aspirations of amateurs who were happy just to appear in print and paid very little for the poems and essays they published. As one would expect, editors often had kind words for amateur contributors. The *Southern Literary Messenger,* for example, boasted that its "CONTRIBUTORS are numerous, embracing Professional and Amateur Writers of the First Distinction." In a column assessing contemporary literary production, the editors of the Cincinnati-based *Ladies' Repository* praised the "literary ability displayed" in several works of history and biography, "written all of them by amateur authors," evidence, according to the editors, that "there is still a vast amount of undeveloped history in every part of the country, inviting the appreciative labors of our writers, while the fields of biography are alike extensive and rich in the most interesting forms of historical matter. Into these it is hoped our non-professional writers will freely enter" ("New York Literary Correspondence," p. 634).

And enter they did. Writers calling themselves amateurs found opportunities in the expanding world of early-nineteenth-century publishing and began developing the stylistic markers that set off their works as the products of amateurs. The South Carolina poet William Gilmore Simms (1806–1870) imagined the amateur as a "gentleman in night-gown and slippers." But he also noted that amateurs presented their tales as told "by one who apologized . . . for this wandering into forbidden grounds—possibly alleging a vacant mind, or an erring mood, for the solitary trespass; and promising if forgiven for this, never, in like manner, to offend again" (p. 14).

Apologies proved useful to amateur and self-published authors, offering an opening gambit that led them before the public. Consider, for example, the preface a writer calling herself Hannah Crafts attached to her unpublished novel, *The Bondwoman's Narrative* (c. 1850s), perhaps the first novel written by an African American woman. "In presenting this record of plain unvarnished facts to a generous public I feel a certain degree of diffidence and self-distrust. I ask myself for the hundredth time How will such a literary venture, coming from a sphere so humble be received?" (p. 3). Crafts uses the few lines of her preface to accomplish several things. She apologizes for coming before the public, but at the same time, she enlists her public's generosity, praising her readers' virtues before they have even begun to read her tale. She also calls attention to her own humble social position and pledges, as do most mid-century amateurs, to confine herself to the facts, to those things about which she can claim a special, experiential knowledge. Experiential knowledge became another mark of the amateur.

CIVIL WAR WRITING

When Simms assessed the state of American authorship in 1844, he singled out the War of 1812 as central to the development of professional writing in the United States. It was no accident, he said, that James Fenimore Cooper's career followed "closely upon the footsteps of war!" (p. 12). The war cut off the supply of British books, and just as the embargo on British goods encouraged domestic manufacture, so the embargo on British ideas encouraged American authors. In some ways, the Civil War played a similar role in the history of amateur authorship, creating a demand for the unvarnished accounts of soldiers' wartime experiences. Books and stories by Union soldiers who were captured and confined in Confederate prisons offer particularly instructive examples of mid-century amateur authorship. Prisoner writers apologized, testifying that they appeared in print only at the urgent "solicitation of friends." "Without any aspira-

tions whatever, to literary notoriety, I have endeavored to give a plain, unvarnished narrative of facts and incidents of prison life, as they occurred, under my observation, during twenty-two months in various rebel prisons," one typical account, written by A. C. Roach, a former prisoner, begins (p. 4).

"I had no thoughts of publishing a book until several weeks after my escape," Willard Glazier confessed. "I kept a diary, or journal, from the time of my capture. After reading portions of it to some of my friends, they persuaded me to amplify and put it in a readable form" (p. vii). To reassure readers that his amplifications had not gone beyond the bounds of his experience, Glazier, like many of his fellow amateurs, made sure to offer a provenance for his literary production. "The rough manuscript was, for the most part, written during my imprisonment at Columbia, sitting on the ground, and writing on my knee. Captain Kelly, 1st Kentucky Cavalry, brought a part of that manuscript through the lines by concealing it in the crown of an old regulation hat. I escaped with the remainder concealed in the lining of my jacket" (pp. vii–viii). He also gave his manuscript an aura of authenticity by describing the nearly heroic measures behind the simplest acts of composition. "I had no pencil of my own," he notes in the middle of an account of a night spent in a swamp. But his companion "had a short piece which he kindly lent me. Having no knife, I was obliged to sharpen it by picking the wood away from the lead with my finger nails" (p. 251). Such details often give immediacy to amateur accounts. And immediacy, not literary polish or philosophical insight, was the chief selling point of amateur tales. As good amateurs, these writers pledged to confine themselves to things they had seen, heard, or felt, leaving the work of describing the war's larger meanings to professional writers.

Working within the bounds of a carefully constructed modesty, former prisoners took their accounts of experience into the postwar literary marketplace. A few prisoners' stories appeared with the imprint of such New York houses as Harper & Brothers, but more were the work of hometown presses and newspaper printing offices—outfits such as the Methodist Book Concern of Cincinnati, the Railroad City Publishing House of Indianapolis, or the Daily Wisconsin Printing House in Milwaukee. Narratives by former prisoners appeared in congressional reports and popular magazines; they appeared as straightforward commercial publications with commissioned illustrations, as bound journalism, as subscription volumes, and as self-published books and cheap pamphlets that former soldiers hawked themselves on street corners and in railroad stations. As Melville's

Ishmael might have remarked, their stories were often just as good as those published in the big commercial houses.

Although some differences between amateurs and professionals may have been clear by the end of the century, questions about the relations between the two remained. Writing in *Scribner's Magazine* in 1893, the novelist William Dean Howells (1837–1920) described the "The Man of Letters as a Man of Business." He called up that older vision of the amateur as the artist outside the market. "People feel that there is something profane, something impious, in taking money for a picture, or a poem, or a statue," he wrote. "Most of all, the artist himself feels this" (p. 429). Business had taken over the arts, Howells wrote. In a better world, artists—even professional artists—retained an amateur's love for their work. It was as amateurs that artists had access to the muses who had been chased from America's noisy commercial culture. The literary world Howells surveyed had not been made to suit the professionals, as Mimin imagined them. Howells looked at a world dominated by hacks and proposed that the best defense of the profession might just be to make peace with its amateurs.

See also Autobiography; Book Publishing; Journals and Diaries; Literary Marketplace; Slave Narratives

BIBLIOGRAPHY
Primary Works
Crafts, Hannah. *The Bondwoman's Narrative.* c. 1850s. Edited by Henry Louis Gates Jr. New York: Warner Books, 2002.

Glazier, Willard W. *The Capture, the Prison Pen, and the Escape; Giving a Complete History of Prison Life in the South.* New York: United States Publishing Company, 1868.

Howells, William Dean. "The Man of Letters as a Man of Business." *Scribner's Magazine* 14 (1893): 429.

Melville, Herman. *Moby-Dick.* 1851. In *Moby-Dick, Billy Budd, and Other Writings.* New York: Library of America, 2000.

Mimin. "Amateur Authors and Small Critics." *United States Magazine and Democratic Review* 17 (1845): 62–63.

"New York Literary Correspondence." *Ladies' Repository: A Monthly Periodical Devoted to Literature, Arts and Religion* 19 (1859): 634.

Roach, A. C. *The Prisoner of War and How Treated.* Indianapolis, Ind.: Railroad City Publishing House, 1865.

Simms, William Gilmore. "International Copyright Law." *Southern Literary Messenger* 10 (1844): 12–14.

Secondary Works
Charvat, William. *The Profession of Authorship in America, 1800–1870.* 1968. New York: Columbia University Press, 1992.

Coultrap-McQuin, Susan. *Doing Literary Business: American Women Writers in the Nineteenth Century.* Chapel Hill: University of North Carolina Press, 1990.

Fabian, Ann. *The Unvarnished Truth: Personal Narratives in Nineteenth-Century America.* Berkeley: University of California Press, 2000.

McGill, Meredith L. *American Literature and the Culture of Reprinting, 1834–1853.* Philadelphia: University of Pennsylvania Press, 2003.

Newbury, Michael. *Figuring Authorship in Antebellum America.* Stanford, Calif.: Stanford University Press, 1997.

Ann Fabian

AMERICAN ENGLISH

When James Monroe was reelected to the presidency in 1820, the United States had been a sovereign nation for more than four decades. It had its own monetary system and its own Constitution and government, but the nation still did not seem to have its own language. For some it was an important question: If no national language existed, should one be created to establish American identity? And if a national language already existed, what were its characteristics? Inseparable from these questions was the relation of American English to British English. Were they one language or two? Should the people of the United States conform to a British standard, or should they form their own? These questions were vigorously debated during the first half of the nineteenth century and continued to generate controversy decades after the Civil War.

As early as the 1780s patriots called for a national language to confirm America's independence from England. Among the first champions of the cause was Noah Webster (1758–1843), a graduate of Yale University and a lawyer, journalist, and teacher who was destined to become preeminent in the history of American English and immortalized in America's dictionaries. In his *Dissertations on the English Language* (1789), published more than a decade before his first dictionary, Webster declares: "Customs, habits, and *language,* as well as government should be national. America should have her *own* distinct from all the world. Such is the policy of other nations, and such must be *our* policy, before the states can be either independent or respectable" (p. 179). Supporters and opponents of Webster's position argued the point in letters, speeches, magazines, and books throughout the early years of the Republic.

By the second decade of the nineteenth century the range of attitudes was clear. Many Americans wanted their language to conform as closely as possible to British English so that British readers might continue readily to comprehend the writings of Americans and vice versa; so that Americans of the future could maintain contact with their literary heritage; and for the continued facility of commercial and cultural exchange between the nations. The distinguished philologist John Pickering (1777–1846), compiler of the first significant collection of Americanisms, *Vocabulary or Collection of Words and Phrases Which Have Been Supposed to Be Peculiar to the United States of America* (1816), repudiated the idea of a unique American language, warned against the natural tendency for that very thing to happen, and cited the "final separation of languages of Spain and Portugal" as an example to be avoided (Baron, p. 34).

Ardent patriots at the other extreme proposed abolishing English altogether, making French or Hebrew the national language, or inventing a new one. The majority of serious commentators took the middle ground, rejecting both colonialist dependence on England and the idea of a separate language. The respected poets Henry Wadsworth Longfellow and John Trumbull, the novelist James Fenimore Cooper, and the poet, editor, and critic James Russell Lowell held views similar to those expressed by John Marshall, chief justice of the Supreme Court, in 1821: "The English language is also ours; and the attempt to change it would be more than Quixotism. The attempt will be to preserve and improve it" (Read, p. 1158). Soon Webster too was no longer calling for a separate language. In 1831, in a letter to the editor of the *Westminster Review,* he wrote: "Our language is English. . . . It is desirable that the language on both sides of the Atlantic should remain the same . . . but some differences must necessarily exist" (Baron, p. 55). On one point all sides agreed: new words were required to denote activities and features of the landscape existing only in America. Thomas Jefferson, the most illustrious defender of innovation, made the case in a letter dated 16 August 1813 to the grammarian John Waldo, thanking him for his *Rudiments of English Grammar* (1811): "The new circumstances under which we are placed, call for new words, new phrases, and for the transfer of old words to new objects." Then putting his principle into practice, he added, "Necessity obliges us to neologize" (13:340, 346), thus transforming the young noun "neologism" (coined in 1803), meaning "a new word,

Noah Webster, c. 1867. Portrait engraving of the author of *American Dictionary of the English Language* and *American Spelling Book.* THE LIBRARY OF CONGRESS

usage, or expression," into a verb meaning "create new words."

AMERICANISMS

The expansion of the English language in America to include thousands of words and phrases not known or current in England raised the vexing question of "Americanisms," a term that a Scotsman, the Reverend John Witherspoon (1723–1794)—a former president of Princeton University, a signer of the Declaration of Independence, and a member of the Continental Congress—claimed to have invented in 1781. In Webster's *American Dictionary of the English Language* (1828), an Americanism is simply "an American idiom." John Russell Bartlett (1805–1886) identified nine classes of Americanisms in the 1859 edition of his *Dictionary of Americanisms: A Glossary of Words and Phrases Usually Regarded as Peculiar to the United States.* According to the *Virginia Literary Museum and Journal of Belles Lettres,* published in 1829–1830, Americanisms were of two kinds: "old words used in a new sense" and "*new* words of indigenous origin"

(Mathews, p. 99). Whether or not they were called Americanisms, several classes of words or phrases that distinguished American English from British English were easily identified. The contact of Americans with different cultures enriched American English by hundreds of words derived from European languages, notably French, Dutch, German, and Spanish. But by far the greatest number of loanwords came from American Indian languages. In *The English Language in America* (1925), George Philip Krapp lists some 250 words of Indian origin, exclusive of proper names. Many remain current: for example such animal names as "caribou," "chipmunk," "hog," "moose," "opossum," "raccoon," "skunk," "woodchuck" (1:165–167).

More likely to be called Americanisms were words and phrases of English origin. H. L. Mencken in *The American Language: An Inquiry into the Development of English in the United States* (1919) at one point lists words that were current in the United States in the nineteenth century but had become obsolete in England, among them "flap-jack," "molasses," "home-spun," "cesspool," "whittle," "hustle," "fall" (for "autumn") (p. 128). Conversely words "in full use in England," such as "yon," "yonder," and "over" (for "too") were becoming obsolete in America (*North American Review,* October 1860, p. 522). Americans did not hesitate to change the meaning of words still current in England. For instance, in nineteenth-century British, "plantation" meant primarily the act of planting seeds or placing plants into soil; it also meant the planting of persons in some locality, synonymous with "colonization." In America "plantation" came quickly to denote not an activity but a place—an estate or large farm. While in England a "creek" was an inlet of the sea, a narrow passage between islands, even a small port, in America the meaning of a rivulet or stream was firmly established by the eighteenth century. "Store" is another case in point. To the British the noun "store" meant a supply of something held for future use, as a store of food or clothing. "Store" carried a connotation of adequacy or abundance, so that if one had a "store" of food that meant the supply was large. In America "store" by the nineteenth century meant what the British called a "shop": a retail establishment where goods were sold. Numerous other words evolved so quickly and completely in America they soon required definition for the British to understand.

Americans were also prone to converting one part of speech to another. As Mencken points out, "The early Americans showed that spacious disregard for linguistic nicety which has characterized their descendants ever since. They reduced verb-phrases to simple verbs, turned verbs into nouns, nouns into verbs, and adjectives into either or both." He cites as examples the reduction of "to convey by deed" and "to lay on the table," which in American legal parlance became simply "to deed" and "to table" (p. 117). Among the slew of nouns that early became verbs are "to author," "to engineer," "to hog," "to scalp," and "to stump." Verbs that became adjectives by, as Mencken says, "shading down suffixes to a barbaric simplicity" are the likes of "classy," "scary," and "tasty" (p. 117).

American inventiveness shone further in forming compounds of English words, demonstrating "the national talent for condensing a complex thought . . . into a vivid and arresting image" (p. 142). Americans ate hoe-cake, corn-dodgers, pop-corn, egg-plant, and pea-nuts; some lived in the back-woods, others in bottom-lands; they cleared under-brush, burned pine-knots during cold-snaps, and traveled by bob-sled. They rough-housed and had housewarmings and spelling-bees. From the frontier steadily moving westward came a flood of expressions that became metaphors: "to cave in," "to bark up the wrong tree," "to take to the woods," "to darken one's door," "to fly off the handle," "to have a hard row to hoe." Political campaigns after the War of 1812 generated new compounds that endured: "gag-rule," "landslide," "dark-horse," "lame-duck," "on-the-fence." Verbs current in Andrew Jackson's administrations (1828–1836)—"to bolt," "to lobby," "to straddle"—remained staples of political talk. The gold rush of 1849 brought "prospector," "pan-out," "flash in the pan," and "strike it rich" into Americans' vocabulary. With the development of the railroads came more new compounds: "box-car," "hand-car," "round-trip," "cow-catcher."

The constant flow into the language of new words and phrases made inevitable a continuous debate about Americanisms. Which were acceptable? Which should be rejected? In the United States the arguments were exacerbated by the steady barrage of British criticism of American speech. The need to retaliate after defeat in two wars no doubt accounts in part for the savage attacks in the nineteenth century by English quarterlies and English travelers in the United States. But even observers who were most sympathetic to the Republic and were prepared to take a friendly interest in the new country made unfavorable comments. After visiting America in 1837–1838, Captain Frederick Marryat, a British naval officer and novelist, wondered at "how very debased the language has become in a short period in America" (Mathews, p. 131). He admired in American metaphors "an energy which is very remarkable" (p. 139) but noted that, while "their lower classes are more intelligible than ours," the "higher classes" often lapsed from the standard of the "well-educated English" (p. 131).

Hostile critics routinely denounced departures from British usage as barbarisms, corruptions, vulgarisms, and perversions. In *Men and Manners in America* (1833), for instance, Thomas Hamilton says: "The privilege of barbarizing the King's English is assumed by all ranks and conditions of men . . . . They assume unlimited liberty in the use of *expect, reckon, guess* and *calculate*" when what they mean is "think," "believe," or "suppose" (Mencken, p. 24). Marryat and other Englishmen were impressed by the prevalence of the all-purpose verb "to fix," which Godfrey Thomas Vigne identified in 1832 as meaning "to be done, made, mixed, mended, bespoken, hired, ordered, arranged, procured, finished, lent or given" (Mencken, p. 26). Such American substitutes for British words as "rooster" for "cock"—which by the 1820s had become a vulgar term for the male sex organ—"boss" for "master," and "help" for "servant" were also viewed with contempt, as was the promiscuous use of "lady" and "gentleman" applied to men and women of all ranks and conditions—all made more disagreeable by the "nasal twang" English travelers professed to hear everywhere in the United States. In *The Life and Adventures of Martin Chuzzlewit* (1843), Charles Dickens puts the defense of America into the tobacco-stained mouth of an uncouth braggart politician, while the most cultured American character delivers criticism of his or her countrymen's manners and speech.

Americans did not stop reading Dickens's novels, but they defended themselves in other ways. Writers in the *North American Review* accused British observers of fabricating the American speech they criticized. One claimed that the novelist Frances (Fanny) Trollope, in her popular travel book *Domestic Manners of the Americans* (1832), put into the mouths of Americans "English vulgarism[s] unknown in any part of the United States" (January 1833, p. 14). Others noted that British writers used many verbs, such as "advocate," "immigrate," and "progress," that they stigmatized as Americanisms, and that they perpetrated their own neologisms—"guardianize," "gutturality," "heathendom" (January 1847, p. 186)—and even more cumbersome and ridiculous constructions the likes of "cacodemonize," meaning "demonize," and "evangelizationeer," meaning "evangelist." These American critics pointed out that often words and phrases "charged as being new-invented barbarities of ours were mostly drawn from the pure wells of English undefiled, and had happened to be preserved in America while they were lost in England" (January 1833, p. 20). James Russell Lowell (1819–1891)

mounts a detailed and lengthy defense of what he calls the Yankee dialect in the introduction to the second series of *The Biglow Papers* (1867), hoping to show that "the Yankee often has antiquity and very respectable literary authority on his side" (p. 217).

American writers, including those with strong ties to England, defended American English in positive ways, by praising it and using it. Lowell urged American writers to seek language "at its living sources," in "our popular idiom . . . racy with life and vigor, and originality" (p. 214). He prophesied that the United States would be "past all question . . . the great home and centre" of the English language. In "The American Scholar" (1837) Ralph Waldo Emerson (1803–1882) declares, "We have listened too long to the courtly muses of Europe" (p. 47); he pronounces the style of Alexander Pope, Samuel Johnson, and Edward Gibbon "cold and pedantic" (p. 46), declares that "Life is our dictionary" (p. 39), and exhorts American writers to celebrate "the near, the low, the common" (p. 45) in the language of everyday life. The genteel narrator of James Fenimore Cooper's (1789–1851) Leatherstocking Tales uses American words and colloquialisms without comment. His vocabulary in chapter 6 of *The Pioneers* (1823), describing a local doctor, includes "butternut," "home-spun," "jobber," "meetinghouse," "one-horse sleigh," "settlement," "to shoot up," and "to break the ice."

DEVELOPMENT OF STANDARD AMERICAN ENGLISH

Americans made their most important, far-reaching defense by promoting American English as one language, uniform throughout the country. Many prominent men, including John Adams, John Marshall, and James Fenimore Cooper, all of whom rejected the idea of a separate American language, concurred with Noah Webster's belief that "our political harmony is . . . concerned in a uniformity of language" (*Dissertations*, p. 20). Both English and American observers noted that differences in the speech of regions and classes were much greater in England than in the United States. Still the peculiarities of idiom and pronunciation marking speech in New England, the South, and the West were feared as sources of linguistic corruption and threats to national unity. The expansion of the United States to the Pacific Ocean, the arrival in the antebellum years of thousands of immigrants, and internal strife foreshadowing the Civil War made ever more urgent the need for one language to unify the nation.

The importance placed on a uniform language at once raised the question of establishing a standard.

By what authority was a standard to be created and implemented? The one sustained effort to legislate uniformity was made by William S. Cardell (1780–1828), a grammarian who in 1820 proposed an American Academy of Language and Belles Lettres to establish the forms of good usage and thus, as he told Thomas Jefferson in a letter, to "maintain, as far as practicable, an English standard of writing and pronunciation, correct, fixed, and uniform, throughout our extensive territory" (Baron, p. 101). Cardell envisioned an American equivalent of the venerable Académie Française, or French Academy, founded in 1635 by Cardinal Richelieu to establish and disseminate a standard language, to supplant regional dialects, and to publish an official exhaustive dictionary. Many leading citizens supported these aims, but no organization like the French Academy, which at the end of the twentieth century was publishing the ninth edition of its exhaustive dictionary, ever developed in the United States.

Webster remained aloof from Cardell's efforts, which failed after three years, but his *American Dictionary of the English Language,* published in 1828 and revised twice in his lifetime, became the single most important work in the development of Standard American English. Preceded by his *American Spelling Book; or, First Part of the Grammatical Institute of the English Language* (1787), his *American Spelling Book, Containing the Rudiments of the English Language, for the Use of Schools in the United States* (1804), and his *Compendious Dictionary of the English Language* (1806), Webster's monumental two-volume work contained definitions of some seventy thousand words, including thousands appearing for the first time in any dictionary (Simpson, p. 141). In the preface to the *American Dictionary,* Webster states his aim "to ascertain the true principle of the language, in its orthography and structure; to purify it from some palpable errors, and reduce the number of its anomalies, thus giving it more regularity and consistency in its forms, both of words and sentences; and in this manner to furnish a standard of our vernacular tongue."

Webster opposed any standard created by British authority or by a privileged class of Americans. He favored a standard based on "the *rules of the language itself,* and the *general practice of the nation*" (*Dissertations,* p. 27); he sought a closer connection between spoken and written language; but his lifelong effort to eradicate localisms indicates a qualified acceptance of the usages of the common people as a standard. Other writers who were more conservative on language looked for their standard to "the class of highest cultivation as exerted especially through the medium of literature" (*North American Review,*

January 1867, p. 53), "not the usage of the majority, but of the learned" (*North American Review,* July 1849, p. 98). Washington Irving warned that "any deviation on our part from the best London usage will be liable to be considered as a provincialism" (Read, p. 1165). In *Notions of the Americans* (1828), James Fenimore Cooper claimed that "the people of the United States . . . speak, as a body, an incomparably better English than the people of the Mother country" (pp. 361–362), but he was an exacting critic of the American penchant for euphemism (polite deflation), affectation (linguistic pretense), and "turgid abuse of terms" (*American Democrat,* p. 110). In his chapter "On Language" in *The American Democrat* (1838), Cooper cites departures from British definitions, calling them "popular abuses of significations." For instance, Americans use "park" when they mean "square," "pond" when they mean "lake," and "creek" when they mean "stream." "In pronunciation," Cooper says, "the faults are still more numerous" (p. 111), and he recommends the British pronunciation of "clerk" (clark), "gold" (goold), "lieutenant" (levtenant), and other words as being "more in conformity with polite usage" (p. 112).

Noah Webster came as close as any one person to creating the authority that determines correct usage. But in the absence of an academy or a court, schools were essential in forming and maintaining a national standard. As early as 1789, Webster declared that "nothing but the establishment of schools and some uniformity in the use of books, can annihilate differences in speaking and preserve the purity of the American tongue" (*Dissertations,* p. 19). In providing teachers and shaping the course of study, New England led the way as the region with the most elementary schools, grammar schools, and private academies as well as with the first two American universities, Harvard (1636) and Yale (1701). Of the standard textbooks studied by millions of children in the nineteenth century, the most nationalistic were Webster's *American Spelling Books,* followed by his *Elementary Spelling Book* (1829), which were designed to promote "a uniform national language" (Krapp 1:17). By the 1820s Webster had abandoned his promotion of phonetic spelling, but he established the simplified spellings that distinguish American from British usage, for example, "ax," "wagon," "mold," "medieval," "program," "mask," "check," and "traveled" instead of "axe," "waggon," "mould," "mediaeval," "programme," "masque," "cheque," and "travelled"; and the removal of "u" from "honour," "favour," "neighbour," and the like.

Despite such support for American English, Lindley Murray's *English Grammar, Adapted to the*

Different Classes of Learners, first published in 1795 and based on the British grammar of Robert Lowth, bishop of London, remained the preferred school text for more than fifty years. Murray's belief that the standard of good English should be formed on "the practice of the best and most correct writers . . . corroborated by general usage" (Baron, p. 145) was shared by other American grammarians of the period, such as Samuel Kirkham, Goold Brown, and William Chauncey Fowler, who likewise sought to regulate language through rules and exercises. Grammarians differed about the legitimacy of certain words but uniformly condemned as substandard such locutions as "don't know as," "had went," and "us girls go." Some coinages—"funeralize," "happify," "questionize," "publishment"—were generally reviled before they expired. Other favorite targets of purists became accepted English by the end of the century. For instance, "talented" was at first reviled by both British and American grammarians because it was used as a past participle but did not derive from a verb. Although "talented" was widely regarded as an Americanism, in fact it was coined in England early in the seventeenth century, then fell into obscurity there while it was used with greater frequency in the United States. In 1855 the American Charles Astor Bristed defended it in "The English Language in America," saying that "it is of little use to inveigh against such words" (Mencken, p. 70), and by 1911 it had been sanctioned within the pages of the *Oxford English Dictionary* and inculcated in the speech of both nations. "Reliable," "influential," "lengthy," "jeopardize," and numerous other words have a similar history.

For decades schoolchildren all over the United States studied the "best and most correct writers" in William Holmes McGuffey's Eclectic Reader series, which also contained pronunciation tables and exercises in articulation. Many of the prose selections, drawn from "the purest fountains of English literature," were by British writers of the eighteenth century. The 1853 edition of McGuffey's *Fifth Eclectic Reader* included selections by Joseph Addison, Edmund Burke, Oliver Goldsmith, David Hume, Samuel Johnson, and Robert Walpole. Political writings of Benjamin Franklin, Patrick Henry, and Daniel Webster and seven essays by Washington Irving represented American prose.

An article called "Expression in America" in the May 1857 issue of *Harper's New Monthly Magazine* emphasized the authority of teachers and ministers in promoting a uniform standard of good usage: "Our schools, colleges, and churches are to decide the speech of the new generations, and our popular education is our national academy" (p. 845). *Harper's*

itself—a periodical with a large national circulation, publishing fiction, poetry, and articles of general interest addressed to a wide audience—represented another institution important in forming Americans' linguistic standard. From its first issue in June 1850 the magazine ardently supported the cause of national unity and opposed sectionalism and "barbaric individualism" (January 1861, p. 262). To help readers acquire "a correct knowledge of English" (April 1860, p. 694) and thus to further the goal of "a pure national speech" (May 1857, p. 845), the magazine published reviews and articles that warned against corruption of the language by "verbal inflation" and "stereotyped grandiloquence" (November 1852, p. 780), the bombast of "the spread-eagle style," and the slang and cant generated by newspapers and political campaigns (February 1867, p. 322). Somewhat ironically, perhaps, a large percentage of the literature published in *Harper's* was by English writers, including such superstars as Edward Bulwer-Lytton, Charles Dickens, and William Makepeace Thackeray.

Harper's editors stressed the need of "settling the question now so important to the whole nation: 'What language is to be spoken and written in America?'" (May 1857, p. 845). But by 1850 this question essentially had been answered. The rules of polite usage were well enough fixed to distinguish correct English from the vulgar and unschooled. American and British English would not become separate languages. Prophecies that language in America would become as different from British English as Dutch and Swedish are different from German never came to pass. But American English became clearly distinct from the Standard English of Great Britain by hundreds of well-established differences in vocabulary, idiom, spelling, and pronunciation. By mid-century American English had developed into a rich, unique language born of American inventiveness and the confluence of many cultures, a language flexible and capacious enough to accommodate the constant influx of new words and the controversies they generated, able to contain opposing impulses to expand and to regulate the language. In his essay "America's Mightiest Inheritance," published in 1856 in the newspaper *Life Illustrated,* Walt Whitman extols the American language—"so long in growing, so sturdy and fluent, so appropriate to our America and the genius of its inhabitants."

See also Book Publishing; Colleges; Curricula;
    Dialect; Editors; Education; English Literature;
    Harper's New Monthly Magazine; Literary
    Criticism; Literary Nationalism; Periodicals;
    Publishers; Rhetoric

BIBLIOGRAPHY

Primary Works

Cooper, James Fenimore. *The American Democrat; or, Hints on the Social and Civic Relations of the United States of America*. 1838. Introduction by H. L. Mencken. New York: Knopf, 1931.

Cooper, James Fenimore. *Notions of the Americans: Picked Up by a Travelling Bachelor*. 2 vols. 1828. Edited by Gary Williams. Albany: State University of New York Press, 1991.

Emerson, Ralph Waldo. "The American Scholar." 1837. In *Essays and Journals*. Edited with an introduction by Lewis Mumford. Garden City, N.Y.: Doubleday, 1968.

Harper's New Monthly Magazine. 5, no. 30 (November 1852); 14, no. 84 (May 1857); 20, no. 119 (April 1860); 22, no. 128 (January 1861); 34, no. 201 (February 1867). Brief quotations in the article come from these issues.

Jefferson, Thomas. *The Writings of Thomas Jefferson*. 20 vols. Edited by Andrew A. Lipscomb. Washington, D.C.: Thomas Jefferson Memorial Association of the United States, 1903–1904.

Krapp, George Philip. *The English Language in America*. 2 vols. New York: Century, 1925.

Lowell, James Russell. *The Poetical Works of James Russell Lowell*. Boston: Houghton Mifflin, 1890. Includes both series of *The Biglow Papers*.

Mathews, Mitford M., ed. *The Beginnings of American English: Essays and Comments*. Chicago: University of Chicago Press, 1931.

Mencken, H. L. *The American Language: An Inquiry into the Development of English in the United States*. New York: Knopf, 1919.

North American Review 36, no. 78 (January 1833); 64, no. 134 (January 1847); 69, no. 144 (July 1849); 91, no. 189 (October 1860); 104, no. 214 (January 1867). Brief quotations in the article come from these issues.

Read, Allen Walker. "American Projects for an Academy to Regulate Speech." *PMLA* 51, no. 4 (1936): 1141–1179.

Webster, Noah. *An American Dictionary of the English Language*. 1828. 2 vols. Introduction by Mario Pei. New York: Johnson Reprint Corporation, 1970.

Webster, Noah. *Dissertations on the English Language: With Notes, Historical and Critical, to Which Is Added, by Way of Appendix, an Essay on a Reformed Mode of Spelling, with Dr. Franklin's Arguments on That Subject*. 1789. Introduction by Harry R. Warfel. Gainesville, Fla.: Scholars' Facsimiles and Reprints, 1951.

Whitman, Walt. *New York Dissected: A Sheaf of Recently Discovered Newspaper Articles by the Author of "Leaves of Grass."* Edited by Emory Holloway and Ralph Adimari. New York: Rufus Rockwell Wilson, 1936. Includes the essay "America's Mightiest Inheritance."

Secondary Works

Baron, Dennis E. *Grammar and Good Taste: Reforming the American Language*. New Haven, Conn.: Yale University Press, 1982.

Kramer, Michael P. *Imagining Language in America: From the Revolution to the Civil War*. Princeton, N.J.: Princeton University Press, 1992.

Marckwardt, Albert H. *American English*. 2nd ed. Revised by J. L. Dillard. New York: Oxford University Press, 1980.

Simpson, David. *The Politics of American English, 1776–1850*. New York: Oxford University Press, 1986.

Elsa Nettels

AMERICANS ABROAD

The best-known and most influential works of American travel literature appeared after 1869, when Mark Twain's *Innocents Abroad* appeared to critical and popular acclaim. The *Nation* first published Henry James's writings on the European scene in 1870; his first published volume, *Transatlantic Sketches,* did not appear until five years later. But between 1820 and 1870, travel writings were among the most popular forms of literature read by Americans. The most avidly read works and the largest body of published material concerned the European Continent. Americans had deeply conflicted attitudes about the Old World. It was the source of their civilization, the home of much they wished to emulate. Europe also represented much that Americans despised. As a result of this tension, they produced and consumed a large amount of judgmental literature about Europe. Writers were aware of this and struggled to find a distinctive voice. Twain sought in *Innocents Abroad* to communicate to his readers a sense of travel as if they were experiencing it themselves. Given the sheer volume of published works, it was a challenging task.

Works on other parts of the world were not nearly as popular as European accounts. Fewer Americans traveled to regions like Asia, Africa, and South America. Also there simply was less demand for these works. Americans needed Europe in a way they did not utilize other parts of the world. Europe never represented exclusively the "other" to American audiences. Americans, engaged in a process of self-definition in the early nineteenth century, rejected much of European culture and constructed their own sense of self against it. But they never entirely separated themselves from Western civilization; to be an American was, in part, to be a European. This ambivalence is particularly notable among travelers to Great Britain but is present in those to the Continent as well. Accounts of Asia, other parts of the Americas, and Africa seldom possess this dual quality. They were more completely the "other," so they had less to offer readers as they considered what it meant to be an American. Even so, books and articles about non-European travel were published and read in the 1820–1870 period.

Scanning the travel books and articles penned by Americans over this fifty-year period, one might be led to believe that everyone who boarded a boat published an account of his or her experiences. In fact, only a small fraction did so. These literary representations are an important source of information about Europe and Americans, but they have their limitations. Published writings could not be as candid as private writings. Sexual behavior, gossip, and other titillating matters could not be discussed openly. These taboos explain much of the banality of travel literature. Wary of candor, authors retreated to safe topics: the dimensions of Saint Peter's, the history of Holyrood Castle, contrasts between English and French national character. Nevertheless, the differences between published narratives and "authentic" private jottings can be exaggerated. Letters and diaries were likely to be distributed among friends and family. And books and articles were hardly bereft of opinion: they reveal many of the issues that preoccupied Americans during this period, such as anti-Catholicism, cultural nationalism, and the significance of European revolutions.

WHO, WHAT, WHERE, AND WHY

Records from consular visits, port records, and notices of ships' arrivals and departures indicate that tens of thousands of Americans traveled abroad from 1820 to 1870. Their reasons for doing so were accordingly diverse. Some relocated there entirely, such as the South Carolinian John Izard Middleton, who married the daughter of a Swiss banker and lived in Paris. Expatriates were a tiny fraction of the community abroad, however. The vast majority of travelers returned home at some point, although their reasons for leaving it varied widely. Physicians prescribed salt air and a change of scenery for consumptives and the seriously ill. Business travel propelled thousands of men overseas. The trade-show movement, which culminated in the 1851 Great Exhibition in London that featured the Crystal Palace, signified the growing importance of business travel, although these shows also attracted many tourists.

Many other Americans traveled abroad in pursuit of education. Artists, of course, congregated in Paris, Rome, and Florence to learn painting and sculpture. During the nineteenth century the centers of medical education shifted away from Edinburgh and London to Paris and later on to Germany. Other American visitors studied law, but most simply sought a more advanced education than could be obtained in the United States. In the mid-nineteenth century, this desire spurred an especially intense student emigration to Göttingen and other German universities. Reform-minded Americans sailed overseas to participate in the numerous meetings and conventions that bound together the transatlantic benevolent empire. Missions drew others abroad, and this cohort represented a disproportionate share of travelers to non-European destinations. Tourism, finally, propelled others overseas. Some engaged in a full-fledged grand tour of several months or even years, traveling from city to city and exploiting letters of recommendation to penetrate high society. Others enjoyed a more modest regimen of a few weeks, rushing from capital to capital via diligence, carriage, or rail, their noses never far from their guidebooks.

This last form of travel, perhaps better labeled tourism, became especially popular in the post-1840 period, when the growth of the middle class and the maturation of transoceanic steamships vastly increased the number and diversity of American travelers. The wars of the French Revolution and Napoleonic era had discouraged overseas travel among Americans and Britons. The coming of peace in 1815 inaugurated a rush of travel abroad. Even so, as the rationales for travel listed above suggest, the vast majority of discretionary travelers in the early nineteenth century were men of means. Sailors in the navy and merchant marine constituted the only significant group of working-class travelers in this period. Overseas travel was an expensive endeavor, out of the reach of all but the well-to-do until the middle of the nineteenth century.

As the social class profile of Americans abroad diversified after 1840, so did its gender distribution. More and more women joined their husbands and fathers on their business and leisure excursions. By the 1860s thousands of women and men were sailing and steaming overseas every year. The Civil War interrupted this trend, but Robert E. Lee and Ulysses S. Grant had hardly parted company at Appomattox when rates of travel began to approach antebellum levels; it soon far exceeded them. But the post-1870 differences were also qualitative. Americans encountered the world in different ways than they had before. They evidenced more interest in areas outside Europe, but they increasingly did so through imperial eyes.

Their views of Europe were different as well. Postwar travelers, representatives of a confident, muscular America, believed they had less to learn from Europe than had their predecessors. A voyage there became more a token of gentility, a tourist practice, than a genuine encounter.

Most Americans traveling abroad in 1820–1870 visited Europe. But they distributed their favors unequally. Early in the century travelers tended to follow the route of the conventional British grand tour, with the significant addition of Britain itself. Great Britain was the single most popular destination. Most travelers seem to have ignored the pleas of literary nationalists, who urged Americans to match political independence from Britain with cultural autonomy. What is more, republican Americans displayed an unseemly interest in the trappings of monarchy and aristocracy. There was acute competition to be presented at court. Americans also visited Scotland with great frequency and to a lesser extent Ireland. When Americans visited Ireland after 1840, the experience usually served to confirm anti-Irish and anti-Catholic prejudices.

Beyond Britain, Americans could be found in large numbers in France and Italy north of Naples—again the conventional route of the grand tour. Many travelers also sailed the Rhine and toured parts of Germany. Other corners of Europe were more poorly represented on travelers' itineraries. Spain, the subject of one of the antebellum era's most interesting travel accounts, James Johnston Pettigrew's (1828–1863) *Notes on Spain and the Spaniards* (1861), seems to have been less popular than Germany. Less visited still were eastern Europe, Turkey, and Russia, although a few intrepid folk made their way there every year. The Holy Land and Egypt, which were not significant destinations in the early decades of the century, became popular toward the middle of the century, when accounts such as John Lloyd Stephens's (1805–1852) *Incidents of Travel in Egypt, Arabia Petraea, and the Holy Land* (1837) made these regions seem accessible.

PREPARATION

Women and men had at their disposal a variety of sources designed to help them prepare for their travels. There was the genre of travel literature itself, of course; books purchased and borrowed from libraries as well as the innumerable shorter accounts in newspapers and magazines were invaluable sources of information on transportation, lodging, and sightseeing. So pervasive was this literature, in fact, that it was often hard for travelers to experience a journey abroad as a process of discovery, as travelogues were not shy about telling their readers what they ought to see and what they ought to think about it. For this reason European travel constituted one of the most constructed and ritual-laden practices in nineteenth-century American culture.

Most of the reading material consulted by Americans preparing to travel overseas during the mid-nineteenth century was not domestic but British. Few travelers employed American-authored guidebooks. Americans in Paris favored the guides to the city published annually by Galignani's, the English bookstore. Beginning in the 1830s the most popular travelogues employed by Americans were published by the London house of John Murray (1808–1892). They were comprehensive and accurate (Murray encouraged his readers to write in with corrections). Murray's handbooks stressed practical information, such as stage schedules and rates, notes on passports and currency, hours of operation for museums, palaces, and other attractions, and locations of hotels. But Murray as well as his main rival Baedeker, went beyond the practical. They shaped travelers' experiences by offering interpretations of artworks, comments on national and regional character, and judgments of religion and culture. That all this was offered from a British perspective (in Murray's case) does not seem to have bothered American travelers, whose loyalty to these guides persisted despite the increased availability of American-published books, such as George Palmer Putnam's (1814–1872) *The Tourist in Europe* (1838).

Imaginative literature was a second genre that influenced how Americans confronted the outside world. British works remained more popular than domestic productions during the mid-century period. Shakespeare was the most important touchstone for travelers to England. Nearly as many Americans visited Scotland as England; the main literary lights here were Robert Burns and Sir Walter Scott. Travelers were more likely to take a pilgrimage to Melrose than to Stratford-on-Avon. George Gordon, Lord Byron, was the favored cicerone to Italy; his description of the Vatican appears to have been particularly vivid to judge by how often travelers to the Holy See cited it. Germaine de Staël's (1766–1817) *Corinne* (1807) shaped perspectives toward Italy in a more general way, by offering a morally tinged contrast between North and South. Her *De l'Allemagne* (1810) was less influential if only because Germany was a less-common destination than Italy.

European writing about the United States also shaped travelers' approaches to foreign experiences. Americans raged over the slights of Frances Trollope

(1780–1863) and Basil Hall (1788–1844) regarding their fast-eating, tobacco juice–spitting, money-grubbing ways. Travelers were keenly sensitive about this literature. Their fixation upon mumbling orators in the House of Lords, hordes of beggars in Naples, and Parisian infidelity represented, in part, payback to European critics of the United States. But they also took this literature seriously for its admonitory lessons. They monitored their own behavior closely. Americans abroad strove to be models of republican gentility, possessed of all the qualities of true refinement shorn of European vices. They tried to be sophisticated, believing that even the most obliging European secretly thought they were barely civilized. They also monitored each other against aristocratic envy, which might be interpreted by Europeans as a sign of national weakness. This responsiveness to Old World opinion was powerful testimony in favor of a central charge of critics like Trollope—that of American cultural insecurity vis-à-vis the Old World.

PORTRAYALS BY AND OF AMERICANS ABROAD

These attitudes guaranteed that literary representations of Americans abroad would be unusually complex. Although American journals regularly reviewed European travelogues, the British less often returned the favor. The English tended to dismiss accounts by Americans abroad as crudely patriotic—as, in fact, many of them were. Although the volume of travel writing defies simple distinctions, in general one's portrayal of Americans abroad depended on where the author came down on the question of national exceptionalism. The heirs of John Winthrop tended to represent Americans abroad as virtuous pilgrims in lands of vice, ignorance, poverty, and despotism. Those who endorsed cultural engagement with the Old World were less Manichaean (with a dual worldview, seeing things as either good or evil), although not many were so daring as to grant Europe moral equivalence with the United States. A few writers did tip the moral scales squarely in favor of Europe. William Wells Brown's (1815–1894) *American Fugitive in Europe* (1855) was exceptional in foreshadowing the expatriate literature of the next century, where the sensitive American is at home only away from his or her own shores. Such a view was very much the exception; only a few figures could muster a strong enough sense of alienation to portray it compellingly. Even Frederick Douglass's fugitive writings possess a core of patriotism that makes even such an alienated American a stranger abroad.

Most Americans abroad fell within the poles of expatriate and hyper-patriot. A significant number of travelers found themselves too overawed by what they saw to maintain a pretense of sophistication or hostility. Such is the disarming quality of the best-selling author Bayard Taylor (1825–1878), whose *Views A-foot* (1847) portrays the American as a kind of parched cultural consumer. Other works took this self-consciousness as their point of departure. James Fenimore Cooper's (1789–1851) *Home as Found* (1838) finds Americans returning from Europe lauded as hajji—participants in a pilgrimage, possessed of special qualities by virtue of their contact with the divine. Cooper's portrayal is unusually complicated because, while he sought to make fun of this phenomenon, he clearly believed that a certain class of Americans who had traveled abroad really was more worthy than regular folks. In Augusta Jane Evans's (1835–1909) *Beulah* (1859) there is little sense of travelers returning with a halo; young men fresh from the Continent marry badly, fall into drink, and fritter away their fortunes. Cooper and Evans each applied a jaundiced eye to both aspects of the American abroad. Their American was neither the eager consumer of refinement portrayed by Taylor nor the embittered realist as written by William Wells Brown. "Abroad" was likewise a more complex category, more morally ambivalent than most of their fellow Americans were, in this middle point in the nineteenth century, prepared to admit. Yet both pointed dumbly toward the future, away from the romantic nationalism that inspired many travelers to find in foreign climes the roots of American greatness and uniqueness, toward the uncertain, calculating modernism of James, Twain, and Henry Adams.

See also Education; English Literature; Leisure; Travel Writing; Tourism

BIBLIOGRAPHY
Primary Works
Brown, William Wells. *The American Fugitive in Europe: Sketches of Places and People Abroad.* Boston: John P. Jewett, 1855.

Cooper, James Fenimore. *Home as Found.* 1838. Introduction by Lewis Leary. New York: Capricorn Books, 1961.

Evans, Augusta Jane. *Beulah.* 1859. Edited with an introduction by Elizabeth Fox-Genovese. Baton Rouge: Louisiana State University Press, 1992.

James, Henry, Jr. *Transatlantic Sketches.* Boston: J. R. Osgood, 1875.

Pettigrew, James Johnston. *Notes on Spain and the Spaniards, in the Summer of 1859, with a Glance at Sardinia.* Charleston, S.C.: Evans and Cogswell, 1861.

Putnam, George Palmer. *The Tourist in Europe; or, A Concise Summary of the Various Routes, Objects of Interest, &c. in Great Britain, France, Switzerland, Italy, Germany, Belgium, and Holland.* New York: Wiley and Putnam, 1838.

Staël, Germaine Anne-Louise de. *De l'Allemagne.* 1810. Paris: Charpentier, 1869.

Staël, Madame de. *Corinne; or, Italy.* 1807. Translated and edited by Sylvia Raphael, introduction by John Isbell. New York: Oxford University Press, 1998.

Stevens, John Lloyd. *Incidents of Travel in Egypt, Arabia Petraea, and the Holy Land.* New York: Harper & Brothers, 1837.

Taylor, Bayard. *Views A-foot; or, Europe Seen with a Knapsack and Staff.* Boston: J. Knight, 1848.

Twain, Mark. *The Innocents Abroad.* 1869. Introduction by Mordecai Richler, afterword by David E. E. Sloane. New York: Oxford University Press, 1996.

Secondary Works

Buzard, James. *The Beaten Track: European Tourism, Literature, and the Ways to Culture, 1800–1918.* New York and Oxford: Oxford University Press, 1993.

Kilbride, Daniel. "Travel, Ritual, and National Identity: Planters on the European Tour, 1820–1860." *Journal of Southern History* 69 (2003): 549–584.

Stowe, William W. *Going Abroad: European Travel in Nineteenth-Century American Culture.* Princeton, N.J.: Princeton University Press, 1994.

Vance, William L. *America's Rome.* 2 vols. New Haven, Conn.: Yale University Press, 1989.

Ziff, Larzer. *Return Passages: Great American Travel Writing, 1780–1910.* New Haven, Conn.: Yale University Press, 2000.

Daniel Kilbride

"THE AMERICAN SCHOLAR"

Ralph Waldo Emerson's (1803–1882) famous essay, which has come to be regarded, in Oliver Wendell Holmes's phrase, as "America's intellectual declaration of independence," almost did not happen. Its occasion was the annual Phi Beta Kappa Society lecture at the Harvard College commencement on 31 August 1837, and Emerson was drafted to speak after the society's original choice, an Episcopalian minister named Jonathan Wainwright, declined. The society was probably looking for something more conservative and less provocative than what they got from Emerson, for Wainwright's most recent publication was

a tract titled *Inequality of Individual Wealth—the Ordinance of Providence and Essential to Civilization.* At the least, most of the audience would have expected to hear praise for the venerable traditions of scholarship and learning at Harvard, not to be told that "books are for the scholar's idle times" or that "instead of Man Thinking, we have the bookworm" (pp. 91, 89). Still, there were eager listeners who caught the drift of Emerson's radical notion that the true sources of learning and culture lay within the individual. At their urging he had five hundred copies of his talk printed, at his own expense, rather blandly titled "An Oration, Delivered before the Phi Beta Kappa Society at Cambridge, August 31, 1837." The little pamphlet sold out within a month. When Emerson reprinted it for the 1849 collection *Nature, Addresses, and Lectures,* he changed the title to the more familiar and more accurate "The American Scholar."

By "scholar," it is important to note, he did not primarily mean a haunter of libraries with a narrow range of specialization but rather something like what we might call a public intellectual—that is, a person of learning who by his or her writing plays an active and thoughtful role in society. And, by extension, he speaks to every reader's intellectual life and the roles we all play or should play as "Man Thinking." The "American" part of the title needs qualification too, for except in the somewhat formulaic beginning and a brief (but important) section at the end, Emerson is more concerned with the universal elements of the scholar's education and duties than with any national or nationalistic aspects of his subject.

BACKGROUND AND CONTEXT

Although the invitation came to Emerson just two months before he was to deliver the address, he had been thinking about writing something on "The Duty & Discipline of a Scholar" for at least two years. Characteristically, many of the passages in the address first appeared in his journals during the years and months before its actual composition in the summer of 1837. The topic had broad and deep relevance to his own condition, for he had resigned his formal ministry in 1832 to set out upon his career as a lecturer and author. Leaving the security, the certainty, and the traditions of the Unitarian ministry for the untried world of public and secular discourse gave Emerson ample impetus to ponder his new vocation. His decision, and the essay on the scholar that in some ways grows out of it, also mark a moment of transition in American cultural and literary history, for Emerson is himself a representative man in the shifting of the intellectual and cultural center of gravity from the clergy to the lay intellectual and writer. With the proliferation of lyceums and other lecture venues, magazines, books, and newspapers in the 1840s and 1850s, it was possible for the first time to think of a career in letters that began somewhere else than in the pulpit.

"The American Scholar" was also the first of what we can now see were three major efforts Emerson made to apply the principles he had announced the previous year in his first book, *Nature* (1836), to specific issues and problems in American culture. As the oration takes up the problem of the place of learning and the role of the scholar/writer in American life, "The Divinity School Address," delivered the following year to a much more hostile reception at Harvard, critiques the failures of religion—specifically the errors of Christianity as reflected in the beliefs of New England Unitarianism. And "Self-Reliance," published in 1841, wrestles with the central problem of life for Emerson: the oppositional relationship that exists between society and the individual and the necessity that the individual base his or her life on the promptings of spirit.

This effort by Emerson to address specific social and cultural problems existed in the context of a general sense, shared by many intellectuals, that major reforms were called for in social relations, in institutions, in people themselves. When Emerson had called in 1836, in *Nature,* for people to cease "grop[ing] among the dry bones of the past" and to "demand our own works and laws and worship" (p. 3) he was unwittingly stepping out in front of a parade that would lead in the next decade to radical efforts to reform every aspect of American life, from diet and health to marriage, religion, economic principles, gender relations, and slavery. There was a sense of urgency in the air too in the late summer of 1837, for the country as a whole was plunging into one of the worst financial panics and depressions of the century. To many it seemed that the very fabric of society and the economy itself were at risk. Emerson himself regarded the depression as proof of the folly of America's single-minded pursuit of wealth and material success. "The world has failed," he noted in his journal; it was a propitious time to reassert the claims of the life of the mind.

STRUCTURE AND THEMES

Emerson begins his address with a polite nod to the tradition of such talks on the role and especially the future of learning and the arts in America, but he quickly separates himself from the traditional celebratory and jingoistic tone of such performances. He does not praise American cultural productions but

instead wishes that the "sluggard intellect of this continent" would awake and produce "something better than the exertions of mechanical skill," a clear jibe at the anti-intellectualism and the practical, materialistic bent of American life (p. 81). Then, as he typically does at the beginning of his essays, Emerson attempts to ground his discourse in an appeal to common experience, in this case the sense of incompleteness and isolation that follows upon the specialization of roles in society. He recounts the fable that "the gods, in the beginning, divided man into men, that he might be more helpful to himself." "The fable implies," Emerson goes on, "that the individual to possess himself, must sometimes return from his own labor to embrace all the other laborers. But unfortunately, this original unit, this fountain of power, has been so distributed in multitudes, has been so minutely subdivided and peddled out, that it is spilled into drops, and cannot be gathered." What we have then, in "the *divided* or social state," is a condition in which "Man is thus metamorphosed into a thing, into many things," but is nowhere complete (pp. 82, 83).

In this scheme the ideal of "Man Thinking," that is, the intellectual and creative facets of the individual self, are wrongly delegated to the scholar. But it is worth noting that this fable and Emerson's interpretation of it also link up to the economic developments of the age and in particular to the financial crisis brought on by the panic of 1837. Emerson describes here a kind of transcendental version of what Karl Marx, a few years later in Europe, would call the alienation of labor, the dis-ease brought on by industrialization and specialization, where the worker has no sense of a whole task or a whole product completed because he is relegated to some partial and repetitive function within a large-scale industrial operation. Emerson is not finally concerned with such a materialist economic analysis, but he is responding with some urgency, as so many writers did, to the increasingly complex, urban, and industrial drift of nineteenth-century society.

After this introduction, the first half of the essay is devoted to an elaboration of the principal formative influences on the scholar's development. Still influenced by his preacherly habit of numbering the points of his discourse, Emerson divides this section of the essay with roman numerals to signal the three major influences: nature, books (or what Emerson calls "the mind of the Past"), and action. What is noteworthy about this list, of course, is the demotion of books and formal learning to a secondary position in the hierarchy of influences. Or, conversely, the elevation of nature to the primary position. Of course, those familiar with Emerson's little book *Nature* would not be surprised. And the sense in

The First Parish meetinghouse, where Emerson delivered "The American Scholar" lecture. Lithograph by James Kidder, c. 1830. COURTESY OF THE BOSTON ATHENAEUM

which Emerson thinks of nature as a teacher to the potential scholar, "this school-boy under the bending dome of day" (p. 86), corresponds to the uses of nature—commodity, beauty, language, and discipline—as he enumerates and describes them in *Nature*. Particularly he has in mind the last of these uses, "discipline," by which he means something like "teaching": nature teaches us through its immense richness and variety and invites us to probe and fathom its complexity through our lower intellectual faculty, the Understanding. But nature also appeals to our higher faculty, the Reason, to intuit underlying truths and the divine laws that animate all creation. Referring to the process of sealing an envelope with a wax seal imprinted on the paper, Emerson employs one of his most resonant metaphors to describe the relation between nature and the mind or spirit that brings it forth: "He shall see that nature is the opposite of the soul, answering to it part for part. One is seal, and one is print." And thus, as he concludes, "the ancient precept, 'Know thyself,' and the modern precept, 'study nature,' become at last one maxim" (pp. 86, 87).

The next section of Emerson's discourse takes up the education of the scholar by books ("the mind of the Past"), in what must have been to his auditors the most surprising if not the most perverse part of his address. Not only is this traditional mainstay of education relegated to second place, as it were, but book learning also undergoes further disparagement. The problem of the book, for Emerson, is the same problem that attaches to any doctrine or form; it supplants the original thought or spirit that created it: "The sacredness which attaches to the act of creation,—the act of thought,—is instantly transferred to the record. . . . Instantly, the book becomes noxious. The guide is a tyrant" (pp. 88–89). Books thus become a bar to original thought, and traditional education becomes an exercise in imitation. The right use, indeed the only legitimate use of books is to inspire, to prompt us to think originally or, as Emerson phrases it more boldly, to "read God directly" (p. 91). If this last notion made some in the audience uneasy, as verging on heresy, it would get worse, for Emerson would return to Harvard the following year and, in his speech to the divinity school students, employ this same critique of the book to attack orthodox Christianity and its reliance on a literal interpretation of the Bible.

Lest one think, on the basis of this principle, that one can simply do without books or formal education, Emerson ends this section with an important caveat that puts us all back in the classroom: "Of course, there is a portion of reading quite indispensable to a wise man. History and exact science he must learn by laborious reading." Yet even here, in getting back to basics, Emerson has a dig for Harvard: speaking of colleges, he says, "they can only serve us, when they aim not to drill, but to create" (p. 93). Because the traditional Harvard pedagogy involved endless numbing recitations sections, his implication is clear.

The third influence on the scholar's development is action, and by his emphasis on this requirement Emerson seeks to counter the stereotype, especially common in nineteenth-century America, that intellectuals reside in ivory towers and shirk the rough-and-tumble of ordinary life and work. The ground for the scholar's action is the same principle that Emerson announces in the "Nature" section of the essay: nature and the world correspond to the self and provide the tangible means to both self-knowledge and productive action: "The world,—this shadow of the soul or *other me,* lies wide around. Its attractions are the keys which unlock my thoughts and make me acquainted with myself. I launch eagerly into this resounding tumult" (p. 95). Besides, thought and action participate in what Emerson calls "That great principle of Undulation" or Polarity, by which apparently opposite qualities actually depend upon one another and call one another into being. This principle is "ingrained in every atom" and partakes of the overarching polarity of Power and Form in life, as Emerson would sketch it in "Experience" a few years later (p. 98).

The education of the scholar completed, it remains for Emerson to sketch his duties and to address the larger issue of how to solve the problem of Americans' long-standing sense of cultural inferiority with respect to Europe. His duties are rather easily dispensed with; they are conveyed in a sort of pep talk that Emerson addresses to the audience (and to himself) out of his own experience and hopes for his fledgling career as public intellectual. Though the scholar is liable to suffer disdain, poverty, and solitude in keeping on the right track, eventually he emerges as a hero:

> He is to resist the vulgar prosperity that retrogrades ever to barbarism, by preserving and communicating heroic sentiments, noble biographies, melodious verse, and the conclusions of history. Whatsoever oracles the human heart in all emergencies, in all

solemn hours has uttered as its commentary on the world of actions,—these he shall receive and impart. (Pp. 101–102)

The concluding section of the essay is devoted to an anatomy of the power that the American scholar will need to draw upon to produce this transformative effect on culture. This power comes from a simple yet profound shift in how culture itself is defined and conceived: "This revolution," Emerson says, "is to be wrought by the gradual domestication of the idea of culture. The main enterprise of the world for splendor, for extent, is the upbuilding of a man" (p. 107). In thus locating the source of culture within the individual—a radical "domestication" if ever there was one—Emerson disposes of the principal negative condition that had stood in the way of America's cultural independence and maturity. Suddenly, instead of looking to Europe we could simply look within. The embarrassing disparity between the long history of European cultural production and the paucity of the same in the United States could be transcended or rendered moot by the realization that Culture with a capital "C" did not consist of the monuments and artifacts stored in museums or libraries but in the potential for self-culture within the individual. This is "domestication" in a double sense: domestic as opposed to foreign, and domestic as pertaining to the individual and the internal as opposed to the public and the external. This subtle but profound shift in the conception of the sources, the expression, and the transmission of high culture is what distinguished Emerson's call for American literary independence from the myriad of such pronouncements that preceded it. This is the foundation of Emerson's claim at the beginning of the essay that "our long apprenticeship to the learning of other lands, draws to a close" (p. 81), and his assertion, at the end of the essay, that "We have listened too long to the courtly muses of Europe" (p. 114).

Another sense of this domestication pertains to the subject matter of American art and the artist's treatment of materials. There follows from Emerson's individual basis of culture, which in turn comes from a belief in each person's ability to access the divine and its manifestations in the world, a democratizing and anti-hierarchical turn in the arts. Interestingly Emerson sees this trend as already having happened, not as prospective: "the same movement which effected the elevation of what was called the lowest class in the state, assumed in literature a very marked and as benign an aspect. Instead of the sublime and the beautiful, the near, the low, the common, was explored and poetized" (p. 110). Thus Emerson does not so much predict the radical democratic practice of Walt Whitman and the realists as look back to English poets of the previous century and early-nineteenth-century Romantics: "this idea has inspired the genius of Goldsmith, Burns, Cowper, and in a newer time, of Goethe, Wordsworth, and Carlyle" (p. 112). There is no call yet, as there would be a few years later in "The Poet," for poets to sing specifically American songs celebrating the richness and diversity of the United States, and there are no Americans in Emerson's list of literary models. Instead there is a kind of generic invocation of the ordinary—"the meal in the firkin; the milk in the pan; the ballad in the street; the news of the boat"—none of which has a specifically American valence (p. 111). In fact, that already archaic word "firkin" signals that Emerson is chiefly thinking along pre-existing literary lines, much as his own poetry, for all the radical implications of his theory, remains largely grounded in conventional poetic diction and forms.

Nevertheless, "The American Scholar" gave American intellectuals and would-be writers a firm basis for overcoming their sense of cultural inferiority with respect to Europe and especially England. Neither the immediate prospects for literature nor the materialistic obsessions of contemporary business culture (in which idealistic young people have no choice but to "turn drudges, or die of disgust") were promising, but the long-range outlook, based on nature, self-culture, and a healthy skepticism about received wisdom, was hopeful (p. 114).

See also Education; "Experience"; Literary Nationalism; *Nature;* "The Poet"; "Self-Reliance"; Transcendentalism

BIBLIOGRAPHY
Primary Works
Emerson, Ralph Waldo. "The American Scholar." 1837. In *The Complete Works of Ralph Waldo Emerson,* centenary edition, 12 vols., edited by E. W. Emerson, pp. 81–115. Boston and New York: Houghton Mifflin, 1903.

Emerson, Ralph Waldo. *Nature.* 1836. In *The Complete Works of Ralph Waldo Emerson,* centenary edition, 12 vols., edited by E. W. Emerson, pp. 3–77. Boston and New York: Houghton Mifflin, 1903.

Secondary Works
Buell, Lawrence. *Emerson.* Cambridge, Mass.: Harvard University Press, 2003.

Burkholder, Robert E. "The Radical Emerson: Politics in 'The American Scholar.'" *ESQ: A Journal of the American Renaissance* 34 (1988): 37–57.

Packer, Barbara. *Emerson's Fall: A New Interpretation of the Major Essays.* New York: Continuum, 1982.

Richardson, Robert D., Jr. *Emerson: The Mind on Fire.* Berkeley: University of California Press, 1995.

Robinson, David. *Apostle of Culture: Emerson as Preacher and Lecturer.* Philadelphia: University of Pennsylvania Press, 1982.

Sacks, Kenneth S. *Understanding Emerson: "The American Scholar" and His Struggle for Self-Reliance.* Princeton, N.J.: Princeton University Press, 2003.

Sealts, Merton M., Jr. *Emerson on the Scholar.* Columbia: University of Missouri Press, 1992.

Robert Sattelmeyer

AN APPEAL IN FAVOR OF THAT CLASS OF AMERICANS CALLED AFRICANS

An Appeal in Favor of That Class of Americans Called Africans by Lydia Maria Child (1802–1880) provoked a storm of controversy when published in 1833. A prominent Massachusetts politician hurled the book out of the window with a pair of fire tongs. The Boston Athenaeum rescinded the free library privileges the trustees had conferred on Child. Former patrons among the Boston elite slammed their doors in Child's face and cut her dead in the streets. Most disastrous for a woman who supported herself and her husband with her pen, the sales of her books plummeted. The outrage Child's *Appeal* aroused indicates how deeply entrenched the slave system and the racist ideology upholding it were in the nation's political, economic, and social life—and how much courage the book's thirty-one-year-old author displayed by challenging the "peculiar institution" at the risk of forfeiting her literary popularity and her livelihood.

CHILD'S CAREER BEFORE THE *APPEAL*
Over the nine years since she had risen to fame on the wings of her daring maiden novel, *Hobomok, A Tale of Early Times* (1824), centering around a Puritan woman who marries an Indian and bears him a son, Child had enjoyed intoxicating success. Only a month before the *Appeal* came off the press, the nation's preeminent journal of letters, the *North American Review,* had hailed her as "just the woman we want for the mothers and daughters of the present generation" (July 1833, p. 139). Child had earned this accolade by producing works that filled widely recognized cultural needs: historical fiction that contributed to creating a distinctively American literature; a children's magazine, the *Juvenile Miscellany* (1826–1834), that molded a generation of New England youth; a pair of best-selling

domestic advice books oriented toward women of modest means, *The Frugal Housewife* (1829) and *The Mother's Book* (1831); and a series of women's biographies that offered readers a range of role models suitable for an era of social change.

In tackling the explosive issue of slavery, Child was once again addressing an urgent cultural need, but this time, as she noted in the preface to the *Appeal,* she knew she could expect "ridicule and censure" rather than acclaim (p. 5). Although Child's hitherto adoring public regarded her as a defector for championing the cause of a despised people, a close reader might have discerned presages of the *Appeal* in the intermarriage plot of Hobomok and in her children's writings, where she expressed sympathy for all peoples of color, spoke out against slavery, and introduced ideas of racial equality. One close reader, the abolitionist William Lloyd Garrison (1805–1879), even discerned the bold social criticism embedded in the essays appended to *The Frugal Housewife,* which he pronounced "worthy of the strongest intellect of the most sagacious politician" (*Genius,* p. 6).

It was Garrison who recruited Child in June 1830 to the antislavery movement he was then starting to build. As she later recalled, "He got hold of the strings of my conscience, and pulled me into Reforms" (*Selected Letters,* p. 558). In response, Child dedicated her literary talents to supplying what the new movement lacked: a comprehensive textbook examining the slavery question from every angle—historical, legal, economic, political, racial, and moral. Her research for the project consumed three years, during which she read a staggering array of scholarly and polemical works and mined the weekly newspaper Garrison founded in January 1831, *The Liberator,* for up-to-date information.

THE *APPEAL* AND THE GENRE OF ABOLITIONIST POLEMIC

In designing the *Appeal,* Child could turn to no models for the compendium she envisaged. The closest analogues, both published in 1808, the year England and the United States outlawed the African slave trade, were the British abolitionist Thomas Clarkson's two-volume *History* of the traffic and the long campaign against it, on which Child drew extensively in her first chapter, and the French Enlightenment scholar Henri Grégoire's *An Enquiry concerning the Intellectual and Moral Faculties, and Literature of Negroes,* which formed the basis of her sixth chapter. Of American antislavery tracts, only a handful existed before the *Appeal,* all more limited in focus. The Reverend John Rankin's *Letters on*

American Slavery (1826) provided vivid eyewitness testimony that Child quoted to illustrate the tortures to which slaves were subjected and the sadism "this diabolical system" unleashed in the "slave-owner." The African American David Walker's fiery *Appeal* (1829) and Garrison's *Thoughts on African Colonization* (1832), which together inspired Child's fifth chapter, presented thoroughgoing critiques of the scheme to send the free black population back to Africa, touted as a means of gradually ending slavery.

More ambitious in scope than either its predecessors or its successors, Child's *Appeal* also differs strikingly in style and substance from other white American abolitionist tracts, including the many that bear witness to its influence. Unlike Amos A. Phelps's

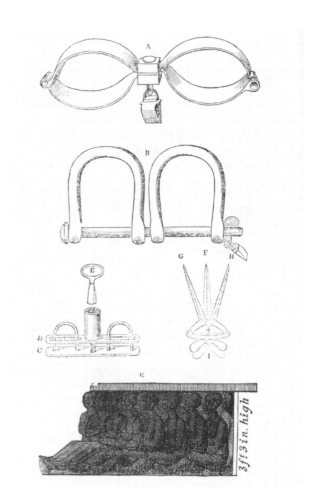

Illustration of instruments of torture and representation of the packing of slaves in the hold of the typical slave ship. From *An Appeal in Favor of That Class of Americans Called Africans.* The original caption read "Th[is] engraving . . . will help to give a vivid idea of the Elysium enjoyed by negroes, during the Middle Passage." GRADUATE LIBRARY, UNIVERSITY OF MICHIGAN

Lectures on Slavery and Its Remedy (1834), William Ellery Channing's *Slavery* (1835), Angelina Grimké's *Appeal to the Christian Women of the South* (1836), and Theodore Dwight Weld's *The Bible against Slavery* (1837), the *Appeal* relies very sparingly on religious and scriptural arguments. Unlike Weld in *American Slavery As It Is* (1839), Child relegates incidents of cruelty to a minor place in the *Appeal*. Unlike Grimké, Child emphasizes rational rather than emotional persuasion, cultivates a political discourse that is more masculine than feminine, and targets a gender-mixed rather than a female audience. And unlike abolitionist tract writers generally, not excepting Richard Hildreth, whose *Despotism in America* (1840) amplifies the *Appeal*'s economic and political analysis, Child looks beyond the issue of slavery to the larger imperative of ending discrimination against free African Americans. In short, the *Appeal*'s most distinctive and enduring feature is its indictment of racism, which governs four out of eight chapters, recurs as a subtheme elsewhere in the book, and shapes Child's argument throughout.

OVERVIEW OF THE *APPEAL*

Organized with flawless logic, Child's pathbreaking textbook on slavery and race moves from past to present, from history to political economy, from fact to argument, from problem to solution. It opens with a "Brief History of Negro Slavery.—Its Inevitable Effect upon All Concerned in It" (chapter 1) and continues with a "Comparative View of Slavery, in Different Ages and Nations" (chapter 2). Occupying almost a third of the volume's two hundred–plus pages, these chapters situate American slavery in a worldwide context that encompasses ancient Israel, Greece, and Rome as well as Africa, the Caribbean, and Latin America. Through a detailed analysis of the laws regulating slavery in the civilizations she covers, Child shows that "modern slavery . . . in all its particulars, is more odious than the ancient; and . . . that the condition of slaves has always been worse just in proportion to the freedom enjoyed by their masters" (p. 36). As the most democratic society in history, the United States has the most stringent slave codes, she underscores, precisely because "slavery is so inconsistent with free institutions, and the spirit of liberty is so contagious under such institutions" that brutal repression is necessary to deter revolt (p. 70). Child also devotes special attention to the ways the laws sustaining slavery systematically "degrade" free people of color, setting them "below the level" of slaves, giving "a positive inducement to violent and vicious white men to oppress and injure people of color" and making "a negro . . . the slave of every white man in

the community" (pp. 62, 50; an insight that would prove even more relevant to the post-Emancipation era, when lynching replaced slavery as a mechanism for keeping African Americans subjugated).

After her geohistorical survey Child explores the economics and politics of the slavery controversy. Chapter 3, "Free Labor and Slave Labor.—Possibility of Safe Emancipation," counters fears that emancipation would entail economic ruin and insurrectionary violence. Abolishing slavery would actually benefit the South economically, Child contends, because free workers perform more efficiently than slaves, as the North's prosperity and the South's backwardness testify. Similarly, she cites evidence that "slavery causes insurrections, while emancipation prevents them," pointing out that the abolition of slavery did not trigger a bloodbath either in the northern states or in other countries and that the notorious St. Domingo uprising had occurred only when the French had tried "to restore slavery" there (p. 80). The real threat to the nation, Child shows in chapter 4, "Influence of Slavery on the Politics of the United States," lies in the South's political dominance and determination to further its own interest at all costs. Thanks to the constitutional clause allowing states to count three-fifths of their slave population in fixing their allotment of congressional seats, the South has acquired "entire control of the national policy" and has used that control "to protect and extend slave power" (pp. 103, 104), Child asserts in an early formulation of what historians call the "slave power thesis."

Having defined the problem, Child turns to the solution. In her pivotal chapter, "Colonization Society, and Anti-Slavery Society," placed at the center of the book, Child examines the contrasting remedies the two organizations propose: gradual emancipation accompanied by repatriation to Africa versus immediate emancipation followed by the bestowal of "equal civil and political rights and privileges with the whites" (p. 130). Since colonizationists and abolitionists disagree primarily on whether prejudice against blacks can and should be overcome, Child devotes the rest of the book to answering that question. Chapters 6 and 7, "Intellect of Negroes" and "Moral Character of Negroes," demolish the rationale for prejudice—the myth of the Negro's biological inferiority and savage past—by resurrecting accounts of Africa's ancient civilizations and recalling numerous modern instances of blacks who have distinguished themselves by their talents. The final chapter, "Prejudices against People of Color, and Our Duties in Relation to This Subject," shifts the focus of critique from the South to the North and from slavery to racism. Concentrating on her native Massachusetts, Child catalogs New Englanders' "unrelenting efforts to keep the colored population in the lowest state of degradation" (p. 187) through such forms of discrimination as employment bans, segregated schools and public facilities, and antimiscegenation laws, which she calls on her compatriots to repudiate.

In all but one respect—her promotion of free labor as an alternative to slavery—Child challenges her readers' deepest cultural assumptions. Here, however, the economic ideology she shares with middle-class northerners blinds her to the parallel tendency of capitalist industry and agribusiness to oppress workers and plunder the environment.

RHETORICAL STRATEGIES

The rhetorical strategies Child devises to win over hostile readers are as varied as the topics she addresses. She herself describes her principal strategy of letting facts speak for themselves: "I . . . state the evidence, and leave [readers] to judge of it, as their hearts and consciences may dictate" (p. 187). The words "evidence" and "judge" indicate that Child seeks to persuade through reason, by bringing readers' "minds . . . to reflect" on the truths she presents (p. 187). "Think of these things wisely," she typically exhorts readers (p. 185). As in this example, Child frequently resorts to direct address, an approach that personalizes her relationship to readers and engages them in a dialogue with her, especially when framed as rhetorical questions: "Let me ask you, candid reader, what you would be, if you labored under the same unnatural circumstances?" (p. 182). By characterizing readers as "candid" or "kind-hearted," she simultaneously disarms them and appeals to their best instincts. Conversely, she admits to having earlier held the very misconceptions and biases she asks readers to renounce: "I once had a very strong prejudice against anti-slavery;—(I am ashamed to think *how* strong—for mere prejudice should never be stubborn,) but a candid examination has convinced me, that I was in error" (p. 134). If she can change, she implies, so can her readers.

Child further disarms readers through humor, as in her complaint that by refusing to act against slavery, New Englanders are behaving like "the man who being asked to work at the pump, because the vessel was going down, answered, 'I am only a passenger'" (p. 120). Her humor often shades into irony, which she uses to question readers' ideological assumptions and expose the absurdity of proslavery arguments. Thus, replying to the claim that slavery has served to Christianize Africans, she comments: "To be violently wrested from his home, and condemned to toil without hope, by Christians, to whom he had done no wrong, was, methinks, a very odd beginning to the

These three extracts from chapter 6, "Intellect of Negroes," illustrate how Child both refutes racist theory and contests racist practices. First, by showing that the ancient Greeks, regarded as the forebears of western civilization, recognized Africa as the source of their religious and scientific knowledge, Child overturns the commonly accepted belief in white European superiority and African inferiority. Second, she predicts that Africans themselves will eventually seize from their European conquerors the power to write their own history and thus negate the racist stereotypes used to denigrate them. Third, she exposes the racial discrimination African Americans face as unjust and ultimately detrimental to the society that wastes their talents.

Why did the ancients represent Minerva as born in Africa,—and why are we told that Atlas there sustained the heavens and the earth, unless they meant to imply that Africa was the centre, from which religious and scientific light had been diffused? . . .

By thousands and thousands, these poor people have died for freedom. They have stabbed themselves for freedom—jumped into the waves for freedom—starved for freedom—fought like very tigers for freedom! But they have been hung, and burned, and shot—and their tyrants have been their historians! When the Africans have writers of their own, we shall hear their efforts for liberty called by the true title of heroism in a glorious cause. . . .

A colored man, however intelligent, is not allowed to pursue any business more lucrative than that of a barber, a shoe-black, or a waiter. . . . It is unjust that a man should, on account of his complexion, be prevented from performing more elevated uses in society. Every citizen ought to have a fair chance to try his fortune in any line of business, which he thinks he has the ability to transact.

Child, *Appeal*, pp. 141, 161–162, 198.

poor negro's course of religious instruction!" (p. 9). Witticisms, anecdotes, metaphors, and analogies punctuate the text, serving not only to enliven a grim subject but to reeducate readers by breaking down accustomed modes of thought and undermining distinctions between white Americans and cultural Others.

Perhaps the most pervasive of the rhetorical strategies Child uses in the *Appeal* are quotations. She deploys them to bolster her own authority, enlist testimony from credible witnesses, advance controversial views through the mouths of reputable spokesmen, and to give voice to the slaves themselves.

INFLUENCE AND LEGACY OF CHILD'S APPEAL

The *Appeal*'s broad sweep, scholarly thoroughness, intellectual depth, and rhetorical power won it an influence unparalleled for an abolitionist tract. It converted to the abolitionist cause a panoply of opinion makers and future political leaders, among them the Unitarian ministers William Ellery Channing and Thomas Wentworth Higginson, the *North American Review* editor John Gorham Palfrey, the orator Wendell Phillips, and the Massachusetts senators Henry Wilson and Charles Sumner. The *Appeal* also emboldened women to assume public roles in anti-slavery ranks, whether by producing tracts of their own, as did Angelina Grimké with her *Appeal to the Christian Women of the South* (1836) and, much later, Harriet Beecher Stowe with her *Key to Uncle Tom's Cabin* (1853), or by defying taboo to lecture to "promiscuous" (gender-mixed) audiences, as did Angelina and Sarah Grimké, Abby Kelley, and Lucy Stone. In less direct ways, the *Appeal* and Child's example generally helped encourage literary figures who had been keeping aloof from the abolitionist movement—such as the transcendentalists Ralph Waldo Emerson, Margaret Fuller, and Henry David Thoreau and the poets James Russell Lowell and Henry Wadsworth Longfellow—to speak and write against slavery. The commitment to eradicating racism that Child expressed in the *Appeal* and acted on in her life encouraged African American writers as well: Frederick Douglass, William Wells Brown, Charlotte Forten, Harriet Jacobs, Frances Ellen Watkins Harper, and Pauline Elizabeth Hopkins all acknowledged Child as an inspiration. "Were she living to-day," wrote Hopkins in 1903, when white supremacy once again ruled the nation, "her trenchant pen would do us yeoman's service in the vexed question of disfranchisement and equality for the Afro-American" (p. 454).

As Hopkins's eulogy suggests, Child's contributions to the struggle against racism extend beyond the *Appeal* and beyond her own time. Over a career of advocacy that lasted until her death in 1880, Child published countless other works for the abolitionist cause—tracts, biographies, newspaper articles, letters to politicians. stories, a novel advocating intermarriage as the solution to America's race problem (*A Romance of the Republic*, 1867), and a primer for the emancipated slaves featuring readings by and about people of African descent (*The Freedmen's Book*, 1865). One of these works, her *Correspondence between Lydia Maria Child and Gov. Wise and Mrs. Mason, of Virginia* (1860), reached a circulation of 300,000. In addition, Child edited both a major abolitionist newspaper, the *National Anti-Slavery Standard* (1841–1843), and a slave narrative now considered a literary classic, Harriet Jacobs's *Incidents in the Life of a Slave Girl* (1861).

The full measure of Child's achievement only becomes apparent, however, in the light of recent scholarly trends she anticipated in the *Appeal*: comparative approaches to the history and sociology of slavery and race, legal analyses of slavery's centrality to the American Constitution and political system, Afrocentric methodologies and studies of European culture's African origins. New research in these fields has confirmed many of Child's key insights, revealing her to be a pioneering scholar as well as a courageous activist for racial equality. Through the *Appeal*, in sum, Child both wrote history and made history—the ultimate mark of a text's cultural significance.

See also Abolitionist Writing; Female Authorship; History; *Incidents in the Life of a Slave Girl; The Liberator;* Religion; Rhetoric; Slave Rebellions; Slavery

BIBLIOGRAPHY

Primary Works

Child, Lydia Maria. *An Appeal in Favor of That Class of Americans Called Africans.* 1833. Edited by Carolyn L. Karcher. Amherst: University of Massachusetts Press, 1996.

Child, Lydia Maria. *Correspondence between Lydia Maria Child and Gov. Wise and Mrs. Mason, of Virginia.* Boston: American Anti-Slavery Society, 1860.

Child, Lydia Maria. *The Freedmen's Book.* 1865. New York: Arno Press, 1968.

Child, Lydia Maria. *A Lydia Maria Child Reader.* Edited by Carolyn L. Karcher. Durham, N.C.: Duke University Press, 1997. Reprints extracts and full texts of many otherwise unavailable articles, editorials, pamphlets, and stories by Child.

Child, Lydia Maria. *Lydia Maria Child: Selected Letters, 1817–1880.* Edited by Milton Meltzer, Patricia G. Holland, and Francine Krasno. Amherst: University of Massachusetts Press, 1982.

Child, Lydia Maria. *A Romance of the Republic.* 1867. Edited by Dana D. Nelson. Lexington: University Press of Kentucky, 1997.

Garrison, William Lloyd. Editorial preface to Child's "Comparative Strength of Male and Female Intellect." *Genius of Universal Emancipation,* 30 October 1829, p. 60.

Hopkins, Pauline E. "Reminiscences of the Life and Times of Lydia Maria Child." *Colored American Magazine* 6 (February, March, and May 1903): 279–284, 353–357, 454–459.

[Mellen, G.] "Works of Mrs. Child." *North American Review* 37 (July 1833): 138–164.

Secondary Works

Clifford, Deborah. *Crusader for Freedom: A Life of Lydia Maria Child.* Boston: Beacon Press, 1992.

Crapol, Edward P., ed. *Women and American Foreign Policy: Lobbyists, Critics, and Insiders.* Westport, Conn.: Greenwood Press, 1987.

Goodman, Paul. *Of One Blood: Abolitionism and the Origins of Racial Equality.* Berkeley: University of California Press, 1998.

Hartnett, Stephen John. *Democratic Dissent and the Cultural Fictions of Antebellum America.* Urbana: University of Illinois Press, 2002.

Karcher, Carolyn L. *The First Woman in the Republic: A Cultural Biography of Lydia Maria Child.* Durham, N.C.: Duke University Press, 1994.

Mills, Bruce. *Cultural Reformations: Lydia Maria Child and the Literature of Reform.* Athens: University of Georgia Press, 1994.

Nelson, Dana D. *National Manhood: Capitalist Citizenship and the Imagined Fraternity of White Men.* Durham, N.C.: Duke University Press, 1998.

Sánchez-Eppler, Karen. *Touching Liberty: Abolition, Feminism, and the Politics of the Body.* Berkeley: University of California Press, 1993.

Sorisio, Carolyn. *Fleshing Out America: Race, Gender, and the Politics of the Body in American Literature, 1833–1879.* Athens: University of Georgia Press, 2002.

Yellin, Jean Fagan. *Women and Sisters: The Antislavery Feminists in American Culture.* New Haven, Conn.: Yale University Press, 1989.

Carolyn L. Karcher

ARCHITECTURE

In the eighteenth century the British were world masters of the architectural handbook, with innumerable volumes published in every shape and size. This stifled the development of an American literature on the subject, as everything was imported: fully twenty-eight English architectural titles of the 1780s and 1790s had arrived in the United States by 1800. The situation began to change at the turn of the nineteenth century with the appearance of Asher Benjamin's (1773–1845) *Country Builder's Assistant* (1797), the first American "pattern book," or builder's guide, in the long-standing British tradition. Such books taught carpenters and homeowners how to build a fashionable house, with text explaining the various illustrations (in plan, elevation, and details). Benjamin had been trained as a builder in Connecticut. As with his six subsequent books, illustrations in the *Assistant* were in the form of engraved copper plates. Published in Boston, these volumes followed (and helped shape) changing architectural fads. The first two copied the Roman orders (Doric, Ionic, Corinthian) of Sir William Chambers and the Adamesque of William Pain—mainstays of America's Federal era, when stylish, attenuated classical forms were grafted onto the heavier, foursquare Georgian house form familiar since colonial times. *The Practical House Carpenter* (1830) and subsequent offerings shifted into Greek Revival, another British mania. *Practical House Carpenter* proved enormously popular, going through more than twenty-one reprintings between 1830 and 1857. Rural craftsmen used it avidly as American towns rapidly expanded during years of phenomenal population growth.

Building on the example of Benjamin was Minard Lafever (1798–1854), a New York carpenter (later a self-proclaimed "architect"), whose five books did more than anything else to spread Greek Revival nationwide. His debut volume, *Young Builder's General Instructor* (1829), borrowed heavily from British precedent in both text and designs. Embarrassed by its inadequacies, he withdrew it from print at considerable personal cost in favor of the improved *Modern Builder's Guide* (1833), his most influential work. Its Greek Revival designs were contributed in part by two architects, the British émigré James Gallier and the New Yorker James Dakin. The Greek theme was continued in the handsome *Beauties of Modern Architecture* (1835). Thanks in part to these portable, easy-to-use publications, Greek Revival spread as far west as California and Oregon.

The steam press fostered a publishing revolution in the 1830s, at exactly the time that new British ideas of the architectural "picturesque"—essentially Romanticism applied to the material world—launched an aesthetic revolution in the United States. An innovative kind of publication would now appear in America: not the old "pattern book" but a "villa book." These had been popular in Britain since the 1790s but now belatedly crossed the sea. Pattern books were aimed primarily at carpenters and only offered a dry text; villa books, with a rich store of pictures and accompanying prose, evoked a bright new lifestyle, intending to establish proper "taste" among the middle class. In quasi-religious language akin to that of other contemporary reform movements, readers were told that the way they embellished their homes spoke volumes about their moral proclivities and had a potentially powerful impact on their families and communities. New York and the Hudson Valley were the crucibles of this new literature, as architects building villas up and down the river partnered with New York publishers to promote their own careers and up-to-date aesthetic visions—all couched in high-minded language about social and familial improvement through architecture.

DAVIS AND DOWNING

The first American villa book was *Rural Residences* (1837–1838) by a New York architect, Alexander Jackson Davis (1803–1892). Owing to an economic downturn, only two sections of a projected six were published, and few of these were sold; the book was nonetheless epochal for the development of American architecture. Instead of the copper-engraved plates of Benjamin and Lafever, here were evocative lithographs (which could be purchased hand-colored for an extra price). Lithography allowed subtleties of light and shade that suggested mood, and homes were increasingly shown surrounded by verdant landscapes. The entire approach was British; indeed the title was borrowed from J. B. Papworth's *Rural Residences* (1818), published in London. But thoughtful attempts were made to adapt English ideas to American conditions, most famously in the promotion of "board-and-batten" construction: vertical siding with wooden strips, or battens, sealing the joints, a method made feasible by America's abundant forests and ubiquitous sawmills.

Davis soon inspired the most important of all nineteenth-century American writers on architecture, Andrew Jackson Downing (1815–1852). Owner of a thriving nursery along the Hudson and editor of the journal *Horticulturist,* Downing was a rabid Anglophile whose house, "Highland Garden" (1838–1839), copied an Elizabethan design (complete with parapets, mullioned windows with label moldings, and a rose window) in an English villa book. Building it and laying out its ornamental grounds whetted his interest in landscape design. In 1841 he published his landmark *Treatise on the Theory and Practice of Landscape Gardening.* As with Davis, who provided the illustrations, his sensibilities were heavily British, and he owed an incalculable debt to John C. Loudon's *Encyclopedia of Cottage, Farm, and Villa Architecture* (1833), published in London. For the first time an American architecture book was copiously illustrated with eighty-eight wood engravings printed integrally with the text, as this new type of printmaking allowed. Compared to the old copperplate pattern books, Downing's publications were small, compact, and affordable, meant to grace the shelves of cottages across the land. Downing quickly became famous as America's tastemaker, with *Landscape Gardening* selling nine thousand copies in twelve years. As his interests turned more and more to pure architecture, he followed it up with *Cottage Residences* (1842) and *The Architecture of Country Houses* (1850).

Downing brilliantly played the role of "apostle of taste." His "Highland Garden" stood as a showpiece for the picturesque, that aesthetic language borrowed from England and Romanticism. Seated at his desk beside a bay window and surrounded by busts of literary greats, he wrote earnestly to the American public in prose both eloquent and persuasive. He took highfalutin British concepts and restated them for a middle- or working-class audience, offering simple, effective examples, as in the famous illustrated contrast in the *Horticulturist* between "A Common Country House" (bald and unadorned) and "The Same, Improved." Downing's career was cut short by his death in a steamboat accident in 1852 as he traveled to Washington, D.C., to superintend the Smithsonian Pleasure Grounds on the Mall.

AGE OF ECLECTICISM

Downing had many eager followers and rivals as publishing expanded in the 1850s, a period that saw nearly ninety American books published on some aspect of architecture, compared to about forty in the decade before. Richard Upjohn (1802–1878), the English-born architect whose Trinity Church (1841–1846) in New York was an icon of the age, popularized its medievalizing, pointed-arch gothic style for small towns nationwide in *Upjohn's Rural Architecture* (1852). The Philadelphia architect Samuel Sloan's (1815–1884) lithographed plates in *The Model Architect* (1852–1853) and *City and Suburban Architecture* (1859) celebrated the tremendous proliferation of accepted styles in the design of houses. He regarded himself as an important pioneer, noting that "American works on architecture are few in number." As only about 20 percent of Sloan's vast architectural output is still standing, his writings assume great importance for architectural historians trying to reconstruct his vanished oeuvre. After the Civil War, Sloan edited the *Architectural Review and American Builder's Journal* (1868–1870), the first periodical in the country devoted entirely to architecture.

An Elizabethan-style villa. Illustration by Philadelphia architect Samuel Sloan from his 1852 book *The Model Architect.* During this era of rapid change, historicism in architecture contrasted strikingly with the novelty of technical innovations such as the railroad. UNIVERSITY OF DELAWARE LIBRARY, NEWARK, DELAWARE

Downing's chief follower was Calvert Vaux (1824–1895), a young architect he brought in tow from England in 1850. They worked as partners until Downing's death. Vaux would later team up with Frederick Law Olmsted—a writer turned landscape designer—to create the immortal "Greensward" plan for New York's Central Park (1857–1858). In 1857 Vaux published *Villas and Cottages,* with thirty-nine buildings illustrated, mostly ones he had built himself for clients along the Hudson. This opened him to charges of "egotism" by the New York reviewer Clarence Cook, whose essay "House Building in America" denounced the whole villa book craze (and Vaux's offering in particular) as borrowing uncritically from the English author John Ruskin, whose ideas about reviving medieval craftsmanship as a means of making nineteenth-century architecture more authentic seemed to him impractical and overintellectualized. Real progress in architecture would come not from villa books with their gratuitous ornament, Cook said, but from careful study of old, vernacular American farmhouses, simple and sincere.

FUNCTIONALISM AND THOREAU

Cook's comments belong to an essentialist (and nativist) strain in American thought on architecture. In the early twenty-first century it is called "form follows function," or functionalism, and it is associated particularly with the jottings of the expatriate sculptor Horatio Greenough (1805–1852) in "American Architecture," published in the *North American Review* (1843), and *Aesthetics at Washington* (1851). Greenough corresponded with Ralph Waldo Emerson regarding "my theory of structure" based austerely on "function" and calling for "the entire and immediate banishment of all make-shift and make-believe." Emerson called these ideas a "beam of sunlight" and borrowed them in his own writing (Kowsky, pp. 86–87). He in turn was quoted by Vaux in *Villas and Cottages.*

Trinity Church, New York City. Engraving c. 1846.
THE LIBRARY OF CONGRESS

Functionalism was encouraged by the constant public dialogue about architectural engineering, then making astounding strides. Charles Ellet's books on American wire suspension bridges (1839–1854), for example, highlighted the fact that exciting architecture need not be historicizing or ornamental at all.

The fiercest essentialist was Emerson's young disciple Henry David Thoreau (1817–1862), whose *Walden* (1854) bears a complex relationship to the villa book craze. Thoreau was surrounded by new villas in the suburbs of Boston, and he critiques them sharply, with their "spacious apartments, clean paint and paper, Rumford fireplace, back plastering, Venetian blinds, copper pump, spring lock, a commodious cellar" (p. 29). He seems to quote Downing's famous advice on how to paint a dwelling—"take up a handful of the earth at your feet, and paint your house that color"—and instantly condemns it. *Walden* has therefore been regarded as a dismissive satire on the villa books, but

actually it adapts, in a sophisticated way, the ideas of those books for radical, transcendentalist purposes. *Walden* has a long introductory chapter, "Economy," much like the didactic prefaces of the villa books. Again like the villa books, it features a wood-engraved frontispiece illustration showing a house designed by the author—in this case his little pond-side dwelling, ten by fifteen feet, which Thoreau took seriously enough to always call a "house," almost never a "cabin" or "hut" as it is called in the early twenty-first century. His itemized list of house-building expenses, amounting to little more than $28, has been taken to be a joke, but some villa books give similar lists with totals not much higher, aimed at an audience of laborers. *Walden* is meant for "poor students," Thoreau notes, and he cleverly co-opts the villa books' language and approach to critique contemporary society and manners.

AN EXPANDING LITERATURE

Thoreau was not the only literary author to use architecture and architectural ideas to telling effect. One thinks of Nathaniel Hawthorne's (1804–1864) *Mosses from an Old Manse* (1846) and *House of the Seven Gables* (1850)—drawing early attention to American colonial architecture, specifically the clapboard frame house of seventeenth-century Massachusetts—and Edgar Allan Poe's (1809–1849) chilling "The Fall of the House of Usher" (1839). Harriet Beecher Stowe (1811–1896) won sympathy for Uncle Tom by describing his log house in the time-honored language of the beloved English cottage, embowered in flowering vines. Washington Irving (1783–1859) went further, building a house for himself that imitated the Dutch colonial architecture he had evoked so vividly in his stories, complete with step gables, shaped chimneys, and two kinds of porch. "Sunnyside" (1835–1837), near Tarrytown, New York, was highly influential on Davis and Downing and still stands in the early twenty-first century as a landmark of the picturesque. In a real sense it advertised Irving to the public, as steamboat travelers on the Hudson could not miss it. In an age when architecture was constantly noticed and discussed, all kinds of promoters used it to advance their causes. P. T. Barnum, for example, erected the wildly flamboyant Moorish-style villa "Iranistan" (1846–1848) in Connecticut to call attention to his New York museum. Guests trekked to the onion dome on top, sat on a circular divan big enough for forty-five people, and viewed the landscape through diamond-shaped windows, each a different color. Awed by the appearance of "Iranistan's" on Barnum's letterhead, the Swedish singer Jenny Lind signed up with him for her sensational American tour in 1850.

Sunnyside. Lithograph by Currier & Ives. Washington Irving's home in the Hudson Valley was designed to reflect the Dutch colonial architecture described in his stories. THE LIBRARY OF CONGRESS

Following suit, literary and newspaper outfits used architecture to advertise themselves, as in the Sun Building (1850–1851) in Baltimore or the Harper & Brothers publishing plant (1854–1855) in New York. Both of these had sumptuously ornate cast-iron facades by James Bogardus (1800–1874), who deserves mention. A technological genius, he took out patents on numerous mechanical devices both before and after a stay in London in 1836–1840. His ferrous (iron) architecture breakthrough swept America after he patented an all-iron building in 1849 and published *Cast Iron Buildings: Their Construction and Advantages* (1856).

As their public role gradually increased, women writers made significant contributions to the contemporary dialogue on architecture. Some of the most eloquent commentators on American building were female travelers, such as Harriet Martineau and Catharine Maria Sedgwick. The Swedish tourist Fredrika Bremer idolized Downing and left invaluable descriptions of his aesthetic lifestyle at "Highland Garden"; Susan A. F. Cooper, daughter of novelist James Fenimore Cooper, voiced opinions on architecture in *Rural Hours* (1850);

and the prolific New Haven, Connecticut, writer Louisa C. H. Tuthill's *History of Architecture from the Earliest Times* (1848) was the first such American publication. With every passing year women were becoming more active in reform movements generally and in publishing books and articles on household improvement. Harriet Beecher Stowe's sister Catharine E. Beecher (1800–1878), founder of Hartford Female Seminary and a subsequent school in Cincinnati, Ohio, argued that women should take control of many aspects of the home and that houses should be rationally designed to suit women's practical needs. Her *Treatise on Domestic Economy* (1841) was annually reprinted through 1856 and was later enlarged, with Harriet's help, into *The American Woman's Home; or, Principles of Domestic Science* (1869).

The fecund architectural ideas of 1820–1870 cast a long shadow, even as the practice of architecture changed greatly with the rise of the university program (starting at the Massachusetts Institute of Technology in 1868), the habit of getting foreign training at the École des Beaux-Arts in Paris, and the proliferation of architectural journals. Downing's published cottage designs were pirated as late as 1883, and his *Landscape Gardening* entered a tenth edition in 1921, nearly seventy years after his death. Davis continued to practice and design into the 1890s. More generally the picturesque flourished in a variety of guises throughout the late nineteenth century, most colorfully as Queen Anne, with its turrets, shaped chimneys, variegated rooflines, and jigsaw work. Even with the coming of modernism, the picturesque remained important, its essentialist and functionalist strain proving highly influential on Frank Lloyd Wright, who began designing in the 1880s. The cottages and villas of 1820–1870 in their leafy landscapes remain significant in the early twenty-first century for they are directly ancestral to the suburban homes that have, by the millions, engulfed the modern American landscape.

See also Americans Abroad; Art; English Literature; Gothic Fiction; Transcendentalism

BIBLIOGRAPHY

Primary Work

Thoreau, Henry David. *Walden.* 1854. New York: Modern Library, 1992.

Secondary Works

Cooledge, Harold N., Jr. *Samuel Sloan, Architect of Philadelphia, 1815–1884.* Philadelphia: University of Pennsylvania Press, 1986.

Crowley, John E. *The Invention of Comfort: Sensibilities and Design in Early Modern Britain and Early America.* Baltimore: Johns Hopkins University Press, 2001.

Gayle, Margot, and Carol Gayle. *Cast-Iron Architecture in America: The Significance of James Bogardus.* New York: Norton, 1998.

Hafertepe, Kenneth, and James F. O'Gorman, eds. *American Architects and Their Books to 1848.* Amherst: University of Massachusetts Press, 2001.

Hitchcock, Henry Russell. *American Architectural Books.* New York: Da Capo, 1976.

Kowsky, Francis R. *Country, Park, and City: The Architecture and Life of Calvert Vaux.* New York: Oxford University Press, 1998.

Maynard, W. Barksdale. *Architecture in the United States, 1800–1850.* New Haven, Conn.: Yale University Press, 2002.

Peck, Amelia, ed. *Alexander Jackson Davis, American Architect, 1803–1892.* New York: Rizzoli, 1992.

Pierson, William H., Jr. *American Buildings and Their Architects: Technology and the Picturesque, the Corporate, and the Early Gothic Styles.* Garden City, N.Y.: Doubleday, 1978.

Reiff, Daniel D. *Houses from Books: Treatises, Pattern Books, and Catalogs in American Architecture, 1738–1950.* University Park: Pennsylvania State University Press, 2000.

Schuyler, David Paul. *Apostle of Taste: Andrew Jackson Downing, 1815–1852.* Baltimore: Johns Hopkins University Press, 1996.

W. Barksdale Maynard

ART

Hailed by the *Edinburgh Review* upon its publication in Britain in 1820 as forming "an era in the literature of the nation to which it belongs," Washington Irving's *The Sketch Book* (1819–1820) established its author as the first successful professional writer in America. *The Sketch Book* presents a miscellaneous assortment of stories, sketches, and essays held together by little more than the rambling inclinations of its bachelor narrator, "Geoffrey Crayon, Gent." In his opening self-description, Crayon characterizes himself as "a lover of the picturesque." Having "wandered through different countries and witnessed the shifting scenes of life," he disavows "the eye of a philosopher" and sees himself as a modern tourist and amateur practitioner of the "sister arts," whose verbal "sketches" are meant simply for the entertainment of friends (p. 745).

Crayon's thumbnail self-portrait gives readers a clearer sense of the actual concerns of his book. "My heart almost fails me," he admits, "at finding how my idle humour has led me aside from the great objects studied by every regular traveler who would make a book." He then compares himself to "an unlucky landscape painter, who had traveled on the continent, but following the bent of his vagrant impulses, had sketched in nooks and corners and bye places" while neglecting "to paint St. Peter's or the Coliseum; the cascade of Terni or the Bay of Naples" (p. 745).

No better assessment of the book's appeal could have been anticipated by an author so consistently attuned to the domestic concerns of an emerging middle-class audience. That audience would award *The Sketch Book* overnight acclaim and enduring influence. In renouncing heroic history while promoting the pastoral and picturesque, helping to shape a taste for the novel, the romantic, the nostalgic and sentimental, Irving (1783–1859) served up a delicious concoction for an increasingly literate and avidly curious public. This public was no longer defined in neoclassical terms—as resolutely masculine, aristocratic, and impersonal. In an age of widening prosperity and vaulting individual achievement, it was now engaged in a quest for cultural moorings. Key to Irving's achievement was his pronounced pictorial sense, bringing to fruition a cultivation of the age-old analogy between literature and painting that had characterized the eighteenth-century British gentleman. Written for a public engaged in capitalist expansion, *The Sketch Book* allowed its readers to luxuriate in fantasies of a traditional society whose members knew their place, while offsetting class and status anxieties through associations with a landed aristocracy.

Thirty-seven years later, Herman Melville (1819–1891) published "The Piazza." Beneath its rather ornate and mannered surface, the story savagely mocked what had by then become a commonplace of American culture. Melville explicitly linked the cult of the picturesque and the quest for home, only to turn this popular version of cultural ideals and aspirations inside out by deconstructing the very nature of illusion and desire. Taking Irvingesque refuge from the modern urban world, his narrator removes to the Berkshires, purchasing an old-fashioned farmhouse fronting Mount Greylock—a "very paradise of painters." As he notes, "the country round about was such a picture, that in berry time no boy climbs hill or crosses vale without coming upon easels planted in every nook, and sun-burnt painters painting there" (p. 1). But alas, the house is without a piazza, that perfect symbol of middle-class pretensions, and the narrator puzzles over which side of the building to construct one, opting for the northern vista of the mountain over a southern exposure to warm breezes. The piazza is, as he tells us, a surrogate for the pew: love of scenery has become a substitute for religious worship. But Melville also aligns aesthetics with politics: his narrator sides with the French king in the democratic revolutions of 1848.

In any case, once situated before a rather austere and alien prospect, he becomes entranced with "some uncertain object I had caught, mysteriously snugged away, to all appearance, in a sort of purpled breast-pocket" (p. 4). The tendency to see the world as a series of carefully composed and suggestively detailed pictures—central to the picturesque aesthetic—provokes him to embark on an "inland voyage to fairy-land." But after toiling up the mountainside, he encounters only "a little, low-storied, grayish cottage, capped, nun-like with a peaked roof," ensconced in a sublime setting, "among fantastic rocks." There he meets a "pale-cheeked girl" named Marianna to whom, after a prolonged silence, he manages only to say, "You must find this view very pleasant" (pp. 8–9).

Her response brings home instead a stark tale of suffering and woe. "Never, never shall I weary of this," she remembers first thinking on coming there. But things are different now. Her subsequent experience has been one of loss, isolation, monotony, and hard labor: "mostly dull woman's work—sitting, sitting, restless sitting" (p. 12). While listening to her, the narrator suddenly recognizes his own abode, far below: "The mirage haze made it appear less a farmhouse than King Charming's palace." Underscoring this moment of acute irony, the girl reveals her long-standing fascination with this vision: "Oh, if I could but once get to yonder house, and but look upon whomever the happy being is that lives there!" In the face of this uncanny revelation, the narrator can only declare, "Enough. Launching my yawl no more for fairy-land, I stick to the piazza. It is my box-royal; and this amphitheatre, my theatre of San Carlo. Yes, the scenery is magical—the illusion so complete." Yet for all his trumped up air of resolution, he must end on a sardonic note, forever after haunted by the girl's face "and many as real a story" (p. 12).

THE DIVIDED WORLD OF THE PICTORIAL MODE

By grappling with the darker, drearier aspects of the brave new world of capitalist expansion, Melville called into question the very home Americans yearned for as a pastoral/nostalgic evasion. For over three decades, what Donald Ringe called "the pictorial mode" dominated American approaches to representation, sugarcoating the pill of progress and undercutting the ideology of the picturesque. Notwithstanding Melville's lonely dissent, the pictorial mode continued to preside over the American cultural establishment for another couple of generations, reaching apotheosis in the publication of the massive two-volume *Picturesque America* in 1872, under the editorship of the venerable William Cullen Bryant (1794–1878). It would be years before the picturesque turned eventually into the byways of kitsch and camp.

Along with Irving and the novelist James Fenimore Cooper (1789–1851), Bryant formed a triad of leading literary pictorialists, canonized in 1971 by Ringe's *Pictorial Mode*. As Ringe took pains to show, the style clearly derived from a theory of how we know the world promoted by the Scottish Common Sense school of moral philosophy, a staple of American higher education in the early national period. Writers like Thomas Reid and Dugald Stewart, widely read by practitioners of the picturesque mode, held that "knowledge of the external world came only through sensation," leaving "nothing in the mind that was not first in the senses" (Ringe, p. 3).

These ideas were derived from the empirical tradition of the English philosopher John Locke. However,

Locke's "simple ideas" suggested an underlying uniformity of perspective. Conversely, the Scottish clergyman Archibald Alison's *Essays on the Nature and Principles of Taste* (1790), not only emphasized the role of associations but based perception as well on the particular experience of the reader or beholder of a natural prospect or work of art in shaping the feelings of beauty and sublimity. Just how a viewer reacted to a landscape depended on whether, for instance, she or he had grown up in the country or the city. Crucial to Alison's model of taste was the capacity to relax attention, suspending rational and analytic faculties and leaving behind practical concerns in order to engage in "a kind of bewitching reverie, through all its store of pleasing or interesting conceptions" (quoted in Ringe, p. 5). One entered a wonderfully restorative half-sleep that allowed free play to memory and affect. Pleasure as well as social prejudice thus took the lead in bringing one to moral insight and even spiritual transport.

The pastoral, along with romance, had long upheld this role of pleasure in western literature and art. In associationism it gained a resourceful ally, imparting color and personal affect. Reliance on the presumed universality of sensation promoted by Lockean empiricism would increasingly be challenged by this emerging subjective dynamic. Nonetheless, for proponents of the picturesque, a commitment to the solidity and uniformity of the natural world continued to hold the upper hand, offering a middle ground between the established categories of the beautiful—grounded in symmetry, serenity, and the social virtues—and the sublime, involving a devotion to wild nature, with its dialectic of terror and transport. Natural objects were necessarily linked, after all, to particular ideas and emotions, providing the foundation for a stable notion of correspondence between nature and spirit. Still, if identification with landscape constituted a kind of "home-coming" for Americans, their feelings remained deeply divided between an earnest search for universal truth and the subjective aesthetic response to the particulars of place and time.

NATURAL RELIGION AND THE IDEOLOGY OF THE PICTURESQUE

Here, indeed, was the foundation for a powerful ideology that naturalized a socially privileged way of interpreting nature, enabling devotees of art and landscape to "forget," as Kenneth Myers put it, that they had actually learned the mental skills enabling them to respond to nature morally and aesthetically (in Miller, *American Iconology,* p. 74). Painting played a central part in this process of naturalizing what had actually been socially constructed. Along with Bryant, Irving, and Cooper, the American romantic painter Thomas Cole (1801–1848), born in England, believed that going into nature afforded the opportunity of listening to the divine monologue. A painting by Cole of a sublime panorama in the Catskills or a poem by Bryant describing a picturesque forest interior turned this religious motive into the leading instigation of landscape representation. Hence Asher B. Durand's (1796–1886) *Kindred Spirits* pictured Bryant and Cole standing together in the Catskill wilderness in what appeared to be a forest chapel. Painted in 1849, following Cole's death, the scene is replete with the imagery of transcendence, suggesting how these two figures assumed a kind of prophetic vocation, seeing themselves—and widely recognized in turn by the public—as truth tellers. Bryant could not have been more explicit about this visionary capacity in his funeral oration for his friend: "The paintings of Cole are of that nature that it hardly transcends the proper use of language to call them acts of religion." And the connection to the character of the artist is naturally invoked, for these paintings "never strike us as strained or forced in character; they teach but what rose spontaneously in the mind of the artists; they were the sincere communications of his own moral and intellectual being" (quoted in McCoubrey, p. 96). In this view, not only was the painting a projection of the artist's genius, but it made landscape the privileged "expression" of moral and spiritual truths. Cole said of waterfalls, for example, that they present both "fixedness and motion—a single existence in which we perceive unceasing change and everlasting duration." Hence "The waterfall may be called the voice of the landscape" (quoted in McCoubrey, p. 105).

But there was another side to this quasi-religious aesthetic. These figures promoted the pictorial mode as a blueprint for society in general. Uvedale Price and Richard Payne Knight, British aestheticians writing at the end of the eighteenth century, had defined the picturesque as a *concordia discors,* or harmony of discords, reconciling liberty with order. American popularizers of the picturesque further conflated aesthetics with politics by associating its mixture of rough and irregular features with the new middle-class effort to balance communal need with an increasingly assertive self-interest, thus reconciling the Jacksonian ideal of the self-made man with the requirements of social stability. For the more conservative members of American society, the all-out battle for wealth and status seemed to threaten all vestiges of traditional order and religious authority; for them the picturesque aesthetic offered a way of containing the explosive force of competitive capitalism.

The Course of Empire: Desolation, **1836.** Painting by Thomas Cole. NEW YORK HISTORICAL SOCIETY, NEW YORK, USA/THE BRIDGEMAN ART LIBRARY

MARKET REVOLUTION AND WARNINGS OF APOCALYPSE

For Cole in particular, the American enterprise appeared to teeter on the brink of apocalypse. As with others still tethered to more traditional ways of seeing the world, the artist believed that history conformed to a continual cycle of rise and fall. The modern idea of progress as a continual upward movement had not fully taken hold. Cole's monumental series *The Course of Empire,* completed in the late 1830s and commissioned by the New York grocer Luman Reed, charted the development of an imaginary civilization (clearly Roman in appearance but in fact a thinly veiled allegory of the United States) from wilderness to pastoral to empire. But in the final two panels of the five-piece sequence, this proud civilization first succumbs to destruction by barbarian hordes, then undergoes nature's inevitable act of reclamation in a vision of *Desolation* that pictures a single column, surrounded by ruins, circled and entwined by vines and tendrils and seen by moonlight. Cole's redolent image of loss and longing resonated with a host of literary examples that manifested not a triumphant but an apocalyptic destiny for the United States, warning Americans in

the age of the common man of the dangers of unbridled materialism and imperialistic pride. Nathaniel Hawthorne's short story "The Ambitious Guest" (1835), Cooper's novel *The Crater* (1847), and even Edgar Allan Poe's "The Fall of the House of Usher" (1839) reflect this pessimism about the consequences of capitalism and democracy, the fear that, in an age of exuberant boundlessness, people could lose their moral bearings.

Cole's extraordinary allegory of inevitable corruption and destruction, coupled with the promise of redemption, was embedded in his very vision of the landscape itself. Typical of this dual message is *Landscape with a Dead Tree* (c. 1828), where the canvas is split into light and dark halves, suggesting a Manichaean struggle between sunlight and storm. The moral emphasis of this dramatic arrangement extends to the blasted tree in the foreground, organizing the entire composition as both a framing device and a way of accentuating the scene's air of contentiousness. The tree serves as a memento mori, or reminder of death; rooted in the earth yet seeming to reach toward the spiritual realm, it encapsulates the human condition, infusing the entire scene with a terrific energy. The sublime hurtle of space the painting depicts suggests the possibility of salvation through escape from the cycles of nature.

TOWARD A PASTORAL BALANCE OF NATURE AND CIVILIZATION

The far quieter images of picturesque prospects Cole increasingly turned to in the 1840s brought his audience back to their moral foundations in a world in which nature and civilization achieved an ideal balance. As early as 1823 James Fenimore Cooper had employed a version of this "middle landscape"—a blend of raw nature, cultivated land, and human habitations—in the opening of *The Pioneers,* the first of the Leatherstocking Tales, to guide his audience's understanding of the proper relationship to nature that must be forged for the American enterprise to succeed. The opening description of the novel anticipates its thematic concerns as a whole. Codified in the panoramic vision offered here—taking in all at once the course of civilization from sublime wilderness to picturesque harmony and pastoral promise—were the efforts of American elites to come to terms with the processes of modernization they themselves were advancing through the many agencies of the marketplace. These included the subjugation of nature through technology and industrialization, the rise of urban life, and the emergence of class consciousness and class conflict.

Moreover, in the works of Cooper as well as Cole we detect some of the earliest versions of environmental and preservationist thinking in the United States. Scenes of the White Mountains, the Berkshires, and the Catskills—the very sort, no doubt, painted by the landscape painters surrounding Melville's narrator in "The Piazza"—proliferated over the next several decades, taking on a deepening aura of nostalgia and idealization by the post–Civil War period. Where Cole's early work had been a warning to a nation he saw as in danger of succumbing to its own hubris, the work of his followers tended to turn apocalypse into millennium, the rise and fall of empires into progress toward perfection, hence testifying to the growing sense that the United States was an exception to the historical rule: rather than decaying, the country was thought to be flowering in the doctrine of Manifest Destiny. Asher B. Durand's grandiose canvas *Progress* (1853) stands along with great works of Frederick Church (1826–1900) like *The Heart of the Andes* (1859) and *Niagra Falls* (1867) as the climax of this confident vision of the course of American civilization. In a single sublime panorama Durand's painting skillfully orchestrates the unfolding of New World history from virgin wilderness to the prospect of a prosperous urban-industrial order, still embosomed in nature. The shift from Cole's *Course of Empire* series to this brilliantly unified image reflects a growing acceptance, clearly evident by the 1850s, of the new market economy and all it entailed.

IDEAL REPRESENTATION AND THE DARKER VISIONS OF AMERICAN LIFE

Meanwhile, the deeper, darker fissures in the American cultural landscape were to be noted only by Melville and a few other intrepid souls. As for American art, there is scarcely a dissonant note to be heard. Painting seems to have largely fulfilled its traditional function (initiated in the humanism of the Renaissance and renewed in neoclassicism) of reinforcing prevailing attitudes through idealization rather than offering critique or subversion—except that now such idealization went hand in hand with painting's ready commodification, as members of the rising middle class became the primary patrons of artists, buying smaller landscapes and genre works for their parlors. The extraordinary demands upon laborers made by the expanding capitalist economy are scarcely to be detected in American genre paintings portraying aspects of everyday life. While southern apologists for slavery might occasionally come up with images of northern "wage slavery," these were confined for the most part to such ephemera as political cartoons. At the same time, northern artists were capable of portraying chattel slavery through the pastoral iconography of benign paternalism.

Melville's dark and foreboding vision of American society is rivaled in the 1850s by only one visual artist, David Gilmore Blythe (1815–1865), of Pittsburgh. Blythe's uncompromising images of street life and his portrayal of urban con men and hard-bitten urchins, drawing heavily on the loose style and satiric characterization of seventeenth-century Dutch and Flemish artists like Adriaen von Ostade and David Teniers the Younger, present a world of anger and aggression, misplaced ambition, stupefying poverty, and anomie. The artist's scenes of everyday life in the Pittsburgh of the 1850s and 1860s stand out in stark relief against the mainstream of American antebellum genre painting, including the work of Francis W. Edmonds (1806–1863), William Sidney Mount (1807–1868), George Caleb Bingham (1811–1879), William Ranney (1813–1857), Lilly Martin Spencer (1822–1902) and Richard Caton Woodville (1825–1855) among a host of others. These genre painters relayed the amusing foibles and fatuities as well as lingering folkways of various American character types. Occasionally concealing political commentary, irony, or sarcasm, they nevertheless steadfastly uphold the optimism of the dominant ideology

***Niagara Falls,* 1867.** Painting by Frederick Edwin Church. NATIONAL GALLERY OF SCOTLAND, EDINBURGH, SCOTLAND/THE BRIDGEMAN ART LIBRARY

of the self-made man. As such they were an easy complement to the pastoral and picturesque vision shaping the antebellum American landscape tradition, often expressing an underlying nostalgia for a way of life rapidly passing away.

A similar set of tendencies was emerging in certain strains of local color writing, which found one important source in Harriet Beecher Stowe's (1811–1896) stories of New England village life, including *The Minister's Wooing* (1859), *Oldtown Folks* (1869), and

Art versus Law, **1859–1860.** Painting by David Gilmore Blythe. © BROOKLYN MUSEUM OF
ART/CORBIS

Poganuc People (1878). In writing *Uncle Tom's Cabin*
(1852), Stowe found that her vocation was "simply
that of a *painter*," her object being "to hold up in the
most lifelike and graphic manner possible Slavery, its
reverses, changes, and the Negro character, which I
have had ample opportunity for studying." As she realized, "There is no arguing with *pictures* and everybody is impressed with them, whether they mean to
be or not" (letter to Gamaliel Bailey, 1851). The pictures she drew in her later work on small-town New
England life were far less melodramatic than those that
transformed *Uncle Tom's Cabin*—Eliza's escape with
her little boy across the ice-choked Ohio River, the
death of Little Eva, Tom beaten to death while praying for the forgiveness of his persecutors—but they

too were certainly effective in engaging an audience
conditioned by the vivid and detailed sketches of
Washington Irving and the pastoral evocations of village life that were such a familiar theme in American
genre painting.

Just how the conventions of the picturesque and
pastoral were carried over into the representation of
everyday life and functioned to conceal the conflict-
ridden nature of American society is evident in
Durand's *Dance of the Haymakers* (1851), a charming
blend of landscape and genre that depicts a paternalistic
agrarian community in upstate New York. The festivi-
ties, benevolently watched over from a respectful distance by the landowner and his wife, are reminiscent
not only of the familiar vision of happy darkies dancing

under the moonlight outside their quarters in the plantation South but also revealingly conjure up association with European peasant society. This reassuring image stands in blithe denial of the condition of virtual serfdom American farmworkers had been reduced to in the Hudson River valley only a decade and a half earlier by the enormous estates owned by such "patroons" as Stephen Van Rensselaer III, the Schuylers, and the Livingstons. The so-called rent wars of the 1840s, in which the "serfs" rose up against their "masters," had finally broken the back of this oppressive system.

In contrast to the blatant idealization and denial of social realities exercised by Durand and many other genre painters from the 1830s into the postbellum period, Blythe offered an uncompromising look at the darkest propensities of human nature, unleashed by urban poverty and degradation. Still, his apparent focus on human nature—betokening an innate conservatism—fell well short of the powerful ideological analysis of American society and its capitalist economy advanced by Melville in his works of the 1850s. In understanding these issues in systemic rather than strictly individual terms, Melville's analysis, albeit fictional, compares with that of his near-contemporary, Karl Marx. And as for landscape representation, Melville's trenchant attack on picturesque and pastoral conventions—as exemplified not only by "The Piazza" but also by "The Encantadas, or Enchanted Isles" (1855)—may find its only clear painterly analogue

in the work of Martin Johnson Heade (1819–1904), an artist whose vision took on definitive form in the 1850s and 1860s. Heade's landscapes, such as *Approaching Storm: Beach near Newport* (1865), and his scenes of jungle and swamp, such as *Brazilian Forest* (1864), herald a new tough-minded ethic that sweeps away all romantic sentiment about nature, paralleling the strenuous antagonism toward the wilds of North America that marks the heroes of the Boston Brahmin Francis Parkman's histories of New World exploration and conquest. Gone is the "rhetoric" of the picturesque and sublime, the literary attributes of drama and oratory, poetry and anecdote, biblical typology and moral allegory, that characterized Hudson River School painting. The commitment to the visual formulas of "character" and "expression," the heroic and hyperbolic style, indeed, all the anthropomorphic qualities imposed on the landscape by the pictorial mode here recede, so that the alien and elusive aspects of nature, now closely observed in all their transitoriness, can come to the fore. Heade's visions of nature bifurcate into the unabashed sensualism and taut formalism of his haystack series, on one hand, and the often unnerving ambiguousness and sometimes outright weirdness of his beach scenes. A work like *Becalmed, Long Island Sound* (1876) evokes the "dumb blankness, full of meaning" of Ishmael's white whale, the sense of a lurking menace that continually fades and reemerges in the beholder's perplexed consciousness.

Summer Showers, c. 1862–1863. Painting by Martin Johnson Heade. © BROOKLYN MUSEUM OF ART/CORBIS

THE QUESTION OF AMERICAN "LUMINISM"

From the 1960s on, a number of scholars of American art designated artists like Heade and the Gloucester, Massachusetts–based painter Fitz Hugh Lane (1804–1865), as well as John Kensett (1816–1872), Sanford Robinson Gifford (1823–1880), and others as "luminists." Luminism was a term taken up most notably by Barbara Novak in her influential *American Painting of the Nineteenth Century: Realism, Idealism, and the American Experience* (1967) and solidified into a movement in the 1980 National Gallery of Art exhibition catalog *American Light: The Luminist Movement, 1850–1875.* Luminist paintings are noteworthy above all for the seemingly palpable presence of light diffused throughout the canvas, enveloping everything in a uniform glow that *may* in certain cases appear numinous or foreboding. As Novak first argued, the artist's presence in luminist paintings is expunged in the collapse of established visual hierarchies—that is, the sometimes unsettling optical effect of giving equal emphasis to every part of the picture plane that is further stressed by the airless atmosphere, minute brushstroke, and glistening surfaces of these works.

There is much to be said for luminism as a pervasive, largely unsystematic tendency not only among American artists during the mid-Victorian period but abroad as well. It makes particular sense in contrasting certain landscape painters like Heade and Lane with artists like Frederick Church and Albert Bierstadt (1830–1902), whose grandiose visions of American and foreign landscapes in the same period extended many of the nationalistic pretensions of the Hudson River School into an imperialistic and operatic mode. Over the years, however, the term "luminism" has lost a good deal of its cachet. Despite Novak's ingenious attempt to link it to New England transcendentalism, art historians were simply unable to tie it down to a consistent set of formal features that could be convincingly correlated with cultural and ideological trends. In order to grasp its significance, we have to look deeper into the underlying dynamics of American culture.

For one thing, the shift away from religious and moral concerns characterizing earlier generations of landscape painters toward a pronounced formalism conveying distinct psychological reverberations—a movement paced by growing interest in exotic environments like the polar regions or the jungles of South and Central America or in what had traditionally been called "desert" places—takes place at a number of levels in American culture from the 1850s and 1860s on. Heade's version of such "symbolistic" painting compares with the more overtly symbolic and obsessive images of Albert Pinkham Ryder (1847–1917) and Ralph Blakelock (1847–1919), working closer to the end of the century. Moreover, Heade's haystacks offer an interesting counterpart to the haystacks of Claude Monet in their preoccupation with changing light and weather effects, which contributed to the unraveling of the old "sister arts" alliance, based on the notion that literature and art were analogous forms of representation. This unraveling took place as effects relaying inward states of mind began to preoccupy painters far more than the traditional focus of art on heroic human events, portrayed in a "high style" of history painting originating in the Renaissance and revived in neoclassicism. The emerging modernist idea that all art should become a law unto itself, much like music in its disconnection from political, social, or moral concerns, was especially evident in the stylistic innovations emerging in Europe during the second half of the century—beginning with the Barbizon School of painting and extending to impressionism and tonalism. From the 1850s on, increasing numbers of American artists went to Europe to study painting, falling under the influence of the latest styles.

THE BOSTON AESTHETIC TRADITION

Such tendencies had actually long been present in American painting, stemming in particular from the work of the painter-poet Washington Allston (1779–1843). Allston stood as nothing less than a fountainhead of the distinctive New England aesthetic tradition. Born into the South Carolina "rice" aristocracy and educated in Newport, Rhode Island, and at Harvard, he returned permanently to Boston in 1818 after establishing his career in England as a history painter. Once home, he became his generation's leading "man of genius," the primary conduit to his contemporaries—especially the nascent Boston Brahmin set—of romantic ideas (above all those of his good friend Samuel Taylor Coleridge) in the nearly two decades before Emerson delivered his epoch-making essay *Nature* (1836). Allston's promotion of romantic theory, though alloyed with certain conservative elements, became a catalyst of change against the dominant empirical model of reality encoded in the pictorial mode. Crucial to his transformation of pictorial style was Coleridge's "coalescence of subject and object," a romantic epistemology that decisively moved visual art away from a preoccupation with mimesis into a world of symbolism and romance.

Accordingly, Allston pushed beyond the long-standing sister arts tradition in which the "heroic" moments depicted in history painting ensured its place at the head of the hierarchy of artistic genres. Allston recast the ideal but essentially imitative subject matter of "monumental" biblical, mythological, or historical

Belshazzar's Feast, **c. 1817–1843.** Painting by Washington Allston. © THE DETROIT INSTITUTE OF ARTS/BRIDGEMAN ART LIBRARY

events into expressive, psychologically charged forms. The artist's later paintings—"cabinet" works for the most part, including ideal landscapes and portraits—evoked elusive moods and soulful states of mind through atmospheric effects conveyed by the visual and tactile qualities of the paint itself (e.g., color, light, and facture or paint surface), so that they challenged his contemporary New England audience to develop new ways of seeing, experiencing, and thinking about the world. The artist's admirers distilled new moral values and civic ideals from Allston's work, which also furnished them a shared form of inner experience.

Serving as a medium of truth between one beholder and the next by way of the material medium of the painting or text, the alembic of the poet or artist's imagination gained priority over conventional meaning or didactic intent. The timeworn topoi of art thus gave ground to a cult of genius, the collective pursuit of originality and personal freedom.

As beholders of Allston's paintings became aware of how meaning was inextricably tied to differences in media (and content to form), they reconfigured the age-old analogy between the visual and the verbal that lay at the heart of the sister arts ideal. As a result, iconography, the conventional connection of motifs with themes and of images with concepts that had constituted the core of the classical doctrine of *ut pictura poesis* ("as a painting, so also a poem"), inevitably receded in importance. Now beholders tended to be stirred less by *what* was represented than by *how* it was imagined. The "poetic" responses of those beholding paintings like Allston's *Moonlit Landscape* (1819) mapped new areas of experience for which music stood as the dominant figure, specifically because of its nonrepresentational character.

Hence, while many cultural figures in Boston lamented Allston's failure over a nearly twenty-six-year period to complete his "masterpiece," the immense history painting *Belshazzar's Feast,* the influence of his personal example, aesthetic ideals, and "musical" reveries went much further. For not only did the artist exemplify the failure of the old sister arts analogy and all it stood for, as epitomized by his titanic struggle with *Belshazzar's Feast;* he fundamentally shaped the religion of art of such figures as Elizabeth Peabody, James Jackson Jarves, and Charles Eliot Norton, while looking forward to the modernist formal experimentation that blossomed at Harvard around the turn of the century and involved such figures as William James and Gertrude Stein, George Santayana and Wallace Stevens. Allston's later art thus instigated for an emerging New England elite the very shift in center of gravity his old friend Washington Irving had accomplished for a new middle-class readership. Unlike Irving, however, whose writings were steeped in nostalgia and grounded in eighteenth-century British models, Allston's contribution to American literary and artistic representation—for all its grounding in tradition—looked forward to twentieth-century developments.

See also Americans Abroad; Labor; Landscape Architecture; *Nature;* Philosophy; Romanticism; Slavery; Transcendentalism; Wilderness

BIBLIOGRAPHY

Primary Works

Alison, Archibald. *Essays on the Nature and Principles of Taste.* 1790. Boston, 1812.

Bryant, William Cullen, James Fenimore Cooper, Washington Irving, et al. *The Home Book of the Picturesque; or, American Scenery, Art, and Literature.* New York: Putnam, 1852.

Bryant, William Cullen, ed. *Picturesque America: The Land We Live In.* 2 vols. New York, 1872–1874.

Irving, Washington. *History, Tales, and Sketches.* Edited by James W. Tuttleton. New York: Library of America, 1983.

Melville, Herman. *The Piazza Tales and Other Prose Pieces, 1839–1860.* Evanston, Ill., and Chicago: Northwestern University Press and the Newberry Library, 1987.

Secondary Works

Burns, Sarah. *Painting the Dark Side: Art and the Gothic Imagination in Nineteenth-Century America.* Berkeley and Los Angeles: University of California Press, 2004.

Burns, Sarah. *Pastoral Inventions: Rural Life in Nineteenth-Century American Art and Culture.* Philadelphia: Temple University Press, 1989.

Chambers, Bruce W., *The World of David Gilmour Blythe, 1815–1865.* Washington, D.C.: Smithsonian Institution Press, 1980.

Conron, John. *American Picturesque.* University Park: Pennsylvania State University Press, 2000.

Gerdts, William H., and Theodore E. Stebbins Jr., eds. *"A Man of Genius": The Art of Washington Allston (1779–1843).* Boston: Museum of Fine Arts, 1979.

Huntington, David C. *The Landscapes of Frederic Edwin Church: Vision of an American Era.* New York: Braziller, 1966.

Johns, Elizabeth. *American Genre Painting: The Politics of Everyday Life.* New Haven, Conn.: Yale University Press, 1991.

Lubin, David M. *Picturing a Nation: Art and Social Change in Nineteenth-Century America.* New Haven, Conn.: Yale University Press, 1994.

McCoubrey, John, ed. *American Art, 1700–1960.* Englewood Cliffs, N.J.: Prentice-Hall, 1965.

Marx, Leo. *The Machine in the Garden: Technology and the Pastoral Ideal in America.* New York: Oxford University Press, 1964.

Miller, Angela. *Empire of the Eye: The Cultural Politics of Landscape Representation, 1825–1875.* Ithaca, N.Y.: Cornell University Press, 1993.

Miller, Angela. "Thomas Cole and Jacksonian America: *The Course of Empire* and Political Allegory." *Prospects: An Annual of American Cultural Studies* 14 (1989): 65–92.

Miller, David C. *Dark Eden: The Swamp in 19th-Century American Culture.* Cambridge, U.K.: Cambridge University Press, 1989.

Miller, David C., ed. *American Iconology: New Approaches to 19th-Century Art and Literature.* New Haven, Conn.: Yale University Press, 1993.

Novak, Barbara. *American Painting of the Nineteenth Century: Realism, Idealism, and the American Experience.* New York: Praeger, 1969.

Novak, Barbara. *Nature and Culture: American Landscape and Painting.* New York: Oxford University Press, 1980.

Peck, H. Daniel. *A World By Itself: The Pastoral Moment in Cooper's Fiction.* New Haven, Conn.: Yale University Press, 1977.

Ringe, Donald. *The Pictorial Mode: Space and Time in the Art of Bryant, Irving and Cooper.* Lexington: University of Kentucky Press, 1971.

Stebbins, Theodore E., Jr. *The Life and Works of Martin Johnson Heade.* New Haven, Conn., and London: Yale University Press, 1975.

Truettner, William H., and Alan Wallach. *Thomas Cole: Landscape into History.* New Haven, Conn., and London: Yale University Press, 1994.

Wilmerding, John, et al. *American Light: The Luminist Movement, 1850–1875.* Washington, D.C.: National Gallery, 1979.

Wolf, Bryan Jay. "All the World's a Code: Art and Ideology in Nineteenth-Century American Painting." *Art Journal* 44 (winter 1984): 328–337.

Wolf, Bryan Jay. *Romantic Re-Vision: Culture and Consciousness in Nineteenth-Century American Painting and Literature.* Chicago: University of Chicago Press, 1981.

David C. Miller

THE ATLANTIC MONTHLY

The *Atlantic Monthly* was born in November 1857, the offspring of a Boston-based Yankee humanism in vigorous middle age. The transcendental fervors of the 1830s and 1840s, the youth of the New England Renaissance, had moderated; but intellectual energy, a tempered idealism, a disposition to challenge the status quo, and optimism about the development of an explicitly American literature remained. These were reflected in active support for abolition, in theological liberalism, and in a growing body of major works of American scholarship and literature written by those living in and around Boston, Cambridge, and Concord. A quarter century later, in the 1880s, the center of intellectual culture and literary publishing would shift to New York, and New England would live out its long Indian summer, lapsing, some would say, into a self-satisfied senescence. But between 1850 and 1870, Boston was, in the semisatirical phrase of Oliver Wendell Holmes (1809–1894), "the Hub of the Universe" (Sedgwick, p. 23).

The culture of Boston, Cambridge, and Concord had already produced several short-lived literary magazines. Ralph Waldo Emerson (1803–1882) had commented that "the measles, the influenza, and the magazine appear to be periodic distempers" among Boston intellectuals and cited his own case and that of James Russell Lowell (1819–1891) as chronic (Letter to Samuel Ward, 24 February 1850). Emerson's own magazine, *The Dial* (1840–1844), influential beyond its small circulation, had cured him of editing but left his enthusiasm for an intellectually iconoclastic periodical intact. In 1831 Edwin Buckingham had initiated the *New-England Magazine,* which published early work by Nathaniel Hawthorne, Oliver Wendell Holmes, Henry Wadsworth Longfellow, and John Greenleaf Whittier. But Buckingham died in 1833, and his magazine followed suit in 1835. With youthful idealism, Lowell and his friend Robert Carter had founded *The Pioneer* in 1843 to promote progressive political reform, high aesthetic standards, and an explicitly American literature. But the intrepid *Pioneer* succumbed after three numbers, leaving Lowell saddled with both debt and a continued conviction of the need for a high-quality literary periodical.

THE FOUNDING

The catalyst that precipitated the *Atlantic* was Francis Henry Underwood (1825–1894), a young man from rural New England who through his activity in the new Free Soil Party, which was formed in 1847–1848 to oppose the extension of slavery into the territories, had been appointed clerk of the Massachusetts Senate. In 1853, hoping to enlist the influence of the New England literary movement in the antislavery cause, Underwood proposed the idea of a magazine to the Boston publisher John Jewett. Jewett, who had recently published *Uncle Tom's Cabin* (1852) and discovered that antislavery literature could be both righteous and remunerative, consented. But recession turned his boom to bankruptcy before the first number could be issued.

Underwood, however, persisted. Securing a job as a reader for the larger publishing house of Phillips, Sampson, & Company, he met sporadically with a group of writers, including Emerson, Holmes, Lowell, and Edwin P. Whipple, to promote his idea. He also cultivated the influence of the firm's most popular author, Harriet Beecher Stowe (1811–1896), who with the other writers convinced the reluctant Moses Dresser Phillips (1813–1859). On 5 May 1857 Phillips convened a dinner at which the magazine was named, its editorial policies defined, and Lowell appointed as editor with Underwood as assistant.

The founders of the *Atlantic,* who included writers and scholars as well as the publisher Phillips, intended it to serve the multiple purposes of culture, politics, and commerce. For both writers and publisher, it was an additional medium for distributing work, cultivating a broader audience, and increasing income. In the 1830s Edgar Allan Poe had hailed the dawning of the age of the magazine, and despite innumerable failures, for the next century magazines transformed the production and distribution of literature and the profession of authorship in the United States. When the *Atlantic* was founded, the average publication run for a book was only fifteen hundred copies. But a successful magazine such as *Harper's New Monthly Magazine,* founded in 1850 by the brothers Harper to promote their book-publishing business, could circulate fifty thousand copies and more twelve times a year. Magazines gave publishers and authors alike the potential to earn significant income before book publication and to develop a much larger readership for their books.

While the *Atlantic* was intended to profit both publisher and authors, it also had multiple cultural missions, articulated particularly by the influential voices of Emerson, Holmes, and Lowell. One mission was Underwood's original purpose of providing a broader platform than the abolitionist newspapers for prominent writers to oppose slavery and its political influences. A second cultural mission of the *Atlantic,* connected with commerce but transcending it, was to promote American writers, particularly from New England. The magazine's title suggested that it was intended to carry on intellectual exchange with Europe. The Boston cultural elite that shaped it rejected a chauvinistic literary nationalism and was in constant contact with its counterparts in England and on the Continent. *Atlantic* book reviews covered a broad range of European publications, and the magazine's editors solicited manuscripts from English authors. But the *Atlantic's* declaration of principles announced that most of the authors would be Americans, and in fact around nine in ten were. By contrast *Harper's New Monthly,* among others, published large quantities of British fiction because it was good quality popular literature with the added advantage that the absence of international copyright law made it cheaper. *Atlantic* fiction and poetry were predominantly American from the start, although writers from other regions complained with some justification that the disproportionate majority was from New England. Nonetheless, *Atlantic* editors cultivated writers from beyond New England, and within nine years a midwesterner, William Dean Howells (1839–1920), was selected as the assistant editor and the presumed successor to the editorship, which in fact he later held from 1871 to 1881.

While the *Atlantic* was no closed circle, it was founded to give voice and influence to the Yankee humanism that had developed in and around Boston by mid-century. The magazine reflected the mission of New England's cultural elite to educate and humanize a developing nation. It represented the Emersonian view that the proper aims of both individual and national life were to develop intellectual breadth and moral character that would guide personal behavior and social policy. The magazine was to provide cultural leadership by developing these values in an increasingly democratic nation focused on expansion and economic development in which the waning of religious orthodoxy was leaving a moral void. The magazine should, its founders believed, promote the best current writing, keep the great canonical works alive, and engage in principled debate on intellectual, political, and aesthetic issues. Like those other contemporary manifestations of the New England cultural mission, universal public education and the lyceum movement for communal education of adults through public lectures by noted persons, the magazine was both to broaden the readership and raise the standards of a liberal, literate culture.

JAMES RUSSELL LOWELL'S EDITORSHIP, 1857–1861

Given the *Atlantic's* missions, Lowell was a logical choice for editor. Both his failed *Pioneer* and his editorship of the *National Anti-Slavery Standard* had tempered his idealism with practical experience that gave Moses Phillips confidence. And Emerson believed that Lowell would be capable of defying the public, thereby providing it with cultural leadership. His two-year editorship of the *Standard* had reflected uncompromising opposition to slavery and its political influence. Lowell was a scholar of Western humanism who had good contacts with contemporary authors and a substantial reputation as a poet. All of this would give the magazine credibility, particularly important at its inception. At thirty-eight, Lowell was still recovering from the devastating deaths of his wife and three of their four children. He had recently reengaged in professional commitments by teaching modern languages at Harvard, and his editorship would divide his attention, but the generous salary of $2,500 a year was attractive.

Lowell issued the first number of the *Atlantic* in November 1857. Successive editors modified the tone and adjusted the balance of the contents, but much of the basic character and format of the magazine during the nineteenth century were established early. Lowell's first issue was typical of its successors in emphasizing literature and book culture. Three short stories and the first installment of a serial novel occupied about a third of the magazine's 128 pages, and all reflected the New England local color realism that was to characterize much *Atlantic* fiction. Half the fictional works were by women. One story was from Stowe, but the other two and the serial were from little-known, young aspirants. Poetry was a major feature, and most was written by established New England poets. That first issue included Emerson's "Days" and "Brahma," works by Whittier and Longfellow, and Lowell's satire on didactic verse. Emerson's "Illusions" and Holmes's "Autocrat of the Breakfast-Table" in different ways represented the reflective literary essay that would be gradually displaced by more journalistic reportage of current affairs.

The cover declared that the *Atlantic* would be "Devoted to Literature, Art, and Politics," and while literature was distinctly primary, current affairs also received attention. Parke Godwin, a New Yorker prominent in developing the first Republican Party platform, had been engaged to write political editorials to run at the end of the magazine, the slot held open closest to publication. Much of the remainder was commentary on literature and art. This included seven pages of "literary notices" in excruciatingly small type in which Charles Eliot Norton, E. P. Whipple, and Lowell reviewed a broad spectrum of current American and European publications. The magazine had the character of Yankee high culture with an earnest dedication to educating the intellect, aesthetic taste, and ethical conscience through liberal inquiry and reasoned debate.

As editor, Lowell worked hard but not always systematically. He sometimes irritated authors with his combination of disorganization, scholarly exactitude, and editorial liberty. He is often remembered for alienating Henry David Thoreau (1817–1862) by editing out a sentence in *The Maine Woods* that pantheistically attributed an immortal soul to pine trees. His generous support to young authors and his willingness to engage the *Atlantic* in controversy are less frequently told tales. In editing the *Atlantic,* Lowell generally practiced the liberal humanistic ideal of open inquiry and principled advocacy, often at some risk. His excision of Thoreau's pantheistic passage, for instance, came during a skirmish between the *Atlantic* and the religious press. Holmes, an Enlightenment rationalist who enjoyed provocation in the person of the Autocrat of the Breakfast-Table, had indicted Calvinism as a barbarous code that produced despair and neurosis by advocating excessive suppression of natural instincts, including the sexual. When the religious press howled, Lowell instead of censoring Holmes humorously advised him to slay one of his critics in order to arm himself with the jawbone of an ass to attack the other Philistines. Lowell again showed willingness to challenge religious orthodoxy when he published a three-part series by the Harvard botanist

The *Atlantic Monthly* office on Tremont Street.
Engraving from *My Mark Twain* by W. D. Howells, 1910.
SPECIAL COLLECTIONS LIBRARY, UNIVERSITY OF MICHIGAN

Asa Gray defending Charles Darwin's theories, probably the earliest authoritative exposition of natural selection and evolution in the United States.

Nor was Lowell reluctant to make his magazine express political opinions offensive to many. Impatient with Godwin's moderate criticisms of the compromises with slavery by President James Buchanan's administration, Lowell appended his own more radical condemnation to one of Godwin's editorials. After Godwin responded to this high-handedness by summarily resigning, Lowell wrote most editorials himself for the rest of his tenure. In a series that Emerson called brilliant, Lowell denounced the moral and political corruption, North and South, caused by slavery. The presidential election of 1860 he saw as the kind of moral turning point that comes "once to every man and nation," offering a choice between an immoral, expedient prosperity on the one hand and respect for the rights of labor and humanity on the other. As secession unfolded, he opposed appeasement of the South and foresaw in the war both rapid Union victory and the abolition of slavery.

JAMES T. FIELDS'S EDITORSHIP, 1861–1871

Lowell's editorship ended as the Civil War began. The *Atlantic's* original publishers, Moses Phillips and his partner Sampson, had both died in 1859, and the magazine, still risky, had been bought for $10,000 by Ticknor and Fields, publishers of Emerson, Hawthorne, Lowell, Thoreau, and others and the proprietors of the Old Corner Bookstore in Boston. Lowell was retained, although Underwood was replaced by William Ticknor's son Howard Ticknor. Gradually, however, the junior partner, James T. Fields (1817–1881), grew restless with Lowell's lack of system and scholarly tastes. By 1861 Fields was ready to try his own hand. The transition was amicable; Lowell continued to contribute, and Fields had no intention of radically changing the magazine Lowell had made influential. But both Fields's personality and his dual position as publisher and editor combined to moderately popularize the *Atlantic* and broaden its readership.

Lowell had been raised a member of the Cambridge intellectual elite and had attended Harvard. Fields, the son of a deceased sea captain from Portsmouth, New Hampshire, came to Boston at thirteen as a clerk at the Old Corner Bookstore and educated himself mainly through the Boston Mercantile Library. Handsome, hearty in manner, inclined to flattery, and totally extroverted, Fields admired writers and wrote verse himself but understood that his talent was for the business of books. By the time he took over the editorship of the *Atlantic* in 1861 at age forty-four, he had become an influential junior partner and had married the charming Annie Adams (1834–1915), who though seventeen years his junior shared his literary and social interests and herself became a talented writer. Over the next decade Fields used the magazine effectively to make his firm America's premier literary publisher and to create a profitable golden age of New England letters.

Fields's talent for promotion served the economic interest not only of his publishing house and the *Atlantic* but also of his authors. In an early form of celebrity publishing, he created the public impression of an *Atlantic* circle of New England Olympians, including Emerson, Holmes, Longfellow, Lowell, Stowe, and Whittier, loyal to the magazine and to Ticknor and Fields. Abolishing the magazine's genteel policy of anonymity, he published their works and their names as regularly as possible, offered their portraits with annual subscriptions, brought out their books in multiple editions, selected sympathetic reviewers, planted reviews and literary gossip in newspapers across the country, featured them in Annie's Charles Street literary salon, and advertised them nationally.

Some critics have held that Fields's promotions corrupted New England literary culture, making it self-congratulatory and closed, but his *Atlantic* does not support this view. Fields affirmed the circle but also widened it. He won back Thoreau, publishing seven of his essays, most of them posthumously. Without Fields's pressure for *Atlantic* serials, Hawthorne probably would not have published his English notebooks or begun the abortive *Dolliver Romance*. But Fields also actively sought new and particularly younger authors. In this effort he was aided by his wife Annie and his quasi-official assistant Thomas Wentworth Higginson (1823–1911), both of whom particularly encouraged women writers. Higginson is often remembered for his equivocal though essentially supportive role as Emily Dickinson's "preceptor," begun when she responded to his *Atlantic* "Letter to a Young Contributor" (April 1862). He is less often remembered for his early support of such largely forgotten writers as Charlotte Hawes, Helen Hunt, Harriet Prescott Spofford, Rose Terry, and Celia Thaxter. Fields himself recognized the power of Rebecca Harding Davis's "Life in the Iron Mills," published it in April 1861, and solicited more.

Fields also demonstrated that neither the *Atlantic* nor Boston culture were closed circles when in 1866 he hired William Dean Howells, a relative unknown from Ohio, as assistant editor with a specific mandate to cultivate new talent. Among those Howells encouraged and Fields published were Thomas Bailey Aldrich (1836–1907; editor of the *Atlantic*, 1881–1890), John DeForest, Bret Harte, Sarah Orne Jewett, and most prolifically Henry James. Importantly Howells himself steadily evolved from Romantic poet to realistic reporter of contemporary social behavior, developing his essential ideas of literary realism and applying them influentially in his prolific book reviews, his editorial choices, and his own contributions.

Atlantic literature under Fields, with Howells's assistance, was predominantly realistic. Writers like Jewett, Stowe, Terry, and Thaxter reflected the best of the New England local color movement, dominated by women. Work by Davis, DeForest, James, and Howells himself consciously subverted the formulas of conventional sentimental fiction and frustrated the romantic expectations of its readers. In nonfiction the journalist James Parton persuaded Fields to move away from the ethereal Emersonian essay toward direct reportage of contemporary life.

While literature was the mainstay of Fields's *Atlantic,* the magazine remained liberal in religion, science, education, and politics as well, generally reflecting an optimistic faith in moral and social progress. Fields refused to add a women's section but published Stowe's long-running domestic series, House and Home Papers, as well as the Chimney Corner series that moderately advocated the basic principles of the nineteenth-century women's movement, including the vote, expanded property rights, equitable divorce laws, and access to education and the professions. Zina Pierce's Cooperative Housekeeping series (1868–1869) proposed more radical reform of women's work and economic rewards in the form of domestic cooperatives. Speculative essays on religion by James Freeman Clarke, Henry James Sr., and David Wasson criticized orthodox Protestant dogma as culturally blind and spoke for a more universal sense of religious and moral truth.

Fields's *Atlantic* portrayed little of the grimness of the Civil War, but the magazine's political views were unequivocal. Early in the war it advocated immediate emancipation. Higginson, a supporter of the radical abolitionist John Brown (1800–1859), contributed sympathetic histories of slave revolts. Both Emerson and Lowell insisted on the need to square the Union cause with the universal laws of moral progress by abolishing slavery. They and others criticized Abraham Lincoln's pragmatic hesitation, but after his assassination they eulogized him as the greatest American and supreme representative of the democratic will.

In the war's aftermath *Atlantic* writers, including Senator Charles Sumner and Frederick Douglass, excoriated President Andrew Johnson, denounced clemency for the rebels, and advocated the Radical Republican program for Reconstruction. Douglass, Higginson, and others declared that former slaves must immediately be granted confiscated land, the vote, and full civic equality enforced by long-term federal occupation. Sumner and the historian George Bancroft, among others, expounded visions of a democratic nation freed of the moral shackles of slavery, manifestly destined to absorb the whole of the American continent into one great plural unit. Emerson, Higginson, and Lowell, while generally sharing this expansive optimism, cautioned that cultural and moral progress must match the geographical and material and that this would require cultural leadership.

By the late 1860s, Fields had grown weary of both the editorship and his business. A lawsuit over royalties brought against him by a disaffected author, Gail Hamilton, had revealed no wrongdoing but was professionally damaging and personally painful. The *Atlantic*'s circulation plummeted in 1870 from a peak of fifty thousand to about thirty-five thousand, partly in a prudish backlash against an 1869 article by Harriet Stowe exposing the incest of George Gordon, Lord Byron. But the publishing house of Fields, Osgood, &

Company, which James Fields had formed with James R. Osgood in 1868 after William Ticknor died in 1864, and the *Atlantic Monthly* had both thrived under his management, offering a comfortable and honorable retirement. On 2 January 1871 Fields resigned his editorship to Howells and sold the company to James Osgood. As publisher and editor, he had promoted the treatment of literature as a commodity, but in doing so he had also expanded the market for good writing and the opportunities for authorship in America.

See also Book Publishing; Boston; Civil War; Editors; Female Authorship; *Harper's New Monthly Magazine;* Literary Criticism; Literary Marketplace; Literary Nationalism; Periodicals; Publishers

BIBLIOGRAPHY
Primary Works
Major primary sources include the editorial correspondence of Lowell and Howells and the publishing archives of Ticknor and Fields in the Houghton Library at Harvard University and volumes of the *Atlantic Monthly* 1857–1870 indexed in *The Atlantic Index* (Boston: Houghton Mifflin, 1889).

Fields, James T. *Yesterdays with Authors.* Boston: J. R. Osgood, 1872.

Howells, William Dean. *Selected Letters.* 6 vols. Edited by George Warren Arms et al. Boston: Twayne, 1979–1983.

Lowell, James Russell. *Letters of James Russell Lowell.* 2 vols. Edited by Charles Eliot Norton. New York: Harper & Brothers, 1894.

Secondary Works
Austin, James C. *Fields of the Atlantic Monthly: Letters to an Editor, 1861–1870.* San Marino, Calif.: Huntington Library, 1953.

Ballou, Ellen B. *The Building of the House: Houghton Mifflin's Formative Years.* Boston: Houghton Mifflin, 1970.

Brooks, Van Wyck. *The Flowering of New England, 1815–1865.* New York: Dutton, 1936.

Brooks, Van Wyck. *New England: Indian Summer, 1865–1915.* New York: Dutton, 1940.

Charvat, William. *The Profession of Authorship in America, 1800–1870.* Edited by Matthew J. Bruccoli. Columbus: Ohio State University Press, 1968.

Duberman, Martin. *James Russell Lowell.* Boston: Houghton Mifflin, 1966.

Howe, M. A. DeWolfe. *The Atlantic Monthly and Its Makers.* Boston: Atlantic Monthly Press, 1919.

McMahon, Helen. *Criticism of Fiction: A Study of Trends in the Atlantic Monthly, 1857–1898.* New York: Bookman, 1952.

Mott, Frank Luther. *A History of American Magazines,* vol. 2, *1850–1865.* Cambridge, Mass.: Harvard University Press, 1938.

Sedgwick, Ellery. *A History of the Atlantic Monthly, 1857–1909: Yankee Humanism at High Tide and Ebb.* Amherst: University of Massachusetts Press, 1994.

Tryon, Warren S. *Parnassus Corner: A Life of James T. Fields, Publisher to the Victorians.* Boston: Houghton Mifflin, 1963.

Ellery Sedgwick

AUTOBIOGRAPHY

An autobiography is a prose narrative about someone's own life. It is generally presumed to be factual, but the way the narrative is shaped, the selections and emphases that must be made by an author, may introduce elements of imaginative invention that reveal something about the author's inner development. If, strictly speaking, there were relatively few "full-dress autobiographies" published in the United States between 1820 and 1870, this half-century was one of the most fertile periods in American literary history for published *autobiographical* writing, which can include diaries, memoirs, lives, histories, journals, narratives, confessions, adventures, recollections, and even novels and poetry. Indeed, many of the most influential texts of the so-called American Renaissance, such as *Walden* (1854) and *Leaves of Grass* (1855), are hybrid literary forms that include strong autobiographical elements but are not, strictly speaking, autobiographies.

Before the 1970s most literary scholars regarded autobiography as a subliterary genre, important primarily as a source—if an unreliable one—of historical and biographical information. The majority of nineteenth-century autobiographers were not professional writers, and their works seldom demonstrated the formal complexity that was expected of literary works in the era of the "New Criticism." The turn toward historically oriented forms of literary scholarship, coupled with the desire to recover the lost voices of women and minority writers, have transformed autobiography into one of the most studied American genres. Nevertheless, the period covered by this essay has not been exhausted. Louis Kaplan's *Bibliography of American Autobiographies* (1961), using relatively strict criteria for inclusion, indicates that this era produced many hundreds of autobiographies, most of which have never been given sustained scholarly attention. Indeed, the field is so large and complex that scholarly treatments tend to focus on a handful of

well-known authors and a few subgenres such as slave and captivity narratives. And studies of American autobiography often conclude with Benjamin Franklin (1706–1790) at the end of the eighteenth century or start with Henry Adams (1838–1918) at the beginning of the twentieth.

The scope and variety of autobiographical publications in nineteenth-century America suggest that the rules of the genre—who could write what for whom—were still emerging in the context of a highly mobile society. Autobiographical writing—if not autobiography proper—flowered in the United States in the mid-nineteenth century as the result of numerous influences, including the ongoing tradition of spiritual self-examination, the expansion of a literate middle class, the spread of popular democracy, a belief in the reality and autonomy of the individual, and the right of that individual to discover a unique destiny. The egocentric qualities of Romanticism in literature and the arts magnified the tendency of Americans to celebrate themselves, to believe that every individual had a story worth telling. And, unique among literary genres, autobiographical writing was accessible to anyone who could write or dictate the story of his or her life. Many autobiographies were written by ministers, politicians, military men, and other professionals, but a substantial portion were written by ordinary people who had an extraordinary story to tell, an injustice to expose, or a cause to promote. There was money to be made too, for the literary marketplace was expanding with the scale of the nation as a whole. The forms of autobiographical writing proliferated in relation to the varied circumstances of their authors, the audiences they wished to reach, and the means by which they were published. Indeed, in this era it is not surprising that autobiographical elements would begin to blend with genres such as the sermon, the novel, the nature study, and the nationalist epic.

If a single characteristic can be said to hold these autobiographical texts of this era together, it is the theme of exploring what it means to be an "American." The United States was still a new nation, and it was struggling to define its purpose and the complementary roles played by its citizens. This presented difficulties for writers who were excluded from the dominant culture's definition of citizenship (in the case of enslaved persons and Native Americans), or who were discouraged from defining a public self except in relation to a spouse or paternal figure (as in the case of women). The nineteenth century was an era in which the authorized autobiographical subject, the life of a representative "white" American man, gave way to challenges from women, African Americans, and other groups whose autobiographical writings

> *Franklin's* Autobiography *established the American upward-mobility narrative in which material success combined with service to the community replaced the contemplation of the state of one's soul that dominated autobiographical writing before the nineteenth century.*

I have been the more particular in this Description of my Journey, & shall be so of my first Entry into that City, that you may in your Mind compare such unlikely Beginning with the Figure I have since made there. I was in my working Dress, my best Cloaths being to come round by Sea. I was dirty from my Journey; my Pockets were stuff'd out with Shirts & Stockings, and I knew no Soul nor where to look for Lodging. I was fatigu'd with Travelling, Rowing, & Want of Rest, I was very hungry; and my whole Stock of Cash consisted of a Dutch Dollar, and about a Shilling in Copper. The latter I gave the People of the Boat for my Passage, who at first refus'd it, on Acct of my Rowing; but I insisted on their taking it, a Man being sometimes more generous when he has but a little Money than when he has plenty, perhaps thro' fear of being thought to have but little. Then I walk'd up the Street, gazing about, till near the Market House I met a Boy with Bread. I had made many a Meal on Bread, & inquiring where he got it, I went immediately to the Baker's he directed me to in second Street; and ask'd for Bisket, intending such as we had in Boston, but they it seems were not made in Philadelphia, then I ask'd for a threepenny Loaf, and was told they had none such: so not considering or knowing the Difference of Money & the greater Cheapness nor the Names of his Bread, I bad him give me three pennyworth of any sort. He gave me accordingly three great Puffy Rolls. I was surpriz'd at the Quantity, but took it, and, having no Room in my Pockets, walk'd off with a Roll under each Arm, & eating the other. Thus I went up Market-Street as far as fourth Street, passing by the Door of Mr Read, my future Wife's Father, when she standing at the Door saw me, & thought I made as I certainly did a most awkward ridiculous Appearance. Then I turn'd and went down Chestnut Street and part of Walnut Street, eating my Roll all the Way, and coming round found myself again at Market street Wharff, near the Boat I came in, to which I went for a Draught of the River Water; and, being fill'd with one of my Rolls, gave the other two to a Woman & her Child that came down the River in the Boat with us and were waiting to go farther.

Benjamin Franklin, *Autobiography* (New York: Library of America, 1994), pp. 1328–1329.

were, by their very existence, a challenge to the conception of who was entitled to a public voice and therefore authorized to be an American. In this sense autobiography played an important role in progressive expansion of the rights promised by the Declaration of Independence and the Constitution—the founding autobiographical documents of the United States—to which many of these marginalized autobiographers appealed in their works.

THE FRANKLINIAN TRADITION

The influence of the *Autobiography of Benjamin Franklin* on American culture is probably greater than any text other than the Bible. It was originally published as Franklin's *Life* in 1791, but the text was not cobbled together into anything resembling its present form until the 1840s. Nevertheless, Franklin's memoir, in its various forms, was surely the most widely disseminated American autobiography of the nineteenth

century. It was adapted, shortly after its initial publication, in dozens of variably priced editions, and practically every would-be autobiographer, including women and slaves, had to reckon with Franklin's model of the bourgeois American self: someone who is born in poverty and obscurity but who manages through hard work and moral virtue to rise to a position of wealth and fame.

The tradition of the spiritual autobiography, which was still vibrant in Franklin's time, focused on the development of the author's relationship with God (see, e.g., Jonathan Edwards's *Personal Narrative*, c. 1740). By the beginning of the nineteenth century, however, the pattern of struggles overcome on the road to salvation was increasingly supplemented, in the American context, by the more secular success narrative, the "rags-to-riches" stories of "self-made men." This pattern would expand through the nineteenth century in America until it became the characteristic mode of self-presentation for nearly every established American (consider the many biographies of Presidents Lincoln and Garfield). Of course, the spiritual journey continued to structure the form of the success narrative, which substitutes the acquisition of capital and status for the infusion of grace. Franklin's escape from poverty and "The Way to Wealth" parallel the escape from sin and the road to salvation. In this sense, wealth is an outward sign of moral virtue, and it is bestowed for the purpose of becoming a benefactor to one's society. Franklin's life—and other lives based on his model—negotiate the tension between the material and the spiritual, the individual and the community, by asserting that self-interest coincides with the interests of society.

The image Franklin established—not without some deviation from the memories of his contemporaries—defined him as what D. H. Lawrence later called "the first dummy American." And Franklin's exemplary life was both liberating and confining to successive generations. He offered the possibility of personal transformation through social mobility, but he also placed responsibility for poverty completely on the individual. His remarkable frankness and self-deprecating humor establishes intimacy—a spirit of equality—with the reader, as if the author is not dressed for a public ball but receiving us in his customary domestic clothing. He adopts a pose of radical honesty and self-knowledge at the service of common public interests. Nevertheless, for all his seeming openness about past "errata," Franklin does not offer the reader much direct insight into his personal feelings: his loves, his hates, the motives that drive his ambition. Franklin also presents a vision of happiness based on wealth and public acclaim at the expense of spiritual or emotional fulfillment. Perhaps the shift to secular autobiography banished the introspectiveness of spiritual self-examination; Thomas Jefferson's (1743–1826) *Autobiography* (1821) is similarly impersonal. In any case, Franklin's autobiography inspired a host of imitators, but it also motivated some writers to subvert his apparent faith in capitalism and American equality, his economic model of success, his concern for appearances over reality, and his apparent neglect of spiritual and emotional reasons for living. For all its influence, some nineteenth-century readers such as Herman Melville (1819–1891) viewed Franklin's autobiography less as a guide for proper conduct than as the deceptive apologia of a con man not all that different from Stephen Burroughs (1765–1840), a notorious Yankee rogue who published his *Memoirs* in 1798.

The Life of P. T. Barnum, Written by Himself (1855)—possibly the second-best-selling American autobiography of the nineteenth century—reflects the influence of Franklin's values and the limitations of his model of the American self. Like Franklin's *Autobiography,* Barnum's *Life* is the story of how a poor boy became a rich and famous man. But Barnum (1810–1891) possesses little of the civic-mindedness of Franklin. At times his *Life* seems like a disconnected compendium of practical jokes and folksy humor mixed with solemn, Franklinesque advice, such as his "rules for success in business." From the beginning, Barnum emphasizes that he was born in an era that was radically different from the eighteenth century. The rules of the economic game had changed. The rapid expansion of cities and industry and an emerging consumer culture called for a new model of success, not based on thrift and humility so much as on conspicuous consumption, visionary speculation, and bombastic advertising. Rather than building the civic infrastructure and cultivating moral virtues, Barnum describes the means by which he hoaxes the American public on an ever-grander scale: liquor, lotteries, Joice Heth, the Fejee Mermaid, Tom Thumb. Ultimately Barnum attributes his triumphs to American characteristics as much as to his own initiative; he expresses this neatly in his dedication: "To the Universal Yankee Nation, of Which I am proud to be one." To some contemporaries, Barnum's *Life* did not represent a rejection of Franklinian values; rather, Barnum was a product of the go-getting marketplace these values encouraged rather than the deeper intellectual and spiritual aspects of the self. For all his claims of hard work, Franklin's autobiography also communicated the value of image over reality in a culture based on capitalist speculation.

THE TRANSCENDENTAL SELF

If the bourgeois self—based on wealth and position—was a speculative bubble by the mid-nineteenth century, then where could the ultimate meaning and purpose of the individual be found? The leading American Romantic intellectual, Ralph Waldo Emerson (1803–1882), called on his fellow Americans in speeches and essays such as "The American Scholar" (1837) and "Self-Reliance" (1841) to throw off the shackles of the past, to become nonconformists, and to live an authentic life. In the act of becoming more truly themselves, unfettered by external influences, American individuals could become more closely connected to each other: the small "self" of the individual could become one with the big "Self" of all human life and experience. This is the essence of Emerson's transcendentalist beliefs. His collection of brief biographies, *Representative Men* (1850), for example, presents the lives of "great men," such as Goethe and Napoleon, whose greatness was emblematic of the larger forces at work in their cultures. They were great

> *Like Franklin, Thoreau is an American pragmatist trying to find the right way to live, but, influenced by Romanticism, Thoreau attempts to recover a more authentic, natural existence by rejecting materialism and the structures of civilization.*
>
> I went to the woods because I wished to live deliberately, to front only the essential facts of life, and see if I could not learn what it had to teach, and not, when I came to die, discover that I had not lived. I did not wish to live what was not life, living is so dear; nor did I wish to practise resignation, unless it was quite necessary. I wanted to live deep and suck out all the marrow of life, to live so sturdily and Spartan-like as to put to rout all that was not life, to cut a broad swath and shave close, to drive life into a corner, and reduce it to its lowest terms, and, if it proved to be mean, why then to get the whole and genuine meanness of it, and publish its meanness to the world; or if it were sublime, to know it by experience, and be able to give a true account of it in my next excursion. For most men, it appears to me, are in a strange uncertainty about it, whether it is of the devil or of God, and have *somewhat hastily* concluded that it is the chief end of man here to "glorify God and enjoy him forever."
>
> Henry David Thoreau, *Walden* (New York: Library of America, 1985), pp. 394–395.

because they focused the virtues of their people. In this manner, transcendentalist autobiography continued Franklin's exemplary project, but it shifted the focus from the external and material to the internal and spiritual.

In *Walden* (1854) Henry David Thoreau (1817–1862) tried to put the ideals of Emerson into practice. He attempts to find the true material and spiritual nature of the self by living in solitude in the woods near Concord, Massachusetts. In effect, Thoreau was intellectualizing the experiences of genuine frontier autobiographers including Davy Crockett and Francis Parkman and high-seas adventurers such as Richard Henry Dana. Based on Thoreau's diaries from the years 1845–1847, *Walden* is divided into chapters on topics such as "Economy," "Brute Neighbors," and "Sounds." It does not cover a lengthy span of Thoreau's life, nor does it adhere strictly to the chronology of events

during his stay at the pond. Instead *Walden* condenses and thematizes his experiences in a manner that equates the seasons of the author's life with the seasons of nature. Although Thoreau begins with the promise to deliver "a simple and sincere account of his own life" (p. 325), he transforms himself into an abstraction of human experience in the context of a seemingly natural environment. Thoreau's autobiography deconstructs his individuality and makes him into a universal man whose personal life is of no consequence to the reader.

Walt Whitman's (1819–1892) autobiographical collection of poems, *Leaves of Grass* (1855), was also inspired by Thoreau's mentor, Emerson. Whitman shares Thoreau's discovery of the self in solitary encounters with nature, but he also images himself as the embodiment and spokesperson for every American: "Through me many long dumb voices / Voices of the interminable generations of slaves" (p. 50). Correspondingly, the frontispiece to the first unsigned edition of *Leaves* presents Whitman not as an aloof, Harvard-educated poet but as a common workman. The book was supposed to represent the spontaneous voice of the American people en masse. Like *Walden*, Whitman's long poem "Song of Myself" does not have a narrative line, but it is organized according to the dialectical cycles of nature—the centrifugal and centripetal, birth and death, and day and night. Unlike Thoreau, Whitman is not concerned with dissolving the distinction between self and place so much as between "self," the individual, and "Self," the common human experience: "Walt Whitman, an American, one of the roughs, a kosmos" (p. 50). Whitman's most autobiographical poetry, like Thoreau's prose, gives the reader little insight into Whitman as an individual human being. If Franklin's autobiography made him the personal exemplar of the bourgeois American, he still stands out as a recognizable historical individual; transcendentalist self-representations, in contrast, eliminated personal specificity—as well as genre boundaries—in favor of national or human representation combined with visionary self-transcendence.

ASSERTING THE RIGHT TO SELFHOOD

It is significant that both Whitman and Thoreau undertook their autobiographical projects on the Fourth of July; they never struggled with the question of whether they had the right to present themselves as representative Americans. Of course, the liberties achieved by Franklin's generation were not extended to everyone in the United States by the mid-nineteenth century. Millions of African Americans were enslaved, and the institution was threatening to expand with the nation into the Far West. Meanwhile,

Neither the Franklianian nor Thoreauvian models of American selfhood were available to enslaved African Americans such as Frederick Douglass. Nevertheless, Douglass's Narrative *weaves together the traditions of spiritual, Enlightenment, and Romantic autobiography.*

You are loosed from your moorings, and are free; I am fast in my chains, and am a slave! You move merrily before the gentle gale, and I sadly before the bloody whip! You are freedom's swift-winged angels, that fly round the world; I am confined in bands of iron! O that I were free! O, that I were on one of your gallant decks, and under your protecting wing! Alas! betwixt me and you, the turbid waters roll. Go on, go on. O that I could also go! Could I but swim! If I could fly! O, why was I born a man, of whom to make a brute! The glad ship is gone; she hides in the dim distance. I am left in the hottest hell of unending slavery. O God, save me! God, deliver me! Let me be free! Is there any God? Why am I a slave? I will run away. I will not stand it. Get caught, or get clear, I'll try it. I had as well die with ague as the fever. I have only one life to lose. I had as well be killed running as die standing.

Only think of it; one hundred miles straight north, and I am free! Try it? Yes! God helping me, I will. It cannot be that I shall live and die a slave. I will take to the water. This very bay shall yet bear me into freedom. The steamboats steered in a north-east course from North Point. I will do the same; and when I get to the head of the bay, I will turn my canoe adrift, and walk straight through Delaware into Pennsylvania. When I get there, I shall not be required to have a pass; I can travel without being disturbed. Let but the first opportunity offer, and, come what will, I am off. Meanwhile, I will try to bear up under the yoke. I am not the only slave in the world. Why should I fret? I can bear as much as any of them. Besides, I am but a boy, and all boys are bound to some one. It may be that my misery in slavery will only increase my happiness when I get free. There is a better day coming.

Frederick Douglass, *Narrative of the Life of Frederick Douglass* (New York: Library of America, 1994), pp. 59–60.

women everywhere were encouraged to remain within the domestic sphere, barred from the professions, and discouraged from engaging in personal publication. In this context, autobiographical writing played an important role in extending the liberal vision of self-determination for these and other marginalized Americans including the destitute and disabled, Native Americans, and immigrants who lived within the expanding borders of the United States.

More than a hundred former slaves, usually men, published narratives of their experiences between 1830 and 1870. Typically these narratives—America's unique contribution to world literature—drew on the spiritual, Enlightenment, and Romantic traditions of autobiographical writing. They showed how slavery as an institution perverted Christianity, destroyed the moral character of the slaveholder, corrupted the principles on which the nation was founded, and severed the strongest emotional ties between human beings. Slave narrators such as Frederick Douglass (1818–1895) and Harriet Jacobs (c. 1813–1897) proved their worthiness to be regarded as citizens by replicating the Franklinian model of self-improvement under great duress.

As Douglass writes in *Narrative of the Life of Frederick Douglass, an American Slave, Written by Himself* (1845), "The argument which he so warmly urged, against my learning to read, only served to inspire me with a desire and determination to learn" (p. 38). Douglass begins his *Narrative* by describing how the slave is excluded from the traditional sources of identity (a birthday, family, marriage, and literacy), but he goes on to describe how he transforms himself in a manner that recalls the Declaration of Independence's characterization of American manhood as the determination to overthrow tyranny: "You have seen how a man was made a slave; you shall see how a slave was made a man" (p. 60). Douglass's fight with Covey the "nigger-breaker" is an iconic moment in which a generalized "slave" becomes a generalized "man." After his escape, he abandons the name "Bailey" for "Douglass" and proclaims himself nothing less than a direct heir of the unfulfilled promise of the Enlightenment and the American Revolution. "Douglass," according to one contemporary, "passed through every gradation of rank comprised in our national make-up, and bears upon his person and upon his soul everything that is American" (Douglass,

p. 132). For all his protestations against American social injustice, Douglass was "a Representative American man—a type of his countrymen" (Douglass, p. 132). Like Franklin, the former colonial subject, Douglass, Jacobs, and many other slave narrators defiantly wrote themselves into existence as exemplary Americans.

The rich tradition of spiritual self-examination, diary keeping, and private, introspective verse was kept alive in the nineteenth century largely by women—consider, for example, the poetry of Emily Dickinson (1830–1886) or the journals of Mary Boykin Chesnut (1823–1886). Women had fewer opportunities to enter the professions, make the social associations, or engage in the adventures (or crimes) that typically led to publication of an autobiographical work. Women were also discouraged from presenting themselves in public, and the culture of domesticity persuaded many women to discount the importance of their own experiences. Although female autobiographers were less numerous than male autobiographers, there are many notable examples of their work, such as *A Narrative of the Life of Mrs. Mary Jemison* (1824) by a woman who had lived among the Seneca Indians for forty years and who was interviewed by James Everett Seaver (1787–1827). Caroline Matilda Kirkland—writing under the pen name/fictional character Mary Clavers—detailed her pioneer experiences with her husband in Michigan in *A New Home—Who'll Follow?* (1839). Lydia Sigourney's (1791–1865) *Letters of Life* (1866) was the first full-length autobiography written by a literary professional in the United States. In order to avoid violating the cultural taboo against public self-revelation, Fanny Fern (Sara Payson Parton, 1811–1872) in *Ruth Hall* (1855) presented her personal experiences as a novel rather than an autobiography and was viciously attacked in the press when her identity was exposed. Quite often, women's autobiographical writings indicate their exclusion from the public sphere by showing how literary professionalism—among other capabilities comparable with those of their male contemporaries—is compatible with traditional domestic responsibilities; in effect, they undermined the Enlightenment and transcendental conception of the American self as solitary, masculine, and universal.

See also Biography; *Narrative of the Life of Frederick Douglass; A New Home—Who'll Follow?;* Slave Narratives; *Walden*

BIBLIOGRAPHY

Primary Works

Barnum, P. T. *The Life of P. T. Barnum, Written by Himself.* 1855. Urbana: University of Illinois Press, 2000.

Douglass, Frederick. *Autobiographies: Narrative of the Life, My Bondage and My Freedom, Life and Times.* New York: Library of America, 1994.

Franklin, Benjamin. *Essays, Articles, Bagatelles, and Letters; Poor Richard's Almanack, Autobiography.* New York: Library of America, 1987.

Thoreau, Henry David. *A Week on the Concord and Merrimack Rivers, Walden, The Maine Woods, Cape Cod.* New York: Library of America, 1985.

Whitman, Walt. *Poetry and Prose.* New York: Library of America, 1982.

Secondary Works

Andrews, William L. *To Tell a Free Story: The First Century of Afro-American Autobiography, 1760–1865.* Urbana: University of Illinois Press, 1986.

Buell, Lawrence. "Autobiography in the American Renaissance." In *American Autobiography: Retrospect and Prospect,* edited by Paul John Eakin, pp. 47–69. Madison: University of Wisconsin Press, 1991.

Cawelti, John G. *Apostles of the Self-Made Man: Changing Concepts of Success in America.* Chicago: University of Chicago Press, 1965.

Couser, G. Thomas. *Altered Egos: Authority in American Autobiography.* New York: Oxford University Press, 1989.

Couser, G. Thomas. *American Autobiography: The Prophetic Mode.* Amherst: University of Massachusetts Press, 1979.

Cox, James M. *Recovering Literature's Lost Ground: Essays in American Autobiography.* Baton Rouge: Louisiana State University Press, 1989.

Fabian, Ann. *The Unvarnished Truth: Personal Narratives in Nineteenth-Century America.* Berkeley: University of California Press, 2000.

Kaplan, Louis, comp., in association with James Tyler Cook, Clinton E. Colby Jr., and Daniel C. Haskell. *A Bibliography of American Autobiographies.* Madison: University of Wisconsin Press, 1961.

Sayre, Robert F., ed. *American Lives: An Anthology of Autobiographical Writing.* Madison: University of Wisconsin Press, 1994.

Shea, Daniel B. *Spiritual Autobiography in Early America.* 1968. Madison: University of Wisconsin Press, 1988.

Spengemann, William C. *The Forms of Autobiography: Episodes in the History of a Literary Genre.* New Haven, Conn.: Yale University Press, 1980.

Steele, Jeffrey. *The Representation of the Self in the American Renaissance.* Chapel Hill: University of North Carolina Press, 1987.

William Pannapacker

THE AUTOCRAT OF
THE BREAKFAST-TABLE

The Autocrat of the Breakfast-Table (1858), an utterly distinctive, landmark work of American nonfiction prose, was born out of the brilliant talk at a series of Boston dinner meetings. These 1857 dinners brought together a constellation of the most eminent representatives of the sudden mid-nineteenth-century "renaissance" of New England literature and culture—Ralph Waldo Emerson, Henry Wadsworth Longfellow, James Russell Lowell, Oliver Wendell Holmes, and John Lothrop Motley, among others—to discuss the founding of an ambitious new journal. Finally Lowell agreed to serve as editor if Holmes would sign on as the magazine's first regular contributor, and the result was the formation of the *Atlantic Monthly*—an enduring and extremely influential organ for the development and promotion of American thought and writing that would serve as the nation's prime intellectual forum for many decades to come. Marking Boston's dominant position in the mid-century cultural landscape and speaking for a distinctive New England vision, the magazine nonetheless became an unavoidable point of reference for writers and thinkers in every region of the country. The *Atlantic*'s godfather, Dr. Holmes, gave it its name and then also contributed the "breakfast-table" essay feature in each issue, beginning with the twelve monthly installments of *The Autocrat of the Breakfast-Table* for 1857–1858. The feature became a huge overnight sensation, captivating a broad readership that assured the new journal's success. For while in these early years the *Atlantic* was the main publishing venue for many of the now canonical literary figures of the New England school—Emerson, Longfellow, Nathaniel Hawthorne, Harriet Beecher Stowe, and John Greenleaf Whittier as well as Holmes and Lowell—it was clear that the "Autocrat" was the journal's main attraction; the *Atlantic*'s stance and tone was from the first defined by and identified with the breakfast-table papers of Dr. Holmes. These enormously popular columns that both recorded and shaped the talk of the town for a large public also transformed Holmes's life—giving the dilettante doctor-writer his sobriquet, the "Autocrat," and making him a household name both in England and in the United States for more than a century.

DR. OLIVER WENDELL HOLMES:
A NATIONAL CHARACTER

A tiny, hyperactive, and hyper-loquacious bundle of energy, Dr. Holmes (not to be confused with his son, Supreme Court Justice Oliver Wendell Holmes Jr.) wanted to play all the parts. His life (1809–1894)

Oliver Wendell Holmes Sr. Photograph by Mathew Brady. THE GRANGER COLLECTION, NEW YORK

spanned most of the nineteenth century, and for much of that time he was recognized by his contemporaries as a national character, even a national institution. Preeminent in American medicine as well as in American literature, he was somehow able to combine the stances of grave scientist and light humorist, sage and jester, traditionalist and progressive, voice of reason and confirmed ironist. Crusading all his life against emerging specialization, the generalist Holmes produced lectures, essays, and poems that placed him at the center of national debates in a surprising range of fields: theology, psychology, and natural science as well as medicine and literature.

The mid-century's best-known doctor, Holmes was one of the fathers of modern American medicine. A professor at and dean of the Harvard Medical School and a major advocate of the revolutionary shift to Parisian "clinical" methods in North America, Holmes addressed and educated his countrymen as the leading spokesman for the medical field at a crucial transitional period in its development. He had studied in Paris and was a key promoter of the "clinical" revolution that mainly worked to clear away the errors and

Illustration by Julian Scott for an 1892 edition of
The Autocrat of the Breakfast-Table. GRADUATE LIBRARY,
UNIVERSITY OF MICHIGAN

era that placed a special value on spoken expression and modes of oral performance, Holmes was much in demand as a traveling public speaker, emerging as the most celebrated after-dinner toastmaster and versifier in his day. He was also one of the trailblazers in opening up the lyceum lecture circuit at mid-century, becoming in that venue both widely popular as one of the first comic lecturers and widely controversial as a proselytizing, scientific voice of reason. Then, with his bustling social life centered around verbal exchanges in drawing rooms, salons, boardinghouses, and elite clubs, he came to be widely celebrated as the most brilliant conversationalist in America's "Age of Conversation." In this role Holmes was a presiding figure at Boston's renowned Saturday Club—where his sense of talk defined the verbal environment for those important monthly conversation meetings that brought together authors such as Emerson, Hawthorne, Longfellow, Whittier, Lowell, Henry James Sr., and Richard Henry Dana Jr.; scientists such as Louis Agassiz and Asa Gray; and historians and scholars such as Francis Parkman, Charles Eliot Norton, William Prescott, and Motley, along with many other prominent figures in business, politics, law, science, literature, and intellectual life.

Holmes's best writing developed out of his explorations of talk form. Print versions of the light, elegant occasional verse he had performed at banquets and public functions brought him his first wide recognition as an author, and he eventually produced some four hundred such works. But Holmes also became known as one of the Fireside Poets for a series of more serious poems memorized by generations of schoolchildren, including "Old Ironsides" (1830), which gave voice to early stirrings of nationalist fervor; "The Chambered Nautilus" (1858), a haunting meditation on intellectual progress; and "The Deacon's Masterpiece; or, The Wonderful 'One-Hoss Shay'" (1858), a humorous romp that reduces Calvinist dogma to absurdity. Turning to prose fiction in later years, Holmes experimented with an early form of literary naturalism in a series of what he called "medicated novels": *Elsie Venner* (1861), *The Guardian Angel* (1867), and *A Mortal Antipathy* (1885). Combining his table-talk wit and personae with aspects of the clinical case history, these novels follow a series of anomalous life stories (involving multiple personalities, repetition compulsions, trauma-induced mental blocks, paralyzing erotic "antipathies," and so on) that pose severe problems of diagnosis for the central doctor/psychologist figures in the stories, raising questions about psychological and physiological determinism and generally challenging conventional thinking about the "normal."

myths of earlier heroic medicine. But he was also associated with many major developments—germ theory, antisepsis, anesthesia, and speculation about the therapeutic uses of doctor-patient dialogue, bedside manner, and humor—that would later lead beyond the impasse of the clinical method's "therapeutic nihilism," making possible key advances in twentieth-century medical treatment. As did Sigmund Freud, Holmes moved in his career from neuro-physiological approaches to verbal and psychological ones, finally developing an experimental, conversational model for diagnosis and therapy that influenced contemporary American psychologists and is still suggestive to medical explorers today.

At the same time, Holmes earned a preeminent place among American literary figures for his work in a variety of verbal forms—from poetry, prose, and public speaking to what was perhaps his main expressive mode: witty, interactive social conversation. In an

But Holmes's works of written table talk are his most important and still vital verbal productions. After the 1857 *Atlantic* meetings with Lowell, when he shifted his primary focus from medicine to literature, Holmes drew upon all of his experiences in social talk at salons, clubs, and lyceums to launch himself seriously into writing with a series of humorous essays presented as multivoiced, interruptive conversations taking place among diverse characters gathered around a boardinghouse breakfast table: *The Autocrat of the Breakfast-Table* (1858), *The Professor at the Breakfast-Table* (1860), and *The Poet at the Breakfast-Table* (1872). By framing his "talk of the town" opinion column as a series of quasi-theatrical spoken dialogues and encounters, and including verse interludes as well as some novelistic plotting in the relations between the speaking characters, Holmes transformed the English essay, giving it a new, dramatic, and dynamic rhetorical form.

RHETORICAL FORM

Rooted in the table talk of the elite dinner clubs or common boardinghouses of nineteenth-century America, just as the early essays of Joseph Addison and Sir Richard Steele had been rooted in the coffeehouse discussions of eighteenth-century England, Holmes's essays were less a form for lyrical reflection or sequential argument than a social experiment, a verbal laboratory for studies of the volatile "associations" among diverse people and diverse ideas. Staging tea-table debates among a wide range of uncomprehending strangers speaking for divergent ideologies in divergent languages, Holmes presented his readers with a carnivalesque festival of verbal pyrotechnics and comic misunderstandings that also developed as a miniaturized, caricatural model of the national conversation in these troubled, divisive years just before the Civil War. These debates thus played out the rational and irrational forces shaping public opinion in this period and made possible some detached reflection on the explosive dynamics of the "public sphere" in mid-nineteenth-century America.

Just two years after Walt Whitman's "Song of Myself" (1855) had introduced his giant Self as a public site in which to gather up the nation's many languages, Holmes in the *Autocrat* introduced his giant Breakfast Table as the site for a potential utopian "conversation of the culture." Though different in so many ways, both Whitman and Holmes, in working to translate interactive social talk into written form, were responding to a felt need to try to counter the ominous breakdown in mid-century discussions and

debates by building texts that could work as print simulacra of an ideal public sphere. This made it possible for readers to imagine themselves to be entering a national arena for dialogue—a dialogue that perhaps could only be realized through the mediation of a written, printed, fictional construct. In an increasingly privatized society, Holmes's print replicas of Saturday Club table talk were an instant sensation, generating a sense of loyal fellowship and intimacy among a huge and diverse readership. Isolated citizens and alienated writers would have been especially receptive to this verbal mode that seems to create its own community, picturing speakers and readers in a close social relation—conversing easily as members of the same family or of the same convivial club.

But Holmes's breakfast table is far from a model of easy cultural coherence. "I was just going to say, when I was interrupted . . ."—the famous first phrase in the first installment of the *Autocrat of the Breakfast-Table*—focuses our attention on the talk element most fundamental to his vision of conversational form: the dynamic moment of "interruption" that allows one speaker to take the floor from another and so makes possible constant changes of voice, tone, and topic. Even the title of *The Autocrat of the Breakfast-Table* foregrounds a sense of conversation as an ongoing struggle between urges to "autocratic" monologism and periodic bursts of revolutionary interruption; here the classic image of totalizing Old World authority—the autocrat—meets the era's prime symbol of democratic decentralization: the American boardinghouse or hotel. And the cap is that even in this reduced realm—of just one small table—no autocrat can hold much sway. At every turn in Holmes's table talk, the efforts of any figure of moral authority—whether the bluntly opinionated Autocrat, the Professor, the Master, or, in the 1880s, the Dictator—to monopolize the conversation, to define its terms or its tastes, to impose Robert's Rules of Order on its debates, or in any way to assert an ominously integrative centralizing power, will always soon be unsettled by explosive outbursts from the Babel of surrounding boardinghouse voices. Miming a sort of perpetual revolution, these conversations give the floor to a succession of "carnival kings"—not only to the title characters but also to the many more minor players speaking for the positions and experiences of diverse classes, genders, ages, regions, specialized professions, political factions, educational backgrounds, and so on. Each develops his or her own hobbyhorse in an over-elaborate personal prose, only to be quickly mocked and dethroned by the rabble constantly waiting on the fringes to interrupt.

In the "Three Johns" passage that opens the third installment of Holmes's Autocrat *papers, the Autocrat takes the everyday experience of social talk as the basis for a groundbreaking and influential vision of the self as a conversation formed out of multiple voices and diverse personalities. In the carnivalesque atmosphere of this interruptive table talk, though, serious psychological speculation mixes with raucous low humor as breakfast-table speakers fight for their share of the conversational pie.*

It is not easy, at the best, for two persons talking together to make the most of each other's thoughts, there are so many of them.

[The company looked as if they wanted an explanation.]

When John and Thomas, for instance, are talking together, it is natural enough that among the six there should be more or less confusion and misapprehension.

[Our landlady turned pale;—no doubt she thought there was a screw loose in my intellects,—and that involved the probable loss of a boarder. . . . Everybody looked up; I believe the old gentleman opposite was afraid I should seize the carving-knife; at any rate, he slid it to one side, as it were carelessly.]

I think, I said, that I can make it plain to Benjamin Franklin here, that there are at least six personalities distinctly to be recognized as taking part in that dialogue between John and Thomas.

Three Johns:

1. The real John; known only to his Maker.
2. John's ideal John; never the real one, and often very unlike him.
3. Thomas's ideal John; never the real John, nor John's John, but often very unlike either.

Three Thomases:

1. The real Thomas.
2. Thomas's ideal Thomas.
3. John's ideal Thomas.

Only one of the three Johns is taxed; only one can be weighed on a platform-balance; but the other two are just as important in the conversation. . . . It follows, that, until a man can be found who knows himself as his Maker knows him, or who sees himself as others see him, there must be at least six persons engaged in every dialogue between the two. Of these, the least important, philosophically speaking, is the one that we have called the real person. No wonder two disputants often get angry, when there are six of them talking and listening all at the same time.

[A very unphilosophical application of the above remarks was made by a young fellow answering to the name of John, who sits near me at the table. A certain basket of peaches, a rare vegetable, little known to boarding-houses, was on its way to me *viâ* this unlettered Johannes. He appropriated the three that remained in the basket, remarking that there was just one apiece for him. I convinced him that his practical inference was hasty and illogical, but in the mean time he had eaten the peaches.]

Holmes, *The Autocrat of the Breakfast-Table*, in *Writings*, 1:52–54.

KEY THEMES

While the *Autocrat* may then reflect a strongly felt desire for some unifying authority, it also speaks forcefully for antebellum America's central ambivalence to such authority. For Holmes the literary conversation does not operate simply as a tour de force of cultural centralization, with a Boston Brahmin from the metropolis, through his definition of "civility," subtly controlling and judging all peripheral languages. Rather, the conversation opens up as an arena of carnivalesque vocal diversity and of sometimes explosive struggles for power. Instead of epitomizing a monolithic vision of the mid-century cultural ideal—serving as the port of entry guiding readers into a newly prescribed "parlor culture"—conversation for Holmes is built upon dialogical breaks, changes in voice and perspective, that take one out of the limits of one's provincial language and home, forcing recognition of the multiplicity of cultures and also serving as a site for possible meetings between these cultures.

Many of Holmes's dialogues turn on the question of provincialism. To be sure, his Autocrat often speaks as the epitome of regional chauvinism—giving Boston its still current title as "hub" of the universe and (in remarks further elaborated in *Elsie Venner*) naming and defining the "Brahmin caste" of intellectuals so often associated with that New England center. But the turns of talk at the breakfast table finally explode that impulse, working to break down the barriers of atomistic individualism, social hierarchy, or local pride. Finally, then, the *Autocrat* embodied for many readers not localism but widely shared national aspirations to sociability, civility, and a cosmopolitan openness. Always the contrarian working in dialogic opposition to dominant trends in the era of the common man, the Autocrat advocates metropolitan urbanity in the face of contemporary ruralism; defends the intellectual as a counter to pragmatic business values; celebrates clubs and talk groups ("Mutual Admiration Societies") as the foundations of a vital culture; and playfully mocks the very idea of the "self-made" man.

Of course a main target of the talk at Holmes's table is the dogma of the Calvinist Church. The humor figures in the boardinghouse erupt with a levity meant to explode the grave truths of the orthodox fathers. The militant voices of scientific rationality at Holmes's table, hailing the rise of man in a modern era, lecture about the need to demolish an irrationalist Calvinist stress on the fall of man that is seen to permeate American culture, blocking emotional growth, intellectual progress, and spiritual development. And in philosophy and psychology, as in theology, Holmes's speakers see the tendency of their talk as working not only to break up monological or monolithic notions of a single truth but also to challenge our conceptions of a singular selfhood. Both the Autocrat and the Professor often point to their own experiences of social conversation—slips of the tongue, repetition compulsions, unconscious plagiarism, déjàvu, and so on—as case studies provoking speculation about the power of subconscious associations to shape or direct streams of thought in what Holmes called "the underground workshop" of the mind, and raising unsettling questions about the role of mechanism or automatism in thought and morals.

The famous "Three Johns" passage that opens the third *Autocrat* paper takes off playfully from another scene of talk to define all mental process as an internal conversation—introducing a notion of multiple personality, or of multivoiced and multilayered consciousness, that would influence Holmes's student William James and later theorists in the "Boston School" of speculative psychology.

Overall, then, Holmes's talk-based works complicate our stereotyped vision of Victorian America as dominated by a settled culture of complacent optimism, leaving us with a very different sense of the spirit of the age and of its genteel culture. Developing out of a continual alternation between opposing voices, which means that every question opens into a multiplicity of possible responses in a process that unsettles fixed standards and involves an almost pathological avoidance of direct statements or conclusions, the multivoiced table-talk writings that made Holmes a major cultural spokesman can be seen as representative expressions of the profound anxieties and indecisions of an "age of uncertainty."

See also The Atlantic Monthly; Fireside Poets; Health and Medicine; Humor; Satire, Burlesque, and Parody

BIBLIOGRAPHY
Primary Work
Holmes, Oliver Wendell. *The Writings of Oliver Wendell Holmes.* 13 vols. Boston: Houghton Mifflin, 1891.

Secondary Works
Gibian, Peter. *Oliver Wendell Holmes and the Culture of Conversation.* New York: Cambridge University Press, 2001.

Tilton, Eleanor M. *Amiable Autocrat: A Biography of Dr. Oliver Wendell Holmes.* New York: Schuman, 1947.

Peter Gibian

BACHELORS AND SPINSTERS

A common theme in American literature of the mid-nineteenth century is a push toward self-realization for both single male and single female characters. Marriage becomes less an expectation and more a reward for the individual who has become developed and fully realized as an individual.

THE SINGLE MAN: "THE PARADISE OF BACHELORS"

Perhaps the most famous short story that depicts a mid-nineteenth-century view of bachelors and spinsters is Herman Melville's (1819–1891) "The Paradise of Bachelors and the Tartarus of Maids" (1855). In this tale the narrator finds that bachelors spend their spare hours in the luxurious surroundings of a gentleman's club. His final assessment of the paradise is:

> It was the very perfection of quiet absorption of good living, good drinking, good feeling, and good talk. We were a band of brothers. Comfort—fraternal, household comfort, was the grand trait of the affair. Also, you could plainly see that these easy-hearted men had no wives or children to give an anxious thought. Almost all of them were travelers too; for bachelors alone can travel freely, and without any twinges of their consciences touching desertion of the fire-side. (P. 1264)

Melville gives a fairly modern version of the bachelor as a free spirit who does not rely on a woman to supply the domestic comforts. Whereas conduct books taught women that their goal was to provide a domestic paradise for their husbands, Melville suggests that this is not necessary, as single men can band together and provide that space for themselves.

Melville's story, like his longer works *Moby-Dick* (1851) and *Typee* (1846), plays on the theme of the single male who is off on a quest of self-discovery and identity formation. As Leslie A. Fiedler and R. W. B. Lewis detail in their work, many male-authored texts of the nineteenth century focused on the theme of a lone male on such a trek. The single life for men was seen as an avenue for maturation, a way to prepare for their lives as adults. This theme plays out in works by most of the canonical (and not coincidentally, male-authored) works of the nineteenth century, including those by Nathaniel Hawthorne (1804–1864) and Mark Twain (Samuel Langhorne Clemens, 1835–1910). Whereas single females were expected to stay at home and learn the domestic arts, single males like Huck Finn were expected to "light out for the Territory" and blaze a new trail.

James Fenimore Cooper's (1789–1851) nonfiction work *Notions of the Americans: Picked Up by a Travelling Bachelor* (1828) states that "perhaps a great majority of the females marry before the age of twenty" (p. 192). Whereas this observation would tend to make modern readers assume that the marriage rate was steady or even high in the mid-nineteenth century, historians like Lee Virginia Chambers-Schiller have shown that marriage rates had begun to decline by the late eighteenth century and continued to do so well into the nineteenth century. Despite Cooper's discussion of married women and men in his nonfiction, his most famous fictional works—the Leatherstocking Tales, which include *The Pioneers* (1823), *The Last of the*

Engraved title page of the first edition of Donald Grant Mitchell's *Reveries of a Bachelor,* **1850.** SPECIAL COLLECTIONS LIBRARY, UNIVERSITY OF MICHIGAN

Mohicans (1826), *The Prairie* (1827), *The Pathfinder* (1840), and *The Deerslayer* (1841)—focus on the solitary Natty Bumppo, the quintessential American bachelor.

In addition to Huck Finn, several other single male characters in nineteenth-century literature are successful at establishing their own identities in the world, at least to a degree. In Hawthorne's work, however, single males are often tortured creatures who are unable to reach their full potential. Consider Arthur Dimmesdale, the adulterous minister in *The Scarlet Letter* (1850); his life is anything but the happy bachelor's existence sometimes presented by Melville. Looking at Melville's depiction of single men and women more closely, one finds that it suggests that a life without marriage turns the world upside down; bachelors enjoy the comforts of the domestic sphere, whereas women are deprived of them to work in the world of commerce. Of course, even in Melville's

story, there is the assumption that men can and do exist in both spheres—the bachelors are able to afford such luxuries. Single women, however, are not able to exist in both worlds. Instead, the story indicates that they must choose either domesticity or industry. In reality, however, women were beginning to find they could have both—by applying their domestic skills in the outside world, as Louisa May Alcott (1832–1888) did in her efforts to help during the Civil War.

THE SINGLE WOMAN: "THE TARTARUS OF MAIDS"

A number of historical surveys try to explain the rise of spinsterhood in the nineteenth century. Nancy F. Cott's *The Bonds of Womanhood: "Women's Sphere" in New England, 1780–1835* discusses the growth of industrialization from cottage industry to factory, covering the influence of millwork on marriage rates. According to Cott, the movement of work outside the home led to a dilemma for women; because their economic choices were broader when they could work outside the home, women faced what Cott terms "marriage trauma." Suddenly women were able to make a choice regarding marriage that included how they felt as well as economic necessity. As Cott notes, some women by the 1820s and 1830s decided that if they could not have the ideal married and domestic life with a man they truly loved they would not marry at all.

This shift continued into the middle and latter half of the century. Chambers-Schiller states that between 1835 and 1875 the percentage of unmarried women, or spinsters, in New England rose from 7.3 percent to 11 percent (p. 3). Not only was this trend due to industrialization and new economic choices for women but it was also partially due to the Civil War. Chambers-Schiller notes, however, that the ratio began to shift in favor of women as early as 1840. As young marriage-aged men went off to fight, the women were left home, and single women soon outnumbered eligible bachelors.

The literature of the time represented spinsters in a variety of ways. The second half of Melville's "The Paradise of Bachelors and the Tartarus of Maids" presents a view of single life for women that is hellish and devoid of any pleasure. The reader might expect that the world of single women will be a pastoral equivalent of the paradise of bachelors. Instead, the narrator must travel past the "bright farms and sunny meadows" (p. 1265) and descend into the world of single women who work in a paper mill. Once inside the mill, he realizes that the women have no joy, no health. Whereas the bachelors have freedom to explore and still return to domestic comfort, the women who work in the mill, the "girls," as the foreman calls them, live a life of own way in the world. This young girl is fittingly called a heroine because her role is precisely analogous to the unrecognized or undervalued youths of fairy tales who perform dazzling exploits and win a place for themselves in the land of happy endings. (P. 11)

As Baym notes, most of the novels written by and for women in this time period include a marriage of the heroine to her suitor. However, often that marriage ends the novel, indicating the importance of the formative power of a single life. For example, Elizabeth Stoddard's 1862 novel *The Morgesons* ends with the revelation that the heroine, Cassandra, who said she would never marry, has done so. Tellingly most of the novels that show single young women who are able to find their autonomy and form an identity independent of the bonds of marriage only end with a mention of the marriage rather than focusing there as the main story line. Likewise one of the most sensational novels of the period, Fanny Fern's (Sara Payson Parton, 1811–1872) *Ruth Hall* (1855), deals with an unmarried woman who is rebellious and savagely independent. Although Ruth Hall refuses to marry at the end, it is important to remember that she is a widow at the start of the work. This automatically removes the label of spinster from the character; having fulfilled her obligation through having married once, the character can have a life of her own at the end. Apparently spinsters were not allowed to be fully successful within the pages of literature.

The prevailing vision of nineteenth-century literature that covers single women has been one that follows Barbara Welter's idea that literature of the period aimed at training women to be good members of the cult of true womanhood. Welter's theory asserted that the ideal, as presented in literature and elsewhere, was for women to live up to what she termed the four cardinal virtues: purity, piety, domesticity, and submissiveness. Ultimately the goal of attaining virtues was a good marriage and a happy household.

Fiction showed characters living up to these ideas. Conduct books and domestic handbooks that instructed women in the domestic arts were also prevalent. One of the most popular magazines of the time, *Godey's Lady's Book*, began in 1830 and had as its goal to entertain and educate the female reader. The magazine combined fashion plates, music sheets, and instructions for how to make common household items along with poetry and some fiction. The magazine was under the helm of the editor Sarah Josepha Hale (1788–1879) until 1877; Hale had originally published *Ladies' Magazine*, which she began in 1828 as a vehicle to advocate for advanced education for women. While she managed to balance the fashion

---

In this quotation from Louisa May Alcott one sees the tension and fear that often accompanied the single life for women. These words open her short fictionalized essay, "Happy Women."

One of the trials of woman-kind is the fear of being an old maid. To escape this dreadful doom, young girls rush into matrimony with a recklessness that astonishes the beholder; never pausing to remember that the loss of liberty, happiness, and self-respect is poorly repaid by the barren honor of being called "Mrs." instead of "Miss."

Alcott, "Happy Women," p. 40.

---

unending toil. The narrator inquires, "Why is it, Sir, that in most factories, female operatives, of whatever age, are indiscriminately called girls, never women?" The answer reveals the stark contrast between unmarried women and the bachelors he encountered earlier:

Oh! As to that—why, I suppose, the fact of their being generally unmarried—that's the reason, I should think. But it never struck me before. For our factory here, we will not have married women; they are apt to be off-and-on too much. We want none but steady workers: twelve hours to the day, day after day, through the three hundred and sixty-five days, excepting Sundays, Thanksgiving, and Fast-days. That's our rule. And so, having no married women, what females we have are rightly enough called girls. (P. 1278)

As Nina Baym notes throughout her book *Woman's Fiction: A Guide to Novels by and about Women in America, 1820–1870,* there was a counterbalance to the male-authored novels that featured the solitary male in search of his true self. Between 1820 and 1870 female authors were outselling their male counterparts with books like E. D. E. N. Southworth's (1819–1899) *The Hidden Hand* (1859). Baym points out that the pattern that dominated women's fiction of the period focuses on a young woman in search of her own identity. The typical pattern, according to Baym, is that:

The many novels all tell, with variations, a single tale. In essence, it is the story of a young girl who is deprived of the supports she had rightly or wrongly depended on to sustain her throughout life and is faced with the necessity of winning her with literature in her new venture at *Godey's*, her view of the magazine as contributing to the education of "true women" is evident in her farewell letter in the December 1877 issue of the magazine: she expressed her hope that *Godey's* had contributed to "the further-ance of their happiness and usefulness in their Divinely-appointed sphere."

Hale also published *Early American Cookery: "The Good Housekeeper"* in 1841. Recipe books and house-hold management books were quite popular during the mid-nineteenth century. Lydia Maria Child (1802–1880), known for her advocacy for the fair treatment of African and Native Americans, also produced a cookbook titled *The American Frugal Housewife* (1835). Such books contributed to the overall trend toward household training for women; even Harriet Beecher Stowe (1811–1896) coedited a household management book, *The American Woman's Home*, in 1869 with Catharine E. Beecher (1800–1878). All of these women were critical of the idea of separate spheres, yet they also created works that were aimed at educating women in household arts, indicating the shift toward higher education for women. Home eco-nomics and higher education for women began in texts that made domestic tasks a matter of household science and economics.

That single women took the skills they were nor-mally expected to utilize in the household and used them outside the home is evident in works like Louisa May Alcott's *Hospital Sketches* (1863). In this memoir, Alcott recounts how she did the thing her protagonist Jo March in *Little Women* (1868–1869) is not allowed to do—serve as a nurse in a hospital dedicated to help-ing soldiers wounded in battle. Alcott, who never mar-ried, recounts how she took the skills that were initially meant to aid in her becoming a good wife and mother to gain employment and aid the wounded. The fact that Jo March will later only be able to sell her hair, her "one beauty" (p. 150), in order to help with the war effort is telling; while single women were being seen as valuable in the outer sphere in professional positions, in fiction that would sell, the women have to be reined in so that they will appear acceptable. That Jo settles down and marries at the end of the work is characteristic of the tension between the realities of the period and the lingering cultural expectations.

Contrasting with Welter's theory is what Chambers-Schiller calls the "cult of single blessed-ness." According to Chambers-Schiller, as the trend in marital rates went down, so did the portrayal of mar-riage at any cost as the ideal. The Civil War contributed to the idea that women could be healthy and productive without being married; not only did the sex ratio change, causing single women to outnumber men, but

women were moving from home education to higher education in college settings. Texts like Catharine Maria Sedgwick's (1789–1867) *Married or Single?* (1857) actually began to advocate that a single life is better than a bad marriage. Instead of only teaching women that their role is always to be a wife and mother, texts began to put the development of the individual for her own sake above that of the develop-ment of the "true woman" fit for marriage. Margaret Fuller's (1810–1850) 1848 exclamation "let them [women] be sea-captains, if you will" (*Woman in the Nineteenth Century*, p. 102) speaks to this notion. Her argument is that women should not be enticed to fit a specific mold in order to find a husband; instead, they should be allowed to develop as their inclinations lead them. As educational opportunities for women grew, so did the literary representations of the single woman who was successful and did not need a husband or family to be fulfilled.

By 1870 educational and economic opportunities had widened considerably, leading to a reality for women that was unlike any they had had before. However, the fiction did not quite live up to the real-ity. Louisa May Alcott was able to say to her fellow single women: "It is not necessary to be a sour, spite-ful spinster, with nothing to do but brew tea, talk scan-dal and tend a pocket-handkerchief. No, the world is full of work, needing all the heads, hearts, and hands we can bring to do it" ("Happy Women," p. 42). Yet she and others like her knew that such images would not lead to the kinds of sales that would allow her to sustain herself. In the end literary representations of single men and single women more closely resemble that of Melville's short story and Alcott's longer fic-tion than they do the reality.

See also Domestic Fiction; Education; Factories; Female Authorship; Individualism and Community; Marriage; *Ruth Hall*

BIBLIOGRAPHY

Primary Works

Alcott, Louisa May. "Happy Women." 1868. In *Louisa May Alcott: Short Stories*. New York: Dover, 1996.

Alcott, Louisa May. *Little Women*. 1868. New York: Signet, 1983.

Cooper, James Fenimore. *Notions of the Americans: Picked Up by a Travelling Bachelor*. 1828. Introduction by Robert E. Spiller. New York: Frederick Unger, 1963.

Fuller, Margaret. *Woman in the Nineteenth Century: An Authoritative Text, Backgrounds, Criticism.* 1855. Edited by Larry J. Reynolds. New York: Norton, 1998.

Melville, Herman. "The Paradise of Bachelors and the Tartarus of Maids." 1855. In *Herman Melville: Pierre, Israel Potter, The Piazza Tales, The Confidence-Man, Uncollected Prose, Billy Budd.* New York: Library Classics of the United States, 1984.

Secondary Works

Baym, Nina. *Women's Fiction: A Guide to Novels by and about Women in America, 1820–1870.* 2nd ed. Urbana: University of Illinois Press, 1993.

Chambers-Schiller, Lee Virginia. *Liberty: A Better Husband; Single Women in America; The Generations of 1780–1840.* New Haven, Conn.: Yale University Press, 1984.

Cott, Nancy F. *The Bonds of Womanhood: "Woman's Sphere" in New England, 1780–1835.* 2nd ed. with a new preface. New Haven, Conn.: Yale University Press, 1977.

Fiedler, Leslie A. *Love and Death in the American Novel.* 1960. Introduction by Charles B. Harris. Normal, Ill.: Dalkey Archive Press, 1997.

Lewis, R. W. B. *The American Adam: Innocence, Tragedy, and Tradition in the Nineteenth Century.* Chicago: University of Chicago Press, 1955.

Welter, Barbara. *Dimity Convictions: The American Woman in the Nineteenth Century.* Athens: Ohio University Press, 1976.

Angelic Rodgers

BALTIMORE

In 1745 Jones' Town, Baltimore Town, and surrounding settlements merged to form the municipality that would eventually become Maryland's largest and most productive city. Baltimore's geographic location enabled it to grow from an obscure port city to an American urban center of culture and commerce. By 1850 Baltimore was America's fourth most populous city and its sixth largest industrial city. This growth rate is a direct reflection of the emergence of industry in American port cities. Once reliant on a mercantile economic system, large American ports developed industrial districts that changed the face of those cities. Instead of strictly moving goods from one port to another, these transitional cities started producing their own goods for sale. Some of Baltimore's major industries were iron and gas production, ship building, canning, financial banking, and textiles. By 1825 Baltimore was the largest flour market in the United States, and over sixty flour mills were in production in or near Baltimore.

As this transition of economies unfolded, Baltimore was in an ideal spot for industrial growth, forty-eight hours closer to the southern markets by boat than New York. The city became the preferred port for trading with the Caribbean and South America. The location was not only well suited for shipping but also for inland trade. The port of Baltimore is located on the Patapsco River estuary, the farthest inlet port on the Chesapeake Bay, 170 miles from the Virginia Capes. Originally, this location was less than ideal for a city competing with other port cities located on or near the Atlantic Ocean. This disadvantage soon turned into a huge advantage for Baltimore, however, when American port cities began competing for trade with the midwestern states, especially Ohio. By sailing all the way to Baltimore, ships were one hundred miles nearer the interior of the United States.

From Baltimore, a single route over the Appalachian Mountains—following the National Pike, the Fredrick Turnpike, and the Cumberland Road—led to the expanding markets in the Ohio Valley. During the nineteenth century, these new markets in West Virginia and the Ohio Valley produced wheat, corn, and raw materials needed for the growing industrial economies in the East, and the major ports like New York, Philadelphia, and Baltimore all vied for their trade. Ohio flour and West Virginia coal and iron helped propel Baltimore into a role as the major exporter of flour to South America. By 1820, the leaders of Baltimore understood their unique situation and were willing to place the city in debt in order to take advantage of their proximity to the West. During the rest of the nineteenth century, city officials financed railroads, canals, and roads to ensure trade and commerce with the midwestern United States moved through Baltimore. One article in the *Baltimore American* stated, "Baltimore should imitate the spider and spread her lines towards every point of the compass, and lodge in the center of them. . . . The present generation are able to pay interest; let the next generation pay the principle" (Olson, p. 560). The Cumberland route was solidified as the preferred route of commerce to the Midwest by the construction of the Baltimore and Ohio Railroad (B&O), which was chartered for carrying freight and passengers in 1827. In 1852 the B&O tracks were the first to reach Wheeling, West Virginia, at the edge of the Ohio River, and in 1857, they were the first tracks from an East Coast city to reach the western gateway of St. Louis, Missouri. The B&O Railroad gave Baltimore

Birds-eye view of Baltimore, c. 1862. At the center of this lithograph is the Washington Monument, designed by Robert Mills and built in 1829. Baltimore's was the first monument to George Washington erected in the United States.
THE LIBRARY OF CONGRESS

an unprecedented advantage for economic and industrial growth in the later half of the nineteenth century.

Besides its vital role in the American economy, Baltimore was also politically important. Before the War of 1812, the British had determined that Baltimore was home to many privateers who were raiding British ships for profit, and the city became a target for attack after the United States and England went to war. The Battle of Baltimore culminated with the British military's unsuccessful attack on Fort McHenry on 13 and 14 September 1814, an event witnessed by Francis Scott Key and celebrated by his poem "The Star-Spangled Banner." This event propelled Baltimore into the national spotlight and endeared the city to citizens of America. For a brief period in the 1830s, Baltimore became the nation's second-largest city.

RACE RELATIONS

Baltimore was the northernmost slave state and developed its own brand of the evil institution. As seen by many historians, slavery in Baltimore was characterized by relatively lax master-slave relationships in which slaves could walk about the town unencumbered. Benjamin Quarles explains, "Slavery in Maryland was more 'enlightened' than in the lower South; town slaves were better fed and less likely to feel the whip than their plantation brothers" (p. 7). Baltimore was also home to one of the largest free black communities in the South. In 1850 there were over twenty-five thousand free blacks in the city, making up 15 percent of the city population. This large population of freed slaves developed churches, unions, and community groups for support.

The abolitionist writer and orator Fredrick Douglass (1818–1895) was a slave in Baltimore during his young life and again later; while in Baltimore, he was a member of the East Baltimore Improvement Society, where he met his future wife, Anna Murray. For Douglass, Baltimore offered an environment that ultimately led to his freedom. As Douglass explains in *Narrative of the Life of Frederick Douglass* (1845), his white slave mistress initially began to teach him to read while he was a young slave in the Auld house, and his education stimulated Douglass to pursue freedom at all costs. After being moved from Baltimore and set to work in several harsh situations, including a year with Edward Covey, a slaveholder with "a very high reputation for breaking young slaves" (Douglass, p. 60), Douglass was sent back to Baltimore and (still a slave) was hired out as an apprentice to earn a wage caulking in the shipyards. Although his wages went to his master, he ultimately was able to hire out his own free time, and he used the money that he earned to finance his eventual escape from slavery, which he managed in 1838 by boarding a Baltimore train bound for Philadelphia. (The former slave and writer-activist Harriet Jacobs [1813–1897] had an uncle, Benjamin, who also escaped slavery, in 1827, using the trains of Baltimore as the means of his flight. Jacobs herself had hoped to take the same route in her flight; however, by the time of her escape in 1842 southern law enforcement had locked down Baltimore's railway stations. Instead of following her uncle's footsteps, she was forced to escape by sailing vessel.)

Historical records show that Douglass was not the only African American to pick up a skilled trade in Baltimore's shipyards. These shipyards provided African Americans jobs as carpenters, caulkers, stevedores, and draymen. The numbers of African American caulkers was so large that in 1838 they organized a union called the Caulker's Association, one of the first black labor unions. The organization dictated high wages and better working conditions. In fact, the historian Bettye C. Thomas claims that African American caulkers in the city's shipyards garnered wages fifty cents higher than their white counterparts.

After the Civil War, African American businessmen established the nation's first black-owned shipyard. The Chesapeake Marine Railway and Dry Dock Company of Baltimore City opened its doors in 1866 and operated with great success for almost twenty years. The company's charter included wording demonstrating that the venture was intended to last for forty years; however, there was a misunderstanding over whether the African American company had purchased the land outright or was leasing the site. The issue went to the courts in 1879. Judges ruled against the claims of the black-owned shipyard and the land was returned to the original white owners in 1884.

In 1820 the American Colonization Society sponsored the first of many ships carrying freed African Americans to new settlements in West Africa. Baltimore took a leading role in this endeavor and tried to create exclusive trading rights with these settlements between 1822 and 1827. Baltimore's monopolistic scheme failed, and the effort illustrates the city's precarious relationship with race in the nineteenth century. On the one hand, many citizens urged the amicable release of slaves, and on the other hand, they were economically tied to the institution. After the failure of the American Colonization Society, the state government established the Maryland Colonization Society, which was separate from the national organization. This society eased fears that Maryland would be limited by the national society's quota on the number of emigrants each state could send to Liberia. William Watkins, the uncle of the black writer and activist Francis E. W. Harper and one of the founders of the Mental and Moral Improvement Society in Baltimore, was one vocal critic of the new state society. Watkins claimed that the colonization of Liberia by freed African Americans had nothing to do with the best interests of African Americans. Instead, it was a scheme to rid America of free blacks. He argues in *Freedom's Journal* (6 July 1827):

> We are appraised that some of the most distinguished of that society (The Maryland Colonization Society), are themselves, Slaveholders! Now, how those men can desire so ardently, and labor so abundantly, for the exaltation of the free people, thousands of whom they have never seen, and feel so little concern for those who are held in bondage by themselves; whose degraded condition is directly under their observation, and immediately within the sphere of their benevolence to ameliorate, is a philanthropy, I confess, unaccountable to me. (Gardner, p. 156)

Under the pseudonym "The Colored Baltimorean," Watkins attacked the colonization plan in abolitionist journals such as the *Genius of Universal Emancipation, The Liberator,* and *Freeman's Journal*. His protests ultimately convinced abolitionists such as William Lloyd Garrison to resist the plan as well.

BALTIMORE AS A CULTURAL CENTER

As Baltimore's population and prosperity grew, the urban core evolved into one of America's premiere cultural centers. Its theater community was one of the largest in the nation, and keeping with the times, Baltimore supported the nineteenth-century interest in lecture series known as the lyceum movement. William Ellery Channing presented his famous sermon on the five tenets of Unitarian Christianity in Baltimore in 1819. In 1857 George Peabody created the Peabody Institute with the goal of developing "a structure that would expose the citizens of Baltimore to the finest in literature, music, the fine arts, and contribute to the formation of literary and scientific taste in the city" (Peabody Institute). Beginning in 1866, the Peabody Institute's new lecture series brought speakers in science, literature, and art to deliver more than thirty lectures a year. The institute also founded the country's first free public noncirculating library in 1866, and in 1868 the Peabody Conservatory of Music opened its inaugural season.

Baltimore was also home to the largest publishing industry in the South. During the early to mid-1800s, New York, Philadelphia, and Baltimore dominated the American publishing industry. Eventually, Philadelphia eclipsed Baltimore as the cities competed for the same markets, and Baltimore receded from its prominence on the national stage. However, it did remain a significant player in the publishing industry of the South. By 1857 half the publishing houses in the South were located in Baltimore. Although the southern publishing industry lagged far behind its northern counterpart, Baltimore (along with Charleston, and New Orleans) was a major distribution hub for the publishing houses in the North, such as Ticknor and Fields. Baltimore's publishing industry was hard hit during the Civil War, however; the historian Warren Tryon has documented that book sales remained fairly normal in the period leading up to the war, "even until April 1861," but "then, suddenly and unexpectedly, they vanished altogether" (p. 329).

BALTIMORE LITERARY FIGURES

Edgar Allan Poe (1809–1849) started his literary career in Baltimore after a brief stint at the U.S. Military Academy at West Point and stayed in the city from 1831 until 1835, where he obtained a license to marry his thirteen-year-old cousin, Virginia Clemm. During this time, Poe also wrote many articles in the Baltimore papers. Some of his work includes publications during this time in the *Southern Literary Messenger* (a new journal out of Richmond, Virginia), including the 1835 gothic tales "Berenice" and "Morella," as well as critical reviews in the *Baltimore Republican* and in the *Baltimore American*. His critiques of the *Southern Literary Messenger* in these Baltimore newspapers reflect Poe's ability to discern quality in the editing profession, and he corresponded with the founding owner of the *Southern Literary Messenger,* Thomas W. White, advising him on his journal and suggesting changes. In one letter, Poe advised White to advertise in the *American* instead of the *Republican* because the *Republican* "is a paper by no means in the hands of the first people here [Baltimore]" (Jackson, p. 252). The correspondence with White led to Poe's appointment as the full-time editor of the *Southern Literary Messenger* in 1835. Although he was discharged from that post early in 1837 and moved to New York and then Philadelphia, he was back in Baltimore at the time of his mysterious death in 1849,

and he is buried at Westminster Presbyterian Church near Camden Yards.

During his time in Baltimore, in 1833, Poe entered a literary contest offered by the *Baltimore Saturday Visitor*. His submission, a group of short stories collectively titled *Tales of the Folio Club*, brought him a fifty-dollar prize, but more importantly, it led to his meeting with the influential Baltimorean literary and publishing figure John P. Kennedy, who became Poe's patron. Kennedy, a former secretary of the navy, wrote two southern novels, *Swallow Barn* (1832), a romance set in rural Virginia in the first quarter of the nineteenth century, and *Horseshoe Robinson* (1835), a Revolutionary War Romeo-and-Juliet romance set in Virginia and the Carolinas. But more significantly, Kennedy was enmeshed in the publishing industry—he was on close terms with White, Henry C. Carey (who published many of James Fennimore Cooper's works), and Washington Irving, and his presence made Baltimore a literary center.

Unlike the black literary figures Frederick Douglass and Harriet Jacobs who had lived in Baltimore as slaves, the writer Frances E. W. Harper (1825–1911) was born in Baltimore into a family of free African Americans. Orphaned three years after her birth, she was raised and educated in Baltimore by her uncle, the abolitionist William Watkins, who enrolled her in the Academy for Negro Youth, a school for free African Americans that he had founded and ran. She published her first book of poetry, *Autumn Leaves,* often called *Forest Leaves* (1845), while living in Baltimore, but she moved to Philadelphia when southern white resentment of the large free African American population in Baltimore reached a fevered pitch.

CONCLUSION

As American economic power increased during the nineteenth century, Baltimore grew from an obscure port town to a bustling urban center. Baltimore's unique position as the largest city in the northernmost slave state on the East Coast helped increase its industrial trade between the North and the South, but this position also placed it in a precarious position at the outset of the Civil War. Leading up to the war, Baltimore's aggressive plans to create efficient trading routes into the American Midwest placed the city on the cusp of becoming America's second city, and its relatively lenient brand of slavery (resulting in, and coexisting with, the largest population of free African Americans in the South), also created an environment that allowed many slaves to escape to the North. During the war, Baltimore's economy ground to a halt and inhibited its future growth. After the Civil War,

Baltimore never regained its prominence as America's next great city; however, the cultural foundation that developed through the growth in the nineteenth century makes Baltimore one of the important cultural cities in this era. After the war, the city was home to the Douglass Institute, where Frederick Douglass delivered a speech on 19 May 1870 to celebrate the Fifteenth Amendment; however, the city did not entirely embrace equality. Maryland, like other southern states, passed Jim Crow segregation laws and prevented total equality of the races until the twentieth century.

See also Blacks; Book Publishing; Literary Marketplace; Maritime Commerce; *Narrative of the Life of Frederick Douglass;* Slavery; Urbanization

BIBLIOGRAPHY

Primary Work

Douglass, Frederick. *Narrative of the Life of Frederick Douglass, an American Slave, Written by Himself.* 1845. In *The Oxford Frederick Douglass Reader,* edited by William L. Andrews, pp. 21–97. New York: Oxford University Press, 1996.

Secondary Works

Bercovitch, Sacvan, ed. *Cambridge History of American Literature.* Vol. 2. New York: Cambridge University Press, 1995.

Blood, Pearle. "Factors in the Economic Development of Baltimore, Maryland." *Economic Geography* 13, no. 2 (1937): 187–208.

French, John C. "Poe and the *Baltimore Saturday Visitor.*" *Modern Language Notes* 33, no. 5 (1918): 257–267.

Gardner, Bettye J. "Opposition to Emigration: A Selected Letter of William Watkins (the Colored Baltimorean)." *Journal of Negro History* 67, no. 2 (1982): 155–158.

Groves, Paul, and Edward Muller. "The Emergence of Industrial Districts in Mid-Nineteenth-Century Baltimore." *Geographical Review* 69, no. 2 (1979): 159–178.

Jackson, David K. "Four of Poe's Critiques in the Baltimore Newspapers." *Modern Language Notes* 50, no. 4 (1935): 251–256.

Mouser, Bruce L. "Baltimore's African Experiment, 1822–1827." *Journal of Negro History* 80, no. 3 (1995): 113–130.

Olson, Sherry H. "Baltimore Imitates the Spider." *Annals of the Association of American Geographers* 69, no. 4 (1979): 557–574.

Peabody Institute. "The Founding of Peabody's Institute." http://www.gtlam.com/archives/api/guide/history/D1.txt.

Quarles, Benjamin. "Douglass' Mind in the Making." *Phylon* 6, no. 1 (1945): 5–12.

Shivers, Frank R., Jr. *Walking in Baltimore: An Intimate Guide to the Old City.* Baltimore: Johns Hopkins University Press, 1995.

Thomas, Bettye C. "A Nineteenth-Century Black-Operated Shipyard, 1866–1884: Reflections upon Its Inception and Ownership." *Journal of Negro History* 59, no. 1 (1974): 1–12.

Tryon, Warren S. "The Publications of Ticknor and Fields in the South, 1840–1865." *Journal of Southern History* 14, no. 3 (1948): 305–330.

Wendell, Barrett. *A Literary History of America.* New York: Scribners, 1900.

Wilson, James Southall. "Poe's Life." Poe Museum online. http://www.poemuseum.org/poes_life/.

Gregory Scott George

BANKING, FINANCE, PANICS, AND DEPRESSIONS

American banking can be traced back to Robert Morris's Bank of North America (1781) or the First Bank of the United States (1791), but the true energy of the United States' banking system came from the state-chartered private banks. Each state had its own chartering requirements—minimum capitalization, length of charter—but all permitted a chartered bank to issue money (notes) in whatever denominations or shapes the bank chose, usually with the founder's picture on one side. Banknotes from these chartered banks were backed by gold and silver (known as "specie") in the vaults. Typically, banks would emit notes based on the reserve of gold and silver. Customers who had banknotes could return their notes at any time and redeem them for gold or silver coin.

In theory, banks could not overissue notes, but in reality, all banks did. And in theory, banks' reserves maintained confidence in the institution, but in reality, it was the reputation of the bank that determined whether it had to hold excessive reserves against anticipated runs. If a single bank refused to redeem its notes in specie, it could have its charter yanked by the state legislature, but if many or all banks simultaneously suspended specie payments, the legislators could do little except warn them not to do it again. When a panic subsided, banks resumed specie payments.

Three other categories of banks existed: free banks, which were banks created under general incorporation laws that did not require special action by the legislature; state banks that were arms of the state government, usually with specific charter require-ments on where their profits went; and private non-chartered banks that could make loans and accept deposits but not issue notes. Of the above institutions, state-chartered private banks, state government banks, free banks, private banks, and the national banks were all permitted to branch (set up offices in other towns under the bank's name and intermix accounts) except where prohibited by the charter. Branch banking was widely adopted in the South, whereas in the North, unit banking remained the norm, meaning that south-ern banks tended on average to be bigger and could more easily serve rural areas and, at the same time, were less vulnerable because branching allowed them to diversify their risk. Northern banks tended to be smaller (aside from those in New York City) and have less protection against economic fluctuations.

The two big exceptions to these generalities were the two Banks of the United States. In 1791 Congress authorized the Bank of the United States (BUS) with a twenty-year charter with a capital stock of $10 million (massive in comparison to state-chartered banks), one-fifth owned by the government. The bank was author-ized to establish branches (which it opened in Boston, New York, Baltimore, and Charleston) and, obviously, to emit notes. However, the BUS's branching provi-sion meant that it had a substantial advantage over all other banks in that it could engage in interstate branching, thereby increasing the use of its notes and further diversifying its risk. In 1811 the BUS's rechar-ter fell victim to growing hostilities between the United States and Britain as, it was asserted, many of the stockholders of the bank were British. The rechar-ter bills failed by one vote in each house.

After the War of 1812, new financial demands on the U.S. government due to war debt led to state banks trying to fill the void by issuing high levels of notes. Circulation expanded from $45 million in bank-notes before the war to $68 million after the war. Prices rose, and many banks had to suspend specie payments. This created new pressures to charter another BUS, and with support from Secretary of the Treasury Alexander Dallas and the merchant Stephen Girard, Congress chartered the Second Bank of the United States in 1816, again with a large capital ($35 million) and the authority to engage in interstate branching. Like the first BUS, the Second BUS served as the repository of government deposits, giving it yet another powerful advantage over all other competitors in that it had a massive deposit base upon which to make loans.

In 1818 international specie drains started to affect the bank's liquidity. The BUS began calling in loans, and predictably, Congress launched investiga-tions. Langdon Cheves (1776–1857), former Speaker of the House, was named the new president. Cheves radically contracted bank obligations as the bank's outstanding notes fell by 50 percent between 1819 and 1820. The United States drifted into its first gen-uine financial panic as banks across the country sus-pended specie payments. As Cheves continued to call in loans, he accentuated the image of the BUS as opposed to the interests of the "common person" and memories of the panic of 1819 later contributed to Jacksonian hostility to the bank.

THE SECOND BANK OF THE UNITED STATES AND THE "BANK WAR"

The Second BUS's branching advantages came under attack by the states when Maryland tried to tax the Baltimore branch, leading to a Supreme Court case, *McCulloch v. Maryland* (1819), in which the Court unanimously ruled that the BUS was constitutional (based on the "necessary and proper" clause). Chief Justice John Marshall, uttering his famous "the power to tax is the power to destroy" phrase, decreed that states could not tax the federal government. In 1823 the Philadelphian Nicholas Biddle (1786–1844) replaced Cheves as president of the BUS. Biddle grad-ually adopted a more expansionist policy and increased annual dividends.

Biddle had an excellent financial mind but also had political ambitions, if not to run for office then to at least control patronage. The BUS, with its many branches, controlled significant numbers of jobs, which were leveraged further by its lending abilities. Biddle wanted to take advantage of the bank's support in Congress to bring the charter bill up for renewal four years early, in 1832, a presidential election year. Counting on the popularity of the BUS to force President Andrew Jackson's (1767–1845) hand, Biddle hoped bringing the vote up early would force Jackson to sign the recharter regardless of his personal views. As the historians like to quip, "Biddle bungled badly." He misjudged the animus Jackson had for banks in general and the political threat his institution pre-sented to Jackson's administration in particular. It is not true, however, that Jackson opposed in principle a national bank, as his own supporters gave him a plan for such an institution in 1833 drawn up by the New York banker Isaac Bronson. Indeed, buried in Jackson's own papers is a plan from his Kitchen Cabinet adviser Amos Kendall for a national bank in 1829—one under the control of the Democrats.

Jackson launched a campaign to kill the "mon-ster," as he called it. Although the bank recharter bill passed, Jackson vetoed it. It passed again, and Jackson vetoed it a second time. Biddle foolishly tried to bring the administration to heel by contracting credit: notes and deposits fell from $44 million in 1832 to $30 million by the end of 1833. The bank's supporters in Congress lacked the votes to override the veto. But Jackson was not finished: he then withdrew the U.S. government deposits in 1833, stripping the bank of one of its most precious advantages, a large pool of money to lend. Jackson further rubbed salt in the wound by depositing the government money in more than twenty state banks, most of them controlled by Democrats.

The BUS charter expired in 1836. But the story did not end there. In 1836 Jackson issued the Specie Circular, an executive order requiring that federal land be paid for in specie. A financial panic ensued in 1837, with the money stock dropping by more than a third (an amount almost identical to the drop in the money supply from 1929 to 1932), and the price level fell 42 percent. By then, Jackson was out and his vice president, Martin Van Buren (1782–1862), was in. Historians have agreed that Jackson's "killing" of the bank, combined with the Specie Circular, set off the panic. It was a story that was internally consistent and had no glaring flaws. But in the late 1960s, the economist Peter Temin (in *The Jacksonian Economy*) found data on international monetary flows that proved that the Texas Revolution interrupted the flow of silver from Mexico, setting off a chain of events that caused the Bank of England to raise interest rates, thus sparking the recession.

Much of the writing—both contemporary and the subsequent scholarly work—surrounding those events has focused on the soundness of the state banking systems without a national "policeman." Most Jacksonians, of course, hated the bank. William Gouge's *Short History of Paper Money* (1833) argued for a return to a specie-only currency—a process he claimed might take ten years. Only Charles Duncombe (*Duncome's Free Banking,* 1841) stood apart from his Jacksonian brethren in advocating a centralized government currency coming from a national bank. Other Jacksonians, like William Leggett, favored open entry into banking (so-called free banking), aware that the country simply could not function on a specie, but warned against the "fetters" of chartered banks. Trying to pin down the Jacksonian position on banking was impossible, as it ranged from a hard-money standard with no banks to support for state banks (but not a national bank) to support for free banking to opposition to all banking.

This has affected the works of historians writing later, like Reginald Charles McGrane (*The Panic of*

1837, 1924), who saw Jackson as ignorant of sound banking principles and blamed him for foolishly destabilizing the system. Fritz Redlich's *The Molding of American Banking: Men and Ideas* (2 vols., 1947, 1951) developed the "soundness school" interpretation that tended to look at the banks solely in terms of their stability, not in terms of their ability to provide capital for economic growth. The bible of money and banking in the Jacksonian period, however, came from a staffer in the Federal Reserve system, Bray Hammond, who viewed Jackson's destruction of the BUS as shortsighted, leading to a flood of banknotes that the BUS would have contained through its informal regulatory policies. But the interpretation one takes out of the Jacksonian era depends almost entirely on which Jacksonians one chooses as representative of Democrats as a whole. In fact, they differed regionally and sectionally, and often their views on money and banking were heavily influenced by the presence of an active Whig opposition in their states or by the absence of any opposition at all.

Despite its dislocations to the rest of the economy, the panic of 1837 had little effect on the book publishing industry or on most of the major literary figures of the day, save Herman Melville (1819–1891), who went to sea in 1840 partly as a result of his personal finances deteriorating due to the economic downturn. James Fenimore Cooper's (1789–1951) *The Bravo* (1831), which predated the panic, included a warning about a European-type financial oligarchy, but he then turned to a series of travel books after the panic. The exception—Cooper's *The American Democrat* (1838)—in fact took the other tack, warning about the dangers of social leveling and the threats such democratization posed to the intellectuals and elites. Ralph Waldo Emerson (1803–1882) was already financially secure, was himself an investor, and seemed somewhat surprised to learn that his investment income dwarfed that which he earned from lectures and publishing. Few literary figures joined the debates over the Second BUS or the panic, nor did the panic seem to have a significant impact on the book trade: in 1755 there were fifty publishers in the colonies, but by 1856 there were 385. More impressive was the sheer number of books appearing, with about a hundred new titles a year appearing between 1830 and 1840, then surging to 879 in 1853, then 1,350 in 1859—increasing during the period of the panic of 1857. New York City accounted for more than one-third of the dollar value of all books published, but points as far away as Cincinnati, Ohio, had over a million dollars in sales.

Meanwhile, as pressure grew for states to charter more banks, the burden on state legislatures increased.

Wall Street, Half Past Two O'Clock, October 13, 1857. Painting by James H. Cafferty and Charles G. Rosenberg, 1858. By mid-afternoon on 13 October, stock prices had hit record lows, forcing the closure of New York City's banks. The banks were not reopened until 12 December. © MUSEUM OF THE CITY OF NEW YORK/CORBIS

Partly to address this development, several states passed "free banking" laws as part of a move toward general incorporation laws. Under most free banking laws, a charter from the state legislature was no longer needed. Instead, the owners of a bank only needed to put up sufficient capital in the form of bonds on deposit with the secretary of state to serve as collateral against failure. Some of the more poorly designed of these laws did not distinguish between par value and market value of the deposited bonds, opening a window of arbitrage that encouraged some unscrupulous owners to wait until the value of the deposited bonds fell and then take off with the deposits. Still other bankers printed excessive numbers of notes redeemable only at branches that were so remote that a wildcat would not go there, hence the term "wildcat banks." States quickly remedied these weaknesses, and the free banking system proved healthy thereafter.

From 1850 until the Civil War, then, banking declined as an issue for many Americans. States such as Arkansas, Wisconsin, and Texas that prohibited banks in the wake of the panic of 1837 found themselves at an economic disadvantage, while their neighbors thrived on the transborder financial activities. Some companies, like George Smith's Wisconsin Marine and Fire Insurance Company, skirted the law by forming nonbanking companies that nevertheless issued money, and by 1860 dozens of corporations (including railroads and cities) issued notes. Nevertheless, far from resulting in a blizzard of money whose value consumers could not determine, the market provided a reliable guide to different currencies in the form of *Dillistin's Bank Note Reporter,* which was regularly updated and which noted the discount of most major notes in the various markets. A discount of more than a percent in *Dillistin's* was usually the kiss of death, and even with collection and shipping costs associated with bundling and returning money to its bank of origin, most notes did not trade at less than half a percent discount in major markets. Put another way, a bank in Philadelphia would give a merchant 99.5 cents on a dollar note from South Carolina.

PUBLISHING, NEWSPAPERS, AND MAILS

The proliferation of banks occurred while the publishing industry itself was rapidly growing and being defined by political developments. Already there were important weekly story papers, like the *Ledger,* which turned out 400,000 papers per week, but most newspapers remained small and local, dedicated mostly to covering local events.

This changed with the creation of the Democratic Party, mostly through the efforts of Martin Van Buren,

who envisioned a national party that could maintain sufficient discipline to keep slavery out of the political debate. To effect this, Van Buren's party structure rewarded loyalists with patronage and relied on a new system of "news" papers to serve as party propaganda organs. The Democrats outright owned many papers and controlled far more in terms of editorial content. Editors freely admitted that newspapers existed only to reinforce Andrew Jackson's views. One modern estimate concluded that fully four-fifths of the nation's papers were blatantly partisan, and other studies even go further, concluding that all were completely partisan. Jackson's opponents had their own papers, usually easily identifiable by names such as the *Arkansas Democrat* or the *Richmond Whig.* At a time when most newspapers lost money on their circulations, party subsidies ensured that the more loyal papers had profits of as much as 40 percent a year during a ten-year period. Printing expenditures by the executive branch of the U.S. government alone rose 75 percent from 1831 to 1841.

The connections between publishing and politics was even closer than may have first appeared. Congress permitted newspapers (virtually campaign literature for incumbents) to be transmitted through the postal system at substantially cheaper rates than other publications. Between 1800 and 1840, the number of newspapers transmitted through the mail rose from under two million to almost forty million, and the postal historian Richard John concluded that if the papers had to pay the same rate as other mail, transmission rates would have been seven hundred times higher. Newspapers traveling through the mail equaled in quantity the number of letters mailed, largely due to the federally subsidized franking privilege of mailing newspapers as part of "government business." Indeed, the government benefits given to newspapers drove publishers away from books and into the more lucrative newspaper business (then to the "dime novels"), leading to an explosion in papers, which by 1840 grew at a rate five times faster than the population. Socially, the implications of this transformation were to further accelerate the "democratization" of the American political structure by providing easy-to-read papers in lieu of deeper—and thicker—hardbound books.

Although few in comparison to the political publications, financial and business newspapers such as *Hunt's Merchant Magazine, De Bow's Review,* the *Farmer's Register,* the *New York Journal of Commerce,* and the *Free Trade Advocate* discussed all matters economic, including banking and financial articles. But if the new political structure favored newspapers over hardbound books, the new dime novel that started to appear in the late 1850s further changed publishing, leading to complaints that the literature markets were oversaturated. These dime novels could pass as newspapers and often received newspaper-like discounts from the U.S. Post Office. Ironically, the system that Martin Van Buren set up to insulate slavery by controlling government—and, therefore, to subsidize newspaper and, now, dime novel transmission through the mail—now became a vehicle for the transmission of abolitionist literature, which often came in the form of cheap tracts. Of course, the major publishing event related to slavery, Harriet Beecher Stowe's (1811–1896) *Uncle Tom's Cabin* (1852), greatly changed both publishing and American attitudes toward slavery. But just as Stowe's book sparked outrage against the Fugitive Slave Law, the panic of 1857 was linking banks, politics, and slavery in a different way, and once again, the publishing industry as a whole suffered little during an economic downturn, with *Putnam's Monthly Magazine*, which failed, being one of the few exceptions.

BANKS, SLAVERY, AND FINANCIAL FLUCTUATIONS

Increasingly, slavery surpassed banking as the central issue of American politics. In the South, banks had indeed supported slavery, making substantial loans to plantation owners both on the value of land and on the value of slaves. But it is a myth that banks ignored industry or manufacturing. Quite the contrary, despite remarkable returns on investment (close to 20 percent), southerners themselves stayed wedded to the cotton culture partially out of familiarity and partially out of the benefits of a power structure that elevated even the poorest whites above slaves. Ironically, the rural nature of the South accelerated efficient banking structures, such as branching, past the unit bank systems of the more heavily populated northern cities. It was the superior branching structure of the South that largely insulated it from the effects of the panic of 1857.

Numerous theories have attributed the panic of 1857 to the fall of grain prices following the Crimean War and the failure of the New York branch of the Ohio Life and Trust Company. In 1990, however, the panic was seen as originating in the *Dred Scott* case, wherein the U.S. Supreme Court destabilized seventy years of American territorial policy by ruling that neither Congress nor the people of a territory could prohibit slavery. This ruling immediately caused the bonds of east-west running railroads to plummet (though not the bonds of north-south running lines) and thus rapidly eroded the asset structure of numerous large banks. The South was less affected by the ruling because its superior branching system provided

a better means of information transmission, thus serving as a circuit breaker for runs. But northern unit banks, lacking as reliable a source of transmission for financial information—not to mention flexibility of assets—suffered disproportionately higher losses.

Contemporaries, however, misread the lessons of the panic, especially in the South where they rightly could have crowed about their banking structure. Instead, advocates of the cotton culture claimed that their plantation system had spared them and that cotton was king. Likewise, in the North, the focus was turned on the tariff, not banking policy. The Civil War intervened before either side accurately analyzed the problems of the panic.

THE CIVIL WAR: BANKING AND FINANCIAL TRANSFORMATION

Secession plunged markets, North and South, into upheaval. After the firing on Fort Sumter, the Confederate States of America immediately confiscated all the gold in Southern banks' vaults, thus destabilizing them. By embargoing cotton, the Confederacy further weakened the position of Southern banks. Abraham Lincoln (1809–1865) delivered the coup with the Emancipation Proclamation, which by freeing the slaves further undercut the asset base of virtually all Southern banks. Had the war ended on 2 January 1863, the Southern banking system still could not have recovered due to the damage that both the Confederate and Union governments had done to the system.

Lincoln's secretary of the treasury, Salmon Chase, concerned about financing the war, devised a new system of banks chartered by the federal government. To obtain a charter, a bank had to purchase U.S. government bonds, thereby assisting the financing of the war. National banks would be given the authority to issue new "national banknotes." To endow those notes with a built-in circulation, Congress affixed a 10 percent tax on the notes of all nonnational banks. State banks still remained in operation (except in the South for several years after the war) but no longer issued their own notes. Congress also authorized the Treasury Department to print $450 million in "greenbacks," which were unbacked notes that would be redeemable in gold at a future date. As might be expected, little literature was directed at banking or finance while the war was in progress.

After the war, deflation set in, bringing calls for new inflationary measures and giving birth to a new political party, the Greenback Party, which ran candidates for president in 1876, 1880, and 1884. The "Greenbackers" urged government to issue new unbacked notes and were soon surpassed as a party by the Populist Party, which favored "free and unlimited silver at 16:1" as a different form of inflation. Until that time, however, national banks again resumed paying specie for notes after 1865, and in 1879 the U.S. government began redeeming greenbacks for gold. Although both the Greenbackers and the "free silver" movement tried to blame the deflation on the government, in fact an international deflation was responsible for falling prices. Nevertheless, the collapse of the southern banking system, combined with the new national bank system—in which new bank charters in the South were unlikely to be given to either the freedmen or to former Confederates—resulted in a de facto shortage of money in the South, whereas the relative shortage of banks in the frontier left a dearth of banking institutions in the West. If government regulations had little to do with precipitating the shortage of circulation, the government did not actively work to increase circulation.

Meanwhile, in the postbellum period, banks that appeared in the new territories relied on symbols of safety to ensure their business. Bank buildings were designed by top architects, adorned with rich wood and fine metals, and located in prime spots in the middle of town to guarantee maximum safety and to add to the value of the bank's real estate. Vaults and safes were prominently displayed to reassure the public that its money was safe. Even after states began to pass sunshine laws requiring banks to issue public statements of their condition, it was these symbols of safety that reassured the "common person" that deposits were safe and the bank itself was solid. Only at century's end were these symbols of safety replaced by government regulations, bank examiners, and deposit insurance.

The publishing industry continued to experience an explosion of cheaper magazines, tracts, and periodicals, even as newspapers moved away from partisan subsidization. Magazines, in particular, saw themselves as social guardians, and encouraged "investigative reporting" on issues important to the public. However, most of the exposé type of reporting, which became the forerunner of the muckrakers, avoided banking and finance as topics. Railroads, trusts, and corrupt politicians proved easier targets. Thus it can be said that during the heyday of controversy over banks and financial panics, not a single prominent work of literature or fiction dealt with the issue as its primary subject.

See also Civil War; Labor; Literary Marketplace; Publishers; Urbanization

BIBLIOGRAPHY
Primary Works
Cooper, James Fennimore. *The American Democrat.* 1838. Indianapolis, Ind.: Liberty Classics, 1981.

Cooper, James Fennimore. *The Bravo.* 1831. New York: P. Collier, 1900.

De Bow's Review (New Orleans).

Dillistin, William H. *Dillistin's Bank Note Reporters and Counterfeit Detectors, 1826–1866: A Bibliography.* New York, 1943.

Duncombe, Charles. *Duncombe's Free Banking: An Essay on Banking, Currency, Finance, Exchanges, and Political Economy.* New York: Sanford, 1841.

Farmer's Register (New York).

Free Trade Advocate (Philadelphia).

Gouge, William. *A Short History of Paper Money and Banking in the United States.* Philadelphia: T. W. Ustick, 1833.

Hunt's Merchant Magazine (New York).

New York Journal of Commerce.

Putnam's Monthly Magazine (New York).

Stowe, Harriet Beecher. *Uncle Tom's Cabin.* 1852. New York: Literary Classics, 1982.

Tucker, George. *The Theory of Money and Banks Investigated.* 1839. New York: Greenwood Press, 1964.

Secondary Works
Calomiris, Charles, and Larry Schweikart. "The Panic of 1857: Origins, Transmission, and Containment." *Journal of Economic History* 51 (December 1991): 807–834.

Dorfman, Joseph. *The Economic Mind in American Civilization, 1606–1865.* Vol. 5. New York: Augustus Kelly, 1966.

Doti, Lynne Pierson, and Larry Schweikart. *Banking in the American West from the Gold Rush to Deregulation.* Norman: University of Oklahoma Press, 1991.

Hammond, Bray. *Banks and Politics in America from the Revolution to the Civil War.* Princeton, N.J.: Princeton University Press, 1970.

John, Richard R. *Spreading the News: The American Postal System from Franklin to Morse.* Cambridge, Mass.: Harvard University Press, 1995.

Leggett, William. *Democratick Editorials: Essays in Jacksonian Political Economy by William Leggett.* Edited by Lawrence White. Indianapolis, Ind.: Liberty Press, 1984.

Lusk, Ralph. *The Life of Ralph Waldo Emerson.* New York: Scribners, 1949.

McGrane, Reginald Charles. *The Panic of 1837: Some Financial Problems of the Jacksonian Era.* Chicago: University of Chicago Press, 1924.

Mitchell, Wesley Clair. *A History of the Greenbacks.* Chicago: University of Chicago Press, 1903.

Perkins, Edwin J. "Lost Opportunities for Compromise in the Bank War: A Reassessment of Jackson's Veto Message." *Business History Review* 61 (winter 1987): 531–550.

Redlich, Fritz. *The Molding of American Banking, Men, and Ideas.* 2 vols. New York: Johnson Reprint Company, 1968.

Ringe, Donald A. *James Fenimore Cooper.* Updated ed. Boston: Twayne, 1988.

Rockoff, Hugh. *The Free Banking Era: A Re-Examination.* New York: Arno Press, 1975.

Rolnick, Arthur J., and Warren Weber. "Banking Instability and Regulation in the U.S. Free Banking Era." *Federal Reserve Bank of Minneapolis Quarterly Review* 9, no. 3 (summer 1985): 2–9.

Schlesinger, Arthur H., Jr. *The Age of Jackson.* Boston: Little, Brown, 1945.

Schweikart, Larry. *Banking in the American South from the Age of Jackson to Reconstruction.* Baton Rouge: Louisiana State University Press, 1987.

Schweikart, Larry. "Jacksonian Ideology, Currency Control, and Central Banking: A Reappraisal." *Historian* 51 (1988): 78–102.

Schweikart, Larry. "U.S. Commercial Banking: A Historiographical Survey." *Business History Review* 65 (1991): 606–661.

Tebbel, John. *A History of Book Publishing in the United States.* Vol. 1, *The Creation of an Industry, 1630–1865.* New York: R. R. Bowker, 1972.

Tebbel, John. *A History of Book Publishing in the United States.* Vol. 2, *The Expansion of an Industry, 1865–1919.* New York: R. R. Bowker, 1975.

Temin, Peter. *The Jacksonian Economy.* New York: Norton, 1969.

Temin, Peter. "The Panic of 1837." *Intermountain Economic Review* 6, no.1 (spring 1975): 1–12.

Unger, Irwin. *The Greenback Era: A Social and Political History of American Finance, 1865–1879.* Princeton, N.J.: Princeton University Press, 1964.

Venit, Abraham. "Isaac Bronson: His Banking Theory and the Financial Controversies of the Jacksonian Period." *Journal of Economic History* 5 (1945): 201–214.

Larry Schweikart

BAPTISTS

The early Baptists who trickled to the American colonies in the seventeenth century were less disposed to creating distinctive doctrines than simply seeking an opportunity to be "faithful and obedient," which they believed was impossible in any of the established churches. Most Baptists were Calvinist in theology.

However, they were more specifically recognized for certain practices: baptism of adults only and then only by immersion; worship inspired by the Holy Spirit and not directed by a set liturgy or prayer book; ministry by "gifts" rather than by hierarchy, with little distinction between clergy and laity; opposition to the use of oaths in court or elsewhere; and, most radically, a belief that no Christian in good conscience could execute the office of civil magistrate.

Over time Baptists articulated their beliefs in the language of freedom: Scriptural freedom asserted that every Christian was free and obligated to study and obey the scripture. Soul freedom affirmed that each believer should deal with God without imposition of creed, direction of clergy, or interference by civil government. Church freedom maintained that local churches were to be free under the Lordship of Christ and should identify their membership, order their work, empower their leadership, or participate (or not) with the larger body of Christ as they determined locally. Religious freedom asserted that the necessity of freedom of religion, freedom for religion, and freedom from religion was absolute. These beliefs made the sacrifice and burden of being Baptist large; consequently, the number of members of the denomination was small in its early days. But in the eighteenth century the Baptists were reinvigorated by their adoption of the "warm" theology of the Great Awakening and by their advocacy of a theology of freedom that fit well with the political inclinations of the Revolutionary era.

From 1820 to 1870 Baptists in America were thus a dynamic force gathering momentum. By 1820 Baptists had left behind their identity as a tiny minority of isolated, independent-minded people who mostly derived from the Puritan traditions of New England. Their new growth was most notable in the old West and the South. In New England and the Middle Atlantic their preachers and leaders were still often among the educated elite. Their published sermons focused on explaining biblical texts, inspiring their congregations, and providing guidance for moral development. In areas of new growth Baptists communicated more frequently in person than in print.

Baptist literary contributions beyond sermons included participating in biblical and theological controversies, shaping ecclesiastical matters (particularly in support of overseas "missions"), and challenging leaders of government and community to maintain strict distance from the internal affairs of religious groups. The latter focus was first expressed around the broad themes of religious liberty and freedom of conscience, especially regarding taxation for support of established religious groups. It was then conceptualized as the doctrine of separation of church and state, which was expressed during the Revolutionary era in the writings of Isaac Backus (1724–1806) in Massachusetts and John Leland (1754–1841) in Virginia. Led by Backus and Leland, Baptists in many locations bartered support for the Revolutionary cause in return for consideration of religious liberty. The ratification of the U.S. Constitution in 1789 and the Bill of Rights in 1791 achieved this most distinctive of Baptist goals. By 1833 it was a doctrine established in every state as well.

By 1820 Baptist literary focus reflected four developments: the adoption of overseas missions as a unifying and energizing force; the success of evangelism and home missions, especially among the marginally educated people of the frontiers and immigrants from Europe; the rapid growth of the Baptist movement into the expanding populations of the new territories; and the growing theological and regional tensions rising among Baptists.

BAPTIST EDUCATION AND PUBLICATION

During this period Baptists developed strong Sabbath school programs to reach and educate children and founded a number of weekday schools, academies, and colleges. Although an attempt to establish a "national college," Columbian College in Washington, D.C. (1821), ultimately failed by mid-century, the founding of Baptist colleges was unusually frequent in this period. Notable examples in the North included such institutions as the Hamilton Literary and Theological Institution, later renamed Colgate University (New York, 1819); Franklin College (Indiana, 1834); the University at Lewisburg, later renamed Bucknell University (Pennsylvania, 1846); and the University of Chicago (1857, reorganized 1891). In the South, Georgetown College (Kentucky, 1829), Wake Forest College (North Carolina, 1834), Richmond College (Virginia, 1840), Mercer University (Georgia, 1837), Howard College (Alabama, 1841), and Baylor College (1856, Baylor University in 1886) were all established. Originally intended to train ministers, these institutions quickly had a much broader impact among the general population. In 1859 the Southern Baptist Theological Seminary was established at Furman University in Greenville, South Carolina, but following the Civil War was moved in 1877 to Louisville, Kentucky.

Baptists also effectively established publication societies, primarily to support the curriculum needs of their educational programs and to print tracts in support of their efforts in evangelism and missions. First organized in 1824 as the Baptist General Tract Society and then later as the American Baptist Publication and Sunday School Society, the Baptist publishing organization was incorporated in 1845 as the American Baptist Publication Society. By 1865 it had established the *National Baptist,* a periodical, and pioneered in publishing multilingual resources for use among immigrant peoples.

To achieve distribution of their materials the Publication Society developed a "colportage program" by which printed materials were transported by colporteurs, a French term meaning "bearers" that was commonly associated with peddlers and purveyors of religious literature. These adventurous agents carried the materials on foot and by horse-drawn wagons and rail. Later this program expanded to include "chapel cars," which were railroad cars outfitted as small churches that included living quarters for missionaries who also delivered printed material to newly developing towns and hamlets near the rail lines. Between 1824 and 1886 the society reported circulating 330,087,724 copies of religious publications.

Baptists, especially Baptist scholars, published widely during this period, but few were broadly received beyond denominational circles. One clear exception was Francis Wayland (1796–1865), Brown University's notable president from 1827 to 1855, whose over seventy published works, most significantly his *Elements of Moral Science* (1836), made important contributions to the then-emerging fields of moral science, political economy, and political philosophy. But if Baptists were limited in their contributions to national literature, their vitality on the frontier and in rural areas made a strong impact on popular thought and values. Communication through sermons and publications serving the needs of those with a rudimentary education encouraged and enabled the Baptist tendency to urge laypersons to aspire to leadership in the church. Also, their emphasis on biblical knowledge and education through Sabbath schools and academies helped to significantly raise literacy among uneducated populations. The colporteurs of the Publication Society, for example, took printed literature and rudimentary education to people in frontier and remote areas with no access to libraries, schools, or regular distribution of literature.

THE CULTURE OF BAPTIST MISSIONS

In this period Baptists developed an ethos—even a significant subculture—around the support of missions and missionaries. Baptist missions were perpetuated by continued distribution of stories about the travels of missionaries. Missionary reports and tales soon developed what might be called a "mythology of Baptist missions." Many who became missionaries were inspired by the tales and reports of mission activity and the mythology of adventure, sacrifice, and noble, godly purpose their commitments reflected. The huge enterprise that mission activity fashioned in this era was fueled by a fusion of religious fervor tinged with the romanticism of the age.

The core, enduring story of missions was generated by the activities of missionaries Adoniram and Ann Haseltine Judson. Adoniram Judson (1788–1850) was reared as a Congregationalist Deist with an emphasis on rationalist thought. Later he experienced a conversion to more evangelical Christian beliefs during the Second Great Awakening, which was a countrywide revival between 1790 and 1820 expanding the personal, emotional, and evangelical religious sentiments first experienced in the mid-eighteenth century. This powerful movement added an urge to humanitarian reform and missions to non-Christians to the personalism of evangelical theology. Judson then attended Andover Seminary, where he determined to be a missionary. Later, while onboard ship to India, Judson, his wife Ann (1789–1826), and their compatriot Luther Rice (1783–1836) all converted to Baptist views. Their shift deprived Congregational missions of a rising star and brought to Baptist missions not only a new and dynamic ambition but also dedicated, talented, and charismatic personalities to lead it. The Judsons established an enduring Christian presence in Burma (Myanmar). As part of their work the Judsons translated portions of the Bible into Burmese languages.

Ann Judson also learned Siamese (Thai) and translated significant biblical texts into that language. Ann became a frequent contributor to American periodicals and publications that communicated stories about her life amidst a culture unknown to most Americans. In this time when women's roles were largely confined to the home, and before the publication of popular magazines, especially women's magazines, her observations, stories, and personal expressions of faith, especially in the face of family loss and tragedy, were eagerly read by a wide audience. Poor health caused her return to the United States in 1822, where she wrote a history of the Burmese work titled *American Baptist Mission to the Burman Empire,* published in 1823.

Work in foreign missions was dangerous, especially for women who faced childbirth and its frequent complications in a primitive environment without medical attention. Judson's experience of loss was typical: Ann Judson died in 1826. Adoniram's second wife, Sarah Hall Boardman (1803–1845), also died in service. Judson met his third wife, Emily Chubbuck (1817–1854), a professional writer, while searching for someone to write Sarah's biography. Emily accomplished

Adinoram Judson. Illustration from *A History of the Baptists* by Thomas Armitage, 1890. GRADUATE LIBRARY, UNIVERSITY OF MICHIGAN

this task before her own death in 1854. The romanticized stories and biographies of the Judsons and, soon, those who followed them in mission service both in America and abroad inspired generations of Baptists and others. Francis Wayland recounted Judson's work in a scholarly tone in *A Memoir of the Life and Labors of the Rev. Adoniram Judson, D.D.* in 1853. And through their missionary reports and writings and the interpretations of them by others in such magazines as the *Baptist Missionary Magazine,* the *Latter Day Luminary* (1818), the *Christian Watchman* (1819), the *Columbian Star* (1822), and the *Religious Herald* (1828), missionaries expanded popular knowledge of the American West and of cultures around the world. Indeed, published and unpublished writings of Baptist missionaries remain the strongest source of Western knowledge about the cultures and social dynamics of Asia, Africa, and elsewhere during this period.

BAPTIST ORGANIZATIONAL LIFE AND CONTROVERSIES

As missions emerged as the common focus of Baptist development, better denominational structure and organization were required. In order to encourage and provide financial support for mission activity, local, regional, and national missionary societies quickly developed. Frequent correspondence between these bodies became the journals of Baptist denominational

Adoniram Judson wrote the following poem after discovering his wife's death, which was followed soon after by the death of his infant daughter, Maria, both in 1826. Judson had been away from home when Ann's death occurred.

And when I came, and saw her not
In all the place around,
They pointed out a grassy spot,
Where she lay underground.
And soon another loved one fled,
And sought her mother's side;
In vain I stayed her drooping head;
She panted, gasped, and died.

Wayland, *A Memoir of the Life and Labors of the Rev. Adoniram Judson*, 1:110.

development. Also, because Baptist churches were independent bodies and were generally protective of their local autonomy, a universally recognized need for guides to Baptist church "order" became urgent. Therefore, this period witnessed the emergence of a number of "church manuals"—volumes that guided church organizational life.

Baptist manuals achieved remarkable circulation among churches in need of direction. The first, William Crowell's (1806–1871) *The Church Member's Manual*, was published in 1847. Francis Wayland offered a somewhat intellectual and theological approach to Baptist practices in *Notes on the Principles and Practices of Baptist Churches* (1857). The New York pastor Edward T. Hiscox (1814–1901) published his *The Baptist Church Directory* in 1859, and James M. Pendleton (1811–1891) likewise published his *Church Manual* in 1867. The latter two works maintained a strong readership well into the twentieth century: by then Pendleton's manual had sold at least 150,000 copies. Hiscox's *Directory* was followed by several additional volumes, including *Principles and Practices for Baptist Churches,* which also enjoyed a long publication history. In the 1960s a volume that drew materials from several of his works was published as *The Hiscox Guide for Baptist Churches,* and in 1995 an expanded, revised, and rewritten work based on his materials was offered as *The New Hiscox Guide for Baptist Churches.*

Despite the unifying focus of missions and the creation of denominational structure to support it, controversy occupied much of Baptist energy in this period. One subject was the mission enterprise itself. The antimissionary Baptists reflected an extreme Calvinist view that because God alone offered salvation, mission attempts were a kind of interference in God's power. Daniel Parker (1781–1844), the movement's most articulate spokesman, published *Views on the Two Seeds Taken from Genesis* in 1826 as the movement's fullest articulation. From 1829 to 1831 he also circulated his beliefs through a journal called the *Church Advocate.*

Another movement, restorationism, grew out of Baptist ranks. It expressed the belief that the true church had become lost through corrupt doctrine and alliances with secular powers. Restorationists asserted that they had re-created apostolic Christianity, or the Christian church of the first generation of Christian believers, directly from the New Testament. Their perspectives were most fully expressed in the works of Barton Warren Stone (1772–1844), Thomas Campbell (1763–1854), and Alexander Campbell (1788–1866). Alexander Campbell was especially effective in articulating his opinions in several journals, notably the *Christian Baptist* (1823–1829) and the *Millennial Harbinger* (1830–1863). Eventually Campbell and his followers rejected Baptist affiliation and formed a new "Campbellite" (later, "Christian," or "Disciples of Christ") denomination.

Partly in response to the Campbellites, the landmarkists claimed a unique historical authenticity for Baptists, tracing an unbroken line directly to the New Testament church. One leader, George Orchard, wrote that Baptists were "the only Christian community which has stood since the times of the Apostles" (p. xviii), thus preserving pure doctrines ever since. The term "landmark" was taken from an essay published in 1854 by James M. Pendleton in Bowling Green, Kentucky, in a pamphlet titled *An Old Landmark Reset.* Other works by Pendleton, James R. Graves (1820–1893), and Amos Cooper Dayton (1813–1865) asserted their claims. Dayton's landmark polemic was in the form of a novel published as *Theodosia Ernest* in 1857.

A number of other controversies regarding church organization, the use of musical instruments, a variety of theological interpretations regarding salvation, the role of humankind in salvation, and other matters also emerged in the period. However, no controversy compared to the debate engendered by slavery. Like the entire American nation, Baptists were subsumed in the debates and controversies leading to the Civil War from the 1830s onward. In 1845 this controversy resulted in the Baptists abandoning the loosely organized "Triennial Convention" structure that had provided the network to unify and support missions, encourage publications, and nurture educational and other joint endeavors since the 1820s. South and North went separate ways.

Baptists were well represented in expressing opinion in print, mostly in denominational journals and publications, arguing all sides of this towering issue in American life. In the South, Richard Furman (1755–1825) articulated views in defense of Christian support of slavery in "Exposition of the Views of the Baptists, Relative to the Coloured Population of the United States" (1823) and other articles published regionally. In his *Elements of Moral Science*, Francis Wayland argued that slavery was inappropriate, but he based his argument on Enlightenment rather than biblical approaches. Wayland, ever anxious about any authoritative body that might interfere in local church prerogatives, sought a middle way on the issue of churches and slavery and searched for allies to protect Baptist organizations from takeover by either abolitionist or proslavery sentiment. Ultimately no compromise was found, and Baptists, like the rest of the nation, were increasingly divided on this issue as the period came to a close.

CONCLUSION

The period 1820–1870 was a formative era for Baptists in the expanding United States. During that time Baptists' central passion was defined; foundations of denominational identity and structure were laid; theological issues were clarified, if not always resolved; and the extraordinary diversity that ultimately came to define Baptists theologically, racially, culturally, and politically appeared. A once-beleaguered minority among American Protestants was becoming a significant majority. As a result, their contributions to cultural and literary life were massive if not immediately recognized. Their most significant leaders, writers, and spokespersons would emerge in the next generations.

See also Calvinism; Evangelicals; Protestantism; Religion

BIBLIOGRAPHY

Primary Works

Orchard, George H. *A Concise History of Foreign Baptists.* Nashville, Tenn.: Graves, Marks and Rutland, 1859.

Wayland, Francis. *Elements of Moral Science.* 1836. 4th ed. Boston: Gould, Kendall, and Lincoln, 1848.

Wayland, Francis. *A Memoir of the Life and Labors of the Rev. Adoniram Judson, D.D.* 2 vols. Boston: Phillips, Sampson, 1853.

Wayland, Francis. *Notes on the Principles and Practices of Baptist Churches.* New York: Sheldon, Blakeman, 1857.

Secondary Works

Brackney, William H., ed. *Baptist Life and Thought, 1600–1980: A Source Book.* Valley Forge, Pa.: Judson Press, 1983.

Copeland, E. Luther. *The Southern Baptist Convention and the Judgment of History: The Taint of an Original Sin.* Lanham, Md.: University Press of America, 1995.

Goen, C. C. *Broken Churches, Broken Nation: Denominational Schisms and the Coming of the American Civil War.* Macon, Ga.: Mercer University Press, 1985.

Goodwin, Everett C. *The New Hiscox Guide for Baptist Churches.* Valley Forge, Pa.: Judson Press, 1995.

Goodwin, Everett C., ed. *Baptists in the Balance: The Tension between Freedom and Responsibility.* Valley Forge, Pa.: Judson Press, 1997.

Leonard, Bill J. *Baptist Ways: A History.* Valley Forge, Pa.: Judson Press. 2003.

Everett C. Goodwin

"BARTLEBY, THE SCRIVENER"

"Bartleby, the Scrivener: A Story of Wall-Street" is one of Herman Melville's most highly acclaimed works of short fiction, along with "Benito Cereno" and the novella *Billy Budd.* "Bartleby" is also one of the most celebrated short stories in American literature. After publishing seven novels between 1846 and 1852, including his magnum opus *Moby-Dick* (1851), Melville (1819–1891) turned to short fiction, writing "Bartleby" and thirteen other stories and sketches between 1853 and 1856. First published in *Putnam's Monthly Magazine* in 1853, "Bartleby" was subsequently published by Dix and Edwards of New York in 1856 in *The Piazza Tales,* a collection of six of Melville's stories.

Readers have been both intrigued and puzzled by Bartleby, the enigmatic and seemingly eccentric clerk of the story. Why does he refuse to work? And what does he want from his employer? In analyzing his character, critics have proposed remarkably diverse interpretations. To some he is a Christ figure; to others a mysterious misfit; to still others he represents the exploited worker, a Thoreau-like practitioner of passive resistance, or even a projection of Melville as alienated author. Readers have also disagreed about the character of the lawyer-narrator. Is he a spineless employer? Or a callous boss? A self-serving hypocrite? Or a compassionate employer whose helpful intentions are frustrated by Bartleby's incurable pathology? Is he a static or dynamic character? Does he understand the story he so artfully tells?

In the early twenty-first century there are two dominant readings of "Bartleby," one of which might be termed psychological and moral and the other economic and ideological. The first, perhaps best articulated by Milton R. Stern and Dan McCall, suggests that Bartleby is, for reasons that are never disclosed, a deeply melancholic soul and that the lawyer is a sensitive and well-meaning employer who recounts, with disarming candor, both his sincere efforts to understand and help his troubled but inscrutable scrivener and his own moral shortcomings. The other dominant reading, which is developed in this essay (see also Gilmore; Kuebrich; and Foley), views Bartleby as a demoralized, exploited worker and the boss as an unreliable narrator who, blinded by his upper-class perspective, is unable to understand the underlying causes of his clerk's unusual behavior.

ECONOMIC CONTEXT

Unlike the first interpretation, the second considers "Bartleby" to be a historicized text, and it emphasizes the importance of placing the story in the context of antebellum capitalism. In the decades prior to Melville's writing of "Bartleby," the United States underwent a complex process of economic transformation. The building of superior surface roads, the introduction of railways, and the invention of the steamship for hauling goods upriver marked a transportation revolution. New forms of labor-saving machinery were developed with the effective use of steam and waterpower. And unprecedented opportunities arose for acquiring and securing capital, made possible by more numerous banks, new insurance companies, and state laws facilitating the creation of business corporations.

These changes in the infrastructure in turn altered the nature of production. Since the Middle Ages, most manufactures had been created by skilled artisans who maintained small shops in or near their homes. A master artisan—a shoemaker or blacksmith, for example—would own his own shop and perhaps be assisted by a journeyman and an apprentice. With the onset of the Industrial Revolution in eighteenth-century Europe and nineteenth-century America, this mode of manufacturing was gradually replaced by entrepreneurs who built large workshops or factories and hired skilled and unskilled workers in increasing numbers, paying them by the hour, day, or piece. For the first time in history, a system of production was established in which masses of workers sold their labor to capitalists who provided the tools needed to produce market goods.

Workers now encountered an impersonal workplace, more tedious work, and less opportunity for advancement. Under the artisanal system, the master knew his workers well. They worked alongside each other, took their meals together, and often lived under the same roof. The master was responsible for training and overseeing those under him, even to the extent of providing for or watching over an apprentice's intellectual and moral development. In contrast, in the emerging industrial order, employers and employees no longer lived and dined together and might not even know each other. Employees became more specialized and less skilled, and their work became more monotonous. In a traditional tailor's shop, a master or his assistant would know how to do every aspect of clothes making; in a new clothing factory, however, a worker might only attach a collar to a shirt or sew on the buttons. Another difference was that workers felt boxed in with little or no chance of rising to a better position or owning their own business. With the older craft system, it was expected that an apprentice would become a journeyman and then go on to become the master of his own shop. In contrast, the new wage laborer was poorly paid and could never expect to amass the necessary wealth to build a factory and employ others. Thus the social mobility and comparatively low degree of social stratification that had characterized life in the northeastern and mid-Atlantic regions during the eighteenth century and early nineteenth century gave way to a more rigid class system.

In "Bartleby" the workplace is not a large shop or factory but a Manhattan law office, yet Melville invests the office with many of the characteristics of the new urban-industrial workplace. New York City's population increased from 124,000 in 1820 to 814,000 in 1860. The population growth resulted in a rapid rise in real estate prices that created a market for tall buildings like those that hem in the lawyer's office. The high cost of space in lower Manhattan also forced workers to search for cheaper housing elsewhere, thus creating the story's austere Wall Street setting that during evenings and Sundays is virtually devoid of human life. The building that houses the law office, described by the lawyer as a space "entirely unhallowed by humanizing domestic associations" (p. 36), further suggests the impersonality of Bartleby's work environment and the loneliness of his life.

Although the lawyer has only four workers, his office mirrors the hierarchical division of labor and impersonality characteristic of the new factory system. The lawyer seems to know his employees only by nickname, and he separates himself from them by screen and partitions, commands them rather than consults with them, and limits their activities to monotonous copying and serving as gofers. There is seemingly no possibility for any of them to become lawyers. At age sixty, Turkey

Lower Broadway in New York City, 1859, with the spire of Trinity Church in the background, shows the tall office buildings referred to in "Bartleby." Melville presumably conceived of the story's law office as being in the rear of a building of this type.
COLLECTION OF THE NEW-YORK HISTORICAL SOCIETY

is still copying documents. Nippers's efforts at practicing law are dismissed by the boss as a case of "diseased ambition" (p. 17). Although Ginger Nut has been placed in the office by his cart-driver father with the hope that he will learn law, there is no evidence that he is receiving any legal training. Instead, finding the office boring, he gladly serves as an errand boy.

The story's omnipresent walls—the Wall Street setting, the tall brick buildings surrounding the office, the folding glass doors and portable screen that divide the office internally, and finally the prison walls—serve as symbols of the growing division between employer and employee and between the capitalist and working classes. They also indicate the barriers that confine the workers to their mind-numbing, poor-paying jobs and prevent their social advancement. In addition they are outward markers of the ideological assumptions that

separate the lawyer from his scriveners, preventing him from understanding them and having genuine compassion for their plight.

IDEOLOGICAL CONTEXT

Melville's primary concern, however, was neither to detail the physical conditions of this new workplace nor to describe the sufferings of the workers but to expose the underlying ideology that legitimated this new system of production. As the old system of small workshops was being displaced by industrial capitalism, supporters and opponents of the change developed rival ideologies to justify their positions. The pro-capitalist position stressed that American workers, unlike their European counterparts, had ample opportunity to achieve a reasonable competence. In an address given to the American Institute of the City of

New York in 1844, Alexander H. H. Stuart maintained that in the United States "no class of our population [is] subsisting on wages of six-pence or a shilling a day!" and that an adequate living was possible for "every man who is disposed to exercise ordinary industry and frugality" (p. 9). For such apologists of capital, the workingman's chief impediments were the age-old sins of laziness, dissipation, and drink; the solution was to embrace the Protestant virtues of industry, thrift, and sobriety.

Advocates for the working class, however, argued that an economic system that made the poor subject to the rich for the necessities of life was unnatural and undemocratic. They maintained that everyone has a God-given right to the property or work necessary for one's livelihood. In the view of Thomas Skidmore, a spokesperson for New York laborers, the wage-labor system was a form of slavery: "He who can feed me, or starve me; give me employment, or bid me wander about in idleness; is my master; and it is but the utmost folly for me to boast of being any thing [sic] but a slave" (p. 388).

As these brief quotations suggest, the change to large-scale production was giving rise to new ideological formations in which the capitalist would assume the benignity of the system, ignore employee complaints, and blame the poverty of workers on their own moral failures. The workers, or at least their more radical spokespeople, with the opposite point of view, would address the inequality in the economy and the workplace, and they would define their dependency as a form of slavery. Both sides would, as is so often the case in American political debate, claim God as an ally.

Ideology, however, especially the dominant ideology, functions at an unconscious level as well as at a conscious level. When an ideology becomes established in a society's institutions and daily practices, it becomes the "natural" or "commonsense" manner of thinking and acting. Almost everyone assumes it is the "right" or "only" way. For instance, if a culture establishes the primacy of property rights, then the workplace will be hierarchical. Employers will feel it is only "reasonable" that they control their workplaces and pay, command, hire, and fire their employees as they please. Under such a system, it does not seem unnatural if the employer is rich and the workers poor or if the employer orders his or her workers around and assigns them menial work and trivial tasks. In contrast, if a society were to emphasize equality in the workplace, the right to meaningful work, and a living wage, then the workplace would be much more democratic. Workers would have more power, and pay would be more equal. It would seem natural that bosses function as coordinators, help with the boring work, and run an occasional errand or two.

If a boss were quickly shifted from a hierarchical to a democratic workplace, he or she would find the new circumstances bewildering, even infuriating, and would demand some explanation for the workers' seeming audacity and insubordination. To a limited extent, the lawyer-narrator in "Bartleby" experiences this disruptive shift because his hierarchical workplace is infiltrated by a worker who begins to protest, albeit quietly, the unfairness of his condition. Accustomed to running his office as he pleases, the lawyer assumes he will treat his new clerk just as he has treated Turkey and Nippers. However, Bartleby, depressed by his tedious work and commodity status, stops taking orders; resisting the injustice of the system, he refuses to cooperate and begins to exercise his own choice—to do as he "prefers." The lawyer is utterly befuddled: How can Bartleby act in such contempt of common usage? Bewilderment turns to exasperation, then anger, and finally he fires his obstinate clerk.

It is hard for readers to understand this ideological conflict between the lawyer and his recalcitrant scrivener because their views are never explicitly presented. The lawyer simply assumes his right to exercise unlimited authority, and Bartleby, although convinced his resistance is justified, appears too depressed to speak or perhaps feels the forces aligned against him are so overwhelming that open protest is futile. However, the story also is perplexing because readers unconsciously subscribe to the same ideology as the lawyer. Living in a society that gives precedence to property rights and thus the rights of employers over those of employees, Americans are conditioned to assume that owners will be much more affluent than their workers, that employers will call the shots, and that their workers will simply comply. One can scarcely imagine a worker saying "No"; and if one does, it is expected that she or he will soon receive a pink slip. In short, as readers, Americans encounter "Bartleby" from the perspective of the culture's dominant ideology regarding employer-employee relations. One shares the lawyer's exasperation and outrage: "What's with this preposterous clerk?" "Shouldn't he be fired immediately?" Melville intends, however, that as a good reader one will slowly come to realize that the ideology consists of ideas and practices based on power rather than reason or right. If one does this, one will have freed his or her mind of its ideological fetters, and one will be able to entertain the possibility that what before seemed the only way to do things may be quite arbitrary and unjust—and as is true of the lawyer's office, quite wasteful of human energy.

A more democratic workplace might prove more natural, fairer, and more productive.

UNCONSCIOUS IDEOLOGY: THE LAWYER'S ASSUMPTIONS

Careful examination of the lawyer's behavior discloses several key assumptions that shape his views of the workplace and workers and prevent him from understanding his employees and addressing the problems that beset his office. Melville directs the reader's attention to this aspect of the story in the episode in which the lawyer first attempts to rid himself of Bartleby: after giving him his full pay plus a severance allowance, the lawyer leaves for the evening, assuming that his unwanted clerk will be gone when he returns to the office in the morning. Notable at this point in the story is the lawyer's use of some form of the word "assume" eleven times, twice italicized for emphasis—a verbal pattern that underscores the gap between the lawyer's desired understanding of Bartleby and Bartleby's actual behavior:

> It was truly a beautiful thought to have assumed Bartleby's departure; but, after all, that assumption was simply my own, and none of Bartleby's. The great point was, not whether I had assumed that he would quit me, but whether he would prefer so to do. He was more a man of preferences than assumptions. (P. 34)

Here the lawyer recognizes that his assumptions about Bartleby may be belied by the facts. What he fails to understand, however, is that he also carries around various class-based assumptions about his clerks and the workplace that are equally erroneous. These beliefs, part of the dominant ideology used to legitimate the new wage-labor system, are so deeply ingrained in the lawyer's consciousness that he conceives of them not as human constructs but as natural laws or common sense. In accentuating the lawyer's assumptions, Melville directs attention to a preconscious dimension of the lawyer's thought that twentieth-century students of ideology, such as Antonio Gramsci and Raymond Williams, speak of as the ideology of the "lived social process" (Williams, p. 109), that is, an unreflective acceptance of some values or beliefs as proper or natural simply because they are given concrete embodiment in one's social world.

Because the lawyer is scarcely aware of these largely unconscious dimensions of his belief and so never articulates them, they must be inferred from the information he unwittingly provides in telling the story. If one attends to the assumptions that underlie his behavior and speech, however, one can identify a set of beliefs that inform his understanding of workers and the workplace—beliefs that legitimate the inequalities inherent in the emerging system of wage-labor capitalism.

The first of these is that the problems of workers are due to vice, poor health, and misfortune. The lawyer never entertains the idea that the dissatisfactions or strange behavior of his clerks may be understandable responses to their monotonous, low-paying, dead-end jobs. The reason Turkey becomes fiery and reckless in the afternoons is simple: he is an alcoholic who drinks too much "red ink" (wine) at lunch (p. 17). Nippers's forenoon nervous tics and irritability are explained by the fact that he is the "victim of two evil powers—ambition and indigestion" (p. 16) and that "nature herself" has endowed him with an "irritable, brandy-like disposition" (p. 18). Bartleby's behavior is imputed to an "organic" psychological ill: an "innate and incurable disorder" (p. 29). Rather than relating the clerks' behavior to their working conditions, the lawyer always points to external factors, thus absolving himself and the wage-labor system of any responsibility.

The second belief is that workers are the servants of the boss. The lawyer feels comfortable exercising a near-despotic power over his clerks. This is evident in his dealings with Bartleby, whom he locates at a desk near his own (but separated by a high screen) so he is "within easy call, in case any trifling thing was to be done" (p. 19). On the third day of Bartleby's employment, the lawyer "abruptly called" to him in "*natural* expectancy of instant compliance" (p. 20, emphasis added). Any idea of equality in the workplace is totally outside the lawyer's consciousness. He thinks it is acceptable to use Bartleby as his personal factotum, and he believes he has the right to do this even though the scriveners are paid only for the pages they copy, and so Bartleby will earn nothing for these additional tasks.

Third is the belief that property rights are supreme. The lawyer feels he has the right to do as he pleases at the workplace; after all, it is his office. When he discovers that Bartleby lives there, he feels no compunction about violating his privacy by unlocking his desk in search of personal information. This intrusion is justified, he tells himself, because "the desk is mine, and its contents too" (p. 28). In a later encounter with his clerk, he challenges Bartleby's de facto claim to a right to live in the office by asserting that his property rights have precedence over Bartleby's need for shelter: "What earthly right have you to stay here? Do you pay any rent? Do you pay my taxes? Or is this property yours?" (p. 35). For the lawyer, the property rights of the rich clearly trump the survival needs of the poor.

That Bartleby is protesting being reduced to little more than a gofer and copying machine is made clear in two instances in which he qualifies his refusal to work—a change brought about by the lawyer suggesting that he considers his clerk to be not just an employee but a fellow human being and even a friend. In the first of these episodes, the lawyer goes beyond his usual appeals to reason or custom, stating, "I feel friendly towards you" (p. 30). Moved by this profession of warmth and equality, Bartleby discloses "the faintest conceivable tremor of . . . [his] white attenuated mouth" and for the first time instead of simply replying "I would prefer not to," he implies that he may become more cooperative in the future: "At *present* I prefer to give no answer" (p. 30, emphasis added). In the second episode, the lawyer assumes his "kindest tone" and actually invites Bartleby to "go home with me now"; in response Bartleby maintains his independence but again hints at lessening his resistance: "No: at present I would prefer not to make any change at all" (p. 41). With good reason, Bartleby remains suspicious of his boss, but at the same time these responses indicate that given adequate respect and fair treatment, he would return to being a productive worker. What Bartleby waits for is clear evidence that the lawyer sees the error of his ways and becomes a more considerate and fair-minded employer. Unfortunately, this does not happen, and so the standoff continues until Bartleby dies.

CONCLUSION

Returning to the questions posed at the beginning of this essay, one can assert that Bartleby is not a Christ figure, an alienated author, or a victim of some obscure psychological malady. His melancholy, given adequate explanation by the story, stems from his being a demoralized worker, and if he practices passive resistance, it is because he recognizes the injustice of the system and decides to oppose it. His lawyer-boss, who proves to be a more complex and puzzling character than his initially mystifying clerk, demonstrates far too much patience and sensitivity to be easily dismissed as a religious hypocrite or callous capitalist. In fact, it is because he is a respectable and compassionate figure that the story is of enduring interest. By investing the lawyer with these positive qualities, Melville crafts a narrative of much greater social significance: he directs attention not to the shortcomings of an individual employer but to the deficiencies of an economic system and its legitimating ideology. The lawyer should be seen as a better-than-average boss. Yet despite his good qualities and intentions, he possesses a limited moral imagination, and he does not significantly improve during the course of the story—a fact

clearly indicated by his still referring to Bartleby in the sequel as a victim of "nature and misfortune" (p. 45) rather than recognizing the true basis of his complaint.

That the lawyer remains a static character despite his need to change calls attention to what it is that restricts his understanding: namely, his "assumptions," that is, the latent ideology he shares with the larger society. Exactly why the lawyer fails to recognize these assumptions as the protectors of class interest remains tantalizingly undetermined. Is the ideology so deeply ingrained in his consciousness that he cannot think in other ways? Or does he refuse to interrogate his habits of mind and conduct because to do so would call into question his privileged position? Or is his behavior a mix of blindness and self-interest? The text does not resolve this issue, but by the end of the story it is clear that "Bartleby" is primarily an account not of an obstinate clerk but of a narrator who fails to acknowledge the exploitative nature of his relationship to his employees.

See also Battle-Pieces; Moby-Dick; Short Story; *Typee*

BIBLIOGRAPHY

Primary Works

Melville, Herman. "Bartleby, the Scrivener: A Story of Wall-Street." 1853. In *The Piazza Tales and Other Prose Pieces, 1839–1860*, edited by Harrison Hayford, Alma A. MacDougall, and G. Thomas Tanselle. Evanston, Ill., and Chicago: Northwestern University Press and the Newberry Library, 1987.

Skidmore, Thomas. *The Rights of Man to Property!* 1829. New York: Burt Franklin, n.d.

Stuart, Alexander H. H. *Anniversary Address before the American Institute of the City of New York*. New York: James Van Norden, 1844.

Secondary Works

American Social History Project. *Who Built America?* Vol. 1. New York: Pantheon, 1989. See pp. 220–267, 318–363.

Foley, Barbara. "From Wall Street to Astor Place: Historicizing Melville's 'Bartleby.'" *American Literature* 72, no. 1 (2000): 87–116.

Gilmore, Michael T. "'Bartleby, the Scrivener' and the Transformation of the Economy." In *American Romanticism and the Marketplace*. Chicago: University of Chicago Press, 1985.

Kuebrich, David. "Melville's Doctrine of Assumptions: The Hidden Ideology of Capitalist Production in "Bartleby." *New England Quarterly* 69, no. 3 (1996): 381–405.

McCall, Dan. *The Silence of Bartleby*. Ithaca, N.Y.: Cornell University Press, 1989.

Stern, Milton R. "Towards 'Bartleby the Scrivener.'" In *The Stoic Strain in American Literature,* edited by Duane J. MacMillan, pp. 19–41. Toronto: University of Toronto Press, 1979.

Williams, Raymond. *Marxism and Literature.* New York: Oxford University Press, 1977.

David Kuebrich

BATTLE-PIECES

Canonized as one of America's most original and profound novelists, Herman Melville (1819–1891) remains underappreciated, and often unrecognized, as a significant American poet. *Battle-Pieces and Aspects of the War,* published in 1866, reflects Melville's intense and anguished engagement with the Civil War. In their variety, density, and experimentalism, the poems of *Battle-Pieces* reveal an ambitious and self-conscious poet who aspires to prophecy as much as to commemoration. *Battle-Pieces* tests the possibilities and limitations of a public and political role for the American poet, its "Supplement," a concluding essay on Reconstruction, in fact suggesting how Melville the poet works out of a specialized sense of "patriotism."

FROM PROSE TO POETRY

Melville was in his late forties when *Battle-Pieces* appeared, and he published the even more ambitious *Clarel,* a "Poem and Pilgrimage in the Holy Land," in 1876. Deciding in his later years largely to abandon novels and stories for poetry, Melville was reacting in part to the failure of mid-nineteenth-century American readers to comprehend or willingly grapple with the complexities of novels such as *Moby-Dick* (1851), *Pierre; or, The Ambiguities* (1852), and *The Confidence-Man* (1857). Nevertheless, continuities between the fiction and the poetry are abundant and telling. The imminence of civil war shrouds the composition and content of *Moby-Dick;* the *Pequod,* American ship of state, sails toward its own apocalyptic destruction throughout the novel, and Ishmael's query in the book's first chapter—"Who aint a slave?" (p. 6)—anticipates Melville's position in *Battle-Pieces* that the Civil War needs to be understood as a singular expression of some more generalized history of human conflict and captivity. Likewise, "Benito Cereno" (1855), a story about a slave mutiny, provides a larger allegory of New World slavery and American blindness to its depravity. *The Confidence-Man* is also a precursor of *Battle-Pieces* in its critique of American idealisms, its

resolutely impersonal presentation of character and event, and the knottiness of its language.

Even the relationship of the lawyer and his employee in "Bartleby, the Scrivener: A Story of Wall-Street" (1853), one of Melville's most renowned short stories, prefigures *Battle-Pieces,* for the lawyer's tentative realization through Bartleby of some "bond of common humanity" generates in him a "fraternal melancholy" (p. 28) that the Civil War poems consistently reproduce. Specifically dedicating *Battle-Pieces* "to the memory of the three hundred thousand" Union dead, Melville also insists on the fraternity of North and South and the fact that "the rebel is wrong, but human yet" (p. 20). Such bonds, however, are hardly the source of any facile celebration of American solidarity. Rather, Melville articulates how sadness and gloom may well be the inevitable offspring of what Ahab in *Moby-Dick* curses as "mortal inter-indebtedness" (p. 471).

The idea for an entire book of Civil War poetry apparently did not take shape in Melville's mind until the end of the war, although some of the poems were written earlier, in the 1860s (the exact order of composition is uncertain). *Battle-Pieces* is a hybrid assembly of texts: its seventy-two poems are framed by a brief prose introduction and a concluding series of "Notes" on the poems and the "Supplement." A first, long group of poems broadly charts the trajectory of the war from the hanging of the insurrectionist John Brown (2 December 1859) through many of the major battles and movements—the First Manassas battle (21 July 1861) in "The March into Virginia"; Shiloh (6 April 1862) in the poem of the same name; Sherman's devastation of Georgia and South Carolina (1864) in "The March to the Sea"—to Robert E. Lee's surrender at Appomattox (9 April 1865) and Abraham Lincoln's assassination (15 April 1865). A second, shorter group of poems, "Verses Inscriptive and Memorial," is primarily elegiac (and reminiscent of the tablets of the dead mariners in the whaleman's chapel in chapter 7 of *Moby-Dick*). Three remaining poems—the long ballad "The Scout toward Aldie," "Lee in the Capitol," and "A Meditation"—complete the text.

Melville assiduously followed news of the war, and a number of the poems of *Battle-Pieces* derive from his readings in periodicals such as *Harper's Weekly* and the *Rebellion Record* (an eleven-volume work that purported to serve as a "diary" of the war). In April 1864 Melville visited his cousin Colonel Henry Gansevoort, who was stationed in Vienna, Virginia, with the Thirteenth New York Cavalry. During the visit Melville took part in an unsuccessful scouting expedition in search of the notorious Colonel John Mosby and his Partisan Raiders, a Confederate guerrilla band adept at disrupting Union forces and infrastructure. But despite his familiarity with contemporary events and his brief firsthand battleground experience, Melville's Civil War poems are uninterested in merely transcribing history or personal experience ("The Scout toward Aldie" is the only poem in *Battle-Pieces* based on Melville's war experience as such, and he is not a participant in the poem's narrative). The poems are intended, rather, to present "the strife as a memory" (p. v), and they call attention to themselves as art, not reportage. "Battle-pieces" itself denoted for Melville's era the specific genre of painting and engravings of battle scenes, and several of his own poems ("The Coming Storm" and "Formerly a Slave," for example) are explicit responses to artwork he had experienced. *Battle-Pieces* deliberately reimagines its source material as a means of exploring America's mission and destiny and human history generally. In "Lee in the Capitol," for example, based on Lee's February 1866 appearance before the Reconstruction Committee of Congress, Melville gives the vanquished general an imagined speech in which Lee espouses a doctrine of magnanimity toward the South in accord with Melville's own counsel in the supplement.

Battle-Pieces proved less accessible for its initial readers and critics than other significant poetic treatments of the Civil War in the 1860s—for example, James Russell Lowell's "Ode Recited at the Harvard Commemoration" (21 July 1865) and Walt Whitman's *Drum-Taps* (1865). *Battle-Pieces*'s shifting perspectives, heavy allusiveness, sometimes crabbed style and obscure thought, and generally unromanticized picture of the war left many readers bewildered. As Melville's cousin Kate Gansevoort confessed, "It is too deep for my comprehension" (Garner, p. 440). An early review chided *Battle-Pieces* for its "great crudities" and found its poetry "epileptic" and "fearful" (Garner, p. 441). "Nature," Charles Eliot Norton averred of Melville in the *Nation* (6 September 1866), "did not make him a poet" (Robertson-Lorant, p. 496). In a more damning review in the *Atlantic Monthly* (February 1967), William Dean Howells complained about *Battle-Pieces*'s "negative virtues of originality" (Robertson-Lorant, p. 496) and the poetry's lack of feeling and outright obliviousness to the human; for Howells, *Battle-Pieces* is a poetry of "phantasms" and "vagaries" (Robertson-Lorant, p. 496), and like Norton, he seems incapable of viewing Melville's alleged poetic infelicities as part of a deliberate aesthetic appropriate to the attempt to poeticize the nation's bloody war experience. Contemporary critics have praised *Battle-Pieces* for many of the

reasons that its original critics reviled it—its difficulty, its compression, its attempt to find new language and form commensurate to the barbarity of the war. Melville has been identified as a proto-modernist and is now frequently taken to be the most significant nineteenth-century American poet after Whitman and Emily Dickinson. Still, the text has yet to attract a wide readership, even among academicians.

VISIONARY TECHNIQUES

Battle-Pieces remains challenging and disconcerting for many reasons. Melville never relinquishes his conviction that "the glory of the war falls short of its pathos" (p. 242), and his poems are as likely to be about failure as triumph. "What like a bullet can undeceive" (p. 90), Melville might write in the requiem that is "Shiloh," but the trauma of war often unmakes the self rather than illuminating or strengthening it. The "idiot-pain" (p. 130) that afflicts the captive of "In the Prison Pen" makes thought and memory impossible. "Self," Melville says of the "college colonel" of the poem of the same name, "he has long disclaimed," and whatever "truth" came to him during his ordeals goes unspecified (p. 131). The soldiers of "The March into Virginia" are "enlightened by the vollied glare" of gunfire only at the moment they perish, and those who live and succeed to the "throe of Second Manassas" are rendered "like to adamant" (p. 60), the process of war for them one of hardening and petrification.

Part of the considerable achievement of *Battle-Pieces,* however, is its multiplicity of perspectives, a democratic technique that suggests how no record of the war can be definitive or complete. Both commoners and luminaries contribute to the design of *Battle-Pieces;* Melville is as interested in the war's prisoners as in its generals. The successive poems "The Cumberland," "In the Turret," "The Temeraire," and "A Utilitarian View of the *Monitor*'s Fight" collectively provide a concise, shifting narrative about the evolution of naval battle that contextualizes the significance of the new ironclads, the Northern *Monitor* and the Southern *Merrimac,* and the new havoc they make possible. "Donelson" considers the war from the civilian perspective as a variety of "eager" and "anxious" (p. 68) Yankees gather about a bulletin board at several times during a week in February 1862 to obtain news about a pivotal Tennessee battle.

The perspective, however, that the modern reader might find conspicuously absent in *Battle-Pieces* is that of the nineteenth-century African American. Melville's poems pay little attention to slavery, and only in "Formerly a Slave," based on a portrait by Elihu Vedder that Melville saw at the National

Lithograph of the Battle of Shiloh, 1862. The bloody Civil War battle of Shiloh, with nearly 24,000 casualties in two days, shocked the nation and inspired a variety of literary responses, of which Melville's requiem is widely considered the most compelling. THE LIBRARY OF CONGRESS

Academy of Design in 1865, does he make an African American the poem's center. The woman does not signify much for Melville in and of herself. Rather she serves as an emblem of "prophetic cheer" that forecasts the "good withheld from her" arriving for her "children's children" (p. 157). Melville himself opposed slavery without advocating abolitionism. Although concerned in the supplement for "the future of the freed slaves," he nonetheless believes that it is the larger "future of the whole country" that "urges a paramount claim upon our anxiety" (p. 243), and "Formerly a Slave" reflects this position.

Battle-Pieces also acutely identifies the terrifying uniqueness of the Civil War and its new technologies of destruction. In "A Utilitarian View of the *Monitor's* Fight" the "anvil-din" of the battle between the *Monitor* and the *Merrimac* establishes a dispassionate, mechanical warfare determined by "crank, / Pivot, and screw, / And calculations of caloric" (p. 89). Such technology requires a new kind of poetry, Melville argues:

a "plain" verse "More ponderous than nimble" that underplays "rhyme's barbaric cymbal" (p. 89). Yet the Civil War for Melville is also analogous to earlier wars (the English Wars of the Roses, the War of Heaven in Milton's 1667 *Paradise Lost*), and American battle-grounds can appear to Melville as biblical wildernesses (especially in "The Armies of the Wilderness"). Such resemblances devastatingly critique American Manifest Destiny, the belief not only in territorial expansion but in boundless individual opportunity as well, by suggesting the course of American history is as much regressive as progressive. In "The House-Top," a poem about the 1863 New York draft riots, Melville in fact chronicles how, on the basis of recent American history, "man rebounds whole aeons back in nature" (p. 108).

The fear that the war cannot be known or apprehended through language and poetry lurks throughout *Battle-Pieces*. "None can narrate that strife in the pines" (p. 120), says Melville in "The Armies of the

Wilderness"; his "entangled rhyme / But hints at the maze of war" (p. 120). The last line of the last poem of *Battle-Pieces*, "A Meditation," appropriately concludes with an image of silent victors—as if silence were in fact the most eloquent possible response to the maze of war. "Silence is the only Voice of our God" (p. 204), Melville actually wrote in *Pierre*.

Yet the Melville of *Battle-Pieces* still retains allegiance to an idea of America as "the world's fairest hope" (p. 53). In "America," the poem that concludes the first sequence of *Battle-Pieces*, a prophetic Melville personifies America as a maternal figure silenced by the fury of the war; by the end of the poem, however, she awakens from an awful dream vision and, with "Law on her brow and empire in her eyes" (p. 163) symbolizes a calmer, graver, purified future. In the supplement Melville works even more explicitly to reconcile North and South as Reconstruction becomes a measure of "the sincerity of our faith in democracy." In a voice of moderation and candor, Melville cautions against "misapplied" Northern "exultation" (p. 241) and asks that a "generosity of sentiment" (p. 243) be extended to the South. Recovering some belief in both "Progress" and "Humanity," he concludes *Battle-Pieces* with the hope that the "terrible historic tragedy" of the Civil War "may not have been enacted without instructing our whole beloved country through terror and pity" (p. 246).

See also "Bartleby, the Scrivener"; "Benito Cereno"; Civil War; *The Confidence-Man; Moby-Dick*

BIBLIOGRAPHY
Primary Works
Melville, Herman. "Bartleby, the Scrivener: A Story of Wall-Street." 1853. In *The Piazza Tales and Other Prose Pieces 1839–1860*. Evanston, Ill., and Chicago: Northwestern University Press and the Newberry Library, 1987.

Melville, Herman. *Battle-Pieces and Aspects of the War: Civil War Poems*. 1866. Foreword by James M. McPherson, introduction by Richard H. Cox and Paul M. Dowling. Amherst, N.Y.: Prometheus Books, 2001. Interpretive essays accompanying the text include Richard H. Cox's "A Careful Disorderliness: The Organization of *Battle-Pieces*," Helen Vendler's "Melville and the Lyric of History," and Rosanna Warren's "Dark Knowledge: Melville's Poems of the Civil War."

Melville, Herman. *Moby-Dick; or, The Whale*. 1851. Evanston, Ill., and Chicago: Northwestern University Press and the Newberry Library, 1988.

Melville, Herman. *Pierre; or, The Ambiguities*. 1853. Evanston, Ill., and Chicago: Northwestern University Press and the Newberry Library, 1971.

Secondary Works
Buell, Lawrence. "Melville the Poet." In *The Cambridge Companion to Herman Melville*, edited by Robert S. Levine, pp. 135–156. New York: Cambridge University Press, 1998.

Cohen, Hennig. "Introduction." In *Battle-Pieces*, edited by Hennig Cohen, pp. 11–28. New York: Thomas Yoseloff, 1963.

Garner, Stanton. *The Civil War World of Herman Melville*. Lawrence: University Press of Kansas, 1993.

Parker, Hershel. *Herman Melville: A Biography*. Vol. 2, *1851–1891*. Baltimore: Johns Hopkins University Press, 2002.

Robertson-Lorant, Laurie. *Melville: A Biography*. New York: Clarkson Potter, 1996.

Rogin, Michael Paul. *Subversive Genealogy: The Politics and Art of Herman Melville*. Berkeley: University of California Press, 1985.

Shurr, William H. "Melville's Poems: The Late Agenda." In *A Companion to Melville Studies*, edited by John Bryant, pp. 351–374. Westport, Conn.: Greenwood Press, 1986.

Michael Berthold

"BENITO CERENO"

Herman Melville's long story "Benito Cereno," which first appeared serially in the numbers of *Putnam's Monthly Magazine* for October, November, and December 1855 and which reappeared in Melville's *The Piazza Tales* (1856), has come to be regarded not only as one of the author's most important works but as one of the most important American fictional works of the nineteenth century. The plot of the story is based on a real-life incident described in the published recollections of an American ship captain: Amasa Delano's *Narrative of Voyages and Travels in the Northern and Southern Hemispheres* (1817). In 1805 Delano encountered a Spanish slave ship, the *Tryal*, at the island of St. Maria, off the coast of Chile. Observing that the vessel was in a state of disrepair and that blacks onboard far outnumbered whites, Delano boarded the *Tryal* and conferred with its captain, Benito Cereno, who informed him that fierce storms were responsible for both the sad condition of the vessel and the small number of Spanish crewmen. After spending several hours with Cereno, who was closely accompanied at all times by a black servant, Delano left the ship to return to his own vessel, the *Perseverance*.

But as Delano was entering his longboat, the Spanish captain suddenly jumped into it, whereupon the blacks on the *Tryal* revealed themselves to have been secretly in control of the vessel while Delano was aboard. After learning from Cereno that the blacks had revolted against their Spanish masters and killed their owner and many of the Spanish crewmen, Delano offered his own crewmen a reward for taking the *Tryal,* which was subsequently captured. Some of the slaves were killed in the assault, and Delano had to protect those left alive from the vengeance of the Spaniards, including Cereno, who later accused Delano of being a "pirate" (Delano, p. 329) for attempting to lay claim to the vessel and its human cargo. Delano's narrative ends with transcripts of various "official documents" connected with the later trial of the surviving slaves, including the depositions of both Cereno and Delano and an account of the sentences meted out to the blacks by the Spanish authorities. The ringleaders of the revolt were to be hanged, after having their bodies dragged to the gibbet at the tails of mules. Their heads were then to be placed on poles and their bodies burned to ashes.

Melville's retelling of this grisly story consists of three parts: an extended account of Delano's initial visit to the Spanish ship, narrated in third person from Delano's unenlightened perspective; a greatly altered version of the deposition given by Benito Cereno at the trial; and an entirely fictional final conversation between Delano and Cereno, in which Delano admits that his failure to grasp the truth of his situation saved his life. In creating his story, Melville also changed the name of Cereno's and Delano's ships to the *San Dominick* and *Bachelor's Delight,* respectively; backdated the episode to 1799; combined Mure, Cereno's servant, and Babo, the leader of the revolt, into a single character named Babo; greatly embellished the character of Delano (instilling in him, for example, the false fear that Cereno rather than Babo is plotting against him); invented several key incidents; eliminated the final wrangling between Cereno and Delano over the rights to the Spanish ship; and added a final, fictitious account of Cereno's death, portrayed as caused directly by the stresses of his experience. Attempting to encourage Cereno at the end of the story, Delano assures the Spanish captain that he is "saved" and asks what has cast such a "shadow" upon him? "The negro," replies Cereno, terminating the conversation ("Benito Cereno," p. 116).

Noting Melville's apparent linking of Babo with Iago, the villain of Shakespeare's *Othello* (who, like Babo, refuses to speak a word after he is convicted) and observing Melville's initial characterization of Delano as failing to appreciate the human capacity for "malign evil" (p. 47), the earliest interpreters of "Benito Cereno" saw the story as focusing primarily on that capacity. They viewed Babo and his black compatriots as Melville's symbols of human violence and cruelty, Cereno as a symbol of moral awareness, and Delano as a symbol of moral ignorance. This reading prompted criticism of the story in some quarters, as Melville was accused of manifesting an inattention to the moral complexities of his own literary materials when he ignored the fact that the "evil" Babo was the leader of slaves understandably seeking to obtain their freedom. Melville also was accused of showing a disturbing disregard for the topicality of his materials when, in a tale about slavery, he failed to treat the issue of most importance to Americans in 1855.

Later critics have clearly demonstrated, however, that in writing "Benito Cereno," Melville was neither ignoring moral complications nor evading contemporary issues. Though his tale underscores human depravity, it cites slavery as a key illustration, focusing as well on mid-century theories of America's "Manifest Destiny." Moreover, its emphasis on the human capacity for evil is itself a direct response to contemporary developments in American intellectual history.

"BENITO CERENO" AND SLAVERY

Melville's early mention of the *San Dominick*'s stern piece, "intricately carved with the arms of Castile and Leon" (p. 49), and later notation that the ship's original figurehead was an image of Christopher Columbus (details missing from his source) transform Cereno's vessel into a symbol of the Spanish Empire in the New World. They also remind readers that slavery was introduced into the Western Hemisphere by Columbus, acting for Spain. Melville's many references to Catholicism (including his early comparison of the figures seen moving on the *San Dominick* to the "Black Friars" [p. 48] of the Dominican order) similarly underscore the role of both the Catholic Church and the Dominicans in sponsoring slavery in the New World. Finally, Melville's nearby comparison of Benito Cereno to Holy Roman Emperor Charles V invokes the Spanish monarch who, at the behest of the church, first approved the importation of African slaves into the Western Hemisphere.

Yet Melville does more in "Benito Cereno" than link the *San Dominick* and its captain to Spain's imperialism and sponsorship of slavery. He also reminds his readers that Spain's once mighty empire had been reduced to pitiful fragments by 1855. Near the outset of his story Melville calls attention to the *San Dominick*'s tattered tops and moldering forecastle, assigning the vessel to the class of "superseded Acapulco treasure-ships, or retired frigates of the Spanish king's navy, which . . . under a decline of masters, preserved signs of former state" (p. 48). Moreover, by comparing the "manner" of the "tottering" Benito Cereno to that of Charles V, "just previous to the anchoritish retirement of that monarch from the throne" (p. 53)—and thus reminding one that Charles eventually retired from his monarchical duties "broken in health and spirits" (Stirling, p. 80; noted in Franklin, "Apparent Symbol")—Melville makes Cereno a further symbol of a declining Spanish Empire. By way of his plot, Melville also reminds one that Spain's empire had declined largely because of a series of violent slave and anticolonial revolutions. Melville changed the name of Cereno's vessel to the *San Dominick* to invoke not merely the Dominican sponsors of slavery but also the violent slave revolt that occurred on the island of Santo Domingo in the late eighteenth century. He also backdated Delano's adventure to the 1790s, the years in which this revolt occurred, to make the Santo Domingo allusion more plain.

Having recalled the history of slave revolt in the Spanish territories, Melville goes on to underscore the potential for further rebellion, particularly in the United States. Melville's recognition that the problem of slavery was not limited to the Spanish territories is clear from the American Delano's offer to buy Babo from Cereno—and from the fact that, when Babo jumps into Delano's boat at the end of the story, it is Delano who, in attempting to thwart Babo's purposes, "grind[s] the prostrate negro" (p. 99). Equally telling is Delano's confidence in the cheerful servility of slaves, a linchpin of the South's rationale for maintaining slavery. Melville's story clearly conveys his opinion that, like the Spanish variety, American slavery was an evil that liberty-loving human beings could be expected to resist.

To be sure, the blacks on the *San Dominick* commit violent acts. But Melville attributes these to the repressive bonds and brutalizing effects of slavery. Noting Melville's linking of Babo with Iago, one early critic insisted that the blacks on the *San Dominick* manifest a "motiveless malignity." Yet the deposition with which "Benito Cereno" ends states plainly that they decided to kill their owner Alexandro Aranda (who was onboard the vessel) and the other Spaniards so as to improve their chances of obtaining "liberty" in Africa (p. 106). Moreover, by reversing the normal dynamics of slavery, by making Babo in effect the merciless black "master" of the white Cereno, Melville highlights the potential for violence in the master-slave relationship, regardless of who is master and who slave. The tableau on the stern piece of the *San Dominick* underscores this point by portraying a "dark satyr in a mask, holding his foot on the neck of a prostrate figure, likewise masked" (p. 49). To be sure, Melville portrays Babo as amply "malign" and his fellow blacks as quite vindictive. Yet these depictions were meant to underscore for all Americans, including both southern slaveholders and northern liberals, the fact that slavery produced violence, not good-humored loyalty. In "Benito Cereno," Melville challenges both the happy image of slavery promoted by certain of its apologists and the docile image of slaves promoted by certain of its opponents. Through his account of Babo's masquerade, he characterizes the "contentment" of slaves as a charade, a veneer overlaying violence.

Some of Melville's critics have suggested that his emphasis on Aranda's relaxed policy toward his slaves (he allowed them to sleep on deck without fetters, believing they were "tractable" [p. 104]) and their brutal reaction to that policy might have encouraged southern slaveholders to view blacks as innately violent and to intensify their oppression of them. Yet Melville would hardly have endorsed such a response to his story, since he clearly sought in "Benito Cereno" not to portray blacks as violent by nature but to depict the violence induced by slavery in the enslavers and enslaved of any race. In his allegorical work *Mardi* (1849), Melville characterized slavery as "a blot, foul as the crater-pool of hell" and predicted that, because of slavery, the southern savannas might one day "prove battle-fields" (pp. 533, 534). His views had obviously not changed when he wrote "Benito Cereno" in the summer of 1854. The blacks on the *San Dominick* are not portrayed as either sympathetic victims or noble freedom fighters. They are portrayed as the merciless perpetrators of heinous acts. Yet, speaking for Melville, Delano accurately observes at one point that slavery "breeds ugly passions in man" (p. 88). If Babo and his fellows are violent, slavery is to blame. If southern slaveholders were to intensify slavery, even more violence would result.

In the final conversation of "Benito Cereno," Cereno, having become all too aware of the black capacity for violence, attributes his gloom to "the negro." Melville, however, encourages one to look beyond the black violence on both Santo Domingo and the *San Dominick* to its source: the unnatural constraints of slavery. At the end of "Benito Cereno," Babo may be dead and his rebellion crushed, but his severed head continues to look sternly toward the graves of Aranda and Cereno. Melville's point is inescapable. So long as slavery exists, the potential for violence remains.

"BENITO CERENO" AND MANIFEST DESTINY

Besides grappling with the slavery question, Melville's tale also carefully treats the issue of Manifest Destiny—particularly mid-nineteenth-century arguments for American intervention in Latin America, which contrasted the energy, libertarianism, and efficiency of

In this memorable passage from "Benito Cereno," in which Babo deftly reminds Cereno of what will happen to him if he answers Delano's naive questions truthfully, Melville simultaneously underscores the violence inherent in the master-slave relationship, America's mimicry of an "inquisitorial" Spain, and the human capacity for viciousness. In a prefatory passage conveying Delano's attitude toward blacks and typifying the ironic strategy the author employs throughout "Benito Cereno," Melville presents a black stereotype that is directly challenged by the "barbarous" scene that follows. Missing from Delano's Narrative, the scene is entirely Melville's creation:

Most negroes are natural valets and hair-dressers; taking to the comb and brush congenially as to the castanets, and flourishing them apparently with almost equal satisfaction. There is, too, a smooth tact about them in this employment, with a marvelous, noiseless, gliding briskness, not ungraceful in its way, singularly pleasing to behold, and still more so to be the manipulated subject of. And above all is the great gift of good humor. Not the mere grin or laugh is here meant. Those were unsuitable. But a certain easy cheerfulness, harmonious in every glance and gesture; as though God had set the whole negro to some pleasant tune. . . .

[Babo] searched among the razors, as for the sharpest, and having found it, gave it an additional edge by expertly stropping it. . . . He then made a gesture as if to begin, but midway stood suspended for an instant, one hand elevating the razor, the other professionally dabbling among the bubbling suds on the Spaniard's lank neck. Not unaffected by the close sight of the gleaming steel, Don Benito nervously shuddered. . . .

"Now, master," [Babo] said . . . , pressing the head gently further back into the crotch of the chair; "now master," and the steel glanced nigh the throat.

Again Don Benito faintly shuddered.

"You must not shake so, master.—See, Don Amasa, master always shakes when I shave him. And yet master knows I never yet have drawn blood, though it's true, if master will shake so, I may some of these times. . . . And now, Don Amasa, please go on with your talk about the gale, and all that, master can hear, and between times master can answer."

"Ah, yes, these gales," said Captain Delano; "but the more I think of your voyage, Don Benito, the more I wonder, not at the gales, terrible as they must have been, but at the disastrous interval following them. For here, by your account, have you been these two months and more getting from Cape Horn to St. Maria, a distance which I myself, with a good wind, have sailed in a few days. True, you had calms, and long ones, but to be becalmed for two months, that is, at least, unusual. Why, Don Benito, had almost any other gentleman told me such a story, I should have been half disposed to a little incredulity."

Here an involuntary expression came over the Spaniard . . . , and whether it was the start he gave or a sudden gawky roll of the hull in the calm, or a momentary unsteadiness of the servant's hand; however it was, just then the razor drew blood.

Melville, "Benito Cereno," pp. 83–86.

Americans with the supposed weakness, despotism, and disorderliness of the Spanish. "Cuba," an 1853 *Putnam's* article, insisted that Americans were "an enlightened, progressive race, the Spaniards the extreme reverse"; described America as a "powerful and prosperous country" and Spain as a "weak nation, tottering toward ruin"; characterized Cuba, the sole Spanish dependency left in the New World, as suffering under a "despotic and even brutal administration"; and insisted that annexation of Cuba would allow liberty-loving Americans to "assert political, religious, and commercial freedom" on the island (pp. 5, 10, 13–16).

Melville's story provides a brilliant critique of such ideas. Amasa Delano, Melville's representative American, complains about the "noisy confusion" (p. 54) aboard the *San Dominick*, attributing this confusion to Cereno's impotence as a commander. Soon after, he also develops a plan to take control of the vessel, thus mirroring the thinking of expansionist Americans eager to replace a weakened Spain in the Caribbean. Yet Melville questions the motives of his "liberty-loving" contemporaries by characterizing American expansionism as mercenary. The author notes that Delano's sailors are persuaded to take the *San Dominick* by the promise of material reward. He also renamed Delano's ship the *Bachelor's Delight* after the ship of a famous English buccaneer and christened Delano's boat *Rover* so as to characterize Manifest Destiny as a kind of piracy. Meanwhile Delano's offer to buy Babo midway through the story underscores the nonlibertarian aspect of American expansionism, which was promoted with special energy by southerners eager to expand American slavery to the south.

By thus negatively characterizing Manifest Destiny, Melville sought, more broadly, to invalidate the distinction, crucial to American expansionists, between American expansionism and the colonialism of Spain. The author of "Annexation," another *Putnam's* article, distinguished American expansionism from "conquest," contrasting the "open, generous, equitable international policy" of the United States (p. 184) with the "sinister and iniquitous proceedings" of European states (p. 191). Delano can cheerfully plot to take over the *San Dominick* because he similarly believes there is a significant "difference" between "the idea of Don Benito's darkly pre-ordaining Captain Delano's fate, and Captain Delano's lightly arranging Don Benito's" (p. 70). Yet Melville's emphasis on Delano's blithe imperialism suggests that, in planning to invade Cuba and take control of the rest of Latin America, America was simply taking over where Spain had left off.

Melville's Catholic imagery may have been another way of emphasizing this point. In the mid-1850s Americans were particularly fearful of Catholicism, as the victories of the Know Nothing Party in 1854 and 1855 demonstrated. Moreover, when envisioning Catholicism, Americans tended to focus on the Spanish Inquisition, which typified for many the bigotry and authoritarianism of "popery." Yet in one of the most powerful scenes in "Benito Cereno," a scene replete with inquisitorial images in which Babo shaves Cereno, Delano actually functions as the inquisitor, pumping Cereno for information. He has in fact been "inquiring" all day long, attempting to distinguish good from evil on the *San Dominick.* Yet his biases have caused him to be as unreliable a judge of these matters as the Spanish inquisitors were thought to be. In particular, his brand of paternalistic white racism has wrongly persuaded him that Babo's blacks are too docile to pose a threat, while national prejudice has made him wrongly suspect the "dark Spaniard" Cereno. A blind and biased inquisitor, Delano is Melville's ingenious way of suggesting that at a time when Americans were especially critical of Spanish Catholicism, they themselves were becoming involved not merely in an imperialist enterprise but in a dogmatic crusade.

In "Benito Cereno" Melville also suggests that both would be unsuccessful. When the confused

Delano is thrown a mysterious knot by a Spanish sailor said to resemble "an Egyptian priest, making Gordian knots for the temple of Ammon" (p. 76), he is implicitly linked with Alexander the Great, who visited the temple of Ammon at the beginning of his military career and, finding there the Gordian knot, believed to be unravelable only by the one who would conquer Asia, simply cut the knot and marched off to his first series of conquests. Unable to unravel his own knot, Delano simply hands it to an elderly Negro, who drops it overboard. Clearly suggesting that Delano is no Alexander, the episode also suggests that Americans were far less likely than Alexander to successfully establish an empire. Delano believes that, as an energetic American, he can succeed where the "weak" Cereno has failed. But Melville calls Delano's confidence into question by comparing Cereno to "an invalid courtier tottering about London streets in the time of the plague" (p. 58), thus invoking an example of Anglo-Saxon weakness. Delano eventually realizes that Cereno's weakness has resulted mainly from his horrifying experiences and the stresses he has undergone for many weeks. And once America embarked on its own imperialist venture, it might well find itself similarly exhausted.

Delano also believes that, as a good-hearted American, he is under the protection of "some one above" (p. 77). So did many Americans feel that a providentially blessed America would succeed where Spanish Catholics had failed. Yet in "Benito Cereno," Melville calls such confidence into question by portraying as unfounded the similar confidence of Spain. The drowned Juan Robles, who dies "making acts of contrition" (p. 107), and the dead Don Joaquin (accidentally killed by Delano's Americans), who intended to present a jewel to "our Lady of Mercy in Lima" to "attest his gratitude . . . for the safe conclusion of his . . . voyage from Spain" (p. 113), seem to have been forsaken by their popish divinities. And Melville seems to have felt that, however blessed Americans might feel in 1855, their confidence in a divine sanction for American expansionism might well prove one day to have been misplaced.

Near the end of "Benito Cereno," Melville notes that Babo chalked the saying "Follow your leader" below the bones of the dead Aranda, lashed to the prow of the *San Dominick,* as a warning to the surviving Spanish sailors (p. 99). "Follow your leader," whisper these bones to the American sailors who invade the *San Dominick.* "Follow your leader!" shouts Delano's mate in reply (p. 102). By way of such details, Melville not only underscores the imperialist resemblance between America and Spain but also suggests that the destiny that seemed most "manifest" for

America was eventually to join with Spain in the non-select company of failed colonial powers.

"BENITO CERENO" AND HUMAN DEPRAVITY

If the earliest critics of Melville's story were wrong to imply that, in writing it, he showed little interest in such contemporary issues as slavery and Manifest Destiny, they were right to suggest that he had a broader concern with human depravity. Moreover, this concern too stemmed from his awareness of contemporary American thinking.

Delano's oft-expressed (and obviously misguided) confidence in the "docility" (pp. 63, 84, 92), "cheerfulness" (p. 83), and "affection" (pp. 51, 52) of blacks is likely meant to represent, for instance, the optimistic view of certain northern abolitionists, including Harriet Beecher Stowe (1811–1896), who argued in *Uncle Tom's Cabin* (1852) that freeing slaves could not possibly induce violence since blacks were by nature so peaceful. Melville found many proofs to the contrary in Delano's *Narrative*. Yet in writing "Benito Cereno" he actually heightened the savagery of Babo's blacks, adding to the story, for example, the grim figurehead of Aranda's bones. By altering the date of Delano's adventure and changing the name of Cereno's vessel to the *San Dominick,* he also invoked a specific historical example of black violence. Finally, he also attributes to Delano's character a number of observations about black docility that are directly challenged by specific disclosures in Cereno's deposition. Whereas Delano praises the Negro's abilities as "body-servant," for example (p. 52), the deposition notes that José, Aranda's personal attendant, brutally stabbed his master after the latter had been dragged to the deck. And whereas Melville, adopting Delano's perspective, describes blacks as "natural valets and hair-dressers" (p. 83), his shaving scene utterly demolishes that notion.

Melville emphasized the violence of Aranda's blacks not merely, then, to demonstrate the evil effects of slavery but also to counter the notion that blacks were less violent than other human beings. He did not, however, wish to portray them as more violent. In an important conversation with Cereno, Delano points to the "hybrid" Francesco, Cereno's mulatto steward, as likely proof that the mixing of white and black "bloods" produces a product superior to the "full-blooded" black (p. 88). Delano's remark and Melville's nearby references to both a "Nubian sculptor finishing off a white statue-head" (p. 87) and the "sculptured porters of black marble guarding the porches of Egyptian tombs" (p. 92) represent precise allusions to Josiah Nott (1804–1873) and George Gliddon's (1809–1857) *Types of Mankind,* a massive ethnological compendium published in 1854. Nott was a southerner determined to prove that the mental and moral deficiencies of the Negro could be demonstrated scientifically; Gliddon was a retired Egyptologist eager to buttress Nott's arguments by highlighting the antiquity of racial differences. Gliddon included reproductions of numerous Egyptian and Nubian paintings and sculptures; Nott insisted that "even a small trace of white blood in the negro improves him in . . . morality" (p. 68).

In "Benito Cereno" one later learns, however, that Francesco was no more moral than the "full-blooded" Babo. He was in fact a ringleader of revolt and a willing follower of Babo's brutal lead. Moreover, if Francesco's behavior calls Nott's theory of white moral superiority into question, so does the behavior of Cereno's Spaniards following the retaking of the *San Dominick.* Melville notes in the deposition that during the night following the recapture, these sailors brutally killed several Negroes who were "shackled to the ring-bolts on deck" (p. 114). The behavior of Delano's American sailors is no less brutal, for a number of Babo's blacks are "mangled" during the recapture, when the "sealing-spears and cutlasses" of the Americans cross the "hatchets and hand-spikes of their foes" (p. 102). Clearly if Babo's blacks are guilty of viciousness, both the Spanish and the American whites are all too willing to "follow their lead."

Melville further emphasizes the universal human capacity for violence by way of Delano's observation that the black women on the *San Dominick* manifest "pure tenderness and love" (p. 73)—and his accompanying recollection of the African explorer John Ledyard's high opinion of female morality. Ledyard's words were these: "Among all nations, . . . women . . . are the same kind, civil, obliging, humane, tender beings," "performing more good actions than [men]" ("American Travelers," p. 565). In the deposition, Cereno notes, however, that the black women on the *San Dominick* were "satisfied at the death of their master, Don Alexandro; that, had the negroes not restrained them, they would have tortured to death, instead of simply killing, the Spaniards slain by command of the negro Babo" (p. 112). Thus does Melville suggest that brutality is not foreign to any portion of humanity.

Melville made this point partly in response to both the pre-Darwinian evolutionists and their orthodox Christian opponents, who regularly emphasized the human moral capacity that was thought to clearly distinguish human beings from animals. The *Putnam's* reviewer of *Types of Mankind* insisted that "a man is a man all the world over, and nowhere a monkey or a hippopotamus." For this writer, man was "inconvertably separated from every other organism, by . . . his mind and his heart, which place[d] him . . . at the head of creation" ("Is Man One or Many?" pp. 5–6, 14). Yet by way of his emphasis on a universal human depravity, combined with his persistent use of animal imagery in describing human behavior—his description, for example, of Negro women as "leopardesses," of Babo as "snakishly writhing up" from the bottom of Delano's boat, and of Delano's American marauders as "submerged sword-fish" menacing "shoals of black-fish" (pp. 73, 99, 102)—Melville implies that the gulf between men and beasts is far from vast.

By underscoring a general human depravity, he also responded to another issue in contemporary American thought. Fearing that Cereno and Babo might be conspiring against him, Delano comforts himself by asking, "Who ever heard of a white . . . so far a renegade as to apostatize from his very species almost, by leaguing in against it with negroes?" (p. 75). Melville apparently realized that *Types of Mankind* was one of many contributions to a mid-century argument regarding the "unity" of the human race. The English ethnologist James Prichard had portrayed the race as a single "species" in several books in the 1840s; he was opposed by Robert Knox in *The Races of Men*, published in 1850, and by Nott and Gliddon, who meant by "types" the various species into which humankind was divided. Readers of "Benito Cereno" had also seen two Scripture-based defenses of human unity—"Is Man One or Many?" and "Are All Men Descended from Adam?"—in the *Putnam's* numbers for July 1854 and January 1855. Both articles suggested that human beings were united by a spiritual capacity denied to lesser creatures.

In "Benito Cereno," Melville unenthusiastically aligned himself with the "unity" party by suggesting that humankind was undeniably "one"—in its disturbing capacity for "malign evil." In the conversation with which Melville's story ends, Delano blithely encourages Cereno to "forget" his horrifying experiences (p. 116), while Cereno tersely insists that he cannot. Clearly Melville wanted his readers not to forget the multiple brutalities depicted in "Benito Cereno": of slavery, of slave revolt, of men and women, blacks and whites, Spaniards and Americans. He was obviously aware that an overly intimate acquaintance with human depravity could be destructive of life and hope—and that an unawareness of this trait could help one survive. Cereno dies of his experience while Delano survives his, partly because of his ability to ignore its gloomy implications. But an author who throughout his career endorsed the facing of grim realities clearly preferred the more informed perspective of Cereno.

See also Battle-Pieces; The Confidence-Man; Manifest Destiny; *Moby-Dick;* Nautical Literature; Slave Rebellions; Slavery; *Typee*

BIBLIOGRAPHY
Primary Works
"American Travelers." *Putnam's Monthly Magazine* 5 (June 1855): 561–576.

"Annexation." *Putnam's Monthly Magazine* 3 (February 1854): 183–194.

"Cuba." *Putnam's Monthly Magazine* 1 (June 1853): 3–16.

Delano, Amasa. *A Narrative of Voyages and Travels, in the Northern and Southern Hemispheres: Comprising Three Voyages Round the World; Together with a Voyage of Survey and Discovery, in the Pacific Ocean and Oriental Islands.* 1817. New York: Praeger, 1970.

"Is Man One or Many?" *Putnam's Monthly Magazine* 4 (July 1854): 1–14.

Melville, Herman. "Benito Cereno." 1855. In *The Piazza Tales and Other Prose Pieces,* edited by Harrison Hayford, Alma A. MacDougall, and G. Thomas Tanselle, pp. 46–117. Evanston, Ill., and Chicago: Northwestern University Press and Newberry Library, 1987.

Melville, Herman. *"Mardi" and "A Voyage Thither."* Edited by Harrison Hayford, Hershel Parker, and G. Thomas Tanselle. Evanston, Ill., and Chicago: Northwestern University Press and Newberry Library, 1970.

Nott, J. C., and George R. Gliddon. *Types of Mankind: or, Ethnological Researches, Based upon the Ancient Monuments, Paintings, Sculptures, and Crania of Races, and upon Their Natural, Geographical, Philological, and Biblical History.* Philadelphia: Lippincott, Grambo, and Company, 1854.

Stirling, William. *The Cloister Life of the Emperor Charles the Fifth.* 3rd ed. London: J. W. Parker and Son, 1852.

Secondary Works
Adler, Joyce Sparer. "Benito Cereno: Slavery and Violence in the Americas." In her *War in Melville's Imagination,* pp. 88–110. New York: New York University Press, 1981.

Burkholder, Robert E., ed. *Critical Essays on Herman Melville's "Benito Cereno."* New York: G. K. Hall, 1992. Includes essays listed in this bibliography by Joyce Sparer Adler, Allan Moore Emery, H. Bruce Franklin, Gloria Horsley-Meacham, Sidney Kaplan, Joseph Schiffman, Eric Sundquist, Charles Swann, and Kermit Vanderbilt.

Emery, Allan Moore. "'Benito Cereno' and Manifest Destiny." *Nineteenth-Century Fiction* 39 (June 1984): 48–68.

Emery, Allan Moore. "The Topicality of Depravity in 'Benito Cereno.'" *American Literature* 55 (October 1983):

316–331. Reprinted in *Melville's Short Novels,* edited by Dan McCall, pp. 303–316. New York: Norton, 2002.

Feltenstein, Rosalie. "Melville's 'Benito Cereno.'" *American Literature* 19 (November 1947): 245–255.

Fisher, Marvin. *Going Under: Melville's Short Fiction and the American 1850s.* Baton Rouge: Louisiana State University Press, 1977. See pp. 104–117.

Fogle, Richard Harter. *Melville's Shorter Tales.* Norman: University of Oklahoma Press, 1960. See pp. 116–147.

Franklin, H. Bruce. "'Apparent Symbol of Despotic Command': Melville's 'Benito Cereno.'" *New England Quarterly* 34 (November 1961): 462–477.

Franklin, H. Bruce. "Slavery and Empire: Melville's 'Benito Cereno.'" In *Melville's Evermoving Dawn: Centennial Essays,* edited by John Bryant and Robert Milder, pp. 147–161. Kent, Ohio: Kent State University Press, 1997.

Horsley-Meacham, Gloria. "The Monastic Slaver: Images and Meaning in 'Benito Cereno.'" *New England Quarterly* 56 (June 1983): 261–266.

Kaplan, Sidney. "Herman Melville and the American National Sin: The Meaning of 'Benito Cereno.'" *Journal of Negro History* 57 (1957): 12–27.

McCall, Dan, ed. *Melville's Short Novels.* New York: Norton, 2002.

Rogin, Michael Paul. *Subversive Genealogy: The Politics and Art of Herman Melville.* New York: Knopf, 1983. See pp. 208–220. Reprinted in *Melville's Short Novels,* edited by Dan McCall, pp. 317–329. New York: Norton, 2002.

Schiffman, Joseph. "Critical Problems in Melville's 'Benito Cereno.'" *Modern Language Quarterly* 11 (September 1950): 317–324.

Sundquist, Eric. "'Benito Cereno' and New World Slavery." In *Reconstructing American Literary History,* edited by Sacvan Bercovitch, pp. 93–122. Cambridge, Mass.: Harvard University Press, 1986.

Swann, Charles. "Melville's De(con)struction of the Southern Reader." *Literature and History* 12 (1986): 3–15.

Vanderbilt, Kermit. "'Benito Cereno': Melville's Fable of Black Complicity." *Southern Review* 12 (1976): 311–322.

Allan Moore Emery

THE BIBLE

The decade of the 1820s was a watershed moment for publishing in America. Whereas a print run of two thousand copies of a book was the industry standard before 1820, a number of factors coalesced during the ensuing decade to enable publishers to print several hundred thousand copies of a title if they wished. Improvements in publishing technologies such as papermaking, power printing, and stereotyping all contributed to this change, as did key cultural shifts in American society, such as rising literacy rates, a push by various ideologies that moved the activity of reading from a luxury to a necessity, and better transportation networks to help disseminate printed material. These diverse factors worked together to make the United States a society that was increasingly formed, framed, and fractured by the power of print.

Towering above the massive growth in American printed material was the country's single most important and prevalent printed text, the Christian Bible. The Bible was the most produced, most widely distributed, and most read title during the middle part of the 1800s. Simply put, it was the most common book in America during this period.

As early as the late 1820s, the American Bible Society—a voluntary society founded in 1816 with the goal of providing a Bible to all those who did not own one—made a concerted effort to place a Bible in every household in America. In 1829 they termed this effort their "First General Supply," and although they did not accomplish their goal, the society did print over a million Bibles over the next three years for the purposes of general distribution, an absolutely unprecedented and staggering number of books to come from an American publisher of the time. So important was this goal of getting Bibles into the hands of every American that the society sponsored three more "general supplies" before the end of the century.

Along with the American Bible Society, a host of other American publishers helped saturate the United States with Bibles. By the 1840s nearly two hundred different publishers in almost fifty different cities across the nation had produced over 350 different Bible editions. No single book came close to the kind of effort and attention American publishers placed on producing and distributing Bibles. Such a deep level of textual saturation showed itself to great effect in almost every area of American life whether it be politics, literature, education, recreation, law, or science. For example, politicians not only invoked biblical phrases in their speeches but pointed to the book itself as pivotal to American attitudes and actions. The writings and oratory of Abraham Lincoln provide ample examples. In his Second Inaugural Address, Lincoln invoked biblical content with phrases like "let us judge not that we be not judged" and also pointed to the importance of the book itself when he stated that both Northerners and Southerners "read the same Bible, and pray to the same God."

The Bible's presence made itself felt throughout the American literary writing of the time. Before 1820 many American Christians eschewed fiction as an evil influence on its readers, but by the 1830s certain denominations such as the Universalists and Episcopalians were tempering their remarks about novel reading and even encouraging writers in their ranks to transpose biblical characters, stories, and messages into the plots of their novels. Other denominations would follow, and by the 1850s one of the best-selling novels of the decade, Joseph Holt Ingraham's *The Prince of the House of David* (1854), sported Jesus as a leading character.

Authors throughout this period used biblical stories and phraseology as a kind of cultural anchor in their own works. They were able to allude to the biblical narrative—or how that narrative was worded in the King James Version of the Bible—with an unabashed fluency and confidence. Readers were so familiar with certain biblical stories, characters, and passages that authors could build upon these narratives in their own works without feeling any need to point out the biblical roots of their thinking. Frederick Douglass could write of weeping "near the rivers of Babylon" and Harriet Beecher Stowe could underline the Christlike character of Tom in *Uncle Tom's Cabin* (1852) by lacing his conversation with unattributed biblical allusions, knowing that their readers would know the parts of the Bible they were so freely referencing. Stowe was not the only writer of women's fiction in the period to fill her works with biblical quotations and allusions. Best-selling authors such as Susan Warner, E. D. E. N. Southworth, and Maria Cummins all packed their fiction with biblical phrases and imagery.

Because of the mass popularity of the Bible itself and the narratives it spawned, historians have long liked to refer to early Americans as "A People of the Book." What is lost in such a broad characterization is the critical fact that the Bible as it was printed and read in the United States was never a simple, uniform entity. The Bible may have had a core text—and even that core text was subject to wide variation—but it also was disseminated in the colonies and then the states in different English translations, in varied styles of type, and with different commentaries, illustrations, and bindings. Such differences significantly complicate any understanding of the Bible's place in American culture.

EDITIONS OF THE BIBLE IN EARLY AMERICA

The English Bible was first printed in the United States in 1777. Before that date the Bible was held by royal copyright, and only certain British printers were allowed to produce the book. The American Revolution would change this practice. As the colonies broke off from England, American publishers found themselves free of the restrictions imposed by the royal copyright. If they had the substantial resources to produce a Bible edition, American publishers now found themselves free to do so.

Once it began to be printed in the United States, the Bible soon underwent a great many textual revisions and changes in format, as different editors and publishers appropriated it to meet a wide range of changing ideological and economic demands. By 1820 American publishers had already produced nearly 300 different editions of the Bible, and by 1870 the number of different editions had increased to almost 1,900 in the English language alone. The Bible's myriad mutations played an enormous and often ignored role in determining its place in the hearts and minds of Americans. It is essential to realize that the Bible for nineteenth-century Americans was not in its purest sense a single book. It was a book whose core text was constantly adapted and repackaged to meet a wide range of needs in American religious, intellectual, and consumer cultures.

One of the most noticeable differences among Bible editions in the mid-nineteenth century is the way they were formatted. Bibles came in all shapes and sizes in this period, with all manner of bindings and illustrations. Beginning in the 1820s pocket Bibles became a common fixture among American Protestants as the larger quarto and folio formats diversified into the ever more popular and smaller octavo and duodecimo editions. Bibles grew smaller so that everyone from ladies who wished to carry them in their purses to sailors who wanted to stow them among the few personal items they carried on voyages might be able to avail themselves of the Holy Scripture.

Bibles in this period grew larger as well. As Bible editions multiplied, so did the number of American households that owned more than one Bible. Different Bible editions could serve different purposes, and by the 1840s Bibles had begun to be used as markers of gentility and middle-class refinement. Americans came increasingly to display large, expensive family Bibles—often weighing as much as fifteen pounds—in their parlors to show that they were both pious and affluent.

Many Bible editions in this period came to hold an ever-growing number of textual notes and illustrations. In 1846 the firm of Harper & Brothers utilized a new technology called electrotyping that allowed them to produce a beautiful family Bible edition that sported over 1,600, mostly black-and-white, illustrations. Up to that time the most heavily illustrated Bible editions to be found in America had contained somewhere around 200 pictures. By the 1870s Bible publishers were advertising Bible editions with 2,000 illustrations and over 100,000 marginal references and readings. Bible editions had moved from simply containing the Holy Scripture to becoming more like biblical encyclopedias that contained concordances, cross-references, biblical commentary, and essays on everything from biblical history to ancient botany.

Biblical illustrations also became one of the great distinguishing marks of elegant American Bible editions. Most of the time such illustrations were simply used to accent various biblical stories or scenes, but illustrations could have grave theological import as well. By the 1820s American Bible publishers were using illustrations to underline the authenticity of the biblical text by including pictures of ancient tablets that supposedly were inscribed with ancient versions of the Scriptures and maps detailing the most minute aspects of the Holy Land's geography and topography. The sentiments of William Thomson (1806–1894), an American missionary and writer in the Middle East, underscored the theological power of biblical illustrations and cartography when he wrote that the Holy Land was one "vast tablet whereupon God's messages to men have been drawn, and graven deep in living characters by the Great Publisher of glad tidings, to be seen and read [by] all to the end of time. The Land and the Book—with reverence be it said—constitute the entire and all perfect text, and should be studied together" (1:1).

As scholars argued over issues of biblical chronology, how the ancient languages were being translated, and how reliable the ancient manuscripts were in the first place, the Bible through its maps and pictures gave readers the assurance that sites such as the town of Bethlehem, the river Jordan, and the Mount of Calvary were actual locations that stood as tangible proof that the Bible was true and that the events reported in it did in fact take place. With the rise of certain biblical schools of European thinking in the opening decades of the nineteenth century, thinking which eventually coalesced into a biblical branch of interpretation known as the Higher Criticism, the trustworthiness of the biblical narrative became an ever greater question. One strategy to address such doubts became biblical illustrations and an emphasis on Holy Land geography, which reminded readers that the places where Jesus was born, was baptized, and was executed actually existed. The implication of such illustrations was simple: just as the Holy Land actually existed, so must have Jesus.

AMERICAN BIBLE TRANSLATIONS

American Bible editions in the nineteenth century could also differ significantly in the area of translation. American publishers produced Bibles throughout the nineteenth century in a host of different languages. The tremendous influx of immigrants from Europe, which became especially noticeable in the 1820s, created a market for Bibles in languages as diverse as Dutch, French, Italian, German, and Welsh. Often these European Bible editions were printed in a dual language format with one language on one page set against the English translation of the scriptures on the facing page. Thus Bibles were not only used for religious purposes but for educational ones as well. Immigrants could work at improving their English skills by reading from Bibles with this format.

American religious publishing also had a long tradition of reaching out to Native American populations through the printing of Bibles, hymnbooks, and grammars in Native American languages. By 1870 missionaries to the Native Americans had worked with publishers to produce translations of the New Testament in languages such as Cherokee, Sioux, Cree, Micmac, Mohawk, and Chippewa.

During the 1820–1870 period American English translations also began to diversify at an unprecedented rate. Prior to 1820 only a single new translation of the Holy Scripture in English had been completed by an American. This particular edition was the product of decades of labor by Charles Thomson (1729–1824), a long-term secretary of the Continental Congress, who spent the final years of his life working to translate the Septuagint (a Greek version of the scriptures) into English. He completed his Bible translation in 1808, predating the next American English translation by fifteen years.

What is important in Thomson's effort is the way in which he foreshadowed the concerns of almost every nineteenth-century translator who came after him. He had an abiding interest in the original texts of scripture and the original meanings of those texts. For Thomson, original texts and meanings were strictly a matter of timing. He wished to find the oldest reliable texts and then find the most reliable scholarship on how the words in these texts might best be translated into the nineteenth-century American idiom. He argued that the Septuagint offered an older account of the Old Testament than any available Hebrew manuscript, and thus his translation would be more accurate because it was based on the biblical manuscript most proximate to the actual events it related.

Between 1820 and 1870 no less than twenty-three Americans would translate over thirty new portions of

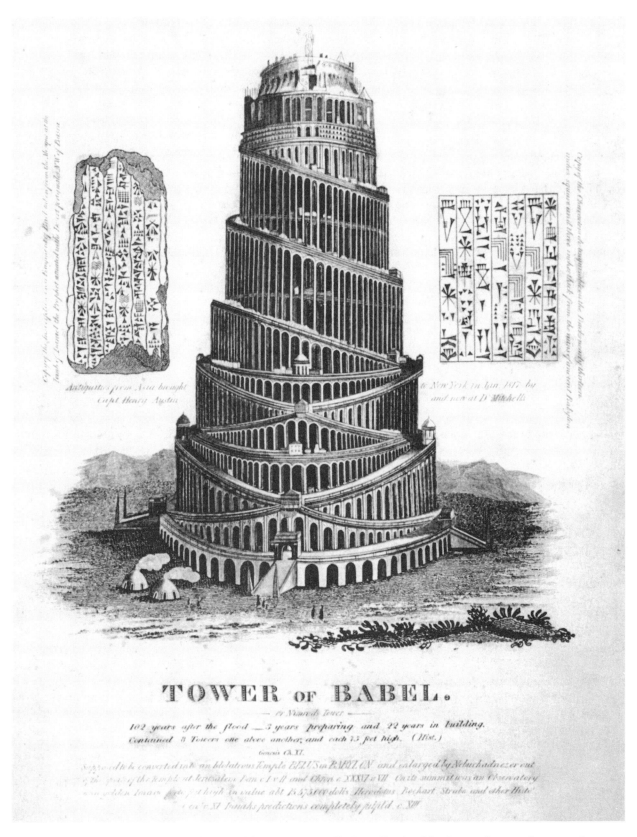

The Tower of Babel with cuneiform tablets purportedly inscribed with the ancient Hebrew scriptures.
Illustration from J. Holbrook's 1818 edition of the Bible, published in Brattleboro, Vermont. THE YALE COLLECTION OF AMERICAN
LITERATURE, BEINECKE RARE BOOK AND MANUSCRIPT LIBRARY

the Bible into English. Although driven by different reasons, the core values of using the most original texts and discovering the most original meanings lay at the root of almost every one of these translations.

A driving interest in the first texts of scripture created a flurry of translation work among Unitarians in the United States in the 1820s, the same decade that they emerged as their own denomination. Unitarianism was fundamentally defined by a theological belief that instead of there being a threefold Godhead, or Trinity, made up of the Father, Son, and Holy Spirit, the Bible taught that God was clearly preeminent and that Jesus his Son and the Holy Spirit were nowhere near his equal. Unitarians turned to producing their own translations of the Bible to prove their point of view concerning the Godhead. Formidable Unitarian scholars such as George R. Noyes, John Gorham Palfrey, and Andrews Norton would produce a series of translations from the 1820s through the 1850s bent on challenging the biblical basis for believing in the doctrine of the Trinity. These translators worked tirelessly to show that every biblical verse that might be used to support the doctrine of the Trinity was spurious and could be found nowhere in the most ancient biblical sources.

The Unitarians, however, had no corner on the market for using translation work to argue for various aspects of doctrinal clarity. The most popular Protestant alternative to the King James Version to be found prior to 1870 was a translation of the New Testament made by the religious revivalist and reformer Alexander Campbell (1788–1866).

Campbell had traveled extensively in the back countries of Ohio, Indiana, Virginia, Kentucky, and Tennessee, preaching a gospel based on the vision of the Christian Church found in the "primitive" first-century church of the New Testament. Eschewing creeds as untrustworthy and divisive, Campbell founded a new denomination he called the Christian Church—later known as the Disciples of Christ—which became the fastest-growing denomination in mid-nineteenth-century America, numbering some 200,000 members by 1860. To make his argument that the pattern of the true Christian church could only be discovered in the New Testament and not in Christian traditions or creeds, Campbell worked on his own translation of the New Testament, which he titled *The Sacred Writings of the Apostles and Evangelists of Jesus Christ, Commonly Styled the New Testament* (1826).

The Sacred Writings is a translation work notable for two reasons. First, Campbell used it to clear up the heavily contested debate of the period on whether true believers could be baptized as children or whether they needed to be baptized as adults. Many denominations of the day believed that God alone predestined—or chose—who was to be saved and who was not. Such denominations most frequently baptized infants, signaling their admission into a relationship with God that they would then have to consummate through their own faithful actions throughout their lives. Infant baptism emphasized God's initiative in extending His grace to humankind.

Other denominations, such as Campbell's, put the emphasis on individuals having total free will and the ability to choose for or against salvation on their own. Those who chose a belief in Jesus Christ as their savior got baptized as adults, signaling their allegiance to Jesus as people old enough and knowledgeable enough to appreciate what they were choosing when they proclaimed that they were Christians. Adult baptism emphasized human volition in the process of salvation.

Campbell used his version to argue his view that adult baptism by immersion was the practice of the primitive Christian church and was therefore the most correct and orthodox church doctrine. To argue this stance he translated the Greek word for "baptize" as "immerse." By making this change Campbell clarified just what John had done when Jesus came to him to be baptized in the Jordan River, and in so doing, Campbell renamed John the Baptist as "John the Immerser."

Second, Campbell's translation could lay claim to being the first modern-language Bible translation to appear in America. Campbell knew that many of his less-educated followers had trouble with the archaic language and cadences of the preeminently popular King James Version of the scriptures, a version which had first been translated two centuries earlier, in 1611, and was written in the language of Shakespeare, Elizabethan English. So Campbell worked hard in his New Testament to simplify the Bible's language. He replaced outdated word forms with more common, contemporary counterparts. He dropped the "eth" off verbs, turning "doeth" to "does" and "keepeth" to "keeps." He also helped readers by printing his Bible in single-column format without the traditional chapter and verse markings, so that the text itself might be less distracting and easier to read.

In the end, however, neither the desire for greater doctrinal clarity or a more understandable idiom moved Americans away from their most highly favored translation of the Bible, the King James Version, which would remain by far the most dominant translation of the scriptures found in the United States long into the twentieth century. It is important to note, however, that many of the translators who worked on new forms of the scriptures in the nineteenth century lay the groundwork for the translations that would eventually eclipse the popularity of the King James Version.

THE BIBLE AND CATHOLICISM

Although the King James Version reigned supreme as the favorite Bible translation for American Protestants throughout the nineteenth century, American Catholics had a different view of the proper Bible translation altogether. The Catholic Douai Bible differed from Protestant Bibles in two significant ways: it was approved by the Holy Catholic Church while the King James Version held no such imprimatur, and it was filled with officially sanctioned commentary. Many King James Versions, particularly those produced by the millions by the American Bible Society, were published "without note or comment." Catholics held that such bare Bibles were dangerous for Catholic youth because it taught them that private biblical interpretation was acceptable, thus degrading the central importance of the interpretative role of the Catholic Church's priesthood and hierarchy. The conflict between the two Bible translations might have been largely intellectual on one level, but its practical applications were felt most forcefully in a series of conflicts that broke out across the United States concerning the role of the Bible in the public school classroom.

By the 1820s the Bible had almost completely receded from its role as a pivotal text in teaching reading and writing. Only in rural areas did the practice persist of pupils bringing whatever books they had (most often the Bible) to school in order to use them as textbooks. In most cases the Bible had been relegated to daily or twice-daily devotional reading in schools because of the vast influx of schoolbooks and grammars. The issue thus centered on which Bible version was to be read in those daily or twice-daily readings.

Protestants insisted the King James Version was the most prevalent Bible translation in the land, and the land was predominantly Protestant. Catholics strenuously objected to this kind of sectarianism, and the issue came to a head in the 1840s in both Philadelphia and New York City. While Catholic leaders began to argue forcefully that if Catholics were in public schools they should only be subjected to devotional reading from an approved Catholic Bible, other issues began to be layered into the argument. Most prominent among these was a feeling that Catholics not only represented a renegade and dangerously antidemocratic religion (there could be no democracy when the pope could dictate whatever he wished and Catholics were forced to obey) but that they were also largely German, Irish, and Catholic immigrants who were flooding the country and taking jobs away from workers who were already in the United States.

Such anti-immigration sentiment became thoroughly mixed with the Bible-reading issue in the public schools. Those who considered themselves Americans of sufficiently long standing came to see the Bible-reading issue as largely symbolic of the immigrant Catholic threat to American democracy in general and American education in particular. So heated did the debates become that in 1844 riots ostensibly over the use of the Bible in American educational life broke out in Philadelphia. Catholics shot Protestants in the street, and in turn Protestants burned Catholic churches, schools, and whole blocks of Catholic homes. Riots also threatened to take over New York City, but the city's mayor called out the state militia after Catholic leaders promised that they would defend their churches and their property with all necessary force if they were threatened by Protestant mobs.

In the end the riots and debates over Bible reading in the schools changed little before 1870. The King James Version continued to be the translation of choice in the schools, but the debates and violence surrounding the issue brought forth important changes in American education toward the close of the century, most noticeably the founding of a parallel Catholic school system that would eventually spread to touch almost every part of the country.

Another significant result of these debates was the growth of Catholic publishing in the country. As the Bible controversy heated up in the 1820s and 1840s, Catholics came to realize that they would need their own editions of the Holy Scripture available if they were going to demand that American Catholics use only Church-sanctioned copies of the Bible in schools and elsewhere. Thus, beginning in the 1840s Catholic publishers began to print new editions of the Douai Bible in the United States, and Catholic scholars in America such as Bishop Francis Kenrick even began to work on new vernacular translations, which they eventually hoped would gain the Catholic Church's approval for use in the United States. Such approval would not take place until the next century, but the significant impetus for new translation work among Catholics began in this period.

THE BIBLE AND OTHER NON-PROTESTANT RELIGIONS

It should be noted that other religious traditions had their own versions of the Holy Scripture. Among these traditions was the growing American Jewish population. In 1845 Isaac Leeser (1806–1868), a German-born scholar and printer, began translating the

Pentateuch into English for American Jewish communities. In the same year he founded the Jewish Publication Society, which would make his translation, as well as other important Jewish material, available in America from an American publisher. By 1853 he had completed his translation of the entire Jewish Old Testament. Jewish publishing would grow slowly in the decades to come, but that it had found a presence at all during these middle nineteenth-century years positioned it to play an important role in the education and cohesion of various Jewish communities throughout the United States.

It might well be impossible to overestimate the importance of the Bible in nineteenth-century American culture. It was so much a part of the warp and woof of almost every aspect of American intellectual thought and cultural life that its influence was felt in every area of American society. Within this massively pervasive influence, however, it is important to remember that the Bible in America was not a static, monolithic entity. It changed with the times as it helped change the times. To even attempt an understanding of the role of the Bible in nineteenth-century American culture, one must first come to terms with the vast diversity of Bible editions to be found throughout the nation during the period. Such a course of study will serve to convince even the most casual observer that nineteenth-century Americans were not only a People of the Book, but a People of the Books.

See also Book Publishing; Catholics; Evangelicals; Protestantism; Publishers; Religion; Religious Magazines; Unitarians

BIBLIOGRAPHY

Secondary Works

Cmiel, Kenneth. *Democratic Eloquence: The Fight Over Popular Speech in Nineteenth-Century America*. New York: William Morrow, 1990.

Gutjahr, Paul C. *An American Bible: A History of the Good Book in the United States, 1777–1880*. Stanford, Calif.: Stanford University Press, 1999.

Gutjahr, Paul C. "Sacred Texts in the United States." *Book History* 4 (2001): 335–370.

Hatch, Nathan O., and Mark A. Noll, eds. *The Bible in America: Essays in Cultural History*. New York: Oxford University Press, 1982.

Hills, Margaret T. *The English Bible in America: A Bibliography of Editions of the Bible and the New Testament Published in America 1777–1957*. New York: American Bible Society, 1962.

Nord, David Paul. "The Evangelical Origins of Mass Media in America, 1815–1835." *Journalism Monographs* 88 (May 1984): 1–30.

O'Callaghan, E. B. *A List of Editions of the Holy Scriptures and Parts Thereof Printed in America previous to 1860*. Albany, New York: Munsell and Rowland, 1861.

Reynolds, David S. *Faith in Fiction: The Emergence of Religious Literature in America*. Cambridge, Mass.: Harvard University Press, 1981.

Sussman, Lance J. *Isaac Leeser and the Making of American Judaism*. Detroit: Wayne State University Press, 1995.

Thomson, William McClure. *The Land and the Book*. 3 vols. New York: Harper & Brothers, 1880–1886.

Wosh, Peter J. *Spreading the Word: The Bible Business in Nineteenth-Century America*. Ithaca, N.Y.: Cornell University Press, 1994.

Paul C. Gutjahr

"THE BIG BEAR OF ARKANSAS"

Indebted to both the oral tradition and the literary culture, "The Big Bear of Arkansas" is a short story of considerable sophistication. Its author, Thomas Bangs Thorpe (1815–1878), first published the work in the *Spirit of the Times* (27 March 1841), the sporting weekly edited by William T. Porter (1809–1858) where much of the best contemporary humor appeared. Porter reprinted Thorpe's tale in an anthology whose title emphasizes its preeminence: *The Big Bear of Arkansas and Other Sketches, Illustrative of Characters and Incidents in the South and Southwest* (1845). Thorpe republished the story himself in a collection of his tales and sketches, *The Hive of "The Bee-Hunter"* (1854). He belongs to a group of American authors active during the middle third of the nineteenth century and known as the humorists of the Old Southwest. This group, which included Augustus Baldwin Longstreet (1790–1870) and George Washington Harris (1814–1869), has become so closely identified with Thorpe's tale that it is sometimes called the Big Bear School of literature.

REVISIONS AND TARGET AUDIENCE

"The Big Bear of Arkansas" has been frequently anthologized in collections of American humor, frontier literature, and classic American short stories. Typically, the anthologies reprint the 1854 text, but this revision masks some of the complexities of the original periodical version. Porter revised the story for inclusion in his collection of sketches, and Thorpe, using Porter's text as his source, revised it again for inclusion in *The Hive of "The Bee-Hunter."* The tale was originally written for the sporting crowd; the revised version better suits the more genteel book-buying public. Through their revisions Porter and Thorpe eliminated much of the story's dialect and raciness. In "The Text, Tradition, and Themes of 'The Big Bear of Arkansas,'" J. A. Leo Lemay comments, "In general, what Thorpe did to the text of 'The Big Bear of Arkansas' in revising it could justly be compared to a pedantic school-marm's corrections of Mark Twain's colloquial prose" (p. 323). The best text is the 1841 *Spirit of the Times* version.

NARRATIVE FRAME AND VOICE

Like the other humorists of the Old Southwest, Thorpe was fascinated with folk speech yet hesitant to give over his narrative completely to some loose-limbed, slack-jawed rustic. Consequently, he structured his story as a frame tale, which allowed him to begin it in a voice not dissimilar to his own, that of an urbane southern gentleman, and then to indulge his interest in folk speech partway through the story by handing the narrative reins over to Jim Doggett, a gregarious Arkansas bear hunter. The gentility of the outside narrator's voice thus frames the inside narrator's down-home twang.

"The Big Bear of Arkansas" begins in New Orleans as passengers board a northbound Mississippi steamboat. Thorpe depicts the steamboat as a microcosm of the world, an idea that recalls the traditional motif of the ship of fools and anticipates the depiction of a Mississippi steamboat by Herman Melville (1819–1891) in *The Confidence-Man* (1857). The sophisticated outside narrator emphasizes that reading faces in a crowd of people resembles the process of reading a written text, an idea Edgar Allan Poe (1809–1849) had pointed out the year before in his short story "The Man of the Crowd" (1840). Thorpe's narrator distinguishes himself from the loud-talking rabble by describing his sedate and solitary act of reading the latest newspaper.

His reading is disturbed by the sound of an ear-piercing Indian war whoop, which is uttered by none other than Jim Doggett, a man better known by his sobriquet, "Big Bear of Arkansas." Doggett has thus taken the name of his prey. His loud whoop shows that he has taken on Native American characteristics as well. Like so many legendary American frontiersmen, Jim Doggett is a hybrid, a mongrel, a man with one foot in civilization and the other in the wilderness. His personality and charm cause others aboard the steamboat to gather around him. His voice is so alluring that he even draws the urbane narrator's attention away from his newspaper.

The story develops as fellow steamboat passengers ask a series of questions and Doggett responds with characteristic tall talk. His responses bristle with memorable phrases. They ask about Arkansas ("the creation State, the finishing-up country; a State where the *sile* runs down to the centre of the 'arth, and government gives you a title to every inch of it"), mosquitoes ("give them a fair chance for a few months, and you will get as much above noticing them as an alligator"), and the plentifulness of bears in Arkansas ("about as plenty as blackberries, and a little plentifuller"). Eventually, they prompt him to tell a bear-hunting story. From this point, Jim Doggett completely takes over the narration and proceeds to tell the story of "the greatest bar was killed that ever lived, *none excepted*" (pp. 1537, 1540).

A MYTHIC TALE

As Doggett tells his tale, it takes on elements of a mythic adventure. The bear possesses an almost supernatural ability to evade capture despite Doggett's multiple attempts to slay it. Sometimes the bear seems to possess shape-shifting powers. At other times it becomes a reflection of Jim Doggett himself. "I would see that bar in every thing I did," Doggett explains at one point (p. 1542). He and the bear are doppelgängers, doubles for each other. The hunter and the hunted almost become one. Of the bear, Doggett says, "I loved him like a brother" (p. 1542). His statement anticipates the love and respect and brotherhood Santiago feels for the great fish he catches in *The Old Man and the Sea* (1952), the classic novella by Ernest Hemingway (1899–1961). In another instance, the bear, as Doggett remarks, seems almost the devil himself. Its unstoppability looks forward to other such manifestations in American popular culture. At one point in the story, the great bear walks "*through the fence* like a falling tree would through a cobweb" (p. 1544), an image that adumbrates Arnold Schwarzenegger's character effortlessly walking through a wall in *The Terminator* (1984).

As it turns out, Doggett never actually shoots or kills the bear. Instead Thorpe deliberately undercuts the hunter's heroism. When the bear makes its final approach, Doggett, his pants around his ankles, is taking a squat in the woods. He explains that "before I had really gathered myself up, I heard the old varmint groaning in a thicket near by, like a thousand sinners, and by the time I reached him he was a corpse" (p. 1544). Doggett concludes his story on a somber note: "My private opinion is, that that bar was an *unhuntable bear, and died when his time come*" (p. 1545).

The outside narrator's voice returns to put the finishing touches on the scene. "When the story was ended, our hero sat some minutes with his auditors in a grave silence; I saw there was a mystery to him connected with the bear whose death he had just related, that had evidently made a strong impression on his mind" (p. 1545). This statement reinforces the sense of melancholy in Doggett's closing words.

CRITICAL RECEPTION AND INFLUENCE

Lemay has recognized connections between "The Big Bear of Arkansas" and early American promotion literature, has identified many biblical echoes in the story, has linked Jim Doggett to such legendary American folk heroes as Davy Crockett and Mike Fink, and has traced the story's prominent motifs to the tall tale tradition. Unlike many similar texts in the American literary tradition, "The Big Bear of Arkansas" ends on an elegiac note. The bear's death ultimately symbolizes the passing of the American wilderness.

"The Big Bear of Arkansas" influenced many major figures in American literature. Thorpe's humor, setting, and dialect were a major inspiration for Mark Twain (1835–1910). Among twentieth-century authors, William Faulkner (1897–1962) reflects Thorpe's influence. Much as Thorpe does in "The Big Bear of Arkansas," Faulkner, generally speaking, uses multiple voices within an individual work to articulate the complexity of its themes and ideas. Specifically, Thorpe's tale had a profound impact on Faulkner's "The Bear" (1942), which reiterates its imagery, tone, and symbolism. "The Big Bear of Arkansas" forms a nexus in American literary history. It echoes early American literature and anticipates the alienation and sense of loss that form such an important aspect of literary modernism.

See also Humor; Tall Tales

BIBLIOGRAPHY

Primary Work

Thorpe, Thomas Bangs. "The Big Bear of Arkansas." 1841. In *The Norton Anthology of American Literature,* vol. 1, 2nd ed., edited by Nina Baym et al., pp. 1535–1545. New York: Norton, 1985.

Secondary Works

Blair, Walter. "The Technique of 'The Big Bear of Arkansas.'" *Southwest Review* 28 (1943): 426–435.

Current-Garcia, Eugene. "'Mr. Spirit' and 'The Big Bear of Arkansas': A Note on the Genesis of Southwestern Sporting and Humor Literature." *American Literature* 27 (1955): 332–346.

Current-Garcia, Eugene. "Thomas Bangs Thorpe and the Literature of the Ante-Bellum Southwestern Frontier." *Louisiana Historical Quarterly* 39 (1956): 199–222.

Justus, James H. *Fetching the Old Southwest: Humorous Writing from Longstreet to Twain.* Columbia: University of Missouri Press, 2004.

Lemay, J. A. Leo. "The Text, Tradition, and Themes of 'The Big Bear of Arkansas.'" *American Literature* 47 (1975): 321–342.

Simoneaux, Katherine G. "Symbolism in Thorpe's 'The Big Bear of Arkansas.'" *Arkansas Historical Quarterly* 25 (1966): 240–247.

Slotkin, Richard. *Regeneration through Violence: The Mythology of the American Frontier, 1600–1860.* Middletown, Conn.: Wesleyan University Press, 1973.

Utley, Francis Lee, Lynn Z. Bloom, and Arthur F. Kinney, eds. *Bear, Man, and God: Seven Approaches to William Faulkner's "The Bear."* New York: Random House, 1964.

Kevin J. Hayes

BIOGRAPHY

Between 1820 and 1870, authors and critics in the United States began to redefine the purposes and meanings of biography, a genre so popular that several magazines identified an American "biographical mania." Before 1820 Americans who discussed biography had divided into two camps. Most biographers and some critics recommended biography for promoting civic virtue among a rising generation and proclaiming America's republican experiment to the world. Other critics, but few American biographers, echoed the English critic Samuel Johnson: a subject's "character" was found in his "domestic privacies," not in the public deeds that republican ideology would highlight. After 1820 the links between biography and "character"—the reader's and the subject's—were transformed in new cultural and critical contexts. A rapidly expanding print culture vastly increased the volume of biographical production, in forms ranging from books to paperbound tracts and periodical articles. At the same time, biography became a significant vehicle for narrating and interpreting the nation's history and particularly for contesting who merited inclusion in that history. By the Civil War era, American biographical critics were arguing that illuminating the subject's character artistically mattered more than providing models for readers to emulate, but few biographers followed their dictates.

INCULCATING "CHARACTER"

Authors and critics had long celebrated biography's instructive power: the life of a worthy subject could encourage readers' imitation or inspire them to higher values and virtuous action. An emphasis on republican instruction was specific to the post-Revolutionary American context. Biographies of American notables between 1790 and 1820 emphasized subjects' civic virtue—devotion to the nation above individual interest, simplicity of style in contrast to aristocratic pretension. Character was revealed on the public stage, whether the battlefield or the councils of state. As early as the 1820s, however, biography helped promulgate new definitions of character, particularly gendered notions associated with a rising northeastern middle class. An 1831 writer recommended that young people read "the lives of *self made men*" for "the several steps by which they arrived at eminent usefulness" (Civis, p. 281). Such biographies proliferated in several forms. Benjamin Franklin's *Autobiography* became the model for the sketches in Henry Howe's collection *Memoirs of the Most Eminent American Mechanics* (1839) and similar works. Freeman Hunt's New York monthly, the *Merchant's Magazine and Commercial Review,* regularly ran brief lives of self-made merchants between 1839 and 1846 for the benefit of the thousands of young clerks thronging the metropolis in search of economic advancement. Whereas lives of merchants glorified commercial professions by suggesting that eminent businessmen retained an ethic of public service, biographical sketches of artisans offered a more ambiguous message. On the one hand, books such as *Lives of Distinguished Shoemakers* (1849) celebrated "manual toil as the true discipline of a man" (p. iii). On the other, they tended to share with merchant biographies an emphasis on self-education and self-making and took as subjects men who had left manual labor for more elevated intellectual or professional pursuits. The most famous American biographer of self-made men was William Makepeace Thayer, a former Congregational pastor whose books included *The Poor Boy and Merchant Prince* (an 1857 manual for young men that took lessons from the life of the manufacturing entrepreneur Amos Lawrence), *The Bobbin Boy* (1860, a life of the Massachusetts governor Nathaniel Banks), *The Printer Boy; or, How Ben Franklin Made His Mark* (1860), and *The Pioneer Boy, and How He Became President* (1863, about Abraham Lincoln).

Biographies of eminent women offered a range of cultural messages. The lives of women renowned for intellectual or literary achievement, such as Madame Germaine de Staël, empowered women readers to pursue their own intellectual development, often in reading groups or correspondence with other women. Numerous biographies told of women distinguished for benevolent work. Ann Haseltine Judson, a missionary to Burma, became more famous after her death than she had been in life thanks to a best-selling memoir by James D. Knowles and other biographies. Lives of Judson, Isabella Graham (who had founded charitable organizations through successful fundraising), and kindred spirits provided models of heroic womanhood and authority in the public realm. In contrast, the popular biographies of European queens served largely to reinforce an ideology of domesticity: authors generally presented political power and femininity as incompatible and queens such as Elizabeth I as mannish perversions rather than figures to be admired.

For both men and women, religious biography—probably the most widely disseminated category of biographies in nineteenth-century America—aimed to shape readers' character as Christians. Some religious biographies were the literary handiwork of the subjects' friends or ministers, who wanted to memorialize a person (often a woman) noted for piety; these books might be locally published or adopted by a regional or national publisher. Others were the product of religious tract societies or the American Sunday-School Union. These organizations reprinted biographies first published by English tract societies and published newly written lives of American subjects. Inverting biography's usual mission to "record the incidents connected with the life of some *distinguished individual,*" many religious memoirs told the lives of little-known subjects, whose very typicality could serve as the best inspiration for similarly ordinary readers (Clark, p. 3). Biographical sketches of exemplary Christians also appeared frequently in religious magazines and newspapers.

Tract societies were the most prolific, but far from the only, organizations that employed biography to create and mobilize imagined communities of readers. For abolitionist societies and publishers, the testimony recorded in the pages of slave narratives was the harshest literary indictment of the South's "peculiar institution." Although narrative and biography differed—"narratives" tended to be first-person accounts of a series of adventures or experiences (such as Indian captivity narratives) rather than full life stories—the authors and publishers of slave narratives, most famously Frederick Douglass's *Narrative of the Life of Frederick Douglass, an American Slave* (1845), capitalized on the power of individual experience that gave biography much of its appeal. Political parties, which developed their own networks of publishers and newspapers in the 1830s and 1840s, used biography to promote not only presidential candidates but also larger political and social ideologies. Democrats' biographers portrayed candidates whose industry had raised them to candidacy within the political party, an ostensibly democratic institution. Their Whig rivals, who argued that party loyalty forced men to sacrifice independent judgment, depicted Whig candidates as men above party, elevated to leadership by innate qualities. At the same time, biographers of both parties emphasized candidates' devotion to the Union, implying that the party system itself had become a bulwark of the republic and an institution of republican education for a rising generation of men.

INTERPRETING AMERICAN HISTORY

If the presentation of characters—and different notions of "character"—for readers' emulation and for the promotion of various collective identities was one major purpose of biography, the definition and elaboration of American history was the other. Through biography, American writers offered multiple interpretations of the nation's past. The first generation of American historical biographers, who included Jeremy Belknap (*American Biography,* 1794), John Marshall (*The Life of George Washington,* 1804–1807), and William Wirt (*Sketches of the Life and Character of Patrick Henry,* 1817), all sought to tell the nation's story through individual lives. After 1820, as most states and even some localities founded historical societies, their successors emphasized the centrality of documentary research for historical scholarship. Jared Sparks (1789–1866), a former Unitarian minister and editor of the *North American Review,* became a leader among these mostly New England historians. Sparks argued for a clear distinction between "truth" (gleaned from research in written documents) and "tradition" (usually oral lore, passed down by subjects' descendants and acquaintances). Tradition, Sparks argued, had no place in serious historical or biographical writing.

The *Library of American Biography,* which Sparks edited in twenty-five volumes (1834–1848), revealed not only his ideas about the genre but also shifting visions of American history. As Sparks explained the project in his journal on 28 July 1832, "The purpose is to select some of the most prominent lives, from the first settlement of the country down to the present time. . . . The series will thus serve as in some degree a connected history of the country, as well as to illustrate the character and acts of some of the most illustrious men in the nation" (Adams 2:189). Sparks expected his authors to consult original sources but not to write biographies in the "life and letters" form replete with long documentary extracts. Instead he wanted easily readable narrative so that the volumes would sell. The first ten volumes (1834–1838) testified to the New England interpretation of American history dominant in the 1830s. Most of the authors in this "first series" of the *Library* were Harvard graduates like Sparks; the twenty-six subjects were predominantly New England figures, from Puritan times to the Revolutionary era and the early Republic. Many authors evinced a Unitarian, Whig bias: critical of Puritan theology and practice, troubled by Anglo-American (especially proto-Jacksonian) treatment of Native Americans, virtually silent about matters south of Pennsylvania. The second "series" (1844–1848) was different. Perhaps because historical societies now existed in southern and western states, Sparks engaged writers from across the nation, who wrote on subjects from every region. As a result these fifteen volumes told a different story, of a United States comprised of diverse local histories and individuals whose local or state eminence had contributed to building the nation.

By the 1840s too, other historical biographers used scholarly methods to challenge the narrative that Sparks and his New England compatriots had built. Some writers sought to broaden the range of biographical subjects. The New York historian William Leete Stone (1792–1844) wrote biographies of the Iroquois leaders Joseph Brant (1838) and Red-Jacket (1841), traveling as far as Montreal and Quebec for documents and employing an early form of ethnography in describing Native American customs and family structures. Stone argued that Anglo-American historians, and even the public documents in which they might seek "truth," distorted the true history of Native Americans. As a corrective, he published long extracts from Brant's own manuscripts. He also compared his method to those employed in John Marshall's *Life of Washington,* Thomas Moore's *Life of Byron,* and John Gibson Lockhart's *Life of Sir Walter Scott*—placing Native American subjects within an Anglo-American biographical tradition. To write the three-volume *Women of the American Revolution* (1848–1850), Elizabeth F. Ellet (1812–1877) collected documentary records of her subjects but found that women's contributions had often gone unrecorded in writing. Therefore she turned to descendants of her potential subjects for information, even as she recognized the difficulties of substantiating their family "traditions." Ellet aimed to elevate the Revolutionary-era women through the medium of historical biography and to connect two literary worlds: scholarly historical writing, often perceived as men's domain, and domestic literature that focused on women's struggles and influence.

Southern biographers of the 1840s and 1850s went further, not merely proposing additions to the national pantheon but arguing that the surfeit of New England biography skewed Americans' comprehension of the national past. William Gilmore Simms (1806–1870), the foremost southern writer and editor, penned lives of Francis Marion and other South Carolinians and pungent biographical criticism in his *Southern Quarterly Review*. Southerners' historical indifference, Simms lamented, had ceded the field: "Our histories are slurred over by Yankee historians, the most important truths suppressed; our heroes receive but cold applause. Shall the warm and generous nature owe the record of its virtues, its uncalculating patriotism, its noble self-sacrifice, its oratory or its valor to the cold and frigid biographies of the unsympathising bigot of another and a too hostile region?" (p. 197). Sectional lines also emerged in the response to New Yorker Henry Stephens Randall's sympathetic *Life of Thomas Jefferson* (1857–1858): southern reviewers embraced this biography of their native son, while northern critics faulted Randall's Democratic bias and even his writing style.

In the mid-1850s Herman Melville (1819–1891) employed another genre—fictionalized personal narrative—to criticize Sparksian biography. In 1853 Melville had commented on biography in his short story "Bartleby," whose narrator laments, "I believe that no materials exist, for a full and satisfactory biography of this man. . . . Bartleby was one of those beings of whom nothing is ascertainable, except from the original sources, and, in his case, those are very small" (p. 3). Israel Potter, a veteran of the battle of Bunker Hill who became a London chair maker and dictated his life story to a Providence printer, had left more. Melville used Potter's 1824 "narrative" as the basis for *Israel Potter: His Fifty Years of Exile* (1855). Dedicating the book to "His Highness the Bunker-Hill Monument," Melville wrote that ordinary men like Potter were missing from "the volumes of Sparks." The monument, he argued, was truly America's "Great Biographer: the national commemorator of such of the anonymous privates of June 17, 1775, who may never have received other requital than the solid reward of your granite" (pp. 3–5). Even if *Israel Potter* was largely Melville's invention, the novelist echoed the questions that Stone, Ellet, Simms, and other contemporaries were asking: whose life stories biography ought to capture, and whether an insistence on documentary evidence excised some Americans from their rightful place in history.

DEFINING BIOGRAPHY AS "LITERATURE"

In the 1840s and 1850s, critics in several American literary magazines argued that most biographies were defective as literature. Their criticism, derived from English Romantic arguments, imagined biography differently than did most Americans who wrote and read in the genre. To authors and readers, biography was either a didactic instrument of character formation or a branch of history. When earlier American critics had discussed the literary properties of biography, they had emphasized its distinction from the novel: biography offered rational, instructive amusement that fiction did not. Historians in Sparks's vein emphasized the quest for documentary truth more than any literary rules for presenting subjects' character. Few Americans wrote literary biography, the lives of American authors, in the vein of Lockhart's *Life of Scott*. But after 1840 literary critics on both sides of the Atlantic increasingly took issue with biographical practice.

Several of their complaints seem at first glance contradictory. On the one hand, critics defended the privacy of the subject against the prurient curiosity of the reader or the hack biographer. On the other, they faulted biographers for lapsing into eulogy that told too little of the subject, a lament that dated back to the eighteenth century. Romantic critics of biography offered another path, founded on different definitions of "truth" and "character." Truth now meant "truth to life": a sense of the subject's individuality. Only a biographer who wrote *con amore*—a phrase also used to describe the true poet's relationship to his subject—could capture what critics now called the "inner man." As Thomas Carlyle wrote and many American critics echoed,

> If an individual is really of consequence enough to have his life and character recorded for public remembrance, . . . the public ought to be made acquainted with all the inward springs and relations of his character. . . . In one word, what and how produced was the effect of society on him? and what and how produced was his effect on society?" (Quoted in "A Biographer at Work," p. 222)

The biographer's responsibility lay in interpretation, not merely the collection of documentation or anecdote. English and American critics of the 1850s defined biography writing as literary artistry that required craftsmanship in arranging materials, vivid depiction of character and scene, and appreciation of the subject's character and accomplishment.

James Parton (1822–1891), a New York journalist for Nathaniel Parker Willis's *Home Journal*, did not immediately seem the sort of writer to meet the critics' standards. His first biography, *The Life of Horace Greeley*, which appeared in 1855 (a year before he married the novelist and fellow journalist Sara Payson Willis Eldredge, known to readers as "Fanny Fern"), displayed literary talent but resembled the myriad lives of self-made men written for aspiring youth. His second, *The Life and Times of Aaron Burr* (1857), became the most controversial biography of the 1850s: critics divided over whether Parton's brisk narrative presented a balanced portrait of a still-mysterious character or palliated the faults of a bad man in order to sell books. Parton's three-volume *Life of Andrew Jackson* (1860) established his reputation as America's premier biographer—indeed, the first American author known *as* a biographer. The hallmarks of his style included deep research in documentary and published sources (the *Life of Jackson* opened with a thirteen-page annotated bibliography) and animated prose that owed something to his journalistic roots.

Several critics noted that Parton pioneered an approach appropriate to telling an *American* life story. They suggested, too, that Parton wrote *con amore*, seeking the "inner man" as Romantic critics prescribed. This approach was most evident in Parton's long, interpretive articles on notable American politicians and entrepreneurs of the previous generation, which appeared in the venerable *North American Review* in the mid-1860s. At the same time, Parton's fame as a biographer afforded opportunities to write in other corners of the genre. For Robert Bonner's *New York Ledger,* he wrote brief, often didactic articles about famous men and women. He continued his career in American historical biography with a two-volume life of Benjamin Franklin (1864). He also capitalized on the fascination with Civil War commanders with *General Butler in New Orleans* (1863), a book not unlike the emerging "dime biographies" of contemporary figures published by the dime-novel publishers Beadle and Adams.

After the Civil War, biography in the United States remained as diverse as it had been for the previous half century. Critics might desire works of literary polish and interpretive depth, but far more biographies adhered to familiar formulas. Didactic works continued to target aspiring self-made men and religious strivers, political parties still produced biographies of presidential candidates, and historians wrote the "lives and times" of historical figures. Beginning in the late 1860s, subscription publishing companies promoted several new sorts of biographical production, all with antebellum roots. Thick compendia of brief life sketches, including several volumes edited by Parton, reached back to collections about self-made men or eminent women but increasingly emphasized celebrity as much as instruction. The lives of Civil War generals, most famously Ulysses Grant's 1885 *Memoirs,* helped place the recent conflict into the nation's historical narrative. And ornately bound compendia of local history and biography, the so-called mug books that were compiled for hundreds of midwestern and western counties in the last quarter of the century, provided a site for ordinary individuals to have their achievements (and sometimes their pictures) recorded for posterity. Americans' "biographical mania" showed no signs of decline.

See also Book Publishing; Civil War; Education; English Literature; History; Literary Criticism; Political Parties; Religion

BIBLIOGRAPHY
Primary Works
Adams, Herbert Baxter. *The Life and Writings of Jared Sparks.* 2 vols. Boston: Houghton, Mifflin and Co. 1893.

"A Biographer at Work." *New Englander* 25 (April 1866): 218–227.

[Civis.] "Art. XII.—Biography." *American Annals of Education and Instruction, and Journal of Literary Institutions* 1 (June 1831): 281.

Clark, John A. *The Young Disciple: or, A Memoir of Anzonetta R. Peters.* Philadelphia: William Marshall, 1837.

Lives of Distinguished Shoemakers. Portland, Maine: Davis and Southworth, 1849.

Melville, Herman. "Bartleby." 1853. In *Piazza Tales and Other Prose Pieces, 1839–1860.* Edited by Harrison Hayford, Hershel Parker, and G. Thomas Tanselle. Evanston, Ill.: Northwestern University Press, 1987.

Melville, Herman. *Israel Potter: His Fifty Years of Exile.* New York: G. P. Putnam, 1855.

Simms, William Gilmore. "Kennedy's *Life of Wirt.*" *Southern Quarterly Review* 17 (April 1850): 192–236.

Sparks, Jared, ed. *Library of American Biography.* 25 vols. Boston: Little, Brown, 1834–1848.

Secondary Works
Altick, Richard D. *Lives and Letters: A History of Literary Biography in England and America.* New York: Knopf, 1969.

Cafarelli, Annette Wheeler. *Prose in the Age of Poets: Romanticism and Biographical Narrative from Johnson to De Quincey.* Philadelphia: University of Pennsylvania Press, 1990.

Casper, Scott E. *Constructing American Lives: Biography and Culture in Nineteenth-Century America.* Chapel Hill: University of North Carolina Press, 1999.

Cockshut, A. O. J. *Truth to Life: The Art of Biography in the Nineteenth Century.* New York: Harcourt Brace Jovanovich, 1974.

Fabian, Ann. *The Unvarnished Truth: Personal Narrative in Nineteenth-Century America.* Berkeley: University of California Press, 1999.

Reed, Joseph W., Jr. *English Biography in the Early Nineteenth Century, 1801–1838.* New Haven, Conn.: Yale University Press, 1966.

Scott E. Casper

"THE BIRTH-MARK"

Nathaniel Hawthorne (1804–1864) is perhaps best known for his novels of the 1850s, *The Scarlet Letter* (1850), *The House of the Seven Gables* (1851), and *The Blithedale Romance* (1852). Yet in the two decades before this creative outpouring, Hawthorne was busy composing some of the most famous short stories written by an American author. Titles such as "The Minister's Black Veil" and "The Shaker Bridal," both of which were originally published in *The Token,* found their way into *Twice-Told Tales* (1837, 1842), Hawthorne's first collection of short stories. Years later he took several stories that had previously appeared in literary journals such as the *New-England Magazine* and compiled them into *Mosses from an Old Manse* (1846), a volume that many readers, antebellum as well as contemporary, believe includes some of his greatest short works, for example, "Rappaccini's Daughter," "Young Goodman Brown," and "The Birth-mark." In fact, no less a reader than Herman Melville (1819–1891) composed a paean to this collection in his 1850 essay "Hawthorne and His Mosses," which, even though it has as much if not more to say about Melville's claims to originality and Shakespearean genius as it does about Hawthorne's stories, lavishes this praise upon the author of "The Old Apple Dealer": "Hawthorne is here almost alone in his generation,—at least, in the artistic manifestation of things" (p. 242).

One might reasonably argue that Hawthorne, far from being alone, keeps company with that other famous short-story writer of the period, Edgar Allan Poe (1809–1849). Together they share a literary penchant for the gothic, an interest in popular science, and a continued fascination with the proposition that, in the infamous words of Poe, "the death of a beautiful woman is, unquestionably, the most poetical topic in the world" (p. 184). When it comes to dying women—and here one thinks of Poe's Ligeia and

Nathaniel Hawthorne. Photograph from a carte de visite. THE ART ARCHIVE/CULVER PICTURES

Berenice and Hawthorne's Beatrice ("Rappaccini's Daughter") and Georgiana—the two are experts. In addition to which, like Poe, Hawthorne is profoundly interested in writing stories that self-consciously reflect upon "the artistic manifestation of things." Hawthorne's protagonists are often creators of some sort, whether sculptors, scientists, or artists, as in the case of Owen Warland of "The Artist of the Beautiful," about whom the narrator writes, "Alas, that the artist, whether in poetry or whatever other material, may not content himself with the inward enjoyment of the Beautiful, but must chase the flitting mystery beyond the verge of his ethereal domain, and crush its frail being in seizing it with a material grasp!" (p. 916). The violence done to nature by art, the search for perfect form at the expense of one's human relationships, and the tension between the artistic ideal of the human body and the reality of that flawed, and often female, body, are themes that run throughout Hawthorne's short stories. And because his stories are about the production of art, they are also stories about and admonitions to the artist himself. Time and again Hawthorne composes allegories of his own artistic production, desire, and what Melville identified as that "great power of blackness [which] derives its force from its appeals to that Calvinistic sense of Innate Depravity and Original Sin" ("Hawthorne and His Mosses," p. 243). Although Hawthorne acknowledges and even applauds the commitment that goes into the artist's desire for great art, more often than not he sees art as a powerful enticement away from the real and toward the unattainable ideal, away from generosity and toward hubris, away from the warmth of human beings and toward "a sensation of moral cold, that makes the spirit shiver" (p. 917). To what extent Hawthorne's own literary artistry is complicit in the very depravity, egotism, and absence of sympathy that he wishes to critique is a central question in many of his most memorable texts.

READING GEORGIANA'S BIRTHMARK

"The Birth-mark," first published in the *Pioneer* in March 1843, represents a particularly effective and sustained consideration of precisely these aesthetic issues and others of more cultural import. The plot is relatively simple. Aylmer, a scientist whose experiments are notable more for failing than succeeding, marries Georgiana, who, though perfect in every other way, has a birthmark he desperately wants to remove. Georgiana, unsurprisingly, is not as keen as Aylmer on this procedure, although as the story unfolds, she becomes as psychically afflicted by the birthmark as he. In the course of experimenting upon his wife, Aylmer adds yet another failure to his list, and Georgiana dies in the process of having the birthmark removed.

What is so powerful about this story? First is Hawthorne's portrayal of Aylmer's monomania, a psychological state whose characteristics were being formulated in the antebellum period by the American psychiatrist Isaac Ray. In his 1838 *A Treatise on the Medical Jurisprudence of Insanity*, Ray argues that "the mind is not observed to have lost any of its original vigor, [and] the patient suffers from delusion concerning one topic" (Smith, p. 38). Hawthorne describes Aylmer's monomaniacal state of mind as "the tyrannizing influence acquired by one idea over his mind" (p. 767). Monomaniacs, it is known, populate American fiction (think of Ahab and the narrators of Poe's "The Black Cat" and "The Tell-Tale Heart"), and Aylmer is not Hawthorne's only specimen (Hollingsworth in *The Blithedale Romance,* Chillingworth in *The Scarlet Letter,* Rappaccini, Richard Digby in "The Man of Adamant," and many others). Aylmer's particular version of monomania is fascinating because the "one topic" that obsesses him is his wife's birthmark. And as

Hawthorne represents it, it is not just any birthmark. This "singular mark" wears "a tint of deeper crimson," bears "not a little similarity to the human hand," and signifies endlessly (p. 765). In the course of only a few pages, the hand is referred to as "the Bloody Hand," "the Crimson Hand," and "the odious Hand" and is likened to a "fairy sign-manual" (pp. 765, 766, 767). The hand, in other words, is a text not unlike the scarlet letter or the white whale, about which Ahab says, "he tasks me; he heaps me" (p. 164). Like Moby-Dick, the birthmark, both the physical mark and the story itself, begs to be read.

One should begin with the mark on Georgiana's body. Aylmer seizes upon the mark as evidence of the following: "it was the fatal flaw of humanity"; it "expressed the ineludible gripe in which mortality clutches the highest and purest of earthly mould"; it was "the symbol of imperfection" (p. 766). Such a reading, then, permits him to transform Georgiana into the subject of a scientific experiment, which is precisely what the narrator warns readers about in the opening paragraph: "He had devoted himself too unreservedly to scientific studies, ever to be weaned from them by any second passion. His love for his young wife might prove the stronger of the two; but it could only be by intertwining itself with his love of science" (p. 764). Being the ideal wife, Georgiana comes to loathe the birthmark as much as her husband does and is desperate to do whatever it takes to get "the spectral Hand" (p. 766) removed and thereby regain Aylmer's love.

Aylmer gets the hand but loses Georgiana. He is "the man of science" (p. 779) whose commitment to knowledge and perfection becomes a mechanism for his egotism and cruelty, destroying everything in its path. But why would anyone get so worked up about a birthmark? Aylmer's interpretation of the birthmark as malevolent certainly aids and abets his scientific claims over it, and yet his readings are clearly informed by other aspects of the birthmark that are related to gender. Indeed, this is the second reason for the power of the story. The birthmark (both mark and story) oozes feminine sexuality. It seems no coincidence that Aylmer is not bothered by it during their courtship, but "very soon after their marriage" (p. 764), and presumably after they have had sexual intercourse, he is. The birthmark is crimson and bloody, signifying menstruation and a loss of virginity. It is also connected to Georgiana's emotions, more particularly "its tiny grasp appeared to have caught hold of Georgiana's heart" (p. 767). The stereotypical divide between reason and feeling is here represented and undermined by the two central characters. Hawthorne reveals the unbridled passion at the core of Aylmer's allegedly rational dedication to science, and Georgiana, the one who blushes, reddens, and "burst[s] into tears" (p. 775) in typical sentimental fashion, is also the one who reads Aylmer's scientific journals, questions him about the drugs he is administering to her, and knows that she is dying well before Aylmer has a clue (even though he has had many clues as to the potentially disastrous consequences of his elixirs).

A key reason, then, that Aylmer wants to erase the birthmark is that it signifies a sexuality with which he is deeply uncomfortable. Unlike the true woman of antebellum domestic ideology, whose qualities include—according to the historian Barbara Welter's influential essay "The Cult of True Womanhood"—piety, submission, domesticity, and most importantly for the purposes of "The Birth-mark," purity, Georgiana is a sexualized being, and the birthmark registers "every pulse of emotion that throbbed within her heart" (p. 766). If that were not problematic enough, it also signals a wifely submission that is incomplete. Georgiana's birthmark gives away her interior state because it records "any shifting emotion," whether that be "momentary anger" (p. 765), sadness, or fear, such as when she is so white at the prospect of beginning the experiment that the birthmark "intense[ly] glows," Aylmer "convulsive[ly] shudders," and she faints (p. 769).

The birthmark, therefore, not only becomes the mechanism through which Aylmer's aversion to Georgiana's sexuality gets played out but represents something of her that is wholly outside of his control (and hers too, but that does not matter much from Aylmer's point of view). The most obvious way to put this point is to say that she comes to him with a mark that he has not made. That Georgiana's mother (or father) has made it, or that "our great Creative Mother" (p. 769) might have made it, is irrelevant. The fact is that someone has been there before him, so he must destroy it and thereby remake her in his desired image à la Pygmalion, a text to which Hawthorne's refers (p. 768). The problem for Aylmer, though, runs deeper. Not only is the birthmark beyond his control, it controls him, and this configuration of power represents the antithesis of all that an antebellum domestic household should be.

Of course Georgiana is the victim of the story, but Hawthorne brilliantly represents how the birthmark (and her husband's obsession with it) victimizes Aylmer. It is important to remember that "its shape bore not a little similarity to the human hand" (p. 765). In an almost comic way, as Aylmer furiously tries to erase that hand-shaped mark, hands, parts of hands, and the verbs used to describe what hands do start appearing throughout the text. For example,

Aylmer tells Georgiana that the birthmark "had taken a pretty firm hold of my fancy" (p. 767). About Aylmer's scientific pursuits the narrator writes, "he handled physical details, as if there were nothing beyond them" and "in his grasp, the veriest clod of earth assumed a soul" (p. 774). Aylmer's hands are everywhere: Georgiana "returned the goblet to his hand" (p. 778); she read "a large folio from her husband's own hand" (p. 774); he "seized her arm with a gripe that left the print of his fingers upon it" (p. 776). "The Birth-mark" represents a power struggle between man and wife in which the man demands that the wife give up something that she herself does not exactly own. The birthmark is both hers and something over which she has no control, and as such, even with the best will in the world (which Georgiana has), she cannot lose it.

Being unable to divest herself of the birthmark can be read in multiple ways, one of which is as evidence of the fact of female sexuality. Another way, however, to think about the necessary visibility of the birthmark is in terms of property and antebellum marriage law. William Blackstone, whose legal decisions about marriage in the eighteenth century laid the groundwork for U.S. marriage laws, maintained that when a woman married, she became a *femme couverte,* or a covered woman. Although there were exceptions, as a general rule her property became her husband's, and she did too. That Hawthorne and Sophia Peabody had married (and happily so) less than a year before he wrote "The Birth-mark" provides biographical evidence to suggest that issues of marriage and property (and sex) were on Hawthorne's mind. Interestingly "The Birth-mark" seems to question the extent to which a woman can become the property of her husband by endowing Georgiana with a physical property that is so "deeply interwoven, as it were, with the texture and substance of her face" (p. 765) that when asked to give it up, she cannot. To read the story this way is to see Hawthorne challenging some fundamental assumptions of domestic ideology. There are some things that a woman simply cannot and should not be asked to give up.

READING HAWTHORNE'S "THE BIRTH-MARK"

"The Birth-mark" is at once a fascinating study of monomania and its potentially gothic implications for domestic relations, and yet the third reason for the continued critical interest in this short story has more to do with its representation of literary production. Once again, the shape of the birthmark is significant. Hawthorne's narrator and the characters in the story tirelessly call attention to the fact that the

In this passage from "The Birth-mark," Georgiana reads Aylmer's scientific record. Several points should be noted. First, Aylmer is an author. Second, Georgiana responds to his writings both as an ideal woman (she loves him even more for his ambitions) and as a transgressive woman (she begins to question his judgment). Third, the presence of hands is an inextricable part of the narrative, just as Georgiana's birthmark is an inalienable part of herself.

But, to Georgiana, the most engrossing volume was a large folio from her husband's own hand, in which he had recorded every experiment of his scientific career, with its original aim, the methods adopted for its development, and its final success or failure, with the circumstances to which either event was attributable. The book, in truth, was both the history and emblem of his ardent, ambitious, imaginative, yet practical and laborious, life. He handled physical details, as if there were nothing beyond them. . . . In his grasp, the veriest clod of earth assumed a soul. Georgiana, as she read, reverenced Aylmer, and loved him more profoundly than ever, but with a less entire dependence on his judgment than heretofore. Much as he had accomplished, she could not but observe that his most splendid successes were almost invariably failures, if compared with the ideal at which he aimed. His brightest diamonds were the merest pebbles, and felt to be so by himself, in comparison with the inestimable gems which lay hidden beyond his reach. The volume, rich with achievements that had won renown for its author, was yet as melancholy a record as ever mortal hand had penned.

Hawthorne, *Tales and Sketches*, pp. 774–775.

birthmark is in the shape of a hand. Aylmer is a scientist, but he is also, quite literally, a writer, an "author" whose volume "rich with achievements . . . was yet as melancholy a record as ever mortal hand had penned" (p. 775). Georgiana reads his works, which are testimonies of failure, presaging her own demise. Whereas the scientist-author does not foresee the consequences of his experiments, the unlikeliest character in the story does. That is Aminadab, Aylmer's "under-worker," who "seemed to represent man's physical nature." A fully embodied creature with "vast strength" and "indescribable earthiness," he understands how Aylmer's attacks on Georgiana's body spell doom. He remarks, "If she were my wife, I'd never part with that birth-mark" (p. 770). Aminadab comprehends the inextricability of Georgiana and her mark. To marry her is, on some level, to marry the birthmark. To divorce her from her mark is to kill her.

Aylmer is an author figure who reads "the fairy-sign manual" of the birthmark as evidence of his own need to write an even better manual, presumably one with no marks. And one with no women. In attempting to erase the hand on Georgiana's cheek, Aylmer wants to re-create Georgiana, only this time immaculately. There will be no reproduction, with its blood and messiness, but only production, with its calculation and rationality. What issues from this logic, which Mary Shelley had examined only twelve years before, is a model of male creation, dependent upon though deadly to the female body. Aylmer becomes, like so many of Hawthorne's scientists-artists gone mad, incapable of love, of community, of sympathy. As an allegory of the potential consequences of authorship, "The Birth-mark" seems to suggest that writing itself is a dangerous proposition for all concerned. In writing an allegory of the perversions of the creative process, Hawthorne acknowledges the philosophical lures of Aylmer's search for perfection and yet protects himself from repeating the unpardonable sins that go along with just such a pursuit. This reading maintains that the pleasures of "The Birth-mark" are the result of the exquisite self-consciousness that Hawthorne's writing brings to bear on the issue of writing itself. It is, ironically enough, an allegory of the dangers of allegory. This is a topic about which Hawthorne eloquently wrote in an introductory and certainly autobiographical note to "Rappaccini's Daughter." The narrator states that the story one is about to read is M. de l'Aubepiné's, whose writings "might have won him greater reputation but for an inveterate love of allegory, which is apt to invest his plots and characters with the aspect of scenery and people in the clouds, and to steal away the human warmth out of his conceptions" (p. 975). Aylmer's fear and loathing of Georgiana's birthmark, and his concomitant desire to erase it, meets its match in Hawthorne's compulsion to erase the model of authorship that is getting represented in "The Birth-mark." After all, Aylmer is, if nothing else, an allegorist who plunders Georgiana's humanity under the guise of scientific knowledge. Hawthorne represents his self-consciousness about the dangers of allegory through the literary mode he knows best and fears most—allegory (think of "The Celestial Rail-road" and "Egotism; or, The Bosom-Serpent," whose subtitle is "From the Unpublished 'Allegories of the Heart'").

In just a few pages "The Birth-mark" presents an account of antebellum domestic relations gone so awry so fast that readers continue to try to figure out how Hawthorne does it and what it means. Such an interpretive pursuit follows the author's lead, for even Hawthorne himself was sometimes perplexed by his own stories. In an 1854 letter to his publisher, James T. Fields, Hawthorne observes, "Upon my honor, I am not quite sure that I entirely comprehend my own meaning in some of these blasted allegories" (Crowley, p. 522). Does Hawthorne's story represent a critique of nineteenth-century conventions of marriage (no woman should be asked to give up essential aspects of herself when marrying) or an endorsement of the doctrine of separate spheres (if only Aylmer had stayed in the laboratory and kept Georgiana out of it)? Is the human "stain" (p. 765)—to invoke provocatively the title of Philip Roth's 2000 novel of hidden racial identity—of the birthmark a sign of a racialized identity about which Aylmer was unaware when he "washed the stain of acids from his fingers and persuaded a beautiful woman to become his wife" (p. 764)? Like Melville's Moby-Dick, the birthmark, whose waning is described at the end of Hawthorne's story as "the stain of the rainbow fading out of the sky" (p. 779), is erased at one's peril. To interpret the birthmark as the monomaniac Aylmer does is to make a natural object "fatal" (pp. 776, 779, 780). Indeed, such an interpretive move occurs both in Moby-Dick ("The Birth-mark" is one of the most heavily marked tales in Melville's copy of Mosses from an Old Manse, according to Richard Brodhead, even though he does not discuss it in "Hawthorne and His Mosses"), and in Billy Budd (published posthumously in 1924), when Vere calls Billy "fated boy" (p. 350) at the moment of Claggart's death. In fact, Billy's stutter is explicitly compared to Georgiana's birthmark in the following passage: "Like the beautiful woman in one of Hawthorne's minor tales, there was just one thing amiss in him. No visible blemish indeed, as with the lady; no, but an occasional liability to a vocal defect" (p. 302). Like Georgiana, Billy is condemned to die by an act of ghastly interpretation. The power of Hawthorne's story, for Melville and for readers, continues to serve as a warning to writers who dare to tread in allegorical waters and to readers whose interpretations are required and regarded with suspicion.

See also Calvinism; Feminism; Gothic Fiction; "Hawthorne and His Mosses"; Marriage; Popular Science; Psychology; Sexuality and the Body

BIBLIOGRAPHY
Primary Works

Crowley, J. Donald. "Historical Commentary." In *The Centenary Edition of the Works of Nathaniel Hawthorne*, edited by William Charvat, Roy Harvey Pearce, and Claude M. Simpson. Vol. 10, *Mosses from an Old Manse*, edited by J. Donald Crowley and Fredson Bowers. Columbus: Ohio State University Press, 1974.

Hawthorne, Nathaniel. *Tales and Sketches.* New York: Library of America, 1982. All page citations to Hawthorne works refer to this edition.

Melville, Herman. *Billy Budd and Other Stories.* New York: Penguin, 1986.

Melville, Herman. "Hawthorne and His Mosses." 1850. In *The Piazza Tales and Other Prose Pieces, 1839–1860*, edited by Harrison Hayford, Alma A. MacDougall, and G. Thomas Tanselle. Evanston, Ill.: Northwestern University Press, 1987.

Melville, Herman. *Moby-Dick; or, The Whale.* 1851. Edited by Harrison Hayford, Hershel Parker, and G. Thomas Tanselle. Evanston, Ill.: Northwestern University Press, 1988.

Poe, Edgar Allan Poe. "The Philosophy of Composition." 1846. In *The Complete Poetry and Selected Criticism of Edgar Allan Poe*, edited and with an introduction by Allen Tate. New York: Meridian, 1986.

Secondary Works

Baym, Nina. *The Shape of Hawthorne's Career.* Ithaca, N.Y.: Cornell University Press, 1976.

Brodhead, Richard H. *The School of Hawthorne.* Chicago: University of Chicago Press, 1986.

Elbert, Monika. "The Surveillance of Woman's Body in Hawthorne's Short Stories." *Women's Studies* 33 (2004): 23–46.

Fetterley, Judith, "Woman Beware Science: 'The Birthmark.'" In *The Scarlet Letter and Other Writings*, edited by Leland S. Person. New York: Norton, 2004.

Herbert, T. Walter. *Dearest Beloved: The Hawthornes and the Making of the Middle-Class Family.* Berkeley: University of California Press, 1993.

Pfister, Joel. *The Production of Personal Life: Class, Gender, and the Psychological in Hawthorne's Fiction.* Stanford, Calif.: Stanford University Press, 1991.

Smith, Henry Nash. *Democracy and the Novel: Popular Resistance to Classic American Writers.* Oxford: Oxford University Press, 1978.

Weinstein, Cindy. *Family, Kinship, and Sympathy in Nineteenth-Century American Literature.* Cambridge, U.K., and New York: Cambridge University Press, 2004.

Weinstein, Cindy. *The Literature of Labor and the Labors of Literature: Allegory in Nineteenth-Century American Fiction.* Cambridge, U.K.: Cambridge University Press, 1995.

Welter, Barbara. *Dimity Convictions: The American Woman in the Nineteenth Century.* Athens: Ohio University Press, 1978.

Cindy Weinstein

BLACKS

Any discussion of blacks as a racial group, whether examined under the guise of science or the humanities, must be framed by a consideration of the historical construction of the term in the Western imagination. Certainly Europeans were not the first to contrast their lighter skin against the darker skin of Africans and other people of color. However, the explosion of fifteenth-century European exploration spawned the construction and the solidification of Western paradigms of a racialized black-white human dichotomy. While continental Africans drew boundaries of group identity along kinship and ethnic lines, the arrival of trade-seeking Europeans along the coast of Africa would dramatically alter the way Africans negotiated identity. On the continent itself, Africans were for the most part able to maintain the integrity of their ethnic groups. Increasingly, however, they faced a European economic and military presence that sought to reduce them to a monolithic African-black identity. Just as Europeans would name the native people of America "Indians" and then treat them as a single racial entity, they developed a racial rhetoric that marked Africans as a single people. Through European discourse, Africans became blacks, and this racial designation would have more severe implications for those who were stolen away to the New World than for those remaining on the continent. Transported Africans were dispersed into enslaved communities that comprised slaves from various ethnic African groups. Consequently continental alliances could not be reproduced, and African people in the New World were forced to shape a new concept of selfhood. The concept that emerged was not free from the influence of European captors who came to understand themselves as white primarily through their negotiation of a black presence.

Black population of the United States: Slaves versus free blacks, 1820–1860

Year	Free	Slave	Total
1820	233,634	1,538,022	1,771,656
1830	319,599	2,009,043	2,328,642
1840	386,293	2,487,355	2,873,648
1850	434,495	3,204,313	3,638,808
1860	488,070	3,953,760	4,441,830

SOURCE: U.S. Bureau of the Census.

Like Africans, early Europeans did not imagine themselves a people unified by a shared skin color. Europeans identified themselves along ethnic or national lines: Greeks no more considered themselves racially connected to Swedes than the Ibo and Ashanti of West Africa considered themselves bound by color. Histories of the various people and nations of pre-imperialist Europe show clearly that they found no particular marker of racial connectedness in whiteness. In fact, throughout the literature of Europeans one finds distinctions made between fairer-skinned northern and western Europeans and their darker southern and eastern neighbors. Through the construction of Americanness, however, whiteness was conferred upon Americans of European descent, and blackness was presumed synonymous with African ancestry. By the close of the seventeenth century in America, blacks were defined as a distinct race in the discourse of national identity. The lines of black and white became entrenched as America's expanding plantation economy found itself increasingly in need of free labor. With laws throughout the colonies confirming the place of blacks as slaves and servitude their lifelong and inherited condition, blacks in America quickly became a new race and a new class. Despite the reality of black and white unions before and after these laws and despite the small but evident population of free blacks in America, blacks came to symbolize the antithesis of Americanness. Blacks represented the absence of freedom guaranteed to whites; they symbolized human degradation and the absence of opportunity granted to whites.

That Africans did not arrive in America with a concept of self rooted in perceptions of skin color is evident in a number of autobiographical accounts of Africans in the New World. Among these, the 1789 autobiography *The Interesting Narrative of the Life of Olaudah Equiano* offers a detailed account of the kinship ties that remained with Equiano from his early childhood in Africa. While the veracity of Equiano's African memories has been questioned by some scholars, his account of life among native Africans nevertheless demonstrates the social and political alliances that existed among them. His narrative takes readers into the cultural world of a people whose identity had not yet been informed by European racialized constructs. As such, the narrative highlights a cultural identity that arose not out of African people's notion of themselves as black but rather as a people defined by ties of kinship, family, and nation.

Ironically, early black writers found the seeds of black racial identity in white racialized readings of the Bible. They and their literary descendants accepted the contention that the biblical figure Ham was the ancestor of Africans. The Bible identifies Ham as one of Noah's three sons (Gen. 5:32) and Egypt as the land of Ham (Ps. 78:51, 105:23). According to the racist discourse that grew out of the transatlantic slave trade, the curse inflicted on Ham for his sin against Noah defined the course of history for Ham's descendants. While this seems a despairing entrance into the community of humankind, early black writers and activists appropriated this biblical connection between Africanity and Christianity—but not without revisiting the actual Scripture and revising the paradigm. According to the story told in Genesis, Ham looks upon his father, Noah, who is drunk and naked. For this show of disrespect, Ham is cursed. Proslavery advocates embraced the story of Ham's curse, arguing that this biblical proclamation defined the generational place of blacks (Ham's presumed descendants) as servants to their white brothers. The point of departure for black readers of the Bible was the presumption of who precisely had been cursed. This was emphasized by the black Episcopal minister Alexander Crummell (1819–1898) in his 1850 essay "The Negro Race Not under a Curse." Crummell highlighted the misreading of this Scripture by many of his fellow white clergy, pointing out that it was not Ham who was inflicted with the curse of bondage but his son Canaan. With this clarification, black activists like Crummell asserted the connection of Africa to biblical antiquity and the history of civilization.

While America's prevailing black-white dichotomy of race originated in the white imagination, whites did not always see Africans simply as blacks. Early European traders recognized Africans according to their native group connections, and even early American slaveholders frequently expressed particular favor or disfavor for certain groups of Africans. However, by the close of the eighteenth century, whites had constructed a regularized racial vocabulary to signal the slave population. Of varied and distinct ethnic backgrounds, blacks in the New World found themselves referred to interchangeably as Africans, Ethiopians, Egyptians, Negroes, and blacks. This interchangeable vocabulary would be taken up by Africans and their descendants in America to forge an identity of self from a people whose histories had been otherwise disparate.

The works of early black authors such as Phillis Wheatley (1753?–1784), Prince Hall (1748–1807), and David Walker (1785–1830) especially exemplify this transformation. Wheatley, who was captured and sold into slavery when she was about seven or eight, alternates racial descriptions of herself and fellow black Americans. From her description of herself as an Ethiop from the land of "Egyptian gloom" ("To the University of Cambridge in New-England," p. 15) to her repeated reference to herself as the African muse, Wheatley demonstrates the linguistic transformation of self precipitated by the transatlantic slave trade. Any memory of her pre-slave self becomes buried in the racialized discourse of the master. While she remembers her native home and her parents, she emerges into adulthood seeing herself connected to fellow blacks on the continent that is her new home.

Wheatley's eighteenth-century contemporary Prince Hall also reveals in his writings the question of identity that blacks in the New World teased out. Hall, the founder of the secret society Prince Hall Masons, vacillated in his use of the terms "African" and "Ethiopian" as he addressed his black fellows of the African Lodge in 1797. Hall highlights the still-fluctuating vocabulary used to refer to first-generation African slaves and slaves of African descent. Hall's and Wheatley's references to blacks as a race demonstrate the formation of a black consciousness in America that struggled to connect Africans in the New World. In particular, their identification of Africans as Ethiopians and Egyptians and their emphasis on the significance of these ancient people in biblical history represent what would become a widespread cultural discourse of identity among African Americans. While the common use of "Egyptian" and "Ethiopian" to describe blacks subsided by the middle of the nineteenth century in America, those terms that substituted—Negroes, blacks, colored—are no less suggestive of a people united through a common modern experience and an ancient spiritual history. Nineteenth-century black writers and thinkers were as fervent as their black predecessors in their belief of a common ancient African past. To this end, the biblical promise of Psalms 68:31 that "Princes shall come out of Egypt; Ethiopia shall soon stretch out her hands unto God" became a defining discourse of identity for many nineteenth-century black leaders. In writings by early nineteenth-century activists such as Maria Stewart, Alexander Crummell, and David Walker, references to the Psalms verse can be found. The promise of this ancient passage came to signify the common destiny of the disparate groups of Africans who emerged into a race of people in the New World. Blacks were the Ethiopians destined to meet the favor of God and emerge out of bondage.

Before the United States ended its legal sanction of the African slave trade in 1808, the slave population was increasingly comprised of blacks born in America. Because the slave trade continued illegally to the dawn of the Civil War, the influence of native-born Africans on the slave population in America was long-standing. This continued importation of native Africans might have reminded generations of blacks of their ancestral ties to Africa; however, nineteenth-century black activists were primarily concerned with the condition and united interest of fellow blacks in the United States. Blacks appropriated and reworked America's racialized reading of the Bible and translated their common oppression into a rhetoric of racial identity and purpose. Whether free or on the plantation, antebellum blacks had come to define themselves as a race of people. This perception was not without its complications, for the notion of a distinct black race was compromised before seventeenth-century slave laws locked blacks into perpetual slavery.

BLACKS IN THE WHITE LITERARY IMAGINATION

From the time blacks arrived in Virginia as indentured servants in 1619 to the end of the seventeenth century, marriages between blacks and whites and blacks and Native Americans foretold the complex cultural and racial influences that shaped the identity of Africans in America when their status would be legally transformed to that of slaves. Laws enacted in the early colonies to prohibit unions between blacks and whites were designed to both clearly define the slave population as black and prevent racial mixing that would cloud the definition of whiteness. These laws represented a failed effort at the very moment of their inception, and as evidenced by the significant numbers of mulattos in the slave population at the end of the Civil War, these laws did not deter those white men who decided that female slaves could be forced into sex as well as servitude. Despite the prevalence of slaves who were living testaments to the fallibility of racist rhetoric and laws, the language of race prevailed.

One's blackness was not confirmed necessarily by the manifestation of dark skin but ultimately by lineage to one of African descent. Likewise, the appearance of white skin was not enough to confirm one's whiteness. In early America, however, blackness was assumed a very real marker of race, and it was a matter of great concern for some of America's most celebrated founding founders. Some colonial thinkers expressed sympathy for the enslaved Africans, but most expressed their anxiety and uncertainty over the threat posed by blacks living among whites. From Cotton Mather's (1663–1728) 1706 speculative essay "The Negro Christianized" to Thomas Jefferson's (1743–1826) 1787 *Notes on the State of Virginia,* one sees the persistent struggle of whites to clearly define Africans and their place. Jefferson's presumed scientific account of blacks is particularly striking for its resonance throughout antebellum proslavery rhetoric as well as its survival into the postbellum caricatures of

newly freed blacks. Jefferson defines Africans as a race, separate from and inferior to whites, and he expresses his deep conviction that blacks, whether free or enslaved, pose a threat to both the race (whites) and the nation. Most provocative is his depiction of blacks as a species of uncertain classification, void of meaningful depth of thought and emotion. This characterization would find its way into countless discourses on the rightness of black enslavement in the nineteenth century. Moreover, these racialized constructs of blackness found their way into the fictional sketches of early nineteenth-century white authors. In Washington Irving's (1783–1859) celebrated short story "The Legend of Sleepy Hollow" (published in the 1819–1820 collection *The Sketch Book*), Irving includes a sketch of local blacks in a tale that otherwise focuses on a fictional white backwoods community. His characterization of the local blacks, particularly the black messenger who is sent to deliver Ichabod's invitation, as a simpleminded, party-loving coxcomb, echoes the portrait of blacks painted in Jefferson's work.

Similarly, in *The Last of the Mohicans* (1826), the second in his series of Leatherstocking Tales, James Fenimore Cooper (1789–1851) embeds a narrative layer that hints at the threat of black blood infiltrating and diluting white purity. Cooper develops this subnarrative through the character Cora, the darker-skinned of the two sibling heroines. While Cora is a model of female virtue and sensibilities, her darkness is persistently cast against the fair skin of her sister and of the novel's hero, Hawkeye, who repeatedly reminds his companions that he is of pure white ancestry. Cora and Alice share the same father, a Scotsman; however, Cora's mother, deceased at the start of the novel, was the offspring of a West Indian planter and a slave mother. Although Cora is the more serious and endearing of the sisters and is loved equally by her father, her fate is a maidenly death. Cora's death and her burial alongside Uncas, the last rightful prince of the Mohican nation, symbolize the impossibility of generational race mixing in the emerging white American landscape that Cooper envisions. Cora further represents the tragic mulatto heroine, a prevalent figure in nineteenth-century fictional explorations of miscegenation. She, like most of her fictional contemporaries, can be awarded no other fate than death, particularly at the hands of white authors who cannot imagine a world not clearly divided into white and black. The survival of the mulatto, especially in a thriving regenerating environment, would undermine prevailing presumptions that whiteness is clearly identifiable. The fictional death of the mulatto restores racial and social order: blacks remain confirmed outsiders, and white privilege and purity are protected from those who might falsely assume whiteness.

Even in the fiction of sympathetic white abolitionists, generational mulatto survival was unimaginable. Though generally as beautiful and intelligent as their white counterparts, these characters inevitably succumb to their tragic flaw—being the product of miscegenation. The nineteenth-century abolitionist and women's rights activist Lydia Maria Child (1802–1880) offers an example of this formulaic narrative in her 1843 short story "Slavery's Pleasant Homes." Rosa, the mulatto heroine in this sketch, dies after successive beatings by her jealous slave master, and her mulatto lover, George, after confessing to killing Rosa's murderer, is hanged. The story offers a tragic depiction of slavery's evil, but it ends with the reassuring restoration of slaves and whites to their separate places. The story hints at no marital intentions for the remaining mulattos at the end of the sketch. Contrastingly, in *Uncle Tom's Cabin* (1852), one of America's most celebrated abolitionist texts, Harriet Beecher Stowe (1811–1896) grants her mulatto protagonists life and regeneration. Stowe grants this deviation and yet assures her white readers that miscegenation will not threaten white purity. This she manages through the strategic relocation of the mulatto couple, George and Eliza. They survive their trials and find themselves looking hopefully to the future; however, their future awaits them not in America but in Liberia. Stowe relocates the couple to the black nation-state, where they will presumably contribute to Liberia's rise to prominence. As for the unambiguously black in the narrative, they remain in America. Uncle Tom has died by the novel's end, but his children choose to remain in the South, loyal to the young white master who has guarded over them.

Popularized depictions of blacks as lighthearted, childlike servants served the rhetoric of many proslavery advocates. By the mid-1800s, however, the reality of Haiti's successful slave revolt and insurgencies such as Nat Turner's 1831 rebellion in Virginia and Denmark Vesey's 1822 uprising in South Carolina incited more serious and threatening images of blacks in the imaginations of white writers. These revolts signaled the tenuous power relationship between master and slave, and they revealed the hyperbole in idyllic representations of the paternalistic master looking over his plantation estate and his dependent, fun-loving slave charges. As Herman Melville (1819–1891) suggested in his 1855 fictionalization of a slave revolt at sea, when presented with a viable opportunity for freedom, the seemingly docile slave can be moved to inexorable acts of violence and deception. "Benito Cereno" is the tale of an insurrection led by the seemingly faithful slave Babo, who leads the transported Africans in the overthrow of the white captain, Don Benito Cereno, and his white crew. Babo symbolizes the haunting image of blacks that lay just beneath the surface of the reassuring images of black docility painted by writers like Irving and Cooper. Intelligent and calculating, Babo hints at the slave's dormant but ever-present spirit of independence and, most alarmingly, its unpredictable potential for unleashing. Blacks like Babo would be painted as merciless killers, and as in Melville's tale, they would come to symbolize the violent, uncontrolled black threatening white civility, safety, and prosperity. The images of Melville's fictional insurrectionist, Babo, and Stowe's pacifist, Uncle Tom, capture the contrasting discourse of blackness in the white imagination. It is a contrast that hints at the dichotomy of white desire and white fear—the desire to lord over a needful, compliant black underling and the fear of the vengeful, noncompliant spirit that lurks so close to the surface.

BLACK VISIONS OF BLACKNESS

Herman Melville's fictional depiction of the savage, freedom-seeking black deviates significantly from a similar tale of a slave insurrection at sea published two years earlier. *The Heroic Slave,* Frederick Douglass's (1818–1895) 1853 fictionalization of an actual slave insurrection, constructs a black hero whose use of violence is judicious. Douglass's hero is named for the real-life insurrectionist Madison Washington, who led the successful overthrow of a slave ship destined to deliver him, along with other slaves, to a New Orleans slave port. While Douglass's heroic liberator does not shrink from the use of violence, he manages to orchestrate an insurrection that leaves only two whites dead. He does not seek reckless revenge but rather holds the whites captive until the slaves have secured their freedom. Douglass's restrained hero is a deliberate construction, answering white anxieties about their safety in a nation of free blacks. Similarly, in Frank Webb's novel *The Garies and Their Friends* (1857), Webb does not shrink from showing his black characters resorting to violence against their white persecutors. In a pivotal episode, members of this fictional middle-class black community find themselves threatened by a white immigrant mob. Although Webb has framed his fictional black characters around mid-nineteenth-century paradigms of middle-class gentility, they energetically embrace arms to protect themselves and their community.

Webb, like Douglass, must perform a delicate juggling act: while asserting the revolutionary spirit of his black characters, he must be careful not to paint them as irrational and easily provoked to violence. Webb's success in this regard is due in great part to his choice of leader. Although the hardworking Mr. Ellis would have seemed a likely choice to lead his community against the murderous white mob, Webb elects the wealthy black entrepreneur Mr. Walters. Walters, the wealthiest black man in the community, offers his lavish home as a fortress during the violence. He further stands as the central organizing force in the community's efforts to defend itself. A man of intelligence and means, acquainted with the conventions and sensibilities esteemed in Anglo-American society, Walters is reminiscent of the stately patriarchs who thoughtfully led colonists into resistance against their mother country. Madison Washington and Mr. Walters dispel representations of blacks as recklessly violent and lacking in foresight; however, it is through Webb's fictional hero that one finds the nationalist visionary. Mr. Walters leads his community through the crisis of the race riot, but his significance to the community is far-reaching. Walters is wealthy, but he is not the Emersonian individualist. He is a man in and of the community, and his hope is to see young black boys like Kinch and Charlie mature into men of means, able to take care of themselves and offer aid to others. Walters is committed to helping fellow blacks, for he understands that even free blacks in the North must band together to find economic and social prosperity.

In his novel *Blake; or, The Huts of America,* Martin R. Delany (1812–1885) echoes Frank Webb's nationalist message. Delany was well known in abolitionist circles for his interest in a black nation-state. This was a vision that Delany held into the post-Emancipation era. Published in 1859, *Blake* allows Delany a prewar fictional journey to a campaign for emancipation that sprang from a visionary slave. Delany's hero-insurrectionist does not limit his plans to the local population; instead Blake has devised a strategy to unite slaves beyond the borders of the United States. The success of Blake's insurrection extends beyond just the freedom of a handful of slaves. Blake's vision promises freedom for all blacks in bondage and further promises the foundation of an international alliance of blacks.

Without trepidation, nineteenth-century black authors were willing to paint their male heroes in the image of stereotypical physical blackness. Dark-skinned and wooly haired, heroes such as Madison Washington, Mr. Walters, and Blake are unmistakably black by the conventions of their time. Ironically, however, this confirmation of blackness is not so generously awarded black fictional heroines. In general, early black writers resisted giving fictional life to unambiguously black female heroines. As in the case

of Madison Washington's fictional wife, black heroines were often left absent of any detailed physical description. In other cases, such as the wife of Delany's hero, Blake, they were noted for their distinctness from both blacks and whites. Nineteenth-century fiction by blacks often echoed the tragic mulatto figure of white-authored works, and the female protagonist was usually sacrificed for this role. In William Wells Brown's (1815–1884) controversial 1853 novel *Clotel,* the heroine, Clotel, highlights the often melodramatic end these women met. In Brown's narrative, Clotel and her sister, Althesa, are the offspring of Thomas Jefferson and his mulatto servant Currer. Mother and daughters will meet tragic ends, and the one surviving granddaughter of the Jefferson-Currer union relocates to France in hopes of a viable homeland. Similarly, in Harriet Wilson's (1808–c. 1870) *Our Nig* (1859) and Hannah Crafts's *Bondwoman's Narrative* (c. 1850s), the authors relate stories of mulatto protagonists who suffer alienation and abuse that lead to their early deaths.

It is in postwar narratives that black authors began to represent their mulatto heroines more optimistically. The tragic mulatto heroine would not disappear in post–Civil War black literature and would survive into the twentieth century. However, as demonstrated in Frances E. W. Harper's (1825–1911) *Minnie's Sacrifice* (1869), black authors began to expand the literary possibilities for these heroines. Even though Minnie dies an early death, this mulatto heroine has not suffered the alienation of her fictional predecessors. This narrative phenomenon became more prevalent in the late nineteenth century, but Webb's antebellum novel prefigures this shift. Although Mrs. Garie, the main mulatto protagonist, meets a tragic and violent end, her near-white daughter, Emily, marries into the black Ellis household and becomes a happy member of the thriving black Philadelphia community. As Harper's later nineteenth-century works demonstrate, mulatto heroines were no longer restricted to symbolic representations of the sins of the master. Like Minnie, they came to represent the integral place of all shades of black in shaping the story of those in America who fell under the monolithic identity called black.

See also "Benito Cereno"; *Clotel;* Miscegenation; Slavery

BIBLIOGRAPHY

Primary Work

Wheatley, Phillis. *Collected Works of Phillis Wheatley.* Edited by John Shields. New York: Oxford University Press, 1988.

Secondary Works

Appiah, Kwame Anthony. *In My Father's House: Africa in the Philosophy of Culture.* New York: Oxford University Press, 1992.

Davis, F. James. *Who Is Black? One Nation's Definition.* University Park: Pennsylvania State University Press, 1991.

Eltis, David, Stephen D. Behrendt, and David Richardson. "Patterns in the Transatlantic Slave Trade, 1662–1867: New Indications of African Origins of Slaves Arriving in the Americas." In *Black Imagination and the Middle Passage,* edited by Maria Diedrich, pp. 21–32. New York: Oxford University Press, 1999.

Fanon, Frantz. *Black Skin, White Masks.* Translated by Charles Lam Markmann. New York: Grove Press, 1967.

Ferber, Abby L. *White Man Falling: Race, Gender, and White Supremacy.* New York: Rowman and Littlefield, 1999.

Franklin, John Hope, and Alfred A. Moss Jr. *From Slavery to Freedom.* 6th ed. New York: McGraw-Hill, 1988.

Fredrickson, George M. *The Black Image in the White Mind.* Hanover, N.H.: Wesleyan University Press, 1987.

Gossett, Thomas F. *Race: The History of an Idea in America.* New ed. New York: Oxford University Press, 1997.

Higginbotham, A. Leon, Jr. *In the Matter of Color.* New York: Oxford University Press, 1980.

hooks, bell. "Representations of Whiteness." In her *Black Looks: Race and Representation,* pp. 165–178. Boston: South End Press, 1992.

Lipsitz, George. *The Possessive Investment in Whiteness.* Philadelphia: Temple University Press, 1998.

Morrison, Toni. *Playing in the Dark: Whiteness and the Literary Imagination.* New York: Vintage, 1992.

Nelson, Dana D. *The Word in Black and White: Reading "Race" in American Literature, 1638–1867.* New York: Oxford University Press, 1993.

Roediger, David R. *The Wages of Whiteness: Race and the Making of the American Working Class.* New York: Verso, 1993.

Sollors, Werner. *Neither Black nor White Yet Both.* Cambridge, Mass.: Harvard University Press, 1997.

Webster, Yehudi O. *The Racialization of America.* New York: St. Martin's Press, 1992.

West, Elizabeth J. "Black Female Protagonists and the Abstruse Racialized Self in Antebellum African American Fiction." *Womanist* 3, no. 2, and 4, no. 1 (2001–2002): 50–56.

Williamson, Joel. *New People: Miscegenation and Mulattoes in the United States.* Baton Rouge: Louisiana State University Press, 1995.

Elizabeth J. West

BLAKE

The first though fragmentary appearance in 1859 of *Blake; or, The Huts of America,* by Martin R. Delany (1812–1885), marks an important milestone in the development of the literature of black America: it is the first novel by a black writer published in the United States. The historical significance of the novel has been somewhat obscured, in part by a complicated publication history. The novel is significant, however, not only for its place in literary history but also for the way its literary themes are interwoven with complex commentary on wide-ranging social debates of the time and for the polemical ideas its prominent author espouses in the novel.

COMPLEXITIES IN PUBLICATION AND PLOT

The complexity surrounding *Blake* arises in part from its idiosyncratic publication history. The novel's incomplete debut came with the January 1859 issue of the *Anglo-African Magazine.* In that issue excerpts from chapters 28, 29, and 30 appear, and an introduction details the novel as spanning eighty chapters. The following issue, February 1859, provides the first chapters of the novel, and chapters continued to appear monthly until July 1859, when publication ceased abruptly with chapter 23. More than two years later, in November 1861, the magazine, by then called the *Weekly Anglo-African,* began a serial publication of *Blake* which started with the first chapters and continued straight through with subsequent chapters until the serialization presumably ended with the novel's conclusion sometime late in May 1862; however, the final issues of the magazine are missing, and thus the novel remains incomplete. The latest surviving issue of the magazine carries the novel through chapter 74, leaving scholars to estimate, based upon the *Anglo-African's* early information about the novel, that six chapters are missing. Still without its concluding chapters, *Blake* was eventually published in 1970 with an introduction by Floyd J. Miller; this was its first publication in book form.

Just as *Blake's* complicated publication history has evoked scholarly investigation and conversation, so too has the complex nature of the narrative itself allowed for a range of interpretation, due in part to the novel's breadth of content and theme that draws from Delany's personal experiences as well as from slave narratives and other literary forms. The novel opens with the sale of the slave Maggie and her subsequent removal to Cuba by her father and owner, Colonel Stephen Franks. Following Maggie's departure for Cuba, her husband and the protagonist of the novel,

Martin R. Delany. © CORBIS

Carolus Henrico Blacus, known by his slave name of Henry Holland, returns to the Franks' plantation from a business expedition made on the colonel's behalf and finds his wife gone. Although Henry too has been living as a slave, readers come to know that he is a West Indian who was enslaved under false pretenses. Upon discovering Maggie's sale, Henry realizes that life as a slave is no longer possible for him, so he runs away, beginning a campaign throughout the South in which he lays the foundation for a slave revolt. The first part of the novel ends with Henry's completion of his travels through the southern United States and his plans to journey to Cuba. In the second part of the novel, Henry, now known as Blake, arrives in Cuba and orchestrates his wife's freedom. Then, with the help of the historically famous Cuban liberation poet Placido, Blake extends the scope of his planned insurrection into Cuba by planning the overthrow of the Cuban government in order to prevent the United States from annexing Cuba as a slave territory.

THE PAN-AFRICAN COMMUNITY

The broad geographic scope of the novel—from the United States to Canada to Cuba to Africa—signals the importance of the Pan-African community, one of the themes upon which scholars most widely comment. An overarching goal of Blake's travels is the unification of the black community, for he envisions the power and potential of racial unity bringing about radical political change: the cessation of slavery, including the suppression of U.S. attempts to annex Cuba. Blake's attempts to unite the larger black community commence more locally in the southern United States with his efforts to create a network of black insurrectionists located throughout the slaveholding South. While Maggie's sale immediately instigates Henry's efforts, several contemporary political debates inform the larger range of his mission of uniting those blacks held in the bondage of slavery. For Delany, the emergence in the 1850s of arguments advocating the reopening of the African slave trade provided a backdrop for the examination of the possibility of violent revolt by slaves. Although only a minority of the southern population supported a reopening of international slave trade, the issue had several prominent and outspoken advocates, including the editors and political activists James D. B. DeBow and Leonidas W. Spratt as well as Governor James Adams of South Carolina. The Southern Commercial Conventions (1855–1859) became primary forums for discussing the topic. Proponents argued that reviving the international slave trade would lower the costs of slaves, thereby raising the profits from products of slave labor, further cementing slavery's position in the South. *Blake* enters this discussion by emphasizing the urgency of ridding the nation completely of all forms and vestiges of slavery, by violence if necessary. A second important political context of the novel is the United States Supreme Court's *Dred Scott* decision in 1857 that held that blacks were not citizens and could not be assured of freedom even in states in which slavery was illegal. This ruling provides a significant backdrop for Delany's almost separatist call for a unified black revolt: in light of the failure of white laws, blacks may have to choose violence as the only means to attaining their freedom. In *Blake*, Delany reaffirms that black freedom will have to be primarily the result of black effort, without the aid of white abolitionists or the white legal system.

While the first part of the novel focuses on Henry's efforts to organize the black community in the southern United States, the Pan-African schematics of the novel reach much further. When *Blake* first appeared in 1859, conflicts over the annexation of Cuba were changing the debates raging over slavery. Due in part to philosophies of manifest destiny held by some Americans, the 1850s spawned a movement aimed at the U.S. acquisition of Cuba. As early as 1848 President James K. Polk, supported by annexationists

This speech, taken from Blake's sixty-first chapter, "The Grand Council," follows the Cuban poet Placido's discourse on the wealth and resources of Africa and its people. The speaker, Madame Cordora, a wealthy and influential Cuban mulatta, expresses her new understanding of the importance of black initiative and a Pan-African vision for the leaders of the uprising:

Although I thought I had no prejudices, I never before felt as proud of my black as I did of my white blood. I can readily see that the blacks compose an important element in the commercial and social relations of the world. Thank God for even this night's demonstrations, if we do no more. How sensibly I feel, that a people never entertain proper opinions of themselves until they begin to act for themselves.

Delany, Blake, p. 262.

in Cuba eager to secure slavery's hold within Cuba as well as U.S. planters, attempted to purchase Cuba from Spain, an offer the United States repeated in 1854. After annexation Cuba was expected to be an extension of the American South, expanding the interests of slavers. For those invested in the push to expand slavery, Cuban annexation was justified in part as a response to the potential "Africanization" of Cuba, an increase in the freedoms allowed blacks living there. In Blake, Delany draws upon the controversy surrounding the Cuban debate, depicting the time as being strategic for unified black action. As the "Commander in Chief of the Army of Emancipation" (p. 256), Blake capitalizes upon the political instability of Cuba in order to stage an armed rebellion aimed at instituting a new government by the blacks themselves.

Delany's inclusion of the debates surrounding Cuban annexation gestures toward his belief in the importance of solidarity among the African diaspora: only by looking out for the interests of the entire African community will any plans for uplift succeed. Delany highlights this concept in the novel in a scene in which a meeting of the key members of the "Army of Emancipation" occurs. One of the attendees, Madame Cordora, an affluent mulatta, questions Placido's use of the term "Ethiopia's sons," remarking, "Although identified together, we are not all Ethiopians" (p. 260). Delany here uses Placido to emphasize the ways in which the conditions of all members of the African race are inherently woven together. Placido clarifies his position for Madame Cordora by explaining that "colored persons, whatever the complexion, can only obtain an equality with whites by the descendants of Africa of unmixed blood. . . . The instant that an equality of the blacks with the whites is admitted, we being the descendants of the two, must be acknowledged the equals of both" (pp. 260, 261). Additionally Placido demonstrates the extent of Delany's Pan-African vision by proceeding to outline the rich resources found in Africa, describing that, once these resources are correctly utilized, the African "race and country will at once rise to the first magnitude of importance" (p. 261). These comments pointedly lay the philosophical foundation for the culmination of Delany's Pan-African proposal: emigration to Africa. Early in the 1850s Delany advocated emigration to Central or South America with the foundation of a new "black" nation as opposed to the more prevalent push for emigration to Liberia, which was rejected by other African American leaders as well; however, after a trip to Africa in 1859 and 1860, Delany began to make plans for establishing an African settlement, a place for the permanent unification of the African community under black leadership as suggested in Blake.

LEADING THE RACE

Black leadership is an important and recurring theme for Delany; therefore it is not accidental that in his novel he utilizes a fully black, educated leader in Blake to unite the African diaspora. Although Delany agreed with other African American and abolitionist activists that African Americans were in need of leaders who would encourage the recovery of mental and moral stamina lost through the degradation of slavery, he disagreed about how best to reach those goals. Delany believed strongly in the prominence of black leadership. For Delany, efforts aimed at black uplift should be instigated and sustained primarily by blacks themselves, as he fictionalizes in Blake; white abolitionists should have a secondary role.

Delany's characterization of Blake as a "fully black" revolutionist works on several levels. Engaged in debates with other prominent African American leaders, such as Frederick Douglass (1818–1895), over the leadership qualities most needed to represent the race, Delany may have fictionalized his assertions in Blake. Some critics, such as Robert S. Levine, have proposed that Blake's racial status argues for the fitness of the fully black Delany to himself be the representative leader for African Americans. Placido's comments on the important role of Africans of "unmixed blood" emphasize a belief in the need for leaders of unmixed blood to guide the race.

A DISTINCT RESPONSE

On another level Delany's use of a hero of unmixed blood also counters abolitionist literary stereotypes of his time that often portrayed mulatto rather than racially pure blacks as having the skills and characteristics needed for leadership. In fact, rather than a response to general literary stereotypes, Delany's *Blake* may specifically be a response to the popularity and acceptance received by Harriet Beecher Stowe's *Uncle Tom's Cabin* (1852). In *Blake*, Delany revises the portrayal of black manhood given by Stowe (1811–1896) by allowing his fully black hero to participate in a violent response to the oppression of slavery. While Stowe avoids characterizations of insurrection and violence, Delany, in *Blake*, recasts the most notable slave revolt in the United States, Nat Turner's bloody rebellion of 1831, and broadens the scope of the insurrection to suggest that the growing population of black slaves could be a formidable foe if organized and coalesced into a unified army. Among other points of contention, Delany also questions Stowe's portrayal of "white" religion as a means of bringing comfort to blacks, but instead of dismissing religion altogether, Delany allows Blake to question religion and ultimately to revise the religious thinking espoused by the white community—in effect, to formulate his own religious beliefs.

Delany's response to the portrayal of religion in *Uncle Tom's Cabin* illustrates his approach to other American social issues facing blacks: African Americans must chart their own course and actively participate in meeting the social, political, and moral challenges facing their community. While the nonextant status of the novel's ending problematizes certain elements of interpretation, other thematics are clear. In *Blake*, Delany suggests that whether responding to a corrupt economic system or to a moral system that values intemperance and a lack of self-control among slaves, African Americans must evaluate societal mores in order to construct beliefs and philosophies that will meet the specific needs of their community. The primacy of communal goals is emphasized by the final words of the last extant chapter of the novel. One of the female members of Blake's inner circle of black leaders exclaims, "My lot is cast with that of my race, whether for weal or woe" (p. 313). Her comments spark the haunting reply that ends the novel: "Woe be unto those devils of whites, I say!" (p. 313). These comments encapsulate the heart of *Blake*'s message of the imperative need for black community and black leadership.

See also Abolitionist Writing; Blacks; Borders; *The Confessions of Nat Turner;* Manifest Destiny; Proslavery Writing; Slave Narratives; Slave Rebellions; Slavery; *Uncle Tom's Cabin*

BIBLIOGRAPHY

Primary Work

Delany, Martin R. *Blake; or, The Huts of America.* 1859, 1861–1862. Boston: Beacon Press, 1970.

Secondary Works

Bernstein, Barton J. "Southern Politics and Attempts to Reopen the African Slave Trade." *Journal of Negro History* 51, no. 1 (1966): 16–35.

Ernest, John. "The White Gap and the Approaching Storm: Martin R. Delany's *Blake.*" In his *Resistance and Reformation in Nineteenth-Century African-American Literature: Brown, Wilson, Jacobs, Delany, Douglass, and Harper,* pp. 109–139. Jackson: University Press of Mississippi, 1995.

Levine, Robert S. *Martin Delany, Frederick Douglass, and the Politics of Representative Identity.* Chapel Hill: University of North Carolina Press, 1997.

Miller, Floyd J. "Introduction." In *Blake; or, The Huts of America,* by Martin R. Delany, pp. xi–xxix. Boston: Beacon Press, 1970.

Okker, Patricia. "William Gilmore Simms, Martin R. Delany, and Serial/Sectional Politics." In her *Social Stories: The Magazine Novel in Nineteenth-Century America,* pp. 79–108. Charlottesville: University of Virginia Press, 2003.

Reid-Pharr, Robert. "Violent Ambiguity: Martin Delany, Bourgeois Sadomasochism, and the Production of a Black National Masculinity." In *Representing Black Men,* edited by Marcellus Blount and George P. Cunningham, pp. 73–94. New York: Routledge, 1996.

Sundquist, Eric J. "Melville, Delany, and New World Slavery." In his *To Wake the Nations: Race in the Making of American Literature,* pp. 135–224. Cambridge, Mass.: Belknap Press of Harvard University Press, 1993.

Sundquist, Eric J. "Slavery, Revolution, and the American Renaissance." In *The American Renaissance Reconsidered: Selected Papers from the English Institute, 1982–83,* edited by Walter Benn Michaels and Donald E. Pease, pp. 1–33. Baltimore: Johns Hopkins University Press, 1985.

Shelley R. Block

THE BLITHEDALE ROMANCE

Nathaniel Hawthorne's *The Blithedale Romance* (1852) is complex in form and content, and a key reason for its complexity is the intriguing relationship between Hawthorne (1804–1864) and Miles Coverdale, the bachelor-poet narrator who describes his membership in the utopian community of Blithedale "twelve long years" (p. 837) after it occurred. This is the only novel that Hawthorne wrote with a first-person narrator, and because he spent seven months at Brook Farm, a cooperative community begun in 1841 in West Roxbury, Massachusetts, he thereby encourages readers to identify him with Coverdale.

Hawthorne's depiction of Coverdale is, however, intimate and detached, sympathetic and ironic. He exposes his narrator's faults—a paralyzing self-absorption, a tendency to inspect and probe the hearts and minds of other persons, an inability to sustain genuine commitments—as well as his appealing qualities of stumbling humor, earnest if sometimes awkward sincerity, and, for a time at least, hopefulness that the world can be made new through communities grounded in socialist values and principles. The novel's complicated point of view and its subtle, shifting tone make the question of Hawthorne's attitudes toward Brook Farm and social reform both fascinating and elusive, suggestive yet difficult to pin down—which is how Hawthorne wanted it.

HAWTHORNE, BROOK FARM, AND REFORM

Hawthorne's *Twice-Told Tales,* a collection of eighteen stories that had appeared in periodicals, was published in March 1837. He sent a copy to the educator and writer Elizabeth Peabody, who was friendly with the Mannings (the family of Hawthorne's mother) in Salem, Massachusetts, and in November 1837 the thirty-three-year-old struggling short story writer made his first call on the Peabody family. He met Elizabeth's sister, Sophia, whom he courted and to whom he became secretly engaged.

Hawthorne became intent on finding work that would enable him to marry Sophia and enjoy extended periods of time to concentrate on his literary art. From 1839 to 1840 he held a position in the Boston Custom House, but he resigned (the work was tedious) in November 1840. In this same month he decided to join the Brook Farm community, which the Unitarian minister and scholar George Ripley and other reformers planned to establish in the West Roxbury countryside, a few miles outside Boston.

Ripley was also one of the founders of the Transcendental Club. Begun in 1836 as Hedge's Club—the name derived from F. H. Hedge, a scholar and Unitarian minister from Maine—its members included Ralph Waldo Emerson, the minister and reformer Theodore Parker, the writer Margaret Fuller, the teacher-philosopher Amos Bronson Alcott, and others whom Hawthorne knew.

Hawthorne's relation to transcendentalism was marginal. But he was familiar with transcendentalists and their activities in Boston, Concord, and Cambridge, and thus he was in a prime position to consider and reflect upon the reform movements and utopian experiments that many were discussing and debating in the area. Hawthorne introduces and explores a host of transcendentalist-inspired ideas and projects in the utopian setting he presents in *The Blithedale Romance,* most notably women's rights and prison reform.

The "woman question" had emerged as a by-product of antislavery agitation. When the abolitionists Angelina and Sarah Grimké of South Carolina were ridiculed and mobbed in the 1830s for presuming to speak in public, they were obliged to proclaim and defend their rights as women. The attacks on the Grimkés' "unnatural" behavior have affinities with the harsh terms that Hollingsworth uses in *The Blithedale Romance* to indict women who stray from functioning as man's sympathizer and helpmate.

Prison reform engaged such stalwart figures as the writer and abolitionist Samuel Gridley Howe and Theodore Parker, both of whom made recommendations for improving prisons and transforming criminals into upright citizens. Hollingsworth shares their concerns, though Hawthorne does not specify the type of prison reform that his vehement but rigid character espouses. Exactly what Hollingsworth wants matters less to Hawthorne than the fact that this liberal reformer cannot tolerate opposition or disagreement.

The reformers of Hawthorne's era who launched utopian communities, fought against slavery, campaigned for women's rights, and advocated prison reform made American society better than it was. But for Hawthorne, reform all too frequently led to fanaticism and exploitation of others, as Hollingsworth's conduct reveals. It brought with it, he believed, disturbing consequences for persons and their relationships that reformers failed to anticipate and cared little about.

HAWTHORNE'S EXPERIENCES AT BROOK FARM

Soon after Hawthorne arrived at Brook Farm on 12 April 1841, he and the others were busy chopping and carrying wood, cutting hay, and plowing and planting the fields. In his first letter to Sophia,

13 April 1841, Hawthorne assured her, "Think that I am gone before, to prepare a home for my Dove, and will return for her, all in good time" (*Letters,* p. 527). He signed his first letter to his sisters Elizabeth and Louisa (who were unsympathetic to his Brook Farm foray), "Nath. Hawthorne, Ploughman" (*Letters,* p. 540). He said he enjoyed the countryside, the routine, and the fellowship. He marveled at the tasks he accomplished, exclaiming in a 16 April letter to Sophia, "Thy husband has milked a cow!!!" (*Letters,* p. 531).

Hawthorne's signs of discontent are evident early, however, as when he apologized to Sophia on 22 April for his "abominable" handwriting—the result of having chopped wood and turned a grindstone for long hours. "It is an endless surprise to me," he admitted, "how much work there is to be done in the world" (*Letters,* p. 533). On 1 June, Hawthorne confessed that he had been "too busy to write thee a long letter. . . . I think this present life of mine gives me an antipathy to pen and ink, even more than my Custom House experience did" (*Letters,* p. 545); and he went on to bemoan the amount of fatiguing labor.

"Thou and I must form other plans for ourselves," Hawthorne said to Sophia in a 22 August letter, "for I can see few or no signs that Providence purposes to give us a home here" (*Letters,* p. 563). In several letters to Sophia he referred to his bondage and enslavement at Brook Farm, and in one, 3 September, he went so far as to declare that "the real Me was never an associate of the community" (*Letters,* p. 567).

By August, Hawthorne had become a boarder, paying his own way (four dollars per week), and he thereby freed himself from manual labor. He spent the first three weeks of September at home in Salem but was back at Brook Farm for a few final weeks. Hawthorne left Brook Farm for good in November and returned to Salem. In July 1842 he married Sophia and settled in the Old Manse in Concord. After several years there, in October 1845, Hawthorne, Sophia, and their daughter Una (born in 1844) moved

Brook Farm, 1844. Painting by Josiah Wolcott. THE MASSACHUSETTS HISTORICAL SOCIETY

to Salem, and in April 1846 he accepted an appointment as surveyor in the Salem Custom House, where he served for three years. During the period 1850–1852—the peak of his career—Hawthorne completed *The Scarlet Letter, The House of the Seven Gables,* and *The Blithedale Romance,* as well as the story collection *The Snow-Image, and Other Twice-Told Tales.*

We think of these first three works as novels, but Hawthorne's own term, as he noted in the prefaces he wrote for each of them, was "romance." To an extent Hawthorne sought to invoke and develop the elements of the traditional romance associated with chivalry, magic, and legend, a story in verse or in prose that presents strange events in a remote or enchanted setting or landscape. But he found the term valuable for the freedom it allowed in contrast to the tradition of the novel. As he explains in his preface to *The House of the Seven Gables,* a novel "is presumed to aim at a very minute fidelity, not merely to the possible, but to the probable and ordinary course of man's experience." A romance, while it be faithful to "the truth of the human heart—has fairly a right to present that truth under circumstances . . . of the writer's own choosing or creation. . . . he may so manage his atmospherical medium as to bring out or mellow the lights and deepen and enrich the shadows of the picture" (*Novels,* p. 351).

Novel and romance are not really, for Hawthorne, opposed to or radically at odds with one another. "Romance" for him opened up possibilities for risk-taking and exploration, for strategic indulgence of the strange, supernatural, and seemingly impossible, if these would lend greater dramatic power to his narrative. Hawthorne took what the novel offered—the expansiveness of the form, the focus on character, the unfolding of a plot amid familiar kinds of locales and scenes—even as he dared to break free from its constraints, making forays into fanciful and allegorical dimensions of plot, character, and implication.

The English edition of *The Blithedale Romance* was published by Chapman and Hall on 7 July 1852; the American edition was published by the Boston firm of Ticknor, Reed, and Fields on July 14. Ticknor's first printing of 5,000 copies sold out, and the book went into a second printing of 2,350 copies in late July. But interest in it then declined. Hawthorne's meager record of achievement after *The Blithedale Romance* deeply disappointed him, and the slowing sales of his books exacerbated his lifelong worries about money, leading him to fear he would die in a poorhouse.

BROOK FARM IN *THE BLITHEDALE ROMANCE*

When Hawthorne wrote *The Blithedale Romance* he drew upon his own experiences in 1841 and his observations of Brook Farm's history in the years after he departed from it, especially the phase when its members aligned themselves with the utopian principles of Charles Fourier, a French socialist. The central figure in promoting Fourierism in the United States was the journalist Albert Brisbane. He outlined Fourier's ideas in *Social Destiny of Man* (1840), *A Concise Exposition of the Doctrine of Association* (1843), and in a regular column for Horace Greeley's paper, the *New York Tribune,* from 1842 to 1844.

Fourier emphasized not the city, town, or single farm or farms but rather the "phalanx," a well-organized community of sixteen hundred persons, and the "phalanstery," a large building where life would be centered. He favored a multiple division of labor with many tasks and occupations and with each person belonging to thirty to forty work groups. No person would spend much time in any one group, and no particular job therefore would become onerous. The precise planning of work, formation of work teams, timetables—these were features of community life that Brook Farm had not previously adopted.

The Brook Farm members shifted to Fourierism because the community was in financial trouble. There was no local market for its trade goods, and the cost of the interest payments on loans was a heavy burden. Something drastic had to be done, and by early 1843 the community was already diversifying work to make it more productive and profitable, requiring sixty hours of labor per week from each adult, planning a central building, and initiating efforts at fund-raising.

The final blow to Brook Farm came on the evening of 3 March 1846 when fire destroyed the phalanstery just as it neared completion. This project had begun in summer 1844; the building was 175 feet in length and three stories high, with a dining hall designed to seat 300–400 persons, and it was paid for by a loan of $7,000 at high interest. There was no insurance policy, and the financial loss was devastating. Ripley and his wife left in September 1847, and the Brook Farm Association was dissolved the next month.

In Hawthorne's preface, where he identifies his novel as a "romance," he states that his "present concern with the Socialist community is merely to establish a theatre, a little removed from the highway of ordinary travel," upon which his characters can act without "too close a comparison with the actual events of real lives." He states that Brook Farm was "certainly, the most romantic episode" of his life; it was "essentially a day-dream, and yet a fact" and hence offers "an available foothold between fiction and reality" (*Novels*, p. 633–634).

Prompted by the preface, Hawthorne's readers have often assumed that his fictional characters are modeled on real people. One scholar has remarked with dismay that readers have been unable to resist the temptation "to find prototypes in the Brook Farm community for the characters in *The Blithedale Romance*" (Crane, p. lxxv). But this temptation is built into the novel from the preface forward, as Hawthorne/Coverdale refers to Emerson, Fuller, transcendentalism, *The Dial*, Fourier, mesmerism, lyceum meetings, the *North American Review*, the California gold rush, the Mormon leader Joseph Smith, the literary critic Rufus Griswold, the Hungarian revolutionary Lajos Kossuth, and many other real persons and events. These references strongly imply that the novel's action should be interpreted in relation to the history of the 1840s and early 1850s—as though the imagined characters of *The Blithedale Romance* inhabit the world where Hawthorne and his readers reside.

Critics have worked diligently, for example, to locate the real-life model for Hollingsworth and have proposed a dozen or more possibilities, including George Ripley, Albert Brisbane, and Theodore Parker. The source for Hollingsworth may not have been a person whom Hawthorne knew at Brook Farm but rather someone whom many there admired—Charles Fourier. Hawthorne and his wife, Sophia, read Fourier's work in summer 1844, and a year later she complained that it was "abominable, immoral, religious, and void of all delicate sentiment." She added: "To make as much money and luxury and enjoyment out of man's lowest passions as possible,—this is the aim and end of his system. . . . My husband read the whole volume, and was entirely disgusted" (J. Hawthorne 1:268–269). In *The Blithedale Romance,* however, Hollingsworth himself—fiercely committed to his reform and no one else's—pronounces an angry judgment on Fourier, echoing the words that Sophia used in her letter.

Hawthorne believed that reformers like Hollingsworth crave to take possession of others and neutralize their individual agency. This skeptical view helps to account for the presence in *The Blithedale Romance* of mesmerism, a theory and practice of possession, influence, and domination that captivated as well as alarmed Hawthorne. The Austrian physician Franz Mesmer (1734–1815) described his theory of "animal magnetism" in the late eighteenth century, and the term "mesmerism" was associated with various forms of spiritualism, séances, and hypnotic experiments and cures. According to Hawthorne, mesmerists, while claiming they produced spiritual, physical, and emotional benefits, were in truth penetrating to the innermost sanctuary of the self, which no one should presume to violate.

As for Zenobia, some critics have confidently maintained that she is based on Margaret Fuller even as others have insisted she is not. Fuller did take part in early discussions about Brook Farm and visited it regularly. She conducted "conversations" there about the rights of women, and she possessed a self-dramatizing personality that Hawthorne may have drawn upon for his characterization of Zenobia. Some scholars have claimed that Hawthorne reveals his disdain for Fuller by engineering a dreadful fate for Zenobia. Those who have made this argument have cited Hawthorne's hostile portrait in his notebook, where he depicts Fuller as "a great humbug" (*Notebooks* 14:155–157). But this does not displace the fact that Zenobia is the most striking character in *The Blithedale Romance*. She has a radiant aura and acute intelligence yet lacks insight into the effects of her power on others and its meanings and implications for herself. Hawthorne represents Zenobia as a woman for whom independence is crucial yet who longs to defer to Hollingsworth and ally herself with his zealously prosecuted reform.

Hawthorne's use of the first-person form gives a degree of complication and depth to the characters of *The Blithedale Romance* that neither *The Scarlet Letter* nor *The House of the Seven Gables* possesses. The reader is drawn not only to explore the motives and moods of Zenobia, Hollingsworth, and Priscilla but must do so while also appraising the point of view (by turns insightful and blind, perceptive and self-deluded) of Coverdale, and beyond that, the point of view of the author himself. What Hawthorne composed is a novel that both tantalizes and at times frustrates the reader because the characters and meanings of the book do not stand still for study. Everything seems to be there for our inspection, yet then it all fades or blurs, like memories slipping away, and we have to struggle to regain the clarity of vision and understanding that for a few moments we thought we had. There is an extreme craft in the novel's operation that Hawthorne may have found both absorbing and disquieting. After *The Blithedale Romance* appeared, he set aside novel writing for nearly a decade, and critics have judged the book that broke his silence, *The Marble Faun* (1860), a mixed success at best.

CRITICAL RECEPTION

Hawthorne's most acute reader in the nineteenth century was Henry James, and in his 1879 book on Hawthorne for the English Men of Letters series, James both extols and criticizes *The Blithedale*

Romance. He singles out Zenobia as "the nearest approach" that Hawthorne made in all of his fiction "to the complete creation of a *person*" (p. 106). Yet James contends that the Blithedale community is too sketchy to serve as a sufficient context for the novel's characters, who remain too little related to Brook Farm/Blithedale and its ideals and goals: "The brethren of Brook Farm should have held themselves slighted rather than misrepresented, and have regretted that the admirable genius who for a while was numbered among them should have treated their institution mainly as a perch for starting upon an imaginative flight" (p. 108).

Following James's lead, later critics also expressed reservations about *The Blithedale Romance.* The influential literary and cultural historian Vernon Louis Parrington, in *Main Currents in American Thought* (1927–1930), judged the novel "thin and unreal" and summed up Hawthorne as "the extreme and finest expression of the refined alienation from reality that in the end palsied the creative mind of New England" (1:448, 450). In their book-length studies, Newton Arvin (1929) and Mark Van Doren (1949) reached similarly negative conclusions.

In *Politics and the Novel* (1957), Irving Howe moved the discussion forward by demonstrating that Hawthorne is not taking a position for or against Brook Farm/Blithedale. Instead, through the first-person narrator Coverdale, he is exploring what it meant to him as a setting that dramatizes the allure and peril of reform. As Howe implies, Hawthorne discloses his doubts about projects for social change but also his understanding of the desires that produce them, desires that are intensely real yet in conflict with others that are equally real and more powerful.

As Nina Baym has argued, Hawthorne's characters yearn to be more or other than they are, but when given an opportunity they replicate themselves in the new environment. They simultaneously flee from and return to the framework of the society that formed them and the basic structures of their personalities. "Though the characters in *The Blithedale Romance* seek to fashion "a new system of shared values and a new mode of serious purpose," says Richard H. Brodhead, they "belong to the world they oppose, so that the society they create ends by repeating and intensifying the features of the one they resist" (p. 99).

The most provocative critical studies of *The Blithedale Romance* since 1980 have focused on sexuality and gender. John N. Miller, for instance, has examined the dynamics of eroticism in the text. Hawthorne, he concludes, demonstrates that "erotic aspirations and desires generate an intense, insatiable yearning—an emptiness or incompleteness when such yearning remains unfulfilled, yet also, paradoxically, a fear of fulfillment and a self-tormenting pleasure in denying oneself one's objects of desire" (pp. 8–9). Benjamin Scott Grossberg, in a related analysis, has inquired into the conjunction of the novel and "a society whose sexual definitions" at mid-century "were crystallizing" (p. 7). "Rather than succumb to the new identities 'homosexual' and 'heterosexual,' rather than see himself as one of these odd, new, discrete animals," Coverdale seeks "to make Blithedale a community apart from them. Coverdale's Blithedale is a place of queer desire and queer gender, a place where the discrete categories of man, woman, heterosexual and homosexual are set up to be undermined" (p. 7).

The Blithedale Romance is distinctive among Hawthorne's work for its intersecting personal and political themes, its complex ironies, and its cast of characters, whose situations compel us yet whose motivations and feelings we feel we never entirely understand. Through this profound novel, Hawthorne scrutinizes the meanings of vocation and purposeful work; the relationship between the sexes; the responsibility of intellectuals for social change; the desire that many persons share for a life better than the one they have experienced; the disenchantment that follows when reformers realize they have not achieved their goals; and, perhaps most disquietingly of all, the mystery of persons and their relationships.

See also "The Birth-mark"; *The House of the Seven Gables;* Reform; The Romance; *The Scarlet Letter;* Transcendentalism; Utopian Communities

BIBLIOGRAPHY
Primary Works
Hawthorne, Nathaniel. *The French and Italian Notebooks.* Edited by Thomas Woodson. The Centenary Edition of the Works of Nathaniel Hawthorne, vol. 14. Columbus: Ohio State University Press, 1980.

Hawthorne, Nathaniel. *Letters, 1813–1843.* Edited by Thomas Woodson. The Centenary Edition of the Works of Nathaniel Hawthorne, vol. 15. Columbus: Ohio State University Press, 1984.

Hawthorne, Nathaniel. *Novels.* New York: Library of America, 1983.

Secondary Works
Arvin, Newton. *Hawthorne.* Boston: Little, Brown, 1929.

Baym, Nina. *The Shape of Hawthorne's Career.* Ithaca, N.Y.: Cornell University Press, 1976.

Berlant, Lauren. "Fantasies of Utopia in *The Blithedale Romance*." *American Literary History* 1, no. 1 (1989): 30–62.

Brodhead, Richard H. *Hawthorne, Melville, and the Novel.* Chicago: University of Chicago Press, 1976.

Crane, Maurice Aaron. "A Textual and Critical Edition of Hawthorne's *Blithedale Romance*." Ph.D. diss., University of Illinois, 1953.

Grossberg, Benjamin Scott. "'The Tender Passion Was Very Rife among Us': Coverdale's Queer Utopia and *The Blithedale Romance*." *Studies in American Fiction* 28, no. 1 (2000): 3–25.

Guarneri, Carl. *The Utopian Alternative: Fourierism in Nineteenth-Century America.* Ithaca, N.Y.: Cornell University Press, 1991.

Hawthorne, Julian. *Nathaniel Hawthorne and His Wife: A Biography.* 2 vols. Boston: Houghton Mifflin, 1884.

Howe, Irving, *Politics and the Novel.* Cleveland: World, 1957.

Hutner, Gordon. *Secrets and Sympathy: Forms of Disclosure in Hawthorne's Novels.* Athens: University of Georgia Press, 1988.

James, Henry. *Hawthorne.* 1879. Ithaca, N.Y.: Cornell University Press, 1966.

Levine, Robert S. *Conspiracy and Romance: Studies in Brockden Brown, Cooper, Hawthorne, and Melville.* Cambridge, U.K., and New York: Cambridge University Press, 1989.

Miller, Edwin Haviland. *Salem Is My Dwelling Place: A Life of Nathaniel Hawthorne.* Iowa City: University of Iowa Press, 1991.

Miller, John N. "Eros and Ideology: At the Heart of Hawthorne's 'Blithedale.'" *Nineteenth-Century Literature* 55, no. 1 (2000): 1–21.

Mitchell, Thomas R. *Hawthorne's Fuller Mystery.* Amherst: University of Massachusetts Press, 1998.

Myerson, Joel. *Brook Farm: An Annotated Bibliography and Resources Guide.* New York: Garland, 1978.

Myerson, Joel, ed. *The Brook Farm Book: A Collection of First-Hand Accounts of the Community.* New York: Garland, 1987.

Parrington, Vernon Louis. *Main Currents in American Thought.* 1927–1930. 3 vols. New York: Harcourt, Brace, and World, 1958.

Van Doren, Mark. *Nathaniel Hawthorne: A Critical Biography.* 1949. New York: Viking, 1966.

William E. Cain

THE BONDWOMAN'S NARRATIVE

The Bondwoman's Narrative is a literary work recounting the life of a young slave and her escape from slavery to freedom. It was probably written in the late 1850s by an author identified as "Hannah Crafts," identified on the title page as "a Fugitive Slave Recently Escaped from North Carolina." The work remained in manuscript until 2002 when, having been recovered and investigated by Professor Henry Louis Gates Jr., it was first published. Its origins are obscure. Nevertheless it is a work that has important implications for understanding antebellum American literary and cultural history.

The young slave whose experiences are chronicled in *The Bondwoman's Narrative* is herself named Hannah, portrayed for much of the text as a relatively privileged slave, almost white in complexion and for the most part mildly treated. The author uses Hannah's privileged status, however, in ways intended to highlight the cruelty of slavery as a system and its power to corrupt slaves and slaveholders alike.

The story begins in Hannah's childhood. Already eager for knowledge and for virtue, she is fortunate to encounter "Aunt Hetty" and "Uncle Siah," an aging white couple who, recognizing her abilities, teach her to read while leading her to Christianity. They do so at great risk to themselves and, ultimately discovered, are driven from their home in retaliation for their kindness to a slave.

Following this revealing episode Hannah embarks on her first major adventure. Her master is to marry, and the bride is soon to arrive. The text describes Hannah's situation as a slave, the author pausing to tell what is essentially a ghost story, recounting the prolonged, excruciating death of a slave woman forcibly suspended from a tree, her spirit, according to legend, continuing to haunt the household through the tree's creaking and groaning. The story is a digression but nevertheless dramatizes slavery's cruel possibilities and the brutality inherent in the system. Following this the tale returns to the action as the bride arrives, accompanied by, among others, Mr. Trappe, a lawyer and a villain.

The bride is beautiful and kind, and she also has a secret, known to Trappe. Her mother was a slave, and Trappe has been blackmailing her to maintain the secret. Faced with a threat from Trappe to break his silence, and encouraged by Hannah, she decides to flee. Hannah joins her in the attempt. The two encounter great trials, and the attempt does not succeed. They are captured, imprisoned, and ultimately returned to Hannah's master's house, where Trappe threatens to remand the young woman to slavery. In her anguish she ruptures a blood vessel and dies. Hannah is sold to a slave trader.

With the sale, Hannah begins her second adventure. As the trader drives her to market, his wagon crashes. The trader is killed, but Hannah is rescued, coming under the care of a slaveholding couple, Mr. and Mrs. Henry. Though Hannah reveals her slave status, they treat her more as a patient and a guest. As Hannah notes, their own slaves are treated fairly too. Here again the work includes several digressions, including the story of a young couple who desire to wed and, facing forcible separation—the groom, from another plantation, is to be sold away—escape to the North.

The young lovers had invited Hannah to join them, but she had refused, despite having been severely disappointed by Mrs. Henry. Happy in the household, she has asked Mrs. Henry to purchase her—the trader's heirs have asserted a claim of their own. Mrs. Henry cannot because of a promise she had earlier made to her father. A slave trader, he had come to feel guilty and had, on his deathbed, demanded a solemn promise from his daughter that she would neither buy nor sell a slave. Despite the benefit to Hannah, Mrs. Henry will keep her word. Instead, and in keeping with the peculiar morality of a slaveholding society, she will arrange with Hannah's legal owner to transfer her to a friend and distant relative, Mrs. Wheeler of North Carolina, known to be a kind and considerate mistress.

The transfer inaugurates the third and final phase of Hannah's story. Mrs. Wheeler is the wife of a leading politician and, despite Mrs. Henry's impression, a spoiled and demanding mistress. Initially she takes Hannah to Washington, D.C., where Hannah observes her efforts, and those of her husband, to win preferment in a viciously competitive arena. Hannah's job is to ensure that Mrs. Wheeler will be appropriately presentable in this difficult world—to dress her hair, provide her cosmetics, and manage her dress, almost never to Mrs. Wheeler's satisfaction. There is one episode, both comic and portentous, in which Hannah buys a powder for Mrs. Wheeler that has the unexpected effect of turning the woman's face from white to black. Although the effect is quickly reversed, Mrs. Wheeler becomes an object of scandal and ridicule, and Hannah becomes an object of Mrs. Wheeler's wrath.

Upon the Wheelers' return to North Carolina, the anger comes out. Here Hannah has her first encounter with what she sees as the worst of the plantation South and its brutalized people. Out of spite Mrs. Wheeler has sentenced Hannah to work as a field slave and to be forcibly wed to one of the other slaves. Taken to the quarters, Hannah, repulsed by her surroundings, is viciously attacked by another woman. Fleeing, she decides to escape.

Hannah has a perilous escape, knowing she is being pursued. She spends a brief period in the company of a young brother and sister trying to make their way from South Carolina. The sister is ill and soon dies. Hannah travels on with the brother, but when they are spotted he is shot and killed. Hannah manages to get away and fortunately encounters Aunt Hetty, her early benefactor, who assists her in completing her journey. She sails north, learning en route that the villainous Trappe has suffered a violent end. The story ends with Hannah free, reunited with her mother, married, and embarked on a career as a teacher.

WHO WAS HANNAH CRAFTS?

There is much about *The Bondwoman's Narrative* that has been both uncertain and controversial. Some of the greatest controversy has focused on the question of authorship: Who was Hannah Crafts? Some scholars have tended to take the title page at its word, despite the fact that it has hitherto been impossible to locate a "Hannah Crafts" in the historical record. Identifying Crafts as a fugitive slave, they have also accepted *The Bondwoman's Narrative* as one of the first works by a female fugitive, roughly contemporary with Harriet Jacobs's *Incidents in the Life of a Slave Girl* (1861).

Uncertainty also exists about the extent to which the work is autobiographical. There is some evidence that parts of the book could have been written by a fugitive familiar with at least some of what the work recounts, especially in its geographical references and, even more, in regard to the Wheelers. John Wheeler was a prominent North Carolina slaveholder and politician. The *Narrative*'s portrayal has at least some connection with what is known about the historical Wheelers, although how much is subject to debate.

But the character of the work itself further complicates such questions. The text of *The Bondwoman's Narrative* draws heavily on a wide variety of literary sources, in recognizable and identifiable ways, to create its portrait of Hannah the slave. Antebellum America produced many fugitive slave autobiographies; in none was the role of literary antecedents so pervasive. Thus even scholars who accept the identity of Hannah Crafts as a fugitive slave and recognize the story's autobiographical possibilities tend to view *The Bondwoman's Narrative* as less an autobiography than a work of fiction, in which facts are enhanced with themes and motifs designed for maximum literary effect.

Because of the work's clearly novelistic features, other scholars have suggested alternative possibilities regarding its authorship. These have included identifying "Hannah Crafts" as a pseudonym adopted by a free woman of color, living in the North, attempting a work of antislavery fiction using first-person narration. Whether fugitive or free, of course, the author would join Harriet E. Wilson—whose *Our Nig,* the fictional autobiography of a New England free woman appeared in 1859—as a pioneering African American female novelist. Some also have suggested that the author might have been white—like such writers as Richard Hildreth in *The Slave, or Memoirs of Archy Moore* (1836) and Mattie Griffith in *Autobiography of a Female Slave* (1856)—using a black voice for antislavery purposes. Most scholars believe, however, that internal evidence, especially in regard to characterization and setting, is inconsistent with such a view.

For the present, both the authorship and the autobiographical dimensions of the work remain unclear. So, it should be noted, does the question of why the manuscript failed to achieve publication in its time. There is little about either the story or its possible authorship to provide a definitive answer.

THE PROBLEM OF SOURCES

Whatever its background, however, *The Bondwoman's Narrative* does draw on a pattern of sources and allusions that are essential to understanding its literary and historical significance. First, and despite its distinctiveness, *The Bondwoman's Narrative* does have notable connections to the tradition of autobiographies written by fugitive slaves. Working mainly within the abolitionist movement, these fugitives used narratives of their lives to expose the brutality of slavery. Such writers as Frederick Douglass, Henry Bibb, William Wells Brown, Harriet Jacobs, and William and Ellen Craft were themselves prominent abolitionists, speaking widely and providing firsthand testimony to buttress abolitionism's key arguments. There has even been speculation that the author of *The Bondwoman's Narrative,* if writing under a pseudonym, chose "Hannah Crafts" deliberately to echo the name of the highly popular fugitive Ellen Craft.

Their narratives had literary as well as ideological impact. As the autobiographical tradition evolved, shaped by its political purposes as well as by its creators' experiences, it developed certain clear conventions. These included accounts of the writer's growing desire for freedom, episodes of physical and psychological

brutality along with those revealing slaveholder callousness and licentiousness, and harrowing tales of escape. These conventions also included creating direct responses to proslavery arguments developing at this same time, using the fugitives' experiences to undermine slavery's defense.

The Bondwoman's Narrative helps to emphasize the appeal of these conventions for antislavery thought as, like most abolitionist fiction—including Richard Hildreth's and Mattie Griffith's novels, Harriet Beecher Stowe's *Uncle Tom's Cabin* (1852), and William Wells Brown's *Clotel; or, The President's Daughter* (1853)—it draws heavily on them. Hannah's quest for literacy, her agonizing efforts to escape, the portraits of kindly and cruel whites, of angry mistresses, all had precedents in the autobiographical literature. And the work shows a clear awareness of the terms of the antebellum debate over slavery, including a subtle understanding of pro- and antislavery arguments alike. The debate is openly addressed at several points, as it was in most slave narratives.

Some critics have raised reservations about *The Bondwoman's Narrative*'s tendency to stress Hannah's elitism, epitomized by her revulsion at being forced by Mrs. Wheeler to live among the field slaves, even to marry one. But statements of personal distinctiveness, even superiority, appeared in many narratives, including, for example, those of Douglass and Brown. There was nothing unique about the *Narrative*'s Hannah.

Again, however, *The Bondwoman's Narrative* is a work in which autobiographical traditions are synthesized with conventions and motifs drawn from more general antebellum literary practices. The author shows a close familiarity with traditions of American sentimentalism. These traditions played an important role in other abolitionist fiction, including Stowe's *Uncle Tom's Cabin* and Brown's *Clotel,* texts that themselves probably influenced *The Bondwoman's Narrative.* The ill-fated bride and mistress, driven to death by the evil Trappe (a perfect sentimental villain), is closely modeled on the sentimental heroine—beautiful, sensitive, virtuous, and condemned to an early death. Hannah, like Brown's Clotel and Mattie Griffith's female slave, draws much of her poignancy from her devotion to sentimental ideals and from the trials she faces in trying to maintain those ideals in the hostile world of slavery.

Some elements in the work are reminiscent of popular motifs from gothic fiction, especially in such stories as the legend of the haunted tree. But some of the most noted sources for the *Narrative* come from nineteenth-century British fiction, well known in

Taken by the Wheelers to North Carolina, Hannah is overwhelmed by the brutal world of plantation slavery and seeks to make its impact on slaves clear to her readers:

Isn't it a strange state to be like them. To shuffle up and down the lanes unfamiliar with the flowers, and in utter darkness as to the meaning of Nature's various hieroglyphical symbols, so abundant on the trees, the skies, in the leaves of grass, and everywhere. To see people ride in carriages, to hear such names as freedom, heaven, hope and happiness and not to have the least idea how it must seem to ride, any more than what the experience of these blessed names would be. It must be a strange state to be prized just according to the firmness of your joints, the strength of your sinews, and your capability of endurance. To be made to feel that you have no business here, there, or anywhere except just to work—work—work—And yet to know that you are here somehow, with once in a great while like a straggling ray in a dark place a faint aspiration for something better, or gli with a glimpse, a mere glimpse of something beyond. It must be a strange state to feel that in the judgement of those above you you are scarcely human, and to fear that their opinion is more than half right, that you really are assimilated to the brutes, that the horses, dogs and cattle have quite as many priveledges, and are probably your equals or it may be your superiors in knowledge, that even your shape is questionable as belonging to that order of superior beings whose delicacy you offend.

It must be strange to live in a world of civilisation, and, elegance, and refinement, and yet know nothing about either, yet that is the way with multitudes and with none more than the slaves. The Constitution that asserts the right of freedom and equality to all mankind is a sealed book to them, and so is the Bible, that tells how Christ died for all; the bond as well as the free.

Crafts, *The Bondwoman's Narrative*, p. 201.

America, especially from the novels of such writers as Charles Dickens and Charlotte Brontë. Some of its passages and characters draw heavily on these sources,

particularly Dickens's *Bleak House* (1852–1853) and Brontë's *Jane Eyre* (1847), another fictional "autobiography." Whoever wrote *The Bondwoman's Narrative* was thus familiar with a wide array of sources, political, intellectual, and literary.

SIGNIFICANCE

In its intricacy, *The Bondwoman's Narrative* is a valuable document for understanding antebellum American history. If the author was indeed a fugitive slave, then it would certainly be of great intrinsic significance. Not only would it add to the expanding corpus of antebellum African American literary work, but it also would highlight the complexities of slavery and the slave community. Its fugitive author would probably have represented a layer in slave society that remains inadequately understood but one that was distinctly present. This was that small class of literate slaves who interpreted the outside world to the larger slave community, helping to engender political and cultural perspectives fundamental to African American political and community development in the South both before and after Emancipation.

Even if the author was free, however, the work would also highlight the important role of literary activity in antebellum African American society. Historians have long noted this role, especially among free people of color. Free communities, North and South, placed great emphasis on literature and literary life, writing poems, stories, and other pieces they hoped could serve as weapons in the battle against discrimination. They founded newspapers, contributed to antislavery periodicals, and formed literary societies that served as central arenas for cultural and political affairs. As much as any other group of Americans, they expressed faith in the power of literature to change the society. "Hannah Crafts" showed that same faith, deliberately presenting her novel as an instrument in the antislavery cause.

But the very uncertainty of the novel's origins contributes to its significance as a literary and historical document. *The Bondwoman's Narrative* underlines the richness of the abolitionist literary tradition, including that represented by the large body of slave narratives. Because it builds such strong bridges to an array of literary sources, the text indicates the degree to which familiar abolitionist forms also participated in broader literary currents and the resonance between abolitionist work and more general concerns in antebellum America.

It also represents a sense on the part of its author that an African American voice, especially a fugitive voice, mattered in the fight against slavery. Scholars have only recently appreciated the importance of such a voice to abolitionism—and of authentic voices generally to an increasingly democratic American public sphere. The author of *The Bondwoman's Narrative* shows a great faith in such a view, and in doing so helps to reveal more fully the characteristics and transformations that shaped antebellum American life.

See also Abolitionist Writing; *Clotel;* English Literature; Gothic Fiction; *Incidents in the Life of a Slave Girl;* Literacy; *Our Nig;* Slave Narratives; *Uncle Tom's Cabin*

BIBLIOGRAPHY

Primary Work

Crafts, Hannah. *The Bondwoman's Narrative*. Edited by Henry Louis Gates Jr. New York: Warner Books, 2002.

Secondary Works

Andrews, William L. *To Tell a Free Story: The First Century of Afro-American Autobiography*. Urbana: University of Illinois Press, 1986.

Bruce, Dickson D., Jr. *The Origins of African American Literature, 1680–1865*. Charlottesville: University of Virginia Press, 2001.

Davis, Charles T., and Henry Louis Gates Jr., eds. *The Slave's Narrative*. New York: Oxford University Press, 1985.

Foster, Frances Smith. *Written by Herself: Literary Production by African American Women, 1746–1892*. Bloomington: Indiana University Press, 1993.

Gates, Henry Louis, Jr., and Hollis Robbins, eds. *In Search of Hannah Crafts: Critical Essays on* The Bondwoman's Narrative. New York: Basic Books, 2004.

Jeffrey, Julie Roy. *The Great Silent Army of Abolitionism: Ordinary Women in the Antislavery Movement*. Chapel Hill: University of North Carolina Press, 1998.

Peterson, Carla L. *Doers of the Word: African-American Women Speakers and Writers in the North (1830–1880)*. New York: Oxford University Press, 1995.

Stauffer, John. *The Black Hearts of Men: Radical Abolitionists and the Transformation of Race*. Cambridge, Mass.: Harvard University Press, 2002.

Tompkins, Jane P. *Sensational Designs: The Cultural Work of American Fiction, 1790–1860*. New York: Oxford University Press, 1985.

Dickson D. Bruce Jr.

BOOK AND PERIODICAL ILLUSTRATION

Between 1820 and 1870, technological developments gave rise to the mass production of images in America. The changes during this fifty-year period were dramatic. In 1820 periodical illustrations were for the most part crude and perfunctory. Illustrated gift books were circulated, by those who could afford them, as tokens of friendship on special occasions. Otherwise, book illustrations were mostly confined to frontispieces, and what would later be called illustrated books were almost nonexistent. Yet by 1870 profusely illustrated children's books and scientific books were commonplace. Popular fiction almost required illustrations in order to sell. Illustrated monthly magazines such as *Harper's New Monthly Magazine* and *Appleton's Journal* circulated in runs of 200,000 or more copies. Travel articles especially drew great interest, illustrating sections of the country and the world that most readers had never seen before. Illustrators such as Harry Fenn (1845–1911) became nationally known brand names, whose contributions to books and periodicals were widely advertised. Meanwhile, beginning in the 1850s and rising to prominence with the Civil War, pictorial journalism emerged. Weekly illustrated papers included high-quality images of battles, spectacular disasters, and other current events as well as images of civic buildings and other engineering and technical accomplishments. Certain images, such as that of Abraham Lincoln's funeral train in 1865, became so widely circulated as to be known to virtually every American. Though photomechanical reproduction would not gain widespread use until the 1880s, America was, by 1870, well on its way to becoming a culture of images.

METAL-PLATE INTAGLIO ENGRAVINGS IN GIFT BOOKS AND PERIODICALS

Before the 1840s, most printed images in America were created through intaglio printing from metal plates, whereby a plate is etched or engraved so that ink remains in the recessed areas after the plate is inked and wiped. ("Intaglio" is a word from Italian meaning "engraved" or "cut.") When the plate comes into contact with paper, under pressure, ink is forced from the recesses to create an image. Though intaglio printing produces detailed, high-quality images, the process is not suited for high-volume reproduction for several reasons: it requires pressure; the plates must be wiped between each impression, and wiping wears down the metal; and, perhaps most important, it does not fit with the letterpress method that was used for commerical printing of text. Intaglio plates retain ink in the recesses, while letterpress is a relief process that retains ink on raised surfaces. Intaglio prints thus cannot be integrated with letterpress to produce book and periodical illustration. Intaglio prints must instead be printed on separate pages, often on special paper. This makes the printing process comparatively slow and expensive and not suited for runs in large numbers.

Thus, much of the book illustration of the period took the form of what are now called "gift books" and "annuals." These were literary miscellanies, lavishly illustrated and intended not primarily as reading material but rather as gifts, often called "tokens," "souvenirs," or "keepsakes." Their literary content was generally unremarkable, and publishers of gift books and annuals often engaged in questionable practices such as publishing a new work under a name already established by another publisher or republishing an existing book under a new name, with only minor changes to the plates or the contents. As a result, by the 1840s such books had a poor reputation among American publishers, although many are highly valued by modern-day collectors.

Beginning in 1830 *Godey's Lady's Book* pioneered the use of fashion plates—mostly intaglio prints from metal plates, showing clothing fashions of the day. These images were then known as "embellishments," not "illustrations." As the historian Frank Luther Mott remarks, the images "did not illustrate the text. The text illustrated them" (1:591). By the mid-1830s, each issue of *Godey's* featured numerous embellishments, including one per issue that was hand-colored, or "illuminated." The publisher referred proudly to "our corps of one hundred and fifty female colorers" (Mott 1:591). In addition to pictures of outrageous hoopskirts and other fashions, the colored embellishments often portrayed flower arrangements. Other magazines of the period, such as *Burton's Gentleman's Magazine,* included line and stipple portraits of actors and actresses in costume. *Graham's Magazine* likewise often included pictures of dramatics scenes. During this period, the plates were very expensive. In the 1830s a publisher might pay more for one new plate than for all of an issue's literary contents. To save money, secondhand plates were often purchased from British periodicals.

ENDGRAIN WOODCUT RELIEF ENGRAVING

Starting in England at the end of the eighteenth century, a technological revolution in printing began, a development that offered many advantages over intaglio printing and that would find its fullest expression in American books and periodicals fifty years later. The so-called "white-line" or woodcut process pioneered by Thomas Bewick (1753–1828) involved the

October bonnet and collar fashions for 1838. Illustration from *Godey's Lady's Book.* BRITISH MUSEUM/ BRIDGEMAN ART LIBRARY.

creation of relief plates engraved on the endgrain of boxwood blocks. Small blocks produced by sawing against the tight grain of Turkish boxwood are extremely hard. When polished, the endgrain provides an excellent surface for engraving. Lines incised with a graver on such surfaces appear in white, on a black background, in the resulting print. The hard wood lends itself to the type of detailed, fine work that was previously only associated with intaglio printing from metal. In addition, the wood is hard enough to withstand many thousands of impressions on a press, and, since the blocks produce relief prints, they can be set directly onto a plate alongside typeface. The first great work that Bewick produced through this method was *A General History of Quadrupeds,* first published in 1790, which includes more than two hundred images integrated with type and which is considered a landmark in printing. It is said that King George III would not believe Bewick's images were from woodcuts until he was shown the blocks.

In America, Bewick's method was copied by Alexander Anderson (1775–1870), a New Yorker who produced a copy of *Quadrupeds* published in 1804. Though the images in that book are generally not as good as those in Bewick's, Anderson quickly became proficient with the endgrain woodcut relief method, producing blocks for, among other works, editions of Noah Webster's dictionary and for various publications of the American Tract Society. By the 1840s Americans began to take the technological lead from the British in printing from woodcuts. One notable work, *Harper's Illuminated and New Pictorial Bible*, published by Harper & Brothers in 1846, included nearly sixteen hundred illustrations and made extensive use of a process called electrotyping, whereby a mold was made from a plate that included both letterpress and woodcuts. (The initial mold was made in wax. A galvanic battery was then used to coat the wax mold in copper, which was in turn backed with metal to produce a durable and finely detailed relief plate.)

With the widespread use of "electros," as they were called, in the 1840s, began the rise of illustrated books and periodicals in America. Notable illustrated books from this period include *The Big Bear of Arkansas and Other Sketches* (1845), edited by William Trotter Porter (1809–1858), featuring a title story by Thomas Bangs Thorpe (1815–1878) and woodcut prints from drawings by Felix O. C. Darley (1821–1888); an 1848 edition of *The Sketch Book of Geoffrey Crayon* by Washington Irving (1783–1859), also illustrated by Darley; and the 1853 edition of *Uncle Tom's Cabin* by Harriet Beecher Stowe (1811–1896), which included 117 illustrations by Hammatt Billings (1818–1874), who had created the seven drawings that appeared in the novel's 1852 first edition (although dated 1853, the "Illustrated Edition" was actually rushed to market at the end of 1852, to be sold for the Christmas trade, and was wildly popular).

HARPER'S MONTHLY AND THE RISE OF THE ILLUSTRATED MONTHLIES

In 1850 Harper & Brothers issued the first number of *Harper's New Monthly Magazine* (known as *Harper's Monthly*), a publishing venture designed to take advantage of the maturing print technologies. The magazine distinguished itself with a quantity of woodcut illustrations considered lavish for the time.

Dr. Livingstone in Africa. Newspaper illustration, c. 1857. Interest in the exploits of Scottish missionary David Livingstone, which was spurred by the publication of his multivolume *Missionary Travels and Researches in South Africa*, was further heightened by articles illustrated with dramatic scenes such as this one. © CORBIS

Circulation rose from 7,500 in 1850 to more than 100,000 in less than three years. The owners bought thirty-five steam-powered presses (so-called Adams presses, developed in Boston) to meet rapidly rising circulation demands. Though the magazine started as an "eclectic," reprinting mainly pirated texts from English authors, illustrated with original woodcuts, by 1853 it was beginning to "Americanize" its content.

One notable contributor was David Hunter Strother (1816–1888), who authored travel articles about the American South, illustrated from his own drawings, under the pen name "Porte Crayon." (Strother's pseudonym was a nod to Washington Irving, Strother's hero. Born in Berkley Springs, [West] Virginia, Strother proposed to do for the Shenandoah Valley what Irving had done for the Hudson River Valley.) Strother's humorous articles about hunting and sporting in Virginia were so well received that, shortly after his first contribution appeared in 1853, he received a standing commission from the magazine. By the end of the 1850s he was its highest paid contributor, and the popularity of his articles is credited with helping raise the magazine's circulation from 100,000 in 1853 to over 200,000 by the start of the Civil War. The success of *Harper's Monthly* inspired competitors. By 1870 *Scribner's Monthly* and *Appleton's Journal* had emerged, ushering in the era of the illustrated magazine, which would see its heyday in the 1880s.

The popularity of Strother's work says something about the appeal of illustrated monthlies in the years around the Civil War. The staple of these magazines was illustrated travel writing, featuring views of places most readers would never see for themselves. The magazines capitalized on Victorian readers' growing interest in distant regions of America and the world. Strother's works, for example, appeared at a time of growing sectarian tension, when northeasterners were increasingly interested in the South. Likewise, alongside Strother's domestic travel pieces, *Harper's* published articles from the far reaches of the British empire, at a time when England was establishing control over vast parts of the globe. For example, volume 16 (1858), the same volume that includes Strother's

President Lincolns' Funeral Procession in New York City. Illustration from *Harper's Weekly,* 1865. © CORBIS

"A Winter in the South," includes "Livingstone's Travels in South Africa," "An American in Constantinople," and "Hasheesh and the Hasheesh-Eaters"—all of which articles are profusely illustrated. The growing prevalence of woodcut illustrations was thus an important influence on—and was in turn influenced by—Americans' evolving conception of the nation, and of their place in the world.

PICTORIAL JOURNALISM

The first edition of *Frank Leslie's Illustrated Newspaper* appeared in New York in December 1855. This was not the first American illustrated weekly, but it was the first to achieve national prominence, and it ushered in the era of pictorial journalism. Leslie (1821–1880) was born in England and in the 1840s worked as head of the engraving department for the *Illustrated London News,* founded in 1842. (Leslie's given name was Henry Carter; he adopted his *nom de crayon* when he moved to London as a teenager.) Leslie's great innovation in New York was to perfect a system that allowed large woodcut blocks to be produced quickly. The system involved brass bolts and latches designed for the back of small boxwood blocks, so that those blocks could be locked together. Boxwood is a shrub or small tree, so blocks sawn from the endgrain were necessarily very small—usually no more than two-and-a-half or three inches square. Leslie's system allowed engravers to lock numerous blocks together in a larger grid, upon which an artist could draw his design. The grid could then be disassembled and the time-consuming work of engraving could be farmed out on smaller blocks to a team of engravers. The blocks were then reassembled, and the engraved lines from block to block were smoothed out and made consistent. Through this system, large images of recent events could be brought to press in a timely fashion.

Less than two years after Leslie founded his newspaper, the Harper brothers began a weekly to compete with it, using the same methods. *Harper's Weekly* would go on to dominate the market and to make celebrities of some of its illustrators, most notably of the caricaturist Thomas Nast (1840–1902), whose work would come to influence the course of New York and national politics. The illustrated weeklies focused on current events and news. They delved into political affairs that were generally avoided by the more aloof and apolitical monthlies. As events precipitated the American Civil War, demand for illustrated accounts of those events drove circulation of the illustrated weeklies. At the height of the war, *Harper's* had as many as a dozen artists in the field, often under fire. Their sketches would be sent to New York by courier, to be reproduced by the weekly's engraving staff. The *Harper's* war illustrators included Winslow Homer (1836–1910), who launched his career as a war artist and went on to become an influential illustrator and painter.

See also Book Publishing; Gift Books and Annuals; *Godey's Lady's Book; Harper's New Monthly Magazine;* Literary Marketplace; Periodicals; Pictorial Weeklies

BIBLIOGRAPHY

Primary Works

Bowker, Richard Rogers. "Great American Industries VII: The Printed Book." *Harper's New Monthly Magazine* 75 (July 1887): 165–188.

Linton, William J. "Art in Engraving on Wood." *Atlantic Monthly* 43 (June 1879): 705–715.

Secondary Works

Brown, Joshua. *Beyond the Lines: Pictorial Reporting, Everyday Life, and the Crisis of Gilded-Age America.* Berkeley: University of California Press, 2002.

Hamilton, Sinclair. *Early American Book Illustrators and Wood Engravers, 1670–1870: A Catalogue of a Collection of American Books, Illustrated for the Most Part with Woodcuts and Wood Engravings in the Princeton University Library.* Princeton, N.J.: Princeton University Library, 1958.

Horning, Clarence P., and Fridolf Johnson. *200 Years of American Graphic Art.* New York: Braziller, 1976.

Ivins, William M., Jr. *Prints and Visual Communication.* Cambridge, Mass.: Harvard University Press, 1953.

Mott, Frank Luther. *A History of American Magazines.* Vol. 1, *1741–1850.* Vol. 2, *1850–1865.* Vol. 3, *1865–1885.* Vol. 4, *1885–1905.* Cambridge, Mass.: Harvard University Press, 1938–1967.

Rainey, Sue. "Wood Engraving in America." In Sue Rainey and Mildred Abraham, *"Embellished with Numerous Engravings": The Works of American Illustrators and Wood Engravers, 1670–1880,* pp. 7–29. Charlottesville: Department of Rare Books, University of Virginia Library, 1986.

Wakeman, Geoffrey. *Victorian Book Illustration: The Technical Revolution.* Detroit: Gale, 1973.

Kevin E. O'Donnell

BOOK PUBLISHING

At the beginning of the nineteenth century, publishing in the United States was primarily the work of small, local printers or booksellers; by the time of the Civil War, publishing had become a modern business,

The Hoe rotary press. GETTY IMAGES

largely concentrated in a small number of major publishing centers catering to a national market. This transformation was made possible by three major factors: important innovations in print technology, enabling publishers for the first time to print large numbers of books quickly and inexpensively; improvements in roads, waterways, and, especially, the introduction and rapid expansion of railways, making possible much wider distribution of books to a national rather than a local market; and the continued expansion of the consumer market, which was a result of both a growing literate audience with the means and the leisure to buy books and the institutionalization of reading in the United States through schools and churches.

THE GROWTH OF AN INDUSTRY

The size and economic significance of the book publishing industry increased steadily throughout the period 1820–1870. Between 1830 and 1842, about 100 books per year were issued by U.S. publishers; by 1853 the number had jumped to 879; and by 1860 more than 1,300 American books were published. On the eve of the Civil War, there were four hundred publishing firms in the United States. John Tebbel has estimated the gross value of books manufactured and sold in the United States in 1820 at $2.5 million (with schoolbooks accounting for the largest single category, at $750,000); a decade later, in 1830, the gross value is estimated to have been $3.5 million; for 1840

the value was $5.5 million; for 1850, $12.5 million; and for 1856, $16 million, with New York publishers alone representing $6 million. Throughout the period (and in fact well into the twentieth century), the publishing industry as a whole cultivated a self-image as a genteel, often family-run, enterprise self-consciously performing the important civic duty of disseminating knowledge to the nation; yet the publishing industry was also a volatile, risky, and at times even cutthroat business—more volatile, perhaps, before the Civil War, but with increasingly high economic stakes throughout the century. While several major publishing houses established before the war thrived and endured (in several cases, to the present day), many other publishers were buffeted by the economic depressions of 1837 and 1857, by the disruptions of the war, or were simply unable to compete in the business and failed.

At the beginning of the period considered here (1820), publishers in the United States were printing works by British authors over those by American authors by a ratio of more than two to one. The United States was only at this moment beginning to produce any major writers (Washington Irving and James Fenimore Cooper were the nation's first successful professional writers with genuinely international reputations); moreover, British works, unprotected by international copyright, were not only better known to U.S. readers but also cheaper for U.S. publishers to print. In 1834 the average cost for a single volume by an American author was $1.20; by a foreign author, $.75. Nevertheless, over the next several decades the ratio of British- to American-authored works shifted steadily in the other direction, reaching a roughly equal balance around 1840, and by 1856 the ratio was roughly seventy to thirty in favor of American-authored books. Gradually U.S. writers reaped the benefits of America simply having a much larger market, which was drawn to native products: by the mid-1850s best-selling books in England sold in the neighborhood of ten thousand copies, compared to numbers reaching fifty thousand in the United States. Moreover, by 1860, school textbooks comprised the single largest category of books published in the United States (about 30 percent to 40 percent of the total market), and American schools preferred American texts, such as Noah Webster's numerous readers, spelling and grammar books, and dictionaries.

THE CENTRALIZATION OF THE INDUSTRY

As the publishing industry grew, it became increasingly centralized. The Philadelphia publisher Mathew Carey was the first to successfully enter into large-scale book production and distribution. His firm dominated the publishing industry of the 1820s, but New York publishing houses soon followed its example. In the first decade of the nineteenth century, almost half the works of American fiction were printed outside of New York, Philadelphia, and Boston; but by the 1840s, only 8 percent were published outside of these cities, New York having by this time surpassed Philadelphia as the leading publishing center, with Boston remaining third in importance. Before the Civil War, only modest publishing enterprises existed in the South, in such cities as Richmond, Virginia, and Charleston, South Carolina; and Cincinnati, Ohio, emerged as an important early western publishing center—by 1850 it was just behind Boston. In the decades after the Civil War, New York extended its domination of the publishing industry, though Boston and Philadelphia continued to support large, enduring publishing establishments, and Chicago surpassed Cincinnati as the major publishing center in the West.

Although many publishers in the United States had begun as retail booksellers, with the expansion and centralization of the publishing industry, major publishing houses gave up the retail component of their businesses almost entirely and concentrated on large-scale wholesale production and wide distribution. The Philadelphia firm of Carey and Lea shut down its retail business in 1830; and the dominant New York publishing house, Harper's, succeeded in part because it eschewed the retail business right from the time of its establishment in 1817. Boston firms,

slower in expanding into the national market, also retained their retail components longer.

Harper's was the predominant U.S. publishing house through the Civil War years, establishing a very strong base with textbook publishing as well as relying on periodical publication and on reprinting uncopyrighted popular British works. Other major New York houses established before the Civil War and that continued to thrive in the decades after the war (though house names tended to shift over time) include Appleton's (established 1831), John Wiley and Sons (established 1814), G. P. Putnam (established 1836), Dodd, Mead, and Company (established 1839), Scribner's (established 1846), and Edward Dutton (established 1852). Among enduring Philadelphia publishing houses, Lippincott (established 1836) was second to the Carey firm in importance. Boston emerged as a leading publisher of belles lettres, the most important houses being Little and Brown (established 1837), Ticknor and Fields (established 1832), and, somewhat later, Houghton (established 1864). While many of these houses vied for the popular writers of the day, especially as fiction became increasingly popular, they also realized the necessity of establishing more reliable business with textbooks, religious works, scientific writing, and the like, and over time each publisher tended to establish its specialty. Several publishers (such as Harper's, Ticknor and Fields, and Putnam) also capitalized on the magazine boom that began in the second quarter of the century and published magazines whose contents complemented their book lists.

ADVANCES IN PRINT TECHNOLOGY

The technology of book publishing had changed little since the fifteenth century; then, in the first decades of the nineteenth century, several dramatic improvements revolutionized printing and made possible the emergence of the modern publishing industry. Isaac Adams developed the steam-driven flatbed press in the early 1830s, which immediately made printing both faster and easier. In 1847 Robert Hoe further improved upon Adams's flatbed press by inventing the steam-powered cylinder press. Hoe's first press used four impression cylinders and could make eight thousand impressions per hour; by the end of the Civil War, rotary presses using ten cylinders could make fifteen thousand impressions per hour. Also crucial to the modernization of publishing was the invention of stereotype (1811) and then electrotype (1841) plates. These were simply metal molds of set type that could then be stored and reused for subsequent printings. Setting type had been a labor-intensive, skilled job, and once an edition was printed, the type had to be broken up to be reused; creating another edition meant having to reset the type from scratch. With stereotyping and electrotyping, subsequent editions could be produced quickly and inexpensively; the plates were portable and storable and could also be sold; moreover, they also took much of the risk out of estimating the appropriate size of a first printing. After 1865 curved stereotype plates were developed to accommodate cylinder presses.

Papermaking also became faster and cheaper during this period. By the 1830s papermaking machines began to employ belts and cylinders that allowed for the production of paper in the form of a continuous roll rather than as single sheets; and after the 1850s paper itself was being produced from inexpensive wood pulp rather than the more expensive cotton and linen rags. The actual binding and manufacturing of books was also made cheaper and more efficient, beginning before mid-century and extending through the 1870s, by the mechanization of paper cutting and folding, gluing, marbling, gilding, and embossing.

CHEAP BOOKS, FANCY BOOKS

As the book market expanded and the technology improved, publishers early began to produce multiple editions of the same book, at varying prices, for different markets, ranging from very inexpensive paper- or cardboard-bound editions to elaborately bound and gilt-edged editions of the highest quality, exhibiting the state of the art of book production. The first "paperback revolution" took place in the 1840s, by which time the United States had the largest literate population in the world. The publication of cheap books was stimulated by the frantic competition among publishers for profits from the reprinting of popular foreign works unprotected by international copyright and was enabled by the transformation of print technology (in particular the cylinder press) that allowed for the very rapid publication of large-volume, low-cost books. The boundaries between books and periodicals began to blur when, in 1841 and 1842, New York's competing weekly periodicals *Brother Jonathan* and the *New World,* which had both been serially reprinting "pirated" British novels, now began to produce entire novels sold as "extras" or "supplements" to their regular weekly issues. Sold on the streets with colorful paper covers, or sent through the mail without covers (and so taking advantage of postage regulations that distinguished between books and newspapers), these mass-market books sold for twenty-five cents. As competition heated up, other periodical publishers and book publishers entered the fray (in some cases issuing cheap editions of the same novel simultaneously); soon entire paperbound novels were selling for as little as six cents, severely threatening the entire publishing industry (as well as drastically diminishing the already constrained market for U.S. authors). Only changes in postal regulations implemented in 1844 brought this paperback war to a halt. There was again a market for cheap paperbound books inaugurated in 1860 by "Beadle's Dime Novels," for which demand grew steadily, even during the Civil War when they (and other cheap paperbound books) were popular in the military camps. After a brief lull in the popularity of cheap books, a new wave of low-cost book production, both hardbound and paperback, began in the 1870s.

At the other end of book-production technology, the "gift books" and "souvenirs" that were in vogue in the 1830s and 1840s (and which, like the cheap "supplements," also tended to blur the boundaries between books and periodicals) featured elaborate, state-of-the-art bindings, illustrations, and printing, at prices within reach of the growing genteel middle class. Although well-known writers sometimes contributed to these gift books, they were clearly less important as texts than they were as artifacts of genteel culture and showcases for bookmaking arts. Publishers also printed elaborately bound and embossed, gilt-edged, and illustrated editions of selected individual works, from Bibles to poetry. Harper's tremendously ambitious *Harper's Illustrated Bible,* published serially in fifty-four parts (1843–1846), was an important early demonstration of the marketability of elaborately illustrated books, though developments in illustration ultimately had a greater impact on magazines than on book production.

BOOK DISTRIBUTION

At the beginning of the nineteenth century, Philadelphia, New York, and Boston were the three largest cities in the United States. Because publishing was largely a local enterprise before 1820, it is not surprising that the largest cities were also the largest producers of books. More extended book distribution was hampered at this time by difficult and unreliable roadways, and so, until mid-century, distribution of goods depended heavily on waterways. This was a significant factor in the steady rise of Philadelphia and New York as major publishing centers, with their combination of deep harbors and their access to navigable inland waterways enabling them to reach both coastal and inland markets. Philadelphia tended to dominate the southern market, New York the western market. The completion of the Erie Canal in 1825 was a major advance in the reliable and timely distribution of goods into the West, and it especially benefited the rise of New York as a publishing center. Boston was the third major publishing center, with a strong, highly literate local market and a good harbor for expanded coastal trade, but it was hampered by its lack of navigable rivers inland. In the West, Cincinnati's situation on the Ohio River made it the leading western publishing center until after the Civil War. Waterways were not reliably accessible year-round, however, and winter freezes largely constrained extended book distribution to seasonal cycles.

The introduction of the railroad was therefore crucial to the extension of affordable and dependable distribution of goods beyond local markets, and the rapid expansion of the railways after the 1840s was crucial to the consolidation and nationalization of the publishing industry. Prior to mid-century, Boston publishers had been quite slow to engage in wholesale publishing and extended distribution, and they tended to retain the identity of local printers and retailers, competing more with each other for the local retail trade than with New York and Philadelphia publishers for a more extended, national market. The development of the railways, however, and particularly the extension of railways beyond the Alleghenies as of 1850, was an important factor in the reemergence of Boston as a major publishing center. The first transcontinental railroad, completed in 1869, of course dramatically transformed accessibility to the emerging Far West at the very end of the period under consideration here.

Publishers were slow to advertise their products before the Civil War, except for trade circulars and modest notices in papers and in the back pages of their own books. Beyond these, publishers relied primarily on reviews to promote their books, and this singular reliance tended to corrupt reviews and reviewing, with publishers pressuring reviewers to "puff" their books. As late as the 1870s, even major publishing houses were typically spending only around one hundred dollars to promote a book. Advertising was perhaps constrained not only by the volatility of the business and the narrow profit margins but also by the industry's self-cultivated image that publishers were genteel public servants. Thus, even when they did begin to advertise, their ads were conservative and staid.

BOOK CONTRACTS

At the beginning of the period under consideration, publisher-author relations were quite variable. Because most publishers were still also retailers, generally undercapitalized and competing for relatively small local markets, they were not inclined to take significant risks on authors. The simplest publishing arrangement, then, was one in which the author bore the financial risks and simply employed the publisher to manufacture and sell books. Under this arrangement, the author saw a profit only if and when production costs were met. This arrangement, of course, required the author himself to have sufficient capital to publish the book. In some cases, the publisher allowed the author to charge manufacturing costs against sales, but if sales were insufficient to recoup production costs the author was still indebted to the publisher for the balance. Washington Irving (1783–1859) and James Fenimore Cooper (1789–1851), the first U.S. writers to demonstrate the economic viability of authorship, reaped considerable benefit from underwriting the cost of manufacture while retaining the rights and also owning the plates for their books. Well into the mid-century, such successful authors as Henry Wadsworth Longfellow (1807–1882) also chose to underwrite and thus retain control of the publication of their works, confident that they could recoup costs and ultimately realize a greater profit. For other authors, however, such arrangements were prohibitive or highly risky. When Henry David Thoreau (1817–1862) was unable to find a publisher willing to risk the costs of producing his first book, *A Week on the Concord and Merrimack Rivers* (1849), he was persuaded to undertake the financial responsibility himself; but four years later Thoreau owed his publisher $290 for unsold copies.

Balancing the economic risks more evenly between author and publisher was the "half-profits" agreement, by which the author and publisher split both the costs (and therefore the risks) of production and also the profits on sales. When publishers were sufficiently well capitalized and anticipated strong sales, they were willing to undertake the entire risk of production and distribution costs in exchange for publishing rights, in which case they paid authors a commission, or royalty, on sales, usually set from 10 percent to 15 percent of the retail sales prices. When the Boston publisher John P. Jewett agreed to publish *Uncle Tom's Cabin* (1852), he offered Harriet Beecher Stowe (1811–1896) a choice between a half-profits contract or a 10 percent royalty on retail sales. Stowe, advised not to risk her own capital, accepted the royalty contract; as it turned out, Stowe ended up accepting 10 percent rather than half the profits of the best-selling book of the century—over 300,000 copies in its first year. By the end of the 1850s, however, as the publishing industry grew and became more centralized, royalty agreements became the standardized and mutually preferable contractual arrangement between publisher and author.

COPYRIGHT

Until the beginning of the twentieth century, U.S. copyright laws regarded printed materials as essentially public property, the private rights to which were ceded to authors or publishers only temporarily and with numerous constraints. The first national American copyright law, in 1790, protected only U.S. citizens and residents, and these copyrights could be held for only fourteen years, renewable for another fourteen years if the author was still living at the expiration of the first fourteen-year term. In 1831 copyright was redefined as heritable property, and the initial term was extended to twenty-eight years. Subsequently the term of copyright was extended still further. While copyright was perceived from the very beginning as an incentive for the publication and dissemination of learning and culture, this same interest in the public dissemination of knowledge was invoked in limiting individual property rights in print material. Most legal, economic, and commercial printed materials could not be copyrighted at all. The Supreme Court case of *Clayton v. Stone* (1829) confirmed that materials printed in newspapers were public property and could not be copyrighted. This principle was implicitly extended to magazine literature as well—regarded as equally ephemeral and equally public—and so newspaper and magazine literature was widely reprinted without permissions or payments. While such reprinting kept costs down and so served the interests of periodical publishers and consumers alike, it of course worked to the great disadvantage of U.S. authors and those periodicals that were paying increasingly substantial fees for original material. The 1834 Supreme Court decision *Wheaton v. Peters* reinforced the underlying public right to printed materials as a matter of public interest, even as market forces continued to exert pressure in favor of increased copyright protections. The 1854 Supreme Court decision *Stowe v. Thomas* established very narrow rights even for literary matter printed in book form: when Harriet Beecher Stowe brought suit against an unauthorized (American) translation into German of *Uncle Tom's Cabin,* the court determined that only the exact words of a printed text were protected by copyright; an author's rights did not extend to translations (or to any other "original" appropriation, whether as a play or a parlor game or decorated plates). Not until 1870 did Congress grant to authors the legal rights to the dramatization and translation of their published works.

Although the absence of international copyright became an increasingly contentious issue after the 1830s, no international copyright law was passed until 1891. The mass market for literature that emerged in the decades prior to the Civil War depended heavily on the cheap reprinting of pirated foreign materials unprotected by international copyright. While the availability of uncopyrighted foreign texts was crucial to the growth of several leading publishing houses—most notably Harper's—and therefore contributed to the increasing consolidation and centralization of the publishing industry, it was also the case that this same lack of copyright protection enabled any printer or publisher to participate in the production of cheap reprints, and so the absence of international copyright laws also acted as a counterforce to the centralizing process, enabling the persistence of decentralized, local printers. Opposition to international copyright laws was cast in political and ideological, as well as economic, terms: the absence of international copyright laws facilitated the dissemination of information, knowledge, and culture that promoted an informed, democratic citizenry. In political terms, opposition to international copyright was part of a more comprehensive resistance to centralized government and so constituted one of several issues dividing the decentralizing Jacksonian Democrats and the federalist Whigs.

Another important source of resistance to international copyright came from almost all of those who labored in the actual production of books (printers and typesetters, binders, papermakers, and so forth), who feared that such laws would severely diminish the publication of cheap reprints on which their continued employment largely depended. In the debates over international copyright, then, the interests of U.S. authors tended to be opposed to those of publishers, laborers, and consumers. U.S. (and British) authors advocated strenuously for international copyright laws through most of the century, petitioning Congress repeatedly from the 1830s through the 1850s, but to no avail. Petitions to Congress were renewed after the Civil War, and Congress engaged in serious debate about international copyright from 1870 to 1873, but nearly twenty more years would pass before an international copyright law was finally enacted. Especially before the Civil War, advocates of international copyright argued that the absence of such laws placed U.S. writers at an unfair disadvantage with publishers. International copyright law was thus represented not as a matter of fairness to foreign writers but as a matter of American literary nationalism. They argued that international copyright would not only protect the rights of U.S. authors but, by making American works more marketable, also help break American dependence on British culture. Of course, the lack of international copyright could cut both ways. Between 1841 and 1846, 382 American books were printed in England without permissions or payments to authors, and by the late 1860s U.S. writers began to complain about British piracy of American works—but before the Civil War this was not yet a significant component of the arguments in support of international copyright. Most publishers opposed international copyright laws, arguing not only on behalf of their own economic interest but also that of U.S. consumers. Publishers also recognized, however, that the absence of international copyright created a highly competitive, risky, and nearly anarchic market for foreign reprints, and so they came to practice an informal means of self-regulation, referred to as the "courtesy of the trade," by which any publisher who announced in print its intention to bring out an edition of a foreign work would be granted proprietary rights to it by other publishing houses. And in order to secure the privileges of the first American printing, publishers sometimes voluntarily paid foreign authors for their manuscripts or their cooperation. These trade "courtesies" were unenforceable and only partially successful (the cheap book wars of the 1840s between book publishers and newspaper "supplement" reprints of foreign works made such courtesies entirely impracticable), but they continued to be widely honored in the years after the Civil War.

See also Dime Novels; Editors; Gift Books and Annuals; Literary Marketplace; Periodicals; Publishers

BIBLIOGRAPHY
Secondary Works
Ballou, Ellen. *The Building of the House: Houghton Mifflin's Formative Years*. Boston: Houghton Mifflin, 1970.

Barnes, James J. *Authors, Publishers, and Politicians: The Quest for an Anglo-American Copyright Agreement, 1815–1854*. Columbus: Ohio State University Press, 1974.

Brown, Richard D. *Knowledge Is Power: The Diffusion of Information in Early America, 1700–1865*. New York: Oxford University Press, 1989.

Charvat, William. *Literary Publishing in America, 1790–1850*. 1959. Amherst: University of Massachusetts Press, 1993.

Charvat, William. *The Profession of Authorship in America, 1800–1870*. 1968. Edited by Matthew J. Bruccoli. New York: Columbia University Press, 1992.

Dzwonkoski, Peter, ed. *American Literary Publishing Houses, 1638–1899*. Detroit: Gale, 1986.

Exman, Eugene. *The House of Harper: One Hundred and Fifty Years of Publishing*. New York: Harper and Row, 1967.

Hackenberg, Michael, ed. *Getting the Books Out: Papers of the Chicago Conference on the Book in Nineteenth-Century America*. Washington, D.C.: Library of Congress, Center for the Book, 1987.

Hamilton, Sinclair. *Early American Book Illustrators and Wood Engravers, 1670–1870*. Princeton, N.J.: Princeton University Press, 1958.

Joyce, Donald Franklin. *Gatekeepers of Black Culture: Black-Owned Book Publishing in the United States, 1817–1981*. Westport, Conn.: Greenwood Press, 1983.

Lehmann-Haupt, Hellmut, Lawrence C. Wroth, and Rollo G. Silver. *The Book in America: A History of the Making and Selling of Books in the United States*. 2nd ed., rev. and enl. New York: Bowker, 1951.

Madison, Charles Allan. *Book Publishing in America*. New York: McGraw-Hill, 1966.

McGill, Meredith. *American Literature and the Culture of Reprinting, 1834–1853*. Philadelphia: University of Pennsylvania Press, 2003.

Mott, Frank Luther. *Golden Multitudes: The Story of Best Sellers in the United States*. New York: Macmillan, 1947.

Schick, Frank L. *The Paperbound Book in America: The History of Paperbacks and Their European Background*. New York: Bowker, 1958.

Tebbel, John. *A History of Book Publishing in the United States*. Vol. 1, *The Creation of an Industry, 1630–1865*. New York: Bowker, 1972.

Tebbel, John. *A History of Book Publishing in the United States*. Vol. 2, *The Expansion of an Industry, 1865–1919*. New York: Bowker, 1975.

Thompson, Ralph. *American Literary Annuals and Gift Books, 1825–1865*. New York: H. W. Wilson, 1936.

Winship, Michael. *American Literary Publishing in the Mid-Nineteenth Century: The Business of Ticknor and Fields*. Cambridge, U.K.: Cambridge University Press, 1995.

Zboray, Ronald J. *A Fictive People: Antebellum Economic Development and the American Reading Public*. New York: Oxford University Press, 1993.

Steven Fink

BORDERS

From the U.S. war cry in the mid-1840s over disputed British and American territory in the Pacific Northwest—"Fifty-Four Forty or Fight!"—to the westward extension of the Mason-Dixon Line separating slave from free states, boundaries and borders of various sorts preoccupy the nation during the antebellum decades. Debated, fought over, and painstakingly delineated on maps and charts, boundaries lie at the heart of major political decisions and prove fundamental to a host of social and economic issues. Paramount among such issues are the expansion of national borders as fresh territories are either annexed by diplomatic treaty or conquered outright, the relocation of eastern tribes to west of the Mississippi through the Indian Removal Act of 1830, the intensification of regionalism, the westward recession of the edge of settlement, and debate over whether new states added to the union should be slaveholding or free. As the nation approaches nothing less than a cataclysmic civil war to resolve many of these issues, and as antebellum boundaries remain in flux, their vulnerable, culturally constructed character lies close to the surface. It is not, then, especially surprising that much of the literature of this period becomes preoccupied with various borders that are said to mark insides and outsides, clearcut beginnings and endings, the limits of territorial jurisdictions, and the outermost edges of the nation itself.

THE FRONTIER

A major antebellum border is of course the frontier. Throughout the antebellum decades the idea of a frontier edge where settlement is said to end, and where "wilderness" is assumed to spread into raw, unsettled space, remains a fundamental aspect of the national sense of geography, with a long history extending back to earliest colonial settlement. William Bradford (1590–1657), governor of the Plymouth Bay Colony throughout most of its early development, invokes the idea of a frontier of civilization in his *Of Plymouth Plantation* (c. 1650), in which "all the civil parts of the world" emerge in stark contrast to a "hideous and desolate wilderness" of "savage hue" where "wild beasts and wild men" are presumed to roam (p. 62).

Scholars and historians such as David Laurence, John R. Stilgoe, and Robert E. Abrams have come to emphasize that terms such as "wilderness," "savage," and "civil parts" register European concepts and values projected into New World topography. As used by a writer like Bradford, the phrase "hideous and desolate wilderness" refers to a pre–New England landscape that in alternative accounts by Giovanni da Verrazzano, Samuel de Champlain, and other European explorers actually emerges as thickly populated by native tribes, whose villages and agricultural clearings dot the Atlantic coastland from the Saco River to Narragansett Bay. The initial colonial division of New World space into a fundamental difference between white "settlement" and "desolate wilderness," with a frontier edge falling between "civil" and "wild" worlds, erases the prior history of tribal cultures on the so-called desolate side of the border while apparently clearing the ground for unimpeded colonial possession. The frontier thus emerges as a problematic

and ideologically charged, if highly significant, concept in North American colonial history.

Rooted in colonial interests and attitudes, the idea of the frontier remains widely influential in antebellum literature and culture, although considerable ambivalence is often expressed about its westward recession and eventual disappearance. On the one hand, the American frontier ostensibly marks the advancing edge of civilized structure and order, and registers the triumph of a nation whose Manifest Destiny, according to the phrase coined by John L. O'Sullivan in 1845, is to expand across the continent, bringing the benefits of civilization to raw, wild land. In commenting on this transformative process, Alexis de Tocqueville (1805–1859) refers in *Democracy in America* (1835) to a great "march" of civilization into wilderness, "turning the course of rivers, peopling solitudes, and subduing nature" (2:74).

Throughout the antebellum decades, however, American writers and artists often lament even as they affirm the militant "march" of settlement behind an advancing frontier. Thomas Cole (1801–1848), the celebrated Hudson River School landscape painter, writes in his "Essay on American Scenery" (1836) that "although an enlightened and increasing people" have "wrought changes that seem magical" across a once uncultivated land, as "civilization" has taken hold, the "sublimity of the wilderness"—"perhaps the most impressive" characteristic of "American scenery"— threatens to "pass away" (pp. 3–19).

A presumed edge of the "wild" that is conceived as withdrawing lamentably away from and yet marking the triumphant expansion of settled, organized space, the frontier thus becomes an ambivalently perceived border, on alternative sides of which allegiances become split between the allure of the vanishing wilderness and the advance of civilization. Over the years, literary critics and art historians ranging from Leo Marx to Angela Miller have emphasized the way the American pastoral ideal, with its roots in poetry by Theocritus and in Virgil's *Eclogues,* emerges in much antebellum writing and painting as the strategy of choice to resolve such ambivalence. Pastoralism, that is to say, appears to soften the sharp distinction between settlement and wilderness through the envisagement of what Marx, in *The Machine in the Garden,* calls a "middle landscape" falling between and yet harmonizing the "opposed worlds" of "civilization" and "unimproved, raw nature" (pp. 22–31). In *Walden* (1854), for example, Henry David Thoreau (1817–1862) strives to maintain equilibrium between wild and civilized worlds by reading classics in the open air, building a shelter open to summer breezes, dressing simply, and avoiding needless luxuries. Similarly, in a number of Cole's paintings in the 1830s and 1840s, a "pastoral moment," as Angela Miller observes in *The Empire of the Eye,* seems deliberately "poised between the extremities of wilderness and overcivilization" (pp. 51–52).

Often in such works, however, the "pastoral moment" seems at best fleeting and provisional: an arcadian idyll doomed by the railroad, the factory, and the whole inexorable momentum of the Industrial Revolution eventually to disappear. At the other end of an ostensibly balanced "middle" terrain between "overcivilization" and "wilderness," the vocabulary of American pastoralism projects concepts such as "the primitive," "savagery," and "the wild" into unreclaimed space in ways that have grown suspicious to a later generation of scholars. The "pastoral moment," that is to say, seems to take shape in the midst of what Henry Nash Smith, in a critique of his own influential earlier book, *Virgin Land,* terms a series of "social stages" presumed to be modulating from "savagery" toward an "increasing level of complexity." At bottom, Smith emphasizes, to perceive the nineteenth-century American landscape in this way is to continue to project so-called free, primitive space—ostensibly inhabited, much as Bradford writes in 1630, by "wild men"—to the far side of a moving frontier, effectually obscuring the prior presence there of "nonwhite races," their own cultures, and their own complex relationship to the land ("Symbol and Idea in *Virgin Land,*" p. 28).

Although the idea of the frontier as a boundary between primitive space and civilized, more advanced space dominates a considerable amount of antebellum writing, such a boundary is sometimes questioned by antebellum authors themselves. Nathaniel Hawthorne's (1804–1864) novels, tales, and sketches of early colonial American life, for example, frequently blur the distinction between wilderness and settlement, nature and culture. The frontier may seem to divide civil from wild space, but Hawthorne suggests that when colonial settlers visit or gaze into the forest, they persist in perceiving it through the lens of their own cultural assumptions. In "Young Goodman Brown" (1846), for example, Hawthorne's protagonist crosses the threshold into the wilderness with his mind so heavily steeped in European forest folklore that he remains on the lookout for devils, witches, and black magic, ever ready, in the shadowy obscurity, to imagine a twig assuming life as a satanic snake or to hear the wilderness laughing at him in the rustle of the wind. Can creatures of human history, steeped in all sorts of unexamined prejudices and biases, ever truly claim to cross the frontier into primitive nature? Significantly,

Hawthorne cautions in "The New Adam and Eve" (1843) that "we, who have been born into the world's artificial system, can never adequately know how little in our present state and circumstances is natural, and how much is merely the interpolation of the perverted mind and heart of man" (p. 237).

However fundamental it may be to U.S. geography and sense of space, the idea of a frontier edge where culture ends and pure nature begins turns problematic for a writer like Hawthorne. A tale such as "Young Goodman Brown," in which nature becomes the projective backdrop of "the perverted mind and heart of man," anticipates the observation by the noted cultural and political theorist Theodor Adorno (1903–1969) that "the image of undistorted nature" is likely to arise "only in distortion, as its opposite" (p. 95).

AMERICAN REGIONALISM

In addition to a frontier edge ostensibly marking a clear-cut distinction between culturally organized and purely natural space, the antebellum landscape sometimes appears, from another perspective, to become regionalized into recognizable sections and localities. Elizabeth Johns observes that as early as the 1780s regional stereotypes—the Yankee sharper, for example, or the tall Kentuckian—begin to codify into what she calls an "efficient roster" of regional differences for "ordering" the nation (p. 12). But although these differences become especially sharp, acrimonious, and intense throughout the 1850s as Northerners and Southerners, increasingly divided over slavery, warily eyed the admission of western states into the union as slaveholding or free, historians ranging from David Potter to Edward L. Ayers generally emphasize that in the early antebellum period, regionalism is less severe. A balance between local interests and representative federal government becomes an especially important principle of the Whig Party, and prominent Whig politicians such as Daniel Webster (1782–1852) and Henry Clay (1777–1852) craft federal legislation based on mutual compromise and negotiation in the interest of the whole nation. In American schoolrooms, moreover, textbooks such as S. G. Goodrich's *The Child's Book of American Geography* (1831) foster concrete attachments to immediate, local regions since these are presumed to provide the very foundation for attachment to the nation as a whole. The assumption, derived from Scottish common sense philosophy, is that the mind first obtains knowledge of the world in concrete, immediate form, moving, so to speak, up a ladder from immediacy of environment and particularity of scene toward larger loyalties and more abstract entities such as the nation as a whole.

Regionalism no doubt intensifies as the nation approaches the Civil War. Travel literature by Northern writers such as Frederick Law Olmsted (1822–1903) and John Stevens Cabot Abbott (1805–1877) not only exoticizes the South, making it seem strange, deviant, and peculiar, but also portrays the South in negative terms against which the North emerges as fostering values of thrift, industriousness, and hard work which slaveholding is assumed to undermine. In particular, the "New England . . . model" of individual freedom, self-reliance, and small village life, as Harriet Beecher Stowe's (1811–1896) husband, Reverend Calvin Stowe, writes in the December 1849 issue of *Godey's Lady's Book,* is assumed to have "originated most of that which is really valuable in the social and political condition of the United States" (p. 459). In reaction, white Southerners cobble together an alternative national identity based on the contrast of agrarian to industrial values, the romanticization of plantation life, and even the assumed superiority of graceful Southern speech to harsh, grating Yankeeisms. Throughout this period, the West, often given to promoting itself as the one region where sectionalism is transcended, and where the expansionary destiny of the nation lies, is nevertheless jealously targeted by both North and South. Southern politicians and landowners promote the extension of slave-based agriculture into western lands and states. In contrast, in an 1850 speech that reveals the underlying sectarian bias even of a stalwart proponent of compromise and federal union, Daniel Webster envisages pioneer "descendants of New England" spreading thrift, industry, and the "Pilgrim" way from the "Alleghenies" across the "Rocky Mountains" to the "shores of the Pacific" (pp. 222–223).

The tendency of the "West" to locate itself beyond narrow regionalism, and yet to become alternatively defined on northern and southern terms, while its center of gravity gradually shifts from the Ohio Valley to beyond the Mississippi, underscores the complex and fluid history which regional divisions simplify. How hard and fast are antebellum regional borders, and how homogeneous and well defined are the regions that appear to take shape within them? Historians often emphasize the ambiguous and fluctuating character of regional boundaries and, to a certain degree, the imaginatively constructed character of places like New England that novels such as Catharine Maria Sedgwick's (1789–1867) *A New-England Tale* (1822), or travelogues such as Timothy Dwight's (1752–1817) *Travels in New-England and*

As acrimony between the North and South intensified in the approach to the Civil War, writers from across the Mason-Dixon Line often exaggerated the virtues of their own respective regions. Theodore Parker's remarks epitomize the rhetorical excesses sometimes spawned by antebellum regionalism.

Whence come the men of superior education who occupy the Pulpits, exercise the professions of Law and Medicine, or fill the chairs of the Professors in the Colleges of the Union? Almost all from the North. . . . Whence come the distinguished authors of America? . . . All from the free states; north of Mason and Dixon's line.

Theodore Parker, *Letter to the People of the United States Touching the Matter of Slavery* (Boston: J. Munroe, 1848), pp. 63–64.

New-York (1821–1822), envision, celebrate, and appear to define. For example, as Stephen Nissenbaum points out, although Dwight's text, with its idealization of New England village life, is a precursor of the later promotion of the New England village by Reverend Calvin Stowe and others, Dwight falsifies the New England past. He erroneously endows the New England village, whose graceful white houses are theoretically arranged around a central, sociable "common," with a long colonial history that is in fact belied by actual historical research. Such research discloses an early New England population actually scattered throughout hamlets and isolated farms, with very few central village "greens" dotting the landscape, and houses painted in a variety of colors rather than in decorous, uniform white (Nissenbaum, pp. 48–52).

In addition, regional boundaries as understood by antebellum Americans actually shift, overlap, or prove uncertain on closer analysis. What, for example, constitutes the authentic "South"? Edward L. Ayers points out that by the 1830s, Virginians and Carolinians, presuming themselves to be the inhabitants of the true if dying "South," warily eye the flow of money and population westward into Alabama and Mississippi, which are considered to be raw, uncouth regions, devoid of gentility, and basically unsouthern (pp. 68–69). Moreover, the cultural life of New York City and New England on the one hand is marked by rivalry and on the other hand remains intimately linked as numerous New Englanders, from the writer William Cullen Bryant (1794–1878) to the painter Frederick Church (1826–1900), become prominent in New York City publishing and art while sustaining strong New England ties.

The relationship between North and South itself proves, on closer analysis, to remain equivocal and ambiguous even as acrimony intensifies and lines seem sharply drawn in the approach to Civil War. The *Massachusetts Quarterly Review* self-righteously affirms New England values and chastises the South as a region of moral decadence. But in "Chiefly about War Matters" (1862), Hawthorne darkly links the economic and social histories of New England and the South. At bottom they are entangled in one another. Hawthorne goes so far as to emphasize that one and the same *Mayflower* brought both Pilgrims to Plymouth Rock and slaves to Virginia: a "monstrous birth," he proposes, of religious idealism and yet American slavery out of a single mother ship such that "two such portents never sprang from an identical source before" (p. 319).

Along border states, an entangled, intertwined, and equivocal sense of reality especially prevails. In Maryland, for example, close kinship ties conflict with dictates of conscience as brothers and cousins join opposing Union and Confederate armies, eventually to face one another in some of the bloodiest battles of the war. Rebecca Harding Davis (1831–1910) recalls that "on the border of West Virginia," "opinions clashed" in "every village," households were torn apart, and many suffered the anguish of seeing "the great question from both sides" (*Bits of Gossip*, pp. 109, 166). The anguish of living in the ambivalent borderland between divided worlds is best emphasized in Davis's story "David Gaunt," published in 1862 in the *Atlantic Monthly*. Set in the northwest Virginia hills close to the Ohio and Pennsylvania borders, Davis's story recounts how the devoutly religious daughter of a Confederate sympathizer falls in love with a Union officer given to doubting God, and how, after joining the Union cause, an idealistic Methodist preacher finds himself bound by duty to shoot the very father of the woman he loves. Little remains clear-cut in this borderland narrative of multiple ties, duties, and affections that refuse to accord with one another. Such a tale of incongruous allegiances and crisscrossed feelings along a troubled border throws into question the stark delineations that appear to divide alternative regions—and alternative human worlds—so precisely and emphatically on geometrically stable maps.

TRANSNATIONALISM AND THE BLURRED EDGE OF NATIONHOOD

Historians and literary scholars assert that the borders and edges of American nationhood itself turned troubled, unsettled, and equivocal throughout the antebellum decades. On the face of it, to be sure, this seems to be a period characterized by an aggressively expanding—scarcely a blurred and troubled—national edge as fresh territories are successively absorbed into the U.S. republic. In the wake of warfare between Mexico and incoming Anglo-American settlers, for example, Texas declares itself to be an independent republic in 1836 and is then annexed to the union at the invitation of President James Polk in 1845. A subsequent U.S. victory over Mexico in the war of 1846–1848 leads to the acquisition of California and New Mexico through the Treaty of Guadalupe Hidalgo in 1848. From the late 1840s through the 1850s, Southern slaveholders in particular press for the conquest and annexation of Spanish-held Cuba, and at times the dream of a Greater South expands still further to include a vast slave empire encompassing the entire Southern Hemisphere. In the Pacific Northwest, after a crisis in British-U.S. relations that almost leads to open warfare over the disputed Oregon Territory, the U.S. border is at last fixed by an 1846 treaty at forty-nine degrees latitude north, and the Oregon Territory is officially admitted into the Union by act of Congress on 14 August 1848.

Yet the very expansion of national borders to include territories and populations once outside the federal republic produces, at bottom, a complex national geography of multiple languages and mixed ethnicity even as immigrant Irish laborers flood into East Coast cities such as Boston and New York and as Germans settle farther west. Lured by the discovery of gold in 1848, moreover, South Americans and Australians, Hawaiians, Chinese, and New Englanders pour into California, while by 1855 a good half of the population of New York City actually consists of the foreign-born (Bridges, p. 55). In reaction, precisely as the U.S. population swells and the borders of the nation expand westward and southward into Spanish-speaking territories, antiforeign sentiment intensifies among American nativists. Rising out of this groundswell of nativist sentiment, the "Know-Nothing" or "American" Party of the 1850s—originally a secret fraternal society whose members are sworn to say that they "know nothing" when asked about it—eventually manages to elect more than a hundred U.S. congressmen committed to anti-Catholic, anti-immigrant policies.

A time of unprecedented expansion and immigration is thus accompanied by increasing anxiety over the social and cultural identity of the nation. What does it ultimately mean to be an "American"? Policing the borders of "American-ness" becomes a major preoccupation of journalists, essayists, and historians, magazine editors, and art publishers even as immigrant laborers pour into cities like New York, and as the boundaries of the nation spread into territories inhabited by numerous native tribes and into the Spanish-speaking Southwest. In reaction, artists employed by Currier & Ives—a significant number of them actually foreign-born—are encouraged to paint standardized, all-American scenes of village lanes with picket fences and of middle-class families out in their carriages for a Sunday drive. Through such standardized scenes, what Bryan F. Le Beau terms a "common" visual "vocabulary" that claims to represent "the nation" finds its way into picture-book collections and popular lithography (p. 7). In addition, what Reginald Horsman identifies as a powerful strain of "American . . . Anglo-Saxonism," defining white Americans as a "superior race" fated to triumph over "inferior races" (p. 2), influences political oratory, contemporary journalism, and new scientific disciplines claiming to make precise racial divisions based on skull measurements and other physical factors.

American Anglo-Saxonism is accompanied by a widespread fear of racial and cultural miscegenation. In *Transamerican Literary Relations,* Anna Brickhouse observes how just such an obsession with cultural, linguistic, and racial purity, along with a consequent fear of cultural and racial mixture, becomes especially directed by Anglo-American writers against the neighboring French- and Spanish-speaking cultures of Mexico, the Caribbean, and the Southern Hemisphere. William Hickling Prescott (1796–1859), for example, in his three-volume *History of the Conquest of Mexico* (1843), is disturbed by the "dark," "doubtful," and mixed character of Mexico's "native races" as well as by the very language that they speak: a decadent Spanish unfortunately bastardized, he believes, by native Indian colloquialisms and jarring sounds (1:482, 53, 207). And in spite of its abolitionist theme, Harriet Beecher Stowe's celebrated novel *Uncle Tom's Cabin* (1852) seeks to affirm clear-cut racial distinctions even though the racial origins of the blond, blue-eyed Augustine St. Claire and his dark twin brother, Alfred, are revealed to be ambiguous when the novel shifts its setting to New Orleans, gateway to the West Indies.

Thus even as American Anglo-Saxonism prevails, a counter-reality of racial and cultural mixture haunts and troubles antebellum U.S. writing. At times, indeed, the focus of certain writers is directly upon an intermixed but by no means harmonious national

space whose fundamental character cannot be fixed and framed. John Rollin Ridge's *The Life and Adventures of Joaquín Murieta* (1854), for example, the first known Native American novel, discloses a California of conflicting alliances and ethnic communities at odds with one another: what emerges is an unsettled space of white nativist mobs, Tejon Indians, and, at one point, the shaky alliance of Indians and Mexican Americans provisionally forged by the bandit Murieta to resist Anglo-American power and oppression. Herman Melville's (1819–1891) *The Confidence-Man* (1857) envisages a Mississippi riverboat world of "Sioux," "Mormon," and "mulatto" passengers, "French Jews" and "Santa Fé traders" (p. 6). In this riverboat world of transient strangers all from somewhere else, immediate social exchange is haunted by underlying paranoia and mistrust. In phraseology characteristic of the worst fears spawned by such unstable gatherings of strangers, Lyman Beecher (1775–1863), father of Harriet Beecher Stowe, warns that especially in "the great West," where a population from "all the States of the Union" and from a multitude of "nations" is "rushing in like the waters of the flood," no "homogeneous public sentiment can be formed" (pp. 15–16).

Beecher's remarks notwithstanding, antebellum American authors sometimes endorse the emergence of a modern social space of increased immigration and cross-cultural exchange. In his famous 1852 speech, "The Meaning of July Fourth for the Negro," Frederick Douglass (1818–1895) celebrates the fact that

> no nation can now shut itself up from the surrounding world. . . . Long established customs . . . could formerly fence themselves in. . . . But a change has now come over the affairs of mankind. Walled cities and empires have become unfashionable. The arm of commerce has borne away the gates of the strong city. . . . Oceans no longer divide, but link nations together. . . . Space is comparatively annihilated. (Pp. 128–129)

Such "comparatively annihilated" space of porous national borders fosters a new cosmopolitanism. Even as U.S. nativism gives rise to the Know-Nothing Party, antebellum writing often eagerly bestrides geographic borders. Douglass's own travels throughout the British Isles from 1845 to 1847, for example, provide him with an out-of-the-country perspective from which to critique U.S. institutions—especially slavery and American racism—in letters and essays written from an international vantage point. In the three volumes of *The Talisman* (1828–1830), William Cullen Bryant (1794–1878) collaborates with Gulian C. Verplanck (1786–1870) and Robert C. Sands (1799–1832) to create the Anglo-American narrator Francis

Life in the Country: The Morning Ride, c. **1859.** Lithograph by Louis Maurer, published by Currier & Ives. In an era of increasing immigration and the expansion of national borders into the Spanish-speaking Southwest, scenes such as this dominated popular lithography. They portrayed a standardized, stereotypic America while ignoring the influx of foreign-born laborers into East Coast cities and the mixed Asian, Spanish-speaking, and Anglo-American populations of regions such as California. THE LIBRARY OF CONGRESS

Herbert, whose travels cater to a growing public appetite to learn about foreign cultures and peoples, albeit in an exoticized and sometimes condescending form. Margaret Fuller's "Dispatches" from Europe to the *New-York Daily Tribune* from 1846 to 1849 range from vivid portraiture of Scottish scenery to descriptions of Italy in the throes of revolution. Edgar Allan Poe's tales are often set abroad. Emily Dickinson's poems are full of wide-ranging allusions and references that escape a provincially "New England" frame of reference.

Indeed, whereas scholars and literary historians once sought to disclose a distinguishably New World voice in mid-nineteenth-century American writing, scholarship tends to emphasize the way such writing is often best situated within a much broader context. Paul Giles, for example, explores the complex interaction and reciprocity of British and American writing and culture, with special attention to the transatlantic

vantage point assumed in works such as Washington Irving's *The Sketch-Book* (1819–1820) and many of Herman Melville's sketches and tales of the 1850s. Moreover, Anna Brickhouse reveals the way mid-nineteenth-century American writing is often best studied within a transamerican, multilingual framework including not only the United States but also Latin America and the French- and Spanish-speaking Caribbean. Timothy Powell addresses what he terms "a fluid, infinitely complicated . . . dialogue" of voices and literatures spawned by America's multicultural history, the powerful U.S. "will to monocultural unity" notwithstanding (pp. 22–23). In *Border Matters: Remapping American Cultural Studies,* José David Saldívar sets the keynote for such criticism by challenging scholarship that locates American studies too tidily within a national framework assumed to be homogenous and stable.

THE LIMITS OF THE MAP

In the final analysis, to explore the various borderlines that appear to organize U.S. geography during the antebellum decades—the frontier, sectional distinctions between different regions, the edge of nationhood itself—is to encounter a significant discrepancy between the divisions of mapped space and a considerably more complex cultural reality. This is scarcely to deny the undeniable historical force of borders that are fought over, carefully delineated on maps and charts, policed, defended, or extended. Borders and the nations and regions that they define can exert enormous influence over the way human beings think about space, determine who owns what, and even perceive one another. Humanly constructed borders and boundaries, however, as Thoreau emphasizes in "Walking" (1852), are by no means natural, inevitable, and timeless features of topography. Thoreau tells us that on a leisurely afternoon walk, he deliberately zigzags this way and that in defiance of the very boundaries of properties that he has professionally surveyed, and quite often, he points out, the most zealously respected borders cannot actually be seen by the naked eye. In *Culture and Imperialism*, Edward W. Said emphasizes that throughout history, what appear to be separate cultural geographies have "always overlapped" or become entangled in "one another" through reciprocal "influence, crossing," and, "of course, conflict" (p. 331).

In the antebellum United States, however, geographic borders prove to be frail and problematic in an especially noticeable sense: that is, they remain in dramatic flux, and they are often as recently and suddenly established as the rectangular townships and squares projected by nineteenth-century federal cartography into wild forest and desert, or as the 1846 agreement between Great Britain and the United States fixing the disputed American border at forty-nine degrees latitude north. This overlay of recently mapped U.S. space upon lands that may have been inhabited by native tribes for thousands of years, or regarded as British and Mexican just a few years earlier, helps to explain why antebellum American borders are often the sites of anxiety, debate, and conflict. It may be true that ongoing tension between borders, on the one hand, and the constantly transgressive flow of immigration and cultural influence across them, on the other, is widespread throughout history. But an underlying ambivalence toward the power and yet the porousness and contingency of borders emerges with particular intensity in the antebellum United States.

See also Americans Abroad; Ethnology; Exploration and Discovery; Indian Wars and Dispossession; Nature; Spanish Speakers and Early "Latino" Expression

BIBLIOGRAPHY
Primary Works

Beecher, Lyman. *A Plea for the West*. Cincinnati: Truman and Smith, 1835.

Bradford, William. *Of Plymouth Plantation, 1620–1647*. 1650. Edited by Samuel Eliot Morison. New York: Knopf, 1952.

Cole, Thomas. "Essay on American Scenery." 1836. In *Thomas Cole: The Collected Essays and Prose Sketches*, edited by Marshall Tymn, pp. 3–19. Saint Paul, Minn.: John Colet Press, 1980.

Davis, Rebecca Harding. *Bits of Gossip*. Boston: Houghton Mifflin, 1904.

Davis, Rebecca Harding. "David Gaunt." *Atlantic Monthly* 10 (1862): 257–271, 403–422.

Dwight, Timothy. *Travels in New-England and New-York*. New Haven, Conn.: Dwight, 1821–1822.

Douglass, Frederick. "The Meaning of July Fourth for the Negro." 1852. In *The Oxford Frederick Douglass Reader*, edited by William L. Andrews, pp. 108–130. Oxford and New York: Oxford University Press, 1996.

Fuller, Margaret. *New-York Daily Tribune* Dispatches. 1846–1849. In *The Portable Margaret Fuller*, edited by Mary Kelley. New York: Penguin, 1994.

Goodrich, Samuel Griswold. *The Child's Book of American Geography*. Boston: Waitt and Dow, 1831.

Hawthorne, Nathaniel. "Chiefly about War Matters." 1862. In *The Works of Nathaniel Hawthorne*, vol. 12, pp. 299–345. Boston and New York: Houghton Mifflin, 1883.

Hawthorne, Nathaniel. "The New Adam and Eve" and "Young Goodman Brown." 1843, 1846. In *The Centenary Edition of the Works of Nathaniel Hawthorne*, vol. 10, edited by William Charvat, Roy Harvey Pearce, and Claude M. Simpson, pp. 247–267, 74–90. Columbus: Ohio State University Press, 1974.

Melville, Herman. *The Confidence-Man*. 1857. Edited by Hershel Parker. New York: Norton, 1971.

Prescott, William Hickling. *History of the Conquest of Mexico, with a Preliminary View of the Ancient Mexican Civilization and the Life of the Conquerer, Hernando Cortes*. 3 vols. New York: Harper & Brothers, 1843.

Ridge, John Rollin. *The Life and Adventures of Joaquín Murieta, the Celebrated California Bandit*. 1854. Norman: University of Oklahoma Press, 1955.

Sedgwick, Catharine Maria. *A New-England Tale*. New York: E. Bliss and White, 1822.

Stowe, Calvin E. "The New England Forefathers' Day." *Godey's Lady's Book* 39 (1849): 457.

Stowe, Harriet Beecher. *Uncle Tom's Cabin*. 1852. New York: Collier Books, 1962.

Thoreau, Henry David. *Walden*. 1854. Edited by J. Lyndon Shanley. Princeton, N.J.: Princeton University Press, 1971.

Thoreau, Henry David. "Walking." 1852. In *The Writings of Henry David Thoreau*, vol. 9, pp. 251–304. Boston and New York: Houghton Mifflin, 1894–1895.

Toqueville, Alexis de. *Democracy in America*. 1835. 2 vols. Edited by Phillips Bradley. Translated by Henry Reeve. New York: Knopf, 1945.

Webster, Daniel. Speech given to the Pilgrim Festival in 1850. In *The Writings and Speeches of Daniel Webster*, vol. 4, pp. 217–226. Boston: Little, Brown, 1903.

Secondary Works

Abrams, Robert E. *Landscape and Ideology in American Renaissance Literature: Topographies of Skepticism*. Cambridge, U.K., and New York: Cambridge University Press, 2004.

Adorno, Theodor. *Minima Moralia: Reflections from Damaged Life*. Translated by E. F. N. Jephcott. London: Verso, 1978.

Ayers, Edward L. "What We Talk about When We Talk about the South." In Edward L. Ayers, Peter Onuf, Patricia Nelson Limerick, and Stephen Nissenbaum, *All Over the Map: Rethinking American Regions*, pp. 62–82. Baltimore: Johns Hopkins University Press, 1996.

Brickhouse, Anna. *Transamerican Literary Relations and the Nineteenth-Century Public Sphere*. Cambridge, U.K., and New York: Cambridge University Press, 2004.

Bridges, Amy. *A City in the Republic: Antebellum New York and the Origins of Machine Politics*. Cambridge, U.K., and New York: Cambridge University Press, 1984.

Giles, Paul. *Transatlantic Insurrections: British Culture and the Formation of American Literature, 1730–1860*. Philadelphia: University of Pennsylvania Press, 2001.

Giles, Paul. *Virtual Americas: Transnational Fictions and the Transatlantic Imaginary*. Durham, N.C.: Duke University Press, 2002.

Grant, Susan-Mary. *North over South: Northern Nationalism and American Identity in the Antebellum Era*. Lawrence: University Press of Kansas, 2000.

Horsman, Reginald. *Race and Manifest Destiny: The Origins of American Racial Anglo-Saxonism*. Cambridge, Mass.: Harvard University Press, 1981.

Johns, Elizabeth. *American Genre Painting: The Politics of Everyday Life*. New Haven, Conn.: Yale University Press, 1991.

Laurence, David. "William Bradford's American Sublime." *PMLA* 102 (1987): 55–65.

Le Beau, Bryan F. *Currier and Ives: America Imagined*. Washington: Smithsonian Institution Press, 2001.

Marx, Leo. *The Machine in the Garden: Technology and the Pastoral Ideal in America*. New York: Oxford University Press, 1964.

Miller, Angela. *The Empire of the Eye: Landscape Representation and American Cultural Politics, 1825–1875*. Ithaca, N.Y.: Cornell University Press, 1993.

Nissenbaum, Stephen. "New England as Region and Nation." In Edward L. Ayers, Peter Onuf, Patricia Nelson Limerick, and Stephen Nissenbaum, *All Over the Map: Rethinking American Regions*, pp. 38–61. Baltimore: Johns Hopkins University Press, 1996.

Potter, David M. *The South and Sectional Conflict*. Baton Rouge: Lousiana State University Press, 1968.

Powell, Timothy B. *Ruthless Democracy: A Multicultural Interpretation of the American Renaissance*. Princeton, N.J.: Princeton University Press, 2000.

Said, Edward W. *Culture and Imperialism*. New York: Knopf, 1993.

Saldívar, José David. *Border Matters: Remapping American Cultural Studies*. Berkeley: University of California Press, 1997.

Smith, Henry Nash. "Symbol and Idea in *Virgin Land*." In *Ideology and Classic American Literature*, edited by Sacvan Bercovitch and Myra Jehlen. Cambridge, U.K., and New York: Cambridge University Press, 1986.

Smith, Henry Nash. *Virgin Land: The American West as Symbol and Myth*. Cambridge, Mass.: Harvard University Press, 1950.

Stilgoe, John R. *Common Landscape of America, 1580 to 1845*. New Haven, Conn.: Yale University Press, 1982.

Robert E. Abrams

BOSTON

In 1869 the nation's greatest war needed a suitably grand symbolic closure. Where better than in Boston, the city associated with agitating for the abolition of slavery? So on the afternoon of 15 June, the Irish immigrant bandleader Patrick Gilmore, who had composed *When Johnny Comes Marching Home* in 1863, kicked off the Great Peace Jubilee, the world's largest musical event to date. Before an audience of over fifty thousand, he had assembled one thousand instrumentalists and ten thousand chorus members to accompany scores of soloists performing patriotic airs and European classics. Between pieces, distinguished speakers held forth. Oliver Wendell Holmes's "Hymn of Peace" acknowledged the surrounding sonic tsunami: "Let the loud tempest of voices reply,— / Roll its long surge like the earth-shaking main!" (2:66). Even Ralph Waldo Emerson, there with his daughter, "was charmed with the spectacle, and with the great human voice of the chorus" (1:524). He was not alone. "I am for the present the fifty-thousandth part of an enormous emotion!" William Dean Howells reported in the *Atlantic Monthly* two months later (p. 247). He winced, however, at what others deemed a high point: in time to the famed "Anvil Chorus" of Verdi's opera *Il Trovatore,* a hundred red-shirted Boston firemen banged anvils while bells rang and cannons fired. "Brothers, once more," Holmes had proclaimed. After four years of war and as many of an ensuing uneasy occupation, Americans could resume hammering out their common destiny.

CITY OF ENTERPRISE

The Peace Jubilee crowned a half century of enterprise that had shaped Boston since its chartering as a city in 1822. "Our proper business is improvement," Daniel Webster had asserted in view of the city in his 1825 Bunker Hill Monument address. "Let us develop the resources of our land, call forth its powers, build up its institutions, promote all its great interests," he urged, with an eye toward linking the Revolution's civic achievements through war with his audience's socio-economic ambitions in peacetime. Let us "see whether we also, in our day and generation," he concluded, "may not perform something worthy to be remembered" (p. 40).

What Bostonians accomplished was indeed memorable. An "enterprising elite" adventured worldwide commercial links during the late eighteenth century, pioneered integrated production in massive factories in the 1810s and 1820s, and inaugurated intensive rail service that would make the city the region's economic hub by the 1830s and 1840s. Drawing upon business loans from large capital pools secured in banks via eleemosynary trusts like the Massachusetts General Hospital, elite families expanded family fortunes at mid-century through nationwide investments. The elite held no monopoly upon enterprise, though. Much of the early impetus for public improvements in health, welfare, schooling, and firefighting and for massive real estate projects, like Faneuil Hall Market's renewal, emerged from the so-called middling interests who elected Josiah Quincy mayor successively from 1823 to 1829. Together, they and the elite combined aggressive wealth-getting with a commitment to social and civic betterment that made Boston world famous for its genteel beneficence.

Such public-spirited enterprise accompanied rapid growth. Migrants swarmed in, some escaping the overpopulation in Boston's rural hinterland and others fleeing famine and political turmoil in Europe. Beginning at 43,298 in 1820, the population soared by 1850 to 136,881 and by 1870 to just over a quarter of a million. How would they all fit into the tiny peninsular city, precariously tied to the mainland by a narrow neck? Already unhealthily overcrowded in the 1820s, Boston could only expand outward. To do this, city fathers first cut down hills to fill the shoreline's many coves, then in the 1850s steam-shoveled suburban gravel into the Back Bay, widening the neck out of existence. The new acreage still did not relieve population pressure and consequent environmental degradation. "Coughing, and the ancient pastime of hawking . . . are the principle amusements of this cold city," the satirist George Horatio Derby pronounced in 1865 (p. 139). Because of continued overcrowding, many in the middle class moved to the suburbs, commuting to and from work. Boston had become a thriving metropolitan hub with spokes jutting deeply inland.

THE INFRASTRUCTURE OF PRINT

In its growth the city far outpaced other New England municipalities by dominating intraregional and northern transoceanic information flows. Prior to transatlantic cable service (1866), ship-bound European news—intercepted out-of-harbor by news brokers in rowboats—often came first to Boston. From there European culture filtered out to the region via reprint vehicles like *Littell's Living Age* (1844–1896). Indeed, the information hegemony benefited publishing. During the 1820s the number of book-trade firms shot up by 123 percent, roughly three times faster than the population. As early as 1833 the book trade surpassed other industries in its capital investment in machinery, while it accounted for about 90 percent of the value of its region's publishing.

As publishing boomed, its character changed. Earlier, printing and bookbinding firms clustered downtown in small-scale artisanal shops that combined home, work, and retail operations. By 1845 printing workplaces had become factory-like; workers now lived on the periphery, often near bridges or railroad terminals, affording easy access to opportunities elsewhere. By mid-century most printing tasks had degraded into repetitive machine-tending, booksellers had moved into specialized retail stores, and publishers had become primarily investors in literary properties who might only hire jobbers for printing and binding work.

State Street, Boston, 1837. Engraving after a drawing by William Henry Bartlett. © BETTMANN/CORBIS

LITERARY ENTREPRENEURS

Out of the industrializing 1840s new literary entrepreneurs emerged who specialized in cheap American novels or other original pamphlets. The German-born Frederick Gleason manufactured engravings of American scenes before publishing regionally oriented original novels, many of them by native authors. A string of successful newspapers followed, including in 1846 the story paper *Flag of Union* and, in 1851, the *Pictorial Drawing Room Companion*, the country's first illustrated weekly. By contrast, George W. Redding emerged from retailing: he started as a newsboy, then became a New York newspaper distributor, periodical depot proprietor, and publisher of pamphlets like *Easy Nat; or, Boston Bars and Boston Boys* (1844).

Publishers like these looked upon their products as mere plastic beneath the entrepreneurial hand, as John Townsend Trowbridge, who wrote for them, made plain in his *Martin Merrivale: His "X" Mark* (1853). "You see, our readers want everything condensed, rapid, dramatic," a cheap editor advises the book's hero, an aspiring author. "Take any ordinary novel, and cut it down one-half, and it'll be twice as good as it was before" (p. 247). Real-life publishers like Gleason went even farther in shaping their properties, publishing them variously as pamphlets, newspaper serials, playbooks.

LITERARY GENTRIFICATION

Memory of Boston's cheap literary entrepreneurs has faded before that of their so-called genteel counterparts, exemplified by the *Atlantic Monthly* (1857–1932) and its contributors. Emerson, Holmes, Henry Wadsworth Longfellow, James Russell Lowell, Charles Eliot Norton, Harriet Beecher Stowe, and John Greenleaf Whittier—the persisting familiarity of many of the names testifies to Boston's enduring success in associating itself with the period's best literature.

It had not always been that way. Successful literary magazines were long in coming, for example. The *North American Review* (1815–1940), the most notable early one, staunchly imitated British essay-laden counterparts, while the Unitarian *Christian Examiner* (1824–1869) did only little better within its theological parameters. The promise of the *New England Magazine* (1831–1834), with its distinguished list of local contributors on the cusp of the American Renaissance, was cut short by its editor's untimely death in 1833. Among quickly fading successors were Nathan Hale Jr.'s *Boston Miscellany* (1842–1843), combining features of a ladies' magazine with a genteel literary monthly, James Russell Lowell's *The Pioneer* (1843), filled with high-minded contributions, and Emerson's *The Dial* (1840–1844), the flagship venue for the transcendentalists.

Literary book publishing fared little better. The city throughout the period ranked third behind New York City and Philadelphia—the "axis" (Charvat, p. 26) of nationally oriented literary book production versus the Boston parochialism that favored local talent. Samuel G. Goodrich gained a small fortune with his "Peter Parley" children's books, and money could be made from reference works (especially in law and medicine), textbooks, and histories, such as the scholar-politician George Bancroft's ten-volume national overview and the sometime western travelogue writer Francis Parkman's work on the English-French struggle for colonial North America. Less remunerative were controversial social and religious works, at least until 1852 with Stowe's *Uncle Tom's Cabin*. By that time John P. Jewett, the book's publisher, was joined by other firms, like Phillips, Sampson, who aimed for a broader mass market but who eschewed the crass commercialism of the cheap publishers. Boston literary publishing was at last awakening, but under a banner of enterprising gentility.

No firm better represents the trend than Ticknor and Fields, founded in 1832. Partner James T. Fields slowly built a very "literary" list that catered to middle-class pretensions toward refinement as he eventually moved toward uniform edition binding, an early example of product branding. The African American schoolteacher Charlotte Forten recorded in her diary several gifts of the firm's imprints identified solely by their characteristic covers, as in her 7 March 1858 entry: "Miss U. came in, and very kindly gave me Mrs. Browning in blue and gold. Miss S. gave me Whittier, in the same" (Grimké, p. 291). The firm soared to prominence when it became Longfellow's publisher in 1846 and thereafter put Fireside Poets like him on the map. Though the firm did not venture as much into novel publishing, it scored a minor hit with Nathaniel Hawthorne's *Scarlet Letter* in 1850. Fields presided over these successes from his curtained room in the firm's Old Corner Bookstore, where he held lively court with Boston literati. The salonlike atmosphere extended to Fields's home, where Annie Adams Fields, after their 1854 marriage, used her influence to shape local literary culture.

PRESCIENT, BUT PREMATURE

For all this enterprise, the city's literary reputation remained higher than its receipts from publishing. Augustine Joseph Hickey Duganne hit at this in his *Parnassus in Pillory* (1851):

> Of Fame's broad temple Boston keeps the portal,
> And Boston bards alone are dubbed immortal:
> Even though her dingy bookstores, it is said,
> Are one great sepulchre of "sheeted dead."
>
> *(P. 202)*

In other words, despite Boston's imperative intellectual claims, most books by local authors stood on the shelves. Indeed, despite the mid-century Longfellow and *Uncle Tom* surge, Boston publishing hopelessly lost, as Philadelphia did, to New York City.

It is not hard to explain why, for New York simply used its advantageous transportation to dominate the national market. Stakes were always higher there than in Boston, which had increasingly to compete with New York in the western and southern parts of its own region. As if that were not enough, Boston tended to produce literature that was more "advanced" than could yet be widely accepted in other places, whether this emerged from Harvard moral philosophers, the city's many reformers, or, on the aesthetic front, from transcendentalists.

Yet the lag in acceptance somewhat accounts for the paradox of high regard with few sales: many avant-garde trends in antebellum Boston literary culture would move toward the postbellum national mainstream. After all, in 1865 abolitionism was written into the Thirteenth Amendment. The emergence of a liberal Protestant united front also made Unitarian moral philosophy more acceptable, as its social-science flavor came increasingly to inform (and moderate) earlier reformism. Even transcendental individualism seemed more at home among postbellum capitalists. Not to be overlooked either was New England's influence, through precedent and personnel, upon state school systems beyond the Hudson. That is how the Schoolroom Poets (William Cullen Bryant, Holmes, Longfellow, Lowell, and John Greenleaf Whittier, among others) got their collective name, after all. In short, Gilded Age America assimilated once-spurned antebellum New England as its own, but by that time the creative vigor was gone, as was Boston publishers' economic wherewithal. Moreover, postbellum Boston's "gendering of letters" (Duffy, p. 91) as masculine had caused the reputations of once prominent local women writers to fade before that of their genteel male counterparts.

"SCRIBBLING WOMEN"

When Hawthorne complained in 1855 about the "mob of scribbling women" (p. 304) who competed with him in the literary marketplace, he necessarily targeted among them the numerous nationally reputed female authors who published in, hailed from, or had come to live in Boston. By the time Hawthorne wrote his now infamous words, Lydia Maria Child (*Letters from New York,* 1843–1845), Julia Ward Howe (*Passion Flowers,* 1854), Margaret Fuller (*Woman in the Nineteenth Century,* 1845), and Harriet Beecher Stowe (*Uncle Tom's Cabin,* 1852), had made their mark upon American literature. The "mob" grew larger still when Caroline W. H. Dall (*The College, the Market, and the Court,* 1867), Louisa May Alcott (*Little Women,* 1868–1869), Elizabeth Stuart Phelps (*The Gates Ajar,* 1868), and Mary Abigail Dodge (*Country Living and Country Thinking,* 1862) made their names during or after the Civil War. These eclectic and prolific authors, who were caught up at some time in their lives by the era's spirit of reform, are today regarded for their abolitionist and proto-feminist vision.

PUBLIC LECTURES

Beyond authorship, women exercised their intellectual might at Boston's many lyceum and lecture halls that began to emerge by 1830. "Ladies who have a passion for attending lectures," Charles Dickens wrote in his *American Notes* (1842), "are to be found among all classes and all conditions" (p. 65). With the "ladies," of course, came male escorts equally enamored with the sights and sounds of lecturing. As Dickens observed, audiences were diverse but mainly composed of upper and middling occupational groups in their forties or younger. So popular were lectures that the city provided at least twenty-six courses during the 1838–1839 winter season alone. This form of entertainment thrived until the Civil War, after which locally sponsored attractions eventually gave way to nationally syndicated affairs.

During the heyday of lecture-going, the most prestigious institutions included the Boston Society for the Diffusion of Useful Knowledge and the Boston Lyceum, both initiated in 1829, and the Lowell Institute, begun in 1839. Together they sponsored, among well-known naturalists, lawyers, and clergymen, American literati such as Emerson, Lowell, Fields, Howells, and the novelist Richard Henry Dana Jr. Sundry speakers were featured by library associations, churches, and benevolent, mechanics', and mercantile societies that opened their doors to the public for a small fee or gratis, and also by entrepreneurs who rented halls and charged admission. Voices of mesmerists, phrenologists, botanists, spiritualists, and above all reformers filled the air. The abolitionists Theodore Parker and Angelina Grimké, the temperance advocate John B. Gough, and the women's rights activist Lucy Stone, among others, made themselves heard.

REFORM

A bustling platform for outspoken reformers, Boston nourished several influential related publications and institutions. Some underscored the city's commitment to intellectual uplift. As the first secretary of the Massachusetts Board of Education established in 1837, Horace Mann published twelve widely received annual reports (1837–1848) and the *Common School Journal* (1838–1851), both reflecting his tireless efforts to rehabilitate the state's failing school system. Library reform culminated in state legislation in 1848 authorizing the city to support a repository, namely the Boston Public Library, which opened in 1854. Other reforms addressed social problems. The Boston Prison Discipline Society's reports (1826–1854), Dorothea Dix's *A Memorial to the Massachusetts Legislature* (1843), and Charles Spear's magazine *The Prisoner's Friend* (1845–1861) advocated more humane treatment of the insane and criminals. Bostonians also tackled alcoholism, from sponsoring the first Massachusetts Temperance Society meeting in 1813 to inviting Washingtonians to hold a spectacular parade in 1844—all publicized through print. Indeed, local publishers put forth more than thirty-five different temperance periodicals between the years 1820 and 1870, with titles like *Zion's Herald* (1823–1828) and *National Philanthropist and Investigator and Genius of Temperance* (1829–1830).

Above all, Boston became a center of abolitionism. William Lloyd Garrison, instrumental in founding the New England Anti-Slavery Society (1832) and the American Anti-Slavery Society (1833–1870), published *The Liberator* (1831–1865), a weekly calling for the immediate abolition of slavery. Soon after *The Liberator*'s first issue, Lydia Maria Child, a novelist and founding member of the Boston Female Anti-Slavery Society that published the gift annual *The Liberty Bell* (1839–1858), brought forth her own "immediatist" *Appeal in Favor of That Class of Americans Called Africans* (1833). Abolitionism thereafter streamed from Boston's presses.

OTHER BOSTONIANS

The racial discourses running through Bostonian debates over slavery touched upon two groups with

In an article titled "Literary and Social Boston," which appeared in Harper's New Monthly Magazine in 1881, George P. Lathrop wistfully looks back upon the now faded cultural ferment of the antebellum years.

In the quickening of thought and the refinement of manners that set in, the smallness and compactness of Boston were advantages. It was a little city; a city of gardens and solid brick houses and stores; cheerful, quiet, unsophisticated; with a fringe of wharves along the bay that supplied the picturesque additions of a successful sea-port, and surrounded by villages smaller than itself, of which Cambridge was an important but rather remote one. . . . In such a place impressions spread rapidly; theories were infectious; phrenology, Unitarianism, vegetarianism, emancipation, Transcendentalism, worked their way from street to street like an epidemic. A new course of study or a new thought was as exciting as news of a European war could have been. A lady remembers meeting another on Tremont Street during the full glow of the Emerson lecture epoch, and exclaiming, "Oh, there's a new idea! Have you heard it?"

"Don't talk to me of ideas," retorted her friend; "I'm so full of them now that I can't make room for a single new one."

George P. Lathrop, "Literary and Social Boston," *Harper's New Monthly Magazine,* February 1881, p. 383.

diverging and sometimes opposing fates. These were African Americans and Catholic Irish immigrants.

Blacks had been in Boston since colonial days, but the population remained fairly small, hovering at around two thousand until 1860. Nominally free since 1783, black Bostonians still faced severe statutory, customary, residential, and economic discrimination. Some, like David Walker in his *Appeal* (1829), explicitly linked slavery with larger patterns of racism, as he called on his "coloured brethren" (p. 62) to act immediately toward ending both. Others, like the schoolteacher Susan Paul in her *Memoir of James Jackson* (1835), a recently deceased seven-year-old pupil of

hers, urged the rising generation to combat prejudice. By the time she wrote, several "black abolitionists" had emerged, notably William C. Nell, who assisted in editing *The Liberator* and campaigned to desegregate Boston's schools (1855). Despite civil rights successes like this and those concerning interracial marriages, segregated transportation, and voting blockages, as late as March 1860 John Swett Rock could still ask in *The Liberator,* "Is Boston anti-slavery?" (Levesque, p. 112). To make his case for the negative, he pointed to persisting ghettoization, unrelieved segregation in public accommodations, stereotyping on the city's two black-face minstrel stages, and rapidly worsening job prospects. The Civil War brought only halting advances, such as that which occurred in 1863 through the efforts of the influential Massachusetts secretary of state messenger Lewis Hayden (to be elected in 1865 as the nation's first black state representative) to commission an African American fighting unit.

Slow progress with symbolic gains also characterized Boston's Irish. In the wake of the 1846 potato famine, the arrival of impoverished and unskilled Irish immigrants on a heretofore unimaginable scale—by 1855 they accounted for about a third of the population—challenged beneficent Bostonian enterprise. How should the city deal with the perceived upsurge in urban maladies, not the least of which was being so stubbornly indifferent to Protestant norms? These perceptions fueled the powerful nativist movement that crested in 1854 with anti-Catholic "Know-Nothings" gaining control of state government. Their initiatives ultimately fell apart, as did the party, thanks partly to the success of Irish leaders—through churchmen, effective news organs like Patrick Donahoe's *Pilot* (1836–1857), and word of mouth in Irish social associations—in restraining community outrage. Separatism worked in this, but it would take the forced integration of Civil War military service finally to allow Boston's Irish to move toward acculturation.

It was, after all, an Irish bandleader who organized and led the 1869 Peace Jubilee before an audience that included blacks, immigrants, women, Yankee workers, middling folk, literati, and Brahmins alike. Clearly the local spirit of enterprise that helped rid the nation of slavery was giving way, however gradually, to a new civic pluralism.

See also Abolitionist Writing; *The Atlantic Monthly;* Book Publishing; Editors; Irish; *The Liberator;* Literary Criticism; Literary Marketplace; Lyceums; Transcendentalism

BIBLIOGRAPHY

Primary Works

Derby, George Horatio. *The Squibob Papers*. New York: Carleton, 1865.

Dickens, Charles. *American Notes for General Circulation*. New York: Harper & Brothers, 1842.

Duganne, Augustine Joseph Hickey. *Parnassus in Pillory; A Satire*. New York: Adriance, Sherman, 1851.

Emerson, Ellen Tucker. *The Letters of Ellen Tucker Emerson*. Vol. 1. Edited by Edith W. Gregg. Kent, Ohio: Kent State University Press, 1982.

Grimké, Charlotte Forten. *The Journals of Charlotte Forten Grimké*. Edited by Brenda Stevenson. New York: Oxford University Press, 1988.

Hawthorne, Nathaniel. "Nathaniel Hawthorne to William D. Ticknor, Jan. 9, 1855." In *The Letters, 1853–1856*, edited by William Charvat, Roy Harvey Pearse, and Claude M. Simpson, p. 304. The Centenary Edition of the Works of Nathaniel Hawthorne, volume 17. Columbus: Ohio University Press, 1962–1997.

Holmes, Oliver Wendell. *The Poetical Works of Oliver Wendell Holmes*. 3 vols. Boston: Houghton Mifflin, 1893.

Howells, William Dean. "Jubilee Days." *Atlantic Monthly* 24 (August 1869): 245–254.

Trowbridge, John Townsend. *Martin Merrivale: His "X" Mark*. Boston: Phillips, Sampson, 1853.

Walker, David. *David Walker's Appeal, in Four Articles, Together with a Preamble to the Coloured Citizens of the World, but in Particular, and Very Expressly, to Those of the United States of America*. 1929. Rev. ed. Edited by Sean Wilentz. New York: Hill and Wang, 1995.

Webster, Daniel. *An Address Delivered at the Laying of the Corner Stone of the Bunker Hill Monument*. 3rd ed. Boston: Cummings, Hilliard, 1825.

Secondary Works

Blouin, Francis X., Jr. *The Boston Region, 1810–1850: A Study of Urbanization*. Ann Arbor, Mich.: UMI Research Press, 1980.

Brooks, Van Wyck. *Literature in New England: The Flowering of New England, 1815–1865; New England: Indian Summer, 1865–1915*. Garden City, N.Y.: Garden City, 1944.

Buell, Lawrence. *New England Literary Culture: From Revolution through Renaissance*. New York: Cambridge University Press, 1986.

Charvat, William. *Literary Publishing in America, 1790–1850*. 1959. Amherst: University of Massachusetts Press, 1993.

Crocker, Matthew H. *The Magic of the Many: Josiah Quincy and the Rise of Mass Politics in Boston, 1800–1830*. Amherst: University of Massachusetts Press, 1999.

Dalzell, Robert F., Jr. *Enterprising Elite: The Boston Associates and the World They Made*. Cambridge, Mass.: Harvard University Press, 1987.

Duffy, Timothy P. "The Gender of Letters: Charles Eliot Norton and the Decline of the Amateur Intellectual Tradition." *New England Quarterly* 69 (1996): 91–109.

Hall, Peter Dobkin. *The Organization of American Culture, 1700–1900: Private Institutions, Elites, and the Origins of American Nationality*. New York: New York University Press, 1982.

Handlin, Oscar. *Boston's Immigrants [1790–1880]: A Study in Acculturation*. Rev. ed. Cambridge, Mass.: Belknap Press of Harvard University Press, 1959.

Horton, James Oliver, and Lois E. Horton. *Black Bostonians: Family Life and Community Struggle in the Antebellum North*. Rev. ed. New York: Holmes and Meier, 1999.

Howe, Daniel Walker. *The Unitarian Conscience: Harvard Moral Philosophy, 1805–1861*. Cambridge, Mass.: Harvard University Press, 1970.

Kaestle, Carl F. *Pillars of the Republic: Common Schools and American Society, 1780–1860*. New York: Hill and Wang, 1983.

Levesque, George A. *Black Boston: African American Life and Culture in Urban America, 1750–1860*. New York: Garland, 1994.

O'Connor, Thomas H. *The Boston Irish: A Political History*. Boston: Northeastern University Press, 1995.

Pred, Allan. *Urban Growth and City Systems in the United States, 1840–1860*. Cambridge, Mass.: Harvard University Press, 1980.

Robboy, Stanley J., and Anita W. Robboy. "Lewis Hayden: From Fugitive to Statesman." *New England Quarterly* 46 (1973): 591–613.

Schwarzlose, Richard Allen. *The Nation's Newsbrokers*. 2 vols. Evanston, Ill.: Northwestern University Press, 1989–1990.

Scott, Donald M. "The Popular Lecture and the Creation of a Public in Mid-Nineteenth-Century America." *Journal of American History* 66 (1980): 791–809.

Tryon, Warren S. *Parnassus Corner: A Life of James T. Fields, Publisher to the Victorians*. Boston: Houghton Mifflin, 1963.

Walters, Ronald G. *American Reformers, 1815–1860*. New York: Hill and Wang, 1978

Whitehill, Walter Muir. *Boston: A Topographical History*. 2nd ed. Cambridge, Mass.: Harvard University Press, 1968.

Winsor, Justin. *The Memorial History of Boston, including Suffolk County, Massachusetts, 1630–1880.* 4 vols. Boston: Ticknor, 1881.

Zboray, Ronald J. *A Fictive People: Antebellum Economic Development and the American Reading Public.* New York: Oxford University Press, 1993.

Zboray, Ronald J., and Mary Saracino Zboray. "The Boston Book Trades, 1789–1850: A Statistical and Geographical Analysis." In *Entrepreneurs: The Boston Business Community, 1700–1850,* edited by Conrad Edick Wright and Kathryn P. Viens, pp. 210–267. Boston: Massachusetts Historical Society, 1997.

Zboray, Ronald J., and Mary Saracino Zboray. *Literary Dollars and Social Sense: A People's History of the Mass Market Book.* New York: Routledge, 2005.

Ronald J. Zboray
Mary Saracino Zboray

BROOK FARM

See The Blithedale Romance; Transcendentalism; Utopian Communities

THE CALIFORNIA
AND OREGON TRAIL

See The Oregon Trail

CALIFORNIA GOLD RUSH

Gold was discovered in California by the carpenter James Marshall on a fork of the American River in January 1848. The effect of the discovery was electric, triggering a stampede of miners from around the world headed to California to find instant wealth. What made the California gold rush a significant social—and literary—event was not simply the $400 million in gold extracted by miners between 1849 and 1855. It was the carnivalesque atmosphere of swagger, heightened expectation, and boomtown hokum that characterized the tens of thousands of young, self-styled "Argonauts" who poured into a remote Pacific maritime province recently wrested from Mexico in the Mexican-American War. The gold rush inspired more written documents than any other nineteenth-century historical event except the Civil War. The bibliographer Gary Kurutz has cataloged over seven hundred individual documents published in the five years from 1848 to 1853. Gold rush writing included fiction, plays, diaries, essays, letters, song lyrics, and satiric squibs written by authors of various nationalities. It provided a vivid, on-the-ground response to life in frontier California, one that embodied imaginative extremes and often fluctuated between exultation and sour disillusionment.

The gold rush was assessed in divergent, even contradictory ways from the start, both by the miners themselves and by outside observers. Initial exuberance about golden prospects in California was often quickly tempered by the sobering realities of cholera, sickness, bad weather, exorbitant prices, fleas, and the demands of hard, repetitive manual labor. Glowing reports of riches in the Golden State were matched by dispirited letters home from impoverished or homesick miners or by disparaging criticism from outside observers. Henry David Thoreau, for instance, was appalled by the spectacle of thousands of miners scrambling for gold. "The hog that *roots* his own living would be ashamed of such company," he noted in his journal in 1852. "Going to California. It is only 3,000 miles nearer to Hell" (p. 317).

The people writing about the gold rush in the 1850s had been translated from conditions of relative stability to social chaos. The boom-and-bust mentality of San Francisco, along with its rapid settlement and polyglot mixing of cultures, helped sponsor a literature that tended to stress the novel and the picturesque. The literary historian Franklin Walker has pointed out that the emphasis was on lawlessness rather than law, gambling rather than the slow accrual of a fortune, the prostitute with a heart of gold rather than the pioneer mother, the abandoned orphan rather than the extended family with solicitous relatives. Although various promotional tracts and pictorial letter sheets portrayed images of the "industrious" miner, that character did not capture writers' imaginations.

POETRY, FICTION, AND DRAMA

Gold rush writing included all the major literary genres, but poetry tended to be undistinguished in early California, characterized by either belabored dialect poems or self-consciously literary celebrations of the landscape by California "songsters." The variously bawdy and maudlin lyrics of such gold rush songs as "Seeing the Elephant," "Sweet Betsey from Pike," and "Ho! For California!" however, provide a rich record of poetic sentiment and satire.

In fiction, the one notable work inspired by the mining camps was John Rollin Ridge's (1827–1867) sensationalist romance *The Life and Adventures of Joaquín Murieta, the Celebrated California Bandit* (1854), which was the first novel published by an American Indian (Ridge was half Cherokee). An action-packed potboiler, *Joaquín Murieta* suggests the uneasy, often indiscriminately violent interracial relations of miners on an ethnically diverse frontier. The novel's landscape of isolated arroyos and campfire canyons matches the sensationalistic plot twists of daring disguises and quick getaways—followed, ultimately, by the decapitation of the novel's hero and the public display of his severed head in a jar.

Gold rush drama embodied the love of melodrama and action displayed in *Joaquín Murieta*. The popular melodramas and farces of the day, such as *A Live Woman in the Mines; or, Pike County Ahead* (1857) by Alonzo Delano (1806–1874) and *Fast Folks; or, The Early Days of California* (1858) by Joseph Nunes (1818–1904), are more historical curiosities than fully realized plays. Yet these works feature a wild and wooly western vernacular indebted to the Southwest humorists, and they possess a kind of rough-and-ready impudence that can still beguile. Delano's *A Live Woman in the Mines*, for instance, comically presents hardships faced by the miners, even starvation. When the food runs out in camp, the men dine on rats and boots. As a last resort they tie the last piece of pork to a string; each man swallows the pork, then pulls it out and passes it on.

NONFICTIONAL NARRATIVES

The true imaginative wealth of the gold rush resides in its nonfictional prose: diaries, letters, journals, memoirs, government documents, and personal narratives. Gold rush writing frequently addressed practical matters such as the arduous travel to and from California, the price of meals or hardware, and claim disputes. Yet in the best works this very emphasis on the demands of everyday life—on the mud, fleas, and open-air autopsies in the camps—contributes to the rough-and-tumble piquancy of these memoirs. The best mining camp narratives, such as Louise Clappe's

Sergeant James H. Carson, a Virginia native, arrived in Monterey, California, with his army regiment just after the Mexican-American War ended. He deserted while on furlough to prospect for gold from 1848 to 1850. He struck it rich at what was soon called Carson's Creek, but not before contracting a severe bout of rheumatism for which he was hospitalized for eighteen months and "lost the use of his speech." In 1852, from his sickbed, he furnished readers with an account of his experiences in the gold diggings. First published as a series of thirty-three articles in the Stockton, California, newspaper the San Joaquin Republican, *the editors noted "an abandon in [his] style, . . . a broad humor, and a liberal soul . . . , which are characteristics peculiarly Californian." Carson died in April 1853, a month before his wife and daughter arrived in California.*

Yes, Billy, I can see you yet, just as you stood before me on that sunny 10th of May, looking so much like the devil, with that great bag of the Tempter on your back! Then he told me it was gold, . . . not in dust or scales, but in pieces ranging in size from that of a pea to hen's egg; and, says he, "this is only what I picked out with a knife." . . . a frenzy seized my soul; unbidden my legs performed some entirely new movements of Polka steps—I took several—houses were too small for me to stay in; I was soon in the street in search of the necessary outfits; piles of gold rose up before me at every step; castles of marble, . . . thousands of slaves, bowing to my beck and call; myriads of fair virgins contending with each other for my love, were among the fancies of my fevered imagination. The Rothschilds, Girard, and Astors appeared to me but poor people: in short, I had a very violent attack of the *Gold Fever"*

Carson, *Bright Gem of the Western Seas*, p. 3.

(1819–1906) *The Shirley Letters* (1854–1855), blend satire and appreciation in unexpected ways. Writing under the nom de plume "Dame Shirley," Clappe wrote a series of twenty-three letters from two high-country camps in the upper reaches of the Feather River to her stay-at-home sister in Massachusetts. The primitive living conditions startled her eastern notions of decorum:

Illustration from *Three Years in California* by Walter Colton, 1850. Emphasizing the opportunistic nature of many forty-niners. CLEMENTS LIBRARY, UNIVERSITY OF MICHIGAN

How would you like to winter in such an abode?—in a place where there are no newspapers, no churches, lectures, concerts or theaters; no fresh books, no shopping, calling nor gossiping little tea-drinkings; no parties, no balls, no picnics, no *tableaux,* no charades, no latest fashions, no daily mail, (we have an express once a month) no promenades, no rides, nor drives; no vegetables but potatoes and onions, no milk, no eggs, no *nothing?* (P. 50)

Yet just when conditions seem most crude and unredeemable, Clappe adds a characteristic sparkle of candor and mischief. "Now I expect to be very happy here. This strange, odd life, fascinates me" (p. 50).

Clappe did not gloss over the ugliness and the prejudice she encountered in the camps. She was sometimes insensitive in her portrayal of California Indians, seeing them as degraded savages who fell disappointingly short of "the glorious forest heroes that live in the Leatherstocking Tales" (p. 12). But she was exhilarated by the cultural heterogeneity of the mining camps, and her letters offer a unique blend of sympathetic social portraiture and literate satire. (Both Bret Harte and Mark Twain seem to have found inspiration in Clappe's letters for some of their best-known stories without acknowledging their origin.) *The Shirley Letters* creates a narrative of rejuvenation. In her last letter Clappe states that it is no longer a "feeble and half-dying invalid" but a "perfectly healthy" woman who will miss the mines: "I *like* this wild and barbarous life; I leave it with regret" (pp. 178–179).

A number of other American gold rush narratives are worthy of note, including Walter Colton's *Three Years in California* (1850); Edward Gould Buffum's *Six Months in the Gold Mines* (1850); Alonzo Delano's *Life on the Plains and among the Diggings* (1854); Eliza Farnham's *California In-Doors and Out* (1856); *The Life and Adventures of James P. Beckwourth* (1856), the as-told-to autobiography of an African American fur trapper and mountain man; John Letts's *California Illustrated* (1852); and Mary Jane Megquier's letters from 1849 to 1856, collected in *Apron Full of Gold* (1949).

Realistic prose accounts of the gold rush were often less well known at the time than the work of frontier humorists like Alonzo Delano and George Horatio Derby. Delano published works under his legal name in the East, but he presented himself as the long-nosed character Old Block in San Francisco. He wrote popular whimsical sketches, or "whittlings from his Pen-Knife" (p. 32), of western types like the miner and the gambler, for San Francisco's *Pacific News.* These articles were collected in two books, *Pen Knife Sketches; or, Chips of the Old Block* in 1853 and *Old Block's Sketch Book; or, Tales of California Life* in 1856.

George Horatio Derby (1823–1861), whom Mark Twain called "the first of the great modern humorists," was a caricaturist and U.S. Army topographical engineer assigned to California in the early 1850s, after service in the Mexican-American War. He wrote under the pseudonyms John Phoenix and John P. Squibob and became famous as a wag and practical joker. His letters, squibs, and burlesques, which often struck a pose of urbane absurdity, appeared in various California newspapers. His occasional prose was collected in two volumes, *Phoenixiana; or, Sketches and Burlesques* (1855), which went through some twenty-six printings, and the posthumous *Squibob Papers* (1865).

TWAIN, HARTE, AND POST-FRONTIER FICTION

The writings of Derby, Delano, Ridge, Clappe, and others helped lodge the California gold rush in the American imagination. In the 1860s and 1870s a second generation of authors that included Twain, Harte, Joaquin Miller, Charles Warren Stoddard, Ina Coolbrith, and Prentice Mulford helped transform the gold rush into mythic history and eclipsed the work of those who had preceded them. The *Overland Monthly* catalyzed the influence of this later group of writers and was arguably the most important literary periodical ever published in California. Founded in San Francisco in 1868 by a local bookseller and former miner named Anton Roman, the *Overland Monthly* was designed to encourage emigration to California, yet the magazine actually eulogized the romantic frontier days eclipsed by modern life after the Civil War. Although he never actually published in the *Overland Monthly,* Mark Twain (1835–1910) captivated his eastern audience with the local color of California subject matter in November 1865, when he published his short story "Jim Smiley and His Jumping Frog" (later retitled "The Celebrated Jumping Frog of Calaveras County") in the New York *Saturday Press.* A parody of a tall tale, in which a nameless confidence man outwits the con man Jim Smiley in one of the animal contests of which miners were so fond, Twain's story made literary capital out of subliterate frontier humor and established his talent for simultaneously celebrating and satirizing the vigorous, misspelled slang of the western mining frontier.

More than any other writer, Bret Harte (1836–1902) was responsible for creating the legendary, larger-than-life image of the gold rush. He did so by transforming squalid mining camps into robust mythical communities inhabited by a citizenry that looked intrepid and stouthearted in hindsight. Harte's "The Luck of Roaring Camp," which was published without a signature in the second issue of the *Overland Monthly,* was an overnight sensation and helped make Harte a household name by the early 1870s. Stories such as "The Luck of Roaring Camp" (1868), "The Outcasts of Poker Flat" (1869), and "Tennessee's Partner" (1869) feature a cast of endearing character types: grizzled sentimentalists (Kentuck and Stumpy), debonair gamblers (John Oakhurst and Jack Hamlin), young innocents (Piney Woods and the Luck), and golden-hearted but fallen women like Mother Shipton and the Duchess.

Harte's stories are filled with violence and degradation. In "The Luck of Roaring Camp" the baby's mother, Cherokee Sal, is an Indian prostitute who died during childbirth; at the end of "The Outcasts," John Oakhurst has committed suicide and the reader is left contemplating an image of the corpses of two frozen women. What keeps Harte's stories from becoming truly terrifying or morally ambivalent, however, is his ability, in Kevin Starr's words, to create mythic history by depicting the gold rush as "quaint comedy and sentimental melodrama, already possessing the charm of antiquity." Harte's narrative voice creates a warmhearted, ameliorating safeguard against violence. He highlights the tender emotions that lurk unexpectedly beneath the hardened shells of his characters and thus prepares his reader for the moral transformations these characters undergo.

Although the heyday of prospecting for gold in California was relatively short-lived, it nevertheless proved to be an irresistible literary subject. Both firsthand accounts of the gold rush and retrospective, reimagined versions of that era like those of Harte and Twain provide an impressive panoply of literary responses whose aesthetic complexity and documentary insight has still not been fully appreciated.

See also "The Celebrated Jumping Frog of Calaveras County"; Humor; Tall Tales

BIBLIOGRAPHY

Primary Works

Carson, James H. *Early Recollections of the Mines, and a Description of the Great Tulare Valley.* Stockton, Calif.: *San Joaquin Republican,* 1852. Reprinted as *Bright Gem of the Western Seas: California, 1846–1852.* Edited by

Peter Browning. Lafayette, Calif.: Great West Books, 1991.

Delano, Alonzo. *Pen Knife Sketches; or, Chips of the Old Block*. Sacramento: Published at the Union Office, 1853.

Shirley, Dame [Louise Amelia Knapp Smith Clappe]. *The Shirley Letters from the California Mines, 1951–1852*. Edited with introduction by Marlene Smith-Baranzini. Berkeley: Heyday Books, 1998.

Thoreau, Henry David. *The Writings of Henry David Thoreau, Volume 4: 1851–1852*. Edited by Leonard N. Neufeldt and Nancy Craig Simmons. Princeton, N.J.: Princeton University Press, 1992.

Secondary Works

Brands, H. W. *The Age of Gold: The California Gold Rush and the New American Dream*. New York: Doubleday, 2002.

Dwyer, Richard A., and Richard E. Lingenfelter, eds. *Songs of the Gold Rush*. Berkeley: University of California Press, 1964.

Fender, Stephen. *Plotting the Golden West: American Literature and the Rhetoric of the California Trail*. New York: Cambridge University Press, 1981.

Holliday, J. S. *Rush for Riches: Gold Fever and the Making of California*. Oakland and Berkeley: Oakland Museum of California and University of California Press, 1999.

Holliday, J. S. *The World Rushed In: The California Gold Rush Experience*. New York: Simon and Schuster, 1981.

Johnson, Susan Lee. *Roaring Camp: The Social World of the California Gold Rush*. New York: Norton, 2000.

Kowalewski, Michael, ed. *Gold Rush: A Literary Exploration*. Berkeley: Heyday Books in conjunction with the California Council for the Humanities, 1997.

Kowalewski, Michael, ed. *Reading the West: New Essays on the Literature of the American West*. New York: Cambridge University Press, 1996.

Kurutz, Gary F. *The California Gold Rush: A Descriptive Bibliography of Books and Pamphlets Covering the Years 1848–1853*. San Francisco: Book Club of California, 1997.

Perry, Claire. *Pacific Arcadia: Images of California, 1600–1915*. New York: Oxford University Press, 1999.

Rohrbough, Malcolm. *Days of Gold*. Berkeley: University of California Press, 1997.

Starr, Kevin. *Americans and the California Dream, 1850–1915*. New York: Oxford University Press, 1973.

Starr, Kevin, and Richard J. Orsi, eds. *Rooted in Barbarous Soil: People, Culture, and Community in Gold Rush California*. Berkeley: California Historical Society and University of California Press, 2000.

Walker, Franklin. *San Francisco's Literary Frontier*. New York: Knopf, 1939.

Michael Kowalewski

CALVINISM

The term "Calvinism" is applied to the teachings linked to John Calvin (1509–1564), a French theologian and church reformer, whose *Institutes of the Christian Religion* (1536) provided the five basic doctrines of the Protestant churches and Reformed tradition: (1) total depravity—the "complete corruption of humanity resulting from Original Sin"; (2) unconditional election—"the predestined salvation or damnation of every individual"; (3) irresistible grace—necessary for conversion but available to the "elect" only; (4) perseverance of the saints—"the enduring justification and righteousness of the converted"; and (5) limited atonement—"Christ's gift of life through His death but only for those already predestined for heaven" (Elliott, p. 187). In short, Calvin stressed the sovereignty of a deliberate God and denied the innately depraved individual all agency.

Calvinistic faith flourished in early America. The Pilgrims, under the leadership of Governor William Bradford (1590–1657), planted it in New England in November of 1620. Only ten years later, roughly one thousand Puritans, led by John Winthrop (1588–1649), set sail for Massachusetts Bay. Particular Baptists removed it to Virginia, Massachusetts, and Providence, Rhode Island. George Fox's (1624–1691) Quakers, whom the church historian Sydney Ahlstrom characterized as the "most important and enduring manifestation of Puritan radicalism in either England or America" (p. 176), brought it to Rhode Island and Pennsylvania. The Dutch Reformed transferred their "predominately Puritan" ethic (p. 253) to New York, New Jersey, and Maryland. The Scotch and Scotch-Irish Presbyterians introduced their faith to the Carolinas and parts of Georgia. By 1730 Puritan Calvinism represented a firmly established theology in the soon-to-be United States. Its ideological and rhetorical legacy for American culture and literature proved both profound and multifaceted.

PURITAN IDEOLOGY

With its emphasis on predestination and simultaneous insistence on the indistinguishability of the "elect" (the "invisible church"), Calvinist theology might have led to the erosion of standards and values. To prevent this from occurring and to help their congregations cope with the uncertainty of unconditional election, seventeenth-century New England Puritan ministers introduced the doctrine of preparationism or "covenant theology." Covenant theology substituted divine decree as the basis for election with a compact between God and his worshipers. In exchange for absolute obedience, God allowed human beings to prepare for grace. Preparation, however, did not guarantee election. Rather, it demanded from the believer a display of a heretofore unseen degree of self-reflection, paradoxically paired with a relatively large portion of self-confidence. To doubt one's election was indicative of the lack of grace and revealed vulnerability to the temptations of the devil. To act as one saw fit was equally disgraceful, as human beings' reliance on the moral faculty was not only misleading but also presumptuous. In order to gain certainty of salvation or *certituto salutis,* then, Puritans had to follow their "effectual calling" or *fides efficax:* they had to dedicate their lives to the glorification of God.

Based on their readings of the Bible, the Puritans believed that there were two ways to answer the effectual calling. On the one hand, they could follow their "general (effectual) calling" and further God's glory by worshiping his creation—that is, by heeding Christ's dictum to love their fellow human beings. "Thou shalt love the Lord thy God with all thy heart, and with all thy soul, and with all thy mind. This is the first and great commandment. The second is like unto it, Thou shalt love thy neighbour like thyself" (Matthew 22:37–39). On the other hand, they were encouraged to follow their "particular (effectual) calling" and demonstrate their love and usefulness for others by thriving in their vocation. In theory, then, Puritan theology considered all legal occupations equal. It measured the public utility and worth of individuals by their dedication to their predestined vocation and not in terms of social status.

Although the Puritans' covenant withered and finally collapsed in the mid-eighteenth century, its biblical theme stipulating grace for reciprocal altruism, an ascetic work ethic, and disregard for class differences persisted. Even Benjamin Franklin (1706–1790), a paragon of the American Enlightenment who dismissed revealed religion, epitomized Puritan precepts. In his *Autobiography* (1791), Franklin boasted his "modesty and . . . disinterestedness" (p. 87) and his "industry and frugality" (p. 41), which, if paired with "respect to all" (p. 93), proved a "means of obtaining wealth and distinction" (p. 91). Franklin set for himself the "arduous project of arriving at moral perfection" (p. 94) and strove to perform "the most acceptable service of God, [that is,] . . . doing good to man" (p. 92). Thus, Franklin's *Autobiography* reflected the Calvinist belief that God helped those

---

As the Puritan clergyman John Winthrop, professor of the Andover Theological Seminary, Harriet Beecher Stowe, E. A. Park, and Mark Twain suggest, Puritan Calvinism left tangible and intangible legacies.

God Almighty in His most holy and wise providence, hath so disposed of the condition of mankind, as in all times some must be rich, some poor, some high and eminent in power and dignity; others mean and in subjection.

(Winthrop, p. 101)

[Edwards] sawed the great dam and let out the whole waters of discussion all over New England, and that free discussion led to all the shades of opinion in modern days . . . yet Waldo Emerson and Theodore Parker were the last results of the current set in motion by Jonathan Edwards.

(Harriet Beecher Stowe, Oldtown Folks, *quoted in Gura, "Jonathan Edwards in American Literature," p. 153)*

The metaphysics of New England Theology is such as the yeomen of our fields drank down for the sincere milk of the word. It is the metaphysics of common sense. . . . The New England system is not only scriptural, but is scriptural science.

(E. A. Park, "New England Theology," 1852; quoted in Noll, America's God, *p. 225)*

I wallowed and reeked with Jonathan in his insane debauch; rose immediately refreshed and fine at 10 this morning, but with a strange and haunting sense of having been on a three days' tear with a drunken lunatic.

(Mark Twain, quoted in Gura, "Jonathan Edwards in American Literature," p. 153)

---

who helped themselves and other members of the "imagined community" (see Anderson).

Puritan millennial thought also figured prominently in later American literature and culture. Its ideology underlay not only the writings of nineteenth-century progressive reformers such as Catherine Maria Sedgwick, Harriet Beecher Stowe, Maria Cummins, and Elizabeth Stuart Phelps, but also the work of proexpansionist thinkers such as John O'Sullivan, editor of the *United States Democratic Review* and author of "The Great Nation of Futurity" (1839). Puritan millennialism was grounded in the readings of the New Testament, especially the books of Matthew (24:29–31), Mark (13:24–27), and Luke (21:25–28). These passages foreshadowed Christ's return, or his Second Coming, to earth and his subsequent one-thousand-year (hence millennial) reign of peace. Millennialists in the seventeenth and eighteenth centuries split into two camps: premillennialists such as Cotton Mather, who believed that Christ's return would precede the age of peace, prosperity, and triumph of the church, and postmillennialists such as Daniel Whitby, Jonathan Edwards, Joseph Bellamy, and Samuel Hopkins, who held that Christ's Second Coming directly followed the expansion of civil and religious American values on earth ("civil millennialism") and hailed Judgment Day and Satan's return.

Intricately connected with notions of civil millennialism and Manifest Destiny was the Calvinist assumption that the priest, as the truth-seeker of an elect elite, had access to an objective reality—an absolute, metaphysical Truth. While Martin Luther granted access to objective reality through a literal and rational reading of only the Bible, Calvin entrusted human beings with a limited allegorical reading of the "Word of God." However, not until the revolutionary writings of Jonathan Edwards (1703–1758) was nature read as a "diffusion of [God] into time and space" (Miller, p. 603). Edwards believed that, under the effects of grace, human beings could experience a mystical union with the divine induced by nature: "God's excellency, His wisdom, His purity and love, seemed to appear in everything: the sun, moon and stars; in the clouds, and blue sky; in the grass, flowers, trees; in the water, and all nature" (Edwards, p. 179). Yet Edwards was very careful to point out that the mysticization of nature neither denied original sin nor questioned God's absolute sovereignty. As his sermon *God Glorified in the Work of Redemption, by the Greatness of Man's Dependence upon Him, in the Whole of It* (1731) and his later works, including *Careful and Strict Enquiry into Notions of . . . Freedom of Will* (1754) and *The Great Christian Doctrine of Original Sin Defended* (1758), made patently clear, "natural man" was "corrupt and his self-reliance is reliance on evil" (Miller, p. 605). Only free grace—experienced by a select few who had attained a "full and constant sense of the absolute sovereignty of God, and a delight in that sovereignty" (Edwards, p. 186–187)—could save human beings and expose them to the supernatural light described in *A Divine and Supernatural Light, Immediately Imparted to the Soul by the Spirit of God, Shown to Be Both a Scriptural and Rational Doctrine* (1734).

Edwards's cosmology bridged Puritan and Enlightenment discourses when it reinterpreted the world as a place suffused with both God's presence and divine truth. Both Calvinism and the emerging theories of evolution, such as Robert Chambers's *Vestiges of the Natural History of Creation* (1844), believed in natural hierarchies governed by an "inexorable sovereignty" or "impersonal law"; they agreed that evil, or the struggle for survival, was "an integral part of that reality"; and, most important, they accepted as true an objective, common-sensical, reality to be discovered by the spiritually graceful or physically fit (Dawson, p. 512). The precarious combination of spiritual and physical superiority facilitated the objectification of the encountered "other" (at home and abroad) and aided territorial expansion.

PURITAN AESTHETICS

The Calvinist aesthetic reflected the Puritan penchant to view the world in terms of dichotomies: depravity vs. innocence, predestination vs. free will, self vs. other, type vs. antitype. Followed by the jeremiad and the conversion narrative, perhaps the most distinctive rhetorical strategy that informed Puritan writing was the typological reading of the Bible. Typology is a form of allegorical reading in which Old Testament "types" are interpreted as prefigurations of future "antitypes." A type, as literary scholar William G. Madsen explains, is (1) strictly historical; (2) "looks forward in time" and foreshadows the appearance rather than essence of an event; (3) can represent "natural objects"; (4) must differ from and resemble their antitype; and (5) is not recognized as such by neither the "actors of a typical event nor the authors of their history" (Lowance, p. 20). Samuel Danforth's *A Brief Recognition of New-England's Errand into Wilderness* (1671), for example, interpreted the Puritans' settlement in the "new world" and construction of the "city upon a hill" as the antitype to Moses's exodus from Egypt and the subsequent arrival of the "holy nation" at Mount Sinai. Broadly speaking, notions of Manifest Destiny and American exceptionalism that developed in the nineteenth century owe much to this typological tradition.

The Puritan jeremiad was a form of oration that "recalled the courage and piety of the founders," denounced social evils of a backslidden generation, and exhorted believers to return to their original, innocent ways (Elliott, p. 257). The term "jeremiad" derives from the Old Testament prophet Jeremiah, who urged the house of Israel to live up to the terms of the covenant, return to "holiness," and prevent damnation and the fall of Judah. The Puritan jeremiad consisted of four parts: the doctrine—a passage taken from the Old or New Testaments; the explication, or "reasons," in which the doctrine was explained in its biblical context; the "uses" that stressed the community's misapplication of the doctrine; and a final part that might be called "prescription," in which the preacher explained what the community must do to renew the covenant. In his "An Indian's Looking Glass for the White Man" (1833), William Apess, a Pequot, adopts the four-part model of the puritan jeremiad to exhort his white Christian readers to return to righteousness by loving all "skins of color" (p. 97).

The jeremiad, however, targeted community members only. In order to become a member, applicants had to undergo an "elaborate preparation" or conversion "process" of six psychological stages, outlined by the Puritan clergyman Thomas Hooker: "contrition, humiliation, vocation, implantation, exaltation, and possession" (Elliott, p. 201). The completion of each of these stages was subject to public scrutiny and assured both convert and community of the truthfulness of the endeavor. Although secular versions of the jeremiad occur occasionally (e.g., in Henry David Thoreau's *Walden*), conversion narratives abounded in the nineteenth century. Works such as Susan Warner's *The Wide, Wide World* (1850), Nathaniel Hawthorne's *The Marble Faun* (1860), or Harriet Jacobs's *Incidents in the Life of a Slave Girl* (1861) continued this tradition as they subjected the convert's experience to the scrutiny of their "imagined [print] community."

LEGACY

It might be useful to situate Calvinist and anti-Calvinist literature during the nineteenth century as a latter-day expression of the Augustinian-Pelagian tradition, or controversy, that characterizes Christianity more broadly. Saint Augustine of Hippo (354–430), author of *Confessions* and *City of God*, was a staunch defender of the orthodox belief in original sin, predestination, and divine grace (and, logically, inequality). His theological opponent, the Romano-British monk Pelagius (c. 355–c. 425), asserted that there is no original sin, that human beings have free will, and that divine grace is universal. In the fifth century, Saint Augustine openly declared Pelagianism a heresy, but, as the emergence of Unitarianism in the early nineteenth century shows, Pelagian sentiments survived. In fact, as much as Calvinism is seen as "a Renaissance representative of the Augustinian point of view" (Harmon, p. 75), Unitarianism, which believes in salvation by character, is a post-Renaissance version of the Pelagian point of view.

Susan Warner's (1819–1895) best-selling *The Wide, Wide World*, for example, falls ideologically and

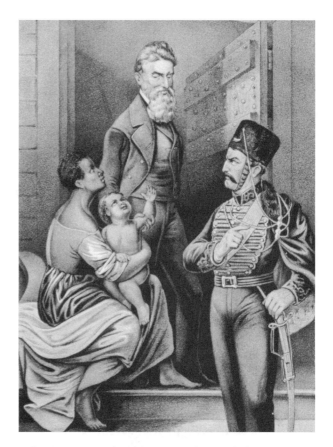

John Brown—The Martyr. Lithograph by Currier & Ives, c. 1870. Brown's uncompromising stance on the issue of slavery is generally regarded in part as the product of his strict Calvinist upbringing. Following his execution, he was regarded by many as a martyr to the cause of abolition. THE LIBRARY OF CONGRESS.

aesthetically within the Augustinian and Calvinist tradition. Warner used what literary scholar Sharon Kim has identified as "Puritan realism"—that is, "a strictly literal, historical world, with the biblical type indicating a literal, spiritual reality within it" (p. 785)—to propagate the concepts of innate depravity, predestination, and divine grace. When one of the novel's characters, Ellen Montgomery, inquires after the meaning of the biblical phrase "He that loveth father or mother more than me is not worthy of me," her mother replies that if Ellen's "heart were not hardened by sin" and if she knew God, she would indeed love him more than her mother (Warner, p. 38). Mrs. Montgomery says, "*You cannot help it*, I know, my dear," and explains that Ellen cannot be saved "except by His *grace* who has promised to change the hearts of *his* people—to take away the heart of stone and give them a heart of flesh" (p. 38, emphases added). Like Warner, Nathaniel Hawthorne's (1804–1864) "great power of blackness . . . derives its force from its appeals to that Calvinistic sense of Innate Depravity and Original Sin, from whose visitations, in some shape or other, no deeply thinking mind is always and wholly free" (Melville, "Hawthorne and His Mosses," p. 1035). Hawthorne's prose, however, is more equivocal than Warner's. In his preface to *The House of the Seven Gables* (1851), Hawthorne hails his belief in original sin and predestination. The novel's moral, he proclaims, is

> that the wrong-doing of one generation lives into the successive ones, and, divesting itself of every temporary advantage, becomes a pure and uncontrollable mischief; and he would feel its singular gratification, if this Romance might effectually convince mankind (or, indeed, any one man) of the folly of tumbling down an avalanche of ill-gotten gold, or real estate, on the heads of an unfortunate posterity, thereby to maim and crush them, until the accumulated mass shall be scattered abroad in its original atoms. (P. 2)

The novel's happy ending, of course, calls this "moral" into question. The moral reverberates in Hawthorne's fictionalized treatment of the failure of Brook Farm in *The Blithedale Romance* (1852). That novel exposes the innate selfishness and depravity of acclaimed philanthropists. Various analyses of Hawthorne's short stories corroborate the claim that Hawthorne's work expresses the belief in innate depravity and predestination. However, close readings of his more ambivalent if not agnostic writing—such as "Young Goodman Brown" (1835) and *The Scarlet Letter* (1850)—in combination with a more recent study of Hawthorne's use of Puritan typology give pause to such an interpretation. The literary scholar Bill Christophersen contends that "whereas [Cotton] Mather . . . used biblical allusions to demonstrate Providence at work, Hawthorne uses them to question Providence" (p. 615). Perhaps, Melville had it right in the first place and "this Man of Mosses takes great delight in hoodwinking the world,—at least, with respect to himself" ("Hawthorne and His Mosses," p. 1041).

More than any other canonized writer, Herman Melville (1819–1891) wrestled with the concepts of original sin, predestination, and divine grace. Echoing Edwards, Melville's writing expressed the belief in original sin. Billy Budd, the young and handsome sailor of Melville's posthumously published novel *Billy Budd, Foretopman* (1924) epitomized "essential innocence" (p. 1425). He is pitted against John Claggart, who represents the naturally "malign" (p. 1394). Similarly, the eternally good Pierre Glendinning in *Pierre; or, The Ambiguities* (1852) struggles to worship God by loving his supposed sister and thus fulfilling

the stipulations of the covenant. Worship, Ishmael explains in *Moby-Dick* (1851), is "—to do the will of God—*that* is worship. And what is the will of God?—to do to my fellow man what I would have my fellow man do to me—*that* is the will of God" (p. 57). God, however, does not reward Pierre's struggles. His mother disowns him, his friends abandon him, his lover and sister die, and he meets death with a "scornful innocence rest[ing] on [his] lips" (*Pierre; or, The Ambiguities*, p. 420).

Pierre's "scornful innocence" stands for the perhaps most central dilemma in Melville's fiction. Human beings who strive to live up to the terms of the covenant, worship God, and acknowledge His absolute sovereignty cannot "delight in that sovereignty" as Jonathan Edwards had suggested. Rather than find "that unfailing comfort" in the fact that "it's all predestinated" (*Moby-Dick*, p. 145), they struggle "all alone"—for example, Pierre as well as the title character in "Bartleby the Scrivener: A Story of Wall-Street" (1853) and Ahab in *Moby-Dick*—to escape the "walls" of Providence while their peers passively witness and listen "in a dumbness like that of a seated congregation of believers in hell listening to the clergyman's announcement of his Calvinistic text" (*Billy Budd*, p. 1420).

Resorting to "Puritan realism" to infuse Bartleby's death with a meaning beyond the literal, to indict God of his injustice, and ask the ultimate question, the narrator, who "at leisure intervals" reads "Edwards on the Will" (p. 1061), explains that Bartleby rests "[w]ith kings and counsellors" (p. 1068). The biblical passage taken from Job 3:14 continues in verses 18, 19, and 23: "There the prisoners rest together; they hear not the voice of the oppressor. The small and the great are there; and the servant is free from his master. . . . *Why is light given to a man whose way is hid, and whom God has hedged in?*" (emphasis added).

Slightly more agnostic in his treatment of the Puritan legacy, Oliver Wendell Holmes's (1809–1894) poem "The Deacon's Masterpiece; or, The Wonderful 'One-Hoss Shay'" (1858) questions the validity, timelessness, and endurance of the Puritan construction of objective reality.

Lying within the Pelagian tradition, Harriet Beecher Stowe's (1811–1896) *Uncle Tom's Cabin; or, Life among the Lowly* (1852), *Dred: A Tale of the Great Dismal Swamp* (1856), and *The Minister's Wooing* (1859) deconstruct the notion of innate depravity and predestination in favor of the Unitarian idea of "salvation by character." Untainted by original sin, Stowe's characters Evangeline and Uncle Tom are paragons of virtue—innately innocent and relentlessly good.

The reaction against the tenets of Puritan Calvinism culminated in the writings of Walt Whitman (1819–1892) and the transcendentalists, who deified nature and man and made the concepts of original sin, predestination, and divine grace obsolete. In "Song of Myself" in *Leaves of Grass* (first published in 1855), Whitman substituted the concept of God as an outside force with Emerson's idea of the "Over-Soul"—a force that permeates matter, the origin and destination of all things. For Whitman, the deification of nature prompted a fundamental reinterpretation of the character and stipulations of covenant theology. Rather than worship God by answering the effectual calling, Whitman worshiped God by denying sin and indulging and actively participating in God's creation. Albeit in less radical ways, the transcendentalists added texture to the idea of human beings as free-thinking, untainted, and independent parts and particles of divine creation.

While a majority of Unitarians and active abolitionists such as Ralph Waldo Emerson, Henry David Thoreau, Catherine Maria Sedgwick, and Lydia Maria Child strove to deconstruct the notions of original sin, predestination, and divine grace altogether, African American and Native American writers such as Harriet Jacobs, David Walker, and Robert Benjamin Lewis successfully appropriated Puritan typology for their own ends. As the historian Albert Raboteau has summarized scholarly observations in this area, "for the black Christian . . . the imagery [Puritan typology] was reversed: the Middle Passage had brought his people to Egypt land, where they suffered bondage under Pharaoh. White Christians saw themselves as a new Israel; slaves identified themselves as old" (p. 251). In his *Walker's Appeal, in Four Articles, Together with a Preamble to the Coloured Citizens of the World* (1829), David Walker (1785–1830) admonished his readers that God had his "ears continually open to the cries, tears and groans of his oppressed people; and . . . will at one day appear fully in behalf of the oppressed, and arrest the progress of the avaricious oppressors" as he did with "hundreds and thousands of Egyptians" (pp. 180–181). He clarified, "the Egyptians . . . a gang of *devils*, . . . having gotten possession of the Lord's people, treated them *nearly* as cruel as *Christian Americans* do us, at the present day" (p. 183). Robert Benjamin Lewis, son of an African American and Native American couple, expressed similar sentiments in *Light and Truth; Collected from The Bible and Ancient and Modern History Containing the Universal History of the Colored and the Indian Race, from the Creation of the World to the Present Time*

(1836): "We ['"Mulattoes," "Quadroons," "Mestizos," "Sambos," "Mangroons," and "Indian tribes"] are all one, and oppressed in this land of boasted Liberty and Freedom. 'But wo unto them by whom it cometh'" (p. 400).

While writers like Walker, Lewis, and the poet Phillis Wheatley awaited a new exodus, Harriet Jacobs (1813–1897) used the elaborate formula of the Puritan conversion narrative to demonstrate that she had experienced divine grace and had become one of the elect. Accordingly, Jacobs examined her life in the psychological stage of "contrition" through the reflections of her fictional narrator Linda Brent in *Incidents in the Life of a Slave Girl*. She experiences "humiliation" as she admits to having sinned and wonders if the "wise purpose of God was leading [her] through such thorny paths, and whether still darker says are in store for [her]" (p. 20). Her grandmother—whose "characteristic piety" and delight in God's sovereignty allowed her to weather the loss of her granddaughter with the words "God's will be done"—represents the demure Christian ideal to which Linda Brent could aspire in the stage of "vocation" (p. 21). Jacobs's appropriation of Puritan aesthetics and the narrator's manifest belief in Puritan ideology situate her firmly in the Puritan-Calvinist tradition of nineteenth-century American writing.

See also The Bible; Protestantism; Puritans; Religion; Unitarians

BIBLIOGRAPHY
Primary Works

Apess, William. "An Indian's Looking-Glass for the White Man." 1833. In *A Son of the Forest and Other Writings*, edited by Barry O'Connell, pp. 95–101. Amherst: University of Massachusetts Press, 1997.

Edwards, Jonathan. "Personal Narrative." In *The Norton Anthology of American Literature*, shorter 4th ed., edited by Nina Baym et al., pp. 177–187. New York: Norton, 1995.

Franklin, Benjamin. *The Autobiography and Other Writings*. 1791. New York: Signet, 1961.

Hawthorne, Nathaniel. *The Blithedale Romance*. 1852. New York: Norton, 1978.

Hawthorne, Nathaniel. *The House of the Seven Gables*. 1851. Columbus: Ohio State University Press, 1963.

Hawthorne, Nathaniel. *The Scarlet Letter*. 1850. New York: Norton, 1968.

Hawthorne, Nathaniel. "Young Goodman Brown." 1835. In *The Norton Anthology of American Literature*, shorter 4th ed., edited by Nina Baym et al., pp. 576–577. New York: Norton, 1995.

Lewis, Robert Benjamin. *Light and Truth; Collected from the Bible and Ancient and Modern History Containing the Universal History of the Colored and the Indian Race, from the Creation of the World to the Present Time.* 1836. Boston: Committee of Colored Gentlemen, 1844.

Holmes, Oliver Wendell. "The Deacon's Masterpiece; or, The Wonderful 'One-Hoss Shay.'" In "The Autocrat of the Breakfast-Table," *Atlantic Monthly,* September 1858, pp. 496–497.

Jacobs, Harriet. *Incidents in the Life of a Slave Girl.* 1861. Cambridge, Mass.: Harvard University Press, 1987.

Melville, Herman. "Bartleby, the Scrivener: A Story of Wall-Street." 1853. In *The Norton Anthology of American Literature,* shorter 4th ed., edited by Nina Baym et al., pp. 1043–1068. New York: Norton, 1995.

Melville, Herman. "Hawthorne and His Mosses." 1850. In *The Norton Anthology of American Literature,* shorter 4th ed., edited by Nina Baym et al., pp. 1032–1043. New York: Norton, 1995.

Melville, Herman. *Moby-Dick.* 1851. New York: Norton, 2002.

Melville, Herman. *Pierre; or, The Ambiguities; Israel Potter: His Fifty Years of Exile; The Piazza Tales; The Confidence-Man: His Masquerade; Uncollected Prose; Billy Budd, Sailor (An Inside Narrative).* New York: Library of America, 1984.

O'Sullivan, John. "The Great Nation of Futurity." *The United States Democratic Review* 6, no. 23 (1839): 426–430.

Stowe, Harriet Beecher. *Uncle Tom's Cabin.* 1852. Edited by Elizabeth Ammons. New York: Norton, 1994.

Walker, David. *David Walker's Appeal, in Four Articles, Together with a Preamble to the Coloured Citizens of the World.* 1829. In *The Norton Anthology of African American Literature,* edited by Henry Louis Gates Jr. and Nellie Y. McKay, pp. 179–190. New York: Norton, 1997.

Warner, Susan. *The Wide, Wide World.* 1850. New York: Feminist Press, 1987.

Winthrop, John. "A Model of Christian Charity." In *The Norton Anthology of American Literature,* shorter 4th ed., edited by Nina Baym et al., pp. 101–112. New York: Norton, 1995.

Whitman, Walt. *Leaves of Grass.* 1855. New York: Vintage Books, 1992. Includes both the original and deathbed edition.

Secondary Works

Ahlstrom, Sydney E. *A Religious History of the American People.* New Haven, Conn., and London: Yale University Press, 1972.

Anderson, Benedict. *Imagined Communities: Reflections on the Origin and Spread of Nationalism.* London: Verso, 1983.

Christophersen, Bill. "Agnostic Tensions in Hawthorne's Short Stories." *American Literature* 72, no. 3 (2000): 595–624.

Dawson, Jan C. "Puritanism in American Thought and Society: 1865–1910." *New England Quarterly* 53, no. 4 (1980): 508–526.

Elliott, Emory. "New England Puritan Literature." In *The Cambridge History of American Literature,* vol. 1, *1590–1820,* edited by Sacvan Bercovitch, pp. 169–306. Cambridge, U.K.: Cambridge University Press, 1994.

Glaude, Eddie S. *Exodus! Religion, Race, and Nation in Nineteenth-Century Black America.* Chicago: University of Chicago Press, 2000.

Gura, Philip F. "Jonathan Edwards in American Literature." *Early American Literature* 39, no. 1 (2004): 147–166.

Harmon, William and C. Hugh Holman. *A Handbook to Literature.* 7th ed. Upper Saddle River, N.J.: Prentice-Hall, 1996.

Herbert, Thomas Walter. *Moby Dick and Calvinism: A World Dismantled.* New Brunswick, N.J.: Rutgers University Press, 1977.

Kim, Sharon. "Puritan Realism: *The Wide, Wide World* and *Robinson Crusoe.*" *American Literature* 75, no. 4 (2003): 783–811.

Lowance, Mason I. *The Language of Canaan: Metaphor and Symbol in New England from the Puritans to the Transcendentalists.* Cambridge, Mass.: Harvard University Press, 1980.

Miller, Perry. "Jonathan Edwards to Emerson." *New England Quarterly* 13, no. 4 (1940): 589–617.

Noll, Mark A. *America's God: From Jonathan Edwards to Abraham Lincoln.* Oxford: Oxford University Press, 2002.

Raboteau, Albert J. *Slave Religion: The "Invisible Institution" in the Antebellum South.* Oxford: Oxford University Press, 1978.

Weber, Max. *Die protestantische Ethik und der "Geist" des Kapitalismus* [The Protestant ethic and the spirit of capitalism]. Weinheim, Germany: Beltz Athenaeum, 2000.

Merit Kaschig

CANADA

In 1820 Canada was little more than a patchwork of British colonies. The following decades, however, would bring great change to British North America. Rebellions in the late 1830s led the British authorities to join the colonies of Upper and Lower Canada, now Ontario and Quebec, into a united Province of Canada. During the next decade London gradually repealed the legislation that had allowed its North American colonies to enjoy preferential access to the British and West Indian markets, and internal autonomy was granted in return. Economic disruption and widespread discontent ensued and British North America desperately sought to reorient its foreign trade toward the United States. Nevertheless, by the mid-1860s it became increasingly clear that the various British North American colonies would have to work together for the purposes of trade and protection. After much deliberation and with the approval of Great Britain, the Province of Canada and the maritime colonies of Nova Scotia and New Brunswick entered into a federal union in 1867. By 1871, with the admission of British Columbia, the Dominion of Canada stretched from the Atlantic to the Pacific. But the new nation was not yet fully independent; Britain would retain control of its external affairs until 1931.

Under British stewardship Canada's relationship with the United States experienced a number of ups and downs during the antebellum age. After the War of 1812, which was fought between the United States and Great Britain over, among other things, maritime rights and trade policies, peace returned to the North American continent. By the 1830s and 1840s, however, tensions arising from boundary disputes along the Maine–New Brunswick border and in the Pacific Northwest brought Britain and the United States to the edge of war. Diplomacy nonetheless prevailed and a short-lived era of Anglo-American harmony followed the signature of the Oregon Boundary Treaty of 1846, which divided the Oregon Territory along the forty-ninth parallel between Britain and the United States. Britain concluded a comprehensive trade agreement—the so-called Reciprocity Treaty—with the United States on behalf of British North America in 1854, and Canadian-American trade soared during the decade that followed. But the outbreak of the Civil War renewed tensions between Great Britain and the United States and, once again, Canada would pay the price for Anglo-American squabbling. Upset by British support for the Confederacy, Congress repealed the Reciprocity Treaty in 1866 and for a time Washington turned a blind eye to the activities of the Fenian Brotherhood, a group of Irish American terrorists who launched a series of ill-fated raids on British North America. By doing so, the Fenians hoped to divert British forces away from Ireland, where they planned to foment an uprising. Tensions simmered along the Canadian-American border until the 1871 Treaty of Washington, which settled the Alabama claims made by the U.S. government against Britain's part in outfitting Confederate cruisers to fight against the Union. The treaty normalized relations between Britain and the United States.

In the nineteenth century the general American perception of Canada was negative and, to a large extent, uninformed. Anglophobia and anti-Catholic nativism, for instance, were common during this period and they influenced domestic perceptions of Canada. As a result, many Americans saw the British North American colonies as proxies for what they believed were two of the greatest external threats to the new republic: British imperialism and Roman Catholicism. The issue of slavery, which dominated antebellum discourse, also colored attitudes toward Canada. Indeed, as a haven for fugitive slaves, British North America gained the respect of many abolitionists but drew the ire of slaveholders.

THE BRITISH PROXY

During the antebellum age anti-British sentiment was founded on a rejection of hereditary privilege, deference, and militarism, which Americans saw as the social and political foundations of British society. Anti-British rhetoric affirmed America's faith in republicanism and democracy, but it also reflected widespread concerns regarding British attempts to check the nation's expansion and influence. In this sense, the very existence of a series of British colonies along America's northern frontier was seen as an affront to American values, a threat to American security, and an obstacle to Manifest Destiny.

Most nineteenth-century Americans viewed British institutions, and monarchy in particular, as archaic and tyrannical. Their survival rested, it seemed, on military repression. British North America was seen as a case in point because only the heavy hand of the British military—whose presence on the North American continent also threatened and contained Young America—was thought to keep Canada in Britain's orbit. The Michigan-born writer and artist Charles Lanman (1819–1895), for instance, bristled at the sight of Montreal's British garrison. "One of the most striking peculiarities of this city," he wrote in 1848, "is the fact that everybody has to live, walk and sleep at the point of a bayonet. Military quarters are stationed in various portions of the city, and soldiers meet you at every corner, marching to and fro, invariably puffed up with ignorance and vanity" (p. 117).

As far as most American observers were concerned Canada was destined to be annexed by the United States, or, at the very least, to gain complete independence from Britain. Accordingly, many Americans were angered and puzzled by the emergence of a transcontinental British dominion as their northern neighbor. They could not understand Canada's loyalty to Great Britain and saw the new nation as a fundamentally unnatural and hostile entity. In 1867 Maine's

Republican governor, Joshua L. Chamberlain (1828–1914), warned that the federation of British North America was "part of a great conspiracy against Liberty on this youthful continent" (Warner, p. 66).

In the antebellum era Anglophobia, annexationism, and protectionist sentiment shared a deep intimacy. Indeed, American manufacturing interests often used anti-British rhetoric to promote high tariffs against British and Canadian products. They argued that shutting Canadian goods out of the American market would ruin the British North American economy, which in turn would hasten Canada's entry into the Union.

Nevertheless, a number of Americans were lukewarm, if not downright hostile, to the idea of bringing Canada into the Union. Many Southerners, for instance, favored free trade with British North America because they feared that economic collapse in the Canadas might bring some or all of the British North American colonies into the Union, thereby upsetting the fragile balance between free and slave states.

THE CATHOLIC THEOCRACY

The United States experienced a burst of anti-Catholic nativism in the mid-nineteenth century. Large-scale Catholic immigration was changing the nation's urban landscape and many Americans worried that these apparently unassimilable newcomers threatened America's Protestant values and republican institutions. Anti-Catholic enmity was generally directed at Irish immigrants; nevertheless, for many Americans, Canada also embodied the menace of Roman Catholicism. Indeed, since the seventeenth century, Protestant America had feared that a Catholic theocracy was forming on the shores of the St. Lawrence. It is hardly surprising, therefore, that the antebellum era's most important nativist document, *The Awful Disclosures of Maria Monk* (1836), took aim at Quebec's Roman Catholic Church. Ghostwritten by a New York Protestant minister, Monk's best-selling book—300,000 copies were sold prior to the Civil War—was a fabricated tale that claimed to be the true experiences of a nun who had escaped from a Montreal convent. The book's wild allegations of sexual abuse and infanticide helped spark the Know-Nothing uproar of the 1840s and 1850s, doing for nativism what *Uncle Tom's Cabin* would later do for the abolitionist movement (Castillo, pp. 49–50).

A more subtle form of anti-Catholic rhetoric could be found in the work of the historian Francis Parkman (1823–1893). In his books on the history of the French regime in Canada, New France emerged as the embodiment of reaction, and its failings were also those of Roman Catholicism and autocracy. Parkman was undoubtedly awed by the exploits of French explorers like Samuel de Champlain and Cavelier de La Salle, but he did not believe that their heroism could redeem a society so thoroughly corrupted by despotism.

Invariably described as a swarthy, ignorant, backward, and priest-ridden people, French Canadians served as convenient foils for anti-Catholic rhetoric. "The population which we had seen the last two days," remarked the transcendentalist writer Henry David Thoreau (1817–1862) during an 1850 tour of rural Quebec, "appeared very inferior, intellectually and even physically, to that of New England. In some respects they were incredibly filthy. It was evident that they had not advanced since the settlement of the country, that they were quite behind the age, and fairly represented their ancestors in Normandy a thousand years ago" (pp. 59–60). The Roman Catholic Church's aversion to liberty and enlightenment, Thoreau and others insisted, was largely responsible for French Canadian backwardness. This sort of bigotry dogged the hundreds of thousands of French Canadian immigrants who settled in the northern United States after 1840.

Nevertheless, anti-Catholic nativism was entirely absent from what was undoubtedly the most popular nineteenth-century work of fiction to deal with a Canadian theme: the poet Henry Wadsworth Longfellow's (1807–1882) *Evangeline: A Tale of Acadie* (1847). The epic poem told the story of two young lovers separated by the Acadian Expulsion of 1755 and was quite sympathetic in its treatment of Roman Catholics. Longfellow, to be sure, held nativism in low regard. His cosmopolitan conception of "a national literature . . . embracing French, Spanish, Irish, English, Scotch, and German peculiarities" (quoted in Seelye, p. 30) was at odds, however, with the forceful nationalism that characterized mid-nineteenth-century American literature.

THE CANADIAN CANAAN

Slavery, which was largely unsuited to Canadian agriculture, first fell into disuse as British North American courts refused to be involved in the pursuit of fugitives, and was officially abolished in the British Empire in 1833. Abolitionist sentiment ran high in nineteenth-century Canada, and Britain refused to extradite the fugitive American slaves that had sought refuge in its North American colonies. British North America was accordingly seen as a haven for African Americans, many of whom fled to Canada through the

Henry David Thoreau visited Lower Canada, now Quebec, in 1850. Like many antebellum travelers, he found two features of Canadian life particularly unsettling: the British military presence and French Canadian Catholicism.

What makes the United States government, on the whole, more tolerable,—I mean for us lucky white men,—is the fact that there is so much less government with us. Here it is only once in a month or a year that a man *needs* remember that institution; and those who go to Congress can play the game of the Kilkenny cats there without fatal consequences to those who stay at home,— their term is so short: but in Canada you are reminded of the government every day. It parades itself before you. It is not content to be the servant, but will be the master; and every day it goes out to the Plains of Abraham or to the Champ de Mars and exhibits itself and its tools. Everywhere there appeared an attempt to make and to preserve trivial and otherwise transient distinctions. In the streets of Montreal and Quebec you met not only with the soldiers in red, and shuffling priests in unmistakable black and white, with Sisters of Charity gone into mourning for their deceased relative,—not to mention the nuns of various orders depending on the fashion of a tear, of whom you heard,—but youths belonging to some seminary or other, wearing coats edged with white, who looked as if their expanding hearts were already repressed with a piece of tape. In short, the inhabitants of Canada appeared to be suffering between two fires,—the soldiery and the priesthood.

Thoreau, *A Yankee in Canada*, pp. 77–78.

Underground Railroad. Several thousand fugitives settled in Upper Canada, especially after the Fugitive Slave Act of 1850 made the Northern states unsafe for escapees. Most would return to the United States after the Civil War.

Canadians, to be sure, shared the general patterns of prejudice found in the free states. Nevertheless, most fugitive narratives were unflagging in their praise of the Canadian haven and scarcely mentioned the prejudice and segregation that black refugees encountered

in British North America (Winks, pp. 241, 251). Likewise, a number of African American leaders were enthusiastic supporters of Canadian resettlement. Unlike the Liberian colonization schemes promoted by the American Colonization Society, which were essentially experiments in deportation, the resettlement of free blacks in the British provinces, particularly in Upper Canada, promised equality and prosperity in North America.

A number of white abolitionists were equally enthusiastic about the Canadian haven and helped fund a variety of education and resettlement schemes in Upper Canada. These programs bolstered abolitionist claims that blacks could be trained to enjoy freedom and that they might even prosper through cooperative activity (Winks, p. 157). The Quaker abolitionist Benjamin Lundy (1789–1839), who visited Upper Canada in 1832, was particularly impressed with the province as a location to resettle manumitted slaves. In Upper Canada, he wrote in his diary, "every citizen, without distinction of color or caste, is entitled to all the privileges and immunities that the most favored individual can claim." "Our colored people," he concluded, would thrive in the British province: "The country in question will be very suitable for them, particularly those north of the Carolinas, if they choose to locate themselves therein" (pp. 114, 132).

Canadian policy and sentiment regarding fugitive slaves infuriated many Southerners. Senator Thomas Hart Benton (1782–1858) of Missouri, for instance, complained that the British North American colonies were lands "where abolitionism is the policy of the government, the voice of the law, and the spirit of the people" (Winks, p. 173). To discourage escape to the "Canadian Canaan," slaves were kept in ignorance of British North America. Masters warned their slaves that they would perish in Canada's harsh climate—the belief that Canada was a desolate, frozen wasteland was firmly entrenched in the American mind—and that French Canadians worshipped idols and killed black men on sight (Winks, p. 238).

The antebellum vision of Canada, though generally negative, was hardly univocal. The British provinces, indeed, embodied different things to different people. For some, they were the distant outposts of popery and British imperialism, whereas for others, they were a haven for fugitive slaves. In the end, however, American judgments regarding British North America had little to do with objective reality. They merely reflected domestic concerns regarding slavery, immigration, and expansion.

See also Abolitionist Writing; Borders; Catholics; Democracy; Slavery

BIBLIOGRAPHY

Primary Works

Lanman, Charles. *A Tour to the River Saguenay, in Lower Canada*. Philadelphia: Carey and Hart, 1848.

Longfellow, Henry Wadsworth. *Evangeline: A Tale of Acadie*. Boston: William D. Ticknor, 1847.

Lundy, Benjamin. "The Diary of Benjamin Lundy Written During his Journey to Upper Canada, January 1832, edited with notes and an introduction by Fred Landon." Ontrario Historical Society *Papers and Records* 19 (1922): 110–133.

Thoreau, Henry David. *A Yankee in Canada, with Anti-Slavery and Reform Papers*. Boston: Ticknor and Fields, 1866.

Secondary Works

Castillo, Dennis. "The Enduring Legacy of Maria Monk." *American Catholic Studies* 112 (2001): 49–59.

Doyle, James. *North of America: Images of Canada in the Literature of the United States, 1775–1900*. Toronto: ECW Press, 1983.

Seelye, John. "Attic Shape: Dusting off *Evangeline*." *Virginia Quarterly Review* 60 (1984): 21–44.

Stewart, Gordon T. *The American Response to Canada since 1776*. East Lansing: Michigan State University Press, 1992.

Stuart, Reginald C. *United States Expansionism and British North America, 1775–1871*. Chapel Hill: University of North Carolina Press, 1988.

Warner, Donald F. *The Idea of Continental Union: Agitation for the Annexation of Canada to the United States, 1849–1893*. Lexington: University of Kentucky Press, 1960.

Winks, Robin W. *The Blacks in Canada: A History*. 2nd ed. Montreal and Buffalo, N.Y.: McGill-Queen's University Press, 1997.

Damien-Claude Bélanger

CAPTIVITY NARRATIVES

The long history of captivity on the North American continent begins before the successive waves of European exploration that occurred toward the end of the fifteenth century. For many Native American people, captivity was a common occurrence within the context of warfare. Accounts of captivity, however, began to form a distinctive genre in Western literature when European explorers and colonizers recorded tales of capture and return. These initial accounts included oral or written retellings by native people of their own histories—stories of war, captivity, sacrifice, or adoption—that were subsequently translated into European texts by the colonizers who read or heard them.

For Europeans, captivity represented both a romantic, exoticized experience—in which the captive might outwit or charm his or her captors—and a time of intense physical and psychological (and often spiritual) suffering. Alvar Nuñez Cabeza de Vaca, a Spanish explorer and colonizer, spent seven years in various captivities and described conditions of near-starvation and abjection at the hands of his early captors. Yet his 1542 text, translated as *Castaways*, recounts his practice as a spiritual and physical healer among his later captors. The celebrated story of Pocahontas and John Smith first appeared in Smith's 1624 work *The Generall Historie of Virginia*. Readers of Cabeza de Vaca's Spanish narrative or Smith's *Historie,* while differentiated by language, region, and religion, found a new species of travel writing. A key element of that genre is its claim to an authoritative description of the "new" people in the "New World." These descriptions constitute an early form of ethnography in which the captive simultaneously portrays and interprets a captor's practices. Ethnographic elements, including details of the captors' physical appearances and their rituals and ceremonies, social organizations, and means of subsistence, deferred objections about the narratives' credibility and assured readers that, while entertaining, the story was also true.

These early texts assert the direct connection between the captive's authentic experiences and his or her authority to tell the tale. Yet as the genre developed, the tension between the narratives' ethnographic description and their personal testimony produced ambiguous texts. The most popular captivity narrative of the American colonial period, Mary Rowlandson's *The Sovereignty and Goodness of God* (1682), displays this tension. Many scholars think that Increase Mather, a leading Puritan minister, exercised heavy editorial influence over the woman's text and is responsible for its mix of religious instruction and cultural polemic against "those Barbarous Creatures" (p. 70). As the genre developed, composers and sponsors of captivity narratives sought to accomplish multiple goals: to entertain readers with tales of exotic, newly "discovered" lands; to "sell" those lands through colonization projects to their metropolitan audiences; to seek funding for the projects' expansion; to report on cultural differences and "new" peoples; to reinforce religious conviction; to support warfare; and notably, to establish themselves as authorities for the interpretation of cross-cultural encounters.

"FACTIVE" AND "FICTIVE" NARRATIVES

Throughout the eighteenth century, captivity narratives reflected the transitions in North American political and cultural conditions, especially conflict. Warfare produced two of the most notable later-eighteenth-century captivity stories, those of Jemima Howe and Maria Kittle. Howe's and Kittle's stories employ first-person narration by a pathetic female captive who emphasizes the loss of family members, home, and sense of personal security. Both narratives illustrate the problem of determining authorship. Howe's editors employed an outright impersonation of her voice. Anne Eliza Bleecker's *The History of Maria Kittle* (1793) has been considered the first "captivity romance," but scholarship indicates that Maria Kittle may have been an actual captive. As these and later narratives indicate, the genre developed as a hybrid species, part historical writing and part novel. Kathryn Derounian-Stodola notes in "The Indian Captivity Narratives of Mary Rowlandson and Olive Oatman: Case Studies in the Continuity, Evolution, and Exploitation of Literary Discourse" that this "factive" and "fictive" divide informs almost all captivity narratives, but by the nineteenth century the divide grew in response to multiple cultural pressures.

One of these imperatives was a call for writers to fashion a history of the early Republic. These calls for a history for the new nation resulted in a turn to "native" sources, and colonial captivity tales helped to shape a national literature. Earlier captivities served as models for the Barbary captivities of the 1790s, such as Royall Tyler's *The Algerine Captive* (1797), Susanna Rowson's *Slaves in Algiers* (1794), and early-nineteenth-century tales of white Christians enslaved by Muslim North Africans. Newspaper accounts linked the captivities on the high seas with the captivities on the western frontiers and thereby reinforced readers' sense that American, Christian, and especially female captives needed to be defended from "Tawnies" and "Turks" alike.

Nineteenth-century captivity accounts extended the rhetorical practices, historical claims, and literary imagery that characterized earlier works. For example, several authors wrote versions of the 1697 Hannah Duston captivity. Duston's story is unusual because she escaped and she killed and scalped her captors. Duston had been taken by a group of Abenakis who raided her home in Haverhill, Massachusetts, in the spring of 1697. The first version of her story was printed in Cotton Mather's sermon "Humiliations Follow'd with Deliverances" shortly after her return. Timothy Dwight (*Travels in New-England and New-York*, 1821–1822), John Greenleaf Whittier ("A Mother's Revenge," in *Legends of New England*,

1831), Benjamin Mirick (*A History of Haverhill, Massachusetts*, 1832), Nathaniel Hawthorne ("The Heroism of Thomas Duston," 1836), and Henry David Thoreau (*A Week on the Concord and the Merrimack*, 1849) wrote versions of Duston's story, and their writings variously construct Duston as victimized, deluded, or vengeful. Historical facts concerning captivity, especially the captivity of women, were often transmuted into historical romance in such novels as Harriet Cheney's *A Peep at the Pilgrims in Sixteen Hundred Thirty-Six: A Tale of Olden Times* (1824) and Catherine Maria Sedgwick's *Hope Leslie; or, Early Times in Massachusetts* (1827). In these romances "captivity provides the metaphorical structure for women's life narratives" (Castiglia, p. 163).

KEY FIGURES: SUFFERING WOMEN

The figure of the victimized woman, in the tradition of sensationalism and sentimentality, "convert[ed] that Indian captivity narrative into another eighteenth-century fiction: the novel of seduction" (Derounian-Stodola, *Women's Indian Captivity Narratives*, p. xxiii). Nineteenth-century texts followed suit while employing improved engraving technologies to produce lurid representations of the captive's plight. Paul Baepler's *White Slaves, African Masters* (1999), a collection of Barbary captivities, reproduces many illustrations from the texts, including the representative "bare-breasted and enchained" (p. 148) Mary Velnet, a figure both pathetic and titillating. This sensationalism, as Jane Tompkins has noted, is a hallmark of nineteenth-century American literature: the figure of the suffering female body mobilized popular sentiment for a variety of political, religious, and commercial goals, including abolition, westward expansionism, Christian proselytizing, and profits for the press.

Although not all captivity narratives considered female captives, women's stories represented an inordinately large proportion of the genre, which raises important issues for scholars who argue that the American captivity narrative is the first truly American literary genre. Contrary to Leslie Fiedler's famous critical argument that American literature emerges from an originary emphasis on heroic male homosocial bonds, captivity narratives emphasize a multicultural and cross-cultural founding myth based on the figures of captive women among native peoples. As well the captive woman came to represent a complex figure of negotiation and indeterminacy: readers could never know what actually happened during captivity, and they were free to "read in" their assumptions about both captors and captives.

This ideological work underwrites the narratives that turn from locales in New England and the mid-Atlantic regions to the lands appropriated during the various Indian wars of the earlier part of the century. Mary Godfrey's *An Authentic Narrative of the Seminole War; and of the Miraculous Escape of Mary Godfrey, and Her Four Female Children* (1836) tells the story of one victim of these wars and contains an interesting episode in which an escaped slave aids Godfrey and her daughters. As Derounian-Stodola notes in *Women's Indian Captivity Narratives*, "Whether or not Mary Godfrey existed in the historical record is irrelevant and currently unknown" (p. 215), but the narrative can be located within the popular literature favoring abolition. Harriet Jacobs's popular 1861 text *Incidents in the Life of a Slave Girl* combines captivity and slave narrative conventions into a powerful abolitionist critique, particularly in both genres' emphasis on the violently fragmented family.

The unusual *Narrative of Mrs. Mary Jemison* (1824) also begins with the image of the destroyed family. Taken as a young girl during the French and Indian War, Jemison remained with her captors, eventually marrying twice, both times to Seneca men with whom she had several children. Her narrative shares the problematic issue of authorship with the earlier narratives produced by impersonating male editors and composers; in Jemison's case, her "amanuensis" was James E. Seaver, a local historian who lived near Jemison in Genesee, New York. June Namias notes that it is impossible to determine which sections of the narrative were verbatim transcripts of Jemison's own words (Jemison could not write) and which were Seaver's creative productions. It seems safe to say that the appendices and political commentary on the Revolutionary War, in which Jemison and her community played a part, are Seaver's own interpolations.

Significantly, Jemison's narrative appeared at a time when debates raged in newspapers and in Congress over the right of the U.S. government to "remove" Native Americans, notably the Cherokees, from their traditional lands. Intermittent warfare between the U.S. Army and the Cherokees, Choctaws, and Creeks disrupted the policies of "civilization and assimilation" initially promulgated by George Washington's administration in the 1790s. Mary Jemison represented a model of transculturation (or reverse assimilation, from the white European perspective), and Seaver's text confounded racist assumptions concerning Native American cultures. His rendition of Mary Jemison's words depicts Native American communities in which some individuals exhibit honorable and admirable behaviors while others commit acts of barbarity. The narrative therefore gave readers an account of Native American (here, mostly Seneca) social formations as complex as the "civilized" white society within which, presumably, most of the text's readers lived.

A majority of nineteenth-century captivity narratives, told from the point of view of white captives, reject the sympathetic, or at least complex, portrayals of Indians found in Jemison's account. The popular *Captivity of the Oatman Girls: Being an Interesting Narrative of Life among the Apache and Mohave Indians* (1857) purported to be the first-person narrative of Olive Oatman. Oatman's likeness, complete with the facial tattoos she received during her captivity, appeared opposite the title page of one early edition and seemed to authenticate the account. The Oatman family had been traveling west to resettle with a religious group led by James C. Brewster, a repudiated Mormon. In February 1851 the party was attacked by Yavapais in New Mexico. Olive Oatman and her sister were captured; only Olive survived the four years of captivity. In 1856 Oatman was ransomed and, with her brother, who had escaped the massacre, made her way to California. While in California, Oatman met the Reverend R. B. Stratton, who wrote down Oatman's story and prepared it for publication. The story proved enormously popular: it was one of the first extended accounts of Native American life in the Southwest, and several editions followed immediately on the 1857 first edition of five thousand copies. By 1859 there were four editions with a total press run of twenty-four thousand copies (Stratton, p. x). Apart from its ethnographic component, the Oatman captivity draws on many fictional conventions from the period, including the gothic novel's foreshadowing of doom in Mr. Oatman's prescience about an impending attack. Its didacticism, directed toward children, echoes the domestic fiction and child-rearing manuals of contemporaries such as Lydia Maria Child and Catharine Beecher.

A later narrative, Sarah Wakefield's *Six Weeks in the Sioux Tepees: A Narrative of Indian Captivity* (1864) presents an unusually spirited defense of Native Americans from the point of view of a female captive of the Dakota wars. Derounian-Stodola notes that Wakefield "took her cue in developing a radical Christianity" (*Women's Indian Captivity Narratives*, p. 237), and Wakefield writes her account explicitly to protest the executions of innocent natives (including her protector, Chaska) and implicitly to counter gossip that she had sexual relations with Chaska, behaving as his "wife." Wakefield's account must be viewed in the context of the Civil War; for Wakefield, the moral basis for Abraham Lincoln's emancipation of African

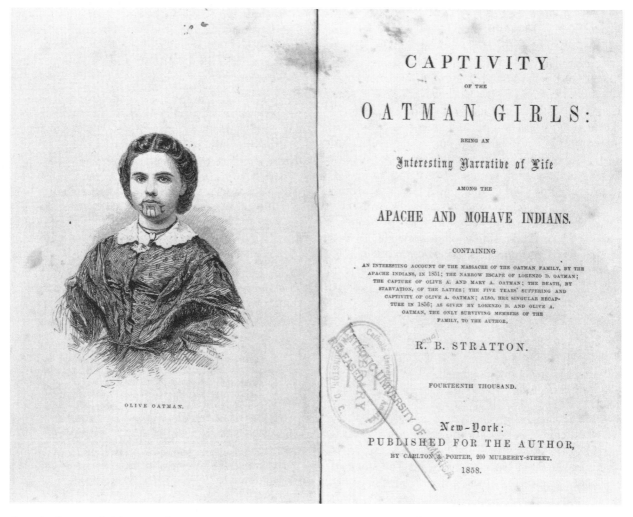

Frontispiece and title page for an 1858 printing of *Captivity of the Oatman Girls.* Olive Oatman is shown here with her tatooed face. © CORBIS

Americans should be extended to include more honorable dealings with the natives. Her narrative attempts to critique the adventure tales and public policy whose images of Native Americans as subhuman savages provided ready ideological scapegoats for western expansionism.

EXTENDING THE USES OF CAPTIVITY

Although didacticism had been an important element in the genre since Mary Rowlandson's preface exhorted her readers to "peruse, ponder, and from hence lay up something from the experience of another" (p. 67), nineteenth-century authors and publishers of captivity narratives employed various formats to expand and exploit the genre's potential for ideological reinforcement. Both missionary tracts and anthologies produced more—and more gruesome—lessons for readers, especially children, to "ponder."

In *The Stolen Boy: A Story, Founded on Facts, by Mrs. Hofland* (1830), young readers encountered Manuel, who was stolen as he visited his wealthy father's stables. Invoking earlier sensationalist imagery, the narrative recapitulates in horrific detail the torture of a Choctaw captive while simultaneously assuring readers, "nor will we afflict our young readers, or our own feelings, with one word on so revolting a theme" (p. 73). The narrative consistently touts the advantages of being "born of christian parents" and compares the admirable behavior of young Manuel with the "vices of [the] misguided" Uswega, son of Manuel's captor (p. 59). *The Book for Children* (1842), a pamphlet in yellow wrappers with crudely rendered woodcuts, exemplifies juvenilia with captivity motifs. Using the simple rhymes of early spelling guides, *The Book* presents the story of Enos Done, a boy deprived of education because of his captivity. Children were to measure their "favorable opportunities" against Enos's sad lot. Similarly, *The Bible Boy Taken Captive by the Indians* (1845) describes Joseph, the "Bible Boy" captive, who converts his Indian friend Light Foot, who himself goes on to become a missionary.

Actual missionary societies seized on the proselytizing potential of captivity narratives for adults as well. Gary Ebersole argues that some of the narratives of the early nineteenth century represent "a defensive effort by conservative Protestants to counter the rise of a broad cultural movement loosely based on a spiritualizing of nature" (p. 151), and he cites as an example of this movement Thomas Baldwin's *Narrative of the Massacre of My Wife and Children* (1835), a tale that emphasizes the captive Baldwin's isolation, his similarity to Job, and the moral lessons to be gained from deep affliction. *The Little Osage Captive: An Authentic Narrative* (1822) relied on contemporary sentimentalizing of suffering children to advance the missionary project of Christian conversion, and it unambiguously links treatment of Native Americans with abolitionist images of slavery's brutality. Most of these captivity narratives emphasized the captive's reliance on God's intervention: their daily suffering, when relieved, was attributed to God's mercy, albeit working through his mortal instruments.

More secular captivity accounts presented a range of attitudes toward the native peoples in the texts. Some accounts argued for the eradication of Indian traditions and the complete assimilation of native peoples into white culture. One such account is the *Narrative of the Captivity and Adventures of John Tanner . . . during Thirty Years Residence among the Indians: In the Interior of North America* (1830), which provides detailed ethnographic information of the people among whom Tanner lived for extended periods and includes the intriguing final note that three of Tanner's children continued to live among the Indians. John Dunn Hunter's *Manners and Customs of Several Indian Tribes . . .* (1823) distinguishes among several groups of Indians, comparing some favorably against others. Hunter also makes the point that whites who were raised by Indians "seldom afterwards abandon" their customs; this "going native" motif haunts all captivity narratives, and it is important to note that the Jemison narrative of a transculturated white was published one year after Hunter's popular account. Another use of captivity conventions is found in Miss Harrington's *Narrative of the Barbarous Treatment of Two Unfortunate Females . . .* (1842), which emphatically counters abolitionist sentiment with a tale of two white women who were captured by "Two Runaway Blacks." The narrative hints broadly that the women were repeatedly tortured and raped

by one of their captors, "the principal instigator," who was subsequently captured and burned at the stake.

If individual captivity tales were intended as evangelizing tracts, anti- or pro-abolitionist polemics, ethnographic studies, war propaganda, and guides to proper domestic behavior, their collection into anthologies often obscured these original aims. Once collected into texts with captivities from diverse historical periods and localities, single captivities each became one element in a concatenation of stories purportedly gathered for historical edification but most likely published for quick commercial gains. In Samuel G. Drake's popular *Indian Captivities; or, Life in the Wigwams* (1851), readers found captivities ranging from 1528 to 1836, but of the thirty-one captivities, only two occurred in the nineteenth century. Colonial collections served as sources for later anthologies such as Drake's, Samuel Metcalf's *A Collection of Some of the Most Interesting Narratives of Indian Warfare in the West . . .* (1821), the anonymous *Indian Anecdotes and Barbarities* (1837), William V. Moore's *Indian Wars of the United States, from the Discovery to the Present Time: From the Best Authorities* (1840), and John Frost's *Heroic Women of the West: Comprising Thrilling Examples of Courage, Fortitude, Devotedness, and Self-Sacrifice, among the Pioneer Mothers of the Western Country* (1854). ("William V. Moore" was a pseudonym of John Frost.) As the title of Frost's collection makes evident, the genre continued to emphasize the experiences of female captives well into the nineteenth century.

The continuing emphasis on female captivity produced a peculiarly American version of the gothic captivity, the "convent tale." The two best-known convent captivities are Rebecca Reed's *Six Months in a Convent; or, The Narrative of Rebecca Theresa Reed* (1835) and Maria Monk's *Awful Disclosures of the Hotel Dieu Nunnery* (1836). In these books the women report their incarceration, deprivation, and humiliation in Catholic convents. The abuses detailed by Reed, combined with local newspaper accounts of "escaped" nuns, led to the notorious incident in which "forty rioters dressed like Indians" attacked and burned the Ursuline convent in Charlestown, Massachusetts. Monk, who later was revealed to be a prostitute, similarly describes the harsh punishments inflicted by mother superiors on young girls and, more damning, the sexual exploitation of the girls by priests. These captivity narratives both shaped and were shaped by the anti-Catholic, anti-immigrant biases of the Protestant communities, elites, and working people in Massachusetts. They exemplify the continuing power of the image of the captive to instruct, inform, and compel to action the readers of captivity narratives.

See also Autobiography; Children's and Adolescent Literature; Ethnology; *Hope Leslie; Incidents in the Life of a Slave Girl;* Indians; Indian Wars and Dispossession; Wilderness

BIBLIOGRAPHY

Primary Works

The Affecting History of the Dreadful Distresses of Frederic Manheim's Family . . . . 1794. Edited by Wilcomb E. Washburn. Garland Library of Narratives of North American Indian Captivities, 111 vols. New York: Garland, 1977.

Baepler, Paul, ed. *White Slaves, African Masters: An Anthology of American Barbary Captivity Narratives.* Chicago: University of Chicago Press, 1999.

The Bible Boy Taken Captive by the Indians. Written for the American Sunday-School Union and revised by the Committee for Publication. Philadelphia: American Sunday-School Union, 1845.

Bleecker, Ann Eliza. *The History of Maria Kittle.* 1793. Edited by Wilcomb E. Washburn. Garland Library of Narratives of North American Indian Captivities, 111 vols. New York: Garland, 1978.

The Book for Children. New York: H. E., 1842.

Cabeza de Vaca, Alvar Nuñez. *Castaways.* 1542. Translated by Frances M. López-Morillas, edited by Enrique Pupo-Walker. Berkeley: University of California Press, 1993.

Cheney, Harriet Vaughan. *A Peep at the Pilgrims in Sixteen Hundred Thirty-Six: A Tale of Olden Times.* 2 vols. Boston: Wells and Lilly, 1824.

Cornelius, Elias. *The Little Osage Captive: An Authentic Narrative.* Boston: Samuel T. Armstrong and Crocker and Brewster; New York: John P. Haven, 1822.

Drake, Samuel G. *Indian Captivities; or, Life in the Wigwams.* Auburn, N.Y.: Derby and Miller, 1851.

Frost, John. *Heroic Women of the West: Comprising Thrilling Examples of Courage, Fortitude, Devotedness, and Self-Sacrifice, among the Pioneer Mothers of the Western Country.* Philadelphia: A. Hart, 1854.

Hofland, Mrs. [Barbara Wreaks Hoole Hofland]. *The Stolen Boy: A Story, Founded on Facts, by Mrs. Hofland.* New York: W. B. Gilley, 1830.

Indian Anecdotes and Barbarities. Barre, Mass.: Albert Alden, 1837.

Jacobs, Harriet. *Incidents in the Life of a Slave Girl.* Edited by L. Maria Child. 1861. Edited by Jean Fagan Yellin. Cambridge, Mass.: Harvard University Press, 1987.

Metcalf, Samuel. *A Collection of Some of the Most Interesting Narratives of Indian Warfare in the West, Containing an Account of the Adventures of Colonel Daniel Boone . . .* Lexington, Ky.: William G. Hunt, 1821.

Moore, William V. [John Frost]. *Indian Wars of the United States, from the Discovery to the Present Time: From the Best Authorities.* Philadelphia: R. W. Pomeroy, 1840.

Rowlandson, Mary. *The Sovereignty and Goodness of God, Together with the Faithfulness of His Promises Displayed.* 1682. Edited by Neal Salisbury. Boston: Bedford Books, 1997.

Rowson, Susanna. *Slaves in Algiers; or, A Struggle for Freedom: A Play, Interspersed with Songs, in Three Acts.* Philadelphia: Wrigley and Berriman, 1794.

Schultz, Nancy Lusignan, ed. *Veil of Fear: Nineteenth-Century Convent Tales by Rebecca Reed and Maria Monk.* West Lafayette, Ind.: NotaBell Books and Purdue University Press, 1999.

Seaver, James E. *A Narrative of Mrs. Mary Jemison.* 1824. Edited by June Namias. Norman: University of Oklahoma Press. 1992.

Sedgwick, Catherine Maria. *Hope Leslie; or, Early Times in Massachusetts.* 1827. Introduction by Mary Kelley. New Brunswick, N.J.: Rutgers University Press. 1984.

Smith, John. *Generall Historie of Virginia.* 1624. In *The Complete Works of Captain John Smith (1580–1631),* 3 vols., edited by Philip Barbour. Chapel Hill: Institute for Early American History and Culture and University of North Carolina Press, 1986.

Stratton, Royal B. *Captivity of the Oatman Girls.* 1857. Lincoln: University of Nebraska Press, 1983.

Tyler, Royall. *The Algerine Captive.* Walpole, N.H.: David Carlisle, 1797.

Wakefield, Sarah F. *Six Weeks in the Sioux Tepees: A Narrative of Indian Captivity.* 1864. Edited by June Namias. Norman: University of Oklahoma Press, 1997.

Secondary Works

Burnham, Michelle. *Captivity and Sentiment: Cultural Exchange in American Literature, 1682–1861.* Hanover, N.H.: University Press of New England, 1997.

Castiglia, Christopher. *Bound and Determined: Captivity, Culture-Crossing, and White Womanhood from Mary Rowlandson to Patty Hearst.* Chicago: University of Chicago Press, 1996.

Derounian-Stodola, Kathryn Zabelle. "The Indian Captivity Narratives of Mary Rowlandson and Olive Oatman: Case Studies in the Continuity, Evolution, and Exploitation of Literary Discourse." *Studies in the Literary Imagination* 27 (1994): 33–46.

Derounian-Stodola, Kathryn Zabelle. *Women's Indian Captivity Narratives.* New York: Penguin, 1998.

Derounian-Stodola, Kathryn Zabelle, and James Levernier, eds. *The Indian Captivity Narrative, 1550–1900.* New York: Twayne, 1993.

Ebersole, Gary L. *Captured by Texts: Puritan to Post-Modern Images of Indian Captivity.* Charlottesville: University Press of Virginia, 1995.

Namias, June. *White Captives: Gender and Ethnicity on the American Frontier.* Norman: University of Oklahoma Press, 1993.

Perdue, Theda, and Michael D. Green. *The Cherokee Removal: A Brief History with Documents.* Boston and New York: Bedford, 1995.

Sayre, Gordon M. *American Captivity Narratives.* Boston and New York: Houghton Mifflin, 2000.

Strong, Pauline Turner. *Captive Selves, Captivating Others: The Politics and Poetics of Colonial American Captivity Narratives.* Boulder, Colo.: Westview Press, 1999.

Tompkins, Jane. *Sensational Designs: The Cultural Work of American Fiction.* New York: Oxford University Press, 1987.

Lorrayne Carroll

CATHOLICS

In the period 1820–1870 Catholicism became the single-largest individual religious denomination in the United States, although by 1850 American Protestants counted together outnumbered American Catholics by two to one. The growth of American Catholicism can be seen in the fact that while in 1826 there were 250,000 Catholics in the United States, by 1865 there were 3.5 million. In part the numbers swelled due to the high number of conversions: 700,000 from 1813 to 1893. In 1835 Alexis de Tocqueville (1805–1859) commented on the large number of conversions to Roman Catholicism among Americans, noting in his magisterial study *Democracy in America* that Americans, who were otherwise governed by individualism in their civil lives, welcomed a religion that exhibited discipline and unity.

AN IMMIGRANT CHURCH

The increase in the population of American Catholics was also driven by natural population growth and by a formidable influx of Catholic immigrants. These immigrants came principally from Ireland, especially at the time of the Great Potato Famine (1845–1849). In spite of their poverty and lack of marketable skills Irish immigrants had an advantage over Catholic immigrants from other countries. They could speak English—even if their education in other respects was lacking due to the severe privations imposed upon

In 1835 the French observer Alexis de Tocqueville commented on the relationship between Catholicism and American democracy:

The Catholic religion has erroneously been regarded as the natural enemy of democracy. Among the various sects of Christians, Catholicism seems to me, on the contrary, to be one of the most favorable to equality of condition among men.

Alexis de Tocqueville, *Democracy in America*, 2 vols., edited by Phillips Bradley (New York: Knopf, 1956), 1:300.

them by English rule. Nonetheless, in 1850 over 75 percent of the Irish Catholic population of America could read and write English. All the same, these immigrants tended to be employed in unskilled jobs—manual labor for the men, household duties for the women. The effect of this was that relatively few Irish Americans before 1870 had risen into the middle class. Most were poor members of the working class, and for this reason these immigrant Catholics were regarded with condescension and sometimes with contempt by the Protestant establishment.

Prior to 1820 the Catholic population of the United States largely comprised Anglo, French, and Hispanic peoples. The French had come to New England from Quebec and the Acadians from Nova Scotia, New Brunswick, and Prince Edward Island, from which they were exiled in 1755 and 1758 to various parts of the American seaboard from Maine to Georgia, the most famous settlement occurring in what is now Louisiana. Henry Wadsworth Longfellow (1807–1882) depicted the expulsion of the Acadians in his long narrative poem *Evangeline* (1847). In that well-known poem a young Acadian woman searches for the man who, abruptly exiled from his homeland, had been separated from her on her wedding day. She finds him at last while serving as a Sister of Mercy in Philadelphia in the late 1790s. Longfellow associated Evangeline's Franco-Catholicism with a pastoral, European stability, of which he felt the lack in American society.

Following the Mexican-American War (1846–1848) there was a huge influx of Hispanic Catholics into the United States, many of whom had had merely a sporadic contact with the clergy. A series of reforms soon followed, led by missionary leaders like

Jean B. Lamy (1814–1888), who regularized the practice of the faith in the American Southwest. Regular contact with priests was indispensable to the practice of Catholicism, in the saying of Mass and in the administering of the sacraments such as the Eucharist, for example, through which Catholics in the Southwest and elsewhere believed themselves brought miraculously and materially into the presence of God. There were other significant immigrant groups including German Catholics, who began to arrive in the 1830s. They arrived with better work skills and more education than the Irish, and they tended to come from more prosperous backgrounds. Other Catholic immigrant groups in the period included the Italians and the Poles, both of whom brought with them church-related ethnic practices.

Prior to the building of Catholic schools the doctrinal knowledge of most immigrant Catholics was rudimentary and often heterodox. The solution to this problem adopted by the American bishops—preeminently John Hughes (1797–1864), bishop and then archbishop of New York (1842–1864)—was to build seminaries in which to train a knowledgeable clergy and to build schools and colleges for all Catholics. An example was Fordham College, which opened in 1841 and which went on to become a distinguished university. Hughes was concerned that public education in the mid-nineteenth century in the United States was tinged with a Protestant ethos, which would eventually undermine Catholic culture. In a similar spirit he and other American bishops developed a network of parishes not only as places of worship but also as social, cultural, and to some extent political gathering places for what was rapidly becoming a large American subculture.

At the head of this subculture were the Irish, who formed a hegemony of bishops in America so that by the end of the nineteenth century two out of three bishops were of Irish descent. With some exceptions these Irish American bishops tended to be authoritarian and anti-intellectual administrators. The essayist and novelist Orestes Brownson (1803–1876), the most important American Catholic writer in the period from 1820 to 1870, complained that American Catholics were too insular and too suspicious of non-Catholic culture and that in this respect they reflected the worst aspects of their European origins in countries where there had been an intermingling of church and state. Such cultural isolation, Brownson argued in an article in *Brownson's Quarterly Review* in April 1847, merely intensified an existing prejudice against Catholics that saw them excluded from honor and wealth.

Orestes A. Brownson.

CATHOLICS AND MAINSTREAM AMERICAN CULTURE

As exemplified by Brownson, American Catholics in mid-nineteenth-century America tended to be partisan and unyielding in their claim of possessing the true faith. Mr. Howard in Brownson's novel *Charles Elwood; or, The Infidel Converted* (1840), for example, suggests that Protestantism is not a religion in itself but merely what remains of Catholicism. Brownson's novel *The Spirit-Rapper* (1854) took aim at the widespread appeal of spiritualism, seeing it as both foolish and, at bottom, demonic. A conspicuous source of difference between Catholics and other American Christians was the special worship of Mary. On the one hand women were elevated in the eyes of Catholics by Mary's role as the mother of Jesus, but on the other hand Mary's virginity seemed to subordinate married women. Thus, although the family was at the top of Catholic social values, married women were assigned a role in Catholic culture that was inferior to celibate women in religious orders. Both groups of women were in turn subordinated to men. As Brownson put it in *The American Republic* (1865), men were created as the heads or intellects of women.

Although Harriet Beecher Stowe (1811–1896) in her novel *Agnes of Sorrento* (1862) praised the communal aspects of Catholicism in contrast to Protestant individualism, many other Americans looked askance at the influx of Catholics into their society in the nineteenth century. The pope was viewed as an intrusive force in American life, and this, together with the poverty and rough behavior of many Irish immigrants who soon set up their own drinking establishments, eventually gave rise to anti-Catholic incidents in a number of eastern cities. In the 1830s and 1840s the nativist movement, including the anti-Catholic weekly *The Protestant,* helped to foment reaction against Catholic institutions. For example, in 1834 an Ursuline convent in Charlestown, Massachusetts, was burned by nativists. In the 1850s the Know-Nothing Party, a nativist group, joined the fray against Catholics. Spurious, allegedly autobiographical books depicting the sexual exploitation of nuns by priests fed the flames, such as Ned Buntline's *The Jesuit's Daughter: A Novel for Americans to Read* (1854), Rebecca Reed's *Six Months in a Convent* (1835), and Maria Monk's scandalous best-seller, *The Awful Disclosures of Maria Monk* (1836). These books suggested that not only were priests unlikely to be able to keep their vows of celibacy but that they were hypocritical and predatory in pretending to do so.

At a more sophisticated level there is the implicit anti-Catholicism of Edgar Allan Poe's (1809–1849) "The Pit and the Pendulum" (1843), in which the horrors of the Spanish Inquisition are portrayed. Poe plays on the common American Protestant association between Catholic Europe, superstition, and clerical corruption. In Nathaniel Hawthorne's (1804–1864) novel *The Marble Faun* (1860), Catholic Italy is viewed skeptically, especially regarding the practice of the sacrament of confession, which is depicted in its dispensing of forgiveness as dulling the conscience and discouraging the renunciation of evil. In his *French and Italian Note-Books* (1858) Hawthorne laments the superstition of the Italians, as in their fear of the evil eye—a belief, he adds, that is frequently found in monasteries. In *Italian Journeys* (1867) the novelist William Dean Howells (1837–1920) characterizes the rituals that he witnessed in the Vatican as tedious and vacuous and as led by haughty and sinister-looking prelates. Like Hawthorne, Howells comments on the superstitiousness of the Catholics he encountered in Italy. In the novella "Benito Cereno" (1855), Herman Melville (1819–1891) depicts Catholics as addressing votive prayers not to God or to Christ but to Mary, the mother of Jesus. A young Spanish nobleman, Don Joaquin, marquez de Aramboalaza, pledges that in return for a safe ocean passage to Peru he will deposit a jewel at the feet of Our Lady of Mercy in Lima.

While Melville records the matter objectively, he captures the view of many American Protestants at the time that Catholics were idolatrous and superstitious in focusing their piety on Mary and the saints and, even more egregiously, on statues. Even more significantly perhaps from the point of view of Melville's attitude toward such Catholic practices, Don Joaquin is killed before reaching his destination.

Realizing that Catholics were viewed negatively by many other Americans, some Catholic writers responded with popular novels designed to make Catholicism more attractive than it had been to non-Catholic American readers. As Willard Thorp has documented, between 1829 and 1865 there were almost fifty novels published in which their authors attempted to clear up misconceptions about Catholicism and in which a proper way for Catholics to relate to the American cultural mainstream was suggested. One of the most influential of these popular novelists was Mary Sadlier (1820–1903), who as a young woman in 1844 emigrated from Ireland to Montreal and there married James Sadlier, who managed the Canadian branch of his family's New York publishing house. Sadlier began publishing her novels through the firm, and some fourteen years later the couple moved to New York City, where they established a successful Catholic newspaper, *The Tablet.* In New York the Sadliers became influential members of the Catholic community and Sadlier became friends with Orestes Brownson.

Most of Sadlier's readers were Irish Catholic women. In addition to depicting Catholicism, Sadlier conveyed the flavor of Irish American speech and customs so that at times readers like Brownson were sometimes unclear as to where religion began and Irish culture left off. From reading novels like *Bessy Conway; or, The Irish Girl in America* (1865), Catholic readers learned how to achieve success in the workplace while not succumbing to the largely Protestant culture that dominated that workplace. Where the temptations were too great, her central characters were advised to leave and head westward, where society was more open, less rigidly organized, than in the eastern cities. Sadlier was a strong advocate of Catholic schools, hospitals, and charitable agencies. In a similar vein, in *Willy Burke; or, The Irish Orphan in America* (1850), Sadlier sets out to undermine the assumption that in order to achieve success in America one had to be Protestant. *The Blakes and the Flanagans: A Tale of Irish Life in the United States* (1855) explores the lure of the American dream of success in tension with the demands of the family and condemns the Blake family for sacrificing the family to success. The Flanagans, on the other hand, reconcile success and virtue by organizing a successful family business. For Catholics the family was valued as having been created by God and was regarded as intermediate between the individual and society. The family was a shelter against being assimilated by the larger society and the most appropriate environment in which to practice virtue and to strive for religious salvation. In this respect the Catholic ethos emphasized something distinct from the traditional American Puritan or Calvinistic theology in which the individual encounter with God paralleled an equally individual pursuit of material success. Nevertheless, Sadlier's characters reflect the difficulty of centering on the family amid the poverty that characterized Catholic immigrant life at this time, by which marginal employment often made it difficult for family members to be together.

Another well-known Catholic popular novelist in the mid-nineteenth century was Charles Pise (1801–1866), a priest and writer who, unlike Sadlier, had been born in the United States. Pise, who was elected a chaplain to the U.S. Senate in 1832, the first of his faith to be so installed, argued for the compatibility of American republican ideals and those of the Catholic faith. He depicted characters who were more genteel than those presented by Sadlier and who articulated their faith for a literate, non-Catholic audience, rationalizing the Catholic practice of venerating the saints, for example, as an honoring of great persons. Typically Pise's novels, like Brownson's, emphasized apologetics in scenic clashes of ideas in which doubters are convinced and conversions follow.

Pitched at a higher intellectual and cultural level than Sadlier's novels, Orestes Brownson's fiction, including *Charles Elwood, the Spirit-Rapper* (1854), and *The Convert* (1857), centered on the philosophical principle that Catholic theology fundamentally expressed reality. If Catholicity was indeed from God, Brownson argued in *The Convert*, an autobiographical novel that anticipated John Henry Newman's *Apologia pro vita sua* (1864), then God as the author of reality would protect Catholicism from illusion. In *Charles Elwood*, Brownson erected a narrative superstructure that thinly veiled the work's didactic purpose. The novel is basically composed of a series of debates in which Elwood, an admirer of John Locke and of empiricism, slowly approaches Catholic belief both through his reason and intuition, a faculty that, as an ex-transcendentalist, Brownson regarded as cognitive rather than emotional. In contrast Brownson portrayed Protestantism as comparatively emotional rather than rational and philosophical. In *Charles Elwood*, Brownson suggested that in any void left by Christianity, a void that spiritualism and a diluted and amorphous Protestantism appeared to Brownson to be filling in the second half of the nineteenth century, the irrational and the absurd would find fertile ground. Brownson also ridiculed the growing ascendancy of the idea of progress across the whole American cultural spectrum since he believed it was unconnected to a teleological framework (such as Catholicism provided) that would give meaning to the concept of progress by pointing to an absolute end, so that steps toward that end could thereby be assessed.

CATHOLICISM AND AMERICAN DEMOCRATIC IDEALISM

Like Brownson, another of the nineteenth century's most influential Catholic essayists, Isaac Hecker (1819–1888), had been associated with the transcendentalist movement and was a convert to Catholicism. In contrast to many other Catholics who looked askance at thought that had not received the blessing of the church, Brownson and Hecker, who had both begun as American Protestants, were accustomed to an open society, at least one that was more open than the European countries from which the large numbers of Catholic immigrants had come. Brownson was scathing in his attack on the intellectual xenophobia of the Catholic Church in America, particularly when contrasted with what he perceived as the rich intellectual heritage of Catholicism over the ages. In an article published in *Brownson's Quarterly Review* in July 1861 he observed that nowhere in the church's history could he find a period in which the leaders of the church had displayed so great a dread of intellect as in nineteenth-century America. For Brownson the vitality of Catholicism had been strongest when the surrounding culture had been replete with intellectual, especially moral and theological, controversy.

Although in their intellectual sophistication and openness to culture in the broadest sense Brownson and Hecker may not have been typical of the thinking of the Catholic population around them, they did present Catholicism to the wider community as an intellectually respectable religion, and in time their influence on American Catholic thought was appreciated by those in the fledgling Catholic intellectual community in the second half of the nineteenth century and subsequently by later generations of American Catholics. Both Brownson and Hecker emphasized the compatibility of Catholic faith and reason, arguing that the supernatural tenets of their faith were not irrational but were, rather, beyond reason and in some respects beyond the reach of science. Indeed, Brownson argued that there was no inherent conflict between Catholicism and science—that the findings of science had to be accommodated by religion but also that science needed to hold to its own area of knowledge and not drift into philosophy and theology. For this reason he was skeptical of some of the philosophical and religious inferences that were drawn by those looking at Charles Darwin's findings. On the whole, however, Brownson affirmed science and other fields of knowledge as contributing to one's knowledge of reality, a reality that could ultimately be traced back to God. For this reason he was impatient with Catholics who saw these other aspects of culture as irrelevant to them as Catholic Christians. The project of American civilization, he made clear, was one that Catholics ought to make their own, both in order to know more about the immensity of the creativity of God and also as a project to which they could, steeped in the writings of thinkers like Thomas Aquinas, contribute valuable philosophical and moral direction.

The openness that both Hecker and Brownson valued in American society was part of their commitment to American constitutional ideals. Though it may have seemed a doubtful claim to some readers at the time, in 1835 Tocqueville in *Democracy in America* concluded that, among all of the religious denominations in the United States, Catholics were the most likely to embrace democratic ideals. This was, he explained, because except for the distinction between the clergy and lay people, all below the level of the priest were regarded as equal before God. Protestantism, Tocqueville added, tended to make its adherents independent and individualistic rather than equal. Freed from the sort of European society in which religion had bonded with royalty and with the aristocracy, Tocqueville concluded, Catholics in America would quite naturally embrace democracy in a society in which there was a separation of church and state, a separation that both Brownson and Hecker affirmed. A further incentive pointed out by Tocqueville was that most American Catholics in the mid-nineteenth century were poor and so had little to gain from supporting a society in which hierarchical privilege reigned. Brownson and Hecker urged Catholics to participate fully in the democratic process, incorporating into American society those principles in Catholicism that were universal rather than sectarian, principles that would benefit the whole population in clarifying and supporting the essential dignity and rights of human beings. In this matter Brownson regretted that in its inner workings his church frequently failed to adopt democratic principles—principles that, he felt, need not have endangered the preservation of the faith. Instead, he lamented, the clergy tended to deny freedom, especially free discussion, to its members because of a rigidly hierarchical ecclesiastical culture.

In *Questions of the Soul* (1855) and *Aspirations of Nature* (1857), Hecker pursued many of the issues related to Catholicism and democracy that his friend Brownson found absorbing. Indeed, Hecker contended that the Catholic view of what human beings were was not only useful to American society but indispensable for it to thrive as a democracy. Affirming, like Brownson, the compatibility of Catholicism and reason, Hecker maintained that if Christianity was true, then the shaping of American society according to its principles must benefit that society in terms of its overall good. Carrying into his Catholic beliefs the optimistic view of human nature he had acquired as a transcendentalist, Hecker believed that the legacy of Calvinistic Protestantism undermined the assumptions about human goodness and reason that underlay the U.S. Constitution. His eventual rejection of transcendentalism, on the other hand (a rejection that he shared with Brownson), arose from what he viewed as a blurred distinction between the individual as capable of transcendental understanding and the objective, ontological reality of God as creator and sustaining power of the cosmos.

In spite of the robust ideological advocacy of democratic ideals by Brownson, Hecker, and other Catholic intellectuals at the time, Catholic attitudes wavered somewhat in connection with slavery. In the 1850s Brownson had no insurmountable moral difficulty with the Fugitive Slave Law, just as Archbishop John Hughes of New York failed to declare himself an abolitionist. Nonetheless, with the beginning of the Civil War in 1861, Brownson, feeling himself forced to choose, declared himself opposed to slavery and in favor of emancipation. The issue would not be resolved for many American Catholics until well into the twentieth century following the Second Vatican Council. In the 1960s the public opposition of most American Catholic leaders to racism and to economic and social as well as political discrimination would be trenchantly and influentially articulated by American Catholic writers like Dorothy Day, Thomas Merton, and Daniel Berrigan, who articulated a fuller understanding of the racial implications of American constitutional ideals than had been expressed by Catholic thinkers in the nineteenth century.

See also Democracy in America; Immigration; Irish; Political Parties; Protestantism; Science; Transcendentalism

BIBLIOGRAPHY

Primary Works

Brownson, Orestes. *The Works of Orestes A. Brownson.* 1882–1907. Edited by Henry F. Brownson. New York: AMS Press, 1966.

Hawthorne, Nathaniel. *Passages from the French and Italian Note-Books of Nathaniel Hawthorne.* 1858. London: Strahan, 1871.

Hecker, Isaac. *Aspirations of Nature.* New York: James B. Kirker, 1857.

Hecker, Isaac. *Questions of the Soul.* New York: Appleton, 1855.

Howells, William Dean. *Italian Journeys.* 1867. Evanston, Ill.: Marlboro Press/Northwestern University Press, 1999.

Tocqueville, Alexis de. *Democracy in America.* 1835, 1840. Edited by Phillips Bradley. New York: Knopf, 1956.

Secondary Works

Fisher, James T. *Catholics in America.* New York: Oxford University Press, 2000.

Franchot, Jenny. *Roads to Rome: The Antebellum Protestant Encounter with Catholicism.* Berkeley and Los Angeles: University of California Press, 1994.

Griffin, Susan M. *Anti-Catholicism and Nineteenth-Century Fiction.* New York: Cambridge University Press, 2004.

Hennesey, James. *American Catholics: A History of the Roman Catholic Community in the United States.* New York: Oxford University Press, 1981.

Labrie, Ross. *The Catholic Imagination in American Literature.* Columbia: University of Missouri Press, 2001.

McDannell, Colleen. *The Christian Home in Victorian America, 1840–1900.* Bloomington: University of Indiana Press, 1986.

Taves, Ann. *Household of Faith: Roman Catholic Devotions in Mid-Nineteenth-Century America.* Notre Dame, Ind.: University of Notre Dame Press, 1986.

Thorp, Willard. *Catholic Novelists in Defense of Their Faith, 1829–1865.* New York: Arno Press, 1978.

Ross Labrie

"THE CELEBRATED JUMPING FROG OF CALAVERAS COUNTY"

The story of Jim Smiley's jumping frog has been from the first and continues to be a staple of Mark Twain's reputation as a humorist and teller of tall tales par excellence. Twain (Samuel L. Clemens, 1835–1910) composed the sketch in 1865 while working (intermittently)

as a journalist in and around San Francisco. By his own testimony, he had heard a version of the story early in 1865 during a sojourn in the mining camps of Jackass Hill and Angel's Camp in northern California with Jim and William Gillis—brothers of Steve Gillis, a close friend and fellow newspaperman (a compositor) from Twain's days on the *Virginia City Territorial Enterprise*. While confined by rainy weather with Jim Gillis and others at Angels Camp, Twain heard (while no doubt reciprocating with stories of his own) a number of tall tales that, as his notebook entries from the time make clear, provided inspiration for later writings. Among these was one recorded in his notebook as follows: "Coleman with his jumping frog—bet stranger $50—stranger had no frog, & C got him one—in the meantime stranger filled C's frog full of shot & he couldn't jump—the stranger's frog won" (*Mark Twain's Notebooks and Journals,* p. 80). The actual teller of the tale is often identified as Ben Coon, whom Twain mentions in his notebook: "Met Ben Coon, Ill [probably meaning Illinois] river pilot here" (p. 75), but Twain did not make the connection explicit. What he did later make explicit was a connection between Coon and the character Twain would develop as "good-natured, garrulous old Simon Wheeler" ("The 'Jumping Frog' in English," p. 589), the fictional narrator of the jumping frog story, who made his first appearance in a newspaper piece titled "An Unbiased Criticism" that Twain published in the *Californian* in March 1865, soon after his return from Jackass Hill and Angel's Camp.

VERSIONS OF THE JUMPING FROG STORY

During the eight-month interval between Twain's return to San Francisco from the mining camps and his submission of the jumping frog story for publication, he made two unsuccessful beginnings at writing the narrative (both evidently from September or early October 1865) that were preserved in manuscript form and much later (1981) published in the second volume of *Early Tales and Sketches.* In the first of these, titled "The Only Reliable Account of the Celebrated Jumping Frog of Calaveras County," Twain sets the story in the California mining camp of Boomerang. This fragment describes Boomerang in detail and introduces Simon Wheeler as prospective narrator but does not manage to include any speech by Wheeler or anything at all about the jumping frog. A second effort, titled "Angel's Camp Constable," again set in Boomerang, has Wheeler tell about the title character, Constable Bilgewater (a name that Twain would later resurrect in *Adventures of Huckleberry Finn,* 1885), but again does not arrive at any portion of the jumping frog story itself. Finally, in October 1865, apparently prodded by continuing requests from Artemus Ward (the literary pseudonym of Charles Farrar Browne) to contribute to a book Ward was compiling, Twain managed to get on track and produce the story he published as "Jim Smiley and His Jumping Frog."

In middle to late October Twain dispatched the story to New York, where Ward's publisher was located, but it arrived too late for inclusion in Ward's book. The publisher, George Carleton, passed "Jim Smiley and His Jumping Frog" along to Henry Clapp, publisher of the *New York Saturday Press,* where it appeared on 18 November 1865. This first published version of the story, retaining (like the abortive manuscript versions) "the village of Boomerang" as its setting, takes the form of a letter addressed to "Mr. A. Ward" and uses the now-familiar frame story in which the unnamed narrator looks up "fat and bald-headed" ("Three Versions," p. 282) Simon Wheeler to inquire, in this case at Ward's instigation, for Rev. Leonidas W. Smiley, only to find himself trapped into listening to a meandering story about Jim Smiley instead—a result that the narrator suspects of being a practical joke played by Ward. The story wanders through accounts of Smiley's betting on dogs, cats, chickens, birds, even "straddle-bugs," and most remarkably, on the imminent death of Parson Walker's wife before reaching the more detailed episodes of the "fifteen-minute nag," the "bull-pup" Andrew Jackson, and at long last, the prize jumping frog "Dan'l Webster"—only to trail off with the narrator's hasty departure in order to avoid hearing any additional seemingly pointless tales about Jim Smiley's adventures.

Soon after its initial publication, "Jim Smiley and His Jumping Frog" was reprinted in a number of other newspapers and magazines. It quickly became a principal vehicle for spreading Twain's growing West Coast reputation to the eastern states. A San Francisco magazine, the *Californian,* published a revised version of the story, retitled "The Celebrated Jumping Frog of Calaveras County," in December 1865, and two years later Charles Henry Webb, the former editor of the *Californian* (who had by then, like Twain, moved to the East Coast) arranged to have it serve as the cornerstone of Twain's first book, a collection of short works titled *The Celebrated Jumping Frog of Calaveras County and Other Sketches* (1867). This revised version of the jumping frog story changes the location of the story's action from "the village of Boomerang" to "Angel's Camp," the name of the actual place where Twain evidently first heard the story. It also drops both the epistolary form and the specific reference to Artemus Ward—referring instead to "a friend of mine" ("Celebrated Jumping Frog," p. 7) as the joker who sends the narrator on his fool's errand. In addition, there are revisions from the earlier published version in the direction of increased dialect in Wheeler's narration, giving his narrative style a more distinctive "local color" flavor.

The final major revision of the story occurred when it was republished by the American Publishing Company in 1875 in a subscription book, *Mark Twain's Sketches, New and Old.* In this reworking, Twain again made changes to increase the distinctiveness of Simon Wheeler's vocabulary and pronunciation, giving him a more coherent and clearly identifiable "voice." He also altered the frame narrator's character slightly to make him more of an objective, amused observer. In "Jim Smiley and His Jumping Frog," the narrator at the end responds to Wheeler's offer to tell about Jim Smiley and his "yaller one-eyed cow that didn't have no tail only just a short stump like a bannanner" with the impatient, if good-natured, exclamation, "O, curse Smiley and his afflicted cow" ("Three Versions," p. 288). The "Celebrated Jumping Frog" version closes with a similar epithet, changing "curse" to "hang." The "Notorious Jumping Frog," on the other hand, demonstrating Twain's growing mastery of the storytelling art, renders the narrator as ironic rather than exasperated: "lacking both time and inclination, I did not wait to hear about the afflicted cow, but took my leave" ("The 'Jumping Frog' in English," p. 594).

In *Sketches, New and Old,* the jumping frog story is accompanied by a French translation of the story from *Revue des Deux Mondes* (possibly an early cause for Twain's distaste for things French) and by Twain's doubly comic retranslation back into English—the whole accumulated mass bearing the title "The 'Jumping Frog' in English. Then in French. Then Clawed Back into a Civilized Language Once More by Patient, Unremunerated Toil." By this means Twain found an opportunity to satirize the difficulty of preserving the nuances of a literary work during translation to another language as well as to showcase ironically the international popularity of what had by then became his signature story. The focus on a labored relation between English and French can be seen as a precursor to the "Why don't a Frenchman talk like a man?" conversation between Jim and Huck in chapter 14 of *Adventures of Huckleberry Finn.* An example of that strained relation occurs in the story's principal punch line: "I don't see no p'ints about that frog that's any better'n any other frog" in the "Notorious Jumping Frog" becomes "I no saw not that that frog had nothing of better than each frog" in Twain's retranslation from the French. And "he set the frog down and took out after that feller, but he never ketched him" becomes "he deposited his frog

The jumping frog as Daniel Webster. Two images, one a portrait of nineteenth-century statesman Daniel Webster, the other an illustration of the jumping frog as drawn by True Williams for *Mark Twain's Sketches, New and Old* (1875), show a facial resemblance, no doubt centered in Webster's habitual gravity of expression, that Twain may have had in mind when he named Jim Smiley's frog "Dan'l Webster." DANIEL WEBSTER PHOTOGRAPH, THE LIBRARY OF CONGRESS; ILLUSTRATION FROM *THE CELEBRATED JUMPING FROG* COURTESY OF CLEMENTS LIBRARY, UNIVERSITY OF MICHIGAN

by the earth and ran after that individual, but he not him caught never" ("The 'Jumping Frog' in English," p. 603).

Further exploiting the immense popularity of the jumping frog story, Twain later included it in several additional collections. He also published "Private History of the 'Jumping Frog' Story" in the *North American Review* in 1894. Here Twain recounts the deadpan telling of the story by the man from whom he professes to have actually heard it. Though he does not identify the teller, he accurately specifies the time and place of the telling as Angels Camp in 1865 and identifies the event itself (i.e., the fateful encounter between Jim Smiley and the stranger) as having occurred in Calaveras County in 1849. He then further complicates the "Frog's" genealogy (and the relation between fact and fiction) by acknowledging (satirically) a predecessor text from ancient Greece. The "Private History" includes the greater part of the "Notorious Jumping Frog" text plus a "translation" of the ancient Greek version and an excerpt from the "retranslation" from French previously published in *Sketches, New and Old*. The "Greek" story is a very straightforward telling of the jumping frog anecdote— with no "fifteen-minute nags," bull-pups, straddle-bugs, or incompetent, dialect-speaking narrators—in

which Jim Smiley becomes a Boeotian and the stranger who bests him is an Athenian.

THE "P'INTS" OF THE JUMPING FROG STORY

Probably the most important factor in the jumping frog's success is simply Twain's overwhelmingly effective sense of humor. In this respect the sketch, for all its seeming offhandedness, is notably dense, containing within its brief compass a remarkable number of amusing incidents, each causally but deftly given its due in the course of the dual narratives presented by the frame narrator and, within his narrative, Simon Wheeler. These include the securing of the frame narrator as a literally captive audience by Wheeler, who "backed me into a corner and blockaded me there with his chair" ("The 'Jumping Frog' in English," p. 589), the catalog of Jim Smiley's gambling adventures (such as his betting on the effectiveness of Parson Walker's sermons or his willingness to follow a straddle-bug "to Mexico" to settle a bet), the proposed bet with Parson Walker about his wife's health, the glorious career of the extraordinarily trained "fifteen-minute nag," the story of the resourceful but eventually tragic bull-pup Andrew Jackson, the jumping frog incident itself, and finally, the story of the "yaller one-eyed cow," which manages to be funny without even being told.

A somewhat less visible but nonetheless compelling aspect of Twain's narrative is the degree to which he succeeds in telling what is actually a tightly structured story while making it seem entirely artless. Simon Wheeler's narrative seems at first to be no story at all but just a rambling expostulation on the peculiar habits of Jim Smiley, which itself is only a digression from consideration of the Reverend Leonidas Smiley, who is purportedly the real object of interest. The name Smiley makes Wheeler think of Jim Smiley, and the reminiscence about Jim's obsession with betting makes him think of the particular incident of Parson Walker's wife, which is not really a story but merely an anecdote about a specific conversational exchange. From there Wheeler's narrative broadens into the story of the fifteen-minute nag, which has character development (of the horse) but no ending. But then the train of thought moves to the story of Andrew Jackson, who has still more personality than the horse, underscored by the fact that he has a name and by Wheeler's expression of sorrow at the outcome of Andrew Jackson's last fight, as well as his judgment that "he would have made a name for hisself if he'd lived, for the stuff was in him and he had genius" ("The 'Jumping Frog' in English," p. 591). The Andrew Jackson episode also includes a reversal of fortune in which the trickster is tricked, as Andrew Jackson's technique of defeating his adversary by merely holding onto his hind leg becomes his undoing when he faces a dog whose legs have been "sawed off in a circular saw" ("The 'Jumping Frog' in English," p. 591). At last Wheeler arrives, as if by chance, at the climactic story of Dan'l Webster, the jumping frog—only to have the value of that story denied in the amusingly and carefully prepared-for anticlimax of the narrator's flight in the face of Wheeler's promise of further Jim Smiley episodes.

An important element in the jumping frog story's artful artlessness is its narrator, Simon Wheeler. It is interesting to note that in Twain's preparation for the story Wheeler had already made four appearances—two newspaper pieces and two manuscript versions of the story—before any portion of the jumping frog narrative itself (other than the plot outline in Twain's notebook entry) is known to have come into being. The evidence is strong that Twain regarded the narrative mode as crucial to the success of the story. In fact, one might say that the core idea for Twain's sketch is as much his conception of Simon Wheeler as narrator as it is the anecdote of Jim Smiley and his well-trained jumping frog. That conception can be seen in Twain's 1894 "Private History of the 'Jumping Frog' Story" in his recollection, whether real or fanciful, of the actual teller of the story when he first heard it:

> He was a dull person, and ignorant; he had no gift as a story-teller, and no invention; in his mouth this episode was merely history—history and statistics; and the gravest sort of history, too; he was entirely serious, for he was dealing with what to him were austere facts, and they interested him solely because they were facts; he was drawing on his memory, not his mind; he saw no humor in his tale. ("Private History," p. 153)

This description of the Simon Wheeler prototype tallies closely with Twain's advice on the right method for telling a humorous story given in his essay "How to Tell a Story," published in the next year (1895). Here Twain identifies the "humorous story" as distinctively American, as opposed to the English "comic story" and the French "witty story." He says, "The humorous story may be spun out to great length, and may wander around as much as it pleases, and arrive nowhere in particular" (p. 201)—a description perfectly tailored to the narrative method of Twain's jumping frog story. As for the teller of the humorous story, he must convey his material "gravely": "the teller does his best to conceal the fact that he even dimly suspects that there is anything funny about it" (p. 201). This storytelling mode, no doubt reflecting Twain's own very successful method for telling humorous stories on the lecture circuit, fits Simon Wheeler precisely, except that in Wheeler's case, the art is all his creator's. He is a kind of idiot savant who tells a hugely amusing story without at all trying to do so.

LIVING WITH THE FROG

When Henry Clapp published "Jim Smiley and His Jumping Frog" in the *Saturday Press* in late 1865, it was not Twain's first exposure in the East. He was in fact already beginning to become well known before its publication. In autumn 1865 the *New York Round Table* published a praiseful assessment of Twain's work, which, as it happened, was reprinted in the *San Francisco Dramatic Chronicle* at about the same time as he was mailing the jumping frog manuscript to New York. Clearly gratified by the positive response to his work, he wrote to his brother Orion Clemens (19 October 1865) that he had experienced "a 'call' to literature, of a low order—i.e. humorous" (*Mark Twain's Letters*, p. 322). He continued, "It is only now, when editors of standard literary papers in the distant east give me high praise, & who do not know me & cannot of course be blinded by the glamour of partiality, that I really begin to believe there must be something in it" (p. 323). He evidently felt himself at this moment poised for a breakthrough, and when "Jim Smiley and His Jumping Frog" was published in New York a month later and was widely praised and reprinted, he must have known that his opportunity had come. Indeed, he perhaps could hardly believe his good fortune. He wrote to his mother and sister on 20 January 1866, "To think that after writing many an article a man might be excused for thinking tolerably good, those New York people should single out a villainous backwoods sketch to compliment me on!" (*Mark Twain's Letters*, p. 327). But it is unlikely that Twain was actually fooled about the literary value of his jumping frog story. It may have been "a villainous backwoods sketch" when he heard it at Angels Camp early in 1865 and recorded its outline in his notebook, but by the time he had worked through the technical considerations that he recognized as necessary for giving it the most effective presentation, it had become a work of considerable craftsmanship.

A measure of the degree to which the average reader of the late nineteenth century could be expected to be familiar with Twain's story occurs in William Dean Howells's (1837–1920) *The Rise of Silas Lapham* (1885), in which the title character's daughter Penelope, a young woman noted for her keen wit, ridicules the possibility of an opposing point of view with the main punch line (what Twain, in "How to Tell a Story," refers to as the "nub") from the jumping frog story: "I don't see any p'ints about that frog that's any better than any other frog" (Howells, p. 80). The story of the jumping frog remains a staple of American culture because its author, turning his own fascination with the culture of the mining camps into something distinctive and yet universally recognizable (as he did with numerous other cultures that he encountered), elevated Jim Smiley, the ill-fated gambler, and Simon Wheeler, the artlessly compelling storyteller, to a level that transcends cultural differences.

See also Humor; Tall Tales

BIBLIOGRAPHY

Primary Works

Howells, William Dean. *The Rise of Silas Lapham.* 1885. New York: New American Library, 1963.

Twain, Mark. "The Celebrated Jumping Frog of Calaveras County." 1867. In *The Celebrated Jumping Frog of Calaveras County and Other Sketches,* pp. 7–19. New York: Oxford University Press, 1996.

Twain, Mark. "How to Tell a Story." 1895. In *Mark Twain: Collected Tales, Sketches, Speeches, and Essays, 1891–1910,* pp. 201–206. New York: Library of America, 1992.

Twain, Mark. "The 'Jumping Frog' in English. Then in French. Then Clawed Back into a Civilized Language Once More by Patient, Unremunerated Toil." 1875. In *Mark Twain: Collected Tales, Sketches, Speeches, and Essays, 1852–1890,* pp. 588–603. New York: Library of America, 1992.

Twain, Mark. *Mark Twain's Letters.* Vol. 1, *1853–1866.* Edited by Edgar Marquess Branch, Michael B. Frank, and Kenneth M. Sanderson. Berkeley: University of California Press, 1988.

Twain, Mark. *Mark Twain's Notebooks and Journals.* Vol. 1, *1855–1873.* Edited by Frederick Anderson, Michael B. Frank, and Kenneth M. Sanderson. Berkeley: University of California Press, 1975.

Twain, Mark. "Private History of the 'Jumping Frog' Story." 1894. In *Mark Twain: Collected Tales, Sketches, Speeches, and Essays, 1891–1910,* pp. 152–160. New York: Library of America, 1992.

Twain, Mark. "Three Versions of the Jumping Frog" ["The Only Reliable Account of the Celebrated Jumping Frog of Calaveras County," "Angel's Camp Constable," and "Jim Smiley and His Jumping Frog"]. In *Early Tales and Sketches, 1864–65,* edited by Edgar Marquess Branch, Robert H. Hirst, and Harriet Elinor Smith, pp. 262–288. Berkeley: University of California Press, 1981.

Secondary Works

Branch, Edgar Marquess. *The Literary Apprenticeship of Mark Twain.* Urbana: University of Illinois Press, 1950.

Branch, Edgar Marquess. "'My Voice Is Still for Setchell': A Background Study of 'Jim Smiley and His Jumping Frog.'" *PMLA* 82 (1967): 591–601.

Cox, James M. *Mark Twain: The Fate of Humor.* Princeton, N.J.: Princeton University Press, 1966.

Kaplan, Justin. *Mr. Clemens and Mark Twain, a Biography.* New York: Simon and Schuster, 1966.

Krause, Sydney J. "The Art and Satire of Twain's 'Jumping Frog' Story." *American Quarterly* 16 (winter 1964): 562–576.

Lynn, Kenneth S. *Mark Twain and Southwestern Humor.* Boston: Little, Brown, 1959.

Steinbrink, Jeffrey. *Getting to Be Mark Twain.* Berkeley: University of California Press, 1991.

Wilson, James D. *A Reader's Guide to the Short Stories of Mark Twain.* Boston: G. K. Hall, 1987.

James S. Leonard

CHARLESTON

The story of Charleston's literary scene during the period between 1820 and 1870 is the story of William Gilmore Simms (1806–1870), advocate for slavery, native of the city, and the South's preeminent man of letters at that time. Although Simms is best known for such historical fiction about South Carolina as *Woodcraft* (1854), a Revolutionary War romance, and *The Cassique of Kiawah* (1859), set in the colonial period, he had his hand in every aspect of literary life imaginable in Charleston, from the theater scene to the compilation of a miscellany of the writings of prominent citizens to the publication of several notable periodicals. Moreover, Simms's career serves as a reflection of important changes in the identity of Charleston as the city's attention shifted from national to sectional matters due to developments on the political scene and population shifts during the half century.

CHARLESTON THEATER

Charleston began the nineteenth century more aligned with cities in the North and even Europe than with other cities in the South. It served as one of the four major theater centers in America along with New York, Philadelphia, and Boston in the first quarter of the century, and in 1821 it was the fifth-largest city in America. The theater scene in Charleston peaked before 1825. Although citizens were still interested in attending performances after that date, the quality of management and productions suffered as the city experienced several periods of depression during the decade. While Charleston struggled to maintain its reputation as one of the dominant cultural centers in the nation, sectional issues arose with the Vesey Slave Rebellion in 1822, after a free black was accused of organizing a conspiracy to murder whites in Charleston, and the dominance of the nullification question between 1828 and 1834, with the South Carolinian and U.S. vice president John C. Calhoun (1782–1850) taking the position that states have the right to nullify laws enacted by the federal government to which they object. Moreover, population growth in Charleston began to slow around 1830 as more people moved west and other cotton states developed. The Old Charleston Theatre was sold to the Medical College of South Carolina in 1833. What followed was the low point in the city's theatrical history as pantomime, circuses, and musical performances overshadowed dramatic productions for four years before the company found a new permanent home. Despite another bout of economic depression, the New Charleston Theater opened in 1837 with William Gilmore Simms giving the dedicatory address.

Simms was a prolific playwright, but much of his involvement in the theater scene was as a spokesperson.

Charleston, 1851. Lithograph by William Hill. FROM THE COLLECTIONS OF THE SOUTH CAROLINA HISTORICAL SOCIETY

Only one of his plays, *Michael Bonham,* was ever produced in Charleston. The play, which encouraged the annexation of Texas as a slave state, was performed at a benefit for Calhoun's memorial in 1855, twelve years after it was written. Simms wrote an ode to Calhoun, which was read on the occasion. *Norman Maurice,* often considered Simms's best play, which was written in 1851 and deals favorably with the admission of new slave states, was never performed. His dramas fit the general political movement from national to sectional interests that took place in Charleston between 1825 and the beginning of the war. Perhaps Simms's dramatic work was not readily received because it ran counter to a general decrease of the performance of political plays in the city during this period. In addition, with the exception of the years 1842–1847, when William C. Forbes managed the theater, more emphasis was placed on importing talent than performing original plays by residents. The theater continued to operate until the verge of war in 1861.

THE CHARLESTON BOOK

In the late 1830s a trend of anthologies from individual American cities began to emerge. Not to be outdone by Boston, New York, Philadelphia, or Baltimore, the Charleston bookseller and Reform Jewish leader Samuel Hart Sr. decided in 1841 that his city needed an anthology of its own. Charleston was at a pivotal moment, concerned with sectional issues but still attempting to maintain its reputation as a dominant city on the national scene, having slipped that year to the position of sixth-largest city in the country. Despite a period of growth for the city as international markets began to rise, Charleston, still preoccupied with agricultural pursuits, struggled economically: only 2.5 percent of the population engaged in industry, and strife over the extension of slavery kept Charleston ideologically separate from most other major cities.

Hart chose Simms at the age of thirty-five to be the editor of his project, although his name never actually appears within its pages. As a professional writer, he did not contribute to a collection of work intended for amateurs. Participants were limited to Simms's contemporaries. They include such notables as Hugh Swinton Legaré, acting secretary of state under President Tyler; the popular playwright John Blake White; and J. D. B. De Bow, who would soon leave for New Orleans to edit the proslavery *De Bow's Review.* Sectional interests are most readily apparent in an essay titled "The Necessity of a Southern Literature" by Daniel K. Whitaker, from whom Simms would later take over the helm of the *Southern Quarterly Review.* Ultimately the anthology was not the success that Hart and Simms had hoped. With less consistent growth rates, a smaller middle class, lower literacy rates, a less densely populated area, and a general lack of accessibility when compared to other major cities, it is not surprising that Charleston's anthology failed to attract enough subscribers when it was published in 1845 to issue subsequent volumes.

CHARLESTON PERIODICALS

Despite any disappointment that *The Charleston Book* may have brought, Simms pressed forward with his plans to forge a strong literary community. He began his own magazine, the *Southern and Western Monthly Magazine and Review,* often simply called "Simms's magazine," in January 1845. His stated plan was to explore the natural political and industrial alliance between the South and the West. The rush westward continued throughout the 1840s, and by the next decade 41 percent of South Carolinians were living out of state. Meanwhile, sectionalism continued to thrive as Charleston was outpaced by Southern and Northern rivals and citizens faced the reality that Charleston would not be considered a major American city much longer. Many of the articles in "Simms's magazine," written by Simms himself, are focused on the issue of slavery. He could not keep up the dual role of editor and primary contributor for very long, and in December 1845 the magazine merged with the *Southern Literary Messenger,* published in Richmond, Virginia. Although Simms had his hand in many of the periodicals emanating from Charleston during this decade, his next major venture was assuming the editorship in 1849 of the *Southern Quarterly Review,* which had relocated to Charleston from New Orleans shortly after its creation. The periodical was devoted to the defense of slavery and advocacy of states' rights. The 1850 crisis in the slavery debate and Simms's own proslavery convictions kept sectional issues central to the magazine. He maintained the role of editor through 1855 of what is often considered the best Southern review before the war due to its accurate portrayal of Southern beliefs and values.

Two years later Simms found himself at the center of the group of intellectuals that met regularly at John Russell's bookstore. Russell agreed to finance a publication created by the group that would bear his own name. Along with the younger poets Henry Timrod (1828–1867) and Paul Hayne (1830–1886), who would edit the periodical, Simms wrote the majority of *Russell's Magazine.* In many ways the publication was specific to life in Charleston and could be considered a local magazine. However, Hayne's first editorial stated the publication's aim to be the "expression of Southern thought and feeling" (Mott, p. 489). By the time the last number was issued in 1860, Charleston was twenty-second in population and eighty-fifth in manufacturing in the nation. Despite its per capita wealth of 3.5 times the Northern mean, the city was expanding at a much slower rate than Boston or New York and could no longer compete. Its intellectual population was less diverse, less cosmopolitan, and less representative of the population of the United States than it had been at the beginning of the century. However, the city had earned its title as the "Capital of Southern Civilization," and it is only fitting that the secessionist movement and the first shots of the Civil War would originate in Charleston. *Russell's Magazine* is considered the best of the Charleston monthlies and would have likely continued to thrive if it were not for the sectional crisis that distracted the already small reading public and diverted the attention of the contributors. It would not be until the 1910s or 1920s that such a collection of talent would assemble again in the South.

What followed in the five years after the end of *Russell's Magazine* was as devastating to Simms personally as it was to others in Charleston and the South. Despite having his plantation gutted, library burned, and slaves freed by the end of the Civil War, Simms set out for New York in late 1865 to salvage the only thing he had left, his literary reputation. Simms's younger friend Paul Hayne gave tribute to his mentor on his passing in 1870. Simms's death marked the end of an era in the literary history of Charleston.

See also Periodicals; Proslavery Writing; Slave Rebellions; Slavery

BIBLIOGRAPHY

Primary Work

Simms, William Gilmore, ed. *The Charleston Book: A Miscellany in Prose and Verse.* 1845. Spartanburg, S.C.: Reprint Co., 1983.

Secondary Works

Guilds, John Caldwell, ed. *"Long Years of Neglect": The Work and Reputation of William Gilmore Simms.* Fayetteville: University of Arkansas Press, 1988.

Mott, Frank Luther. *A History of American Magazines.* Cambridge, Mass.: Harvard University Press, 1938–1968.

O'Brien, Michael, and David Moltke-Hansen, eds. *Intellectual Life in Antebellum Charleston.* Knoxville: University of Tennessee Press, 1986.

Watson, Charles S. *Antebellum Charleston Dramatists.* University: University of Alabama Press, 1976.

Wimsatt, Mary Ann. "William Gilmore Simms." In *The History of Southern Literature,* edited by Louis D. Rubin Jr. et al., pp. 108–117. Baton Rouge: Louisiana State University Press, 1985.

Natalie Collins Trice

CHEROKEE MEMORIALS

Among most Native American nations east of the Mississippi, an esteemed quality of political leadership has historically been a leader's ability to convince community members of the rightness of her or his ideas. Persuasion is valued above coercion; a bullying leader generally loses the mandate of leadership. The eloquent body of political literature from eastern Native American nations is a testament to this social and rhetorical ethic, for these speeches, letters, laws, and petitions often place a fundamental value on bringing audiences and writers and speakers to a middle ground of mutual respect and understanding, even when simultaneously challenging racism, land theft, and political oppression. The nineteenth-century Cherokee memorials to the U.S. Congress—diplomatic petitions that invoked this reciprocal relationship through ethical, legal, and empathetic appeals—are insightful illustrations of the political concepts and values of the Cherokee Republic and powerfully contrast the difference between Cherokee and U.S. articulations of nation-to-nation relationships and their associated obligations and responsibilities.

CHEROKEE STRUGGLES IN THE NINETEENTH CENTURY

While Cherokees had long defended their lands against a wide range of interlopers, from indigenous nations such as the Choctaws, Shawnees, and Chickasaws to European powers, it was the aggressive and diplomatically immature United States that posed the greatest challenge to the Cherokee Nation in clearly and concisely communicating a mutually intelligible language of sovereignty and diplomacy. It was also a time of extraordinary internal cultural change that included the codification of a written syllabary of the Cherokee language, the political centralization of autonomous towns to a republican form of government, the eclipsing of women's formal political influence, the increasingly economic dependence on black slavery among wealthy Cherokee planters, and the growing influence of Euro-Western social mores. Some of these changes, such as the syllabary and the political unification, were adopted to ensure that Cherokees throughout the Nation could more effectively and efficiently communicate with one another, especially in the face of ever-increasing oppression. Other changes, however, worked toward the economic and political benefit of a small group of privileged Cherokee men, thus distancing the clan-based authority of women and the human struggles of African Americans from the public sphere.

The dangers of the time emerged from a long history over Cherokee land rights in the southern Appalachian Mountains, which include parts of present-day Georgia, the Carolinas, Tennessee, Kentucky, Alabama, West Virginia, and Virginia. The American Revolution had devastated the Cherokees. Much of the colonists' anger toward Great Britain was rooted less in unfair taxation than in antagonism to the Royal Proclamation of 1763, which, prompted in part by a bloody war against the Cherokees, affirmed the crown's recognition of Native American claims to the lands west of the Appalachians, with the intent of placing a permanent barrier to the westward flood of settlers. Many U.S. leaders—George Washington and Thomas Jefferson among them—were land speculators, and their revolutionary ambitions were motivated as much by land hunger as by desire for freedom from British authority. When the battle lines were drawn, many Cherokee towns were on the side of the British, who, while always unreliable allies, made overtures toward respecting Native American territorial integrity. Yet when the war was over and most Cherokee towns were in ruins, the terms of the nation's first formal agreement with the fledgling United States—the 1785 Treaty of Hopewell—set the stage for later troubles.

Although the Cherokees had lost vast tracts of land during the long resistance, the Treaty of Hopewell was concerned less with taking more lands than with establishing a recognizable boundary for Cherokee land title that was to be protected by the United States and its citizenry. This boundary, however, included lands that were claimed by the state of Georgia, and Georgians flouted the treaty protections. The wave of white squatters continued in spite of numerous Cherokee protests and was exacerbated by the inability (or unwillingness) of U.S. agents to intervene. In an 1802 deal with the federal government Georgia gave up some lands through assurances that the United States would work to vacate the Cherokee title to other lands within Georgia's claimed boundaries, and this further emboldened the state's increasing aggression against Cherokee sovereignty.

The Cherokees were not passive victims—they responded forcefully and eloquently. Though overwhelmingly outnumbered in their own homelands, the nation in 1827 adopted a written constitution that affirmed the Cherokees' unwavering determination to remain on their ancestral lands and to fully exercise both cultural and political self-determination. The year 1828 saw the launch of the *Cherokee Phoenix,* a bilingual national newspaper that included powerful editorials by Elias Boudinot (1800–1839) and others that publicized the Cherokee fight for sovereignty. These actions enraged Georgia authorities, who responded by extending state law over the contested lands and declaring all Cherokee legal authority extinguished.

In 1830, under the active encouragement of the Indian fighter turned president Andrew Jackson, Congress narrowly passed the Indian Removal Act, under which terms Cherokees and other tribal nations in the East were to be expelled from their lands and relocated to the "Indian Territory" in what is now Oklahoma. Emboldened by Jackson's hard-line stance and the discovery of gold in the Cherokee mountains, Georgia increased its campaign of land seizures, political harassment, censorship of the press, and ultimately, state-sponsored terrorism that encouraged brutal attacks on individual Cherokees (including beatings, rapes, and murders) and threatened the national leadership and white allies with injury and imprisonment. In 1838, after U.S. treaty commissioners arranged for a fraudulent land cession treaty with a small group of self-appointed Cherokee representatives (the 1835 Treaty of New Echota), the majority of the sixteen-thousand-strong nation was driven by federal troops, members of the Georgia militia, and lawless white squatters into concentration camps, from which they were moved onto the thousand-mile journey westward. This expulsion, commonly known as the Trail of Tears, resulted in the deaths of up to a third or more of the nation from disease, abuse, hunger, exposure, exhaustion, and despair. Although the Cherokee Nation ultimately survived, the removal remains one of the most devastating events in Cherokee history.

CHEROKEE POLITICS AND THE MEMORIALS

The Cherokee memorials provide a striking picture of the peoples' struggle to maintain their nationhood during this traumatic period. Cherokees submitted a number of memorials to the U.S. Congress, each with the express intent of convincing U.S. political leaders to reverse the Indian Removal Act and its conditions (and after 1835 to repudiate the illegitimate Treaty of New Echota), to recognize Cherokee sovereignty, and perhaps most pointedly, to honor the United States's

The Trail of Tears, 1838, **1942.** Painting by Robert Lindneux of the forced journey to Indian Territory, during which over four thousand Cherokees died. Lindneux's illustration is the most renowned; no contemporary depictions are known to have survived. THE GRANGER COLLECTION, NEW YORK

own avowed political and religious ideals. These documents were written firmly within the communal context of Cherokee diplomatic rhetoric, highlighting the necessity of empathy and reason in creating harmonious relations between Cherokees and whites.

There were many memorials over the decade-long removal struggle, and most followed a similar rhetorical pattern of nation-to-nation engagement, affirmation of higher principles, and invocations of accountability. As official governmental petitions, the documents clearly represent the Cherokee position that they are engaged in a strong and mutually respectful government-to-government relationship and that they firmly comprehend the political rights and responsibilities implied by such a treaty-protected relationship.

Each memorial begins with an address to the U.S. Senate and House that acknowledges the memorialists' position as official representatives for the Cherokee Nation. The petitions then generally move into a brief account of the abuses and outrages

being experienced by the Cherokee Nation, along with a reminder to the U.S. lawmakers that they are responsible for maintaining a legal and moral relationship of protection to the Cherokees, as in an 1834 memorial:

> They [the memorialists] respectfully represent that their rights, being stipulated by numerous solemn treaties which guaranteed to them protection, and guarded, as they supposed, by laws enacted by Congress, they had hoped that the approach of danger would be prevented by the interposition of the power of the Executive, charged with the execution of treaties and laws, and that when their rights should come in question, they would be finally and authoritatively decided by the Judiciary, whose decrees it would be the duty of the Executive to see carried into effect. For many years, these their just hopes were not disappointed. (Ross, p. 290)

Similarly, in an 1836 memorial and protest of the nation to Congress, the memorialists assert that there has been a long relationship between the two governments, and it is one that the United States has repeatedly affirmed, to the cultural benefit of Cherokees:

> It would be useless to recapitulate the numerous provisions for the security and protection of the rights of the Cherokees, to be found in the various treaties between their nation and the United States. The Cherokees were happy and prosperous under a scrupulous observance of treaty stipulations by the Government of the United States, and from the fostering hand extended over them, they made rapid advances in civilization, morals, and in the arts and sciences. Little did they anticipate that when taught to think and feel as the American citizen, and to have with him a common interest, they were to be *despoiled by their guardian*, to become strangers and wanderers in the land of their fathers, forced to return to the savage life, and to seek a new home in the wilds of the far west, and that without their consent. (Ross, pp. 427–428)

The leaders of the Cherokee Nation of this time placed great faith in the promises of Euro-Western "civilization," which included education in the English language, familiarity with a classical education, and conversion to Christianity, but they did not do so in order to surrender their nation's sovereignty or identity. Rather, their embrace of Euro-Western values was to more effectively protect and affirm Cherokee distinctiveness in a way that was recognizable to their most powerful and aggressive neighbors. As Maureen Konkle observes, "The claim to 'civilization' and 'progress' must be understood in context—as a material but also temporal claim, a claim to history on their own terms" (p. 77). If, as international law of the time asserted, "savages" had no claim to the land, then the Cherokees would join the ranks of "civilized" nations and draw on the rights implied therein.

The memorials, as both chronicles of facts and analyses of principles, generally move into discussions of moral and legal philosophy regarding the exact relationship between the Cherokee Nation and the United States, specifically regarding the inherent rights and responsibilities of Cherokee nationhood and the illegitimate claims of the state of Georgia over Cherokee territories, interspersed with examples of outrages committed against both the Cherokee government and individual Cherokee citizens. These examples generally include names of both victims and perpetrators, giving a deeply human dimension to their struggle that highlights the drafters' intimate awareness of their people's difficulties. Throughout the memorials are appeals to the basic good nature of white Americans and numerous biblical allusions to justice and fairness, each located in such a way as to emphasize as much as possible both the necessity and the practicability of reversing the brutalizing policies.

The closing words of the memorials are particularly poignant appeals to the fundamental nobility and human sympathies of their American neighbors, thus representing the most cherished founding ideals of the United States as the primary barrier between Cherokee survival and destruction. In one of numerous 1835 memorials, the drafters end this way:

> They respectfully pray that measures may be adopted by your honorable bodies to vindicate the faith of treaties, to preserve to them their rights guaranteed by those treaties, to arrest the hand of rapine now stretched forth to despoil them of their homes and possessions, and to save them from being driven out to perish from starvation and misery, if not condemned even to a speedier death, by the ruthless spoiler. (Ross, p. 317)

In 1836, when the Cherokees had become significantly more imperiled, the memorial is even more impassioned in its closing appeal:

> The Cherokees cannot resist the power of the United States, and should they be driven from their Native American land, then will they look in melancholy sadness upon the golden chain presented by President Washington to the Cherokee people as emblematical of the brightness and purity of the friendship between the United States and the Cherokee nation. (Ross, p. 444)

Although the memorials ultimately did not sway enough political or public opinion to prompt a reversal of U.S. removal policies, the documents were not failures. Many included long lists of signatures of Cherokee citizens (the 1835 memorial above included 15,546 names), demonstrating a communitywide familiarity with the issues and endorsement of the documents' positions. They explicitly engaged the concept of Cherokee nationhood from within; they did not simply react to ideas imposed from without. Though generally drafted by a small group of delegates, the memorials represented, as much as possible, the collective voice and position of the Cherokee people, most of whom were literate in either English or Cherokee and were well aware of their nation's struggle through the editorials and articles published in the *Cherokee Phoenix*.

These documents were thus as much about bringing the community together as they were about advocating the community's concerns to outsiders. They were oriented toward sharing the political struggles of all Cherokees and demonstrated an awareness of a leader's obligations to his or her people. It was a principle of leadership that encompassed more than just the Cherokee delegates: as the United States had taken upon itself the responsibility of leadership and protection, its representatives too were held to a high standard of accountability to the Cherokee people. The memorials, then, stand as more than simply documents of protest: they are eloquent testaments to the covenant of trust, respect, and responsibility between nations and a poignant reminder of the need for principled attention by all parties to the terms of that covenant.

See also Indians; Indian Wars and Dispossession; Native American Literature; Trail of Tears

BIBLIOGRAPHY

Primary Works

Ross, John. *The Papers of Chief John Ross.* Vol. 1. Edited by Gary E. Moulton. Norman: University of Oklahoma Press, 1985.

U.S. Congress, House of Representatives. "Memorial of a Delegation of the Cherokee Tribe of Indians." 9 January 1832. 22nd Cong., 1st sess., doc. no. 45. U.S. House of Representatives.

Secondary Works

Konkle, Maureen. *Writing Indian Nations: Native Intellectuals and the Politics of Historiography, 1827–1863.* Chapel Hill: University of North Carolina Press, 2004.

Perdue, Theda, and Michael D. Green, eds. *The Cherokee Removal: A Brief History with Documents.* New York: Bedford/St. Martin's Press, 1995.

Daniel Heath Justice

CHILDHOOD

The stage of life referred to as "childhood" is not a fixed notion but is instead a concept defined largely by the dominant concerns, needs, and values of a given cultural and historical context. What it means to be a child changes as society changes. How children are portrayed in literary texts of a given period and what recommendations are documented regarding the actual treatment of children become ways to examine the major issues and events of that particular historical time and place. According to Caroline Levander and Carol Singley in *The American Child: A Cultural Studies Reader,* the child is "not only a biological fact but a cultural construct that encodes the complex, ever-shifting logic of a given group . . . and reveals much about its inner workings" (p. 4). The period between 1820 and 1870 in American history is one of the richest for examining changes in attitudes about childhood and studying the child as a vehicle that reveals the struggles and inner workings of an emerging nation. Summarizing the early- and mid-nineteenth-

century shifts in understanding childhood, Ralph Waldo Emerson (1803–1882) commented, "There grew a certain tenderness on the people not before remarked. Children had been repressed and in the background; now they were considered, cosseted and pampered" (*Complete Works* 10:325). Emerson's observation not only refers to the growing interest in nurturing children that characterized these decades but alludes to broader meanings as well.

In the years following the American Revolution, childhood became a useful site for debate about changing theological beliefs regarding human nature and served as an allegorical tool for exploring the challenges faced by the newly formed, independent Republic separated from its parental monarch. The portrayal and treatment of the child became an important tool for reflecting and conveying the fundamental transition from harsh puritanical, authoritarian rule of colonial America to more egalitarian and participatory democracy of the Jacksonian era; a transition apparent in church, government, and even in the microcosm of the family. No longer "repressed and in the background," Americans were exploring what would be required of governing themselves while respecting the common good and solidifying a diverse nation (Emerson, *Complete Works* 10:325). A new concept of citizenry was emerging and with it new ideas about raising children who would fulfill the role of democratic citizens guided by conscience—able to be self-governing yet unified. Moreover, in theological matters, beliefs in original sin and infant depravity, dominant in seventeenth- and eighteenth-century Calvinism, were giving way to more moderate viewpoints about human nature, specifically regarding souls of infants and children. By the early 1800s children were considered to be morally neutral, not evil, and by mid-century, Romantic notions of the child's innate goodness had emerged in the writings of Unitarians and transcendentalists respectively. In an unprecedented way, major and lesser-known American authors of early and mid-century incorporated children as significant characters in novels and stories, while childhood itself both served as subject matter and appeared in figurative language and rhetorical devices in imaginative literature as well.

Additionally, literature and periodicals were written and published for children. With increasing literacy rates, the reading of magazines, stories, and informational books became a commonplace activity for children and family gatherings, whereas in earlier times reading the Bible or religious tracts had been the predominant, if not exclusive, literacy activity for children and adults. As the connection was made between nation building and child rearing, large numbers of advice manuals were published and sold between 1820 and 1870.

In the previous century parents received guidance on raising their children from sermons and authorities on religious doctrine; by the nineteenth century sources of information had broadened and came from more liberal religious teachers as well as from secular writers on child rearing and domestic management. This advice literature incorporated and represented the opinions of physicians and educators as well as mothers and fathers themselves, who at least to some extent were influenced by the philosophy of John Locke (1632–1704) and, to a lesser degree, by Jean-Jacques Rousseau's *Emile* (1762). American parents and educators found in the work of Locke especially and Rousseau (1712–1788) more controversially explanations of the critical role that environment plays in shaping the malleable, growing child. Such views were compatible with the hope of cultivating conscientious children for future citizenship in a republican society.

LITERARY REPRESENTATIONS OF CHILDHOOD

With religious and political change as a thematic focus, major writers of the nineteenth century, such as Nathaniel Hawthorne (1804–1864), Harriet Beecher Stowe (1811–1896), Mark Twain (1835–1910), Walt Whitman (1819–1892), Ralph Waldo Emerson, Henry David Thoreau (1817–1862), and Henry Wadsworth Longfellow (1807–1882) employed the child figure in some fashion in their work, usually emphasizing the redemptive and innocent nature and presence of the child while also acknowledging the rebellious and resistant capacities of children. Most widely recognized among texts by these authors in which children appear as central characters are Nathaniel Hawthorne's "The Gentle Boy" (1832), "Little Annie's Ramble" (1834), and *The Scarlet Letter* (1850); Harriett Beecher Stowe's *Uncle Tom's Cabin* (1852); and Mark Twain's "The Story of the Bad Little Boy" (1865) and "The Story of the Good Little Boy" (1870), forerunners to his *The Adventures of Tom Sawyer* (1876) and later *Adventures of Huckleberry Finn* (1885). Perhaps no child characters of the nineteenth century are discussed more extensively in critical scholarship than Hawthorne's Pearl, Stowe's Little Eva and Topsy, and Twain's Tom Sawyer and Huck Finn. The proliferation of comment is not surprising because these characters embody so clearly three essential and frequently expressed themes, sometimes contradictory, related to the portrayal of children in fiction of this period: children possess higher moral insight and integrity that challenges the status quo; children die dramatically and with redemptive flair; and children behave rebelliously or uncontrollably as symbolic voices against the social injustices of their historical settings, whether it be against the abuses and bigotry of New

England Puritanism or slavery. Child "saintliness" and early death as described by Anne Trensky (1975) or their cunning misbehavior as discussed by Daneen Wardrop (2000) and Franny Nudelman (1997) are two general characterizations of children in early- to mid-century fiction. Each child prototype carries significant symbolic reference to numerous and timely controversial issues having to do with beliefs in innate neutrality or purity replacing the eroding dogma of original sin; the corruptive aspect of urban industrialization and expanding commerce, where good cannot survive without a price; the abolitionists' debates and discussions about inhumane and unjust treatment of slaves and Native Americans; and paradoxically, the persistent need to instill the value of conformity to support a threatened national identity during this time.

ANGELIC AND INSPIRATIONAL CHILDREN

Nathaniel Hawthorne's child characters Ilbrahim in "The Gentle Boy" and Pearl in *The Scarlet Letter* function as outcasts from their restrictive and judgmental New England Puritan communities of the seventeenth century. Each endures ridicule for different reasons. Ilbrahim is a child of Quaker heritage among intolerant and condemning Puritans, and Pearl's illegitimate status renders her little identity in the eyes of the Puritans beyond that of the manifestation of her mother's stigma as adulteress. In both texts the child becomes a method for Hawthorne to display his ambivalent position about human nature and to explore the questions regarding the extent to which children inherit the sins of their parents. At the same time, Pearl and Ilbrahim also show endearing and genuine tenderness and playfulness that provide joy and comfort to adults and soften the impact of their persecution. Pearl and Ilbrahim meet different fates. Ilbrahim dies a martyr to the narrowness of a community intolerant of his different "sect." He suffers as well from the death of his birth father; the abandonment by his biological mother, an eccentric Quaker; and the inadequacies and ambivalences of his adoptive parents. Ilbrahim's death suggests the fundamental possibility of evil associated with religious and doctrinal fanaticism, while Pearl survives and, as the character in the novel least repressed or oppressed, embodies redemption or hope for a broader, open future.

What is generally understood is that Hawthorne modeled Pearl on his observations of his daughter, Una, and that Pearl provides evidence for the strong influences of discussions he had with friends and family about children's education and development. Hawthorne's wife, Sophia, expressed interest in transcendentalist ideas of the period, although Hawthorne

Eva and Topsy. Lithograph by Louisa Corbaux, c. 1852. Both characters from *Uncle Tom's Cabin* exemplify the nineteenth-century view of the moral superiority of children. THE LIBRARY OF CONGRESS

was reluctant to fully embrace the assumptions of essential human goodness and child innocence that Ralph Waldo Emerson expresses in his work, especially in his essay *Nature* (1836), and to which Henry David Thoreau alludes in *Walden* (1854). However, Hawthorne had many opportunities to participate in discussions about transcendentalism and to be familiar with the work of educational progressives of the period. Sophia's two sisters, Elizabeth Peabody and Mary Peabody Mann, wife of the noted advocate of public education, Horace Mann, were teachers and authors of numerous texts about children, including the widely read *Moral Culture of Infancy and Kindergarten Guide* (1863). Hawthorne had a genuine interest in and fascination with actual children as well as fictive ones, and he wrote several books specifically for children: *The Whole History of Grandfather's Chair* (1840), *Tanglewood Tales* (1853), and *A Wonder Book for Boys and Girls* (1851). In fact, "Little Annie's Ramble" first appeared in 1835 in an annually published gift book for children (also read by adults), *Youth's Keepsake: A Christmas and New Year's Gift for*

Young People. In this story of a five-year-old girl who accompanies a man on a journey through a small town, Hawthorne captures what might be read as his ultimate statement of the child's compelling, almost mystical impact. The adult narrator says of his time spent with the child that he is revived, "After drinking from those fountains of still fresh existence, we shall return into the crowd . . . to struggle on and do our part in life . . . with a kinder and purer heart, and a spirit more lightly wise" (pp. 121–129).

Anne Tropp Trensky calls the character Little Eva in *Uncle Tom's Cabin* a "quintessential saintly child—an unequivocally pure savior" ("The Saintly Child," p. 392). Harriet Beecher Stowe, deploying the sentimentality characteristic of the period and especially associated with child and childlike figures (e.g., Uncle Tom), portrays children as voices of wisdom and redemptive insight. Stowe distinguishes Eva from other children by describing her as having a "dreamy earnestness" and noting "the deep spiritual gravity" of her eyes (p. 161). Like Hawthorne's Annie, Eva has a profound and transforming impact on those around her, particularly as she nears her death and expresses deep compassion for the suffering of slaves and contempt for the injustices they endure. Eva is a voice for Christian humanitarianism and assures the uncontrollable and self-depreciating slave child, Topsy, that Jesus loves her even in her bondage. Eva is the vehicle for Stowe's abolitionist statement, which, as Jane Tompkins suggests, is softened and made palatable by the use of child characters and their tear-jerking deaths or the heart-wrenching plight of a slave mother attempting to prevent the sale of and separation from her young son. Stowe's child characters are covert instruments of social critique and are designed in their domestic innocence and purity as tools of persuasion to elicit sympathy.

Often, these divine children die, further underscoring the idea that the corrupt world is no place for them to thrive. The frequent depiction of child death was especially poignant and effective rhetorically because actual infant and child mortality rates in the nineteenth century were extremely high. Many families suffered from the actual deaths of their children. Readers empathized with and sought solace in fictive descriptions of angelic children who were taken from earth where, as Fanny Fern (Sara Payson Willis Parton, 1811–1872) says of her character "Dear Little Charley" in *Fern Leaves from Fanny's Port-Folio* (1853), "you were . . . out of place" (p. 120). Children of redemptive virtue who retain their innocence or succumb to death in the face of society's hostility are also portrayed in Susan Warner's best-seller *The Wide, Wide World* (1850), Timothy Shay Arthur's *The Angel of the Household* (1854), Elizabeth Oakes Smith's *The Newsboy* (1854), Maria Cummins's *The Lamplighter* (1854), Martha Finley's *Elsie Dinsmore* (1868), and Louisa May Alcott's *Little Women* (1868–1869). Twenty-first-century readers may think of these texts as designed for child audiences, yet nineteenth-century readers of all ages, especially women, enjoyed these books.

CHILDREN AND NATURE

Transcendentalist writers and thinkers such as Ralph Waldo Emerson and Henry David Thoreau saw the child as aligned with essential divine energies of nature. Not only did the child represent a model of integrity, purity, and an unaccommodating "self-reliance" to which adults should aspire, but in its youthfulness possessed a vitality of the senses, a freshness, that these writers saw as an important quality in having direct, authentic experiences with the divine vitality in daily life. "Children appear to me as raw as the fresh fungi on a fence rail," Thoreau wrote in his journal (*Journal* 1:85). Similarly, he wrote in 1851,

"The senses of children are unprofaned" (*Journal* 3:291). It was the clarity and purity of the senses that Thoreau revered as the avenue to living a "fresh" and creative life. Because observation of the natural world confirms the cycles of new life followed by growth, degeneration, and regeneration, both Thoreau and Emerson saw human life as adhering to this natural rhythm. The child, literally, was new life and symbolically represented to the transcendentalist writers the possibility of inspired self-regeneration at any chronological age. Hence, in his 1836 essay *Nature* not only does Emerson write about the importance of accessing the inward source of new inspiration, but he also emphasizes that when adults live close to nature they live a "perpetual youth"; they "retain the spirit of infancy even into the era of manhood" (p. 498).

Apart from his theoretical reverence, Emerson suffered immense personal loss when his own young son, Waldo, died in 1842. Emerson was forced by this tragic event to reexamine his understanding of nature and childhood. His 1846 poem "Threnody" was written in honor of his son and reflects some of his modifications. Instead of perceiving the child as perfectly unified with natural, "self-reliant" life, Emerson elevated the child above nature to a state so pure and open to divine intuitions that it is, in fact, vulnerable to the grosser natural world (pp. 699–706). Waldo's death affected Emerson and Thoreau to the extent that both writers began in their later work to acknowledge that although the child, "the feeblest babe," may indeed represent "a channel through which the tremendous energies stream" (Emerson, *Journals* 8:223), the mature adult has the benefit of experience to mix with inspiration, so maturation is not entirely a disadvantage. Thoreau's poem "Manhood" refers to "the man, the long-lived child . . . I love to contemplate the mature soul of lesser innocence, Who hath traveled far on life's dusty road" ("Manhood," p. 634).

Another transcendentalist, Amos Bronson Alcott, a teacher of young children and father of Louisa May Alcott, wrote extensive journals and texts from the 1820s through the 1840s about his teaching philosophy and observations of children. His beliefs that children must be allowed to pursue the spontaneity of their divine natures were radical to the point of being impractical, especially in the eyes of many conservative parents, and Alcott was dismissed from several teaching positions. Nevertheless, progressive educators and writers of the period, such as Peabody, Mary and Horace Mann, and Emerson, admired and encouraged Alcott's deep commitment to describing and respecting the spiritual quality of children. In a similar vein, Walt Whitman's poetry also exalts the higher spiritual and intuitive status of the child. In "There Was a Child Went Forth" (1855), Whitman describes the child's capacity to merge with and assimilate the vast world of experience. Fundamentally, Whitman echoes the Lockean perspective that learning comes from direct experience through the senses and, similar to Thoreau and Emerson, suggests that the child's senses and intuitions are particularly acute for generating new perspectives. In "Song of Myself" (1855), Whitman suggests that the child's insight and knowledge is just as valid as the adult's, and he uses the child as the rhetorical vehicle for diminishing authoritarianism in favor of an egalitarian spirit. When the voice of a child poses the question, "What is the grass?" the poet responds, "How could I answer the child? I do not know what it is any more than he" (p. 665).

NAUGHTY CHILDREN

Finally, no discussion of early- and mid-nineteenth-century literary representations of children would be complete without mention of the "bad boy" prototype. Although associated with dime novels and work of the later decades of the century, the depiction of children as rambunctious, mischievous, and slightly criminal appeared by mid-century as reaction to the prevalence of fiction portraying holy and esteemed child characters and allusions. There had been a proliferation of American Sunday School Union publications for children in the early decades describing excessively pious children whose dedication to their religion brought rewards to themselves and to their families or, in contrast, portrayed naughty children who brought downfall and shame to their lives and those around them. Obviously, these texts were designed to teach the benefits of good and moral living and the hazards of wrongdoing. The bad-boy genre, however, had a broader focus and attempted to dilute the sweet sentimentalizing about childhood by presenting children in a more realistic light. In *The Story of a Bad Boy* (1869) by Thomas Bailey Aldrich, the narrator says, "I was really not a cherub . . . I was a real boy" (pp. 7–8). Aldrich's use of the word "cherub" is particularly significant, since Lydia Maria Child's *The Mother's Book* (1831), which sets the stage for an onslaught of domestic guidebooks on the importance of mothering and diligent nurturance of the tender body, mind, and spirit of the innocent and impressionable child, describes the child as "the little cherub."

Advice literature of the time built the case for child rearing to be taken seriously. While middle-class white children certainly benefited from such attention, there were also growing populations of abandoned and poor "street children," especially in

In addition to being a well-known abolitionist, Lydia Maria Child also wrote on domestic issues and childrearing. In The Mother's Book, *Child discusses the importance of mothers guiding the education and development of their children.*

It is a great mistake to think that education is *finished* when young people leave school. Education is never finished. Half the character is formed after we cease to learn lessons from books; and at that active and eager age it is formed with a rapidity and strength absolutely startling to think of. Do you ask what forms it? I answer the everyday conversation they hear, the habits they witness, and the people they are taught to respect. Sentiments thrown out in jest, or carelessness, and perhaps forgotten by the speaker as soon as uttered, often sink deeply into the youthful mind, and have a powerful influence on future character. This is true in very early childhood; and it is peculiarly true at the period when youth is just ripening into manhood. Employ what teachers we may, the influences at home *will* have the mightiest influences in education. Schoolmasters may cultivate the *intellect;* but the things said and done at home are busy agents in forming the *affections;* and the latter have infinitely more important consequences than the former.

Child, *The Mother's Book,* p. 146.

expanding urban areas. By the 1840s and 1850s, the problem of petty crimes and vagrancy among children in New York was perceived as a threat to civility and predictions of a growing "dangerous" underclass began to proliferate. Philanthropic efforts were begun to save children. Charles Loring Brace established the Children's Aid Society in 1853, and actions were taken to get children off the street and into facilities where they would receive adult supervision and care. Horatio Alger's *Ragged Dick; or, Street Life in New York,* published in 1867, popularized the struggles of urban underclass children and their relentless efforts to improve themselves and rise above a life of poverty, actually as much through luck and the intervention of benevolent wealthy strangers as through their own cunning and hard work. Alger's writing was certainly one version of presenting the bad-child-turned-successful formula and served to construct the didactic message linking social mobility to honest effort in a democratic society.

Bad-boy fiction conveyed other viewpoints as well. It also provided a way to glorify the nonconforming, precocious independent child whose less than stellar behavior was more an insightful act of resistance to societal restraint than it was a sign of maliciousness. Furthermore, the bad boy, in his refusal to be civilized and grown up, was a nineteenth-century manifestation of the Peter Pan complex, and this reluctance to comply was communicated as particularly American. Even before *Tom Sawyer* and *Huck Finn*, Mark Twain published "The Story of the Bad Little Boy" and "The Story of the Good Little Boy." These stories were some of the first examples of the bad-boy genre and were parodies of sentimental fiction that contained the usual trajectory of reward promised pious, well-behaved children explicit particularly in the Sunday school series. But Twain reverses the trajectory: the bad boy is seen as justified in his unruliness, and the good boy endures more pain than reward for his propriety.

LITERATURE FOR CHILDREN AND ADVICE LITERATURE ON CHILD REARING

Attitudes toward real children changed drastically in the nineteenth century. Whereas references to children in poetry and diaries of previous centuries focused mainly on birth and death in baptism or funeral elegies emphasizing the child's salvation, by the nineteenth century attention began to be directed to the quality of a child's upbringing and the experience of childhood itself. This attitude had emerged as a logical extension of eighteenth-century sermons about parents' responsibilities in helping their children consciously adopt Christian practices for redemption of the child's innate sinfulness and then extended to an understanding that children are indeed malleable and could be shaped in ways that promoted moral conscience and good character as was necessary, particularly in the national context of political uncertainties and change. The modern understanding of childhood as an important life stage took hold in the early 1800s, perhaps because for the first time in history, childhood was embraced as a period of preparation for adult life and children were viewed as responsive to a variety of adult influences. The breaking of the child's will through harsh discipline and even beatings to the point of death in rare cases in the 1600s and 1700s shifted to gentler approaches that emphasized cultivating a relationship of nurturance, trust, and guidance aimed at building, not breaking, the child's character and spirit.

Since Ann Douglas coined the phrase "the cult of motherhood" in her 1976 book *The Feminization of American Culture,* much scholarly attention has been given to studying connections between nineteenth-century domestic advice literature and literary texts produced for children as well as its influence on major literary work for adult readers, such as *The Scarlet Letter* or *Uncle Tom's Cabin.* The critical role of the mother in the child's care and education, the movement away from the use of corporeal punishment in favor of instilling an internalized self-restraint in the child through firm but gentle parental correction, and the importance given the role of play and entertainment are three basic themes appearing repeatedly as recommendations for raising children with strong self discipline and initiative in addition to nurturing in them the awareness and capacity to make constructive social contribution. Two early secular child-care publications that had wide influence on parents and teachers and on subsequent advice authors were *Thoughts upon the Mode of Education Proper in a Republic* (1784) by Benjamin Rush (1746–1813) and *Treatise on the Physical and Medical Treatment of Children* (1825) by William Potts Dewees (1768–1841). Rush and Dewees, both physicians, emphasized good physical and mental health in children and early cultivation of a social consciousness to the extent that the child must understand his or her purpose in life to be one of contribution to community functioning even if it entailed the sacrifice of personal advantage or whim. With the breakdown of the father's autocratic rule of the family prevalent during colonial times, the mother assumed a more central role in the management of the home and children throughout the 1800s. Motherhood was a personal as well as patriotic duty for women to take seriously, and from 1830 through 1850, an extensive list of books with this message was published. Most influential in this category were *The Mother's Book* (1831) by Lydia Maria Child, *Home* (1835) by Catherine Sedgwick, *Letters to Mothers* (1839) by Lydia Sigourney, and *Treatise on Domestic Economy* (1841) by Catherine Beecher. Later, in 1869, Catherine Beecher (1800–1878) and her sister Harriet Beecher Stowe published *The American Woman's Home; or, Principles of Domestic Science Being a Guide to the Formation and Maintenance of Economical, Healthful, Beautiful, and Christian Homes.* The lengthy title bespeaks the comprehensive duty of women to "form" and "maintain" the domestic sphere, which of course included the care of children and from which men had less and less influence because they were preoccupied by demands in the public, not private, realm. These books were written by and for women, yet men also published significant contributions on child rearing. In 1847 Horace Bushnell wrote *Views of Christian Nurture,* and as early as 1833 a small version of *The Mother at Home* by John Abbott was published, to be published again in 1852.

In the wake of such attentiveness to raising children, the market for books and periodicals for children and youth exploded in the early and mid-1800s. Lydia Maria Child (1802–1880), a prolific writer and abolitionist, started publishing the magazine *Juvenile Miscellany* in 1826. The periodical, although intensely popular for awhile, was discontinued in 1834, when subscriptions fell drastically in protest of Child's outspoken opposition to slavery. Samuel Griswold Goodrich (1793–1860) began publishing the series of *Tales of Peter Parley about America* in 1827, followed by his publication of *Parley's Magazine.* Later Goodrich solicited the help of writers such as Nathaniel Hawthorne, Henry Wadsworth Longfellow, Lydia Maria Child, Catherine Sedgwick, and Oliver Wendell Holmes to contribute to a gift book called *The Token* that was released each year from 1827 to 1842. Jacob Abbott, already widely known for his child rearing advice, wrote a series of popular books focused on a central child character, Rollo.

For the most part, children's literature, whether fictional or factual, had a didactic flavor and was geared to promote a unified national identity and instill a sense of morally inspired character in nineteenth-century youth. Scholarly work examining children's literature grew exponentially in the late twentieth century and considers gender role divisions in addition to social class, moral, and political messages embedded in these texts. Without doubt, the modern understanding of childhood as a developmentally significant time began in the decades of the early and middle nineteenth century. With greater attention devoted to nurturing children and by conceptualizing childhood as a formative life stage, the period from 1820 to 1850 viewed children as resources to be cultivated with the goal of securing a strong and unified democratic citizenry. Fiction and nonfiction of the period portrayed the child as a site of opportunity and hope, filled with wisdom and promise for a better future in a new nation valuing good character and persistent self-improvement.

See also Children's and Adolescent Literature; Domestic Fiction; Education; Marriage; Reform; Romanticism; *The Scarlet Letter; Uncle Tom's Cabin*

BIBLIOGRAPHY
Primary Works
Aldrich, Thomas Bailey. *The Story of a Bad Boy.* 1869. Hanover, N.H.: University Press of New England, 1976.

Alger, Horatio. *Ragged Dick; or, Street Life in New York with the Boot-Blacks.* 1867. Introduction by Alan Trachtenberg. New York: Penguin Books, 1990.

Child, Lydia Maria. *The Mother's Book.* 1831. New York: Arno, 1972.

Emerson, Ralph Waldo. *The Complete Works of Ralph Waldo Emerson.* Centenary ed., 12 vols., edited by Edward Waldo Emerson. Boston: Houghton Mifflin, 1903.

Emerson, Ralph Waldo. *Journals and Miscellaneous Notebooks.* 10 vols., edited by William Gilman. Cambridge, Mass.: Harvard University Press, 1960– 1966.

Emerson, Ralph Waldo. *Nature.* 1836. In *Norton Anthology of American Literature,* 6th ed., shorter version, edited by Nina Baym, pp. 1072–1101. New York: Norton, 2002.

Fern, Fanny. *Fern Leaves from Fanny's Port-Folio.* 1853. Auburn, N.Y.: Miller, Orton, and Mulligan, 1854.

Hawthorne, Nathaniel. *Twice-Told Tales.* The Centenary Edition of the Works of Nathaniel Hawthorne, volume 9. Columbus: Ohio University Press, 1974.

Stowe, Harriet Beecher. *Uncle Tom's Cabin; or, Life among the Lowly.* 1852. Introduction by Jane Smiley. New York: Modern Library, 2001.

Thoreau, Henry David. *The Journal of Henry David Thoreau.* 14 vols. Edited by Bradford Torrey and Francis Allen. Boston: Houghton Mifflin, 1906.

Thoreau, Henry David. "Manhood." In *Henry David Thoreau: Collected Essays and Poems,* edited by Robert F. Sayre. New York: Library of America, 2001.

Whitman, Walt. *Leaves of Grass and Other Writings.* 1855. Edited by Michael Moon. New York: Norton, 2002.

Secondary Works
Avery, Gillian. *Behold the Child: American Children and Their Books, 1621–1922.* Baltimore, Md.: Johns Hopkins University Press, 1994.

Brodhead, Richard H. "Sparing the Rod: Discipline and Fiction in Antebellum America." In *Culture of Letters: Scenes of Reading and Writing in Nineteenth-Century America,* edited by Richard H. Brodhead. Chicago: University of Chicago Press, 1993.

Douglas, Ann. *The Feminization of American Culture.* 1976. New York: Farrar, Straus and Giroux, 1998.

Levander, Caroline, and Carol Singley, eds. *The American Child: A Cultural Studies Reader.* New Brunswick, N.J.: Rutgers University Press, 2003.

MacLeod, Anne Scott. *American Childhood: Essays on Children's Literature of the Nineteenth and Twentieth Centuries.* Athens: University of Georgia Press, 1994.

Nudelman, Franny. "'Emblem and Product of Sin': The Poisoned Child in *The Scarlet Letter* and Domestic Advice Literature." *Yale Journal of Criticism* 10, no. 1 (1997): 193–213.

Price, Kenneth M., and Susan Belasco Smith, eds. *Periodical Literature in Nineteenth-Century America.* Charlottesville: University Press of Virginia, 1995.

Reinier, Jacqueline S. *From Virtue to Character: American Childhood, 1775–1850.* New York: Twayne, 1996.

Singley, Carol J. "Building a Nation, Building a Family: Adoption in Nineteenth-Century American Children's Literature." In *Adoption in America: Historical Perspectives,* edited by E. Wayne Carp. Ann Arbor: University of Michigan Press, 2002.

Tompkins, Jane P. *Sensational Designs: The Cultural Work of American Fiction, 1790–1860.* New York: Oxford University Press, 1986.

Trensky, Anne Tropp. "The Bad Boy in Nineteenth-Century American Fiction." *Georgia Review* 27 (winter 1973): 503–517.

Trensky, Anne Tropp. "The Saintly Child in Nineteenth-Century American Fiction." *Prospects: Annual of American Cultural Studies* 1 (1975): 389–413.

Wardrop, Daneen. "Hawthorne's Revisioning of 'The Little Cherub': Pearl and Nineteenth-Century Childrearing Manuals." *National Hawthorne Review* 26 (2000): 18–32.

Nancy D. Chase

CHILDREN'S AND ADOLESCENT LITERATURE

At the end of a long, hard-fought war, Britain's American colonies became an independent, self-governed nation, the United States of America. British recognition of this new reality, however, was equivocal. At war with Napoleon, Britain intervened in U.S. sea trade and impressed American sailors (calling them deserters from Britain's navy) into service on British ships. The United States declared war on Britain in 1812.

While the War of 1812 had only minor political and territorial effects, it transformed the American psyche. It loosed a powerful nationalism, which colored all of American social history in the first half of the nineteenth century. Americans were aggressively proud of their country, eager to underscore their differences from—and superiority to—the Old World, in particular of course, Britain.

American children's literature was born of this fervent nationalism. While books for children existed in the earliest settlements in America, most were instructional—primers, catechisms, spelling books, geographies, and the like. Storybooks were few and almost always imported, principally from England. By 1820, however, these arrangements seemed unsatisfactory. When nineteenth-century Americans contemplated the future, pride and anxiety alike told them that the Republic's survival depended upon the moral character of the next generation and that sound republican values could not be learned from the literature of old, class-ridden societies. There must be an American literature for American children.

What publishers provided—quite promptly—fell into roughly three categories: schoolbooks, Sunday school books, and nonschool fiction. Differences among them were superficial until at least 1850. All might impart useful knowledge, but the strongest motive in any literature for children, school or nonschool, fiction or nonfiction, was moral instruction: reading must improve the reader. Children's books of all kinds purveyed a Protestant, conventional moralism, with sectarian divisions blurred to ensure broad salability and difficult political and social problems evaded for the same reason. The intended audience was Protestant, literate but not highly educated, and middle class—which is to say, it was most Americans of the time.

FICTION

Unquestionably the strongest influence on early American children's fiction was the work of Maria Edgeworth (1767–1849), often called the first English classic writer for children. Edgeworth's popular tales for children matched the American taste for realistic narrative and clear moral messages. Daughter of the educational theorist Richard Edgeworth, she shared her father's views on child nurture, advocating firm but gentle discipline, rational explanation, and reading taught through realistic, morally instructive stories entertainingly written. Their theories, set out in an essay jointly produced, *Practical Education* (1798), had great influence on American thinking about children and the literature written for them. The eldest of her father's numerous children (by four wives), Maria was deeply involved in all aspects of their upbringing, including reading. *The Parent's Assistant* (1796), a collection of stories she wrote for her step-siblings, became a landmark of moralistic literature for children and the premier model for early American writers of juvenile fiction. Though Maria's stories were indeed entertaining, their justification lay in their moral instructiveness. No author before mid-century recommended fiction purely for entertainment; in fact, fanciful tales were suspect. Authors understood that. "When I tell you stories of things that never happened," one told his child readers in 1836, "my real design is to give you lessons of importance" (Goodrich, *Peter Parley's Book of Fables,* p. 6).

Fiction provided models of both the moral character Americans wanted in their children and of the child nurture that would produce it. Teaching by example rather than precept (though the books were full of precepts) and by explanation rather than punishment and encouraging children to review their mistakes and learn from them—these were the recommended methods. Children's stories opposed corporal punishment and, except for a few produced by sectarian presses, did not hold that children were born sinful. For all the moral seriousness of these works, they were rarely harsh in their approach to children. American authors wrote to instruct children, certainly, but also to tutor parents in gentle (though firm) child nurture.

It was not an exciting literature, nor was it meant to be. After all, a great many Americans of the time disapproved of fiction for any reader because it was "untrue." Only a moral mission justified writing stories for children, and authors embraced that mission to the exclusion of most other elements of fiction. Staid, domestic tales centered on child, parent, and the small transactions of a middle-class family life dominated the literature at least until mid-century.

The market for children's books proved good, as it was for most print. Literacy rates were high in the nineteenth century thanks to the common schools, and reading was by far the most available form of both education and entertainment for Americans. In the course of the first half of the century, the nature of reading and of its public changed greatly. As access to print expanded, reading shifted from intensive—reading a few books many times over (in America, the Bible)—to extensive, that is, wider reading with fewer iterations. And the reading public was no longer an economic or educational elite but as broad as the literate population—which was very broad indeed. The 1840 census put overall American literacy at 78 percent; for whites, 91 percent. Though children's

literature had a special mission, it also was simply part of the larger picture.

AUTHORS

If readers were eager and available, so were writers. While it was nearly impossible until the last decades of the nineteenth century for an author to make a living "by the pen," writing could eke out a skimpy income from other sources: thus the goodly number of women and clergymen who wrote for every kind of publication—book or magazine, for child or adult readers. For women, authorship was a welcome addition to the short list of occupations open to them. And despite conventional opinion, there were many who needed to make their own way—women who were single or inadequately supported, widowed, or divorced. (Sarah Josepha Hale, editor of *Godey's Lady's Book,* and Sara Parton, a.k.a. "Fanny Fern," an immensely popular columnist for the *New York Ledger,* were both divorced.) Clergymen and schoolmasters, reasonably well educated but badly paid, also seized their opportunities. As a group, writers for children were white, Protestant, educated, middle-class, and usually of the Northeast.

Most children's authors of the pre–Civil War period are long forgotten, though a literary historian might recognize the name Jacob Abbott (1803–1879). A respected educator, Abbott flourished in a second career as an author of didactic fiction for children. Probably his best-known publications were twenty-eight books about Rollo (1832–) as he grew from age five to near-adulthood. Rollo's family life, education, and moral development were models for American families to emulate. As tastes changed toward the end of the century, the Rollo stories became scorned examples of a preachy, outdated literature, but in the antebellum period they were not only typical but popular. Later, and more fun, were Abbott's 1850s Franconia stories. In these he was still teaching but less to adults and more to children, where his gifts as a teacher shone.

Probably the most financially successful children's author of the period was Samuel Griswold Goodrich, "Peter Parley" (1793–1860)—tireless author, publisher, and compiler of fiction, textbooks, histories, mythologies, astronomy books, geographies, and two periodicals for children, all overpoweringly moralistic. Goodrich was an exception to the rule; he did make a good living producing works for children. Some 170 titles, about 7 million of them sold by 1856, made him a wealthy man. But however popular and financially rewarding, Goodrich's work was all "slip-slop," according to Nathaniel Hawthorne (1804–1864). And indeed, in his 1856 *Recollections of a Lifetime*, Goodrich himself acknowledged that he had not written for the ages: "I have written too much and done nothing really well" (2:333–334) he said mournfully (and accurately).

It was a little ungrateful of Hawthorne to be so critical. Goodrich published some of Hawthorne's early stories in his family annual the *Token*, hired him to compile material for *Peter Parley's Universal History* (1837), and commissioned him to write other works well before the young author's success as a serious novelist. Hawthorne awoke to the possibilities of the children's literary market and wrote four historical works for children, *Grandfather's Chair*, *Famous Old People*, *The Liberty Tree*, and *Biographical Stories for Children*, all published between 1840 and 1842, but they did not make him rich. *The Scarlet Letter*, which did make Hawthorne's name if not his fortune, was not published until 1850. In 1852 and 1853, respectively, he brought out two children's books still well known, *A Wonder-Book for Girls and Boys* and *Tanglewood Tales for Girls and Boys*. Here he rewrote selected Greek myths in nineteenth-century style—that is to say, moralistically and sentimentally, befitting contemporary taste. It was Hawthorne's version of the King Midas story, for example, in which the wretched king turns his daughter into gold and so repents his greed. (In the classic version, the gods' gift makes it impossible for him to eat and he begs to be released.) Even with their coating of moralism, though, Hawthorne's retold myths lifted children's fiction out of the narrow prison of the usual instructive story. These tales survived well beyond the nineteenth century for the same reason the myths themselves have survived—they were interesting.

Yet it would be a mistake to think that children did not read the more standard fare written for them. Most young readers had little to choose from. Public libraries were still in the future, and while itinerant peddlers always carried children's books, few families—let alone children—had money to buy them. Only the Sunday school library regularly provided books, especially in the early decades. The American Sunday-School Union (ASSU), representing all the major Protestant sects, poured out small, well-illustrated books of didactic fiction, supplying Sunday schools all over the nation. The books were determinedly nonsectarian. A Committee of Publication reviewed every manuscript to avoid sectarian—and all other—controversy, producing books that were thoroughly moralistic, doctrinally bland, and widely acceptable. Since the Sunday school library was the only source of books for many children, child readers in the early nineteenth century certainly read them; the ASSU was a major publisher for children right up to the Civil War.

PERIODICALS

Transportation and printing improvements from the 1820s on created a boom in publishing of all kinds. Periodicals, deliverable by railroad to more and more communities, became enormously popular. Every town had a newspaper—often more than one—locally produced and sold, but weeklies, monthlies, bimonthlies, and annuals arrived by post, which meant by railway.

Samuel G. Goodrich made a career of children's literature at a time when American juvenile literature was in its infancy. He was a publisher, editor, and author of schoolbooks, children's periodicals, and books of fiction. In the absence of more systematic data, his estimates of the expansion of the children's book field in America are generally accepted. In his Recollections of a Lifetime *(1856), he says that in 1820 only 30 percent of all books published in America were authored by Americans; 70 percent were by British authors. By 1850 that balance had been reversed, largely because of the huge production of schoolbooks by American authors. He gives no figures for children's fiction, but the pattern seems to have been much the same. Goodrich's memoirs of his thirty years in the juvenile book field tell the story.*

In casting my mind backward over the last thirty years—and comparing the past with the present, duly noting the amazing advances made in every thing which belongs to the comfort, the intelligence, the luxury of society—there is no point in which these are more striking than in the books for children and youth. Let any one who wishes to comprehend this matter, go to . . . a juvenile bookstore . . . and behold the teeming shelves—comprising almost every topic within the range of human knowledge, treated in an attraction of style and every art of embellishment—and let him remember that nineteen twentieths of these works have come into existence within the last thirty years.

Samuel G. Goodrich, *Recollections of a Lifetime*, p. 21.

Periodicals varied in content, from those dealing with farm and domestic economy to such journals as the *Knickerbocker Magazine* and the *Atlantic Monthly.* Most family periodicals included some juvenile fare, and from time to time periodicals especially for children appeared—and disappeared. One of the early successes was the *Juvenile Miscellany,* published from 1826 to 1834 and edited by Lydia Maria Child (1802–1880). Some of the best-known women writers of the time were contributors—Child herself, Lydia Sigourney, Sarah Josepha Hale, Eliza Follen—forgotten now, but literary lights of their time. The magazine died soon after the 1833 publication of Child's brilliant abolitionist essay *An Appeal in Favor of That Class of Americans Called Africans.* Samuel Goodrich edited *Parley's Magazine* (1833), which merged with *Merry's Museum* in 1844 and lasted until 1872 under that title. Since most mainstream children's fare carefully avoided the slavery issue, abolitionists established two outspokenly antislavery journals for children, the *Slave's Friend* and the *Youth's Emancipator,* in the 1830s. The first lasted two years, the second less than one.

By far the longest-lived of any early-nineteenth-century periodical aimed at a young audience was the *Youth's Companion* (*YC*), which began publication in 1827 and survived until 1929. Nathaniel Willis (1780–1870), founding editor, described his intended magazine in a prospectus sure to appeal to potential subscribers. It would be, he said, "a small weekly journal, which should entertain . . . children and insensibly instruct them" ("Prospectus," p. 1). It certainly instructed; how "insensibly" is debatable. Despite its name, the *YC* format was that of a family weekly, with some material clearly meant for children but much that also spoke to adults. The tone was evangelical in the early years of publication; later, in accord with changing tastes, the editors shifted the journal's emphasis to a more generalized moralism. The *YC* was socially conservative; the magazine vigorously supported the temperance movement, but it never discussed slavery.

No sharp distinction existed between literature for children and for adolescents for most of the nineteenth century. Society loosely classed anyone up to about fifteen as a child. Jo March, who is fifteen at the beginning of *Little Women* (1868–1869) refers to herself as a child, though she is (reluctantly) on the verge of adulthood. That some children's books addressed adolescents seems clear when stories discuss work choices, domestic skills, business practice, and occasionally even the management of servants (the latter was rare, as were servants in America). But of course it must also be remembered that some of these matters might be relevant to youngsters as young as twelve. Any number of books, for example, warned boys against a sailor's life, which could begin at a very early age. Moreover, the authors believed that, like moral values, habits of industry were best formed early. Stories showed quiet little girls learning domestic tasks, and Jacob Abbott frequently instructed young boys in good labor and business practices.

TEXTBOOKS

Before the latter decades of the nineteenth century, textbooks were not tightly age graded and for good reason. Common schools in the antebellum years were not graded; they were one-room, one-teacher classrooms, serving students from three and four years old up to sixteen and seventeen. Though textbooks existed and were used in urban and private schools, in the rural common schools (which means most of them) books of any kind were entirely hit or miss. Neither the rural families nor the schools could afford to buy textbooks as a matter of course. Children used whatever books their families owned—very few usually—whether they were well adapted to their age or not. Aside from the Bible, which was often used as a reading text, the book likeliest to be found in common schools was Noah Webster's Blue-Back Speller, a few copies per school being shared around by all the scholars.

Next to the *Speller* in ubiquity were the McGuffey *Eclectic Readers,* which came on the market in 1836. These were graded in order of difficulty from the primer through six reading books. They were composed of short pieces, some written for the books but most excerpted from prose and poetry by well-known authors, the prose sometimes reworked by the editors. Like all schoolbooks of the time, they were strongly Protestant and moralistic and thoroughly allergic to controversy. Heavily marketed by their publisher, Truman and Smith, they were used in schools well into the twentieth century.

The ever-energetic Samuel Goodrich also published textbooks, most of them written by hired hands, all of them reflecting their publisher's cultural biases. Latin America and Asia were wholly written off for their misguided religious beliefs; Hawthorne's project, *Parley's Universal History on the Basis of Geography* (1837), blandly stated that "no country has ever been happy or well governed where Mohammedanism prevailed."

Louise Alcott, The Children's Friend. Illustration by Lizbeth B. Comins from Ednah Cheney's 1888 biography.
© BETTMANN/CORBIS

CHANGES

At mid-century, children's literature began a shift that would accelerate in the post–Civil War period. Fiction, whether published in books or periodicals, took on some of the drama and sentimentality already popular in adult literature. New authors also expanded the narrow range of children's stories to encompass some of the social concerns of an urbanizing, industrializing society. Cities, chronic poverty, immigration, crime—none of these appeared in children's fiction of earlier times. By the 1850s and 1860s they were commonplace.

But the greatest impact on children's literature came from the popular fiction that flooded the country after 1850. In a marketplace teeming with story papers and other cheap periodicals offering "sensational" fiction, to say nothing of the immensely popular dime and "half-dime" novels of the 1860s, young readers eagerly abandoned the sober fare of the past. Boys of all classes devoured pulp literature—which was not of course meant for them—because it was absorbing and exciting, however ill written. Girls were drawn to sentimental romances—when they could get them—and they read their brothers' books too.

Middle-class parents were not content. Surely children should not read lurid accounts of improbable adventures of daredevils and desperadoes with guns and horsewhips and romantic (though chaste) yearnings toward the fair sex. Surely sentimental romances were a danger to young girls. Surely there could be fiction written for children that was interesting and even exciting enough to hold a child's attention yet moral, moderate, and nonviolent.

Thus the stage was set for William Taylor Adams, "Oliver Optic" (1822–1897), and all who followed him into the rewarding world of formula fiction series books for the juvenile market. Adams was not unique in producing formula stories or series, either, but he judged shrewdly the audience he was wooing. He contrived adventure tales (thrilling perhaps but never lurid); he published the books in series; and he wrote prolifically. He also targeted his readers: the Boat Club Series, for example, was not aimed at newsboys. Adams, Horatio Alger Jr., "Sophie May," Edward S. Ellis, and many other hack writers through the 1860s and beyond dished out easily read, predictable but exciting, morally high-minded stories. The books were tamer than the trash they were meant to displace, but children liked them and parents tolerated them.

But only just: these mass-merchandised products woke no great enthusiasm among the genteel middle classes. Mediocre at best, acceptable because of what they were not—that is, not sensational, not violent, not totally implausible—juvenile series books were not as bad as the trash, but neither were they good. What parents wanted for their children, and particularly for their girls—what they were waiting for, though they did not know it—was Louisa May Alcott (1832–1888).

Alcott had published two novels, some "sketches" and many stories in magazines, and was editing a children's magazine when Thomas Niles, chief editor in a Boston publishing house, asked her to write a "girls' book." Reluctantly she agreed, and in 1868 Little Women was published. The book was an immediate—and enormous—success, as was its sequel, Good Wives (1869). Now combined in one volume (titled Little Women) the book is still read a century and a half later. The form Alcott chose was that of the domestic novel that had dominated American fiction for forty years, but Alcott's was not a watered-down replica of the standard domestic novel. The straightforward, colloquial prose and the autobiographical nature of the story, which made its characters individual, believable, and memorable, had powerful appeal for young readers. The book was funny, sad, serious, lighthearted, and of course moralistic, like all 1860s writing. For all the period feeling of the novel, the characterizations in Little Women still speak to girls. The portrayal of Jo was far more complex and heartfelt than anything offered to young readers up to that time. Little Women had then and still has its critics, but most scholars of children's literature agree that it was the work that marked the beginning of "real" literature for children.

See also Childhood; Courtship; Dime Novels; Domestic Novel; Literacy

BIBLIOGRAPHY
Primary Works
Abbott, Jacob. *Rollo at School*. Boston: T. H. Carter, 1839.

Adams, William Taylor [Oliver Optic]. *All Aboard*. New York: Hurst & Company, 1855.

Alcott, Louisa May. *Little Women*. 1868–1869. Edited by Anne Hiebert Alton. Petersborough, Ontario: Broadview, 2001.

Child, Lydia Maria. *Flowers for Children*. 3 vols. New York: C. S. Francis & Company, 1844, 1845, 1847.

Follen, Eliza Lee. *Made-up Stories*. Boston: Whittemore, Niles, & Hall, 1856.

Goodrich, Samuel Griswold [Peter Parley]. *Peter Parley's Book of Fables*. Hartford, Conn.: White, Dwier, 1836.

Goodrich, Samuel Griswold [Peter Parley]. *Peter Parley's Juvenile Tales*. Rev. ed. Cincinnati, Ohio: Applegate, 1851.

Goodrich, Samuel Griswold *Recollections of a Lifetime*. 2 vols. New York: Miller, Orton, and Mulligan, 1856.

Parton, Sara [Fanny Fern]. *Little Ferns for Fanny's Little Friends*. Auburn, N.Y.: Derby & Miller, 1854.

Sedgwick, Catherine Maria. *A Love Token for Children*. New York: Harper & Brothers, 1838.

Tuthill, Mrs. Louise C. *Anything for Sport*. Boston: William Crosby & H. P. Nichols, 1846.

Willis, Nathaniel. "Prospectus." *Youth's Companion*, 16 April 1827, p. 1.

Willis, Nathaniel, publisher and ed. *Youth's Companion*. Weekly publication, New York, 1827–1860.

Secondary Works
Baym, Nina. *Novels, Readers, and Reviewers*. Ithaca, N.Y.: Cornell University Press, 1984.

Baym, Nina. *Woman's Fiction: A Guide to Novels by and about Women in America, 1820–1870*. Ithaca, N.Y.: Cornell University Press, 1978.

Davidson, Cathy N. *Revolution and the Word: The Rise of the Novel in America*. New York: Oxford University Press, 1986.

Kaestle, Carl F. *Pillars of the Republic: Common Schools and American Society, 1780–1860*. Eric Foner, consulting editor. New York: Hill and Wang, 1983.

MacLeod, Anne Scott. *A Moral Tale: Children's Fiction and American Culture, 1820–1860*. Hamden, Conn.: Archon Books, 1975.

Nye, Russel. *The Unembarrassed Muse: The Popular Arts in America*. New York: Dial Press, 1970.

Rice, Edwin W. *The Sunday-School Movement and the American Sunday-School Union: 1817–1917*. Philadelphia: American Sunday-School Union, 1917.

Zboray, Ronald J. *A Fictive People: Antebellum Economic Development and the American Reading Public*. New York: Oxford University Press, 1993.

Anne Scott MacLeod

CHINESE

By the middle of the nineteenth century the economy, sovereignty, and stability of China were in disarray. The defeat in the two Opium Wars, against the British (1839–1842) and the British and French (1856–1860), fought predominantly to stop the entry of opium into China, forced China to legalize the import of opium and sanction Christian missionary activity; it also led to the European and American control of major Chinese ports. Almost simultaneously, several internal rebellions to overthrow the ruling Ch'ing dynasty further impoverished the country, especially the southern provinces, as war repeatedly ravaged the countryside. The Taiping Rebellion (1851–1864) was especially devastating. In addition to the twenty to thirty million lives lost as a direct result of the armed conflict, millions of Chinese suffered through numerous famines and damaging floods as dams and fields were either raided or destroyed by full-fledged armies or small bands of rebels.

It should come as no surprise, then, that the opportunity to escape extreme poverty—through the 1848 discovery of gold in California and the promise of work and superior wages in Gold Mountain, as America was known in China—attracted a growing number of Chinese to the western shore of the United States, from 325 in 1849 to 20,026 in 1852 (Takaki, p. 79). Usually unable to pay for their own voyage, most of the Chinese came to America through the credit system, where the migrant had to reimburse a Chinese broker or merchant for the ticket for passage plus interest and expenses through his labor in California. Since Gold Mountain was early on seen as a place to earn money and not to reside, most of the workers did not or could not afford to bring their wives and families. As a result, early Chinese communities in America consisted overwhelmingly of men. Until the 1870s the majority of the few Chinese women who came to the United States were prostitutes who, tricked into false marriages or sold by their parents, found themselves "in a condition of debt peonage, under contracts" to repay food and passage to her "master/mistress" (Takaki, p. 121). By 1880, however, the percentage of prostitutes had greatly decreased as more women married and more wives were brought over to join their husbands. It is worth noting that Chinese emigration to Hawaii differed greatly than that to the mainland. The majority of Chinese who traveled to Hawaii were contract laborers who were made to repay their debt by working on sugar plantations. Whereas single men predominantly migrated to America, whole families were encouraged to travel to Hawaii not only to make life more comfortable for workers but also to expand at no great cost the number of possible workers on the plantations.

RECEPTION OF CHINESE IMMIGRANTS

On mainland America, the first contacts between Chinese and white Americans were usually amiable; the Chinese provided needed labor and were coming from an intriguing country at a time when anything Oriental was seen as novel, amusing, and desirable. As more Chinese emigrated, however, the reception quickly changed from one of curiosity and benevolence to one of ridicule and the view that they were a nuisance. On the rapidly developing West Coast, more Chinese laborers meant more competition for Irish and other poor white workers. In northeastern cities, the menial jobs and the squalor in which the Chinese were forced to live relegated them to a status as inferior creatures to be scorned. Across the country, racism and derogatory stereotypes would dictate how the Chinese were perceived and treated.

As early as 1852 the California state legislature catered to white miners' concerns about Chinese competition and instituted a foreign miners' license tax; although the law was not exclusively directed at them, only Chinese were consistently made to pay a mining license tax that increased repeatedly and arbitrarily. A year later the disenfranchised status of Chinese was confirmed when California's Supreme Court reversed a guilty verdict of a man who killed a Chinese, declaring that Chinese could not be trusted as witnesses in a court of law. Thus it came about that in California, cheating and assaulting a Chinese, from pulling his queue (a hairstyle consisting of a shaved front and long ponytail in the back that became a symbol of pride and of Chinese

Chinese miners. Illustration from *Harper's Weekly,* 3 October 1857. THE LIBRARY OF CONGRESS

culture for the Chinese and one of ridicule for Americans who likened Chinese queues to the tails of rats) to murdering him were now committed with impunity.

As the reception and consideration of Chinese workers deteriorated, so did opinions of them. On the West Coast, because of racist views of their appearance, the predominantly migrant Chinese were soon perceived to be sneaky and inscrutable bachelors responsible for the moral decline of white women and for the advent of prostitution. They could not be assimilated, were dishonest heathens, stole jobs from white workers, and drove down wages. The misconception that all Chinese were transient sojourners who did not contribute to the U.S. economy further worsened their image; in reality, only 47 percent of Chinese who entered the United States between 1850 and 1882 returned to China, a percentage quite comparable to that of European immigrants (Takaki, pp. 116, 11). By the mid-1850s in the eastern United States, where many Chinese sailors had settled, Chinese and beggary, heathenism, gambling,

and opium addiction had become closely associated in people's minds. Chinese association with poor Irish immigrants (many Chinese men married Irish women) provided further proof to many of their inherent inferiority. China was seen as a fallen power that had refused to change for four thousand years; compared to the growing and energetic United States it was something to be pitied at best and exploited at worst. As John Kuo Wei Tchen has noted, "Race, physiognomy, phrenology, and character were becoming so intertwined that the views of Chinese as equals or as people to be admired and respected were becoming less and less possible" in the United States (p. 217).

CHINESE LABOR

If the perception of Chinese was decidedly negative, their labor was still in great demand. Between 1862 and 1869 nine to ten thousand Chinese worked on the western section of the transcontinental railroad; as a result of the insufferable working conditions, at least a thousand died. During the construction more and more Chinese were employed to replace Irish crews; compared to the Irish, the Chinese were seen as more industrious, soberer, and less demanding. After the completion of the railroad many Chinese established themselves near the new railroad towns and turned to farming, fishing, factory work (particularly cigar making and in woolen mills), or laundering, a non-threatening occupation normally reserved for women where Chinese were usually tolerated but still not free from abuse. Frustrated by the increasing demands of Irish and African American workers, American businessmen imported Chinese laborers specifically to toil in the fields of the South or break strikes in New England manufactures; due to the reputation they had gained doing railroad work as meek, docile, and beasts of burden, the Chinese were brought to the United States to displace malcontent workers and teach them their place: this is arguably one of the first instances of the model minority myth being applied to Asian Americans. Seen by the industrialists as cheap labor and by the predominantly poor white working class as strikebreakers and takers of jobs, the Chinese were further alienated and reviled. Both views of the Chinese were reinforced and facilitated by their isolation, forced in many cases by city ordinances, racism, continued threats of violence, and lack of judicial or political recourse.

RACISM

The severe recession of the 1870s, along with incendiary speeches by anti-Chinese demagogues and racist representations (see, for example, Tchen, Matsukawa, and Moon for further discussions of Chinese in cartoons, advertising, and songs), pushed many Americans to protest more openly what they believed to be the cause of economic demise: cheap Chinese labor. Cartoons likening Chinese to rats, advertisements for starch that pictured unemployed Chinese launderers and happy white families, and songs like the anonymous "John Chinaman" (1855) helped to portray the Chinese as vermin who threatened to take the country away from hardworking Americans. "John Chinaman" sings about various stereotypes and how the Chinese, through their own volition, have failed to assimilate. To John Chinaman, America—the presumed singer—regrets being so welcoming because it had originally

> thought you'd open wide your ports. . . .
> I thought you'd cut your queue off, John, . . .
> But I find you'll lie and steal too— . . .
> For our gold is all you're after, John.
> *(Moon, pp. 36–37)*

Indeed, (white) America is sad to attest that because of John Chinaman's dishonesty, cultural attachment, diet of "rats and puppies," thieving, and greed, he will never become a true American nor a welcomed guest. The Chinese, in this and similar popular songs, are sneaky opportunists who scheme and lie in order to claim America's resources. In addition to the fear that Chinese would break down the labor system and bring white Americans to starve, many worried about a massive emigration, possibly armed, of Chinese who would take over the land (referred to as "yellow peril") and about the possible miscegenation with an inferior race. This anti-Chinese sentiment lead to numerous lynchings and riots against the Chinese and their communities, brought about by the passage of the 1875 Page Law, which banned the immigration of Chinese contract laborers and the importation of Chinese women for immoral purposes and culminated in the Chinese Exclusion Act of 1882, which prohibited all Chinese laborers from immigrating to the United States. The Exclusion Act was not an effective solution for the lack of jobs; at .002 percent of the nation's population, Chinese laborers did not pose a real threat to the white workforce. The immigration ban did, however, lessen the tensions between the working and governing classes and appeased the concerns of nativists who wanted to maintain a white America. The act was renewed in 1892, and in 1902 Chinese immigration was made permanently illegal; the act would not be repealed until 1943 as China became an American ally in World War II.

THE CHINESE IN AMERICAN LITERATURE

To help Chinese deal with white people and provide them with a voice and language Americans would understand, Wong Sam and assistants published *An English-Chinese Phrase Book* (1875), which was distributed for free at Wells Fargo offices in towns where Chinese Americans lived. The bilingual phrase book announces that it "contain[s] strategy and tactics for business and criminal law" and includes such phrases as "The price is too high," "He defrauded me out of my salary," "He tried to assassinate me," "I understand how to work. Have you any work for me to take home to do?" and "I will leave you when my month is up" (Wong, pp. 94–110).

While the difficulties of the Chinese in being admitted into American society and overcoming the stereotypes of being submissive, inscrutable, and unassimilable may be hinted at in the phrase book, they are quite apparent in the earliest fiction featuring Chinese characters. Although anti-Chinese sentiment was widespread by the time Ambrose Bierce,

Joaquin Miller, and Bret Harte published their first stories, the three western frontier colorists, as William F. Wu points out, refrained from "depict[ing] the Chinese immigrants as a threat, instead taking more tolerant or even sympathetic positions" (p. 13). The early stories show Chinese as individuals who participate in the everyday life of the West and who too often become victims of senseless violence and/or unveiled hostility "because they were foreigners, and of another race, religion, and color, and worked for what wages they could get" (Harte, "Wan Lee, the Pagan," p. 136). Even in stories depicting some Chinese as good and kind, however, stereotypes are often used to describe them or to contrast the exceptional protagonist with the base and most widely known type of Chinese.

The cynical journalist and satirist Ambrose Bierce (1842–1914?), in such early stories as "The Haunted Valley" (1871) and "The Night-Doings at 'Deadman's'" (1877), makes no effort to portray Chinese characters in a positive light but instead emphatically criticizes and condemns the violence and hostility directed at them. Bierce's unsympathetic characterization of Chinese characters should not be read as an example of Sinophobia, or fear and intolerance of Chinese; Bierce was commonly known as being one of the worst misanthropes of his time and "frequently wrote pieces where none of the characters were very likeable" (Wu, p. 23). Rather, anti-Chinese violence and prejudice are used in Bierce's stories to illustrate how malicious and excessive people had become. Joaquin Miller (1837–1913) takes a different approach in presenting the sole Chinese protagonist in his first novel, *First Fam'lies of the Sierras* (1876). The "Byron of the Rockies," as Miller was known for his poetry of the West, portrays Washee-Washee as a laundryman who occasionally steals, is unambiguously amoral, and ends up as an opium addict; nevertheless, as Wu points out, Washee-Washee does not pose a real threat to white Americans as his "character is that of a playful rascal, annoying but less than an object of real hatred" (p. 24). Chinese launderers are as much a part of the western landscape as gold miners and mountains, and, Miller argues, should be left unharmed.

By comparison, the local colorist Bret Harte (1806–1902) represents Chinese protagonists who are not free from stereotypes but who are more complex and sympathetic than what was normally portrayed in the popular press. In "An Episode of Fiddletown" (1873), "Wan Lee, the Pagan" (1874), and *Gabriel Conroy* (1875–1876), Harte's Chinese characters "are all presented as loyal and skillful,

yet sometimes uncooperative" (Wu, p. 14). In "Wan Lee, the Pagan" the narrator presents three distinct characters: Hop Sing is a refined old friend who has no equals among the "Christian traders of San Francisco"; Wang is a silent court juggler who can conjure up a baby among other "weird, mysterious, and astounding" feats; and Wan Lee is a ten-year-old mischievous trickster (pp. 125–126). Following an evening at Hop Sing's where Wang conjures a one-year-old Wan Lee, the narrator becomes the infant's godfather. Nine years later, Hop Sing sends the boy away from San Francisco, asking the narrator to save him "from the hands of the younger members of your Christian and highly civilized race who attend the enlightened schools" (p. 128). Away from the city, the young Wan Lee becomes a loyal and trusted servant, albeit with a penchant for trickery. Upon his return to San Francisco, the narrator fails to remember Hop Sing's warning and regards Wan Lee's avoidance of "crowded public streets" as "superstitious premonition" rather than as a realistic fear of violence (p. 135). A few months later, riots and anti-Chinese violence erupt in the city, and Wan Lee is stoned to death by a "mob of half-grown boys and Christian school children" (p. 137). In this story Harte calls attention to the religious hypocrisy of some white Americans and decries violence toward the Chinese. Ironically, however, it was the stereotypical name "Hop Sing" that was picked up to name the Chinese cook in the popular American western television series *Bonanza* in the 1960s.

The most popular piece of the time, however, was Harte's short poem "Plain Language from Truthful James" (1870), also known as "The Heathen Chinee." The poem, which was the inspiration for numerous songs, presents two white men playing cards with a Chinese man who pretends not to understand the game. Despite the white men's constant cheating, the Chinese keeps winning until, frustrated, one of them "went for that heathen Chinee" exclaiming, "'We are ruined by Chinese cheap labor'" (p. 216). The white men's hypocrisy, the similarities between the white men and the Chinese, and the irony of the white men being out-cheated were unfortunately lost on many readers, and, much to the chagrin of Harte, the stereotype of the conniving and devious Chinese was perpetuated on account of his poem.

The American reading public would have to wait until 1887 to read a first-person narrative written by a Chinese. Yan Phou Lee's (b. 1861) autobiography *When I Was a Boy in China* not only depicts, as the title infers, the author's life in China but also offers many insights into the American experience from a hybrid Chinese American perspective.

See also California Gold Rush; Ethnology; Foreigners; Immigration; Labor; Orientalism; San Francisco

BIBLIOGRAPHY
Primary Works

Harte, Bret. "Plain Language from Truthful James." 1870. In his *The Luck of Roaring Camp and Other Writings,* pp. 215–216. New York: Penguin, 2001.

Harte, Bret. "Wan Lee, the Pagan." 1874. In his *The Luck of Roaring Camp and Other Writings,* pp. 123–137. New York: Penguin, 2001.

Wong Sam and Assistants. *An English-Chinese Phrase Book.* 1875. In *The Big Aiiieeeee! An Anthology of Chinese American and Japanese American Literature,* edited by Jeffery Paul Chan et al., pp. 94–110. New York: Meridian, 1991.

Secondary Works

Matsukawa, Yuko. "Representing the Oriental in Nineteenth-Century Trade Cards." In *Re/Collecting Early Asian America: Essays in Cultural History,* edited by Josephine Lee, Imogene L. Lim, and Yuko Matsukawa, pp. 200–217. Philadelphia: Temple University Press, 2002.

Moon, Krystyn R. *Yellowface: Creating the Chinese in American Popular Music and Performance, 1850s–1920s.* New Brunswick, N.J.: Rutgers University Press, 2005.

Takaki, Ronald. *Strangers from a Different Shore: A History of Asian Americans.* Rev. ed. Boston: Back Bay, 1998.

Tchen, John Kuo Wei. *New York before Chinatown: Orientalism and the Shaping of American Culture, 1776–1882.* Baltimore: Johns Hopkins University Press, 1999.

Wu, William F. *The Yellow Peril: Chinese Americans in American Fiction 1850–1940.* Hamden, Conn.: Archon, 1982.

Nikolas Huot

CINCINNATI

Following its founding in 1788, expansive development characterized the first forty years of Cincinnati's history. Citizens, aware of their city's growing prosperity, began to refer to Cincinnati as the Athens of the West and as the Queen of the West or simply the Queen City. In 1819, commenting on this rapid expansion, an article in the *Inquisitor and Cincinnati Advertiser* stated, "The City is, indeed, justly styled the fair Queen of the West: distinquished [*sic*] for

order, enterprise, public spirit, and liberality, she stands the wonder of an admiring world" (Cincinnati Museum). In much the same spirit, Henry Wadsworth Longfellow wrote a poem entitled "Catawba Wine" (1854) that honored the city's beautiful vineyards:

> And this Song of the Vine,
> This greeting of mine,
> The winds and the birds shall deliver,
> To the Queen of the West,
> In her garlands dressed,
> On the banks of the Beautiful River.
> *(Cincinnati Museum)*

A CHARGED ARENA

Because of its importance as a river town and to the Underground Railroad movement, Cincinnati was seen as an economically and culturally diverse city. Just across the river from the slave state Kentucky, Cincinnati had such a large black community that a runaway slave could blend in without being noticed. White abolitionists, freed blacks, and others associated with the Underground Railroad could then provide them with food, shelter, and safety. Cincinnati's location also encouraged trade, increase in population, and real estate development. This increase in population was a result of the influx of immigrants into the city. In 1850 nearly half, or 51,171 out of the 115,438 Cincinnati residents, were foreigners (Hastings, p. 455). Plentiful work attracted many different ethnic and racial immigrants, the largest being Germans and freed African Americans.

The publication of Harriet Beecher Stowe's *Uncle Tom's Cabin* in 1851–1852 and passage of the Fugitive Slave Law in 1850 contributed to the domestically and internationally racially charged arena in which Cincinnati existed. According to James Walvin,

> The Fugitive Slave Law stated that any federal marshal who did not arrest an alleged runaway slave could be fined $1,000. People suspected of being a runaway slave could be arrested without warrant and turned over to a claimant on nothing more than his sworn testimony of ownership. A suspected black slave could not ask for a jury trial nor testify on his or her behalf. Any person aiding a runaway slave by providing shelter, food, or any other form of assistance was liable to six months' imprisonment and a $1,000 fine. (P. 29)

This law especially affected Cincinnati due to the influx of runaway slaves to the city. As David F. Ericson has observed, dynamic political, social, and cultural transformations brought on by the impending sectional division of the Civil War—with Cincinnati very divided on slavery issues—prompted racial as well as moral issues (pp. 121–123).

LITERARY INTEREST AND ATTENTION

The appeal of Cincinnati often drew writers and orators. The attraction of authors to the area resulted in public lectures, some of which addressed the fiery issue of slavery from opposite sides of the question, with each side finding a receptive audience in Cincinnati. The proslavery apologist Alexander Kinmont (1799–1838) lectured in Cincinnati from 1837 to 1838; his ideology included what was called "romantic racialism," a patriarchal/familial model that sought to justify slavery as a benevolent institution for "civilizing" slaves (Hedrick, p. 9). Another established essayist and lecturer was Ralph Waldo Emerson (1803–1882), whose visits in 1850 are recorded in the archives of the Literary Club of Cincinnati. Emerson's lectures were praised for his "high idealism and his fearless independence of thought" (Hastings, p. 445). By 1857 he had procured a place in Cincinnati cultural life and had become a strong intellectual force in the community. Emerson's last trip to Cincinnati was in 1867.

Moving to Cincinnati with her family in 1832 when her father became head of the Presbyterian Lane Theological Seminary (founded in 1830), Harriet Beecher Stowe (1811–1896) became a literary force in the Queen City. In 1836 she married Calvin Stowe, a professor in her father's seminary. The seminary became known for a fierce disagreement between its board of directors and the student/faculty body when the university wanted to endorse abolition but the board of directors disagreed. The subsequent decline in enrollment caused severe financial hardship on the Beecher/Stowe family, and finances served as an additional impetus for the prodigious literary output of Stowe's author wife.

As Joan Hedrick notes, Stowe "used the written word as a vehicle for religious, social, and political purposes" (p. 1). Her topics ranged from domestic culture and politics to male debauchery and incest, resting finally on the issue of racism. Stowe's first stories were written for a group of Cincinnati's notable citizens called the Semi-Colon Club. Stowe transgressed the boundary between public and private spheres for women with the advent of "parlor writing," which when published reached a wide public and in turn promoted social change.

What promoted the most change and resulted in one of the most influential pieces of literature in American history was *Uncle Tom's Cabin*, a domestic fiction depicting the evil of slavery upon the moral conscience of the proslavery South, which Stowe wrote soon after she moved to Maine from Cincinnati in 1850. This book was published serially in the *National Era* for nearly a year, from 5 June 1851 to 1 April 1852. The impact of the book on the nation's conscience was astounding. When Stowe visited the White House in 1862, Abraham Lincoln is said to have greeted her by saying, "So you're the little woman who

Bird's eye view of Cincinnati, c. 1850. GETTY IMAGES

wrote the book that started this great war" (Hedrick, pp. 7–8). *Uncle Tom's Cabin* affected not only American audiences but foreign observers as well. Even after Emancipation, Stowe's characterizations of black people continued to be an issue. Her "shrewd sketches of regional types" exposed existing stereotypes of African Americans, including generalizations describing their "childlike dependence" (Hedrick, p. 9).

Even though *Uncle Tom's Cabin* was not published until 1851, abolitionist writing was not new to the Cincinnati scene. In 1836 the office that housed the abolitionist paper *The Philanthropist* was broken into and vandalized. Stowe's brother, the Presbyterian minister Henry Ward Beecher, was acting as editor of the paper while James G. Birney was away. When Birney refused to cease publication, some of the most prominent residents of Cincinnati threatened to form a mob (Hedrick, p. 5). According to Peter H. Clark the abolitionist and lecturer Wendell Phillips was likewise threatened by a mob. These racist acts prompted Stowe to write some of her first public remarks regarding slavery in 1836 in a letter she wrote to the editor of the *Cincinnati Journal and Western Luminary* (Hedrick, p. 5).

Other literature, both pro- and antislavery, was catalyzed by the internationally riveting case of Margaret Garner, a fugitive slave, who with her husband Robert and their children fled from Maplewood Farm and its adjacent plantation in Richwood, Kentucky, across the icy Ohio River into Ohio on 28 January 1856. Surrounded by a U.S. marshal's party, Margaret killed her daughter to keep her from slavery. She was put on trial in Cincinnati, not, ironically, for killing her child but for theft of her child—"property" under the terms of the Fugitive Slave Law. After a month-long trial filled with contentious border politics involving governors of both Ohio and Kentucky, the Garners were remanded to their slaveholders and then sold to Mississippi. Margaret died of typhus in 1856. Her story was widely debated in pro- and antislavery journalism. The proslavery novel *Abolitionism Unveiled; or, Its Origin, Progress, and Pernicious Tendency Fully Developed* (1856) by the Kentuckian Henry Field James contained a version of Garner's murder (Weisenburger, p. 264), but the story soon disappeared from Southern consciousness. It became a legend in the North, spawning poems in *The Liberator* and including two ghost story versions (e.g., *Chattanooga* [1858] by John Jolliffe; Weisenburger, p. 272). More recently there has been a resurgence in southern consciousness—and controversy—about the story. The Nobel Prize–winner Toni Morrison based *Beloved* (1998) on the tale of Margaret Garner. The

opera houses in Detroit, Philadelphia, and Cincinnati commissioned the opera *Margaret Garner*, with Morrison as librettist and the grammy award–winning composer Richard Danielpour as composer. In 2005 it debuted in Cincinnati to full houses and battling editorials about the Margaret Garner story.

The citizens of Cincinnati also expressed their interest in art and music. The prodigality and regional qualities of Cincinnati's culture largely came from its accessible location on the Ohio River. With Ohio on one side and Kentucky on the other, Cincinnati conjoined the colloquial style of the frontier West with the aristocratic and proslavery attitudes of the South to produce a curious blend. In 1851, when a National Portrait Gallery was established, it contained "a collection of notable portraits of distinguished early Americans" (Hastings, pp. 451–452).With the true panache of the city, these portraits—including Beethoven, Schubert, and Mozart—hung in the beer gardens across the canal.

JOURNALISM

To say that journalism during the antebellum years was a synonym for Cincinnati itself would not be to exaggerate. In 1834 the *American Quarterly Review* of Andover, Massachusetts, wrote: "Cincinnati now commands in a considerable measure the literary resources of the western valley. . . New York is too deeply imbued with the commercial spirit ever to become the literary center of the country . . . Boston is too far from the southern, western, and even central portions of the country" (Mott 1:386).

From 1820 to 1870 journalism established itself on the forefront of Cincinnati's literary scene. The increase of population and location of the city partially caused this rapid growth of journalism, but what predominantly spurred this emergence was the tumultuous nature of pre–Civil War Cincinnati. Home to both abolitionists and proslavery advocates, Cincinnati seeped with controversy. Given the religious, racial, and political tensions prevalent here, journalists and writers alike rose to the occasion.

Journalism gave Cincinnati, the Athens of the West, a voice to give back to the East. Local humor and regional color were displayed through journalistic endeavors. Numerous literary publications representing the regional character of Cincinnati appeared in the first third of the century. In early 1821 a semimonthly, the *Olio*, was founded. This newspaper contained "contributions of such industrious collectors of local history as Robert T. Lytle, Dennis McHenry, John H.

James, Lewis Noble, and a number of other well-known writers of that time" (Nelson and Runk, p. 257). A year later the actor Sol Smith (1801–1869) established the *Independent Press;* the popularity of this newspaper can be attributed to its satirical drawings and humorous remarks. That same year John P. Foote (1783–1865) introduced the *Cincinnati Literary Gazette.* It also gained widespread attention as a result of its notable literature. As with the *Olio,* much of its information is related to local history, and historians to this day reference it. It also contains some of the first articles written by Benjanim Drake (1794–1841), "who proved himself one of the most industrious local writers of the time" (Nelson and Runk, p. 258).

Writers and journalists continued to undertake measures to demonstrate the flavor of Cincinnati through literature and journalism. In July 1827 the *Western Monthly Review* appeared with Reverend Timothy Flint (1780–1840) as editor. According to Frank Luther Mott, Flint wrote most of the magazine himself and was "a good interpreter of the West and gave it some literary and critical quality" (p. 387). Its success was short-lived, and it was eventually united with the *Cincinnati Mirror,* which was edited by a renowned writer of his time, W. D. Gallagher (1808–1894). Gallagher's nature poetry was collected in three volumes entitled *Erato* (1835–1837), and in 1841 he edited *Selections from Poetical Literature of the West,* a regional anthology. Gallagher also edited the *Western Literary Journal and Monthly Review.* According to S. B. Nelson and J. M. Runk, "It was a magazine of considerable pretension and real excellence—the largest, until then, established in the West" (p. 262). Almost a decade later, the *Evening Post,* a daily noted for its reviews of art, surfaced. Also advocating Cincinnati as the Athens of the West was a journal called the *Great West.* "The title was as captivating as it was suggestive of a wide field. . . . a strong corps of Cincinnati editors, and all prominent writers throughout the Mississippi Valley, were engaged as paid contributors" (Nelson and Runk, p. 264). The *Genius of the West* and the *Gem,* both edited by Howard Dunham and founded in the 1850s, focused on the music and literature of the time. Among those who contributed were the popular New England poet Alice Cary and Gallagher. All of these publications sought to establish Cincinnati as a cultural and political center of the West.

Cincinnati was a hotbed of politics and controversy in this period, so many of its publications were charged with political sentiment. In 1828 *Truth's Advocate,* a monthly, was published in the political interest of the Kentucky orator and statesman Henry Clay (1777–1852), whose compromise stances on slavery did much to shape pre–Civil War policy. The *Democratic Intelligencer,* which supported John McLean for president, was founded in 1834. The *Chronicle* was established in 1830 as "an anti-slavery Whig organ, but stopping short of abolitionism" (Nelson and Runk, p. 262). This newspaper published Harriet Beecher Stowe's first story in 1835. A few years later a Whig paper, the *Republikaner,* surfaced and became "for ten years the principal appendage of this party in the western States" (Nelson and Runk, p. 261). Its editor, Emil Klauprecht (1815–1896), also wrote several novels as well as a historical work on Ohio.

Because of the large influx of German immigrants to Cincinnati, German newspapers were prominent. The publishers, editors, and subscription lists consisted mostly of foreigners, but the turmoil of the time often directed their efforts toward politics. The *Weltbürger,* which appeared in 1834, was originally anti-Democratic, but it was eventually renamed *Der Deutsche Franklin* and encouraged what would turn out to be the successful presidential campaign of the Dutch descendant and Democrat Martin Van Buren. (Van Buren, who had been Andrew Jackson's vice president, would eventually leave the Democratic Party because of his antislavery sentiments.) Perhaps a better-written Democrat paper was the *Volksblatt* (1836–1840), which Nelson and Runk believe served as a basis for future high standards in Cincinnati journalism. In 1837 the views of the opposing Whig Party surfaced in *Westlicher Merkur.*

Religious publications were another important part of Cincinnati journalism. Because of Cincinnati's location and variance of opinions, many religious publications at that time capitalized on the political as well as religious tensions prevalent among its citizens. The *Cincinnati Journal,* an anti-Catholic and antislavery newspaper, was published in 1830. A year later the *Baptist Weekly Journal of the Mississippi Valley* was founded. It still exists today as the *Journal and Messenger* and is one of the six oldest remaining Baptist publications. The Book Concern, a publishing company associated with the Methodist Episcopal Church, founded the *Western Christian Advocate* in 1834. In 1841 the *Ladies Repository* was founded by the Book Concern. According to Mott, "Its material was highly moralized, and was written largely by ministers; the verse was furnished by the Cary sisters, the ubiquitous Mrs. Sigourney . . . with several ballads contributed by . . . Martin F. Tupper, S.C.L., F.R.S." (1:388). The Unitarians founded the *Western Messenger* in 1835 "under the patronage of the Unitarians of the West" (Nelson and Runk, p. 262). This paper printed contributions from the New England transcendentalists Emerson, Margaret Fuller, Jones Very, and other eastern authors, with a liberal inclusion of British writing (Mott 1:387–388). The first Catholic newspaper, the *Wahrheits Freund*, made its debut in 1837, and another German-language periodical, *Der Protestant*, was established shortly thereafter. The Methodist paper *Der Christliche Apologete* followed in 1838. Its editor, Wilhelm Nast, also founded the *Sonntag-Schule Glocke*, a juvenile paper.

Whether locally, politically, or religiously affiliated, the majority of Cincinnati's nineteenth-century newspapers ceased to exist or lost their individuality by being merged with other publications. Nonetheless the history of journalism in Cincinnati is important to its culture and helps to define a distinctive city and its people. As Mott explains:

> Cincinnati's ambitious publication efforts grew not so much out of the difficulty of getting eastern periodicals, or the desire (so prominent in the South) to be independent of New York and Boston, as out of the aspiration to create, immediately and impressively, a full-blown civilization, with all its appurtenances and cultivation and refinement. Cincinnati, with its educational institutions, printing presses, churches, and libraries—Cincinnati, the Athens of the West—would lead the way to culture. (1:386)

See also Abolitionist Writing; Death; Periodicals; Political Parties; Proslavery Writing; Religion; *Uncle Tom's Cabin;* Underground Railroad

BIBLIOGRAPHY

Primary Work
Stowe, Harriet Beecher. *The Oxford Harriet Beecher Stowe Reader.* Edited by Joan D. Hedrick. New York: Oxford University Press, 1999.

Secondary Works
Cincinnati Museum Center at Union Terminal. Cincinnati Historical Society Library. http://www.cincymuseum.org/cmc/collection/.

Clark, Peter H. *The Black Brigade of Cincinnati.* 1864. New York: Arno Press, 1969.

Ericson, David F. *The Debate over Slavery: Antislavery and Proslavery Liberalism in Antebellum America.* New York: New York University Press, 2000.

Hastings, Louise. "Emerson in Cincinnati." *New England Quarterly* 11 (1938): 443–469.

Hedrick, Joan D., ed. *The Oxford Harriet Beecher Stowe Reader.* New York: Oxford University Press, 1999.

Johnston, John. "Ohio Was Free, Not Safe." (Cincinnati) *Enquirer,* 1 August 2004. Available at http://www.cincinnati.con/freetime/nurfc/slavery_urailroad.html.

Mott, Frank Luther. *A History of American Magazines.* Vols. 1 and 2. Cambridge, Mass.: Harvard University Press, 1939.

Nelson, S. B., and J. M. Runk. *The History of Cincinnati and Hamilton County, Ohio.* Cincinnati: S. B. Nelson, 1894. Available at *www.heritagepursuit.com/Hamilton/HamiltonIndex.htm.*

Walvin, James. *The Slave Trade.* New York: Sutton, 1999.

Weisenburger, Steven. *Modern Media.* New York: Hill and Wang, 1998.

LeAnne Garner

CIRCUSES AND SPECTACLES

Circuses and spectacles must stand at the center of any substantive discussion of nineteenth-century American popular culture. The circus, an itinerant entertainment comprising the exhibition of animals and the performances of skilled entertainers within rings, first appeared in America in 1793. The commercial display of spectacles, the exhibition of persons, animals, or objects possessed of unusual characteristics, first appeared in American museums perhaps as early as 1810. Although some early-nineteenth-century circuses featured displays of human or animal spectacles, the two entertainment forms did not fully merge until after the Civil War, when tented troupes consistently carried "museums" or "sideshows" of spectacles along with their traditional circus exhibitions.

It is important to note that the transportation and market revolutions, as much as the creative minds of showmen, afforded larger numbers of nineteenth-century Americans the opportunity to patronize these performances. Indeed, by the postbellum period, the spread of rail lines across America allowed leading showmen to undertake national tours that brought their outfits into the rural West and South. Previously, the poor character of the nation's road system had made extensive tours of the American backcountry an arduous undertaking for circus companies because they almost all ambulated by wagon prior to the Civil War. By the 1870s a person living outside a railroad town in rural Mississippi had the chance to see the same show that had just finished a stand in New York or Washington, D.C. Moreover, the growth of a cash-based economy helped make professional entertainment a purchasable commodity, thereby encouraging increasing numbers of Americans to turn out whenever a show raised a big top in their home towns. All of these factors aided the rise of the circus to its position as the nation's premier form of mass entertainment by the end of the nineteenth century.

Still, the circus's key contribution to the development of an American, rather than regional, popular culture involved more than just the exhibitions themselves. Circus owners and advertisers made their own singular contribution to the language of nineteenth-century America as they produced innumerable pamphlets, couriers, heralds, and posters replete with vivid and hyperbolic textual descriptions of their acts and exhibits. In doing so, they helped make exaggeration a key component of American advertising. In addition, showmen like P. T. Barnum (1810–1891) produced best-selling biographies that detailed both their rise to power and the roles that their most famous exhibits played in their success. The creative minds behind the display and marketing of the nation's circuses and spectacles altered the nation's vocabulary as much as they did its entertainment.

P. T. BARNUM AND THE CREATION OF THE AMERICAN SPECTACLE

No single individual did more to popularize spectacles than the circus proprietor, museum owner, and author Phineas Taylor Barnum. P. T. Barnum was born in Bethel, Connecticut, in 1810 to a farm family, but he rejected an agrarian life in favor of the merchant business. As a young man, he worked as a shop clerk and a lottery manager. After a brief career as a newspaper editor, Barnum abandoned conventional commercial pursuits in favor of a life of an entertainment impresario. His career in this profession eventually saw him assume the role of the nation's leading showman. His heady success stemmed from a variety of factors, but perhaps none were more important than his fundamental understanding that nineteenth-century Americans had a seemingly insatiable appetite for spectacles that exploited issues of race, natural history, and corporeal difference.

Barnum's first major marketing and entertainment triumph came in 1835 when he purchased an elderly African American woman named Joice Heth. Upon initial examination, Heth seemed no different than any other wizened, superannuated slave woman, but her putative history made her a potentially profitable attraction. According to her Philadelphia-based owners, she was 161 years old and had been the nursemaid of George Washington. Perhaps convinced by a seemingly authentic bill of sale bearing the date of 1727, Barnum bought Heth for one thousand dollars and put her on display in New York. To garner public attention, the showman issued a pamphlet detailing her purported biography, and Gotham crowds flocked to see her. Barnum then took her on tour throughout New England and continued to show her until her death in 1836.

Yet even after her passing, Barnum continued to make use of her profitability as a curiosity. Upon her death, Barnum engaged a doctor to perform an autopsy on her. The physician concluded after conducting his examination that she could not have been as old as was claimed, thus bringing Barnum's reputation for veracity into question. Regardless, Barnum's public image hardly suffered, and in any event, he began to focus on efforts to find a grander stage upon which to display his attractions.

In 1841 Barnum began negotiating for the purchase of a New York City institution, Scudder's American Museum. Unlike more rarefied establishments that shared the same appellation, Scudder's "Museum" featured little in the way of truly edifying specimens of natural history. Rather, it offered a hodgepodge of cheap curiosities, second-rate performers, and lectures of dubious educational value. Despite these manifest flaws, Barnum bought the museum, renamed it Barnum's American Museum, and opened for business on 1 January 1842. He quickly moved to improve its holdings, adding trained canines, a group of Native American performers, and a number of obese, towering, and diminutive persons, and put them all on public display.

Later that year, Barnum bought a most unusual new specimen for his museum. The "Fejee Mermaid," a desiccated object consisting of an hominid's upper body and a fishlike tail below the torso, had supposedly emerged from the waters off Fiji before ending up in England, Boston, and finally, in the hands of Barnum. Barnum helped spread the word of his new attraction by printing up thousands of inexpensive but detailed pamphlets trumpeting its singular wonders. The resulting sensation brought thousands of visitors through his museum. Patrons stood in front of the display, stared at the specimen, and argued about whether it was a genuine marvel of natural history or a clever fraud. As had been the case with the age of Joice Heth, the actual authenticity of the Fejee Mermaid mattered little as long as Barnum's pockets were lined in the process. Incidentally, in later years, Barnum would concede that his mermaid "specimen" was a fake.

But Barnum's greatest antebellum sensation could not be called a fake or a fraud. In late 1842 Barnum learned that a midget four-year-old boy named Charles Stratton (1838–1883), who appeared perfectly normal in all respects except his tiny proportions, dwelled in his home state of Connecticut. Barnum quickly came to a contractual arrangement with the boy's parents, dubbed him "General Tom Thumb," and put him on display in the museum. Stratton gave speeches and performed as a variety of characters in the museum's lecture hall. The following year, Barnum took Stratton to England, creating much excitement among the populace of London. In fact, the crowning achievement of this English tour seemingly destroying Barnum's fortunes as a showman along with his place of business. But rather than allowing these catastrophes to drive him from the entertainment profession, the ever-resourceful Barnum once again shifted his resources and focus to an industry he had worked in during the 1830s, the circus business.

CIRCUS, MENAGERIES, AND MUSEUMS

The first traveling shows of significance in the early nineteenth century were menageries, or outfits that displayed exotic animals. By the 1830s circus troupes began to challenge menageries for the entertainment monies of Americans. These early circuses were small affairs that moved overland in caravans of wagons or, less commonly, by steamboat. The staffs of these shows were small and their performances were modest in scope. When Barnum traveled with Aaron Turner's wagon circus from 1836 to 1838, he performed multiple roles by selling tickets and by keeping the outfit's books. And when the show raised its canvas tent, it featured only a handful of entertainers, all of whom performed within a single ring.

Yet by this time, some showmen began to offer shows that featured the exhibitions of wild animals and the performances of clowns, riders, and acrobats. This fusion of both genres won wide public acclaim, as perspicacious impresarios quickly learned that if they displayed their wild animals prior to their circus performances, religious-minded patrons would turn out to see the wonders of God's animal creation and then depart before the main show got underway. In this way, churchgoers could avoid viewing performers wearing skimpy outfits and listening to clowns cracking off-color jokes.

The Civil War disrupted the ability of these shows to undertake national tours but by 1865 showmen began to carry their troupes into the South and West once again. Initially, the touring method featured by these shows differed little than the approach taken by their antebellum predecessors. They planned their tour routes in the hopes of moving between ten and fifteen miles between daily stands, assuming favorable weather and road conditions. These shows sought audiences where they could find them, raising their single tents in both larger towns and at country crossroads.

In 1871, however, P. T. Barnum and two other leading showmen conceived of a new way of transporting and presenting a circus performance. Rather than moving by wagon, these men put their new show on rails and routed their troupes through the nation's cities and growing railroad towns. The more efficient mode of movement aside, rail transport would allow the outfit to carry and display more attractions and curiosities than

P. T. Barnum with Charles Stratton (General Tom Thumb). Undated photograph. © BETTMANN/CORBIS

came when Stratton performed for Queen Victoria at Buckingham Palace. "Tom Thumb" had brought Barnum international acclaim and made him America's most influential entertainment magnate.

Significantly, even those unable to see Barnum's attractions had a chance to learn about them from the pen of Barnum himself. In 1855 he published the first of his two autobiographies, *The Life of P. T. Barnum.* In the volume, Barnum tells of his Yankee upbringing as well as his successes with Heth, the Fejee Mermaid, the American Museum, and Tom Thumb. Barnum would follow this work with a second autobiography, *Struggles and Triumphs* (1869). Both books were best-sellers that went through several printings.

Sadly, Barnum's collection of attractions was largely lost in two disastrous conflagrations. His museum, a veritable New York landmark, burned down in 1865 and its replacement burned in 1868,

P. T. Barnum's mammoth tent. Illustration from *Gleason's Pictorial Drawing Room Companion,* c. 1851. THE LIBRARY OF CONGRESS

any prior show. In fact, "P. T. Barnum's Great Traveling Museum, Menagerie, Caravan, and Hippodrome" featured three interconnected but separate canvas enclosures: a museum tent, a menagerie tent, and finally, a main circus tent. Although Barnum's competitors felt certain the operation would financially collapse from its high overhead costs, the show enjoyed a highly profitable season. Unsurprisingly, the three-tent presentation became the industry standard by 1872.

To attract both the literate and illiterate to their performances, showmen distributed textually dense handbills to curious readers and pasted up colorful posters in the communities where they were scheduled to appear. In both cases, advertisers used artful exaggeration and seemingly erudite language to give their shows an air of excitement and an elevated character. Hence, an image of a hippopotamus on a circus poster invariably came described as "The Blood-Sweating Behemoth of Holy Writ," a reference to the giant creature described in the Book of Job. Similarly, circus scribes gave a simple ballet performance a rarefied air by calling it a "grand terpsichorean divertissement." Lastly, showmen claimed that their traveling sideshows,

or "Museums," would contain not objects of transparent fraudulence but rather the "choicest excerpts from the realms of Zoology, Ornithology, Geology, Ichthyology, Conchology, Entomology, Anthropology, Mechanics, [and] Numismatics." The fact that the majority of individuals who read such descriptions probably had no idea what most of these categories comprised mattered less than the fact that the exhibitions sounded edifying and therefore morally upright. Notwithstanding issues of morality, the traveling circus remained the nation's leading commercial entertainment until the 1920s, when motion pictures and professional sports began to erode its popularity.

Arguably, the most important impact that circuses and spectacles had on nineteenth-century America stemmed from their ability to expand the cultural horizons of millions of Americans who had not ventured beyond the confines of their own counties, much less the bounds of their nation. Nineteenth-century circuses carried exotic animals and amazing performers into the American backcountry at a time when zoos were nonexistent. In much the same way, spectacles like Barnum's FeJee Mermaid forced those that set their eyes upon it to ponder the existence of a creature that seemed to defy the laws of nature. With their carefully phrased yet often exaggerated descriptions of their achievements and exhibits alike, the written works of industry advertisers and impresarios further contributed to this challenge to the conventional, known, and understood aspects of life. In sum, circuses and spectacles pushed the boundaries of American popular culture and helped set the stage for the entertainment excesses and media saturation of the century that followed.

See also Autobiography; Satire, Burlesque, and Parody; Theater

BIBLIOGRAPHY

Primary Works

Barnum, P. T. *Struggles and Triumphs: or, Forty Years' Recollections of P. T. Barnum.* Hartford, Conn.: J. B. Burr, 1869.

Coup, W. C. *Sawdust and Spangles: Stories and Secrets of the Circus.* Washington, D.C.: Paul A. Ruddell, 1901.

Robinson, Gil. *Old Wagon Show Days.* Cincinnati: Brockwell, 1925.

Secondary Works

Adams, Bluford. *E Pluribus Barnum: The Great Showman and the Making of U.S. Popular Culture.* Minneapolis: University of Minnesota Press, 1997.

Bogdan, Robert. *Freak Show: Presenting Human Oddities for Amusement and Profit.* Chicago: University of Chicago Press, 1988.

Bondeson, Jan. *The Feejee Mermaid and Other Essays in Natural and Unnatural History.* Ithaca, N.Y.: Cornell University Press, 1999.

Carlyon, David. *Dan Rice: The Most Famous Man You've Never Heard Of.* New York: Public Affairs, 2001.

Dennett, Andrea Stulman. *Weird and Wonderful: The Dime Museum in America.* New York: New York University Press, 1997.

Greenberg, Kenneth S. "The Nose, the Lie, and the Duel." In his *Honor and Slavery: Lies, Duels, Noses, Masks, Dressing as a Woman, Gifts, Strangers, Humanitarianism, Death, Slave Rebellions, the Proslavery Argument, Baseball, Hunting, and Gambling in the Old South,* pp. 3–23. Princeton, N.J.: Princeton University Press, 1996.

Harris, Neil. *Humbug: The Art of P. T. Barnum.* Boston: Little, Brown, 1973.

Reiss, Benjamin. *The Showman and the Slave: Race, Death, and Memory in Barnum's America.* Cambridge, Mass.: Harvard University Press, 2001.

Thayer, Stuart. *Traveling Showmen: The American Circus before the Civil War.* Detroit: Astley and Ricketts, 1997.

Thomson, Rosemary Garland, ed. *Freakery: Cultural Spectacles of the Extraordinary Body.* New York: New York University Press, 1996.

Wallace, Irving. *The Fabulous Showman: The Life and Times of P. T. Barnum.* New York: Knopf, 1959.

Gregory J. Renoff

"CIVIL DISOBEDIENCE"

See "Resistance to Civil Government"

CIVIL WAR

The Civil War was the greatest transforming event in American culture. Its memories continue to haunt and inspire people, and it is impossible to imagine what the United States would look like today had it never happened. With some 620,000 deaths, more Americans died in the conflict than in all other wars combined until Vietnam. More than 10 percent of the population was directly involved, and almost every American had a close friend or family member who was killed or maimed in the war. The largest expenditure in a few Southern states after the war was payment for prosthetic limbs to its veterans. The war brought a centralized nation-state, a national income tax, conscription, and the emergence of large bureaucratic and regimented organizations in both the public and private sectors.

Slavery was of course the root of the war. But from the nation's founding (when the process of gradual emancipation began in the North) until 1850, the North and South agreed on a series of compromises that prevented the powder keg of slavery from exploding. The first compromise followed the crisis in 1819 over Missouri entering the Union as a slave state, which erupted "like a firebell in the night," as Thomas Jefferson put it (*Life and Selected Writings,* p. 698). It was the first major crisis over slavery, and it shattered a tacit agreement between the two regions that had been in place since the Constitution. Under the terms of the agreement, the North would not interfere with slavery in Southern states, and the South would recognize slavery as an evil that should be discouraged and eventually abolished whenever it was safe and feasible to do so. The agreement reflected the belief, shared by most of the Founding Fathers and framers of the Constitution, that slavery was wrong, the equivalent of America's "original sin," according to James Madison (quoted in Mellon, p. 158).

The Missouri crisis established the basic debates over slavery that persisted until the Civil War. During the controversy, the New York congressman James Tallmadge included an amendment that provided for gradual emancipation of Missouri's slaves, much as other Northern states had done. Northerners worried that if slavery became legally entrenched in Missouri, it would spread throughout the West. Rufus King, another New Yorker, was the first politician to apply a "higher law" to slavery; he stated that any law upholding slavery was "absolutely void, because [it is] contrary to the law of nature, which is the law of God" (Ernst, p. 372). The higher-law thesis would become a central rhetorical weapon in the writings of immediate abolitionists (those advocating an immediate end to slavery), including *Freedom's Journal* (1827–1829), the nation's first black newspaper; David Walker's *Walker's Appeal, in Four Articles, Together with a Preamble to the Coloured Citizens of the World* (1829); William Lloyd Garrison's *Liberator* (1831–1865); and the organs of the American Anti-Slavery Society and the Liberty Party, the nation's first abolitionist party. Ralph Waldo Emerson, Henry David Thoreau, Frederick Douglass, and Harriet Beecher Stowe all based their antislavery arguments on the higher-law thesis.

Southerners responded to the Missouri crisis by saying that Congress had no power to exclude slavery even in unorganized territories. They worried about losing representation in Congress, and with cotton production and slave prices on the rise, they became much more belligerent in their quest for national power and their defense of slavery. Restricting slavery, they said, implied eventual emancipation and racial equality. By the 1830s most Southern writers had abandoned the beliefs of their forefathers and viewed slavery as a positive good for masters, slaves, and society at large. Implicit in their proslavery rhetoric was their assumption that blacks were subhuman, more akin to domesticated animals than to humans.

The Missouri crisis was in essence a battle over the western frontier, which each side sought to control. In the compromise, which averted disunion and war, Missouri entered the Union as a slave state; but slavery was excluded from the remaining, unsettled portions of the Louisiana Territory north of 36° 30′ north latitude, the same latitude as the southern border of Missouri.

The frontier became the imaginative site where the battle over slavery and the future of America got played out. It was also a site occupied by Native Americans, who in the minds of Northern and Southern whites, needed to vanish to pave the way for American expansion. Some of the most popular and critical works of American literature beginning in the 1820s took as their setting the frontier, from James Fenimore Cooper's Leatherstocking Tales (1823–1841) and Lydia Maria Child's stories and novel *Hobomok: A Tale of Early Times* (1824) to Caroline Kirkland's *A New Home—Who'll Follow?* (1839) and the southerner William Gilmore Simms's fiction. The frontier became the site where writers explored the "rules of coexistence" between racially diverse groups of people, according to the cultural critic Jane Tompkins (p. 119). For many American writers, the frontier would determine the fate of America; it would also distinguish American from European literature, which had no comparable interracial frontier to draw on.

Political debates over slavery and the frontier were averted for more than twenty years after the Missouri Compromise, until 1845, when Texas entered the Union as a slave state. This period of illusory calm stemmed from two factors. First, from 1819 until 1845 there was no new territorial expansion, and under the terms of the Missouri Compromise, existing territories petitioned for statehood in pairs, with one free and one slave state entering the Union together. Second, from 1836 to 1844, the so-called gag rules automatically tabled all abolitionist petitions in Congress and effectively prevented explosive debates on the subject of slavery.

The annexation of Texas in early 1845 outraged northerners. John Quincy Adams, the last living Founding Father and a staunch antislavery congressman, described it as a "calamity" in his diary: "the day passes, and leaves scarcely a distinct trace upon the memory of anything, and precisely because . . . the heaviest calamity that ever befell myself and my country was this day consummated" (p. 574). As Adams anticipated, the annexation of Texas provoked hostilities with Mexico, which led in 1846 to the Mexican-American War. The war was perpetrated by southerners including President James K. Polk, and their sympathizers, in order to acquire more slave territory. It virtually doubled the size of the Union, bringing in California and the entire Southwest. Protests occurred throughout the North. Henry David Thoreau abandoned society for Walden Pond on 4 July 1845, partly in response to Southern belligerence. And the Free-Soil Party emerged out of the Liberty Party, offering a more conservative and inclusive alternative to the Liberty Party's radical platform. Free-Soilers sought to prohibit the further spread of slavery, which they hoped would lead to its ultimate extinction. The Liberty Party advocated an immediate end to slavery and was the party of choice among Northern blacks, including Frederick Douglass, James McCune Smith, and Henry Highland Garnet. But by the late 1840s, members also accepted violent resistance to slavery.

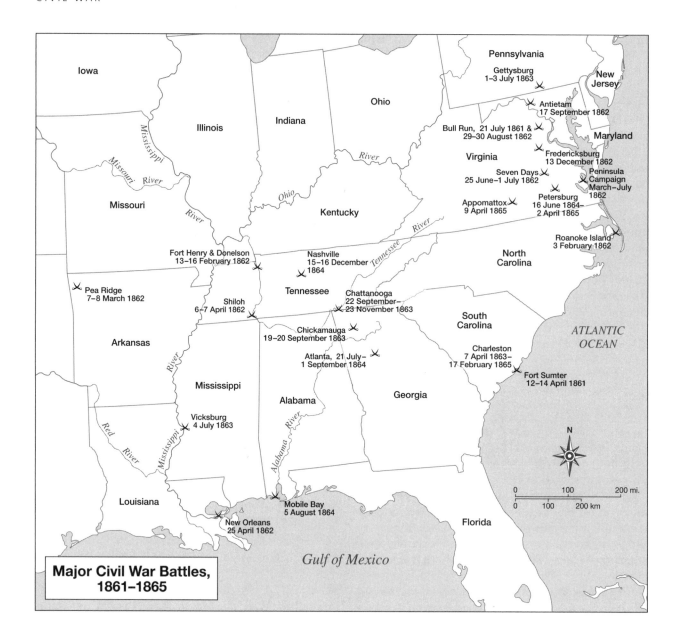

Major Civil War Battles, 1861–1865

THE FAILURE OF COMPROMISE

In the wake of the Mexican-American War the nation was on the verge of civil war, which was averted only by the Compromise of 1850. The compromise consisted of five basic parts, the most onerous of which was a stringent fugitive slave law that denied suspected fugitives the right to a jury trial and virtually legitimated slave stealing. The Fugitive Slave Law converted countless northerners to the antislavery cause. In their eyes the law put the federal government in the business of manhunting. And since all citizens could now be required to hunt down suspected fugitives, northerners could no longer wash their hands of slavery. The Fugitive Slave law inspired Harriet Beecher Stowe (1811–1896) to write *Uncle Tom's Cabin; or, Life among the Lowly* (1852); and these two pieces of writing—the legislation and the novel—greatly exacerbated sectional hostilities and led to secession and war.

The Compromise of 1850 achieved the opposite of its intentions. Americans were increasingly *unwilling* to compromise, or to accept limits, the rule of law, and traditional boundaries. It is not coincidental that Herman Melville published one of the nation's great novels, *Moby-Dick* (1851), in the immediate wake of the Compromise of 1850. It highlights the costs of denying limits, ignoring rules, and seeking to vanquish all opposing, unknown forces in life. The black abolitionist James McCune Smith (1813–1865), who was one of the foremost intellectuals of the era, appreciated the political symbolism of the novel. Writing to his friend Frederick Douglass in Douglass's newspaper, he likened the *Pequod,* the whaling ship in *Moby-Dick,* to the ship of state in American politics. Captain Ahab, the ship's captain, like the leaders of America, were in pursuit of the wrong thing: the white whale, symbol of all evil, on the one hand; whiteness and respect for white laws on the other hand. The leaders of both settings, said McCune Smith, were thus sacrificing "the one thing needed in each society—HUMAN BROTHERHOOD—and the belief that all men are by nature free and equal" (quoted in Stauffer, p. 66). By ignoring the multiracial makeup of their country, American leaders were following the plight of the *Pequod,* in McCune Smith's estimation, and were heading toward destruction and death. His letter to Douglass, titled "Horoscope," was more accurate than he knew.

In effect civil war broke out even before the explosions shook Fort Sumter in April 1861. Small battles erupted when slave catchers attempted to arrest fugitives, and there were casualties at Boston and Christiana, Pennsylvania. In 1854 Congress passed the Kansas-Nebraska Act, which opened the northern territories of Kansas and Nebraska and repealed the Missouri Compromise, creating a battleground in Kansas. The Kansas Territory erupted in guerrilla-style civil war from 1855 to 1858 and led to the founding of the Republican Party, the demise of the Whig Party, and the destabilization of the two-party system. In 1857 the Supreme Court declared the Republican Party unconstitutional in the infamous *Dred Scott v. Sandford* case. In his opinion Chief Justice Roger Taney, a Southern slave owner, argued that Congress had no power to legislate slavery in territories or states; that blacks were "beings of an inferior order . . . so far inferior that they had no rights which the white man was bound to respect; and that the negro might justly and lawfully be reduced to slavery for his benefit" (quoted in Finkelman, p. 61). In the wake of the *Dred Scott* decision, numerous black writers abandoned their faith in American ideals and advocated emigration.

The last spark leading to disunion was John Brown's raid on the federal arsenal at Harpers Ferry, Virginia, in October 1859, shortly before the 1860 presidential election. Brown's small army of sixteen whites and five blacks, and his "provisional constitution" that would govern those areas he hoped to liberate from slavery, terrified the South. The insurgents were captured, convicted of treason and murder, and Brown was sentenced to hang on 2 November. Although Abraham Lincoln and other Republicans sought to distance themselves from Brown, most southerners believed that he symbolized the spirit of the Republican Party and the North in general. While northerners considered Brown a madman and murderer, they also called him a martyr

and respected his principled actions. During his imprisonment and trial, his prison writings (among the most powerful of the genre) were distributed throughout the North. The sympathetic outpouring for him, led by Lydia Maria Child, Thoreau, and Emerson, who said that Brown would "make the gallows like the cross" (quoted in Stauffer, p. 37), possibly helped Lincoln get elected. And in the immediate wake of Lincoln's election, Southern states began seceding.

The road to disunion contained some of America's most memorable literature: the essays of Ralph Waldo Emerson and Margaret Fuller; the autobiographical writings of Henry David Thoreau, Frederick Douglass, Harriet Jacobs, and John Quincy Adams; the poetry of Walt Whitman, Emily Dickinson, and Henry Wadsworth Longfellow; the speeches of Douglass, Lincoln, Charles Sumner, Theodore Parker, and Daniel Webster; the journalism of William Lloyd Garrison, Horace Greeley, and Douglass; and the fiction of Stowe, Child, Fanny Fern, Melville, Edgar Allan Poe, and Nathaniel Hawthorne. Not all of these writers responded directly to sectional tensions; they often wrote in symbolic language, addressing the irreconcilable hopes and utopian ideals, as well as the costs, of American dreaming.

THE WAR AND ITS CONSEQUENCES

As Lincoln famously said in his second inaugural in March 1865, each side "read[s] the same bible, and pray[s] to the same God; and each invokes His aid against the other" (p. 450). Well before the war, each side believed in a vision, sanctioned by God, of what the good society looked like. And each side fought and was willing to sacrifice everything to preserve its respective vision. For the South, this vision was the agrarian way of life, supported and upheld by slavery and governed by "natural aristocrats" who would create an eventual empire of slavery. Southern leaders borrowed from Aristotle, who articulated a natural slave ideal based on the premise that some men were born to rule and others to do the basic work of society. The North's vision of the good society was the free labor ideal, premised on the assumption that one could begin a career as an employee or apprentice and through hard work and the acquisition of a craft eventually become an independent artisan or entrepreneur and employ the next generation. Each vision threatened the other: northerners believed that southerners sought to extend slavery into every territory and state. And southerners thought that the North sought to abolish slavery throughout the nation.

What neither side understood was that the economic and industrial forces unleashed by the war not only helped to destroy slavery (through the manufacture of weapons, equipment, and railroads); they hastened the end of the free labor ideal. By waging total war to defend an older America, the North assured the demise of its own society as well as that of the agrarian and aristocratic South. Thus, one of the tragic ironies of the war, as the historian Eric Foner has noted, was that "each side fought to defend a distinct vision of the good society, but each vision was destroyed by the very struggle to preserve it" (p. 33).

Herman Melville (1819–1891) was one of the few Northern writers who understood such transforming effects of the war. In his poem from *Battle-Pieces and Aspects of the War* (1866), "The Conflict of Convictions," he points to the transformation of the nation:

> Power unanointed may come—
> Dominion (unsought by the free)
> And the Iron Dome,
> Stronger for stress and strain,
> Fling her huge shadow athwart the main;
> But the Founders' dream shall flee.
>
> (P. 17)

The power of the federal government, here symbolized by the "Iron Dome," would fling her shadow across the Main Streets of America and impose unprecedented dominion on communities and towns, thus destroying the founders' dream of a loose confederation of states and a decentralized government.

The transformation of culture by the war was reflected in the very language that Americans used to define themselves: before the war they referred to themselves in the plural case ("the United States of America *are* . . ."); after the war they used the singular ("the United States of America *is* . . ."). The change of case reflected a much greater cultural transformation, from a weak to powerful central government, from small shops to big business, and unrestricted capitalist expansion at levels that were previously unimaginable.

During the four years of war, few of the nation's prominent white male writers were productive. Nathaniel Hawthorne (1804–1864) captured the war's relationship to established male writers in a letter to a friend in 1862: "I feel as if the great convulsion were going to make an epoch in our literature as in everything else (if it does not annihilate all), and that when we emerge from the war-cloud, there will be another and better . . . class of writers than the one I belong to" (quoted in Masur, p. 177). He worked in vain to complete three novels during the war, but they remained unfinished when he died in 1864. "War continues to interrupt my literary industry," he wrote a year before his death; "and I am afraid it will be long before Romances are in request again, even if I could

write one" (*Letters*, p. 427). Ralph Waldo Emerson (1803–1882) likewise published little during the war. Walt Whitman (1819–1892), who worked as a nurse during the war, captured a sense of the futility of representing it in prose, as he wrote in his 1875 memoir, *Memoranda during the War:* "The real war will never get in the books" (quoted in Masur, p. 281). The normally prolific output of William Gilmore Simms (1806–1870) dwindled to one short novel during the four years of conflict. "I am literally doing nothing in letters," he confided to a friend. "It will need a year of peace to bring me back to that calm mood which Literature demands. . . . Literature, poetry especially, is effectually overwhelmed by the drums, & the cavalry, and the shouting" (quoted in Masur, pp. 213, 218).

Some scholars, especially the critics Edmund Wilson and Daniel Aaron, have taken these comments and the paucity of writings by white literary men as emblematic of *all* literature during the war. "The period of the American Civil War was not one in which *belles lettres* flourished," Wilson argued (p. ix). For Aaron, the war remained "unwritten": although "one would expect writers, the 'antennae of the race,' to say something revealing about the meaning, if not the causes, of the War," with "a few notable exceptions, they did not" (p. xviii).

There was, however, an enormous outpouring of popular literature during the four years of war, as the historian Alice Fahs has emphasized. Additionally, African American writers, from black soldiers to Frederick Douglass and Martin Delany, were enormously productive during the conflict, especially in essays and speeches; and Harriet Jacobs published her brilliant slave narrative, *Incidents in the Life of a Slave Girl,* in 1861. Women writers from Stowe and Child to Louisa May Alcott and Rebecca Harding Davis produced significant work, including Davis's masterpiece, *Life in the Iron Mills* (1861), and Alcott's *Little Women* (1868–1869), which became, after *Uncle Tom's Cabin,* the most successful novel of the nineteenth century and remained influential through the twentieth century.

From the end of the war until the 1880s, however, there was a dwindling of war-related publications. African American literary works published in the 1850s greatly exceeded the works published between 1867 and 1876, a period of legal freedom in which only two novels were published and slave narratives dwindled to a trickle. While black writers grappled with the problem of how to understand and represent freedom, many whites simply wanted to forget the conflict. As early as 1866, a subscription book publisher argued that people were "tired of being importuned to buy various Histories of the War" (quoted in Fahs, p. 313). *Harper's Weekly*, which had published hundreds of Civil War stories during the war, virtually abandoned the war as a topic or setting in the entire decade of the 1870s. As the publisher James Henry Harper noted, "the public was tired of reading about the war" (quoted in Fahs, p. 313).

The desire—indeed the need—to forget the conflict manifested itself in a disdain for professional soldiers. The *Army and Navy Journal* complained in 1883 that since the war, the designation of "soldier" seemed "to be a synonym for all that is degrading and low, and whenever" people meet someone "bearing it they cannot forbear showing their contempt" (quoted in Linderman, p. 272). Veterans themselves sought to forget, and a widespread disillusionment, or "void of disorientation," set in after the war. The Civil War historian Bruce Catton explained the collective feeling of veterans in these terms: they "lost something; if not life itself, then the dreams or illusions of youth which once seemed to give life its meaning. . . . Like Adam, they had been cast out of the enchanted garden, leaving innocence behind" (p. 159). This sense of loss affected the entire generation that lived through the war. The resurgence of interest in the war in the 1880s and 1890s came from a younger generation, which understood the war through memories and stories rather than experience. Yet the ways in which they understood and represented reality had been profoundly changed by the war.

Thus, the transformation of American literature after the war did not occur suddenly; it happened gradually, and did not become prominent until the 1880s, during the resurgence of interest in the war. A shift in the zeitgeist, or collective identity of America, had demanded a reconceptualization of what American literature should be, what forms it took, and what was deemed acceptable. The changes can be summarized in four broad categories: (1) the ascendancy of fiction; (2) the rise of realism; (3) the displacement of God; and (4) the masculinization of society.

THE ASCENDANCY OF FICTION

From the Revolution to the Civil War, American statesmen and leaders were fearful of fiction. They accurately understood its subversive power: fiction empowered individuals; it catered to people's passions, fancies, and whims, which threatened republican ideas of order and rationality. At least through President Andrew Jackson's administration, politicians were quite vocal in their belief that fiction threatened the very fabric of society and led to chaos, licentiousness, destruction, and revolution. Jefferson captured

the prevailing sentiment in 1818 when he referred to the novel as "poison":

> When this poison infects the mind, it destroys its tone and revolts it against wholesome reading. Reason and fact, plain and unadorned, are rejected. Nothing can engage attention unless dressed in all the figments of fancy, and nothing so bedecked comes amiss. The result is a bloated imagination, sickly judgment, and disgust towards all the real business of life. (*Writings*, pp. 1411–1412)

The nation's cultural gatekeepers were correct in fearing that fiction would fuel ambition, the bane of republican government, and threaten to subvert the existing hierarchy. Fiction offered people a way to imagine themselves anew. It gave them new visions, hopes, and dreams for transforming themselves as they read in books about everyday people who resembled them.

As a result of this attack, writers claimed that their prose was truthful in spirit if not in fact. They passed their novels off as nonfiction, referring to them as "narratives," "true" stories, or travelogues. From the Revolution until the Civil War, most of the nation's prominent writers—from Hector St. John Crevecoeur and Susanna Rowson to Charlotte Temple, Hannah Foster, Washington Irving, Cooper, Melville, and Stowe—suggested that their fiction was history or truthful representations of how things really were. (Melville, by beginning the narrative of *Moby-Dick* with the suggestion, "Call me Ishmael," raised questions about the veracity of the narrator; from a marketing point of view, it was a bad strategy, for his novel did not sell well.)

Early critics of the novel were in one sense prophetic in their fears that the novel would tear the nation asunder by unleashing passions that would be ungovernable. When Stowe met Lincoln at the White House in 1862, the president is said to have greeted her with the words: "So you're the little woman who wrote the book that started this great war!" Lincoln was not the only one who believed that Stowe's novel was one of the causes of the Civil War. The social forces that led to war also brought the art of *Uncle Tom's Cabin*. Mark Twain (1835–1910) went so far as to blame the war on Sir Walter Scott, whose romances southerners had devoured throughout the antebellum era. Scott, Twain argued in *Life on the Mississippi* (1883),

> sets the world in love with dreams and phantoms; with decayed and swinish forms of religion; with decayed and degraded systems of government; with the sillinesses and emptinesses, sham grandeurs, sham gauds, and sham chivalries of a brainless and worthless long-vanished society. He did measureless harm. . . . Sir Walter had so large a hand in making Southern character, as it existed

before the war, that he is in great measure responsible for the war. (P. 327)

After the Civil War, writers no longer apologized for their fiction or tried to pass it off as nonfiction. And cultural gatekeepers no longer had a moral problem with fiction per se. In a sense one could say that before the war, writers aspired to the condition of history and wrote "people's history"—a history of their new nation focusing on the little people. After the war, writers aspired to the condition of fiction; they dispensed with material facts in order to get at psychological truths and to understand the surreal apocalypse of war. Louisa May Alcott (1832–1888), one of the most popular writers after the war, marks the transition; *Little Women* is a war novel focusing on the home front, and it does not apologize for its fictional form. By contrast, before the war, one of the nation's most popular writers, James Fenimore Cooper (1789–1851), defined himself as a historian and was generally read as such. And Stowe, in the last chapter of *Uncle Tom's Cabin*, sought to add legitimacy to her novel by asserting that "the separate incidents that compose the narrative are, to a very great extent, authentic, occurring, many of them, either under [Stowe's] own observation, or that of her personal friends" (p. 618). Soon after *Uncle Tom's Cabin* was published, Stowe published *A Key to Uncle Tom's Cabin: Presenting the Original Facts and Documents upon Which the Story Is Founded, Together with Corroborative Statements Verifying the Truth of the Work* (1853), which corroborated with "facts and documents" her fictional story.

The ascendancy of fiction, and the commercial success of writers like Alcott, whose royalties far outstripped those of Cooper, related as well to the rise of a literary hierarchy during and after the war. The literary marketplace was divided into three forms of fiction: sensational fiction, which was published in story papers and dime novels (that cost a dime to purchase); domestic fiction, which resembled the narratives published before the war; and "high" or "highbrow" literature, which was published, often serially, in such prestigious magazines as the *Atlantic Monthly*. The emergence of a rigid literary hierarchy was part of a larger cultural hierarchy brought on by the war. The new marketplace also provided many more outlets for writers to make a living from their work than had existed in the antebellum era.

THE RISE OF REALISM

The effects of the war also helped to destroy romantic and sentimental modes of writing, whereby writers sought to ennoble their readers, offer ideal visions of society, and avoid the seamy side of life. Realism, which first emerged in France in the 1830s as a term signifying a general rejection in the visual arts of academic models and "studio" work, emphasized firsthand experience and direct observation in a material world. Realism coincided with the rise of a regimented, corporate society; it sought to depict life in its daily, unheroic, and unsentimental rhythms. Realism rejected the bourgeois emphasis on stability, security, and middle-class values and focused on working-class or morally problematic protagonists.

Rebecca Harding Davis's (1831–1910) novella *Life in the Iron Mills* coincided with the firing on Fort Sumter and is sometimes referred to as one of the first works of American realism. Her novella highlights the exploitation of laborers that would only get worse after the war. The name of her protagonist, Hugh Wolfe, suggests his identity. He seems more like an animal, a beast of burden, than a human. Despite his poverty and lack of education, he creates beautiful sculpture out of the waste in the iron mill where he works. Yet he is no moralist in the traditional sense: he drinks and steals, and commits suicide while in jail. Yet these crimes are not considered moral transgressions: "But was there right or wrong for such as he?" the narrator asks of Hugh Wolfe. "What was right? And who had ever taught him?" (p. 68).

The popular and critical success of Mark Twain's *Adventures of Huckleberry Finn* (1885),written in the vernacular voice of a poor uneducated boy, would have been unthinkable before the war. While many antebellum writers experimented with dialect, their narrators were educated moralists. Stowe uses dialect throughout *Uncle Tom's Cabin;* but her narrator is a sentimental moralist. After the war such sentimentalism and overt moralism was increasingly treated with disdain by writers ranging from Davis and Twain to Henry James, William Dean Howells, Sarah Orne Jewett, and Edith Wharton.

With so many people having needlessly died in the conflict, irony and the abridgment of hope, moral certainty, and illusion became an acceptable, even desirable, mode of telling stories. Melville's line in *Battle-Pieces*, "what like a bullet can undeceive," foreshadows the shattering of illusion and the rise of irony as a way to understand the world (p. 63). Irony replaced the loss of moral certainty. After the war, reformers increasingly concluded that "moral certainty" was something they "should sacrifice a little of in exchange for order," as Louis Menand has noted (p. 59). It is no coincidence that Melville and Hawthorne, the great ironists of the 1840s and 1850s, were also opposed to war and the moral certainties on which it was based. Hawthorne longed for peace

"The Battle of Gaines's Mill and Its Preliminaries." Illustration from the article in the *Century,* 1885. GRADUATE LIBRARY, UNIVERSITY OF MICHIGAN.

throughout the war, even at the cost of letting the Confederacy remain a separate nation with slavery still intact: "Amputation [disunion] seems to me much the better plan, and all we ought to fight for is the liberty of selecting the point where our diseased members [the South] shall be lopt off" (quoted in Masur, pp. 165–166). In *Battle-Pieces,* Melville characterized the war spirit in the poem "Misgivings," saying, "Nature's dark side is heeded now" (p. 13). And in the last poem of the collection, "A Meditation," the poet describes how

> . . . something of a strange remorse
> Rebelled against the sanctioned sin of blood,
> And Christian wars of natural brotherhood.
>
> *(P. 241)*

DISPLACEMENT OF GOD

The war created a profound crisis of faith in the collective consciousness of Americans. This crisis can be seen in the shift of soldiers' attitudes from the beginning to the end of the war. As the historian Gerald Linderman has shown in his 1987 book, *Embattled Courage: The Experience of Combat in the American Civil War,* Northern and Southern soldiers believed at the beginning of the war that with faith in God, coupled with courage, they would survive and conquer the enemy. But as the war dragged on, soldiers became disillusioned and no longer believed that God would protect them. They increasingly felt like objects rather than actors in events; and by war's end many had become fatalists. Soldiers on both sides reenlisted in the last year of the war in order to gain a thirty-day furlough, in which they could see loved ones before returning to battle and probable death. This displacement of God is understandable when one recognizes that most Americans in both the North and South defined the war in apocalyptic terms. With the end of the war, it was as though the apocalypse had come, but the new age was nowhere in sight.

In antebellum writings as diverse as *Uncle Tom's Cabin, Moby-Dick, The Scarlet Letter,* and the Leatherstocking Tales, God interferes with and affects the affairs of the world. He is everywhere in *Uncle Tom's Cabin,* which sold more copies than any other book in the nineteenth century save the Bible. Uncle Tom is a Christlike hero whose death will, the narrator predicts, redeem the sins of the nation. Even in works by Melville, in which the narrator has a much more nuanced attitude toward God, central characters such as Ahab in *Moby-Dick* see themselves as prophets fulfilling providential destiny.

After the war, writers increasingly began to secularize religious language rather than dispense with religious tropes altogether. The opening lines of Davis's *Life in the Iron Mills* offers a good example. The narrator describes a town filled with smoke, rolling "sullenly in slow folds from the great chimneys of the iron-foundries," settling in "slimy pools on the muddy streets" and seeping into the homes. "Here, inside," the narrator continues, "is a little broken figure of an angel pointing upward from the mantel-shelf; but even its wings are covered with smoke and black" (pp. 39–40). In iron mills, she suggests, the wings of angels get broken, much as the hopes of men are destroyed; the emblems of God have been cloaked with the smoke and grit by an indifferent world.

The opening pages of *Huckleberry Finn* similarly invert antebellum conceptions of God and spirituality. Huck hates being "sivilized" and rejects Christian morality. When Miss Watson tells him that Tom Sawyer will go to hell, Huck responds that he wants to go there as well. And in the climactic scene in the novel, Huck vows, "All right, then, I'll *go* to hell," after tearing up the letter he has written that upholds the law and reveals the whereabouts of the fugitive Jim (p. 223).

Frederick Douglass (1818–1895), often referred to as a "representative American" because he transformed himself from the poorest of the poor (a slave) to an independent entrepreneur (newspaperman and orator), was representative in his attitudes toward God as well. From his first speeches in 1841 through the Civil War, he frequently called on God to help him and his nation, even though he rejected conventional doctrines and denominations. Like other black and white abolitionists, Douglass drew from scripture and sought to "come out" from corrupt institutions and churches. Throughout the 1850s he defined himself as a prophet and millennialist and treated the Declaration of Independence, Constitution, and Bible as sacred texts. The principles of the Declaration of Independence, if fulfilled, "would release every slave in the world and prepare the earth for a millennium of righteousness and peace," he argued, adding, "I believe in the millennium" (*Frederick Douglass Papers,* pp. 529, 553). He likened the war to Revelations 12, where Michael and his angels battle against Satan. But

after the war he gradually abandoned his faith in God as immanent or indwelling. A heaven on earth increasingly seemed to him a dangerous illusion. He became more secular in his worldview and no longer believed that God could change the world or affect the laws of nature. In his third autobiography, *The Life and Times of Frederick Douglass* (1881, revised in 1892), he castigated blacks for believing that they could procure "help from the Almighty." By remaining true to their faith, blacks were "false to fact" and thus to history, he argued. Material facts and the laws of nature now trumped "all the prayers of Christendom" (p. 480).

THE MASCULINIZATION OF SOCIETY

The Civil War was the nation's first "total war," and it penetrated the home as well as the battlefield. The mentality of war destroyed the status of the domestic sphere as a sacred site that would ennoble and nurture its inhabitants. Women increasingly sought to participate in the battles of life along with men, in part as a means to gain power and basic rights.

As a result of the war, a crisis of manhood occurred among Northern white men from 1860 to 1870, which coincided with the dwindling output among New England men who had been prominent and prolific writers before the war. During the same decade, especially during the war years, women's writings burgeoned. "Woman has now taken to her pen . . . and is flourishing it with a vengeance," wrote a journalist in *Frank Leslie's Illustrated* on 10 October 1863 (quoted in Young, p. 7).

The crisis came to a head in 1869, when Stowe published "The True Story of Lady Byron's Life" in the *Atlantic Monthly,* followed by *Lady Byron Vindicated: A History of the Byron Controversy* in 1870. In these works Stowe attacked Lord Byron, accusing him of incest with his half sister, among other sins, and championing her friend Lady Byron as one of Europe's great intellectuals and literary figures. The male backlash was virtually unprecedented in American literature. The *Atlantic,* which catered primarily to literary men, lost fifteen thousand subscribers in the immediate wake of Stowe's article. Throughout the country, newspaper and magazine editors excoriated Stowe. Lord Byron had long been viewed as a symbol of the male liberator and freedom fighter par excellence. For numerous male readers, to attack Byron was tantamount to attacking the mass of Northern men who had fought in the war to save their nation.

The male backlash against Stowe reflected changes in literature and culture. The backlash was "a symptom of the polarization of literature along gender lines" that became especially prominent after the war, according to Stowe's biographer Joan Hedrick (p. 370). Stowe's attack on Lord Byron occurred at the end of a decade in which concepts of manhood were in a state of flux and would ultimately become codified in the 1880s by proponents of American realism and an embrace of masculine virtue.

John William De Forest's (1826–1906) Civil War novel, *Miss Ravenel's Conversion from Secession to Loyalty* (1867), a loosely autobiographical book based on his wartime experience, explored these new meanings of manhood. In the novel De Forest distinguished between Northern and Southern manhood; while the former is superior, it is not without its genteel, feminine qualities, which he viewed as problematic. But fortunately the war accelerated Northern combativeness and martial vigor, resulting in a healthier mixture of physical strength and moral fortitude, coupled with virtue, that constituted the essential ingredients of the "redeemed" nation's manhood. "The old innocence of the peaceable New England farmer and mechanic had disappeared from these war-seared visages and had been succeeded by an expression of hardened combativeness, not a little brutal," the narrator says happily (p. 248). And the novel's protagonist, Edward Colburne, has similarly been transformed: "He is a better and stronger man for having fought three years, out-facing death and suffering. Like the nation, he has developed and learned his powers" (p. 468).

Alcott brilliantly captured the emerging masculinization of culture in her two war novels, *Hospital Sketches* (1863) and *Little Women* (1868). In each book, her female protagonists become, in effect, men. More than virtually any other writer of her era, Alcott understood the crisis of manhood caused by the war; and she transformed herself and her leading characters into masculine women for profit, opportunity, and the good of society. While Lillie Ravenel, the female protagonist of *Miss Ravenel's Conversion,* learns to love and appreciate Northern manhood, Alcott and her characters become like men in order to vanquish their enemies, redeem their nation, and assert their independence. And she acknowledges that sentimentality can be dangerous, even fatal, in war. In effect, a war mentality had invaded her domestic sphere, and Alcott responded as a man.

This new masculinist ethos, which became widespread in the 1880s, is one of the defining aspects of realism. But affirmations of a martial ideal and the attack on sentimentalism were already in place in 1870, especially by a new generation of writers. Emerson and Hawthorne understood that the Civil War would create a new, realistic, and masculine form

of representation. De Forest partly attributed the war to a crisis of gender, while also lauding its effects on Northern men. Alcott saw the war as a means to reconcile men and women, North and South. She attacked the corrupt influences of masculinity, especially men's efforts to control, govern, and exploit women, by creating masculine men. In a sense, she borrowed from her war experiences and affirmed a battlefield code, becoming like the enemy in order to subdue him. With the vast economic transformation after the Civil War and the ever-increasing exploitation of labor, war had become an apt metaphor for life.

See also Abolitionist Writing; *Battle-Pieces; The Liberator;* Proslavery Writing; Slave Narratives; Slave Rebellions; Slavery; *Uncle Tom's Cabin*

BIBLIOGRAPHY

Primary Works

Adams, John Quincy. *The Diary of John Quincy Adams, 1794–1845.* New York: Longmans, Green, 1928.

Alcott, Louisa May. *Hospital Sketches.* 1863. New York: Bedford/St. Martin's, 2004.

Alcott, Louisa May. *Little Women.* 1868–1869. Edited by Elaine Showalter. New York: Penguin, 1989.

Davis, Rebecca Harding. *Life in the Iron Mills.* 1861. Edited by Cecelia Tichi. Boston: Bedford/St. Martin's, 1998.

De Forest, John William. *Miss Ravenel's Conversion from Secession to Loyalty.* 1867. Edited by Gary Scharnhorst. New York: Penguin, 2000.

Douglass, Frederick. *The Frederick Douglass Papers.* Series 1, vol. 3. Edited by John Blassingame. New Haven, Conn.: Yale University Press, 1985.

Douglass, Frederick. *Life and Times of Frederick Douglass.* 1881. Rev. ed. 1892. New York: Collier, 1962.

Finkelman, Paul. *Dred Scott v. Sandford: A Brief History with Documents.* Boston: Bedford/St. Martins, 1997.

Hawthorne, Nathaniel. *The Letters, 1857–1864.* Edited by Thomas Woodson et al. Centenary Edition of the Works of Nathaniel Hawthorne, volume 18. Columbus: Ohio State University Press, 1987.

Jefferson, Thomas. *The Life and Selected Writings of Thomas Jefferson.* Edited by Adrienne Koch and William Peden. New York: Modern Library, 1944.

Jefferson, Thomas. *Writings.* Edited by Merrill Peterson. New York: Library of America, 1984.

Lincoln, Abraham. *Selected Speeches and Writings.* New York: Library of America, 1992.

Masur, Louis P., ed. *The Real War Will Never Get in the Books: Selections from Writers during the Civil War.* New York: Oxford University Press, 1993.

Melville, Herman. *Battle-Pieces and Aspects of the War.* 1866. New York: Da Capo Press, 1995.

Stowe, Harriet Beecher. *A Key to Uncle Tom's Cabin: Presenting the Original Facts and Documents upon Which the Story Is Founded, Together with Corroborative Statements Verifying the Truth of the Work.* 1853. Bedford, Mass.: Applewood, 1998.

Stowe, Harriet Beecher. *Lady Byron Vindicated: A History of the Byron Controversy.* Boston: Fields, Osgood, 1870.

Stowe, Harriet Beecher. "The True Story of Lady Byron's Life." *Atlantic Monthly,* September 1869.

Stowe, Harriet Beecher. *Uncle Tom's Cabin; or, Life among the Lowly.* 1852. Edited by Ann Douglas. New York: Penguin, 1986.

Thoreau, Henry David. *Walden and Civil Disobedience.* 1854, 1849. New York: Penguin, 1983.

Twain, Mark. *Adventures of Huckleberry Finn.* 1885. Edited by Thomas Cooley. New York: Norton, 1999.

Twain, Mark. *Life on the Mississippi.* 1883. New York: Penguin, 1986.

Walker, David. *David Walker's Appeal, in Four Articles, Together with a Preamble to the Coloured Citizens of the World, but in Particular, and Very Expressly, to Those of the United States of America.* 1829. New York: Hill and Wang, 1994.

Whitman, Walt. *The Portable Walt Whitman.* Edited by Mark Van Doren. New York: Penguin, 1973.

Secondary Works

Aaron, Daniel. *The Unwritten War: American Writers and the Civil War.* New York: Knopf, 1973.

Blight, David W. *Race and Reunion: The Civil War in American Memory.* Cambridge, Mass.: Harvard University Press, 2001.

Brodhead, Richard H. *Cultures of Letters: Scenes of Reading and Writing in Nineteenth-Century America.* Chicago: University of Chicago Press, 1993.

Catton, Bruce. *Reflections on the Civil War.* Garden City, N.Y.: Doubleday, 1981.

Crane, Gregg D. *Race, Citizenship, and Law in American Literature.* Cambridge, U.K.: Cambridge University Press, 2002.

Davis, David Brion. *Challenging the Boundaries of Slavery.* Cambridge, Mass.: Harvard University Press, 2003.

Donald, David Herbert. *Lincoln.* New York: Simon and Schuster, 1995.

Ernst, Robert. *Rufus King: American Federalist.* Chapel Hill: University of North Carolina Press, 1968.

Fahs, Alice. *The Imagined Civil War: Popular Literature of the North and South, 1861–1865.* Chapel Hill: University of North Carolina Press, 2001.

Foner, Eric. *Politics and Ideology in the Age of the Civil War.* New York: Oxford University Press, 1980.

Freehling, William W. *The Road to Disunion: Secessionists at Bay, 1776–1854.* New York: Oxford University Press, 1990.

Gates, Henry Louis, Jr. "The Trope of a New Negro and the Reconstruction of the Image of the Black." In *The New American Studies: Essays from Representations,* edited by Philip Fisher, pp. 319–345. Berkeley: University of California Press, 1991.

Hedrick, Joan D. *Harriet Beecher Stowe: A Life.* New York: Oxford University Press, 1994.

Linderman, Gerald F. *Embattled Courage: The Experience of Combat in the American Civil War.* New York: Free Press, 1987.

McPherson, James M. *Ordeal by Fire: The Civil War and Reconstruction.* 2nd ed. New York: McGraw-Hill, 1992.

Mellon, Matthew T. *Early American Views on Negro Slavery.* Boston: Meador, 1934.

Menand, Louis. "John Brown's Body." *Raritan* 22, no. 2 (2002): 59.

Potter, David M. *The Impending Crisis, 1848–1861.* New York: Harper and Row, 1976.

Rohrbach, Augusta. *Truth Stranger Than Fiction: Race, Realism, and the U.S. Literary Marketplace.* New York: Palgrave, 2002.

Samuels, Shirley. *Facing America: Iconography and the Civil War.* New York: Oxford University Press, 2004.

Silber, Nina. *The Romance of Reunion: Northerners and the South, 1865–1900.* Chapel Hill: University of North Carolina Press, 1993.

Sizer, Lyde Cullen. *The Political Work of Northern Women Writers and the Civil War, 1850–1872.* Chapel Hill: University of North Carolina Press, 2000.

Slotkin, Richard. *The Fatal Environment: The Myth of the Frontier in the Age of Industrialization, 1800–1890.* Middletown, Conn.: Wesleyan University Press, 1986.

Stauffer, John. *The Black Hearts of Men: Radical Abolitionists and the Transformation of Race.* Cambridge, Mass.: Harvard University Press, 2002.

Tompkins, Jane. *Sensational Designs: The Cultural Work of American Fiction, 1790–1860.* New York: Oxford University Press, 1985.

Trachtenberg, Alan. *The Incorporation of America: Culture and Society in the Gilded Age.* New York: Hill and Wang, 1982.

Wilson, Edmund. *Patriotic Gore: Studies in the Literature of the American Civil War.* 1962. New York: Norton, 1994.

Young, Elizabeth. *Disarming the Nation: Women's Writing and the American Civil War.* Chicago: University of Chicago Press, 1999.

John Stauffer

CLASSICAL LITERATURE

"Come Muse migrate from Greece and Ionia," Walt Whitman urges in his 1871 poem "Song of the Exposition," producing a new twist to the traditional epic invocation. He points to America as a new and worthier subject for poets than "that matter of Troy" and other "immensely overpaid accounts" (p. 158); using the language of American mercantilism, he repudiates classical models for representing the New World. On the opposite end of the spectrum in his stance toward classicism stands Edgar Allan Poe, displaying awe, veneration, and heartfelt gratitude toward "the glory that was Greece / and the grandeur that was Rome" in his well-known sonnet of 1831 "To Helen" (p. 62). These fluctuating, ambivalent attitudes toward the classical tradition as embodied by its literatures are to a large degree representative of nineteenth-century America.

AMERICA AND THE CLASSICAL TRADITION

The two great Western traditions, the Judeo-Christian and the Greco-Roman, retained a pervasive influence on American culture in the nineteenth century, although Americans displayed characteristically ambiguous feelings about the power of the Old World over the New. A Judeo-Christian outlook formed the ideological basis of nineteenth-century America, with its strong Protestant heritage and growing evangelical movement, but nonetheless the Greco-Roman tradition survived through the educated American's immersion in classical literatures, both in the original and in translation. The importance in high culture of classical thought—be it ancient writing, art, and architecture or later representations and allusions—was another reason for its remarkable influence. From the beginning of "America" as it was conceived of and settled by Europeans, the classical picture parallels and complements the vision of the new continent as an Edenic garden, beginning with the Puritan notion of America as the New Canaan. The new continent was regarded as a place that offered a return to the Golden Age, a place akin to the Garden of the Hesperides, the Isles of the Blessed, Atlantis, or a new Arcadia; its explorers and settlers were compared to classical heroes. The first important piece of English poetry produced on the American continent was a notable verse translation of Ovid's *Metamorphoses* by the poet

George Sandys in 1626, written while Sandys resided in Virginia. The Muses, migrating to the New World, brought with them a robust classical tradition—in education, politics, oratory, law, history, literature, and the arts.

The Republic of the United States was, after all, consciously modeled by the Founding Fathers on the Roman Republic, complete with a capital city built to echo Rome, an enduring iconography of Latin mottos on official seals, public buildings resembling classical temples, and a goddess called Liberty. In the sphere of neoclassicism itself, the 1820s mark a turning away from Rome to Greece in architecture, art, literature, and scholarship. Within the United States, the Greek revival superseded the "Roman republican" style, symbolically equated with the politics of Thomas Jefferson (1743–1826). The French emperor Napoleon's (1769–1821) lavish use of ancient Roman symbols to bolster his imperial conquests made a younger generation of Americans uneasy about the thin line separating republic from empire, while classical Greece inspired admiration as the cradle of the democratic city-state. Homer was now regarded as a truer epic poet than Virgil, and in tribute William Munford of Virginia produced the first American verse translation of the *Iliad* in 1848. Americans were also eager to praise and aid the modern Greeks in their struggle for independence, which furnished material not only for U.S. newspapers but also the literary production of the philhellenic English Romantic poets, particularly George Gordon, Lord Byron (1788–1824), who did much to popularize an interest in Greece in Britain and America. On the whole it was democratic Periclean Athens that was considered the model for the United States, but Sparta was also evoked, largely due to the popularity of Plutarch's *Lycurgus,* an account of the legendary Spartan lawgiver's reforms of the Spartan monarchy by establishing a senate and instituting laws to ensure that Spartans cultivated honesty; simple, healthy, and vigorous living; and military prowess. In this context Sparta could be seen to offer an ideal for the early American Republic, visible in Samuel Adams's wish that Boston would become a "Christian Sparta" (p. 673). In antiquity Sparta was the main rival of Athens and the victor in the Peloponnesian War between the two states and their allies (431–404 B.C.). Unlike urban, democratic Athens, Sparta was a feudal monarchy with a large population of oppressed serfs, called helots, working the land and often rising in rebellion. A certain loose parallel could be drawn between the American North and South, and in the nineteenth century southerners invoked Sparta to defend their agrarian way of life and their peculiar institution, pointing to the importance of slavery in classical antiquity. As the Civil War approached they might raise comparisons to Thermopylae. At the pass of Thermopylae in 480 BC, a small band of Spartans under Leonidas defended the entry to Greece against a huge Persian army; they were defeated, but ultimately the united Greeks were able to prevail against the invaders, and the battle of Thermopylae became famous as a glorious instance of patriotism. Stephen Crane in *The Red Badge of Courage* (1895), written three decades after the Civil War, imagines his young protagonist first thinking of the war in terms of "a Greeklike struggle" and "Homeric," so that his mother "disappointed him by saying nothing whatever about returning with his shield or on it" (pp. 5, 6). A New England farm boy's familiarity with them offers a clear indication of the prevalence of these classical tropes.

EDUCATION

The classical influence is most clearly visible in the male-dominated spheres of art and architecture, serious literature, philosophy, and school curricula. Educated men received a more or less solid grounding in the classics, as the curriculum of most high schools and colleges centered to a large extent on classical literature in Greek and Latin. Though the teaching of works in Latin and Greek focused heavily on grammar and translation rather than context, so that many college graduates still preferred to read the classics in English translation, they were nevertheless exposed to classical languages and literatures in the original. The authors most often taught were Homer, Virgil, Ovid, Aesop, Cicero, Horace, Thucydides, Xenophon, and the Greek dramatists. Familiarity with classical literatures still entailed learning two dead languages, traditionally part of an elitist male education, a process that excluded women and the lower classes. Hence Booker T. Washington points to "the craze for Greek and Latin learning" among black Americans in the Reconstruction period and their "feeling that a knowledge, however little, of the Greek and Latin languages would make one a very superior human being, something bordering almost on the supernatural" (pp. 57–58). And although throughout the nineteenth century debate raged over the usefulness of a classical education, the *Yale College Reports* of 1828, in defining the aims and methods of the classical college, strengthened the status quo and helped retain the British-inspired emphasis on the predominance of the classics in college, even as American universities were turning toward the German model of higher education. Indeed the first professor of Greek at Harvard, the twenty-one-year-old Edward Everett (1794–1865), repaired to Germany for an intensive course of study (lasting more than four years) that would enable him

A fragment of John Greenleaf Whittier's poem "Snow-Bound: A Winter Idyl" (1866) describes a young village schoolmaster retelling the classical tales.

Or mirth-provoking versions told
Of classic legends rare and old,
Wherein the scenes of Greece and Rome
Had all the commonplace of home,
And little seemed at best the odds
'Twixt Yankee peddlars and old gods;
Where Pindus-born Araxus took
The guise of any grist-mill brook,
And dread Olympus at his will
Became a huckleberry hill.

John Greenleaf Whittier, "Snow-Bound: A Winter Idyl," in *Norton Anthology of American Literature*, 4th ed., edited by Nina Baym et al. (New York: Norton, 1994), vol. 1, p. 1419.

to return to Boston in 1820 to take up the work of instilling rigorous classical scholarship in Harvard students and propagating the classical languages and literatures to a general audience in his popular public lectures. A move in the 1820s to give precedence to Greek over Latin in American schools died a quiet death, and Latin remained the more studied and better-known language. Charles Anthon of Columbia University brought out a notable critical edition of Horace in 1830, but the United States was not ready for advanced classical scholarship, and it was Anthon's *Classical Dictionary* (1841), a lexicon of Greco-Roman places and figures, that was the most appreciated and used of his scholarly efforts.

With the establishment of such rigorous elite women's colleges as Vassar (1865), Wellesley (1875), and Smith (1875), middle-class women were offered classics programs similar to those of male colleges. In general, however, nineteenth-century women received less schooling, of which the classics made up only a small part. Walter J. Ong has argued that the grueling task of learning Latin and Greek in Renaissance colleges was the equivalent of an initiation rite for upper-class boys, marking their entrance into the tough outside world of men and separating them from the vernacular home and the domestic influence of women, a distinction still maintained in the nineteenth-century English-speaking world. The learning of Latin and Greek was traditionally seen as peculiarly masculine, outside the woman's sphere, and a woman learning the classical languages with their literature and myths was often considered a violation of femininity.

Even Almira Phelps, vice principal of Troy Female Seminary, a well-known, progressive girls' school in New York State, in her popular, frequently reprinted educational volume *The Fireside Friend; or, Female Student* (1840) shows a reluctance to tackle the subject of classical mythology, but she does so because the myths "are so interwoven with ancient classic literature, and so frequently alluded to, by modern writers, especially some of the best English poets, that an acquaintance with these fictions seems necessary, to those who aim at a knowledge of general literature" (p. 151). Thomas Bulfinch makes precisely the same point in his preface to *The Age of Fable* (1855), his ever-popular retelling of the Greek and Roman myths, when he assures that his book is for the reader "of either sex, who wishes to comprehend the allusions so frequently made by public speakers, lecturers, essayists, and poets, and those which occur in polite conversation" (p. viii). Any upwardly mobile American needed at least a superficial acquaintance with the classics to keep up appearances of cultural literacy.

POLITICS, LAW, ORATORY

A classical education gave direction and purpose to several generations of lawyers whose oratory informed the political life of the young Republic. John Quincy Adams (1767–1848) and Daniel Webster (1782–1852) are supreme examples of classically trained political orators working in the first half of the nineteenth century, heirs to the oratory of Demosthenes and Cicero. In a younger generation, prominent figures such as the great Bostonian lawyer Rufus Choate, the Supreme Court judge Joseph Story, the chancellor of New York James Kent, and the secretary of state Edward Livingston all testified to the importance of classical literature in their daily lives and careers. Horace, Cicero, Virgil, Plutarch, Livy, Sallust, Tacitus, Thucydides, and Plato were their guiding lights. After 1825 classicism began to wane as a determining factor in American intellectual thought, and the role of the lawyer in Jacksonian America shifted toward specialization and more narrow concerns, moving away from the lofty ideal of lawyers as public intellectuals and ideological guardians of the Republic. The classical influence remained strong in the South and elsewhere could still work indirectly, as when Abraham Lincoln (1809–1865), following such classically informed orators as Jefferson and Webster, became part of an important Ciceronian model in American politics.

On a more popular level, the classical tradition can be seen in Caleb Bingham's *The Columbian Orator* (1797), a standard nineteenth-century schoolboys' handbook notable for furnishing the young Frederick Douglass with his first lessons in rhetoric in 1830, before he escaped from slavery and began his career as orator and abolitionist. The book includes five classical orations—by Socrates, Cato, Cicero, and two Roman generals—in its selection of speeches, dialogues, and poems. Bingham includes a poem titled "Lines Spoken at a School-Exhibition, by a Little Boy Seven Years Old" that mentions Cicero and Demosthenes with familiarity, thus demonstrating the endurance of these two great models of oratory.

LITERATURE

Through its association with high culture—the art, languages, and literature of ancient Greece and Rome, the art and poetry of the European Renaissance and Baroque—the classical tradition represented a conservative, past-oriented, stable element in American culture. On the one hand, the nineteenth-century tendency to stress the "Apollonian" and proto-Christian side of classical antiquity complements the age's idealized picture of the noble, temperate, dignified world of classical antiquity, in particular Greece. On the other hand, the classical literatures, through their use of ancient history and traditional myths, their open treatment of sexuality, and their disruptive grappling with the dark side of the human psyche, could provide writers with a medium through which to question and subvert the dominant values of nineteenth-century America. The major authors of the American Renaissance or Romantic period—such as Nathaniel Hawthorne (1804–1864) in his novels *The Blithedale Romance* (1852) and *The Marble Faun* (1860) or Herman Melville (1819–1891) in *Moby-Dick* (1851) and *Pierre* (1852)—use classical allusions as a kind of symbolic shorthand, highlighting themes and motifs, adding symbolic resonance to contemporary subject matter, setting up intertextual correspondences. They also use classical allusions as a way to signal subversive or forbidden material, such as a rebellion against the accepted norms of American society, a questioning of Christianity, or a celebration of sexuality. Hawthorne was classically trained at Bowdoin College, whereas Melville was self-taught through intensive reading in Shakespeare and translated classics, but both were steeped in an appreciation of classical literatures. The transcendentalists Ralph Waldo Emerson (1803–1882) and Henry David Thoreau (1817–1862) also show the influence of classical reading in their works.

With the mid-century emergence of a huge though unsophisticated readership, the classical world reached this widening public in a variety of ways—

Study for the Dream of Arcadia, **1838.** Painting by Thomas Cole. The American painter's depiction of what was considered the early human stage of Arcadian simplicity and closeness to nature suggests Hawthorne's ideas of Arcadia in *The Marble Faun.* © NEW YORK HISTORICAL SOCIETY, NEW YORK/BRIDGEMAN ART LIBRARY

through lexicons and handbooks such as Anthon's and Bulfinch's; through retellings of the myths for children, such as Hawthorne's *A Wonder-Book for Girls and Boys* (1852) and *Tanglewood Tales* (1853) or Charles Kingsley's (1819–1875) *The Heroes* (1857); through significant allusions in contemporary literature; and through the medium of the increasingly popular visual arts. Reproductions and imitations of classical statues and old masters exposed larger numbers of middle-class Americans of both sexes to the legacy of the Greco-Roman world while more and more were also traveling to Europe to view the real thing. Literary and popular journals, such as *The Dial,* the *Southern Literary Messenger,* the *Nation,* the *New Monthly,* the *Atlantic Monthly,* and even *Godey's Lady's Book,* paid respectful attention to classical literature by publishing reviews of translations and publications on classical literature and art as well as travel accounts, poems, and stories inspired by antiquity. Clearly the classical literatures and the Greco-Roman tradition were part of Americans' program for self-education and self-improvement. However, although colleges taught the great Athenian dramatists, these did not

appear on the American stage until the late nineteenth century. The tragedies of Sophocles, Aeschylus, and Euripides were considered too dark and immoral for the American public. Dominated by melodrama for most of the century, the professional theater presented classical antiquity through the medium of Shakespeare and a few romantic tragedies; for example, Robert Montgomery Bird's (1806–1854) story of Spartacus, titled *The Gladiator* (1831), was based on Plutarch and Appian and written as a popular vehicle for Edwin Forrest (1806–1872), the leading actor in Jacksonian America. Plutarch was indeed one of the most popular and influential classical writers, much read in translation. Emerson himself wrote a laudatory essay on Plutarch in 1870.

Insofar as middle-class women increasingly entered the cultural marketplace as consumers and producers of art and literature, they saw classical literature both as an outmoded and immoral tradition, unsuitable for a Christian nation and a country looking toward a millennial future, and as part of a hitherto elitist masculine preserve, permeating all of Western culture and hence to be mastered if women wished to prove their intellectual parity with men. The mid-century ushered in the Victorian image of woman as chaste upholder of religion, spirituality, and the finer aspects of life in a materialistic and brutally commercial society. This perception of woman's betterment through Christianity—stressed, for instance, in the influential Sarah Josepha Hale's (1788–1879) lexicon of famous women, *Woman's Record* (1853)—can well explain women writers' indifference or hostility to classical literatures.

At the other end of the nineteenth-century spectrum stand those women who gained a masculine education, often through the encouragement of their fathers, and hence imbibed an understanding and appreciation of the classics. Margaret Fuller (1810–1850), Elizabeth Peabody (1804–1894), and Lydia Maria Child (1802–1880) represent women writers of the transcendentalist circle who were notably concerned with questions of religion, philosophy, education, and art, striving to keep up with contemporary European scholarly achievements and to present them to a wider American public. They were active in making the classical tradition accessible to larger numbers of Americans, particularly women, through lectures, conversational classes, articles, and historical fiction (such as Child's novel of 1836, *Philothea*, set in Periclean Athens). Elizabeth Stoddard (1823–1902) uses allusions to classical literature in her New England domestic novel *The Morgesons* (1862) to ironically stress her heroine's lack of a classical education, cultural ignorance, and growing realization of sexuality. For the popular southern writer Augusta Jane Evans (1835–1909), classical allusions in *Macaria* (1864) and in her best-seller *St. Elmo* (1866) underscore the moral superiority and prodigious learning of her female protagonists; Evans was clearly catering to a culture-hungry reading public. Classical allusions could sell, as Harriet Beecher Stowe (1811–1896) recognized when she penned her amusing short story "Olympiana." This satiric sketch of the Greek gods and goddesses as a squabbling Victorian family, published in 1839 in *Godey's Lady's Book*, serves as a humorous advertisement for the popular journal when Zeus himself declares it worthy of Olympian patronage.

ART, FASHION, AND ARCHITECTURE

The classical world represented valuable cultural capital, made most visible in the important domain of classical sculpture, considered in the nineteenth century to represent the apogee of art and the model for the innumerable statues and statuettes that decorated the public and domestic spaces of Victorian America. Hiram Powers, Horatio Greenough, Thomas Crawford,

William Wetmore Story, Harriet Hosmer, Edmonia Lewis, and other American neoclassical sculptors spent many years in Italy, making copious use of classical literatures for subjects of their idealized statues and busts, such as Crawford's *Orpheus and Cerberus* (1838–1843), Hosmer's *Medusa* (1854), or Story's *Cleopatra* (1869). Part of the impact of these artworks derived from the viewers' acquaintance with the underlying classical context. The sculptors could count on the public's understanding of their classical allusions, even if these were filtered through later art or literature, as when Alfred, Lord Tennyson's (1850–1892) poem provided the inspiration for Hosmer's *Oenone* (1855).

These neoclassical sculptures found a home within neoclassical buildings springing up all over the United States. The Greek Revival became the first national style and dominated American architecture from about 1820 to 1860, just when the classical style of dress initiated by the French Revolution gave way to the Victorian or gothic mode of heavily structured clothes and expanding crinolines, and the rage for classical furniture waned. The classical style did remain important for monumental public buildings, while American gothic gradually took over in the sphere of domestic architecture. The distinction between classical and gothic was important, for it paralleled the contrast between paganism and Christianity, Hellenism and Hebraism. In America the struggle between classical and gothic in architecture and fashion was also a contention between two ways of viewing the United States, either as heir to Greek democracy and the Roman Republic or as the New Canaan and a leading light among Christian nations. Despite such countercurrents, the classical literatures, filtered through literary and artistic allusions, kept hold of the American imagination. "The glory that was Greece and the grandeur that was Rome" cast a diminished light but lived on in the culture of Victorian America.

See also Architecture; Art; Colleges; Curricula; Education; Female Authorship; Manhood; Oratory; "Plymouth Rock Oration"; Proslavery Writing; Transcendentalism

BIBLIOGRAPHY
Primary Works
Adams, Samuel. "Samuel Adams to John Scollay, 30 Dec. 1780." In vol. 1 of *The Writings of Samuel Adams*, 4 vols., edited by Harry Alonzo Cushing. New York: Putnam's, 1904–1908.

Bingham, Caleb. *The Columbian Orator*. 1797. Edited by David W. Blight. New York: New York University Press, 1998.

Bulfinch, Thomas. *The Age of Fable.* 1855. In *Bulfinch's Mythology.* New York: Gramercy, 1979.

Crane, Stephen. *The Red Badge of Courage.* 1895. In *Great Short Works of Stephen Crane.* New York: Perennial, 2004.

Phelps, Almira. *The Fireside Friend; or, Female Student: Being Advice to Young Ladies on the Important Subject of Education.* Boston: Marsh, Capen, Lyon, and Webb, 1840.

Poe, Edgar Allan. "To Helen." 1831. In *Edgar Allan Poe: Poetry and Tales.* New York: Library of America, 1984.

Washington, Booker T. *Up from Slavery: An Autobiography.* 1901. Garden City, N.Y.: Doubleday, 1963.

Whitman, Walt. "Song of the Exposition" (1871). In *Leaves of Grass,* 6th ed. Boston: James R. Osgood, 1881.

Yale College. *Reports on the Course of Instruction in Yale College.* New Haven, Conn.: Howe, 1828.

Secondary Works

Cooper, Wendy A. *Classical Taste in America, 1800–1840.* Baltimore and New York: Baltimore Museum of Art and Abbeville Press, 1993.

Ferguson, Robert A. *Law and Letters in American Culture.* Cambridge, Mass.: Harvard University Press, 1984.

Jones, Howard Mumford. *O Strange New World: American Culture; The Formative Years.* New York: Viking, 1964.

Larrabee, Stephen A. *Hellas Observed: The American Experience of Greece, 1775–1865.* New York: New York University Press, 1957.

McManus, Barbara. *Classics and Feminism: Gendering the Classics.* New York: Twayne, 1997.

Nye, Russel Blaine. *The Cultural Life of the New Nation, 1776–1830.* New York: Harper, 1960.

Nye, Russel Blaine. *Society and Culture in America, 1830–1860.* New York: Harper and Row, 1974.

Ong, Walter J. "Latin Language Study as a Renaissance Puberty Rite." In *Rhetoric, Romance, and Technology: Studies in the Interaction of Expression and Culture,* pp. 113–141. Ithaca, N.Y.: Cornell University Press, 1971.

Rawson, Elizabeth. "Appendix: Note on the United States." In *The Spartan Tradition in European Thought,* pp. 368–370. Oxford: Clarendon Press, 1969.

Reinhold, Meyer. *Classica Americana: The Greek and Roman Heritage in the United States.* Detroit: Wayne State University Press, 1984.

Richardson, Robert D., Jr. *Myth and Literature in the American Renaissance.* Bloomington: Indiana University Press, 1978.

Vance, William L. *America's Rome.* Vol. 1, *Classical Rome.* New Haven, Conn.: Yale University Press, 1989.

Winterer, Caroline. *The Culture of Classicism: Ancient Greece and Rome in American Intellectual Life,* 1780–1910. Baltimore: Johns Hopkins University Press, 2002.

Elżbieta Foeller-Pituch

CLOTEL

Clotel; or, The President's Daughter, by William Wells Brown (c. 1814–1884), is the first novel published by an African American. It was published in London in 1853 because the British were generally considered more sympathetic than the Americans to the plight of African American slaves during pre–Civil War times. Throughout the nineteenth century, it was difficult for black novelists to get a book published in the United States. There was usually insufficient capital for blacks to run their own publishing firms, and white firms were reluctant to endorse black writers, fearing to alienate their white audiences and to lose money from books written by and at least in part aimed toward a minority population. Two of these came out during the 1850s, soon after *Clotel.* One, Harriet Wilson's *Our Nig* (1859), would remain largely unread in book form during its own time, and the other, Hannah Crafts's *The Bondwoman's Narrative* (c. 1850s), was not published as a book until the twenty-first century. Only *Clotel* would influence the course of fiction during the nineteenth century, as it was eventually republished in America in several different versions, for the first time in 1864 as part of the publisher James Redpath's Books for the Camp Fire series for Union soldiers.

CLOTEL'S PLOT AND THEMATIC INNOVATIONS

Although *Clotel, Our Nig,* and *The Bondwoman's Narrative* are all considered important in the early twenty-first century, it was *Clotel* that provided the model for writers of African American fiction in the nineteenth century. *Clotel* tells the tale of five African American women living in the antebellum South who lose their freedom through the betrayal of southern white men and the American legal system. The beautiful slave Currer is left to the auction block when Thomas Jefferson, her slave owner, deserts her and his daughters by her to pursue his political ambition. The same fate occurs to Currer's daughter, Clotel; the white man who is her quasi-husband abandons her to slavery in order to pursue his political ambitions. Slavery is also the fate of Currer's granddaughters, Ellen and Jane, when their mother, Althesa (Clotel's sister), and her white husband die of fever.

Clotel's story line emerges in plot pieces that serve to articulate and rearticulate several antislavery

Frontispiece to the first edition of *Clotel*. This classic scene of a tragic mulatto jumping off a bridge to die (and be free) rather than be enslaved became a standard in later mulatto fiction as well.

themes. *Clotel* marks the beginning of the "tragic mulatto" theme in African American fiction. The novel also denotes the beginning of the use by African American fiction writers of central American political events to dramatize the underlying hypocrisy of democratic principles in the face of African American slavery. Finally, as a result of the predominance of theme over plot in *Clotel*, Brown set the pace for formal innovations in the structure of the novel. In contrast to traditional British standards of plot unity and mimesis—that art should present an imitation of real life—Brown unabashedly brought into his text actual newspaper accounts, full-scale borrowings from other literary texts, and texts from actual sermons. *Clotel* was openly and even daringly grounded in events of the time that blew the lid off ideal notions of American equality. Like Herman Melville's (1819–1891) *Moby-Dick* (1851), Brown's book did not maintain the illusion that it was a self-contained mirror of reality; the reader is persistently bombarded by different forms of discourse—fiction, factual accounts, narrative intrusions including his own attached prefatory slave narrative—

that privilege the message of the text over the concept of a seamless fiction. But unlike Melville, Brown kept his heterogeneous or patchwork discourse more squarely focused on the "now" of his own time.

Although Brown's unorthodox manner of combining fact, fiction, and external literary sources was not only innovative but also influential for later African American authors, it has ultimately led to an open questioning of Brown's own originality, based on the fact that he borrowed heavily from the white abolitionist Lydia Maria Child's (1802–1880) short story "The Quadroons." "The Quadroons" appeared in the Boston Female Anti-Slavery Society's annual gift book, *The Liberty Bell*, in 1842. Although Brown's position as father of African American fiction would suggest that any challenge to his originality should be taken seriously, literary originality itself is often a matter of shifting historical perspective. Nevertheless, Brown shows his originality as he penetrates to the heart of traumatized black female identity. Also, quite unlike Child's "The Quadroons," Brown's *Clotel* serves as a powerfully original jeremiad against the self-destructive shortcomings of an American democracy devoted to retaining African American slavery.

THE TRAGIC MULATTO THEME

Clotel begins a long-term tradition in African American fiction, the theme of the tragic mulatto. During the African American nadir of 1877–1920, when the political backlash against black Americans was at its height, the tragic mulatto theme developed fully into a set of conventions whose central plot element concerned mixed-race, near-white heroes or heroines who discovered, to their horror, that they were not completely white as they had previously thought but instead had at least a drop of black blood. This revelation led either to acceptance or denial of a mixed-race self.

It is important to mention that black writers were not the only writers in the nineteenth century to employ the theme of the tragic mulatto. Mark Twain, for example, in *Puddn'head Wilson* (1894) structured his novel around the fate of near-white African Americans. Even some racists used the form to depict mulattos as physiologically degenerate. They capitalized on irrational fears of ethnic difference by warning a general white populace that the consequence of intimate relations with "inferior" black people would be a degenerate hybrid species. Thomas Dixon Jr.'s *The Clansman: An Historical Romance of the Ku Klux Klan* (1905) is probably the most notorious of these racist fictions, especially because it became the basis of D. W. Griffith's 1915 film *The Birth of a Nation*. This fear of miscegenation is satirized in an 1864 cartoon in *Harper's Weekly*, "The Miscegenation Ball," that portrays leading Republicans at Abraham Lincoln's New York headquarters dancing with caricatures of voluptuous young black women. The cartoon makes the point negatively that black women were reduced to the level of "property," whose sexual virtue could be compromised at any time by white men's desire.

Female virtue under siege and without protection was almost a given in the tragic mulatto novel and is the issue at the core of Brown's depiction of the fate of his five mixed-race heroines in *Clotel*. As the novel begins, Currer, abandoned by her famous white lover, Thomas Jefferson, is about to be sold in a slave auction in Richmond, Virginia, along with her two daughters by Jefferson. The point is clearly made that despite Currer's near-white skin, initial guardianship under a white man's protection, and subsequent cultural education superior to that of most enslaved African Americans, there is no legal protection for her in mid-nineteenth-century American society. Currer

has tried to gain freedom from slavery for her two near-white daughters, Clotel and Althesa, by "bring[ing] her daughters up as [implicitly white] ladies" (p. 64). Hoping to secure for them the protection of white men, she has encouraged them to attend a "Negro ball," where "a majority of the attendants are often whites" (p. 64).

The fear of, and fascination with, such balls shows the complicated sexual dynamics of the process by which white southern men might form loving relationships with black women yet fail to protect them from the ravages of slavery. Their options, after all, were limited, since the southern slavery system looked severely askance at white men marrying black women. Even if they wanted to, white southern men could not afford to challenge the southern slavery system, which was the source of their own power and social status.

The problem for black women was not only that they were black but also that they were women. Throughout the nineteenth century in America, even white single women who had sexual relations before marriage were considered "fallen," and in the principal mode of women's representation during the 1850s—the domestic or woman's novel, such as *The Wide, Wide World* (1850) by Susan Warner (Elizabeth Wetherell)—the fate of fallen women was horrific: such women were shunned or even expected to commit suicide after their indiscretions, even if the compromise was brought about by rape.

At least white women had some modicum of independence and social identity in mid-century America by which they could actively seek their own protection. Without the privilege of marriage, black women had no means to protect themselves from their white plantation masters or anybody else. They were caught in an impossible social bind: having little or no control over their own sexual fates, they were held to the same standards of judgment as those who did. What Currer hopes to accomplish by sending her daughters to the Negro ball is to save their sexual virtue and keep them from enslavement. She has these hopes even in the face of her own rejection by Jefferson.

In fact, as the novel begins, Currer seems to have accomplished her purpose, at least for one of her daughters. On the slave block in Richmond, Clotel is actually purchased by Horatio Green, the wealthy young white man who fell in love with her at the Negro ball. Although he keeps her in a cottage behind his house and does not marry her, they have a loving relationship, which early on produces a child. For Clotel, it is as though they are married. But just as Jefferson had abandoned Currer for the sake of his political ambitions, Green also abandons Clotel when he feels the pull of politics. He leaves her to the mercy of his jealous wife (whom he had married to serve that ambition) and hence to the fate of re-enslavement.

Another apparent option for freedom from sexual taint is presented in the subplot concerning Currer's other daughter, Althesa, who gets sold a second time on the slave block in New Orleans but is rescued by a young white physician formerly from Vermont. These two do marry and have two daughters, Ellen and Jane, and all is well until both parents die of yellow fever. Enter the seemingly infallible low-life class of slave catchers, who ferret out hidden racial identity. It turns out that Althesa, through some predictable snag in the law, was never manumitted (formally emancipated from slavery). Because according to the law she was still a slave when she died, her daughters, Ellen and Jane—who in true tragic mulatto fashion were unaware of their own black blood—are also legally slaves. Rather late in the novel, Brown develops the tragic mulatto theme most fully in the fates of Ellen and Jane: Ellen, revealed as mixed-race and not in control of her future, takes poison to avoid sexual compromise, and Jane, her potential lover killed by her master, dies of a broken heart.

In these last two sorrowful deaths of the tragic mulatto, Brown exposes the sexual economy of the South, where black women—even near-white black women—were made universally available to the sexual advances of white men. And though a white man might play the game of marriage with a black woman who appeared white, he would never challenge the slavery system, and his own power and social status, by making that marriage legal.

CLOTEL AND JEFFERSONIAN DEMOCRACY

When *Clotel* was published in the United States, the subtitle "A Tale of the Southern States" was substituted for the original "or, The President's Daughter." "The President's Daughter" referred to Brown's use in *Clotel* of the rumor circulating in a number of publications in the late 1830s—and subsequently proven to be true—that Thomas Jefferson had children from a relationship with a slave mistress. Such an imputation did not sit well with an American public proud of Jefferson's untarnished reputation. This was exactly Brown's point. Jefferson's public position as the champion of American liberty, versus Jefferson's personal position as a Virginian planter who held slaves, could not have presented a better subject matter for Brown's fictional jeremiad. For how could Thomas Jefferson, the third president of the United States (1801–1809) and the major drafter of the Declaration of Independence (1776), hold slaves and, worse yet,

be a party to the sexual compromise of a black woman in his relation with a slave mistress? The opening lines of the Declaration of Independence—"We hold these truths to be self-evident: that all men are created equal"—may not have explicitly referred to women, but it is usually thought to refer to all humankind.

One explanation for the paradox of Jefferson was that he lived in Virginia, and Virginia was considered the jewel in the crown of southern aristocracy. Here, it was thought, were the descendants of British royalty who had immigrated to the United States but retained their divine right to rule over lesser laborers. Jefferson was obviously torn: as an American dissenter to British rule, he felt the strong pull of the "self-evident" truth that all persons were created equal—but he was still a Virginian, and so he felt entitled to hold slaves.

Brown treats Virginia as the epitome of a slave state and then finds an opposing region in New England and sets up the opposition in two contending myths of America's origin. If, on the face of it, the question of origin seems unimportant, Brown suggests that origin myths influence strongly America's sense of itself, which in turn is an influence on the making of American policy.

Brown's two origin myths, in New England and Virginia, follow the almost simultaneous arrival of two ships. One, the *Mayflower,* landed in New England and aboard it were "great and good men" who practiced "Justice, mercy, humanity [and] respect for the rights of all" (p. 187). This, Brown proclaims, is "the good genius of America" (p. 188). Brown means genius here in the same sense as "genie," the attendant spirit that informs America's inclination toward freedom. The other landing, "far in the South-east" was of a "low rakish ship . . . freighted with the elements of unmixed evil" and bringing "the first cargo of slaves on their way to Jamestown, Virginia" (p. 188). The opposition in American culture that exists between these two events is too profound for Brown not to re-summarize:

> Behold the May-flower anchored at Plymouth Rock, the slave-ship in James River. Each a parent, one of the prosperous, labour-honouring, law-sustaining institutions of the North; the other the mother of slavery, idleness, lynch-law, ignorance, unpaid labour, poverty, and dueling, despotism, the ceaseless swing of the whip, and the peculiar institutions of the South. (P. 188)

By juxtaposing Virginia to New England, Brown wants to expose the cruelty behind the genesis of slavery in America's South. Just as significantly, he wants to open up a gap in the imagination of America where slavery does not exist; New England becomes for

Brown a metaphorical space for America to imagine itself without bigotry.

Despite this powerful image of a founding New England, slavery-free, for Brown as he expresses his views in *Clotel*, the ideal of freedom in America was inherently tainted by the coexistence of African American slavery. Jefferson was the perfect representation of that, and at the time of Brown's composition of *Clotel*, Brown had every reason to think that the policies of the American government were irrevocably invested in slavery.

Brown makes precisely this point in *Clotel*. Toward the end of the novel, Clotel is recaptured after her escape from slavery in Vicksburg, Mississippi, when she returns to Virginia to find her daughter. Clotel's recapture takes place shortly after the 1831 Nat Turner revolt, a bloody uprising during which approximately sixty whites were slaughtered. Turner and thirty other blacks were hanged as a result, and Brown uses this incident to explain how a hyper sense of vigilance and near-panic among whites makes Clotel's recapture in Virginia or anywhere in the South almost inevitable. Not nearly so clear is the question of why Clotel ends up in a slave prison in Washington, D.C., which is usually considered the symbolic site of American democracy and freedom.

Symbolically, at least, Clotel is in prison in Washington, D.C., because of the 1850 Fugitive Slave Law, which compelled any white person, North or South, to turn in a fugitive slave on penalty of fines or even imprisonment. Although the Fugitive Slave Law does not fall within the fictional time frame of Brown's novel, it does fall within the time frame of his composition of *Clotel*, and it clearly influences the political theme of the novel. Brown uses the Nat Turner revolt as a contemporary stand-in for the later law. When he writes "the Free States are equally bound with the Slave States to suppress any insurrectionary movement that may take place among the slaves," he is writing about the binding obligation between northern and southern states, which became much more inflexible after the 1850 Fugitive Slave Law.

Clotel escapes from the slave prison in Washington only to find herself immobilized on a bridge over the Potomac River, caught between the Virginia side, swarming with men who are keen to arrest her, and the Washington side, blocked by slave catchers. It is Clotel's status as a fugitive slave imprisoned "midway between the capitol at Washington and the President's house" (p. 216) in Washington, D.C., that provides Brown with a fictional analogue for Washington's congressional reenslavement of all

African Americans as a result of the 1850 Fugitive Slave Law. In the end, Clotel leaps off the bridge into freedom, an episode that would have profound echoes in African American fiction. Brown's ironic chapter title for Clotel's demise, "Death Is Freedom," collapses the options for American blacks to live free in America. Also, Brown's point is clear that the treatment of fugitive slaves in the "free" district of Washington, D.C., recapitulates the paradox of Jefferson, whose commitment to American freedom did not interfere with his enslavement of African Americans.

FORM AND ORIGINALITY IN *CLOTEL*

Robert S. Levine describes the plot structure of *Clotel* as a pastiche or bricolage, an elegant way of saying that Brown cuts and pastes into his novel many different forms of discourse, such as newspaper articles, real-life sermons, and most pertinent to the question of Brown's originality in *Clotel*, major sections of Lydia Maria Child's story "The Quadroons." Regarding Brown's use of Child's text, Levine suggests that it "*is* useful to think of Brown as a kind of plagiarist," but one who justifiably "steals the texts of a culture that steals black bodies" (p. 6).

For Levine, the structural concept of cutting and pasting leads naturally to the question of plagiarism, but structure and content can be separated to examine the degree of originality in each. *Clotel*'s plot resembles an innovative mode of visual representation that Brown admired—the panorama. The panorama, an art form patented in Ireland in 1787, was at its height of popularity in the mid-nineteenth century. When he lived in England, Brown created a panorama covering slave life along the Mississippi River after seeing a panorama of the Mississippi that excluded African Americans. Panoramas, coming from the Greek words *pan* (all) and *horama* (view), exhibited geographical vistas on a continuous horizontal screen that was unrolled slowly before an audience. At a time when tourism was a popular commodity, panoramas provided a form of what Roberta J. M. Olson calls "virtual travel."

Brown actually uses this concept of "virtual travel" as a structural device in *Clotel*, as the novel fans out to distribute Brown's near-white heroines throughout the various regions of the South—Richmond, Virginia; New Orleans, Louisiana; Natchez and Vicksburg, Mississippi; and the regionally ambiguous Washington, D.C. Pieces of Child's story are interspersed at various points along the geographical continuum of Brown's larger story of the slavery panorama, which is tied thematically in *Clotel* to the argument that black women are not safe anywhere they are in the South, or even in Vermont, for that matter.

The lingering question of Brown's originality in his use of "The Quadroons" is not an isolated one in the canon of nineteenth-century American literature. After all, other important authors in nineteenth-century America borrowed liberally from outside sources—Herman Melville (1819–1891), for example, in his use of Amasa Delano's *Narrative of Voyages and Travels in the Northern and Southern Hemispheres* for his story "Benito Cereno." It can be argued that just as Melville shows his originality through brilliant transformations of a source, Brown also invokes Child's text principally to transform it.

Child's text was romantic and sentimental, written for a gift book intended to decorate parlor tables. A careful comparison of Brown's subtle word changes will yield numerous examples of his resistance to Child's sentimentality, but one will serve here to establish the point. When Clotel's lover abandons her and her child after their fiction of marriage outside the law, Child emphasizes one trait prominently, the passion that Clotel feels. Brown adds that although Clotel "was [Horatio's] slave; [and] her bones, and sinews, had been purchased by his gold, yet she had the heart of a true woman" (p. 112). Though seemingly minor, Brown's inclusion of the phrase "true woman" in his addition is actually quite radical. Throughout the nineteenth century, the phrase "true woman" signified female chastity and purity as well as domesticity. Stunningly, Brown gives Clotel the title "true woman" although she has been sexually compromised.

Brown's radical inclusion of black women among the virtuous, his deft use of the tragic mulatto theme to attack southern morals, and the way that his novel serves as an ardent jeremiad against American democracy makes *Clotel; or, The President's Daughter* an early testament to the enduring genius of African American fiction writers.

See also Abolitionist Writing; Blacks; Compromise of 1850 and Fugitive Slave Law; Miscegenation; Slavery

BIBLIOGRAPHY

Primary Work

Brown, William Wells. *Clotel; or, The President's Daughter.* 1853. Introduction and notes by William Edward Farrison. New York: Citadel Press, 1969.

Secondary Works

Andrews, William A. "The Novelization of Voice in Early African American Narrative." *PMLA* 105 (1990): 23–34.

Berzon, Judith R. *Neither White Nor Black: The Mulatto Character in American Fiction.* New York: New York University Press, 1978.

Farrison, William Edward. "Introduction" and notes. In *Clotel; or, The President's Daughter.* New York: Citadel Press, 1969.

Farrison, William Edward. *William Wells Brown: Author and Reformer.* Chicago: University of Chicago Press, 1969.

Levine, Robert S. "Introduction." In *Clotel; or, The President's Daughter.* Edited by Robert S. Levine. Boston: Bedford/St. Martin's, 2000.

Lewis, Richard O. "Literary Conventions in the Novels of William Wells Brown." *CLA Journal* 29 (1985): 129–156.

Mulvey, Christopher. "The Fugitive Self and the New World of the North: William Wells Brown's Discovery of America." In *The Black Columbiad: Defining Moments in African American Literature and Culture,* edited by Werner Sollors and Maria Diedrich, pp. 99–111. Cambridge, Mass.: Harvard University Press, 1994.

Olson, Roberta J. M. "Panorama." *ArtLex Art Dictionary.* http://www.artlex.com.

Sánchez-Eppler, Karen. "Bodily Bonds: The Intersecting Rhetorics of Feminism and Abolition." In *The Culture of Sentiment: Race, Gender, and Sentiment in Nineteenth-Century America,* edited by Shirley Samuels, pp. 92–114. New York: Oxford University Press, 1992.

Stepto, Robert B. *From behind the Veil: A Study of Afro-American Narrative.* Urbana: University of Illinois Press, 1979.

Janet Gabler-Hover

COLLEGES

The half century after 1820 was the heyday of the classical college in American higher education. It was also characterized by the proliferation of denominational colleges. Both these developments took shape in the 1820s.

Although instruction in Latin (primarily) and Greek had been the core of the curriculum for the colonial colleges, standards had deteriorated by 1800. Latin ceased to be the language of instruction, and the dominance of the ancients was vigorously challenged as undemocratic in the early Republic. However, experiments with modern languages such as French and

Italian invariably failed, and the classical pedagogy—the teaching of Latin and Greek—was gradually rehabilitated, with considerably greater emphasis on Greek. This refurbished course of study was emphatically defended by Yale College against proponents of more modern or practical subjects. The *Yale College Reports* of 1828 defined the aims and methods of the classical college, which became the standard across American colleges.

Denominational colleges also became entrenched during the 1820s, as minority religious groups reacted against existing, often state-sanctioned colleges, most often dominated by dogmatic Presbyterians. As states relaxed barriers to chartering colleges, each denomination or splinter defensively founded colleges to educate its own flocks. The classical course and denominational sponsorship, however, convey little of the nature of college education. The ancient languages were but one component of the collegiate experience. And as ministerial preparation was confined to theological seminaries, the standard classical course was basically secular, even if offered in a Christian ambiance. Moreover although denominational colleges multiplied everywhere, collegiate education developed distinct regional traditions. In the East the original colonial colleges spearheaded an academic development that introduced more subjects and more learned teachers. In the South, led by North and South Carolina and Virginia, state-sponsored universities became the dominant institutions. And beyond the Appalachians—the West for all practical purposes—denominational colleges sprouted in the wake of the advancing frontier.

This pattern was altered appreciably after 1850 without dislodging the hegemony of the classical course. Now the leading institutions of the East added schools of science and graduate study to accommodate the growth of knowledge. The western colleges sought to include more kinds of instruction for a broader clientele, including women, thus becoming "multipurpose colleges." In the South, however, innovation was largely smothered by the catastrophe of the Civil War. The years from 1820 to 1870 thus form a coherent era when the classical college was the characteristic form of American higher education.

THE CLASSICAL COLLEGE

Student learning took place through recitations, lectures, written and oral exercises, and activities outside the curriculum. The classical college is best known for the first of these, the unfortunate recitations, easily the most stultifying element. Students typically "recited" on three subjects per term, five or six days per week.

Latin and Greek were standard for the first three years. Mathematics was intermittently the third subject, with geography, philosophy, and science for upperclassmen interspersed as well. Students were expected to prepare the day's lesson immediately before the recitation. In class they merely recited the expected answers when called upon and were graded accordingly by the tutors. Tutors, or later instructors, conducted most recitations through the junior year, but professors taught the seniors. "Mental discipline," as extolled in the *Yale Reports,* may have been the only benefit of this regimen: the classical authors were read in disjointed excerpts, and the emphasis was on grammar not content; other subjects demanded chiefly rote memorization.

By the junior year not only did the recitation subjects become more interesting but students also attended lectures by the professors. Most science was taught this way during the junior and senior years. The number and variety of lectures depended on the resources of the college—the number of professors and their areas of competence—and thus varied far more than recitations across institutions.

The classical college placed considerable emphasis on writing and speaking, and here students seemed to recognize the importance of developing such skills. Writing exercises were usually based on classical subjects. Sophomores and juniors typically gave "declamations"—histrionic speeches based on classical models; and juniors and seniors engaged in stylized disputations. The most adept students were rewarded with parts in the commencement ceremonies—the culmination of the college experience.

Perhaps the greatest psychological impact of the classical college resulted from its structure rather than the academic course. Each class went through the course of study as a unit, taking the same subjects and participating in the same activities for four years. This in itself engendered strong bonds, but the cumulative effect was more powerful still. The freshman year was something like boot camp, where "newies" were ridiculed and persecuted, especially by the sophomores. The latter, having learned the ropes, became for that year the most rowdy of the classes. Juniors faced the heaviest academic load and behaved somewhat more maturely, in part to distinguish themselves from the overbearing sophomores. "Dignity" is the term most often applied by contemporaries to seniors, who assumed increasing aloofness from the ruckus of campus life as they focused their efforts on elaborate preparations for commencement. Thus despite its shortcomings, the classical college instilled a deep sense of camaraderie, accomplishment, loyalty, and maturity in its graduates. This picture of the classical college best fits institutions in the Northeast and a few southern universities, but elsewhere smaller and poorer denominational colleges largely sought to emulate this model.

LITERATURE AND THE COLLEGES: FACULTY

"Literature" in the early nineteenth century was an inclusive term, not in the least confined to imaginative writings. Samuel Miller in his compendium *A Brief Retrospect of the Eighteenth Century* (1803) devoted a long section to the contributions to the Republic of letters by the United States, a nation "lately become Literary" (2:330–410). By literary he meant virtually all types of writing for an educated audience—philosophy, history, biography, romances and novels, poetry, drama, and the kind of essays that filled literary and political journals. He included colleges in his discussion of literary institutions, and indeed, they were often called "literary seminaries" in this era, chiefly for their association with classical literature, rhetoric, and philosophy but not for any connection with modern literature.

Efforts to secure a place in the curriculum for literature in modern languages were few and far from successful before 1870. The teaching of modern languages was a dismal failure, eventually farmed out to private instructors. In addition, the *Yale Reports* emphatically held that modern languages were inferior to Greek and Latin for instilling mental discipline. Hence, an underlying enthusiasm for literature, broadly construed, was channeled to other outlets.

One early-nineteenth-century attempt to constitute the republic of letters in America was the Anthology Society in Boston, a group of professionals and would-be intellectuals who met regularly and published a monthly review. One Anthology stalwart, John Kirkland (1770–1840), became president of Harvard (1810–1828); a younger recruit, George Ticknor (1791–1871), resolved to become a man of letters. In 1815 Ticknor embarked for Germany to imbibe true scholarship, and the following year Kirkland offered him the first endowed professorship in modern languages at an American college. Ticknor's travails at Harvard illustrate the obstacles facing literature. He chafed under the rigid protocol of the classical college and sought in vain to reform it. He succeeded only in his own domain. He organized the department of modern languages on the basis of proficiency instead of classes, and himself delivered lectures on the history of Spanish literature. When Ticknor retired in 1835 to become an independent man of letters, the Smith Professorship of Modern Languages was filled first by Henry Wadsworth Longfellow (who held the post in 1835–1854) and then by James Russell Lowell (1855–1886), making it a distinguished but isolated outpost for literature in the colleges.

Pioneering attempts to teach English literature lacked such continuity. James Marsh (1794–1842), one of the boldest reformers of the 1820s as president of the University of Vermont (1826–1833), attempted to include English in a new-model curriculum. Only

A nineteenth-century engraving of Harvard College and the Yard. © BETTMANN/CORBIS

in the late 1830s did it appear to have been taught as lectures to juniors, and this practice was intermittently continued. Also in the 1830s, Henry Reed (1808–1854) was appointed professor of English literature at the University of Pennsylvania (1835–1854). Both Marsh and Reed contributed to literary studies. Marsh introduced Samuel Taylor Coleridge's *Aids to Reflection* (1829), which was influential in U.S. literature, to American readers. Reed's collected lectures constitute an impressive body of criticism, although they were only published posthumously (1855). Reed also developed a direct relationship with English letters, befriending and serving as the American agent for William Wordsworth.

If a single theme links Ticknor, Marsh, and Reed it would be Romantic nationalism. These doctrines gave literature a special significance of manifesting the unconscious mind of a people or race. Reed was particularly aggressive in his interpretation of Anglo-Saxonism, and Ticknor leaned heavily on national character to explain French and Spanish literature. Due to such racial roots, Marsh and Reed saw the study of English literature as a fundamentally moral subject that should be taught to collegians in order to connect them with their heritage.

This Romantic impulse seems to have waned after Reed's ship sunk on a return voyage from England in 1854. Instead, the next generation found in philology—historical and comparative linguistics—the justification for studying English in the college course. Philology traces its roots to Johann Gottfried von Herder (1744–1803) and German Romanticism, but it found its way into the college classroom by imitating the classical languages. Francis A. March (1825–1911), who began teaching English at Lafayette College in 1855, set an example by teaching his subject as Greek was taught; that is, giving minute attention to grammar, etymology, and linguistic history but neglecting the meaning of literary works themselves. The transposing of the philological approach to English literature implied a historical focus that seldom advanced beyond William Shakespeare or John Donne. It only reached college classrooms at the end of this era in the teaching of Moses Coit Tyler (1835–1900) at Michigan and Francis Child (1825–1896) at Harvard. Philology better characterizes the professionalization of the discipline after 1870.

LITERATURE AND THE COLLEGE: STUDENTS

In relation to questions of literature, students were left to pursue the interests and activities that most appealed to them on their own initiative. The image that students had of themselves was that of budding gentlemen, a role that implied the capacity to speak eloquently and knowingly on issues of the day and to be conversant with literature—again, broadly understood. But such things were only touched upon obliquely in junior or senior studies. Students needed to cultivate these qualities among themselves.

Their chief means for such self-improvement were the literary societies. These institutions were begun in the colonial colleges and persisted on some campuses into the twentieth century. However, the years of their greatest influence stretched from about 1815 to the Civil War, with the zenith for the Northeast in the 1830s. Although arrangements at each campus were unique, literary societies were a staple of the classical college, officially sanctioned by the institution. Most colleges had two societies, and often every student would belong to one or the other. Competition between the societies was fierce, but largely indirect. Each sought to outperform the other in recruitment, campus recognition, and awards. But the societies focused internally on the intellectual interests of their member students. Before the 1830s, literary societies were virtually the only approved outlet for extracurricular activities; but after that decade, the growth of other outlets, especially fraternities, eroded the campus influence of the societies, at least in the Northeast.

Literary societies were entirely run by students. Besides conducting long business meetings according to parliamentary procedures, their chief activities were to provide a forum for public speaking and to maintain a library. Public speaking included the delivery of orations and the reading of essays, all written by the students themselves, but greatest interest was on conducting formal debates. The debates were heavily focused on current affairs. They gave students the opportunity to express views on the pressing issues of the day, including slavery, tariffs, foreign policy, or preserving the Union. Literary or philosophical questions seem to have been addressed less frequently. However, literary interests were fulfilled instead through the libraries.

The building of library collections was a major effort of most literary societies from 1820 onward. Book purchases often accounted for a substantial part of their expenditures, and they also sought donations. The 1830s and 1840s were the peak for this endeavor in the Northeast, but activity in southern and western societies was unabated until the Civil War. By 1840 society libraries at the older colleges contained more books than the college libraries—and far more useful books as well. College libraries consisted largely of antiquated Latin or theological tomes, and they tended to be open only a few hours per week. The society libraries owned canonical authors and eighteenth-century English writers, but they also purchased contemporary literature. The most popular volumes were the Waverly Scottish border romance novels of Sir Walter Scott (1771–1832). The historian Thomas Harding notes that one society even debated "is the moral and literary influence of the Waverly novels beneficial?" (p. 77). James Fenimore Cooper (1789–1851) and Washington Irving (1783–1859) were the American writers most read, and Lord Byron (1788–1824) captured the imagination of collegians for some time. Overall, novels were the largest holding, although the libraries also had substantial collections of drama, poetry, biography, history, essays, and travel books. The more affluent societies maintained subscriptions to the major literary journals of the United States and Great Britain (*North American Review, Knickerbocker, Blackwood's Magazine, Edinburgh Review*). Without doubt, the libraries were heavily used by students—for leisure reading and to gather material for writings and debates.

The literary societies filled a large lacuna in collegiate education and were so recognized by the colleges. A mirror image of the classroom, the societies were entirely student run, engaged with current affairs, and connected as well with contemporary literature. The societies thus tended to be linked with students' own literary enterprises.

The *Yale Literary Magazine,* founded in 1836, was the first continuous student publication. Previously at Yale and elsewhere, student attempts at literary publications appeared and disappeared, seldom achieving more than a few successive volumes. At Union College in Schenectady, New York, for example, some eleven publications were launched from 1807 to 1854 before the *Unionian* achieved some continuity (1854–1871). The second oldest college literary magazine, the *Nassau Literary Magazine* at Princeton, was begun in 1842. Most of the successful magazines were cooperative efforts between the rival literary societies, a model set by Yale. Their contributions seemed to oscillate between the aspirations of collegians to emulate popular essayists and the attraction of portraying aspects of college life. Since they were independently financed, reader interest seems to have pulled them toward the latter subjects.

The popularity of student literary magazines spread rapidly after 1850 and was only dampened temporarily by the Civil War. One of the most ambitious undertakings, however, was a casualty of the war. In 1859 the *University Quarterly* (originally called the *Undergraduate*) was organized at Yale as a compendium of writings by collegians and professional students throughout the country, and a few studying in Europe. By 1861 it was receiving contributions from "associations" at twenty-eight colleges, mostly in New England, but at least five from the Midwest. The *Quarterly* published four fat issues of essays and campus news reports in 1860 and in 1861 before contributions evaporated with the war. In even so brief a history, the *Quarterly* is testimony to the widespread literary impulse of collegians. Not surprisingly, the impulse revived all the stronger after the war. The 1869 Yale graduate Lyman Bagg estimated that by 1870 more than fifty colleges had regular student publications.

LITERATURE AND THE COLLEGES: AUTHORS

Given the intense student enthusiasm for literature in the classical colleges, how did the colleges affect American literature? The question might be answered in different ways. If one were able to chart the careers of collegiate literati, many would be found who became men of letters in nineteenth-century terms and were recognized as such by contemporaries. For example, consider the three young men most responsible for sustaining the *Nassau Lit* in the 1840s: Theodore L. Cuyler, George H. Boker, and Charles G. Leland. Unknown and unread in the early twenty-first century, Cuyler was a prolific author of books and articles on spiritual themes; Boker wrote two volumes of poems and eleven plays; and Leland wrote widely in a number of areas but became best known for German-dialect ballads. For these writers, and no doubt many others, there was continuity between literary activities in college and subsequent literary pursuits.

The picture changes, however, if one considers the most widely read and enduring American authors. For these figures two patterns stand out: either college had little or no apparent effect on their writings or they are associated with the Harvard-Cambridge milieu. In the first group, Herman Melville, John Greenleaf Whittier, Mark Twain, Walt Whitman, and (much earlier) Washington Irving never attended college. William Cullen Bryant spent one year at Williams, and a young James Fenimore Cooper lasted almost two at Yale before being expelled. In the South, Henry Timrod attended the University of Georgia for a single year, and Edgar Allan Poe did the same at the University of Virginia. Timrod and Poe apparently valued their studies and would have attended longer but for financial constraints. One might add Emily Dickinson, who endured one year of evangelical pressure with the founder Mary Lyon at Mount Holyoke. It would be difficult to generalize from these idiosyncratic talents; but the remarkable fact is the absence of literary talents graduating from all the other classical colleges. Henry Wadsworth Longfellow and Nathaniel Hawthorne are only partial exceptions. They graduated from Bowdoin in the same class (1828), but both fell into the Harvard-Cambridge orbit—Longfellow as a professor and Hawthorne as a resident of nearby Concord.

In contrast, Harvard graduates form a literary pantheon. Ralph Waldo Emerson and Henry David Thoreau promoted transcendentalism from Concord. Oliver Wendell Holmes, James Russell Lowell, and later Henry Adams first distinguished themselves as students. Horatio Alger Jr. was a Harvard graduate (1852), although he wrote his famous rags-to-riches novels after the Civil War. If one lowers the bar somewhat, there are more literary Harvardians like Richard Henry Dana Jr. and Edward Everett Hale. Moreover, judging from their biographies, all these writers seem to have been shaped to some extent by their Harvard experiences, despite its faults. The rigorous writing instruction of longtime rhetoric professor Edward Tyrell Channing has been widely noted. Lowell, although rusticated (sent to the country) his senior year, edited a student literary magazine and was elected class poet. Henry Adams, who claimed in his 1918 *The Education of Henry Adams* that his Harvard education had been worthless, made an exception for his interaction with Professor Lowell; furthermore, he was elected class orator—the highest honor a class could bestow. Clearly Harvard sustained an elevated and sophisticated literary culture. The ambient culture of Boston-Cambridge-Concord was certainly one factor. Another might well be the prevalence of Unitarianism rather than the evangelical Protestantism that prevailed at most other colleges. Also, the presence of Ticknor, Longfellow, and Lowell as Smith Professors of Modern Languages at Harvard recurs as a vital influence.

As a tentative conclusion, it seems that the literary activities of classical colleges tended for the most part to promote the kind of superficial eloquence that flourished in mid- and late-nineteenth-century America. Students, for all their enthusiasm, seldom transcended the conventional taste and thinking of their contemporaries. Harvard did somewhat better through closer contact with European thought, by harboring the nation's largest faculty and by mixing with a rich local culture; that is, Harvard promoted enduring contributions to American literature in spite of clinging to the conventions of a classical college until the end of this era.

See also Classical Literature; Curricula; Education; English Literature; Fireside Poets; Religion; Rhetoric

BIBLIOGRAPHY
Primary Works
Adams, Henry. *The Education of Henry Adams: An Autobiography.* New York: Houghton Mifflin, 1918.

Bagg, Lyman. *Four Years at Yale: By a Graduate of '69.* New Haven, Conn.: Chatfield, 1871.

Looney, J. Jefferson, ed. *College as It Is; or, The Collegian's Manual in 1853.* Princeton, N.J.: Princeton University Libraries, 1996.

Miller, Samuel. *A Brief Retrospect of the Eighteenth Century.* 2 vols. New York: T. and J. Swords, 1803.

Yale College. *Reports on the Course of Instruction in Yale College.* New Haven, Conn.: Howe, 1828.

Secondary Works
Geiger, Roger L. "The Reformation of the Colleges in the Early Republic, 1800–1820." *History of Universities* 16, no. 2 (2001): 129–182.

Geiger, Roger L., ed. *The American College in the Nineteenth Century.* Nashville, Tenn.: Vanderbilt University Press, 2000.

Graff, Gerald. *Professing Literature: An Institutional History.* Chicago: University of Chicago Press, 1987.

Harding, Thomas S. *College Literary Societies: Their Contribution to Higher Education in the United States, 1815–1876.* New York: Pageant Press, 1971.

Schrum, Ethan D. "Henry Reed and the Development of English Studies in Antebellum American Higher Education." Ms. in progress, University of Pennsylvania.

Turner, James. *Language, Religion, Knowledge: Past and Present.* Notre Dame, Ind.: University of Notre Dame Press, 2003.

Tyack, David. *George Ticknor and the Boston Brahmins.* Cambridge, Mass.: Harvard University Press, 1967.

Roger L. Geiger

COMPROMISE OF 1850 AND FUGITIVE SLAVE LAW

The Compromise of 1850 and the Fugitive Slave Law that constituted one of its provisions were controversial federal laws intended to pacify the slaveholding South but that outraged northern abolitionists and ultimately helped provoke the Civil War. The compromise was necessitated by the U.S. annexation of

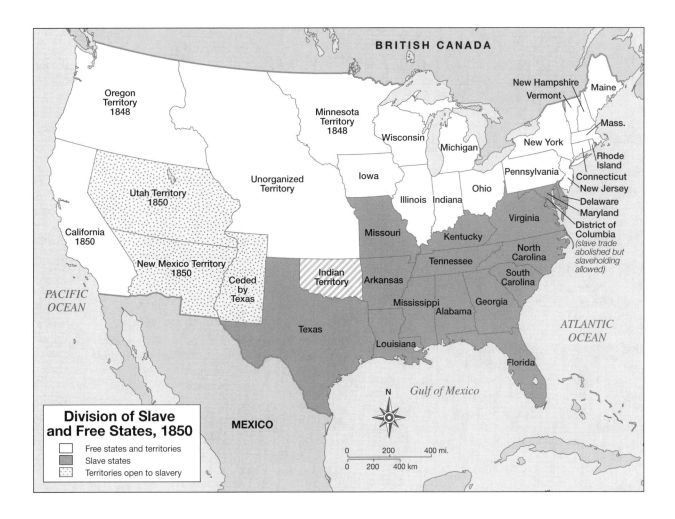

BRITISH CANADA

Oregon
Territory
1848

Minnesota
Territory
1848

Wisconsin

Michigan

New Hampshire
Vermont
Maine

Mass.

New York

Rhode
Island
Connecticut
New Jersey
Delaware
Maryland
District of
Columbia
(slave trade
abolished but
slaveholding
allowed)

Pennsylvania

Utah Territory
1850

Unorganized
Territory

Iowa

Ohio

Illinois Indiana

California
1850

New Mexico Territory
1850

Ceded
by
Texas

Indian
Territory

Missouri

Arkansas

Kentucky

Tennessee

Virginia

North
Carolina

South
Carolina

PACIFIC
OCEAN

Mississippi

Alabama

Georgia

ATLANTIC
OCEAN

Texas

Louisiana

Florida

Gulf of Mexico

N

MEXICO

**Division of Slave
and Free States, 1850**

☐ Free states and territories
■ Slave states
⋮ Territories open to slavery

0   200   400 mi.
0   200   400 km

territory stretching from Texas to California after the Mexican-American War (1846–1848). While this national expansion confirmed the Manifest Destiny ideology that claimed that God intended America to extend "from sea to shining sea," it posed a significant political problem. Since 1820 a precarious balance had been achieved between free (nonslaveholding) and slave states. This balance had been established by the Missouri Compromise, which legislated that slavery would not be allowed to spread above the Mason-Dixon line, roughly equivalent to the 36°30′ parallel, nor would slavery be prevented below it. Ruled by this law, the growth of the nation in the early nineteenth century—including the admission of Missouri and Maine in 1820 and the annexation of Texas in 1845 and the Oregon Territory in 1848—was monitored by a strict division of slavery in the South and freedom in the North. The Compromise of 1820 sought to allow the United States to continue to function as a united nation by satisfying both the North and the South and thus to defer the political and ethical dilemmas posed by the practice of slavery in a nation founded upon the phrase "all men are created equal."

In 1850 the political balance was upset as the number of free states was allowed to exceed the number of slave states. The United States was eager to admit California as a state after the discovery of gold in 1848, but the Wilmot Proviso (1846) prevented slavery anywhere in the new territory gained from Mexico. Thus California could only be admitted as a free state. Southerners viewed the resulting imbalance as a threat to their very way of life; they feared that the federal government would soon be dominated by an antislavery agenda. John C. Calhoun (1782–1850), senator from South Carolina, argued that it was necessary to "satisfy the States belonging to the Southern section that they can remain in the Union consistently with their honor and their safety. . . . Nothing else can, with any certainty, finally and for ever settle the question at issue, terminate agitation, and save the Union" (pp. 559, 572). The Compromise of 1850 sought to pacify the South in several ways. The admission of California was balanced by the fact that the Utah and New Mexico territories were allowed to determine their own free or slave status through popular sovereignty. But the farthest-reaching aspect of the compromise was the inclusion of the Fugitive Slave Law, a law intended to prevent southern unrest but which resulted in outrage and indignation in the North.

FUGITIVE SLAVE LAW

The Fugitive Slave Law was only one element of the Compromise of 1850, but it provoked the most passionate response. The law was intended to placate southern concerns about the spread of antislavery sympathies into the federal government; ironically the public outcry over the law resulted in the abolitionist movement gaining a more prominent political role than it had had previously. The Fugitive Slave Law essentially ruled that fugitive slaves or slaves who had escaped into free northern states were still subject to southern slave laws. They could legally be recaptured and returned to the South as slaves. In other words, the law required northern states, even those that had ruled slavery illegal, to abide by southern laws that declared slavery legal. Moreover, the law contained conspicuously corrupt provisions such as those that denied accused fugitive slaves the right to testify in their own defense or the right to trial by jury. Instead the law appointed commissioners to oversee the trials, who were compensated $5 for freeing a fugitive but $10 for returning one to the South.

Northerners were particularly outraged over the Fugitive Slave Law's ruling that they were required to assist in the capture and return of escaped slaves. In states like Vermont and Massachusetts, which had abolished slavery in the eighteenth century, the idea that their citizens were required by federal law to turn in escaped slaves was repulsive. Northern free blacks were particularly alarmed that the law did not contain allowances for those blacks who were not escaped slaves; blacks who had lived their entire lives as free citizens could easily be captured and "returned" to a slavery they had never before experienced. Thousands of free blacks and fugitive slaves fled to Canada, no longer secure in the protection of the free states. Several northern states witnessed the formation of "vigilance committees" designed to intervene, with violence if necessary, to prevent blacks from being seized by southern slave catchers. The Underground Railroad, a secret alliance of abolitionists who assisted slaves in their flight to freedom, faced greater danger even as the activity on the railroad increased in response to the new law.

REACTIONS AND CONSEQUENCES

Reactions to the Compromise of 1850 and the Fugitive Slave Law exacerbated rather than relieved the growing divisions between the North and the South. In an effort to mollify the South, politicians alienated the North and transformed many whites who had previously considered themselves unaffected by slavery into fervent abolitionists. Abolitionist leaders were outspoken in their condemnation of the law, no one more so than Frederick Douglass (1818–1895), a former slave who had achieved national prominence as the editor of an antislavery newspaper. In the speech "What to the Slave Is the Fourth of July?" (1852), Douglass declared that "slavery has been nationalized in its more horrible and revolting form": "By that act, Mason & Dixon's line has been obliterated; New York has become as Virginia; and the power to hold, hunt, and sell men, women, and children as slaves remains no longer a mere state institution, but is now an institution of the whole United States" (p. 121). After 1850 Douglass began to consider the possibility that the abolition of slavery could only be achieved through the violation of the law. In 1853 Douglass authored *The Heroic Slave*, a fictionalized account of the life of Madison Washington, a slave who led a revolt in 1841 against the slave traders who held him captive. By explaining Washington's motives, Douglass explored the justification behind violent resistance and gave voice to his own frustration over the Fugitive Slave Law.

One northerner strongly affected by the Fugitive Slave Law was Harriet Beecher Stowe (1811–1896). Stowe argued that the law called everyone, even women and children, to act in defense of freedom. Her own response took the form of the novel *Uncle Tom's Cabin* (1851–1852), which portrayed the horrific experiences of slavery in graphic detail. Through the sympathetic slave character Uncle Tom, Stowe sought to sway public opinion against southern slavery. But Stowe did not limit her novel to the South; instead the novel moves equally between North and South, demonstrating how slavery affects the entire nation. Stowe took particular care to depict white northerners like Mary Bird and the Quaker Rachel Halliday, who assist fugitive slaves and consciously violate the Fugitive Slave Law. In the novel, Mrs. Bird argues persuasively that the Fugitive Slave Law is "a shameful, wicked, abominable law, and I'll break it, for one, the first chance. . . . I don't know anything about politics, but I can read my Bible; and there I see that I must feed the hungry, clothe the naked, and comfort the desolate; and that Bible I mean to follow" (p. 144). Through her portraits of these characters, Stowe sought to provide a model of behavior for northern whites, encouraging them to subvert the law in any way that they could. *Uncle Tom's Cabin* was an overnight sensation, selling over 300,000 copies in one year. As the most popular novel of the nineteenth

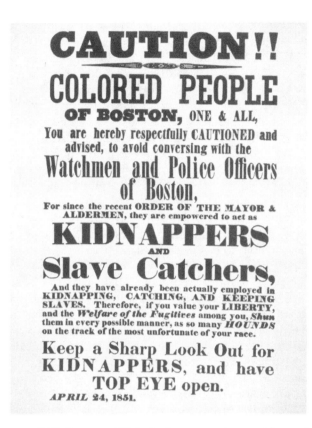

CAUTION!!

COLORED PEOPLE

OF BOSTON, ONE & ALL,

You are hereby respectfully CAUTIONED and advised, to avoid conversing with the

Watchmen and Police Officers of Boston,

For since the recent ORDER OF THE MAYOR & ALDERMEN, they are empowered to act as

KIDNAPPERS

AND

Slave Catchers,

And they have already been actually employed in KIDNAPPING, CATCHING, AND KEEPING SLAVES. Therefore, if you value your LIBERTY, and the *Welfare of the Fugitives* among you, *Shun* them in every possible manner, as so many *HOUNDS* on the track of the most unfortunate of your race.

Keep a Sharp Look Out for KIDNAPPERS, and have TOP EYE open.

APRIL 24, 1851.

Handbill, Boston, 1851. Resistance to the provisions of the Compromise of 1850 concerning the return of fugitive slaves was particularly strong among abolitionists in Boston, who defied the laws and in many cases attempted to prevent officials from apprehending suspected fugitives. THE LIBRARY OF CONGRESS

century, *Uncle Tom's Cabin* influenced countless readers in their opinions about the Fugitive Slave Law and its impact upon slaves seeking freedom.

The consequences of the Fugitive Slave Law were also powerfully captured in slave narratives, autobiographical accounts of the experience of slavery that gained popularity in the nineteenth century. Slave narratives published after 1850 describe how the Fugitive Slave Law affected even slaves who had achieved their freedom. In *Incidents in the Life of a Slave Girl* (1861), Harriet Jacobs (1813–1897) writes that the law unleashed a "reign of terror" over northern blacks: "I lived in a state of anxiety. . . . I was, in fact, a slave in New York, as subject to slave laws as I had been in a Slave State. Strange incongruity in a State called free!" (pp. 147, 150). In *Running a Thousand Miles for Freedom* (1860), William Craft describes how he and his wife Ellen achieved a daring escape: Ellen, who was light skinned, posed as a white, male slave owner,

while William posed as her slave. In this way they traveled from Georgia to Pennsylvania. But their freedom was short-lived because accounts of their escape had made them celebrities, and they were targeted by the slave catchers empowered by the Fugitive Slave Law. The Crafts joined many other prominent black writers and intellectuals who fled to England to escape the constant threat of recapture.

Despite the power and popularity of literary critiques like these, the Compromise of 1850 and the Fugitive Slave Law continued to have long-lasting political effects. The Kansas-Nebraska Act of 1854 further eroded the efficacy of the Mason-Dixon Line by allowing those two territories to decide by popular sovereignty whether or not to allow slavery. Proslavery and antislavery supporters flooded into Kansas to decide the vote, causing a violent conflagration known as "Bleeding Kansas" that resulted in numerous deaths, provoked John Brown's raid upon Harpers Ferry, Virginia, and foreshadowed the coming war. In 1857 the Fugitive Slave Law was put to a legal test during the *Dred Scott* case. Scott was a slave whose owner had moved to Illinois and Wisconsin, where slavery was prohibited. Scott sued, arguing that he and his wife should be considered free due to their residence in free territories. But the U.S. Supreme Court decided against Scott's claim and upheld the premise of the Fugitive Slave Law that even free states were subject to the laws of slavery. The opinion of Roger B. Taney, the chief justice of the Supreme Court, went far beyond the issue of Scott's freedom and declared that blacks were "beings of an inferior order, and altogether unfit to associate with the white race, either in social or political relations; and so far inferior, that they had no rights which the white man was bound to respect; and that the negro might justly and lawfully be reduced to slavery for his benefit" (Lowance, p. 459). The Court declared that blacks were not American citizens and thus not included in the rights declared by the Declaration of Independence: "The general words [all men are created equal] would seem to embrace the whole human family. . . . But it is too clear for dispute, that the enslaved African race were not intended to be included, and formed no part of the people who framed and adopted this declaration" (p. 461). Furthermore, the *Dred Scott* case ruled once and for all that the Missouri Compromise of 1820 was unconstitutional and that no legal limits could be placed upon slavery.

It was in the aftermath of the Compromise of 1850 and the Fugitive Slave Law that Abraham Lincoln made his now famous statement that "a house divided against itself cannot stand." He astutely recognized that in the decade between the Compromise of 1850 and the presidential election of 1860, when Lincoln was elected to the presidency, the nation had become more divided than ever before. The laws that sought to rectify these divisions by allowing slavery to persist and even expand across the nation only worked to cause further antagonism and disagreement. The political legacy of the Compromise of 1850 and the Fugitive Slave Law is arguably the Civil War itself, the final solution to the long question of slavery's place in a free society.

See also Abolitionist Writing; Blacks; Civil War; *Clotel; Incidents in the Life of a Slave Girl;* Slavery; *Uncle Tom's Cabin*

BIBLIOGRAPHY

Primary Works

Calhoun, John C. "Speech on the Slavery Question, 4 March 1850." In *The Works of John C. Calhoun*, vol. 4, edited by Richard K. Crallé, pp. 542–573. New York: D. Appleton, 1853–1856.

Craft, William. *Running a Thousand Miles for Freedom.* 1860. Baton Rouge: Louisiana State University Press, 1999.

Douglass, Frederick. "What to the Slave Is the Fourth of July?" 1852. In *The Oxford Frederick Douglass Reader,* edited by William L. Andrews, pp. 108–130. New York: Oxford University Press, 1996.

Lowance, Mason I., Jr., ed. "Fugitive Slave Law (1850) and *Dred Scott v. Sanford* (1856)." In *A House Divided: The Antebellum Slavery Debates in America, 1776–1865,* pp. 26–30, 458–462. Princeton, N.J.: Princeton University Press, 2003.

Jacobs, Harriet. *Incidents in the Life of a Slave Girl.* 1861. Edited by Nellie Y. McKay and Frances Smith Foster. New York: Norton, 2001.

Stowe, Harriet Beecher. *Uncle Tom's Cabin; or, Life among the Lowly.* 1851–1852. New York: Penguin, 1981.

Secondary Works

Buckmaster, Henrietta. *Let My People Go: The Story of the Underground Railroad and the Growth of the Abolition Movement.* 1941. Columbia: University of South Carolina Press, 1992.

Hamilton, Holman. *Prologue to Conflict: The Crisis and Compromise of 1850.* Lexington: University of Kentucky Press, 1964.

Holt, Michael F. *The Political Crises of the 1850s.* New York: Wiley, 1978.

Sewell, Richard H. *A House Divided: Sectionalism and Civil War, 1848–1865.* Baltimore: Johns Hopkins University Press, 1988.

Desirée Henderson

CONCORD, MASSACHUSETTS

Concord, Massachusetts, less than twenty miles northwest of Boston, is justifiably one of the most famous towns in the United States, if not in the world. It is rare when circumstances align themselves and historical forces converge in a small town to create an event of exceptional historical importance, but just that has occurred on numerous occasions in the long history of Concord. Residents of the town saw at close range the political revolution that founded the country and then the cultural revolution in the decades prior to and immediately following the Civil War that played a large role in defining the sort of country the United States would be. Concord—famous as the ultimate destination of Paul Revere on his midnight ride in April 1775 and as the geographical home of New England transcendentalism—is the ideal American town, more actual than Colonial Williamsburg or Disney's "Main Street, USA" but also subject to a similar sort of nostalgia about small-town life and the quaintness of America's rural past.

PURITANS AND REVOLUTIONARIES: CONCORD'S FOREGROUND

For centuries before the arrival of Europeans, the area known as Concord, but called "Musketaquid" ("marsh-grass river") by the Native Americans, was a prime fishing and hunting ground of the Massachusetts tribe of Algonquins who lived there. It is the place where the Sudbury and Assabet rivers converge to form the Concord River. In the early seventeenth century, the Indians who had prospered for so long in a place rich in fish and wildlife were reduced to a remnant band by low birthrates and disease, especially a devastating outbreak of smallpox in 1633.

Enter Simon Willard (1605–1676), a former soldier and businessman from Kent, who arrived in the Massachusetts Bay Colony in May 1634, settled in Cambridge, and probably spent a good portion of his first year exploring the land to the west of the settlements of Cambridge and Watertown, then the edge of the "civilized" part of the colony. Perhaps he saw in the land some of the qualities that had sustained the Native Americans for so long, but whatever it was that motivated him—and no doubt profit was not too far from the top of the list—Willard approached several wealthy investors to join him, and with them he petitioned the General Court for a new town. The Court granted the petitioners six square miles of land on 3 September 1635.

One of the investors called upon by Simon Willard was the Puritan minister Peter Bulkeley (1583–1659), a wealthy and well-connected graduate of St. John's

The central part of Concord, 1839. Engraving from *Historical Collections of Massachusetts* by John Warner Barber, 1848. THE BRIDGEMAN ART LIBRARY

College, Cambridge, and minister of the parish church in Odell, Bedfordshire. Bulkeley emigrated in 1635, as did the Reverend John Jones (c. 1593-c.1665), also a Cambridge graduate and non-conformist minister from Abbots Ripton, Hants, England. The two ministers joined with Willard in his petition. Newly arrived in a colony wracked by various controversies, including the banishment of Roger Williams (c. 1603–1683) to Rhode Island in the winter of 1635–1636, they were inspired to give the town the hopeful name of Concord. Later, Bulkeley's descendant, Ralph Waldo Emerson (1803– 1882), would prize the non-conformist origins of the town, the first in the colony established above the tidewater, and he would state with some pride that the Puritan history of Concord could be distinguished from that of other settlements by the absence of witch trials, ghost sightings, and the whipping of Quakers through the streets.

During the 1770s Concord became the focal point for a great deal of Revolutionary activity. The town, in voting on 26 September 1774 to raise one or more companies of militia to "Stand at a minutes warning in Case of an alarm," would claim to be the first to use the word "minute" in describing these militiamen. Concord was also the meeting place of the first and second Provincial Congresses from the fall of 1774 through the spring of 1775. These congresses ordered the purchase of supplies that were subsequently stored in the town. The British commander,

General Thomas Gage (1721–1787), dispatched troops on 18 April 1775 to confiscate those supplies and arrest patriot leaders. Informing the countryside, and particularly the rebel stronghold of Concord, became the goal of William Dawes (1745–1799) and Paul Revere (1735–1818), who rode from Boston to warn of the advancing British troops. All of this is memorably versified in Henry Wadsworth Longfellow's (1807–1882) poem "The Midnight Ride of Paul Revere," published in *Tales of a Wayside Inn* in 1863. The opening shot of the battle that ensued on 19 April 1775 between Minute Men and British troops at the North Bridge, on Concord's outskirts, was immortalized by Emerson in his 1837 poem "Concord Hymn" as "the shot heard round the world." In 1904 the novelist Henry James (1843–1882) pronounced the fighting at the North Bridge on that day to be "the hinge . . . on which the large revolving future was to turn" (quoted in Wheeler, p. 131).

MAKING MUCH OF HIS OWN PLACE: EMERSON AND CONCORD

One of those who stood with Major Buttrick and the other Concord Minute Men on 19 April 1775 was their chaplain, the Reverend William Emerson, the grandfather of Ralph Waldo Emerson. William Emerson preached a commemorative sermon on the first anniversary of the battle of Concord and subsequently

CONCORD HYMN

In 1837 Ralph Waldo Emerson's step-grandfather, Dr. Ezra Ripley, gave a small piece of land adjacent to his home, the Concord manse (Hawthorne would later dub it the "Old Manse"), on the condition that the donated land be fenced with heavy stone and that a monument commemorating the battle at the North Bridge on 19 April 1775 be erected by 4 July 1837. On the latter date a celebration was held at the site, featuring the dedication of the commemorative stone obelisk, a speech by the local congressman, Samuel Hoar, and lines "by a citizen of Concord," that is, Ralph Waldo Emerson, sung to the tune of "Old Hundred" by those assembled. Emerson later titled these lines "Concord Hymn." To commemorate the centennial of the battle, the town commissioned one of its own, the young and inexperienced sculptor Daniel Chester French, only twenty-five at the time, to create a statue of the Minute Man. French, now best known as the sculptor of the monumental statue of Abraham Lincoln in the Lincoln Memorial in Washington, D.C. (completed in 1919), was favored by Emerson to be the sculptor for the Minute Man monument. When the Minute Man was unveiled on 19 April 1875, the first stanza of Emerson's hymn, with its famous line characterizing the Americans' first shot as "the shot heard round the world," was engraved on its base.

By the rude bridge that arched the flood,
    Their flag to April's breeze unfurled,
Here once the embattled farmers stood
    And fired the shot heard round the world.

The foe long since in silence slept;
    Alike the conqueror silent sleeps;
And Time the ruined bridge has swept
    Down the dark stream which seaward creeps.

On this green bank, by this soft stream,
    We set to-day a votive stone;
That memory may their deed redeem,
    When, like our sires, our sons are gone.

Spirit, that made those heroes dare
    To die, and leave their children free,
Bid Time and Nature gently spare
    The shaft we raise to them and thee.

Emerson, *Complete Works* 9:158–159.

Emerson attempted without success to locate their grandfather's grave, although there is an impressive brick marker on an empty grave in Concord's Hill Burial Ground. The Emerson family was also related to Peter Bulkeley through the marriage of Joseph Emerson, a baker from Mendon, Massachusetts, to Peter's granddaughter, Elizabeth Bulkeley. So Ralph Waldo Emerson, born in Boston, had a deep ancestral connection to Concord, and while growing up, he often traveled to the village to visit at the Old Manse with his grandmother, Phebe Bliss Emerson, who had married her late husband's successor in the Concord pulpit, Dr. Ezra Ripley. It is really because of Ralph Waldo Emerson's fame as a writer, lecturer, thinker, and reformer, and the attention he brought to the place he thought of as his ancestral home, that the village became a cultural mecca in the nineteenth century. Concord remains a place of spiritual and cultural pilgrimage.

Emerson, whose father, William, had been an influential minister of the First Church (Unitarian) in Boston, and who held the prestigious pulpit of the Second Church himself from 1829 to 1832, was thrown into a spiritual and vocational crisis by a series of events that began with the death of his young wife, Ellen Tucker Emerson, in February 1831. This soon led to his resignation from the Second Church and a trip to western Europe to, in part, work out his crisis of vocation. When he returned from Europe, declaring on the ship back that his goal in life was to be naturalist, Emerson began to make plans to move his mother and himself to Concord. Perhaps his search for a useable past in his ancestral home and his move there in October 1834 were part of his vocational crisis. In any case, the move to Concord seemed to contribute to Emerson's successful transition to a life as a lecturer, writer, and public intellectual.

The first fruit of this transition was the address Emerson delivered and subsequently published on the history of Concord, "A Historical Discourse, Delivered to the Citizens of Concord, 12th September, 1835." The occasion of that address was an opportunity for Emerson to merge personal history with the history of the town, thus creating an identification between himself and his ancestral home that exists to this day. Moreover, the address allowed Emerson, at the outset of his career as a public intellectual, to define an ideal of action based on principle that he recognized in those involved in what he called those "two great epochs of public principle, the Planting and the Revolution of the colony" ("Historical Discourse at Concord," p. 85). The speech may also have been Emerson's first reading of national history, and perhaps

died from fever in Rutland, Vermont, on his way home from Fort Ticonderoga in 1776. In 1831 his grandsons Ralph Waldo Emerson and Charles Chauncy by implication all history, in terms of the individual, a theme that Emerson would work and rework throughout his career.

The importance of Concord as a sort of symbolic base for Emerson's identity is hinted at in his correspondence with Lydia Jackson, the young woman from Plymouth, Massachusetts, whom he planned to marry in September 1835. Less than a year after moving to Concord, Emerson wrote to Lydia regarding her preference to live in Plymouth, close to her own family and friends, after their nuptials. He argued that his removal from Concord "would cripple me of some important resources," and later, in a journal entry, he associated his ancestral home with the resources that inspired the great poets of history: "Make much of your own place. The stars & celestial awning that overhang our simple Concord walks & discourses are as brave as those that were visible to Coleridge as he talked or Dryden or Ben Jonson & Shakspear or Chaucer & Petrarch & Boccac[c]io when they met" (*Journals and Miscellaneous Notebooks* 5:83).

Emerson did make much of his own place. In the months after his move to Concord he and his mother lived as guests of his grandparents at the Old Manse, but his proposal to Lydia Jackson and the new circumstances it presented required new accommodations, so he bought a house built by Charles Coolidge in 1828 where the Cambridge Turnpike branched off from the Lexington Road, less than half a mile from the town center. The Emersons sometimes called it the Coolidge House or Coolidge Castle. There Emerson entertained the great and near-great, raised a family, dutifully kept his journal and wrote his books, and there he returned after all of the speaking tours that saw him deliver approximately fifteen hundred lectures from the 1830s until 1881. Concord itself provided plenty of opportunity for Emerson's talents as a lecturer. The Concord Lyceum, founded in 1828 as an outgrowth of the Concord Academy's Friday declamations, hosted ninety-eight lectures by Emerson alone and nineteen more by Henry David Thoreau (1817–1862). Among those who also lectured there were the Harvard scientist Louis Agassiz; members of Emerson's transcendentalist circle, including Orestes Brownson, Theodore Parker, and Jones Very; and authors such as Richard Henry Dana Jr., Oliver Wendell Holmes, and James Russell Lowell.

THOREAU'S COUNTRY

Emerson universalized the town, making it more important as symbol than as specific place, but Thoreau believed that the particulars of the place mattered, and by writing about Concord as a particular place he universalized it for the world in ways that Emerson could not. Thoreau may have had even more claim to an identification with Concord than his benefactor, one-time mentor, and sometime friend Emerson did; he was the only "Concord writer" who was actually a native of the town. He was born there on 12 July 1817 and was educated first in Concord's public schools and then, beginning in 1828, at the prestigious Concord Academy. This was a financial sacrifice for his father, who supported the family with a Concord-based pencil-making business. The town school committee subsequently hired Thoreau to teach in the public school when he graduated from Harvard in 1837. When he resigned from that position later that year, he and his brother John opened a private school in the vacant Concord Academy building that operated until John's sudden death from tetanus in 1842.

Thoreau rarely left the Concord area during his short life. In the spring of 1843, Emerson arranged for Thoreau to live with his brother William Emerson on Staten Island and tutor his children, an experiment that lasted just six months because of Thoreau's chronic homesickness. His subsequent trips away from home—the most extended were to Canada and then, near the end of his life, to Minnesota—were comparatively much shorter. Thoreau's parochial preference for Concord and his unquestionable identification with it caused Emerson to complain of his lack of cosmopolitanism in his 1862 eulogy and to suggest that Thoreau might have had difficulty with those whose views he found unacceptable because they were not born in Concord but had the "unspeakable misfortune to be born in London, or Paris, or Rome."

Perhaps Thoreau's attachment to his hometown was in part the result of his intimate knowledge of it, which was only enhanced by his work as a surveyor in the area. While keeping school in 1840 he purchased surveying equipment in order to make lessons in mathematics more practical for his students, but eventually surveying became a relatively steady source of income for him.

The most famous incidents of Thoreau's life, and the writings associated with them, are, like the man himself, inextricably linked to Concord. In March 1845 Thoreau's friend and fellow Concord resident William Ellery Channing II (1817–1901), known as Ellery Channing, wrote to Thoreau from New York City to suggest that he build himself a hut at Walden Pond on the outskirts of Concord and begin the process of devouring himself alive. Since Emerson had, just the preceding fall, bought a number of acres on the shores of the sixty-one-acre pond for a woodlot, and since it would be some time before the largely denuded acreage, heavily cut by a previous owner, would serve its intended purpose for Emerson, he allowed Thoreau to squat there. Thoreau began almost immediately to prepare the house site, built his famous hut for the grand sum of $28.50, and moved there on 4 July 1845. He lived there rather famously on twenty-seven cents a week until 6 September 1847, leaving to take up residence in Emerson's house in the village, while his benefactor was off on an extended European lecture tour. While at the pond Thoreau finished his first book, *A Week on the Concord and Merrimack Rivers* (1849); took his first trip to the wilderness of Maine, climbed Mt. Katahdin, and wrote an essay about it; and wrote much of the first draft of his most famous book, *Walden,* which was eventually published in 1854. *Walden* is a book that identifies the most rewarding way to live with a space beyond the village limits of Concord; in his short chapter on "The Village" he depicts the town as the site of a kind of torture, a place from which to escape to the vastness and freedom of the woods. A much more positive view of the village and its material development can be found in the writings of one of Thoreau's Concord contemporaries, Edward Jarvis (1803–1884). Robert A. Gross has identified Jarvis's *Traditions and Reminiscences of Concord* as "a massive refutation of *Walden*'s jeremiad on the division of labor and its dehumanization of Thoreau's townsmen" ("The Most Estimable Place," p. 6).

In July 1846, while living at the pond, Thoreau was arrested on the main street of Concord by the town tax collector, constable, and jailer, Sam Staples. Staples apparently asked Thoreau when he would pay his poll tax and even offered to pay it for him. Thoreau, however, said that he did not plan to pay it as a matter of principle, not wishing to support a government that condoned slavery, and he was led off to the jail. Late that evening, while Thoreau languished, drinking the hot chocolate provided by Staples, someone paid his tax very much against his desires and, by the next afternoon, he was off to the Concord countryside to pick huckleberries. Thoreau later delivered a two-part lecture on the incident at the Concord Lyceum, which was subsequently published as "Resistance to Civil Government" in 1849. Perhaps better known by the title it was given after Thoreau's death, "Civil Disobedience," this essay that one might say originated in the Concord jail has had a profound impact on national and world history through its influence on Mohandas K. Gandhi (1869–1948), who led the movement to free India from British colonial rule, and Dr. Martin Luther King Jr. (1929–1968), the leader of the movement for civil rights for African Americans. As for Thoreau's "persecutor," apparently

arresting the town troublemaker had no negative effect on Sam Staples, who was so popular with his fellow Concordians that he was elected to the state legislature in 1847.

Of course, the origins of "Civil Disobedience" also point up the importance of reform in nineteenth-century Concord. Thoreau himself is thought to have provided sanctuary for escaped slaves as part of the Underground Railroad. His mother and sisters, along with female members of the Emerson and Alcott households, among many others, were prominent in the Concord Female Antislavery Society, one of the most active such societies. The militant abolitionist John Brown (1800–1859) visited Concord twice. In March 1857 he met with Emerson, Thoreau, Franklin Benjamin Sanborn (1831–1917), and Ellery Channing. During a lecture at the Concord Town Hall, Brown showed a Bowie knife he had taken from a Missouri border ruffian. He returned to Concord in May 1859, just five months before his ill-fated raid on the federal arsenal at Harpers Ferry. Thoreau spoke in Brown's defense at a public meeting that he called on 30 October 1859 at Town Hall, ringing the bell himself when the town's selectmen refused to announce the meeting, and on 2 December 1859, the day Brown was hanged, Thoreau conducted a memorial service for Brown in Concord. To suggest that Thoreau was taking a chance with his advocacy for Brown, and to show that Concord was not the safe haven it might appear to us to have been, deputies of the U.S. Senate were dispatched there in April 1860 to arrest Sanborn and take him to Washington, D.C., where he, as one of Brown's confidantes, would be required to testify. A crowd that included Emerson and other prominent citizens of the town physically stopped the marshals from taking Sanborn. The next day a favorable court decision relieved Sanborn from being compelled to testify.

THE EMERSONIAN CIRCLE

Emerson's presence in Concord from 1834 onward and his increasing fame drew many people to the town. Amos Bronson Alcott (1799–1888) enjoyed the friendship and moral support (and sometimes the financial aid) of Emerson from their initial meeting in the summer of 1835. Alcott moved to Concord with his wife and three daughters after a number of failed attempts to keep experimental schools in Connecticut, Philadelphia, and Boston. His plan was to support his family through farming, but Alcott was never really able to provide sufficiently for his household. That task eventually fell to his daughter Louisa May Alcott (1832–1888) once her own career as a writer and editor of children's literature, author of anonymous blood-and-thunder tales for the pulp magazines, and writer of best-sellers like *Little Women* (1868–1869) began to take off. The Alcotts lived at "Hillside" (Hawthorne later renamed it "The Wayside")—bought for them by the family of Alcott's wife, Abba May, and kept in her name to protect it and the family's welfare from Alcott's many creditors—from 1845 until 1852. From 1858 until 1877, the family lived at Orchard House. It was there that Louisa May Alcott wrote *Little Women,* and it was there, in 1879, that her father, prompted by a visit from William Torrey Harris (1835–1909), editor of the *Journal of Speculative Philosophy,* founded the Concord School of Philosophy, devoted to discussion of transcendental philosophy, when he sponsored a five-week session of conversations at Orchard House. A second session of the school was held at the Hillside Chapel, next to Alcott's home. The fourth session in 1882 was momentous because it followed the death of Emerson by only a few months and marked the last time Alcott himself would lecture, since he suffered a paralytic stroke only a few months after the session. A total of nine sessions of the school were held between 1879 and the year of Alcott's death, 1888.

Nathaniel Hawthorne (1804–1864) bought what he called the Wayside from the Alcotts in 1852. He lived there briefly with his family before leaving for an extended stay in Europe from 1853 until 1860. From 1860 until Hawthorne's death, the Hawthorne family lived in Concord, next-door neighbors to the Alcotts. But Hawthorne's initial stay in Concord had come much earlier. After he and Sophia Peabody (1809–1871) were married at the bookstore of Sophia's sister, the editor and transcendentalist Elizabeth Palmer Peabody (1804–1894), in Boston on 9 July 1842, they drove the same day to Concord to begin what would be a happy three years' residence at the Old Manse. When Emerson lived there in 1834 and 1835, he finished the first draft of his first book, *Nature* (1836), in the upstairs study. Hawthorne, who was actually the first to call the house the "Old Manse," meaning a minister's home, wrote a great deal about the house and surrounding countryside in his journals and in the collection of stories, *Mosses from an Old Manse,* which he published in 1846. The Manse may be the only place in the United States, or perhaps anywhere, where two different writers penned part of their literary masterpieces in the same room.

Of course visitors like Margaret Fuller (1810–1850) and other transcendentalists were commonplace in Concord in the 1840s and 1850s. Ellery Channing, who was married to Fuller's sister, Ellen, lived in Concord for seven years, beginning in 1846, during which time he became Thoreau's walking companion and closest friend. After the death of his wife in September 1856, Channing moved back to Concord permanently. His poetry may best be characterized by Thoreau's pronouncement that he was "all genius, not talent." Channing's life, at the end, is oddly intertwined with that of another Concordian, Franklin Benjamin Sanborn, who in 1891 took in the elderly and indigent Channing as a houseguest in order to record and collect his reminiscences of Thoreau and Emerson. Sanborn had first visited Concord in 1854 as a Harvard student, when he came to call on Emerson. A few months later he moved to the town permanently after being invited to take over the school once kept by Henry and John Thoreau. Eventually Sanborn became a prominent editor and biographer of the transcendentalists, but he deserves as much or more notice for his work as a pioneer of social science. He established the first college course in social science at Cornell University, where he was a special lecturer from 1885 until 1888. He was also instrumental in getting Annie Sullivan (1866–1936), who later became famous as "the miracle worker" who taught Helen Keller (1880–1968), into the Perkins Institute for the Blind.

Given its geographical location and its important role in American culture, Concord has continued to be a place associated with genius and with controversy. Some of that controversy over proposed development in the area near Walden Pond is admirably reported in W. Barksdale Maynard's *Walden Pond: A History.* Concord also remains very much a place of pilgrimage. One such pilgrimage is described in John Hanson Mitchell's *Walking toward Walden: A Pilgrimage in Search of Place* (1995), the story of a fifteen-mile hike taken by Mitchell and two friends in October 1994 through the woods around Concord to Authors' Ridge in Sleepy Hollow Cemetery, where Thoreaus, Emersons, Hawthornes, and Alcotts are buried. The book is a meditation on history and change, the meaning of place, and the way in which these Concord writers continue to speak to us so long after they lived. It is a book that eloquently represents and explicitly states the meaning of Concord. Mitchell writes,

> Concord is America's metaphor for itself, an epicenter, a quintessential place, a vision, a dream, an imaginary landscape in which ideas converge, and then break up and spread into the world beyond. To go there is to be swept into a vortex, to be part of a great circle of time in which past is present and present is future. (Pp. 6–7)

See also Harpers Ferry; *Little Women;* Lyceums; "Resistance to Civil Government"; Transcendentalism; Unitarians; Utopian Communities; *Walden*

BIBLIOGRAPHY

Primary Works

Emerson, Ralph Waldo. *The Complete Works of Ralph Waldo Emerson.* 12 vols. Edited by Edward Waldo Emerson. Boston: Houghton Mifflin, 1903–1904.

Emerson, Edward Waldo. *Emerson in Concord: A Memoir.* Boston and New York: Houghton Mifflin, 1889.

Emerson, Ralph Waldo. "A Historical Discourse, Delivered Before the Citizens of Concord, 12th September, 1835. On the Second Centennial Anniversary of the Incorporation of the Town." Concord: G. F. Bemis, 1835. Reprinted as "Historical Discourse at Concord," in *Complete Works,* 11:27–86.

Emerson, Ralph Waldo. *The Journals and Miscellaneous Notebooks of Ralph Waldo Emerson.* 16 vols. Edited by William H. Gilman, et al. Cambridge, Mass.: Harvard University Press, 1960–1982.

Jarvis, Edward. *Traditions and Reminiscences of Concord, Massachusetts, 1779–1878.* Edited by Sarah Chapin. Amherst: University of Massachusetts Press, 1993.

Shattuck, Lemuel. *A History of the Town of Concord: Middlesex County, Massachusetts, From Its Earliest Settlement to 1832.* Boston: Russell, Odiorne, 1835.

Secondary Works

Burkholder, Robert E. "Emerson and the West: Concord, the *Historical Discourse,* and Beyond." *Nineteenth Century Studies* 4 (1990): 93–103.

Concord Free Public Library. "'Earth's Eye': An Online Exhibition of Walden Pond Images." http://www.concordnet.org/library/scollect/Walden/Walden.htm.

Concord Free Public Library. "Emerson in Concord: An Exhibition in Celebration of the 200th Anniversary of the Birth of Ralph Waldo Emerson." http://www.concordnet.org/library/scollect/Emerson_Celebration/Opening_page.htm.

Concord Free Public Library. "Henry Thoreau Land and Property Surveys." http://www.concordnet.org/library/scollect/Thoreau_surveys/Thoreau_surveys.htm.

Foster, David R. *Thoreau's Country: Journey through a Transformed Landscape.* Cambridge, Mass.: Harvard University Press, 1999.

Gross, Robert A. "Commemorating Concord." *Common-Place* 4 (October 2003). Available at http://www.common-place.org/vol-04/no-01/gross/.

Gross, Robert A. *The Minutemen and Their World.* New York: Hill and Wang, 1976.

Gross, Robert A. "'The Most Estimable Place in All the World': A Debate on Progress in Nineteenth-Century Concord." In *Studies in the American Renaissance,* edited by Joel Myerson. Boston: Twayne, 1978.

Gross, Robert A. "Transcendentalism and Urbanism: Concord, Boston, and the Wider World." *Journal of American Studies* 18 (1984): 361–381.

Maynard, W. Barksdale. *Walden Pond: A History.* New York: Oxford University Press, 2004.

Mitchell, John Hanson. *Walking towards Walden: A Pilgrimage in Search of Place.* Reading, Mass.: Addison-Wesley, 1995.

Nadenicek, Daniel Joseph. "Sleepy Hollow Cemetery: Philosophy Made Substance." *Emerson Society Papers* 5 (spring 1994): 1–2, 8.

Neufeldt, Leonard N. "'The Fields of My Fathers' and Emerson's Literary Vocation." *American Transcendental Quarterly,* no. 31 (summer 1970): supplement, pp. 3–9.

Petrulionis, Sandra Harbert. "'Swelling That Great Tide of Humanity': The Concord, Massachusetts, Female Anti-Slavery Society." *New England Quarterly* 74 (September 2001): 385–418.

Scudder, Townsend. *Concord: American Town.* Boston: Little, Brown, 1947.

Wheeler, Ruth Winifred Robinson. *Concord: Climate for Freedom.* Concord, Mass.: Concord Antiquarian Society, 1967.

Robert E. Burkholder

THE CONFESSIONS OF NAT TURNER

On 21 August 1831 the black minister Nat Turner (1800–1831) raised a brief but bloody slave insurrection in Southampton County, Virginia. In about two days' time, Turner and a small band of slaves and free blacks killed fifty-five white people, including many women and children. Hundreds of local militiamen and vigilantes from Virginia and nearby North Carolina responded to crush the insurrection, killing many of the participants plus dozens of innocent blacks. Surviving participants were captured and tried immediately; many were sentenced to death, with the exception of Turner, who evaded capture for two months. He was eventually found and then executed on 11 November 1831.

THE *CONFESSIONS*: BACKGROUND AND CONTENT

While Turner waited in a jail cell for his perfunctory trial, Thomas R. Gray (d. 1845), an attorney, visited him and recorded his account of the insurrection. Gray entered Turner's confession as evidence at his trial and then published the account as a pamphlet after his execution. Although numerous personal and newspaper accounts of the insurrection survive, Gray's pamphlet is the only document that purports to record Turner's first-person account of the reasons for and the events of the insurrection. Thus Gray's account has often been accepted as the most authentic description of the insurrection.

But authenticity in this case is a complex issue. As a slaveholder and a resident of Southampton County, Gray had no reason to present an objective depiction of Turner or his motives for raising the insurrection. On the contrary, Gray appears to portray Turner in a way calculated both to mitigate the insurrection's impact and to sell numerous copies of the pamphlet. He overtly characterizes Turner as a "gloomy fanatic" (p. 304), and he argues that the insurrection was an isolated event solely instigated by Turner's religious fanaticism and thus not a response to slavery as an institution. Gray contends that his own reason for making Turner's narrative public is to allay fears that another insurrection may occur in the immediate future, ameliorating the "greatly excited public mind" (p. 303).

To relate Turner's confession, Gray takes an unusual rhetorical position. He claims that, "without being questioned at all, [Turner] commenced his narrative in the following words" (p. 306). This statement implies, first, that Turner gave his story freely and honestly and, second, that Gray transcribed Turner's story verbatim, suggesting that he acted solely as an amanuensis. But the text of the confession suggests that neither of these qualifications is accurate. While nothing about the narrative suggests that Gray coerced Turner into telling his story, Gray structures the narrative to emphasize Turner's religious convictions and the insurrection's vindictive violence, portraying Turner as fanatical and bloodthirsty. Also, the voice Gray represents as Turner's speaks not as an uneducated slave would but as an educated lawyer would. For example, the first line supposedly in Turner's voice reads, "Sir—you have asked me to give a history of the motives which induced me to undertake the late insurrection, as you call it" (p. 306). The disconnect here between the voice purportedly speaking and the language used destabilizes the pamphlet's claim to authenticity.

Yet even if not credibly authentic, Gray's pamphlet represents Turner provocatively. Rather than simply recounting the events of the insurrection, the narrative delves into Turner's character, beginning with a rendering of events from his childhood that, in Gray's account, led him to believe that he had a gift for prophecy. Gray records Turner as describing himself as uncommonly intelligent. He claims to have learned to read with no assistance, and he says that religion "principally occupied my thoughts" (p. 307). He also says that he had a natural talent for planning and leadership, so that, even when he was a child, the other black children expected him to plan their "roguery" because of his "superior judgment" (p. 307).

When he grew older, according to Gray's depiction, Turner determined that he should live as an ascetic, separating himself from society and fasting and praying. One day, he claims to have heard the voice of "the spirit that spoke to prophets in former days" (p. 308). He felt himself to be "ordained for some great purpose" (p. 308), and he began to minister to blacks in the community. On one occasion, he escaped from his overseer for thirty days but surprised the other slaves and ostensibly proved his faith by returning voluntarily. After his return he heard voices, saw visions, and found supernatural signs with more frequency. He shocked the community at one time by baptizing a white man, Ethelred T. Brantley.

Turner's ministry culminated in a vision he claims to have seen on 12 May 1828. Gray records him as saying, "The Spirit instantly appeared to me and said the Serpent was loosened, and Christ had laid down the yoke he had borne for the sins of men, and that I should take it on and fight against the Serpent, for the time was fast approaching when the first should be last and last should be first" (p. 310). In the narrative, Gray asks Turner if he feels that he was mistaken about his vision, to which Turner replies enigmatically, "Was not Christ crucified?" (p. 310). A solar eclipse in 1830 convinced Turner that the time had come when he should fight against the serpent, presumably white slaveholders.

To accomplish his mission, Turner tells Gray he took four other slaves into his confidence, and they planned to commence their murderous work at the home of Turner's master, Joseph Travis. They stipulated that "until we had armed and equipped ourselves, and gathered sufficient force, neither age nor sex was to be spared" (p. 311). At the Travis family home, Turner and his men murdered the family, "five in number" (p. 311), in their beds, including Putnam Moore, Travis's apprentice and Turner's legal owner. Gray highlights two events in the account of the events at the Travis home that portray Turner as both impotent and bloodthirsty. First, Turner was incapable of killing Mr. Travis, and second, after forgetting to kill a sleeping infant, Turner sent one of his followers back into the home to kill it. After murdering the

THE

CONFESSIONS

OF

NAT TURNER,

THE LEADER OF THE LATE

INSURRECTION IN SOUTHAMPTON, VA.

As fully and voluntarily made to

THOMAS R. GRAY,

In the prison where he was confined, and acknowledged by
him to be such when read before the Court of Southampton; with the certificate, under seal of
the Court convened at Jerusalem,
Nov. 5, 1831, for his trial.

ALSO, AN AUTHENTIC

ACCOUNT OF THE WHOLE INSURRECTION,

WITH LISTS OF THE WHITES WHO WERE MURDERED,

AND OF THE NEGROES BROUGHT BEFORE THE COURT OF
SOUTHAMPTON, AND THERE SENTENCED, &c.

Baltimore:

PUBLISHED BY THOMAS R. GRAY.

Lucas & Deaver, print.

1831.

Title page of the original edition of *The Confessions of Nat Turner.* CLEMENTS LIBRARY, UNIVERSITY OF MICHIGAN

Travis family, Turner and his followers repeated the process at several other homes, gathering recruits, horses, and weapons. At the height of the insurrection, Turner's followers numbered more than fifty armed men, most on horseback. While his followers killed as many as fifty-five white people, Turner himself killed only one person, Margaret Whitehead, a young girl.

By the afternoon of 22 August, the insurrection was discovered and a general alarm sounded. An initial skirmish with hastily assembled militiamen dispersed many of Turner's followers. He and the remaining force retreated to an abandoned homestead under cover of darkness. At daybreak, a larger militia force attacked, killing or capturing Turner's remaining followers. Only Turner managed to escape. For more than two months he hid in various locations near the Travis home, until discovered by Benjamin Phipps on 31 October and delivered to the authorities for trial.

NAT TURNER'S REBELLION AND THE SLAVE DEBATE

After relating Turner's account of the insurrection, Gray describes his own apprehension of him in terms that demonstrate the insurrection's effect on slaveholders and betrays Gray's personal attitude toward Turner: "The calm, deliberate composure with which he spoke of his late deeds and intentions, the expression of his fiend-like face when excited by enthusiasm, still bearing the stains of the blood of helpless innocence about him; clothed with rags and covered with chains; yet daring to raise his manacled hands to heaven, with a spirit soaring above the attributes of man; I looked on him and my blood curdled in my veins" (p. 317). Gray's visceral reaction to Turner suggests the panic the insurrection caused among whites throughout the slaveholding areas of the United States.

The response to Turner's insurrection reveals the complexity of slavery in American history. Immediately, a wave of violent hysteria gripped the region as hundreds of whites directed their outrage at innocent blacks. The extent of the panic may be glimpsed in *Incidents in the Life of a Slave Girl* (1861) by Harriet Jacobs (1813–1897), in which a white mob searches Jacobs's grandmother's home. As a result of the insurrection, the Virginia legislature debated a bill to abolish slavery out of respect for public safety, but the measure failed. Instead, virtually every slaveholding state soon passed repressive laws forbidding slaves to meet for religious purposes or to be educated. Turner's insurrection was the only successful slave rebellion in the United States—two other rebellions, planned by Gabriel Prosser and Denmark Vesey,

respectively, were discovered before they began—but American slaveholders were aware of the Haitian revolution of 1791 during which slaves massacred their white masters and assumed control of the national government. The Haitian revolution instilled a deep paranoia in American slaveholders, which Turner's insurrection actualized.

Turner's insurrection occurred at a critical moment for the growing abolitionist movement in the United States. David Walker's (1785–1830) *Appeal,* a militant pamphlet urging slaves to overthrow their masters, had appeared in 1829. A few months before the insurrection, William Lloyd Garrison (1805–1879) had begun publishing *The Liberator,* a radical abolitionist newspaper. The insurrection lent credibility to the nascent abolitionist movement's claim that slaves desired liberty as much as any other Americans. Between 1831 and 1861 tension between slaveholding states and anti-slaveholding states escalated, reaching a climax with John Brown's raid on the U.S. armory at Harpers Ferry, Virginia (now West Virginia), in October 1859. Influenced by Turner's insurrection, Brown intended to use the weapons in the armory to outfit a mass rebellion of American slaves against their masters.

For many fugitive slaves and other members of the abolitionist movement, Turner became a hero. For example, William Wells Brown (c. 1814–1884), a fugitive slave and author of *Clotel* (1853), the first novel published by an African American, described Nat Turner in messianic terms in his history of prominent African Americans, *The Black Man* (1863). Turner's insurrection also inspired several nineteenth-century novels, including Harriet Beecher Stowe's (1811–1896) *Dred: A Tale of the Great Dismal Swamp* (1856). Unlike the submissive Uncle Tom of her earlier novel, Dred defies white slaveholders by escaping his master and plotting an insurrection. The plot is eventually discovered and aborted, but the character Dred prophesies imminent dissolution, presaging the Civil War. Literary portrayals of Turner ranged from mythic and heroic to deranged and monstrous, reflecting the various sentiments of the individual writers toward either slavery in particular or African Americans in general.

MODERNIST PORTRAYALS

Although Turner figured prominently in popular discourse in the nineteenth century, he fell into relative obscurity until 1967. In that year, as the civil rights movement moved into a more militant phase, two radically different portrayals of Turner emerged. In *Ol' Prophet Nat,* Daniel Panger adopted Turner's voice to describe slavery as a moral outrage and to explain the inherent urge to freedom in terms that echoed integrationist rhetoric. In *The Confessions of Nat Turner*, William Styron adopted Turner's voice to probe Turner's psychology, attempting through fiction to understand what caused one specific slave out of millions to attempt an insurrection. Styron thus depicted Turner as manic and sexually obsessed with the girl he killed, Margaret Whitehead. Styron's book became a critical success—winning the Pulitzer Prize for fiction in 1968—and a source of great controversy. Many black intellectuals resented that Styron, a white southerner, presumed to understand a black man's psyche; even more, they resented the implication that a historical event represented as an act of black heroism could be portrayed as a glorified act of sexual aggression against white women. These and other objections were articulated in the 1968 collection *William Styron's Nat Turner: Ten Black Writers Respond*. Curiously, while the essays in this collection attack Turner's characterization, the editors included Gray's account as an appendix.

The conflicting representations of Turner may in fact be a product of Gray's account of Turner's confessions. Gray set a precedent of adopting Turner's voice to serve his own complex purposes. Since no direct, unmitigated first-person account of Turner's motives and his role in the insurrection exists, his actual purpose remains open to conjecture.

See also Abolitionist Writing; *An Appeal in Favor of That Class of Americans Called Africans;* Crime and Punishment; History; Slave Rebellions; Slavery

BIBLIOGRAPHY

Primary Works
Bouvé, Pauline Carrington Rust. *Their Shadows Before*. Boston: Small, Maynard, 1899.

Brown, William Wells. *The Black Man: His Antecedents, His Genius, and His Achievements*. 1863. New York: Kraus Reprint, 1969.

Edmonds, Randolph. *"The Nat Turner Story": Six Plays for a Negro Theater*. Boston: Walter H. Baker, 1934.

Gray, Thomas R. *The Confessions of Nat Turner*. 1831. In *The Southampton Slave Revolt of 1831: A Compilation of Source Material,* edited by Henry I Tragle. Amherst: University of Massachusetts Press, 1971.

James, G. P. R. *The Old Dominion; or, The Southampton Massacre*. 1856. London: G. Routledge and Sons, 1903.

Panger, Daniel. *Ol' Prophet Nat*. Winston-Salem, N.C.: J. F. Blair, 1967.

Stowe, Harriet Beecher. *Dred: A Tale of the Great Dismal Swamp*. 1856. New York: Penguin, 2000.

Styron, William. *The Confessions of Nat Turner*. New York: Random House, 1967.

Tieran, Mary Spear. *Homoselle*. Boston: J. R. Osgood, 1881.

Secondary Works
Burnett, Charles, director. *A Troublesome Property*. Film. San Francisco: California Newsreel, 2002.

Davis, Mary Kemp. *Nat Turner before the Bar of Judgment*. Baton Rouge: Louisiana State University Press, 1999.

French, Scot. *The Rebellious Slave: Nat Turner in American Memory*. New York: Houghton Mifflin, 2004.

Genovese, Eugene D. *From Rebellion to Revolution: Afro-American Slave Revolts and the Making of the Modern World*. Baton Rouge: Louisiana State University Press, 1979.

David A. Davis

THE CONFIDENCE-MAN

Some literary critics have reckoned Herman Melville's (1819–1891) *The Confidence-Man: His Masquerade* (1857) the author's "second best" book, after *Moby-Dick* (1851); it is certainly one of his most provocative and problematic. *The Confidence-Man* bears little resemblance to Melville's sea epic, at any rate. Unlike Ishmael, the third-person narrator is detached and almost antiseptically cryptic. Except for those three chapters (14, 33, and 44) where he steps outside of his narrative to address the reader directly, the narrator retires behind his "smoky" prose, deals in cunning ambiguities and double purposes, and offers his readers precious little help in untangling the snarled intricacies of his highly episodic narrative. One knows that the story takes place on April Fools' Day on a Mississippi riverboat named the *Fidèle* somewhere above Cairo, Illinois. One knows as well that the boat stops occasionally to discharge and take on a wide array of passengers and that in an oddly disorganized way these travelers constitute a diverse sampling of that "multiform pilgrim species, man" (p. 9). Beyond that, the reader cannot be very sure about much of anything that happens in the book.

The title implies that the confidence man is a single figure, but individual readers must decide whether that figure is one character or several and, if the latter, how many disguises he assumes. On four occasions, one schemer attempts to swindle another confidence man, and one has to determine which figure is engaged in the central masquerade. Is the "man in cream-colors" (p. 3), a deaf mute who writes passages of scripture on his slate in the opening chapter, one of the avatars of the confidence man? If so, he seems to be indifferent to conning anyone out of anything. Is Black Guinea, the crippled Negro who plays his tambourine and begs for the stray coins passengers might toss his way, the same figure as the man with the weed who follows upon Guinea's exit? The narrator does nothing to clarify these uncertainties. More to the point, what is this novel (if it is a novel) all about? Ahab's purposes in *Moby-Dick* may be quite mad, but at least they are unmistakable. The confidence man, by contrast, seems equally interested in conning his fellow passengers out of a few pennies, a major investment, or the price of a shave. It is more certain that *The Confidence-Man* is some sort of social and philosophical satire, but for many readers the extent and object of that satire may be murky, indeed. A description of the genesis and background of this book may help to clarify some, but by no means all, of these mysteries.

GENESIS

The phrase "confidence man" entered the English language on 8 July 1849. A *New York Herald* article titled "Arrest of the Confidence Man" described the duping of numerous New Yorkers, including one Thomas McDonald, by a man whose supposed name was "William Thompson." The man approached the targets of his swindle and bluntly asked, "Have you confidence in me to trust me with your watch until tomorrow?" Like other unwary victims, McDonald, supposing some joke involving friends of his, had given the stranger his watch. As luck would have it, he spotted the swindler weeks later and had him arrested. The original confidence man instantly became a topic for commentary. One journalist compared the criminal to a Wall Street broker, and Melville's friend Evert Duyckinck, writing in the pages of the *Literary World* in August 1849, observed that the success of these appeals to confidence testifies to the charitable humanity of the average American. Melville himself no doubt read the original *Herald* article, for in his novel the cosmopolitan offers to hold the watch of the skeptic Pitch, but at the time Melville was involved in writing *White Jacket* (1850) and at any rate apparently did not immediately see anything literary in the figure. The same criminal, now calling himself "Samuel Willis," was apprehended in 1855 in Albany, New York. This time his ploy involved pretending prior acquaintance with a jeweler, introducing himself as a fellow Freemason; he managed to persuade the man to give him six or seven dollars.

The 1855 reemergence of the confidence man occurred when Melville was casting about for literary material, and once again the figure received some

In most of his longer works, Herman Melville used sources to flesh out narratives that were at least in part based on his own experience. Melville had a natural respect for the "fact," but he was accustomed to alter or otherwise embellish his sources in order to dramatize what he might call the "significances" of actual occurrences. Almost always, Melville, stylistically at least, improved the prose sources from which he borrowed. The passages below reprint excerpts from a brief newspaper article Melville was undoubtedly familiar with, though he may have read a reprinted piece that appeared in the Springfield Republican *on 5 May 1855. In any event, the resurfacing in 1855 of the "original" confidence man, who was first apprehended on the streets of New York City in 1849, evidently stimulated him to write a full-length novel about this figure and, more generally, about confidence games and venality abroad in the land.*

He called into a jewelry store on Broadway and said to the proprietor: "How do you do, Mr. Myers?" Receiving no reply, he added "Don't you know me?" to which Mr. M. replied that he did not. "My name is Samuel Willis. You are mistaken, for I have met you three or four times." He then said he had something of a private nature to communicate to Mr. Myers and that he wished to see him alone. The two men walked to the end of the counter, when Willis said to Myers, "I guess you are a Mason,"—to which Myers replied that he was—when Willis asked him if he would not give a brother a shilling if he needed it. By some shrewd management, Myers was induced to give him six or seven dollars.

(Anonymous, "The Original Confidence Man in Town," Albany Evening Journal, 28 April 1855)

"How do you do, Mr. Roberts?"

"Eh?"

"Don't you know me?"

"No, certainly." . . .

"If I remember, you are a mason, Mr. Roberts?"

"Yes, yes."

Averting himself a moment, as to recover from a return of agitation, the stranger grasped the other's hand; "and would you not loan a brother a shilling if he needed it?"

(Melville, The Confidence-Man: His Masquerade, chap. 4, p. 21)

attention in newspaper and magazine articles that the author probably read. Melville was certainly familiar with at least some of these reports and with the second swindle, for in chapter 4 of *The Confidence-Man* he has John Ringman "renew" his acquaintance with Mr. Roberts and claim to be a fellow Mason. What separated the confidence man from other swindlers and made him known as a true "original" was his blunt appeal for the confidence of potential victims (without reference to get-rich-quick schemes, miracle cures, and the like) and his apparent indifference to both the risks he took and the amount of money he might gain as a consequence. Melville several times has his own confidence man, in one or another disguise, make overtures that recall the original prototype, but the part of a voluble apostle of confidence is mostly reserved for the role of Frank Goodman, the cosmopolitan, who dominates the final half of the book. It was in this manifestation of the confidence man that Melville sought to create a true literary original.

The author insists in chapter 44 that if one means something more than mere oddity by the word "original," then original characters are scarce indeed—he instances Hamlet, Don Quixote, and Milton's Satan as examples of true originals—and he further acknowledges that such a character is more often found than created: "Where does any novelist pick up any character? For the most part, in town, to be sure" (p. 238). A truly unique character is more than "singular," or rare, however—"while characters, merely singular, imply but singular forms so to speak, original ones, truly so, imply original instincts" (p. 239). He elaborates the comparison: an original character "is like a revolving Drummond light," that rays away from itself, "everything is lit by it. . . . there follows, upon the adequate conception of such a character, an effect, in its way, akin to that which in Genesis attends upon the beginning of things" (p. 239). Melville's thoughts here were recorded well after he began his novel, and they seem to testify to the high literary ambitions he eventually had for his title character. At the outset, though, his own conception of the confidence man appears to have been as the timely vehicle for a rich and sardonic social satire.

SOCIAL BACKGROUND

After the disappointing sales and reviews of *Moby-Dick* and *Pierre* (1852), Melville had turned to magazine writing, and there is, to use Leon Howard's word, something very "magazinish" about *The Confidence-Man*. Melville freely interpolates five freestanding tales into his novel, and the main narrative itself moves by fits and starts toward some uncertain conclusion; the encounters between and among characters are highly dramatized, the subject matter is topical, and at least at first blush there appears to be very little of the "weighty" writing that had been his ambition in earlier novels but that he had deliberately avoided his most recent novel, the serialized historical fiction *Israel Potter* (1855). Potentially, if it too had been serialized, *The Confidence-Man* could have been extended indefinitely, with Melville having his central figure don yet another disguise and practice yet another familiar deception. The narrator surveys at his leisure the rich variety of characters who populate the decks of a Mississippi riverboat and who sometimes yield and sometimes resist the importuning of a glad-handing stranger anxious to sell them a bill of goods. The opening chapter rather overtly dramatizes the terms of moral and social conflict Melville meant to examine. The deaf-mute man in cream colors writes upon a slate for all to see passages from 1 Corinthians ("Charity thinketh no evil," "Charity believeth all things"); as if in answer, the boat's barber hangs over his door "NO TRUST." The barber means that he will accept no credit for his services, but Melville clearly intends to convey a broader skepticism about placing one's confidence in a stranger. It is between those two poles that Melville meant to enact his drama of faith and skepticism. Each encounter between the confidence man and his potential victim (sometimes, ironically, yet another con man who has his own designs upon him) poses what Melville would call in *Billy Budd* a "moral emergency." Each successive confidence game is a lose-lose situation. If a passenger resists the appeals of the schemer, he might be deemed callous, unfeeling, or misanthropic. If he falls for the ploy, the man is gullible, idealistic, and foolish.

The original confidence man may have provided Melville with the germ for his novel, but confidence men and confidence games abounded in antebellum America. The author might also have drawn on literary antecedents as well as didactic and polemical tracts in fleshing out his book. James Fenimore Cooper in *Home as Found* (1838) and Charles Dickens in *Life and Adventures of Martin Chuzzlewit* (1843) dealt with certain kinds of land fraud in the United States; Augustus Baldwin Longstreet in *Georgia Scenes* (1835) and Johnson Jones Hooper's *Some Adventures of Simon Suggs* (1846) supplied their sketches with criminal schemes and schemers in colorfully humorous ways; and a multitude of "reformed" swindlers (including gamblers, counterfeiters, Wall Street brokers, and the like) detailed in their autobiographies the sorts of deceptions they had practiced before they were redeemed from that wayward life. However he came by the information, Melville was familiar enough with the schemes and argot of the underworld to

Mississippi riverboats. Lithograph by Currier & Ives, c. 1866. In *The Confidence-Man,* Melville portrays the various petty crimes and misrepresentations that occurred on mid-nineteenth-century Mississippi riverboats. GETTY IMAGES

create in *The Confidence-Man* an atmosphere of venality, chicanery, and double-dealing that is at once comic and vaguely sinister.

From the very beginning Melville surveys the types and practices of swindlers abroad in the land. The man in cream colors may or may not be a confidence man, but at any rate the deaf and dumb act was a familiar ruse—the Yankee peddler William Avery Rockefeller, the father of John D. Rockefeller, had used that tactic more than once. Melville has the president of the Black Rapids Coal Company offer the college sophomore a chance to invest in "New Jerusalem." He also makes casual reference to gambling, counterfeiting, bandits, pickpockets, and sham charities dedicated to "international improvement." The herb doctor's "Omni-Balsamic Reinvigorator" and his "Samaritan Pain Dissuader" promise quick relief from pain and suffering. The man in gray claims to have invented the "Protean easy-chair," which will comfort the most restless body and perhaps soothe the "most tormented conscience." In her introduction to a 1954

edition of the novel, Elizabeth Foster suggests the natural cure-all may have reference to the once-popular "Dr. Brandreth's Pills" and the "Protean easy-chair" may be a send-up of a reclining chair a Philadelphia manufacturer displayed at the Crystal Palace in 1851. The representative of the "Philosophical Intelligence Office" was also a familiar type; an intelligence office was an antebellum employment agency, and cartoons and jokes concerning the dubious practice of promising to supply one with a laborer or apprentice for an advance fee often appeared in magazines and newspapers.

In sum, Melville presents in *The Confidence-Man* a veritable rogue's gallery of impostors and swindlers who prey upon the unwary sympathies or desires of fellow passengers. The author refers at least casually to nearly every shady scheme of the time, and he seasons his narrative of self-fashioning and double-dealing with underworld slang. The name Charlie Noble itself is a punning contradiction—a "charlie" in nineteenth-century parlance was a thimblerigger, or cheat, and anything but "noble." The comic encounter between the cosmopolitan and the barber in chapter 42 is a tissue of such puns. Almost as a dare, the cosmopolitan asks the barber if he is able to "shave" (that is, "cheat") him; the barber replies, "No broker more so, sir" (p. 226) (a "broker" was a pandering retailer, or Yankee peddler). From that point forward, their conversation is a battle of wits interlarded with puns on such underworld terms as "customer" (a victim), "barber" (any sort of cheat, but more usually a gossipy kind), "lather" (smooth talk), and "brush up" (flattery). In the end, the cosmopolitan prevails, for he convinces the barber to take down his sign of "NO TRUST" and then exits without paying for his shave.

PHILOSOPHICAL AND LITERARY QUESTIONS

Considered as social satire, *The Confidence-Man* is an antic and freewheeling comedy. One discerning contemporary reviewer recognized that the book did not abide by novelistic conventions and that it was a mistake to read it in that way. Instead, he described it as a "Rabelaisian patchwork": "The oddities of thought, felicities of expression, and wit, humor, and rollicking inspirations are as abundant and original as in any of the productions of this most remarkable writer" (Leyda 2:570). Melville attempted to capitalize upon a contemporary interest in the original confidence man and to provide an olio of shams and deceptions that might be practiced on the streets of New York or on a riverboat on the Mississippi. To that degree, he succeeded in delivering the sort of social satire that is most comprehensible and most retrievable when viewed through the lens of American history. But Melville, as he almost always did in his better books, also probed his material for what he called in a letter to Nathaniel Hawthorne their "significances." Modern readers have tended to be more alert to the sly depth and intricacy of Melville's ambiguities than to those moments, frequent enough, when he straightforwardly addressed his own era and dealt with popular issues and concerns. Even so, Melville's deep-diving intelligence and his own high literary aspirations are not without their historical interest.

Particularly in the latter half of the novel, the confidence man, in the guise of the cosmopolitan, appears far less interested in bilking his victims for petty cash than in serving as an evangelist of confidence itself. Virtually every character the cosmopolitan encounters dramatically embodies the paradoxes of human nature. The Missouri bachelor, Pitch, fancies himself a skeptic, but he finds he has "unwittingly been betrayed into being an unphilosophical dupe" (p. 129). Charlie Noble, a confidence man himself, means to ask Frank

Goodman for a loan, but when Frank is the first to make application for charity, Charlie Noble undergoes a radical transformation: "Out of old materials sprang a new creature. Cadmus glided into the snake" (p. 180). Similarly, the novel's grandly spiritual transcendentalist figures Egbert and Mark Winsome are at length revealed to be "practical" mystics—self-serving, hard-hearted, and callous. The boat's barber, as already noted, suspends his customary practice of "no trust" and is perplexed by his own lapse into confidence. The old farmer in the concluding chapter of the novel is presented as a perfectly innocent Christian, "untainted by the world, because ignorant of it" (p. 241). His purchase of a door lock, a counterfeit detector, and a money belt, however, contradicts his professed faith in a benevolent and superintending Providence.

The upshot of these transformations, Melville seems to be saying, is that human nature itself is something of a masquerade, and deceivers may themselves be self-deceived. Declared misanthropes are discovered to be secret philanthropists. Would-be "boon companions" are in fact conniving enemies. Transcendentalists are really Yankee peddlers. Professing Christians are, unknown even to themselves, unbelievers. It is in this sense that Melville's satire broadens out and dramatically discloses the "caprices" of the human heart. More than once, the author suggests that literature itself may be something of a confidence game. In chapter 14 he has his narrator observe that readers demand consistent characters but at the same time know that in view of the "inconsistencies" of human nature human personality is past finding out. The superficial or beguiling novelist, who by representing human character always in a clear light "leaves it to be inferred that he clearly knows all about it" (p. 70), is in fact practicing a swindle on his readers. Likewise, in chapter 33, Melville says that "it is with fiction as with religion"; the common reader wants "another world, and yet one to which we feel the tie" (p. 183).

Taken together, these comments, and many like them, express Melville's objection to the literary culture of his day, and that culture is also an object of satire. Various critics and scholars have detected satiric portraits of many nineteenth-century literary figures in the pages of *The Confidence-Man,* from Ralph Waldo Emerson, Henry David Thoreau, and Edgar Allan Poe to Horace Greeley, Fannie Kemble, Bayard Taylor, and Joel Barlow. One may push this line of reasoning too far, and it is probably more judicious to think of certain characters aboard the *Fidèle* as "type exponents" of literary figures, to use Harrison Hayford's phrase (p. 350). One does know, at any rate, that Melville was deliberately satirizing the writing of James T. Hall and in particular his account of the Indian-hater Colonel John Moredock in chapter 26, "Containing the Metaphysics of Indian Hating." The story of China Aster has unmistakable reference to a homiletic journal for children by that name, and Melville displays his particular disgust for the sort of pabulum that passes for moral instruction. The more secure point is that Melville was, if not satirizing, certainly registering his contempt for a literary culture that seemed to play fast and loose with its reader's fears and hopes and to foster attitudes toward life that were neither realistic nor prudent.

Finally, there is the question of faith in the book, an ingredient that probably has less to do with the religious ethos of America than it does with Melville's own religious uncertainties. At all events, a book that begins with passages from St. Paul and ends with the cosmopolitan and the old farmer puzzling over disturbing statements in the Apocrypha, while the whole narrative takes place on a riverboat not so coincidentally named the *Fidèle*, is not wholly preoccupied with secular concerns. In fact, some critics have tended to read *The Confidence-Man* as a religious, or perhaps as an antireligious, allegory in which the title character is actually Satan. Such a reading may be too stark. Nevertheless, Melville does seem to be conflating the sorts of confidence one offers or withholds on deck with the sort of faith upon which the old man and the cosmopolitan meditate in the boat's library at the conclusion of the book. The old man remarks how comforting it is to trust "in that Power which is alike able and willing to protect us when we cannot ourselves" (p. 250). The cosmopolitan assents to the sentiment, but Melville has shown throughout his novel how vulnerable and ambiguous faith of any sort might be.

See also Battle-Pieces; Confidence Men; *Moby-Dick;* Religion; Satire, Burlesque, and Parody; *Typee*

BIBLIOGRAPHY

Primary Works

Anonymous. "The Original Confidence Man in Town." *Albany Evening Journal,* 28 April 1855. Reprinted in *The Confidence-Man,* edited by Hershel Parker, pp. 228–229. Norton critical edition. New York: Norton, 1971.

Melville, Herman. *The Confidence-Man: His Masquerade.* 1851. Edited by Harrison Hayford, Hershel Parker, and G. Thomas Tanselle. Evanston, Ill.: Northwestern University Press and the Newberry Library, 1987. Quotations from the novel in the text are from this edition.

Secondary Works

Bergmann, Johannes Dietrich. "The Original Confidence Man: The Development of the American Confidence Man in the Sources and Backgrounds of Herman Melville's *The Confidence-Man: His Masquerade.*" Ph.D. diss., University of Connecticut, 1968.

Foster, Elizabeth S. Introduction to *The Confidence-Man: His Masquerade,* by Herman Melville. New York: Hendricks House, 1954.

Halttunen, Karen. *Confidence Men and Painted Women: A Study of Middle-Class Culture in America, 1830–1870.* New Haven, Conn.: Yale University Press, 1982.

Hayford, Harrison. "Poe in *The Confidence-Man.*" *Nineteenth-Century Fiction* 14 (1959): 207–218. Reprinted in *The Confidence-Man,* edited by Hershel Parker, pp. 344–353. Norton critical edition. New York: Norton, 1971.

Howard, Leon. *Herman Melville: A Biography.* Berkeley and Los Angeles: University of California Press, 1951.

Kuhlmann, Susan. *Knave, Fool, and Genius: The Confidence Man as He Appears in Nineteenth-Century American Fiction.* Chapel Hill: University of North Carolina Press, 1973.

Lenz, William E. *Fast Talk and Flush Times: The Confidence Man as a Literary Convention.* Columbia: University of Missouri Press, 1985.

Leyda, Jay. *The Melville Log: A Documentary Life of Herman Melville.* 2 vols. New York: Harcourt, Brace, 1951.

Lindberg, Gary. *The Confidence Man in American Literature.* New York: Oxford University Press, 1982.

Quirk, Tom. *Melville's Confidence Man: From Knave to Knight.* Columbia: University of Missouri Press, 1982.

Trimpi, Helen P. *Melville's Confidence Men and American Politics in the 1850s.* Hamden, Conn.: Archon, 1987.

Wadlington, Warwick. *The Confidence Game in American Literature.* Princeton, N.J.: Princeton University Press, 1975.

Tom Quirk

CONFIDENCE MEN

In "Diddling Considered as One of the Exact Sciences" (1843), Edgar Allan Poe argues: "Man is an animal that diddles, and there is *no* animal that diddles *but* man. . . . To diddle is his destiny. 'Man was made to mourn,' says the poet. But not so:—he was made to diddle. This is his aim—his object—his *end.* And for this reason when a man's diddled we say he's '*done*'" (p. 869). To Poe, diddling is a fundamental human behavior. To be a man is to lie, cheat, steal, and misrepresent; every man is essentially a diddling confidence man, seeking the confidence of others for his own profit and amusement. Poe exposes the characteristics of confidence men in his definition of diddling and reveals their alignment with antebellum cultural values: "Diddling, rightly considered, is a compound, of which the ingredients are minuteness, interest, perseverance, ingenuity, audacity, *nonchalance*, originality, impertinence, and *grin*" (pp. 869– 870). In many ways, Poe sums up the love-hate relationship that Americans have with confidence men. For confidence men ambiguously represent shared national values. Americans admire success, expertise, and imagination. Americans are trusting and like to be considered trustworthy. But since the Pilgrims arrived on the *Mayflower* (1620), Americans have recognized that the devil has been active in the New World. And the problem of ascertaining identity—especially moral identity and intention—in a landscape without clear markers of class or lineage has become increasingly problematic. Americans want to trust everyone, to believe in the democratic promise that all people are equally good and equally engaged in cooperative and progressive personal and communal development. Americans want to believe in a Jeffersonian meritocracy of good individuals rising to leadership and receiving just rewards. Yet Americans suspect that often within the hearts of strangers (and sometimes within the hearts of close associates) lurks the very devil himself, waiting to spring upon one and rob one of his or her goods and good faith. Americans want to be trusting but do not want to be gulled.

HISTORICAL, MYTHICAL, AND LITERARY SOURCES

The confidence man inhabits a liminal space in American culture between faith and doubt, reality and appearance, truth and falseness. He owes fealty to a myriad of dissembling ancestors, including Hermes, Loki, Coyote, Satan, Till Eulenspiegel, the Elizabethan fool, and countless seducers and conycatchers (swindlers), all of which represent forces of social disorder. His American lineage might seem to begin with explorers' accounts of the New World, for Christopher Columbus, John Smith, and the writers of numerous promotional tracts insisted that their Old World readers have perfect confidence in the unbelievable (and often fictional) wonders of the New World they described. Exaggeration of the bounty of the New World and misrepresentation of the ease of its harvest often went hand in hand with the cardinal motive for exploration and settlement. As William Penn (1644–1718) clearly explained in *A Further Account of the Province of Pennsylvania* (1685), the enterprise was designed so that "those that are Adventurers, or incline to be so, may imploy their Money, to a fair and secure Profit" (quoted in Wayne Franklin, p. 101).

Despite its Puritan beginnings, the New World was populated by legions of shape-shifters and mischief-makers. William Bradford (1590–1657), who recorded the Pilgrims' struggles at Plymouth Plantation, is certainly disturbed by the presence of individuals who misrepresent themselves, their motives, or what Bradford takes to be God's truth. He comes to believe that John Lyford, for example, is a scoundrel who pretends to be a minister; identity is fluid, and it is impossible at Plymouth to verify or deny Lyford's professional claims (see Bradford, pp. 146–169). In the seventeenth and eighteenth centuries, writers from John Winthrop (1588–1649) to Cotton Mather (1663–1728) cataloged the infamous exploits of New World tricksters; Mather, in *Magnalia Christi Americana* (1702), warns against various ruses of counterfeit priests in the chapter called "Wolves in Sheeps' Cloathing" (chap. 5, 2:537–551).

FROM SELF-PROMOTION TO SELF-CREATION

By the time Benjamin Franklin (1706–1790) published his *Autobiography* in 1791, the line separating historical record from imaginative literature—and absolute morality from moral relativism—had become blurred, the act of writing less a search for God's eternal truth and more a temporal performance of situational morality. Franklin can argue that a minister named Hemphill who plagiarizes sermons is neither a wolf in sheep's clothing nor a confidence man: "I rather approv'd his giving us good Sermons compos'd by others, than bad ones of his own Manufacture" (p. 168). Whether writing as Silence Dogood, Poor Richard, or the hero of the *Autobiography,* Franklin confidently assumes various fictional personae in the service of doing good, in a style that is at once detached, self-reflexive, and humorous. Franklin points directly to the development of the American confidence man: he delights in self-caricature, viewing the self as a fictive construction; he expresses a new relativism toward morality through humor; he reveals an excitement in the power of language; and he demonstrates the drive to create symbols of national identity.

It is a short step from the image of Franklin leaving his lamp on to give the citizens of Philadelphia the impression that he is laboring far into the night to the popularity of images of the shrewd and shifty Yankee, the wily Davy Crockett, and the boisterous Brom Bones of Washington Irving's (1783–1859) "The Legend of Sleepy Hollow." Shrewdness and comic detachment are paramount in tales of Mike Fink, Nimrod Wildfire, Sam Slick, Jack Downing, Hosea Biglow, and Major Jones, rough and tumble regional characters appearing in the pages of magazines such as William T. Porter's *Spirit of the Times*. Sharpers, swindlers, tricksters, counterfeiters, diddlers, and horse swappers overran the antebellum landscape, suggesting that they had humorously interpreted Poor Richard's proverb "God helps them that help themselves" (Franklin, n.p.) to mean that they should help themselves to the wealth of others by tricks, cons, or fast talk. Shifty characters such as Augustus B. Longstreet's horse-swapping Yellow Blossom, Joseph G. Baldwin's "Ovid Bolus, Esq.," George Washington Harris's Sut Lovingood, and Johnson Jones Hooper's Simon Suggs dominate the frontier "flush times" and humorously give voice to its contradictions.

THE CONFIDENCE MAN AS
A LITERARY CONVENTION

The term "confidence man" first appears in public discourse in 1849 as a description of what the *New York Literary World* called "a new species of the Jeremy Diddler" (Melville, p. 227). Less than ten years later, in a review of Herman Melville's (1819–1991) novel *The Confidence-Man* (1857), the confidence man is recognizable as "one of the indigenous characters who has figured long in our journals, courts, and cities" (Melville, p. 270). The confidence man has evolved into a localized American version of the archetypal trickster, a figure that developed through the interaction of fictional and historical sources—witness the cultural prominence of Davy Crockett, who in one tale trades a single coonskin for ten successive bottles of rum and who in reality became a congressman and then a hero martyred at the Alamo, and P. T. Barnum (1810–1891), who promoted scores of self-proclaimed "humbugs," such as the Feejee Mermaid yet who made and lost several very real fortunes—and remains in the American mind as a cultural as well as a literary convention. These blurred outlines have led to differing scholarly points of view. Gary Lindberg in *The Confidence Man in American Literature* argues that the confidence man is a "covert cultural hero for Americans" (p. 3). William E. Lenz in *Fast Talk and Flush Times* concludes that the confidence man "personifies the ambiguities of the new country in a nonthreatening form" (p. 20). And Kathleen De Grave in *Swindler, Spy, Rebel* reminds one that confidence women joined the confidence men, "women who used disguise, deception, and manipulation to become human" (p. 245). Despite these varieties of interpretation, clearly nineteenth-century Americans admired the confidence man's intuition, imagination, self-confidence,

and inspired smooth talk yet condemned his dishonesty, misrepresentation, self-serving greed, and felonious fast talk. In his popular autobiography, Barnum insisted, "When people expect to get 'something for nothing' they are sure to be cheated, and generally deserve to be" (quoted in Harris, p. 54).

In 1845 Johnson Jones Hooper's (1815–1862) *Some Adventures of Captain Simon Suggs* codified the American confidence man in a mock campaign biography that pokes fun at the standard democratic genre of self-promotion as it also suggests that in a democratic society, any man—even the most dishonest— may offer himself for political office. In fact, as Hooper's narrator explains of Simon:

> His whole ethical system lies snugly in his favourite aphorism—"It is good to be shifty in a new country"—which means that it is right and proper that one should live as merrily and as comfortably as possible at the expense of others; and of the practicability of this in particular instances, the Captain's whole life has been a long series of the most convincing illustrations. (P. 12)

As articulated by Simon Suggs, the American confidence man abuses the confidence of everyone he meets for personal profit. At the same time, his "snaps" expose a pattern of faith betrayed that mirrors the antebellum cycle of boom and bust. His escapades form a checklist of confidence gambits: Suggs begins playing at cards, then speculates in frontier lands, then impersonates in turn a politician, a military hero, a fearless Indian fighter, and a reformed sinner at a revivalist camp meeting.

In a typical adventure, Suggs travels to a gambling house in Tuscaloosa, where he confidently assumes the identity of one General Thomas Witherspoon, a wealthy hog farmer from Kentucky, who had never been seen by anyone at the gambling hall, including Witherspoon's own nephew. The gentlemen engaged in cards and dice ("a large proportion members of the legislature" [p. 55]) represent the discrepancy between public appearance and private practice; these men are hypocrites and deserve to be conned. By the end of the evening "General Witherspoon" has won and lost $1,500, subjected the general's nephew to a thorough cross-examination to verify the nephew's identity (and thereby his own), borrowed several hundred additional dollars from this nephew, and treated the entire company to a champagne-and-oyster supper on the general's credit, guaranteeing the whole lot by the promise of the general's hogs supposedly arriving to be sold tomorrow.

> "Gentlemen," said he "I'm devilish glad to see you all, and much obleeged to you, besides. You are the finest people I ever was amongst, and treat me

The relationship between social history and literary history was especially close in the nineteenth century, as authors such as Washington Irving, Edgar Allan Poe, Johnson Jones Hooper, and Herman Melville enjoyed blurring the distinction between truth and fiction. Popular culture and elite culture often cross-fertilized one another, as witness the almost simultaneous appearance in a New York newspaper and a literary journal of the "confidence man" figure in 1849. Even in these relatively factual, objective accounts, a deep American ambivalence about the need for confidence and the anxiety of distrust is readily apparent.

Arrest of the Confidence Man

For the last few months a man has been traveling about the city, known as the "Confidence Man;" that is, he would go up to a perfect stranger in the street, and being a man of genteel appearance, would easily command an interview. Upon this interview he would say, after some little conversation, "have you confidence in me to trust me with your watch until tomorrow;" the stranger, at this novel request, supposing him to be some old acquaintance, not at the moment recollected, allows him to take the watch, thus placing "confidence" in the honesty of the stranger, who walks off laughing, and the other, supposing it to be a joke, allows him to do so.

(New York Herald, *8 July 1849*)

The New Species of Jeremy Diddler

It is not the worst thing that can be said of a country that it gives birth to a confidence man. . . . "That one poor swindler, like the one under arrest, should have been able to drive so considerable a trade on an appeal to so simple a quality as the confidence of man in man, shows that all virtue and humanity of nature is not entirely extinct in the nineteenth century. It is a good thing, and speaks well for human nature, that, at this late day, in spite of all the hardening of civilization and all the warning of newspapers, men *can be swindled.*"

(Literary World, *18 August 1849*)

Melville, *The Confidence-Man: His Masquerade*, pp. 227–228.

a d—d sight better than they do at home"—which was a fact! "Hows'ever, I'm a poor hand to speak, but here's wishing luck to you all"—and then wickedly seeming to blunder in his little speech— "and if I forgit you, I'll be d—d if you'll ever forgit me!" (Pp. 66–67)

The narrative dramatizes not only the fluidity of identity but also the mercurial nature of flush-times life. Everyone in Hooper's world is a gambler, tossing the dice in a frenzy of speculation, manipulation, or legerdemain. Legislators, military officers, bank directors, Indian agents, revival preachers, even fathers—all are dishonest. Proven false, they are humorously, subversively, violently fleeced. They will, as Suggs swears, never forget him. And the brilliance of Suggs's performance is that, like thousands of Americans held up as paragons of Franklinian success, he quite literally makes his fortune out of nothing. In a comic form that distances the reader from the rude vernacular action, nineteenth-century Americans admired the skill with which Suggs revealed the greed and desire at the heart of the American Dream.

Herman Melville, in *The Confidence-Man* (1857), suggests that cynicism and distrust are turning that dream into a nightmare. The avatars of the confidence man have become travelers on a symbolic American ship of fools, the *Fidèle*. The mute in cream colors sets the novel's ironic tone by writing a slogan on a slate, "Charity thinketh no evil" (p. 2), which is canceled by the barber, who posts his motto at the novel's end, "No trust" (p. 194). Within these parameters the reader is ricocheted between faith and doubt as character after character makes an appeal for confidence that seems legitimate and worthy of trust and then has that appeal narratively undermined as a possible confidence trick. How can reality be determined based solely on appearance? What is an adequate basis for identifying truth and falsehood? Is every appeal for confidence really a confidence game?

To Melville, the confidence man's humor is at root bitter. His narrator plays a game of fast and loose with the reader, replacing the comforting frame technique of Hooper's humorous snaps with a narrative structure that denies certainty of intention and suggests that all relationships are essentially dishonest. Is Black Guinea a man to pity or a confidence man? Does the man with a wooden leg in fact have a wooden leg? Are these characters deserving of confidence? If they are strangers, how can one tell? Is the agent of the Black Rapids Coal Company trustworthy? How about the man in gray, ostensibly soliciting funds for the Seminole Widow and Orphan Asylum? The herb doctor, the Philosophical Intelligence Office agent, and finally the cosmopolitan all perform an elaborate masquerade on April Fools' Day. The purpose of their tricks seems no longer to expose the greedy and unscrupulous in a comic catharsis but to imprison the reader in an elaborate funhouse of distorting cultural mirrors. Melville dramatizes doubts of the American promise of plenty that would soon erupt in the Civil War.

TO THE GILDED AGE AND BEYOND

The Civil War effectively derailed the American confidence man. Humor, detachment, and self-caricature were no longer effective mechanisms to explain or resolve American cultural anxieties. The pursuit of happiness, democratic freedom, rugged individualism, and Franklinian industriousness seemed a vast confidence trick. In the following years, authors including Mark Twain, William Faulkner, F. Scott Fitzgerald, Nathanael West, Thomas Pynchon, and Louise Erdrich would reimagine the confidence man as trickster, jester, and victim. The confidence man's nineteenth-century masquerade had concluded with the flush times.

See also The Confidence-Man; Humor; Satire, Burlesque, and Parody

BIBLIOGRAPHY
Primary Works
Barnum, P. T. *The Life of P. T. Barnum, Written by Himself.* New York: Redfield, 1855.

Bradford, William. *Of Plymouth Plantation 1620–1647 by William Bradford.* Edited by Samuel Eliot Morison. New York: Knopf, 1966.

Franklin, Benjamin. *The Autobiography of Benjamin Franklin.* 1791. Edited by Leonard W. Labaree et al. New Haven, Conn.: Yale University Press, 1964.

Franklin, Benjamin. *Poor Richard's Almanack: Being the Choicest Morsels of Wit and Wisdom Written during the Thirty Years of the Almanack's Publication by Dr. Benjamin Franklin of Philadelphia.* Mount Vernon, N.Y.: Peter Pauper Press, 1936.

Hooper, Johnson Jones. 1845. *Some Adventures of Captain Simon Suggs.* Upper Saddle River, N.J.: Literature Press/Gregg Press, 1970.

Mather, Cotton. *Magnalia Christi Americana; or, The Ecclesiastical History of New-England, from Its First Planting, in the Year 1620, unto the Year of Our Lord 1698.* 1702. 2 vols. New York: Russell and Russell, 1967.

Melville, Herman. *The Confidence-Man: His Masquerade.* 1857. Edited by Hershel Parker. New York: Norton, 1971.

Poe, Edgar Allan. "Diddling Considered as One of the Exact Sciences." 1843. In *Collected Works of Edgar Allan Poe,* edited by Thomas Ollive Mabbott. Cambridge, Mass.: Belknap Press of Harvard University Press, 1978.

Secondary Works
Bergmann, Johannes Dietrich. "The Original Confidence Man." *American Quarterly* 21 (1969): 561–577.

Blair, John G. *The Confidence Man in Modern Fiction: A Rogue's Gallery with Six Portraits.* New York: Barnes and Noble, 1979.

De Grave, Kathleen. *Swindler, Spy, Rebel: The Confidence Woman in Nineteenth-Century America.* Columbia and London: University of Missouri Press, 1995.

Franklin, Wayne. *Discoverers, Explorers, Settlers: The Diligent Writers of Early America.* Chicago: University of Chicago Press, 1979.

Halttunen, Karen. *Confidence Men and Painted Women: A Study of Middle-Class Culture in America, 1830–1870.* New Haven, Conn.: Yale University Press, 1982.

Harris, Neil. *Humbug: The Art of P. T. Barnum.* Boston: Little, Brown, 1973.

Kuhlmann, Susan. *Knave, Fool, and Genius: The Confidence Man as He Appears in Nineteenth-Century American Fiction.* Chapel Hill: University of North Carolina Press, 1973.

Lenz, William E. *Fast Talk and Flush Times: The Confidence Man as a Literary Convention.* Columbia: University of Missouri Press, 1985.

Lindberg, Gary. *The Confidence Man in American Literature.* New York: Oxford University Press, 1982.

Maurer, David W. *The American Confidence Man.* Springfield, Ill.: Charles C. Thomas, 1974.

Wadlington, Warwick. *The Confidence Game in American Literature.* Princeton, N.J.: Princeton University Press, 1975.

William E. Lenz

COPYRIGHT

See Book Publishing

COURTSHIP

In traditional courtship stories, hero and heroine meet, fall in love, overcome misunderstandings or other obstacles, and, just as the curtain falls, marry each other. A courtship plot is predictable, but that does not mean it has no deeper significance. Quite the contrary: courtship stories are windows through which we can examine key values of a society and discover ways that those values are changing or being challenged. On the surface, courtship is intimately personal, but each story of individual desire and fulfillment is enacted within a particular social context, and every society is deeply invested in who marries whom. In nineteenth-century American literature, novels with courtship plots come most often from the established societies of the South and the Northeast. Courtship is defined and practiced by the privileged classes within a given society, and it is those groups that are most deeply concerned with what happens to property and family identity as people marry. Central to all courtships, whether the issue is confronted directly or not, is the value of women's chastity. The connotations of the term "courtship" are significant: they are linked to "courtly" behavior ("courts" are complex mixes of people maneuvering for favor), to genteel class traditions, and to a pattern of specific rituals followed to bring about a desired result.

Marginalized groups do not possess the leisure, property, and social standing required to participate fully in genteel courtship as defined by the privileged classes. Slaves, by law, could not enter into binding marriage contracts. Laborers, immigrants, and paupers, who could and almost always did marry, are nevertheless not included in the groups that define courtship. Precisely because courtship is a marker of "civilized" society and individual class standing, however, authors writing from the margins frequently adopt the privileged language of courtship as they work to "class up" the group they represent. African American authors of antebellum slave narratives and of novels before and after the war often portray their characters' love stories with the traditional language of courtship, and writers who depict the westward movement sometimes show the struggle of characters to maintain the genteel ideals and behavior associated with courtship in the "civilized" regions of the country.

Courtship is an intense period of unstable and volatile transition during which individuals move from one family formation to another. When authors write courtship stories, they dramatize the transitional space between single and married life and identify how various family and community groups are invested in the outcome of the courtship. By looking at both the courting couple and other characters who have a stake in the courtship, we can discover the secret strategies of the most obvious plot in the world.

COURTSHIP WITHIN THE PLANTATION ARISTOCRACY

In the antebellum South, the small planter class's control of everything from aristocratic manners to slave labor was predicated on a strict patriarchal model. For a southern girl, courtship practices governed her passage from belle to matron. For her family, this passage was critical to assuring the smooth transfer of property

Cover of sheet music for the song "I'd Offer Thee This Hand of Mine," 1848. The genteel nature of traditional concepts of courtship is emphasized here. THE LIBRARY OF CONGRESS

(especially land and slaves) from one privileged family to another and within the planter class as a whole, to perpetuating and reinforcing the strict system of race, gender, and class hierarchy. Antebellum novels about the South, then, give their authors' perspectives on how these hierarchical values could be reinforced, renegotiated, or challenged within the drama of courtship.

Caroline Lee Hentz (1800–1856) is best known for *The Planter's Northern Bride* (1854), a novel she wrote as a proslavery response to Harriet Beecher Stowe's *Uncle Tom's Cabin* (1852). Hentz's story is one of many written throughout the nineteenth century in which a character representing the northern perspective courts and marries a character with a southern outlook, thereby dramatizing the victory of one or another point of view, or, especially after the Civil War, the possibility of a reconciliation of the divided portions of the country. Hentz's *Eoline; or, Magnolia Vale* (1852) is set entirely in the South, and while it romanticizes many aspects of southern life, it also depicts realistic elements of courtship. Slaveholding families kept strict watch over their daughters, and all encounters with suitors were to be chaperoned; the plantation patriarch exerted authority over whom and when his children married. Eoline's father demands her obedience to him, expecting her to marry the neighbor's son Horace, as the families have planned for years, in order to cement friendship and consolidate property. But Eoline refuses to be a wholly submissive daughter, insisting on her right to marry only someone she loves. Her father believes that "in a struggle for power, for a father to yield to a child was monstrous, unnatural; it was an outrage upon social regulations, an infringement of the Divine law" (p. 32). Eoline leaves home to teach rather than submit to the arranged marriage, shocking her father because of the damage to the family name caused by her choice. She rejects the courtship plan laid out for her by her family and by the planter society, but her rebellion is limited. While on her own, she fortuitously falls in love with Horace all by herself. Their second courtship is patterned more along the lines of northern courtships, as the couple's romance grows away from the close watch of their families. But since Eoline chooses to marry the man her father had selected for her in the first place, Hentz suggests, allowing daughters an increased degree of freedom in courtship will not in the end damage the planter class's control.

The Hidden Hand (1859), by E. D. E. N. Southworth (1819–1899), includes several courtship plots, all set in the antebellum South. As in Hentz's novel, these plots turn on patriarchal efforts to maintain control of courtship and marriage. But because Southworth was not protective of the slaveholding class and in fact held strong antislavery views, her plots are far more daring than Hentz's. The two heroines, Capitola and Clara, enjoy a double wedding at the end of the novel, but their paths through courtship are quite different. Capitola, who is far more interested in adventure than in romance, marries a childhood friend almost as an afterthought. Their courtship, perfunctory though it seems next to Clara's dramatic romance, is carried out in socially approved ways, with letters and visits. Since Herbert Grayson is the nephew of Capitola's guardian, Capitola, like Eoline, marries a man who has the full approval of her male guardian. Capitola's detachment from her own love story is the primary challenge to courtship tradition, which holds that a woman is naturally and deeply invested in her romantic life. The gentler heroine Clara bears out this expectation, as throughout the novel she focuses on

maintaining her betrothal to Traverse in the face of ominous obstacles. Her courtship with Traverse is approved of by her father, and after her father's death she carries with her the banner of his endorsement. This banner enables her to stand up in a public courtroom to claim her engagement, to withstand efforts of the evil LeNoirs to force her into marriage and thus seize her property, and to flee from her legal guardian. Southworth's courtships follow accepted patterns of romantic interaction, but the heroines appropriate patriarchal authority for themselves, taking charge of their courtships, protecting their own sexual purity, and finally bestowing their property as they choose. The marriages partly cross class lines, with the suitors playing the Cinderella role: Capitola is an heiress and Clara is quite wealthy, while Herbert and Traverse both work their way up into the respected professional ranks, Herbert in the military and Traverse as a physician. Seen against the conservatism of Hentz's fiction, Southworth's courtship stories appear progressive: she gives her energetic heroines much more freedom of movement and authority over their own lives and demands that the heroes work for a living.

SLAVERY AND THE IMPOSSIBILITY OF HAPPY ENDINGS

Slave narratives and abolitionist texts written by contemporaries of Hentz and Southworth provide painful testimony of what it meant to be denied the rights to protect one's chastity, to work, to court, and to marry. Antislavery literature often draws on the language of romantic love both to assert the humanity of black Americans and to draw out the sympathy of readers who were well trained to react empathetically to courtship plots and to expect happy endings to follow hardship. In his novel *Clotel; or, The President's Daughter* (1853), William Wells Brown (c. 1814–1884) blends realistic depictions of the brutality of slavery, especially the sexual oppression of women, with complex courtship plots, most of which end in disaster. Brown does offer readers a happy ending when one couple is reunited and married in Europe. This happy ending emphasizes that no such marriage is possible in the United States because both characters are slaves under the laws of their native land. In her autobiographical *Incidents in the Life of a Slave Girl* (1861), Harriet Jacobs (1813–1897) depicts a young slave, Linda Brent, who futilely falls in love with a free black man: "Why does the slave ever love? Why allow the tendrils of the heart to twine around objects that may at any moment be wrenched away by the hand of violence? . . . Youth will be youth. I loved, and I indulged the hope that the dark clouds around me would turn out a bright lining" (p. 41). Instead of being rewarded with a "bright lining," Linda must fight off her predatory master, who crushes her hopes of marrying her loved one. Linda eventually chooses to become the mistress of a white man who is not her master because that relationship allows her a small amount of self-determination. Under the laws of slavery, this is the closest she can come to courting and marrying; happy endings are illegal for slaves.

CHRISTIAN COURTSHIP IN THE NORTH

Courtship stories set in the northern sections of the country reveal a different complex of concerns and values. Northern communities were concerned with the rapid changes brought by waves of immigrants, by the growth of cities, and by the boom-and-bust economy that could suddenly create or destroy wealth. Young people had far more mobility than in the South, both in terms of location and in terms of socioeconomic status. These cultural characteristics were seen as coming into conflict with the core values of evangelical Christianity: a personal experience of religion, long-suffering, self-sacrifice, and faithfulness. In secular terms, these values play out in a strong work ethic and a scorn for, or even fear of, "fashionable society." The transitional space of courtship was almost always entangled with questions of faith, work, and duty to God.

Maria Susanna Cummins (1827–1866) provides an excellent example of such a courtship in *The Lamplighter* (1854). While the first half of the novel focuses on the heroine Gertrude's development from unruly child to ideal young woman, the second half dwells on the superiority of her Christian life to the fashionable, materialistic, selfish world that looks down on her because of her (apparently) humble origins. Like that of Capitola in *The Hidden Hand*, her courtship grows from a childhood friendship and is carried out largely through letter writing because the suitor is making his way in the world. By the time Willie returns home, having established himself in business, Gertrude has become a beautiful young woman, and each fears the other has been lured away by the glittering fashionable world. The series of misunderstandings is resolved, and the narrator brings them together at last with a summary of how an ideal courtship should work: "With heart pressed to heart, they pour in each other's ear the tale of a mutual affection, planted in infancy, nourished in youth, fostered and strengthened amid separation and absence, and perfected through trial, to bless and sanctify every year of their after life" (p. 409). The Christian values they hold dear have protected their love for one another and have also ensured their material well-being. Capitola is catapulted into fabulous wealth, but

Cummins's northern story values solid middle-class status instead.

In *Barriers Burned Away* (1872), set in Chicago, Edward Payson Roe (1838–1888) emphasizes the same set of northern values we see in Cummins but introduces a new element into courtship that became increasingly prominent after the Civil War: the conflict of a woman's personal ambition with her desire for love and marriage. In Roe's story, Dennis Fleet, a hard-working Christian hero, courts the daughter of wealthy German immigrants. Christine is absorbed in high society, scornful of Dennis, and in quest of personal fame as an artist. But a series of events, culminating in the fire of 1871, humbles her, and she embraces the Christian faith, gives up fashion and ambition, and accepts Dennis's proposal.

COURTSHIP AND WOMEN'S CAREERS

Other authors are less eager to sacrifice women's ambition on the altar of marriage. For Augusta Jane Evans (1835–1909), a deeply prosouthern writer, ambitious heroines with northern values of work and evangelical Christianity struggle mightily throughout their courtships to reconcile their desire for fame with their investment in the conservative ideal of women's subservient role in marriage. The heroines of her novels *Beulah* (1859) and *St. Elmo* (1866) finally accept marriages defined much like Christine's, but their "happy endings" are intertwined with grief over the sacrifice of their career ambitions. St. Elmo's beloved Edna faints during the wedding, and her husband then announces: "To-day I snap the fetters of your literary bondage. There shall be no more books written! No more study, no more toil, no more anxiety, no more heart-aches! . . . You belong solely to me now, and I will take care of the life you have nearly destroyed in your inordinate ambition" (p. 65).

Inevitably, courtships began to raise the possibility of women combining marriage and career instead of being forced to choose between them. Elizabeth Stuart Phelps (1844–1911) tests out such a courtship in *The Story of Avis* (1877). Avis has sworn not to marry in order to develop her talent for painting, but she is won over by Philip when he promises that she will be able to continue practicing her art after their marriage: "I do not want your work, or your individuality. I refuse to accept any such sacrifice from the woman I love." Avis responds, "I have wondered sometimes if there were such a man in the world" (pp. 107–108). But this "happy ending" is the beginning of unhappiness. Between Philip's inability to live up to his promises and the daily grind of keeping house and caring for children, Avis fails as an artist and the marriage itself barely survives.

THE ENDURING VALUE OF COURTSHIP PLOTS

The conventional courtship plot, because of its predictable elements, provides an excellent glimpse into competing cultural values of a given time period and region. The problem of dual-career marriage, treated so pessimistically by Phelps, remains significant, even though such marriages are now the norm rather than the radical exception. In the nineteenth century, miscegenation was taboo and could rarely lead to a happy ending. *Our Nig; or, Sketches from the Life of a Free Black*, by Harriet E. Wilson (1825–1900), opens with such a story. Frado's mother, Mag, seduced and abandoned by a white man, is rejected by her community. Her only choice for survival is to marry the black man Jim. She is shocked at first, but "he prevailed; they married. You can philosophize, gentle reader, upon the impropriety of such unions, and preach dozens of sermons on the evils of amalgamation. Want is a more powerful philosopher and preacher" (p. 13). As time went on, interracial dating and marriage became a central issue in courtship plots and eventually led to happy endings.

Again, only slowly did writers begin to question a central assumption of the conventional courtship plot: the sexual purity of the heroine. Various negotiations of the sexual double standard began to emerge at the end of the nineteenth century and continued for decades afterward. Romance plots in the late twentieth and early twenty-first centuries began to challenge the cultural authority of heterosexual courtship, paralleling the contemporary debate about gay marriage. A careful reading of nineteenth-century novels will uncover the beginnings of this conflict, as same-sex friendships are sacrificed to marriage, often to the grief of the abandoned friend. For example, in *The Undiscovered Country* (1880), by William Dean Howells (1837–1920), the social butterfly Phillips is strongly attracted to the hero Ford and is dismayed when Ford's marriage puts an end to the (mostly one-sided) friendship.

Over time, some conflicts become anachronistic while others become more central, and with each succeeding generation of writers, new value conflicts come to the center. Through courtship and marriage, we learn whether something ought to be sacrificed or rejected and whether apparently irreconcilable differences might be settled by a happy ending.

See also Abolitionist Writing; Domestic Fiction; Evangelicals; Fashion; Feminism; Marriage; Miscegenation; Sexuality and the Body; Slave Narratives; Proslavery Writing

BIBLIOGRAPHY
Primary Works

Brown, William Wells. *Clotel; or, The President's Daughter: A Narrative of Slave Life in the United States*. 1853. Edited by M. Giulia Fabi. New York: Penguin, 2003.

Cummins, Maria Susanna. *The Lamplighter*. 1854. Edited by Nina Baym. New Brunswick, N.J.: Rutgers University Press, 1988.

Evans, Augusta Jane. *Beulah*. 1859. Edited by Elizabeth Fox-Genovese. Baton Rouge: Louisiana State University Press, 1992.

Evans, Augusta Jane. *St. Elmo*. 1866. Tuscaloosa: University of Alabama Press, 1992.

Hentz, Caroline. *Eoline; or, Magnolia Vale*. Philadelphia: T. B. Peterson, 1852.

Howells, William Dean. *The Undiscovered Country*. Boston: Houghton Mifflin, 1880.

Jacobs, Harriet A. *Incidents in the Life of a Slave Girl*. 1861. New York: Penguin, 2000.

Phelps, Elizabeth Stuart. *The Story of Avis*. 1877. Edited by Carol Farley Kessler. New Brunswick, N.J.: Rutgers University Press, 1985.

Roe, Edward Payson. *Barriers Burned Away*. 1872. Upper Saddle River, N.J.: Literature House, 1970.

Southworth, E. D. E. N. *The Hidden Hand: or, Capitola the Madcap*. 1859. Edited by Joanne Dobson. New Brunswick, N.J.: Rutgers University Press, 1988.

Wilson, Harriet E. *Our Nig; or, Sketches from the Life of a Free Black*. 1859. Edited by Henry Louis Gates Jr. 2nd ed. New York: Vintage, 1983.

Secondary Works

Boone, Joseph Allen. *Tradition Counter Tradition: Love and the Form of Fiction*. Chicago: University of Chicago Press, 1987.

Diedrich, Maria. "'My Love Is Black as Yours Is Fair': Premarital Love and Sexuality in the Antebellum Slave Narrative." *Phylon* 47, no. 3 (1986): 238–247.

duCille, Ann. *The Coupling Convention: Sex, Text, and Tradition in Black Women's Fiction*. New York: Oxford University Press, 1993.

Leach, William. *True Love and Perfect Union: The Feminist Reform of Sex and Society*. New York: Basic Books, 1980.

Lystra, Karen. *Searching the Heart: Women, Men, and Romantic Love in Nineteenth-Century America*. New York: Oxford University Press, 1989.

Rothman, Ellen K. *Hands and Hearts: A History of Courtship in America*. New York: Basic Books, 1984.

Tracey, Karen. *Plots and Proposals: American Women's Fiction, 1850–1890.* Urbana: University of Illinois Press, 2000.

Karen Tracey

CRIME AND PUNISHMENT

Scenes of transgressions and consequences inform Western cultural discourse going back to the first story of humankind in the Bible, so it is not surprising that crime and punishment form the basis of a number of literary works in the mid-nineteenth century. Under this rubric one finds memorable criminals such as the narrator of "The Tell-Tale Heart" by Edgar Allan Poe (1809–1849), scenes of imprisonment in fictions such as "Bartleby, the Scrivener" and *Billy Budd* by Herman Melville (1819–1891), and women described in fictions by Lydia Maria Child (1802–1880) and Catharine Sedgwick (1789–1867) who find themselves unjustly incarcerated. Perhaps one of the most celebrated literary efforts to document crime and punishment occurs in *The Scarlet Letter* by Nathaniel Hawthorne (1804–1864). The story of Hester Prynne begins at the prison door with a crowd of men and women, apparently waiting. The narrator provides a historical footnote to accompany the scene: "The founders of a new colony, whatever Utopia of human virtue and happiness they might originally project, have invariably recognized it among their earliest practical necessities to allot a portion of the virgin soil as a cemetery, and another portion as the site of a prison" (p. 53). The inevitability of death and punishment mark their incorporation into both the Puritan community and this narrative of Hester's complex relation to those who punish her. Likewise, crime and its consequences occupied the minds of American reformers and writers during the antebellum period.

Eager to demonstrate the success of the republican revolution, Americans in the late eighteenth century and early nineteenth century worked toward reconfiguring a criminal justice system deemed inefficient and cruel in its procedures and punishments. Some abjured the death penalty as despotic, linking it with monarchy. Many reformers considered corporal punishments inhumane, preferring to effect a program of work and solitude for the convict as a means of rehabilitating character and habit. Supporting methods used in particular prisons, prison associations in Philadelphia (formed in the 1780s), Boston (1826), and New York (1844) advocated rehabilitating prisoners by instruction, silent reflection, and work. They differed over whether to allow convicts to see one another in the penitentiary, how to incorporate study of the Bible and other texts, whether to promote solitary or congregate work, and whether to depend on convict labor to subsidize the penitentiary. Even Americans not involved with criminal procedures or reforms read about crimes, trials, prisons, and disciplinary methods in periodicals and in sensational, sentimental, and realist fictions.

CULTURAL INFLUENCES ON PRISON REFORM

Antebellum anxieties about crimes reflected general unease concerning social change, including immigration, slavery, and class mobility. Carroll Smith-Rosenberg explains that the difficulties of establishing social cohesion for a mobile, increasingly diverse population prompted Jacksonian reformers in cities to develop institutional mechanisms of preventing crime, notably almshouses and workhouses. Prisoners were disproportionately black, Indian, and immigrant, groups assumed more likely to be deviant. As David Rothman discerns, whether fears of increasing crimes and ideas about predispositions toward criminal behavior were justified by actual numbers or not remains an open question because statistics from the period are suspect.

Penitentiary reforms were also affected by other cultural formations, including other reform movements, theological arguments about sin, emerging social scientific theories of moral character, and the national project of information diffusion. Whitney Cross describes how diverse religious sects promoted contradictory doctrines concerning free will and the sovereignty of God. Religious groups joined with philanthropists to advocate regulating the social environment in ways that would appropriately shape individual moral character. The Second Great Awakening (beginning in the 1790s and at its height from 1822 to 1844) encouraged the formation of missionary organizations and tract societies, which in turn supported institutions for the prevention and amelioration of poverty, unemployment, and juvenile delinquency.

Concerned citizens in the antebellum period pressed for new laws regarding abolition, women's rights, temperance, and prison discipline. Reformers were enjoined to employ a spirit of sympathy in their benevolence. In an 1811 speech to the Humane Society of Massachusetts, Lemuel Shaw, who was appointed in 1830 as chief justice of the Supreme Judicial Court of Massachusetts, promoted "a habitual compassion for the wants and sufferings of others" (p. 6) as the necessary motivation for reformers. The Philadelphia publisher and bookseller Mathew Carey, whose politics exiled him to France from his native

Cold shower bath depicted in "Torture and Homicide in an American State Prison," *Harper's Weekly,* **18 December 1858.** Originally captioned "The Negro convict, More, showered to death." The article exposed abuses at Auburn State Prison in New York.
© CORBIS

Ireland before he immigrated to the United States, argued in 1833 that those better off had a duty to help those less fortunate. Poverty could lead to prison, and once debtors were imprisoned, they were forced to subsist on charity (as were their families, who were left destitute), a situation that lasted until 1840, according to Frank Carlton, when "nearly every Northern State had practically abolished this relic of barbarism" (p. 344).

Some reformers argued that environmental influences produced crimes. In a column in the abolitionist newspaper the *National Anti-Slavery Standard,* the activist and journalist Lydia Maria Child described visiting New York's Blackwell's Island prison in 1842. She responded to a companion's inquiry of "Would

you have them [the prisoners] prey on society?" by affirming "I am troubled that society has preyed upon *them.* I will not enter into an argument about the right of society to punish these sinners; but I say she made them sinners" (pp. 202–203). She posits that similar instincts motivate the soldier killing Indians, the frontier resident vindicating an insult, and a New York professional shooting someone who accuses him of dishonor, but that society nominates the first (Andrew Jackson) for the presidency, hails the second for bravery, and hangs the third. Sara Payson Willis Parton (1811–1872), writing as Fanny Fern about Blackwell's Island in 1858, pointedly asked readers if they were any less guilty in being "politic enough to commit only those [crimes] that a short-sighted, unequal human law sanctions?" (p. 305). She criticized the inefficacy of prison discipline: "I don't believe the way to restore a man's lost self-respect is to degrade him before his fellow creatures; to brand him, and chain him, and poke him up to show his points, like a hyena in a menagerie. No wonder that he growls at you, and grows vicious" (p. 306).

Reformers closely connected with institutions expressed greater confidence in penal techniques, arguing that because instinctive emotions influenced some to do good and others to transgress, habitual offenders ought to be carefully controlled. In her footnote to a criminal psychology text published in 1846, Eliza Farnham, women's matron at Sing Sing, describes "the inheritance of propensities" leading to "criminal indulgence" (p. 28). The book's author, M. B. Sampson, blames its possible biological cause: "a defective form of brain" (p. 7).

Most reformers were optimistic about the power of a controlled environment to improve individuals. The early nineteenth century witnessed a reading revolution, a popular lyceum movement, and a general disposition of Americans toward self-improvement and social progress. Richard Brown characterizes the diffusion of information during this period as "a great national enterprise," for the "seemingly inexhaustible market for this sort of personal improvement information . . . was driven by a popular desire to enjoy such material and psychological benefits as gentility afforded" (pp. 289, 274). Society's interest in encouraging moral improvement included developing rehabilitation methods in prisons to stop recidivism.

ORIGINS OF THE PENITENTIARY IN THE UNITED STATES

While the century witnessed a number of innovations relevant to the topics of crime and punishment, including establishing metropolitan police forces along with specialized detective units, the most celebrated landmarks of reform involved the construction of penitentiaries by various states in the Northeast. The transformation from prison to penitentiary began with eighteenth-century experiments and arguments advocated by Benjamin Rush and others in Philadelphia, where Eastern State Penitentiary, designed by John Haviland, was built in 1821–1823. New York also developed penal techniques and facilities, instituting a contract labor system in Auburn penitentiary in 1819; convicts worked silently in groups during the day and slept in solitary cells. Auburn's brief experiment with solitary cells permitting some convicts to work separately in the early 1820s was abandoned as unworkable, likely due to the poor conditions of the cells.

By 1828 the congregate Auburn penitentiary turned a profit, but its system of contract labor invited criticism from prisoners, most notably regarding the physical punishments employed to increase productivity. The ex-convict William Coffey's first-person account, *Inside Out; or, An Interior View of the New-York State Prison* (1823), indicted harsh disciplinary methods used during his incarceration and called for separating prisoners instead of requiring convict labor, a recommendation agreeing with the conclusions of an 1822 New York Senate report on prisons. Two works by Horace Lane, *The Wandering Boy, Careless Sailor* (1839) and *Five Years in State's Prison* (1835), respectively a first-person didactic account of his criminal life and a dialogue between two prisoners of Auburn and Sing Sing, also explore the inefficacy of corporal punishment.

Many reformers also objected to harsh corporal punishments as a way of forcing convicts to work. Philadelphia's inspector Richard Vaux, a frequent critic, argued in 1855: "It is believed that the congregation of convicts during their incarceration for crime-punishment, and their sale to the highest bidder as human machines, out of which profit is to be made, is of far greater evil to society, than society yet fully comprehends" (Staples, p. 33). Convicts were subdued with straitjackets, iron gags, the lash, and the cold shower-bath, punishments applied frequently in New York penitentiaries to improve productivity. Proponents of extreme punishments sometimes depicted blacks, immigrants, Indians, and certain white recidivists as more likely to be inured to pain, an argument also advanced by slaveholders. John W. Edmonds, a judge who founded the New York Prison Association in 1844, was one of many humanitarians opposed to flogging, which was finally outlawed by New York penitentiaries in 1847.

On 16 January 1843 the New York State inspectors of the state prison at Auburn reported to the New York State Senate on "reforms" in treatment of prisoners:

Within the last year the former mode of punishing the convicts, by whipping for infringement of the rules of the prison, has been almost wholly abandoned, and as a substitute the application of cold water in the form of showering or pouring upon the naked head and body has been adopted; and we are convinced that in a very great majority of cases it has the desired effect of subduing the disobedient and refractory, while at the same time the self respect of the man is preserved.

New York State Inspectors of the State Prison at Auburn, "Annual Report," 1843, p. 2.

THE MODEL AMERICAN PENITENTIARY

Officials and philanthropists in the first half of the century built, managed, and theorized about penitentiaries based on principles of separation and solitary confinement. Americans acknowledged European predecessors, including Césare Beccaria, who argued that "it is better to prevent crimes than to punish them" (pp. 104–105) and John Howard, whose writings improved British prisons. Elizabeth Fry's work in British prisons and Alexander Maconochie's in Australian institutions were also lauded by Americans. The 10 April 1847 issue of the *Literary World* praised Fry as having "gone forth with a mission to complete the unfinished labor of Howard," reminding readers that "our own country is taking the lead, most honorably, in this humane science" ("Review of Memoirs," p. 226).

Penitentiaries provided architectural and programmatic models for visitors who wished to observe reforms in action. Scott Christianson describes the "inspection avenues" that allowed officials and visitors to Auburn to secretly observe convicts at work. Approved visitors to Eastern State, colloquially termed "Cherry Hill" because of its site in a former cherry orchard, were permitted to engage solitary inmates in conversations focused on moral rehabilitation. Norman Johnston argues that "over three hundred prisons worldwide show the direct or indirect imprint of

Haviland's Philadelphia and Trenton prisons. It is on the basis of both contributions that Cherry Hill must be considered the most influential prison ever built and arguably the American building most widely imitated in Europe and Asia in the nineteenth century" (p. 105).

Touring the United States in the early 1830s as representatives of the French government, Gustave de Beaumont and Alexis de Tocqueville (who would also produce *Democracy in America* from this visit) reported on the American models of penal discipline in *On the Penitentiary System in the United States and Its Application to France* (1833); they were succeeded in 1837 by their countrymen Frédéric-Auguste Demetz and Guillaume-Abel Blouet and the Spaniard Ramón de la Sagra, who visited in the mid-1830s. Visitors noted that prison discipline societies associated with the penitentiaries emphasized the virtues of their own system and the vices of the other. Eastern State's solitary system, with individual cells used for work, contemplation, and sleeping, was more expensive to administer and appeared to induce mental degeneration in some inmates. The congregate Auburn system was profitable but appeared less humanitarian in its reliance on corporal punishments and on independent contractors to supervise silent convict laborers. As Beaumont and Tocqueville state, "the Philadelphia system produces more honest men, and that of New York more obedient citizens" (p. 60).

HUMANITARIAN INTERVENTIONS

In 1841 Dorothea Dix (1802–1887), a schoolteacher and a writer of childrens' didactic literature, became an advocate for prisoners and the mentally ill after teaching a Sunday school class for women in an East Cambridge jail. In 1843, after surveying conditions for the incarcerated and institutionalized in the state, she reported her findings to the Massachusetts legislature, and in subsequent legislative addresses she identified abuses in other states' facilities. In *Remarks on Prisons and Prison Discipline in the United States* (1845), Dix connected rehabilitating criminals and diminishing poverty as "the two great questions" and argued for making paupers "useful" citizens and for paying convicts for work to help them improve habits and conscience (p. 5).

The reformer Samuel Gridley Howe (1801–1876) noted in 1846 that the debate between the supporters of separate and congregate establishments reflected cultural differences between Europeans, who were reluctant to endorse corporal punishment, preferring the Philadelphia system, while most Americans approved the profitable Auburn system. Howe counted the Americans Francis Lieber (1800–1872) and Dorothea Dix as recommending Eastern State, while George Combe and Charles Dickens, visiting from Britain, were horrified by the degenerative effects of solitary confinement there.

Others also kept prisons in the public eye. Chaplains, philanthropists, and officials reported on penitentiaries in publications issued by prison discipline societies; excerpts from such reports and from related books were often reprinted in reviews appearing in popular periodicals. Francis Lieber, a German immigrant and professor of political science who translated Beaumont and Tocqueville's report on penitentiaries into English, later wrote his own book on the subject. In an 1847 book on prison discipline, the American Francis Gray responded to Howe's 1846 book, which had expressed a preference for solitary confinement, by arguing on behalf of the congregate Auburn system. John Luckey, a chaplain, published *Life in Sing Sing* in 1860, a brief history documenting how moral instruction improved several convicts.

In the mid-1840s Eliza Farnham and Georgiana Bruce reorganized the previously badly managed women's prison at Mount Pleasant, associated with Sing Sing. Nicole Hahn Rafter notes that their educational program permitted some conversation and allowed fictional texts. Barbara Packer notes that, during Farnham and Bruce's four-year tenure, the prominent transcendentalist Margaret Fuller (1810–1850) read excerpts from prisoners' journals sent by Bruce. With Caroline Sturgis and W. H. Channing, Fuller visited Mount Pleasant in fall 1844 and motivated friends to donate books to supplement religious tracts; the same year she spent Christmas with the female convicts.

SENTIMENTAL DEPICTIONS

Other writers also advocated for prisoners by noting how economic circumstances drive individuals to crime, the cruelty of particular punishments, and the poor prospects for released convicts. As noted above, Lydia Maria Child advocated improvements in the criminal justice system in her journalism. In her story "The Irish Heart: A True Story," published in *Fact and Fiction* (1846), she tells of the young Irish immigrant James, unfairly sentenced as a forger to Sing Sing, which fails to provide him with adequate skills to earn a living; upon release he receives tools and other help from the New York Prison Association. In the same anthology's "Rosenglory," Child describes Susan, a domestic servant corrupted by one employer's son who later steals money from another employer for not paying her wages. Susan is sent to prison and later receives assistance from a home for discharged women convicts. In Harriet Beecher Stowe's (1811–1896) *Uncle Tom's Cabin* (serialized in 1851–1852), Marie St. Clare sends her slave Rosa to be whipped in a New Orleans jail despite her sister-in-law Ophelia's protests that to put a girl under a man's lash degrades her body and soul.

Other writers represented more positive views of how the law protects the innocent, emphasizing the speedy, efficient resolution of crimes. Catharine Sedgwick was involved with the Women's Prison Association and the Isaac Hopper Home for discharged women prisoners. She alluded to the unfortunate situation of the innocent convict in her novel *Married or Single?* (1857), in which Alice Clifford visits her brother Max in the Tombs because he has been falsely indicted for forgery. After Alice spends a night in a jail cell adjacent to his, Max is acquitted because several individuals help Alice prove his innocence at trial. Horatio Alger's (1832–1899) prototypical rags-to-riches tale *Ragged Dick* (1868) contains a subplot detailing how a fellow boarder steals Dick's bankbook; tipped off by the victim, the police set a trap for the thief, who is arrested, convicted, and sentenced to nine months on Blackwell's Island.

SENSATIONALIZING CRIME

As Andie Tucher notes, American periodicals began printing crime news in 1820, shortly after certain London papers started columns reporting petty crimes. Economic fluctuations encouraged the editors James Gordon Bennett of the *New York Herald* and Horace Greeley of the *New York Tribune* to develop a newspaper readership among the working class by castigating greedy, fraudulent entrepreneurs and corrupt politicians as well as alleged murderers and thieves. Periodicals printed descriptions of jails and prisons based on reporters' visits and collected reports of domestic and foreign crimes. The *National Police Gazette* (published 1845 to 1933 and claiming a circulation of forty thousand readers in its first decade) described famous crimes in history and noted recent crimes reported in the popular press in the United States and abroad. The *Gazette* summarized criminal trials, editorialized about political crimes, and printed articles about historical and contemporary criminals; the editor, George Wilkes, also published the latter in pamphlet form some reprinted decades later. Patricia Cline Cohen argues that newspaper articles about the clerk Richard Robinson, acquitted for the alleged murder of his lover, the New York prostitute Helen Jewett, in 1836, increased sales of the papers and fueled competition in the 1840s by retailing obsessions about sex and death.

Sensational, dime, and western novels incorporated lurid details also used in newspaper crime stories. According to David Reynolds and Kimberly Gladman, the first American city novel was George Lippard's *The Quaker City; or, The Monks of Monk Hall: A Romance of Philadelphia Life* (1844–1845). Inspired by Eugène Sue's *Mystères de Paris, The Quaker City* describes upstanding citizens and criminals conspiring to seduce young women. Reynolds characterizes journalistic aspects of the prolific George Foster's *New York in Slices* (1849), *Fifteen Minutes around New York* (1854), and *New York Naked* (1854) as "realistic exposés" of everyday life in the city. George Thompson's many novels, including *Venus in Boston* (1849) and *City Crimes* (1849), lasciviously describe the degenerative effects of drinking and promiscuous sexual habits, unveiling seemingly virtuous individuals as deviants working closely with vicious criminal gangs. Dime novels, including some published in Erastus Beadle's series beginning in 1860, and some westerns were also criticized as morally pernicious. Bret Harte's "The Luck of Roaring Camp" (1868) more optimistically depicts the rehabilitation of those inclined toward transgression in plotting how a baby civilizes miners on the frontier.

REPRESENTING CRIME AND PUNISHMENT

In addition to the works already cited, images of incarceration and punishment appear in a number of other texts, including Indian captivity narratives and Revolution-era captivity narratives such as Thomas Dring's *Recollections of the Jersey Prison Ship* (1829); narratives of slavery, including Harriet Jacobs's *Incidents in the Life of a Slave Girl* (1861) and Harriet Wilson's novel *Our Nig* (1859); and anti-Catholic convent literature, such as Rebecca Reed's *Six Months in a Convent* (1835) and satires of the latter such as *Six Months in a House of Correction* (1835). After Henry David Thoreau resisted paying his poll tax in protest of the Mexican-American War, he described his night in the Concord jail in "Resistance to Civil Government" (1849).

Several American fiction writers refer to issues associated with historical and contemporary practices of crime and punishment, and some criticize contemporary reforms and reformers. Edgar Allan Poe's fictions represent transgressive anxieties and fears of incarceration; particularly chilling are depictions of murder in "The Tell-Tale Heart" (1843) and of an old man who "is the type and the genius of deep crime" (p. 272) in London, depicted in "The Man of the Crowd" (1840). In the first American detective stories, Poe describes Auguste Dupin's ratiocination in solving criminal cases in "The Murders in the Rue

Morgue" (1841), "The Purloined Letter" (1844), and "The Mystery of Marie Roget" (1842–1843).

Nathaniel Hawthorne's works are more critical of criminal stereotypes and reform motivations. "Endicott and the Red Cross" (1838) and *The Scarlet Letter* (1850) characterize the cruelty of Puritan punishments directed at those who are different (Episcopalians, women, Indians). *The House of Seven Gables* (1851) denounces social conventions falsely accusing Clifford Pyncheon, foreigners, deviants, women, and the poor of transgressive behaviors. *The Blithedale Romance* (1852) suggests that reforms focused on moral rehabilitation fail in representing Hollingsworth's "impracticable plan for the reformation of criminals through an appeal to their higher instincts" (p. 36).

Herman Melville mentions the prison reformer Elizabeth Fry in *The Confidence-Man* (1857) and François Eugéne Vidocq, the French criminal turned detective, in *White-Jacket* (1850) and *Moby-Dick* (1851). Melville's other fictions note the imprisoning aspects of civilizing society (*Typee*, 1846) and colonialism (*Omoo*, 1847; *Mardi*, 1849). Images of captivity recur in *Redburn* (1849), *The Piazza Tales* (1856), and *Israel Potter* (1855), as protagonists experience diverse forms of captivity on land and sea. The last scenes of "Bartleby, the Scrivener" (1853) and *Pierre* (1852) take place in the Tombs, a New York jail, and in *Billy Budd* (1924) the title character is summarily executed in a hasty trial at sea.

Foreshadowing naturalistic depictions of crime and punishment, *Life in the Iron Mills* (1861), by Rebecca Harding Davis (1831–1910), depicts the wretched circumstances endured by poor ironworkers, who labor like convicts in that their lives and work are constrained by those in authority. In the novella, Deb picks the pocket of the rich observer who admires her cousin Hugh's ironwork, an action resulting in Hugh's conviction as a thief after he tries to return the money. Davis portrays the inevitable, cruel punishment heaped on the honest worker. Like Hawthorne and Melville, she suggests that Americans countenance social and economic inequalities as the byproduct of entrepreneurial spirit. Decades of investment in penitentiary programs and thousands of words endorsing moral rehabilitation in the antebellum period reflect and reconfigure reform ideals as inextricably tied to ideas of American progress.

See also Individualism and Community; *Life in the Iron Mills;* Psychology; Reform; Sensational Fiction

BIBLIOGRAPHY

Primary Works

Beaumont, Gustave de, and Alexis de Tocqueville. *On the Penitentiary System in the United States and Its Application to France*. Translated by Francis Lieber. Philadelphia: Carey, Lea, and Blanchard, 1833.

Beccaria, Césare. *Essay on Crimes and Punishment*. Translated by E. D. Ingraham. Philadelphia: H. Nicklin, 1819. http://www.fordham.edu/halsall/mod/18beccaria.html.

Carey, Mathew. *Appeal to the Wealthy of the Land*. 2nd ed. Philadelphia: L. Johnson, 1833.

Child, Lydia Maria. *Fact and Fiction: A Collection of Stories*. New York: C. S. Francis, 1846.

Child, Lydia Maria. *Letters from New York*. 1845. Freeport, N.Y.: Books for Libraries, 1970.

Dix, Dorothea. *Remarks on Prisons and Prison Discipline in the United States*. Boston: Munroe and Francis, 1845.

Farnham, Eliza. Preface to *The Rationale of Crime*, by M. B. Sampson. New York and Philadelphia: D. Appleton and George S. Appleton, 1846.

Fern, Fanny. *Ruth Hall and Other Writings*. Edited by Joyce W. Warren. New Brunswick, N.J.: Rutgers University Press, 1991.

Hawthorne, Nathaniel. *The Blithedale Romance*. 1852. Columbus: Ohio State University Press, 1964.

Hawthorne, Nathaniel. *The Scarlet Letter*. 1850. Edited by Ross Murfin. Boston: Bedford Books, 1991.

"Review of Memoirs of Mrs. Elizabeth Fry." *Literary World*, 10 April 1847, pp. 226–227.

Poe, Edgar Allan. *Great Short Works of Edgar Allan Poe*. Edited by G. R. Thompson. New York: Harper and Row, 1970.

Sampson, M. B. *The Rationale of Crime, and Its Appropriate Treatment*. New York and Philadelphia: D. Appleton and George S. Appleton, 1846.

Sedgwick, Catharine. *Married or Single?* New York: Harper, 1857.

Shaw, Lemuel. *A Discourse Delivered before the Members of the Humane Society of Massachusetts, 11 June 1811*. Boston: John Eliot, 1811.

Six Months in a House of Correction; or, The Narrative of Dorah Mahony. 1835. Boston: Benjamin B. Mussey, 1835.

Secondary Works

Brown, Richard. *Knowledge Is Power: The Diffusion of Information in Early America, 1700–1865*. New York: Oxford University Press, 1989.

Carlton, Frank. "Abolition of the Imprisonment for Debt in the United States." *Yale Review* 17 (November 1908): 339–344.

Christianson, Scott. *With Liberty for Some: 500 Years of Imprisonment in America*. Boston: Northeastern University Press, 1998.

Cohen, Patricia Cline. *The Murder of Helen Jewett: The Life and Death of a Prostitute in Nineteenth-Century New York*. New York: Knopf, 1998.

Colatrella, Carol. *Literature and Moral Reform: Melville and the Discipline of Reading*. Gainesville: University Press of Florida, 2002.

Cross, Whitney R. *The Burned-Over District: The Social and Intellectual History of Enthusiastic Religion in Western New York, 1800–1850*. New York: Harper and Row, 1950.

Davis, David Brion. *Homicide in American Fiction 1798–1860*. Ithaca, N.Y.: Cornell University Press, 1957.

Friedman, Lawrence M. *Crime and Punishment in American History*. New York: Basic, 1993.

Johnston, Norman, with Kenneth Finkel and Jeffrey A. Cohen. *Eastern State Penitentiary: Crucible of Good Intentions*. Philadelphia: Philadelphia Museum of Art, 1994.

Masur, Louis P. *Rites of Execution: Capital Punishment and the Transformation of American Culture*. New York: Oxford University Press, 1989.

Packer, Barbara. "Diaspora." In *Cambridge History of American Literature*, vol. 2, *1820–1865*, edited by Sacvan Bercovitch, pp. 495–547. Cambridge, U.K.: Cambridge University Press, 1995.

Rafter, Nicole Hahn. *Partial Justice: Women, Prisons, and Social Control*. 2nd ed. New Brunswick, N.J.: Transaction, 1990.

Reynolds, David S. *Beneath the American Renaissance: The Subversive Imagination in the Age of Emerson and Melville*. Cambridge, Mass.: Harvard University Press, 1989.

Reynolds, David S., and Kimberly R. Gladman. "Introduction." In *Venus in Boston and Other Tales of Nineteenth-Century City Life*, by George Thompson, pp. ix–liv. Amherst: University of Massachusetts Press, 2002.

Rothman, David J. "Perfecting the Prison." In *The Oxford History of the Prison: The Practice of Punishment in Western Society*, edited by Norval Morris and David J. Rothman. New York: Oxford University Press, 1998.

Smith-Rosenberg, Carroll. *Religion and the Rise of the American City: The New York City Mission Movement, 1812–1870*. Ithaca, N.Y.: Cornell University Press, 1971.

Staples, William G. *Castles of Our Conscience: Social Control and the American State, 1800–1985*. New Brunswick, N.J.: Rutgers University Press, 1990.

Thomas, Brook. *Cross-Examinations of Law and Literature: Cooper, Hawthorne, Stowe, and Melville*. Cambridge, U.K.: Cambridge University Press, 1987.

Tucher, Andie. *Froth and Scum: Truth, Beauty, Goodness, and the Ax-Murder in America's First Mass Medium*. Chapel Hill: University of North Carolina Press, 1994.

Carol Colatrella

CROSS-DRESSING

If the American nation and American literature shared an infancy in the late eighteenth century, then we might look at the nineteenth century as an adolescence and coming-of-age. American literature achieved both fertility and emotional intensity in the nineteenth century and reflected a restlessness evident in the American population. Just as the Missouri Compromise of 1820 marked the dividing line between Southern slave and Northern free territories, it simultaneously divided "settled" territories in the East from "Indian" territories in the West. These dividing lines were also transgression lines; the invisibility of state lines (other than on a map or as represented by geographical features, such as the Ohio River, which themselves became symbolic of division and transgression) served as an apt metaphor for American anxieties about how cultural categories were to be policed—anxieties about intermarriage and miscegenation, for example. This geography of racial tension was echoed in American gender relations: Sarah Bartley Smith, also in 1820, tested the line drawn for women between the private and public spheres by playing "the first transvestite Hamlet" at New York City's Park Theatre (Shattuck, p. 37); just a year later, the first American college for women was established in Waterford, New York. As contemporary critics look back over American literature's nineteenth-century adolescence, one literary type emerges again and again: the cross-dresser.

Cross-dressing—generally understood as the practice of one sex wearing clothes traditionally assigned to the other, but expandable to include the crossing of other cultural categories through dress—was not new or specific to American literature or culture. Literarily, the American cross-dressed character had ancestors not only in European literature accepted as germinal to American letters, such as Greek dramas, Medieval romances and saints' lives, Elizabethan plays, and European novels (such as *Don Quijote* [1605] and *The Fortunes and Misfortunes of the Famous Moll Flanders* [1722]), but also in Native American and African American folklores. As Marjorie Garber has noted, "at times of national strife or social change . . . aspects of dress often become emblematic of political position" (p. 22), and cross-dressers therefore often signify unstable positions, symbolically embodying societal conflicts. The figure of the cross-dresser in American literature emerges simultaneously as male and female, native and colonist, captive and free, and represents conflicts central to American identities.

SHAKESPEAREAN CROSS-DRESSING AND THE AMERICAN STAGE

Though in America Shakespearean actresses had been playing since the mid-1700s—not only women's roles, such as Portia in *Merchant of Venice,* but also men's roles, such as Hal in *Henry IV*—the demand for "breeches parts" (roles played by women in men's clothing) became respectable in the early part of the nineteenth century. Charlotte Cushman (1816–1876, who was famous for portrayals of both Rosalind in *As You Like It* and Romeo in *Romeo and Juliet,* and also played Oberon from *A Midsummer Night's Dream*), Fanny Kemble (1809–1893, who played Portia), and Ellen Tree Kean (1805–1880, who performed Viola from *Twelfth Night,* in addition to Romeo and Rosalind) are some of the actresses who played Shakespearean transvestite roles in the early 1800s. Cushman was especially known for these roles; one of the early Shakespearean exports to England from America, she was often praised in London for her masculine verisimilitude. Many of these actresses also played cross-dressed roles in works by American authors.

Shakespearean themes of cross-cultural and cross-gender investigation are abundant in the above-listed repertoires, as well as in other works performed in America during the period, such as *Othello, The Tempest,* and *The Taming of the Shrew.* Shakespeare and his plays represented these cultural themes to an American audience, allowing it to wrestle with the meaning and mission of America—which may account, in part, for Shakespeare's status as a "best-seller" in the new republic (Mott, p. 305). In contrast with English theater, from the inception performances of Shakespeare's plays in America relied on a mixed cast of men and women; in America, then, while one direction of cross-dressing (from actor to heroine) was lost to audiences, the cross in the other direction (from actress/heroine to male alter ego) was emphasized. No doubt this fact reflected a certain willingness in the colonies to explore expanded roles for women in the new republic and also helped to foster the dialogue about that expanded role. American Shakespearean actresses, in confronting stereotypes about women in the theater, gradually began to

transform American theatergoing into a genteel activity—one suitable for respectable women (Shattuck, p. 98). Women's expanded roles in the theater as actresses and audience members allowed audiences to work through cultural anxieties as women's roles expanded in other directions—for example, as mothers became responsible for religious education and moral authority within the home (Davidson, p. 13).

THE AMERICAN CROSS-DRESSING NOVEL

Shakespearean theater was a tremendous force in America, and it had an observable impact on conversations about race, class, and gender—not exclusively, but especially in the pages of American novels. Novelist Catharine Maria Sedgwick (1789–1867), for example, was a close friend of Fanny Kemble's and drew on Shakespeare's Rosalind for one of the characters in her widely acclaimed novel *Hope Leslie* (1827). Indeed, the cross-dressed page, Rosa (whose male alter ego is Roslyn), is only one of several characters who cross-dress over the course of the novel—two others being the lead female characters, Hope (an English immigrant) and Magawisca (an Indian princess). Magawisca is one party in a chiasmatic exchange of clothing between herself and Hope's tutor, Cradock, which facilitates her escape from an unjust imprisonment at the hands of the Puritans—a plot device that stands on its head the traditional Indian captivity narrative relating the imprisonment and escape of white colonials from Indian captives.

Like Shakespearean theater, the Indian captivity narrative was an important source for novels drawing the cross-dressed character. While often depicting heroines such as Mary Rowlandson (c. 1636–1711), who adhered in the extreme to traditional European gender roles, the Indian captivity narrative also related the cautionary tales of intriguing figures like Mary Jemison (1743–1833), who remained with her Indian "captors" by choice after it was possible for her to return. James Everett Seaver's (1787–1827) introductory description of Jemison relates Jemison's masculine qualities—such as the ownership of a house, barn, and considerable livestock—to her style of dress, which is both cross-cultural (a pair of moccasins) and cross-gender (a man's shirt). Earlier narratives by explorers like Jacques Marquette (1637–1675) and Pierre François Xavier de Charlevoix (1682–1761) related a Native American gender system more fluid than the European, and American authors like Sedgwick and also James Fenimore Cooper (1789–1851) drew on these texts in their tales of the American frontier. The clash of gender systems is visible in Cooper's *Last of the Mohicans* (1826) in the character of psalmodist David Gamut—a precursor to

Sedgwick's Cradock—who is feminized by Cooper and initially ridiculed by Hawkeye until his unusual gifts so impress the Hurons that he is allowed to pass freely in and out of their camp, thus facilitating the rescue of the women captives. Gamut is feminized throughout the novel and exhibits some qualities associated with the "berdache," or two-spirit, members of certain Native American tribes, and his cross-cultural dress late in the novel marks him as a traverser of many cultural categories.

Another kind of captivity narrative, the slave narrative was also a source for American novelists who created cross-dressed characters—most notably, perhaps, the escape of William and Ellen Craft (1821–1900, 1826–1891), as told in their book *Running a Thousand Miles for Freedom; or, The Escape of William and Ellen Craft from Slavery* (1860) and circulated widely in the abolitionist press starting in 1849. William and Ellen managed their escape by using a disguise for light-skinned Ellen, who wore a man's suit and invalid's veil and passed for an ailing white slave owner, with husband William passing as her slave. The story was extremely popular in the press and a drawing of Ellen in disguise was widely distributed. The Crafts' story was compelling enough to foster similar plots in several novels, including Harriet Beecher Stowe's *Uncle Tom's Cabin: or, Life Among the Lowly* (1852), William Wells Brown's *Clotel; or, The President's Daughter* (1853), and Hannah Crafts's *The Bondwoman's Narrative* (c. 1850s); indeed, there is speculation that the author of *The Bondwoman's Narrative* may have drawn on the story of her own escape, inspired by Ellen Craft's disguise (Crafts, p. xxii). In all of these stories, boundaries of race, class, and gender are crossed simultaneously to give the disguise its effectiveness; in two of them, the female-to-male cross by the heroine (Eliza in *Uncle Tom's Cabin* and Clotel in *Clotel*) is countered by a male-to-female cross (by baby Harry in *Uncle Tom's Cabin* and by George in *Clotel*). As in the novels of Sedgwick and Cooper, cross-dressing in Stowe's, Brown's, and Crafts's novels is associated with escape from a captivity representative of diverse cultural constraints.

Whereas escapes from captivity are depicted in these earlier novels, however, gender itself is the prison to be escaped in works in circulation during and after the Civil War: *The Hidden Hand* (published serially in 1859, as a book in 1888), by E. D. E. N. Southworth (1819–1899); *Little Women* (1868–1869), by Louisa May Alcott (1832–1888); and a host of novels published during the period—a trend in fiction reflecting significant numbers of historical women who cross-dressed to fight in the Civil War (see Young,

pp. 132, 340). Southworth's antebellum novel, in contrast with those described above, uses slave characters mostly as a comic backdrop; Capitola's cross-dressing at the start of the novel is likewise comic, though it also creates sympathy for the heroine, who is orphaned and must pass as a newsboy to survive on the streets. Capitola puts the cross behind her at the start of the novel and heads out to her grandfather's Southern plantation, obscuring issues of both gender and race as she goes.

In contrast, Jo March's cross-gendered identification and appearance in *Little Women* are developed over the course of the novel and are rendered most visible by her efforts to support the Civil War against slavery. Within the first few pages of the novel, we learn that Jo laments the fact of her sex and wishes to be a man so that she can fight on the Union side with her father. Like Kemble, Cushman, and Kean, Alcott stands the Shakespearean tradition on its head by having Jo write plays in order to play the swashbuckling

Ellen Craft, c. 1851. Craft and her husband William Craft fled slavery by posing as a white male slaveholder (Ellen) and his slave (William). Their slave narrative was published as *Running a Thousand Miles for Freedom; or, The Escape of William and Ellen Craft from Slavery* (1860). THE GRANGER COLLECTION

male roles herself, with the boots, foil, and doublet that are her "chief treasures" (p. 17). Though all the March sisters adopt male pseudonyms for the family newspaper, *The Pickwick Portfolio,* only Jo later goes on to do so in actually publishing her gothic thrillers. Like Joan of Arc and other cross-dressing female saints (and Alcott herself, as well) Jo sacrifices her hair for the martial cause, selling it to bring her injured father home from the fighting. Jo is the only one of the sisters to leave the March home to strike out on her own, taking a governess position and circulating her writing in New York City; it is here that she determines to put aside the gothic thrillers, but she continues in her "masculine" profession of writing to the novel's end, where her poem brings her lover to her so that she may tell him she is determined "to "help to earn the home" (p. 367). Alcott's treatment of Jo is an exceptional innovation of the cross-dressing tradition in that it begins to develop the possibility of "cross"-dressing as true self-expression—in other words, the possibility that the clothes of the "other" may, in truth, be one's own best attire. In her postbellum novel, Alcott attempts to create a postwar reconstruction of gender in line with the goals of postslavery Reconstruction legislation passed as she wrote and published *Little Women.*

The novels described here all contain characters who come of age in a world of fractured identities, the real condition in which Americans found themselves. Represented in these texts is the idea that as American youth come to consciousness about the human condition, they must learn not only to traverse territories of race, class, and gender but also to some extent to contain these fractured territories of identity. In *Disarming the Nation: Women's Writing and the American Civil War,* Elizabeth Young discerns a central Civil War metaphor in nineteenth-century fiction, representing fractured geographic, social, and psychological regions often represented in a language of captivity, disguise, and escape. While the term "cross-dressing" is generally understood as having to do with sex and gender, the scope is clearly much larger, with many more cultural boundaries crossed—a series of symbolic jail-breaks within the pages of American novels, often represented and facilitated through cross-dressing. As these cross-dressed characters come of age, then, they show us that part of what it means to be a full-fledged American is that disguise, betrayal, desire, and self-revelation are unavoidable; these are part of the human condition in America, where so many cultures interact and intertwine. A comforting structure of wholeness that holds these fractured territories together, the novel as book becomes, like Lincoln's trope of the "house united," representative

of a human family made up of fractured identities (Young, pp. 26–27). The cross-dressed character within the novel, then, is the book within a book, within whose "covers" is contained all of the myriad identities and desires of the American people, embodying the conflicts and deceptions but also the truths of fiction—the book whose cover we judge, but whose content we must read if we are to know the American family.

See also The Bondwoman's Narrative; Captivity Narratives; Civil War; English Literature; *The Hidden Hand; Hope Leslie;* Indians; *Little Women;* Slave Narratives; Theater

BIBLIOGRAPHY

Primary Works

Alcott, Louisa May. *Little Women.* 1868–1869. New York: Penguin Books, 1989.

Brown, William Wells. *Clotel; or, The President's Daughter: A Narrative of Slave Life in the United States.* 1853. Edited by Robert S. Levine. Boston: Bedford/St. Martin's, 2000.

Cervantes, Miguel de. *Don Quijote.* 1605. Translated by Burton Raffel and edited by Diana de Armas Wilson. New York: W. W. Norton, 1999.

Cooper, James Fennimore. *Last of the Mohicans.* 1826. New York: Penguin Books, 1986.

Craft, William and Ellen. *Running a Thousand Miles for Freedom; or, The Escape of William and Ellen Craft from Slavery.* 1860. Athens: University of Georgia Press, 1999.

Crafts, Hannah. *The Bondwoman's Narrative.* c. 1850s. Edited by Henry Louis Gates Jr. New York: Warner Books, 2002.

Defoe, Daniel. *The Fortunes and Misfortunes of the Famous Moll Flanders.* 1722. Middlesex, U.K.: Penguin, 1980.

Derounian-Stodola, Kathryn Zabelle, ed. *Women's Indian Captivity Narratives.* New York: Penguin, 1998.

Sedgwick, Catharine Maria. *Hope Leslie.* 1827. Edited and with an introduction by Mary Kelley. New Brunswick, N.J.: Rutgers University Press, 1987.

Shakespeare, William. *The Riverside Shakespeare.* 2nd ed. Boston: Houghton Mifflin Company, 1997.

Southworth, E. D. E. N. *The Hidden Hand.* 1859. Oxford: Oxford University Press, 1997.

Stowe, Harriet Beecher. *Uncle Tom's Cabin: or, Life among the Lowly.* 1852. Edited by Ann Douglas. New York: Penguin Books, 1986.

Secondary Works

Bullough, Vern L., and Bonnie Bullough. *Cross Dressing, Sex, and Gender.* Philadelphia: University of Pennsylvania Press, 1993.

Davidson, Cathy N. *Revolution and the Word: The Rise of the Novel in America.* New York: Oxford University Press, 1986.

Garber, Marjorie. *Vested Interests: Cross-Dressing and Cultural Anxiety.* New York: Routledge, 1992.

Mott, Frank Luther. *Golden Multitudes: The Story of Best Sellers in the United States.* New York: Macmillan, 1947.

Shattuck, Charles H. *Shakespeare on the American Stage: From the Hallams to Edwin Booth.* Washington, D.C.: Folger Shakespeare Library, 1976.

Young, Elizabeth. *Disarming the Nation: Women's Writing and the American Civil War.* Chicago: University of Chicago Press, 1999.

Mary Lamb Shelden

"CROSSING BROOKLYN FERRY"

"Crossing Brooklyn Ferry" has long been regarded as one of Walt Whitman's greatest poems. It shows Whitman (1819–1892) at his most optimistic, yet also at his most reflective, as he uses local and biographical detail to express transcendental ideas. The poem appeared for the first time in the 1856 (second) edition of *Leaves of Grass* in a somewhat different form and with the title "Sun-Down Poem." This first version's eleven sections, while notably different from the final nine-section revision in the 1881 edition of *Leaves of Grass*, contains much of the language that appears in later versions. The main themes are present from the earliest versions: life, death and immortality, general optimism, and joy in the daily details of life in the cities of New York and Brooklyn (New York was not consolidated into its present five boroughs until 1 January 1898).

WHITMAN AND FERRIES

In a memoir of his earliest years in Brooklyn, "Old Brooklyn Days," Whitman recalls ferry rides he took in early childhood (*Complete Poetry*, p. 1282). In *Specimen Days,* in a piece titled "My Passion for Ferries," he describes how he has come to be "identified with the Fulton ferry," which connected Brooklyn to Manhattan and which he rode "almost daily" in the 1850s and 1860s; he states that he has "always had a passion for ferries: to me they afford inimitable, streaming, never-failing, living poems" (*Complete Poetry*, pp. 700–701). Whitman also discusses ferries in several of his early pieces of journalism. In 1847 he wrote a piece for the *Brooklyn Eagle* called "The Philosophy of Ferries," a humorous description of the behavior of passengers on the various ferries that connected Brooklyn and New York. Two years later he described another trip in detail in the tenth installment of "Letters from a Travelling Bachelor" in the December 1849 issue of the *New-York Sunday Dispatch.*

"Crossing Brooklyn Ferry" draws on this December 1849 newspaper piece. The trip takes place in winter (the poem mentions the "Twelfth-month sea-gulls," l. 28) and at the same time of day, late afternoon ("sun there half an hour high," l. 2), but the poem reverses the direction: the newspaper piece describes a trip from Manhattan to Brooklyn, whereas the ferry in the poem moves from Brooklyn to Manhattan. Changing the direction expands the trip's meaning: it is no longer merely a ten-minute commute from Manhattan back home to Brooklyn but a journey that parallels the direction of the sun throughout the day (as the original title, "Sun-Down Poem," suggests), a journey from life through death into an eternal future that is also eternally present. The newspaper piece goes into great detail about the human passengers, their behavior and appearance; the poem mentions them but prefers to detail the physical scene on the water and on either shore.

SYMBOLS, THEMES, AND TECHNIQUES

One of the most interesting features of the poem, one it shares with "Song of Myself" and other major works, is the speaker's direct address to those who will live after him. Whitman's joy in his surroundings is so great and transformative that he shares it not only with those who will read his words during his lifetime but also with those who will read them in the distant future. In the seventh installment of the "Letters from a Travelling Bachelor," from 25 November 1849, Whitman tries out the same view, wondering what future generations will make of the Croton Reservoir at Forty-second Street and Fifth Avenue (current site of the New York Public Library). He describes a late afternoon "jaunt" to watch a summer sunset from the top of its walls and says:

> A hundred years hence, I often imagine, what an appearance that walk will present, on a fine summer afternoon! You and I, reader, and quite all the people who are now alive, won't be much thought of then; but the world will be just as jolly, and the sun will shine as bright, and the rivers off there—the Hudson on one side and the East on the other—will slap along their green waves, precisely as now; and other eyes will look upon them about the same as we do. ("Letters," pp. 336–337)

Whitman takes the situation of the viewer on land between two rivers, thinking of how that view will persist a century or more in the future, and makes it the situation of the speaker on the water, between the cities of Brooklyn and New York, speculating on exactly the same idea. But in the poem he addresses not an imaginary companion on a contemporary stroll but the generations who will come long after him.

Whitman turns his gaze and his address in many directions in "Crossing Brooklyn Ferry," with apostrophes to the tide, the waves, the clouds, the sun, even the rail he leans on as he rides. Sections 2, 3, 6, and 9 in particular feature catalogs; the one in section 9 is particularly notable for its exhortation of the ingredients of the natural scene to keep on doing what they are doing.

The poem relies on the physical realities of New York and Brooklyn, the river between them, the sights of the harbor and the movement of the ferry. It may seem strange, then, that none of the later revisions of the poem mention the construction of the Brooklyn Bridge, which began in 1869 and continued, with national attention to its progress, until it opened to the public formally on 24 May 1883. Any ferry trips Whitman would have taken during that period would have been overshadowed by the bridge. He includes it in a list of great public works in "Song of the Exposition" (1876), and mentions the part of the bridge that was standing in 1878 in "Manhattan from the Bay," collected in *Specimen Days,* but, as Richard Haw has noted, pays no particular attention to it, as he did to other technological achievements and public projects. For the purposes of this poem, the ferry is all he needs. He may have felt that the ferry linked him to ancient myths of immortality and that the bridge was an unnecessary distraction. In fact, he had other opinions about the very idea of a bridge. The tenth number of his "Letters from a Travelling Bachelor," from December 1849, concludes with these remarks:

> We notice there is much talk, just at present, of a bridge to Brooklyn. Nonsense. There is no need of such a bridge, while there are incessantly plying such boats as the Manhattan, the Wyandance, and the Montauk. If there be any spare energy, let it be applied to improving the indifferent accommodations at Catherine Ferry, and the wretchedness of that at Jackson Street. Also, to completing the proposed lines from the bottoms of Montague Street and Bridge Street. (P. 352)

In temporal terms, Whitman sees no use for a bridge while there are so many ferries taking care of the transportation needs of the two cities, and in spiritual terms, he does not number the bridge among the

"silent, beautiful ministers" that "furnish [their] parts toward the soul." His poem, for all its particularities about the harbor, is not a chronicle of the realities of harbor phenomena. It is instead an epic reworking of an ordinary episode.

Whitman's transposition of the thoughts of this type of immortality from the lip of the reservoir to the deck of a ferry plying between two cities connects his poem to all the significance attached to ferries shuttling the dead between the earth and the underworld. The critic Bettina Knapp has linked Whitman's ferry to the Egyptian "Solar bark" of the dead that transported the souls of the dead to the underworld (p. 147). But of course, unlike these mythic ferries, which bring the dead one way only, Whitman's Brooklyn ferry goes back and forth and can carry the same people—or their descendants—in either direction. This is a different type of immortality, manifested through the repeated phenomena of daily life that show forth eternity.

THE POEM

"Crossing Brooklyn Ferry" has nine sections. The five lines of the first begin with an apostrophe to a few of the physical phenomena he invokes: the flood-tide, the clouds in the western sky, the crowds on the ferry, and "you that shall cross from shore to shore years hence" (*Complete Poetry,* p. 308). This brief opening stanza states the poem's main themes: the physical phenomena of the harbor, including the "hundreds and hundreds" of passengers "that cross, returning home" (p. 308), and the speaker's claim of connection to the future riders/readers of whom he is thinking. From here on, the speaker will establish his connection to the harbor, his contemporaries, and the future.

The second section puts forth the theory behind the poem: an overall "simple, compact, well-joined scheme" (p. 308) of the universe precipitates out individual phenomena and individual humans who can see and appreciate them. Two brief catalogues state the idea and give examples, ending again with those who will cross the river in the future, and the things they too will see.

The long third section is addressed directly to those who will come after and begins with the assertion, "It avails not, time nor place—distance avails not" (p. 308), making the central point that "I am with you" (p. 308), enumerating many of the poem's central images: the gull, the sun on the water, the ships coming into the harbor, the waves, the storehouses on one side of the river, a tug with two barges, and the foundry fires on the other side of the river. This is not merely a visual catalog of the harbor sights, however, because the items begin with "Just as you . . ." or "I too," cementing the connection (p. 309). The fourth section restates his enjoyment of it all, including the people, to whom he feels close, even to those who will come after: "Others the same—others who look back on me because I look'd forward to them" (p. 310).

The fifth section, at the poem's structural center, asks the central question: "What is it then between us? / What is the count of the scores or hundreds of years between us?" (p. 310). It makes no difference, he says. He too was "struck from the float" (p. 310), and his individual consciousness comes to him from his body. This idea pervades Whitman's work, and here he joins it to an obliteration of time in the face of common origins (the "float") and common experience.

The sixth section establishes a connection through vices as well as virtues, beginning with an invocation of "dark patches" (p. 311) that fell on him as well as the ones who currently read him—echoing the "flicker of black" that the foundry fires throw "down into the clefts of streets" in the third section (p. 310). He insists that readers identify with him as fully as possible, putting forth all the ways in which he was just like those who will read him in the future, even in life's less admirable and forthright respects. Insisting that he too, as well as his readers, knew "what it [was] to be evil" (p. 311), he catalogs some undesirable behavior, including "hot wishes I dared not speak" (p. 311) and behavior like "the wolf, the snake, the hog" (p. 311). The speaker himself may actually be guilty of each of these things, or he may be mentioning general categories of "evil" as part of a confession of collective guilt, yet another way of solidifying the connection of present to future. He was one of the crowd, he insists, playing "the part that still looks back on the actor or actress" (p. 311).

The seventh section is another direct address to future readers, and it assumes that his readers are thinking of him: "What thoughts you have of me now, I had as much of you" (p. 311), amplified this time by the addition of the possibility that he may somehow still be present, "enjoying this . . . as good as looking at you now, for all you cannot see me" (pp. 311–312), an echo of the closing lines of "Song of Myself" and "So Long."

The eighth section begins with a sigh of appreciation: "Ah, what can ever be more stately and admirable to me than mast-hemm'd Manhattan?" (p. 312). It moves on to intensify the connection between the reader and speaker, invoking the attraction, the tie between him and others, "Which fuses me into you now, and pours my meaning into you" (p. 312). After this frankly coital image, the connection is firmly established: "We understand then do we not?" (p. 312).

The ninth and final section urges the phenomena he has already mentioned—the tide, the waves, clouds, current and future passengers, masts of Manhattan and hills of Brooklyn, the ships, the sea birds, ending with the foundry fires and their shadows—to continue doing their work in the overall scheme. This recapitulates the poem's main themes, with a triumphant shift into the imperative. Whitman's own embodied consciousness both connects him to generations ahead and separates him from the phenomena and people he sees. Without being atomized—"disintegrated," as he says in the second section—and apart from the whole, he would have no individual consciousness and no ability to seek out connection. But the last six lines, addressed to the cities and the phenomena he sees, shift into the first person plural. As he says in the last four lines:

> We use you, and do not cast you aside—we plant
>   you permanently within us,
> We fathom you not—we love you—there is per-
>   fection in you also
> You furnish your parts toward eternity,
> Great or small, you furnish your parts toward the
>   soul
>
> (P. 313)

These lines suggest that connection has, at least in some measure, been achieved.

TRANSCENDENTALIST CONNECTIONS

Whitman's ideas about an all-encompassing film, a "float" from which the individual being is "struck," and the irresistible attraction between individuals, all expressed in "Crossing Brooklyn Ferry" and other poems, echo Ralph Waldo Emerson's 1841 essay, "The Over-Soul." Emerson (1803–1882) also uses the image of a river:

> As with events, so is it with thoughts. When I watch that flowing river, which, out of regions I see not, pours for a season its streams into me, I see that I am a pensioner; not a cause, but a surprised spectator of this ethereal water; that I desire and look up, and put myself in the attitude of reception, but from some alien energy the visions come. (P. 385)

The poem's insistence on an all-encompassing matrix from which individual souls are precipitated is also foreshadowed by Emerson when he says, "The soul circumscribes all things. . . . In like manner it abolishes time and space" (p. 387), as Emerson also foreshadows the irresistible attraction Whitman feels between these individual souls: "I am certified of a common nature, and these other souls, these separated selves, draw me as nothing else can" (p. 390).

Whitman's admiration of Emerson cannot be underestimated, and his eager adoption of a basically transcendental approach to life and poetry place him among the exemplars of Emerson's ideas. When Emerson praised the first edition of *Leaves of Grass,* Whitman reprinted the letter and kept it with him for years. In its insistence on the existence of transcendental forces in the universe, and its related insistence on the ability of individual humans to be formed out of and return to this source, "Crossing Brooklyn Ferry" carries out the same self-exploratory agenda as "Song of Myself," "When Lilacs Last in the Dooryard Bloom'd," and "Out of the Cradle Endlessly Rocking." Whitman's point of departure for investigations of eternal truth is his own physical being, and all of these poems demonstrate how this exploration happens. He both explores and celebrates himself, setting himself forth as an example of how this sort of exploration happens.

See also Leaves of Grass; New York; "Out of the Cradle Endlessly Rocking"; "Song of Myself"; Urbanization; "When Lilacs Last in the Dooryard Bloom'd"

BIBLIOGRAPHY
Primary Works
Emerson, Ralph Waldo. *Essays and Lectures.* Edited by Joel Porte. New York: Library of America, 1983.

Whitman, Walt. *Complete Poetry and Collected Prose.* Edited by Justin Kaplan. New York: Library of America, 1982. Includes "Crossing Brooklyn Ferry," "Old Brooklyn Days," and *Specimen Days.*

Whitman, Walt. "Letters from a Travelling Bachelor." 1849. In *The Historic Whitman,* edited by Joseph Jay Rubin. University Park: Pennsylvania State University Press. 1973.

Whitman, Walt. "The Philosophy of Ferries." 1847. In *The Uncollected Poetry and Prose of Walt Whitman,* 2 vols., edited by Emory Holloway. Garden City, N.Y.: Doubleday, 1921. Reprint, New York: P. Smith, 1932.

Whitman, Walt. *The Uncollected Poetry and Prose of Walt Whitman.* 2 vols. Edited by Emory Holloway. New York: Doubleday, 1921. Reprint, New York: P. Smith, 1932.

Secondary Works
Coffman, Stanley K. "'Crossing Brooklyn Ferry': A Note on the Catalogue Technique in Whitman's Poetry." *Modern Philology* 51 (May 1954): 225–232.

Dougherty, James. *Walt Whitman and the Citizen's Eye.* Baton Rouge: Louisiana State University Press, 1993.

Gilbert, Roger. "From Anxiety to Power: Grammar and Crisis in 'Crossing Brooklyn Ferry.'" *Nineteenth-Century Literature* 42, no. 3 (1987): 339–361.

Haw, Richard. "American History/American Memory: Reevaluating Walt Whitman's Relationship with the Brooklyn Bridge." *Journal of American Studies* 38, no. 1 (2004): 1–22.

Kim, Hoyoung. "Emerson's 'The Over-Soul' and Whitman's 'Crossing Brooklyn Ferry': Intertextual Continuities and Discontinuities." *Nineteenth Century Literature in English* 2 (1999): 273–289.

Knapp, Bettina. *Walt Whitman.* New York: Continuum, 1993.

Kummings, Donald D., ed. *Approaches to Teaching Whitman's Leaves of Grass.* New York: MLA, 1990.

Thomas, M. Wynn. *The Lunar Light of Whitman's Poetry.* Cambridge, Mass.: Harvard University Press, 1987.

Patricia Spence Rudden

CURRICULA

From 1820 to 1870, curricula in higher education shifted from a focus on oral to written discourse, in part as a result of the Industrial Revolution. The increased access to printed materials, rising literacy rates, and reliance on the written word to conduct political, economic, and legal business effected changes in educational curricula and pedagogy. By the end of the century, American education replaced the oratorical training necessary for students interested in ministry and civic leadership positions with a specialized disciplinary curricula designed for emerging professional careers. While school curricula and the ideologies behind them obviously influenced literary production, the relationship between instruction and authorship was especially close during this period; a stint at school teaching was part of the preparation of most of the important authors of the period, including Ralph Waldo Emerson, Margaret Fuller, Fanny Fern, Henry David Thoreau, Herman Melville, and Walt Whitman.

PRIMARY SCHOOL INSTRUCTION
Throughout the period under discussion, high schools and colleges shared similar curricula and pedagogical trends. However, primary school instruction was defined by a handful of textbooks that established the basis for a "chauvinistic nationalism" and literary heritage, which went unchallenged well into the twentieth century.

One of the best known was the text that was commonly known as the Blue-Back Speller—the first part of *A Grammatical Institute of the English Language* (1783) by Noah Webster (1758–1843). It was common in America until 1900 and, as described by Arthur Applebee in *Tradition and Reform in the Teaching of English: A History,* it "combined under one cover alphabet, primer, speller, and reader, using materials which were unabashedly adult and didactic" (p. 3). Created in part to unify education and culture, Webster's *Grammatical Institute* also included a grammar and a reader, neither of which ever attained the success of Webster's speller but, nevertheless, established the pattern for all subsequent grammar-school texts. Grammar was considered a primary school subject, a prerequisite for study at the college level but not a subject actually studied there. In 1819 the College of New Jersey (later Princeton) first asked incoming students to demonstrate competence in English grammar. By 1860 most colleges had adopted similar requirements, which relegated the study of grammar to the lower schools. By 1850 *Murray's English Grammar* (first published in England in 1795) had gone through two hundred editions and enjoyed widespread adoption in American lower schools.

Of note, Webster's *An American Selection of Lessons in Reading and Speaking* (the third part of *Grammatical Institute* and first published in 1787) secularizes school curriculum by selecting patriotic texts useful for improving spoken discourse. However, not until 1830 did secular concerns outnumber religious readings and lessons in primary school readers. During the time period under consideration, belletristic literature was rarely adopted as the primary text for reading instruction—not until the 1880s would the study of literature become an accepted pedagogical method for primary reading instruction. Instead, students were assigned selections that reflected a Protestant work ethic. Within this tradition, we find the enormously popular *Eclectic Reader,* better known as the McGuffey reader—a six-volume series first published in 1836 by William Holmes McGuffey (1800–1873). Universally adopted in America for fifty years, the McGuffey readers included short (one- to two-page) lessons sequentially ordered according to difficulty. Volumes five and six also included short belletristic selections. The McGuffey readers stressed reading aloud and included topics associated with elocution instruction. Collectively, Webster's and McGuffey's texts established both the educational theories and subject matter that defined American primary school education and dictated text production for decades to come.

A page from one of McGuffey's *Eclectic Reader* books, c. 1840. THE GRANGER COLLECTION, NEW YORK.

ELOCUTION

Originally a part of the classical rhetorical canon—invention, arrangement, style, memory, and delivery—training in elocution remained a distinct field of study during the nineteenth century. Introduced into the curriculum in order to prepare students training to become lawyers, ministers, and political leaders, the elocutionary movement in America derived from the strong British tradition. The first American influence upon teachers and texts of the period was *Philosophy of the Human Voice* (1827) by James Rush (1786–1869). It provided an introduction to the scientific components of speech, adding a discussion of vocal production to traditional discussions of delivery and gesture. The Rush system spawned many American texts, and followers of Rush represented diverse fields: rhetoric, science, medicine, education, and theater. Like Rush, the Reverend Ebenezer Porter (1772–1834), Bartlett Professor of Sacred Rhetoric in

Andover Seminary, was a pioneer teacher and textbook writer interested in the physiology of elocution; his sphere of influence extended far beyond theological circles. Porter, too, was interested in the scientific aspects of speech. His 1827 treatise *Analysis of the Principles of Rhetorical Delivery as Applied in Reading and Speaking* was adopted at colleges such as Amherst, Brown, Dartmouth, Georgia, Gettysburg, Hampden-Sydney, Middlebury, Mount Holyoke, and Wesleyan. The shortened version of that work designed for lower-school instruction, *The Rhetorical Reader* (1831), was adopted by schools in every state in the union.

The separation of rhetoric and elocution is obvious by 1830, when Yale appointed Erasmus D. North as instructor of elocution, and Harvard hired Jonathan Barber to teach a scientific method of elocution. By 1850 "Rhetoric and Oratory" was replaced by the term "Rhetoric and Belles Lettres," and although declamations, disputations, and training in rhetoric had traditionally been part of the American curriculum, not until the nineteenth century were endowed chairs established and speech training organized into a separate course or combined with composition instruction. In 1842 and 1843 Amherst offered a freshman course entitled Elements of Orthoepy and Elocutions, supplemented by weekly exercises in composition and declamation. At the same time, the University of Alabama offered a freshman-level course called Elocution, which required students to compose and publicly deliver weekly exercises in Latin and English. As late as 1861 Harvard offered a class entitled Elocution, which included lessons in orthoepy, expression, action, rhetorical analysis, and reading; and the same year Yale offered a sophomore-level class entitled Elocution, Declamation, and Composition. However, the majority of elocution teachers were itinerant lecturers who often gave private lessons at area educational institutions and occasionally established private schools of elocution. William Russell (1798–1873), the author of *The American Elocutionist* (1844), and James Murdoch founded the School of Practical Rhetoric and Oratory in 1844 in Boston, and J. W. Shoemaker (1842–1880) established the National School of Elocution and Oratory in Philadelphia in 1866. The public looked to oratory and elocution as a means for social advancement. Notably, in his youth, Frederick Douglass purchased an edition of *The Columbian Orator* (1797) by Caleb Bingham (1757–1817), a popular elocution textbook. Douglass studied the collected famous speeches and rules of oratory in order to find his own voice.

Elocutionary training was included in the lower schools, as well. In addition to Porter's *The Rhetorical Reader*, the McGuffey Readers acknowledged elocutionary instruction, and Russell, the first editor of the *American Journal of Education* (1826–1829), was particularly interested in the improvement of "expressive faculties" in the lower grades—evidenced in his treatises written for grammar school teachers. Although elocution as a school subject was displaced by 1875, because of its tendency to become artificial and exhibitionist, the American elocutionists from 1820 to 1870 made significant contributions to what would become the field of speech education.

RHETORIC AND COMPOSITION

In *Writing Instruction in Nineteenth-Century American Colleges,* James Berlin identifies three strands of nineteenth-century rhetoric within American education: classical (based on Greek and Roman oratorical practice), psychological-epistemological (deriving from Scottish common sense realism, the rejection of Aristotelian philosophy, and belletristic concerns), and romantic (which places the act of reading and writing at the center of knowledge). By 1820 the classical tradition was in demise as Americans came to value education that was scientific, practical, and personal. And by the end of the nineteenth century, the term "rhetoric" became synonymous for writing instruction.

The first half of the nineteenth century witnessed the publication of few American works on rhetoric. Colleges and universities relied heavily on British texts, particularly Hugh Blair's *Lectures on Rhetoric and Belles Lettres* (published and brought to America in 1783 and reprinted in Philadelphia in 1784), George Campbell's *Philosophy of Rhetoric* (published in 1776 and reprinted in America in 1818), Richard Whately's *Elements of Rhetoric* (1828), and Lord Henry Home Kames's *Elements of Criticism* (1762). Best known as an influential source for the rhetoric of Blair, Campbell, and Whately, Kames's text went through over thirty American editions and was widely adopted in American colleges during this period. One other Scottish belletristic rhetoric, Alexander Jamieson's *A Grammar of Rhetoric and Polite Literature* (1818), was enormously popular from 1820 until about 1880, going through sixty editions.

Blair's *Lectures on Rhetoric and Belles Lettres* was enormously popular prior to the Civil War. Not a systematic treatment of classical rhetoric but rather a collection of opinions on literary composition and criticism, *Lectures* addressed taste, style, language, eloquence, and belletristic compositions. Often imitated, Blair's categorizations and codification of rhetorical principles were prevalent within college curricula. His dismissal of invention and attention to style led to the widespread study of belletristic literature. After 1820 Campbell's *Philosophy of Rhetoric* became a strong competitor of Blair's *Lectures*. Although designed for rhetorical oratory, Campbell's work applied equally to written discourse and was widely adopted as a composition text. Campbell discussed logic, grammar, and style extensively, and his treatment of usage was, for a time, universally adopted in American schools.

Addressing both oral and written discourse, Whately's *Elements of Rhetoric* immediately rivaled the popularity of Blair and Campbell in the American colleges but was used in conjunction with those texts rather than supplanting them. Adopted as late as 1880, Whately restored to rhetoric the Aristotelian emphasis on logic. Uninterested in belletristic rhetoric, he devoted much attention to invention and arrangement, insisting that students must be given assignments that they find interesting and that fall within their range of abilities. Until after the Civil War, no original American rhetoric text appeared—only imitators of Blair, Campbell, and Whately.

A Practical System of Rhetoric; or, The Principles and Rules of Style: Inferred from Examples of Writing (1827) by Samuel P. Newman (1797–1842) was the first commercially successful American rhetoric designed specifically as a textbook. A rhetoric of written criticism, Newman's work focused on style and criticism—and clearly followed Blair's belletristic tradition. Within this tradition, Edward T. Channing (1790–1856), holder of the Boylston Chair at Harvard, 1819–1851, is noteworthy. Although Channing's *Lectures Read to the Seniors in Harvard College* (1856) never enjoyed widespread adoption, the publication of his work, which focuses on the writer rather than orator, marks the end of the dominance of classical rhetoric in America. Channing is perhaps best known as the influential teacher of students such as Thoreau, Emerson, Oliver Wendell Holmes, and James Russell Lowell. Channing supplemented his courses in rhetoric with informal evening meetings in which his students read and discussed English poetry.

The most notable shift in curricula during this time concerns the institutionalization of composition instruction. Alexander Bain, the Scottish professor of moral philosophy, psychologist, and the first holder of the chair of English and Logic at Aberdeen University, published *English Composition and Rhetoric: A Manual* (1866) to introduce his rustic Scottish students to paragraph unity, topic sentences, and the modes of discourse. Widely adopted, emulated, and (mis)appropriated in American schools, Bain's work is often blamed for establishing a reductive view of current-traditional rhetoric in America, which was practiced throughout the twentieth century.

George Payne Quackenbos (1826–1881) was perhaps the first American rhetorician to synthesize the British imports and to deliver pedagogical advice in a practical manner. In *Advanced Course of Composition and Rhetoric: A Series of Practical Lessons on the Origin, History, and Peculiarities of the English Language* (1854), Quackenbos included discussions of the belletristic tradition, composition advice based on Campbell's conception of faculty psychology, and an exhaustive section on grammar (a practical subject not normally included in the more theoretical rhetoric texts characterizing the time). Along with Bain and less influential American contemporary Henry Noble Day (1808–1890), author of *Elements of the Art of Rhetoric* (1850), Quackenbos was one of the first rhetoricians to make the modes of discourse a fundamental component of composition instruction.

EDUCATION FOR FEMALE STUDENTS

The educational move from oratory to composition instruction benefited women's education in three important ways: Belletristic rhetoric's focus on taste and literary style (as opposed to eloquence) better suited nineteenth-century perceptions of womanhood. Suggesting that rhetoric fell within the realm of womanhood, belletristic education offered examples of women's conversation as models of excellent prose. Technological advancements—cheaper ink and paper—refuted arguments claiming that the education of women was an expensive extravagance. And rising middle-class parents were often eager to educate their daughters so that they might obtain jobs in respectable teaching fields and raise the socioeconomic status of the family (Wright and Halloran, pp. 234–235). Although the education of women was becoming socially acceptable during this time, women were still educated in the "rhetoric of use" or "culture of service." Female students were not introduced to traditional modes of public speaking—although they often engaged in the practice of reading aloud their written works in class, as was the case with the students of the educator Catharine Beecher (1800–1878). Women also were trained in drama and debate, whereby they inadvertently received oratorical training. Essentially, viewed as ill-suited to oratory and social advancement and well-suited to nurturing young children, women were trained to teach formulaic, unimaginative lessons in what later became current-traditional rhetoric. The career of the prolific and commercially successful Fanny Fern (the pen name of Sara Payson Willis Parton, 1811–1872) provides a notable exception to prescribed female roles. Educated at Catharine

Beecher's Female Seminary in Hartford, Connecticut, Fern became the first woman newspaper columnist in America.

Advocates for women's equal right to education made early inroads during this period. Oberlin College stands out as one notable success in the early access of women to higher education. In 1833 Oberlin admitted 38 women out of 101 total students into its first college class, and, in 1835 it established the first female literary society in the American colleges—the Young Ladies' Association.

In 1839 the essayist and social reformer Margaret Fuller (1810–1850), formerly a teacher at Amos Bronson Alcott's Temple School and the Greene Street School in Providence, began a series of public "Conversations" targeting socially active and intellectual women in the Boston area. An accomplished teacher in the transcendentalist tradition, Fuller provided a venue in which women could intimately explore intellectual interests and freely discuss social reform. Spanning five years and expanding the discussion format of Elizabeth Palmer Peabody's earlier lecture series, Fuller's Conversations attracted more than two hundred women and addressed a wide range of topics, such as Greek myths and the fine arts. Many leaders of the feminist movement, including Julia Ward Howe, participated in Fuller's feminist venture.

TRANSCENDENTAL EDUCATION AND THE TEMPLE SCHOOL

From about 1836 to 1860, the American transcendental movement thrived in New England. Initiated as a reform effort of the Unitarian church, a small group of intellectuals in Concord, Massachusetts, developed instead their own philosophies of individual integrity and explored connections among spiritual, social, and the intellectual consciousness. Transcendentalism adopted tenets of Neoplatonism, German idealistic philosophy, and Eastern religious teachings. Influenced by philosopher Immanuel Kant's "transcendental" ideas and expanding upon William Ellery Channing's belief in an indwelling God, the transcendentalists rejected Lockean empiricism and instead embraced intuitive thought. Recognizable figures associated with this literary and philosophical movement include Frederic Henry Hedge, Amos Bronson Alcott, Margaret Fuller, Ralph Waldo Emerson, and Henry David Thoreau.

Self-educated, Amos Bronson Alcott (1799–1888) boldly embodied the transcendentalist's ideals. In 1834 Alcott opened a school for thirty elementary-age boys and girls in the Masonic Temple in Boston.

The transcendentalists' optimistic emphasis on individualism, self-reliance, and rejection of traditional authority formed the cornerstone of Alcott's Temple School. Working with Peabody and Fuller, Alcott adopted a pedagogy based on Socratic dialogue and established a curriculum that included not only the traditional triumvirate of reading, writing, and arithmetic, but also instruction in art, music, exercise, and student government. Abandoning traditional exercises in rote memorization, Alcott designed a curriculum promoting the physical, mental, and spiritual development of his pupils. Although Boston newspapers proclaimed Temple School one of the best common schools in the United States, ultimately the school failed because Alcott's teaching methods fell far afield of mainstream education.

LITERARY AND DEBATING SOCIETIES

Extracurricular activities—in the form of debating and literary societies—fostered an appreciation for literature and provided students the opportunity to polish English composition skills. College courses focused on improving student's Latin and Greek. Although both high school and college students were expected to read widely on their own time, the classical curriculum of most schools did not view English literature as a subject worthy of academic instruction. In fact, the libraries of the literary societies were often the only campus source for contemporary fiction, poetry, biography, or drama. In the literary and debate societies, students addressed contemporary political and philosophical issues and often hosted controversial speakers. For example, at the invitation of student groups, Emerson—although officially banned from campus—spoke at Williams College three times. But the primary focus of the societies from 1820 until their eventual decline was disputation and debate.

The forensic disputation and extempore speech (defined as well-prepared but not yet delivered or memorized papers) were well cultivated in the debating societies. Unlike classroom exercises, which strictly followed Latin syllogistics, the disputations characterizing the societies were delivered in English, included the adoption of emotional proofs and decreased reliance on syllogism as the primary logical appeal. The debating societies held participants to such a high standard that, by 1837, Columbia College felt no need to replicate the societies' efforts and dropped all extemporaneous exercises and debate from the curriculum.

The college model of literary and debating societies was adopted by college preparatory schools. The study of literature was relegated to extracurricular societies until after 1870, following the publication of works such as *Culture and Anarchy: An Essay in Political and Social Criticism* (1869) by Matthew Arnold (1822–1888). Arnold, a school inspector in addition to his more famous roles as poet and critic, argued that through the study of culture, public education could maintain traditional values and serve as an agent of social control. Although Arnold did not claim authority for vernacular studies, his argument was appropriated as a rationale for incorporating the realm of literary and debating societies into mainstream curricula.

THE RISE OF PHILOLOGY AND LITERATURE

"The flowering of New England," as Van Wyck Brooks terms the period from 1815 to 1865, fostered the development of a uniquely American literature and the establishment of America's educational legacy. Harvard, in particular, provided the curricular and pedagogical blueprint guiding American higher education. At Harvard, the curriculum was divided along the lines of religion and philosophy, mathematics and science, rhetoric and oratory, and classical and modern languages. Placing great emphasis on the study of languages (and accompanying literature), many well-known writers and critics of the period taught at Harvard—publishing scholars who did not confine their literary interests to the classroom. Unlike their predecessors, the Harvard-educated elite of the nineteenth century became professor-scholars, not ministers. Henry Wadsworth Longfellow (1807–1882), James Russell Lowell (1819–1891), and Oliver Wendell Holmes (1809–1894)—the Brahmin Poets (as the patrician, Harvard-educated class was known)—held positions at Harvard and augmented traditional rote lessons to include stimulating discussions of literature. From 1836 to 1854 Longfellow served as Smith Professor of Modern Languages, and his home—Craigie House—became a meeting place for students, as well as literary and philosophical figures, including Emerson, Nathaniel Hawthorne, Julia Ward Howe, and Charles Sumner. Before coming to Harvard, Longfellow had been the first professor of modern languages at Bowdoin College, where he wrote his own text for the course—because none existed. Following Longfellow's retirement from Harvard, Charles Russell Lowell assumed the professorship of modern languages and gained respect not only as a poet but as a critic and educator, as well. The poet Oliver Wendell Holmes established an impressive academic career, first serving as professor of anatomy and physiology at Dartmouth College (1839–1840), then dean of the Harvard Medical School (1847–1853) and Parkman Professor of Anatomy and Physiology at Harvard

(1847–1882). The study of literature, previously subsumed within courses on rhetoric and language, was coming to the foreground.

The career of the Harvard professor Francis James Child (1825–1896) most clearly represents the rise of philological studies in American education. Harvard appointed Child the Boylston Professor of Rhetoric and Oratory in 1851, following the retirement of Edward T. Channing. Although holding the preeminent American chair in rhetoric, Child, inspired by German ideals of scholarship, rejected classical rhetoric and instead lectured passionately on the understanding and appreciation of great literature. When Johns Hopkins offered Child a professorship of literature in 1876, Harvard retained Child by naming him professor of English, a position he held until his death in 1896. Child established himself as a literary scholar, specializing in philological and historical study of literature and, subsequently, transformed a struggling elective subject into a major discipline. Under Child's influence, rhetoric was relegated to first-year composition classes, and literary studies became the focus of American English departments.

James Rolfe is credited for introducing the study of literature into the high school curriculum. From 1848 to 1858 Rolfe taught literature within three different high school districts, and eventually his work drew Child's attention. After receiving an honorary A.M. degree from Harvard in 1859, Rolfe became principle of Cambridge High School in 1862, where he regulated the study of literature, united literary study and philology, and rooted the study of literature within the classical tradition. He adopted a formal method of pedagogy, stressing rote memorization of rules and facts.

During the latter half of the period under consideration, Charles Dexter Cleveland's *A Compendium of English Literature* (1847) enjoyed widespread adoption in the high schools. Manuals of literary history, which included short articles on English authors, answered college student demand for study in English literature. Arranged chronologically and including no actual works of literature, these essays were designed for rote memorization and recitation. Thomas B. Shaw's *Outlines of English Literature* (originally published in 1849) was the most widely adopted of these manuals in the American colleges. By 1870 the high school study of literature (joined with philology and studied within the classical tradition) was considered an intellectually rigorous curriculum. Child and Rolfe were instrumental in establishing literature as a legitimate course of study in American schools.

EDUCATION DURING THE CIVIL WAR AND THE MORRILL LAND GRANT ACT

Initially, higher education paid little attention to threats of civil war. Even during the war, many colleges continued to hold classes and sustain university business as long as possible. The effects of war on individual institutions varied, depending on the proximity of schools to the front lines, declining enrollments, and finances. Curriculum varied little, and course offerings at most institutions remained constant during the war, depending on faculty availability.

Following the war, the prewar trend to provide increased funding for developing agricultural and mechanical-sciences curricula continued—assisted in great part by the Morrill Land Grant Act of 1862, which was signed into effect by President Abraham Lincoln during the Civil War. Named after its sponsor, Vermont representative Justin S. Morrill, the legislation was additionally entitled "An Act donating Public Lands to the several States and Territories which may provide Colleges for the Benefit of Agriculture and the Mechanic Arts." It provided each state with thirty thousand acres for each senator and representative in Congress under the census of 1860. The states were to sell the land and apply the interest on receipts toward

> the endowment, support, and maintenance of at least one college where the leading object shall be, without excluding other scientific and classical studies and including military tactics, to teach such branches of learning as are related to agriculture and the mechanic arts, in such manner as the legislature of the States may respectively prescribe, in order to promote the liberal and practical education of the industrial classes in the pursuits and professions of life. (Quoted in Cowley and Williams, p. 121)

Answering a century-long national call for blending technical and academic instruction (first introduced by Benjamin Franklin in 1749), the Morrill Land Grant Act altered the trajectory of American higher education. This legislation established institutions capable of expanding elective curricula to train students for work in new disciplines and occupations, some of which were unforeseeable in the 1860s.

CONCLUSION

Educational curricula from 1820 to 1870 are critical in understanding the origins of contemporary American disciplinary studies; yet, this period in American education is understudied. Archival resources from the period—including institutional data, school-reform reports, lecture notes, student writings, class plans, society minutes, committee reports, local school legislation, and so forth—await discovery and analysis.

See also Colleges; Education; Literacy; Oratory; Rhetoric

BIBLIOGRAPHY

Secondary Works

Applebee, Arthur. *Tradition and Reform in the Teaching of English: A History.* Urbana, Ill.: National Council of Teachers of English, 1974.

Berlin, James A. *Writing Instruction in Nineteenth-Century American Colleges.* Carbondale: Southern Illinois University Press, 1984.

Brooks, Van Wyck. *The Flowering of New England, 1815–1865.* New York: Dutton, 1936.

Cowley, W. H., and Don Williams. *International and Historical Roots of Higher Education.* New York: Garland, 1991.

Golden, James L., and Edward P. J. Corbett. *The Rhetoric of Blair, Campbell, and Whately.* Carbondale: Southern Illinois University Press, 1990.

Guthrie, Warren. "The Development of Rhetorical Theory in America, 1635–1850: The Domination of the English Rhetorics." *Speech Monographs* 15 (1948): 61–71.

Johnson, Nan. *Nineteenth-Century Rhetoric in North America.* Carbondale: Southern Illinois University Press, 1991.

Kitzhaber, Albert R. *Rhetoric in American Colleges, 1850–1900.* Dallas, Tex.: Southern Methodist University Press, 1990.

Schultz, Lucille M. *The Young Composers: Composition's Beginnings in Nineteenth-Century Schools.* Carbondale: Southern Illinois University Press, 1999.

Stewart, Donald C. "Two Model Teachers and the Harvardization of English Departments." In *The Rhetorical Tradition and Modern Writing,* edited by James J. Murphy, pp. 118–129. New York: Modern Library Association of America, 1982.

Wallace, Karl R., et al., eds. *History of Speech Education in America: Background Studies.* New York: Appleton-Century-Crofts, 1954.

Wright, Elizabethada A., and S. Michael Halloran. "From Rhetoric to Composition: The Teaching of Writing in America to 1900." In *A Short History of Writing Instruction: From Ancient Greece to Modern America,* edited by James J. Murphy, pp. 213–246. Mahwah, N.J.: Erlbaum, 2001.

Lynée Lewis Gaillet

"THE CUSTOM-HOUSE"

When Nathaniel Hawthorne's (1804–1864) *The Scarlet Letter* first appeared in March 1850, "The Custom-House" gained more attention than the story of Hester Prynne that the sketch purports to introduce. The local press took sides over Hawthorne's portraits of the men who served under his authority as the chief officer of the Salem Custom House from 1846 to 1849. Newspapers aligned with the Democratic Party considered the portrayals humorous and harmless. Those aligned with the Whigs, however, found them scandalous, and they derided Hawthorne for disparaging the characters of good public servants. Both sides nonetheless understood that Hawthorne's motive in writing the satirical portraits was revenge for having been removed from his position. Commissioned as surveyor of custom in April 1846 by Democratic president James K. Polk, Hawthorne was sent packing three months after Whig president Zachary Taylor took office in March 1849. Were it not for his having been charged by some Whigs in Salem with misusing his position to the advantage of Democrats, a charge that apparently had some validity, Hawthorne might have retained his office and not written his most famous novel. Be that as it may, in "The Custom-House," he generally and mirthfully refers to his dismissal but only alludes to the ensuing controversy that raged in the press across the nation. Why all the fuss? And what does it have to do with the sketch that announces itself as "INTRODUCTORY TO 'THE SCARLET LETTER'"?

In addition to believing he had been falsely charged with wrongdoing, Hawthorne was distressed over losing a steady income. Before assuming his office at the Custom House, he had spent the first three years of married life at the Old Manse in Concord, Massachusetts, publishing numerous tales in magazines, which never paid enough to support himself, Sophia, and their daughter. His *Twice-Told Tales* (1837, 1842), was no longer selling, and his next collection of short fiction, *Mosses from an Old Manse* (1846), which appeared just before he began duties at the Custom House, offered little promise of financial reward, inasmuch as American readers preferred novels and Hawthorne had been unable to write one. Since he had earlier lost a large sum of money invested in the Brook Farm experiment and was in debt, he had, during the last year at the Old

The custom house in Salem, Massachusetts, engraving, c. 1871. © CORBIS

Manse, successfully urged friends with political connections to have President Polk appoint him to a governmental position.

With the prospect of losing that position, Hawthorne wrote a letter to his poet friend Henry Wadsworth Longfellow in which he promised literary revenge, and he couched the "vitriol" his pen would let drop in the context of his belonging to the tribe of sacred poets that should be immune to the vagaries of politics and therefore safe in the patronage system under which he had been appointed. Because neither his fellow citizens of Salem nor the U.S. government appeared to pay any respect to him as a writer, Hawthorne evidently decided to avenge himself by exhibiting the power of his pen in ways both somewhat petty and quite profound.

CHARACTERS

The petty seems obvious enough. While his repeated self-deprecation in "The Custom-House" and its overall genial tone and humor might seem to disguise the bitterness over losing his job, the descriptions of his native town, the federal eagle perched aloft on the Custom House, and most of the employees in it constitute a vindictive attack. As Hawthorne presents matters, Salem has declined from its one-time commercial preeminence, with the wharf dilapidated and former rich merchants faded into memory. The inhabitants, through inbreeding, have devolved into complacent provinciality and forsaken the enterprising spirit and vigor that once defined them, leading Hawthorne to declare that, as far as he can be of influence, his children "shall strike their roots into unaccustomed earth" (p. 12). The disparagement of Salem extends to the U.S. government in the symbol of the eagle, which seems to promise maternal protection but which, with its clutch of barbed arrows and fierce beak, Hawthorne envisions as a menacing threat.

Yet the lengthy satire on Custom House employees actually represents the depth of Hawthorne's vengeance as well as his regret, even guilt, for having felt the need to accept "Devil's wages" (p. 39) for employment at the Custom House, where "neither the front nor the back entrance . . . opens on the road to Paradise" (p. 13). Distant from the squabbles between Democrats and Whigs in the 1840s, it is scarcely a surprise that the satirical portrayals caused Hawthorne to be defamed in many newspapers. By and large he somewhat gently though clearly presents the Custom House workers as a collection of ineffectual, doddering old fools. More specifically he singles out two officials for especial condemnation and one for reserved praise. The first represents the commercial essence of the Custom House bureaucracy, for in his mathematically acute understanding of how it functions, he appears not so much human as machine-like, the "main-spring" of the system to which he is "thoroughly adapted," the one who keeps "its variously revolving wheels in motion" (p. 24). The second is the "patriarch" of the Custom House, "so perfect" from the point of view of his "animal" characteristics, "so shallow" from the vantage of his possessing anything remotely resembling the human. A sensualist by default, the old Inspector resembles a "cock" or "clarion," suggesting the sexual drive responsible for his wearing out three wives in producing twenty children. His taste for meals eaten decades ago still remains in juicy detail on his tongue. Although Hawthorne claims "perfect contentment" with the "animal nature" of the Inspector, initially welcoming him as a change of diet from transcendental neighbors at the Old Manse, he emphatically reduces him to an "absolute nonentity": for "he had no soul, no heart, no mind" (pp. 17–18).

Except for two young men, one who secretly writes poetry and the other who occasionally talks with Hawthorne about literature, the only figure at the Custom House for whom Hawthorne reserves some praise is the Collector, General Miller, who won laurels for gallantry at the battle of Lundy's Lane during the War of 1812. Now aged, barely able to climb the steps leading to his office where he mostly sleeps, Miller has outlived his usefulness and therefore seems aligned with other old men who lend a decayed, death-in-life atmosphere to the Custom House. But Miller rises above the others in Hawthorne's estimation, because he "was as much out of place as an old sword—now rusty, but which had flashed once in the battle's front, and showed still a bright gleam along its blade—would have been, among the inkstands, paper-folders, and mahogany rulers, on the Deputy Collector's desk" (p. 23).

Being out of place, Miller is like Hawthorne, who may not yet have earned the literary fame he desires but who as he writes the sketch has rededicated himself to an early ambition to create literary works equal to those of England's greatest authors. Hence he conceives that, in dreaming about his heroic past, Miller "lived a more real life within his thoughts than amid the unappropriate environment of the Collector's office" (p. 23). The lengthy discussion of him thus prepares for a pivotal juncture in the sketch, when the deepest and most critically important subject emerges from its previous obscurity—Hawthorne's advocating the cultural primacy of art in a country that by and large discounted products of imagination to the level of insignificant commodities.

LITERARY MANIFESTO

Accordingly, because he takes pride in himself as an artist, Hawthorne discovers the subject for a novel in his being fired from his post at the Custom House; and in this discovery, he transforms the petty motive of wreaking revenge into a profound cultural critique that extends beyond himself. His Puritan ancestors would no doubt think that he has brought discredit on the family tree for being a writer of "story-books," but "strong traits of their nature have intertwined themselves" (p. 10) with his; and out of that strength, he affirms opposition to a puritan tradition that demeaned the value of imagination and its artistic expressions. Instead of persecuting Quakers and sending supposed witches to the gallows, as did his forebears, Hawthorne vilifies a nation intent on persecuting not only him but also art itself. The persecution of Hester occurs in seventeenth-century Boston, and yet the link between Hawthorne and her, the art that defines them, is unmistakable.

When Hawthorne places the scarlet letter on his breast, he identifies himself with Hester. Her "A" symbolizes adultery, and his "A" symbolizes art, just as her shame and pride over those respective significations are his. Her adultery is literal, his figural—he has betrayed his pledge to art in exchange for "Devil's wages" at the Custom House. Her shame is public in the same way that his being fired from office receives nationwide exposure. Her pride lies in creating the luxuriant letter "A," demonstrating a spiteful response to a political system that has stigmatized her. Hawthorne's pride reveals itself in admitting to his "unmanly" dependence on governmental support and resuming his pledge to authorship, a vow resulting in a vengeful castigation of an America that has spurned both him and the high calling of art. Both Hester and Hawthorne transform their adultery, she through her art and community service, he through her story for a country that, despite its devaluation of art, might in some measure finally embrace it.

Hawthorne pretends that he did not mind being unknown in the Custom House as an author or having his name stenciled on packaged commodities rather than emblazoned on the spines of books. But when he mentions Geoffrey Chaucer and Robert Burns and when he calls Surveyor Pue his "official ancestor," all three of whom served as customhouse officers under the British Crown, he clearly casts aside his unimaginative Puritan ancestors and adopts these authors and their Old World tradition of honoring art. This strategy not only supports his resolve to become again a "literary man" but also explains why he creates Hester as an artist. Having no American artist in New England history with whom to connect himself, Hawthorne supplies one, and in a manner at once lamenting and vengeful; for he will associate Hester's art with an Anglo-Catholic tradition strictly anathema to Puritans in England and America.

The point of that association becomes apparent in the lethargy, sensuality, and rundown materialism on the first floor depicted in "The Custom-House." The snores and old jokes of the aged officers, undeserving to be summoned for "apostolic errands" as were Christ's disciples (p. 7), and the accounts of savory meals eaten long ago by the Collector represent the moribund condition of Salem and its antipathy to creativity from which Hawthorne must remove himself. Thus the importance of the shift that occurs midway through the sketch. In a line perhaps more memorable than any in his works, Hawthorne suddenly announces: "But the past was not dead" (p. 27). Proceeding to the second story of the Custom House, he fails to find any documents that lead back to the Cromwellian Protectorate in England (1652–1659), but he discovers, actually creates, the scarlet letter and Surveyor Pue's account of Hester. Herein lies the fictionalized inception of the novel, and it will turn out to be one that looks back, as Hawthorne imagines, to the pivotal stage in New England history coinciding with the civil war in England (1642–1649).

Although the reference to the protectorate might seem innocent or arbitrary, it serves two crucial functions. First, it subtly indicates the measure of Hawthorne's denunciation of the anti-aesthetic Puritan tradition that continues to exert influence in nineteenth-century America. Second, it joins with other references in "The Custom-House" to revolutionary moments with which Hawthorne cleverly plays. Historical recollection helps. Not long before being chosen Lord Protector, Oliver Cromwell had been the general of the parliamentary army fighting against the Royalist forces of Charles I. Cromwell's army delighted in destroying statuary, stained-glass windows, and other iconographic features of English churches associated with Roman Catholicism. In the scarlet letter tale, Hawthorne takes sides against his Puritan ancestors' support of such iconoclasm by associating Hester and Pearl with Anglo-Catholic art endorsed by Queen Elizabeth and the House of Stewart that succeeded her. As if that association were not an adequate demonstration of his opposition to the Puritans, he also associates himself with Charles I. For the mention of the protectorate likewise includes a glance at the regicide preceding it. When Hawthorne invokes the image of the guillotine and claims that his head was "the first that fell" (p. 41), that he becomes the "DECAPITATED SURVEYOR" (p. 43) upon being ousted from the Custom House, he connects his beheading with that of Charles I that, as it were, occurs offstage prior to the midnight scaffold scene in the scarlet letter tale.

To be sure, the guillotine resonates more obviously with historical events closer to Hawthorne's moment of writing. A French device, it calls to mind the regicide of Louis XVI and the Reign of Terror during the revolution beginning in France in 1789. More contemporaneously to Hawthorne's moment of writing, it alludes to the 1848 revolution in France as well as to the revolutionary events in Italy and Hungary at roughly the same time. Revolution itself would appear to be Hawthorne's chief point, and thus he wryly refers to Zachary Taylor's election to the presidency in 1848 as a revolution. Even though this peaceful succession of administrations in America somewhat belies Hawthorne's revolutionary impulses in writing *The Scarlet Letter,* literary historians readily grant that Hawthorne successfully avenged himself for losing his job. Less clear but indisputable emerge the suggestions, whether in "The Custom-House" or the scarlet letter tale, that the loss of his official head allowed him to regain his literary one and thereby to advocate the preeminent value of art for any culture worthy of the name.

While at the Custom House, of course, he cannot fulfill his promise to Jonathan Pue to write ("I will!") the story of Hester Prynne. The surroundings have caused his imagination to become a "tarnished mirror," so unlike the creative reflections provoked by "that invigorating charm of Nature, which used to give me such freshness and activity of thought, the moment that I stepped across the threshold of the Old Manse" (pp. 34, 35). Even the atmospheric medium of his domestic study at night, dimly illuminated by moonbeams and a faintly glowing fire, affectively establishing a perceptual "neutral territory," fails to inspire Hawthorne to write the kind of fiction for which he is known, a "romance" located "somewhere between the real world and fairy-land, where the Actual and the Imaginary may meet, and each imbue itself with the nature of the other" (p. 36). Despite Hawthorne's protesting that, instead of flinging himself into the past, it would have been a "wiser effort . . . to diffuse thought and imagination through the opaque substance" of the "petty and wearisome incidents, and ordinary characters" in the Custom House, that a "better book than I shall ever write was there," such a "page of life" is precisely what inhibits him (p. 37). Only after readopting something like the self-reliance preached by Ralph Waldo Emerson can Hawthorne polish the mirror of his imagination and

earn a respectable living from his pen rather than accept gold from the U.S. treasury or seek nuggets in the hills and streams of California, as many Americans were rushing to do.

As he draws "The Custom-House" to a close, Hawthorne can now declare, "My forgiveness to my enemies! For I am in the realm of quiet!" (p. 44). His vengeance is complete. He has exposed the custom of the country for what it is: materialistic, small-minded, and culturally decadent. He has disinherited himself from a Puritan tradition antithetical to imaginative writing. He has purged himself, through vengeance and confession, of his guilt for having relied on the charity of a government oblivious to the cultural value of literature. Along the way he has amply suggested a transmutation of the vengeance by recovering an inheritance from pen-and-ink forebears across the Atlantic, all the way back to Chaucer and thus, by implication, to the papacy and monarchies of Europe that over the centuries patronized artists. That transmutation obviously involves his relating the discovery of Surveyor Pue's sheets of foolscap and the scarlet letter fabric, a conventional device of authors that ostensibly explains the real-life basis for the fictional tale that follows. That tale, largely focused on a woman in mid-seventeenth-century Boston, would seem to have nothing to do with Hawthorne in mid-nineteenth-century Salem. But the careful and informed reader will notice that Hawthorne allows the first-generation Puritans, remembering the aesthetic refinement of England during and prior to the Elizabethan period, to accept and even demand Hester's art, whereas the succeeding generations that he construes as fanatical will not. Laboring under the influence of those succeeding puritanical generations, Hawthorne rebels against it, declares himself a "citizen of somewhere else" (p. 44), and prepares to ally himself with Hester, the maternal origin of American art whom he imagines as a worthier protectress than the federal eagle. Consequently he must bid goodbye to Salem; and it surely strikes him as a bittersweet farewell, as he concludes "The Custom-House" with the half-jocular, half-serious hope that the people of his hometown might remember him as the author of a story commemorating the town pump. No small irony in the ongoing ironies of history has ensued: the Salem that once spurned him eventually reclaimed its citizen of somewhere else as its favorite son and mostly because of *The Scarlet Letter.*

See also The Blithedale Romance; The House of the Seven Gables; The Scarlet Letter; "Young Goodman Brown"

BIBLIOGRAPHY

Primary Work

Hawthorne, Nathaniel. *The Scarlet Letter*. 1850. In *The Centenary Edition of the Works of Nathaniel Hawthorne*, edited by William Charvat et al. Vol. 1. Columbus: Ohio State University Press, 1962.

Secondary Works

Anderson, Douglas. "Jefferson, Hawthorne, and 'The Custom-House.'" *Nineteenth-Century Literature* 46 (1991): 309–326.

Baym, Nina. "The Romantic *Malgré Lui:* Hawthorne in 'The Custom-House.'" *ESQ: A Journal of the American Renaissance* 10 (1973): 1425.

Berner, Robert L. "A Key to 'The Custom-House.'" *ATQ* 41 (1979): 33–43.

Brumm, Ursula. "Hawthorne's 'The Custom-House' and the Problem of Point of View in Historical Fiction." *Anglica* 93 (1975): 391–412.

Cox, James M. "*The Scarlet Letter:* Through the Old Manse and the Custom House." *Virginia Quarterly Review* 51 (1975): 432–447.

Dolis, John. "Hawthorne's Circe: Turning Water to (S)wine." *Nathaniel Hawthorne Review* 24 (spring 1998): 36–45.

Eakin, Paul John. "Hawthorne's Imagination and the Structure of 'The Custom-House.'" *American Literature* 43 (1971): 346–358.

Green, Carlanda. "'The Custom-House': Hawthorne's Dark Wood of Error." *New England Quarterly* 53 (1980): 184–195.

Lee, A. Robert. "'Like a Dream behind Me': Hawthorne's 'The Custom-House' and *The Scarlet Letter*." In *Nathaniel Hawthorne: New Critical Essays*, edited by A. Robert Lee, pp. 48–67. London and Totowa, N.J.: Vision Press and Barnes and Noble, 1982.

MacShane, Frank. "The House of the Dead: Hawthorne's 'Custom House' and *The Scarlet Letter*." *New England Quarterly* 35 (1962): 93–101.

McCall, Dan. "The Design of Hawthorne's 'Custom-House.'" *Nineteenth-Century Fiction* 21 (1967): 349–358.

Mellow, James R. *Nathaniel Hawthorne in His Times*. Boston: Houghton Mifflin, 1980.

Nissenbaum, Stephen. "The Firing of Nathaniel Hawthorne." *Essex Institute Historical Collections* 114 (1978): 57–86.

Pease, Donald. "Hawthorne's Discovery of a Pre-Revolutionary Past." In his *Visionary Compacts: American Renaissance Writings in Cultural Context*, pp. 49–80. Madison: University of Wisconsin Press, 1987.

Reynolds, Larry J. "*The Scarlet Letter* and Revolutions Abroad." In his *European Revolutions and the American Literary Renaissance*, pp. 79–96. New Haven, Conn.: Yale University Press, 1988.

Tew, Arnold G. "Hawthorne's P. P.: Behind the Comic Mask." *Nathaniel Hawthorne Review* 20 (spring 1994): 18–23.

Tomc, Sandra. "'The Sanctity of the Priesthood': Hawthorne's 'Custom-House.'" *ESQ: A Journal of the American Renaissance* 39 (1993): 161–184.

Turner, Arlin. *Nathaniel Hawthorne: A Biography*. New York: Oxford University Press, 1980.

Van Deusen, Marshall. "Narrative Tone in 'The Custom-House' and *The Scarlet Letter*." *Nineteenth-Century Fiction* 21 (1966): 61–71.

Frederick Newberry

DEATH

Death haunts American literature. Upon even a cursory sampling of works by Nathaniel Hawthorne, Herman Melville, Edgar Allan Poe, Harriet Beecher Stowe, Walt Whitman, or any of the other major writers of the nineteenth century, readers will trip over coffins, bump up against ghosts, hear voices from beyond the grave, and witness the shock of people buried alive, though these writers did not have a monopoly on the corpse and its afterlife. Popular works from the period, ranging from sentimental literature to sensational novels and from religious fiction to African American slave narratives, also fed a compulsive cultural imagination obsessed with death. With the carnage associated with places like Fredericksburg, Cold Harbor, and other Civil War battlefields, the American public was confronted by the dead and the dying on an unprecedented scale. But even before the eruption of hostilities between North and South, death was firmly lodged in the nation's literature, its psychological hold expressive of troubling political and social dynamics.

How is one to understand this morbid fascination with death? While the nation's fratricidal conflict killed more white Americans than any previous conflict, the body count in American literature both precedes and extends beyond the anxieties and mourning associated with the war years of 1861 through 1865. Even as one guards against reducing the obsession with death to a specific historical conflict, one must likewise prevent the tremendous literary energy lavished on death scenes and corpses from being simply abstracted and

explained as some universal fascination with the inevitable. One must examine the ideological factors that gave death such resonance in American culture in the nineteenth century. Such factors are at once political, gendered, and national in nature and can be grouped into three general lines of inquiry: death as an anxious expression about the decay of the American Republic, the corpse as a specifically female body that resounds with uncertainties about the status of women in an era of public reform, and the afterlife as an eerie commentary on citizenship and freedom.

DEATH AND POLITICAL DECAY

Sucked into the whirlpool at the end of *Moby-Dick; or, The Whale* (1851) by Herman Melville (1819–1891), the whaling ship vanishes with all its crew save one sailor named Ishmael. An elaborate metaphor for the ship of state, the *Pequod* sinks, carrying with it a diverse crew that, like the United States, had been united around a single quest—to hunt the white whale. Only one object bubbles to the surface, escaping the vortex: a coffin carved by a reformed cannibal named Queequeg. Ishmael clings to this coffin even as he abandons the memory of Queequeg, his loving companion. The friendship between the two men represents the best impulses of democracy, including equality and a heartfelt commitment to others. The political significance of their homosocial bond is heightened early in the novel with Ishmael's famous comparison that "Queequeg was George Washington cannibalistically developed" (p. 847). But by the novel's final page the comparison becomes an empty one as Ishmael floats on the husk intended for his friend's dead body. So, too, in an era of sectional division over slavery, the national promise encapsulated by the mythic Washington seems hollowed out, devoid of true meaning.

Ishmael's forgetting Queequeg typifies the malady of the post-Revolutionary generation that struggled to preserve the traditions and ideals of its forefathers. What would happen to democratic ideals and republican virtue now that the heroes of 1776 had faded into memory and as that memory itself faded? The deaths of Thomas Jefferson and John Adams, each on the Fourth of July 1826, poignantly staged the crisis confronting the citizens who inherited a nation from their political fathers. Would the nation die along with those men? The intense divisions over issues such as tariffs, territorial expansion, and most crucially, slavery seemed to indicate that the ship of state was indeed headed for dangerous waters and that this new country would not long outlast its dead founders.

For these reasons the body count of founding fathers must have been alarming for many nineteenth-century readers. As he wrote about the glories of national history, James Fenimore Cooper (1789–1851) found himself forced to confront the fact that the past was dead, never more to return. Although his romance of the American Revolution, *The Spy: A Tale of Neutral Ground* (1821), ends with a strengthened union as families from North and South unite in marriage, the final pages of this novel also witness the death of Harvey Birch, the patriot who worked selflessly for the American cause. He dies alone, deprived of human companionship, his national ardor a fragile relic of an almost forgotten past. When the novel was reissued in 1849 as the sectional crisis over slavery intensified, Cooper wondered aloud in his introduction whether the story of Washington could still exercise the mythic force to keep the nation intact. It seemed that the dead might really be dead, unable to offer the post-Revolutionary generation any advice about how to safeguard the political life of the new nation.

When in 1823 Cooper brought forth Natty Bumppo, his most famous hero, in the first in the series of novels that would be called the Leatherstocking Tales, Washington died yet another death in ways that deepened the gloom over the possibilities of interracial democracy. Much as Melville pairs Queequeg and Ishmael in a politically and erotically charged union, Cooper's white scout and his Indian chief, Chingachgook, commit themselves to a deeply felt companionship in *The Pioneers; or, The Sources of the Susquehanna: A Descriptive Tale* (1823). Wearing around his neck a silver medallion emblazoned with an image of Washington, Chingachgook symbolically recognizes the national paternal authority that in Cooper's world makes equality among men possible. Often given as part of treaty ceremonies between the federal government and Indian tribes, this medallion is brought into view by Chingachgook only "on great and solemn occasions" (p. 406), most notably his own death. As the flames of a wildfire swirl around his body, Chingachgook dies unadorned save for this icon of national promise. Washington's symbolic body becomes fuel for the fire. Although the chief's stoic resolve to his own fate participates in a voluntaristic logic that represented Native Americans as acceding to their own disappearance, *The Pioneers* also communicates a darker lesson in which fatherly law seems ready to perish as well.

Yet not all writers expressed loss or remorse over the death of America's paternal ancestors. In *The Scarlet Letter* (1850) and *The House of the Seven Gables* (1851), both by Nathaniel Hawthorne (1804–1864), men and women express a different sort of longing: if only the dead would die and stay dead. In "The Custom-House," his introduction to *The Scarlet Letter*, Hawthorne feels oppressed by the burden of the past, weighted down by the memory that his Puritan ancestors were "conspicuous in the martyrdom of the witches" (p. 126) that has made seventeenth-century Salem so notorious. Moreover, Hawthorne confesses to feeling judged by his stern progenitors for being nothing more than an "idler" and a "writer of story-books" (p. 127). It is thus not without some satisfaction that the strangulating influence of such forefathers is put to death when the novelist turns his attention to the Salem of his day. In *The House of the Seven Gables* the harsh Puritan strain remains ascendant, now embodied in the person of Judge Pyncheon, who uses the law's authority to harass his poorer relations. But in a scene dripping with sarcasm, Hawthorne's narrator badgers the judge, asking him repeatedly why he does not move, lest he miss a political meeting at which he is to be the guest of honor. The answer is that the judge is a corpse, having choked on his own blood. A hereditary gag reflex is the cause; the dead come back to kill the descendents who most resemble them. While disastrous for the judge, the murderous claims of the past are good news to the Pyncheon cousins, who have been suffering from both the judge's schemes and the psychological burden of family history.

For the citizens represented by the crew on Melville's ship of state, Cooper's frontier scouts, and Hawthorne's shopkeepers, death occasioned a sense of grieving as the bereaved often felt cut off from the political traditions that had secured the health and vitality of the nation. At the same time, however, death provided hints of liberation, suggesting that the post-Revolutionary generation could be freed from conventions and practices that had persisted since America's founding. Like Ralph Waldo Emerson (1803–1882) in his essay *Nature* (1836), antebellum citizens could ask irreverently, "Why should we grope among the dry bones of the past?" (p. 7).

THE BEAUTIFUL CORPSE

Tragic as the deaths of the founding fathers may have been, no death in the nineteenth century was as traumatic as the passing of Evangeline in the antislavery novel *Uncle Tom's Cabin; or, Life among the Lowly* (1852) by Harriet Beecher Stowe (1811–1896). Tens of thousands of readers were deeply moved by the death of this sainted child, and many even shed real tears as they watched little Eva waste away, imparting with her dying gasp millennial lessons about love, goodness, and perfect equality. Her death represents the height of American sentimentalism, a deeply emotional style that has been vilified for falsifying social reality even as it has been acclaimed for its affective power in changing attitudes and reorienting sensibilities. Certainly there is something troubling about a novel in which the death of a pampered slave owner's daughter threatens to overshadow—and sentimentalize—the historical actuality of racial bondage in the United States. Almost as certainly, however, the sentimental plea of *Uncle Tom's Cabin* caused many northern readers to feel personally and passionately about an issue—the abolition of slavery—that to many had no doubt seemed remote and distant. While it is difficult to settle this debate definitively, it is undeniable that the death of little Eva carries a political charge. On her deathbed this sinless child provides a glimpse of heaven on earth, a utopian world of pure equality based on love. As her slaveholding father comments, such a "little child is your only true democrat" (p. 211).

Eva's death fits within a larger cultural framework that idealized women and girls as the spiritual communicants of a pure social order. It was precisely their supposed proximity to death that allowed female trance mediums and clairvoyants to regale audiences with mystical pronouncements about abolition, women's rights, and eternal peace. Like Stowe's Eva, these women seemed barely embodied, hovering close to death, cultivating an aura of heavenly disconnection in which their near transcendence of earthly trappings left them free to glimpse vaster political truths that so surely eluded a world marred by slavery and other forms of injustice. Because they communicated with departed beings from the "other side," spiritualized women, such as those who practiced spirit rapping, gained access to public venues—lecture halls, abolitionist meetings,

and reform conventions—previously denied to them. In addition to Stowe, prominent women activists and early feminists such as Amy Post showed an interest in the political reformist possibilities emerging mystically from the afterlife. Death, it seemed, promised a liberation unavailable in an earthly sphere contaminated by slavery and the subjugation of women. Once within a trance and insensible to the commotion of the terrestrial world, the female medium inhabited a shadowy and sentimental realm whose glorious freedom she shared with audiences at public séances. Women's participation in the public sphere of nineteenth-century America was thus organized around a contradiction: women can take part in public life only by approximating death. *Uncle Tom's Cabin* illustrates this contradiction perfectly as slaveholders and slaves alike are moved to follow Eva's living example of brotherly—and sisterly—love only once the girl dies. The power of sentimentalism to move and affect readers, in turn, pivots on the morbid faith that problems in this world could best be solved by attending to otherworldly voices channeled through girls and young women.

In 1846 Edgar Allan Poe (1809–1849) wrote that "the death . . . of a beautiful woman is, unquestionably, the most poetical topic in the world" (p. 19). Poe's remark suggests the particular resonance attached to women in a culture that sentimentalized death and dying. Hawthorne's Miles Coverdale, the narrator of *The Blithedale Romance* (1852), no doubt models the attitude of many men who viewed this spiritual fad with a combination of distrust, contempt, and fear. Based on Hawthorne's own experiences at Brook Farm, a mid-century utopian experiment that included supporters of women's rights, abolitionists, and spiritualists, *The Blithedale Romance* is an erotically charged novel of voyeurism and betrayal that lavishes attention on women's bodies. Mediums, reformers, and frauds flit in and out of the novel, appearing on public stages and making appeals to the afterlife in order to ground their pronouncements in a mystical authority. While the young clairvoyant Priscilla certainly attracts her share of male interest, nobody is more subject to the public eye than Zenobia, a striking woman renowned for her intellect, reformist zeal, and literary talent. But Zenobia never garners so much attention as when she is a corpse.

In a scene rife with overtones of necrophilia, the men of the community drag her dead body from a river, puncturing the corpse with a hooked pole and grappling with her arms in an attempt to make a body affected by rigor mortis appear docile and penitent. Zenobia preeminently is a public woman (since the novel was first published her portrait has drawn comparisons to Margaret Fuller) who pays the ultimate price for disregarding social strictures that relegate women to private spheres. As Hawthorne implies in several instances, when Zenobia is alive, Coverdale is threatened by his own erotic desire for her. Is it possible that he really feels attracted to an unruly woman who does not know her place? But death allows him to sidestep this uncomfortable question without forcing him to give up his desire. Her dead body makes no feminist protests and is powerless to evade the invasive gaze of men like Coverdale, except that Hawthorne adds an ironic wrinkle to his narrator's morbid satisfaction: Zenobia's corpse itself remains recalcitrant, refusing to abide by notions of feminine propriety. Having retrieved the body from the river, the men of Blithedale determine that its posture is inappropriate, bearing an attitude of "immitigable defiance" (p. 837). But because rigor mortis has set in, they are powerless to alter her body's posture; in the most graphic way, the dead woman cannot be bent to their will.

Death, when conjoined with femininity, is the picture of acquiescence. Yet the corpse also houses uncontrolled and rebellious indications that not all bodies abide by earthly restraints.

FREEDOM AND DEATH

In other words, death implies a passport to freedom. Patrick Henry's famous challenge to British colonial authority—"Give me liberty or give me death"—is critically reworked in African American slave narratives, poetry, and fiction to stake a defiant posture against American slavery. Indeed the climax to the first African American novel, *Clotel; or, The President's Daughter* (1853) by William Wells Brown (c. 1814–1884), comes in a chapter titled "Death Is Freedom." How exactly does death liberate? In the case of Brown's heroine, a quadroon slave who can trace her bloodline back to Thomas Jefferson, suicide frees her from the institutional proscriptions that make her body the property of another. Pursued by slave catchers and with nowhere to turn, Clotel takes her own life by jumping into the rushing waters of the Potomac that flow by the nation's capitol. An abolitionist verse by Grace Greenwood (1823–1904), absorbed by Brown into his novel, memorializes the event with bitter irony: "To freedom she leaped, through drowning and death— / Hurrah for country! hurrah!" (p. 222). Clotel's status as a slave

The Modern Medea. Wood engraving after the painting by Thomas Noble, from *Harpers Magazine,* 18 May 1867, depicts Margaret Garner, an escaped slave who killed two of her children rather than see them returned to slavery. ©CORBIS

woman's daughter is meaningless in the culturally life-less vacuum that death provides. Her suicide radically divorces her from legal and racial contexts that legitimate bondage. Clotel finds peace in an eternal, final freedom that exists apart from the sociohistorical currents that give meaning to everyday life. Death radically abstracts her from history; indeed American freedom recognizes only an abstract identity.

Although perhaps extreme in its gothic sensationalism, Clotel's leap readily tallies with scenes of suicide, infanticide, and murderous longing in African American writing and abolitionist poetry and fiction. Morbid fantasies exerted an almost phantasmic hold upon antebellum audiences, especially after 1856, when the slave Margaret Garner killed her two-year-old daughter rather than see her fall into the clutches of slave catchers. But even before this much-publicized tragedy, deathly tropes were common to mid-century African American writing, including slave narratives by William Wells Brown and Lunsford Lane as well as Hannah Crafts's *The Bondwoman's Narrative,* an African American novel written in the 1850s but lost to readers until its discovery at the beginning of the twenty-first century. In *Narrative of the Life and Adventures of Henry Bibb, an American Slave* (1849), for instance, Henry Bibb (1815–1854) finds solace in imagining his wife's death. Because he has been unable to rescue her from southern bondage, he prefers to think of his wife as no longer among the living, freeing him—but not her—from the painful attachments that threaten his sense of liberty. Her death would leave him free; the fantasy of her death permits him to construct, in self-negating terms, an identity that, like Clotel liberated by the cessation of being, neither suffers nor enjoys any earthly entanglements. But whereas Clotel takes her own life, Bibb sacrifices the memory of his wife, thereby escaping the fatal implications of American freedom.

In order for death to secure liberty, it must produce a political identity that is both steeped in the isolation of abstraction and unswerving in its forgetting of all cultural contexts, including one's family, friends, and past. Freedom demands social death. Clotel, Bibb, and the other heroes and heroines of antislavery literature, who ponder suicide and see liberty as residing only in the afterlife, construe freedom as befitting only a lifeless political subject, a figuratively bloodless person who knows neither memory nor embodiment. Frederick Douglass (1818–1895), the great antislavery orator and black leader, was not immune to this deathly political rhetoric either. His *Narrative of the Life of Frederick Douglass, an American Slave* (1845) invokes Patrick Henry's morbid trope, but by the time of his second autobiography, *My Bondage and My Freedom* (1855), Douglass had come to see the need of moving beyond absolute political formulas based on an extreme all-or-nothing logic. Quoting Henry's dictum of "liberty or death," Douglass implies in this later work that this expression is "incomparably more sublime" when "*practically* asserted by men accustomed to the lash and chain—men whose sensibilities must have become more or less deadened by their bondage" (p. 312). Because Douglass's claim to freedom never forgets the institutional history of its own origin, never outstrips whips or fetters, his political identity exceeds standard American formulas linking death and liberty. In effect Douglass's freedom is practical and worldly, not abstract and eternal. Consequently Douglass moves beyond death to think about an experience of citizenship rooted in life and memory, no matter how traumatic or pained.

See also The Blithedale Romance; Cincinnati; Civil War; *Clotel;* Gothic Fiction; *The House of the Seven Gables;* Leatherstocking Tales; *Moby-Dick;* Mourning; Slave Narratives; Slavery; *Uncle Tom's Cabin*

BIBLIOGRAPHY

Primary Works

Bibb, Henry. *Narrative of the Life and Adventures of Henry Bibb, an American Slave.* 1849. In *Slave Narratives,* edited by William L. Andrews and Henry Louis Gates Jr., pp. 425–566. New York: Library of America, 2000.

Brown, William Wells. *Clotel; or, The President's Daughter: A Narrative of Slave Life in the United States.* 1853. New York: Citadel Press, 1969.

Brown, William Wells. *Narrative of William W. Brown, a Fugitive Slave.* 1847. In *Slave Narratives,* edited by William L. Andrews and Henry Louis Gates Jr., pp. 369–423. New York: Library of America, 2000.

Cooper, James Fenimore. *The Pioneers; or, The Sources of the Susquehanna: A Descriptive Tale.* 1823. In *The Leatherstocking Tales,* vol. 1, edited by Blake Nevius, pp. 1–465. New York: Library of America, 1985.

Cooper, James Fenimore. *The Spy: A Tale of Neutral Ground.* 1821. New York: AMS Press, 2002.

Crafts, Hannah. *The Bondwoman's Narrative.* c. 1850s. Edited by Henry Louis Gates Jr. New York: Warner Books, 2002.

Douglass, Frederick. *My Bondage and My Freedom.* 1855. In *Autobiographies,* edited by Henry Louis Gates Jr., pp. 103–452. New York: Library of America, 1994.

Douglass, Frederick. *Narrative of the Life of Frederick Douglass, an American Slave.* 1845. In *Autobiographies,* edited by Henry Louis Gates Jr., pp. 1–102. New York: Library of America, 1994.

Emerson, Ralph Waldo. *Nature.* 1836. In *Essays and Lectures,* edited by Joel Porte, pp. 9–49. New York: Library of America, 1983.

Hawthorne, Nathaniel. *The Blithedale Romance.* 1852. In *Novels,* edited by Millicent Bell, pp. 629–848. New York: Library of America, 1983.

Hawthorne, Nathaniel. *The House of the Seven Gables.* 1851. In *Novels,* edited by Millicent Bell, pp. 347–627. New York: Library of America, 1983.

Hawthorne, Nathaniel. *The Scarlet Letter.* 1850. In *Novels,* edited by Millicent Bell, pp. 115–345. New York: Library of America, 1983.

Lane, Lunsford. *The Narrative of Lunsford Lane, Formerly of Raleigh, N.C.* 1842. In *Five Slave Narratives: A Compendium,* edited by William Loren Katz. New York: Arno Press, 1968.

Melville, Herman. *Moby-Dick; or, The Whale.* 1851. In *Redburn, His First Voyage; White-Jacket; or, The World in a Man-of-War; Moby-Dick; or, The Whale,* edited by G. Thomas Tanselle, pp. 771–1408. New York: Library of America, 1983.

Poe, Edgar Allan. "The Philosophy of Composition." 1846. In *Essays and Reviews,* edited by G. R. Thompson, pp. 13–25. New York: Library of America, 1984.

Stowe, Harriet Beecher. *Uncle Tom's Cabin; or, Life among the Lowly.* 1852. In *Three Novels,* edited by Kathryn Kish Sklar, pp. 1–519. New York: Library of America, 1982.

Secondary Works

Andrews, William L. *To Tell a Free Story: The First Century of Afro-American Autobiography, 1760–1865.* Urbana: University of Illinois Press, 1986.

Bercovitch, Sacan. *The Office of the Scarlet Letter.* Baltimore: Johns Hopkins University Press, 1991.

Gates, Henry Louis, Jr., and Hollis Robbins. *In Search of Hannah Crafts: Critical Essays on the Bondwoman's Narrative.* New York: Basic Books, 2004.

Goddu, Teresa. *Gothic America: Narrative, History, and Nation.* New York: Columbia University Press, 1997.

Laderman, Gary. *The Sacred Remains: American Attitudes toward Death, 1799–1883.* New Haven, Conn.: Yale University Press, 1996.

Levine, Robert S. *Martin Delany, Frederick Douglass, and the Politics of Representative Identity.* Chapel Hill: University of North Carolina Press, 1997.

Sundquist, Eric J. *To Wake the Nations: Race in the Making of American Literature.* Cambridge, Mass: Harvard University Press, 1993.

Tompkins, Jane. *Sensational Designs: The Cultural Work of American Fiction, 1790–1860.* New York: Oxford University Press, 1985.

Weisenburger, Steven. *Modern Medea: A Family Story of Slavery and Child-Murder from the Old South.* New York: Hill and Wang, 1998.

Russ Castronovo

DECLARATION OF SENTIMENTS

Arguably the most significant document to call for the advancement of women in nineteenth-century America, the Declaration of Sentiments was made famous at the first Woman's Rights Convention, held in Seneca Falls, New York, on 19 and 20 July 1848. Drafted by the then thirty-two-year-old Elizabeth Cady Stanton (1815–1902), the declaration outlined a series of grievances resulting from the disenfranchisement of women and proposed eleven resolutions arguing that women had the right to equality in all aspects of their lives, including the right to vote. Despite the declaration's symbolic significance, however, it would be seventy-two years later that women finally won the right to vote.

The events leading up to the 1848 convention date back to 1840, when Stanton, a new bride, attended the World Anti-Slavery Convention in London. There she met Lucretia Mott (1793–1880), a Quaker reformer and abolitionist who, along with Stanton and other women delegates, had been denied a seat at the convention. Incensed and humiliated by the ban, which remained in effect even after appeals by convention delegates William Lloyd Garrison and Wendell Phillips, Stanton and Mott discussed plans to hold a public assembly to advance the rights of women. After her return to the United States, however, Stanton started a family, and the meeting plans were put on hold. Eight years after the London convention and following the passage of New York's much-debated Married Woman's Property Rights Act, Stanton attended a small social gathering near her home in Seneca Falls, where she laid out her list of grievances about the treatment of women in society. The group of five women agreed that the time was ripe for the convention that Stanton and Mott had envisioned in London. The women convened the convention just six days later at the Wesleyan Chapel in Seneca Falls. Hoping to attract a large crowd, they placed an ad in the local newspaper announcing a convention to discuss the social, civil, and religious condition of women and promoting Mott as the keynote speaker.

The convention organizers had a long history of feminist thought on which to draw: Mary

Our Roll of Honor

Containing all the

Signatures to the "Declaration of Sentiments"

Set Forth by the First

Woman's Rights Convention,

held at

Seneca Falls, New York

July 19-20, 1848

LADIES:

Lucretia Mott	Sophronia Taylor	Rachel D. Bonnel
Harriet Cady Eaton	Cynthia Davis	Betsey Tewksbury
Margaret Pryor	Hannah Plant	Rhoda Palmer
Elizabeth Cady Stanton	Lucy Jones	Margaret Jenkins
Eunice Newton Foote	Sarah Whitney	Cynthia Fuller
Mary Ann M'Clintock	Mary H. Hallowell	Mary Martin
Margaret Schooley	Elizabeth Conklin	P. A. Culvert
Martha C. Wright	Sally Pitcher	Susan R. Doty
Jane C. Hunt	Mary Conklin	Rebecca Race
Amy Post	Susan Quinn	Sarah A. Mosher
Catherine F. Stebbins	Mary S. Mirror	Mary E. Vail
Mary Ann Frink	Phebe King	Lucy Spalding
Lydia Mount	Julia Ann Drake	Lovina Latham
Delia Mathews	Charlotte Woodward	Sarah Smith
Catherine C. Paine	Martha Underhill	Eliza Martin
Elizabeth W. M'Clintock	Dorothy Mathews	Maria E. Wilbur
Malvina Seymour	Eunice Barker	Elizabeth D. Smith
Phebe Mosher	Sarah R. Woods	Caroline Barker
Catherine Shaw	Lydia Gild	Ann Porter
Deborah Scott	Sarah Hoffman	Experience Gibbs
Sarah Hallowell	Elizabeth Leslie	Antoinette E. Segur
Mary M'Clintock	Martha Ridley	Hannah J. Latham
Mary Gilbert		Sarah Sisson

GENTLEMEN:

Richard P. Hunt	William S. Dell	Nathan J. Milliken
Samuel D. Tillman	James Mott	S. E. Woodworth
Justin Williams	William Burroughs	Edward F. Underhill
Elisha Foote	Robert Smallbridge	George W. Pryor
Frederick Douglass	Jacob Mathews	Joel Bunker
Henry W. Seymour	Charles L. Hoskins	Isaac VanTassel
Henry Seymour	Thomas M'Clintock	Thomas Dell
David Spalding	Saron Phillips	E. W. Capron
William G. Barker	Jacob P. Chamberlain	Stephen Shear
Elias J. Doty	Jonathan Metcalf	Henry Hatley
John Jones		Azaliah Schooley

"Our Roll of Honor." Card listing the signatories to the Declaration of Sentiments promulgated at the Seneca Falls Convention, 1848. THE LIBRARY OF CONGRESS

Wollstonecraft's (1759–1797) *Vindication of the Rights of Women* had been published in 1792, Sarah Grimké's (1792–1873) *Letters on the Equality of the Sexes* was released in 1838, and Margaret Fuller's (1810–1850) *Woman in the Nineteenth Century* appeared in 1845. Although some states had passed legislation granting women property rights, women still had no legal entitlement to their wages or to their children in the event of a divorce. It was illegal for women to testify against their husbands in a court of law, and most professions—

with the exception of teaching and publishing—were still closed to women. There was also a double standard in place with respect to morality; women were expected to remain chaste until marriage, while promiscuity among men was widely tolerated.

Much to the surprise of Stanton and Mott, the convention drew some three hundred people from miles around. Among those in attendance were forty men, including the abolitionist and former slave

The Declaration of Sentiments, excerpted below, contains a list of eighteen injustices that were unique to women, ranging from the systemic oppression that resulted from the absence of legal and voting rights to the lack of economic freedom and educational opportunities.

When, in the course of human events, it becomes necessary for one portion of the family of man to assume among the people of the earth a position different from that which they have hitherto occupied, but one to which the laws of nature and of nature's God entitle them, a decent respect to the opinions of mankind requires that they should declare the causes that impel them to such a course.

We hold these truths to be self-evident: that all men and women are created equal; that they are endowed by their Creator with certain inalienable rights; that among these are life, liberty, and the pursuit of happiness; that to secure these rights governments are instituted, deriving their just powers from the consent of the governed. Whenever any form of government becomes destructive of these ends, it is the right of those who suffer from it to refuse allegiance to it, and to insist upon the institution of a new government, laying its foundation on such principles, and organizing its powers in such form, as to them shall seem most likely to effect their safety and happiness. . . .

The history of mankind is a history of repeated injuries and usurpations on the part of man toward woman, having in direct object the establishment of an absolute tyranny over her. . . .

He has never permitted her to exercise her inalienable right to the elective franchise. . . .

He has made her, if married, in the eye of the law, civilly dead.

He has taken from her all right in property, even to the wages she earns. . . .

He has so framed the laws of divorce, as to what shall be the proper causes and, in case of separation, to whom the guardianship of the children shall be given, as to be wholly regardless of the happiness of the women—the law, in all cases, going upon a false supposition of the supremacy of man and giving all power into his hands. . . .

He has monopolized nearly all the profitable employments, and from those she is permitted to follow, she receives but a scanty remuneration. . . . He has denied her the facilities for obtaining a thorough education, all colleges being closed against her.

He allows her in church, as well as state, but a subordinate position, claiming apostolic authority for her exclusion from the ministry, and, with some exceptions, from any public participation in the affairs of the church.

He has created a false public sentiment by giving to the world a different code of morals for men and women, by which moral delinquencies which exclude women from society are not only tolerated but deemed of little account in man.

He has usurped the prerogative of Jehovah himself, claiming it as his right to assign for her a sphere of action, when that belongs to her conscience and to her God.

He has endeavored, in every way that he could, to destroy her confidence in her own powers, to lessen her self-respect, and to make her willing to lead a dependent and abject life.

Now, in view of this entire disfranchisement of one-half the people of this country, their social and religious degradation, in view of the unjust laws above mentioned, and because women do feel themselves aggrieved, oppressed, and fraudulently deprived of their most sacred rights, we insist that they have immediate admission to all the rights and privileges which belong to them as citizens of the United States. . . .

Resolved, That such laws as conflict, in any way, with the true and substantial happiness of woman, are contrary to the great precept of nature and of no validity, for this is "superior in obligation to any other."

Resolved, that all laws which prevent woman from occupying such a station in society as her conscience shall dictate, or which place her in a position inferior to that of man, are contrary to the great precept of nature and therefore of no force or authority.

Resolved, that woman is man's equal, was intended to be so by the Creator, and the highest good of the race demands that she should be recognized as such.

Resolved, that the women of this country ought to be enlightened in regard to the laws under which they live, that they may no longer publish their degradation by declaring themselves satisfied with their present position, nor their ignorance, by asserting that they have all the rights they want.

Resolved, that inasmuch as man, while claiming for himself intellectual superiority, does accord to woman moral superiority, it is preeminently his duty to encourage her to speak and teach, as she has an opportunity, in all religious assemblies.

Resolved, that the same amount of virtue, delicacy, and refinement of behavior that is required of woman in the social state also be required of man, and the same transgressions should be visited with equal severity on both man and woman. . . .

Resolved, that woman has too long rested satisfied in the circumscribed limits which corrupt customs and a perverted application of the Scriptures have marked out for her, and that it is time she should move in the enlarged sphere which her great Creator has assigned her.

Resolved, that it is the duty of the women of this country to secure to themselves their sacred right to the elective franchise.

Resolved, that the equality of human rights results necessarily from the fact of the identity of the race in capabilities and responsibilities.

Resolved, that the speedy success of our cause depends upon the zealous and untiring efforts of both men and women for the overthrow of the monopoly of the pulpit, and for the securing to woman an equal participation with men in the various trades, professions, and commerce.

Resolved, therefore, that, being invested by the Creator with the same capabilities and same consciousness of responsibility for their exercise, it is demonstrably the right and duty of woman, equally with man, to promote every righteous cause by every righteous means; and especially in regard to the great subjects of morals and religion, it is self-evidently her right to participate with her brother in teaching them, both in private and in public, by writing and by speaking, by any instrumentalities proper to be used, and in any assemblies proper to be held; and this being a self-evident truth growing out of the divinely implanted principles of human nature, any custom or authority adverse to it, whether modern or wearing the hoary sanction of antiquity, is to be regarded as a self-evident falsehood, and at war with mankind.

U.S. Department of State, International Information Programs, Declaration of Sentiments and Resolutions, http://usinfo.state.gov/usa/women/rights/sentimnt.htm.

Frederick Douglass (1818–1895). It was there that the Declaration of Sentiments, drafted by Stanton, was introduced. Modeled on the Declaration of Independence, the Declaration of Sentiments proposed reforms in all areas of women's lives.

On the first day of the convention, attendees debated the contents of the declaration, discussed the wisdom of allowing men to sign it, and deliberated the merits of its eleven resolutions. Stanton began the declaration with the proposition that "all men and women are created equal." This assertion underscored the point that, rather than being all-inclusive, the language in the Declaration of Independence had explicitly excluded women. The Declaration of Sentiments sought to illustrate this discrepancy in the earlier document and its application to the female half of the population, for many of the liberties outlined there simply had no standing when applied to women's lives. Included in the Declaration of Sentiments was a list of eighteen injustices endured by women, ranging from the lack of equal educational opportunities and the denial of the right to vote to the exclusion of public participation in the affairs of the church. It also protested unequal wages and employment opportunities. After Stanton

read the declaration paragraph by paragraph, it was amended and adopted unanimously.

The second day of the convention focused on a discussion of the declaration's eleven resolutions. With the exception of the ninth proclamation, demanding the vote for women, the resolutions passed unanimously. After an impassioned appeal by Douglass, however, the suffrage resolution passed by a slim margin. One hundred people—sixty-eight women and thirty-two men—signed the final draft of the declaration.

The Seneca Falls Convention generated widespread ridicule and even hostility, primarily from religious leaders and the press. An article in the *Philadelphia Public Ledger and Daily Transcript* (26 September 1848) opined that, unlike the Seneca Falls women, the women of Philadelphia were "celebrated for discretion, modesty, and unfeigned diffidence" rather than "standing out for woman's rights." After all, the writer reasoned, "A woman is nobody. A wife is everything. A pretty girl is equal to ten thousand men, and a mother is, next to God, all powerful. . . . The ladies of Philadelphia, therefore . . . are resolved to maintain their rights as Wives, Belles, Virgins and Mothers, and not as Women" (Stanton, Anthony, and Gage, p. 804). Another article, appearing in the 1 August 1848 issue of the *Rochester Democrat,* derided the "absurdity" of the convention: "This great effort seemed to bring out some new, impracticable, absurd and ridiculous proposition and the greater its absurdity the better" (Viewpoint). Another newspaper reported that the convention constituted "the most shocking and unnatural incident ever recorded in the history of womanity" (Gurko, p. 103).

Recognizing the potential to further publicize her cause, Stanton responded to the "printed challenges" to the Declaration of Sentiments in the 14 September 1848 *National Reformer:*

> There is no danger of this question dying for want of notice. . . . But one might suppose from the articles that you find in some papers, that there were editors so ignorant as to believe that the Chief object of these recent Conventions was to seat every lord at the head of a cradle, and to clothe every woman in her lord's attire. . . . For those who do not yet understand the real objects of our recent Conventions at Rochester and Seneca Falls, I would state that we did not meet to discuss fashions, customs, or dress, the rights or duties of man, nor the property of the sexes changing positions, but simply our own inalienable rights, our duties, our true sphere. If God has assigned a sphere to man and one to woman, we claim the right to judge ourselves of His design in reference to *us,* and we accord to man the same privilege. (Stanton, Anthony, and Gage, p. 806)

Not all of the press coverage was negative, however. Douglass, who was editor of the *Rochester North Star,* wrote that the Declaration of Sentiments should be regarded as the basis of a grand movement for attaining the civil, social, political, and religious rights of women.

> We should not do justice to our own convictions, or to the excellent persons connected with this infant movement, if we did not in this connection offer a few remarks on the general subject which the Convention met to consider and the objects they seek to attain. In doing so, we are not insensible that the bare mention of this truly important subject in any other than terms of contemptuous ridicule and scornful disfavor, is likely to excite against us the fury of bigotry and the folly of prejudice. A discussion of the rights of animals would be regarded with far more complacency by many of what are called the "wise" and the "good" of our land, than would a discussion of the rights of women. . . . While it is impossible for us to go into this subject at length, and dispose of the various objections which are often urged against such a doctrine as that of female equality, we are free to say that in respect to political rights, we hold woman to be justly entitled to all we claim for man. . . . Our doctrine is that "right is of no sex." We therefore bid the women engaged in this movement our humble Godspeed. (Stanton, Anthony, and Gage, pp. 74–75)

Although it would be seventy-two years before women finally won the vote, the 1848 Seneca Falls Convention had set the wheels in motion. Regrettably, only one of the original signers of the Declaration of Sentiments, Charlotte Woodward Pierce, survived long enough to cast her ballot in the 1920 national election. She was ninety-one years old.

In 1851 Stanton joined forces with Susan B. Anthony, and the two devoted much of the remainder of their lives to fighting discrimination against women. Without question, however, it was Stanton's Declaration of Sentiments that first politicized the issues that would take center stage in the struggle to attain equality for women.

See also Democracy; Female Authorship; Feminism; *Letters on the Equality of the Sexes;* Reform; Seneca Falls Convention; Suffrage; *Woman in the Nineteenth Century;* Young America

BIBLIOGRAPHY

Primary Works

DuBois, Ellen Carol, ed. *The Elizabeth Cady Stanton–Susan B. Anthony Reader: Correspondence, Writings, Speeches.* Rev. ed. Boston: Northeastern University Press, 1992.

Stanton, Elizabeth Cady. *Address of Mrs. Elizabeth Cady Stanton, Delivered at Seneca Falls & Rochester, N.Y. July 19th & August 2d, 1848.* New York: Robert J. Johnston, 1870.

Stanton, Elizabeth Cady, Susan B. Anthony, and Matilda Joslyn Gage, eds. *History of Woman Suffrage.* 3 vols. New York: Fowler & Wells, 1881–1886.

Secondary Works

Gurko, Miriam. *The Ladies of Seneca Falls: The Birth of the Women's Rights Movement.* New York: Macmillan, 1974.

"Viewpoint: A Historic Opportunity." http://www.now.org.

Ward, Geoffrey C., and Ken Burns. *Not for Ourselves Alone: The Story of Elizabeth Cady Stanton and Susan B. Anthony: An Illustrated History.* New York: Knopf, 1999.

Denise D. Knight

DEMOCRACY

In the October 1837 inaugural issue of the *United States Magazine and Democratic Review,* an antebellum journal dedicated to strengthening democracy in politics and literature, the editor John O'Sullivan (1813–1895) expressed the democratic thrust of the era when he announced that "all history has to be

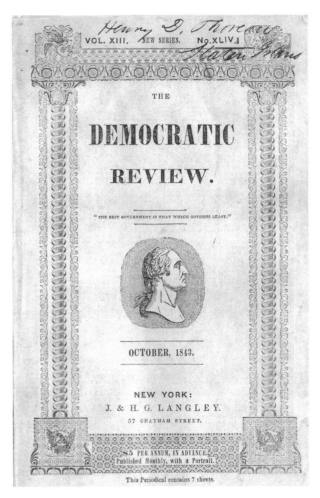

Title page of *The Democratic Review,* October 1843, signed by Henry David Thoreau. COURTESY OF THE CONCORD FREE PUBLIC LIBRARY

re-written; political science and the whole scope of all moral truth have to be considered and illustrated in the light of the democratic principle" (p. 14). In the early decades of the nineteenth century, the "democratic principle" was defined by a resurgence of interest in the promises of the Declaration of Independence as the foundational statement of American freedom, liberty, and equality. The *Democratic Review,* as it was more commonly called, saw the creation of a national literature as the most "potent influence" (p. 14) in reviving the principles of democracy and in advancing America as a nation that might realize the "glorious destiny of its future" (p. 13).

As suggested in O'Sullivan's first editorial, 1837 is a signal year in the rhetoric of American nationalism, during which a renewed interest in revitalizing American culture was displayed by a literature infused with democracy. This is also the year of Ralph Waldo

Emerson's (1803–1882) "American Scholar" address to the Phi Beta Kappa Society at Harvard, in which he denounces European literary tradition in favor of a sense of newness and youth in American books. Emerson asks young scholars to take up the project of renewing American democracy by creating a literature that breaks with "the courtly muses of Europe" and moves away from antiquated political and social thought. For Emerson, seizing the freedom to "speak our own minds" means that "a nation of men [*sic*] will for the first time exist" in American letters and culture (pp. 104–105).

Orations on American patriotism in the antebellum era, such as one delivered at Brown University in 1840 by Thomas Kennicutt, a popular New England lecturer, displayed this Emersonian insistence that it was the "duty of literary men of our country" to revive the "democratic principle in civil society" (Kennicutt, p. 5). Writers of the early and mid-nineteenth century were thus charged with the responsibility of promoting a political and cultural revolution through the creation of a literature that would best express the spirit of a young America destined to spread democracy throughout the world.

JACKSONIAN DEMOCRACY AND YOUNG AMERICA

Andrew Jackson (1767–1845), who served two terms as the seventh U.S. president from 1828 to 1836, was significant in defining the terms of democracy in the early nineteenth century. Jackson and his followers portrayed the Democratic Party and its policies as progressive and egalitarian in contrast to what they characterized as the antidemocratic aristocracy of the Whigs. In his claims to represent the American electorate and to advance democracy, Jackson embodied this democratic impulse, declaring himself a man of the people. For Jackson, the "people" were not rising capitalists, leaders of business and industry, or entrepreneurs; instead, Jackson understood "the people" to be mechanics, laborers, and farmers. Under Jackson, the concept of a popular or majority rule took hold; Democrats denounced elitism and aristocratic pretensions, heralding instead the rights of the citizenry, insisting that the will of the people be represented by their elected leaders. By most historical accounts, Jackson is seen as largely responsible for effecting this political and cultural transformation of the United States from a republic, governed by an elect few, to a democracy. Jackson persuaded Americans that sovereign power resided in them—that they would control the governing process by deciding questions of constitutionality, law, and representation through the ballot box.

Many writers, philosophers, and activists were also convinced by Jackson's rhetoric of democracy, believing that more concern for the rights of common individuals would yield a more inclusive political and cultural environment receptive to the ideals of a younger generation of Americans. Emerson, for example, calls for young scholars to transform themselves into "Man Thinking," "free even to the definition of freedom" (p. 97). For Emerson, this movement toward self-rule, wherein individuals treat each other as "sovereign state[s]," reflects the embodiment of "an analogous political movement," the impulse in Jacksonian democracy in which "new importance [is] given to the single person" (p. 103). The political and intellectual trend that Emerson recognizes was animated by a group of literary critics in New York who aligned themselves with the more liberal faction of the Democratic Party. This group of critics and writers became known as Young America, and the earliest members included the prominent New York City activists and editors Cornelius Mathews, Evert Augustus Duyckinck, William A. Jones, and the *Democratic Review* editor John O'Sullivan.

At the intersection of political sentiments and the production of literature in antebellum America, the *Democratic Review* had two primary aims: to give liberal intellectuals a voice to effect political and social change and to promote a democratic American literature that would better represent the interests of the proletariat. Young Americans, encouraged by O'Sullivan to muse overtly on the connections between art and liberty, were attempting to realize the promises of social equality, interpreting democracy as a harmonization of the actual condition of individuals in society with their acknowledged rights as citizens. In an 1842 article in the *Democratic Review,* "Democracy and Literature," O'Sullivan makes clear his intention to publish work in favor of literary democratic freedom: "Literature is not only the natural ally of freedom, political or religious; but also affords the firmest bulwark . . . to protect the interests of freedom" (p. 196). Through the *Democratic Review,* O'Sullivan was attempting to create a community of revolutionary intellectuals, like Nathaniel Hawthorne (1804–1864) and Walt Whitman (1819–1892), as literary agents for social change.

THE LITERATURE OF YOUNG AMERICA

During his tenure at the *Democratic Review* from its inception in 1837 until Evert Duyckinck (1816–1878) took over the magazine in 1846, O'Sullivan published the bulk of Hawthorne's stories, housed Whitman's earliest major publications, included many of James

Fenimore Cooper's (1789–1851) writings, provided an outlet for abolitionist writers Catharine Maria Sedgwick (1789–1867) and John Greenleaf Whittier (1807–1892), and even published work by Edgar Allan Poe (1809–1849), although the latter frequently voiced his critique of the Democratic Party. Having just published his *Twice-Told Tales,* 1837 is a watershed year for Hawthorne as well, as he begins to publish most of his work in the *Democratic Review,* including the short story "Rappaccini's Daughter" and nearly all the stories later collected in *Mosses from an Old Manse* (1846). Hawthorne was particularly influential in inspiring other writers to join the cause of Young America's democratic revolution, most notably a young Herman Melville (1819–1891), who praised Hawthorne's *Mosses* as the greatest work of fiction by an American in his 1850 tribute "Hawthorne and His Mosses," which appeared in the *Literary World.*

The influence of Young America and the milieu of the *Democratic Review* can be seen in some of Hawthorne's better-known novels, such as *The Scarlet Letter* (1850) and *The House of the Seven Gables* (1851). In his introduction to *The Scarlet Letter,* "The Custom-House," Hawthorne's description of himself as a "Locofoco Surveyor" suggests his sympathies with the Jacksonian faction of the Democratic Party in his use of the term "locofoco," derived from the name of the matches used to relight the 1835 meeting of New York Democrats after dissenters turned off the lamps. Salem Whigs later accused Hawthorne of locofoco activity and released him from his governmental post, resulting in Hawthorne's sense of alienation as suggested in his declaration, at the end of the "The Custom-House," of himself as a "citizen of somewhere else" (p. 157). Similarly, in *The House of the Seven Gables,* Hawthorne expresses a distrust of the influences of the past that closely echoes Emerson's ideas about the need to move beyond the authority of an older period. Through Holgrave, a character who symbolizes the reformist tendency of the era, Hawthorne articulates the Emersonian imperative for society to reject "Dead Men's forms and creeds" in order for a younger generation to have a "proper influence on our own world" (pp. 509, 510). In Holgrave, Hawthorne presents an archetype of the ideals and vision of a Young America struggling to redefine the promises of democracy.

The *Democratic Review* also provided an early forum for Whitman's writing in the 1840s and 1850s; Whitman seemed to inherently understand O'Sullivan's push for a literary democracy as seen in his insistence that a nation's literature must emanate from its political beliefs and practices. Whitman reiterated the platform of Young America almost to the letter, calling for the younger generation to usurp the old in order to revive American democracy. In addition to his pieces in the *Democratic Review,* Whitman's musings on democracy were printed in the *Brooklyn Daily Eagle,* a journal already enjoying a strong standing among newspapers in New York and throughout the country when Whitman took over as editor in 1846. In an editorial this same year, "Perpetuity of the Democratic Spirit," (*Gathering of the Forces* 1:6–9) Whitman speaks as the voice of the people seeking to regenerate the democracy envisioned by Thomas Jefferson (1743–1826) and his contemporaries: "We stand here the inheritors of their principles and opposed to the same foe—the foe of equal rights. Democracy must conquer again as it did then—and more certainly than it did then" (p. 9). As seen in these editorials, and throughout his poetry, Whitman's understanding of democracy takes on religious significance as a sense of faith that transcends and endures despite political movements and systems; for Whitman, the "true Democratic spirit is endued [*sic*] with immortal life and strength" (p. 7).

Whitman's 1855 preface to his collection of poems *Leaves of Grass* highlights his Jacksonian understanding of the importance of "the common people" and their "deathless attachment to freedom" in defining the true "genius of the United States" (p. 450). As seen in the poem's tributes to ordinary people and objects, *Leaves of Grass* displays Whitman's vision of a democratic art form that fused the desire for political democracy with an egalitarian concern for the experiences of everyday people. In *Leaves,* Whitman also declared independence from traditional poetic forms and subjects, pioneering a free verse style that rejected conventional patterns of rhyme and meter. Although his mixture of the sacred and the profane in *Leaves* distanced and offended many nineteenth-century readers, poets and critics have since noted the importance of Whitman's unconventional style in exhibiting Emerson's call for literary independence. For Whitman, the poet was the voice of this patriotism, incarnating the people and their quest for liberty, thus embodying the Young American movement for the "transcendant [*sic*] and new" (*Leaves,* p. 452). Whitman's poet is one of the masses, a "bard . . . commensurate with a people" (p. 450), serving their interests by being the "voice and exposition" of their quest for political liberty (p. 459). Just as Emerson's "American Scholar" address influenced a new generation of Americans to be forward-looking in developing a literature to express the democratic spirit of the nation, Whitman's 1855 preface to *Leaves* served as a manifesto for a new American poetry that would supplant outdated traditions.

Whitman's optimistic view of democratic transcendence resonates with the democratic vision of John Greenleaf Whittier, who wrote for the *Democratic Review* a decade earlier. The journal published a significant amount of Whittier's work, including the poem "Democracy," first published in the *Review* in 1841 and later collected in *Lays of My Home, and Other Poems* in 1843). Whittier's abolitionist, anticapitalist, and pro-labor beliefs can be seen in his vision of a democracy that sees with an "impartial eye" through which "fade the lines of caste and birth!" Whittier's democratic vision unites the "groaning multitudes of earth" who under its benevolent eye become "equal in their suffering." Democracy for Whittier has a transformative effect, erasing class and racial boundaries so that there are no divisions between "prince or peasant—slave or lord— / Pale priest, or swarthy artisan." Democracy's eye sees beyond what Whittier refers to as "all disguise, form, place or name" and instead "lookest on *the man* within" (p. 63). As demonstrated in this poem and throughout his active political and literary life, Whittier's understanding of the necessity for a democracy that represents people of all social strata provides another response to Emerson's plea that American writers embrace the everyday experiences of commonplace people. Whittier's optimistic rejuvenation of democracy, however, recognizes the existence of vast social inequalities that were plaguing the United States and threatening its cohesion.

DEMOCRACY FOR ALL?

The 1840s and 1850s witnessed significant political and cultural changes concurrent with the Young American call for equality, as seen in the strengthening of reform movements that focused on denouncing materialism and organizing efforts to correct social and economic abuses. This reformist impulse in American culture and literature, however, raised debates about the meaning of liberty and freedom in a democratic society. Many reformers believed that Jacksonian policies and practices excluded women, African Americans, and Native Americans from the democratic vision of Young America.

The late Jacksonian era is characterized by the expansion of the United States both domestically—nearly a doubling of its spatial domain—and abroad, as America pursued territorial and economic advantages in places like Hawaii, Cuba, and China. This expansionism fulfilled the dream of Jacksonian Democrats, embodied in the concept of Manifest Destiny. John O'Sullivan first coined the infamous phrase in his article "Annexation" in the *Democratic Review* in July/August 1845. For O'Sullivan and other Jacksonian democrats, the acquisition of land was crucial for the success of a new and distinctly American political and economic system. Writers of this era espoused a belief in Manifest Destiny as part of the democratic mission of Americanism; Whitman, for example, argues for the importance of the West as a site for democracy in his 1847 article "Where the Great Stretch of Power Must be Wielded." Whitman expresses the sentiment of the era when he claims that the West—"the boundless democratic free West!"—represents the future of American progress and liberty (*Gathering*, p. 25). Jacksonian Democrats believed that territorial expansion would foster harmonious relations by uniting people across geographical boundaries; expansionism, in this sense, would bring about the spread of democracy.

Many scholars have noted that Jacksonian expansionism displays antiabolitionist tendencies and racial fears that fueled the acquisition and conquest of lands. As early as Jackson's first term in the 1820s, the issues of slavery and of Indian removal animated questions about American democracy. Outspoken critiques of America's mobile quest for democracy can be seen throughout the literature of the mid-century. For example, John Rollin Ridge's 1854 novel *The Life and Adventures of Joaquín Murieta, the Celebrated California Bandit* demonstrates Ridge's firsthand understanding of Jacksonian Indian removal. Ridge's Cherokee family fought with arms and in the courts against such policies before ultimately signing treaties that led to their eventual removal on the Trail of Tears, which claimed the lives of more than four thousand Cherokees on their trek westward. Ridge's novel represents an important response to the colonization impulse frequently overlooked in studies of the literary democracy of Young America. Women writers such as Fanny Fern (Sara Payson Willis Parton, 1811–1872), Lydia Maria Child (1802–1880), Catharine Maria Sedgwick, and Harriet Beecher Stowe (1811–1896), among many others, also fictionalized their experiences of exclusion from the promises of democratic equality. They were influenced in part by the first woman's rights convention in Seneca Falls, New York, in 1848. Organized by the abolitionists Elizabeth Cady Stanton (1815–1902), Lucretia Mott (1793–1880), and other Quaker women, the Seneca Falls Convention called for social and civic equality between women and men. Stanton's Declaration of Sentiments remains a significant document of the rights of women; modeled after the Declaration of Independence, this pivotal piece of literature from the convention lists the injustices done to women by men, much as the earlier Declaration listed the grievances of the colonists against British rule. The resolutions adopted at the convention included a call for suffrage, which would enable women to secure for themselves the promises of democracy.

One of the fewer than fifty men present at Seneca Falls was the ex-slave and abolitionist Frederick Douglass (1818–1895). Douglass wrote and spoke widely on the topic of equality for African Americans in the 1850s and 1860s, depicting the vast inequalities between blacks and whites in the United States as bringing about the degeneration of America's proclaimed national values and ideals. In one such speech, delivered in Corinthian Hall in Rochester, New York, on 5 July 1852, Douglass characterizes America as a young nation at the "beginning of [a] national career." He invokes the rhetoric of Young America to argue for a resurgence in the democratic ideals upon which the nation was founded—democratic ideals that might ultimately "be shrouded in gloom" if the enslavement of blacks continued ("Oration," pp. 4–5). Douglass also invokes the language of the Declaration of Independence as a reminder of the democratic principles of the nation's founding, encouraging white Americans to "stand by those principles," which he describes as the "ringbolt to the chain of your nation's destiny" (p. 9). The fundamental question Douglass asks of his white audience is: "What have I, or those I represent, to do with your national independence? Are the great principles of freedom and of natural justice embodied in that Declaration of Independence extended to us?" (p. 14). In so asking, Douglass makes clear the disparity between whites and blacks, brought about largely because of American slavery. In this speech, he ultimately rejects the Fourth of July as "yours not mine," declaring the memorial a hypocrisy on the democratic principles of liberty and equality (p. 15). Throughout his life and career, Douglass insisted that the emancipation from slavery was fundamental to the full realization of American democracy; anything less, for Douglass, was a mockery of America's discourse on equal rights. He was ambivalent, though, on the speediest means to achieving this democracy, initially imploring African American men to enlist during the Civil War, for example, yet later withdrawing his support of enlistment because he believed black men were not being recognized as soldiers equal to whites. This sense of ambivalence about the promises of democracy can be seen in the literature of a second-generation Young American, Herman Melville, whose novel *Moby-Dick* (1851) displays both assenting and antagonistic responses to Young America's democratic nationalism.

DEMOCRATIC TENSIONS AND THE WHITE WHALE

Literary democracy underwent another shift in the 1840s when Evert Duyckinck became the literary editor of the *Democratic Review*. Duyckinck had a conspicuous part in this second wave of Young

Americanism, heralding a series published through Wiley and Putnam, a prominent New York publishing house where he was also an editor, called the Library of American Books. In this series, Duyckinck attempted to realize his democratic literary vision, publishing a wide range of affordable paperback editions of works by popular and lesser known writers including Hawthorne, Whittier, the early feminist writer Margaret Fuller (1810–1850), and Caroline Matilda Kirkland (1801–1864), who wrote about the American West. This series was important for the advancement of Duyckinck's populist ideology and the democratization of literature because it encouraged the publication of first-rate books at affordable prices in order to reach the widest possible audience.

In Duyckinck, Melville found a Young American role model and encouragement for the unrefined writing of his early novels, *Typee* (1846), *Omoo* (1847), and *Mardi* (1849). Although Duyckinck hailed the latter, in particular, as purely original, he found Melville's vision in *Moby-Dick* too far beyond the pale of his own democratic idealism to accept, instead issuing an aggressive and devastating review of the novel in the *Literary World* in 1852. *Moby-Dick* suggests the influence of Duyckinck's Young American teachings on Melville's nationalism. This is particularly evident at the end of chapter 26 ("Knights and Squires"), which has been read as Melville's defense of Jacksonian democracy. Echoing the work of Emerson and Whitman, Melville lauds the laboring class as infused with a "democratic dignity" and appeals to a "democratic God"—the "centre and circumference of all democracy"—as the bearer of the "Spirit of Equality" (pp. 126–127). However, *Moby-Dick* also reflects Melville's pessimism and cynicism about American politics and culture, as suggested in the chapter "The Whiteness of the Whale." This chapter ends with Melville's musing on the "centre and circumference" of democracy, symbolized here in the white whale, as duplicitous, perhaps merely one of the "subtle deceits" lacking in real substance (p. 212).

In prophesying the unfulfilled promises of democracy, *Moby-Dick* suggests Melville's awareness of the racial and imperialist rhetoric underscoring the era's democratic proclamations. Melville was writing the final drafts of *Moby-Dick* in 1850 when the Fugitive Slave Law extended the rights of white slave owners by requiring citizens to assist in the return of fugitive slaves. Read in this context, the novel suggests that Melville's democracy requires a dismantling of racist institutions and laws—a point of view not held by more moderate Young Americans. Melville's critique of Young America's softening ideology can be seen more overtly in the "Young America in Literature"

chapter of his next novel, *Pierre* (1852), which barely disguises Melville's dislike of the fickle editorial world represented by Duyckinck. Although it disturbed Melville's contemporaries, *Moby-Dick* nonetheless confirmed Young America's belief that literature needed to have democracy at its core.

RECONSTRUCTING DEMOCRACY

Reconstruction policies after the Civil War suggest a failure to achieve democratic equality; the 1860s and 1870s, for example, saw the veto of bills that would have granted greater freedom and equality to African Americans, and despite laws against segregation and the passage of the Fifteenth Amendment, which guaranteed enfranchisement of African Americans, racial discrimination was still widespread, economic advancement for blacks still limited, and the struggle for female suffrage unresolved. In *Democratic Vistas* (1871), his indictment of American materialism, Whitman diagnoses the problems plaguing America as stemming from a hypocrisy at the core of its nationalism and once again calls for "a new founded literature" to breathe a "recuperative" breath into "these lamentable conditions" (*Leaves*, p. 477). The older Whitman held onto his vision of political and literary democracy, pleading for a nationalism that would "prove itself beyond cavil" and grow out of a "great original literature . . . to become the justification and reliance . . . of American democracy" (pp. 470–471). As suggested in Whitman's musings on America's new vistas, although Young American politics receded, the cultural impact of democracy continued to be a pervasive influence on the creation of a national literature—a literature of hope and independence.

See also Democracy in America; Individualism and Community; Reform; Utopian Communities; Young America

BIBLIOGRAPHY

Primary Works

Douglass, Frederick. *Narrative of the Life of Frederick Douglass, An American Slave.* 1845. New York: Penguin, 1982.

Douglass, Frederick. "Oration Delivered in Corinthian Hall, Rochester." Rochester, N.Y.: Lee, Mann and Co, 1852.

Emerson, Ralph Waldo. "The American Scholar." 1837. In *Selected Essays.* New York: Penguin, 1982.

Hawthorne, Nathaniel. *Collected Novels: Fanshawe, The Scarlet Letter, The House of the Seven Gables, The Blithedale Romance, The Marble Faun.* New York: Library of America, 1983.

Kennicutt, Thomas. "Oration Delivered before the Society of United Brothers at Brown University in 1840." Providence, R.I.: Knowles and Vose Printers, 1840.

Melville, Herman. *Moby-Dick.* 1851. New York: Penguin, 1992.

Melville, Herman. *Shorter Works.* New York: Literary Classics, 1984.

Proceedings of the Woman's Rights Convention of 1848. New York: R. J. Johnston, 1870.

The United States Magazine and Democratic Review 1, no. 1 (October 1837).

The United States Magazine and Democratic Review 11, no. 50 (August 1842).

Whitman, Walt. *The Gathering of the Forces.* 2 vols. New York: G. P. Putnam's Sons, 1920.

Whitman, Walt. *I Sit and Look Out: Editorials from the Brooklyn Daily Times.* Selected and edited by Emory Holloway and Vernolian Schwarz. New York: Columbia University Press, 1932.

Whitman, Walt. *Leaves of Grass and Selected Prose.* 1855. Edited by Lawrence Buell. New York: Modern Library, 1981.

Whittier, John Greenleaf. *Lays of My Home, and Other Poems.* Boston: W. D. Ticknor, 1843.

Secondary Works

Budick, Emily Miller. *Nineteenth-Century American Romance: Genre and the Construction of Democratic Culture.* New York: Twayne Publishers, 1996.

Burstein, Andrew. *Sentimental Democracy: The Evolution of America's Romantic Self-Image.* New York: Hill and Wang, 1999.

Dimock, Wai-Chee. *Empire for Liberty: Melville and the Poetics of Individualism.* Princeton, N.J.: Princeton University Press, 1989.

Fredricks, Nancy. *Melville's Art of Democracy.* Athens: University of Georgia Press, 1995.

Herbert, T. Walker, Jr. *Marquesan Encounters: Melville and the Meaning of Civilization.* Cambridge, Mass.: Harvard University Press, 1980.

Hietala, Thomas R. *Manifest Design: Anxious Aggrandizement in Late Jacksonian America.* Ithaca, N.Y.: Cornell University Press, 1985.

Karcher, Carolyn L. *Shadow Over the Promised Land: Slavery, Race, and Violence in Melville's America.* Baton Rouge: Louisiana State University Press, 1980.

Matthiessen, F. O. *The American Renaissance: Art and Expression in the Age of Emerson and Whitman.* 1941. New York: Oxford University Press, 1968.

Powell, Timothy B. *Ruthless Democracy: A Multicultural Interpretation of the American Renaissance.* Princeton, N.J.: Princeton University Press, 2000.

Remini, Robert V. *Andrew Jackson and the Course of American Democracy, 1833–1845.* New York: Harper and Row, 1984.

Reynolds, David S. *Beneath the American Renaissance: The Subversive Imagination in the Age of Emerson and Melville.* New York: Knopf, 1988.

Rogin, Michael Paul. *Fathers and Children: Andrew Jackson and the Subjugation of the American Indian.* 1975. New Brunswick, N.J.: Transaction Publishers, 1991.

Rogin, Michael Paul. *Subversive Genealogy: The Politics and Art of Herman Melville.* New York: Knopf, 1983.

Satz, Ronald N. *American Indian Policy in the Jacksonian Era.* Lincoln: University of Nebraska Press, 1975.

Stafford, John. *The Literary Criticism of "Young America": A Study in the Relationship of Politics and Literature, 1837–1850.* New York: Russell and Russell, 1952.

Widmer, Edward L. *Young America: The Flowering of Democracy in New York City.* New York: Oxford University Press, 1999.

Julie Prebel

DEMOCRACY IN AMERICA

The work that remains to this day the most profound and prescient account of democratic culture in the United States was written not by a native son born and bred in the ways of democracy but by a French aristocrat—a sympathetic outsider—named Alexis Charles Henri Maurice Clérel de Tocqueville (1805–1859). Tocqueville first conceived the idea for his great *De la Democratie en Amerique* (commonly translated as *Democracy in America*) during an eighteenth-month sojourn to the United States in 1831–1832. The purpose of Tocqueville's trip, which he undertook in the company of a close friend, Gustave de Beaumont, was to study the federal prison system, a project that led the two researchers as far west as Green Bay (now in the state of Wisconsin), as far north as Quebec, Canada, and as far south as New Orleans. The results of this research were published in France in 1833, at which time Tocqueville had also begun to work on *Democracy in America*. The first volume of *Democracy in America* was published in 1835 to significant acclaim both in France and abroad; the second volume, which completed the work, appeared five years later in 1840. (The first English translations of the volumes were published in 1835 and 1840 by Henry C. Reeve.) Tocqueville's masterwork deftly combines an exacting empirical analysis of democratic institutions in America (both local and federal) with a visionary "phenomenology" of the characteristic habits and sentiments underpinning democratic life. In his celebratory review of 1840, the great English social and political philosopher John Stuart Mill praised

Alexis de Tocqueville. AP/WIDE WORLD PHOTOS

Tocqueville's work as the "first philosophical book ever written on Democracy . . . the essential doctrines of which it is not likely that any future speculations will subvert" (p. 156). For Mill, Tocqueville's *Democracy in America* signals "a new era in the scientific study of politics" (p. 156).

TOCQUEVILLE'S INTENTION

Tocqueville experienced the advent of modern democracy as a profoundly religious phenomenon. "Everywhere," writes Tocqueville, "the various incidents in the lives of peoples are seen to turn to the profit of democracy . . . as blind instruments in the hands of God" (p. 6). Tocqueville confesses to writing *Democracy in America* under "pressure of a sort of religious terror" (p. 6) induced by the dizzying pace of democratic development in Europe and North America. To oppose democracy is to "struggle against God himself" (p. 7), and yet, like the biblical Jacob, Tocqueville proves himself a subtle wrestler, at once obedient and defiant. Democracy is "already strong enough that it cannot be suspended," but "not yet rapid enough to despair of directing it" (p. 7). The aim of Tocqueville's work is to remind those nations inflamed by the divine spirit of democracy that its fate resides in the ideas and

actions of human beings. A healthy democracy must be willing "to regulate its movements, to substitute little by little the science of affairs for its inexperience, and knowledge of its true interests for its blind instincts" (p. 7). Tocqueville is often severe with democracy, but always in the manner of a nurturing friend who understands the improving influence of spirited criticism. In Tocqueville's words, "it is because I [am] not an adversary of democracy that I [wish] to be sincere with it" (p. 400). Tocqueville's account of the promise and peril of democratic culture in the United States reminds us that true friends of democracy refuse to flatter its weaknesses.

EQUALITY OF CONDITIONS

What distinguishes democracy for Tocqueville is the "equality of conditions" (p. 6) fostered by America's political, legal, commercial, and educational institutions. Equality of conditions promotes freedom primarily defined as economic opportunity, which promises to all citizens (regardless of social standing) equal access to the circumstances and means for achieving security, prosperity, and general well-being. Whereas class boundaries in aristocratic societies are "very distinct and immobile" (p. 483), the equality of conditions that prevail in democracies allows an unprecedented degree of movement and interaction between kinds and classes of people. Tocqueville frequently remarks the astonishing tempo of American life, the "continual movement" inspired by the promise and possibility that "reigns in the heart of a democratic society" (p. 403).

INDIVIDUALISM

Equality of conditions, in bringing citizens from all walks of life into closer relation, would appear to encourage consensus and community. However, Tocqueville feels that as freedom of opportunity increases, the "bond of human affections is extended and loosened" (p. 483). As social identities and attachments are broken apart by economic mobility, there emerges a large population of restless individuals who, having procured "enough enlightenment and goods to be able to be self-sufficient," develop the damaging "habit of always considering themselves in isolation" (p. 484). Tocqueville calls this peculiar feature of American democracy "individualism," which inclines toward (but is not the same as) selfishness. Whereas selfishness expresses "a passionate and exaggerated love of self that brings man to relate everything to himself alone," individualism is "a reflective and peaceable sentiment that disposes each citizen to . . . withdraw to one side with his family and friends" (p. 482). As a form of regard limited to the interests of those who are immediately present—one's family and friends—individualism seriously inhibits the formation of a genuinely civic or public consciousness. Individualism results from the turbulence of a democratic culture in which the tempo of movement and change is so accelerated that the "fabric of time is torn at every moment and the trace of generations is effaced" (p. 483). Equality of conditions, precisely in expanding freedom of opportunity, gently makes "each man forget his ancestors . . . and threatens finally to confine him wholly in the solitude of his own heart" (p. 484).

LOVE OF WELL-BEING

The individualism encouraged by equality of conditions is animated by a distinctive passion or love. Tocqueville remarks that of "all the passions that equality gives birth to or favors, there is one . . . that it sets in the hearts of all men at the same time: the love of well-being" (p. 422). This passion develops in the American environment as an obsessive desire to accumulate material wealth. "The taste for material enjoyments," Tocqueville writes, "must be considered the first source of this secret restiveness revealed in the actions of Americans and of the inconstancy of which they give daily examples" (p. 512). The extraordinary pace of American democracy is driven by a restive population of individuals who define freedom "possessively" as economic consumption. Such persons conceive well-being not as a condition of spiritual or contemplative repose but as the ceaseless pursuit of material goods aimed at "satisfying the least needs of the body" (p. 506). Americans "dream constantly of the [material] goods they do not have" (p. 511) and pass rapidly from desire to desire, possession to possession. Tocqueville speaks of the American who constructs a home for retirement and then "sells it while the roof is being laid," who "embraces a profession and quits it. He settles in a place from which he departs soon after." In this way, Americans pursue their vague desires "here and there within the vast limits of the United States" (p. 512).

This agitated quest for material well-being may look and feel like freedom, but for Tocqueville it expresses the tyranny of an anxiety peculiar to the middle-class disposition of American democracy: an excessive fear of mortality and death. "He who has confined his heart solely to the search for the goods of this world," Tocqueville observes, "is always in a hurry. . . . In addition to the goods that he possesses, at each instant he imagines a thousand others that death will prevent him from enjoying if he does not hasten" (p. 512). Equality of conditions arouses in all persons empowering sentiments of hope, prosperity, and happiness, but the boundlessness of these sentiments induces a sharp sense of mortality that both inflames and frustrates desire. This torment maintains the democratic soul in a condition of "unceasing trepidation" that compels the individual to "change his designs and his place at every moment" (p. 512).

DEATH OF THE MIND AND SOUL

Tocqueville's description of the desperate materialism that drives American democracy concludes with a pointed warning: an excessive passion for material pleasures "soon disposes men to believe that all is nothing but matter" (p. 519). America threatens to evolve a culture driven solely by frantic and fantastic efforts to improve "the goods of the body" (p. 521) with little regard for the needs and care of the mind and soul. In fact, American democracy encourages a practical "body-centered" ethos that increasingly denies any distinction or difference between intellectual or spiritual desires and pleasures of the flesh. Tocqueville's provocative claim that no country in the world is "less occupied with philosophy than the United States" (p. 403) accentuates the aggressive materialism of a democratic culture that refuses to honor the *vita contemplativa* or "life of the mind" as a valuable human endeavor. The restive pursuit of material well-being emphasizes speed, efficiency, and execution as distinguishing marks of prestige and success. The example of America convinces Tocqueville that "there is nothing less fit for meditation than the interior of a democratic society," for "where does one find the calm necessary to the profound combinations of the intellect?" (p. 434). Where equality of conditions is defined first and foremost as freedom of economic opportunity, an "excessive value" is assigned to "rapid sparks and superficial conceptions" (p. 435) tailored to material concerns of time saving and cost cutting. "For minds so disposed," says Tocqueville, "every new method that leads to wealth by a shorter path . . . every discovery that facilitates pleasures and augments them seems to be the most magnificent effort of human intelligence" (p. 436).

UTILITY

In general, Tocqueville finds little tolerance in America for the mind's "profound, slow work" (p. 435) and very few individuals who risk cultivating a genuinely impractical, unworldly passion for contemplation. The "transcendent lights of the human mind" waver uncertainly in the glare of America's "unparalleled energy toward application" (p. 437). Tocqueville would not be surprised that American culture would later give rise to a philosophic method called "pragmatism" that values mind according to its efficacy as an instrument for achieving practical results.

As mind and imagination in America are oriented almost exclusively toward practical power, so the "taste for the useful predominates over the love of the beautiful" (p. 439). To the degree that Americans admire beauty they wish it to be useful, as when a sailor remarks to Tocqueville that the "art of navigation makes such rapid progress daily that the most beautiful ship would soon become almost useless if its existence were prolonged beyond a few years" (p. 428). What we today call "planned obsolescence" was readily apparent to Tocqueville, who noted that in order to satisfy the ceaseless demand for material goods, American artisans were compelled "to make many imperfect things very rapidly" (p. 441). These same artisans also refined the modern art of advertising in ascribing to their products "brilliant qualities that they do not have" (p. 441). Even the development of language in America reflects an "industrial taste"(p. 435) that readily substitutes the terminology of commerce for the language of philosophy and religion. In the United States, there would appear to be "no power on earth that can prevent the growing equality of conditions from bringing the human spirit toward searching for the useful and from disposing each citizen to shrink within himself" (p. 503).

STATE OF THE ARTS

What is the condition of the fine arts in a democratic culture that channels the "principal effort of the soul" (pp. 458–459) ever more insistently toward the material, the worldly, the human? For Tocqueville, a democracy that identifies human success with material well-being threatens to extend the commercial spirit into all modes of human activity, including architecture, music, painting, and poetry. The fine arts in America are never free of the democratic pressure to be relevant or useful, a predicament (and tragedy) superbly illustrated in Nathaniel Hawthorne's story "The Artist of the Beautiful." Tocqueville observes that the fine arts turn irresistibly from depictions of the soul to representations of the body, from "sentiments and ideas" to "motions and sensations" (p. 442). This indulgence of the material and physical finds confirmation in the American enthusiasm for theater, which Tocqueville considers the taste "most natural to democratic peoples" (p. 467). "Most of those who attend the acting on the stage," Tocqueville continues, "do not seek pleasures of the mind, but lively emotions of the heart. They do not expect to find a work of literature but a spectacle" (pp. 467–468). Spectators in democratic societies, subdued by the "practical, contested, and monotonous" routines of commerce, develop a compensatory need (satisfied by theater) for "lively and rapid emotions, sudden clarity, brilliant truths or errors" (p. 448). The public taste for titillating spectacle influences dramatic style, which becomes at once more sentimental and more aggressive, "overloaded, and soft, and almost always bold and vehement" (p. 449). A theater that caters to this taste aims "to astonish rather than to please" (p. 449). Tocqueville's censure of the democratic taste for theater seems even more relevant today when we consider the spectacles of extremity and excess routinely dramatized (to much acclaim!) in television and film.

DIVINING WHITMAN

Tocqueville's observation on the state of poetry in democracies is remarkable for anticipating the emergence of an American poet whose verse Tocqueville never read. The visionary quality of Tocqueville's exposition of democratic culture is nowhere more evident than in his divination of Walt Whitman (1819–1892), whose great song of democracy, *Leaves of Grass,* would not appear until 1855.

Tocqueville begins his discussion of poetry by confessing his own attachment to an aristocratic or "Platonic" conception of the poetic as the "search for and depiction of the ideal," the aim of which is to "adorn" the real or true so as to "offer a superior image to the mind" (p. 458). On this view, which seeks to "maintain the human mind in faith" (p. 459), poetry is a movement of transcendence or "going beyond" that illuminates the human in relation to eternal ideals of nature or the divine. The equality of conditions obtaining in democracies, however, weakens the sense of transcendence or "taste for the ideal" (p. 458) that sustains poetry in aristocratic cultures. The secular disposition of democratic societies "brings the imagination of poets back to earth and confines them to the visible and real world" (p. 459). Democracy seems to Tocqueville to move inexorably toward anthropocentrism (human-centeredness), turning the mind skeptically "away from all that is external to man to fix it only on man" (p. 460). Equality, therefore, "in establishing itself on the earth, dries up most of the old sources of poetry" (p. 460). What, then, are the new or fresh sources of poetry in the American democracy?

Tocqueville remarks two characteristics of the American people which, combined in the figure of Walt Whitman, express a distinctly American poetic vision. First, although Americans are enthusiastic admirers of nature "they only become really animated at the sight of themselves" (p. 460); indeed, nature mirrors the glory of American democracy. Secondly, Americans "scarcely worry about what has been, but they willingly dream of what will be. . . . Democracy, which closes the past to poetry, opens the future to it"

(p. 460). The American democratic vision expresses a profound self-absorption, but not in the sense of a fixed or complacent worship of the past or present. On the contrary, this vision opens always toward the horizon, casting forward the ideal of an ever-progressing democratic future.

The practical form of this ideal (utility is *always* sovereign in America!) is an aggressive "expansionist" effort of cultivation and settlement. The eyes of the American people, writes Tocqueville, are filled with visions of themselves advancing across the wilderness, "draining swamps, straightening rivers, peopling the solitude, and subduing nature" (p. 461). Ultimately it is the nation itself, the expansion of American democracy into geographic space, that provides a fresh source of stimulation for poetry. As Whitman triumphantly proclaims in the 1855 preface to *Leaves of Grass,* the "United States themselves are essentially the greatest poem. . . . Here at last is something in the doings of man that corresponds with the broadcast doings of the day and night. Here is not merely a nation but a teeming nation of nations" (p. 5). The poet equal to the task of representing America's magnitude, Whitman writes, "incarnates its geography and natural life and rivers and lakes. . . . When the long Atlantic coast stretches longer and the Pacific coast stretches longer he easily stretches with them north or south. He spans between them also from east to west and reflects what is between them" (p. 7). Whitman certainly admires nature, but his highest admiration is reserved for his own prowess in what might be called poetic calisthenics.

Tocqueville's descriptions illuminate the complex character of a democratic people whose devout materialism and skeptical worldliness erodes, but does not extinguish, religious faith: "equality does not shake religions, it simplifies them" (p. 459). The simplifying effect of equality is a gentle compulsion to transfer religious sentiment to the *image* of democracy as possessing divine or transcendent value. Significantly, this sublime image of democracy promotes in the culture at large a strong emphasis on unity and homogeneity at the expense of individuality. In light of the abstract glow of the democratic ideal, the American people "form nothing more than a vast democracy of which each citizen is a people" (p. 461).

In a passage that vividly foreshadows the temper of Whitman's famous poem "Song of Myself," Tocqueville (writing in the first person) reveals the primary source of poetry in America: "I have no need to travel through heaven and earth to discover a marvelous object full of contrasts, of infinite greatness and pettiness. . . . I have only to consider myself" (p. 462). Tocqueville's uncanny approximation of one of Whitman's best-known

phrases—"I contain multitudes"—is linked to an important irony. The self imagined in Tocqueville's passage (and exulted in Whitman's poetry) appears concrete and definite, but in truth it is thoroughly formal or abstract, not so much substance as pure potentiality. The grave danger here is that amorphous sentiments of an impersonal democratic self impose an "idea of unity" that, "although it destroys human individuality . . . will have secret charms for men who live in democracy" (p. 426). Tocqueville's name for this seductive charm is "pantheism," an immoderate sentiment of equality that opposes division and singularity and thus the liberty of discrete individuals. Is it possible that the allure of Whitman's poetry lies precisely in its pantheistic vision of nature equalized in the poet's (to borrow Tocqueville's phrase) "immense being" (p. 426)? Tocqueville sees in pantheism a fatal attraction that must be resisted in order to preserve a healthy tension in democratic life between equality and liberty; indeed, "all who remain enamored of the genuine greatness of man should unite and do combat against it" (p. 426). It would seem, then, that a healthy democratic culture must be prepared to wage war against the alluring influence of its greatest poet.

RELIGION

Tocqueville argues that at the heart of American democracy lies a great tension of opposing sentiments. Equality of conditions promotes rapid secularization, implanting in Americans an almost "instinctive incredulity about the supernatural" (p. 408). However, Americans remain a fundamentally religious people. "It is religion that gave birth to the Anglo-American societies," Tocqueville recalls, and "one must never forget this; in the United States religion is therefore intermingled with all national habits" (pp. 405–406). Although the feverish pursuit of material wealth inclines Americans very much "toward the earth," the persistence among them of religious sentiment inspires "passing, distracted glances toward Heaven" (p. 430). Tocqueville observes the importance placed on the weekly Sabbath, at which time the "industrial life of the nation seems suspended" and "the soul finally comes back into possession of itself" (p. 517). At such moments, the American "steals away from himself . . . into an ideal world in which all is great, pure, eternal" (p. 517).

In a culture where individuals habitually seek the quickest practical route to power and wealth it is necessary, Tocqueville asserts, to "detain the human mind in theory" (p. 438) if we wish to preserve our "most sublime faculties" (p. 519). The threatened atrophy of these faculties requires all persons concerned with the health of democracy to cultivate "a taste for the infinite, a sentiment of greatness, and a love of immaterial pleasures" (p. 519). These saving sentiments of transcendence need not be attached to any particular religious tradition or orthodoxy, since there is no religion in the world "that does not place man's desires beyond and above earthly goods" (p. 419). Where democracy has cultivated an excessive love of material pleasures, the supreme importance of religion or spiritualism lies in opposing materialism. The persistence of religious sentiment in America proves that satisfaction of material pleasures is never adequate to the extent of human desire: "the human heart is vaster than one supposes; it can at once contain a taste for the goods of the earth and a love of those of Heaven" (p. 520).

TOCQUEVILLE'S GREAT FEAR

Tocqueville suggests that a healthy democratic culture will nurture in the souls of its citizens a vital awareness of the tension between the limited (and limiting) goods of this world and the transcending sentiments of an "exalted and almost fierce spiritualism" (p. 510). Preserving this tension secures the integrity of religion's polemical effort to "purify, regulate, and restrain the too ardent and too exclusive taste for well-being" (p. 422). Tocqueville fears, however, that the stability of this crucial tension is threatened by a mild democratic ethos that "does not corrupt souls, but softens them and in the end quietly loosens all their tensions" (p. 509). The implication here is that if the decisive tension between materialism and spiritualism, commerce and religion, is allowed to perish—if defenders of this tension disappear—then religion will lose its principal critical function. In such circumstances, religious sentiment will be thoroughly domesticated, annexed to the practical, and harnessed to material ambition as its accomplice and servant. Tocqueville foresees the cynicism and hypocrisy of public officials who exploit the eased tension between material well-being and religious sentiment by flattering the "dogma of the immortality of the soul . . . every day as if they themselves believed it" (p. 521).

The root cause of this softening of tension lies in the fundamental democratic principle of equality. The opposition between materialism and spiritualism preserves a hierarchy of value (typical of aristocratic societies) that assigns superior dignity to a life of contemplative leisure as opposed to a life consumed by labor and business. Such hierarchical determinations of value deeply offend the democratic ideal of equality. Tocqueville notes the "immortal hatred, more and more afire, which animates democratic peoples against the slightest privileges" (p. 645). Democratic sentiment

yearns for a fluid condition free of decisive commitments and tensions, and thus free of the moral burden of discriminating between higher and lower, noble and base. The loosening of such moral distinctions, symptomatic of the dissolving tension between materialism and spiritualism, portends a culture of listless tolerance "where nothing seems any longer to be forbidden or permitted, or honest or shameful, or true or false" (p. 12). Most importantly, Tocqueville discerns in this general loosening of tensions and distinctions the collapse of those particularities that "preserve for the individual the little independence, force, and originality that remain to him" (p. 672). Equality of conditions exerts upon individuals an intense pressure to abandon principled commitments for a ceaseless process of self-revision that honors equality by avoiding settled judgments. For Tocqueville, such a culture brings to view an "innumerable crowd composed of similar beings, in which nothing is elevated and nothing lowered" (p. 674). Tocqueville confides that this "universal uniformity" is what most "saddens and chills me" (p. 674) as it leaves democracy vulnerable to a soft tyranny of the majority. Democracy marks for Tocqueville the providential trend of modern history, but the issue of democracy remains very much in our hands: "Nations of our day cannot have it that conditions within them are not equal; but it depends on them whether equality leads them to servitude or freedom, to enlightenment or barbarism, to prosperity or misery" (p. 676).

See also Democracy; Individualism and Community; *Leaves of Grass*

BIBLIOGRAPHY

Primary Works

Tocqueville, Alexis de. *Democracy in America*. 1835, 1840. Edited and translated by Harvey C. Mansfield and Delba Winthrop. Chicago: University of Chicago Press, 2000.

Whitman, Walt. *Leaves of Grass*. 1855. New York: Penguin, 1986.

Secondary Works

Bellah, Robert N., et al. *Habits of the Heart: Individualism and Commitment in American Life*. Berkeley: University of California Press, 1985.

Jardin, Andre. *Tocqueville: A Biography*. Translated by Lydia Davis with Robert Hemenway. New York: Farrar, Straus and Giroux, 1988.

Lawler, Peter Augustine, ed. *Tocqueville's Political Science: Classic Essays*. New York: Garland, 1992.

Lerner, Max. *Tocqueville and American Civilization*. New York: Harper and Row, 1969.

THE DIAL

Lively, Jack. *The Social and Political Thought of Alexis de Tocqueville.* Oxford: Clarendon Press, 1962.

Manent, Pierre. *Tocqueville and the Nature of Democracy.* Translated by John Waggoner. Lanham, Md.: Rowman and Littlefield, 1996.

Mill, John Stuart. "De Tocqueville on Democracy in America [II]." In *Essays on Politics And Society,* vol. 18 of *Collected Works of John Stuart Mill,* edited by J. M. Robson, pp. 153–204. Toronto: University of Toronto Press, 1977.

Mitchell, Joshua. *The Fragility of Freedom: Tocqueville on Religion, Democracy, and the American Future.* Chicago: University of Chicago Press, 1995.

Schleifer, James T. *The Making of Tocqueville's Democracy in America.* Chapel Hill: University of North Carolina Press, 1980.

Siedentop, L. A. *Tocqueville.* Oxford: Oxford University Press, 1994.

Wolin, Sheldon S. *Tocqueville between Two Worlds.* Princeton, N.J.: Princeton University Press, 2001.

David K. Heckerl

THE DIAL

In his inaugural address to readers in the first issue of *The Dial: A Magazine for Literature, Philosophy, and Religion,* Ralph Waldo Emerson (1803–1882) alludes to a revolution whose members share "no external organization, no badge, no creed, no name [and] . . . do not vote, or print, or even meet together [or] . . . know each other's faces or names" (1.1.2). These comments are perhaps rhetorically disingenuous when one recalls that Emerson knew the faces and names of many of the revolutionaries, and the *The Dial* was itself the outgrowth of an "external organization" that made this revolution a reality for many New Englanders—the Transcendental Club. *The Dial* was supposed to be the voice of this loose cadre of liberal Unitarian ministers, intellectuals, writers, and social radicals who met sporadically from 1836 to 1840, but by the time the first issue was released in the summer of 1840, the group had already expired and the magazine became the project of a handful of its members—mainly Emerson and Margaret Fuller (1810–1850). Nevertheless, for the next four years, *The Dial* would function as the most recognizable voice for transcendentalism in New England, publishing book reviews, musings on art, poetry, selections from Confucian and Buddhist texts, feminist tracts, quasi-journalistic pieces about transcendentalist activities, theological discourse, sonnets, lectures, travelogues, German works in translation, and some difficult-to-categorize writing.

By most standards of publishing *The Dial* was an embarrassing failure, but the magazine remains relevant today as the most valuable primary text for studying the transcendentalist movement. The entire history of transcendentalism seems to filter through its 2,172 pages. Fuller, Emerson, and Henry David Thoreau (1817–1862) all served as editors and published extensively in its pages. Emerson had only recently published *Nature* (1836), "The American Scholar" (1837), and "The Divinity School Address" (1838) when he began editing and writing for *The Dial.* Thoreau, then in his mid-twenties, was gaining confidence as a writer by regularly contributing to the magazine. George Ripley (1802–1880), one of the founding members of the transcendentalist Brook Farm commune later satirized in Nathaniel Hawthorne's *Blithedale Romance* (1852), served as *The Dial*'s first managing editor. The educator Amos Bronson Alcott (1799–1888)—founder of the other transcendentalist commune, Fruitlands—wrote a column for *The Dial* called "Orphic Sayings." Lesser-known Transcendental Club alumni like Frederic Henry Hedge, James Freeman Clarke, Theodore Parker, John Sullivan Dwight, Elizabeth Hoar, Sarah Ripley, Elizabeth Palmer Peabody, Jones Very, William Ellery Channing, and Christopher Pearse Cranch all contributed to the magazine as well.

LIFE CYCLE

The Dial was officially born in July 1840, when its first issue, or "number," was released to the public, but the idea for a journal had been circulating since the first meetings of the Transcendental Club. The discussion group was founded by Frederic Henry Hedge (1805–1890), with Emerson's help, to refresh the contemporary discourse on religion and philosophy. Many of its members were dissatisfied with the dominance of John Locke's empiricism in philosophical and theological discussions, which privileged knowledge gained through the senses over inborn knowledge and inspiration. Many were also appalled at the institutional cowardice of Unitarianism—an unwillingness to grapple with important theological issues. Included among its fluxional membership were all of the people who would later edit and produce *The Dial*—Emerson, Fuller, Ripley, and Peabody. In the four years before the first issue, there had been numerous private discussions among group members about starting a journal—Hedge in particular was keen to make the journal a reality—but the subject was not officially broached until the 18 September 1839 meeting, when the group discussed "the subject of a Journal designed as the organ of views more in accordance with the Soul" (Alcott, p. 249). Amos Bronson Alcott

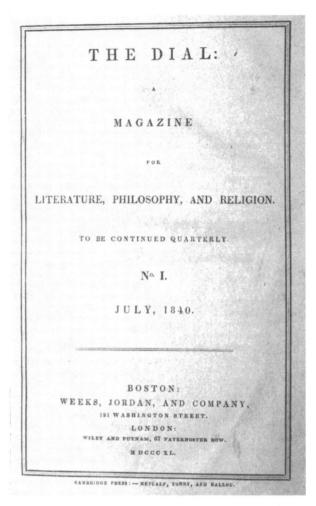

THE DIAL: ·

A

MAGAZINE

FOR

LITERATURE, PHILOSOPHY, AND RELIGION.

TO BE CONTINUED QUARTERLY.

No. I.

JULY, 1840.

BOSTON:
WEEKS, JORDAN, AND COMPANY,
121 WASHINGTON STREET.
LONDON:
WILEY AND PUTNAM, 67 PATERNOSTER ROW.
MDCCC XL.

CAMBRIDGE PRESS:—METCALF, TORRY, AND BALLOU.

Cover of the inaugural issue of *The Dial*, 1840.
COURTESY OF THE CONCORD FREE PUBLIC LIBRARY

proposed to call it "The Dial," borrowing the title of a collection of his own musings he was assembling at the time. Emerson was the natural first choice for editor, but the famously reticent writer backed away from the project initially, assuring his brother William, "I will never be editor" (*Letters* 2:225). After Hedge returned to his pulpit in Maine for the winter that year, Emerson invited Fuller to be editor, and she accepted.

Although birthed by the Transcendental Club, *The Dial* maintained a loose, often tenuous association with the group. Throughout the winter of 1839–1840, Fuller solicited pieces for the journal but found club alumni surprisingly reluctant to participate. Hedge wrote Fuller expressing surprise at the suddenness of the publication. Other members like James Freeman Clarke (1810–1888) and William Henry Channing (1810–1884) made vague promises of assistance. Emerson and Ripley seemed willing to lend concrete

assistance, however, and Emerson secured an agreement from Little and Brown to publish the magazine. Even before the first issue appeared, Fuller and Emerson were mostly on their own, which meant that the Transcendental Club's original hopes of creating a journal that represented its dissenting theology would never be realized. From the first, *The Dial* was primarily a literary magazine driven by only a handful of Transcendental Club members, though many others—including Hedge—would eventually contribute to it.

Two distinct editorial regimes would oversee *The Dial*—Fuller's, which lasted until the spring of 1842, and Emerson's, which spanned roughly the last two years of publication. Fuller's tenure saw the release of the shaky first issue—a critical bomb—and six more successful subsequent numbers before she resigned in March 1842, citing the continued insolvency of the magazine and her own ill health as reasons. Fuller never received a salary for her work; she taught school and gave private lessons to support herself, and the strain of balancing these responsibilities weighed considerably on her. She nevertheless managed to shepherd *The Dial* through its formative years, establishing a regular circulation and cultivating an eager pool of contributors. Emerson, who had served as coeditor throughout the first two years, took over in the spring of 1842. He presided over a period of dwindling subscriptions and continued insolvency balanced by numerous positive reviews. The overall quality of the magazine had improved and contributions now overflowed the space that required filling in the magazine.

But the magazine failed to catch on with the public, and this proved to be a fatal flaw. The last two years of *The Dial* were marked by constant anxiety over its future. When Emerson took over as editor in 1842 there were about three hundred names on the subscription list. A year later the number had dropped to 220. Financial failure was inevitable. In the spring of 1842, when Fuller left, the magazine was barely breaking even, and Emerson's tenure did not improve *The Dial*'s financial fortunes. In 1843 Elizabeth Peabody audited the magazine's accounts only to learn that the income from subscriptions did not even cover the cost of the paper it was printed on. Emerson was grimly aware of the task he had undertaken. In a letter written to Thomas Carlyle in July 1842, Emerson admits to "petty literary patriotism" in his decision to take over editing *The Dial*, acknowledging that he "took charge of our thankless little Dial, here, without subscribers enough to pay even a publisher, much less any laborer; it has no penny for editor or contributor, nothing but abuse in the newspapers, or, at best, silence" (p. 323). In the fall of 1843 Emerson was helping to support the magazine with his own money.

Reviews for *The Dial* were mixed throughout its existence. It provoked strong negative reactions from some who thought it was a profane or even ludicrous publication. The first issue was greeted with scorn by many of the major newspapers of the day or was ignored altogether. The *Boston Times* (17 July) called it one of the most "ridiculous productions of the age," describing its synthesis of German mysticism and pantheism as "unintelligible as the confusion of tongues at Babel." The *Philadelphia Gazette* complained about the "ravings of Alcott and his fellow zanies" and *The Knickerbocker* (August 1840), the United States's premier literary magazine, said that the magazine's intelligent ideas were buried in wordy prose. Alcott's "ravings" in his "Orphic Sayings" column attracted the largest measure of negative press, generating numerous parodies that were published throughout the country (Myerson, p. 51).

The Dial received better reviews during its last two years of publication under Emerson, though interest in the magazine among reviewers dropped off considerably. When the final issue appeared in April 1844, only one newspaper, the *New-York Daily Tribune*, reviewed it.

THE CONTRIBUTORS

Despite its persistent insolvency and disappointing fade-out, *The Dial* did manage to publish sixteen issues between July 1840 and April 1844—introducing more than 350 pieces of writing from 42 writers into the literary marketplace and creating a temporary outlet for one of the nation's most dynamic literary communities. The magazine's rhythm of publication was certainly erratic—appearing sometimes quarterly, sometimes monthly—but *The Dial* appeared on average once every three months during its forty-six-month life span. The magazine did not make any of its contributors into literary stars, but viewed retrospectively, its confluence of literary talent is remarkable. *The Dial* published seventy-six pieces by Emerson, including poetry, essays, reviews, and lectures. Some of the pieces, like his essays "Transcendentalism" (1840) and "Thoughts on Modern Literature" (1840) are well known; others, like his ode to the Persian poet Saadi (1842) and his fawning celebration of the dirt farmer over the bureaucrat, "Agriculture of Massachusetts" (1842), reveal the breadth—and perhaps also the limitations—of Emerson's eclecticism. Thoreau, who would depart for Walden Pond a year after the final issue was printed, was already working out some of his major themes. His essay "Natural History of Massachusetts" (1842) reveals an early passion for the details of scientific naturalism that would occupy him during the last decade of his life. Similarly,

his presentation of selections from Hindu, Confucian, and Buddhist texts reveals an interest in Eastern philosophy that would find its way into both *A Week on the Concord and Merrimack Rivers* (1849) and *Walden* (1854). He contributed twenty-six verifiable pieces in all, including poetry—notably "Rumors from an Aeolian Harp" (1842), "Sympathy" (1840), and "Friendship" (1841)—and a translation from Greek of "The Prometheus Bound" (1843).

Some of *The Dial*'s most faithful contributors are seldom read or studied today except as background to the more famous transcendentalists. William Ellery Channing, the restless nephew of the famous Unitarian minister of the same name, filled *The Dial*'s pages with more than forty poems, making him the most prolific contributor behind Emerson and Fuller. Channing married Fuller's sister Ellen in 1841 and, with Emerson's help, in that same year published *Poems,* a collection that Edgar Allan Poe criticized as mostly "utter and irredeemable nonsense" (p. 113). Caroline Sturgis, Margaret Fuller's best friend, contributed more than twenty poems, and Christopher Pearse Cranch contributed eighteen. The Unitarian minister Theodore Parker (1810–1860) was *The Dial*'s theological backbone, filling 257 pages, most of it about theology or religious history.

The contributions of women to the magazine were impressive. Women were at the core of *The Dial*'s financial and editorial management, and a quarter of the contributing writers were female. Despite this considerable presence, however, only two explicitly feminist pieces can be found in *The Dial*—Sophia Ripley's "Woman" (1841) and Margaret Fuller's "The Great Lawsuit: Man *Versus* Men, Woman *Versus* Women" (1843). Fuller's piece was expanded and published in book form under the title *Woman in the Nineteenth Century* in 1845 and is a foundational text of American feminism.

CONTENTS

From the first issue, *The Dial* revealed a boldly transcendentalist character, which was better expressed through its poetry than its prose. The transcendentalists regarded the true poet as inspired, able to pierce the veil of the ordinary to apprehend the spiritual truths that lie underneath. In this vein, Emerson's poem "The Problem" (1840) proclaims

> The word by seers or sibyls told,
> In groves of oak, or fanes of gold,
> Still floats upon the morning wind,
> Still whispers to the willing mind.
>
> *(1.1.123)*

Some of the lesser-known contributors to the first issue of *The Dial* were among its most faithfully "transcendentalist." Cranch's poem "To the Aurora Borealis" (1840) endows the Northern Lights with a hidden spiritual essence, summoning out the

> . . . *inner* light
> That hath hid its purer ray
> Through the lapses of the day—
> Then like thee, thou Northern Morn,
> Instincts which we deemed unborn,
> Gushing from their hidden source
> Mount upon their heavenward course.
>
> *(1.1.12)*

In "The River" (January 1843), Ellery Channing proclaims "There is an inward voice, that in the stream / Sends forth its spirit to the listening ear," and the promise of perfection is upheld in Ellen Sturgis Hooper's "I Slept, and Dreamed That Life Was Beauty" (1840), whose narrator awakens to find that life is duty, only to reaffirm the ethereal, Romantic ideal a few lines later at the end of the poem.

The Dial's metaphysical poetics were often interrupted by more temporal concerns. Social reformism was a consistent theme—especially the philosophy of Charles Fourier, a French socialist whose ideas were circulating in the United States thanks to Albert Brisbane's *Social Destiny of Man* (1840). Fourier advocated the construction of vast single-dwelling communes called "phalanxes" that would gradually and peacefully destroy competitive capitalism. Emerson wrote a short review of Brisbane's book, proclaiming, "The name of Fourier may be placed at the head of modern thinkers" (1.1.265–266). Emerson and Peabody both contributed pieces on Fourierism, and Emerson wrote about "The English Reformers." The transcendentalist experiments in communal living also registered in *The Dial*. Peabody and Charles Lane both wrote quasi-journalistic articles about the Brook Farm commune (a year after *The Dial* folded, the residents of Brook Farm adopted a Fourieristic charter). Lane also contributed a piece on the Fruitlands commune, which he helped establish with Alcott, and a piece titled "A Day with the Shakers"—each chronicling his personal experiments with communalism.

Unitarian politics and theology were consistent themes in *The Dial,* which maintained a theological temperature that hovered somewhere between liberal Unitarianism and a tentative pre-Whitman brand of "pantheism." By 1841 Theodore Parker was a household word in Unitarian circles for weighing in on the pamphlet debate between George Ripley and Andrews Norton over the veracity of "miracles" in the scriptures— a debate Emerson had touched off in his incendiary address to Harvard's Divinity School in 1838, wherein he challenged the role of miracles in the Christian tradition. Parker's reputation as a transcendentalist was further cemented by his 1841 sermon "A Discourse on the Transient and Permanent in Christianity," which denied the authority of miracles in the Old and New Testaments. *The Dial* preserves traces of these debates in Parker's essay "The Divine Presence in Nature and in the Soul" (July 1840), which describes God in nearly pantheistic terms, with "the fullness of the divine energy flow[ing] inexhaustibly into the crystal of the rock, the juices of the plant, the splendor of the stars, the life of the Bee and Behemoth" (1.1.59). All men were endowed with inspiration, writes Parker, but in varying degrees, with Jesus possessing the greatest measure of this quality, more even than "Moses, Zoroaster, Socrates or the sages" (1.1.65). William Dexter Wilson may have had Parker in mind in his April 1841 *Dial* essay "The Unitarian Movement in New England" when he identified the "Pantheists" along with Trinitarianism and Unitarianism as the three major religious movements of his time, predicting that pantheism "will never prevail" (1.4.433). Ripley's "Letter to a Theological Student" in the October 1840 *Dial* suggests his own distemper with Unitarianism, when he warns against pursuing theology to confirm already held beliefs instead of advocating an open mind. Truth should be pursued "in a magnificent procession, in which all Sciences and Arts are pressing forward to truth" (1.2.186), he declares. Parker echoes these sentiments in "Thoughts on Theology" in the April 1842 issue: "The more Light, the freer, the more profound and searching the investigation, why the better; the sooner a false theory is exploded and a new one induced from the observed facts, the better also. In theology the opposite rule seems often to prevail" (2.4.448).

The Dial was also filled with less deliberative explications of transcendentalist "theology." The lucid explications of transcendentalist history and theology by Ripley, Parker, and Wilson were balanced by representations from the movement's cosmic-silly side. In just thirteen pages, the former soldier William Batchelder Greene's rambling January 1842 "First Principles" pontificates on Love, Destiny, Freedom, Matter, Beauty, Justice, Harmony, and the Soul in short chapters filled with inchoate declarations like "the Stream flows between its banks, according to Love" (2.3.273) or "Beauty, Justice, and Harmony, always accompany Life, yet they do not constitute life; but, if life be manifested, they are attributes of that manifestation" (2.3.284). Even less coherent are Alcott's "Orphic Sayings," also organized into minichapters. "Choice implies apostasy," he declares in his section titled "Choice" in *The Dial*'s inaugural issue. "The pure, unfallen soul is above choice. Her life is unbroken, synthetic; she is a law to herself, and finds no lust in her members warring against the instincts of conscience" (1.1.88).

The classical predilections of the *Dial* contributors are apparent in nearly every issue. "I have promised to write to you from Italy of the Italians," writes Samuel Gray Ward in the January 1841 issue. "Not of those of to-day, late and imperfectly ripened fruits of the great tree, beneath which the nations once feasted in the shade, but of the great ones who represent the June day in the garden of the world" (1.3.386). *The Dial's* writers were eager to demonstrate their knowledge of "the great ones," from Sarah Clarke's poem "Dante" (July 1840) to Thoreau's revival of a Greek "minor poet" in "Anacreon" (April 1843). Transcendentalist eclecticism and exoticism are also on display in *The Dial.* Emerson's contributions to the "Ethnical Scriptures" section included the "Sayings of Confucius" (July 1842), whereas Thoreau excerpted the Hindu "Laws of Menu" (January 1843) and "The Preaching of the Buddha" (January 1844). More than anything actually written *about* religion in the pages of *The Dial,* these snippets of Eastern "scripture" suggest how far the magazine's circle had drifted from the main Unitarian fold on the issue of divine inspiration.

Despite its intellectual eclecticism and universalist pretensions, *The Dial* preserves a snapshot of a fairly localized cultural phenomenon. Most of the contributors and editors lived in or near Concord, Massachusetts, and together they represented a cozy coterie of friends, neighbors, fellow ministers, spouses, cousins, and close relations. Most of the contributors knew either Fuller or Emerson, and their work was often solicited directly by one or the other. Taken with all of its limitations, *The Dial* was likely the first truly independent literary magazine in the country, and its four volumes represent the most valuable primary collection of transcendentalist texts available today.

See also Literary Marketplace; Periodicals; Transcendentalism

BIBLIOGRAPHY

Primary Works

Alcott, A. Bronson. "Diary July-December 1839." Harvard Library, Harvard University.

Emerson, Ralph Waldo. *The Correspondence of Emerson and Carlyle.* Edited by Joseph Slater. New York: Columbia University Press, 1964.

Emerson, Ralph Waldo. *The Letters of Ralph Waldo Emerson.* 6 vols. Edited by Ralph L. Rusk. New York: Columbia University Press, 1939.

The Dial: A Magazine for Literature, Philosophy, and Religion. 4 vols. New York: Russell & Russell, 1961.

Citations in the text give volume number, issue number, and page number.

Poe, Edgar Allan. "Our Amateur Poets. No. III.—William Ellery Channing." *Graham's Magazine* 23 (August 1843): 113–117.

Secondary Works

Cady, Lyman V. "Thoreau's Quotations from the Confucian Books in *Walden.*" *American Literature* 33, no. 1 (1961): 20–32.

Cameron, Thompson. "John Locke and New England Transcendentalism." *New England Quarterly* 35, no. 4 (1962): 435–457.

Cooke, George Willis. *An Historical and Biographical Introduction to Accompany* The Dial. 2 vols. New York: Russell & Russell, 1961.

Grodzins, Dean, and Joel Myerson. "The Preaching Record of Theodore Parker." *Studies in the American Renaissance* (1994): 55–122.

Hennessy, Helen. "*The Dial:* Its Poetry and Poetic Criticism." *New England Quarterly* 31, no. 1 (1958): 66–87.

Myerson, Joel. *The New England Transcendentalists and The Dial: A History of the Magazine and Its Contributors.* Rutherford, N.J.: Fairleigh Dickinson University Press, 1980.

Richardson, Robert D. *Emerson: The Mind on Fire: A Biography.* Berkeley: University of California Press, 1995.

Daniel R. Vollaro

DIALECT

"Dialect" is a loaded word that presupposes a correct language against which to posit the cultural deficiency of the deviant speaker. Yet throughout the nineteenth century, American discussion of the nation's vernacular language varieties returned again and again to the notion that any border between standard and nonstandard discourse was fundamentally unstable. The post-Revolutionary period had established a strong emphasis on language as an organ of civic order and national unity, which helps to account for a continuing paradox in discussions of American speech—the simultaneous opinions that the United States had no dialects, at least compared to the British model, and that the regional features which were detectable threatened wholesale national fragmentation and cultural collapse. An explanation for this paradox is offered by Charles A. Bristed in his groundbreaking essay "The English Language in America" (1855): "The English provincialisms *keep their place;* they are confined to their own localities, and do not encroach on the metropolitan model. The American provincialisms are more equally distributed

> What we regard as distortions of our mother-tongue are more offensive to us than the widest diversities between it and unallied languages; and we regard a fellow-citizen who speaks a marked provincial English with a contempt and aversion, which we do not bestow upon the foreigner who speaks no English at all.
>
> Marsh, *Lectures on the English Language*, p. 677.

through all classes and localities, and though some of them may not rise above a certain level of society, others are heard everywhere" (pp. 61–62).

Discussion of dialect often moved in this way toward broader analysis of the sociopolitical consequences of American independence and democracy: the restlessness of social mobility that made Alexis de Tocqueville warn of instability, abstraction, and ambiguity in American speech; the postcolonial anxiety that American English was itself merely a dialect, and a deteriorating one according to Henry Alford in *A Plea for the Queen's English* (1863); and the effects of ethnic intermixture and of the racial oppression that led to the Civil War.

The 1820–1870 period was a major one in the formation and dominance of English in America, a period when regional distinctions within American English became readily identifiable and were used by writers and public speakers alike. The earlier fear that dialects would diverge into mutually unintelligible varieties and the lexicographical efforts of Noah Webster to impose a single national language based on an idealized version of New England speech gave way to a new acceptance of regional folk dialects by politicians in the 1820s and 1830s, when the rise of democracy as a political ideology directed attention to lower-class speech varieties. American writers focused as never before on what they perceived to be the grammatical peculiarities and, most obviously, the pronunciation of the nation's many regional, ethnic, and social dialects, which they attempted to represent in purportedly phonetic spelling. Novelists began to include dialect-speaking characters in their novels, though it was the literary sketch, the short story, and to a lesser extent the poem in which dialect tended to thrive. The uses of dialect ranged from those of protest, in which writers divorced from centers of power found political voice, to much more conservative efforts to burlesque dialect, thus making outlandish

speech imply the educational, social, and even biological inferiority of the imagined speaker. The tone of dialect writing may have been predominantly humorous, but behind it lay pronounced anxieties over class hierarchies, over racial and ethnic identity, and over regional relations. Speaking generally, dialect writing can be thought of as a literature of internal conflict between different cultures and political causes.

ETHNICITY AND CULTURAL CONFLICT

The literary emphasis on differences within English undoubtedly diverted attention from the continuing presence—and disappearance—of non-English languages in the United States, thus helping to establish English as the national language without official recognition at the federal level. Rather than simply masking non-English languages, however, the literary appearance of dialect could also register the influence of "foreign" discourse, thus suggesting that the regional characteristics of American English may have emerged from contact with speakers of other languages, not just from British settlement patterns. In his introduction to the *Dictionary of Americanisms* (1848), John Bartlett believed that German would "leave behind it an almost imperishable dialect as a memento of its existence" (p. xvi), as would Norwegian, Welsh, French, Spanish, and Native American languages. Traces of this ethnic variation, and the cultural contact it implies, can be found in the attempted transcriptions of Irish and Scots English in Hugh Henry Brackenridge's novel *Modern Chivalry* (1792–1815); in representations of Native American, black, and Irish English in William Gilmore Simms's novel *The Yemassee* (1835); in the "German-English" dialect poetry of Charles G. Leland (which announces the interest in ethnic dialect writing later in the century); and in the pidgin English of *The Chainbearer* (1845) by James Fenimore Cooper (1789–1851).

Cooper's novels are excellent places to see the politics of dialect at work, as David Simpson argues in his noteworthy critical study *The Politics of American English*. Pitting Cooper against Noah Webster's linguistic homogenizing and against the transcendentalists' tendency to stress the spiritual unity of all language, Simpson argues that novels such as *The Pioneers* (1823) and *The Deerslayer* (1841) place their thematic weight on representations of American English as a collection of competing dialects— vocational, racial, and regional—which reflect the multiple social and cultural conflicts within the nation. Cooper thus refuses simply to target dialect as inferior language that represents cultural and moral debasement. The figure of Natty Bumppo emerges from the cacophony of the Leatherstocking Tales to become an important example of the traditionally "ungrammatical" character whose language obeys natural laws that encode higher moral values. Cooper's focus on the varieties of vernacular discourse is found in a less-developed form in Robert Montgomery Bird's *Nick of the Woods* (1837)—which features various southern dialects and Quaker English as well as some black and Native American speech—and in more sophisticated ways in the works of northeastern and southwestern humor that attracted international attention in the 1830s. Like Cooper's novel *Satanstoe* (1845), which detects in the distinction between New England and New York speech profound racial, educational, and moral differences (all to the detriment of New England), these humorous works juxtaposed different social registers of speech while simultaneously contemplating the politics of regional difference, especially as the Civil War approached.

NORTHEASTERN AND SOUTHWESTERN HUMOR

Rustic Yankee speech had been employed for political commentary as early as the 1760s and was common on the stage in humorous portrayals of the stock Yankee figure. George W. Arnold is commonly credited with bringing the political and the humorous together in the mid-1820s in his "Joe Strickland" letters, published in numerous eastern newspapers and written in an alleged Yankee speech (one replete with comic misspellings as well as attempts at regional grammar and phonology) as the lighthearted medium of social satire. The mildly colloquial Maine vernacular of Seba Smith's "Jack Downing" letters became popular in the 1830s as a marker of plain talk that employed self-mocking humor to launch political critiques of the Maine legislature and later of Jacksonian national politics. This northeastern literary tradition was accessed by women writers too, with Frances M. Whitcher's "Widow Bedott" sketches using rustic Yankee ironically to satirize gender relations and to promote feminist causes. Perhaps the best-known example of a politicized use of New England speech was the *Biglow Papers* by James Russell Lowell (1819–1891), which in two series (collected in 1848 and 1867) opposed the expansionism of the Mexican-American War and supported the Union cause in the Civil War. Hosea Biglow is a Massachusetts farmer whose rustic dialect poetry is imagined by Lowell as a "divinely illiterate" language of the heart with a moral power that outstrips the effete standard language of Biglow's fictional editor (the pedantic parson Homer Wilbur) and that opposes a range of corrupt political discourses advocating belligerent nationalism, slavery,

and secession. In his introduction to the second series of the *Papers*, Lowell aligns his ideas with a Romantic tradition of valuing a certain variety of lowly speech that embodies the virtues of an Anglo-Saxon past rather than valuing nonstandard language per se. Hence Lowell ironically uses a dialect-speaking soldier as the wrongheaded spokesman for Manifest Destiny and exhibits a distaste for the encroaching slang of popular culture.

Humorously political dialect writing may have emerged in the North but it became most self-conscious and sophisticated in writings from the South. The tradition of southwestern humor, much of which appeared in William T. Porter's magazine the *Spirit of the Times* between 1831 and 1861, was produced quite often by gentlemanly professionals, though its class values were far from stable. Augustus Baldwin Longstreet's collection of sketches *Georgia Scenes* (1835) helped pioneer a device prevalent in subsequent dialect writing, whereby the standard, implicitly educated language of the narrator "frames" the dialect speech. If the intent of linguistic polarization in works such as *Georgia Scenes* and Johnson Jones Hooper's *Some Adventures of Captain Simon Suggs* (1845) was to satirize Jacksonian democracy by targeting the alleged violence and irresponsibility of its lower-class voices, then the effect is often one in which the over-refinement of the polite language gets submerged by the attractive energy of the rural dialect. In T. B. Thorpe's "The Big Bear of Arkansas" (1841) the compelling vernacular ousts the frame language almost completely to create a subjective reality rich with unconscious significance concerning humans' relationship with the natural world. Joseph G. Baldwin's "Ovid Bolus, Esquire," from *The Flush Times of Alabama and Mississippi* (1853), is a remarkably complex contemplation of the links between the hyperbolic tallness of vernacular talk and the socioeconomic inflation of the Jacksonian era as well as a virtual treatise on the power within language to outstrip and manipulate the world it purports to represent—a thematic correlative of the stress that nonstandard spelling places on the conventional, and thus pliable, nature of words. Whether in plays such as James Kirke Paulding's *The Lion of the West* (1830) or in writings by and about the backwoods politician Davy Crockett, the Southwest became humorously associated with the densely metaphorical exaggeration of tall talk, the valuing of big words for their own sakes. This implied a broader definition of dialect not simply as a representation of colloquial speech but as an attitude toward language itself, an attitude typically described as a product of the sublime landscape of the West and the rampant individualism of its frontier freedoms.

THE CIVIL WAR AND BLACK ENGLISH

Miscommunication between speakers of different varieties of a purportedly common tongue is a staple of dialect humor. Little surprise, then, that this kind of writing became the perfect medium for replaying the political differences that culminated in the Civil War. The second wave of dialect humorists of the 1850s and 1860s often deemphasized regional speech in their creation of burlesque languages that forced humor from bad grammar, mixed metaphor, ludicrous misuse of words (malapropism), and unintentional puns, all underscored by the running joke of incorrect spelling. This "misspelling bee" was partly a reaction against strong cultural pressure toward uniform spelling, though the growth of this writing during the Civil War suggests a need for unconventional languages to translate the shock of national conflict. Often dropping the frame device altogether, these humorists emphasized the limited literacy of their narrators and characters, representing their personae in imagined acts of (mis)writing, not speaking, which became a means to satirize the ignorance and ineptitude of opposing political factions. David Ross Locke's "Petroleum V. Nasby" sketches, for instance, attacked the Confederacy ironically by ventriloquizing its voice, while Charles Henry Smith's "Bill Arp" returned the compliment in a parodic southern speech disastrously sympathetic with the North. Of particular note in the southwestern tradition is *Sut Lovingood's Yarns* (1867) by George Washington Harris (1814–1869), which presents a purportedly Tennessean dialect that becomes almost unreadable in its subversion of conventional literacy. In the voice of white poverty, Sut's violent attacks radiate beyond the occasional target of the North to include the agents of decorum, logic, education, and civilization itself.

A challenge of reading dialect is to decide how far the literary representation distorts speech to champion or demean the speaker, how far it regularizes speech patterns to make the dialect seem more distinct than it was, and how far it represents genuine evidence for linguistic history. This challenge is pronounced with regard to representations of black English, always pressured by the weight of racist ideology. The genre of the ex-slave narrative tended to eschew dialect because of the humanizing implications of mastering the standard language and because ludicrously inaccurate parodies of black speech featured prominently in the tradition of blackface minstrelsy (remarkably popular in the North and South by the 1840s) and in proslavery agitation in the antebellum era. Both of these traditions tended to rationalize black subordination by staging linguistic ineptitude to imply the ignorance, immaturity, and mental inferiority of African Americans. Yet the representation of dialect to inscribe

black-white difference may have been a reaction to racial closeness as well. Strong evidence, especially in the writings of visitors to the South such as Charles Lyell, Charles Dickens, and Frances Kemble, suggests that whites learned black English, with the implication that white southern speech may have been influenced by black English—a point that became much more contentious after the war. Many white Americans were clearly aware of distinct forms of black English by the early eighteenth century, though the mid-nineteenth century saw the real emergence of allegedly black speech in mainstream literature: in Cooper's *The Spy* (1821) and *Satanstoe*, in William Gilmore Simms's novels and stories, in Harriet Beecher Stowe's *Uncle Tom's Cabin* (1851–1852), and in Edgar Allan Poe's story "The Gold-Bug" (1843). The linguist J. L. Dillard has argued that the speech of Poe's character Jupiter contains a number of integral features of black English and may suggest the widespread existence of a Creole language beyond the Gullah spoken on the Sea Islands of Georgia and the Carolinas. The ambivalence in well-meaning white reactions to black English can be glimpsed in Stowe's novel as well as in William Francis Allen's discussion of Gullah in his introduction to *Slave Songs of the United States* (1867). Stowe's attempted spelling of black English is largely inconsistent and stereotypical, yet the novel still recognizes the capacity of African Americans to mask meaning through ambiguous expression—a particular skill of the character Topsy. Allen attributes the "foreignness" of Gullah to a decay, simplification, and corruption of English, but he also recognizes in black dialect a resistance to conventional representation, a tendency for speech patterns to vary tremendously from one plantation to another and between different speakers, an endless capacity to improvise on and resignify English, and a possible survival of African words.

By 1870 dialect had become a crucial aspect of American literary language. Regional speech types were established and recognizable, white writers were grappling with the difference of black English, western speech was drawing widespread attention in the early stories of Mark Twain and Bret Harte, the so-called local color movement had emerged in the New England works of Stowe, and scientific philologists such as William Dwight Whitney were beginning to argue relativistically that all languages were really dialects. The stage was set for the Gilded Age craze for dialect writing, a craze that would only intensify the social, cultural, and racial anxieties with which the representation of dialect had emerged.

See also American English; Blacks; Civil War; Ethnology; Leatherstocking Tales; Proslavery

Writing; Satire, Burlesque, and Parody; Tall Tales

BIBLIOGRAPHY

Primary Works

Bartlett, John Russell. *The Dictionary of Americanisms.* 1848. New York: Crescent, 1989.

Bristed, Charles Astor. "The English Language in America." In *Cambridge Essays, Contributed by Members of the University,* pp. 57–78. London: J. W. Parker, 1855.

Marsh, George Perkins. *Lectures on the English Language.* New York: Scribner, 1860.

Secondary Works

Bailey, Richard W. *Nineteenth-Century English.* Ann Arbor: University of Michigan Press, 1996.

Blair, Walter. *Native American Humor (1800–1900).* New York: American Book Company, 1937.

Blair, Walter, and Hamlin Hill. *America's Humor: From Poor Richard to Doonesbury.* New York: Oxford University Press, 1978.

Cmiel, Kenneth. "'A Broad Fluid Language of Democracy': Discovering the American Idiom." *Journal of American History* 79 (December 1992): 913–936.

Cmiel, Kenneth. *Democratic Eloquence: The Fight over Popular Speech in Nineteenth-Century America.* New York: William Morrow, 1990.

Dillard, J. L. *Black English: Its History and Usage in the United States.* New York: Random House, 1972.

Gates, Henry Louis, Jr. "Dis and Dat: Dialect and the Descent." In his *Figures in Black: Words, Signs, and the "Racial" Self,* pp. 167–189. Oxford: Oxford University Press, 1987.

Gustafson, Thomas. *Representative Words: Politics, Literature, and the American Language, 1776–1865.* Cambridge, U.K.: Cambridge University Press, 1992.

Lynn, Kenneth. *Mark Twain and Southwestern Humor.* Boston: Little, Brown, 1959.

Read, Allen Walker. "The World of Joe Strickland." *Journal of American Folklore* 76 (1963): 277–308.

Schmitz, Neil. "Tall Tale, Tall Talk: Pursuing the Lie in Jacksonian Literature." In *On Humor: The Best from "American Literature,"* edited by Louis J. Budd and Edwin H. Cady, pp. 190–210. Durham, N.C.: Duke University Press, 1992.

Shell, Marc. "Babel in America; or, The Politics of Language Diversity in the United States." *Critical Inquiry* 20 (1993): 103–127.

Simpson, David. *The Politics of American English, 1776–1850.* Oxford: Oxford University Press, 1986.

Gavin Jones

DIME NOVELS

The firm of Beadle & Company published the first dime novel, *Malaeska, the Indian Wife of the White Hunter,* by Mrs. Ann S. Stephens, in 1860. The firm (its name would change to Beadle & Adams in 1872) was run by two brothers from Buffalo, New York, Irwin Beadle (1826–1882) and Erastus Beadle (1821–1894), who in 1859 moved to New York City and began publishing brief pocket-size paperback books on a variety of topics, such as *Beadle's Dime Debater, Beadle's Dime Base-ball Player,* and *Beadle's Dime Book of Verses.*

In early June 1860 the brothers applied the "dime" formula to fiction and announced Stephens's work under the slogan: "Books for the Million! A Dollar Book for a Dime!" *Malaeska* was not an original work but had appeared in serial form in the *Ladies' Companion;* Stephens, far from being an unknown, was a prolific author and well-known literary professional who received $250 from the Beadles for the rights to the novella. The "dime novel," as the format came to be known, caught on rapidly. *Malaeska* sold ten thousand copies in its first appearance in the Beadle series. Only four months later, Edward Ellis's *Seth Jones,* issue number 8 in the *Beadle Dime Novel Library,* would sell 60,000 copies on its first appearance (and almost 500,000 overall), and sales only escalated from there. This success bred imitators. George Munro, who worked for the Beadles, started his own competing firm, and George's brother, Norman Munro, followed suit. While many competitors arose, there were five firms that published dime novels for significant periods of time: Beadle & Company (Beadle & Adams); George Munro; Norman Munro; Frank Tousey; and Street & Smith.

THE POPULARITY OF DIME NOVELS

Dime novels did not represent a new type of writing but rather a new kind of book and a new approach to the process of selling and distributing fiction. What was most notable about dime novels was reflected in their name—the low price—which made them accessible to a much wider audience of potential readers. In 1860, when the Beadles published the first dime novel, books of a comparable length, if they were sold in a cloth or leather binding (in the early twenty-first century thought of as "hardcover"), would have cost close to a dollar. Even the inexpensive paper-covered fiction of the 1840s and 1850s, written by popular, sensationalist authors like Ned Buntline, George Lippard, and Justin Jones, most often cost between twenty-five and fifty cents per volume. The Beadles' great innovation was to publish works of fiction in a

Cover of *The Lost Trail.* One of Beadle's dime novels, 1864. BROWN RARE BOOKS AND SPECIAL COLLECTIONS DIVISION, THE LIBRARY OF CONGRESS

standard format at regular intervals (roughly every two weeks) at a standard price in a size that made for easy distribution through the mail.

The dime novels of the 1860s were paperbound books of around one hundred pages that measured four by six inches and had covers of colored paper (the most common colors were yellow and salmon). The early issues of the dime novel series did not have cover illustrations, but soon images depicting particularly exciting scenes from the novels were emblazoned on the covers. The low price was a substantial part of dime novels' appeal, as they were affordable to poorer (and younger) readers who would not have been able to buy clothbound books (the average daily wage for a laborer in the 1840s and 1850s was around a dollar a day, but younger workers would not have earned that much). The small size of the dime novels was also part of their appeal, as they were lightweight and

extremely portable; their size also made them easy to conceal from disapproving parents and teachers.

Before the Beadles' innovation, cheap publication was a difficult business because the narrow profit margins on cheap books required large volume in order to make the business profitable and it was thought that there were not enough American readers to generate such sales. The issue was not, however, the small number of readers—the United States had one of the highest literacy rates in the world in the nineteenth century—but rather the difficulty and expense of distributing books to them. The Beadles saved money on cheap paper and small type, their production methods capitalized on technological advances in printing, and the absence of an international copyright agreement meant that they could pirate works by European authors without paying for them. But they also took advantage of a loophole in U.S. postal rates: it was prohibitively expensive to send books through the mail, but periodicals—publications that were issued at regular intervals—qualified for a much lower rate. This difference in postage was intended to allow for the easy circulation of newspapers, which were thought to be essential to the political life of the young Republic.

By issuing their dime novels regularly, dime novel publishers qualified for the lower rate that applied to periodicals and thus were able to let the U.S. Postal Service do their distributing for them through the mail. Readers generally paid for a book in advance, then the publisher sent the book out postage due; the buyer paid the postage upon receipt. While capitalizing on postal distribution, Beadle & Company in 1864 also formed a partnership with the nascent American News Company, which distributed dime novels to newsstands and bookstores. (The publishers of dime novels played a cat-and-mouse game with the Postal Service over the question of postage rates over the last half of the nineteenth century, ultimately losing their exemption.) As such, dime novels constitute a particularly useful example for the study of the growth of the mass-culture industry in the United States. Dime novels also offer a useful case for an examination of the creation of literary celebrity; authors such as Ned Buntline (E. Z. C. Judson, 1823–1886) and Horatio Alger Jr. (1832–1899) and characters including Buffalo Bill, Old Sleuth, and Nick Carter gained fame through dime novels (Ned Buntline published his first Buffalo Bill story in 1869).

The original audience for dime novels was adult readers, primarily men, although there would later be dime novel series aimed at female readers. Part of the early success of the genre can be attributed to the market provided by soldiers fighting in the Civil War.

Beadle, Munro, and other publishers shipped thousands of dime novels to Union army camps, creating a taste for the novels that persisted after 1865. Over time, however, the audience that came to be most strongly associated with dime novels in the public imagination was boys, prompting periodic panics over the books' "corrupting influence," including Anthony Comstock's crusades in the 1880s. It is likely, though, that early dime novels were read by everyone in the family, as they rarely contained any material that would have been considered morally questionable. Indeed the prominent critic William Everett wrote in the *North American Review* (1864) of the Beadle publications that they were "without exception . . . unobjectionable morally, whatever fault be found with their literary style and composition. They do not even obscurely pander to vice, or excite the passions" (p. 308). This view would change over time, however, as dime novels changed in physical format, came to be increasingly associated with juvenile readers, and were distributed more often from newsstand sales rather than through the mail. Regardless of the debates about dime novels' morality, they were astonishingly popular. No exact publication records exist for any of the publishers of dime novels, but Everett estimated that in 1864 there were five million dime novels in circulation that had been produced by the Beadle firm alone, not counting the output of its competitors.

DIME NOVELS AS A GENRE

It is difficult to characterize dime novels as a distinct genre of literature because the dime novel was primarily an innovation in production, packaging, distribution, and marketing rather than a new literary form. As was the case with *Malaeska*, many dime novels were texts that had previously been published elsewhere; indeed, Beadle & Adams republished some stories as many as fourteen times, often under different titles or in different series. Many of the early dime novels were westerns, which is what most readers think of when they hear the term "dime novel." Instead of being typical westerns, however, many dime novels of the 1860s were actually American historical adventures in the tradition of James Fenimore Cooper (1789–1851) and William Gilmore Simms (1806–1870), set not on the high plains of the West but in the forests of the East and the swamps of the South as well as on the high seas (seafaring stories were extremely popular). Because many of the early dime novels were reissues of texts that had previously appeared elsewhere, they tended to deal with historical subjects, particularly the Revolutionary and post-Revolutionary periods and the War of 1812. But many of these sensational stories featured more contemporaneous settings, such as California during the gold rush;

in Texas, particularly during the years of the Texas Republic and the Mexican-American War; and in the mountain West during the heyday of the fur trade.

The primary literary effect that these novels strove for was excitement, with fights, captures, escapes, and reunions crowded improbably close together, all focused around the exploits of a rugged and always prepared male hero, with multiple plot lines being tied up neatly (but suddenly) in the final chapter. A passage from Edward S. Ellis's *Seth Jones; or, The Captives of the Frontier* (1860), which is set on the frontier of western New York in the 1780s, is indicative of their typical style:

> All the savages sprung to their feet, and one held his tomahawk, ready to brain the captive Ina, in case they could not retain her. Another leaped toward Seth, but his surprise was great, when the man in turn sprung nimbly to his feet, and this surprise became unbounded when, doubling himself like a ball, Seth struck him with tremendous force in the stomach, knocking him instantly senseless. Quick as thought, Graham felled the savage standing over Ina, and seizing her in his arms, plunged into the woods, setting up a loud shout at the same instant. The scene now became desperate. Haldidge and Haverland, fired almost to madness, rushed forward, and the former added his own yells to those of the savages. Ten minutes after, not an Indian was in sight. (Brown, p. 231)

Along with such "blood-and-thunder" effects, many dime novels also often incorporated regional dialect, frequently for humorous or satirical effect, in the tradition of the southwestern humorists like Simms and Davy Crockett. Seth Jones, for instance, in the eponymous novel, speaks in typical Yankee dialect when a Mohawk captor takes away his rifle: "I'll lend that to you awhile, provided you return it all right. Mind, you be keerful now, 'cause that ar' gun cost something down in New Hampshire" (Brown, p. 199).

Given their subject matter and setting, dime novels are useful sources for examining nineteenth-century attitudes about the wilderness and encroaching civilization, the frontier, masculinity and individualism, and race and ethnicity, particularly within the context of westward expansion. (Later dime novels were more likely to be set in cities, to have detectives as heroes rather than trappers or Texas Rangers, and to reflect current news events in their plots.) With their sensational plots, dime novels played a large role in shaping a popular image of the western frontier as a place of lawlessness and violence and provided a popular and sensationalized mass cultural account of the process of Manifest Destiny.

See also Book Publishing; Literacy; Literary Marketplace; Publishers

BIBLIOGRAPHY

Primary Works

Brown, Bill, ed. *Reading the West: An Anthology of Dime Westerns.* Boston: Bedford, 1997.

"Dime Novels and Penny Dreadfuls." http://www-sul. stanford.edu/depts/dp/pennies/home.html.

Secondary Works

Cox, J. Randolph. *The Dime Novel Companion: A Source Book.* Westport, Conn.: Greenwood Press, 2000.

Denning, Michael. *Mechanic Accents: Dime Novels and Working-Class Culture in America.* London and New York: Verso, 1987.

Everett, William. "Critical Notices: Beadle's Dime Books." *North American Review* (July 1864): 303–309.

Johannsen, Albert. *The House of Beadle and Adams and Its Dime and Nickel Novels: The Story of a Vanished Literature.* 3 vols. Foreword by John T. McIntyre. Norman: University of Oklahoma Press, 1950–1962. Available at http://www.niulib.niu.edu/badndp/bibindex.html.

Noel, Mary. *Villains Galore: The Heyday of the Popular Story Weekly.* New York: Macmillan, 1954.

Pearson, Edmund Lester. *Dime Novels; or, Following an Old Trail in Popular Literature.* Boston: Little, Brown, 1929.

Smith, Henry Nash. *Virgin Land: The American West as Symbol and Myth.* Cambridge, Mass.: Harvard University Press, 1950.

Streeby, Shelley. *American Sensations: Class, Empire, and the Production of Popular Culture.* Berkeley: University of California Press, 2002.

Sullivan, Larry E., and Lydia Cushman Schurman, eds. *Pioneers, Passionate Ladies, and Private Eyes: Dime Novels, Series Books, and Paperbacks.* New York: Haworth, 1996.

Paul J. Erickson

DOMESTIC FICTION

"Domestic fiction" is a term used to describe a body of popular narrative literature written by, for, and about women that flourished during the mid-nineteenth century. Also called "woman's fiction" by the critic Nina Baym, who was one of the first scholars to study the genre in great detail, this literature focuses on the daily domestic lives of young, mostly middle-class white girls as they grow into womanhood. The plots of domestic fiction deliver didactic life lessons that members of the dominant culture considered useful in preparing nineteenth-century female readers for their lives as adult women. The life lessons conveyed in this fiction mirror the Protestant Christian values of the time and usually subscribe to what Barbara Welter has termed "the cult of True Womanhood," a nineteenth-century cultural ideal of femininity that upheld the four virtues of purity, piety, domesticity, and submission.

SOCIAL AND CULTURAL HISTORY

Historians have often characterized the nineteenth-century United States using the paradigm of "separate spheres," the notion that gender differences between men and women relegated them to different social, economic, and cultural roles. While cultural and social history is more complex than such a paradigm allows, and men's and women's lives probably functioned a bit more fluidly, this concept is useful for understanding domestic fiction. From the 1820s through the 1860s, advice and gift books, children's textbooks, household manuals, periodicals, and popular fiction, including domestic fiction, reinforced the ideology of separate spheres, which held that a proper woman's place was at home, tending to the spiritual, emotional, physical, and moral needs of her husband and children. As Nancy Cott has argued, the image of the "lady" served as a model of femininity for the age. The ideal of the True Woman persisted in the popular imagination, and women writers and characters of the nineteenth century were often judged on their adherence to these values.

In reality, of course, the ideal of separate spheres was inaccessible to those whose economic circumstances prevented its practice. Many women worked in factories or as servants or slaves and certainly could not conform to the ideal of a True Woman that circulated in print any more than women's lives today resemble those of "Cosmo girls" on magazine covers. Thus, although the cultural icon of the True Woman saturated mid-nineteenth-century popular media as a universal and achievable Christian imperative, it ignored the realities of class status. Many women, including women of color, lacked access to resources that would enable them to practice this ideal. For example, enslaved women could not control the way their masters used their bodies, which were also commodities and unprotected by the sanctity of home. Denied homes of their own and ownership of their own bodies, enslaved women could not educate and nurture their children, care for their husbands (marriage among slaves was forbidden in many states), or practice Christianity. Submission, one of the four cardinal virtues of the True Woman, according to Welter, meant something entirely different in the context of slavery, for instance. Indeed, domesticity reinforced the link between black women and their physical bodies even as it functioned in an opposite manner for white women. As Gillian Brown observes, by making housework transcendent—separating white housekeepers from the products and processes of their labor, and disciplining their bodies into invisibility—domestic ideology divested white women of their corporeality, circumscribing their movements and possibilities in the world.

Nonetheless, the concepts of separate spheres and True Womanhood had important socioeconomic and cultural functions in the context of the era. Some aspects of nineteenth-century women's lives may have particularly suited them for the pursuit of piety. Women were largely responsible for care of the sick and preparation of the bodies of the dead; at a very young age, women of this time would have lost friends and family to death in childbirth or through incurable diseases such as consumption (tuberculosis). Christianity, as several critics have observed, is the ultimate democracy—the disempowered on earth are delivered into an equitable and even triumphant afterlife. Another socioeconomic function of True Womanhood and the notion of separate spheres, as Nancy Cott notes, is the rise of mercantile capitalism, which transformed the family from a self-supporting unit to one reliant on a larger market economy, which increasingly necessitated men's work outside of the home. The division of the culture into separate spheres, at least in the popular and historical imagination, may have evolved as a result of men's employment outside of the home and the need for the nation's moral and spiritual values to flourish in safety. The reliance on the marketplace may have led to an imagined split between workplace and home because the workplace functioned according to the arbitrary rules of capitalism, whereas the home could operate from a Christian worldview.

Several critics have argued that True Womanhood offered many benefits to women privileged to deploy it as a strategy. Cott and others have noted that domesticity gave women a vocation with intrinsic value outside of the shifting market. That is, Christian piety, moral character, and the care and education of children became a meaningful profession that united many white, middle-class women with common values and gave them what many historians characterize as "influence" over their husbands and sons. In her *Treatise on Domestic Economy* (1841), Catharine Beecher (1800–1878) argued that women were accomplishing "the greatest work that ever was committed to human responsibility" (p. 14). Separate-sphere ideology led not merely to women's confinement in the home but to women's increasing solidarity outside of the home in their work with churches and reform organizations. Women organized for causes such as temperance, self-

improvement, and the abolition of prostitution and slavery. One might even argue that this organization of white, middle-class women with shared concerns and values laid a foundation for the Seneca Falls Convention in 1848 to discuss the condition and rights of women, concerns encapsulated in Elizabeth Cady Stanton's (1815–1902) Declaration of Sentiments. However, it can also be argued that domestic ideology represented another form of imperialism in its focus on the values and lives of certain women at the expense of others.

LITERARY HISTORY

The typical plot of a domestic novel is comparable to the familiar Cinderella story, according to Nina Baym, who argues that these narratives recount the protagonist's trials and eventual triumph. Following the loss of her mother and often both parents, the main character, a young or adolescent girl, embarks on a voyage of self-discovery, usually within a circumscribed domestic sphere. Finding herself alone, powerless, and without parental love and guidance, the heroine faces cruel, selfish, or immoral adversaries as she struggles to retain the Christian values inculcated by her mother, a True Woman. Through trial after trial, the protagonist slowly acquires the qualities of True Womanhood and recognizes their centrality to her survival and success. The story usually ends when she has sufficiently mastered the arts of True Womanhood. Often, this moment coincides with finding the love of a kind, fiscally sound, and morally upright man, whose support ensures the heroine a home of her own. Critics disagree about the extent to which this typical ending undermines the message of self-sufficiency, resourcefulness, and the importance of women's education that these novels undoubtedly relay.

Nathaniel Hawthorne (1804–1864) famously made a frustrated comment on the "d——d mob of scribbling women," a reference to women writers of domestic fiction whose hold on popular taste assured their commercial success. These women writers, including Susan Warner (1819–1885), Fanny Fern (pseudonym of Sara Parton; 1811–1872), Harriet Beecher Stowe (1811–1896), Maria Susanna Cummins (1827–1866), E. D. E. N. Southworth (1819–1899), and Elizabeth Stuart Phelps (1844–1911), widely known practitioners of the genre, treated the so-called woman's sphere—the home—with gravity and even realism. By the late nineteenth century, however, many literary critics, including Henry James (1843–1916) and William Dean Howells (1837–1920), agreed with Hawthorne's assessment and considered domestic fiction "romantic." The genre then fell out of favor—and print—and went generally unnoticed or was dismissed as "sentimental" by literary critics. This trend continued well into the twentieth century, as the foundation of literature as an academic discipline emphasized aesthetic complexity and literary formalism over historical and cultural approaches. Herbert Ross Brown acknowledged the enormous influence of the genre in *The Sentimental Novel in America, 1789–1860* (1959), although his characterization of these novels as unrealistic escapism reiterated the common view. Finally, in the 1970s and 1980s, feminist critics in the academy revived domestic fiction as part of the expansion of the literary canon and the project of recovering "lost" works written by women.

In a 1977 study that examined the split between elite and popular literary culture, Ann Douglas sparked renewed interest in domestic fiction. Douglas pronounced the genre guilty of "debased religiosity" and "sentimental peddling of Christian belief" (p. 6) and held its practitioners responsible for the subsequent devaluation of so-called feminine values throughout the nineteenth and twentieth centuries. However, Douglas was the first to consider domestic fiction in such detail. Her study maintained that the genre was historically and vitally important for an understanding of Victorian culture and modern readers' own immersion in contemporary mass culture. The following year Nina Baym answered Douglas's indictment of nineteenth-century "sentimental" values with *Woman's Fiction*, a survey of the genre and several of its key authors. While Douglas dismissed the values conveyed by these works, including passivity, Christianity, and self-sacrifice, Baym viewed the heroines of domestic fiction as intelligent, resourceful, and courageous. Instead of vilifying the home and the values associated with it, Baym insisted that the writers of domestic fiction viewed the home as a crucial alternative to American capitalism and industrialization. Baym discusses the heroine in domestic fiction in contrast to two other feminine types, the passive woman and the "thoroughly modern" woman. The former is characterized by her incompetence, fear, and undeveloped emotional and intellectual capabilities; the latter is demanding, selfish, and enamored of luxury, money, and power. While the heroines of domestic fiction are not flawless, Baym argues, they do possess the strength, courage, and wit to endure adversity in practical and resourceful ways. Baym views domesticity and its concomitant values of Christianity and love as a support system for women's strengths, desires, and fulfillment. Her book shifted scholars' understanding of the American literary canon away from its focus on what Baym herself had called in an earlier article "melodramas of beset manhood" and paved the way for a generation of feminist critics, including Judith Fetterley, Sharon Harris, and Annette Kolodny, whose renewed interest in the genre continues to influence the way we read American literature.

In 1984 Mary Kelley published *Private Woman, Public Stage*, which considers twelve women authors of nineteenth-century domestic fiction whom Kelley dubs "literary domestics": Caroline Howard Gilman, Maria Cummins, Caroline Lee Hentz, Mary Jane Homes, Maria McIntosh, Sarah Parton (Fanny Fern), Catharine Maria Sedgwick, E. D. E. N. Southworth, Harriet Beecher Stowe, Mary Virginia Terhune, Susan Warner, and Augusta Evans Wilson. Relying on the personal papers of these authors, ten of whom chose public, nontraditional, and intellectual lives out of economic necessity, Kelley argues that all found writing at odds with domestic ideals. Comparing the personal histories of these women novelists with the novels they produced, Kelley is less optimistic than Baym about the role domesticity played. Kelley maintains that these authors compromised their work in the struggle to reconcile social expectations of women and women writers with their own sense of purpose so they could earn their living. She argues that women were second-class citizens even within the home but that the market demanded their complicity with domesticity. Writers of domestic fiction, therefore, were able to extend their roles as women into the public realm specifically because they were viewed as performing proper women's work. In some ways, Kelley suggests, they broadened the sphere of women's influence by speaking to the world beyond the home. In 1990 Susan Coultrap-McQuin extended Kelley's argument with a study of "gentleman publishers" of domestic fiction, editors who assumed guardianship of these women and their works and whose loyal patronage assisted them to financial success.

Jane Tompkins, however, took a more radical view of domestic fiction in her groundbreaking book *Sensational Designs: The Cultural Work of American Fiction, 1790–1860* (1985). Furthering both Douglas's and Baym's arguments about the central role of popular fiction in culture, Tompkins shifts attention away from aesthetic concerns ("But is it any good?") and focuses instead on the "designs" popular novels had on their audiences. This rhetorical and critical strategy, which relied on nineteenth-century readers' responses and an awareness of the historical context for the novels' production, enabled a new kind of discussion about the genre. Tompkins argues forcefully that this fiction traded in stereotypes and sentimentalism for the purpose of moving its audiences to action. In compelling chapters about Stowe's *Uncle Tom's Cabin* (1852) and Warner's *The Wide, Wide World* (1851), Tompkins advances the notion of "sentimental

A domestic scene. From chapter 61 of the 1890 English edition of Susan Warner's *The Wide, Wide World.* WAYNE STATE UNIVERSITY LIBRARY SYSTEM

the domestic novel may represent the replacement of one form of imperialism with another. A collection of essays edited by Shirley Samuels, *The Culture of Sentiment: Race, Gender, and Sentimentality in Nineteenth-Century America* (1992), follows Tompkins in considering sentimentalism as a cultural phenomenon. However, Samuels's volume advances the ways that sentimentalism, which domestic fiction often deployed, depended on the representation and circulation not simply of ideals but of specific bodies marked by gender, race, and class. If, as Tompkins argues, this fiction attempts to move its audience to feeling and, through feeling, to action, then Samuels's collection examines how these important differences in bodies might influence feeling and impact action. Essays in this collection consider the politics and aesthetics of the convergence of sentimentalism and race within a specific historical context, which previous critics had not made a primary category of analysis.

PRACTITIONERS OF DOMESTIC FICTION

Catharine Maria Sedgwick (1789–1867) may have inaugurated the genre of the domestic novel with *A New-England Tale* (1822), which focuses on women characters in domestic settings and delivers a moral lesson. Like most novels in this genre, the orphaned heroine relies on her inner resources, including piety, industry, and intelligence, to rise above her situation and even support herself as a schoolteacher. However, the story ends with marriage to a wealthy widower, who purchases the heroine's childhood home, which she had lost earlier in the novel through the deaths and bankruptcy of her parents. While the novel follows the Cinderella story of rags to riches via a wealthy husband, it also emphasizes the role of education, independence, and morality for women's success. Sedgwick followed this first novel with many others like it, including *Redwood* (1824), *Clarence* (1830), and *The Linwoods* (1835). Her most important novel, *Hope Leslie* (1827), is a historical novel that considers women's roles in early Puritan Massachusetts. Although not purely domestic fiction, the novel focuses on three strong and motherless female characters, each of whom represents one aspect of True Womanhood.

Published in 1851, Susan Warner's *The Wide, Wide World,* the first American book to sell over a million copies, epitomizes the genre of domestic fiction. Contemporary reviews praised its delineation of character, its wholesome purpose and religious feeling, and its avoidance of sensationalism. The narrative follows Ellen Montgomery, a privileged and beloved child until the illness and death of her mother, as she learns the values of hard work, humility, and Christian self-sacrifice at the

power," a concept that influenced the next decades of criticism on American domestic fiction. Tompkins's basic point is that domestic fiction is feminist and political; its central goal, she contends, is to revolutionize the world from a woman's viewpoint. For the authors of domestic fiction, the home is neither escape nor refuge but a model of how a truly democratic world should be organized—with women at the helm. In Tompkins's reading, the Christian and feminine values of submission linked with the cultural ideal of True Womanhood become strategies for achieving godliness and ultimate power.

Tompkins's important argument does not accommodate the inherent biases of True Womanhood. One might ask from which woman's point of view the world should be reorganized. As the black abolitionist Sojourner Truth (c. 1797–1883) famously asked, "And ar'n't *I* a woman?" The revolutionary aims of hands of her cruel and ironically named Aunt Fortune, who lives on a working farm. Befriended by a kind neighbor, the angelic Alice Humphreys, a True Woman who closely resembles Ellen's mother, Ellen finds spiritual and emotional comfort and guidance. In the Humphreys's home, Alice's brother John, a minister, essentially educates Ellen for the role of his wife, prescribing courses of reading in philosophy, language, and the Bible and reinforcing the importance of piety, purity, and submission. Perhaps Ellen's biggest challenge is acquiring the art of self-discipline, made even more difficult by the emotionally wrenching nature of her trials while in the care of tyrannical and exacting guardians. Critical response to the preponderance of tears in the novel has run the gamut from frustration to feminist acceptance. Nina Baym argues that the novel enables the expression of grief that accrues to powerlessness, while Jane Tompkins finds that only through the mastery of emotion can the heroine ally herself with true authority, God. Also problematic in this novel is the role that the highly masculinized John Humphreys plays in Ellen's education and survival. That is, the heroine exhibits not the qualities Baym lauds, resourcefulness and intelligence, but what Tompkins describes as the complete "extinction of her personality" (p. 600) through obedience to masculine and godly authority.

Maria Susanna Cummins's *The Lamplighter* (1854) enjoyed enormous popularity, selling forty thousand copies in the first month of publication alone. Cummins's Gerty is less dependent and passive than Ellen, although she certainly must learn self-discipline. In a tale set in urban Boston, the orphaned heroine cares for the aging Mr. Flint until his death, when she is taken in by the kind, wealthy, and unobservant Emily Graham, who arranges for her education. The novel depicts a wide range of working- and middle-class characters who gain success based on their merit, including the heroine herself, who becomes a teacher. The outspoken, high-spirited, passionate, and impulsive Gerty, unlike Warner's Ellen, marries a man who is her equal at novel's end. Although Cummins's sympathetic characters are undoubtedly Christians, the story emphasizes the values of domesticity and industry, informed by life and educational experience, as most important. Similarly, Fanny Fern's *Ruth Hall* (1854), a thinly veiled autobiography of the author (Sara Parton), emphasizes the heroine's industry and resourcefulness as a writer struggling to support and retain custody of her children despite her cruel and stingy relatives. While Christianity is a given, these novels cite education and intelligent use of their wits as most central for women's survival in a masculine world.

Serialized in the antislavery newspaper *National Era* in 1851 and 1852, Harriet Beecher Stowe's *Uncle Tom's Cabin; or, Life among the Lowly* was published in two volumes in 1852 and became the best-selling novel of the century. This narrative traces the stories of two slaves, Tom and Eliza, as they are forced deeper into slavery. Although the novel follows a different plot than typical domestic fiction, Stowe is generally considered the most important contributor to the genre, and her work embraces the values of maternal-based Christianity and True Womanhood fundamentally. *Uncle Tom's Cabin*, written as a response to the Fugitive Slave Act of 1850, which permitted escaped slaves to be captured from nonslaveholding states and returned to their masters, considers slavery as a moral problem that right-thinking Christians are obligated to address through feeling and action. In its treatment of Tom, a passive, loving Christian black man, and Eliza, a young slave mother frantic to save her child and preserve her family, the novel demonstrates slavery's serious threat to the values of motherhood, Christianity, democracy, and the home. Stowe accomplishes her goals through frequent sentimental addresses that ask both male and female readers to consider the question "How would you feel?" and at the same time she deploys sentimental plot structures that show the evils of slavery, including its destruction of families and the depredation of the morals of both slaves and slaveholders.

Jane Tompkins argues that the novel's twinned heroes, the white child Eva and the black slave Tom, enact the sentimental conviction that death is the ultimate victory. By drawing a parallel to the suffering and crucifixion of Christ, the suffering and deaths of the innocent Eva and Tom reminded nineteenth-century readers of the power of Christianity to change the world. Stowe's novel, Tompkins argues, hinges on the power of religious and emotional conversion to transform the course of history by placing women and their values at the center of the sociopolitical world, represented by the pacifist Quaker household of Rachel Halliday. Subsequent critics have questioned Stowe's vision, which, through its representation of black bodies as commodities, seems to leave racialized structures of power intact.

In 1859 two books of domestic fiction appeared that seem to critique domestic ideology and its possibilities for reform: E. D. E. N. Southworth's wildly popular *The Hidden Hand; or, Capitola the Madcap*, published serially in the *New York Ledger*, and Harriet E. Wilson's virtually unknown *Our Nig; or, Sketches from the Life of a Free Black, in a Two-Story White House, North, Showing that Slavery's Shadows Fall Even There.* Southworth's novel is often considered a parody of domestic fiction in that its heroine seems to mock True

Womanhood by overplaying purity, piety, submission, and domesticity as a strategy to catch the villains that beset her. Like most heroines of domestic fiction, Capitola is orphaned, but she dresses as a newsboy to earn her living on the New York streets, where girls are not permitted (or advised) to work. Rescued by a grumpy "uncle," and raised in his southern mansion, Capitola, who does not realize she is an heiress, encounters a series of villains determined to get their hands on her money. Bored by domestic life and undaunted by bands of robbers, Indians, and would-be rapists, Capitola cross-dresses, rages, impersonates, and even fights a duel in her determination to save her reputation, create a just world, and have adventures. Although Southworth's witty and resourceful "Cap" seems to challenge previous models of domestic heroism, she does eventually marry and settle down, and the text reinforces the powerlessness of women central to all domestic fiction. *The Hidden Hand,* although comic, chronicles a sobering array of dangers that women faced: arrest, imprisonment, institutionalization, seduction, rape, forced marriage, submission to unfair laws, ruined reputations, poverty, isolation, exposure to the whims of white male authority, and even slavery. As with many other examples of the genre, the novel often ignores the race and class politics that enable Capitola's heroism and success.

Harriet E. Wilson's fictionalized autobiography *Our Nig* provides an important perspective on domestic fiction. Written to earn money for its ailing and poverty-stricken author, the novel traces the story of Frado, a mixed-race child abandoned by her white mother upon her father's death. Sold into indentured servitude, Frado is repeatedly and cruelly abused, both physically and emotionally, by her white mistress, Mrs. Bellmont, and her mistress's daughter. Although Mr. Bellmont and his sons are sympathetic, they are also ineffectual, like most men in domestic fiction. Like other heroines, Frado exhibits industry, seeks education, and devotes herself to her Bible. However, her staunch piety and drive for self-improvement are no match for the physical and economic hardships she faces from a life of incessant servitude. Unlike other domestic novels, *Our Nig* ends not with marriage but with the deserted and then widowed and penniless Frado struggling to support her child and avoid the workhouse. Wilson's story provides an important critique of domestic fiction, highlighting the race and class inequities inherent in but ignored by the genre and its critics. By depicting a heroine who possesses all of the qualities of a True Woman and yet is unable to triumph over her trials, Wilson characterizes domesticity as a white and middle-class ideal, an impossibility for free black women.

Domestic fiction continued to flourish throughout the 1860s in the publication of Augusta Evans Wilson's *St. Elmo* (1866), Elizabeth Stuart Phelps's *The Gates Ajar* (1868), and Louisa May Alcott's *Little Women* (1868–1869). Increasingly, however, authors experimented with different kinds of heroines, sometimes known as the "new woman." Described by Frances B. Cogan as the "all-American girl," this heroine, like Alcott's Jo March (or even Southworth's Capitola), is intelligent, physically fit, self-sufficient, and far less interested in self-sacrifice. Cogan locates the emergence of this heroine in women on the Oregon Trail, schoolteachers, and even in the many self-sufficient, prolific women writers behind domestic fiction. By the 1870s, however, domestic fiction as a generic form seemed to have played itself out. Considered romantic and unrealistic by critics such as Henry James and William Dean Howells, domestic novels were replaced by so-called realist and local color fiction. The Cinderella plots of domestic fiction were inadequate to explain an increasingly complex society and its rapidly growing and diverse population of readers.

See also Female Authorship; *The Gates Ajar; The Hidden Hand; Little Women; Our Nig; Ruth Hall;* Sentimentalism; *Uncle Tom's Cabin; The Wide, Wide World*

BIBLIOGRAPHY
Primary Works

Beecher, Catharine. *A Treatise on Domestic Economy.* 1841. Edited by Kathryn Kish Sklar. New York: Schocken, 1977.

Cummins, Maria S. *The Lamplighter.* 1854. Edited by Nina Baym. New Brunswick, N.J.: Rutgers University Press, 1988.

Fern, Fanny. *Ruth Hall and Other Writings.* 1854. Edited by Joyce W. Warren. New Brunswick, N.J.: Rutgers University Press, 1986.

Sedgwick, Catharine Maria. *A New-England Tale.* 1822. Edited by Susan K. Harris. New York: Penguin, 2003.

Southworth, E. D. E. N. *The Hidden Hand; or, Capitola the Madcap.* 1859. Edited by Joanne Dobson. New Brunswick, N.J.: Rutgers University Press, 1988. First published serially in the *New York Ledger.*

Warner, Susan. *The Wide, Wide World.* 1851. New York: Feminist Press at CUNY, 1987.

Wilson, Harriet E. *Our Nig; or, Sketches from the Life of a Free Black, in a Two-Story White House, North, Showing that Slavery's Shadows Fall Even There.* 1859. Edited by P. Gabrielle Foreman and Reginald H. Pitts. New York: Penguin, 2005.

Secondary Works

Bauer, Dale M., and Philip Gould, eds. *The Cambridge Companion to Nineteenth-Century American Women's Writing.* New York: Cambridge University Press, 2001.

Baym, Nina. "Melodramas of Beset Manhood: How Theories of American Fiction Exclude Women Authors." *American Quarterly* 33, no. 2 (1981): 123–139.

Baym, Nina. *Woman's Fiction: A Guide to Novels by and about Women in America, 1820–1870.* Ithaca, N.Y.: Cornell University Press, 1978.

Brown, Gillian. *Domestic Individualism: Imagining Self in Nineteenth-Century America.* Berkeley: University of California Press, 1990.

Brown, Herbert Ross. *The Sentimental Novel in America, 1789–1860.* New York: Pageant, 1959.

Cogan, Frances B. *All-American Girl: The Ideal of Real Womanhood in Mid-Nineteenth-Century America.* Athens: University of Georgia Press, 1989.

Cott, Nancy F. *The Bonds of Womanhood: "Woman's Sphere" in New England, 1780–1835.* New Haven, Conn.: Yale University Press, 1977.

Coultrap-McQuin, Susan. *Doing Literary Business: American Women Writers in the Nineteenth Century.* Chapel Hill: University of North Carolina Press, 1990.

Douglas, Ann. *The Feminization of American Culture.* New York: Anchor, 1977.

Fetterley, Judith. "Commentary: Nineteeth-Century American Women Writers and the Politics of Recovery." *American Literary History* 6, no. 3 (1994): 600–611.

Fetterley, Judith, ed. *Provisions: A Reader from Nineteenth-Century American Women.* Bloomington: Indiana University Press, 1985.

Fetterley, Judith, and Joan Schulz. "A *MELUS* Dialogue: The Status of Women Authors in American Literature Anthologies." *MELUS* 9, no. 3 (1982): 3–17.

Harris, Sharon M. "Early American Women's Self-Creating Acts." *Resources for American Literary Study* 19, no. 2 (1993): 223–245.

Harris, Sharon M. "'A New Era in Female History': Nineteenth-Century U.S. Women Writers." *American Literature: A Journal of Literary History, Criticism, and Bibliography* 74, no. 3 (2002): 603–618.

Kelley, Mary. *Private Woman, Public Stage: Literary Domesticity in Nineteenth-Century America.* 1984. Chapel Hill: University of North Carolina Press, 2002.

Kolodny, Annette. "Dancing through the Minefield: Some Observations of the Theory, Practice, and Politics of a Feminist Literary Criticism." *Feminist Studies* 6 (1980): 1–25.

Kolodny, Annette. "A Map for Rereading: or, Gender and the Interpretation of Literary Texts." *New Literary History: A Journal of Theory and Interpretation* 11, no. 3 (1980): 451–467.

Logan, Lisa. "*Uncle Tom's Cabin* and Conventional Nineteenth-Century Domestic Ideology." In *Approaches to Teaching Stowe's Uncle Tom's Cabin,* edited by Elizabeth Ammons and Susan Belasco, pp. 46–56. New York: Modern Language Association, 2000.

Ryan, Mary P. *The Empire of the Mother: American Writing about Domesticity, 1830–1860.* New York: Harrington Park Press, 1985.

Samuels, Shirley, ed. *The Culture of Sentiment: Race, Gender, and Sentimentality in Nineteenth-Century America.* New York: Oxford University Press, 1992.

Tompkins, Jane. *Sensational Designs: The Cultural Work of American Fiction, 1790–1860.* New York: Oxford University Press, 1985.

Welter, Barbara. "The Cult of True Womanhood: 1820–1860." *American Quarterly* 18 (1966): 151–174.

Wood, Ann Douglas. "The 'scribbling Women' and Fanny Fern: Why Women Wrote." *American Quarterly* 23, no. 1 (1971): 3–24.

Lisa M. Logan

DRED SCOTT V. SANDFORD

Dred Scott v. Sandford (1857) was the Supreme Court's most important decision in the years leading up to the Civil War. Jurisprudentially the decision had relatively little long-term impact. However its short-term political impact was enormous. It generated hundreds of newspaper editorials and countless speeches by politicians. In 1858 two senatorial candidates in Illinois—the incumbent Stephen A. Douglas and the challenger Abraham Lincoln—vigorously analyzed the case, as well as the issue of extending slavery into the territories, in the famous Lincoln-Douglas debates. In 1860 Horace Greeley, the editor of the *New York Tribune* and the most important Republican journalist, published a pamphlet edition of the majority opinion of Chief Justice Roger Brooke Taney (1777–1864) and the dissent of Associate Justice Benjamin Robbins Curtis. Predominantly antislavery, the Republicans distributed tens of thousands of copies of these two opinions as a campaign document. Republicans hated Taney's opinion and believed that distributing it would help bring out the vote in the election that year.

DRED SCOTT'S ROAD TO THE COURT

Dred Scott (1795–1858) was a Virginia-born slave. His master, Peter Blow, took him to Missouri in 1827 and, in 1833, sold him to Captain John Emerson, a U.S. Army surgeon. In December of that year Emerson took Dred Scott to his post at Fort Armstrong at

Scott and his wife (below) and their daughters (above). Front page of *Frank Leslie's Illustrated Newspaper,* New York, 27 June 1857, discussing the Dred Scott case. GETTY IMAGES

Territory would apply to the new territory, and the laws of the Michigan Territory also prohibited slavery. Thus under a variety of federal and territorial laws, slaves could not be legally held in bondage at Fort Snelling.

Despite these laws Scott was held as a slave in Fort Snelling from 1836 to 1838. While there he married Harriet Robinson in a ceremony performed by the local Indian agent, who also served as a justice of the peace. This marriage might be construed as indicating that Scott was free because slaves could not be legally married. Over the next few years the Scotts lived in Louisiana, Missouri, and once again in the Wisconsin Territory. In 1843 Emerson died and ownership of the Scotts passed to his widow, Irene Sanford Emerson. For the next three years the Scotts were rented out to various temporary masters.

SUING FOR FREEDOM

In 1846 Scott tried to purchase his freedom, but Irene Emerson refused. Scott then sued for his freedom and after various delays, a jury in 1850 declared him free, basing its judgment on a series of precedents dating from 1824, in which Missouri courts had held that if a master took a slave to a free state, that slave became free. However, in 1852 the Missouri Supreme Court reversed these precedents, asserting that the free states had "been possessed with a dark and fell spirit in relation to slavery" (Finkelman, *Dred Scott,* p. 22), and thus Missouri would no longer recognize the free state law that did not recognize slavery.

The case should have ended there, but at this point Irene Emerson remarried (ironically to an abolitionist physician and politician in Massachusetts) and transferred ownership of Scott to her brother, John F. A. Sanford, who lived in New York. (The Supreme Court clerk would misspell his name as "Sandford," and it appears that way in the case.) Scott, now claiming to be a citizen of Missouri, sued Sanford in federal court under what is known as "diversity jurisdiction." "Diversity" of citizenship means that the involved parties are residents of different states, and diversity jurisdiction provides that suits between them be heard in federal court.

In response to this suit, Sanford argued that Scott could not sue in diversity because "Dred Scott is not a citizen of the State of Missouri, as alleged in his declaration, because he is a negro of African descent; his ancestors were of pure African blood, and were brought into this country and sold as negro slaves" (Finkelman, *Dred Scott,* p. 25). U.S. District Judge Robert W. Wells rejected this argument, asserting that if Scott was free he had the right to sue in federal court.

Rock Island, Illinois. Slavery was illegal in Illinois and had Scott tried to gain his freedom then, presumably an Illinois court would have granted it. Illinois was generally hostile to free blacks, but at the same time the state would probably not have allowed anyone, even an army officer, to keep a slave in the state for a long period of time. Scott, however, did not seek his freedom in Illinois, and in May 1836 Emerson took him to Fort Snelling in what today is Minnesota and at the time was part of the Wisconsin Territory.

The Northwest Ordinance of 1787 had banned slavery in the Northwest Territory, including Wisconsin and part of Minnesota. The Missouri Compromise, passed in 1820, had banned slavery in the territories north of Missouri, which included all parts of Minnesota not covered by the Northwest Ordinance. In addition the Wisconsin Enabling Act, which created the Wisconsin Territory, declared that the laws of the Michigan

After hearing the case, however, Wells ruled against Scott, finding that the federal court in Missouri should follow the decisions of the Missouri Supreme Court on the status of blacks in Missouri. Scott remained a slave.

His lawyers then appealed to the United States Supreme Court. The Court twice heard arguments in the case before deciding on 6 March 1857 that Scott was still a slave. The date of the announcement was significant. It came two days after the inauguration of President James Buchanan. In his inaugural address on 4 March, Buchanan had taken note of the controversy over slavery in the territories and urged Americans to accept the forthcoming decision by the Supreme Court.

THE SUPREME COURT DECISION

The Supreme Court's response to Dred Scott's freedom claim was extraordinary. For the first time in the history of the Court all nine justices wrote opinions. In total the case consumes more than 250 pages of volume 60 of *United States Reports*. Chief Justice Taney's opinion of the Court was 54 pages long; Justice Curtis answered him with a 70-page dissent.

By a seven-to-two vote the Court rejected Scott's freedom claims. Chief Justice Taney reached four major conclusions: (1) that blacks, even if free, could never sue in federal court under diversity jurisdiction because blacks, even if citizens of the states in which they lived, were not citizens of the United States; (2) that Congress lacked the power to pass general laws for the regulation of the territories; (3) that Congress specifically could not ban slavery in the territories because this would constitute taking private property without just compensation; (4) that the Missouri Compromise, which had operated for more than thirty-five years, was unconstitutional.

Not every justice in the majority agreed with all these conclusions. Justice Samuel Nelson of New York, for example, wanted to deny Scott's claim on the very narrow ground that the federal courts were bound to follow state law on the status of people within any state, and thus whatever claim to freedom Scott might have had from living in Illinois or the Wisconsin Territory was lost when he returned to Missouri. Justice John Catron of Tennessee agreed that Congress could not ban slavery in the territories, but rejected the claim that Congress had no power to pass general legislation for the territories. But despite differences among the majority justices, all agreed that Scott was to remain a slave.

CHIEF JUSTICE TANEY'S OPINION

Taney's opinion shocked many northerners. While most northern whites at this time held various prejudices against blacks, many were stunned by the conclusion that blacks were without any rights under the Constitution. Taney's language was indeed harsh and jarring. Hoping to appeal to widely held hostility toward blacks, Taney argued that race was the key to American citizenship. While almost all white southerners accepted these ideas of race, many northerners—and probably a majority of the members of the new Republican Party—no longer blindly accepted race as a reason for denying people fundamental rights. Thus Taney's language stunned many northerners when he wrote,

> The question is simply this: Can a negro, whose ancestors were imported into this country, and sold as slaves, become a member of the political community formed and brought into existence by the Constitution of the United States, and as such become entitled to all the rights, and privileges, and immunities, guarantied by that instrument to the citizen? (Finkelman, *Dred Scott*, pp. 57–58)

Taney attemped to support these claims with an appeal to history—what we might today call the "intentions of the framers."

To bolster his claims he provided a detailed analysis of colonial statutes that discriminated against blacks. He asserted that colonial laws such as the Massachusetts Act from 1705 proved "the degraded condition of this unhappy race" at the time of the Revolution (Finkelman, *Dred Scott*, p. 62). He further appealed to the memory of the founders by citing the Declaration of Independence, only to argue that it did not apply to blacks. Taney quoted the Declaration's assertion that "all men are created equal" but then asserted that "it is too clear for dispute, that the enslaved African race were not intended to be included, and formed no part of the people who framed and adopted this declaration" (Finkelman, *Dred Scott*, p. 63). He proved this assertion, at least to his own satisfaction, by an odd appeal to patriotism and the historical memory of the founders. He argued that the equality language of the Declaration could not have applied to blacks because

> the conduct of the distinguished men who framed the Declaration of Independence would have been utterly and flagrantly inconsistent with the principles they asserted; and instead of the sympathy of mankind, to which they so confidently appeared, they would have deserved and received universal rebuke and reprobation. (Finkelman, *Dred Scott*, p. 63)

He went on to claim that "the men who framed this declaration were great men—high in literary acquirements—high in their sense of honor, and incapable of asserting principles inconsistent with those on which they were acting." Thus, because some of the founders—such as Thomas Jefferson—owned slaves, it was not possible to imagine, according to Taney's view, that blacks could ever be considered members of the body politic that created the United States. This history lesson of course ignored the many black soldiers who fought in the Revolutionary War. It also ignored what historians call the "first emancipation," which led to an end to slavery in the North during and after the Revolution.

Moving from the Declaration to the Constitution, Taney continued to use a narrowly constructed view of history and of the framers to support his conclusions about black citizenship. Thus he completely ignored the fact that free black men had voted in most of the northern states, as well as some southern states, at the time of the ratification of the Constitution in 1789. Nevertheless, tying his analysis to a flawed historical perspective, Taney declared that African Americans

> are not included, and were not intended to be included, under the word "citizens" in the Constitution, and can therefore claim none of the rights and privileges which that instrument provides for and secures to citizens of the United States. On the contrary, they were at that time considered as a subordinate and inferior class of beings, who had been subjugated by the dominant race, and, whether emancipated or not, yet remained subject to their authority, and had no rights or privileges but such as those who held the power and Government might choose to grant them. (Finkelman, *Dred Scott,* p. 58)

Taney tied his historical analysis to an explicit appeal to what legal scholars later identified as original intent, originalism, or the intentions of the framers. He argued that Americans had to follow the intent of those who wrote the Constitution and that

> no one, we presume, supposes that any change in public opinion or feeling, in relation to this unfortunate race, in the civilized nations of Europe or in this country, should induce the court to give to the words of the Constitution a more liberal construction in their favor than they were intended to bear when the instrument was framed and adopted. (Finkelman, *Dred Scott,* p. 68)

This argument seemed to acknowledge that many northerners and Europeans no longer accepted the legitimacy of slavery. Some, such as abolitionists and members of the new Republican Party, might even favor equality. But Taney in effect denied the legitimacy of such views, at least when it came to constitutional law.

Even northern whites who did not believe in racial equality were uncomfortable with this conclusion. By this time blacks could vote on equal terms with whites in five New England states and had some voting rights in three other states. Everywhere in the North blacks were able to hold property, enter various professions, attend schools, sign contracts, and sue and be sued. In all but three states (Indiana, Illinois, and California) they could testify against whites in court. Surely they were not without rights even if their rights might be restricted. But Taney said otherwise. Under *Dred Scott* a free black citizen of, say, Massachusetts who was kidnapped and taken to a slave state would be unable to sue in federal court to regain freedom. Such a possibility outraged many northerners.

Even more shocking was Taney's conclusion that the Missouri Compromise was unconstitutional. This was only the second time in its history that the Court had declared an act of Congress unconstitutional. The first, *Marbury v. Madison* (1803), had involved a single minor provision of an elaborate law. *Dred Scott,* however, engaged a major federal statute that had been key to regulating settlement of the territories for more than a generation. Moreover, as Justices John McLean and Benjamin Robbins Curtis stressed in their dissents, the principle of regulating the territories—and banning slavery in the territories—predated the Constitution itself. In 1787 the Congress under the Articles of Confederation had banned slavery in the Northwest Territory. Shortly after ratification of the Constitution, Congress readopted the Northwest Ordinance, confirming its power to regulate the territories. In the Missouri Compromise, Congress in 1820 also regulated the territories and banned slavery in some of them. Since then, as the dissents noted, Congress had repeatedly regulated the territories, allowing slavery in some and not in others.

Surely these many congressional acts could not have been unconstitutional. Many former delegates to the Constitutional Convention had been in the Congress that readopted the Northwest Ordinance. George Washington, a signer of the Constitution, had also signed this bill into law. President James Monroe, who signed the Missouri Compromise bill, had been a delegate to Virginia's ratifying convention. Surely all these founders of the nation in Congress and the executive branch could not have so completely misunderstood the powers of the federal legislature. This in any event is what McLean, Curtis, and many northerners thought, but Taney and a majority of the Court judged otherwise.

IN THE COURT OF PUBLIC OPINION

The public response to Taney's opinion and to the two dissents was at one level predictable. Northern Democrats were relieved, believing the issue of slavery in the territories would no longer disrupt politics. Their political opponents in the North had built an entirely new political party—the Republican Party—around opposition to slavery in the territories. They could no longer, so northern Democrats believed, fight to stop slavery in the territories without seeming to oppose the Constitution. This would vanquish the Republicans and leave the field open for sweeping Democratic victories in the next elections.

Southerners were for the most part gleeful. On 10 March 1857, the Richmond *Enquirer* happily noted that "the *nation* has achieved a triumph, *sectionalism* has been rebuked, and abolitionism has been staggered and stunned." The paper concluded, "And thus it is, that reason and right, justice and truth, always triumph over passion and prejudice, ignorance and envy" (Finkelman, *Dred Scott,* p. 130). The New Orleans *Daily Picayune* asserted on 21 March 1857 that the decision "clears away the mists through which many honest men have distorted views of the rights of the Southern people." The paper was pleased with a decision that "gives the sanction of established law, and the guarantees of the constitution, for all that the South has insisted upon in the recent struggles, and forces her adversaries to surrender their political organization against her rights, or assume openly the position of agitators against the constitution." As such it was "a heavy blow to Black Republicanism" (Finkelman, *Dred Scott,* p. 132).

Republicans rejected this analysis. They pointed out over and over again that Chief Justice Taney had said Dred Scott, as a black, had no right to sue in federal court. If that was so then there was no case before the Supreme Court, and Taney's conclusions about the validity of the Missouri Compromise were *dicta* that had no value or force. In its 7 March 1857 issue the *New York Tribune* concluded, "This decision . . . is entitled to just so much moral weight as would be the judgment of a majority of those congregated in any Washington bar-room. It is a *dictum* prescribed by the stump to the bench—the Bowie-knife sticking in the stump ready for instant use if needed." In his 1858 senatorial campaign Lincoln argued that the decision was part of a conspiracy by Presidents Franklin Pierce and James Buchanan, Chief Justice Taney, and Senator Stephan A. Douglas to nationalize slavery.

Abraham Lincoln continued to make these arguments after 1858, and in 1860 northern voters overwhelmingly supported him, giving him an electoral vote majority, as well as a popular vote plurality, that put him in the White House. Six years later Republican majorities in the House of Representatives and the Senate would pass the Fourteenth Amendment, and on 9 July 1868 the states would ratify it. The amendment made all people born in the United States—without regard to race or ancestry—citizens of the nation. This formally reversed the decision that Roger Brooke Taney had written.

See also Abolitionist Writing; Blacks; Compromise of 1850 and Fugitive Slave Law; Proslavery Writing; Slave Narratives; Slavery

BIBLIOGRAPHY

Primary Work

Finkelman, Paul. *Dred Scott v. Sandford: A Brief History with Documents.* Boston: Bedford Books, 1997.

Secondary Works

Ehrlich, Walter. *They Have No Rights: Dred Scott's Struggle for Freedom.* Westport, Conn.: Greenwood Press, 1979.

Fehrenbacher, Don E. *The Dred Scott Case: Its Significance in American Law and Politics.* New York: Oxford University Press, 1978. Winner of the 1979 Pulitzer Prize in history.

Finkelman, Paul. *An Imperfect Union: Slavery, Federalism, and Comity.* Chapel Hill: University of North Carolina Press, 1981.

Hyman, Harold M., and William M. Wiecek. *Equal Justice under Law: Constitutional Development, 1835–1875.* New York: Harper, 1982.

Paul Finkelman

ECONOMY

See Banking, Finance, Panics, and Depressions

EDITORS

Whether suggesting revisions of a manuscript for book publication, choosing the contents of a magazine, or assigning a writer or reporter a story, an editor always serves as a mediator—between an author and a publisher or between an author and a reader. This mediating role was especially crucial in the period 1820–1870 as authors and editors alike tried to navigate the chaotic and unstable world of the book and periodical industries. To successfully appeal to all their constituents—readers, writers, and publishers—nineteenth-century editors needed a wide variety of literary and business skills. Part author, part literary critic, part entrepreneur, nineteenth-century editors have rarely enjoyed the kind of attention paid to writers themselves; nonetheless editors of all kinds—magazine, book, and even newspaper editors—contributed to the development of American literature in the antebellum period.

FROM AVOCATION TO PROFESSION

The role of editors changed dramatically in the period 1820–1870. Like their eighteenth-century predecessors, such as Isaiah Thomas, Noah Webster, and Mathew Carey, periodical editors in the 1820s likely envisioned their work as a hobby, even an intermittent one. With few readers and even fewer contributors,

magazines during this early period rarely survived even a year, and the vast majority of editing work consisted of cutting and pasting excerpts from other sources, often without attribution. Opportunities for editors in the book industry were likewise extremely limited in the 1820s. Book publishing was still a local industry, and editing had not yet emerged as a distinct occupation. Many local book publishers did work now recognized as editorial in nature, of course, but these same people often served as printers, publishers, and booksellers as well.

By 1870, however, growth within both the book and periodical industries made editing a viable, even necessary, profession. According to Frank Luther Mott's estimates, there were probably around one hundred magazines in the United States in 1825, virtually all as local productions with limited circulations. In the early 1820s, for instance, the *North American Review* had only five or six hundred subscribers, and the *Saturday Evening Post,* one of the more successful literary weeklies of the decade, boasted a circulation of just three or four thousand (Mott 1:200, 4:674). By the end of the period, however, the overall condition of the periodical industry had changed dramatically. By 1870 Mott estimates more than 1,200 periodicals and some periodicals of the 1850s and 1860s—including *Godey's Lady's Book* and *Peterson's Magazine*—enjoyed circulations of more than 100,000. Most successful was probably the *New York Ledger,* with 400,000 subscribers in 1860 (Mott 2:359).

The book industry experienced similar growth between 1820 and 1870. Just a few years before this period, for example, James Harper (1795–1869) and

John Harper (1797–1875), both in their early twenties, opened a small printing shop in New York. Within a few decades, they, along with two other brothers, had established one of the most successful publishing dynasties in American literary history. Although the enormous success of Harpers was hardly typical, it does suggest not only the overall growth of the industry but also the development of national rather than local firms. By 1870 some of the most important national publishing firms of the century were thriving, including not only Harpers but also Ticknor and Fields and Houghton, Mifflin and Co. The monetary value of books published and sold in the United States likewise increased. According to John Tebbel's estimates, the value of books manufactured and sold in the nation in the mid-1850s stood at $16 million, up from $2.5 million in 1820 (1:221).

These two growing industries were largely intertwined throughout this period. Published books were reviewed in periodicals, for example, and many authors chose dual publication, with their work appearing first in periodicals and then in books. Some editors, such as Charles Frederick Briggs (1804–1877) (editor of *Putnam's Monthly*), moreover, edited periodicals that were directly linked with the publishing firms that owned them (in Briggs's case, G. P. Putnam's). Other editors who managed periodicals owned by publishing firms include Fletcher Harper's (1806–1877) work with *Harper's New Monthly Magazine* (owned by publishing firm Harper & Brothers) and William C. Richards's work with the *Southern Literary Gazette*. Recognizing the potential power of a book publishing and periodical collaboration, Richards formed a partnership with a Charleston printer, Joseph Walker, with the goal of publishing in book form fiction that had initially appeared in the *Gazette*. Although the partnership of Richards and Walker was short-lived, it attests to the interdependence of the book and periodical industries.

Given the growth and increasing complexity of these industries, it is hardly surprising that editors took on new importance during this period. Although most periodical editors continued to rely on reprinted material from other sources, many editors took on new responsibilities, including establishing editorial policy, soliciting authors, reading manuscripts, and writing material. The growing importance of editorial work is suggested by the dramatic success of editor-publishers such as James T. Fields (1817–1881). In the early 1830s in Boston, a young Fields was working as a clerk for a local bookstore owner and sometimes publisher, William D. Ticknor (1810–1864). Within a decade Fields was a partner in the publishing firm, and he was soon negotiating terms with such writers as Henry

Wadsworth Longfellow, Nathaniel Hawthorne, Henry David Thoreau, and Ralph Waldo Emerson. But with the potential editorial successes came the risk of failure. In September 1869, for example, when Fields published Harriet Beecher Stowe's essay accusing Lord Byron of incest in the *Atlantic Monthly*, the magazine lost thousands of outraged readers.

Antebellum editors adopted various models for their work. Like Fields, many antebellum editors served as both editors and publishers for their periodicals or publishing firms. David Ruggles (1810–1849), for example, was founder, publisher, and editor of the African American newspaper *Mirror of Liberty*, as was Charles J. Peterson (1819–1887) with *Peterson's Magazine*, the popular women's magazine. Fluid roles between editor and publisher were even more common within the book industry. As publisher-editor of his own book firm, for example, George Palmer Putnam (1814–1872) worked directly with authors, choosing manuscripts for his list and encouraging particular projects. Whereas some editors, like Robert Bonner of the enormously popular *New York Ledger*, enjoyed very long editorial careers, many others viewed editing as a temporary assignment. Edgar Allan Poe (1809–1849), Ralph Waldo Emerson (1803–1882), William Gilmore Simms (1806–1870),

James T. Fields. COURTESY OF THE BOSTON ATHENAEUM

and Caroline Matilda Kirkland (1801–1864) are just a few of the many authors who turned to editing at least occasionally, often with hopes both of supplementing the salaries they earned as authors and of shaping the public's perception of literature and American authorship. Still others created positions that are best understood as contributing editors. Aware of their appeal to readers, many publishers identified popular writers as "editors" of their magazines. The popular poet Lydia Sigourney (1791–1865) was at times listed as one of the editors of *Godey's Lady's Book*, for example, even though her only responsibility to the magazine was to provide poetry.

Editors continued to face serious challenges during this period. Within the periodical industry, editors struggled under heavy workloads and insufficient salaries. As Ellery Sedgwick describes, the *Atlantic Monthly* editor James Russell Lowell (1819–1891) often worked fifteen-hour days, reading manuscripts, corresponding with contributors, soliciting authors, writing literary notices, and reading proofs. At one point, Lowell complained that 150 unanswered letters piled on his desk. Despite such efforts, Lowell did not earn enough from editing to support himself. In addition to the $2,500 annual salary he received for editing the *Atlantic Monthly*, Lowell also earned $1,800 for a full-time teaching position at Harvard (Sedgwick, pp. 34, 45–46). Lowell's difficulties regarding workload and salary were hardly atypical. At various points in his career, William Gilmore Simms served as editor of six different periodicals. Although attracted to the idea of editing a southern magazine as a way of promoting southern literature, he repeatedly left his editorial positions in dismay at the lack of adequate remuneration, the overwhelming workload, and the difficulty of success. Near the end of his tenure as editor of the *Southern Quarterly Review*, Simms confided to a friend: "I need not say how little time is left me for thinking and living. I do not live. I grub, and grub is my portion—my reward" (Guilds, p. 159).

CONSOLIDATION AND DIVERSITY

One of the most remarkable facts about this period in publishing was that it was a time of both intense consolidation and diversity. Major national journals and publishing firms were established within the literary centers of Boston, Philadelphia, and New York, and editors working within this context experienced a degree of literary and cultural authority that their eighteenth-century predecessors could not have imagined.

At the same time, however, the book and periodical industries were expanding well beyond the northeast urban triangle. This diversity—both geographically

and topically—can be suggested by noting just a few of the countless periodicals established during this period. In 1825, for example, the socialist community of New Harmony, Indiana, founded the *New-Harmony Gazette* with the famous reformer Frances Wright serving as one of its editors. Just a few years after that journal was founded, the Indian agent Henry Rowe Schoolcraft launched *Muzzeniegun* in Sault Ste. Marie, Michigan. A manuscript paper that circulated widely, *Muzzeniegun* focused on documenting Ojibwa culture, and Schoolcraft depended greatly on the assistance of his Ojibwa wife, Jane Johnston Schoolcraft, and her family. Thousands of miles away in San Francisco, J. MacDonough Foard and Rollin M. Daggett founded the *Golden Era* in 1852, a literary weekly that published the work of Bret Harte and Mark Twain. Precisely because these efforts required relatively little financial investment (compared with publishing books), editors were able to launch countless periodicals, literally throughout the entire United States and on almost every imaginable topic.

For many of the same reasons, a significant number of women and minorities became editors during this period, thus beginning a long tradition of women's and minority editing and publishing in the United States. In general, the book industry was less hospitable to women and minority editors during this period than was the book industry. A notable exception is the African Methodist Episcopal Book Concern, which was established in 1817, just a year after the A.M.E. Church was founded. Under the direction of its editors, known as General Book Stewards, the A.M.E. Book Concern published several books related to the church, including its governing laws and a hymnal, and both a monthly and weekly periodical.

Relatively few minority editors worked within the book industry, but the periodical industry proved much more open, especially with antislavery periodicals. In 1827 the first newspaper edited by and for African Americans appeared under the title *Freedom's Journal*, with John Brown Russwurm and Samuel E. Cornish as editors. Other important African American editors during this period include Frederick Douglass (with *North Star, Frederick Douglass' Paper*, and *Douglass' Monthly*), Thomas Hamilton (*Anglo-African Magazine* and the *Weekly Anglo-African*), George Hogarth (*African Methodist Episcopal Church Magazine*), and David Ruggles (*Mirror of Liberty*).

In addition to providing news and opinions about the abolitionist movement, many of these African American editors also offered a wide range of reading material. Russwurm and Cornish, for example, editors of *Freedom's Journal*, also published entertaining and informative pieces, including poetry, general interest essays, and biographical sketches of famous blacks. *Frederick Douglass' Paper* likewise included book reviews, poetry, fiction, and slave narratives. In terms of literary offerings, Thomas Hamilton's *Anglo-African Magazine* is especially notable. Although the magazine was short-lived, Hamilton had a definite talent for promoting African American writers, and he published the work of such authors as Frances Ellen Watkins (later Harper) and Martin Robinson Delany.

Many other racial and ethnic minorities also assumed editorial positions in the periodical industry. Important early Native American editors include Elias Boudinot with the *Cherokee Phoenix*, who published material in both English and Cherokee, and William Potter Ross with the *Cherokee Advocate*. Within the Spanish-language press, important editors include Victoriano Alemán and Eusebio Juan Gómez, who in 1846 founded *La Patria*, a successful journal published in New Orleans but distributed in places such as Baton Rouge, Havana, Mexico City, and New York City. Also notable is the work of José María Vigil, who founded *El Nuevo Mundo* in San Francisco in 1864. Like *La Patria*, *El Nuevo Mundo* boasted wide circulation, with sales offices in Peru, Colombia, and New York.

Similar periodicals published in other languages or English-language periodicals directed to specific ethnic groups were generally more local, and their existence was shaped by the immigration patterns into the United States. Boston and New York, for instance, each had a thriving Irish press, Milwaukee boasted a strong German press, and the Dano-Norwegian and Scandinavian press was focused primarily in Wisconsin and Minnesota. Although the editors of these publications are far less studied in the early twenty-first century than, say, Emerson or Lowell, they attest to the wide-ranging influence editors held throughout the nineteenth century. Indeed these editors, often immigrants themselves, provided their readers with information not only about native culture but also about the United States and the local communities in which they lived. As such, these editors helped their readers establish their place in American culture.

Even as it supported the work of minority editors, the periodical industry was also quite open to the work of women. Most famous is Margaret Fuller (1810–1850), who served as the first editor of *The Dial*, a small but influential journal associated with New England's Symposium or Transcendentalist Club. First issued in July 1840, *The Dial* was created as a means of expressing the ideas of the individuals associated with the club, including Emerson, Orestes Augustus Brownson, and Thoreau. Like many editors of small literary journals of the time, Fuller had difficulty finding material, and she was forced to write a large portion of the magazine herself. But Fuller is also remembered as an editor committed to free expression of ideas, even ones with which she disagreed, and she published the work of new and established authors alike.

Fuller's editorship was long regarded as an anomaly in the history of nineteenth-century editing, but many other women also worked successfully as editors. Women's magazines proved especially eager to boast women editors. Sarah Josepha Hale's (1788–1879) career is particularly noteworthy. After serving as editor of a small literary magazine for women for nine years, Hale accepted Louis Godey's offer to edit *Godey's Lady's Book*. For the next four decades, Hale shaped the *Lady's Book* into one of the most popular and influential magazines in antebellum America. As editor of the *Lady's Book*, Hale published the work of many of the nation's mportant writers, including Poe, Emerson, Simms, and Stowe.

Although few editors—male or female—could boast careers as long or as successful as Hale's, many other women pursued editing positions at a variety

Sarah Josepha Hale.

of magazines. Some of the more notable women editors of this period include Elizabeth Cady Stanton (1815–1902) with the women's rights journal the *Revolution,* Caroline Matilda Kirkland with *Sartain's Union Magazine of Literature and Art,* and Mary Ann Shadd (later Cary) with the *Provincial Freeman,* a newspaper published in Toronto for African Americans living in Canada.

EDITORS AND POLITICS

As these examples suggest, many editors defined their careers in political terms. Most famous are the editors associated with the antislavery movement, including William Lloyd Garrison (with *The Liberator*), Gamaliel Bailey (*National Era*), Thomas Hamilton (*Anglo-African Magazine*), and Frederick Douglass (*North Star, Frederick Douglass' Paper, Douglass' Monthly*). Also important were the many editors who tackled the issue of women's rights: Amelia Bloomer (*Lily*), Elizabeth Cady Stanton (*Revolution*), and Paulina Wright Davis (*Una*), to name just a few. These periodicals were not isolated from their more literary counterparts. On the contrary, these editors frequently published literature that supported their political aims, including, for example, Stowe's *Uncle Tom's Cabin,* which first appeared in Gamaliel Bailey's antislavery weekly newspaper.

Whereas engaging with politics allowed these editors to advance, coverage of political matters proved troubling for many others. Fearful of offending readers at a time of deep political divisions, many editors vowed to avoid partisan politics altogether. Those unwilling to avoid the controversies surrounding them frequently suffered the consequences of angry readers. Lydia Maria Child (1802–1880), for instance, lost many supporters of the *Juvenile Miscellany* when she began including antislavery pieces in the children's magazine and when her own book *An Appeal in Favor of That Class of Americans Called Africans* was published. Reaction to Child's political involvement was so strong that she was forced to resign as editor of the *Juvenile Miscellany,* which she had founded.

EDITOR AS LITERARY FIGURE

Perhaps even more so than with politics, antebellum editors exerted their influence over literary matters, helping to shape not only the careers of individual authors but also more generally the development of American literature. Throughout her editorship of *Godey's Lady's Book,* for instance, Hale used the pages of her magazine, including her own columns, to promote women authors. Similarly, in the late 1850s and 1860s, Lowell and later Fields used their positions as

editor of the *Atlantic Monthly* to support literary realism. Under Fields's watch, the *Atlantic* published early realistic texts, such as Rebecca Harding Davis's *Life in the Iron Mills,* as well as many reviews supportive of literary realism, reviews largely written by William Dean Howells, who was assistant editor at the time.

One of the reasons editors were able to influence literary culture so much during the antebellum period was that the vast majority of editors were themselves accomplished authors. Although there were exceptions—Robert Bonner with the *New York Ledger* had a background in printing, not literature— the typical antebellum editor in both the periodical and book industries was a man or woman of letters. Lowell, for example, had already established himself as a member of Boston's cultural elite as a poet, critic, and essayist when he accepted the position as first editor of the *Atlantic Monthly.* Likewise, Hale was a published poet and novelist before assuming the editor's post at the *Ladies' Magazine* in 1828, and she continued to write after she moved on to *Godey's Lady's Book,* publishing more than two dozen single-authored books (including poetry, fiction, and nonfiction) as well as many other edited books such as poetry anthologies and collections of letters. Other figures used editing positions as a way of testing or developing their literary inclinations. Walt Whitman's (1819–1892) editorial stints at papers such as the *New York Aurora* were brief, but he developed many of his innovative poetic techniques while working as a journalist and editor.

SUPPORT OF AMERICAN LITERATURE

One of the most important developments in the period 1820–1870 was the increasing support of American literature. With the United States denying copyright protection for foreign authors until 1891, many editors and publishers initially favored foreign texts, but some antebellum editors actively supported American literature. Even before he founded his own firm, while serving as a junior partner in Ticknor & Company, for instance, Fields was recruiting American writers, including Oliver Wendell Holmes, John Greenleaf Whittier, and Longfellow. Evert Duyckinck (1816–1878), likewise, served as series literary editor of Library of American Books, an impressive book series published by Wiley and Putnam that included works by Herman Melville, Fuller, Hawthorne, and Poe. Magazine editors, too, boasted their support of American literature, sometimes even competing with one another as to which magazine was the most "American." Because they enjoyed large circulations and were thus able to offer generous rates to their contributors, editors at popular magazines often offered the most generous financial arrangements for authors. Hale, for example, enacted several policies that supported recognition of American authorship as a profession: she accepted only original submissions and strongly favored American authors, she rejected the tradition of anonymous contributions and encouraged attribution, and she supported an author's right to be paid.

In addition to shaping particular author's careers, antebellum book editors also influenced the public's perception—and consumption—of American literature. Particularly notable is the editorial work associated with gift books, which first appeared in the 1820s and remained popular until the Civil War. Gift books such as *The Ladies' Wreath, Affection's Gift,* the *Gem,* and *Friendship's Token* were designed primarily for holiday gift giving. Most gift annuals consisted of miscellaneous moral and polite literature, compiled by an editor, but others focused on particular subjects—such as mourning—or were linked directly with social causes, particularly the antislavery movement. Designed as parlor ornaments as much as reading material, these gift annuals were lavishly illustrated and printed. Editors of these gift books—including T. S. Arthur, Lydia Sigourney, Nathaniel P. Willis, Samuel Griswold Goodrich, and Eliza Leslie—were frequently writers or magazine editors as well.

Although they typically lacked the visual extravagance of true gift annuals, literary anthologies of the antebellum period also necessitated strong editors. Some of the most important anthologies of the antebellum period include Rufus Wilmot Griswold's *The Poets and Poetry of America* (first issued in 1842) and *The Female Poets of America* (1849), Thomas Buchanan Read's *The Female Poets of America* (1849), Caroline May's *The American Female Poets* (1848), and Evert and George Duyckinck's *Cyclopaedia of American Literature* (1855). Like so many of the periodical editors who worked in or influenced the book industry, these anthology editors also had strong ties to the periodical world. Rufus Wilmot Griswold (1815–1857), for example, was a journalist, editor of *Graham's Magazine,* and Poe's editor and literary executor. Likewise, the Duyckinck brothers edited New York's *Literary World,* an innovative weekly founded in 1847 that offered detailed discussion of current books, and Read was a poet whose works appeared in both book form and in magazines such as *Peterson's,* the *Atlantic Monthly,* and *Lippincott's.* These anthologies were designed to appeal to popular tastes but nonetheless represent some of the first attempts to define American literary traditions.

Although they did not have the literary authority of major editors like Griswold and the Duyckinck brothers, editors of small local periodicals also influenced the public's reception of literature. Precisely because they were designed to provide general family reading, such periodicals—including local newspapers, small family magazines, even farming periodicals—often included some literary contents in their pages. While the editors of these periodicals are now largely forgotten, they no doubt participated in the public's knowledge and perception of nineteenth-century American literature.

EDITOR-AUTHOR RELATIONSHIPS

Although the most famous author-editor relations in American literature would emerge in subsequent periods (Thomas Wentworth Higginson and Mabel L. Todd's editing of Emily Dickinson's poems, for example, or Arthur Henry's handling of Theodore Dreiser's *Sister Carrie*), many editors were actively involved in shaping the works and careers of the authors with whom they worked. Editors' relationships with authors varied widely. Some authors complained of editors who mutilated their work and others portrayed their editors as patron saints. Many authors and editors had relationships in which business and personal matters intertwined. Correspondence between authors and their editors, for example, frequently shifts between contract negotiations and social invitations and friendly queries about spouses and children.

But not all author-editor relationships remained so friendly. Most notable—and most notorious—is Griswold's handling of Poe's works. Editor of *Graham's Magazine* for several years in the early 1840s and of the *International Monthly Magazine* in the early 1850s, Griswold was named Poe's literary executor when Poe died in 1849. Soon after Poe's death, Griswold published both an edition of Poe's works and a scathing biography. Most damaging to Poe's reputation was Griswold's handling—and forgery—of Poe's correspondence. Although Griswold's presentation of Poe influenced numerous subsequent biographies, scholars have exposed Griswold's forgeries and the overall self-serving nature of his work.

Other editors served writers far better. Fields, for example, convinced Hawthorne to abandon his plans for a collection of stories titled "Old Time Legends" and urged him instead to expand one of those legends, titled *The Scarlet Letter,* into a novel. E. D. E. N. Southworth (1819–1899), author of over sixty novels, likewise benefited from the work of her editor-publisher Robert Bonner, whom she described as a virtual savior. As Southworth recalled in a letter to Bonner:

"The first day that you entered my little cottage, was a day, blessed beyond all the other days of my life. I had some genius in popular writing; but not one bit of business tact and my pen was the prey of whoever chose to seize it. . . . You have made my life prosperous and happy. Every improved circumstance around me, every comfort in my home, every attainment of my children, speak of your kindness and liberality to us" (Coultrap-McQuin, p. 50). Although Southworth's praise for her editor was unusually laudatory, it nonetheless attests to the power and influence of nineteenth-century editors.

See also The Atlantic Monthly; Book Publishing; *The Dial;* Gift Books and Annuals; *Harper's New Monthly Magazine;* Literary Marketplace; Periodicals; Publishers

BIBLIOGRAPHY

Secondary Works

Chielens, Edward E., ed. *American Literary Magazines: The Eighteenth and Nineteenth Centuries.* New York: Greenwood, 1986.

Coultrap-McQuin, Susan. *Doing Literary Business: American Women Writers in the Nineteenth Century.* Chapel Hill: University of North Carolina Press, 1990.

Cyganowski, Carol Klimick. *Magazine Editors and Professional Authors in Nineteenth-Century America: The Genteel Tradition and the American Dream.* New York: Garland, 1988.

Daniel, Walter C. *Black Journals of the United States.* Westport, Conn.: Greenwood, 1982.

Fishkin, Shelley Fisher. *From Fact to Fiction: Journalism and Imaginative Writing in America.* Baltimore: Johns Hopkins University Press, 1985.

Greenspan, Ezra. *George Palmer Putnam: Representative American Publisher.* University Park: Pennsylvania State University Press, 2000.

Gruesz, Kirsten Silva. *Ambassadors of Culture: The Transamerican Origins of Latino Writing.* Princeton, N.J.: Princeton University Press, 2002.

Guilds, John Caldwell. *Simms: A Literary Life.* Fayetteville: University of Arkansas Press, 1992.

Joyce, Donald Franklin. *Black Book Publishers in the United States: A Historical Dictionary of the Presses, 1817–1990.* New York: Greenwood, 1991.

Lehuu, Isabelle. *Carnival on the Page: Popular Print Media in Antebellum America.* Chapel Hill: University of North Carolina Press, 2000.

McGill, Meredith L. *American Literature and the Culture of Reprinting, 1834–1853.* Philadelphia: University of Pennsylvania Press, 2003.

Mott, Frank Luther. *A History of American Magazines.* 5 vols. Cambridge, Mass.: Harvard University Press, 1938–1968.

Okker, Patricia. *Our Sister Editors: Sarah J. Hale and the Tradition of Nineteenth-Century American Women Editors.* Athens: University of Georgia Press, 1995.

Sedgwick, Ellery. *The "Atlantic Monthly," 1857–1909: Yankee Humanism at High Tide and Ebb.* Amherst: University of Massachusetts Press, 1994.

Tebbel, John. *A History of Book Publishing in the United States.* 4 vols. New York: R. R. Bowker, 1972–1981.

Patricia Okker

EDUCATION

The history of American education reflects the history of the nation as a whole. It represents the best intentions and principles of a democratic people but is plagued by the same problems and contentiousness that are characteristic of a free society. Despite the heated debates as to the form education should take, particularly for children, Americans created a system that would introduce millions of children to the joys of literature. During the colonial period the ethnic and religious diversity of settlements was expressed in schools. From New England's ambitious system of "public" primary and secondary schools to the middle colonies' religious and private schools to the South's tradition of home tutors, the colonists had tried it all.

Diverse educational experiments seemed to make sense at the time, but following the American Revolution they were found to be inadequate in a number of ways. Americans realized their sons and daughters needed an education that would prepare them for civic responsibilities in the new Republic and provide them with the skills and values necessary to become successful. Moreover, the new nation needed an educational system that would be "within the reach of all," not just the fortunate few who by virtue of their birth had access to good schools. "Universal" public education certainly would not be achieved during the nineteenth century, but the idea of free public education was launched in that era.

The common school appeared to be the answer to the educational needs of the new Republic. Initially supported by generous federal land grants to states under provisions of the Northwest Ordinance of 1787, these schools were to be maintained and controlled by local communities. In one-room schoolhouses scattered throughout the countryside, children of all ages learned to read, write, and cipher—what some called the three "R's"—reading, 'riting, and 'rithmitic. Moreover, common-school teachers quietly pursued the vision of the Founding Fathers by embracing a curriculum that would nurture a love of God and country as well as the values of hard work, determination, and competition.

THE McGUFFEY READERS

The centerpiece of the common-school curriculum was often a reader—most notably the McGuffey reader. By requiring students to read, memorize, and then recite poetry, literary passages, speeches of Revolutionary War heroes, moralistic tales, and Bible verses, the McGuffey readers helped to nurture a common culture and the basis of a literate society. Although not all common-school children during these years read the *Eclectic Readers* of William Holmes McGuffey (1800–1873), these popular books were representative of the materials available to students. The *Eclectic Readers* sold more than seven million copies by 1850 (Clifton, p. 75). During the middle decades of the nineteenth century they provided the basis of the common-school curriculum in many parts of the country. The original series, published in 1836, was revised slightly in 1857 and then revamped significantly in 1879 (Westerhoff, p. 17).

The *Eclectic First Reader* (1836 edition) contained forty-five selections or lessons. It was illustrated and included a list of new words following each lesson. The *Eclectic Second Reader* was slightly larger and more complex than the first and also included "discussion questions" that could provide the basis for review and examinations. The third reader in the set was more comprehensive with about twice as many selections as the first two. It was designed primarily for the "fifth or sixth grade level." Finally, the fourth and fifth readers were more difficult and were reserved for the most advanced elementary school students. In fact, McGuffey thought these volumes were appropriate for secondary school students. These readers included selections from literary classics, including excerpts from Shakespeare, Dr. Johnson, and "contemporary" writers, such as Alfred, Lord Tennyson, Henry Wadsworth Longfellow, Henry David Thoreau, Nathaniel Hawthorne, and Louisa May Alcott.

THE CURRICULUM: LOVE OF GOD

In addition to classic and contemporary secular literature, the readers also included stories that emphasized the love of God and country. The late-eighteenth- and early-nineteenth-century predecessors of the early

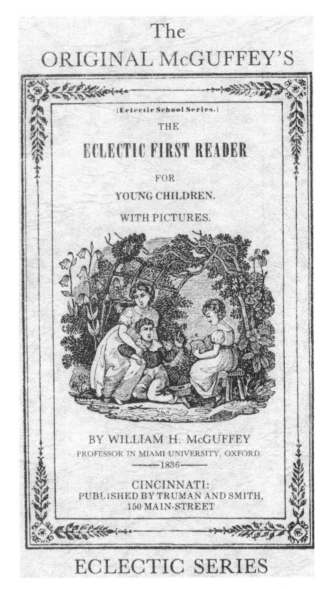

Cover of McGuffey's *Eclectic First Reader*, 1836. The McGuffey readers taught young children how to read and provided an introduction to literature. Approximately 122 million McGuffey books were purchased between 1836 and 1920. COURTESY OF DONALD PARKERSON

readers were the "primers," a term that originally referred to a book of prayers and devotions. The early primers, such as the ubiquitous *New England Primer,* typically included the Lord's Prayer, the Ten Commandments, and a selection of psalms. And since the primer often was the only book a family owned besides the Bible, it usually included an alphabet for instructional purposes.

As early primers evolved from instruments of religious and moral teaching to their more secular function of instructing young children to read, some of their religious content remained. McGuffey's *Eclectic First Reader,* like other readers of this period, placed great emphasis on God and teachings from the Bible. Of the forty-five lessons in this reader, ten directly mentioned God, and another two referred to the Bible. They informed young students that God gave human beings food, clothes, the sun, and the rain. In one lesson, "Thick Shade," students were told that God not only made the shade but also created the rich man and the poor, the dark man and the fair, the wise man and the fool. Moreover, God saw everything, including the good and bad deeds of little children. In "The Little Chimney Sweep," students were warned that to lie was to sin against God. In "Good Advice," students were told that sins must be confessed to God for forgiveness. Finally, children were encouraged to pray at bedtime and were instructed never to use profanity nor drink alcohol (pp. 95, 78, 48, 130).

The McGuffey readers also embraced secular values. Young students were reminded of the secularized axiom "honesty is the best policy." Similarly, temperance was often featured in the readers. In one selection, "The Whiskey Boy," little John got "tipsy every day," and by the age of eight he had become a drunkard. Eventually he was found drunk in the street and was brought to a poorhouse. John had now become a burden to society, and perhaps as punishment for his actions, he died within "two weeks." The lesson ended with the rhetorical question: "How do you think his father felt?" (*Eclectic First Reader,* pp. 143, 141).

THE CURRICULUM: INDIVIDUAL RESPONSIBILITY AND KINDNESS

While religious teachings were important parts of the *Eclectic First Reader,* responsibility was also a major theme of this and more advanced volumes. In fact, this value was the central focus of at least seventeen of the forty-five lessons in the first reader. Other basic themes emphasized here were kindness and obedience.

Kindness was perhaps the most important value presented in the *Eclectic First Reader.* Children were instructed to be kind to animals specifically: cows, oxen, cats, dogs, lame dogs, bluebirds, young birds, goats, bees, and even flies. By understanding that cruelty to animals (and even insects) was a sign of selfishness, children would comprehend the limits of their own self-interest. Indeed there was more to life than what the individual child wanted to do. In "The Cruel Boy," for example, George Craft pulled the wings off a fly. Like many other boys, George found this kind of activity amusing and entertaining. Eventually, however, another boy—a good boy—explained to George that

it was cruel to act in such a way, even if it was "fun" (pp. 78–80).

Building on these ideas, McGuffey introduced the general lesson of kindness to people, especially those who were less fortunate. Specifically the readers mentioned an old man, a sick man, a blind man, and a handicapped war veteran. Finally, McGuffey encouraged kindness to friends, brothers and sisters, and of course teachers (*Eclectic First Reader,* pp. 15–18, 32–34, 96, 106–107, 130–132). By emphasizing the importance of controlling one's self-interest, considering the feelings of others, and avoiding self-indulgent cruelty, McGuffey set the stage for more complex ideas including love of community and love of country. By promoting the idea that one's self-interest must sometimes be subordinated, the principles of civic virtue were developed at a very early age.

THE CURRICULUM: LOVE OF COUNTRY

In the early readers children were taught to obey their parents and teachers. Once these lessons were learned, children would understand the concept of obedience to higher secular authorities, such as the police, the town council, their employers, and even the federal government. Sometimes these lessons were rooted in biblical teachings, but more typically they were expressed in a secular context. If students understood the importance of secular deference, they would be more likely to respect the laws of the land.

As students progressed to more advanced readers, McGuffey gradually introduced another important curricular theme: love of country. Of course, this value reflected the burgeoning nationalism of Americans following the conclusion of the War of 1812. In fact, the term "nationalism" first appeared in American schoolbooks in the early 1820s (Elson, p. 101). Typically the readers took the position that the people of each nation had collective national personalities that differed dramatically from one another. For example, the *Juvenile Mentor,* another popular nineteenth-century reader, included a number of stories that portrayed the cruelty of Spaniards as a national character trait (Elson, p. 101).

This and other stereotypes strengthened nationalism. It also would seem that they helped encourage the strong nativist impulses that have plagued America since the middle of the nineteenth century. In the case of the Spanish, it may also have helped make possible the country's eager acceptance of the Spanish-American War in 1898. The British, however, were an exception. Although anti-British feelings were clearly reflected in some late-eighteenth- and early-nineteenth-century readers, this sentiment gradually diminished by mid-nineteenth century as Americans began to emulate British agricultural and industrial practices. By then American schoolbooks often boasted of British roots, a heritage that provided a glorious past full of "virtue and prestige but purified in the American environment" (Elson, p. 123). Besides the English, the only other national groups portrayed favorably in the early readers were the Scots (for their frugality) and the Swiss. Perhaps because there were relatively few Swiss immigrants to this country and because of their republican heritage, the image persisted. One of their countrymen, William Tell, figured prominently in many readers at this time. His story, the famous episode where he shot an apple off the head of his young son, was seen as both an act of heroism and a defiance of tyranny. In this story, Tell placed service to his country even above parental love. This was a magnificent expression of intense nationalism to be emulated by all true republicans (*McGuffey's Fifth Eclectic Reader*, pp. 219–232).

But while the English, Scots, and Swiss sometimes exhibited positive values, Americans were seen as the most virtuous of all. To reinforce that point, the readers of this period typically included many selections about America's Founding Fathers, such as Thomas Jefferson, George Washington, and Paul Revere. Rousing tales of their accomplishments and inherent values provided an essential element of the common-school reading curriculum. For example, the story of young George Washington and the fabled cherry tree was presented to virtually every schoolchild during this period. The mid-nineteenth-century version of this story was published in *Harper's New Monthly Magazine* in February 1856. In this story George "tried the edge of his new hatchet upon his father's favorite cherry tree . . . (but later confessed) Father, I can not tell a lie: I cut the tree." George's father responded and "tears gushed into his eyes. . . . I had rather lose a thousand trees than find falsehood in my son!" (Abbott, pp. 290–291).

Students were encouraged to celebrate the great success of patriots in the American Revolution, but the violence and divisiveness of that struggle as well as the writings of controversial and "radical" writers were minimized or even omitted from readers. Works by Thomas Paine (1737–1809), for example, were rarely included and then only when prefaced with a warning. One reader devoted an entire lesson to Paine's atheism, noting with outrage that he had claimed in *The Age of Reason* that "the Christian fable (was based on) ancient superstition (and) . . . mythologies" (McGuffey, *Eclectic Fourth Reader*, p. 166). The "exorcism" of Paine from the pantheon of American Founding Fathers by these readers demonstrates their awesome power in defining

and shaping the attitudes and values of nineteenth-century American schoolchildren.

By avoiding conflict and controversy on matters pertaining to God and country, the primary school readers of the mid-nineteenth century promoted a national consensus, however illusionary it may have been. The goal of the curriculum was to create what Benjamin Rush called patriotic "republican machines" (p. 14). That goal met with a great deal of success in common-school classrooms. These ideals, blended into a disciplinary framework that emphasized the values of hard work, achievement, and accountability, reflected the unique republican worldview of nineteenth-century America. In addition the United States was quietly becoming a nation of readers.

THE GRADED SCHOOL

During the second half of the century, it had become clear to educators that a new form of school organization was needed to deal with soaring enrollments and an ethnically diverse student body. The answer was the graded school. These schools also reflected the idea among educators that students of different ages had diverse needs and learning styles. Gradually students were grouped according to grade levels, introduced to a distinctive curriculum, and taught by teachers who had formal training. Despite these organizational changes, however, the basic reading curriculum remained virtually unchanged until the late nineteenth century.

Although the American people embraced the idea of the graded public school, they were slower to accept the concept of the public high school. In fact, most secondary schools during this period were private academies outside the jurisdiction of local school boards. As a result, enrollments in high schools were limited to the wealthy. This tradition was challenged by the landmark Michigan Supreme Court *Kalamazoo* decision of 1872 that allowed high schools to be operated by school districts and funded through taxation.

With the high school now in place, a number of American cities began to embrace the concept of the "educational ladder"—elementary and high schools integrated into unified school districts. In some districts, schools were combined for organizational simplicity, whereas in others each step of the educational ladder was separate—often occupying different buildings. The modern public school was taking shape.

COLLEGES

When graded schools and high schools were ostensibly linked to American colleges and universities, the concept of the educational ladder was complete. American colleges had always been separate from the primary and secondary schools of the nation. Their history, moreover, was very different. As early as 1636 Harvard College emerged as America's first institution of higher learning, followed by the College of William and Mary and Yale in 1693. By the eve of the American Revolution, a number of other important colleges had been established, including the College of New Jersey (Princeton University), the College of Philadelphia (University of Pennsylvania), King's College (Columbia University), Rhode Island College (Brown University), Queens College (Rutgers University), and Dartmouth College. These early institutions focused primarily on the training of clergy, and most had direct religious affiliations.

Between the American Revolution and 1800, a number of institutions of higher learning were established, and during the next half century hundreds of colleges emerged to meet the specific challenges of the nation. For example, the U.S. Military Academy at West Point developed an early engineering program, and Rensselaer Polytechnic Institute focused on science and civil engineering. Similarly a number of medical schools and law schools were established. By the middle of the nineteenth century, several "normal schools," including Mount Holyoke and Troy Female Seminary, were founded to train teachers for America's growing student population. Although most colleges of this era excluded women, Holyoke and Troy enrolled women and established a rigorous academic curriculum. Also notable was Oberlin Collegiate Institute, which was America's first coeducational college and also its first racially integrated institution of higher learning. By the late 1860s, a number of all-black colleges, including Fisk University and Atlanta University, were established to meet the needs of the nation's free African American population.

Institutions of higher learning played an important role in the development of the young Republic but did little to directly promote an appreciation of American literature. Colonial colleges were concerned primarily with the training of ministers. Theology was therefore the centerpiece of the curriculum in even the most prestigious institutions. By the late eighteenth century, as colleges underwent a gradual secularization, there also was a growing emphasis on the classics in Greek and especially Latin, but little if any required reading of more contemporary literature. In addition, other colleges of the early Republic typically had a practical focus such as engineering, medicine, law, or teacher training. The United States was indeed a pragmatic nation that sought to solve the "practical" problems of the day. Reading contemporary literature for fun or interest (or even as a component of a well-rounded education) was simply not the focus of these early schools.

To fill the growing demand for literature in colleges, a number of literary societies were formed beginning in the late 1780s. Students established these literary societies to provide a forum for literary and debating activities. Groups such as Princeton's Whig and Clio Societies provided an important "extracurricular" literary outlet. These societies often purchased their own books and established their own libraries. Members of such societies sometimes lived in their own residence halls. By the late nineteenth century, literary societies were eclipsed by the rise of Greek social fraternities, and by the time of the First World War, only a few survived. Nevertheless, they played an important role in introducing "contemporary" literature to thousands of college students.

ANTI-INTELLECTUALISM IN AMERICA

The pragmatic nature of American higher education was in some ways paralleled by a persistent anti-intellectualism bound up with the ideas of rugged individualism and frontier democracy. Many Americans were either uninterested in "book learning" or actively hostile toward it. In fact, as one intellectual of the time lamented, "It was not the want of learning I consider as a defect, but the contempt of it" (Faragher et al., p. 289). Even in larger cosmopolitan communities such as New York, Boston, and Philadelphia there was surprisingly little general interest in literature. Even though most Americans were literate, their taste in reading gravitated toward trade journals and religious tracts. The *North American Review* had a national circulation of only three thousand. Agricultural journals such as *Northern Farmer* and the *Cultivator*, however, had hundreds of thousands of readers, and the Methodist *Christian Advocate* boasted a circulation of over twenty-five thousand at mid-century (Faragher et al., p. 289).

Literature and literary criticism also took a backseat to the growing "penny press" of this period, so-called because the price of the newspaper typically was one cent. In 1833 the *New York Post* began publishing sensationalist stories that fascinated the American people. Similarly *Police Gazette*'s stories of swindlers, murder, and mayhem often titillated readers. The growth of these newspapers at mid-century was dramatic. On the eve of the American Civil War, one writer noted discouragingly, "No narrative of human depravity or crime can shock or horrify the American reader" (Faragher et al., p. 360).

Of course, there were communities of intellectual activity scattered throughout the country. This growing body of educated men and women eagerly embraced American literature. A handful of novels achieved commercial success. Harriet Beecher Stowe's

Uncle Tom's Cabin (1852) sold more than 300,000 copies in a single year (Faragher et al., p. 421). In addition to converting thousands to the cause of abolition, Stowe (and other women authors) helped transform what was disparagingly called "parlor" literature into an important literary form and attracted thousands of new American readers.

LYCEUMS AND LIBRARIES

Two informal movements influenced Americans' reading habits. The first was the lyceum, and the second was the public library. These two institutions sought to bring culture and literature to the people, and slowly they began to achieve their goals.

The lyceum movement was a system of adult education that emerged during the late 1820s in New England. It was a broad-based and very ambitious enterprise that promoted public education as well as the establishment of libraries and museums. Sometimes seen as the forerunner of the modern university extension system, the lyceum was the educational product of working-class "mechanic institutes" of this period as well as educators and intellectuals such as Josiah Holbrook of Millbury, Massachusetts.

By the 1830s, the lyceum had spread throughout the northern states, bringing speakers on a variety of subjects to small cities and rural communities. The lyceum recruited a number of important figures, such as Daniel Webster, Henry David Thoreau, Oliver Wendell Holmes, Nathaniel Hawthorne, Charles Dickens, William Makepeace Thackeray, William Lloyd Garrison, and Susan B. Anthony. Ralph Waldo Emerson, a regular speaker on the lyceum circuit, delivered more than fifteen hundred lectures to packed houses in twenty states between 1833 and 1860 (Faragher et al., p. 290). The lyceum movement not only provided broad support for public education but also helped nurture an appreciation of literature for hundreds of thousands of Americans.

Throughout this period, books were relatively expensive, and despite improvements in the American standard of living during the nineteenth century, families rarely owned more than a handful of books. As a result, libraries were critical in nurturing an appreciation of literature. There were a number of private subscription libraries established during the colonial period modeled on the Library Company of Philadelphia, which had been organized by Benjamin Franklin. There were subscription libraries in Charleston, South Carolina; New York; and Newport, Rhode Island. Also notable were Boston's Athenaeum and the fabled "coonskin library" established in frontier Ames, Iowa. Free lending libraries, however, were much slower to develop. In 1833 the first of these institutions was established in Peterborough, New Hampshire, and Boston established the first public library in the country supported by a municipal tax at mid-century. It was not until the end of the nineteenth century, however, that libraries became commonplace. This was the result of both philanthropy and a growing sense of civic responsibility in America. Andrew Carnegie, for example, endowed more than seventeen hundred free libraries by 1900 with his generous matching grants. A number of states, led by New Hampshire, mandated that each township support a public library.

CONCLUSION

By formal and informal means, Americans struggled to embrace the new literary world. In addition to reading religious tracts, trade magazines, agricultural journals, and the penny press, Americans were beginning to embrace the great literature of contemporary authors from James Fenimore Cooper to Melville and Hawthorne; from Washington Irving to Stowe, Thoreau, and Walt Whitman. The common school had provided the foundation of literacy in the new Republic and had introduced generations of young Americans to the joys of literature. Colleges and universities did their part as well by building on the traditions of a growing literate culture and nurturing an appreciation of the classics in Greek and Latin. The informal intellectual movements of the lyceum and the emergence of the public lending library brought a greater appreciation of reading to the masses and allowed them access to that literature.

See also Colleges; Curricula; Literacy; Lyceums

BIBLIOGRAPHY

Primary Works

Abbott, John S. C. "George Washington." *Harper's New Monthly Magazine* 12 (February 1856): 289–315.

Burton, Warren. *The District School as It Was.* Boston: T. R. Marvin, 1852.

McGuffey, William H. *The Eclectic First Reader, for Young Children.* 1836. Milford, Mich.: Mott Media, 1982.

McGuffey, William H. *The Eclectic Fourth Reader.* 1838. Milford, Mich.: Mott Media, 1982.

McGuffey, William H. *The Eclectic Second Reader, for Young Children.* 1836. Milford, Mich.: Mott Media, 1982.

McGuffey, William H. *The Eclectic Third Reader.* 1837. Milford, Mich.: Mott Media, 1982.

McGuffey, William H. *McGuffey's Fifth Eclectic Reader.* 1879. Compiled by Alexander Hamilton McGuffey. New York: New American Library, 1962.

"The Old Deluder Law of 1647." In *American Education: An Introduction through Readings,* edited by Tyrus Hillway, p. 200. Boston: Houghton Mifflin, 1964.

Rush, Benjamin. "A Plan for the Establishment of Public Schools and the Diffusion of Knowledge in Pennsylvania." 1789. In *Essays on Education in the Early Republic,* edited by Frederick Rudolph, pp. 3–23. Cambridge, Mass.: Belknap Press of Harvard University Press, 1965.

Taylor, J. Orville. *The District School.* New York: Harper & Brothers, 1834.

Secondary Works

Bailyn, Bernard. *Education in the Forming of American Society: Needs and Opportunities for Study.* Chapel Hill: University of North Carolina Press, 1960.

Clifton, John L. *Ten Famous American Educators.* Columbus, Ga.: R. G. Adams, 1933.

Cohen, Sol, comp. *Education in the United States: A Documentary History.* New York: Random House, 1974.

Cremin, Lawrence A. *American Education: The National Experience, 1783–1876.* New York: Harper and Row, 1980.

Elson, Ruth Miller. *Guardians of Tradition: American Schoolbooks of the Nineteenth Century.* Lincoln: University of Nebraska Press, 1964.

Faragher, John Mack, Mari Jo Buhle, Daniel Czitrom, and Susan H. Armitage. *Out of Many: A History of the American People.* 3rd ed. Upper Saddle River, N.J.: Prentice Hall, 2000.

Ford, Paul Leicester, ed. *The New England Primer: A History of Its Origin and Development.* New York: Teachers College, Columbia University, 1962.

Graff, Harvey J. *The Literacy Myth: Literacy and Social Structure in the Nineteenth-Century City.* New York: Academic Press, 1979.

Katz, Michael B. *The Irony of Early School Reform: Educational Innovation in Mid-Nineteenth Century Massachusetts.* Cambridge, Mass.: Harvard University Press, 1968.

Lockridge, Kenneth A. *Literacy in Colonial New England.* New York: Norton, 1974.

Mosier, Richard. *Making the American Mind: Social and Moral Ideas in the McGuffey Readers.* New York: King's Crown, 1947.

Parkerson, Donald H., and Jo Ann Parkerson. *The Emergence of the Common School in the U.S. Countryside.* Lewiston, N.Y.: E. Mellen Press, 1998.

Parkerson, Donald H., and Jo Ann Parkerson. *Transitions in American Education: A Social History of Teaching.* New York: RoutledgeFalmer, 2001.

Reese, William J. *The Origins of the American High School.* New Haven, Conn.: Yale University Press, 1995.

Spring, Joel. *American Education.* 8th ed. Boston: McGraw-Hill, 1998.

Westerhoff, John H., III. *McGuffey and His Readers.* Milford, Mich.: Mott Media, 1982.

Donald H. Parkerson
Jo Ann Parkerson

ENGLISH LITERATURE

For inhabitants of Britain and the United States in the mid-nineteenth century, the American War of Independence was only two generations past, roughly the same distance in time as the Second World War from those living at the turn of the twenty-first century. It was, in other words, still an active memory within the general culture as well as being an actual memory for the elderly. Furthermore there had been a series of conflicts between these two countries in the early nineteenth century, the most significant of which was the War of 1812 arising out of trade disputes and American anger at the Royal Navy's methods of impressment. These hostilities led to British troops entering Washington and burning the White House to the ground. Heated controversies also erupted over rights to the fur-trading territories of the Pacific Northwest, a saga described in Washington Irving's popular work *Astoria; or, Anecdotes of an Enterprise beyond the Rocky Mountains* (1836, first published with a slightly different title), and over the boundary between Maine and British Canada. Not only were the cultural fortunes of Britain and the United States closely interwoven in the early nineteenth century, then, but also much mutual antipathy existed between the two nations. As Britain was consolidating its own empire, it was becoming increasingly suspicious of the United States partly because of what it regarded as that nation's anarchic principles of democracy and liberty but also because of U.S. potential to become an imperial competitor, an increasingly significant player on the world stage.

In the 1820s Lord George Gordon Byron (1788–1824) was still noting how the republican sensibility had migrated west across the Atlantic, upbraiding George III before a celestial court in *The Vision of Judgment* (1822) in a manner that would have brought smiles to the faces of the Founding Fathers. Indeed Byron's well-known sympathies for American independence induced the London *Times* to complain on

6 November of 1822 that "Lord Byron, who hates his own countrymen and countrywomen, has a prodigious *penchant* for the men and women of America." This old spirit of libertarian radicalism, however, was superseded in the early years of the nineteenth century by more romantic forms of patriotic attachment that tended to use transatlantic comparisons in order to emphasize the superiority of the writer's native culture, either American or British. Accounts of travels to North America by English writers became very popular in Britain at this time, and the success of such narratives was predicated upon their predictability, their tendency to reinforce an existing set of national stereotypes or prejudices rather than to discover anything new. Typifying this conservative mentality was Captain Basil Hall (1788–1844), whose *Travels in North America, in the Years 1827 and 1828* (1829) offers a severely critical account of the American political system, although, as Hall himself admitted: "I have often been so much out of humour with the people amongst whom I was wandering, that I have most perversely derived pleasure from meeting things to find fault with" (1:167).

Mocking Americans became something of a national sport for the British at this time, with *Domestic Manners of the Americans* (1832), written by Frances Trollope (1779–1863), being perhaps the most famous work in this genre. Trollope's narrative is an account of the time she spent between 1827 and 1831 in Cincinnati, Ohio, where she moved with her family in an attempt to reestablish their wealth by selling imported luxury goods after her husband's business in England had failed. *Domestic Manners* represents America as a land of vulgarity and greed, and it concludes that the "total and universal want of manners" in the United States "is so remarkable, that I was constantly endeavouring to account for it" (pp. 39–40). The book also achieved a certain political notoriety among liberal circles in Britain by being published on 19 March 1832, three days before the Reform Bill to enlarge enfranchisement had its third and final reading in the House of Commons. Many Tories in England blamed the democratizing impulse of the electoral reformers on the pernicious effects and example of American republicanism, and the liberal *Edinburgh Review* was not alone in suspecting that Trollope had conspired with her publishers on the timing of her book to make it appear "an express advertisement against the Reform Bill" (July 1832). However this may be, *Domestic Manners* fits within a tradition of travel writing in the first half of the nineteenth century wherein English writers patronize their American cousins as uncouth upstarts who have failed fully to understand the codes of civilized behavior.

DICKENS AND AMERICA

For Charles Dickens (1812–1870), who well knew Trollope's work and its emphasized objection to New World manners, the more pressing reason for hostility toward America was financial in nature. During the

---

In the following representative selection taken from chapter five of Frances Trollope's Domestic Manners of the Americans, *the author describes her residence in Cincinnati:*

The "simple" manner of living in Western America was more distasteful to me from its levelling effects on the manners of the people, than from the personal privations that it rendered necessary; and yet, till I was without them, I was in no degree aware of the many pleasurable sensations derived from the little elegancies and refinements enjoyed by the middle classes in Europe. There were many circumstances, too trifling even for my gossiping pages, which pressed themselves daily and hourly upon us, and which forced us to remember painfully that we were not at home. It requires an abler pen than mine to trace the connection which I am persuaded exists between these deficiencies and the minds and manners of the people. All animal wants are supplied profusely at Cincinnati, and at a very easy rate; but, alas! These go but a little way in the history of a day's enjoyment. The total and universal want of manners, both in males and females, is so remarkable, that I was constantly endeavouring to account for it. It certainly does not proceed from want of intellect: I have listened to much dull and heavy conversation in America, but rarely to any that I could strictly call silly, (if I except the every where privileged class of very young ladies). They appear to me to have clear heads and active intellects; are more ignorant on subjects that are only of conventional value, than on such as are of intrinsic importance; but there is no charm, no grace in their conversation. I very seldom, during my whole stay in the country, heard a sentence elegantly turned, and correctly pronounced from the lips of an American. There is always something either in the expression or the accent that jars the feelings and shocks the taste.

Trollope, *Domestic Manners of the Americans*, pp. 39–40.

---

depression of the late 1830s in the United States, many British companies that had invested heavily in America found the value of their state bonds collapsing, with British investors learning to their cost that neither the American federal government nor taxpayers regarded themselves as responsible for the financial affairs of individual states. One of Dickens's complaints about America in *The Life and Adventures of Martin Chuzzlewit* (published serially in 1843 and 1844) is that, as its hero tells Elijah Pogram, from "disregarding small obligations" Americans "come in regular course to disregard great ones: and so refuse to pay their debts" (p. 508). This double-dealing is associated by Dickens not only with a personal breach of trust but also with the inherent financial instability of the country: one of Martin's English acquaintances tells the story of "Lummy Ned," a man who emigrated to New York to make his fortune but then "lost it all the day after, in six-and-twenty banks as broke" (pp. 213–214). This sense of the United States as a den of financial iniquity would have merged in Dickens's mind with his bitterness regarding the absence of an international copyright agreement, an absence that meant he received no royalties at all from his vast sales in the United States. Indeed he went to America partly to campaign for a change in the law, an issue on which he was supported by Washington Irving and other American authors; but he underestimated the ferocity of the American popular press in defending its territory against what they saw as unjustified levies, particularly levies imposed by that old tax tyrant, Great Britain. Paradoxically, it was the widespread dissemination of Dickens's novels through unauthorized American reprints that brought his huge popularity in the United States during the late 1830s, a popularity he could turn to his financial advantage only through personal appearances and readings. Although the copyright question never surfaces overtly in Dickens's nonfictional *American Notes for General Circulation* (1842) or in *Martin Chuzzlewit*, this perception of the United States as a commercial predator is never far from the author's thoughts.

American Notes maps its version of the United States by constant comparison to English affairs, discovering parallels between the two countries all over the East Coast—the effect of Yale, for example, being "very like that of an old cathedral yard in England" (p. 125)—but finding the American West much more difficult to fit into Anglocentric perspectives. The prairies, complains Dickens, do not give the same "sense of freedom and exhilaration which a Scottish heath inspires, or even our English downs" because of their "very flatness and extent, which [leaves] nothing to the imagination" (p. 226). Since the American West appears not to

Caricature of Charles Dickens. Cover illustration for the French journal *L'Eclipse* by André Gill, 14 June 1868.
THE LIBRARY OF CONGRESS

accord with Dickens's English imagination, he conceptualizes these untamed lands by relating them to the vulgar state of Ireland, another country to the west of England, represented here as a parallel to the barbarous nature of these American frontier territories. On his journey to Cincinnati in the company of pioneers bound farther west, he comes across a village that is "partly American and partly Irish" (p. 204) while in the heart of New York state he encounters "an Irish colony" comprising "hideously ugly old women and very buxom young ones, pigs, dogs, men, children, babies, pots, kettles, dunghills, vile refuse, rank straw, and standing water, all wallowing together in an inseparable heap" (p. 256). The jumble of disparate materials here is akin to the vast flatness of the prairies in that both betoken a threat to the Dickensian predilection for an aesthetic perspective interwoven with recognizable social and spatial hierarchies; thus the Irish, like the

Americans, cannot be fitted into Dickens's sacrosanct domestic categories. On his second visit to the United States in 1867 and 1868, Dickens expressed a more specific hostility toward the "enormous influence" of the "Irish element" (*Dickens on America,* p. 230) in urban centers like New York City, talking of the "depraved condition" (*Dickens on America,* p. 225) of their political culture and linking it with the Fenian explosion, an attempt to free Fenians held as prisoners at the Clerkenwell House of Detention in Clerkenwell, near London, in December 1867.

The negative portrayal of the United States in *Martin Chuzzlewit* is well known, and indeed the novel is dogmatically and compulsively anti-American in its overall style and structure as well as in those episodes actually set in the United States. The burden of the narrative is to expose what Dickens takes to be the hypocritical discrepancy between "saintly semblances" and corrupt self-interest, a discrepancy that manifests itself on a personal level in the characterization of Pecksniff and on a national level through the inflated American conception of its own destiny in the "Valley of Eden" (p. 347). With the relentless urge to crush self-aggrandizing delusions that typified the English Victorian moralist, Dickens seizes upon the fat target of slavery as a prime instance of the American tendency to preach liberty while practicing oppression, mocking that "air of Freedom which carries death to all tyrants, and can never (under any circumstances worth mentioning) be breathed by slaves" (p. 248). This satirical overthrow of constitutional idealism is conceptualized by the author through iconoclastic imagery, as he describes how the "great American eagle, which is always airing itself sky-high in purest aether . . . tumbles down, with draggled wings into the mud" (p. 485). Associated with this idiom of bathos is a thread running throughout the novel designed to interrogate the supposed primacy of "mind over matter," as the author puts it, and thus to elucidate what he takes to be the intellectual failure of transcendentalism and all its works. Dickens's empiricist perspective ridicules the way "Edeners were 'going' to build a superb establishment for the transaction of their business, and had already got so far as to mark out the site: which is a great way in America" (p. 338).

CLOUGH AND TRANSCENDENTALISM

While the more conservative Dickens was skeptical about the idealist aspects of American culture, in his poetry Arthur Hugh Clough (1819–1861) approaches transcendentalism much more sympathetically. Although born in England in 1819, Clough spent six years of his childhood in Charleston, South Carolina, after his father had taken the family to the United States in the winter of 1822–1823. The plan of Clough's father was

to circumvent the economic depression that had followed the Napoleonic Wars in Europe by tapping sources of raw cotton in the American South and exporting it back to England. The family did not settle back in England until 1836, and, though Clough himself was sent back to England for his schooling in 1828, he retained early memories of living by the harbor at Charleston—South Carolina was, of course, then still a slave state—as well as of three summers when the family sojourned in the milder climate of New York. Clough was nicknamed "Yankee" at Rugby School, and his American childhood also ensured that when he traveled to Cambridge, Massachusetts, as an adult in December 1852, Clough was aware in an important sense of returning to the United States rather than encountering that country for the first time. In the 1840s Clough had experienced a tense relationship with the English cultural establishment, resigning his Oxford fellowship in 1848 on the grounds that he felt himself unable in principle to subscribe to the Church of England's Thirty-Nine Articles of Religion, a requirement at that time for all Oxford dons. Meanwhile Clough had met and spent some considerable time with Ralph Waldo Emerson (1803–1882) when the latter visited England in 1848—Emerson, the senior partner by sixteen years, noted in his private journal for 22 December 1848: "'Tis, I think, the most real benefit I have had from my English visit, this genius of Clough (*Journals* 11:64)—and, after Clough's trials and tribulations in English academe had led him to consider emigration, Emerson was quick to write encouraging him to come to Cambridge and assuring him of a plentiful supply of private tutorial work. Emerson, who was a great admirer of Clough's first major poem, *The Bothie of Tober-na-fuosich* (1848; later revised and retitled *The Bothie of Tober-na-Vuolich*), blamed the neglect of his friend on the narrow prejudices of English society, and he also hoped that Clough would assist him with "a catechism of details touching England" (1:316) in relation to his own work, *English Traits* (1856), which he was then writing.

At first Clough was generally enthusiastic about America. He met James Russell Lowell (1819–1891) and his wife on board the *Canada* en route to the United States, and in New England he was welcomed into the Emersonian circle, becoming quickly acquainted with Henry Wadsworth Longfellow, Nathaniel Hawthorne, Henry David Thoreau, Theodore Parker, Harriet Beecher Stowe, William Ellery Channing, and others. Clough also developed some important intellectual friendships, particularly with Lowell and with Charles Eliot Norton (1827–1908), and, even though he soon became weary of Massachusetts and chose to return to

England in 1853, these associations were to have significant repercussions for his subsequent literary career. Clough was indebted to Lowell, in particular, for the first publication of his best-known poem, *Amours de Voyage,* which was written in 1849 but suppressed by the author until Lowell persuaded him to allow it to be published in installments in the new magazine he was editing, the *Atlantic Monthly,* between February and May 1858.

It is clear from *Amours de Voyage* that Clough's work is torn between English and American cultural influences and that his poetry involves a shuttling between alternative transatlantic points of view. The poem itself features a hero wandering forlornly through Europe who is unable ultimately to find within himself either human love or religious faith; and it might be described as a poem that interrogates the notion of transcendentalism since there is a debate here between idealism and materialism, between an idea of neoplatonic "affinity," wherein correspondences are predestined, and mere "juxtaposition," wherein all encounters are seen as random and haphazard. Though he generally admired *Amours de Voyage,* Emerson himself disliked what in a letter to Clough he described as "the baulking end or no end" of the poem, its structural anticlimax whereby the hero Claude and his prospective lover Mary Trevellyn miss each other on their travels; Emerson was appalled that Clough appeared to "waste such power on a broken dream," a sense of disappointment that the American sage deemed "bad enough in life, and inadmissible in poetry" (Clough 2:548). Clough answered indirectly by writing in a letter to Norton that he had "always meant" to organize the poem in this way, and that he "began it with the full intention of its ending so" (2:551). Clough's response here indicates how the English-born poet saw himself not, like Walt Whitman, as Emerson's acolyte or mere follower, but rather as his transatlantic rival and interlocutor.

THE CIVIL WAR

Such authorial dialogues give only an indication of the extent to which English literature and American literature in the mid-nineteenth century were intellectually intertwined. Anthony Trollope (1815–1882), son of Frances, wrote his own account of U.S. manners in *North America* (1862), during the course of which he mentions hearing Emerson lecture in Boston. Although Trollope had feared beforehand "how the star-spangled flag would look when wrapped in a mist of mystic Platonism," he actually found to his surprise that Emerson spoke "with admirable simplicity and truth," being "terse and perspicuous in his sentences,

practical in his advice" (p. 223); for this new generation of visitors, the crude stereotypes promulgated by Trollope's mother no longer seemed sufficient. Anthony Trollope also met Nathaniel Hawthorne (1804–1864) at a dinner in Boston during this visit, and he later wrote a highly perceptive and complimentary critical essay on Hawthorne published in the *North American Review* in 1879.

Trollope's visit to America took place between August 1861 and May 1862, in the shadow of the American Civil War, which had broken out in April 1861. It is probably true to say that this war was the event that changed the cultural balance of power between Britain and the United States permanently. While Britain maintained an official position of neutrality during this conflict, the sympathies of Trollope himself, like those of other English liberals, lay with the North, even though he was suspicious of what he took to be the fanaticism of New England abolitionists. Elizabeth Gaskell, a friend and correspondent of Charles Eliot Norton, similarly supported the Northern states, as did John Stuart Mill and political advocates of free trade such as Richard Cobden and John Bright. There had been considerable support for the antislavery cause in Britain over the previous two decades, with Frederick Douglass (1818–1895) garnering much support during his successful tour of Britain between 1845 and 1847; indeed it was actually his English friends, led by Ellen and Anna Richardson of Newcastle, who raised the funds to purchase Douglass's freedom from Hugh Auld of Maryland in 1846. Harriet Beecher Stowe (1811–1896) was also welcomed enthusiastically by Queen Victoria during a tour of Britain in 1853, when she was presented with a petition containing the signatures of over half a million British women against slavery. This experience later encouraged Stowe to write "A Reply" (1863), addressed to the women of Britain, urging them to raise their voices in protest against the British establishment's tacit support for the Confederacy.

Stowe's wrath was directed not only against open apologists for slavery such as Thomas Carlyle (1795–1881), but also against Lancashire industrialists protective of their vested interests who did not want to see their profitable cotton trade with the American South disrupted, and the London *Times,* which supported the social idea of a Southern aristocracy and feared how the emancipation of slaves in the American South might destabilize British colonial interests in the West Indies. The black uprising in Jamaica in October 1865, when nearly five hundred insurrectionists were massacred by the army on the instructions of Governor E. J. Eyre, seemed to the *Times* to bear out its fears about "the original savageness of the African blood" (13 November 1865). After 1865 when the United States became in constitutional terms (in however problematic a way) a racially mixed and integrated society, the idea of a natural continuum between different branches of the Anglo-Saxon race on either side of the Atlantic became more difficult to sustain. In addition the reconciliation of the different regions of the United States into one strong federal nation marked a decisive stage in the shift of imperial power from Britain to America. The U.S. population had exceeded that of Britain for the first time in the 1840s, and, though Britain in the late nineteenth century remained strong politically and economically, the rapid growth in communications technologies and other forms of national standardization in America after 1865 led inexorably toward its establishment as the world's leading power.

AMERICAN RESPONSES TO ENGLAND

American writers of the mid-nineteenth century viewed their English counterparts with various degrees of enthusiasm, but in each case there was a strong sense of the two cultures being in dialogue with each other. For Washington Irving (1783–1859) in *The Sketch Book* (1819–1820) and *Bracebridge Hall* (1822), the English landscape existed in a continuum with its extension westward across the Atlantic, and he portrayed Shakespeare's Stratford-on-Avon as just as much a part of the American heritage as the Hudson River valley represented in "The Legend of Sleepy Hollow" and "Rip Van Winkle." Emerson famously declared in his 1837 address "The American Scholar" that his countrymen had "listened too long to the courtly muses of Europe" (p. 69), but the desire for such cultural independence arose not out of simple hostility toward England but from a desire to associate the spirit of nationalism with a home environment, a desire Emerson shared with William Wordsworth, Thomas Carlyle, and other British romantic writers by whom he was influenced. Emerson first wrote to Carlyle in 1834 expressing his delight that "one living scholar is self-centred & will be true to himself" (Slater, ed., p. 98) and the two men always remained on friendly terms despite Carlyle's complaint in a letter to his brother in 1862 that Emerson seemed to think of himself as "becoming celestial by emancipating Niggers" (Slater, ed., p. 537). "Each of the masters has some puerility," noted Emerson indulgently in his journal, "as Carlyle his pro-slavery whim" (*Journals* 10:52).

In *English Traits,* his account of a visit to England in 1847 and 1848, Emerson suggests that the British race has fragmented into two parts, with "her liberals in America, and her conservatives at London" (p. 28). This statement testifies to his sense of the vital genealogical continuities (as well as political differences) between the two nations, something mirrored in Henry David Thoreau's *Walden* (1854), which similarly draws on and revises conventions of Elizabethan pastoral. Herman Melville (1819–1891), who was widely read in English literature, particularly that of the Renaissance era, deliberately conceived of *Moby-Dick* (1851) as a response to John Milton's *Paradise Lost,* a transgressive narrative in which vengeance is glorified as Captain Ahab unleashes the destructive potential that is implicit, but never fully licensed, in Milton's Satan. Melville is sometimes thought of as a specifically Anglophobic writer because of his involvement with Evert Duyckinck's Young America movement in the late 1840s and the wariness he expresses toward "alien" England in his famous essay "Hawthorne and His Mosses" (1850). In fact, Melville's enthusiasm for this nationalist program was short-lived and all of Melville's works after *Moby-Dick* treat the English literary inheritance in a respectful if quizzical manner. Melville met with Hawthorne, then serving as American consul in Liverpool, during his visit to Europe in the fall of 1856, and it is odd to think of them walking together on the beach in the unlikely surroundings of Stockport, Lancashire, exchanging views on Calvinist notions of predestination. Hawthorne's own account of English customs, *Our Old Home,* was published in 1863, and in the manuscripts to his unfinished novel about an American claimant, Hawthorne attempts to reconfigure transatlantically his style of romance, with the story turning upon an estate passing from the English to the American branch of a fictional family.

Since the publication in 1941 of F. O. Matthiessen's seminal work *American Renaissance: Art and Expression in the Age of Emerson and Whitman,* American literature between 1820 and 1870 has normally been read within a nationalist context, with Emerson and his compeers conventionally said to have forged an independent culture that could stand apart from English models. However, more recent work on the extent to which English literature itself at this time was shaped by imperial and colonial designs has reintroduced the question of how relationships between English and American literature might be understood within a postcolonial framework, where different traditions develop in uneasy parallels. Such an emphasis was anticipated by the England volume of James Fenimore Cooper's (1789–1851) *Gleanings in Europe,* an account published in 1837 of a trip he had undertaken nine years earlier. In this work Cooper critiques the British ruling classes by arguing that colonial dependencies are essential to the maintenance of English authority—otherwise "she would sink to a second-rate power in twenty years" (p. 257). He comments also on the general ignorance among the English population about American conditions, recollecting how he talked to a man who insisted that "the winters are too long in America to keep sheep" (p. 254), despite the fact that there were at that time, Cooper says, three and a half million sheep in New York state alone. Paradoxically, though, such misunderstandings create breaches that Cooper welcomes, since he wishes to correct the general American tendency to pay too much heed to English views and thus to free Americans from the "mental dependence created by colonial subserviency" (p. 233).

What is interesting here is the way in which Cooper sees America as engaged in a postcolonial struggle with the specters of British cultural authority. Whereas Emerson's lecture "The American Scholar," also published in 1837, is characteristically abstract, representing freedom and self-determination as philosophical necessities, Cooper's treatise is more attuned to the social and material conditions that brought about increased tensions between Britain and the United States in the early nineteenth century. Cooper mentions the War of 1812 as a lingering source of antipathy between the two countries, and he also remarks on British unease at the growing political power of the United States. If the critical direction of Matthiessen's *American Renaissance,* drawing its impetus from an imagined organic unity in the native culture, was inspired by the spirit of Emerson, it might not be too much of an exaggeration to suggest that recent accounts of interactions between British and American literature in the nineteenth century—from John Carlos Rowe, Susan Manning, and others—have taken their cue more from the method of Cooper, with its emphasis on ways in which the national symbolic forms of the United States were shaped both domestically and internationally by a variety of historical circumstances.

See also American English; Americans Abroad; Book Publishing; Democracy; Literary Criticism; Literary Nationalism; Taste; Tourism; Travel Writing; Young America

BIBLIOGRAPHY

Primary Works

Clough, Arthur Hugh. *The Correspondence of Arthur Hugh Clough.* Edited by Frederick L. Mulhauser. 2 vols. Oxford: Clarendon Press, 1957.

Cooper, James Fenimore. *Gleanings in Europe: England.* 1837. Edited by Donald A. Ringe and Kenneth W. Staggs. Albany: State University of New York Press, 1982.

Dickens, Charles. *American Notes for General Circulation.* 1842. Edited by John S. Whitley and Arnold Goldman. Harmondsworth, U.K.: Penguin, 1972.

Dickens, Charles. *Dickens on America and the Americans.* Edited by Michael Slater. Sussex, U.K.: Harvester Press, 1979.

Dickens, Charles. *The Life and Adventures of Martin Chuzzlewit.* 1843–1844. Edited by Patricia Ingham. London: Penguin, 1999.

Emerson, Ralph Waldo. "The American Scholar." 1837. In *The Collected Works of Ralph Waldo Emerson,* vol. 1, Nature, *Addresses, and Lectures,* edited by Alfred R. Ferguson, pp. 49–70. Cambridge, Mass.: Harvard University Press, 1971.

Emerson, Ralph Waldo. *English Traits.* 1856. Edited by Douglas Emory Wilson. Vol. 5 of *The Collected Works of Ralph Waldo Emerson.* Cambridge, Mass.: Harvard University Press, 1994.

Emerson, Ralph Waldo. *The Journals and Miscellaneous Notebooks.* 16 vols. Edited by William H. Gilman et al. Cambridge, Mass.: Harvard University Press, 1960–1982.

Hall, Basil. *Travels in North America, in the Years 1827 and 1828.* 3 vols. Edinburgh: Cadell, 1829.

Slater, Joseph, ed. *The Correspondence of Emerson and Carlyle.* New York: Columbia University Press, 1964.

Trollope, Anthony. *North America.* 1862. Edited by Donald Smalley and Bradford Allen Booth. New York: Knopf, 1951.

Trollope, Frances. *Domestic Manners of the Americans.* 1832. Edited by Pamela Neville-Sington. London: Penguin, 1997.

Secondary Works

Buell, Lawrence. "American Literary Emergence as a Postcolonial Phenomenon." *American Literary History* 4, no. 3 (1992): 411–442.

Dekker, George. *The American Historical Romance.* Cambridge, U.K.: Cambridge University Press, 1987.

Giles, Paul. *Transatlantic Insurrections: British Culture and the Formation of American Literature, 1730–1860.* Philadelphia: University of Pennsylvania Press, 2001.

Gravil, Richard. *Romantic Dialogues: Anglo-American Continuities, 1776–1862.* New York: St. Martin's, 2000.

Grey, Robin. *The Complicity of Imagination: The American Renaissance, Contests of Authority, and Seventeenth-Century English Culture.* Cambridge, U.K.: Cambridge University Press, 1997.

Kasson, Joy S. *Artistic Voyagers: Europe and the American Imagination in the Works of Irving, Allston, Cole, Cooper, and Hawthorne.* Westport, Conn.: Greenwood Press, 1982.

Lease, Benjamin. *Anglo-American Encounters: England and the Rise of American Literature.* Cambridge, U.K.: Cambridge University Press, 1981.

Manning, Susan. *The Puritan-Provincial Vision: Scottish and American Literature in the Nineteenth Century.* Cambridge, U.K.: Cambridge University Press, 1990.

Matthiessen, F. O. *American Renaissance: Art and Expression in the Age of Emerson and Whitman.* New York: Oxford University Press, 1941.

Mulvey, Christopher. *Anglo-American Landscapes: A Study of Nineteenth-Century Anglo-American Travel Literature.* Cambridge, U.K.: Cambridge University Press, 1983.

Mulvey, Christopher. *Transatlantic Manners: Social Patterns in Nineteenth-Century Anglo-American Travel Literature.* Cambridge, U.K.: Cambridge University Press, 1990.

Nevins, Allan, ed. *America through British Eyes.* New York: Oxford University Press, 1948.

Peach, Linden. *British Influence on the Birth of American Literature.* London: Macmillan, 1982.

Rowe, John Carlos. *Literary Culture and U.S. Imperialism: From the Revolution to World War II.* Oxford: Oxford University Press, 2000.

Weisbuch, Robert. *Atlantic Double-Cross: American Literature and British Influence in the Age of Emerson.* Chicago: University of Chicago Press, 1986.

Widmer, Edward L. *Young America: The Flowering of Democracy in New York City.* New York: Oxford University Press, 1999.

Paul Giles

ETHNOLOGY

Today the term "ethnology" refers to cultural anthropology, the comparative and analytical study of cultures. However, the term in nineteenth-century parlance was much more comprehensive. A branch of the natural sciences, ethnology dealt with the division of humans into races as well as their origin, distribution, relations, and characteristics.

Ethnology, or the "natural history of man" as it was called, was in its formative stage during the antebellum period. Its roots were in Europe with the work of the German physiologist Johann Friedrich Blumenbach (1752–1840), who divided humans anatomically into five main races. Nineteenth-century American ethnologists approached their subjects in one of two ways: one approach focused on cultural aspects, particularly language, traditions, and material culture; and the other addressed the biological disparities in humans, principally bone structure, size, and skin color. The respective findings had differing implications for understanding the origin and relationship of the races. The first group, the "environmentalists," attributed racial differences to climatic and other environmental forces. The other camp concluded that the races were so physically different that they could not

possibly have originated as biblically described and therefore each race must have had a separate origin.

Politically, some ethnological findings provided "scientific" justification for slavery, particularly as new states were entering the Union and their status as a slave or free state needed to be defined, and for the treatment of some Native American tribes—their removal, subjugation, and decimation. However, the ethnological implications went beyond these debates to questions of whether the human species was divided into superior and inferior races and whether the account of creation in Genesis was accurate.

This new science of race found an interested American public and became part of the antebellum cultural climate. Ideas derived from ethnological studies—racial theories, Native American tales, excavation reports, missionary descriptions, travel narratives—found an eager audience. They were disseminated in newspapers, magazines, reviews, lectures, governmental reports, and works of fiction and poetry. For many literary writers, the scientific findings and dialogues emerging from ethnology became the creative impetus for popular and canonical works.

CULTURAL APPROACHES TO ETHNOLOGY

Disease, relocation, and extermination of Native Americans created a sense of urgency in many antebellum Americans to record tribes' rapidly disappearing cultures. Albert Gallatin (1761–1849), a statesman and diplomat, began collecting tribal vocabularies in the 1820s and, once retired, devoted himself full-time to philology. In 1826 Gallatin created the first tribal language map and became the first to designate language groups by a comparative method. *A Synopsis of the Indian Tribes . . . in North America* (1836) established him as America's leading ethnologist. His classification of North American Indian languages is the basis on which all later classifications of these languages rely. A product of the Enlightenment and a proponent of the environmental approach, he believed that if Native Americans moved to a more agrarian life, they would advance to a civilized station. Meetings of the New-York Historical Society, of which he was president, served as a forum for papers on Native Americans, thereby encouraging an academic interest. Gallatin also formed the American Ethnological Society in 1842 and served as its president.

Another prominent ethnologist, Lewis Henry Morgan (1818–1881), an attorney by profession, began to research the organization of the Iroquois League in order to duplicate its structure for a secret organization that he had joined. In Albany, New York, he interviewed Tonawanda Seneca chiefs and later visited the Tonawanda reservation for observation in 1845. His interests began with understanding the government and institutions of the Iroquois League and then turned to linguistics, particularly kinship terminology. The fruits of his labor were a series of essays, some delivered as papers at the secret society's chapter meetings and at the New-York Historical Society and published in *The American Review* in 1847. Collected, these essays became the *League of the Ho-de-no-sau-nee, or Iroquois* (1851), still widely read and considered one of the best descriptions of Iroquois society and culture. His later work, *Systems of Consanguinity and Affinity of the Human Family* (1870), created analytical tools that form the basis of modern kinship studies; previously these relationships had been described inaccurately in feudalistic terms.

Henry Rowe Schoolcraft (1793–1864), who spent thirty years with Native Americans, much of it as an Indian agent, recorded the myths, language, and narratives of the Chippewa and other northern tribes, as well as collecting reports from other sources. His wife Jane, the granddaughter of a Chippewa chief, no doubt provided him access and insight into the language and culture. His six-volume *Historical and Statistical Information Respecting the History, Condition and Prospects of the Indian Tribes of the United States* (1851–1857) and two-volume *Algic Researches* (1839) made him an authority on Native Americans at mid-century. Schoolcraft's Anglo-American ethnocentrism, however, clouded his conclusions, such that, as one scholar describes, "the very data his monumental studies provide frequently refute his conclusions" (Mitchell, p. 168). Schoolcraft assumed the cultural and intellectual superiority of the Caucasian race and the eventual subjugation and destruction of the Native American race.

This urgency to preserve Native American cultures before they transformed or completely disappeared spurred amateur collectors by the 1820s, as Lee Clark Mitchell has described. Many self-taught linguists who assembled vocabularies were frontiersmen, boundary commissioners, army personnel, missionaries, and doctors. For example, the Reverend Stephen R. Riggs compiled a series of grammars and vocabularies of northern Plains tribes, published in the 1840s. By the 1840s collectors more commonly recorded the legends and poems of tribes, such as Mary Henderson Eastman's (1880–1887) collection of Dakota Sioux myths. Local societies and museums sprouted up between 1830 and 1880, often as a last effort to preserve disappearing native materials. The underlying assumption, fueled by observation, documentation, and scientific "proof," was the decline and impending extinction of the Native American race.

RACIAL THEORIZING AND STEREOTYPING: THE AMERICAN SCHOOL

Perhaps the most infamous aspect of nineteenth-century ethnology was the "scientific" findings of the American School, which unlike other ethnological theories, posited separate creations for the races, or polygeny. Rather than looking for cultural affinities among peoples, these researchers looked for biological disparities. They built upon the German physiologist Johann Friedrich Blumenbach's cranial classification of the human species into five races: Asian, Aboriginal Indian, Caucasian, Malayan, and Ethiopian. In addition, phrenology, a pseudoscience popular in antebellum America, spread the idea that the shape of the head reflected a person's temperament and moral and intellectual aptitude. Phrenological studies interested intellectuals in the 1820s and were popularized by mid-century. For a set fee one could visit a phrenological establishment, have his or her head read, and receive a phrenological handbook. While the results of the studies were received in the spirit of fun and/or with skepticism, they did serve to proliferate the idea of inherent racial differences. In fact, the December 1850 issue of the *American Whig Review* described Blumenbach's five racial categories: "these have been too trivialized by our phrenological hornbooks to need repetition in this place. Who has not heard of the Caucasian, Ethiopian, Mongolian, Malayan, and American races?" (Horsman, p. 142).

The Philadelphia physician Samuel G. Morton (1799–1851) looked to bone structure for dividing and characterizing humans. Influenced by phrenological studies and Blumenbach's cranial classifications, Morton worked under the assumption that the larger the cranium, the larger the brain, and therefore the greater the intelligence. In fact, Morton includes an essay by the British phrenologist and lecturer George Combe as the appendix to his magnum opus *Crania Americana; or, A Comparative View of the Skulls of Various Aboriginal Nations of North and South America* (1839). In this text, which provided the groundwork for what would become the American School, Morton documents his research of four hundred Native American skulls. He measured internal capacity by filling the skulls with white pepper seed and submitted the skulls to an additional twelve measurements such as longitudinal diameter, horizontal periphery, and facial angles. The book's charts of measurements and lithograph drawings of skulls created the illusion of objectivity and provided the facts for others to use in more overtly political ways. By measuring and comparing ancient and relatively contemporary skulls, Morton concluded that types of races had not changed over the years and thus must have been created separately: "we are left to the reasonable conclusion, that each Race was adapted from the beginning to its peculiar local destination. In other words, it is assumed, that the physical characteristics which distinguish the different Races, are independent of external causes" (p. 3). Morton does not comment directly on the unity or multiplicity of the species; he leaves that for others.

While the explicit racism of Morton's ideas is striking to modern readers, the religious heresy of a separate creation for each race shocked contemporaries. Blumenbach, within the tradition of Enlightenment optimism, believed in the unity of the races of man. One creation for all races was consistent with biblical teachings and with the humanist belief of a Golden Age, a mythical era of peace and prosperity. However, Morton's research showed little difference between ancient and modern skulls. The data from Egyptian monuments, presented in his second book *Crania Aegyptica* (1844), suggested distinct races a short time after the commonly accepted date of the flood, calculated by Archbishop Ussher as 2348 B.C.E. This date left no time for the racial adaptation to climate argued by the environmentalists; therefore, each race must have had a separate origin. Polygenesis was the first American scientific theory to win respect in European circles, thus its name, the American School. This "scientific" refutation of biblical accuracy incited great consternation and was not universally well received in the South, although it provided scientific justification for slavery, as the historian Thomas E. Will has discussed.

Samuel Morton's Crania Americana *provided the groundwork for the American School. While this work does not explicitly state that each race has its own creation, Dr. Morton does argue that races are distinct and adapted to their particular locality from the start; in addition, external circumstances have not affected them. In the essay that begins the book, Morton employs Blumenbach's classification of five races. He then divides humans into twenty-two families, again skirting the issue of separate species. The American Family described below, also called "the barbarous tribes of North America," comprises most of the North American Indians. Here, Morton describes their intellect:*

The intellectual faculties of this great family appear to be of a decidedly inferior cast when compared with those of the Caucasian or Mongolian races. They are not only averse to the restraints of education, but for the most part incapable of a continued process of reasoning on abstract subjects. Their minds seize with avidity on simple truths, while they at once reject whatever requires investigation and analysis. Their proximity, for more than two centuries, to European institutions, has made scarcely any appreciable change in their mode of thinking or their manner of life; and as to their own social condition, they are probably in most respects what they were at the primitive epoch of their existence. They have made few or no improvements in building their houses or their boats; their inventive and imitative faculties appear to be of a very humble grade, nor have they the smallest predilection for the arts or sciences. The long annals of missionary labor and private benefaction bestowed upon them, offer but very few exceptions to the preceding statement, which, on the contrary, is sustained by the combined testimony of almost all practical observers. Even in cases where they have received an ample education, and have remained for many years in civilized society, they lose none of their innate love of their own national usages, which they have almost invariably resumed when chance has left them to choose for themselves. Such has been the experience of the Spanish and Portuguese missionaries in South America, and of the English and their descendants in the northern portion of the continent.

However much the benevolent mind may regret the inaptitude of the Indian for civilization, the affirmative of this question seems to be established beyond a doubt. His moral and physical nature are alike adapted to his position among the races of men, and it is as reasonable to expect the one to be changed as the other. The structure of his mind appears to be different from that of the white man, nor can the two harmonise in their social relations except on the most limited scale. Every one knows, however, that the mind expands by culture; nor can we yet tell how near the Indian would approach the Caucasian after education had been bestowed on a single family through several successive generations.

Morton, *Crania Americana*, pp. 81–82.

Other notable proponents of the American School were Ephraim G. Squier, Louis Agassiz, George Gliddon, and Josiah C. Nott. The latter two popularized Morton's ideas in their books *Types of Mankind* (1854) and *The Indigenous Races of the Earth* (1857). George Gliddon (1809–1857), an Englishman, a former United States vice-consul to Egypt, and a supplier of skulls for Morton, was considered a leading Egyptologist. A flamboyant and popular lecturer, he was a prolific disseminator of the American School's theories, particularly the thesis of Morton's *Aegyptica:* the Egyptians who had built the pyramids were white-skinned and slaves were black-skinned even at that point in history. Josiah C. Nott (1804–1873), a physician from Mobile, Alabama, built upon Morton's work. For example, he credits his personal observations in medicine as "evidence" for the lecture "The Mulatto a Hybrid—Probable Extermination of the Two Races if the Whites and Blacks are Allowed to Intermarry" (1843), which was published in the reputable *American Journal of the Medical Sciences.* While this and other writings attempt to justify slavery, part of Nott's motivations seem to be to taunt the clergy, whom he calls "skunks" in personal correspondence. In *Two Lectures, on the Natural History of the Caucasian and Negro Races* (1844) he argues that the human race must have been descended from many different original pairs.

Another advocate of the American School, Ephraim G. Squier (1821–1888), began his career as a journalist. He introduces and promotes ethnology as "essentially the science of the age" in an article published in *The American Review* (p. 385). Squier asks,

> Do we desire to discover the results which must follow from the blending of men of different races and families? Do we inquire in what consists the superiority of certain families over others; to what extent they may assimilate with, to what repel each other, and how their relations may be adjusted so as to produce the greatest attainable advantage to both? (P. 386)

He responds that America is the ideal place for this study because of its three races living in close proximity. Squier moved to Ohio to begin a newspaper and excavated and wrote about the Native American earthworks that he found in the Mississippi Valley. From tree rings, which he dated as more than eight hundred years old, Squier concluded, "we are compelled to assign them [the earthworks] no inconsiderable antiquity" (Will, p. 26). While not stated explicitly, the evidence of Native Americans in ancient times cast doubt upon the likelihood that all races originated from one pair. But because his anthropological project *Ancient Monuments of the Mississippi Valley* (1848)

was funded by the Smithsonian, Squier was forced to focus on his findings and reign in his speculations on multiple origins.

Louis Agassiz (1807–1873), the renowned Swiss-trained biologist who taught at Harvard, embraced the theory of polygeny. The idea of separate creations of races worked well with his own argument that animal species lived in the distinct provinces in which they had been created. He applied his theory of geographical distribution to race and set forth his argument in three articles (1850–1851) for the Unitarian *Christian Examiner.* The second, "The Diversity of Origin of Human Races," argues that racial distinctions existed from the very beginning—that "an intelligent Creator" adapted each race to its particular locality. Agassiz's support gave credibility and authority to the American School.

Early in the nineteenth century the prevailing racial theory postulated that environmental forces, particularly climate, caused racial differences. By mid-century, the influence of the American School was so pervasive that the April 1850 issue of the *United States Democratic Review* could declare, no doubt with exaggeration, "few or none now seriously adhere to the theory of the *unity* of the races" (Will, p. 28). It would not be until Charles Darwin's *On the Origin of Species* (1859) that the idea of species as always changing would end the reign of the American School.

THE SLAVERY DEBATE

Ethnology provided a justification for slavery at a time when territories were entering the Union and their status as a slave or free state needed to be defined. When Secretary of State John C. Calhoun asked Gliddon in 1844 for scientific justification for slavery, Gliddon readily supplied Morton's *Crania Americana* and *Crania Aegyptica* and several pamphlets of his own. It was just this sort of "scientific" attack upon African Americans that Frederick Douglass (1818–1895) targeted in a commencement address entitled "The Claims of the Negro, Ethnologically Considered" in 1854. He asserted that "the debates in Congress on the Nebraska Bill during the past winter, will show how slaveholders have availed themselves of this doctrine [multiple creations] in support of slaveholding. There is no doubt that the Messrs. Nott, Glidden [*sic*], Morton, Smith and Agassiz were duly consulted by our slavery propagating statesmen" (p. 16). Indicting the subjective nature of the American School's findings, Douglass comments,

> Indeed, ninety-nine out of every hundred of the advocates of a diverse origin of the human family in

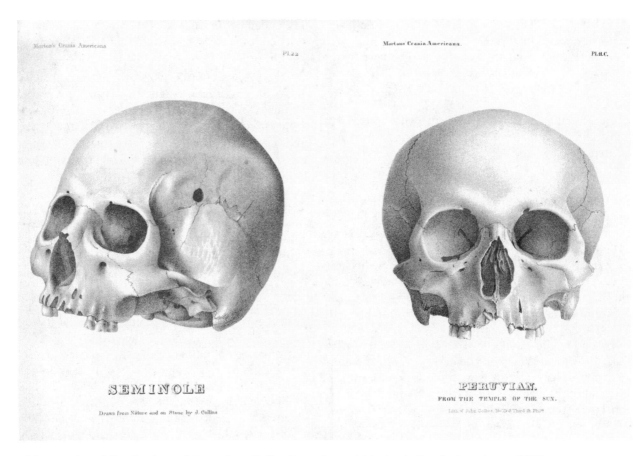

Lithographs of Seminole and Peruvian skulls. From Samuel Morton's *Crania Americana*, 1839. CRANIA AMERICANA, SPECIAL COLLECTIONS, UNIVERSITY OF VIRGINIA LIBRARY.

this country, [who] are among those who hold it to be the privilege of the *Anglo-Saxon* to enslave and oppress the African—and slaveholders . . . have admitted, that the whole argument in defence of slavery, becomes utterly worthless the moment the African is proved to be equally a man with the Anglo-Saxon. The temptation, therefore, to read the negro out of the human family is exceedingly strong, and may account somewhat for the repeated attempts on the part of Southern pretenders to science, to cast a doubt over the Scriptural account of the origin of mankind. . . . Pride and selfishness, combined with mental power, never want for a theory to justify them—and when men oppress their fellow-men, the oppressor ever finds, in the character of the oppressed, a full justification for his oppression. (Pp. 14–15)

Douglass refutes the charges of the American School by first noting scriptural authority, particularly the Bible's account of the origin of humans, and then taking Morton to task, showing his "contempt for Negroes" in his argument to prove ancient Egyptians as distinct from Negroes and for claiming ancient

Egyptians as Caucasian. Douglass's rebuttal uses historical physical descriptions and contemporary philological sources to show "a strong affinity and a direct relationship" between Africans and Egyptians. He goes on to argue that "outward circumstance" (environmentalism) affects physical attributes, noting the similarity between poor Irish and plantation slaves: "The open, uneducated mouth—the long, gaunt arm—the badly formed foot and ankle—the shuffling gait—the retreating forehead and vacant expression—and, their petty quarrels and fights—all reminded me of the plantation, and my own cruelly abused people" (p. 30).

THE INFLUENCE OF ETHNOLOGY ON POPULAR AND CANONICAL WORKS

The American public learned about ethnology from a variety of sources: amateur studies of tribes, governmental reports, philological papers, captivity narratives, excavation reports, as well as popular lectures like Gliddon's Egyptian series. These findings, often scientific in nature, were discussed in articles in newspapers, magazines, and reviews, part of the hub and buzz of daily life. They provided for many contemporary writers subject matter and a creative impetus.

For example, James Fenimore Cooper (1789–1851) found within the Moravian missionary John Heckewelder's *Account of the History, Manners, and Customs of the Indian Nations, Who Once Inhabited Pennsylvania and the Neighboring States* (1819) material on which to base the characterization of the Native Americans in his Leatherstocking Tales (1823–1841). Heckewelder lived with the Delaware Indians, described them sympathetically, and "accepted their national prejudices," according to the historian and anthropologist Paul A. W. Wallace (p. 426). One prejudice, since found unsubstantiated, was against the Iroquois, who supposedly deceived the Delaware into accepting peace and then incited their enemies to attack. Within the novels, Cooper constructs a dichotomy: the perfidious Iroquois versus the noble Delaware. Pathfinder (Leatherstocking) says, "Iroquois—devil—Mingoes—Mengwes, or furies . . . all are pretty much the same. I call all rascals Mingoes" (Wallace, p. 427). Throughout his five-book series, Cooper characterizes the Mingoes (Iroquois) as consistently malign and treacherous, whereas the Delaware Indians Chingachgook and his son Uncas are noble and sympathetic. In *The Pioneers* (1823), Cooper's portrayal of Old Indian John (Chingachgook) as drunk, tragic, and proud—a symbol of a people destined for extinction as white settlements moved in—reflected the overriding assumptions of the day.

While Cooper worked to represent Native Americans with fidelity, Henry Wadsworth Longfellow (1807–1882) was not so concerned with authenticity in *The Song of Hiawatha* (1855). Drawing from Schoolcraft's retelling of Algonquin legends in *Algic Researches,* he substitutes an Iroquois name for the hero Manabozho and modifies and consolidates several stories. Longfellow employs a Finnish epic's meter to suggest the tom-tom beat. The poem concludes with the hero Hiawatha canoeing westward into the setting sun after encouraging his people to welcome European missionaries. Like Cooper, Longfellow celebrates the Indian culture while romanticizing its destruction. *The Song of Hiawatha* was hugely successful, selling eleven thousand copies its first month and thirty thousand in its first five months. It was performed, set to music, extensively reviewed, and parodied. Longfellow's poem is perhaps the best example of the flood of romantic adaptations of Native American tales in the form of poems, novels, plays, and even operas. By mid-century, Native American legends and sentimental poems were staples of periodical literature.

Some writers, however, were consciously trying to document the state and culture of Native American tribes. In 1849 the novelist, magazine editor, and cultural critic Caroline Kirkland (1801–1864) suggested the motivation behind many of these studies:

> We are continually reproached by British writers for the obtuse carelessness with which we are allowing these people [Native Americans], with so much of the heroic element in their lives, and so much of the mysterious in their origin, to go into the annihilation which seems their inevitable fate as civilization advances, without an effort to secure and record all that they are able to communicate respecting themselves. (P. viii)

Amateur ethnographers were documenting vocabularies and stories of tribes, often with great urgency. Mary Eastman's *Dahcotah; or, Life and Legends of the Sioux around Fort Snelling* (1849), in the preface of which Kirkland laments the loss of Native American culture, is one such example.

Henry David Thoreau (1817–1862), too, may be classified as an amateur ethnologist, as he was scouting the Concord environs for Native American arrowheads, pottery shards, and other material culture and researching Native Americans through his voluminous readings. His unpublished Indian Notebooks are twenty-eight hundred manuscript pages filled with excerpts. Seeking firsthand interaction, Thoreau traveled to northern central Maine partly to learn about the Penobscot Indians who still lived and hunted there. He described the trips undertaken in 1846, 1853, and 1857 in three travel essays, posthumously compiled as *The Maine Woods* (1864). These accounts reveal his increasing understanding of native peoples. In his first essay, he described the Penobscot Indians as "sinister and slouching fellows" (p. 78) and as an "ancient and primitive man" soon to be extinct (p. 79). By his third trip and essay, "The Allegash and East Branch," he was more sympathetic toward an acculturated Native American in need of formal education to protect his interests.

Some writers were also addressing and questioning the scientific categorization of the races. Nathaniel Hawthorne's (1804–1864) *The Marble Faun* (1860) entered into the debate regarding the separation of the races, as Michael Louis Merrill has demonstrated. Hawthorne created mystery over the racial composition of certain protagonists. After visiting a Cuvier-inspired exhibit of ethnology at the British Museum, Hawthorne wrote in the *English Notebooks* (1856), "I care little for the varieties of the human race, all that is really important and interesting being found in our own variety" (p. 440). However, he felt compelled to ask readers, in a conclusion after the novel's initial publication, not to spoil the merging of "the real and the fantastic" by demanding to know "how Cuvier would have classified poor Donatello" (Merrill, p. 80). While the racial composition of a faun might seem ridiculous, Kenyon, the novel's expert on race who classifies who is or is not "Anglo-Saxon," asserts that Donatello is an atavism, or racial throwback, and his race is Pelasgic (p. 82). Within the family tree charting the development of races, the Pelasgic race, according to polygenesists, eventually became the modern Caucasian race. However, Donatello's dark complexion and curly hair suggest a passing mulatto in nineteenth-century texts. Hawthorne describes the Praxiteles' fawn that Donatello strikingly resembles: "Neither man nor animal and yet no monster, but a being in whom both races meet on friendly grounds" (Merrill, p. 86). Hawthorne's use of sculpture in the novel is suggestive in that the visual arts were used in the race debates; in fact Frederick Douglass once warned, perhaps facetiously, foreign artists to shield their "every specimen of ancient and modern arts that is chiseled or cast in black" for fear of defacement (Merrill, p. 68).

Contemporary debates on race appeared in southern antebellum literature. Defenders of slavery and the southern way of life responded to Harriet Beecher Stowe's *Uncle Tom's Cabin; or, Life among the Lowly* (1852) with more than twenty novels. As part of their defense, they incorporated existing "research" and assumptions. For example, Mary Eastman's *Aunt Phillis's Cabin; or, Southern Life As It Is* (1852) portrays the security and happiness of slaves on a Virginia plantation and contrasts that scene with escaped slaves exploited in low-paying jobs after being goaded into running away by abolitionists. These escaped slaves, Eastman suggests, do not have the skills and intelligence needed to take care of themselves. In characterizing the title figure, Eastman includes a passage from the popular travel writer Bayard Taylor:

> Those friends of the African race, who point to Egypt as a proof of what that race has done, are wholly mistaken. The only negro features represented in Egyptian sculpture are those of the slaves and captives taken in the Ethiopian wars of the Pharaohs. The temples and pyramids throughout Nubia, as far as Abyssinia, all bear the hieroglyphics of these monarchs. There is no evidence in all the valley of the Nile that the negro race ever attained a higher degree of civilization than is at present exhibited in Congo and Ashantee. I mention this, not from any feeling hostile to that race, but simply to controvert an opinion very prevalent in some parts of the United States. (P. 103)

This assertion that the darker-skinned race was enslaved in ancient Egypt and could not be credited

with a sophisticated civilization is one of many arguments that Eastman wove through her plot. The eponymous Aunt Phillis is lauded greatly for her loyalty to the Weston family; not surprisingly Eastman characterizes her as a mulatto, explaining that "the blood of the freeman and the slave mingled in her veins" (p. 103). In other antebellum novels, this mixing of blood, or miscegenation, could be explosive and sensational, as the critic Janet Gabler-Hover has examined in her study of the figure Hagar. Hagar's ethnic ambiguity allowed white writers to psychologically appropriate blackness with all its cultural baggage while the "pure blood" of their heroines is challenged or compromised.

Research on supposed inherent racial differences and the ensuing debates—as well as philological papers, excavation reports, missionary descriptions, Native American tales, and fieldwork—shaped the popular and literary depictions of the "other" in antebellum America. An understanding of this new science of ethnology, which "proved" the superiority of Caucasians, and of its influence on the culture provides a historical context for race and thereby enables readers to view antebellum texts with greater insight.

See also Abolitionist Writing; Blacks; Indians; Leatherstocking Tales; Popular Science; Proslavery Writing; Science; Slavery

BIBLIOGRAPHY
Primary Works

Douglass, Frederick. "The Claims of the Negro, Ethnologically Considered: An Address Before the Literary Societies of Western Reserve College, at Commencement, July 12, 1854." Rochester, N.Y.: Lee, Mann and Company, Daily American Office, 1854. Library of Congress, Slavery to Freedom: The African-American Pamphlet Collection, 1822–1909, available at http://memory.loc.gov.

Eastman, Mary Henderson. *Aunt Phillis's Cabin; or, Southern Life As It Is.* Philadelphia: Lippincott, Grambo and Company, 1852. University of Virginia Digital Library, Uncle Tom's Cabin and American Culture, available at http://www.iath.virginia.edu/utc/proslav/eastmanhp.html.

Kirkland, Caroline M. Preface to *Dahcotah; or, Life and legends of the Sioux around Fort Snelling,* by Mary Henderson Eastman, pp. v–xi. New York: John Wiley, 1849.

Hawthorne, Nathaniel. *English Notebooks.* 1856. Edited by Thomas Woodson and Bill Ellis. Ohio: Ohio University Press, 1997.

Morton, Samuel George. *Crania Americana; or, A Comparative View of the Skulls of Various Aboriginal*

Nations of North and South America. Philadelphia: J. Dobson, 1839.

Nott, Josiah C. *Two Lectures on the Natural History of Caucasian and Negro Races.* Mobile, Ala.: Dade and Thompson, 1844.

Squier, Ephraim G. "American Ethnology." *The American Review* 16 (April 1849): 385–398.

Thoreau, Henry David. *The Maine Woods.* 1864. Princeton, N.J.: Princeton University Press, 1972, 1983.

Secondary Works

Bieder, Robert E. *Science Encounters the Indian, 1820–1880: The Early Years of American Ethnology.* Norman: University of Oklahoma Press, 1986.

Gabler-Hover, Janet. *Dreaming Black/Writing White: The Hagar Myth in American Cultural History.* Lexington: University Press of Kentucky, 2000.

Horsman, Reginald. *Race and Manifest Destiny: The Origins of American Racial Anglo-Saxonism.* Cambridge, Mass.: Harvard University Press, 1981.

Merrill, Michael Louis. "Race and Romance: Ethnology, Eugenics and the Evolution of the Nineteenth Century Novel." Ph.D. diss., University of California, Los Angeles, 1994.

Mitchell, Lee Clark. *Witnesses to a Vanishing America: The Nineteenth-Century Response.* Princeton, N.J.: Princeton University Press, 1981.

Stanton, William. *The Leopard's Spots: Scientific Attitudes toward Race in America 1815–59.* Chicago: University of Chicago Press, 1960.

Wallace, Paul A. W. "Cooper's Indians." In "James Fenimore Cooper: A Re-Appraisal," special issue, *New York History* 35 (1954): 423–446.

Will, Thomas E. "The American School of Ethnology: Science and Scripture in the Proslavery Argument." *The Southern Historian* 19 (1998): 14–34.

Kelli M. Olson

EVANGELICALS

Evangelical Protestants exerted an enormous cultural influence in nineteenth-century America. In 1791 the population totaled four million, 5 to 10 percent of whom, or less than 400,000, joined any church. By 1870, 40 million people inhabited the United States, 20 percent of whom, or more than eight million, were evangelicals. Methodists and Baptists outnumbered every other denomination, together accounting for two-thirds of Protestants.

The term "evangelical" originates in the Bible, translated from the Greek *euaggellion* and the Anglo-Saxon *godspel,* meaning good news of salvation from sin through faith in the atoning death and resurrection of Jesus Christ. The so-called Great Commission, "Go ye into all the world, and preach the gospel to every creature" (Mark 16:15 KJV), has inspired generations of Christians with confidence in the power of language to transform the world. Protestants first called themselves evangelicals during the Reformation, when Martin Luther's (1483–1546) followers in Germany adopted the name Evangelische Kirche, or Evangelical Church. In addition to his famed ninety-five theses, Luther circulated sermons, tracts, hymns, and broadsides to communicate the gospel.

The name "evangelical" developed a more restrictive meaning during the Great Awakening of the mid-eighteenth century. Self-proclaimed evangelicals reserved the label, which had earlier referred to all Protestants, for a subset of church adherents they approved. Evangelicals distinguished themselves from high church traditionalists, whom they accused of relying on the sacraments instead of the gospel, and from rationalist liberals, whom they charged with denying the gospel's power. Transatlantic revivalists like George Whitefield (1714–1770) and John Wesley (1703–1791) wrote or republished hundreds of periodicals, tracts, books, and hymns to reinforce their preaching. A subsequent wave of revivals, the Second Great Awakening, reached its peak in the 1830s. These revivals stimulated the formation of moral reform societies, many of which employed the press to gain adherents.

Scholars typically emphasize individual conversion as the apex of evangelical experience. Yet conversion marked the first step in a lifelong, communal pilgrimage toward holiness or sanctification, as Christians progressively modeled their lives after Christ's. Printed texts—both those traditionally classed as literature and a much wider array of sermons, histories, memoirs, gift books, Sunday school libraries, periodicals, and hymnals—played a critical role in sustaining and transmitting evangelical values both within evangelical communities and across American culture as a whole.

EVANGELICAL DENOMINATIONS

By the mid-nineteenth century most American Protestants thought of themselves as evangelicals but no less often described themselves as members of a denomination. According to denominational theory, one Christian Church divided into multiple branches, each of which contributed to the growth of the whole. The establishment clause of the First Amendment (1791) prohibited Congress from supporting any particular denomination; every state followed suit in formally disestablishing religion by 1833. Under a new voluntary

A revival meeting, c. 1850. Painting by Jeremiah Paul. Outdoor meetings where sermons were given and converts encouraged were a favored forum for evangelism during the nineteenth and early twentieth centuries. The often animated style of preaching and dramatic behavior of attendees, who often wept, fainted, spoke in tongues, or otherwise reflected spiritual ecstasy, became the hallmarks of such meetings in the popular conception. THE ART ARCHIVE / PRIVATE COLLECTION / LAURIE PLATT WINFREY

principle, denominations developed into fuller institutional dimension in the United States than in Europe.

Evangelical and denominational identities blossomed simultaneously and in tension. Denominational rivalries cut across the shared fabric of evangelicalism, generating fierce polemics around issues such as baptism and free will. Simultaneously, many Protestants hoped that interdenominational unity would hasten the millennium, or thousand-year period prefatory to Christ's Second Coming. More than fifty American and European denominations sent representatives to the first meeting of the Evangelical Alliance, held in London in 1846; an American branch formed in 1867. The alliance promoted fellowship, cooperation, and prayer for united action against the forces opposing evangelical religion—enumerated by the convention as Roman Catholicism, ignorance, strong drink, and an irreligious press.

Evangelical denominations, despite biting antagonisms toward one another, strove to form a united front against common opponents, including Catholics, liberal Protestants, and other sects perceived as unevangelical. Robert Baird (1798–1863), a spokesperson for Presbyterianism and for the nondenominational American Bible Society, American Sunday-School Union, and Evangelical Alliance, used his influential history *Religion in America; or, An Account of the Origin, Progress, Relation to the State, and Present Condition of the Evangelical Churches in the United States, with Notices of the Unevangelical Denominations* (1844) to solidify popular perceptions of difference between what he termed evangelical and unevangelical denominations. According to Baird, evangelicals, those who recognized "Christ as common head," included Protestant Episcopal churches, Congregationalists, Baptists, Presbyterians, German and Dutch Reformed, Methodists, Moravians, Lutherans, United Brethren, Winebrennarians, Mennonists, Quakers, and Baird added "with much hesitation," Disciples (p. 251).

Baird similarly compiled a list of unevangelical denominations, which he defined as those "not ranked with those for whom the whole Bible and only the Bible is a foundation" (p. 270). Although recognizing that not all unevangelical churches shared the "same footing," Baird listed together Roman Catholics, Unitarians, the Christian Connection, Universalists, Swedenborgians, Dunkers, Jews, Rappists, Shakers, Mormons, Atheists, Deists, Socialists, and Fourierists. Not everyone would have compiled the same lists, but Baird's division of the religious world into evangelical and unevangelical segments reflected and perpetuated a perception widely held by self-identified evangelicals.

EVANGELICAL USES OF LITERATURE

Lists of denominations that fell within or without evangelicalism do not tell the whole story of evangelical influence. Although twenty-first-century terminology often confuses the terms "evangelical" and "fundamentalist," nineteenth-century evangelicals were not fundamentalists in the sense of being culturally defensive, frozen in a world withdrawn from the broader milieu. Evangelicals participated in the American literary market both to exert an influence and to appropriate useful resources. Certain individuals, such as Lydia Huntley Sigourney (1791–1865), Harriet Beecher Stowe (1811–1896), and Susan Warner (1819–1885), inhabited both evangelical and nonevangelical literary worlds and attempted to bridge the gap between them.

Evangelicals distinguished between literature written as an end in itself and language calculated to be useful in promoting heavenward progress. Usefulness, more than genre or form, marked texts as evangelical rather than secular. Evangelicals read and wrote literature to influence a scripted action pattern: moving readers forward along a spiritual pilgrimage through this world toward the holiness of heaven. The Protestant Episcopal Lydia Huntley Sigourney's *How to Be Happy* (1833) pairs a children's narrative with instructions to study the text daily to learn to do good. Those who systematically practice the "science of being good and happy . . . are taken to heaven" (p. 118).

In choosing the pilgrimage metaphor from among alternative tropes for the Christian life, evangelicals placed themselves within a narrative framework constructed by the English Puritan John Bunyan's classic, *The Pilgrim's Progress: From This World to That Which Is to Come* (1678), a text more familiar to nineteenth-century readers than virtually any other excepting the Bible. The Congregationalist William Simonds's (pseudonym Walter Aimwell, 1822–1859) *The Pleasant Way* (1841) was one of many texts that retold *Pilgrim's Progress* using contemporary scenes, events, and characters. Even literary works better classed as secular than evangelical, such as the transcendentalist Louisa May Alcott's (1832–1888) *Little Women* (1868–1869), assumed readers' long companionship with Bunyan. *Little Women* opens with Mrs. March advising her daughters to playact Bunyan's story in earnest; several chapter titles allude to stages in the Christian's journey.

Evangelicals who participated in the American literary market worried about the influence exerted by secular literature, particularly novels. An anonymous physician warned in *Confessions and Experience of a Novel Reader* (1855) that the "popular literature" of the day had opened a "floodgate" of "public poison . . . from beneath whose slimy jaws runs a stream of pollution, sending forth its pestilential branches to one great ocean of immorality" (pp. 26–27). Evangelicals criticized secular authors for merely exciting the imagination instead of provoking moral action on behalf of others. Rather than eschew literature altogether, evangelicals wrote and read religious genres envisioned as alternatives to secular fiction. Doctrine reinforced religious truth, memoirs offered models for Christian character formation, science and history explained God's providence, travel narratives encouraged interest in missions, periodicals sustained community awareness, and hymnals unified evangelicals despite denominational divisions.

Many evangelicals also read and wrote fiction, arguing that imagination could be made to serve religious purposes. The Congregationalist Harriet Beecher Stowe's *Uncle Tom's Cabin* (serialized 1851–1852) employed sentimentalism to move its audiences to oppose slavery and oppression. Stowe's use of sentiment reflected certain evangelicals' growing appreciation

---

John Bunyan's The Pilgrim's Progress *(1678) exerted a deeper influence on nineteenth-century literature and culture than did any other text excepting the Bible.*

This book it chalketh out before thine eyes
The man that seeks the everlasting prize:
It shows you whence he comes, whither he goes;
What he leaves undone; also what he does:
It also shows you how he runs and runs
Till he unto the gate of glory comes.

Bunyan, *The Pilgrim's Progress*, p. 21.

> *Ellen, in Susan Warner's* The Wide, Wide World *(1850), uses her Bible and* Pilgrim's Progress *to grow as a Christian and to influence others to become Christians.*

"Wouldn't it be pleasant, while you are lying there and can do nothing,—wouldn't you like to have me read something to you, Mr. Van Brunt? *I* should like to, very much."

"It's just like you," said he gratefully,—"to think of that; but I wouldn't have you be bothered with it."

"It wouldn't indeed. I should like it very much."

"Well, if you've a mind," said he;—"I can't say but it would be a kind o' comfort to keep that grain out o' my head a while. Seems to me I have cut and housed it all three times over already. Read just whatever you have a mind to. If you was to go over a last year's almanac, it would be as good as a fiddle to me."

"I'll do better for you than that, Mr. Van Brunt," said Ellen, laughing in high glee at having gained her point.—She had secretly brought her Pilgrim's Progress with her, and now with marvellous satisfaction drew it forth.

"I ha'n't been as much of a reader as I had ought to," said Mr. Van Brunt, as she opened the book and turned to the first page;—"but, however, I understand my business pretty well and a man can't be every thing to once. Now let's hear what you've got there."

With a throbbing heart, Ellen began; and read, notes and all, till the sound of tramping hoofs and Alice's voice made her break off. It encouraged and delighted her to see that Mr. Van Brunt's attention was perfectly fixed. He lay still, without moving his eyes from her face, till she stopped; then thanking her he declared that was a "first-rate book," and he "should like mainly to hear the hull on it."

From that time Ellen was diligent in her attendance on him. That she might have more time for reading than the old plan gave her, she set off by herself alone some time before the others, of course riding home with them. It cost her a little sometimes, to forego so much of their company; but she never saw the look of grateful pleasure with which she was welcomed without ceasing to regret her self-denial. How Ellen blessed those notes as she went on with her reading! They said exactly what she wanted Mr. Van Brunt to hear, and in the best way, and were too short and simple to interrupt the interest of the story. After a while she ventured to ask if she might read him a chapter in the Bible. He agreed very readily; owning "he hadn't ought to be so long without reading one as he had been." Ellen then made it a rule to herself, without asking any more questions, to end every reading with a chapter in the Bible; and she carefully sought out those that might be most likely to take hold of his judgment or feelings. They took hold of her own very deeply, by the means; what was strong, or tender, before, now seemed to her too mighty to be withstood and Ellen read not only with her lips but with her whole heart the precious words, longing that they might come with their just effect upon Mr. Van Brunt's mind.

Warner, *The Wide, Wide World*, vol. 2, pp. 140–141.

of feeling, as opposed to intellect, as a legitimate, even superior, faculty of religious knowledge that promoted useful action. Readers motivated to feel right necessarily acted to right the inherent wrong of slavery. Stowe portrays Little Eva, Uncle Tom, and the Quaker Rachel Halliday as evangelical Christians and as types of Christ, who achieve Christian victory by exemplifying the Last Supper, crucifixion, and heavenly communion. Simultaneously Stowe warns of God's coming wrath toward professed evangelicals who fail to do what they can against slavery.

Other evangelical fiction similarly offered readers models of Christian pilgrimage. Following in the Calvinist literary tradition of the *exemplum fidei*, Susan Warner's (1819–1885) best-selling *The Wide, Wide World* (1850) traces Ellen's religious growth as she learns to submit to God's will. Encouraged by Christian friends to read her Bible, hymns, and *Pilgrim's Progress*, Ellen makes her way through the world seeking to live as a servant of God. The novel's popularity can be partially explained by Warner's omission of references to particular denominations or doctrines; any evangelical reader could identify with Ellen's struggles and triumphs.

Despite scholars' claims that women's religious fiction weakened orthodox theology, many women used fiction to preach evangelical doctrines. *Stepping*

Heavenward (1869), by the Presbyterian Elizabeth Prentiss (1818–1878), sold over 100,000 copies in the United States during the nineteenth century, besides British, French, and German editions. Formally *Stepping Heavenward* is an imaginative rendering of a young woman's diary. In the unfolding narrative of everyday experiences, Katy takes daily steps heavenward. The text is doctrinally rigorous, privileges intellectual principle over fluctuating feelings, and legitimates women's experiences not by undercutting theology but by imbuing domestic life with theological significance.

LITERARY CRITIQUES OF EVANGELICALS

Just as evangelicals challenged secular dominance of the literary market by writing religious literature, secular literature critiqued evangelical doctrines and practices. Stowe became increasingly critical of Calvinist doctrine in her later works, such as *The Minister's Wooing* (1859) and *Oldtown Folks* (1869), as she turned toward high church Episcopalianism. Similarly, *The Gates Ajar* (1869), by Elizabeth Stuart Phelps (1844–1911), articulates an alternative to Calvinism. As the novel opens, Mary has just learned of the death of her brother Royal. Mary describes herself as a "member of an Evangelical church, in good and regular standing," who questions a God and heaven that seem to her distant and unattractive (p. 10). In contrast to Dr. Bland's exhortation to submit to afflictions sent by Providence, Aunt Winifred encourages Mary that heaven is like happy, domestic life on earth.

Although Stowe and Phelps objected to what they considered austere doctrines, *The Deerslayer* (1841) by James Fenimore Cooper (1789–1851) instead portrays evangelicalism as intellectually vacuous. Raised by Quaker parents who attended Episcopal and Presbyterian churches, Cooper in this novel suggests a more distant relationship to evangelicalism. Hetty Hutter's unquestioning religious faith provides evidence of her feeblemindedness. Cooper contrasts Hetty's purity with the immorality of most other white characters in the novel (excepting Quakers and Moravians) yet ridicules her conviction that reading the Bible to the Hurons will convince them to release their captives. Natty Bumppo is Cooper's ideal; he has little use for the Bible, which he cannot read, but his innate Christian integrity gains the respect of whites and Native Americans.

The most common charge that nineteenth-century literature raises against evangelicals is hypocrisy. "The Celestial Railroad" (1843) by Nathaniel Hawthorne (1804–1864) parodies *Pilgrim's Progress*. Modern pilgrims, who are wealthier, more respectable, and more liberal-minded than those of Bunyan's day, enjoy a faster, more comfortable journey to the Celestial City on the railroad. These pilgrims retain their financial interest in the City of Destruction and employ Christian's adversary, Apollyon, as engineer. A small minority of pilgrims continue to travel on foot—despite the persecutions of the railroad's passengers—but the vast majority of professed pilgrims never complete their heaven-bound journey.

Moby-Dick (1851) by Herman Melville (1819–1891) similarly critiques evangelical inconsistencies. Father Mapple, for example, preaches rigorous duties to God while physically distancing himself from his congregation. The Quaker captains Bildad and Peleg exhibit greed and irreverence, respectively, treating religion as distinct from the practical world and using the Bible to justify paying Ishmael absurdly low wages. An avowed Presbyterian, Ishmael joins Queequeg in pagan worship because this heathen exhibits more Christian kindness than do professed evangelicals.

Whether endorsing or attacking evangelicals, nineteenth-century literature reflects the group's far-reaching cultural influence. As evangelicals used literature to transform the world, they articulated a high moral standard to which critics held them accountable.

See also The Bible; Methodists; Protestantism; Quakers; Religion; Religious Magazines

BIBLIOGRAPHY

Primary Works

Baird, Robert. *Religion in America; or, An Account of the Origin, Progress, Relation to the State, and Present Condition of the Evangelical Churches in the United States, with Notices of the Unevangelical Denominations.* New York: Harper & Brothers, 1844.

Bunyan, John. *The Pilgrim's Progress from This World to That Which Is To Come Delivered under the Similitude of a Dream.* 1678. New York: Macmillan, 1948.

Phelps, Elizabeth Stuart. *The Gates Ajar.* Boston: Fields, Osgood, 1868.

Physician, A. *Confessions and Experience of a Novel Reader.* Chicago: William Stacy, 1855.

Sigourney, Lydia Huntley. *How to Be Happy: Written for the Children of Some Dear Friends.* Hartford, Conn.: D. F. Robinson, 1833.

Warner, Susan. *The Wide, Wide World.* 2 vols. New York: Putnam, 1851.

Secondary Works

Brown, Candy Ann Gunther. "The Spiritual Pilgrimage of Rachel Stearns, 1834–1837: Reinterpreting Women's Religious and Social Experiences in the Methodist

Revivals of Nineteenth-Century America." *Church History* 65 (December 1996): 577–595.

Brown, Candy Gunther. *The Word in the World: Evangelical Writing, Publishing, and Reading in America, 1789-1880*. Chapel Hill: University of North Carolina Press, 2004.

Brumberg, Joan Jacobs. *Mission for Life: The Story of the Family of Adoniram Judson, the Dramatic Events of the First American Foreign Mission, and the Course of Evangelical Religion in the Nineteenth Century*. New York: Macmillan, 1980.

Douglas, Ann. *The Feminization of American Culture*. New York: Doubleday Anchor, 1977.

Fisher, Philip. *Hard Facts: Setting and Form in the American Novel*. New York: Oxford University Press, 1985.

Moore, R. Laurence. *Selling God: American Religion in the Marketplace of Culture*. New York: Oxford University Press, 1994.

Noll, Mark A. *A History of Christianity in the United States and Canada*. Grand Rapids, Mich.: Eerdmans, 1992.

Reynolds, David S. *Faith in Fiction: The Emergence of Religious Literature in America*. Cambridge, Mass.: Harvard University Press, 1981.

Tompkins, Jane. *Sensational Designs: The Cultural Work of American Fiction, 1790–1860*. New York: Oxford University Press, 1985.

Candy Gunther Brown

"EXPERIENCE"

"Experience," from *Essays: Second Series* (1844), is the defining statement of the transitional phase in the career of Ralph Waldo Emerson (1803–1882), flanked on one side by the exorbitant hopefulness of his high transcendentalist period and on the other by the worldly pragmatism of his later years. The title itself is resonant. In his preface to *The American* (1877), Henry James characterizes "the real" as "the things we cannot possibly *not* know, sooner or later, in one way or another." Emerson's "experience" is similarly what the act of living impresses upon us regardless of the innocence or idealism we begin with and the reluctance of the aspiring self to acknowledge defeat or limitation. "I am not the novice I was fourteen, nor yet seven years ago" (p. 491), Emerson confesses late in the essay, distancing himself from *Nature* (1836), "The American Scholar" (1837), and "Self-Reliance" (published in *Essays* in 1841 but incorporating journal entries dating back to the early 1830s), yet also inviting comparison to those and other early writings.

Stephen E. Whicher aptly calls "Experience" "an Interim Report on an Experiment in Self-Reliance" (p. 111). "Where do we find ourselves?" the essay begins (p. 471). Although "Experience" is Emerson's most intimate and candid essay—"I have set my heart on honesty in this chapter" (p. 483), he proclaims as if his other writings had been less than wholly honest—its "I" is a representative figure whose frustrations and doubts are meant to illustrate the radical disjunction between ideal and fact, thought and practical power, and the Soul and its psychic complement, the naturalistic self. Emerson still conceives life as an endless journey—"We wake and find ourselves on a stair: there are stairs below us, which we seem to have ascended; there are stairs above us, many a one, which go upward and out of sight" (p. 471)—but the spiritual upward mobility of "Circles," published only three years earlier, has been replaced by bewilderment and a sense of incapacity. The prophet who formerly urged his audiences to awaken now finds that "sleep lingers all our lifetime about our eyes" (p. 471). In "The Oversoul" (1841) Emerson had figured spiritual power as an upwelling of the "flowing river" of life within the Soul (p. 385). "Experience" returns to the image in tragic counterpoint: "We are like millers on the lower levels of a steam, when the factories above them have exhausted the water. We too fancy that the upper people must have raised their dams" (p. 471).

Emerson's testament to depletion differs from two familiar Romantic analogues, William Wordsworth's "Ode: Intimations of Immortality from Recollections of Early Childhood" (1807), which concerns the loss of visionary power that comes with maturity and socialization, and Samuel Taylor Coleridge's "Dejection: An Ode" (1802), whose subject is psychic depression. Emerson did not believe that the Soul was, or should be, any less accessible to the adult than to the child or that the periodicity of moods, whose tyranny he openly conceded, would eventuate in a chronic diminution of spiritual energy. "Experience" is a confession of disillusion, though its theme of thwarted idealism, of standing at the brink of an empowerment that eludes more than fitful possession, is anticipated by passages in "The Transcendentalist" (1841) and by the prophetic "First Philosophy" journal entry of 1835. "Experience" is not so much a new direction in Emerson's thought as the announcement of a revisionary shift in proportion and tone. Doubts that had always been lurking are openly avowed; vetoes upon transcendentalism's "Saturnalia or excess of Faith" (p. 198) are soberly given their full due.

Some have argued that the death from scarlet fever of Emerson's five-year-old son Waldo in January 1842 contributed heavily to Emerson's chastened mood. Emerson makes use of Waldo's death early in

"Experience" to suggest the dreamlike quality that haunts even the most catastrophic life events. We are stoics perforce, by some horrible decree of fate, Emerson implies in ironic reversal of the benign invulnerability to "disgrace" and "calamity" he had claimed in *Nature*. Waldo's death affected Emerson more than he acknowledged, but no less important to his thought were two other private developments that "Experience" openly, if impersonally, addresses: Emerson's disappointment with the succession of promising disciples—Henry David Thoreau (1817–1862) and the poet William Ellery Channing (1818–1901) among them—who seemed constitutionally doomed to underachievement ("We see young men who owe us a new world . . . , but they never acquit the debt," p. 474) and his frustrations concerning his personal relationships, especially with Margaret Fuller and her friend Caroline Sturgis, which he generalizes into the propositional "Two human beings are like globes, which can touch only in a point" (p. 488).

The year-by-year deferral of the prophesied cultural revolution also eroded Emerson's faith and gave a historical aspect to the drift toward skepticism announced in his lecture series "The Times," delivered in the winter of 1841–1842, in which he conceded the element of truth in the Conservative's case for the fallenness of man and the inertia of social institutions, and in which he deplored his own "double consciousness" ("The Transcendentalist," p. 205), the perpetual bifurcation between the life of the understanding and the life of the Soul. "Experience" develops and causally interrelates these two ideas; it looks at the world from the standpoint of the Conservative's social and metaphysical realpolitik, then, in visceral reaction, labors to reaffirm the claims of free intellect. It is Emerson's mid-career effort to take stock of himself and the world and, so far as he can, to reconstitute faith upon, or at least in full cognizance of, the bedrock of stern, unmalleable fact.

STRUCTURE, LANGUAGE, AND VOICE

Emerson's essays, reputed to lack form, characteristically make their own form. "Experience" begins with a poetic epigraph about the "lords of life" (p. 469), which Emerson returns to enumerate late in the essay: "Illusion, Temperament, Succession, Surface, Surprise, Reality, Subjectiveness" (p. 490). After its opening paragraph "Experience" organizes itself into sections centered around these metaphoric gods of limitation. The primary voice is that of worldly sagacity surveying life as it presents itself when the Soul is in abeyance and internal and external necessity hold sway, though "primary" by no means implies "authoritative" or "final." Writing of temperament, Emerson recasts *Nature's*

image of the "transparent eye-ball" (p. 10) as "a string of beads" whose "many-colored lenses . . . paint the world their own hue, and each shows only what lies in its focus" (p. 473). This recognition of chronic subjectivity is what Emerson later calls "the Fall of Man" (p. 487). Mystic vision, oneness with the All, and the Soul's apprehension of absolute Truth have yielded to a "system of illusions" that confine us within "a prison of glass which we cannot see" and from whose distortions we can seldom, and even then only partially, escape (p. 474).

As the intertextual metaphor of seeing suggests, "Experience" is in dialogue with Emerson's earlier writings, but it is a dialogue of imagination and feeling conducted primarily within established categories of thought. Indeed no essay of Emerson's better illustrates Joel Porte's contention that Emerson "is fundamentally a poet whose meaning lies in his manipulations of language and figure" (p. 94) and whose changes in thought are most dramatically signified by changes of imagery. In "Spiritual Laws" (1841), for example, Emerson had represented an individual's special "*calling* in his character" through

Lydian Emerson with her young son Edward, c. 1847. The death of Emerson's young son Waldo in 1842 contributed to the chastened mood of "Experience."
COURTESY OF THE CONCORD FREE PUBLIC LIBRARY

the figure of "a ship in a river" that "runs against obstructions on every side but one," on which "all obstruction is taken away, and he sweeps serenely over a deepening channel into an infinite sea" (p. 310). In "Experience" the thought reappears, but Emerson's claims have been drastically reduced: "A man is like a bit of Labrador spar, which has no lustre as you turn it in your hand, until you come to a particular angle; then it shows deep and beautiful colors" (p. 477). Success in life, formerly a cultivation of the particular bent of one's genius, has become sleight of hand, a trick of "adroitly" positioning oneself so as to keep one's gift most often to the light. It is not the *propositional* content of Emerson's idea that has changed (human beings have one unique ability) so much as its *affective* content. The infinite has become finite—the organizing idea of the section is "Surface"—and what in "Spiritual Laws" had been a cause for celebration ("There is one direction in which all space is open to [a man]," p. 310) now appears an occasion for lament ("There is no power of expansion in men," p. 477).

In the section on temperament—structurally and tonally a microcosm of the essay—Emerson traces the logic of biological determinism to the point where it calls into question the origin and nature of "the religious sentiment" (p. 474) and seems to condemn human beings to a "sty of sensualism." This is one side of the case, and Emerson concedes that, "on its own level, or in view of nature, temperament is final" (p. 476). But nature—the realm of material causes and effects as grasped by the Understanding—is not the only reality, Emerson argues, and though the Soul may be dormant for long stretches of time, its moments of presence have an authority that overrides the necessitarianism of science and reenthrones Mind, if only temporarily, as the sovereign power in human affairs.

This rhythm of bleak concession, philosophical bottoming out, and urgently affirmative counterstatement governs the structure of "Experience." In the section on surface, the philosophical nadir of the essay, Emerson assumes the weary, illusionless voice of the skeptic, professing (with utter implausiblity) to expect nothing of life and therefore to be thankful for "moderate goods" (p. 480). In truth no one ever expected more of life or was constitutionally less capable of abridging his demand for the ideal. The fact that rankles Emerson, against his early belief, is that nature—"no saint" (p. 481)—seems to honor power and fecundity more than what Mind intuits as the moral law. A chastened Emerson seems ready to accept this lesson and abide within "the kingdom of known cause and effect"; but then in the section on surprise the Soul "with its angel-whispering" (p. 482) temporarily returns, routing the

settled wisdom of the Understanding and alluring the self with a prospect of redeemed seeing and being that will never be steadfastly realized. The only incontestable reality, Emerson concludes from the ebbs and flows of vision, is the doubleness of experienced reality, now exalted, now (for ever longer periods) discouragingly mean, the difference depending not on any virtue or behavior subject to human volition but, like the Calvinist's grace, on "more or less of vital force supplied from the Eternal" (p. 483).

The balance of "Experience" is largely Emerson's attempt to prophesy, even if he cannot substantively imagine, a "new statement" (p. 487) that will incorporate both skepticism and belief and constitute a viable creed for a post-Christian (and now a post-transcendental) age. Emerson's sense of spiritual interregnum recalls that of Thomas Carlyle (1795–1881) in *Sartor Resartus* (1836) a decade earlier, but where Carlyle had leaped to a blustery, indeterminate faith, Emerson is resolute in "hold[ing] hard to this poverty, however scandalous" (p. 490), and using it as the base for renewed ventures into truth. After the philosophical Idealism of his earlier writing, in which consciousness was the primary reality and social institutions its epiphenomenal result, it must have cost Emerson dearly to acknowledge that "the world I converse with in the city and in the farms, is not the world I *think*" and that not much has been "gained by manipular attempts to realize the world of thought" (pp. 491–492). The challenge he girds himself to face ("Never mind the ridicule, never mind the defeat: up again, old heart!") is to bring these disparate worlds into congruence and (throwing off all drowsiness) to abet "the true romance which the world exists to realize"—"the transformation of genius into practical power" (p. 492).

AFTER THE FALL

It is noteworthy that 1844, the year of "Experience," was also the year of "The Young American," Emerson's détente with capitalism, and "Emancipation in the British West Indies," his impassioned, if belated attack upon slavery. Sensitive always to the signs of the times, Emerson felt that great persons must apprehend and align themselves with historical forces, seeing beyond their immediate manifestations to their teleological direction. In its acknowledgment that nature's "darlings, the great, the strong, the beautiful, are not children of our law" (p. 481), "Experience" would seem to imply moral and political quietism, if not outright despair. However Emerson's diminished expectations apply chiefly to the prospects of the individual, whose life is now seen as invariably stunted and incomplete, and to the short-term conformity of events to human ethics. Emerson never doubts the immanence and ultimate beneficence of universal Law, indifferent as it seems to himself or to any private person.

Indeed even as he voices his disenchantments Emerson is feeling his way toward a new belief founded on the replacement of the individual by society and of millennialism by a faith in gradual amelioration. Though the individual is always defeated, the species may at least be sure of measurable, if sometimes pitilessly sacrificial progress. Nature is now understood to operate by what in "The Young American" Emerson calls "a cruel kindness" (p. 218). "It will only save what is worth saving," he adds in the Emancipation address, "and it saves not by compassion, but by power" (p. 117). In 1844 power seemed tilting in the direction of abolition; the historical moment had arrived; and the Negro race had proved itself "worth saving" by showing that, "more than any other," it was "susceptible of rapid civilization" (p. 116). The Irish laborers building American railroads were not so fortunate. Emerson grants the wrongs done them, but he sees the Irish as temporary casualties of a laissez-faire capitalism that, for better or worse—in "Man the Reformer" (1841) it had emphatically been for worse— seems the appointed means for advancing humanity during this particular phase of its development. The short-term consolation is that the children of the Irish will have the benefits of American schools and American opportunity; the long-term consolation is that capitalism itself is destined to evolve peacefully into a "beneficent socialism" (p. 222). Already in 1844, even as Emerson is cataloging the impoverishments of personal and collective experience, he is beginning, as he would say in "Fate" (1860), "to rally on his relation to the Universe, which his ruin benefits," and to "build altars to the Beautiful Necessity" (p. 967).

See also "The American Scholar"; *Nature;* "The Poet"; "Self-Reliance"; Romanticism; Transcendentalism

BIBLIOGRAPHY
Primary Works

Emerson, Ralph Waldo. "Emancipation in the British West Indies." In *The Political Emerson: Essential Writings on Politics and Social Reform,* edited by David M. Robinson. Boston: Beacon Press, 2004.

Emerson, Ralph Waldo. *Essays and Lectures.* Edited by Joel Porte. New York: Library of America, 1983. Quotations from all of Emerson's writings except "Emancipation in the British West Indies" are from this edition.

Emerson, Ralph Waldo. "Experience." In *Essays: Second Series.* Boston: James Munroe, 1844. First publication of "Experience."

Secondary Works

Allen, Gay Wilson. *Waldo Emerson: A Biography.* New York: Viking Press, 1981.

Cameron, Sharon. "Representing Grief: Emerson's 'Experience.'" *Representations,* no. 15 (summer 1986): 15–41.

Jacobson, David. *Emerson's Pragmatic Vision: The Dance of the Eye.* University Park: Pennsylvania State University Press, 1993.

Michael, John. *Emerson and Skepticism: The Cipher of the World.* Baltimore: Johns Hopkins University Press, 1988.

Packer, B. L. *Emerson's Fall: A New Interpretation of the Major Essays.* New York: Continuum, 1982.

Porte, Joel. "The Problem of Emerson." In *Uses of Literature,* edited by Monroe Engel, pp. 85–114. Cambridge, Mass.: Harvard University Press, 1973.

Robinson, David M. *Emerson and the Conduct of Life: Pragmatism and Ethical Purpose in the Later Work.* Cambridge, U.K.: Cambridge University Press, 1993.

Rusk, Ralph L. *The Life of Ralph Waldo Emerson.* New York: Scribners, 1949.

Van Leer, David. *Emerson's Epistemology: The Argument of the Essays.* Cambridge, U.K.: Cambridge University Press, 1986.

Whicher, Stephen E. *Freedom and Fate: An Inner Life of Ralph Waldo Emerson.* Philadelphia: University of Pennsylvania Press, 1953.

Robert Milder

EXPLORATION AND DISCOVERY

European exploration and discovery was transformed during the eighteenth century by what Mary Louise Pratt calls "the knowledge-building project of natural history" (p. 24). A foundation stone of this project was the botanical classificatory system of the Swedish naturalist Carl Linne (Linnaeus), which offered a comprehensive method of arranging all plant species in the world. Equipped with such tools and motivated by a sense of "planetary consciousness," the international scientific expedition "became one of Europe's proudest instruments of expansion" (p. 23). Expeditions such as those of James Cook, George Vancouver, Louis Antoine de Bougainville, and Jean François de Galaup, comte de La Pérouse, included scientific specialists with instructions to gather information of all kinds. Despite an emphasis on international science, it was well understood that marine mapping, the development of navigational tools and techniques, and botanical, zoological, and ethnographic research served to signal, support, and extend the power of the sponsoring states.

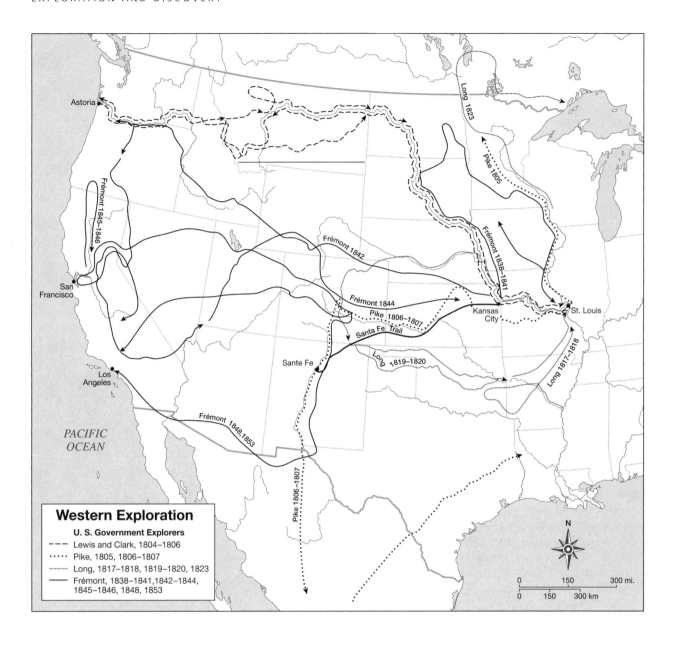

Western Exploration

U. S. Government Explorers

- - - Lewis and Clark, 1804–1806
······· Pike, 1805, 1806–1807
········ Long, 1817–1818, 1819–1820, 1823
——— Frémont, 1838–1841, 1842–1844, 1845–1846, 1848, 1853

EARLY U.S. MILITARY EXPEDITIONS

With these eighteenth-century expeditions as models, President Thomas Jefferson conceived the Lewis and Clark expedition (1804–1806) that traversed the continent between St. Louis and the mouth of the Columbia River. Jefferson's copious instructions echoed those that had guided late-eighteenth-century maritime explorers, imposing on men traveling in small boats, on horseback, and on foot many of the data-gathering ambitions previously sustained by fleets of sailing vessels. This expedition coincided with the Louisiana Purchase, and while it expressed Jefferson's engagement with international science, it also was motivated by the strategic concerns of a new, expanding nation in competition with the imperial designs of Britain,

France, Spain, and Russia. As early as 1786, Jefferson wrote that the United States "must be viewed as the nest from which all America, North and South, is to be peopled" (p. 218). While the British explorers Cook and Vancouver mapped the Pacific coast of North America and British and Canadian fur traders were the first to cross the continent and establish operations on the Pacific, American military exploring expeditions tended to have broader aims, keeping in mind the general public interests of a young, growing country.

Up to the early 1840s, when American settlers began crossing the continent to Oregon and California, exploration was concentrated east of the Rockies and focused on the rivalries with the Spanish in northern

Mexico and the British in Canada. The fur trade was an immediate motivator of reconnaissance, particularly around the Great Lakes. Lieutenant Zebulon Pike (1779–1813) led two expeditions intended to familiarize Americans with the frontiers of Louisiana and to assert U.S. sovereignty. In 1805 Pike explored the headwaters of the Mississippi in present-day Minnesota. In 1806 he ventured into the Southwest, ascending the Arkansas River into the Rocky Mountains in the region of Pike's Peak and the headwaters of the Platte. Pike's reconnaissance of both the Mississippi and the southwestern regions was mostly focused on the immediate strategic interests of the United States, but he also gathered much important geographical information, and his privately published *Report* (1810) had lasting influence on American ideas about the Far West. In particular, according to William H. Goetzmann, he described the region as extremely dry and not suitable for farming; he argued that an easy land passage existed between the Colorado River and California; and he publicized the idea that Santa Fe and northern Mexico afforded many opportunities for trade (pp. 51–52).

Major Stephen Long's (1784–1864) expedition of 1819 ascended the Platte River into the Rockies in the area of Pike's Peak. Long's assessment of the conditions of the high western plains echoed Pike's view that they were not fit for farming, and Long has been blamed for perpetrating the idea of the "Great American Desert." Goetzmann argues, however, that in retrospect Long's assessment of the situation was probably a just one, given the technology of the time (p. 62). Long's greatest contribution is his map of 1821, which was one of a handful that formed the basis of western cartography until the systematic surveys undertaken after the Civil War. His expedition was the first to include civilian scientists, whose data gathering was perhaps parodied in the figure of Dr. Obed Battius in James Fenimore Cooper's *The Prairie* (1827). Cooper's novel also includes a young military man whose self-conscious representation of U.S. interests in the western territories recalls some of the poses struck by Meriwether Lewis and Zebulon Pike in their reports.

EXPLORATION AND COMMERCE

In addition to official expeditions led by army officers, opportunities for trade with northern Mexico, focused on Santa Fe and the fur trade generally, stimulated individuals to investigate the Southwest as well as the central Rocky Mountains. The *Personal Narrative* (1831) of James Ohio Pattie (1804?–1850) recounts his own and his father Sylvestre Pattie's travels as far north as the Yellowstone, as far south as the Gulf of California, and as far west as San Diego, where James Ohio was imprisoned by the Mexican administration. His amazing

story was dictated to Timothy Flint of Cincinnati, an editor and novelist credited with authoring the first "western" and generally with pioneering the West as a subject of fiction and social history. Washington Irving (1783–1859), perhaps the most esteemed American writer of the 1830s, also took on the Far West as a subject in the later part of his literary career. *A Tour on the Prairies* (1835) recounts his own excursion with a corps of Arkansas Rangers. *Astoria* (1836) is a history of John Jacob Astor's American Fur Company, and *The Adventures of Captain Bonneville* (1837) is an account of the Rocky Mountains and the Great Salt Lake area based on Benjamin Bonneville's journals. Zenas Leonard and Joseph Walker, employees of Bonneville, investigated the area of the Great Salt Lake before they crossed the Sierra into California, returning via what came to be known as Walker's Pass, a future emigrant route. In his *Narrative* (1839) Leonard surveys the "vast waste of territory" in the Far West and contemplates "its settlement and civilization" by citizens of the United States. Writers and editors such as Flint and Irving played their part in creating a discourse of the Far West in the popular press. The emigrant wagon trains and then the California gold rush of 1849 would prompt a surge of personal narrative accounts, many finding their way into newspaper and book form.

FRÉMONT AND WILKES

In the early nineteenth century U.S. elected officials were generally reluctant to use public funds for the promotion of science. But the westward flow of emigrants in the 1840s prompted increased sponsorship of exploring expeditions by the American government, and the military figures leading these expeditions played a complex role representing the interests of a country in the process of more than doubling its territory through westward expansion. The ultimate such figure in this period was the dashing John Charles Frémont (1813–1890), who lead expeditions to the Rocky Mountains and to Oregon and California and whose published reports (1842, 1845) presented to thousands of readers a model of heroic American action in the West. Frémont's expeditions are not credited with much original geographical information but rather with systematizing and publicizing the routes to Oregon and California and with articulating a vision of opportunity in those territories. Frémont's heroic persona, at least partly the creation of his wife and editor, Jessie Benton Frémont, is intelligent and romantic, a climber of mountains with a soul that expands on the summit. In addition to inspiring followers, his published reports served as practical guidebooks during the later 1840s. Goetzmann sums him up as "a representative figure of this time whose posture has perhaps more to tell us about the 1840s and 1850s than do his actual achievements" (p. 252).

Upon arriving at the mouth of the Columbia in 1843, Frémont linked his expedition with that of Lieutenant Charles Wilkes (1798–1877), the ambitious leader of the United States Exploring Expedition, which between 1838 and 1842 charted the coasts of Antarctica and large areas of the south and central Pacific ocean. In 1841 Wilkes and his party arrived at the mouth of the Columbia, whence they conducted explorations of the coast as far north as Puget Sound as well as sending parties inland along the Willamette Valley and into California as far as San Francisco. Frémont wrote that he and Wilkes presented "a connected exploration from the Mississippi to the Pacific" (p. 562), and both men shared a vision that a great American state would emerge on the Pacific coast.

The Wilkes expedition is a story unto itself. The first government-sponsored marine exploration had a long gestation in disputes over whether the government ought to be financing such a thing at all, complicated by jurisdictional infighting as the navy resisted the influence and presence of civilian scientific specialists. The expedition was in part an attempt to reduce the dependence of U.S. seafarers on mainly British marine charts. As *Harper's New Monthly Magazine* (1872) explained, "Forty years after the adoption of our national Constitution the United States were, for all maritime and scientific knowledge, wholly dependent on *foreign* governments" (p. 60). Whaling, sealing, and trading interests all condemned the lack of American initiative in the realm of systematic navigational aids. Cultural nationalists professed shame that the United States "stood in humiliating contrast with the whole scientific world," to quote the same *Harper's* article (p. 60). When the expedition departed in 1838, there was an international competition to discover what lay behind the barriers of ice that previous navigators such as James Cook had encountered as they sailed to the extreme south. The expedition succeeded in mapping a portion of the Antarctic coast, but it was the quantities of plant, animal, mineral, and ethnological materials that secured the expedition's popular and scientific success. When the expedition returned, there was initially no facility in any way adequate even to house the extensive collections, let alone catalog or display them. Eventually the expedition's collections came together with the bequest of James Smithson, and a national museum, the Smithsonian Institution, was created. The narrative account of the expeditions (1845), in five volumes written by Wilkes, is burdened with much irrelevant information, and although it sold relatively well and went through more that ten editions, it never captured the American imagination as Frémont's narratives

did. That said, it influenced the sea novels of James Fenimore Cooper and Herman Melville, the latter deriving, among other information, the lineaments of his South Sea character Queequeg, who, according to William Stanton, was "modeled on the New Zealand chief Kotowatowa" (p. 310). The greatest legacy of the Wilkes expedition may have been the realization of the value of scientific exploration to the country as a whole, an understanding that led to vastly increased expenditures on exploration in subsequent decades.

THE AGE OF OFFICIAL SURVEYS

The Army Corps of Topographical Engineers, founded in 1813 and reorganized in 1838, was the platform for much of the official exploration of the West up to the Civil War. Long and Frémont were officers in the corps, as were many other explorers of the territory acquired from Mexico in 1848 and of Oregon, officially annexed in 1846. Mapping of the territory was the corps's primary responsibility, along with assessing economic and scientific features. Such work was later handled by various U.S. Geological Surveys, which themselves became a bureau under that name in 1879, as well as by state-funded enterprises such as the important Geological Survey of California. Information gathered by the army and the later civilian geological surveys informed and fueled the debates that accompanied westward expansion. Following settlement of the boundary with Mexico and then of the Oregon boundary to the north, the demand for accurate geographical and economic information increased, while the western territories became what Goetzmann has called a "vast natural laboratory" for scientists (p. 303).

During the Mexican-American War, William H. Emory (1811–1887), lieutenant in the Topographical Engineers, accompanied General Stephen Watts Kearny on his march from Santa Fe to San Diego. Emory's report, along with his original map of the Southwest, offered a detailed firsthand view of New Mexico and Arizona. A scientist and a curious man, Emory describes country that is "different from scenery in the States," with "singular" geological formations, an unusually limpid atmosphere, and oasis-like river valleys surrounded by forbidding desert pans (pp. 37, 39). As travelers in the Southwest would do increasingly, Emory resorts to new geological theories in order to account for what he sees, noting the visible strata and hypothesizing "some denuding process" that removes softer rocks. Emory was also a pioneer of southwestern archeology, describing and speculating upon the ancient Pecos ruins and the Casas Grandes along the Gila River. The War Department printed ten thousand copies of Emory's report, the size of the printing indicating the extensive interest in this area as well as

A Tributary of the Gila. Lithograph from William H. Emory's *Notes of a Military Reconnoissance,* 1848. Emory's was one of many expeditions to the American West funded by the federal government. These expeditions included scientists and civil engineers who mapped and surveyed the land and were responsible for collecting plants, zoological and geological specimens, and ethnographic information. The reports were widely circulated and introduced many Americans to western landscapes. © CORBIS

asserting that the country acquired in the war was valuable and worth the fight.

Subsequently the Topographical Engineers were employed on railroad surveys and also in relation to the "Mormon War" of 1857, when an expedition led by Joseph Ives and including the geologist John Newberry was "the first party in recorded history to explore the floor of the Grand Canyon" (Goetzmann, p. 308). The vast chasm of the Grand Canyon, exposing thousands of feet of layered rock, offered a kind of map of geological time. Newberry and the geologists who followed after 1860 turned to new theories of geomorphology in order to account for such natural spectacles by means of processes acting over millions of years (volcanism, uplifting, glaciation, erosion). John Wesley Powell's (1834–1902) *Exploration of the Colorado River and Its Canyons* (1875) is both a travelogue and a course in geology. Powell describes the boat trip down the Colorado River and the towering walls above, interspersing explanations as to the origins of the landforms they followed. Clarence King's

(1842–1901) *Mountaineering in the Sierra Nevada* (1872), an account of the valleys and high peaks of the Sierra, also explains the geological history of each awe-inspiring sight. Powell and King, both dashing figures, displace the military man of the Frémont *Reports* with the glamorous and brilliant scientist-adventurer. King's *Mountaineering* springs from his participation in the Geological Survey of California under the direction of Josiah Dwight Whitney. Also emerging from this survey were Whitney's *Geology* (1865), Whitney's *Yosemite Book* (1868), and William H. Brewer's posthumously published (1930) *Up and Down California in 1860–1864.* King's greatest scientific publications, however, are the series of volumes based on the expeditions of the Fortieth Parallel Survey (1867–1869). King's *Systematic Geology* (1878) presents a comprehensive account of the western cordillera and the Great Basin, spanning all the major geological periods in order to offer a systematic understanding of the landscape and resources of the West in terms of the latest scientific theories and techniques.

There was considerable public interest in what these scientists were doing in the West. In addition to his popular book *Mountaineering in the Sierra Nevada,* King published photographs in *Harper's New Monthly Magazine* (Goetzmann, p. 440 n. 5) as well as articles there and in Bret Harte's *Overland Monthly* (Goetzmann, p. 445 n. 5). Powell published articles and engravings in *Scribner's Magazine.* By 1870 photography was portable enough to be part of western surveys, contributing greatly both to scientific reporting and public involvement. Timothy O'sullivan was the photographer on the Fortieth Parallel Survey and on the Wheeler surveys of 1871, 1872, and 1873. The War Department published *Photographs Showing Landscapes, Geological, and Other Features, of Portions of the Western Territory of the United States* (1875), consisting of images by O'Sullivan and William Bell. A notable heir to these nineteenth-century scientist-writers is the literary journalist John McPhee, whose monumental *Annals of the Former World* (1998) extends the fortieth parallel to the Atlantic coast and then follows it westward with modern geologists playing the role of King and his contemporaries.

EXPLORATIONS BEYOND THE STATES

The occasion for the first U.S. explorations of the Arctic region was the disappearance in 1845 of the British explorer Sir John Franklin with his two ships, *Erebus* and *Terror.* The British Admiralty offered a £20,000 reward for Franklin's rescue, and Lady Franklin appealed to President Zachary Taylor for help. Between 1850 and 1873 American expeditions led by Edwin De Haven, Elisha Kent Kane, Isaac Hayes, and Charles Francis Hall set out to find Franklin, in the process mapping the area and gathering various kinds of scientific data. American, British, Russian, and Danish expeditions all worked toward determining whether a feasible Northwest Passage existed, whether there was an unfrozen "Polar Sea," and whether there was an Arctic landmass corresponding to that discovered at the southern pole.

The De Haven expedition retraced the route of the Franklin expedition, spending the winter of 1850–1851 trapped in the moving ice sheets of Lancaster Sound, north of Baffin Island, and sailing for home in August 1851. Elisha Kane (1820–1857), the surgeon on this voyage, organized his own expedition, which sailed in May 1853. Kane explored the western coast of Greenland, sighting a large body of open water that he construed as the polar sea but which proved to be a basin succeeded by the long Kennedy Channel. Kane's astronomical and magnetic observations were much praised. Kane was also a vivid writer, and his *Arctic Explorations*

(1856) was popular. Isaac Hayes (1832–1881), himself a member of the Kane expedition, continued work in northern Greenland and in the strait between Greenland and Ellesmere Island. From a vantage point on the coast of Grinnell Land, Hayes too thought he saw the open polar sea. The belief, though untrue, provided the title for his account of the venture, *The Open Polar Sea: A Narrative of a Voyage of Discovery towards the North Pole* (1867). Prior to his own expedition, Hayes wrote *An Arctic Boat Journey* (1860), capitalizing on the public interest in Arctic exploration to sustain himself as he tried to raise funds for the next voyage.

Charles Francis Hall (1821–1871) led three expeditions between 1860 and 1871. The first two, focused on discovering the fate of the Franklin expedition, turned up many items from the Franklin ship as well as evidence that there were no survivors. Hall's most notable contribution to Arctic exploration and knowledge, however, was his learning to rely on Inuit guides and technology for a series of overland treks. Hall learned some of the Inuit language, and he established long-term relationships with a number of individuals whose knowledge and active assistance enabled his journeys. This aspect of the ventures captured the public imagination, as is evidenced in the title of his own account, *Life with the Esquimaux* (1864), and in the featuring of his two Inuit companions, Ebierbing and Tookoolito, at P. T. Barnum's American Museum in New York and on Hall's own lecture tours. The third expedition, in a steam-powered naval tug, *Polaris,* attempted to extend the explorations of Kane and Hayes along the west coast of Greenland, looking for access to the "Polar Sea." After Hall, interest in the Arctic continued to grow among geographers, scientists, and the general public, culminating in Robert Edwin Peary's twenty years of work, first exploring Greenland and subsequently trekking to the North Pole, where he arrived in 1908.

The publication of Alexander von Humboldt's (1769–1859) massive *Personal Narrative* (1814–1829), the account of his travels and researches in South America, stimulated many great scientists of the next generation, including Charles Darwin. After 1840 the Amazon Basin became a focus of scientific and commercial interest, the latter spurred by the invention of vulcanization, the process whereby natural latex became the useful product rubber. The two most significant U.S. expeditions to South America at mid-century were the U.S. Naval Astronomical Expedition to the Southern Hemisphere in 1849–1852 led by James Melville Gilliss (1811–1865), and the expedition to the Amazon in 1851–1852 led by William Lewis Herndon (1813–1857). The main purpose of the Gilliss expedition was to measure the distance of the earth from the sun by observing the motions of the planet Venus simultaneously from the Southern and Northern Hemispheres. Regrettably, though Gilliss completed his observations in Chile, the complementary ones were neglected in the United States, and so the main scientific purpose was not achieved. Nonetheless Gilliss reported on the geography and economy of Chile in what seems to have been a disinterested spirit (Harrison, p. 186). Herndon's expedition was the most important and widely followed U.S. expedition to South America in the nineteenth century. Herndon descended the length of the Amazon River, after crossing from Lima to the headwaters. According to John P. Harrison, there are many indications that the promoters of this venture had in mind the transplantation of slave agriculture from its threatened practice in the southern United States (pp. 187–190). Whatever the strategic purposes, Herndon traveled for almost a year, covering almost four thousand miles by foot, mule, canoe, and small boat, and his narrative took its place among popular books by the fellow American William Edwards and the Englishman Henry Walter Bates in stimulating scientific and commercial interest in the Amazon. Demand for Herndon's *Exploration of the Valley of the Amazon* (1853) was such that the navy authorized the printing of thirty thousand copies.

In the nineteenth century the figure of the explorer embodied the ambitions of a growing country along with western faith in scientific and technological progress. Horizons beckoned to the west, north, and south. The popular currency of the heroic explorer is perhaps glimpsed in the objections of a skeptical dissident, Henry David Thoreau, who, though he was himself an avid reader of travel books, advised his compatriots that the meaning of the Wilkes expedition to the South Sea was that "there are continents and seas in the moral world . . . yet unexplored," and that one ought to "obey the precept of the old philosopher, and Explore thyself" (pp. 301, 302).

See also Nature; Science; Travel Writing

BIBLIOGRAPHY

Primary Works

Emory, William H. *Lieutenant Emory Reports: A Reprint of W. H. Emory's Notes of a Military Reconnaissance*. Introduction and notes by Ross Calvin. Albuquerque: University of New Mexico Press, 1951.

Frémont, John Charles. *The Expeditions of John Charles Frémont*. Vol. 1, *Travels from 1838 to 1844*. Edited by Donald Jackson and Mary Lee Spence. Urbana: University of Illinois Press, 1970.

Harper's New Monthly Magazine 44 (December 1871 to May 1872). New York: Harper & Brothers.

Thoreau, Henry David. *Walden and Other Writings*. New York: Modern Library, 2000.

Secondary Works

Caswell, John Edwards. *Arctic Frontiers: United States Explorations in the Far North*. Norman: University of Oklahoma Press, 1956.

Goetzman, William H. *Exploration and Empire: The Explorer and the Scientist in the Winning of the American West*. 1966. Austin: Texas Historical Association, 2000.

Greenfield, Bruce. *Narrating Discovery: The Romantic Explorer in American Literature, 1790–1855*. New York: Columbia University Press, 1992.

Harrison, John P. "Science and Politics: Origins and Objectives of Mid-Nineteenth-Century Government Expeditions to Latin America." *Hispanic American Historical Review* 35 (May 1955): 175–202.

Jefferson, Thomas. *The Papers of Thomas Jefferson*. Vol. 9. Edited by Julian P. Boyd. Princeton, N.J.: Princeton University Press, 1954.

Pratt, Mary Louise. *Imperial Eyes: Travel Writing and Transculturation*. London and New York: Routledge, 1992.

Stanton, William. *The Great United States Exploring Expedition of 1838–1842*. Berkeley: University of California Press, 1975.

Bruce Greenfield

FACTORIES

The idea of factories in literature may sound discordant, even antithetical. Factories, after all, involve mechanization and subdivided tasks performed repetitively by low-skilled and often poorly educated workers. On the other hand, literature, in the romantic sense, enables imaginative flights and an expansiveness of human spirit at odds with the mill's confinement and regimentation. American authors considered classic, such as Nathaniel Hawthorne, Walt Whitman, and Emily Dickinson, apparently agreed, since their writings largely ignore the industrial workplace. A notable exception is Herman Melville's (1819–1991) short story "The Paradise of Bachelors and the Tartarus of Maids" (1855), set in a paper mill.

Literary scholars have likewise given little attention to industrialism, publishing few related critical studies. Although classic authors and scholars have mostly overlooked the factory, other nineteenth-century Americans created a large body of literary writings exploring its meaning. These "humbler" authors tended to derive from social strata closer to the factory experience. They were popular, often working-class writers who may themselves have toiled in the mills. They explored industrialism's human side, employing multiple literary genres—novels, short fiction, poetry, and sketches—to respond to the new workplace.

In 1820 the U.S. factory system was just taking hold, having originated within the textile industry, where women and children comprised the majority of workers. Women outnumbered men for several reasons. Because the first factories were spinning mills and spinning had traditionally been women's work, it was natural for them to fill these positions. Also factory work was considered lighter labor, suitable for women and children, who earned lower wages, at a time when men's physical strength was needed on the farms (see Abbott). Well into the mid-nineteenth century, cotton textiles were the predominant factory-made product. In 1850 cotton mills employed 33,150 men and 59,136 women. By 1870 these figures had risen to 42,790 men and 69,637 women. Factories developed in other industries as well by the 1850s, such as the manufacture of paper, iron, and garments. The numbers of all industrial workers rose dramatically from 731,137 men and 225,922 women in 1850 to 2,353,471 men and 353,950 women in 1870.

The literature reflects the dominance of the textile industry and its female workers. Into the later nineteenth century, much more writing about textile mills survives than for other industries, with women authors and characters predominating. The U.S. experience parallels that of Great Britain, where, as Susan Zlotnick argues, female authors played a major role in founding and shaping factory writing. The textile industry enabled, for the first time, the entry of large numbers of women into the public sphere of work. Fictional texts such as Eliza Jane Cate's *Lights and Shadows of Factory Life in New England* (1843), Ariel I. Cummings's *The Factory Girl; or, Gardez la coeur* (1847), and Miss J. A. B.'s *Mary Bean: The Factory Girl* (1850) address many women's issues, including changing gender roles, women's work, and violence against women. Writers tackle such social problems as workers's oppression, class bias, poverty, and child labor. Struggles between

Illustration of young women and children working in Fisher's Patent Label Manufactory, 1857. Factory writing of the nineteenth century reflected the predominance of female workers, frequently focusing on women's issues in addition to concerns such as social inequality and the evils of child labor. TIME LIFE PICTURES/GETTY IMAGES

labor and capital are explored in such texts as Martha Tyler's *A Book without a Title; or, Thrilling Events in the Life of Mira Dana* (1855), the first known American strike novel.

While highbrow writers increasingly eschewed didacticism and sensation, factory literature is often unabashedly moralistic and sensational. Examples include the tractate *The Factory Boy; or, The Child of Providence* (1839) by "a Lady" and the sensational *Over the Brink; or, The Peril of Beauty* (1869) by Jasper Colfax. The circumstances of this literature's publication have also contributed to its neglect. Whereas highbrow literature appeared in established publishers's journals and monographs, factory writing was often published in such ephemeral formats as broadside ballads, workers's periodicals, Sunday school tracts, and pulp novels. Although more readily available to poor, working people in its time, cheap literature was also less likely to be preserved and hence studied by scholars.

Factory literature is much scarcer for the 1820s and 1830s than for later decades because the factory system and publishing industry were still relatively small. One important early text is Thomas Man's pamphlet poem *Picture of a Factory Village* (1833). Man attacks the factory system for abandoning American ideals of freedom and equality and inflicting suffering and ignorance upon workers. The speaker characterizes mill employment as "grinding work," resembling slavery. Another poem questioning factory work's similarity to slave labor, "The Factory Girl" (1833), was published anonymously in a Boston labor paper, the *New England Artisan and Laboring Man's Repository*. The poem belongs to a great tradition of nineteenth-century working-class ballads, many of which were published and preserved in broadsides and labor papers—and probably as many lost. The poem's speaker, a "factory girl," insists that although she must heed the mill's bell, she "cannot be a slave" because she is "so fond of liberty" (9 May 1833).

Women workers found this poem inspiring, reciting portions of it during the 1834 and 1836 strikes in Lowell, Massachusetts.

Literature of the textile industry increased greatly in volume in the 1840s. A remarkable feature of this outpouring was the publication of numerous worker's's periodicals. Early titles, such as the *Lowell Offering* (Lowell, Massachusetts, 1840–1845), *The Operatives's Magazine* (Lowell, 1841–1842), and the *Wampanoag, and Operatives's Journal* (Fall River, Massachusetts, 1842), were designed for workers's edification, entertainment, and cultural enrichment and for informing the public about factory life. Some of the later periodicals, such as the *Manchester Operative* (Lowell and Manchester, New Hampshire, 1844–1845), the *Voice of Industry* (Fitchburg, Lowell, and Boston, Massachusetts, 1845–1848), and the *Factory Girl's Album, and Operatives's Advocate* (Exeter, New Hampshire, 1846–1847), emerged from the Ten-Hour movement, which sought to reduce the twelve- to fourteen-hour workday to ten hours (for more titles, see Ranta, pp. 43–55).

The periodicals offer a rich source for studying the literary treatment of class and industrialism. Often written and edited by workers, they include much short fiction and poetry. The editors and publishers frequently aimed at a female audience and printed many writings both by and for women. Such female-dominated magazines as the *Lowell Offering* are noteworthy for early and searching feminist speculation. The periodicals's representations of industrial work and workers anticipate later-nineteenth-century realist and naturalist writings.

Toward 1850 it becomes easier to find literature associated with other industries, such as those producing paper, iron, and garments. Texts related to the paper industry include Theodore Bang's pulp novel *The Mysteries of Papermill Village* (1845). An example of the city-mysteries fiction popular at the time, the text does not represent mill work but instead satirizes the community's foibles, for example, intemperance, gossip, and greed. Such texts (another is *Fun in a Factory Village*, published anonymously in Worcester, Massachusetts, in 1847), with their focus on street life and vernacular and their raucous humor, furnish rare glimpses into nineteenth-century working-class culture. Two studies that examine the dime novels that developed from such pulp literature are Michael Denning's *Mechanic Accents: Dime Novels and Working-Class Culture in America* and J. Randolph Cox's *Dime Novel Companion: A Source Book*.

In his story representing female paper-mill workers, "The Paradise of Bachelors and the Tartarus of Maids" (1855), Herman Melville addressed women's industrial work, utilizing tropes appearing earlier in factory-girl literature. The liveliness of mill women's culture, however, as seen in the factory periodicals and other writings, is entirely lacking in Melville's representation of silent, suffering workers. Viewing the women as the slaves of the machines, the narrator remarks, "The girls did not so much seem accessory wheels to the general machinery as mere cogs to the wheels" (p. 328). Scholars, including Elizabeth Renker and Elizabeth Freeman, have also noted the antifeminism of Melville's story (see Renker, chap. 3; Freeman). Nonetheless, Melville's critique of the factory system resonates with some labor-paper writings, such as those appearing in the *Voice of Industry*. An article signed by Juliana (probably Huldah J. Stone) expresses scorn for "the Cotton Lords of Lowell" who regard factory women as "there [*sic*] living machinery." The narrator asks whether some mill women have "been so long accustomed to watching machinery that they have actually become dwarfs in intellect—and lost to all sense of their own God-like powers of mind" (Juliana).

Paper-mill workers also appeared in Protestant evangelical tractate literature (small, cheap books issued abundantly by such bodies as the American Sunday-School Union and often intended for young and working-class readers). Anonymously published, *The Mill-Girls* (1862) tells of two young sisters's religious conversion. Laura and Helen Jones, age thirteen and nine, work as ragpickers in Tompkin's paper mill, employment the narrator describes as "one of the most unpleasant and unhealthy tasks that can be well imagined" (p. 6). As in other such texts, the characters begin to prosper once they embrace evangelical Christianity. While religion is presented as the solution to workers's problems, tracts are often quite critical of capitalists for neglecting workers's physical and spiritual needs.

Rebecca Harding Davis (1831–1910) represented the iron industry in her pioneering realist and naturalist novella *Life in the Iron Mills* (1861). In depicting the destruction of Hugh Wolfe, an artistic iron-mill worker, Davis contributed to the tradition of women's factory writing. The garment industry also received literary treatment when sweatshops developed after the sewing machine's introduction in 1846. An anonymously published novel, *Mabel Ross, the Sewing-Girl* (1866), chronicles the hardships of Chicago seamstresses. For meager pay, the women alternate stitching at home with toiling in "workrooms" at rows of sewing machines. The text includes scenes of an unsuccessful strike at one such establishment.

The texts mentioned above represent only a few of the hundreds published before 1870. These examples point to the importance of factory literature's opportunities for working-class and female expression. Although this little-known writing possesses special characteristics, it certainly influenced other American literature as well as women's roles and writing. In their treatment of industrial work and such social problems as poverty and violence, factory writers introduced new subjects and techniques that were developed by later realist and naturalist authors, such as Stephen Crane and Theodore Dreiser.

See also Childhood; Dime Novels; Labor; *Life in the Iron Mills; Lowell Offering;* Progress; Reform; Slavery; Technology; Urbanization

BIBLIOGRAPHY

Primary Works

Eisler, Benita, ed. *The Lowell Offering: Writings by New England Mill Women (1840–1845).* 1977. Reprint, New York: Norton, 1997.

Foner, Philip S., ed. *The Factory Girls: A Collection of Writings on Life and Struggles in the New England Factories of the 1840s by the Factory Girls Themselves.* Urbana: University of Illinois Press, 1977.

Juliana. "Lowell Girls—Standing at the Gate." *Voice of Industry* 2, no. 43 (7 May 1847).

Larcom, Lucy. *A New England Girlhood: Outlined from Memory.* 1889. Boston: Northeastern University Press, 1986.

Melville, Herman. *The Piazza Tales and Other Prose Pieces, 1839–1860.* Evanston, Ill.: Northwestern University Press, 1987.

Robinson, Harriet Hanson. *Loom and Spindle; or, Life among the Early Mill Girls.* Rev. ed. 1898. Kailua, Hawaii: Press Pacifica, 1976.

Secondary Works

Abbott, Edith. "The History of Industrial Employment of Women in the United States: An Introductory Study." *Journal of Political Economy* 14 (1906): 461–501.

Amireh, Amal. *The Factory Girl and the Seamstress: Imagining Gender and Class in Nineteenth-Century American Fiction.* New York: Garland, 2000.

Cox, J. Randolph. *The Dime Novel Companion: A Source Book.* Westport, Conn.: Greenwood Press, 2000.

Denning, Michael. *Mechanic Accents: Dime Novels and Working-Class Culture in America.* Rev. ed. London: Verso, 1998.

Freeman, Elizabeth. "'What Factory Girls Had Power to Do': The Techno-Logic of Working-Class Feminine Publicity in *The Lowell Offering.*" *Arizona Quarterly* 50, no. 2 (1994): 109–128.

Prestridge, Virginia W. *The Worker in American Fiction.* Champaign: Institute of Labor and Industrial Relations, University of Illinois, 1954.

Ranta, Judith A. *Women and Children of the Mills: An Annotated Guide to Nineteenth-Century American Textile Factory Literature.* Westport, Conn.: Greenwood Press, 1999.

Renker, Elizabeth. *Strike through the Mask: Herman Melville and the Scene of Writing.* Baltimore: Johns Hopkins University Press, 1996.

Zlotnick, Susan. *Women, Writing, and the Industrial Revolution.* Baltimore: Johns Hopkins University Press, 1998.

Judith A. Ranta

"THE FALL OF THE HOUSE OF USHER"

"The Fall of the House of Usher" is a landmark in literary history. While telling an eerie tale of gothic horror, Edgar Allan Poe (1809–1849) manages to echo the literary past, embody contemporary ideas and imagery, and anticipate the development of modernism. This short story, which first appeared in *Burton's Gentleman's Magazine* in September 1839, begins as Poe's nameless first-person narrator describes how he feels upon approaching the ancestral mansion of the Usher family where his boyhood friend Roderick Usher lives with his sister Madeline, the last descendants of a formerly grand family. The narrator first sees the house cloaked in shadow and considers it a melancholy sight, but he quickly modifies his reaction: he is overcome by "a sense of insufferable gloom," insufferable because the feeling is "unrelieved by any of that half-pleasurable, because poetic, sentiment, with which the mind usually receives even the sternest natural images of the desolate or terrible" (p. 145). The narrator is obviously used to taking pleasure in both the melancholy and the sublime. His inability to do so as he approaches the Usher mansion disturbs his equanimity. Try as he might he simply cannot achieve the pleasurable feelings he typically enjoys and sees that "no goading of the imagination could torture into aught of the sublime" (p. 145).

Poe's diction in this opening paragraph recalls literary concepts that had become prevalent in the critical discourse during the preceding century, when poets cultivated intense emotions to heighten philosophic contemplation and enhance aesthetic appreciation. Melancholy—"a not unpleasing sadness," in Herman Melville's words—emanates from the contemplation

Recovering his presence of mind after this failure, he dismisses his attempt to adjust the physical world to suit himself as a childish experiment. As he looks at the house again, it seems as if "around the whole mansion and domain there hung an atmosphere peculiar to themselves and their immediate vicinity" (p. 145). Capturing the mansion as it appears to the narrator, Poe uses a method of description Nathaniel Hawthorne used so well: he depicts the ambiguity of individual perception. Poe's narrator sees the mansion enshrouded with a weird vapor but shakes off that impression and redoubles his efforts in order to perceive "the real aspect of the building," which may be best characterized by its profound decrepitude (p. 145).

THE GOTHIC AND POE

The gothic imagery that fills "Usher" reflects a style of literature that had emerged during the late eighteenth century and was flourishing in the early decades of the nineteenth. The large mysterious castle filled with dark corners and secret passageways had been an important feature of gothic literature at least since Horace Walpole's *Castle of Otranto* (1765). Poe explicitly aligns "Usher" with such literature. Upon dismounting from his horse, the story's narrator enters "the Gothic archway of the hall" (p. 146). Once inside a valet leads him through "many dark and intricate passages" (p. 146). Having his narrator enter the mansion through a gothic archway, Poe identifies this short story as a piece of gothic fiction. Furthermore, he establishes a parallel between the narrator's experience and his reader's. Much as the narrator enters the gothic by entering the home, the reader enters the gothic by reading the story. Establishing such a parallel between reader and narrator, Poe incorporates a doppelgänger theme, another motif characteristic of gothic fiction. Poe's "William Wilson" (1839) is the classic story of a double or doppelgänger in the English language, but "Usher" also makes sophisticated use of this motif. Not only does Poe establish a parallel between narrator and reader, he also parallels the narrator and Roderick Usher, Roderick and his sister Madeline, and Roderick and the house itself.

Poe is the last great gothic writer, but his attitude toward the gothic often seems ambiguous. At times, he incorporates gothic elements only to spoof them. "The Raven" (1845), though a great example of the literary gothic, is not without satiric moments. Of course, the use of humor in gothic fiction was not unprecedented. As Benjamin Fisher has observed, humor had frequently been an element of the gothic before Poe's time. "Usher," however,

"The Fall of the House of Usher." Illustration by Arthur Rackham for a 1935 edition of Poe's tales. © BETTMANN/CORBIS

of death or adversity. The sublime, on the other hand, involves the pursuit of beauty in the face of terror. Using these two critical terms, Poe's narrator associates himself with the complex literary impulses they embody. Neither are sufficient to help him understand the appearance of the Usher home, however. When these traditional literary concepts fail him, he tries something new: he attempts to dispel the gloom by changing his physical relation to what he sees. Repositioning himself has quite the opposite effect, however: it only serves to heighten his fear. He now sees an image of the same house made more sinister by its reflection in the dark tarn.

Poe, it seems, has introduced these traditional concepts of late-eighteenth-century verse only to call them into question. Deprived of his usual, poetic way of coping with sadness and fear, the narrator has lost his moorings and must find new methods of dealing with what he encounters. One of these ways, his attempt to change his physical relation to the environment, fails, too.

treats the gothic with profound seriousness. Reading the story, one gets the impression that Poe set out to write the gothic tale to end all gothic tales.

In terms of the relationship of "Usher" to the American literature of its day, Poe's tale differs considerably. The middle third of the nineteenth century was a time of great literary jingoism. Numerous critics clamored for a national literature commensurate with the greatness of the nation and urged American writers to incorporate its mountains and rivers and plains into their work. Poe considered such jingoism, or extreme nationalism, hogwash. The way to make great national literature was not to make it represent the physical and political character of the nation: the way to make great American literature was to make it original. In so doing, it could stand on a world stage. Consequently, Poe seldom felt compelled to use American settings for his fiction. Instead, he frequently set his tales in the dark corners of Europe. "Usher" is no exception. The vault beneath the mansion dates back to "remote feudal times" and thus suggests an indeterminate European setting (p. 150).

CONTEMPORARY VISUAL CULTURE IN "USHER"

Many of Poe's gothic tales have similarly indeterminate time settings, but a bookish reference in "Usher" and the narrator's careful diction help give the story a contemporary setting. In no other tale does Poe describe a character's books in more detail than he does in "Usher." The narrator closely associates Roderick's personal character with the books he reads and lists several specific titles. One of the books is listed as "the Selenography of Brewster" (p. 149). The author Poe names, Sir David Brewster, was best known for his groundbreaking optical experiments. His *Treatise on Optics* (1831) and *Letters on Natural Magic* (1832) offered Poe rich sources of information about various optical phenomena. Poe gives "Usher" a contemporary setting with his reference to Brewster, whose most well-known works were published the same decade "Usher" appeared. Brewster never wrote a book called *Selenography*, however. What Poe had in mind was a work by Charles F. Blunt entitled *Selenographia, a Telescopic View of the Moon's Disc* (1833).

Attributing the *Selenographia* of Blunt to the more well-known Brewster, Poe allows himself to make optical phenomena an important aspect of the story. "Usher" also makes imaginative use of a popular entertainment that created optical illusions for purposes of amusement. As the valet first leads him through the mansion, the narrator describes what he sees: "The carvings of the ceilings, the somber tapestries of the walls, the ebon blackness of the floors, and the phantasmagoric armorial trophies which rattled as I strode" (p. 146). The narrator's use of the adjective "phantasmagoric" to describe the furnishings of the Usher home calls to mind the contemporary phantasmagoria, a popular form of entertainment that used weird noise and lighting effects for the purpose of scaring audiences. Later in the story the word phantasmagoria specifically pertains to Usher's mental state. The narrator speaks of Usher's "phantasmagoric conceptions" and finds books in his library "in strict keeping with this character of phantasm" (p. 149). The narrator finds his own mental state influenced by the home's interior, too:

> I endeavored to believe that much, if not all of what I felt, was due to the phantasmagoric influence of the gloomy furniture of the room—of the dark and tattered draperies, which tortured into motion by the breath of a rising tempest, swayed fitfully to and fro upon the walls, and rustled uneasily about the decorations of the bed. (P. 150)

Much as the producers of contemporary phantasmagoria shows did and much as he had done himself earlier in "Ligeia," Poe uses lighting effects, sound effects, and the semblance of movement in "Usher" to enhance the ghastly nature of the setting. Madeline Usher's reappearance at the story's end resembles the specters depicted in the denouement of a phantasmagoria show, as she is enshrouded with "blood upon her white robes, and the evidence of some bitter struggle upon every portion of her emaciated frame" (p. 152).

Discussing the history of the word phantasmagoria, Terry Castle has used "The Fall of the House of Usher" to show how the term underwent a paradigmatic shift from the external to the internal around the time Poe published the tale. The word originally entered the English language to describe a form of entertainment, but when the popularity of phantasmagoria shows waned, the word stayed in the language to refer to hallucinatory images conjured up by the mind. "Usher" finely captures this shift from the external to the internal. Though Poe uses the adjective "phantasmagoric" to describe home furnishings early in the story, before its end, he is talking about phantasms of the mind.

Poe's reference to Brewster and his use of the word "phantasmagoria" clearly fix the action of "Usher" in the present. The other books Roderick and the narrator read in the story help link past and future. Several of Usher's books describe imaginary journeys to utopias. In *Iter Subterraneum* (1741), for instance, the great Danish writer Baron Ludvig Holberg takes his fictional narrator, Nicholas Klimm, on an imaginary voyage underground to a fantastic place. Tommaso Campanella's *City of the Sun* (1623), another book Roderick reads, describes an ideal utopian society inspired by Plato's vision of the universe. As Priscilla Rice has suggested, Poe's reference to Campanella reinforces important themes of the story. Campanella posited that the health of the individual family reflected the health of the political state in which they lived. Implicitly, the unhealthfulness of the Usher family reflects the decrepitude of their home. The works by Campanella, Holberg, and others suggest that the books Roderick and the narrator read in the present come from the past yet anticipate life in the future.

Thoughts of the future send Roderick into a state of terror. As he tells the narrator: "I dread the events of the future, not in themselves, but in their results. I shudder at the thought of any, even the most trivial, incident, which may operate upon this intolerable agitation of my soul" (p. 148). Roderick's comments are a reflection of his illness, which involves a hypersensitivity to any external stimuli. He can eat only the blandest of foods: mulligatawny has no place at his dinner table. He can tolerate the sound of no musical instruments save the quiet strumming of his own guitar. He exists by keeping himself in extreme stasis, by never trying anything new, never experimenting with anything unfamiliar, never leaving his house. He is an exile in time. Madeline Usher is afflicted with a different condition, but one that has much the same result. She is cataleptic. She literally exists in a state of physical torpor. She, too, seems trapped in an eternal present, never slipping back into a happier past, never going forward to an eternal future.

Roderick and Madeline possess these afflictions as the narrator arrives. Through much of his time in the mansion, their conditions only intensify. Roderick's sensitivity becomes even more acute. Madeline's catalepsy becomes so severe that it seems as if she has died. Her apparent death introduces a catastrophic element of change to Roderick's life. They entomb her in an ancient vault that forms a part of the dungeons from the feudal past. Entombed below the house, Madeline is removed from the present into the realm of the past. But hers, like those of so many other Poe characters, is a premature burial. She escapes her sepulchre to accost her brother. Her reappearance only precipitates the inevitable. She confronts Roderick, and the two die in each others's arms. The narrator flees the house. As he escapes, a huge crack forms in the masonry, and the house collapses into the tarn.

"USHER" AND THE AVANT-GARDE

"The Fall of the House of Usher" would be recognized by many as Poe's finest tale and, indeed, one of the best short stories in the English language. In the introduction to his edition of Poe, Padraic Colum, for example, calls the story "splendid" and names it as one of the "world's best tales" (p. 148). A reprinting of it in the *New York Times* (17 January 1909) to celebrate the centenary of Poe's birth introduced it with the headnote: "Students of Poe and his works hold differing opinions as to which of his tales is entitled to the first place among his prose writings. But certainly a large number of these—and possibly a majority—would give first place to 'The Fall of the House of Usher.'" The tale has inspired numerous other works including Claude Debussy's *La Chute de la Maison d'Usher*, an opera he left unfinished at the time of his death; Jean Epstein's impressionistic film, *La Chute de La Maison d'Usher* (1928); and *The Fall of the House of Usher* (1928), a highly experimental avant-garde short film created by James Sibley Watson Jr. and Melville Webber. The character of Roderick Usher also anticipates many of the protagonists of some of the most influential literary works of the modernist period. Allen Tate sees a little Roderick Usher in such literary characters as Stephen Daedalus, J. Alfred Prufrock, and Mrs. Dalloway. In Poe's story, neither Roderick nor Madeline have a future, but the story itself has had a profound influence on the development of modernism.

Some have claimed more credit for the story's influence on modernist art than it may deserve, however. During the course of the story, Roderick often amuses himself by painting. The narrator describes Roderick's paintings as "pure abstractions" that Roderick "contrived to throw upon his canvas" (p. 152). Roderick Usher is the first abstract expressionist, a few commentators have asserted. Such claims may be more clever than useful, but it is productive to see "Usher" as yet another of Poe's stories that symbolize the life of the artist. Roderick's paintings may identify him as an artist, but his mental and physical condition are more important for understanding his attitude toward art. Roderick is like many authors Poe critiqued in his day: he is afraid of the future. Consequently, he does not experiment; he does not take chances; he does not stray from what is comfortable, from what he already knows. His death in the story parallels the death of any artist who refuses to take risks.

The narrator, however, who alone survives to tell Roderick's tale, survives because he runs from the house. Instead of being immobilized like Roderick, the narrator possesses a dynamic quality that allows him to flee. Closing his narrative, he explains, "I saw the mighty walls rushing asunder—there was a long tumultuous shouting sound like the voice of a thousand waters—and the deep and dank tarn at my feet closed sullenly and silently over the fragments of the '*House of Usher*'" (p. 152). This is no statement of a man struck with terror who has just witnessed the death of a friend and his sister and has just barely escaped from death himself. This is the voice of a meticulous literary artist. The clever simile, the biblical echo (Ezekiel 43:2), the conjoined, alliterative word pairs: all bespeak a meticulous literary craftsmanship. "The Fall of the House of Usher" is the story of two artist figures, Roderick Usher and the narrator, but the narrator is the one Poe wants his readers to emulate. Artistic stasis leads to death. Dynamic experimentation leads to the future.

See also Gothic Fiction; "The Philosophy of Composition"; Short Story

BIBLIOGRAPHY

Primary Work
Poe, Edgar Allan. "The Fall of the House of Usher." *Burton's Gentleman's Magazine* 5 (1839): 145–152.

Secondary Works
Brennan, Matthew C. "Turnerian Topography: The Paintings of Roderick Usher." *Studies in Short Fiction* 27 (1990): 605–607.

Castle, Terry. "Phantasmagoria: Spectral Technology and the Metaphorics of Modern Reverie." *Critical Inquiry* 15 (1988): 26–61.

Colum, Padraic. "Introduction." In *Edgar Allan Poe's Tales of Mystery and Imagination*, edited by Padraic Colum, pp. vii–xiv. London: J. M. Dent, 1908.

Fisher, Benjamin F. "Poe and the Gothic Tradition." In *The Cambridge Companion to Edgar Allan Poe*, edited by Kevin J. Hayes, pp. 72–91. New York: Cambridge University Press, 2002.

Hayes, Kevin J. *Poe and the Printed Word.* New York: Cambridge University Press, 2000.

Howes, Craig. "Burke, Poe, and 'Usher': The Sublime and Rising Woman." *ESQ* 31 (1985): 173–189.

Peeples, Scott. "Poe's 'Constructiveness's and 'The Fall of the House of Usher.'" In *The Cambridge Companion to Edgar Allan Poe*, edited by Kevin J. Hayes, pp. 178–190. New York: Cambridge University Press, 2002.

Rice, Priscilla. "Poe and Campanella." *Edgar Allan Poe Review* 4 (2003): 105–107.

Tate, Allen. "Three Commentaries: Poe, James, and Joyce." *Sewanee Review* 58 (1950): 1–15.

Walker, I. M. "The Legitimate Sources of Terror in 'The Fall of the House of Usher.'" *Modern Language Review* 61 (1966): 585–592.

Kevin J. Hayes

FASHION

Distinguished from dress or costume by its demand for novelty, fashion was of course constantly changing throughout the antebellum period. The highly ornamented dresses of the 1820s, for example, with their enormous sleeves and ankle-length hemlines were replaced by the simpler line of floor-length dress fashionable in the 1830s. But it was more than hemlines and sleeve styles that were changing. Indeed, the antebellum period represents dramatic shifts in the very meaning of fashion and its relationship to other cultural phenomena.

STYLES OF FASHION

Although the specifics of what was fashionable changed from year to year and season to season, scholars typically date the beginning of Victorian fashion as the early 1820s, when women abandoned the previous "empire" or "classical" mode of dress that featured a high waistline and straight skirt. That overall vertical silhouette was dramatically altered with the introduction of Victorian fashion. Indeed, as Valerie Steele has described, Victorian fashion presents the female body as "essentially formed by two cones—the long full, structured skirt and the tailored, boned bodice—intersecting at a narrow and constricted waist" (pp. 51–52).

While this overall Victorian silhouette survived until about 1910, scholars have suggested three distinct periods within Victorian fashion. The 1820s were a time of intense ornamentation. Sleeves were large, and elaborate accessories were popular, including plumed hats, ribbons, ruffles, and fancy jewelry. By the mid-1830s a new more subdued or demure style emerged, which some scholars have characterized as sentimental. Sleeves were tighter, decoration much simpler, and bonnets replaced the elaborate hats of the previous decade. Because the emphasis was on inconspicuous dress and overall self-effacement, the sentimental style appeared in some ways to be antifashion, and indeed it became increasingly popular to critique the power and popularity of fashion itself.

That apparent resistance to fashion gradually eroded by 1850, which marks the beginning of the age of the crinoline, or hoop skirt. Women were increasingly encouraged to find an individual style rather than blindly following the particular conventions of the moment, and fashion was increasingly seen as an acceptable form of performance in the 1850s and 1860s, creating a renewed interest in elaborate dress. Rich fabrics, bright colors, wide sleeves, and elaborate ruffles and flounces were all popular in the 1850s and 1860s. This tendency toward more elaborate dress was certainly aided by the introduction of the sewing machine, which became widely available in the late 1850s.

But as the name "age of crinoline" suggests, these two decades are best remembered for the size of the skirts. To reach the desired circumference (approaching fifteen feet in some cases), women turned to as many as seven separate petticoats. In addition to these petticoats women bore the weight of the skirts themselves, which could include more than twenty-five yards of material. The first crinolines, created with a gauzelike fabric stiffened with starch, actually relieved some of the weight of these enormous skirts. Introduced shortly after the crinoline was the hoop, a cage made of steel wires that eliminated the need for multiple petticoats. These elaborate hoop skirts remained popular throughout much of the 1860s.

MEN'S FASHIONS

In general, fashion was strongly associated with middle-class women's dress, but men's fashion underwent significant change during the antebellum period. In particular, scholars note the dramatically decreased use of bright colors and elaborate decoration in men's fashions, particularly in clothing designated for work, which was increasingly distinguished from men's evening wear. By the mid-nineteenth century the plain, dark business suit dominated middle-class men's fashions. Various commentators have suggested that such changes reflect a dramatic shift in fashion's emphasis. While in previous centuries fashion highlighted the contrast between classes, nineteenth-century fashion emphasized a contrast between men and women.

While men's clothing changed at a far less rapid pace than did women's, contemporary commentators were nonetheless aware of changing fashions for men. The columnist Fanny Fern (Sara Payson Willis Parton, 1811–1872) was particularly critical of many trends. In one 1851 column titled "Thoughts on Dress," for instance, she poked fun at two men at a church service. One was struggling "to get his head in a comfortable position to look over the top of his dickey and see the singers, without cutting his ears off" (p. 217). The other created a "most extraordinary noise—such a

creaking"—simply by loosening his very tightly buttoned vest (p. 217). In another essay, "In the Dumps," Fern again criticized the constricted nature of men's clothing: "Why can't they leave off those detestable stiff collars, stocks, and things, that make them all look like choked chickens, and which hide so many handsomely-turned throats" (p. 287).

FASHION MAGAZINES

Just as men's fashions became increasingly differentiated from women's, so too did the methods of transmitting fashion diverge. Because ready-made clothing for men developed much earlier than standardized dress for women, men's fashions were transmitted largely through tailors and trade journals, such as *Mirror of Fashion.*

Women's fashions, however, were spread directly to individual middle-class women through the fashion magazines that developed during this period. Eighteenth-century and early-nineteenth-century magazines had occasionally commented on fashion, but it wasn't until editors and publishers were able to include elaborate illustrations that true fashion magazines flourished.

And flourish they did. In 1827, following the example of late-eighteenth-century ladies's magazines in France and England, Philadelphia's *Album and Ladies's Weekly Gazette* was the first American magazine to include an illustration of contemporary fashion. Soon afterward came *Godey's Lady's Book,* which was founded in 1830 and became the nation's most popular magazine. Although it had an intellectual and literary focus, its illustrations, especially its fashion plates, which were hand-colored steel engravings, were key to the magazine's success. In some years Louis Godey printed as many as twenty fashion plates in each issue, typically featuring pictures of small groups of women in the latest fashions with their dresses hand-painted in watercolors. Children's fashions were also occasionally included. Although these "embellishments," as they were often called, were expensive, many other magazines followed Godey's success, making fashion plates one of the most popular elements of antebellum magazines. Descriptions of current dress styles, historical essays about fashion, and patterns for fashionable clothing and accessories were also regular features not only in the *Lady's Book* but also in such periodicals as *Ladies's Companion, Peterson's Magazine,* and later, *Demorest's Monthly Magazine* and *Harper's Bazar* (as it was originally spelled). These magazines, some of which boasted national circulations, were particularly influential in bringing fashion to nonurban areas. Although they frequently adapted the displayed styles to suit their own circumstances, most women throughout the United States had access to fashion.

Although such magazines promoted themselves as the best source of the latest fashions, these same magazines virtually always discouraged excessive attention to fashion. When fashionable dress was used to reflect a woman's morality or her aesthetic sense, in other words, it was praised. When used to deceive others or to mask an inferior sense of morality, however, fashion was condemned. One of the greatest dangers posed by fashion, according to *Godey's Lady's Book,* was that it diverted attention away from moral and spiritual self-improvement. As one editorial explained, "Oh! It is grievous to see a being standing upon the threshold of an immortal existence, created for glorious purposes, and with faculties to fulfill them, discussing the merits of a ribbon, or the form of a bow, or the width of a frill, as earnestly as if the happiness of her race, or her soul's salvation depended upon her decision" (January 1839, p. 8).

ANTIFASHION AND DRESS REFORM

These concerns about fashion were much more pronounced in other periodicals and other media. Indeed, fashion was regularly attacked in sermons, medical journals, popular magazines, even fiction, and it was associated with virtually every imaginable offence—physical injury, mental illness, lack of patriotism, immoral behavior, and reckless spending, to name just a few. Although the antifashion reformers included women's rights activists, not all such reformers took a proto-feminist position, and many of those people arguing against fashion's popularity relied on quite restricted notions of feminine modesty and virtue.

While most opponents of fashion were content to voice their opposition, dress reformers not only changed their own style of dress but also encouraged others to do the same. Robert Owen's socialist community in New Harmony, Indiana, was one early attempt at radical dress reform. Owen believed that uniform clothing for all would support his goal of an egalitarian community, and the women of New Harmony were encouraged, though evidently not required, to wear an outfit similar to the men's, consisting of pantaloons and a coat. Somewhat similar styles were adopted at several religious communities, including the Oneida community led by John Humphrey Noyes and Michigan's Beaver Island group of Strangite Mormons. Leaders in the water-cure movement also advocated women's wearing of trousers and created the National Dress Reform Association in 1856.

The most important attempt at dress reform—and the most covered by the contemporary press—involves the actions of a small group of feminists—Elizabeth Smith Miller, Elizabeth Cady Stanton, and Amelia Jenks Bloomer—who walked through Seneca Falls, New York, in 1851 wearing short skirts and pantaloons. The occasion was covered in several newspapers, and hostile cartoons and essays soon spread throughout the popular press. Called at various times "Turkish Trousers" and the "freedom dress," the outfit quickly became known as "bloomers." Although a number of feminist leaders defended the outfit, most soon abandoned it, realizing that it was detracting from their overall political objectives.

FUNCTIONS OF FASHION

The public's heated response to these attempts at dress reform suggest that fashion is not simply about basic essentials of comfort or protection from sun or cold. On the contrary, fashion inevitably carries social and political meanings.

Following the influential work of turn-of-the-century philosophers, most notably Thorstein Veblen, fashion has long been linked with the development of a bourgeois capitalist society. The spread of fashion beyond the aristocracy in the late eighteenth century, then, was the result of the middle class's growing power and its desire both to imitate the aristocracy and to distinguish itself from the lower classes. According to Veblen's *Theory of the Leisure Class* (1899), elaborate fashionable dress was a sign of a woman's leisure, which in turn reflected the economic power of her husband or father. One of the essential functions of fashion, then, is to indicate one's class position.

But as the examples from antebellum America make clear, fashion was not limited to middle- and upper-class women. Diaries from U.S. women in fact demonstrate that working-class women observed and participated in fashion. While they might not have been able to hire a seamstress, as did their middle-class counterparts, they could make their own dresses, often with cheaper fabrics but in styles similar to the latest fashions displayed in women's magazines. In this way fashion could be used to promote social mobility or to mask one's social class.

In addition to class, fashion has been linked with issues of sexuality. For many years antebellum fashion was assumed to be a systemic part of patriarchy that kept women oppressed. The Victorians's long dresses, for example, have been interpreted as evidence of a heightened discomfort with the female body and female sexuality. The corset, likewise, is often associated with keeping women passive and confined.

Bloomers. In this 1850 lithograph, Amelia Jenks Bloomer (right), a young woman, and a girl are shown wearing Bloomer's innovative costume. GETTY IMAGES

More recently, however, historians have questioned these assumptions. Refuting the idea that any one type of clothing is universally seen as natural, comfortable, or erotic, Anne Hollander has shown how both shapeless and tight-fitting clothing, long and short skirts, have all been understood as reflecting—rather than concealing—

the wearer's sexuality. Valerie Steele has likewise challenged the stereotype of Victorian fashion as inherently prudish, arguing that expression of eroticism was an essential feature of Victorian fashion. Indeed, the barely exposed toe, the tight waists, and the low necklines popular were all markers of sexuality in Victorian fashion.

While economic theories of fashion generally portray women as competing with one another for fashionable status, more recent interpretations have begun to explore how fashion can also serve to connect women with one another. The popular fashion plates, for instance, frequently depict women in intimate settings with one another. Much like twentieth- and twenty-first century women who take pleasure in shopping together, these images suggest that fashion can be important components of women's shared culture.

FASHION AND LITERATURE

Because it sometimes suggests an absolute obedience to a superficial standard of beauty rather than an inherent appreciation of aesthetics, fashion has long been portrayed as antithetical to literature. Certainly a number of antebellum writers defined their goals in stark contrast to the practices of fashionable life. In the opening chapter of *Walden* (1854), for instance, Henry David Thoreau (1817–1862) expresses his complete disdain for fashion. Eager for his readers to transform themselves rather than their clothing, Thoreau bemoans Americans's blind obedience to Fashion, who "spins and weaves and cuts with full authority." As Thoreau explains, "The head monkey at Paris puts on a traveller's cap, and all the monkeys in America do the same" (p. 25).

But Thoreau's opposition of fashion with spiritual transformation masks the complex relationship between fashion and literature in the antebellum period. Many writers were aware of the symbolic power of dress, as suggested, for example, by Nathaniel Hawthorne's portrayal of Hester's beautifully embroidered *A* in *The Scarlet Letter* (1850) or Harriet Beecher Stowe's attention to Marie St. Clare's silk dresses, lace, and jewelry in *Uncle Tom's Cabin* (1852). Moreover, many of the period's best-known writers, such as Edgar Allan Poe and Nathaniel Hawthorne, published their work in magazines literally alongside fashion plates. Fashion was also influenced by literature. Capitola Black, the heroine in E. D. E. N. Southworth's *The Hidden Hand* (1859), for example, inspired the "Capitola" hat.

The response of women writers to fashion was particularly diverse. On the one hand is a writer like Ann S. Stephens, a popular novelist and editor who worked for more than fifty years in fashionable magazines such as *Peterson's Magazine, Ladies's Companion,* and her own *Mrs. Stephens's Illustrated New Monthly.* Refusing to accept the idea that fashion was antithetical to art and literature, these magazines repeatedly defined literature and fashion as similar enterprises. As early as 1834, for example, the *Ladies's Companion* published an essay titled "The Dress of Ladies," in which the author compares the "pains, which a lady takes in adorning her person" to the poet's "genius, invention, and taste" (August 1834, p. 193). A later editorial likewise promised readers to "talk over our favorite authors, painters, sculptors, milliners and dressmakers" (January 1838, p. 146). This strong link between fashion and art is also demonstrated by the facts of Stephens's career. Best known for her serial novels that were issued in *Peterson's* from 1848 until her death in 1886, Stephens not only wrote novels attentive to details of fashionable clothing, but she also enjoyed a reputation as a fashionable celebrity.

Other women writers, however, were much more critical of contemporary fashion. In addition to poking fun at men's fashions, for instance, Fanny Fern frequently mocked the ridiculous excesses of fashion, from $40 handkerchiefs to waist laces so tight that a woman "breathes only by rare accident" (pp. 267, 341). In *A New Home—Who'll Follow?* (1839), Caroline Kirkland likewise exposes the worthlessness of paper-soled shoes on the muddy Michigan frontier. In addition to these more comical concerns about fashion, many women writers focused attention on the fashionable belle who spent all of her time and energy maintaining her looks. Emphasizing the corrupt basis of fashionable life, these writers used this familiar figure as a foil to their virtuous heroines. Near the opening of Susan Warner's (1819–1885) *The Wide, Wide World* (1850), for instance, the heroine Ellen meets Mrs. Dunscombe, who will be escorting Ellen as she leaves her mother to live with her aunt. While much of the novel is devoted to Ellen's searching for appropriate mentors, Mrs. Dunscombe is quickly identified as incapable of serving in this capacity. A "lady of the first family and fashion," Mrs. Dunscombe has virtually no sympathy for Ellen and instead complains of Ellen's dress. Mrs. Duncombe's daughter Margaret likewise criticizes Ellen for looking as if she had "come out of the woods," with an unfashionable bonnet and no gloves (pp. 58, 66). While the novel does not completely condemn attention to clothing—indeed one of the novel's most memorable scenes involves an elaborate shopping expedition—it does suggest, as do many other novels of the period, that excessive attention to one's appearance is a mark of inadequate moral development.

One of the most elaborate literary explorations of contemporary fashion was Anna Cora Mowatt's (1819–1870) satiric play *Fashion*, which was first performed in New York in 1845. Like many sentimental novels of the antebellum period, Mowatt presents the fashionable belle Seraphina Tiffany as a foil to the more virtuous Gertrude. But Seraphina's greatest offenses—and those of her equally fashionable mother—are not so much their clothing as their behavior. Filled with foolish ideas of what fashionable life entails, Mrs. Tiffany speaks bad French, praises people who are late, plans balls even though her husband is near bankruptcy, and ultimately is fooled by someone pretending to be a count. As the hero, appropriately named Adam Trueman, declares, not only does fashion require people to "expend all their rapture upon the works of their tailors and dressmakers," it also demands far more dangerous goals. As Trueman explains, fashion is an "agreement between certain persons to live without using their souls! to substitute etiquette for virtue—decorum for purity—manners for morals! to affect a shame for the works of their Creator!" (p. 39). Suggesting the extent to which concerns about fashion extended far beyond simple choices of clothing, Mowatt's play attests to the rich cultural meanings of socially accepted behaviors and dress.

See also Feminism; *Godey's Lady's Book;* Periodicals; Seneca Falls Convention; Sentimentalism; Sexuality and the Body; Theater; Utopian Communities

BIBLIOGRAPHY

Primary Works

Fern, Fanny. *Ruth Hall and Other Writings.* Edited by Joyce W. Warren. New Brunswick, N.J.: Rutgers University Press, 1986.

Mowatt, Anna Cora. *Fashion; or, Life in New York: A Comedy, in Five Acts.* New York: Samuel French, 1849.

Thoreau, Henry David. *Walden.* 1854. Edited by J. Lyndon Shanley. Princeton, N.J.: Princeton University Press, 1971.

Warner, Susan. *The Wide, Wide World.* 1850. New York: Feminist Press, 1987.

Secondary Works

Banner, Lois W. *American Beauty.* New York: Knopf, 1983.

Fischer, Gayle V. *Pantaloons and Power: Nineteenth-Century Dress Reform in the United States.* Kent, Ohio: Kent State University Press, 2001.

Haltunnen, Karen. *Confidence Men and Painted Women: A Study of Middle-Class Culture in America, 1830–1870.* New Haven, Conn.: Yale University Press, 1982.

Hollander, Anne. *Seeing through Clothes.* New York: Viking, 1978.

Lehuu, Isabelle. *Carnival on the Page: Popular Print Media in Antebellum America.* Chapel Hill: University of North Carolina Press, 2000.

Okker, Patricia. "Fashion and the Magazine Novelist: The Case of Ann Stephens." In her *Social Stories: The Magazine Novel in Nineteenth-Century America.* Charlottesville: University of Virginia Press, 2003.

Severa, Joan L. *Dressed for the Photographer: Ordinary Americans and Fashion, 1840–1900.* Kent, Ohio: Kent State University Press, 1995.

Steele, Valerie. *Fashion and Eroticism: Ideals of Feminine Beauty from the Victorian Era to the Jazz Age.* New York: Oxford University Press, 1985.

Wilson, Elizabeth. *Adorned in Dreams: Fashion and Modernity.* London: Virago, 1985.

Zakim, Michael. *Ready-Made Democracy: A History of Men's Dress in the American Republic, 1760–1860.* Chicago: University of Chicago Press, 2003.

Patricia Okker

FEMALE AUTHORSHIP

American women were highly visible as professional writers in the nineteenth century. In fact, male writers often expressed dismay about the popularity of literature by women, particularly at mid-century, when many best-selling novels were authored by women. Nathaniel Hawthorne's often-quoted lament about the "d——d mob of scribbling women," written in a letter to the publisher William D. Ticknor in 1855, captures the frustration that some felt at the prominence of women in the literary marketplace. A look at some statistics about women novelists substantiates the perception that women were prominent in the literary marketplace. Before 1830 about one-third of those who published fiction were women. During antebellum years about 40 percent of novels reviewed were written by women. In the 1850s almost 50 percent of the best-sellers were written by women, including Susan B. Warner's (Elizabeth Wetherall) *The Wide, Wide World* (1851), which quickly sold more than 100,000 copies, and Harriet Beecher Stowe's *Uncle Tom's Cabin* (1852), which sold more than 300,000 copies in its first year alone. In addition to writing novels, women also wrote for newspapers and magazines and were represented in the ranks of poets and nonfiction writers.

The women who earned livings as authors between 1820 and 1870 came from strikingly similar backgrounds. They were primarily, though not exclusively, white, Protestant, middle-class women. They were frequently from New England in the early years and had access to the education and opportunities necessary to develop their literary talents. Economic necessity,

Harriet Beecher Stowe. © BETTMANN/CORBIS

family difficulties, and limited options for earning money first led many of them to begin writing for income. Writing for magazines and newspapers provided many with a better income than they could earn by sewing or teaching. As the century passed, the characteristics of female authors slowly came to reflect the changing ethnic, racial, and religious backgrounds of a nation that had freed its slaves and was moving westward. Nevertheless, the majority of female authors before 1870 continued to be from white, middle-class backgrounds. As wage earners, these women differed from other members of their gender, race, and class. Unlike their female friends and neighbors who lived primarily as wives and mothers, female authors supported or contributed to the support of their families by their incomes.

Though they were writers, they were not free from many of the duties expected of traditional middle-class women. Like other women, female authors were expected to be responsible for doing the housework and caring for children and other family members. Even when there were domestic servants in the household, women often worked beside them. Female authors were also involved in the rounds of visits and social activities that characterized their class. While some women managed all of this on their own, others were fortunate to have family members—husbands, siblings, or other relatives—who helped them out. For example, Augusta Dodge, sister of the writer Mary Abigail Dodge (Gail Hamilton, 1833–1896), took over most of their household tasks. Friendships that developed between female authors were also important for sustaining their efforts.

ATTITUDES TOWARD FEMALE AUTHORSHIP

Female writers in the nineteenth century lived and worked within an ambiguous cultural context of ideas and attitudes related to their gender and their occupation. These attitudes shaped their experiences as writers and their understanding of themselves as writers. For example, no matter what their own beliefs about womanhood were, female authors could not avoid being judged by others and by themselves in relation to the gender expectations of their day. They had to come to terms with the popular, conservative belief in True Womanhood with its expectations that middle-class women ought to focus their lives solely on religious, moral, and domestic matters, leaving business and other worldly affairs to men. Women and men were supposed to have separate spheres of activity and influence. True Women were expected to create a satisfying and uplifting home life for husband and children and to lead their families by Christian example; they were not expected to pursue a career. In response, some writers, like Emma Dorothy Eliza Nevitte (E. D. E. N.) Southworth (1819–1899), one of the most popular writers of the mid-nineteenth century, defended their literary activity by claiming that they were true women as well as authors. Other female authors, like Harriet Beecher Stowe (1811–1896), adopted the more liberal rationale of women's rights advocates and educators that women should bring their special qualities of purity, morality, and nurturance into the world through writing as well as through volunteer work and teaching. Depending on their own personality and circumstances, female authors defended their literary activity by claiming they were True Women despite their profession or by justifying what they were doing as an extension of their woman's role into the world.

Given the success of women, it is clear that attitudes toward gender roles did not stop all women from writing, though those attitudes did shape female authors's thinking about and defense of their careers. The nineteenth-century views of womanhood also shaped the ways in which authors and their works were judged. Literary critics almost always critiqued a woman's literary work by commenting on the gender of the author and the appropriateness of content and

When Mary Abigail Dodge (Gail Hamilton) discovered that her gentleman publisher, James T. Fields, was not compensating her as well as some other authors, she first tried to settle the dispute through discussion. When that did not satisfy her, she pressed for arbitration. She wrote a thinly veiled account of the dispute in A Battle of the Books (1870). In her conclusion, Dodge argues that both male and female authors must put aside their idealistic views of authorship and gender as well as their expectations of generous, fair treatment from the Gentlemen Publishers.

It is the same with women as with men, for in literature as in the gospel, there is neither male nor female. When a woman does any work for which she receives money, she becomes so far a man, and passes immediately and inevitably under the yoke of trade. She has no right to demand a favorable judgment of her work because she is a woman, nor has she the least right to require that chivalry shall come in to help fix or secure her compensation. . . . Under this law there is no sex, no chivalry, no deference, no mercy. There is nothing but supply and demand. Nothing but buy and sell. To him who understands it, and guides himself by it, it is a chariot of state bearing him on to fame and fortune. To him who does not comprehend it and flings himself against it, it is a car of Juggernaut, crushing him beneath its wheels, without passion, but without pity.

Hamilton, A Battle of the Books, pp. 287–288.

style for a female author. Women were most often praised for conforming to established expectations for womanhood. Thus the reviews of the poet Louise Chandler Moulton (1835–1908), for example, included comments on her truthfulness, innocence, and dependence. Women were expected to write like women, yet they were also criticized for doing so. Harriet Prescott Spofford (1835–1921), for example, was criticized for being wordy, even though wordiness was expected of women. The negative reception that Sara Payson Willis Parton (Fanny Fern, 1811–1872) and her story *Ruth Hall* (1855) received from critics is a good example of the harsh criticism women and their literary works could face when they did not conform to gender expectations. She created a scandal by

her "unfeminine" portrayal of relatives who opposed her independent behavior and her literary career.

Despite criticism of their womanhood, female authors persisted in their profession, justified intellectually perhaps by similarities in the concepts of womanhood and authorship. Between 1820 and 1870 the concept of authorship was evolving from that of the "genteel amateur" to the professional writer. The concept of author as genteel amateur without commercial aims, writing only when the spirit moved "him," was compatible with the nineteenth-century ideal of womanhood, safe from and superior to commercial demands. In this vein female authors such as Catharine Maria Sedgwick (1789–1867) insisted that their writing was simply a pastime, not a profession. Like a male author, woman too could write from her home for the pleasure of a respectable audience. Furthermore, she could claim she was especially well suited to provide for her readers the moral and social lessons expected from all authors. Apparently many agreed that authorship and womanhood were similar; male writers were sometimes characterized as "feminine" in their attitudes and work. Nevertheless, the identification of womanhood with authorship was never complete; a female author was always distinguished from the male norm by being labeled "lady author" or "authoress."

Nineteenth-century views of authorship and audience expectations also helped open the profession to women. As an emerging middle-class profession, authorship seemed to express the anxieties of an increasingly industrial and class-conscious society. Thus for many writers authorship was viewed in comparison to manual labor—often as separate from and superior to manual labor. At the same time middle-class women's role in the home was considered separate from and superior to the harsh realities of industrial work. In this regard being an author and a middle-class woman were not too far apart conceptually. Furthermore, as authorship became a profession, all writers were conscious of the mid-nineteenth-century audience for successful work—an audience with expectations that literary works, especially fiction, would reflect middle-class moral and family values. These understandings of authorship and of audience encouraged women to find their voices as authors along with, and often more successfully than, men.

In addition to some compatibility of values between the concepts of womanhood and authorship, female writers also found some familiar values in the literary marketplace of the mid-nineteenth century. In this time period many publishers and editors tried to present themselves in the image of the Gentleman Publisher. Well-known publishers who represented themselves as Gentlemen Publishers included such men as George P. Putnam, Charles Scribner, and James T. Fields. Editors who reflected similar values included Henry Mills Alden, William Dean Howells, and James Russell Lowell. According to the ideal, Gentlemen Publishers were expected to have personal relationships with their authors, expressing paternalism, affection, loyalty, and trust; they were also expected to value good literature above commercial aims, even though they were in business; and finally, they were expected to be moral guardians, protecting their readers from anything offensive and helping to instill good values. Of course, many publishers did not live up to this ideal, and all gentlemen publishers who stayed in business did make money or they would not have survived. What is significant is that the expressed values of the literary marketplace were compatible with many women's own focus on family relationships, noncommercialism, and moral guardianship. Furthermore, the relationship of the Gentleman Publisher to any writer was expected to be like a provider to a family member—a familiar environment for women. In fact, it was this similarity to domestic male-female relationships that Mary Abigail Dodge (Gail Hamilton) so accurately criticized in *A Battle of the Books* (1870) as creating inequitable circumstances for dependent writers (wives) in relationship to their dominant publishers (husbands).

There are scholarly disagreements about how emotionally and intellectually comfortable women were as writers in the mid-nineteenth century, given the ambiguous context of expectations about womanhood and authorship. Some scholars have argued that there was great anxiety expressed by women in their literature and personal writings about the role, opportunities, and fate of the female writer or artist. Thus, despite their successes, writers like Sarah Josepha Hale (1788–1879) and Sara Jane Clarke Lippincott (Grace Greenwood, 1823–1904) could describe themselves as timid, dependent, and domestic, not to be considered as competitors with men in the literary marketplace. Other female authors seemed to try to hide from the public. Catharine Maria Sedgwick and Maria Susanna Cummins (1827–1866) began their careers by writing anonymously, and others, like Mary Virginia Terhune (Marion Harland, 1830–1922), used pseudonyms throughout their careers; both strategies are seen by some scholars as ways in which women expressed ambivalence about their careers and protected their private lives from public scrutiny. These behaviors seem to suggest unease with the public visibility they had (or potentially could have) as writers.

Other scholars have suggested that any "anxiety of authorship" women might have expressed should not be exaggerated. They argue that anxiety did not deter many authors from pursuing their careers with a good deal of self-confidence and pride. By focusing on female authors' successes and the skills that made success possible, such scholars conclude that women were comfortable as writers, even when they protested otherwise and even when they were criticized for what they did. Many, like Rose Terry Cooke (1827–1892) and Mary Abigail Dodge, demonstrated self-esteem by poking fun at themselves and their work. Others demonstrated confidence in the successful strategies they developed as they pursued their writing careers.

AUTHORSHIP AS A PROFESSION

Studies of female authors show that they were serious about their own literary skills. The most successful writers worked to develop their own distinctive literary styles in content and technique. Authors like Mary Abigail Dodge sought advice from other writers early in their careers so that they could learn to write well. During their careers, many authors like E. D. E. N. Southworth, expressed pride in their particular style and defended their own work in comparison to the works of others. Because they were confident about their skills, many women expected to be able to write about what they themselves chose and in a manner that they themselves chose, even when they knew they had to conform to some expectations of length and style. Much correspondence of female authors with their publishers shows they could be angered by editorial changes in their work. Furthermore, Harriet Beecher Stowe and authors like her were confident enough in their own skills to offer encouragement and advice to other writers. Many authors also freely expressed opinions about other people's work to their peers, to editors, and to publishers. In these and other ways, female authors demonstrated pride in their work.

Authorship was a profession built on literary abilities and business skills. When women became writers to earn an income, they entered a world of business relationships that necessitated submitting and revising manuscripts, negotiating fair prices for their efforts, hoping that their work would be presented well to the public, and maintaining connections with publishers for their future work. Correspondence between female authors and their publishers in which the former offer advice about the printing of their work or the marketing and distribution that could lead to greater sales demonstrates women's understanding of the marketplace. Over the course of their careers female authors made judgments about the services of various publishers and editors, changed publishers and editors when they were dissatisfied, and let others know their opinions about those services.

Depending on their personalities and personal experiences, female authors used various interpersonal strategies to conduct the business of their careers. As professionals most of them understood the context of the Gentleman Publisher's marketplace and used it when they could to their own advantage in conducting their business. Many took advantage of the opportunities provided by the emphasis on personal relationships. E. D. E. N. Southworth, for example, used a posture of dependence with her gentleman editor, Robert Bonner, to negotiate continuing and increasing salaries for her work. Harriet Beecher Stowe used a more assertive domestic feminism to negotiate with her gentleman publisher, James T. Fields. Most were savvy enough not to be fooled too often by publishers's protests of economic self-sacrifice. Most knew how to use the ideal of moral guardianship to defend and promote their own work.

It is unclear whether or not the economics of the literary marketplace disadvantaged female authors more than male authors. Both men and women were always at the mercy of publishers's and editors's decisions about the value of their literary work. Early in the century authors were more likely to be asked to share the costs of publishing, which would have been a greater hardship on women who had fewer resources than men. By mid-century, however, when the industry was more stable and lucrative, a percentage of profits was usually given to authors, and the most popular women seem to have received the same percentages as their male counterparts. It is difficult to compare royalties offered because contracts were not consistently used until after the Civil War. In other words, since arrangements were handled individually through correspondence, and records are sparse, it is unclear if female authors were more likely to be paid less than their male counterparts. Women seem to have complained as often as men about poor pay. For both sexes the Gentleman Publisher's practice of trade courtesy discouraged authors from seeking competing offers for their work or from knowing accurately what they should be paid.

Whether or not one measures their successes in comparative economic terms, the most popular female authors were committed to their careers and worked hard, often telling others how hard they worked. Even if they did not begin their careers because of a deep commitment to writing, most of them developed that commitment over time. Thus, even when family circumstances no longer necessitated pursuing a career or when family circumstances made it incredibly difficult to continue, the most successful authors did not give up their careers. In fact, there are many stories of female authors who broke down in exhaustion, dramatically demonstrating their commitment to continuing their careers despite the many difficulties of doing so.

Female authorship became a recognized profession for middle-class women in the nineteenth century. It was a profession based on literary talents and business skills that many women were able to develop. The literary marketplace of the Gentleman Publisher brought women's writings to a broad audience. Nevertheless, despite their successes as authors in this period, they were never free of their society's judgments about them as women. They were always "female" authors.

See also Domestic Fiction; Editors; Feminism; Literary Criticism; Literary Marketplace; Publishers

BIBLIOGRAPHY

Primary Works
Fanny Fern. *Ruth Hall: A Domestic Tale of the Present Time.* New York: Mason Brothers, 1855. Republished as *Ruth Hall and Other Writings,* edited by Joyce W. Warren. New Brunswick, N.J.: Rutgers University Press, 1986.

Hamilton, Gail. *A Battle of the Books.* Cambridge, Mass.: Riverside Press, 1870. Republished in *Gail Hamilton: Selected Writings,* edited by Susan Coultrap-McQuin. New Jersey: Rutgers University Press, 1992.

Wetherall, Elizabeth [Susan Warner]. *The Wide, Wide World.* Putnam, 1851.

Secondary Works
Baym, Nina. *Novels, Readers, and Reviewers: Responses to Fiction in Antebellum America.* Ithaca, N.Y.: Cornell University Press, 1984.

Baym, Nina. *Woman's Fiction: A Guide to Novels by and about Women in America, 1820–1870.* Ithaca, N.Y.: Cornell University Press, 1978.

Buell, Lawrence. *New England Literary Culture: From Revolution through Renaissance.* Cambridge, U.K.: Cambridge University Press, 1986.

Charvat, William. *The Profession of Authorship in America, 1800–1870: The Papers of William Charvat.* Edited by Matthew J. Bruccoli. Columbus: Ohio State University, 1968.

Coultrap-McQuin, Susan. *Doing Literary Business: American Women Writers in the Nineteenth Century.* Chapel Hill: University of North Carolina Press, 1990.

Fetterley, Judith, ed. *Provisions: A Reader from 19th-Century American Women.* Bloomington: Indiana University Press, 1985.

Kelley, Mary. *Private Woman, Public Stage: Literary Domesticity in Nineteenth-Century America.* New York: Oxford University Press, 1984.

Newbury, Michael. *Figuring Authorship in Antebellum America*. Stanford, Calif.: Stanford University Press, 1997.

Railton, Stephen. *Authorship and Audience: Literary Performance in the American Renaissance*. Princeton, N.J.: Princeton University Press, 1991.

Susan Coultrap-McQuin

FEMINISM

Although the term "feminism" was not invented until the 1880s, reform movements aiming to improve women's lives emerged early in the nation's history. At the end of the Revolutionary War, women lived under far more constraints than men. In slavery, to be sure, neither men nor women had rights. But in the free white population, women, governed by the doctrine of coverture—laws defining the status of women during marriage—were transferred from paternal guardianship to their husbands' rule when they married, with no legal access to property, education, children, occupations. Female education was rudimentary at best. Still, marriage was women's most reasonable choice because (except for widows) if unmarried, women had to live in their parents' homes, work as servants in other people's homes, or go into the sex trade.

CULTURAL FEMINISM

In a subsistence farming economy, women's subordination was less visible and more bearable than it would become in the emergent middle-class and urbanizing culture of the post-Revolutionary years. By the 1790s, white women from the middle and upper classes had begun publishing (an activity itself testifying to changes in women's lives) on behalf of such initiatives as female education, access to respectable and decently paying work, the right to keep money and property, liberalized divorce laws, esteem for unmarried women, and participation in public life. These women hoped their work would argue effectively for female mental equality while demonstrating female abilities. Because conventional beliefs that women were weak in mental and moral as well as bodily strength seemed to justify treating them like children, the first feminist literary work aimed to demolish these beliefs. Granting that women could never equal men in physical strength, the early writers decoupled physical from mental strength, accepting the mind-body split established by the seventeenth-century French philosopher René Descartes and dissociating themselves from their own physicality. They drew inspiration from such European feminists as Mary Wollestonecraft, as well as from Enlightenment ideas about human rationality that had been important to American Revolutionary thought.

By 1848, when the first women's rights convention took place at Seneca Falls, New York, the idea of "women's rights" had become familiar across the culture. Among early initiatives, the drive for female education was especially successful, with women's schools springing up across the nation, especially in the northeast. Although not at the same level as good men's schools—even the best were more like high schools than colleges—they turned teaching into a women's profession while producing an ever-larger number of graduates who could read and write well beyond the minimal level. These graduates in turn constituted a market for printed literary goods that women themselves supplied.

The emergence of women writers, the expansion of female education, the development of teaching as a female profession, and the growth of a women's literary market are thus all interconnected expressions of cultural feminism in a capitalizing economy. Women writers became part of the literary landscape, but always as representatives of their gender rather than as individuals. Publishing was a balancing act for each of them, and the suffrage issue became a test case. In 1818, when the great educator Emma Hart Willard (1787–1870) petitioned the New York State legislature for funding to open a girls' school in Troy, New York, she celebrated education's capacity to control women's boisterous, unruly energies. She used herself as an example of how educated women would petition but never seek to vote or hold public office. A quarter century later, however, Margaret Fuller (1810–1850) in "The Great Lawsuit: Man vs. Men and Woman vs. Women" (1843, expanded in 1845 into *Woman in the Nineteenth Century*) said women's needs could never be fairly represented in public policy unless women represented themselves. The Declaration of Sentiments issued by the Seneca Falls Convention openly called for women's suffrage.

But the franchise was not to come about for another seventy years, and some of its opponents were women like Willard and her educator sister, Almira Hart Phelps. Some women firmly believed that women's role in the home was incompatible with any kind of public life; others feared that anti-suffrage sentiment would delay all feminist reform. Thus, many anti-suffrage women—like Willard and Phelps—worked energetically for other women's issues. The anti-suffragist Catharine Esther Beecher (1800–1878), for example, published widely on female education and improving women's lives in the home. Her 1841 *Treatise on*

Representative Women. Lithograph composite of portraits of prominent feminists, c. 1870. Clockwise from top: Lucretia Coffin Mott, Elizabeth Cady Stanton, Mary Livermore, Lydia Maria Child, Susan B. Anthony, and Grace Greenwood. Anna Dickinson is in the middle. THE LIBRARY OF CONGRESS

Domestic Economy, for the Use of Young Ladies at Home, and at School argued that homemaking should be respected as a profession, that women should be trained as homemakers, and that teachers should be trained to train such women. Her curriculum included chemistry, physics, mechanics, anatomy, and physiology among other difficult subjects. She thought reading belles lettres was a waste of time, but to make an impact she chose the printed word.

Whether Beecher's *Treatise* looks feminist to later eyes, it helped further technological education for women and led directly to the founding of the profession of home economics at the end of the nineteenth century, under which aegis women were able to go to college and even become professors. Another powerful anti-suffrage voice was that of Sarah J. Hale (1788–1879), editor in chief of the monthly *Godey's Lady's Book* from 1837 to 1877. Under cover of the women's magazine format, Hale agitated tirelessly for a huge array of goals that would now be recognized as feminist even while she adamantly opposed the vote, sexual freedom for women (for men too), dress reform, and anything else that in her view allowed women to behave or look too much like men. Through her editorials and editorial policies, she nurtured women authors, supported women editors, encouraged female business entrepreneurs, strove to open new professions to women, and espoused modern technologies like the sewing and washing machines to make women's traditional work less laborious. She wrote many different kinds of books, but always with an emphasis on improving women's lot: cookbooks with information about chemistry and nutrition, floras mixing sentimental verses with botanical information. She wanted women to learn astronomy, botany, chemistry, geology, anatomy, and physiology, and she spearheaded a successful campaign in the 1840s for schools that would train women doctors. She feminized this major breakthrough by claiming it was obscene for women to be examined intimately by men. In 1850 she published what she considered her crowning achievement—a thousand-page biographical encyclopedia of famous women throughout history. *Woman's Record; or, Sketches of All Distinguished Women, from "The Beginning" till A.D.* aimed to show how, despite all obstacles, women had managed to leave their mark on history and also how the impact of women in history was increasing and improving as the world became more enlightened and more Christian. "Christian" to Hale meant qualities of compassion and altruism, which she linked to women, whose physical weakness relative to men had always, she claimed, made them more sympathetic to Christian goals.

On account of the many southern subscribers to the *Lady's Book* she opposed abolition, going so far as publicly to criticize abolitionist women for disturbing the peace. In 1853, responding specifically to Harriet Beecher Stowe's *Uncle Tom's Cabin; or, Life among the Lowly* (1852), she published *Liberia; or, Mr. Peyton's Experiments,* a novel endorsing Liberian colonization for free African Americans. The novel has a striking portrayal of a strong African American heroine, Keziah, who, however, can come into her own only in a country of her own—which, Hale insisted, could never be the United States, where racism was simply too entrenched. Whatever one thinks of the politics of this novel, the fact that it was published at all (like Lydia Maria Child's abolitionist *Appeal on Behalf of That Class of Americans Called Africans* [1833] and Stowe's antislavery *Uncle Tom's Cabin*) shows clearly that women expected to publish freely on all sides of even the most explosive political topic.

FICTION

Even if they had not actually been teachers themselves, women who published for other women often wrote like teachers. Simultaneously, they turned to that favorite women's genre, the novel, to reach the largest possible audience, presenting stories in which young women learned how to overcome obstacles, stand on their own two feet, and be respected and admired by all. Far from resenting the commandeering of fictional entertainment for didactic purposes, women apparently loved such books. The first example of this new kind of woman's fiction, Catharine Maria Sedgwick's (1789–1867) *A New-England Tale,* appeared in 1822. Until then, the typical woman's story had been a tearjerking seduction tale in which a naive young girl is taken advantage of by a rogue who woos her, gets her pregnant, and abandons her to shame and early death. The narrative, ostensibly counseling women not to listen to men's flattery, indicated that women were so weak-willed and weak-minded that to listen to flattery was to believe it. In *A New-England Tale,* however, Sedgwick introduced an all-American girl with mental strength, a powerful sense of justice, a capacity for resistance, and—key to her survival in a capitalist culture—a desire to be useful. The orphaned Jane Elton is adopted by an unfeeling aunt who exploits her as an unpaid servant. In time she moves out, takes a teaching job, and gets engaged to an attractive young lawyer who turns out to be a scoundrel. She breaks her engagement without regret when she discovers his true character and prepares for life without marriage. But she marries a young widower with a daughter, a man who respects and admires her, offering her romance, security, and above all friendship.

The formula in these stories of trials and triumph—the woman's novel—featuring energetic and competent protagonists who contributed to the ongoing national (or at least northern) project of modernization propelled hundreds of novels to best-seller status, establishing a standard for sales that almost no novels by men attained. Two examples of the type—Susan Warner's *The Wide, Wide World* (1850) and Maria Susanna Cummins's *The Lamplighter* (1854)—not only sold hundreds of thousands of copies but remained in print until the twentieth century. Diversified by settings and obstacles, and enlivened by a friendly narrative voice, the novels often situated the heroine between two other feminine types, a meek and helpless victim and a selfish, greedy, fashion-crazy "belle." The differences between these characters and the protagonist made an obvious statement about female self-reliance, as well as a statement about female citizenship in the United States. The belle's acquisitive egotism undermines community and squanders resources. The helpless woman, although appealing in her way, counters the so-called cult of true womanhood idealizing purity, piety, passivity, and submissiveness. In this formula fiction, such women are burdens to others and useless to themselves—not true women at all. The heroines, although true women to the core, and certainly pure and pious, are neither passive nor submissive. No fragile, fainting stereotype here: these novels tell women to value inner character, get the best education possible, learn a useful trade, respect women who work for a living, esteem unmarried women, marry men who can be companions, and help other women by setting an example.

The genre attracted a wide range of women authors. E. D. E. N. Southworth's (1819–1899) *The Hidden Hand; or, Capitola the Madcap,* serialized in 1859–1860 and then published as a book in 1888, had an extraordinary success. The heroine, Capitola Black, enters the action as a street urchin in New York City, dressed in boys' clothes. "Because I was a girl," she explains, "there seemed to be nothing but starvation or beggary before me;" then, "all of a sudden, a bright thought struck me; *and I made up my mind to be a boy!*" (p. 40). Discovered accidentally by an uncle from the South, who takes her back to his plantation, she embarks on a career of principled resistance to Southern mores, venturing out to punish oppressors and free victims and, implicitly, impose Yankee values on the backward South. By the end of this joyous, romping, cheerfully subversive story, all wrongs have been righted, and Capitola has married her faithful childhood friend.

Almost a decade later Louisa May Alcott (1832–1888) published *Little Women* (1868), the most loved girls' book in the United States for more than a century.

The characters derived from Alcott's own family and starred Jo March (modeled on Alcott herself) as the heroine who wanted to be a boy. Jo has many setbacks as she learns how to be a woman without sacrificing the essential core of her independent, powerful personality. Eventually, she succeeds as a writer and goes on to marry a kindly professor and run a boys' school. Alcott's point, ultimately, is that the best women are those with the most gumption and internal resistance to the status quo. But there is a kind of sadness in this novel; the different careers available to the two genders show how far women are from occupational equality.

If feminism is about independence and resistance to unjust authority, all these novels are feminist. If feminism is about group consciousness, asserting female solidarity in the face of male tyranny, then the novels' advocacy of mutual respect and esteem among women makes them feminist even though they do not describe formal associations of women agitating for women's rights. Nor do they depict women who want to reform the nation's politics or economy—they want to belong. If persuading women to choose husbands who see them as equals is feminist, these are feminist novels. If living without men is a feminist goal, they are not; at least until toward the end of the Civil War, marriage for the protagonist is the inevitable ending. During the 1860s a few novelists, recognizing that the huge number of men killed made marriage impossible for many women, tried to work out alternatives. Among these, Augusta Jane Evans's *Macaria; or, Altars of Sacrifice* (1864), Harriet Prescott Spofford's *Azarian: An Episode* (1864), and Alcott's *Work: A Story of Experience* (1872) depict female companionship among women who will not marry. *Azarian* comes the closest to what today's literary culture might think of as a lesbian novel.

Possibly, most women's novels eschewed radical feminist plots because their readers were young, white, and middle class. Women who could not or did not read, or who read at basic levels—working-class women, immigrant women, women in slavery—were not likely to absorb these lengthy and self-consciously literary texts that, along with lessons in character formation, aimed to increase reading skills and instill a love for good books. The novels' belles tended to be wealthy, spoiled, and contemptuous of the bookish protagonist, implying that upper-class women were not a target audience either. The novels are full of loyal and interesting servants—in this era all middle-class and even genteelly poor households had servants—but always as secondary characters. The story did not resonate with African American women; the two important published narratives by African American women recovered to date—*Our Nig* (1859) by Harriet Wilson and *Incidents in the Life of a Slave Girl* (1861) by Harriet Jacobs—use the formula to show its irrelevance for women of color.

ABOLITION AND TEMPERANCE

Formal women's rights activism in the United States grew directly out of abolitionism. Both Elizabeth Cady Stanton (1815–1902) and Lucretia Mott (1793–1880), Quaker organizers of the Seneca Falls Convention, turned to women's rights when they were denied seating at an antislavery convention in London because they were women. If abolitionism provided an official venue for feminists to argue their case for women's suffrage, the two reform movements would soon develop a complicated relationship during the periods preceding and following the Civil War. Although Frederick Douglass attended the first meeting of woman suffragists at Seneca Falls, many pre–Civil War abolitionists themselves argued that feminist concerns should be subordinated to the more pressing needs of slavery reform, which temporarily sidelined feminists' attempts to gain women's suffrage. Race also split suffrage issues between white and black women and black men and women. The black activist and writer Frances Watkins Harper (1825–1911), who entitled her late trials and triumph novel *Iola Leroy; or, Shadows Uplifted* (1892) after the pen name of activist Ida B. Wells-Barnett, felt frustrated as early as the American Equal Rights Association Convention of 1869 that black women were especially sidelined from gaining the vote. She fictionalizes this voice in her periodical novel *Minnie's Sacrifice* (1869) when her heroine asks, "'But, Louis, is it not the negro woman's hour also? Has she not as many rights and claims as the negro man?'" (Harper, p. 78; O'Brien, pp. 1–2, 11).

Along with abolitionism, the temperance movement interacted significantly with women's rights. Until recently alcoholism was thought of as weakness of will, not disease; many believed that large numbers of heavy drinkers threatened the nation's moral fiber. As well as moralizing, male reformers decried the toll of heavy drinking on economic productivity while women noted the abuse of wives and children by drunkards. Given the laws of coverture, a married woman could not escape from a drunkard husband nor protect her children, whereas such a husband could abandon his family at will, returning occasionally to confiscate whatever meager wages his wife might have earned. A highly sensationalist literature of inebriation pervaded the working-class press, mostly written by men, appearing in cheap pamphlets and weekly story papers rather than between the covers of a book or in the glossy magazines.

The following excerpt is from a speech by Lucretia Mott, a mother of contemporary feminism:

Woman has been so debased, so crushed, her powers of mind, her very being brought low . . . . woman must avail herself of the increasing means of intelligence, education, and knowledge. She must rise also in a higher sphere of spiritual existence. . . . Then will the time speedily come . . . when the monopoly of the pulpit shall no more oppress her, when marriage shall not be a means of rendering her noble nature subsidiary to man, when there shall be no assumed authority on the one part nor admitted inferiority or subjection on the other.

"'Abuses and Uses of the Bible,' a Sermon delivered at Cherry Street Meeting, Philadelphia, Eleventh Month, Fourth, 1848." Edited from Warthmore Friends Collection MSS 0476, Swarthmore College, Swarthmore, Pennsylvania.

Thus, in the literary world temperance seems more a class than a gender issue; in middle-class woman's fiction, the men's great weakness is financial irresponsibility demonstrated in bad business investments that impoverish their families. The first of many recessions to hit the U.S. economy occurred as a direct result of stock speculation in 1837; with women lacking all legal control over family resources, the melodramatic plot device of a comfortably well-off family suddenly pauperized turns out to be quite realistic.

MEN'S WRITING

That men wrote temperance stories and women, although highly active in the movement, seldom did, raises the reverse question: whether men's writing across the board registers feminist awareness. Certainly, Timothy Shay Arthur's *Ten Nights in a Bar-Room and What I Saw There* (1854) features women as victims of the drunkard's failings, but its solution is prohibition not women's rights. In James Fenimore Cooper's Leatherstocking novels, women—whether powerful or weak—are obstacles to men. Herman Melville's fiction has almost no women characters. Walt Whitman's poems celebrate women as mothers of men. Henry Wadsworth Longfellow's women are good wives or long-suffering ciphers, and Edgar Allan Poe's are victims of violently paranoid fantasies. Margaret Fuller tried to rescue transcendentalism from the exclusively male perspectives of Ralph Waldo Emerson and Henry David Thoreau, insisting that women too had divine souls.

Nathaniel Hawthorne (1804–1864) is the exception. Earlier stories, including "Young Goodman Brown" (1835), "Egotism; or, the Bosom Serpent" (1843), and "The Birth-mark" (1843) often centered on icy male characters whose egotism destroyed the women who loved them; but beginning with *The Scarlet Letter* (1850) he featured the women themselves. The problem as presented in *The Scarlet Letter, The House of the Seven Gables* (1851), *The Blithedale Romance* (1852), and *The Marble Faun* (1860) was that both male egotism and female compassion were inherent and gender-specific. How then could women ever attain true social equality without changing their inner being? If they changed their essential nature, would they still be women? It was Hawthorne's literary habit to raise but not answer questions. His novels proposed small improvements that might make women's lives more bearable, but except for *The Scarlet Letter,* they show women defeated by the struggle to remain loving and yet assert themselves as individuals. His one avowed feminist—Zenobia, in *The Blithedale Romance*—kills herself. This outcome is hardly what women activists hoped for then or look for now, and yet its very bleakness recognizes women's dilemma in a way that no other male writer approached.

See also Abolitionist Writing; Declaration of Sentiments; Domestic Fiction; *The Hidden Hand; Letters on the Equality of the Sexes; Little Women; The Scarlet Letter;* Seneca Falls Convention; Suffrage; Temperance; *Woman in the Nineteenth Century*

BIBLIOGRAPHY

Primary Works

Alcott, Louisa May. *Little Women; or, Meg, Jo, Beth, and Amy.* Boston: Roberts Brothers, 1868.

Beecher, Catharine Esther. *A Treatise on Domestic Economy, for the Use of Young Ladies at Home, and at School.* Boston: Marsh, Capen, Lyon, and Webb, 1841.

Declaration of Sentiments. Seneca Falls Woman's Rights Convention, 1848. Votes for Women: Selections from the National American Woman Suffrage Association Collection, 1848–1921, Library of Congress, Washington, D.C.

Fuller, Margaret. "The Great Lawsuit: Man vs. Men and Woman vs. Women." *The Dial* (July 1843). Expanded into *Woman in the Nineteenth Century.* New York: Greeley and McElrath, 1845.

Hale, Sarah J. *Woman's Record; or, Sketches of All Distinguished Women, from "The Beginning" till* A.D. 1850. New York: Harper & Brothers, 1853.

Harper, Frances Ellen Watkins. *Minnie's Sacrifice.* In *Minnie's Sacrifice; Sowing and Reaping; Trial and Triumph: Three Rediscovered Novels,* edited by Frances Smith Foster, pp. 3–92. Boston: Beacon Press, 1994.

Hawthorne, Nathaniel. *The Scarlet Letter: A Romance.* Boston: Ticknor, Reed, and Fields, 1850.

Sedgwick, Catharine Maria. *A New-England Tale.* New York: Bliss and White, 1822.

Southworth, E. D. E. N. *The Hidden Hand; or, Capitola the Madcap.* 1888. Oxford and New York: Oxford University Press, 1997.

Secondary Works

Bardes, Barbara, and Suzanne Gossett. *Declarations of Independence: Women and Political Power in Nineteenth-Century American Fiction.* New Brunswick, N.J.: Rutgers University Press, 1990.

Baym, Nina. *Feminism and American Literary History: Essays.* New Brunswick, N.J.: Rutgers University Press, 1992.

Baym, Nina. *Woman's Fiction: A Guide to Novels by and about Women in America, 1820–1870.* 2nd ed. Urbana: University of Illinois Press, 1993.

Bushman, Richard L. *The Refinement of America: Persons, Houses, Cities.* New York: Knopf, 1992.

Cott, Nancy F. *The Bonds of Womanhood: "Women's Sphere" in New England, 1780–1835.* 2nd ed. New Haven, Conn.: Yale University Press, 1997.

Epstein, Barbara Leslie. *The Politics of Domesticity: Women, Evangelism, and Temperance in Nineteenth-Century American Thought.* Middletown, Conn.: Wesleyan University Press, 1981.

Lutz, Alma. *Emma Willard: Daughter of Democracy.* Boston: Houghton Mifflin, 1929.

O'Brien, Colleen. "The White Women All Go for Sex: Frances Harper and the Racist *Revolution.*" Unpublished paper, Georgia State University, Atlanta, 11 February 2005.

Okker, Patricia. *Our Sister Editors: Sarah J. Hale and the Tradition of Nineteenth-Century American Women Editors.* Athens: University of Georgia Press, 1995.

O'Neill, William L. *Feminism in America: A History.* 2nd ed. New Brunswick, N.J.: Transaction Publishers, 1989.

Sklar, Kathryn Kish. *Catharine Beecher: A Study in American Domesticity.* New Haven, Conn.: Yale University Press, 1973.

Woody, Thomas. *History of Women's Education in the United States.* Vol. 1. New York and Lancaster, Pa.: Science Press, 1929.

Yellin, Jean Fagan. *Women and Sisters: The Antislavery Feminists in American Culture.* New Haven, Conn.: Yale University Press, 1989.

Zboray, Ronald J. *A Fictive People: Antebellum Economic Development and the American Reading Public.* New York: Oxford University Press, 1993.

Nina Baym

FIRESIDE POETS

"May is a pious fraud of the almanac," complains James Russell Lowell (1819–1891) in "Under the Willows" (1868). Spring seems to have arrived in New England, but then winter suddenly returns, "like crazy Lear," carrying the dead spring in his arms, "her budding breasts and wan dislustred front / With frosty streaks and drifts of his white beard / All overblown." He retreats into his study, "warmly walled with books," where his "wood-fire supplies the sun's defect / Whispering old forest-sagas in its dreams." Sheltered against the unexpected cold outside and comforted by his blazing fireplace inside, the speaker takes a book off his "happy shelf" and creates his own springtime indoors, reading "vernal Chaucer, whose fresh woods / Throb thick with merle and mavis all the year" (*Complete Poetical Works,* p. 383). Never mind that Chaucer's "sweet-showered" April must have been invention, too, a shivering Englishman's memory of his visits to the Mediterranean.

Lowell's poem rehearses a scene one finds, with slight variations, in much of the poetry written in mid-nineteenth-century New England: discouraged by the weather, which, as William James once observed, may change in Boston as many as three times a day, a speaker finds solace and predictability in front of the fireplace, where he, often joining the rest of the family or a circle of congenial friends, will tell a story or read a book. Unsurprisingly, Lowell and three of his colleagues who were also fond of their indoor fires—Henry Wadsworth Longfellow (1807–1882), Oliver Wendell Holmes (1809–1894), and John Greenleaf Whittier (1807–1892)—became known as the "Fireside Poets." Some historians have argued that William Cullen Bryant (1794–1878), who left Massachusetts in 1825 to begin a long and successful career as a newspaper editor in New York, also belonged to, or at least paved the way for, this loose circle of writers.

And a loose circle it was. Superficially at least, Holmes, the witty conversationalist and urbane Harvard doctor, has little in common with Whittier, the humble Quaker and confirmed bachelor from rural Haverill,

James Russell Lowell. THE LIBRARY OF CONGRESS

Massachusetts, who had enjoyed a spotty education at best. Similarly, the Maine-born Longfellow, who studiously kept his political and literary opinions to himself and always refused to speak at public events, seems far removed from the Boston blue-blood diplomat, satirist, and trenchant essayist Lowell. Seen from a modern critical perspective, however, the Fireside Poets—the "worst offenders" in the twentieth-century critic F. O. Matthiessen's catalog of poetic blunderers—all subscribed to similar ideas about the purposes of poetry. For Longfellow and his peers, a poem's proper place was in the home or, more precisely, the parlor. There, a family would listen to the poet's words of wisdom, warmed by his uplifting message as well as by the pleasantly flickering fire before which they had so cheerfully assembled. Poetry should, declared Longfellow, "soothe our worldly passions and inspire us with a love of Heaven and virtue" ("Defence of Poetry," p. 64). While Ralph Waldo Emerson (1803–1882) was busily searching for an American bard to "chaunt our own times and social circumstance," someone to write about "our log-rolling, our stumps and their politics, our fisheries, our Negroes and Indians" (p. 238), Lowell was still invoking the "loftiest muse" who "has ever a household and fireside charm about her" ("Poe," p. 19). The fire in the fireplace was, of course, a metaphor for the poet's imagination, which was to burn brightly especially on cold days but always in a familiar, contained, safely domestic space—in fact, a space often imagined as more feminine than masculine (Roberts, p. 46). Intended to comfort rather than to convert, a typical fireside poem acted as a digestif rather than as a stimulant, allowing the reader to lean back in his rocking chair and get ready for a pleasant nap. Longfellow himself parodied a moment of such postprandial ecstasy in a cartoon drawing of a character he invented for the amusement of his children, Mr. Peter Quince.

POETS AS READERS

That such fantasies about the comforting effect of the "hearth-fire's ruddy glow," in Whittier's phrase (*Snow-Bound*, in *Complete Poetical Works*, p. 490), should haven taken hold at a time when Victorian Americans were plotting ways to get rid of fireplaces altogether seems richly ironical, at least from a modern perspective. (The model house featured in Catherine E. Beecher and Harriet Beecher Stowe's book, *The American Woman's Home*, 1869, included a system of heating and ventilation that supplied hot air from a furnace in the basement to every room.) Considered a major part of the American canon in their own day and a staple in the successive editions of Rufus Griswold's *The Poets and Poetry of America* (1842), the Fireside Poets, pale imitators of the European Romantics, look distinctly minor today: derivative, antiquarian, sentimental, and shallow. The fire that once warmed the cockles of the Victorian American heart is not, the editors of our anthologies agree, the flame that inspires great poetry. Written for literate but not literary Americans, to paraphrase the critic Roy Harvey Pearce, the poems of the firesiders, in which depth was "not far below the surface" (pp. 196–197), had to make way for the much more radical sensibilities expressed in the works of Emerson, Edgar Allan Poe, Walt Whitman, and Emily Dickinson.

But such criticism belittles one of the most salient features of American "fireside poetry," one that might make it worthy of reconsideration today, namely the relentless de-emphasis of the author's sovereign authority over his work. What Pearce found missing in fireside poetry—namely the attempt to challenge or transform, rather than minister to, the common reader—could also be interpreted as a rejection of what the modern social theorist Pierre Bourdieu has called "the field of restricted production" (pp. 17–22). Rather than producing poetry only for other producers of poetry or those aspiring to become such, the firesiders were serious in their appreciation for those "Poets Who Only Read and Listen" (to quote

the title of a poem by Holmes, p. 292). What the fireside in these poems epitomizes is a radically reader-centered poetics, a conception of literature not as the divinely inspired creation of the few but as the shared possession of the many. The poet is, above all, a reader himself, a patient listener to stories told and poems passed on by others.

He appears as such in the dedication to Longfellow's collection *The Seaside and the Fireside* (1850), in which he joins his friends on a twilight walk by the seaside, the grateful recipient of their "words of friendship, comfort, and assistance." He himself is "mostly silent" so as not to disturb them or the ocean with "intrusive talk." When he finally joins his friends (that is to say, his readers) in their home, he does so only after he is sure that no one will object to his presence:

Therefore I hope, as no unwelcome guest,
　　At your warm fireside, when the lamps are lighted,
To have my place reserved among the rest.
　　Nor stand as one unsought and uninvited!
　　　　　　(Complete Poetical Works, *p. 99*)

The three double negations ("no unwelcome"; "nor . . . unsought"; "nor . . . uninvited") underscore the deliberately diminished role the poet has chosen for himself in poems that are, as he wants us to believe, little more than faithful transcriptions of what others have heard, felt, or seen.

Take "The Fire of Drift-Wood: Devereux Farm, near Marblehead," which Longfellow strategically placed at the juncture between the first part ("By the Seaside") and the second part ("By the Fireside") of *The Seaside and the Fireside*, at a point where the ocean meets the land. The poem evokes the memory of a day (29 September 1846, according to Longfellow's journal) that he himself had spent remembering the past. In Longfellow's poem, old friends are assembled round the fireplace in a drafty farmhouse near the harbor of Marblehead, Massachusetts, on a stormy, cold, and damp night, swapping stories about vanished friends and events that took place long ago:

We sat within the farm-house old,
　　Whose windows, looking o'er the bay,
Gave to the sea-breeze, damp and cold,
　　An easy entrance, night and day.
Not far away we saw the port,
　　The strange, old-fashioned, silent town,
The lighthouse, the dismantled fort,
　　The wooden houses, quaint and brown.
We sat and talked until the night,
　　Descending, filled the little room;
Our faces faded from the sight,
　　Our voices only broke the gloom.
　　　　　　(Complete Poetical Works, *pp. 106–107*)

Drawing of Peter Quince by Henry Wadsworth Longfellow. BY PERMISSION OF THE HOUGHTON LIBRARY, HARVARD UNIVERSITY, MS AM 1340 (163)

From the beginning, the distinctions between the inside and the outside, between the sea and the land are porous. Through rattling windows, the sea wind enters the house, where wood taken from "the wreck of stranded ships" (*Complete Poetical Works*, p. 107) is burning in the fireplace. What is implied here—none too subtly, as Longfellow's critics would charge—is the old and familiar idea of life as a seafaring journey and of shipwreck as the fate that may befall everyone. As the philosopher Hans Blumenberg has pointed out, the "harbor is not an alternative to shipwreck"—rather, it is the place where we abandon the pleasures of life (p. 35).

And so it seems in Longfellow's poem. In a room so dark that we seem to be listening to disembodied voices rather than actual people, Longfellow's speakers (as so often in his poetry, he employs the collective "we" rather than the first person singular) sadly reminisce about lost opportunities and long-lost friends ("We spake of many a vanished scene, / Of what we

once had thought and said, / Of what had been, and might have been, / And who was changed, and who was dead" [*Complete Poetical Works*, p. 107]). In the light of the flickering fire, the difference between tenor and vehicle, between actual shipwrecks and the metaphorical ones we suffer in life, becomes irrelevant. And when the friends finally fall silent, the glimmering wood turns into an image also for their aimlessly drifting thoughts. Through the agency of the fire, the outside (the ocean, the wind, and the beach) and the inside (both the inside of the old house and the thoughts of the guests assembled there) become indistinguishable:

> The windows, rattling in their frames,
> The ocean, roaring up the beach,
> The gusty blast, the bickering flames,
> All mingled vaguely in our speech;
> Until they made themselves a part
> Of fancies floating through the brain,
> The long-lost ventures of the heart,
> That send no answers back again.
> O flames that glowed! O hearts that yearned!
> They were indeed too much akin,
> The drift-wood fire without that burned,
> The thoughts that burned and glowed within.
>
> (Complete Poetical Works, *p. 107*)

In a sense, Longfellow's poem describes its own genesis—not as the miraculous product of a "strong poet's" active individual imagination but as the joint re-collection, the collective merging of voices and identities, in which it ultimately does not matter anymore who creates and who responds, who writes and who reads. A fireside poem induces in the reader the same state of heightened awareness and receptivity in which it was first conceived and which it seeks to represent. The "too much akin" in Longfellow's final stanza can be read both as a joke (as if Longfellow were mocking his own transparent image-making here) as well as a less than funny reminder that all fires will eventually burn out, leaving us with little more than charred wood and what Longfellow elsewhere calls "the ashes in our hearts" ("Palingenesis," *Complete Poetical Works*, p. 288).

TEA-TIME FOR THE WITCHES

A similarly melancholy tone informs the long poem that made Whittier famous, *Snow-Bound: A Winter Idyl* (1866). Preceded by a motto taken from Emerson's poem "The Snow-Storm" (first published in 1841), in which "the housemates sit / Around the radiant fireplace, enclosed / In a tumultuous privacy of storm" (p. 414), Whittier's poem recalls two days in the poet's youth, when a roaring blizzard confined his family to their homestead and the world outside changed into an unfamiliar "universe of sky and snow" (p. 487). In the eyes of the child, the transformation was nothing short of frightening:

> No church-bell lent its Christian tone
> To the savage air, no social smoke
> Curled over woods of snow-hung oak.
> A solitude made more intense
> By dreary voicèd elements,
> The shrieking of the mindless wind,
> The moaning tree-boughs swaying blind,
> And on the glass the unmeaning beat
> Of ghostly finger-tips of sleet.
> Beyond the circle of our hearth
> No welcome sound of toil or mirth
> Unbound the spell, and testified
> Of human life and thought outside.
>
> (Complete Poetical Works, *pp. 489–490*)

All the more important becomes the fire that the family builds inside, which they take care to make just right:

> The oaken log, green, huge, and thick,
> And on its top the stout back-stick;
> The knotty forestick laid apart,
> And filled between with curious art
> The ragged brush; then, hovering near,
> We watched the first red blaze appear,
> Heard the sharp crackle, caught the gleam
> On whitewashed wall and sagging beam,
> Until the old, rude-furnished room
> Burst, flower-like, into rosy bloom. . . .
>
> (Complete Poetical Works, *p. 490*)

In a letter to an admirer who wanted to recreate the scene for a pageant in Cleveland, Ohio, Whittier later described exactly what their "hearth" had looked like: "the mantelpiece was at least 10 feet long, and the fire place wide enough to take in a five-foot log. . . . How plainly I can see it all" (*Letters* 3:431). And so could the readers of his poem. The triumphant entry of the blazing fire into the shivering world of Whittier's household changes the scenery both outside and inside. Whittier's speaker watches with fascination how the fire indoors, through the reflection in the window, seems to create its own mirror image outside, thus instantly giving life to the wintry landscape that had seemed so forbidding to the child. Never mind that the characters he imagines congregating out there are witches. Normally scary creatures in fairy tales, they are here shown engaged in a rather mundane activity, "making tea." (If Whittier had chosen the perhaps more appropriate verb "brewing," rather than "making," the scene might have had a different and perhaps more sinister effect.) Remembering an (unidentified) "old rhyme" the child is able to give sense, shape and meaning to the snowy world outside.

At a crucial moment in the narrative, then, the child has become a reader:

> . . . radiant with a mimic flame
> Outside the sparkling drift became,
> And through the bare-boughed lilac-tree
> Our own warm hearth seemed blazing free.
> The crane and pendent trammels showed,
> The Turks' head on the andirons glowed;
> While childish fancy, prompt to tell
> The meaning of the miracle,
> Whispered the old rhyme: *"Under the tree,*
> *When fire outdoors burns merrily,*
> *There the witches are making tea."*
>
> (Complete Poetical Works, *p. 490*)

The "tropic heat" generated by the fire allows the members of Whittier's family and their guests to entertain each other with stories and games. Whittier does not fail to remind us that all the members of the original household, with the exception of the poet and his brother, have since passed away: "The voices of the hearth are still; / Look where we may, the wide earth o'er, / Those lighted faces smile no more" (p. 490).

But *Snow-Bound* is not simply an autobiographical poem (the pronoun "I" appears only fifteen times in 759 lines). Nor is it merely nostalgic. In the poet's imagination, the easygoing companionship in front of the flickering fire hints at the possibility of another form of togetherness that seems particularly relevant now that the Civil War's "bloody trail" has ended. Just as the indoor fire has provided the speaker with a useful image (that other, "mimic fire," that will overcome, at least in the speaker's imagination, the separation of the world indoors from the world outside), so the harmonious gathering of the poet's family before their hearth-fire prefigures a time when the "hell / Of prison-torture" has ended, the chains from "limb and spirit" have been struck and there will be no more differences between black and white, North and South (p. 495). To such harmony of the races the abolitionist Whittier—who was mobbed and stoned for his anti-slavery views in Concord, New Hampshire, in 1835—had devoted most of his life.

ASHES TO ASHES

Obviously, the Fireside Poets did not limit themselves to pleasant chats in front of the domestic hearth. Their poems may be provocatively political (viz Longfellow's early *Poems on Slavery* [1842] and Lowell's *Biglow Papers* [1848]), acidly satirical (Lowell's *Fable for Critics* [1848]), darkly elegiac (Longfellow's "Hawthorne" [1864] and "Three Friends of Mine" [1874], or Lowell's ode on the death of the scientist Louis Agassiz [1873]), or just plain silly (see Holmes's "The Height of the Ridiculous," 1830, in which the poet vows never to write anything funny again after some lines he wrote while in a "merry mood" have "tumbled [his servant] in a fit" [p. 14]). Much of Holmes's poetry seems hopelessly ephemeral today—as the twentieth-century poet Alfred Kreymborg once put it, every other poem seems to be the result of an invitation to dinner—but when he talks about science, for example, he does so with a clear-sightedness we do not, as a rule, find in Emerson. Holmes's most famous poem, "The Chambered Nautilus" (1858), evokes a curious shellfish, a relative of the octopus, which builds its own shell and spends its life adding new chambers to it. In Holmes's hands, in a move reminiscent of metaphysical poetry, the shellfish becomes a metaphor for the self that constantly outgrows the definitions it creates for itself over the course of a life. Holmes routinely warned his medical students that they should not look at their patients the way Agassiz, the dissecting knife in his hand, would look at a fish ("The Morning Visit," in *Poetical Works,* p. 59). But "The Chambered Nautilus," which begins with the speaker raptly gazing at a nautilus's beautiful shell, is based on the provocative premise that there is not much indeed that seems to separate the human from the mollusk: "Build thee more stately mansions," the speaker exhorts the human shellfish, "as the swift seasons roll!" (p. 149).

Such self-deprecation was part of a fireside poet's standard repertoire. Holmes called his poems "toys" in his "Prologue" to *Songs in Many Keys* (1861; Holmes, p. 72) and in "For Whittier's Seventieth Birthday" jokingly compared himself, the author of 1,001 poems, to Scheherazade, but without the threat of death hanging over him to justify his productivity: "I believe that the copies of verses I've spun, / Like Scheherezade's tales, are a thousand and one; / You remember the story,— those mornings in bed,— / 'T was the turn of a copper,—a tale or a head" (p. 250). Lowell shared Holmes's reluctance to engage in self-aggrandizement. Asked for an autograph in Venice, he gave free rein to his feelings of embarrassment: "In this grave presence to record my name / Something within me hangs the head and shirks" (*Complete Poetical Works,* p. 543). For him, as for the rest of the firesiders, poetry was a means to an end, and that end had nothing to do with the kind of self-elevation they found in the writings of the transcendentalists, where, as Holmes unkindly put it in "An After-Dinner Poem" (1843), "Self-inspection sucks its little thumb" (p. 57).

The fire of poetry warms the reader as long as it is burning, but it will inevitably end, as our lives do, in a heap of ashes. For Holmes, the fireside in his old age had become a rather lonely place, where he would sit watching the glimmering fragments of his life, "the spoils of years gone by," as he wrote on 1 March 1888,

in a poem titled "At My Fireside." But even as the sun is setting on his career, Holmes looks up to see around him the breaking of yet another morning:

> Alone, beneath the darkened sky,
>   With saddened heart and unstrung lyre,
> I heap the spoils of years gone by,
> And leave them with a long-drawn sigh,
> Like drift-wood brands that glimmering lie,
>   Before the ashes hide the fire.
> Let not these slow declining days
>   The rosy light of dawn outlast;
> Still round my lonely hearth it plays,
> And gilds the east with borrowed rays,
> While memory's mirrored sunset blaze
>   Flames on the windows of the past.
>
>   (P. 269)

Whittier, too, responded to Longfellow's driftwood poem late in his life. In "Burning Drift-Wood" (1890), the wrecked ships that feed his dying fire are the poems he has written over a lifetime, "the wrecks of passion and desire, / The castles I no more rebuild" (*Complete Poetical Works,* p. 581). But all these losses ultimately do not count because the world has, on the whole, become a better place. Above all, slavery has come to an end. In full assurance of all the good that has happened and is yet to come, old Whittier folds his hands and waits, "as low my fires of drift-wood burn," for the peace which passeth—that much he knew—all poetry.

See also Lyric Poetry; Popular Poetry; *The Song of Hiawatha*

BIBLIOGRAPHY

Primary Works

Emerson, Ralph Waldo. *Selections from Ralph Waldo Emerson.* Edited by Stephen W. Whicher. Boston: Houghton Mifflin, 1957.

Griswold, Rufus Wilmot, ed. *The Poets and Poetry of America.* Philadelphia: Carey and Hart, 1842.

Hollander, John, ed. *American Poetry: The Nineteenth Century.* 2 vols. New York: Library of America, 1993.

Holmes, Oliver Wendell. *The Poetical Works of Oliver Wendell Holmes.* Cambridge edition. Rev. ed. Edited by Eleanor M. Tilton. Boston: Houghton Mifflin, 1975.

Longfellow, Henry Wadsworth. "Defence of Poetry." *The North American Review* 34 (January 1832): 56–78.

Longfellow, Henry Wadsworth. Journal, A.MS, 1 March 1847–31 December 1848, Longfellow Papers, MS Am 1340 (201). Houghton Library, Harvard University.

Longfellow, Henry Wadsworth. *The Complete Poetical Works of Henry Wadsworth Longfellow.* Cambridge edition. Boston: Houghton Mifflin, 1893.

Lowell, James Russell. "Edgar Allan Poe." 1845/1850. In *The Shock of Recognition*, vol. 1, *The Nineteenth Century*, 2nd ed., edited by Edmund Wilson, pp. 5–20. New York: Grosset and Dunlap, 1955.

Lowell, James Russell. *The Complete Poetical Works of James Russell Lowell*. Cabinet edition. 1895. Boston: Houghton, Mifflin, 1903.

Whittier, John Greenleaf. *The Complete Poetical Works of John Greenleaf Whittier*. Cambridge edition. Edited by Horace E. Scudder. Boston: Houghton Mifflin, 1894.

Whittier, John Greenleaf. *The Letters of John Greenleaf Whittier*. 3 vols. Edited by John B. Pickard. Cambridge, Mass.: Belknap, 1975.

Secondary Works

Arms, George. *The Fields Were Green: A New View of Bryant, Whittier, Holmes, Lowell, and Longfellow, with a Selection of Their Poems*. Stanford, Calif.: Stanford University Press, 1953.

Arvin, Newton. *Longfellow: His Life and Work*. Boston: Little, Brown, 1963.

Beecher, Catharine E., and Harriet Beecher Stowe. *The American Woman's Home; or, Principles of Domestic Science; Being a Guide to the Formation and Maintenance of Economical, Healthful, Beautiful, and Christian Homes*. New York: J. B. Ford, 1869.

Blumenberg, Hans. *Shipwreck with Spectator: Paradigm of a Metaphor for Existence*. Translated by Steven Rendall. Cambridge, Mass.: MIT Press, 1997.

Bourdieu, Pierre. "The Market of Symbolic Goods." *Poetics* 14 (1985): 13–44.

Brooks, Van Wyck. *The Flowering of New England*. 1936. New York: E. P. Dutton, 1952.

Charvat, William. *The Profession of Authorship in America, 1800–1870: The Papers of William Charvat*. Edited by Matthew J. Bruccoli. Columbia: Ohio State University Press, 1968.

Duberman, Martin. *James Russell Lowell*. Boston: Beacon, 1966.

Gibian, Peter. *Oliver Wendell Holmes and the Culture of Conversation*. Cambridge, U.K.: Cambridge University Press, 2001.

Golding, Alan. *From Outlaw to Classic: Canons in American Poetry*. Madison: University of Wisconsin Press, 1995.

Gruesz, Silva Kirsten, "Feeling for the Fireside: Longfellow, Lynch, and the Topography of Poetic Power." In *Sentimental Men: Masculinity and the Politics of Affect in American Culture*, edited by Mary Chapman and Glenn Hendler, pp. 43–63. Berkeley: University of California Press, 1999.

Irmscher, Christoph. *Longfellow Redux*. Urbana-Champaign: University of Illinois Press, forthcoming.

Kreymborg, Alfred. *A History of American Poetry: Our Singing Strength*. 1929. New York: Tudor, 1934.

Matthiessen, F. O. "Introduction." In *The Oxford Book of American Verse*, 2nd ed., edited by F. O. Matthiessen, pp. ix–xxxiii. New York: Oxford University Press, 1950.

Pearce, Roy Harvey. *The Continuity of American Poetry*. Princeton, N.J.: Princeton University Press, 1961.

Roberts, Kate. "Fireside Tales to Fireside Chats: The Domestic Hearth." In *The Arts and the American Home, 1890–1930*, edited by Jessica H. Foy and Karal Ann Marling, pp. 44–61. Knoxville: University of Tennessee Press, 1994.

Ruland, Richard, and Malcolm Bradbury. *From Puritanism to Postmodernism: A History of American Literature*. New York: Penguin, 1991.

Tilton, Eleanor M. *Amiable Autocrat: A Biography of Dr. Oliver Wendell Holmes*. New York: Henry Schuman, 1947.

Christoph Irmscher

FOLKLORE

Folklore is that part of a culture learned informally and interpersonally in groups whose members have a common bond. Communities such as a village or urban neighborhood as well as families, ethnic or religious groups, occupations, and regions generate and perpetuate traditions expressing shared values. Transmitted by word of mouth and demonstration, folklore takes many forms, from oral literature (proverbs, songs, tales) and material culture (architecture, crafts, food) to behavior that combines words and body action (superstitions, customs, games).

Folk knowledge was central to the lives of many Americans at the start of the nineteenth century. But institutions arising in the period 1820–1870, such as public schools, sheet music, popular magazines, and factories, would begin to fill the educational, recreational, and material needs once served by folk culture. This time of great change also saw the closing of the frontier, the building of a transcontinental rail system, and a demographic shift from countryside to city, breaking down the isolation that had fostered dependence on folklore for survival and quality of life.

Collectively, writers of the period who had grown up in tradition-based communities must have witnessed this transformation of American society with a mixture of regret and relief. Their literary uses of folklore, whether as the foundation of a work or for "local color," were both an attempt to recapture a vanishing way of life and an acknowledgment of the progress they were experiencing.

With a few exceptions, the serious study of American folklore did not occur until after 1870, as manifested by the establishment of the American Folklore Society in 1888 (along with academically based scholars, early members included Mark Twain, Joel Chandler Harris, Henry Wadsworth Longfellow, James Russell Lowell, and George Washington Cable). Our knowledge of antebellum American folklore thus depends heavily on the work of imaginative writers, with little contemporaneous "scientific" fieldwork documentation to corroborate their reliability. For most of those authors, folklore was grist for the creative mill, not a collection of cultural gems to be accurately recorded.

Early literary uses of folklore can be a valuable resource that allows folklorists to fill in missing information. A methodology for assessing the authenticity of folklore in literature should include consultation of biographical materials to determine under what circumstances the author encountered the lore, and comparison of perceived folk materials with those in later "scientific" collections from the same culture believed to be continuous since the author's time. To literary scholars, on the other hand, folklore is of interest as one source of an author's inspiration and for its contribution to a work's artistic success.

Whereas historical events certainly have had a role in shaping American folklore, geography has been an even stronger influence; it has provided a template for the diversity of the country's population and physical environment. The regional character of American folklore will therefore be the basis for this review of some noteworthy cases of literary use.

THE NORTH

Marking the beginning of the survey period, and also illustrating the "detective work" of analyzing folklore in literature, is Washington Irving's (1783–1859) "Rip Van Winkle" (1819). At first glance, the story seems to be a European fairy legend transplanted to New York State that Irving might have heard from descendants of early Hudson Valley settlers. But the story's endnote hints at a very different source: "The foregoing Tale, one would suspect, had been suggested . . . by a little German superstition about the . . . Kypphäuser [sic] mountain" (p. 57). Living abroad in 1817, Irving met British novelist and folklorist Sir Walter Scott (1771–1832), who encouraged him to explore German folklore. Soon thereafter, while learning German, Irving came across the folktale "Peter Klaus" in either *Volks-Sagen* (1800) by Otmar (Johann Carl Christoph Nachtigal) or *Volks-Sagen, Märchen und Legenden* (1811) by Johann G. Büsching. It concerns a

goatherd who awakens from a twenty-year slumber, after drinking fairy wine on the Kyffhäuser Mountain, to find his village dramatically changed.

Although elements of "Rip Van Winkle" are nearly identical to those in "Peter Klaus," a close reading shows the German tale to be merely Irving's Old World springboard for a distinctly New World work of fiction. Further, mention of possibly genuine Catskill Mountains legends (the bowling ghosts of Henry Hudson's crew and the Postscript's Native American lore) is grafted to the conclusion. Although the main plot of "Rip" thus is not based on American folklore, the discovery of, and comparison with, its source material more clearly reveals Irving's creative contributions in this seminal work of American short fiction. (His other famous story, "The Legend of Sleepy Hollow" [1820], most likely had a similar German inspiration in the headless-horseman Rübezahl legends published by Johann Karl August Musäus.)

Studies of folklore in literature often are by scholars whose literary training and focus has caused them to overlook their subjects's inclusion of material folk culture (which became part of American folklore study in the 1960s). Such is the case with Kevin J. Hayes's *Melville's Folk Roots*, which examines the largely nautical superstitions, legends, tall tales, proverbs, and songs in the works of Herman Melville (1819–1891), mostly acquired firsthand in his early sailing experiences. But Melville did not restrict himself to this verbal lore; some of his richest uses involve traditional food, art, and architecture. For example, chapter 32 of *White-Jacket* (1850) describes a type of sailor's pie called dunderfunk as "made of hard biscuit, hashed and pounded, mixed with beef fat, molasses, and water, and baked brown in a pan . . . in the feeling language of the Down Easter, [it] is certainly 'a cruel nice dish'" (p. 134); chapter 15 of *Moby-Dick* (1851) gives a recipe for New England chowder: "It was made of small juicy clams, scarcely bigger than hazel nuts, mixed with pounded ship biscuit, and salted pork cut up into little flakes; the whole enriched with butter, and plentifully seasoned with pepper and salt" (p. 65). Both dishes create a sense of place, the first on sea to illustrate shipboard resourcefulness with limited stores, the second on land as Nantucket hotel fare.

Chapter 57 of *Moby-Dick* describes the folk art of scrimshaw: "In Nantucket, and New Bedford, and Sag Harbor, you will come across lively sketches of whales and whaling-scenes, graven by the fishermen themselves on Sperm Whale-teeth . . . in their hours of ocean leisure" (p. 269). This occurs as part of a critique of visual depictions of whales, Melville's point being that only artists who have actually seen the

"Rip Van Winkle"

On a level spot in the centre was a company of odd looking personages playing at ninepins. They were dressed in a quaint outlandish fashion— some wore short doublets. . . . By degrees Rip's awe and apprehension subsided. He even ventured, when no eye was fixed upon him, to taste the beverage, which he found had much of the flavour of excellent hollands. . . .

[The villagers] all stared at him with equal marks of surprise, and whenever they cast their eyes upon him, invariably stroked their chins. The constant recurrence of this gesture induced Rip involuntarily to do the same, when to his astonishment he found his beard had grown a foot long!

"Peter Klaus"

Peter . . . came at last to a smoothshaven green, where twelve ancient knights, none of whom spoke a word, were engaged in playing ninepins. . . . [He] saw at once that their . . . slashed doublets belonged to a fashion long past. By degrees his looks grew bolder, and noting . . . a tankard near him filled with wine whose aroma was excellent, he took a draught. . . .

These people only stared at him and fixed their eyes upon his chin. He put his hand unconsciously to his mouth, and to his great surprise found that he had grown a beard at least a foot long.

"Peter Klaus" as published by Otmar, translated by Thomas Roscoe in *The German Novelists* (1826), and reprinted in *A Harvest of World Folk Tales,* edited by Milton Rugoff (New York: Viking, 1949), pp. 371–373.

animal are capable of portraying it accurately (and, by extension, only those who have experienced the world can truly know it). This example of both occupational and regional folklore thus supports one of the author's philosophical themes. Finally, Melville's short story, "I and My Chimney" (1856), revolves around a type of

vernacular building known to architectural historians as the New England Large House (a late-eighteenth-century development of the saltbox). Melville uses the dwelling, modeled on his real-life Berkshire farmhouse, Arrowhead, as a playful, pre-Freudian allegory of emasculation. The narrator's wife wants to tear out the massive central chimney with which he identifies to create a more fashionable hall: "'What!' said I, 'abolish the chimney? To take out the back-bone of anything, wife, is a hazardous affair'" (p. 289).

John Greenleaf Whittier (1807–1892) was both a poet and pioneer folklorist whose *Legends of New-England in Prose and Verse* (1831) and *The Supernaturalism of New England* (1847) were early attempts at preserving his region's "traditionary lore." Although much of his material was gleaned from printed sources, some evidently was taken from oral tradition. It should thus come as no surprise that he incorporated this lore in his poetry. A good example is "Telling the Bees" (1858). In his note to the somber poem the folklorist in him explains, "A remarkable custom, brought from the Old Country, formerly prevailed in the rural districts of New England. On the death of a member of the family, the bees were at once informed of the event, and their hives dressed in mourning. This ceremonial was supposed to be necessary to prevent the swarms from leaving their hives and seeking a new home" (p. 59). Whittier's appreciation of the custom's origin, indicative of the English background of early New England folklore, is confirmed three decades later by British writer Thomas Hardy's description of the same tradition in one of his *Wessex Tales,* "Interlopers at the Knap."

THE SOUTH

A rich vein of folklore runs through the antebellum literature known as "humor of the old Southwest." Southern writers such as David Crockett (and his exploiters), Johnson Jones Hooper, William Tappan Thompson, George Washington Harris, and Thomas Bangs Thorpe broke from British literary models by using rustic speech, characters, and manners to comically portray their region. Allowing for the fictionalization and exaggeration, their works provide valuable insight into America's frontier folkways.

A pioneer of this genre was Augustus Baldwin Longstreet (1790–1870), whose *Georgia Scenes* (1835) is set in Augusta, Georgia, in the 1790s. Teachers then were paid directly by parents, who would withhold pay for the days their children were freely given a holiday. In Longstreet's sketch, "The Turn Out," the pupils barricade themselves in the log schoolhouse and prevent the teacher from entering until he is forced to

Vol. 2.] "GO AHEAD!!" [No. 1.

THE CROCKETT ALMANAC 1839.

An Unexpected Ride on the Horns of an Elk. See Page 25.

Containing Adventures, Exploits, Sprees & Scrapes in the West, & Life and Manners in the Backwoods.

Nashville, Tennessee. Published by Ben Harding. See Page. 2

Cover of the *Crockett Almanac,* 1839. Published from 1835 to 1856, the *Crockett Almanac* presented the fictional adventures of the famed American hero. COURTESY OF TENNESSEE STATE LIBRARY AND ARCHIVES

grant them a holiday. This curious school ritual had its origins in sixteenth-century Britain and is the subject of Anglo-Irish novelist Maria Edgeworth's story, "The Barring Out" (1796). In America, "turn outs" are documented as early as 1702, but *Georgia Scenes* is the first literary treatment, followed by Edward Eggleston's *The Hoosier School-Master* (1871).

Another Longstreet sketch, "The Gander Pulling," features an even more unbelievable, but no less real, tradition. Vaguely inspired by medieval jousting tournaments, this brutal sport of the frontier South and Midwest required contestants to gallop their horses along a track while trying to yank the greased head off a live male goose suspended by the feet from above. Travel writers Henry Bradshaw Fearon and

George William Featherstonhaugh described the sport in the early nineteenth century, but again, *Georgia Scenes* is the first fictionalization, followed by *The Crockett Almanac 1840.*

Perhaps the finest (from the folklorist's perspective) literary use of folklore for the period, if one of the most obscure, is Hardin E. Taliaferro's (1811–1875) *Fisher's River (North Carolina) Scenes and Characters* (1859). The author, a Baptist minister and newspaper editor in Alabama, wrote the book following a visit to his Appalachian home community in Surry County, North Carolina. His recollections of boyhood neighbors emphasize the tradition of storytelling, in particular tall tales, a folktale type favored by many regional humorists (perhaps because it relies on the same hyperbole as do their writings). Taliaferro, however, managed to produce a work of literary merit with few of the genre's usual distortions.

At the same time, *Fisher's River* is a reliable American folklore document for the 1820s, a good half century before the first serious research. Early variants of folktales are told in dialect in the social contexts in which the author originally heard them. He did not even fictionalize the narrators's names (although he chose to hide his own identity with the pen name "Skitt"). These include Larkin Snow, the miller, whose stories entertained customers waiting for their meal to be ground, and gunsmith Uncle Davy Lane, whose "Ride in the Peach-Tree" substitutes a peach pit for the cherry stone used by Baron Munchausen in an eighteenth-century European variant of the hunting yarn. The seed, rammed down the barrel of the narrator's rifle when he runs out of regular ammunition, is fired at a large buck, which then runs off. A few years later, the narrator climbs from a cliff into a peach tree to gather the fruit, only to have the tree, which he discovers to be growing from the shoulders of the same stag, run off with him.

The best nineteenth-century literary portrayals of African American folklore, such as those of Joel Chandler Harris (1848–1908) and Charles Waddell Chesnutt (1858–1932), appeared too late for the period under consideration. Two earlier nonfiction works, however, give a promise of things to come. While *Narrative of the Life of Frederick Douglass, An American Slave, Written by Himself* (1845) was intended as abolitionist polemic, its details of slave culture anticipate the ex-slave oral histories recorded in the 1930s as part of President Franklin Roosevelt's Work Projects Administration. Frederick Douglass (1818–1895) describes the Maryland plantation of Colonel Edward Lloyd as having "the appearance of a country village. All the mechanical operations for all

Hardin E. Taliaferro's Fisher's River *contains a wealth of tall tales the author heard while growing up in the North Carolina mountains in the 1820s. The following is narrated by Larkin Snow, whose "ambition consisted in being the best miller in the land, and in being* number one *in big story-telling." The tale has a European precedent in* The Surprising Adventures of Baron Munchausen *(London, 1785, in which the fast-running animal is a hare) and is first reported for the United States in 1808. In this sketch, Taliaferro also offers insight into the traditional Southern Mountain approach to fox hunting, which dispenses with "riding to the hound."*

He would occasionally feel of his meal—while the old tub-mill would perform its slow revolutions as though it was paid by the year—to see whether it was ground fine enough to suit him. He would then give you one of his peculiar looks . . . and would tell you the story of the

Fast-Running Dog

"You see," said Larkin, "a passel uv fellers cum frum 'bout Rockford, Jonesville, and the Holler to have a fox-hunt, and kep' a-boastin' uv thar fast dogs. I told 'um my little dog Flyin'-jib could beat all thar dogs, and give 'um two in the game. I called him up and showed him to 'um, and you mout a hearn 'um laugh a mile, measured with a 'coonskin and the tail throwed in. I told 'um they'd laugh t'other side o' thar mouths afore it were done. They hooted me.

"We went out with 'bout fifty hounds, and, as good luck would hev it, we started a rale old Virginny red fox, 'bout three hours afore day, on the west side uv Skull Camp Mountain . . . Not fur from Shipp's Muster-ground they passed me, and Flyin'-jib were 'bout half a mile ahead on 'um all, goin' fast as the report of a rifle gun. Passin' through a meader whar thar were a mowin'-scythe with the blade standin' up, Flyin'-jib run chug against it with sich force that it split him wide open frum the eend uv his nose to the tip uv his tale. Thar he lay, and nuver whimpered, tryin' to run right on. I streaked to him, snatched up both sides uv him, slapped 'um together, but were in sich a hurry that I put two feet down and two up. But away he went arter the fox, scootin' jist in that fix. You see, when he got tired runnin' on two feet on one side, he'd whirl over, quick as lightnin', on t'other two, and it seemed ruther to hev increased his verlocity. He cotch the fox on the east side uv Skull Camp, a mile ahead uv the whole kit uv 'um."

Hardin E. Taliaferro ("Skitt"), *Fisher's River (North Carolina) Scenes and Characters* (1859; New York: Arno, 1977), pp. 148–151.

the farms were performed here. The shoemaking . . . the blacksmithing, cartwrighting, coopering, weaving, and grain-grinding, were all performed by the slaves on the home plantation" (p. 37). Slave fare consisted of "coarse corn meal boiled. This was called *mush*. It was put into a large wooden tray or trough, and set down upon the ground. The children were then called, like so many pigs . . . [to] devour the mush; some with oyster-shells, others with pieces of shingle, some with naked hands, and none with spoons" (p. 45).

As protection from whippings, a fellow slave advised Douglass to carry "a certain *root . . . always on my right side*," but in a note the author distances himself from such magico-religious practices: "This superstition is very common among the more ignorant slaves" (pp. 67, 73). Charles Waddell Chesnutt would later fictitiously elaborate, in *The Conjure Woman* (1899), on the empowering sense of control afforded slaves by this African-derived belief system.

Thomas Wentworth Higginson (1823–1911), literary critic, friend of poet Emily Dickinson, abolitionist, and commander of the First South Carolina Volunteers, a Union Army regiment of freed slaves, devotes a chapter of his *Army Life in a Black Regiment* (1870) to the spirituals he jotted down at night in the outfit's Civil War camp. The chapter was first published as an *Atlantic Monthly* article in 1867, the same year field-collected variants of twenty of his thirty-seven songs appeared in *Slave Songs of the United States,* compiled by pioneer folklorists William Francis Allen, Charles Pickard Ware, and Lucy McKim Garrison, a confirmation of their authenticity.

THE WEST

A limited grounding in the culture of the American West typifies the antebellum writers who depicted this region's folklore. A case in point is Henry Wadsworth Longfellow's lengthy poem, *The Song*

Folktales often found their way as fillers into antebellum periodicals such as the Spirit of the Times *and* Yankee Blade, *published in New York and Boston, respectively. As an illustration of westward migration, the following excerpt appeared in the 18 December 1845 issue of the* Cherokee Advocate *of Tahlequah, Oklahoma, under the heading "Indian Fables." Using the pen name "Aesop," the contributor, missionary Samuel Worcester Butler, "accidentally stumbled on" the story among the Cherokees in Oklahoma after their forced removal from Georgia on the Trail of Tears. It is the first American report of "The Tar Baby," made famous by Joel Chandler Harris in* Uncle Remus, His Songs and His Sayings *(1880). The research of folklorist Florence Baer suggests that the folktale was brought from West Africa and that southeastern Indians borrowed it from blacks, perhaps in the eighteenth century.*

"Once upon a time," there was such a severe drought, that all streams of water, and all lakes, were dried up.

In this emergency, the beasts assembled together, to devise means to procure water. It was proposed by one to dig a well. All agreed to do so except the hare. She refused because it would soil her tiny paws.—The rest, however, dug their well, and were fortunate enough to find water. The hare beginning to suffer with thirst, and having no right to the well, was thrown upon her wits to procure water. She determined, as the easiest way, to steal from the public well. The rest of the animals, surprised to find that the hare was so well supplied with water, asked her where she got it. She replied, that she arose betimes in the morning and gathered the dew drops. However, the wolf and the fox suspected her of theft, and hit on the following plan to detect her. They made a wolf of tar and placed it near the well. On the following night the hare came as usual, after her

supply of water. On seeing the tar wolf, she demanded who was there. Receiving no answer, she repeated the demand, threatening to kick the wolf if he did not reply.

She receiving no reply, kicked the wolf, and by this means adhered to the tar and was caught. When the fox and wolf got hold of her, they consulted what it was best to do with her. One proposed cutting her head off. This the hare protested would be useless, as it had often been tried without hurting her. Other methods were proposed for despatching her, all which she said would be useless.

At last it was proposed, to let her loose to perish in a thicket. Upon this the hare affected great uneasiness, and pleaded hard for life. Her enemies however refused to listen, and she was accordingly let loose. As soon however as she was out of reach of her enemies, she gave a whoop, and bounding away, exclaimed, "This is where I live!"

---

of Hiawatha (1855). Sparked by the East's (and his own) Romantic fascination with Native Americans, Longfellow (1807–1882) wrote in an 1854 journal entry, "I have at length hit upon a plan for a poem on the American Indians. . . . It is to weave their beautiful traditions into a whole. I have hit upon a measure, too, which I think the right and only one for such a theme" (S. Longfellow 2:247–248). That measure was the trochaic tetrameter, or "tom-tom" beat, of the *Kalevala*, a Finnish folk epic compiled by Elias Lönnrot (1849, German translation 1852). The traditions Longfellow chose to weave were tales of the Algonquin trickster hero Manabozho, collected in Michigan among the Ojibwa (Chippewa) by Henry Rowe Schoolcraft (1793–1864) and published in his *Algic Researches* (1839). Some tales in that study had been rendered into English by Schoolcraft's half-Ojibwa wife and chief interpreter, Jane Johnston Schoolcraft (Bame-wa-was-ge-zhik-a-quay, 1800–1842). Longfellow said of the

pioneer ethnologist, "I have pored over Mr. Schoolcraft's writings nearly three years before I resolved to appropriate something of them to my own use" (Keiser, p. 192).

As a presentation of Ojibwa mythology, however, Longfellow's poem is less than reliable. One problem is the name of his protagonist. A week after the previously quoted journal entry he wrote, "Work at 'Manabozho'; or, as I think I shall call it, 'Hiawatha' — that being another name for the same personage" (S. Longfellow 2:248). Hiawatha was said to have united the warring tribes of central New York into the Iroquois League around 1570; he had no connection with the more westerly Manabozho. The confusion of the two figures began when Schoolcraft, taking some poetic license himself, read a group of Hiawatha legends and made him into an Ojibwa god. Longfellow compounded the error and further departed from his source material by emphasizing the more creative side of Manabozho's character, that of culture hero. Not all of Longfellow's borrowings were from print, however; Schoolcraft arranged for him to meet Mendoskong, an Ojibwa chief, who supplied firsthand information. This rare early collaboration of a folklorist, folklore informant, and creative writer is remarkable in itself.

The Indians of the Great Plains made a literary appearance as early as 1827 in James Fenimore Cooper's *The Prairie,* a westward extension of his Leatherstocking novels. However, Cooper (1789–1851) had never been within a thousand miles of its Wyoming setting, relying for his details on the 1823 account of Stephen H. Long's expedition to the Rocky Mountains. In contrast, Francis Parkman's (1823–1893) travel narrative, *The Oregon Trail* (1848), offers a realistic (if superficial) eyewitness account of Dakota (Sioux) traditions, especially customs and material culture.

"The Celebrated Jumping Frog of Calaveras County" (1865) launched struggling journalist Mark Twain (1835–1910) into the literary spotlight. Rooted in the Southwestern Humor genre, the story is said to be based on folklore, but the nature of that lore is unclear. In an Angels Camp, California, saloon, Twain heard former steamboat captain Ben Coon tell of a frog-jumping contest. Whether Coon's yarn was a local tall tale or an account of an actual gold miners's recreation, similar stories in California newspapers of the 1850s suggest a tradition of some kind. Although Twain's story paints a less detailed portrait of life in the gold fields than Bret Harte's "The Luck of Roaring Camp" (1868), it did inspire a California tradition of its own: in 1928 the Angels Camp Boosters Club began its annual Calaveras County Fair and Jumping Frog Jubilee.

CONCLUSION

Partly as a response to the disruptions of the Civil War and the nostalgia of the Centennial, the later nineteenth century ushered in a golden age of folklore in American literature. If regional diversity arising from early settlement and the frontier experience can be said to mark the literary use of folklore from 1820 to 1870, the following decades would see for American letters a greater ethnic and gender inclusiveness, revealing more fully the colors and textures of the country's folk-cultural patchwork. Such literary masters of folklore as Mark Twain, Joel Chandler Harris, and George Washington Cable would come into their own, soon followed by the likes of Rowland E. Robinson, Charles Chesnutt, Sarah Orne Jewett, and Kate Chopin. But the antebellum writers of this survey pointed the way, establishing a precedent for using folklore to reconnect American readers to their roots in traditional culture.

See also Blacks; "The Celebrated Jumping Frog of Calaveras County"; Humor; Indians; "The Legend of Sleepy Hollow"; *Moby-Dick;* Oral Tradition; "Rip Van Winkle"; *The Song of Hiawatha;* Tall Tales

BIBLIOGRAPHY
Primary Works
Douglass, Frederick. *Narrative of the Life of Frederick Douglass, an American Slave, Written by Himself.* 1845. In *The Oxford Frederick Douglass Reader,* edited by William L. Andrews, pp. 21–97. New York: Oxford University Press, 1996.

Irving, Washington. "Rip Van Winkle." 1819. In *The Legend of Sleepy Hollow and Other Selections from Washington Irving,* edited by Austin McC. Fox, pp. 39–59. New York: Washington Square Press, 1962.

Melville, Herman. *White Jacket; or, The World in a Man-of-War.* 1851. New York: Grove Press, 1956.

Melville, Herman. *Moby-Dick; or, The Whale.* 1851. New York: Holt, Rinehart and Winston, 1964.

Melville, Herman. "I and My Chimney." 1856. In *Great Short Works of Herman Melville,* edited by Warner Berthoff, pp. 275–302. New York: Harper and Row Perennial Classic, 1966.

Whittier, John Greenleaf. "Telling the Bees." 1858. In *The Complete Poetical Works of John Greenleaf Whittier,* Cambridge Edition, pp. 59–60. Boston and New York: Houghton Mifflin, 1894.

Secondary Works
Brown, Carolyn S. *The Tall Tale in American Folklore and Literature.* Knoxville: University of Tennessee Press, 1987.

Carey, George. "John Greenleaf Whittier and Folklore: The Search for a Traditional American Past." *New York Folklore Quarterly* 27, no. 1 (1971): 113–129.

Cohen, Hennig. "American Literature and American Folklore." In *Our Living Traditions: An Introduction to American Folklore,* edited by Tristram Potter Coffin, pp. 238–247. New York: Basic Books, 1968.

Cuff, Roger Penn. "Mark Twain's Use of California Folklore in His Jumping Frog Story." *Journal of American Folklore* 65, no. 256 (1952): 155–158.

Dorson, Richard M. "The Identification of Folklore in American Literature." *Journal of American Folklore* 70 (1957): 1–8.

Dorson, Richard M. *Jonathan Draws the Long Bow: New England Popular Tales and Legends.* Cambridge, Mass.: Harvard University Press, 1946.

Hayes, Kevin J. *Melville's Folk Roots.* Kent, Ohio: Kent State University Press, 1999.

Jones, Steven Swann. *Folklore and Literature in the United States: An Annotated Bibliography of Studies of Folklore in American Literature.* New York: Garland, 1984.

Keiser, Albert. *The Indian in American Literature.* New York: Oxford University Press, 1933.

Leach, MacEdward. "Folklore in American Regional Literature." *Journal of the Folklore Institute* 3 (1966): 376–397.

Longfellow, Samuel. *Life of Henry Wadsworth Longfellow.* 2 vols. Boston: Ticknor, 1886.

Pochmann, Henry A. "Irving's German Sources in *The Sketch Book*." *Studies in Philology* 27 (1930): 477–507.

Pronechen, Joseph S. "The Making of Hiawatha." *New York Folklore Quarterly* 28, no. 2 (1972): 151–160.

Williams, Cratis D. "Mountain Customs, Social Life, and Folk Yarns in Taliaferro's *Fisher's River Scenes and Characters*." *North Carolina Folklore Journal* 16 (1968): 143–152.

John A. Burrison

FOREIGN CONSPIRACY AGAINST THE LIBERTIES OF THE UNITED STATES

Samuel F. B. Morse (1791–1872) is perhaps best known as the inventor of the telegraph and the "Morse code" that bears his name. Those familiar with American art know him as an accomplished painter of landscapes, portraits, and ambitious history paintings such as the *Gallery of the Louvre* (1831–1832), a six-by-nine-foot panoramic containing thirty-eight miniaturized European old masters's paintings, including works by Leonardo da Vinci, Raphael, and Rembrandt. Morse played a prominent role in the establishment of the National Academy of Design in 1825 and served for more than two decades as its president. Because Morse is admired for these significant contributions to American history and culture, a less-appealing side of his personality is often overlooked: his intolerance toward Catholics and his nativist activism. Morse launched several public attacks on Roman Catholicism, including the publication in 1835 of *Foreign Conspiracy against the Liberties of the United States,* a treatise warning Americans against the political influence of Roman Catholicism. *Foreign Conspiracy* ranks among the most virulent and paranoid of a flurry of anti-Catholic documents published during the antebellum period.

BACKGROUND TO MORSE'S ANTI-CATHOLICISM

Samuel Finley Breese Morse was born 27 April 1791 in Charlestown, Massachusetts. His father, Jedediah Morse, was a Congregational minister and geographer, and Samuel was the eldest of eleven children,

Samuel F. B. Morse. Photograph by Mathew Brady, c. 1850. THE LIBRARY OF CONGRESS

only three of whom survived infancy. After his graduation from Yale College in 1810, Morse was determined to make a name for himself as a painter, and in 1811 he set sail for England to begin his studies at the Royal Academy of Arts in London. He remained in England until 1815, when he returned to the United States. Within a year he met Lucretia Pickering Walker, whom he married in 1818, and he briefly considered careers other than painting, including studying for the Episcopal ministry, invention, and architecture. After his marriage, Morse struggled to support himself as a painter, and the couple had three children. Following his wife's sudden death in 1825, Morse moved to New York, where he became a founder and first president of the National Academy of Design. In 1829 he returned to Europe for another three years to continue his study of European art.

Morse's antipathy to Catholicism had deep roots in his New England boyhood, where a culture of anti-Catholicism had thrived since the region's Puritan settlement and where his father issued pulpit polemics warning his countrymen of the dangers of the Bavarian Illuminati. Morse's antipathy grew under the influence of his friends James Fenimore Cooper (1789–1851) and the anticlerical Marquis de Lafayette. It was to Lafayette that Morse had attributed the statement "American liberty can be destroyed only by Popish clergy," which he often quoted and which was reprinted in Morse's *Confessions of a French Priest* (1837). His experiences studying abroad are pivotal to an understanding of the ideas that form the core of *Foreign Conspiracy.*

The sensuousness and aesthetic beauty of Catholicism appealed to Morse, as his dalliance with conversion to Episcopalianism demonstrated. As a painter Morse was moved by the magnificent art he viewed in Europe, especially the Catholic art of the Italian Renaissance. Many of his paintings were influenced by the study of these old masters, and in paintings such as the *The Chapel of the Virgin at Subiaco* (1830), Morse romanticizes the devotion of Italian peasants praying in the countryside.

However, one episode that took place in Italy in June 1830 may have marked a turning point in his sensibilities. Morse reported in his journal that he had had a "rather disagreeable experience" while watching a papal procession: "I was standing close to the side of the house when, in an instant, without the slightest notice, my hat was struck off to the distance of several yards by a soldier . . . and this courteous manoeuvre was performed with his gun and bayonet, accompanied with curses and taunts and the expression of a demon in his countenance" (1:353). Morse apparently took this insult deeply to heart, writing: "In cases like this there is no redress. The soldier receives his orders to see that all hats are off in this religion of force, and the manner is left to his discretion. . . . There was no excuse for this outrage on all decency, to which every foreigner is liable" (1:353).

From a historical vantage point, this clash with the pope's grenadier appears to have been a life-altering one for Morse. Back in New York, he finished his work on the ambitious *Gallery of the Louvre,* and though he continued to seek commissions as an artist for several more years, by 1832 he had made a career shift, turning his attention to the development of the telegraph. Morse is thought to have conceived of the idea of the telegraph on the ship returning from Europe in 1832. For the second half of his life Morse worked primarily on the telegraph and other inventions.

As Morse drifted away from his career in painting, the mediating influence of Catholic European art receded. During the 1830s he assiduously cultivated his scientific interests, and in this new arena European ideas began to hold considerably less sway. Where Catholic art produced an unavoidable impression on

any artist intent on achieving greatness as a painter, the essentially antimodern nineteenth-century Roman Catholic doctrine was in many ways anathema to the pursuit of science and technology. As the inventor's star rose, he became more overt in his antipathy for Catholicism. During the same period he began experimenting with the invention of the telegraph, Morse published *Foreign Conspiracy,* first during 1834 in the newspaper owned by his brothers, then as a monograph in 1835.

NATIVISM AND *FOREIGN CONSPIRACY*

Morse's personal antipathy toward Catholicism was part of a growing nativist movement in the United States, sparked by increasing numbers of immigrants, mainly from Catholic Ireland. Nativists vowed to protect the interests of "native-born" Americans against newcomers. In fact nativism and anti-Catholicism were only one piece of a broad Anglo-Protestant hegemony in the United States during the 1830s that permitted, among other things, a system of slavery in the South and westward expansion. Within this national context, blacks, Indians, Spanish settlers, and Catholics were systematically excluded from privileges accorded American citizens. Morse's use of the ideology of liberty to protect these privileges is best understood within this broader context.

Because of his European experiences, Morse felt well qualified to write this series of twelve letters under the pen name "Brutus" to expose, as his title indicated, *A Foreign Conspiracy against the Liberties of the United States.* Despite the pseudonym Brutus, a reference to the Roman patriot who murdered the tyrant Julius Caesar, Morse's identity as author was generally well known. The serialization of *Foreign Conspiracy* in the *New York Observer* during 1834 began just weeks after an anti-Catholic incident in Morse's birthplace of Charlestown, Massachusetts: the burning of the Ursuline convent in August 1834. Morse's essay was reprinted in Congregational, Methodist, and Baptist journals and in the leading nativist papers. His first edition sold so well in book form that a second edition appeared almost immediately. *Foreign Conspiracy* was favorably reviewed in such anti-Catholic publications as the *Downfall of Babylon* and the *American Protestant Vindicator.*

During Morse's 1836 run for mayor of New York on a nativist ticket, a fourth edition of *Foreign Conspiracy* appeared, issued by Van Nostrand and Dwight, sponsors of the notorious Canadian "escaped nun" Maria Monk. Morse was resoundingly defeated in the election, with a distant fourth-place finish. He made another unsuccessful bid for the seat in 1841 and then for Congress in 1854. A seventh edition of *Foreign Conspiracy* was issued in 1851, and a final edition appeared after his death.

Foreign Conspiracy and Morse's subsequent work, *Imminent Dangers to the Free Institutions of the United States through Foreign Immigration*—first serialized in the *Journal of Commerce,* then appearing in book form in 1835—linked Catholicism and immigration as clear and present dangers to Americans. The Brutus letters originated in response to Frederick Schlegel's lectures in Vienna in 1828 that warned of the alliance of monarchy and Catholicism. Morse believed that without an effective army to attack America, Austria, and other so-called backward countries had joined with the Catholic Church through the Leopold Association, formed in Vienna in 1829, to win the American West by sending large numbers of immigrants to colonize America. Like his contemporary the Reverend Lyman Beecher, Morse encouraged Protestants to work together and unite against Catholic schools.

Foreign Conspiracy characterized Catholicism as a political system with roots in monarchial Europe, headed by an autocratic temporal ruler. The plot Morse detailed in *Foreign Conspiracy* originates with the Austrian government: "Austria is now acting in this country. She has devised a grand scheme. She has organized a great plan for doing something here" (p. 14). Prince Metternich, according to Morse, "the arch-contriver of plans to stifle liberty," will join forces with Pope Gregory XVI—whose agents are the Jesuits—to attack the United States. Morse elaborated on this collaboration, charging that "Austria has her Jesuit missionaries traveling through the land; she has supplied them with money, and has furnished a fountain for a regular supply" (p. 15). One "fountain" was thought to be the Leopold Association, a group of Austrian and Hungarian Catholics dedicated to missionary work in America.

America's liberty of conscience, liberty of opinion, and liberty of the press, continued Morse, presented a dangerous model to revolutionaries in Europe chafing under monarchial systems. These governments therefore and the Catholic Church were conspiring to destroy America. Since their armies could not cross the Atlantic, Catholic immigrants to America became their weapon. Morse saw evidence of the plot in the growing mob actions in New York, the O'Connell Guards, and in the purported interference of Catholic priests in elections.

Morse's anti-Catholic books attracted the attention of the mentally unstable German student Lewis Clausing, whose claims of persecution by Metternich's

agents, the Jesuits, led to his suicide and to Morse's subsequent publication of *The Proscribed German Student* (1836) and *Confessions of a French Priest* (1837). These texts moved beyond the more overt political concerns of *Foreign Conspiracy* and attacked aspects of Catholicism, such as celibacy and the confessional. Their charges of imprisonment of girls in nunneries echoed the kind of lurid material that was creating best-sellers of such books as Rebecca Reed's (1813–1838) *Six Months in a Convent* (1835) and the Canadian Maria Monk's (1817–1849) *Awful Disclosures* (1836).

Despite its appearance in multiple editions, Morse's *Foreign Conspiracy* was probably far less influential than the best-selling tales of escaped nuns. Reed's narrative is thought to have sold close to 200,000 copies. Monk's story sold 20,000 copies in the first few months after its release, and by the start of the Civil War, 300,000 copies were in circulation. Morse, with his deep affinity for the politics of Monk's book, is alleged to have helped with its publication. The beguiling escaped nun, Maria Monk, who in fact had likely been a Montreal prostitute, fended off several attacks on her credibility, yet Morse continued to be her supporter even once her credibility was worn thin. In 1836 an incredulous James Fenimore Cooper joked that his friend must have a romantic interest in the renegade nun. In a letter to their mutual friend, the sculptor Horatio Greenough, Cooper worried that Morse might be getting too carried away: "I am very much afraid Morse is about to marry a certain Miss Monk. I am afraid the issue of such a celibate as himself and a regular Monk, who, by the way, has also been a *nun,* might prove to be a progeny fit only for the choir of the Sistine Chapel" (3:220). Cooper's joke echoes the fascination with Catholic sexuality that drove much of the pseudo-pornographic anti-Catholic material, such as Monk's narrative. Morse had in fact become extremist in his nativist views.

By 1838 the inventor was deeply involved in demonstrating the telegraph and so did not participate in the 1838 National Academy of Design exhibition. But at least one art critic for the *New-York Commercial Advertiser* satirized his absence this way: "Has 'Brutus' eloped with Maria Monk? or has the author of 'Foreign conspiracies against the liberties of the United States' been kidnapped by emissaries of the Propaganda?" (Johnston). Morse's reputation had clearly suffered in many quarters by his commitment to nativism. During this period he apparently wooed several young ladies with a success rate that matched that of his political campaigns. In 1848 the fifty-seven-year-old Morse married the twenty-six-year-old Sarah Elizabeth Griswold, who was speech and hearing impaired and close to the age of his first wife at her death. Morse persisted in his anti-Catholicism and continued to act as a key figure in the rise of the Know-Nothing Party during the 1850s.

When Morse died on 2 April 1872, the telegraph flashed the news around the world. Yet despite his work in advancing technology, he was far from progressive. Morse was deeply regressive in his political beliefs, serving during the pre–Civil War period as president of the American Society for the Promotion of National Unity, a proslavery society. As his work in *Foreign Conspiracy* demonstrates, Morse was intolerant to the point of paranoia about Catholicism and remained so until the end of his days.

See also Art; Catholics; Foreigners; Immigration; Technology

BIBLIOGRAPHY

Primary Works

Cooper, James Fenimore. *The Letters and Journals of James Fenimore Cooper.* 2 vols. Edited by James Franklin Beard. Cambridge, Mass.: Harvard University Press, 1960.

Morse, Edward Lind, ed. *Samuel F. B. Morse, His Letters and Journals.* 2 vols. 1914. New York: Da Capo Press, 1973–.

Morse, Samuel F. B. *Foreign Conspiracy against the Liberties of the United States.* New York: Leavitt, Lord, 1835.

Schultz, Nancy Lusignan. *Veil of Fear: Nineteenth Century Convent Tales by Rebecca Reed and Maria Monk.* West Lafayette, Ind.: Purdue University Press, 1999.

Secondary Works

Billington, Ray Allen. *The Protestant Crusade, 1800–1860: A Study in the Origins of American Nativism.* New York: Macmillan, 1938.

Johnston, Patricia. "Samuel F. B. Morse's Gallery of the Louvre: Social Tensions in an Ideal World." In *Seeing High and Low: Representing Social Conflict in American Visual Culture,* edited by Patricia Johnston. Berkeley: University of California Press, 2006.

Mabee, Carleton. *The American Leonardo: A Life of Samuel F. B. Morse.* 1943. New York: Octagon, 1969.

Silverman, Kenneth. *Lightning Man: The Accursed Life of Samuel F. B. Morse.* New York: Knopf, 2003.

Nancy Lusignan Schultz

FOREIGNERS

Bigotry against foreigners was rampant in nineteenth-century America, buttressed by patriotic or racial ideas about geography, ethnography, and sociohistorical process. These ideas made it easy to rank foreigners upon a global hierarchical scale, with white U.S citizens and the United States itself stationed at its apex. According to the notion known as American "exceptionalism," the geographical locale of the New World endowed the Republic with a special status and mission. In the seventeenth century the Pilgrims had escaped the tyranny and corruption of the Old World, crossed the Atlantic, and founded a new, uniquely free society, an "empire for liberty" as Thomas Jefferson (1743–1826) phrased it a century and a half later. In its nineteenth-century guise, the sentimental view of the United States was as a bastion of liberty rationalized expansionism. In 1845 the newspaper editor John Louis O'Sullivan termed this imperative the country's "Manifest Destiny," the divinely sanctioned engulfing of territory up to, and perhaps even beyond, the western Pacific shore.

Anti-foreigner sentiment was also based on ethnographical categories widely accepted in a white scientific community that reached from southern physicians who wished to justify slavery to naturalists at Harvard. The most popular, now notorious, text of this group, Josiah Nott and George Gliddon's 1854 *Types of Mankind,* divided the globe and its inhabitants into racial types and privileged Western Europeans or Anglo-Saxons. Another component was the deeply ingrained, pervasive concept of inevitable universal historical progress. The Caucasian race—best represented by its incarnation in the United States—with God's aid had reached the most advanced stage of civilization, after passing through previous "savage" or "barbaric" stages, and was dutifully obliged to pull up those cultural groups or races—aboriginal peoples in Africa or the Pacific Islands, for example—that otherwise would stagnate in their own benightedness.

Fourth-of-July speeches, magazine articles, history textbooks, and travel narratives disseminated these nationally chauvinistic ideas to a receptive U.S. populace. But perhaps the strongest shaping influence came from geography primers, especially those of Peter Parley, the pseudonym of the Boston author and publisher Samuel Goodrich (1793–1860). The Peter Parley series and Goodrich's other textbooks typically mix patriotism and Christian paternalism and continually seesaw between the claimed superiority of U.S. culture and the apparent crudity or deformity of virtually all non-U.S cultures. In *Manners and Customs of the Principal Nations of the Globe* (1845), Goodrich reflects upon the supposed tendency of countries with hot climates to produce indolent citizens:

> Let a person turn round an artificial globe, and mark the countries within the tropics, and observe that there is not one among them all where the spirit of liberty, the light of learning, the love of industry, the

From *First Geography for Children*, 1855. Illustration from Harriet Beecher Stowe's book, showing races of humans. BALDWIN LIBRARY OF HISTORICAL CHILDREN'S LITERATURE, UNIVERSITY OF FLORIDA.

voice of piety, or the arts of refined life, pervade society—and he may then bless Providence that his lot is cast in the chill regions of the Pilgrims. (Pp. 8–11)

Goodrich, to his credit, preferred sociological (however fuzzily adduced) assessment and resisted raw racist ideologies. In fact, at times his grade-school primers could even undercut their own biased simplifications. In *Peter Parley's Tales about the Islands in the Pacific Ocean* (1837) he asserts that the nomadic hunters of New Guinea appear "to be very savage and brutal," but then immediately adds that "the truth is we know but very little about them. . . . Perhaps, after all, if . . . [we] knew these people better, their character would appear different" (pp. 100–101).

In the 1860s textbooks written by professional, academic geographers began to replace Goodrich's juvenile-pedagogical ones, and yet these works, drawing upon the racist ethnographical science in *Types of Mankind* and kindred works, devised hierarchical systems that often outlined racial types more firmly and ethnocentrically than those used in the 1840s or 1850s. Arnold Henry Guyot (1807–1884), a Princeton professor, includes in his 1866 *Physical Geography* a section on "The White Race the Normal or Typical Race," with an accompanying picture depicting the latter "in unrivalled works of the ancient sculptures," and with the text confirming that a "comparison of the different tribes and races of men, reveals the fact of a gradual modification of types, on every side of the central or [Caucasian] highest race, until by insensible degrees, the lowest or most degraded forms of humanity are reached" (quoted in Elson, p. 67). The nonhierarchical, nonracist appreciation of all cultures—which would accord each an intrinsic merit and a complete, holistic development—was not to gain scientific credence until the early years of the twentieth century, in the writings of the U.S. anthropologist Franz Boas (1858–1942), and even then jingoism and anti-immigrant sentiments continued, in the popular mind, to reinforce stereotypes.

THE EUROPEAN WORLD

Patriotic self-regard largely explains the tendency to stereotype foreigners, but insecurity played a role as well. National anxiety about the stability of Protestant, republican culture—especially in the face of massive Irish Catholic immigration in the 1840s and 1850s—induced wholesale xenophobia against all non-Protestant foreigners. There was a widespread anticlerical literature defaming Catholicism and its adherents, often in the form of melodramatic captivity narratives in which an innocent American is made the victim of Spanish priestcraft. The dungeon in Edgar Allan Poe's (1809–1849) famous short story "The Pit and the Pendulum" (1842), for instance, happens to be in Seville, and unknown and unseen agents of the Spanish Inquisition persecute the tale's protagonist. Behind Poe's story are more salacious potboiler novels that depicted the Catholic world as guileful and corrupt. Such lurid sensationalism seems intended for lowbrow audiences, but even more polished and circumspect authors such as James Fenimore Cooper (1789–1851) and Nathaniel Hawthorne (1804–1864)—in *The Bravo* (1831) and *The Marble Faun* (1860), respectively—envisioned Venice and Rome as urban labyrinths given over to conspiratorial plotting. This anti-Catholicism, however, ultimately had less to do with sectarian bias than with an ongoing worry about the New World's vulnerability to the perceived decadent luxury, artifice, or despotism of the Old World. Hawthorne's sister-in-law, Elizabeth Palmer Peabody (1804–1894), was a well-known New England pedagogue who wrote that her textbooks were designed to instruct young Americans "how to dispose the elements of a new world into a truly Christian order" so that the United States would not revert to those types of flawed "institutions, that, with their death-in-life, cumber Asia and Africa, and even Europe," nor "act to-day principles which have rendered desert, and strewed with ruins, regions the most favored on the globe" (p. ii).

The most prolific writer about foreign lands and peoples was Bayard Taylor (1825–1878). Largely forgotten, he was hailed in his own time as the "Great American Traveler." Antebellum readers eagerly followed his footsteps through areas far from the United States: the Middle East, India, Central Africa, Spain, Greece, Sweden, and Russia. Taylor could write with nuance and perception, but a text such as a *Visit to India, China, and Japan, in the Year 1853* (1855) betrays an apparent knee-jerk reaction against cultural difference: the "only taste which the Chinese exhibit to any degree, is a love of the monstrous. That sentiment of harmony, which throbbed like a musical rhythm through the life of the Greeks, never looked out of their oblique eyes. . . . [They] admire whatever

is distorted or unnatural" (pp. 352–353). Taylor's works sold well to a literate middle-class audience, curious about the world's diversity, but diversity was orchestrated to privilege the ethnicity, religion, and political values of the U.S (mainly Anglo-Saxon) white reader. In Taylor's most famous travel text, *Eldorado; or, Adventures in the Path of Empire* (1850), Protestant and western-northern European cultures get to lord it over southern ones, via an image of a colossal, dominant mountain:

> Rising from the level of the sea and the perpetual summer of the tropics, with an unbroken line to the height of eighteen thousand feet, it stands singly above the other ranges with its spotless crown of snow, as some giant, white-haired Northern king might stand among a host of the weak, effeminate sybarites of the South. Orizaba [in Mexico] dwells alone in my memory, as the only perfect type of mountain to be found on the Earth. (2:189)

Given a perceived shared Anglo-Saxon racial and cultural identity, feelings about Britain were ambivalent. Ralph Waldo Emerson (1803–1882) in his *English Traits* (1856) likens Britain to an aged, staid, and conventional parent in contrast to his own seemingly more energetic and youthful country. Meditating on the British aristocracy, Emerson comments that it "shocks republican nerves" and that "England, an old exhausted island, must one day be contented, like other parents, to be strong only in her children" (5:275).

The obverse side to this celebration of American youthfulness was nervousness that the United States did not match up to the glories of European culture. Washington Irving (1783–1859), Cooper, and Hawthorne all waxed nostalgic when musing on Old World sophistication, layered history, and artistic polish. Hawthorne chose Italy as the setting for his 1860 novel *The Marble Faun* not only to exploit his audience's interest in the forbidden spaces and rituals of Catholicism but also because he was genuinely attracted to European cultural richness. In the novel's preface, he writes that no "author, without a trial, can conceive of the difficulty of writing a Romance about a country [the United States] where there is no shadow, no antiquity, no mystery, no picturesque and gloomy wrong" (p. 854). Irving reveled in the exotic mystique of old Moorish Spain in his *The Alhambra* (1832), and in his *The Sketch Book of Geoffrey Crayon* (1819–1820) he fondly depicts Westminster Abbey and other venerable English architectural monuments and scenes. Although Irving at times lightly satirizes British custom, the *Sketch Book* manifests a transatlantic, Anglo-American sensibility and cosmopolitanism, which later would be fully aesthetically realized in the turn-of-the century novels of Henry James (1843–1916), such as *The Wings of the Dove* (1902) and *The Ambassadors* (1903).

The rise of a highly literate middle-class tourist culture was also catered to by a number of texts written by women. Caroline Matilda Kirkland's (1801–1864) travel book *Holidays Abroad; or, Europe from the West* (1849) responds to the lavish artistic thrills to be found in Italy and other European locales. The enticement of a rich antiquity and fear of its Catholic context or associations leads Kirkland, however, to scrupulous restraint. She praises St. Peter's Basilica in Rome as being "sumptuous" but adds that "soul it had none to me" (1:286–287). Margaret Fuller (1810–1850), a New England transcendentalist luminary and friend of Emerson, reporting on the scenes of 1840s revolutionary Italy for the *New-York Daily Tribune,* more astutely saw European sights as being indispensable to historic consciousness: the "thinking American" is a "man who . . . does not wish one seed from the Past to be lost" (p. 411).

THE MIDDLE EAST

Europe was the Old World, but the old Old World, and the original home of Christianity, was the Levant, that is, the Middle East or Holy Land. The geography and history of the Holy Land allured both Bible-reading citizens in the United States and citizens more interested in exotic entertainments. Popular travel writers and novelists—George William Curtis (1824–1892) in *Nile Notes of a Howadji* (1851) and its sequel *The Howadji in Syria* (1852) as well as Maturin Murray Ballou (1820–1895) in *The Circassian Slave; or, The Sultan's Favorite* (1851), for example—titillated the public with romanticized images of a sensual, mysterious Orient. "Damascus is a dream of beauty as you approach it," Curtis wrote in *The Howadji in Syria,* but "the secret charm of that beauty, when you are within the walls, is discovered only by penetrating deeper and farther into its exquisite courts, and gardens, and interiors, as you must strip away the veils and clumsy outer robes to behold the beauty of the Circassian or Georgian slave" (p. 12). Other contemporary works moralized on what seemed to be the result of despotic rule and indulgence. John Ross Browne (1817–1875) in *Yusef; or, The Journey of the Frangi* (1853), for instance, described the harem as a scene "of absolute servitude, and disgusting sensuality" (p. 145). Mark Twain (1835–1910) devoted a large section of his satiric *The Innocents Abroad* (1869) to his trip to the Levant, a region which he mocked as being stalled in time: "They never invent anything, never learn anything" (p. 318).

The most renowned U.S. writer who reported on the scenes and sites of the Holy Land was John Lloyd Stephens (1805–1852). He traveled incognito (and at some personal risk) through the arid and sublime lands of the Old and New Testaments, and the memoir of his arduous experience—*Incidents of Travel in Egypt, Arabia Petræa, and the Holy Land* (1837)—became an overnight hit. For Stephens and other writers (including Herman Melville [1819–1891] in his ethical-metaphysical epic poem *Clarel: A Poem and Pilgrimage in the Holy Land* [1876]), the Levant seemed a hostile, devastated terrain—with the desolate Dead Sea at its center—but also a landscape eerily filled with biblically resonant holy shrines and sites. The latter were forbidden objects of devotional fascination for U.S. Protestants, whose official theology emphasized more abstract, nonphysical forms of religious attachment and focus. Even as they stare intently at the Levant's palpable religious memorials and relics, Stephens and other contemporary U.S. travelers condemn them.

THE OTHER AMERICAS

Stephens's celebrity status was heightened when he published *Incidents of Travel in Central America, Chiapas, and Yucatan* (1841) and its sequel *Incidents of Travel in Yucatan* (1843). These narratives mix the adventure of unearthing ancient, hitherto unseen monuments (unseen by white northern eyes, that is) with scorn for the revolutionary political turmoil of the time. Stephens often viewed Mexican or Central American indigenes with contempt, but he was obsessed by the Spanish conquistadors who had overrun and appropriated their ancestral lands. His feelings are kindred to those of Julia Ward Howe (1819–1910), who wrote in her travel memoir *A Trip to Cuba* (1860) that the "race" of the Spanish rulers has "suffer[ed] and degenerate[d] under the influence of the warm climate" (p. 26). Other works—historical romances such as William Gilmore Simms's (1806–1870) *The Damsel of Darien* (1839)—tantalized Victorian American prudery with forbidden cross-racial sexual relations. In William Hickling Prescott's (1796–1859) massive *History of the Conquest of Mexico* (1843), vulgar sensationalism, but not melodrama, is avoided when the history of the Spanish Conquest is figured as a clash between the iron-willed Hernan Cortés and the melancholic, soft-spoken Aztec leader Montezuma.

These works about Mexico and other Latin American regions were popular in part because of the U.S. audience's prurient regard for Catholicism and alternative New World narratives, but also because the lands south of the border attracted the nation's territorial ambitions. A best-selling novelist of the period, George Lippard (1822–1854), in *Legends of Mexico* (1847) and *'Bel of Praire Eden: A Romance of Mexico* (1848), exploited the nation's expansive interests in Mexico. Although his novels were at times sympathetic to indigenous people who fought against despotic Spaniards, they remained essentially jingoistic in tone.

POLYNESIA

Foreign lands often became the site for a sort of soft pornography. Herman Melville knowingly highlights the antebellum audience's desire for fleshy exotica when, in *Typee: A Peep at Polynesian Life* (1846), his fictionalized account of his stay on the Marquesan island of Nukuheva, he invites the reader to imagine South Sea isles: "What strange visions of outlandish things does the very name [of the Marquesas] spirit up! Naked houris—cannibal banquets—groves of cocoa-nut . . . sunny valleys planted with bread-fruit trees—carved canoes dancing on the flashing blue waters—savage woodlands guarded by horrible idols—*heathenish rites and human sacrifices*" (p. 5). This, though, is a bit of self-conscious, tongue-in-cheek pandering, and in fact *Typee* foregrounds for the attentive reader the limits and hazards of stereotypic depictions.

In *Typee,* Melville excoriates evangelical-minded Christians who saw in the native mostly only a subject for conversion. Hawaii was the focal point for the U.S. missionary movement in the Pacific, what the Reverend Henry T. Cheever (1814–1897) in his popular *Life in the Sandwich Islands* (1851) called the "religious Protestant Heart of the great Ocean" (p. 3). The average U.S. citizen, consequently, would regard the world of the Pacific Islands as an arena for heroic missionaries overthrowing licentiousness, and part of the appeal of Melville's first novel was exactly its scandalous affront to orthodoxy and apparent relishing of native sensuality. Melville, however, refuses to make the natives consistently knowable as either brutal savages or gay-hearted, sexually liberated innocents. The two perspectives cancel each other out, and Melville thereby leaves the reader to ponder the precarious, unstable means of understanding foreignness in the first place.

AFRICA AND THE CARIBBEAN

Of all the major regions or continents addressed thus far, Africa was the one about which the least was known, and yet it also, along with the Caribbean, figured intensely in debates over slavery. Southerners often justified slavery as a fortunate escape from an Africa depicted as a primitive, abject realm. One of the most influential apologetic, proslavery texts was William J. Grayson's (1788–1863) *The Hireling and the Slave* (1856):

> In this new home [of the U.S. south], whate'er
> the negro's fate—
> More blessed his life than in his native state!
> No mummeries dupe, no Fetich charms affright,
> No rites obscene diffuse their moral blight;
> Idolatries, more hateful than the grave,
> With human sacrifice, no more enslave . . .
>
> *(Sundquist, p. 247)*

Such derogatory views were countered in abolitionist literature. Sarah J. Hale (1788–1879) in her antislavery novel *Liberia; or, Mr. Peyton's Experiments* (1853) chronicles the efforts of a group of liberated slaves to build farms and civic communities in Liberia, the African colony founded by expatriate U.S. and British diasporic Africans in the 1840s. Hale, however, still wants to uplift Africa through the hands of Christianized black immigrants rather than recognizing the merits of the native population.

More radical thinkers appalled by racism and slavery emphasized stronger positive images of Africa and its varied people as well as the island sites of the African Diaspora. The bloody 1791 revolt in nearby St. Domingo shocked many U.S., and especially southern, citizens, but some abolitionists endorsed black violence as a political necessity along freedom's road. John Greenleaf Whittier (1807–1892), for example, wrote verses praising the Haitian revolutionary Touissant-Louverture (c. 1743–1803) as a strong patriot of liberty who deserved history's encomiums:

> Dark Haytien! for the time shall come,
> Yea, even now is nigh,
> When, everywhere, thy name shall be
> Redeemed from color's infamy
>
> *(P. 6)*

The most well-known African American asserting the dignity of Caribbean and African cultures was Martin R. Delany (1812–1885), who in a series of texts—from *The Condition, Elevation, Emigration, and Destiny of the Colored People of the United States* (1852) to his novel *Blake; or, The Huts of America* (1859–1862)—advocated the need to found a strong black nation. In his late monograph *Principia of Ethnology: The Origin of Races and Color* (1879), Delany countered the biased view of the geography primers cited earlier: "So far from [being] stupefying and depressing, as popularly taught in our schoolbooks [the African] climate and inhalations of the aroma and odors with which the atmosphere is impregnated, are exciting causes, favorable to intellectual development" (p. 61).

The white-written literary text most highly regarded today as subtly expressing the complexity of the African-Caribbean New World scene is Melville's "Benito Cereno" (1856), a fact-based novella that recounts the story of a revolt on a slave ship, bringing into collision the perspectives of an adroit, cagey African insurrectionist leader, a willfully naive American captain, and a Spanish commander, whose loss of his slave ship to those he would enslave symbolizes an emasculation of Spanish Old World imperial power. It is a New World story purposely constructed to show how the "new" world was deeply shadowed by the histories of the past and the burdens of accumulated inequalities.

U.S. citizens during the antebellum period lauded themselves for their democracy, energy, and moral progressiveness, a triad of virtues all in contrast to the seeming failings of realms and peoples elsewhere: the despotic and effete old European world; the stagnant Levant; the barbaric, heathenish continent of Africa; the sensual and savage islands of the Pacific; and the racially mixed, politically convulsive countries of Latin America. Such distorting stereotypes were culturally powerful because they simultaneously focused both fears and desires, as in the example of Hawthorne's *The Marble Faun*, which depicts Rome's labyrinthine complexity as at once alluring and repulsive. The dissenting views of Melville, Delany, and other critical literary artists and political thinkers are crucial reminders that during a past era of national pomp and self-congratulation no absolute commonality of attitude prevailed. The best imaginative and empathic writers of the age saw beyond the patriotic seduction of New World exceptionalism as they engaged, in travelogues and novels, the surrounding multitudinous world.

See also "Benito Cereno"; *Blake;* Ethnology; Immigration; *The Innocents Abroad;* Irish; Manifest Destiny; Tourism; Travel Writing; *Typee*

BIBLIOGRAPHY

Primary Works

Browne, John Ross. *Yusef; or, The Journey of the Frangi.* New York: Harper & Brothers, 1853.

Cheever, Henry T. *Life in the Sandwich Islands.* New York: A. S. Barnes, 1851.

Curtis, George William. *The Howadji in Syria.* New York: Harper & Brothers, 1852.

Delany, Martin. *Principia of Ethnology: The Origin of Races and Color.* Philadelphia: Harper & Brothers, 1879.

Emerson, Ralph Waldo. *English Traits.* 1856. In *The Complete Works of Ralph Waldo Emerson.* 12 vols. Edited by Edward Waldo Emerson. Boston: Houghton Mifflin, 1903–1904.

Fuller, Margaret. *The Portable Margaret Fuller.* Edited by Mary Kelley. New York: Penguin, 1994.

Goodrich, Samuel. *Manners and Customs of the Principal Nations of the Globe.* Vol. 19 of *Parleys Cabinet Library.* Boston: Bradbury, Soden, 1845.

Goodrich, Samuel. *Peter Parley's Tales about the Islands in the Pacific Ocean.* 1831. Philadelphia: Thomas, Cowperthwait, 1846.

Hawthorne, Nathaniel. *The Marble Faun.* 1860. In *Novels.* New York: Library of America, 1983.

Howe, Julia Ward. *A Trip to Cuba.* Boston: Ticknor and Fields, 1860.

Kirkland, Caroline Matilda. *Holidays Abroad; or, Europe from the West.* 2 vols. New York: Baker and Scribner, 1849.

Melville, Herman. *Typee: A Peep at Polynesian Life.* New York, Wiley and Putnam, 1846.

Nott, Josiah Clark, and George Gliddon. *Types of Mankind.* Philadelphia: J. B. Lippincott, Grambo & Co., 1854.

Peabody, Elizabeth Palmer. *Universal History: Arranged to Illustrate Bem's Charts of Chronology.* New York: Sheldon and Co., 1859.

Taylor, Bayard. *Eldorado; or, Adventures in the Path of Empire.* 2 vols. New York: Putnam, 1850.

Taylor, Bayard. *Visit to India, China, and Japan, in the Year 1853.* New York: Putnam, 1855.

Twain, Mark. *The Innocents Abroad.* Hartford: American Pub. Co., 1869.

Whittier, John Greenleaf. "Toussaint L'Ouverture." In *Haiti and the United States: National Stereotypes and the Literary Imagination,* 2nd ed., edited by J. Michael Dash. New York: St. Martin's, 1997.

Secondary Works

Davis, John. *The Landscape of Belief: Encountering the Holy Land in Nineteenth-Century American Art and Culture.* Princeton, N.J.: Princeton University Press, 1996.

Elson, Ruth Miller. *Guardians of Tradition.* Lincoln: University of Nebraska Press, 1964.

Franchot, Jenny. *Roads to Rome: The Antebellum Protestant Encounter with Catholicism.* Berkeley: University of California Press, 1994.

Gilroy, Paul. *The Black Atlantic: Modernity and Double Consciousness.* Cambridge, Mass.: Harvard University Press, 1993.

Harvey, Bruce A. *American Geographics: U.S. National Narratives and the Representation of the Non-European World, 1830–1865.* Stanford, Calif.: Stanford University Press, 2001.

Herbert, T. Walter, Jr. *Marquesan Encounters: Melville and the Meaning of Civilization.* Cambridge, Mass.: Harvard University Press, 1980.

Kasson, Joy S. *Artistic Voyagers: Europe and the American Imagination in the Works of Irving, Allston, Cole,*

Cooper, and Hawthorne. Westport, Conn.: Greenwood Press, 1982.

Manthorne, Katherine Emma. *Tropical Renaissance: North American Artists Exploring Latin America, 1839–1879.* Washington, D.C.: Smithsonian Institution Press, 1989.

Obenzinger, Hilton. *American Palestine: Melville, Twain, and the Holy Land Mania.* Princeton, N.J.: Princeton University Press, 1999.

Rennie, Neil. *Far-Fetched Facts: The Literature of Travel and the Idea of the South Seas.* Oxford: Clarendon Press and New York: Oxford University Press, 1995.

Sanborn, Geoffrey. *The Sign of the Cannibal: Melville and the Making of a Postcolonial Reader.* Durham, N.C.: Duke University Press, 1998.

Schramer, James, and Donald Ross, eds. *Dictionary of Literary Biography.* Vol. 183, *American Travel Writers, 1776–1864.* Detroit: Gale, 1997.

Schriber, Mary Suzanne. *Writing Home: American Women Abroad, 1830–1920.* Charlottesville: University Press of Virginia, 1997.

Schueller, Malini Johar. *U.S. Orientalisms: Race, Nation, and Gender in Literature, 1790–1890.* Ann Arbor: University of Michigan Press, 1998.

Streeby, Shelley. *American Sensations: Class, Empire, and the Production of Popular Culture.* Berkeley: University of California Press, 2002.

Sundquist, Eric. "The Literature of Expansion and Race." In *The Cambridge History of American Literature,* vol. 2, *Prose Writing, 1820–1865,* pp. 125–328. New York: Cambridge University Press, 1995.

Wertheimer, Eric. *Imagined Empires: Incas, Aztecs, and the New World of American Literature, 1771–1876.* New York: Cambridge University Press, 1999.

Bruce A. Harvey

FREE LOVE

Although the free love movement owed its origin to European intellectual traditions, the phrase "free love," which came to embody its countercultural critique, was the creation of American vernacular speech. Pejorative in intent, its earliest usage seems to have been to describe the close association of Frances Wright (1795–1852) and Robert Dale Owen (1801–1877) and more particularly Nashoba (1826–1829), the racially mixed, manumissionist social experiment Wright founded in Tennessee, popularly known as Fanny Wright's Free Love Colony.

Proponents of social and sexual orthodoxy, like Hubbard Eastman (1809–1891)—who published *Noyesism Unveiled* (1849), a critique of the perfectionist theology and sexual practices of John Humphrey Noyes's (1811–1886) Putney and Oneida Communities that had institutionalized the pantagamic marital form Noyes called "complex marriage"—and John B. Ellis (*Free Love and Its Votaries,* 1870), used the term as a derogatory reference to "promiscuous intercourse of the sexes," "founded in lust," in which "utter freedom . . . is given to the passions" (Ellis, p. 193). Exemplary of this association of free love with vice was the roué's guidebook, the *Directory to the Seraglios in New York, Philadelphia, Boston, and All the Principal Cities of the Union* (1859), compiled by "A Free Loveyer."

By the 1850s, however, the loose coalition of those who advocated an anti-marriage position had begun to call themselves "Free Lovers." "Free lovism" came to be a shorthand way of referring to free love (a complex set of ideas and practices critical of conventional marriage) and its correlative social doctrines. Indicative of this shift in usage was *Bible Communism* (1853), which provided an expository overview of the unique social practice of pantagmy, or "complex marriage" (under which each adult male and adult female was married to every other adult of the opposite sex in their alternative society) of the Oneida Community (1848–1879). *Bible Communism* explicitly equated pantagmy with "free love" and asserted its power as an agent of universal reform and moral purification that would "annihilate the very sources of adultery, whoredom, and all sexual abuse" (p. 128). J. H. Noyes, charismatic founder of the community, even claimed, in his *History of American Socialisms* (1870), that the term "free love" had originated in Oneidan publications around 1849.

ORIGINS OF FREE LOVE

The roots of the free love movement may be traced to the triumph of Protestant evangelicalism in the Second Great Awakening, especially the religious enthusiasm associated with perfectionism (the radical evangelical doctrine that the individual could attain complete freedom from sin during his or her earthly life, absolute "salvation from sin," that is, could be come "perfect") in the 1830s and the rapid spread of spiritualism in the 1840s. Indeed contemporaries often cited the concept of "spiritual affinities" (the quest for an individual's "true" soul mate), a higher and purer form of association between the sexes than terrestrial marriage, as the model for free love. William Hepworth Dixon (1821–1879), a British journalist and editor of the *Athanaeum,* called the doctrine "celestial marriage" and linked it directly to free love in his *Spiritual Wives* (1868). Contemporary dictionaries of Americanisms typically cross-referenced "free love" and "affinity." The

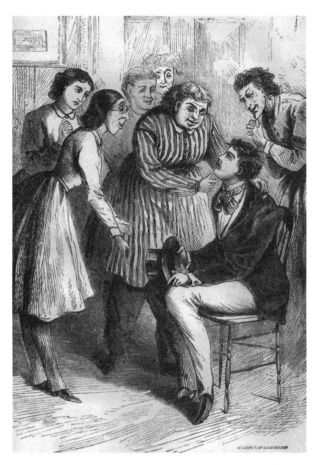

Arrival of a recruit at the Oneida Community.
Nineteenth-century cartoon reproduced in John B. Ellis's
*Free Love and Its Votaries; or, American Socialism Un-
masked,* 1870. ONEIDA COMMUNITY COLLECTION, SPECIAL COLLECTIONS
RESEARCH CENTER, SYRACUSE UNIVERSITY LIBRARY

Swedish mystic and theosophist Emanuel Swedenborg's
(1688–1772) concept of mystical union in *The Delights
of Wisdom Pertaining to Conjugal Love* (1768, 1856),
as popularized by Andrew Jackson Davis (1827–1910)
in "The Seven Phases of Marriage," made the theoretical link most explicitly, as did the sensationalist
*Lenderman's Adventures among the Spiritualists and
Free-Lovers* (1857). Phrenology, the popular pseudoscience that claimed to be able to read character traits
by examining the shape of the skull by touch, also influenced free love. Of particular import here were the
addition of a specific cranial organ as a site of "amativeness" in the 1820s by Johann (Christoph) Gaspar
Spurzheim (1776–1832) and the systematic discrimination of that trait from "philoprogenitiveness." The
distinction of these two phrenological traits validated
free lovers' separation of sex as an expression of love or
to satisfy the desire for bodily pleasure from sexual
intercourse with the primary objective of reproduction.

These ideas were popularized in America by Orson
Fowler and Lorenzo Fowler, especially in the sex-advice
books of the former, like *Amativeness; or, Evils and
Remedies of Excessive and Perverted Sexuality* (1844).

Utopian socialism reinforced unorthodox conceptions of sexual relations, most specifically in the ideas
of Robert Owen (1771–1858), an English philanthropist and founder of the New Harmony community in
Indiana (1825–1827), whose "Declaration of Mental
Independence" (4 July 1826) declared marriage
grounded in private property as one of the chief social
evils and asserted the impossibility of a binding pledge
of lifelong commitment to a single sexual partner. He
also advocated liberalization of divorce laws and equality for women. His son, Robert Dale, in conjunction
with Fanny Wright, continued to advocate these ideas
in the *Free Enquirer* well into the 1830s after the collapse of the community.

The most extensive secular communitarian movement in the antebellum years, Fourierism, was based
on the phalanstery system of the French social thinker
Charles Fourier (1772–1837), who established
"phalanxes" (communal, self-contained, cooperative
societies) in the 1840s. Fourier provided a model for
the later development of free love associations—
Berlin Heights, Ohio (1854–1858); Modern Times,
Brentwood, Long Island, New York (1851–1863); and
Oneida. Although its chief American propagandists—
Albert Brisbane (1809–1890), the leading American
Fourierist and author of *The Social Destiny of Man*
(1840), and Horace Greeley (1811–1872), the activist
editor of the *New York Tribune*—tended to ignore
Fourier's application of the *série passionelle* (his seven
degrees of "passional attraction") to sexual relation-
ships, the French social thinker Victor Antoine
Hennequin (1816–1854) published *Love in the
Phalanstery* (1848, translated by Henry James Sr.),
which provided a frank and succinct summary of
Fourier's radical sexual ideas. Brook Farm (Roxbury,
Massachusetts) was a transcendentalist utopian community from 1841 to 1844 and was reorganized as a
Fourierist community, the Brook Farm Phalanx, from
1844 to 1847. Max Lazarus resided at Brook Farm
during its Fourierist phase and published a major
overview of the Fourierist system in the *Harbinger*
(November and December 1846 and January 1847)
and in 1852 issued *Love vs. Marriage,* which applied
Fourier's ideas directly to American society. The broad
stream of social reform from abolitionism and the first
stirrings of the women's movement to the discursive
debates over divorce, birth control, and abortion contributed to the development of free love thought.
Female antislavery activists analogized the condition
of wives in traditional marriages to that of the

enslaved, as did Sarah Grimké (1792–1873) in her *Letters on the Equality of the Sexes and the Condition of Woman* (1838). Early advocacy of liberal divorce laws as well as the publication of the first American book to openly discuss contraceptive methods—*Moral Physiology* (1830)—were undertaken by Robert Dale Owen. Charles Knowlton (1800–1850), an enlightened physician, produced *The Fruits of Philosophy* (1832), the most popular and thorough canvass of contraceptive methods of the antebellum years. Rational control of reproduction, the social and emotional equality of women, and the quest for more flexible, open systems of sexual association to serve as an alternative to monogamy would comprise the core of the free love program.

DOCTRINES OF FREE LOVE

Wholly a phenomenon of the North and, with the exception of the Oneida Community, largely a decentralized network of like-minded social radicals, the free love movement had two primary centers of activity— Ohio and New York. Consequently the diversity of views and the contradictions of their social positions made for doctrinal inconsistency. For instance, most women's rights advocates were opposed to marriage, believing it to be an institution of patriarchal domination that licensed male sensuality (compulsion of wives to excessive frequency of intercourse, insistence of sexual practices wives found distasteful, and imposition of undesired pregnancy on women), but few women openly supported the radical sexual solutions proposed by the free love movement. Despite the fact that virtually all free lovers were feminists, the movement ironically became the mirror image of the sexual economy of the dominant social order—those who wrote the tracts and gave the lectures, with a few notable exceptions like Mary Gove Nichols (1810–1884) and Victoria Woodhull (1838–1927), were men. Although a central tenet of free love reform was the contention that women should have the absolute right to determine whether, when, and with whom they should have sexual intercourse and the collateral right to decide whether they wished to assume the burden of maternity and, if so, who the father should be, the heart of free love concern revolved around the regulation of male sexuality.

The separation of sexual intercourse from reproduction suggested both the possibility of the redemption and purification of institutionalized marriage (considered by free lovers to be abusive of women and to be a legally sanctioned form of rape or unrestricted lust) and, when coupled with liberalized divorce, the practice of serial monogamy. These two alternatives

James Clay was an individualist anarchist who had resided at both Berlin Heights and Modern Times. This passage is illustrative of the moral seriousness of the free love movement, the doctrine of its romantic wing, and its concern for eugenics.

How frequently have I asked the question, and seldom with a dissenting voice, "Were not your days before marriage the happiest you ever experienced?" Then love was enjoyed in freedom; there were no bonds; and no little act of kindness or courtesy, that could render each other more happy was overlooked. Alike might be the result throughout life in freedom.

In freedom there would be every inducement for each party to be always agreeable, kind, and really good, knowing each of them that it was dependent on such qualities that they have and retain such partners as they desire. And then, too, teach a woman the laws of her being and those of her offspring,—let her know the fact that, as well as her own sins, those of the father of her child are visited on the babe,—and she will seek the purest, the noblest man for the father; which would be a stimulus to induce the males to purify themselves by temperance in all things, and obedience to all of God's laws; and woman alike would be induced to make herself really good, else she could not have the companionship of the best.

James Clay, *A Voice from Prison* (1856), in Stoehr, ed., *Free Love in America: A Documentary History,* pp. 339–340.

divided free lovers into two broad groups—varietists and romantics, the latter of which sought to preserve the sentimentalities of courtship and the tenderness of the honeymoon within the bounds of a reformed marital institution. Thus contrary to the image of exponents of free love in the minds of their opponents, theorizing desire apart from reproduction did not necessarily mean that free lovers validated sexual pleasure; more typically, it prioritized sexual purity (anti-masturbation, opposition to prostitution, self [primarily male] control of the sex drive, and the use of contraception to protect women from excessive childbearing and to promote eugenic reproduction rather than to enhance sexual pleasure) and control of the sexual response.

It is perhaps most accurate to say that free love sexuality found expression along a continuum stretching from those like Andrew Jackson Davis, who, adapting the spiritualist concept of "affinities," advocated readily available divorce and successive exclusive marital relationships until an "eternal union" had been achieved, to J. H. Noyes, who allowed controlled universal sexual association within the Oneida Community based on a postmillennialist perfectionist theology that posited that for believers worldly marriage had ceased to exist. Occupying a middle position, associated with philosophical anarchism that derived from Josiah Warren's (c. 1798–1874) conception of "individual sovereignty" (a form of philosophical anarchism that insisted there should be no restrictions on individual rights; each person would have absolute liberty to act exactly as he or she chose, bearing full personal responsibility for all acts and decisions taken) as practiced at Modern Times, were the universal reformer and social radical Stephen Pearl Andrews (1812–1886) and the hydropathic physician Thomas Low Nichols (1815–1901). Both championed varietism as more honest and purer than conventional marriage; both held a romantic vision of sexuality. Andrews argued in the early 1850s that only love could validate, sanctify, and purify marriage. Loveless marriages (the majority of civil unions) should be subject to immediate dissolution so as to insure emotional liberty. Nichols took a physiological stance in his best-selling *Esoteric Anthropology* (1853), maintaining that variety in love is natural and denouncing exclusive, lifelong marriage as false and unnatural. True marriage could never be established by legal restriction but only by mutual affection and then for only as long as reciprocal desire persisted. For Andrews and Nichols, free love constituted a kind of informal divorce.

Central to free love doctrine was not libertinism but sexual purity achieved through romanticization of intimate relations, responsible personal emotional lives, and rigorous self-control, especially of male sexuality (i.e., putting the health, inclination, and desire of the female first; typically refraining from intercourse during pregnancy, menstruation, or illness rather than insisting on the absolute male prerogative of marital sexual gratification). Mary Gove Nichols, in her *Lectures to Ladies on Anatomy and Physiology* (1842), vigorously condemned masturbation, marital rape, and excessive marital intercourse. Like her husband, she recognized the value of contraception but believed that sexual purity in marriage could best be achieved when the woman determined the frequency of intercourse. J. H. Noyes's system of "complex marriage" mandated an immediate control of male sexuality through "male continence," which required men to refrain from ejaculation during intercourse. Though

this practice reinforced male control of the sex act, it was unique in frankly mandating female sexual pleasure, since Oneidan men were expected to bring their partners to sexual climax. This system also provided a "natural" form of contraception (Noyes rejected the use of artificial devices as "unnatural") and ultimately provided the basis (after 1868) for Oneida's practice of eugenical reproduction ("stirpiculture") that made the community the first experiment in practical eugenics in the United States.

FROM THE FIRST TO THE SECOND WAVE OF FREE LOVERS

Free love agitation may be fairly said to have begun with the establishment of the New Harmony community in 1825, but as a countercultural movement, its first wave achieved its greatest coherence in the period 1840–1860. During these years the literature of free love contravened the conventional understanding of love and championed a variety of alternatives to institutionalized marriage as well as reconceptualizing the physiology of sex and reproduction. Books and periodicals were published, reform organizations established, and alternative communistic communities founded. Examples of free love activity in this period were the Free Convention in Rutland, Vermont (1858), that was called the "Free Love Convention" by the New York press, the Free Love League (club) in New York City (1854–1855), the "varietist list" (a free love personals listing) in the *Social Revolutionist* (1857), and the Progressive Union (*Nichols Journal*, 1854–1857), a national clearing house for "affinities." Though often vilified, free lovers in the 1840s and 1850s were engaged participants in the broad cultural discourse on ideal marriage, sexual hygiene, and the "true" woman. Perhaps most representative of the movement were the debate over love, marriage, and divorce among Henry James Sr., Stephen Pearl Andrews, and Horace Greeley in the *New York Tribune* (1852), and that over divorce between Robert Dale Owen and Greeley in 1860. The first wave of the free love movement ended with the onset of the Civil War; its second wave, less cohesive and more concerned with issues of free speech and eugenics, continued to agitate for sexual freedom in the period 1865–1905.

See also Feminism; Marriage; Reform; Sex Education; Sexuality and the Body; Utopian Communities

BIBLIOGRAPHY
Primary Works
Andrews, Stephen Pearl. *Love, Marriage, and Divorce and the Sovereignty of the Individual.* 1853. New York: Source Books, 1972.

Dixon, William Hepworth. *Spiritual Wives*. 1868. 2 vols. New York: AMS Press, 1971.

Ellis, John B. [pseud.]. *Free Love and Its Votaries; or, American Socialism Unmasked: Being an Historical and Descriptive Account of the Rise and Progress of the Various Free Love Associations in the United States, and of the Effects of Their Vicious Teachings upon American Society*. 1870. New York: AMS Press, 1971.

Noyes, John Humphrey. *History of American Socialisms*. 1870. New York: Hillary House, 1961.

Noyes, John Humphrey. *Male Continence*. 1872. Oneida, N.Y.: Oneida Community Mansion House, 1992.

Oneida Community. *Bible Communism: A Compilation from the Annual Reports and Other Publications of the Oneida Association and Its Branches; Presenting in Connection with Their History, a Summary View of Their Religious and Social Theories*. 1853. Philadelphia: Porcupine Press, 1972.

Secondary Works

Spurlock, John C. *Free Love, Marriage, and Middle-Class Radicalism in America, 1825–1860*. New York: New York University Press, 1988.

Stoehr, Taylor, ed. *Free Love in America: A Documentary History*. New York: AMS Press, 1979.

Louis J. Kern

FRIENDSHIP

In spite of "all the selfishness that chills like east winds the world," Ralph Waldo Emerson (1803–1882) wrote, "the whole human family is bathed with an element of love like a fine ether" (p. 341). He was writing of friendship, in the essay of that name published in *Essays: First Series* (1841), where he praised friendship for its power to "make a young world for me again" (p. 342). Emerson's biographer notes that of all the essays included in this collection, "'Friendship' gave [Emerson] the most pleasure, [and] the most difficulty" (Allen, p. 350). The famously self-reliant sage of Concord may have experienced trouble not only in composing "Friendship" but also in composing his friendships, for, as he confessed in his essay, "Friendship . . . is too good to be believed" (p. 343). Claiming, perhaps hoping, that friendship "cancels the thick walls of individual character, . . . and now makes many one" (p. 343), Emerson also acknowledged that in his own friendships he discovered anew the truth that "all persons underlie the same condition of an infinite remoteness" (p. 344). While "the instinct of affection revives the hope of union with our mates,"

he lamented, "the returning sense of insulation recalls us from the chase" (p. 344).

It should perhaps not be surprising that Emerson, whose most exalted moments were always solitary, should have found friendship a difficult engagement. In his famous description of "perfect exhilaration" recounted in *Nature* (1836), Emerson observes that at the peak of a sublime experience "the name of the nearest friend sounds then foreign and accidental" (p. 10). For Emerson as for many American transcendentalists, true insight occurs when the individual sees past the phenomenal, material world and discerns higher (what Kant called "noumenal") truths. Any other individual, even the closest friend or lover, belongs (from the subject's point of view) to the world of the senses, the inferior world of mere (often false) phenomena. Much as Emerson wished to praise the affections—he called himself "a worshipper of Friendship" (Allen, p. 350)—he wondered whether what he saw in his friends was not mere projection or misperception: "I cannot deny it, O friend," he wrote, "that the vast shadow of the Phenomenal includes thee also in its pied and painted immensity" ("Friendship," p. 344). Surprised by "shades of suspicion and unbelief" (p. 343), Emerson confessed that he doubted the truth of what he saw in his friends.

SOLITARY FRIENDS

Friendship was a primary casualty in a culture so devoted to solitude and the discovery of noumenal truths. There were of course exceptions depicted in American literary culture, solitary men who nevertheless fashioned enduring and heartfelt friendships with other men. Herman Melville's (1819–1891) introspective sailor, Ishmael, who names himself after the biblical outcast, quickly finds himself sharing the bed and the affections of the savage harpooner Queequeg in *Moby-Dick* (1851). James Fenimore Cooper (1789–1851) describes another such man, the frontiersman Hawkeye, who has left European settlements to live in the forest on his own terms. When, at the end of *The Last of the Mohicans* (1826), Hawkeye's companion Chingachgook loses his only son in battle, Hawkeye promises eternal friendship:

> The gifts of our colors may be different, but God has so placed us as to journey in the same path. I have no kin, and I may also say, like you, no people. He was your son, and a red-skin by nature; and it may be that your blood was nearer—but if I ever forget the lad, who has so often fou't at my side in war, and slept at my side in peace, may He who made us all, whatever may be our color or our gifts, forget me! The boy has left us for a time, but, Sagamore, you are not alone! (P. 349)

Still, friendship did not always come easily for a culture identified by what R. W. B. Lewis called the "American Adam," the individual who regarded his society with deep suspicion and who favored solitude. Although Emerson's Concord neighbor, Henry David Thoreau (1817–1862), considered himself as sociable as most people, he often preferred the "sweet and beneficent society in Nature" to the "fancied advantages of human neighborhood" (*Walden*, p. 383). Margaret Fuller (1810–1850) "taxed" her friend Emerson, he complained, "with a certain inhospitality of soul," charging him with aloofness in return for her "sacred" affection (Allen, p. 352). While Fuller prized intimacy rather than social conventions, Emerson, in his journal, was forced to acknowledge the "icy barriers" that surrounded his friendships.

The poet Walt Whitman (1819–1892) might be expected to have had an easier time with friendship, for in "Song of Myself" he had announced himself "mad" for "contact." In the "Calamus" poems of *Leaves of Grass,* most of them first published in 1860, Whitman explored what he called "manly attachment," a friendship between men that blurred the boundaries between *caritas,* or caring, and *eros,* or erotic love. To be sure, the lusty, boastful Whitman of "Song of Myself" seems more careful here, and more defenseless, too, as if the attachment he celebrates is primarily erotic and therefore dangerous; he writes of his "Calamus" poems in "Here the Frailest Leaves of Me" (1860):

> Here the frailest leaves of me, and yet my
> strongest lasting,
> Here I shade and hide my thoughts, I myself do
> not expose them,
> And yet they expose me more than all my other
> poems.
>
> *(P. 112)*

At times Whitman uses the words "lover" and "friend" interchangeably. In "The Base of All Metaphysics" (1871) he claims that beneath all philosophy is the more elemental "dear love of man for his comrade, the attraction of friend to friend" (p. 103).

But even the bold and affectively free Whitman experienced some of the trouble with friendship also observed in Emerson. Like Emerson, Whitman seems to have understood that such powerful emotions as dear friends shared might be projected rather than discerned, that human relations might, finally, be phenomenal and thoroughly unreal. As he writes in "Are You the New Person Drawn Toward Me?" (1860):

> Are you the new person drawn toward me?
> To begin with take warning, I am surely far different from what you suppose;

> Do you suppose you will find in me your ideal?
> . . . .
> Have you no thought, O dreamer, that it may all
> be maya, illusion?
>
> *(P. 105)*

Melville's Ishmael, however, is not troubled by the thought that friendship depends largely on projection. Faced with an invitation to worship with his new friend, the pagan Queequeg, Ishmael considers that the "will of God" would have him "do to my fellow man what I would have my fellow man do to me," in short, to "unite with me in my particular Presbyterian form of worship. Consequently, I must then unite with him in his; ergo, I must turn idolator" (p. 849). Ishmael and Queequeg become "Bosom Friends," a "cosy, loving pair," because Ishmael relinquishes the "sense of insulation" (p. 849) that jeopardizes friendship for Emerson. By letting go of his own sense of identity and the values and prejudices that go with it, Ishmael enters into the feelings of his new friend. Although he understands that he cannot literally do this—that any sympathy with Queequeg is necessarily projection, by nature misleading—he is content to forgo what Emerson called the "thick walls of individual character."

FRIENDSHIP AND SOCIAL REFORM

These epistemological questions regarding friendship—how much of it is real, how much illusion, how to distinguish between the two, whether doing so finally matters—demonstrate that friendship was not simply a private matter between individuals but rather one that had important intellectual consequences for antebellum American thinkers. Many nineteenth-century American friendships grew out of or were the result of larger cultural concerns. The friends Frederick Douglass (1818–1895) made at St. Michael's when he was a seventeen-year-old slave—the fellow slaves for whom, he later recalled, "I felt a friendship as strong as one man can feel for another; for I could have died with them and for them" (p. 274)—became Douglass's "revolutionary conspirators" (p. 280) and joined him in his first, unsuccessful attempt to escape slavery. Their earnestness and loyalty helped Douglass demonstrate that slaves were capable of manly devotion, not merely slavish fidelity to their masters. Harriet Jacobs (1813–1897) demonstrates a more generalized loyalty to her fellow slaves, writing her narrative "to kindle a flame of compassion in your hearts for my sisters who are still in bondage, suffering as I once suffered" (p. 29).

Women's friendships became the occasion for—and grew out of—a variety of organizations arranged around domestic activities like quilting, embroidery, sewing, and reading. Often several activities were

This passage from Frederick Douglass's second autobiography suggests the profound value he attached to his friendships. The passage is particularly interesting in light of Douglass's first autobiography (1845), where he depicts his struggle for emancipation as a series of solitary accomplishments and inspirations like those made famous by Emerson and Franklin.

"For much of the happiness—or absence of misery—with which I passed this year with Mr. Freeland, I am indebted to the genial temper and ardent friendship of my brother slaves. They were, every one of them, manly, generous and brave, yes; I say they were brave, and I will add, fine looking. It is seldom the lot of mortals to have truer and better friends than were the slaves on this farm. It is not uncommon to charge slaves with great treachery toward each other, and to believe them incapable of confiding in each other; but I must say, that I never loved, esteemed, or confided in men, more than I did in these. They were as true as steel, and no band of brothers could have been more loving. There were no mean advantages taken of each other, as is sometimes the case where slaves are situated as we were; no tattling; no giving each other bad names to Mr. Freeland; and no elevating one at the expense of the other. We never undertook to do any thing, of any importance, which was likely to affect each other, without mutual consultation. We were generally a unit, and moved together. Thoughts and sentiments were exchanged between us, which might well be called very incendiary, by oppressors and tyrants; and perhaps the time has not even now come, when it is safe to unfold all the flying suggestions which arise in the minds of intelligent slaves. Several of my friends and brothers, if yet alive, are still in some part of the house of bondage; and though twenty years have passed away, the suspicious malice of slavery might punish them for even listening to my thoughts."

Douglass, *My Bondage and My Freedom*, pp. 268–269.

combined, as when young women took novels to read aloud at quilting bees with their friends. During and following the Civil War, these organizations often took on a more political or civic role, as sewing circles, for example, became venues for raising money for soldiers, widows, and orphans, and as women began to discuss social arrangements at their meetings. Henry James's (1843–1916) 1885 novel *The Bostonians*, set during the years following the war, dramatizes the interconnectedness of reading, political activism, and intimate female friendships. The suffragists Olive and Verena spend the winter preparing for Verena's career as a lecturer for the women's movement, and while their winter is filled with study and discussion, it is also a time of deep personal intimacy:

Olive often sat at the window with her companion before it was time for the lamp. . . . They watched the stellar points come out at last in a colder heaven, and then, shuddering a little, arm in arm, they turned away, with a sense that the winter night was even more cruel than the tyranny of men—turned back to draw curtains and a brighter fire and a glittering tea-tray and more and more talk about the long martyrdom of women, a subject as to which Olive was inexhaustible and really most interesting. There were some nights of deep snowfall, when Charles Street was white and muffled and the doorbell foredoomed to silence, which seemed little islands of lamplight, of enlarged and intensified vision. They read a great deal of history together, and read it ever with the same thought—that of finding confirmation in it for this idea that their sex had suffered inexpressibly, and that at any moment in the course of human affairs the state of the world would have been so much less horrible . . . if women had been able to press down the scale. (P. 168)

Reading Goethe, Olive and Verena learn to renounce social pleasures, but even as they keep their eyes fixed steadily on their political goal, James allows his readers to see that the real drama of his novel is the growing intimacy between these two women.

James had based his story, in part, on the friendship between his sister, Alice James (1850–1892), and Katharine Peabody Loring (1849–1943), which began in social reform but deepened beyond their work as teachers of history. The friendship lasted until the end of Alice's life, as Katharine followed her to England and nursed her through her many illnesses, including breast cancer. In a diary entry just months before her death, Alice wrote this of her loyal friend:

As the ugliest things go to the making of the fairest, it is not wonderful that this unholy granite substance in my breast should be the soil propitious for the perfect flowering of Katharine's unexampled genius for friendship and devotion. The story of her watchfulness, patience and untiring resource cannot be told by my feeble pen, but all the pain and discomfort seem a slender price to pay for all the happiness and peace with which she fills my days. (*Diary*, p. 225)

The Quilting Party. Woodcut, c. 1840–1850. An important social event, the quilting party was an occasion for festive animation, a time for gathering of young and old. © BETTMANN/CORBIS

PRIVATE FRIENDSHIPS

Although many novels of the nineteenth century were written by women, most women wrote in more modest and private genres, and in those forms they memorialized their friendships. Even many nineteenth-century literary texts were formally and substantively indebted to the private intimacies of friendship. Emily Dickinson's (1830–1886) poems, for example, are sometimes hard to distinguish from her letters, which were often cryptic, brief, imagistic, and punctuated in the manner of her poems. Sometimes she included her poems in letters to close friends. And she borrowed the address of the private letter for her poems, which often give the impression that one is eavesdropping on words meant for someone else. Other times her letters and poems were indistinguishable. "Safe in their Alabaster Chambers," now known as Dickinson's poem 216, was originally a letter that the poet sent to her sister-in-law Sue in 1861. Dickinson, who famously kept to her house

after her vision began to fail, carried out her friendships via the written word. This reclusive poet found life in words, as she wrote in poem 1651, "A Word that breathes distinctly, / Has not the power to die," and she found great value in her friendships. "My friends are my estate," she wrote; "forgive me then the avarice to hoard them!" (*Selected Letters*, p. 144).

Dickinson was not the only American writer to borrow the forms used to express private friendships. The epistolary novel, one of the earliest genres of American fiction, was written entirely in letters, thus highlighting the intimate means of communication available to friends. William Hill Brown's (1765–1793) *The Power of Sympathy* (1789), widely regarded as the first American novel, draws on the written disclosures exchanged between friends to tell its sentimental tale of seduction and death. No omniscient narrator is needed in such novels, for friends keep constant watch on each other, share their secrets, narrate their lives and offer advice. In the words of one of Brown's characters, "It is the duty of friends to be interested in all the concerns of one another" (p. 99). The popular seduction novel, whose main plot involved a cautionary tale, often featured a close female friend whose virtuous counsel, if heeded, might have spared the fallen heroine. Even traditional novels, those presided over by an omniscient narrator, drew on the norms of friendship. Among the enormously popular sentimental fiction of the early and mid-nineteenth century, according to Glenn Hendler, the same sympathetic identification that enables private friendships allowed nineteenth-century readers to empathize with and be drawn into the relationships enacted in novels. This strategy is most vividly evident in *Uncle Tom's Cabin* (1852), in which Harriet Beecher Stowe's (1811–1896) narrator exhorts her readers to "pity the mother who has all your affections, and not one legal right to protect, guide, or educate, the child of her bosom!" (p. 384). Although Stowe calls for a political response beyond the limits of her novel, other sentimental novels merely required readers to follow along emotionally and imaginatively, the way they might become involved in the lives of their friends.

In content as well as form, nineteenth-century fiction often concerned itself with intimate friendships. Domestic novels, another best-selling genre, depicted the everyday lives of women, which meant they tended to focus on women's friendships and courtships. And sentimental fiction was likewise deeply engaged in the friendships of its female characters. As Cathy Davidson has remarked, "Diaries of young women describe how part of virtually every day was spent visiting with one's friends and otherwise circulating, very much as do the characters in numerous sentimental novels" (p. 113).

See also Courtship; Domestic Fiction; Individualism and Community; Same-Sex Love; Sentimentalism; Transcendentalism

BIBLIOGRAPHY

Primary Works

Brown, William Hill. *The Power of Sympathy.* 1789. Edited by William S. Kable. Columbus: Ohio State University Press, 1969.

Cooper, James Fenimore. *The Last of the Mohicans.* 1826. Introduction by Richard Slotkin. New York: Penguin Books, 1986.

Dickinson, Emily. *Selected Letters.* Edited by Thomas H. Johnson. Cambridge, Mass.: Belknap Press of Harvard University Press, 1971.

Douglass, Frederick. *My Bondage and My Freedom.* 1855. Introduction by Philip S. Foner. New York: Dover, 1969.

Emerson, Ralph Waldo. "Friendship." 1841. In *Ralph Waldo Emerson: Essays and Lectures,* edited by Joel Porte, pp. 339–354. New York: Library of America, 1983.

Emerson, Ralph Waldo. *Nature.* 1836. In *Ralph Waldo Emerson: Essays and Lectures,* edited by Joel Porte, pp. 5–49. New York: Library of America, 1983.

Jacobs, Harriet A. *Incidents in the Life of a Slave Girl.* 1861. Edited by L. Maria Child with an introduction by Jean Fagan Yellin. Cambridge, Mass.: Harvard University Press, 1987.

James, Alice. *The Death and Letters of Alice James: Selected Correspondence.* Edited by Ruth Bernard Yeazell. Berkeley: University of California Press, 1981.

James, Alice. *The Diary of Alice James.* Edited by Leon Edel. New York: Dodd, Mead, 1964.

James, Henry. *The Bostonians.* 1885. New York: Oxford University Press, 1998.

Melville, Herman. *Moby-Dick.* 1851. In *Redburn, White-Jacket, Moby-Dick.* New York: Library of America, 1983.

Stowe, Harriet Beecher. *Uncle Tom's Cabin.* 1852. Edited by Elizabeth Ammons. New York: Norton, 1994.

Thoreau, Henry David. *Walden.* 1854. In *The Portable Thoreau,* edited by Carl Bode. New York: Viking Penguin, 1977.

Whitman, Walt. *Leaves of Grass and Other Writings.* 2nd ed. New York: Norton, 2002.

Secondary Works

Allen, Gay Wilson. *Waldo Emerson: A Biography.* New York: Viking Press, 1981.

Davidson, Cathy N. *Revolution and the Word: The Rise of the Novel in America.* New York: Oxford University Press, 1986.

Hansen, Karen V. *A Very Social Time: Crafting Community in Antebellum New England.* Berkeley: University of California Press, 1994.

Hendler, Glenn. *Public Sentiments: Structures of Feeling in Nineteenth-Century American Literature.* Chapel Hill: University of North Carolina Press, 2001.

Jabour, Anya. "Albums of Affection: Female Friendship and Coming of Age in Antebellum Virginia." *Virginia Magazine of History and Biography* 107, no. 2 (1999): 125–158.

Katz, Jonathan Ned. "Coming to Terms: Conceptualizing Men's Erotic and Affectional Relations with Men in the United States, 1820–1892." In *A Queer World: The Center for Lesbian and Gay Studies Reader,* edited by Martin Duberman, pp. 216–235. New York: New York University Press, 1997.

Kelly, Catherine E. *In the New England Fashion: Reshaping Women's Lives in the Nineteenth Century.* Ithaca, N.Y.: Cornell University Press, 1999.

Lewis, R. W. B. *The American Adam: Innocence, Tragedy, and Tradition in the Nineteenth Century.* Chicago: University of Chicago Press, 1955.

Marchalonis, Shirley, *Patrons and Protégées: Gender, Friendship, and Writing in Nineteenth-Century America.* New Brunswick, N.J.: Rutgers University Press, 1988.

Richardson, Robert D., Jr. *Emerson: The Mind on Fire.* Berkeley: University of California Press, 1995.

Steele, Jeffrey. "Transcendental Friendship: Emerson, Fuller, and Thoreau." In *The Cambridge Companion to Ralph Waldo Emerson,* edited by Joel Porte and Saundra Morris, pp. 121–139. Cambridge, U.K., and New York: Cambridge University Press, 1999.

Kristin Boudreau

FUR TRADE

During the seventeenth and eighteenth centuries, the fur trade was the primary enterprise fueling both exploration by and competition among European powers in North America. It was also the primary activity through which Europeans interacted with Native Americans, changing permanently the latter's way of life, economy, and relation to their environment. European control over the continent and the trade gradually waned by the end of the eighteenth century, and after the Louisiana Purchase (1803), the Lewis and Clark expedition (1804–1806), and the War of 1812, the stage was set for Americans to appropriate the West. From the 1810s through the 1840s the fur trade remained a major economic stimulus for exploration and expansion, and it would continue to be the primary basis for interaction with native peoples. It would also generate a mythic American figure, the mountain man, and make its presence strongly felt in Romantic literature and art.

DEVELOPING THE MYTH

From economic and historical perspectives, the fur trade was not a romantic enterprise at all but a highly contested, dangerous, and cutthroat business. Throughout most of the period, Americans competed with representatives of the British-owned Hudson's Bay Company in the northern and central Rockies, and within American jurisdiction there were also rival companies and small independent groups vying for dominance. John Jacob Astor, a New York fur merchant who would eventually become the richest man in America, founded (with government encouragement) the Pacific Fur Company in 1810. By sea, he established a trading post, Astoria, at the mouth of the

Columbia River in what is now Oregon and sent a party up the Missouri River and across the Rocky Mountains to rendezvous with the men at Astoria. The War of 1812 led to the failure of this scheme, but reorganized later as the American Fur Company, Astor's men played a dominant role in the trade in the 1820s and 1830s. Their principal rival during the heyday of the trade was the Rocky Mountain Fur Company, begun by William Ashley of Missouri, which often surpassed the American Fur Company in entrepreneurial energy and efficiency. Each summer all parties gathered at a rendezvous in the mountains—part bacchanal, part trade fair—where furs would be collected and supplies distributed for the following season. This system prevailed until the 1840s, when over-trapping and a drop in fur prices on the global market caused the industry to decline.

There were two aspects of the American fur trade in the first half of the nineteenth century that helped to metamorphose what was essentially a brutal and exploitative economic activity into the stuff of legend and popular literature. The first was its setting: in contrast to the earlier continental scope of the fur trade, ranging from the Creek commerce in deer hides in the Southeast to the pursuit of seals and sea otters in the Pacific Northwest, the American fur trade focused on trapping beaver (whose felt ended up as hats on men in American and European cities) in the Rocky Mountains. This rugged and largely unexplored landscape, ranging from northern New Mexico to Montana, fueled a Romantic passion for the sublime, for wilderness in its most extreme, inaccessible, and even dangerous manifestations. Where earlier generations had found beauty in the garden and the cultivated landscape and regarded mountain chains as barriers to trade and as unfit for agriculture, the literary and aesthetic taste of the nineteenth century favored the snowcapped mountain, the barren desert, and the rushing waterfall as sites of primal struggle, contemplation, and even spiritual fulfillment.

The second factor that lent itself to mythologizing was the shift from an Indian-based trapping economy to a white-based one. The Europeans had generally acted as merchants and middlemen, relying on the Indians as a kind of native worker class who would bring their furs to trading posts to exchange for European goods. However destructive of native culture the introduction of trade goods was (especially firearms and liquor), this arrangement tended at least to preserve the Indians's traditional lands. When Americans began pushing toward the headwaters of the Missouri River and the Rocky Mountains to prosecute the fur trade, they did so not only as traders but also as trappers and as year-round residents rather than occasional visitors.

***Fur Traders Descending the Missouri*, c. 1840–1845.** Painting by George Caleb Bingham. © GEOFFREY CLEMENTS/CORBIS

The activity of trapping itself—as opposed to merely trading—brought the mountain men, as they came to be called, into the rugged and romantic landscape of the mountains and also into competition and conflict with the various tribes that claimed these lands as home and hunting grounds. The situation was full of danger and ambiguity for both parties: The Indians, resenting and resisting this intrusion and appropriation of resources by ever-increasing numbers of Americans, often fought back by stripping the isolated trappers of their pelts and equipment or even killing them. At the same time, they desired and became increasingly dependent on manufactured goods and could not afford to alienate the suppliers who established trading posts and conducted the annual rendezvous where furs were exchanged. The white trappers, for their part, were in constant danger of attack, especially from small bands of hunters and warriors roaming outside tribal control. At the same time, their success depended upon their ability to assimilate themselves into native cultures. They adopted the dress and way of life of the Indians and frequently married or at least lived with Indian women.

THE MOUNTAIN MAN IN LITERATURE

While such conflict and assimilation were matters of necessity among the trappers, they also made good copy for popular fiction, in the form of tales of Indian fighting and hairbreadth escapes along with romantic involvements between white men and Indian women. The very first of Beadle's Dime Novels, written by a well-known New York writer and editor, Mrs. Ann S. Stephens, was *Malaeska, the Indian Wife of the White Hunter.* Published in 1860, it sold over 65,000 copies within a few months. The first long catalog of American sights and scenes in Walt Whitman's "Song of Myself" depicts a typically picturesque and romantic image of such an attachment, which Whitman, because he had never traveled to the West,

---

DESCRIPTION OF THE ROCKY MOUNTAIN TRAPPER

The trappers of the Rocky Mountains belong to a "genus" more approximating to the primitive savage than perhaps any other class of civilized man. Their lives being spent in the remote wilderness of the mountains, with no other companion than Nature herself, their habits and character assume a most singular cast of simplicity mingled with ferocity, appearing to take their colouring from the scenes and objects which surround them. Knowing no wants save those of nature, their sole care is to procure sufficient food to support life, and the necessary clothing to protect them from the rigorous climate. This with the assistance of their trusty rifles, they are generally able to effect, but sometimes at the expense of great peril and hardship. When engaged in their avocation, the natural instinct of primitive man is ever alive, for the purpose of guarding against danger and the provision of necessary food.

Keen observers of nature, they rival the beasts of prey in discovering the haunts and habits of game, and in their skill and cunning in capturing it. Constantly exposed to perils of all kinds, they become callous to any feeling of danger, and destroy human as well as animal life with as little scruple and as freely as they expose their own. Of laws, human or divine, they neither know nor care to know. Their wish is their law, and to attain it they do not scruple as to ways and means.

Firm friends and bitter enemies, with them it is "a word and a blow," and the blow often first. They may have good qualities, but they are those of the animal; and people fond of giving hard names call them revengeful, bloodthirsty, drunkards (when the wherewithal is to be had), gamblers, regardless of the laws of *meum* and *tuum*—in fact, "White Indians." However, there are exceptions, and I *have* met honest mountain men. Their animal qualities, however, are undeniable. Strong, active, hardy as bears, daring, expert in the use of their weapons, they are just what uncivilized white man might be supposed to be in a brute state, depending upon his instinct for the support of life. Not a hole or corner in the vast wilderness of the "Far West" but has been ransacked by these hardy men. From the Mississippi to the mouth of the Colorado of the West, from the frozen regions of the North to the Gila in Mexico, the beaver-hunter has set his traps in every creek and stream. All this vast country, but for the daring enterprise of these men, would be even now a *terra incognita* to geographers, as indeed a great portion still is; but there is not an acre that has not been passed and repassed by the trappers in their perilous excursions. The mountains and streams still retain the names assigned to them by the rude hunters; and these alone are the hardy pioneers who have paved the way for the settlement of the western country.

George F. Ruxton, *Adventures in Mexico and the Rocky Mountains* (London: John Murray, 1849), pp. 241–242.

---

could only have derived from popular fiction or illustrations:

> I saw the marriage of the trapper in the open air
>   in the far west, the bride was a red girl,
> Her father and his friends sat near cross-legged
>   and dumbly smoking, they had moccasins to
>   their feet and large thick blankets hanging
>   from their shoulders,
> On a bank lounged the trapper, he was drest
>   mostly in skins, his luxuriant beard and curls
>   protected his neck, he held his bride by the
>   hand,
> She had long eyelashes, her head was bare, her
>   coarse straight locks descended upon her
>   voluptuous limbs and reach'd to her feet.
>   (P. 36)

Many of the men who were drawn to the trade were frontiersmen already accustomed to pushing west into remoter lands and already the subject of legend as hunters, scouts, and Indian fighters. In popular representations there was a tendency, beginning in the 1820s, for the legendary figure of the frontiersman to metamorphose into the trapper and mountain man, a change dramatically portrayed in James Fenimore Cooper's five-volume Leatherstocking Tales. Its hero, Natty Bumppo, is a scout and Indian fighter based in western New York, the scene of *The Pioneers, The Last of the Mohicans,* and *The Deerslayer.* But by the last book chronologically in the series, *The Prairie,* Natty dies far out on the western plains after living his last years as a trapper. The mountain men in turn often became scouts and guides for the army after the heyday of the fur trade and thus prolonged their legends into a new era; the most famous of these was Kit Carson, who became a guide to John C. Frémont's exploring expedition in 1842 and lived on as a dime-novel hero and a major character in Willa Cather's *Death Comes for the Archbishop* (1927).

The fur trade also figured prominently in many works of autobiography and nonfiction, some of which have become at least minor classics of American literature. The most interesting as well as the most sensational autobiography is *The Life and Adventures of James P. Beckwourth* (1856), which was edited (and doubtless embellished) by T. D. Bonner, a New York editor. Beckwourth was an African American born in Virginia who ran away to the West and became one of the most prominent mountain men as well as a chief in the Crow tribe. There were a number of British travelers and adventurers who produced accounts of time spent with the trappers and Indians. Among these, George Frederick Ruxton's *Life in the Far West* (1849) and *Adventures in Mexico and the Rocky Mountains* (1847) are notable for their vividness and the urbanity of their point of view.

The fur trade, the mountain men, and their Indian adversaries are also featured prominently in important nonfiction works about the West from the 1840 and 1850s: Josiah Gregg's *The Commerce of the Prairies* (1844); Francis Parkman's first book, *The California and Oregon Trail* (1849); and Lewis H. Garrard's *Wah-To-Yah, and the Taos Trail* (1850).

But by far the most ambitious attempt by a major writer to memorialize the fur trade and its participants was that of Washington Irving in his two volumes *Astoria* (1836, revised 1849) and *The Adventures of Captain Bonneville* (1837). Irving's aim was twofold: to recuperate his own reputation as an American writer by engaging a distinctively American enterprise after many years of residing in and writing about Europe; and to dramatize the fur trade as a heroic undertaking, especially emphasizing the role of his friend and benefactor John Jacob Astor. Though written with his usual grace and clarity, and full of colorful characters and incidents, Irving's accounts suffer from the fact that he had no firsthand experience (of the sort that, say, Herman Melville had with whaling), and he tended both to romanticize and Europeanize his subjects,

describing nomadic groups of Indians, for example, as "banditti." Neither was it politically astute in Jacksonian America to make a hero of the capitalist Astor rather than the individualist mountain men.

As heroic figures, the latter themselves were supplanted after the Civil War by the cast of characters who people the western. Still, they lived on throughout the twentieth century in popular fiction such as A. B. Guthrie's *The Big Sky* (1947), histories like Bernard De Voto's *Across the Wide Missouri* (1947), and such films as Sidney Pollack's *Jeremiah Johnson* (1972), starring Robert Redford.

See also Biography; Dime Novels; Exploration and Discovery; Leatherstocking Tales; *Leaves of Grass;* Romanticism; Sensational Fiction; Travel Writing; Wilderness

BIBLIOGRAPHY

Primary Work

Whitman, Walt. "Song of Myself." In *Leaves of Grass*. New York: Oxford University Press, 1998.

Secondary Works

Axtell, James. *The Invasion Within: The Contest of Cultures in Colonial North America*. New York and Oxford: Oxford University Press, 1985.

De Voto, Bernard. *Across the Wide Missouri*. Boston: Houghton Mifflin, 1947.

Hafen, Le Roy, ed. *Fur Traders, Trappers, and Mountain Men of the Upper Missouri*. Lincoln: University of Nebraska Press, 1995.

Martin, Calvin. *Keepers of the Game: Indian-Animal Relationships and the Fur Trade*. Berkeley: University of California Press, 1978.

Nash, Roderick. *Wilderness and the American Mind*. New Haven, Conn.: Yale University Press, 1967.

Smith, Henry Nash. *Virgin Land: The American West as Symbol and Myth*. Cambridge, Mass.: Harvard University Press, 1950.

Wishart, David J. *The Fur Trade of the American West, 1807–1840: A Geographical Synthesis*. Lincoln: University of Nebraska Press, 1979.

Robert Sattelmeyer

THE GATES AJAR

Few today may have heard of either the novel *The Gates Ajar* (1868) or its author Elizabeth Stuart Phelps (1844–1911), though it was a best-seller in its time. Nearly 100,000 people had read it in the United States by 1900, and even more in Britain. The novel was later translated into French, German, Dutch, and Italian. *The Gates Ajar* gained entrepreneurial recognition, too, as mourning apparel (such as collars and tippets), cigars, songs, patent medicines, and floral funeral arrangements were named after it, according to Phelps in her autobiography *Chapters from a Life* (1896). The book met an urgent need for hope and consolation of bereaved people everywhere but especially in the United States, where women mourned the loss of their beloved husbands, fathers, brothers, friends, and lovers in the recent and most bloody Civil War (1861–1865). A catastrophic 623,000 soldiers died while 500,000 were wounded and some 30,000 received amputations. Many dead bodies were never buried; hence the bereaved lacked the comforting closure of end-of-life ceremonies.

On the book's title page Phelps quoted the nineteenth-century Swiss novelist and memoirist Madame de Gasparin: "Splendor! Immensity! Eternity! Grand words! Great things! A little definite happiness would be more to the purpose." Phelps provided a means to achieve such "happiness" in her book. Instead of an orthodox abstract heaven, she sought in *The Gates Ajar* to console bereaved Civil War women through her message that their lost loved ones remained spiritually close and readers might expect to rejoin them in a domestic afterlife. Phelps drew upon the domestic regional realism of her mother, Elizabeth Stuart Phelps, whose *The Sunny Side; or, The Country Minister's Wife* (1851), in its depiction of an unending round of household duties, reflected the lives of many of its 100,000 first-year readers. The daughter also followed the domestic sentimentalism (a literary mode evoking sympathy) of her Andover, Massachusetts, neighbor Harriet Beecher Stowe, whose *Uncle Tom's Cabin; or, Life among the Lowly* (1852) engaged more than 100,000 readers in less than a half year with its heart-rending portrayal of mothers black and white aching from the loss of their children through slavery or death, thereby pleading for mothers everywhere. To losses from the ensuing Civil War, Phelps then responded with *The Gates Ajar,* which she cast in the first-person diary entries of orphaned twenty-four-year-old Mary Cabot, who had just lost her brother Roy in the war. Mary finds that "the house feels like a prison" and the telegram words—"'shot dead'—shut [her] up and walled [her] in, as . . . in Hell" (p. 7).

LITERARY PRODUCTION AND RECEPTION

Phelps developed a domestic view of heaven from a focused course of reading, evident in the many allusions to religious and theological authors appearing in *The Gates Ajar* (well-explicated in the introduction and notes by Helen Sootin Smith in the novel's 1964 edition). This reading required "two or three years spent in exceptional solitude" from her own despair over the 22 October 1862 death following the battle at Antietam (17 September) of her dear friend Samuel Hopkins Thompson. She likely wrote *The Gates Ajar*

Elizabeth Stuart Phelps. GRADUATE LIBRARY, UNIVERSITY OF MICHIGAN

from about 1864 to 1866. Although she claims, in *Chapters*, that the novel grew "more of nature than of purpose"—"The angel said unto me 'Write!' and I wrote"—she also acknowledged her "steady and conscientious toil" (pp. 95, 99). She was twenty-two when she completed the work.

Two more years would pass before *The Gates Ajar* reached an audience: the manuscript rested with the Boston publishing firm of Fields, Osgood, notable for its booklist of most of the major nineteenth-century British and American authors. The partner James T. Fields was reluctant to move forward until his wife (the well-known Boston literary hostess Annie Adams Fields) said decidedly, "Take it" (*Chapters*, p. 108). The literary reputation of the twenty-four-year-old Phelps was firmly established by *The Gates Ajar*. By 1884 Houghton Mifflin, which succeeded Fields, Osgood, had run fifty-five printings, and in 1910 Regent Press of New York made the last consecutive printing. It has since been reprinted in 1964 and 2000. The 2000 reprint includes novels continuing Phelps's particularization of a heavenly afterlife, *Beyond the Gates* (1883), in which a woman joins her father, who has been keeping house, and finds the lover she missed in life, and *The Gates Between* (1887), in which a husband assumes a mother's domestic duties and cares for their son as they await her arrival.

Not reprinted and less important is *Within the Gates* (1901), a dramatization of the 1887 novel. James D. Hart in his study *The Popular Book* (1950) lists all four "Gates" books among those most widely read in the United States in the years following their publication.

Contemporary reviews for *The Gates Ajar* were mixed, the least favorable objecting on religious grounds. They complained that Phelps had gone astray in her book, which would do harm; no one could know that heaven would have pianos, statuary, strawberries, and gingersnaps, as Phelps averred. By contrast, more favorable notices stressed Phelps's literary skill. The Scottish novelist Margaret Oliphant, writing in *Blackwood's Magazine* in October 1871, found *The Gates Ajar* to be the first worthy successor to Nathaniel Hawthorne and Harriet Beecher Stowe.

Although reviewers expressed disagreement over the novel's merits, common readers flocked to the book. A mourning manual, the book gave readers ways to cope with losses of family members and of one's very self, since the self may be viewed to be premised upon these family relationships. Readers found in Mary a character who validated their own stages of grieving as they re-experienced initial shock followed by anger, a flood of grief and hopeless despair, then finally being able to let go and move on. Through guidance of Mary by her aunt Winifred, readers might experience in their own reading of *The Gates Ajar* the "exchange of sympathy" that Mary Louise Kete calls "sentimental collaboration" (p. xv).

Likewise, the work of at least three important United States writers also revealed the impact of *The Gates Ajar*. The poetic imagery of Emily Dickinson (1830–1886) seems to have sprung from a source similar to that of Phelps. Barton Levi St. Armand finds that Dickinson and Phelps share a view of heaven as "a very private kind of paradise furnished with very concrete and material wish fulfillment" (p. 128) and that a voice like that of Phelps's Winifred counseled Dickinson's acceptance of the kind of "spiritual materialism" (St. Armand, p. 149) exemplified in *Gates* (p. 84). Howard G. Baetzhold and Joseph B. McCullough have pointed out how, in *Captain Stormfield's Visit to Heaven* (1909), Mark Twain (1835–1910) wrongly claimed that he had "burlesqued" Phelps's book as "a mean little ten-cent heaven about the size of Rhode Island" (p. 130): actually Twain emulated a number of the heavenly features of *The Gates Ajar*, including a critique of contemporary views of a heaven abounding in halos and wings, harps and hymnbooks. And the fiction of Charlotte Perkins Gilman (1860–1935)—who read *The Gates Ajar* in July 1897, as well as many other Phelps

Detail from *News from the War*. This image of a despairing woman might well depict Mary Cabot from Phelps's *Gates Ajar*. It is part of a collage by Winslow Homer that appeared in *Harper's Weekly,* 14 June 1862, consisting of twelve illustrations from Homer's most prolific year of depicting war subjects. THE LIBRARY OF CONGRESS

novels—includes characters who act to enhance the growth of others through their own expression of thought, action, and feeling: Phelps's heroine Winifred anticipates Gilman's heroine Ellador, the wife of Vandyck Jennings in *With Her in Ourland* (1916), in that each enhances the insight of others.

THEMES AND CULTURAL CONTEXTS

The Gates Ajar fomented much religious debate over its spiritualism, a belief in communication with spirits of the dead, and heretical unorthodoxy, discounting human sin and divine punishment. Phelps had read works by the Swedish philosopher Emanuel Swedenborg (1688–1772), whose thought influenced spiritualism. Winifred reveals that she "used to fancy [she] believed in Swedenborg—until [she] read his books" (p. 114), but she recommends to Mary a passage from his *Heaven and Hell* (1758) describing his materialist view of homes in heaven. Later Winifred complains that "the Spiritualistic notion of 'circles' of dead friends revolving over us is . . . intolerable" (p. 148). Though their influence is clear, these passages indicate Phelps's ambivalence concerning spiritualism. Winifred also agrees with the essayist Gail Hamilton (a pseudonym for Mary Abigail Dodge, 1833–1896), who expressed "righteous indignation" for any Bible but the "original Greek" (p. 62). Phelps reports in *Chapters* that some theologians—including her father, Austin Phelps, president and professor of rhetoric and homiletics (the art of preaching) at Andover Theological Seminary—considered her view of heaven heretical. Lisa A. Long argues that Phelps "deftly foregrounded the gap between abstract social systems and beliefs, and the physical and emotional realities of life in [the United States], which crystallized during the Civil War" (p. 83). According to Marcia Ian, Phelps's views overall fit the emergent religious perspective documented by William James's *Varieties of Religious Experience* (1902) of an "affectionate religion," one based in individual feeling and experience rather than rationality, and a "material Protestantism" (p. 36) that evoked emotion by engaging sensory experience of material objects. In her study of figuration in *The Gates Ajar,* Gail K. Smith finds that Phelps "attempts to reconcile the long history of Christian theology, new currents in biblical criticism, the needs of the contemporary believer, and the words of the Bible in a form accessible to the ordinary reader" (p. 124), as for example Winifred's query, "Can't people tell picture from substance, a metaphor from its meaning?" with regard to the concrete though symbolic biblical descriptions of heaven (p. 54).

In contrast to focus upon an afterlife, the nineteenth-century social gospel movement directed believers' attention toward doing God's work on earth. The social gospel, which encompassed belief in the perfectibility of humanity and use of religious faith in the service of social amelioration, especially for the working urban poor, was an element of various utopian movements during the same period, some communitarian, others reformist. These movements overlapped and fed each other, often the same adherents participating in several. *The Gates Ajar* has been considered in this context, too, as Phelps sought in it to effect relief for her largely female and grieving readership, through the lay ministry exemplified in Winifred.

Much of the power that readers responded to in *The Gates Ajar* derived from Phelps's skillful deployment of familiar cultural practices. The rural cemetery movement was a material manifestation of the nineteenth-century religious effort to join heaven to earth and to eradicate dying from earth. Mary refers to the "ivied cross" in the cemetery under which Roy lies with her "dreams," assuring herself that her dreams "will come back to me with him" (p. 127). The cemetery, a landscaped park, became a place for the family to remain united as they gathered at gravesides to commune among themselves: its tasteful natural beauty was expected to refine visitors as it reminded them of heavenly eternity. Even pets lay under gravestones. A religion of love replaced the Calvinist focus upon sin: under Winifred's guidance, Mary comes to realize that loving Roy and loving God are synonymous. Though Phelps parodied the complicated condolence system of exchanges expected to comfort the bereaved and keep the dead in the minds of the living, she acknowledged mourning's ritual attire in Winifred's wearing the white collar and cuffs of half-mourning, customary for a widow of three years, a practice that alerted others to approach her with sympathy.

Not only religious but also secular in its impact, *The Gates Ajar* concerns gender stereotypes, especially women's roles. Phelps attests in *Chapters* that when she was twenty-five (in 1869), she approved the "enfranchisement and elevation of her own sex": "I believe in women," she vowed, "and in their right to their own best possibilities in every department of life" (p. 250). Many critics of the book since the late twentieth century have affirmed its utopian feminist features. For example, the heroine Winifred challenges established patriarchal organization for her own welfare and, though a woman, presumes herself a lay minister. She offers a collaborative model for comforting the grieving, what can only be considered as realizable utopian social reform. In her 1871 essay "The True Woman," Phelps denounced the personality without a self required of that "enormous dummy . . . the 'true woman,'" expected to immerse herself totally in family to the exclusion of any self-care (p. 269). Early in *The Gates Ajar*, Mary bemoans to her diary that Roy "had grown to me, heart of my heart, life of my life. . . . Roy was all there was," her acknowledgment that her own self was buried in Roy (p. 9). Later she confides her sense of a merged self to her aunt Winifred: once in heaven, Mary despairs that she "hasn't talent, nor even a single absorbing taste . . . : what shall she do?" (p. 109). Winifred urges Mary to reveal her own self's feeling to her aunt and, in so doing, find and strengthen her own self: Mary's loss of Roy becomes the occasion for her self-discovery. Later in the novel

Mary fears that she shall never "[sound] her own nature" as has Winifred who "knows the worst of herself, and faces it . . . fairly" (p. 65).

The Gates Ajar reveals Phelps's broad understanding of literary strategies and her astute deployment of them to console her readers, expressed in the familiar voice of a bereaved young woman. Its wide popular appeal derives from the many social practices and issues that Phelps touched upon. Given a belief that heaven would be an improvement over earth, placing social innovations in heaven made a claim for their desirability.

See also Civil War; Death; Domestic Fiction; Female Authorship; Feminism; Mourning; Religion; Sentimentalism; Spiritualism

BIBLIOGRAPHY

Primary Works

Phelps, Elizabeth Stuart. *Chapters from a Life*. Boston: Houghton Mifflin, 1896.

Phelps, Elizabeth Stuart. *The Gates Ajar*. 1868. Edited and with an introduction by Helen Sootin Smith. Cambridge, Mass.: Belknap Press of Harvard University Press, 1964. In-text citations are to this edition.

Phelps, Elizabeth Stuart. *Three Spiritualist Novels: The Gates Ajar (1868), Beyond the Gates (1883), and The Gates Between (1887)*. Introduction by Nina Baym. Urbana: University of Illinois Press, 2000.

Phelps, Elizabeth Stuart. "The True Woman." *Independent* 23, no. 1193 (12 October 1871): 1. Reprinted in *The Story of Avis* (1877). Edited and with an introduction by Carol Farley Kessler. New Brunswick, N.J.: Rutgers University Press, 1985. In-text citations are to the reprinted version.

Secondary Works

Baetzhold, Howard G., and Joseph B. McCullough, eds. *The Bible according to Mark Twain: Irreverent Writings on Eden, Heaven, and the Flood by America's Master Satirist*. Athens: University of Georgia Press, 1995.

Bennett, Mary Angela. *Elizabeth Stuart Phelps*. Philadelphia: University of Pennsylvania Press, 1939.

Hart, James D. *The Popular Book: A History of America's Literary Taste*. New York: Oxford University Press, 1950.

Ian, Marcia. "Psychology and the of Impasse Reason: William James's Religious Experience." *Streams of William James* 4, no. 3 (2002): 34–37.

Kete, Mary Louise. *Sentimental Collaboration: Mourning and Middle-Class Identity in Nineteenth-Century America*. Durham, N.C.: Duke University Press, 2000.

Knight, Denise D., ed. *The Diaries of Charlotte Perkins Gilman*. Vol. 2, *1890–1935*. Charlottesville: University Press of Virginia, 1994.

Long, Lisa A. *Rehabilitating Bodies: Health, History, and the American Civil War.* Philadelphia: University of Pennsylvania Press, 2004.

Oliphant, Margaret. Review of *The Gates Ajar. Blackwood's Magazine* 10 (October 1871): 422–442.

St. Armand, Barton Levi. *Emily Dickinson and Her Culture: The Soul's Society.* New York: Cambridge University Press, 1984.

Schnog, Nancy. "'The Comfort of My Fancying': Loss and Recuperation in *The Gates Ajar.*" *Arizona Quarterly* 49, no. 3 (1993): 127–154.

Smith, Gail K. "From the Seminary to the Parlor: The Popularization of Hermeneutics in *The Gates Ajar.*" *Arizona Quarterly* 54, no. 2 (1998): 99–133.

Carol Farley Kessler

GERMAN SCHOLARSHIP

During the latter half of the eighteenth century, readers in New England and the other seaboard colonies enjoyed German popular literature and political-historical treatises, which were available in the original as well as in translation. Often such literature was pietistic, mystical, and moralistic or religious. The fascination with the rationalistic philosophies of Immanuel Kant (1724–1804) ran parallel to an interest in the biographies of such figures as Frederick the Great (1712–1786), ruler of Prussia from 1740 to 1786, who had challenged the English intellectual base. Friedrich Klopstock's *Der Messias* (1773) was repeatedly published in American magazines. Christoph Wieland's *Oberon* (1780) and the tales of Baron Munchausen earned a place in juvenile and humorous literature. Exemplary Sturm und Drang works such as *The Sorrows of Young Werther* (1774), by Johann von Goethe (1749–1832), were translated frequently and read widely, though the movement itself was misunderstood. Friedrich Schiller (1759–1805) was undoubtedly the most popular German writer this side of the Atlantic, beginning with his *Robbers* (1781), available in British translations, and continuing to his *Kabale und Liebe* (1784) and *Don Carlos* (1787) in Samuel Taylor Coleridge's 1800 translation. Schiller's dramas about political freedom evoked the sympathy of American readers and theatergoers. August Kotzebue's *Menschen und Reue* (1789) garnered broad audiences, as did *Miss Sara Sampson* (1755) and *Emilia Galotti* (1772), by Gotthold Lessing (1729–1781). From the Romantic period, the poignant works of E. T. A. Hoffmann (1776–1822) were an object of fascination. These writers exerted a moderate German literary influence on American writing.

Between 1797 and 1815, the English blockade on the high seas and the war-torn exchanges between the youthful United States and Germany resulted in a waning of this influence, but it reawakened during the post-Napoleonic period beginning in 1820. Later, the revolutions of 1848 triggered the migration of thousands of German intellectuals to America, who prepared the way for the reception of German literature and art on the American scene. Despite a certain puritanical bias on the part of American readers, respect for German poetry and letters in general grew with the political rise of Prussia and further increased in 1870 when unification of the Reich was achieved thanks to Prussia's military prowess.

THE INFLUENCE OF GERMAN EDUCATION

Several factors facilitated the flow of ideas and writing between Germany and the United States. One was the presence of young American students at German universities. Shortly after 1800, during the Napoleonic wars, universities such as those founded by the intellectual giants Wilhelm and Alexander von Humboldt in Berlin gained the world's admiration for their excellence. Harvard men such as George Ticknor (1791–1871), Edward E. Everett (1794–1865), Joseph Cogswell (1786–1871), George Bancroft (1800–1891), and others arrived in Germany to study. In the words of the president of Harvard, John Thornton Kirkland (1778–1840), who engineered scholarships for them, each was to become "an accomplished philologian and Biblical critic, able to expound and defend the Revelation of God" (Pochmann, p. 73). As is the custom in German universities even today, soon after their arrival, these students scattered to other schools. Bancroft left Göttingen for Berlin in 1820, commenting that learning in Germany was done too earnestly, that the scholar was too diligent, that Germany made too much of science and too little of the scientist, and that the whole process was too coldly calculating and impersonal (Pochmann, p. 74). In Berlin Bancroft pursued philological studies under August Böchk, Hermann Hirt, and G. W. F. Hegel (1770–1831), and heard lectures by Friedrich Schleiermacher, Friedrich Savigny, and Wilhelm von Humboldt. Humboldt discussed John Milton, Goethe, Schiller, August Wilhelm von Schlegel and Friedrich von Schlegel, and German literature in general. Twice Bancroft visited Goethe in Weimar.

Throughout their subsequent careers in America, the strong leaven of German culture made these young Americans champions of German scholarship and ideas. They became at once pathfinders in American cultural endeavors and effective agents for the infusion of German ideas. Bancroft's historical writings were inspired by Hegel's philosophy of history, which set the pattern for American historiography, earning him the title "Father of American History."

Prominent German intellectuals received appointments to prestigious universities in the United States. Karl (known in the United States as Charles) Follen (1795–1840) was appointed to Harvard and Georg Blättermann (1788–1850) to the University of Virginia in Charlottesville. Scholars have dwelled on Blättermann's influence on Edgar Allan Poe, who studied under him at Virginia (Pochmann, p. 710). In Richmond, the Virginia legislature mandated German university traditions recommended by Alexander von Humboldt in his lengthy correspondence with Thomas Jefferson; in Massachusetts and in the nation as a whole, the efforts of Horace Mann (1796–1859), the father of American education, on behalf of a public, nonsectarian school system set the tone for American state-funded education.

Mann believed that the Prussian public school system was the solution to the growing social problems of America: it would create a more homogenous population of compliant workers who shared similar opinions and values. It would tame the wild West and settle a restive population. He began proselytizing for compulsory public education, particularly among leaders of industry, suggesting that if they could bring their political influence to bear they could work toward a solution to society's problems while at the same time getting better workers for their factories.

TRANSCENDENTALISM

Perhaps the most important influence exerted by German intellectualism on the American literary scene flowed through New England transcendentalism. Ideals generated by German Romanticism (1797–1832) percolated easily into the writing and thought processes of Ralph Waldo Emerson (1803–1882), even though they were filtered through English writers such as Samuel Taylor Coleridge (1772–1834) and Thomas Carlyle (1795–1881). Kant's theories were transmitted especially through Carlyle. Orestes Brownson (1803–1876) delved into the transcendentalism of the time in an article published in the *Christian Examiner* in 1834. Amos Bronson Alcott (1799–1888) sought to implement tenets of that philosophy in schools of his native rural Connecticut, whereas Elizabeth Peabody (1804–1894) and Margaret Fuller (1810–1850) tried to put similar notions into practice in elementary education. Later, with the help of Theodore Parker and others, the transcendentalist movement expanded into an abolitionist force, drawing on

ideals imbibed from the philosophies of German predecessors.

Karl Follen and another immigrant, Carl Beck (1798–1866), were influential in propagating the German craze, as it was called by those who opposed Germanism in American culture (Pochmann, p. 127). Follen was dismissed from a lectureship at the University of Jena in central Germany for his participation in the *Burschenschaftenbewegung,* a march by German university students in 1817, on the third centennial of the Lutheran revolt, to the Wartburg Castle in Eisenach. The movement spawned by these students later fostered the revolutions of 1848. Follen was threatened by reactionaries and finally left for America. In 1825 he began lecturing at Harvard on topics ranging from jurisprudence to the theories of education of Friedrich Froebel and Johann Pestalozzi, coupled with gymnastics training, or *Turnkunst,* as promoted by Friedrich Ludwig Jahn. Follen married the daughter of a prominent family, Eliza Lee Cabot, which provided him access to the social elite of Boston and advanced his professional career. He was eventually granted a full professorship at Harvard.

Carl Beck, two years younger than Follen, had studied in Berlin, Heidelberg, and Tübingen before coming to America, where he soon became director of the Round Hill School in Northampton, Massachusetts. Like Follen, Beck promoted Jahn's *Turnkunst* and in 1830 opened schools in Philipstown on the Hudson, opposite West Point. Later he became professor of Latin at Harvard.

ECONOMICS AND ENCYCLOPEDIAS

Two additional distinguished immigrants with paramount influence on American thought and literature were Friedrich List and Francis Lieber. List (1789–1846) made his mark in economic theory with his *Outlines of American Political Economy* (1827), which gained fame for defining the "American System," a high-tariff program to make the United States thrive in the face of stiff English competition in world trade. Lieber (1800–1872) became especially well known for his thirteen-volume *Encyclopaedia Americana,* which appeared between 1829 and 1833. Not since Thomas Paine had an author achieved such literary respect in America. In his subsequent *Manual of Political Ethics* (1838–1839), Lieber propounded Kant's political philosophy. Emerson credited Lieber with breaking down the American view that German scholarship produced little more than uninspired dictionaries. Lieber, said Emerson, was "at once man thinking and man acting" (Pochmann, p. 127).

TRANSLATIONS

As the nineteenth century progressed, German literary works in translation began to appear in American libraries. Adelbert von Chamisso's (1781–1838) character Peter Schlemihl and Friedrich de la Motte-Fouqué's Undine in turn inspired folkloric and water spirit figures in American literature. Heinrich Heine (1797–1856) made his way to America through the appreciative efforts of the British writers Matthew Arnold and George Eliot. As entertainment and conversational material, however, the German novel never matched the expectations of the critics, though many light and entertaining books were serialized in American newspapers. In the American South, George Calvert (1803–1889) exerted considerable effort introducing German literature to American readers. After graduating from Harvard, Calvert had lived in Göttingen from January 1824 until September 1825 and had visited with A. W. von Schlegel, the historian Barthold Georg Niebuhr, and other German writers. He had also visited Goethe in Weimar. Calvert's translation of Schiller's *Don Carlos* appeared in 1834. He also published treatises and correspondence between Goethe, Jean Paul, and A. W. von Schlegel. Other German authors were introduced to the American literary scene in the antebellum period by the transcendentalist Unitarian ministers Samuel Osgood, George Ripley, Cyrus A. Bartol, Frederic Henry Hedge, Nathaniel L. Frothingham, and others. *The Nation, Atlantic Monthly, Western Messenger, The Dial, Harbinger, North American Review, New Englander, Century, Harper's,* and other journals published their reviews and critical commentary.

Bayard Taylor's powerful translation of *Faust* in 1870 was a major achievement and was soon followed by others: John Weiss's translation of *Westöstlicher Divan* (1877) and Charles Eliot Norton's editions of correspondence between Goethe and Carlyle (1877). Goethe societies and Goethe schools—for example, those founded by the St. Louis Hegelians—sprang up in cities where German immigration had swelled the population. Monuments, street names, and parks paid homage to Goethe in various cities where his works had been read or performed on stage and where he was honored as a poet. During the Civil War, Gotthold Ephraim Lessing came into his own among American writers with his drama of tolerance, *Nathan der Weise* (1779), partly because of the American race question then being fought over. A translation of Lessing's *Laokoon* (1766) appeared to positive reviews in 1867, following on the heels of E. P. Evans's translation of Adolph Stahr's two-volume *Lessing: His Life and His Works.* Works by Jean Paul (Richter), depicted as the "healthiest" of the German romantics, were translated in the 1860s by Charles T. Brooks.

GERMAN WRITERS IN EUROPE AND AMERICA

Prominent German writers in the early nineteenth century created sharp images of America. Portrayals by Schiller in his *Kabale und Liebe,* in which he describes the fate of the Hessian soldiers, and by Goethe, who depicts willing emigrants in his *Wilhelm Meisters Lehrjahre* (1795–1796), contrast sharply with those in Ferdinand Kürnberger's *Amerikamüde.* While Schiller and Goethe romanticize the political "freedom" the emigrant to America would enjoy, Kürnberger dwells on the new arrival's loss of economic status, emotional support, and cultural identity. The title of his novel refers to someone who is sick and tired of the American experience.

Friedrich Gerstäcker's *Nach America* (1855) and the novels of Charles Sealsfield (the pseudonym of Karl Postl, 1793–1864) were more widely read. Postl published many novels between 1828 and about 1850, several of which, including *Das Cajütenbuch* (1841), had a strong impact on Henry Wadsworth Longfellow (1807–1882), according to that writer. Otto Ruppius (1819–1864), a refugee who came to America in 1848, worked as a journalist in New York and Saint Louis, producing novellas such as *Der Pedlar* (c. 1857) in his spare time. Friedrich Armand Strubberg (1806–1889), a hunter and soldier who used the pen name "Armand," turned out thrillers such as *Sklaverei in Amerika* (1862) and *Der Sprung vom Niagarafälle* (1864) that were popular for a time. Heinrich Baldwin Möllhausen (1825–1905) sometimes merited the title of the "German James Fenimore Cooper": he was more an adventure seeker than a refugee. His novels were readily translated into English. Robert Reitzel (1849–1898) was a publicist of note who propagandized in radical German fashion for *Sozialdemokratie, Arbeiterbewegung, Turnerei,* and *Freimännerei* before hunkering down with his Detroit literary weekly, *Der arme Teufel.*

Writers in the German dialect of Pennsylvania can be credited with a minor influence. Phebe Earle Gibbons (1821–1893), for example, wrote between 1845 and 1882 and published a novel in 1869. Authors of a separatist or pietistic orientation had considerable influence on American literature and on music and art. Large collections of hymns and other religious works were produced by Germans from Pennsylvania to South Carolina and Georgia, appearing notably in the diaries of Moravian missionaries. In addition, there is considerable travel literature that indirectly influenced the American literary mind-set.

Did German literary writers make a significant contribution to American literature? Genuinely German American novelists such as Theodore Dreiser

(*Jennie Gerhardt*, 1911), Willa Cather (*O Pioneers!* 1913), or Sinclair Lewis (*Main Street*, 1920), while sympathetic to the German immigrant, can hardly be said to have been influenced by German writers. These classic American novelists wrote rather *about* the German immigrant but never attributed their style or production *to* the masters of German literature. Thus the effects of German learning (especially literary theory and the "higher criticism" of the Bible) on literary production in the United States is tangential. Even in the case of transcendentalism, it is difficult to say how German literary theory may have affected American literature. That is even more true for Sturm und Drang, classicism, Romanticism, and *Jung Deutschland*.

See also The Bible; Literary Criticism; Philosophy; Religion; Transcendentalism

BIBLIOGRAPHY

Secondary Works

Bauschinger, Sigrid. *The Trumpet of Reform: German Literature in Nineteenth-Century New England.* Translated by Thomas S. Hansen. Columbia, S.C.: Camden House, 1998.

Bickman, Martin. "An Overview of American Transcendentalism." http://www.vcu.edu/engweb/transcendentalism/ideas/definitionbickman.html.

Brooks, Van Wyck, and Otto L. Bettmann. *Our Literary Heritage: A Pictorial History of the Writer in America.* New York: Dutton, 1956.

The Cambridge History of English and American Literature. 1907–1921. Vols. 5, 8, and 14. New York: Bartleby, 2000.

Flanagan, J. T. "The German in American Fiction." In *In the Trek of the Immigrants, Essays Presented to Carl Wittke,* edited by O. Fritiof Ander, pp. 95–113. Rock Island, Ill.: Augustana College Library, 1964.

Galinsky, Hans. "Germany's Literary Impact on America's Contemporary South (1950–1980)." In *A Conversation in the Life of Leland R. Phelps: America and Germany—Literature, Art, and Music,* edited by Frank L. Borchardt and Marion C. Salinger. Durham, N.C.: Duke University, Center for International Studies, 1987.

Galinsky, Hans. "Three Literary Perspectives on the German in America: Immigrant, Homeland, and American Views." In *Eagle in the New World: German Immigration to Texas and America,* edited by Theodore Gish and Richard Spuler, pp. 102–131. College Station: Texas A&M University Press, 1986.

Galinsky, Hans. "Zwei Jahrhunderte amerikanisch-deutsche Literaturbeziehungen (1776–1976)." *Nassauische Annalen* 89 (1978): 49–77.

Hartmann, Thom. "The 'Real School' Is Not Free." http://www.thomhartmann.com/realschool.shtml.

Herminghouse, Patricia A., ed. *Gustav Phillip Körner, Das Deutsche Element in den Vereinigten Staaten von Nordamerika, 1818–1848.* Facsimile reprint. New York: Peter Lang, 1986.

Merrill, Peter G. *German-American Urban Culture: Writers and Theaters in Early Milwaukee.* Madison: University of Wisconsin, 2000.

Pochmann, Henry A. *German Culture in America: Philosophical and Literary Influences, 1600–1900.* Madison: University of Wisconsin Press, 1957.

Schaff, Philip. *America, A Sketch of Its Political, Social, and Religious Character.* 1854. Cambridge, Mass.: Harvard University Press, 1961.

Spiller, Robert E., et al., eds. *Literary History of the United States.* 1946. 2 vols. 4th ed. New York: Macmillan, 1974.

Vogel, Stanley M. *German Literary Influences on the American Transcendentalists.* New Haven, Conn.: Archon Books, 1970.

Wendell, Barrett. *A Literary History of America.* New York: Charles Scribner's Sons, 1900.

LaVern J. Rippley

GETTYSBURG ADDRESS

Abraham Lincoln's (1809–1865) Gettysburg Address is widely recognized as one of the most significant speeches in American history. Just as Lincoln's declaration in June 1858 that "a house divided against itself cannot stand" ("Speech," p. 428) exemplified the state of the nation before the Civil War, the Gettysburg Address captured the spirit of a people seeking to maintain their unity in the face of divisive and destructive violence. Although the Civil War raged for two more years, Lincoln's Gettysburg Address provided Americans with a literary formula for accepting the costs of the war and moving toward the future with resolution and hope.

The Gettysburg Address was delivered on 19 November 1863 during a dedication ceremony that transformed the site of the Battle of Gettysburg into a national war cemetery. The Battle of Gettysburg (1–3 July 1863) is considered one of the bloodiest battles in American history. Historians estimate that fifty-one thousand soldiers were killed, wounded, or captured during the battle, more casualties than any other battle ever fought in North America. It is generally considered a turning point in the Civil War. By 1863 Americans on both the Northern and the Southern sides had come to accept that the initial expectation that the war would be settled quickly with

Abraham Lincoln. Photograph by Alexander Gardner, taken 8 November 1863, eleven days before the Gettysburg Address. © BETTMANN/CORBIS

little bloodshed was mistaken. The Confederate army had already achieved several important military victories, defeating the Union at Bull Run (21 July 1861), Fredericksburg (11–13 December 1862), and Chancellorsville (1–3 May 1863), among others. The Confederate general Robert E. Lee (1807–1870) sought to build upon this advantage by invading the North at Gettysburg, Pennsylvania. But at the Battle of Gettysburg, the tide appeared to turn against the Confederate army, which lost approximately twenty-eight thousand soldiers, including ten thousand men

in one hour during the infamous Pickett's Charge. In the end, the Union commander George Gordon Meade (1815–1872) gained the upper hand, and by 4 July 1863 the Union army had won the battle. But the Union losses were so great—approximately twenty-three thousand men—that it was a dubious honor, and only in retrospect was the victory recognized as a significant achievement for the Union.

The dead of Gettysburg were piled upon the battlefield, quickly decomposing in the hot summer air. Sanitary concerns required an immediate response, so

Four score and seven years ago our fathers brought forth on this continent, a new nation, conceived in Liberty, and dedicated to the proposition that all men are created equal.

Now we are engaged in a great civil war, testing whether that nation, or any nation so conceived and so dedicated, can long endure. We are met on a great battle-field of that war. We have come to dedicate a portion of that field, as a final resting place for those who here gave their lives that that nation might live. It is altogether fitting and proper that we should do this.

But, in a larger sense, we can not dedicate— we can not consecrate—we can not hallow—this ground. The brave men, living and dead, who struggled here, have consecrated it, far above our poor power to add or detract. The world will little note, nor long remember what we say here, but it can never forget what they did here. It is for us the living, rather, to be dedicated here to the unfinished work which they who fought here have thus far so nobly advanced. It is rather for us to be here dedicated to the great task remaining before us—that from these honored dead we take increased devotion to that cause for which they gave the last full measure of devotion—that we here highly resolve that these dead shall not have died in vain—that this nation, under God, shall have a new birth of freedom—and that government of the people, by the people, for the people, shall not perish from the earth.

Lincoln, "Address at the Dedication of Gettysburg National Cemetery," pp. 786–788.

deemed appropriate for an enemy.) But sentiment and politics demanded that the dead be commemorated in a more long-lasting and honorable way. Land was purchased near the battle site and designated as a national cemetery, and thirty-five hundred Union soldiers were reinterred in graves organized in radiating semicircles according to the eighteen states whose soldiers participated in the battle.

Four months after the terrible battle, the Soldiers' Cemetery at Gettysburg (now the Gettysburg National Cemetery) was dedicated with a public ceremony. Fifteen thousand people gathered to participate, including many family members who had lost loved ones in the battle. The central speaker was Edward Everett (1794–1865), a former secretary of state, U.S. senator, and U.S. representative from Massachusetts, who was the most renowned orator in the nation. By the standards of the day, Everett's speech was a masterpiece; nineteenth-century audiences were accustomed to lengthy speeches that employed grandiose, ornate language. Everett's two-hour-long, 13,609-word speech did not fail to satisfy.

By contrast, Lincoln's speech was short and sparse, only 272 words long. Lincoln had been invited to deliver "a few appropriate remarks." He understood that Everett's speech was the main event and his own contribution was the peroration, or summing up. Nevertheless, Lincoln's speech was shockingly brief; he spoke for less than three minutes and sat down before many in the audience had realized he was through. The response to the speech was mixed. Some immediately recognized its power, including Everett, who praised Lincoln for accomplishing with such economy what he himself had required two hours to achieve. Others criticized Lincoln for his bad taste in speaking so briefly and accused him of insulting the memory of the dead. Only in retrospect has Lincoln's speech been understood as both a brilliant work of literature and a revolutionary statement of political philosophy.

THE GETTYSBURG ADDRESS AS LITERATURE

The Gettysburg Address exemplifies the transformative power of language; in 272 words, Lincoln replaced the violence and carnage of the Battle of Gettysburg with a vision of a unified nation committed to equality. Lincoln's brevity and simplistic language is deceptive, giving the impression that the text was extemporaneous. Indeed, since the Gettysburg Address was first delivered, a rumor has spread that Lincoln wrote the speech quickly on the train from Washington, D.C., to Pennsylvania. Contrary to this myth, there are five

the Union dead were initially disposed of in field graves: hastily dug, shallow graves close to where the soldiers fell in battle. (The Confederate dead were simply piled into mass, unmarked graves as was copies of the speech in Lincoln's handwriting; this shows that Lincoln revised the text several times before and after he delivered it in 1863. It is the fifth draft of the speech, known as the "Bliss copy" after its owner Colonel Alexander Bliss, which has become accepted as the standard edition of the text.

Rather than a spontaneous response to the battlefield cemetery, the Gettysburg Address is a precisely crafted literary text that distills Lincoln's complex political ideals to their essence. The multiple drafts of the text are a testament to the care with which Lincoln composed the speech as well as his awareness of the subtle nuance of each word. The Gettysburg Address is often described as a prose poem because of the significance of Lincoln's word choices. In addition, certain lines of the address have a lyrical rhythm and regular structure that evoke the sensibility of poetry, such as: "we can not dedicate—we can not consecrate—we can not hallow." The use of repetition in this phrase creates a rhythm that carries the audience from what they cannot do to what they must do: dedicate themselves to a government "of the people, by the people, for the people." These two phrases occur at the beginning and end of the final paragraph and thus create a unified structure that models through language what the speech seeks to accomplish through politics.

In addition to his ingenious use of rhythm and repetition, Lincoln employs powerful literary imagery, primarily in the form of antithesis or the comparison of opposites such as light/dark or new/old. Lincoln uses antithesis in the juxtaposition of birth and death; although he acknowledges that death occasions the speech, his language evokes images of birth: "brought forth," "conceived," "new birth of freedom." Thus he replaces the grim reality of the dead with the hopeful idea of rebirth and continuity. Similarly, Lincoln links the past and the future, beginning the speech with a look backwards ("Four score and seven years ago") but concluding with a repetition of active verbs that point toward the future: the dead shall not have died in vain, the nation shall have a new birth of freedom, the government shall not perish.

The complex meaning achieved by the few words Lincoln uses also draws attention to the words he did not use: North/South, Union/Confederacy, or slavery. He never mentions Gettysburg or the particulars of the battle. He never mentions the South as either enemy or challenger. It is also striking that he does not mention the other historically significant text of 1863, the Emancipation Proclamation that freed the slaves. By avoiding mention of the specific issues, participants, and events that dominated the war, Lincoln sought to transform them into types, abstract and

idealistic rather than tangible and ordinary. This allows Lincoln to transcend the particulars of the war and focus upon the principles at stake. In a similar way, Lincoln employs general terms rather than proper nouns throughout: *a* civil war, *a* battlefield, *any* nation rather than *the* Civil War, *the* Gettysburg battlefield, *the* United States. This technique reflects Lincoln's knowledge of classical oratorical tradition; inspired by speeches like Pericles' funeral oration for the Athenian dead in 431 B.C.E., Lincoln sought to elevate the dead of Gettysburg into inspirational symbols. In Lincoln's formulation, the dead should be commemorated by the rededication of the living to the principles of equality and unity. Thus America itself becomes the lasting monument to the Civil War dead.

THE GETTYSBURG ADDRESS AS POLITICAL PHILOSOPHY

The Gettysburg Address is one of Lincoln's most revolutionary political speeches. Although he had been invited to simply give his approval to the creation of the Gettysburg National Cemetery, Lincoln took advantage of the time and place to take a stand on the controversial issues that sparked the Civil War. Even though he does not specifically mention slavery or states' rights, the address is understood as a turning point in the development of Lincoln's thinking about these complex political debates.

In the Gettysburg Address, Lincoln turns away from the Constitution as the document that defines the parameters of American policy. Instead, Lincoln embraces the Declaration of Independence and the phrase "all men are created equal" as the cornerstone of the nation. By looking to the declaration for guidance, Lincoln implicitly acknowledges the flaws of the Constitution, such as its provisions for the existence of slavery. The answer to the great "test" the nation is undergoing is a rededication to the original intent of the declaration. The consequences of Lincoln's statements are profound: he acknowledges the incompatibility of slavery and equality and implies that the Constitution must be amended to set the nation back on the correct path, thus anticipating the Thirteenth Amendment, which abolished slavery in 1865.

In his Pulitzer Prize–winning account of the Gettysburg Address, the historian Gary Wills argues that Lincoln's speech was more than just a great work of oratory. Instead, he writes, the Gettysburg Address resulted in a revolutionary reconception of American identity:

> The Gettysburg Address has become an authoritative expression of the American spirit—as

authoritative as the Declaration itself, and perhaps even more influential, since it determines how we read the Declaration. For most people now, the Declaration means what Lincoln told us it means, as a way of correcting the Constitution itself without overthrowing it. . . . By accepting the Gettysburg Address, its concept of a single people dedicated to a proposition, we have been changed. Because of it, we live in a different America. (Pp. 146–147)

THE GETTYSBURG ADDRESS IN AMERICAN MEMORY

The Gettysburg Address is celebrated as a masterpiece of American literature. Although many scholars identify Lincoln's Second Inaugural Address (1865) as his greatest work of oratory and political philosophy, it is the Gettysburg Address that remains foremost in most people's minds when they think of Lincoln. Both the Gettysburg Address and the Second Inaugural are inscribed upon the walls of the Lincoln Memorial in Washington, D.C. The association between the man and his words has worked to elevate both in American memory. As Lincoln's reputation has ascended since his death in 1865, so too have historians, literary critics, and politicians come to recognize the remarkable accomplishment of the Gettysburg Address. Continuing a long-standing tradition, every year innumerable school children across the nation still commit Lincoln's words to memory.

Even as the deaths suffered in 1863 fade from memory, the power of Lincoln's words live on. On 11 September 2002, one year after the attacks on the World Trade Center, New York governor George Pataki participated in a memorial service at Ground Zero. Rather than deliver an original speech about the terrible events of 2001, Pataki chose to read Lincoln's Gettysburg Address. This employment of Lincoln's words suggests that they transcend the specific losses of the Civil War and capture instead a national experience of grief in the face of almost unimaginable violence and loss.

See also Abolitionist Writing; Civil War; Death; Democracy; Oratory; Slavery

BIBLIOGRAPHY

Primary Work

Lincoln, Abraham. "Address at the Dedication of Gettysburg National Cemetery." 1863. In *The Life and Writings of Abraham Lincoln,* edited by Philip Van Doren Stern, with a biographical essay by Philip Van Doren Stern and an introduction by Allan Nevins, pp. 786–788. New York: Modern Library, 1999.

Lincoln, Abraham. "Speech Delivered at Springfield, Illinois." 1858. In *The Life and Writings of Abraham Lincoln,* edited by Philip Van Doren Stern, with a biographical essay by Philip Van Doren Stern and an introduction by Allan Nevins, pp. 428–437. New York: Modern Library, 1999.

Secondary Works

Desjardin, Thomas A. *These Honored Dead: How the Story of Gettysburg Shaped American Memory.* Cambridge, Mass.: Da Capo Press, 2003.

Einhorn, Lois J. *Abraham Lincoln, the Orator: Penetrating the Lincoln Legend.* Westport, Conn.: Greenwood Press, 1992.

Kunhardt, Philip B., Jr. *A New Birth of Freedom: Lincoln at Gettysburg.* Boston: Little, Brown, 1983.

Peterson, Merrill D. *Lincoln in American Memory.* New York: Oxford University Press, 1994.

Wills, Garry. *Lincoln at Gettysburg: The Words That Remade America.* New York: Simon and Schuster, 1992.

Desirée Henderson

GIFT BOOKS AND ANNUALS

During the nineteenth century, and especially between 1830 and 1860, gift books—beautifully designed, illustrated volumes of poetry and prose—were significant components of upper-middle-class reading culture. Created by publishers to be given as gifts or purchased for home library collections, gift books were designed to be seen as well as read and signaled a kind of middle-class taste and respectability that other fiction did not carry. Related to the gift book is the annual. These terms are sometimes used synonymously, with the idea that the annual was produced by publishers of a periodical and advertised at year's end to the periodicals' subscribers. Later in the nineteenth century, however, the term "annual" came to refer to the bound volume of the magazine, sometimes issued with additional illustrations or special features that could be purchased at the year's end. Parents and grandparents would give gift volumes and annuals to children, and other adults would purchase them for family libraries. The illustrations in these volumes provide present-day readers with a sense of the literary and artistic tastes and cultural values of mid-nineteenth-century America. Both the illustrations and the text are sentimental, and pages from gift books repeatedly show tranquil scenes of mothers surrounded by children, creating the impression that nineteenth-century white middle-class homes revolved around well-ordered, mother-centered domestic spheres.

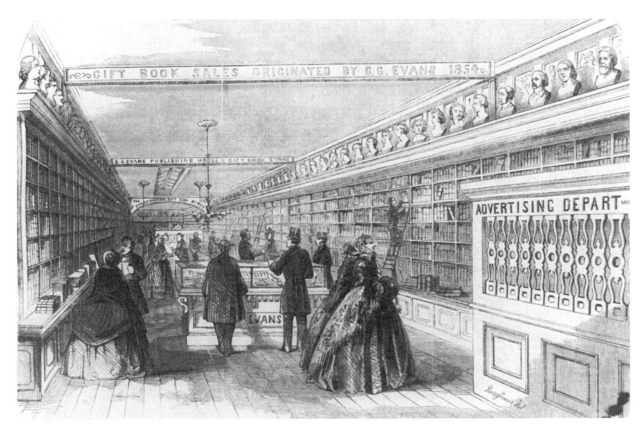

G. G. Evans's gift book store, Philadephia. Engraving from *Frank Leslie's Ilustrated Newspaper,* 31 December 1859. The huge selection of gift books available is apparent in this illustration. THE LIBRARY OF CONGRESS

ILLUSTRATIONS AND DESIGN

The number of illustrations in gift books ranges from four to twelve, although some have as few as one full-page of engraving opposite the title page. Usually these engravings are scattered throughout the book and reflect the themes and content of the text. David S. Lovejoy has studied volumes of *The Token* (first published 1828 in Boston) and the *The Atlantic Souvenir* (1826 in Philadelphia) and argues that these early gift books provide an interesting record of American Romantic painting, marked by the "birth of the New Republic and by those characteristics so prominent in American life in the first half of the nineteenth century: democracy, individualism, sentiment, humor, and an interest in the frontier" (p. 347). Lovejoy discusses the gift-book art of Alvin Fisher (1792–1863), George Loring Brown (1814–1849), and Henry Inman (1801–1846), all of whom produced illustrations for James Fenimore Cooper's work. Thomas Cole's (1801–1848) contributions of powerful landscape scenes to *The Token* are also discussed. Lovejoy points out that John Neal, an art critic writing in the early nineteenth century, reviewed the paintings published in the gift books and argued that much of the

success or failure of illustrations was in the engraving process: "A long life is to be spent in diligent, exact, and laborious work; a long life in very delicate and careful experiment, before [engravers] can hope even to see the finer and more wonderful difficulties of their art" (quoted in Lovejoy, p. 360). Two engravers noted in Lovejoy's piece include E. Gallaudet, who engraved Thomas Cole's *The Whirlwind* for *The Token* in 1837, and W. E. Tucker, who engraved Alvin Fisher's *The Buffalo Hunt* for *The Token* in 1835. The paintings in gift books highlighted the work of significant American artists, and as Lovejoy notes, this "helped to popularize contemporary American painting and carry it into the homes of the people whose history, environment, and character it expressed" (p. 361).

In the 1850s, 1860s, and 1870s, the illustrations included in gift books and annual volumes of periodicals shifted from engravings of landscapes to portraits of human subjects and paintings of domestic scenes. The illustrations and content of *Godey's Lady's Book,* a periodical that ran from 1830 to 1898 under a variety of titles, influenced gift books and annuals. During the second half of the nineteenth century periodicals such as *Harper's New Monthly*

Magazine (1850–1900), *Demorest's* (1865–1890), and *Scribner's Monthly–The Century Illustrated Monthly* (1870–1929) included more illustrations in their publications, and the *Godey's Lady's Book* style of sentimental illustrations of mother and child or child and pet became more prevalent. Bradford K. Peirce's 1850 volume *A Token of Friendship: Gift Book for the Holidays,* for example, includes one illustration by J. Andrews and H. W. Smith titled *The Watcher,* which depicts a young mother or an adolescent girl watching over a baby in a parklike setting. Another illustration in this same volume, titled *Beauty's Bath,* shows a young girl standing on a towel holding a dog. The illustrations in both periodicals and gift books were considered valuable, and sometimes the images were removed and resold individually. During the later decades of the nineteenth century, as lithography (discovered in 1796 by Aloys Senefelder) and chromolithography began to be used more frequently in the place of steel and wood engraving and hand-coloring of plates, more gift volumes were produced with chromolithographs included at the beginning of the books. *The Aldine* (1868–1879), an art periodical, used chromolithographs as "premiums" in annual volumes sold at slightly higher prices. The art included in gift books and annuals influenced fashion and home design, and the art itself was often removed from the volumes and displayed in homes.

Gift books were purchased for special occasions—for birthdays or holidays—or as tokens of courtship or friendship. The design of the book as much as the content was meaningful. Ronald J. Zboray and Mary Saracino Zboray note that many of the books that were given as gifts were not read but were seen as signs of status. Publishers and consumers

> paid particular attention to types of print, binding, and format which not only suggested refinement, but conveyed more intimate messages through the color of leather, quality of paper, beauty of engravings, and selection of themes. . . . the most elaborate experimentation with the book's physical aspect as a selling point can be found in giftbooks sold mainly at Christmas and New Year's when the output of the industry intensified. (P. 605)

The Token and *The Atlantic Souvenir,* which were two of the best-selling, annually produced gift-book titles during the 1830s, eventually merged, and in several subsequent years volumes were titled *The Token and Atlantic Souvenir.* Other titles include *The Opal, The Garland, The Oasis; or, Golden Leaves of Friendship, The Wide Awake Gift: A Know-Nothing Token, Autumn Dreams,* and *The Sapphire.* Many of the volumes published between 1830 and 1860 are quarto-sized (approximately four inches by seven inches) and fairly brief—many just over a hundred pages. The covers are

usually in solid colors—red, blue, or green with gilded titles and designs. The poetry and prose is frequently sentimental, focusing on such subjects as death, dreams, and the innocence of children. A small brown-and-gold volume titled *Autumn Dreams* (1870), by Eppie Bowdre Castlen, a poet from Macon, Georgia, offers an example, with poems such as "Autumn Days," "The Dead Infant," and "All Is Dreary Now." In a poem titled "Fifteen!" Castlen writes

> . . . in all the strength
> Of Womanhood, will I, down Childhood's green,
> Fresh valley, cast my last and ling'ring look.
>
> *(P. 9)*

Not all volumes were as saccharine as Castlen's, and many gift books contained mixtures of poetry and prose.

SENTIMENTALISM AND LITERARY RESPONSES

The sentimentality of the literature in gift books is significant because many writers of the 1850s, 1860s, 1870s, and 1880s both critiqued and made use of the popular interest in sentimental poetry and prose to further their own literary agendas. Jane Tompkins discusses how men who wrote during the American Renaissance resisted the widespread influence of gift-book sentimentality, while women writers such as Harriet Beecher Stowe (1811–1896) and Susan Warner (1819–1885) made use of sentiment in ways that gave them personal, professional, and political agency. Nathaniel Hawthorne's (1804–1864) well-known "damned mob of scribbling women" comment shows his awareness of the popularity of short sentimental pieces written for periodicals and gift books and his position as a writer who, in order to succeed professionally, needed to some extent to use these forms to please the powerful publishing houses. Edgar Allan Poe (1809–1849) and Herman Melville (1819–1891) also explored the gothic aspects of the sentimental and used the popularity of the gift-book form to support their literary careers.

Hawthorne's critique of women's participation in the writing profession and of their successful use of sentimental poetry and prose intersects in interesting ways with Walt Whitman's (1819–1892) publication of *Leaves of Grass,* which first appeared in 1855 and drew on gift-book conventions in its size and title format. This volume also challenged these conventions by addressing sexuality, social classes, racism—aspects of human experience never honestly or fully explored in nineteenth-century gift books. Louisa May Alcott's (1832–1888) novel *Moods* (1864) contrasts Whitman's *Leaves of Grass* with more sentimental publications in an exchange between two young people at the very beginning of their courtship.

Many pieces in the 1855 gift book The Oasis; or, Golden Leaves of Friendship, *are anonymous, but some of the listed contributors include "Mrs. Child," "H. F. Gould," and "Mrs. Hemans." Goodwin Barnby's poem "Give Me the Hand" appears opposite Mrs. Child's moralistic fable about two princesses, "The Palace of Beauty." Both pieces offer a sense of the didacticism and sentimentality that is prevalent in the gift books of this period.*

Give Me the Hand

Give me the hand that is warm, kind, and ready;
Give me the clasp that is calm, true, and steady;
Give me the hand that will never deceive me;
Give me its grasp that I aye may believe thee.
   Soft is the palm of the delicate woman!
   Hard is the hand of the rough, sturdy yeoman!
   Soft palm or hard hand, it matters not—never!
   Give me the grasp that is friendly forever.
Give me the hand that is true as a brother;
Give me the hand that has harmed not another;
Give me the hand that has never forswore it;
Give me its grasp that I aye may adore it.
   Lovely is the palm of the fair, blue-veined maiden!
   Horny the hand of the workman o'erladen!
   Lovely or ugly, it matters not—never!
   Give me the grasp that is friendly forever.
Give me the grasp that is honest and hearty,
Free as the breeze, and unshackled by party;
Let friendship give me the grasps that become her,
Close as the twine of the vines of the summer.
   Give me the hand that is true as a brother;
   Give me the hand that has wronged not another;

   Soft palm or hard hand, it matters not—never!
   Give me the grasp that is friendly forever.

From "The Palace of Beauty"

In ancient times, two little princesses lived in Scotland, one of whom was extremely beautiful, and the other dwarfish, dark-colored, and deformed. One was named Rose, the other Marion. The sisters did not live happily together. Marion hated Rose because she was handsome, and every body praised her. She scowled, and her face absolutely grew black when any one asked her how her pretty little sister Rose did; and once she was so wicked as to cut off all her glossy, golden hair, and throw it on the fire. Poor Rose cried bitterly about it; but she did not scold or strike her sister, for she was an amiable, gentle little being as ever lived. No wonder all the family and all the neighborhood disliked Marion, and no wonder her face grew coarse and uglier every day. The Scotch used to be very superstitious people, and they believed the infant Rose had been blessed by the fairies, to whom she owed her extraordinary beauty and exceeding goodness.

Ferguson, ed., *The Oasis*, pp. 50, 51.

Adam Warwick, a character Alcott possibly modeled after Henry David Thoreau, offers the main character Sylvia two books, saying "in one you will find much falsehood in purple and fine linen, in the other some truth in fig-leaves" (p. 43). The "purple and fine linen" suggests the beautiful and elaborate designs of gift books, with the "fig-leaves" indicating Whitman's bold and groundbreaking use of the physical and the erotic. Later, reinforcing Ronald Zboray's theory that gift books are not read so much as used as props to support courtship, friendship, and kinship rituals, Warwick puts aside *Leaves of Grass:* "Warwick resumed his seat and the 'barbaric yawp,' but seemed to find Truth in demi-toilet less interesting than Youth in a gray gown and round hat, for which his taste is to be commended" (p. 44). In *Adventures of Huckleberry Finn* (1885), Mark Twain (1835–1910) satirizes the sentimental poetry of the 1850s in his description of Emmeline Grangerford's poem "Ode to Stephen

Dowling Bots, Dec'd." (pp. 122–123). Despite these critiques, the sentimental poetry in gift books was widely circulated, and because these books were so frequently given, they influenced literary tastes. They also continue to shape understandings of nineteenth-century culture.

Subtitles used for gift books indicate whether volumes focus on religious, political, or more general subjects, as can be seen in Sarah Josepha Hale's (1788–1879) *The Opal* (1845), subtitled *A Christian Gift for the Holy Days* and designed to be given at Christmas. At other times general titles offer no suggestion of the content of the gift book. For example, *The Garland,* published by Philadelphia's J. B. Lippincott in 1868, indicates merely that it contains "selections from various authors," but all of the poems are religious. John Greenleaf Whittier's (1807–1892) "Gone" appears:

Another hand is beckoning us,
Another call is given;

And glows once more with angel-steps
The path which reaches heaven.

(P. 200)

Henry Wadsworth Longfellow's (1807–1882) "A Psalm of Life" is also printed in this volume:

Tell me not in mournful numbers,
"Life is but an empty dream!"
For the soul is dead that slumbers,
And things are not what they seem.

(P. 110)

James Russell Lowell (1819–1891), who edited the *Atlantic Monthly* from 1857 to 1861, a periodical that shaped regional and national literary tastes, published many pieces by Longfellow, Oliver Wendell Holmes, and Whittier, among others, and although this periodical did not contain as many illustrations as *Harper's* and *Scribner's*, its literary content was certainly reproduced in many gift books and annuals. The presence of so many of the so-called Fireside Poets in the gift books and annuals accounts in some ways for their popular appeal throughout the end of the nineteenth century and into the twentieth. The Fireside Poets' popular presence and the sentimental content and structure of their poetry also helps to explain their marginalization from ongoing academic attention and literary scholarship. Unlike Poe, Hawthorne, and Melville, they did not succeed in critiquing the form as they participated in it. Perhaps because of the earnestness of these poets, late-twentieth- and early-twenty-first-century critics have largely avoided in-depth study of their significance, although more serious consideration of their literary, political, and social contributions is certainly warranted.

POLITICAL AND SOCIAL CAUSES

Some political groups used the popularity of the gift-book form to forward specific causes or special interests. *The Wide Awake Gift: A Know-Nothing Token,* which was published in 1855, supported the Know-Nothing Party, a nativist party that rose to prominence in the middle of the 1850s. The title page states that it is "edited by 'one of 'em'" and also has the motto "Put None but Americans on Guard to-night." The preface continues the nativist theme: "Having culled our bouquet from among the choicest flowers of native Eloquence and Poetry, we lay the Patriotic Offering upon the altar of American Liberty, believing that the incense thereof will prove a 'sweet-smelling savor' in the nostrils of all those who love the aroma of their NATIVE LAND." The editor is not named, but pieces by Ralph Waldo Emerson, Lydia Huntley Sigourney, Henry Wadsworth Longfellow, and William Cullen Bryant appear as representative American pieces alongside "The Star Spangled Banner," the Declaration of Independence, and the Constitution. This volume contains several illustrations, including engravings of portraits of Daniel Webster and Martha Washington, which are signed by the engraver J. C. Buttre.

The abolitionist movement used gift books to circulate antislavery messages, and in one of the most substantive studies of these books, Ralph Thompson argues that the move to didactic and political topics is part of the reason the number of gift books produced decreased toward the end of the century: "The *Liberty Bell* is the last of a dozen major gift-book series, a sort of mistaken attempt to impose a semi-realistic burden upon an essentially romantic literary vehicle" (p. 164). Thompson notes that the *Liberty Bell* was published annually by Maria Weston Chapman and other Boston abolitionists between 1839 and 1857, with breaks in the years 1850, 1853, 1854, and 1859. Poems by Emerson and James Russell Lowell appear in the *Liberty Bell* volumes, and Thompson explains that unlike other annuals, which focused on making gift books an American form that celebrated American writing, the *Liberty Bell* included pieces by British and European writers including Elizabeth Barrett Browning, Alexis de Tocqueville, and Fredrika Bremer. Thompson points out that it is significant that Whittier did not contribute to this publication, although his abolitionist poetry appears in Lydia Maria Child's antislavery gift book *The Oasis,* which was published in Boston in 1834. Other significant antislavery annuals mentioned by Thompson are *The North Star,* published in Philadelphia in 1839, and *Freedom's Gift; or, Sentiments of the Free,* published in Hartford in 1840. Because these gift books were not as well funded as those produced by larger publishing houses, they contain fewer illustrations and their cover designs are less elaborate, although in size, shape, and variety of content, they follow the gift book format.

Some of the smaller, less elaborate gift books were produced for a cause or a charity. *The Harbinger: A May-Gift* provides an example. This text, published in Boston in 1833, is dedicated "to the ladies who have so kindly aided the New England Institution for the Education of the Blind"; pieces include the "Hymn for the Blind" and "Lines Spoken by a Blind Boy." In addition to the poems about blindness, a few of the poems examine the lives of women. These poems, presumably written by the residents of the school for the blind, have a dark, almost sinister humor that contrasts with the other saccharine poems about death and love. "My Aunt" reads,

My aunt! My dear unmarried aunt!
Long years have o'er her flown;

Yet still she strains the aching clasp
That binds her virgin zone.

(P. 44)

The poem goes on to lament the aunt's failure to accept her spinster status. Another poem about a man who murders his wife is titled "The Screeching Lady." Her scream continues to haunt the place where she dies:

it chills the blood in their veins to hear
That terrible voice come shrill and clear.
And the curse, they say, will never more
Pass from the cliffs of that fated shore!

(P. 89)

This gift book does not have any illustrations, and only a few poems are signed.

GENERAL-OCCASION AND CHILDREN'S GIFT BOOKS

Gift books designed for general occasions, rather than for specific holidays, contain mixtures of poetry and prose. *The Oasis; or, Golden Leaves of Friendship,* an 1855 gift volume edited by N. L. Ferguson, explains its purpose in its introduction:

We have culled from many of the flowers, and have endeavored to form such an arrangement of prose and poetry, combined with moral and religious sentiment, as, we trust, will not only amuse and be acceptable to the reader, but that the good impressions left on the mind may have a tendency to elevate, and stimulate, to higher and more intellectual attainments.

Although this volume does not indicate that it is intended for women, many of the articles, stories, and poems focus on women's lives. A poem on the title page reads,

A perfect woman, nobly planned
To warm to comfort, and command,
And yet a spirit, still and bright,
With something of an angel's light.

A short fairy tale signed by Mrs. Child (probably Lydia Maria Child, 1802–1880) and titled "The Palace of Beauty" tells of two little princesses named Rose and Marion. Other titles include "A Dressy Woman," "Economy and Her Daughter," and "Woman, Man's Best Friend." Most are heavy-handedly didactic and seem designed to provide advice about courtship, marriage, and women's duties to their families.

Not all gift books are so obviously didactic. *The Sapphire: A Collection of Graphic and Entertaining Tales, Brilliant Poems and Essays,* edited by Epes Sargent (1813–1880), was published in 1867. A subtitle indicates that the pieces were "gleaned chiefly from fugitive literature of the nineteenth century," and many

of the texts are reproduced from French, German, and English publications of the 1820s and 1830s. Titles include "The Beggar-Girl of the Pont-des-Artes" and "The Bellows-Mender of Lyons." This gift book is part of "The Gem" series produced by John L. Shorey. *The Emerald* is another gift book in this series edited by Sargent.

Gift books were also produced for children. Lydia Maria Child produced several of these, which combined original material with pieces that had been previously published in the *Juvenile Miscellany*. *Flowers for Children* was published in 1844. Child's "The Little White Lamb and the Little Black Lamb" provides an example of her abolitionist writing for children: "God made the white lambs, and the black lambs. God loves them both, and made them to love each other" (p. 133). This gift book combines fiction and nonfiction prose and poetry, and several wood engravings are scattered throughout the volume.

Some of the most interesting details of gift books are not in the published texts or illustrations but in inscriptions that provide evidence that these books really were given as gifts and were read. A copy of *The Harbinger* bears the inscription "presented to Miss Sarah Johnson by her Aunt Caroline Johnson." Dated 25 December 1844, a copy of *The Opal* states in large, elaborately curled letters that it was "presented to Mary Ann Moore by her brother Samuel R. G. Searle." Cliff G. Pope, who evidently owned *Autumn Dreams,* signed and dated his copy several times—in 1877 from Columbus, Georgia; in 1877 from Muscogee County, Georgia; in 1880 from Fulton County, Georgia; and in November 1883 from Atlanta, Georgia. These multiple markers of ownership are all in pencil, but they show that he opened this gift book multiple times and in several places, suggesting either that he was moving to different homes or that the book was small enough to carry with him on his travels. Each inscription names the readers or the intended readers, and two of these inscriptions provide evidence that these books were used to maintain kinship ties through gift rituals.

Gift books and annuals provide important records of how reading material was used to establish and maintain courtship and friendship ties. These beautifully designed volumes also provide insight into shifts in national literary tastes and developments in illustration technology. The popularity and sentimentality of gift books and the uses of these characteristics to further political and cultural agendas are also significant to any study of the print culture of the mid-nineteenth century. These are important artifacts of book history and of literary and national culture, and ongoing study of this form will produce interesting questions and conclusions about their influence in constructing ideas of Americanness, citizenship, notions of the literary and the artistic, and their connections to childhood and womanhood in the United States.

See also Abolitionist Writing; Book and Periodical Illustration; Children's and Adolescent Literature; Fireside Poets; *Leaves of Grass;* Religion; Sentimentalism; Taste

BIBLIOGRAPHY

Primary Works

Alcott, Louisa May. *Moods.* 1864. Edited by Sarah Elbert. New Brunswick, N.J.: Rutgers University Press, 1995.

Castlen, Eppie Bowdre. *Autumn Dreams.* New York: D. Appleton, 1870.

Child, Lydia Maria. *Flowers for Children.* 1844. New York: C. S. Francis, 1854.

Ferguson, N. L., ed. *The Oasis; or, Golden Leaves of Friendship.* Boston: Dayton and Wentworth, 1855.

The Garland: Selections from Various Authors. Philadelphia: J. B. Lippincott, 1868.

Hale, Sarah Josepha. *The Opal: A Christian Gift for the Holy Days.* Illustrated by J. G. Chapman. New York: J. G. Riker, 1845.

The Harbinger: A May-Gift. Boston: Carter, Hendee, 1833.

Peirce, Bradford K. *The Token of Friendship: A Gift Book for the Holidays.* Boston: Charles H. Peirce, 1850.

Sargent, Epes. *The Sapphire: A Collection of Graphic and Entertaining Tales, Brilliant Poems, and Essays.* Boston: John L. Shorey, 1867.

Twain, Mark. *Adventures of Huckleberry Finn.* 1885. Norton critical edition. Edited by Thomas Cooley. New York: Norton, 1999.

The Wide-Awake Gift: A Know-Nothing Token for 1855. New York: J. C. Derby; Boston: Phillips, Sampson; Cincinnati: H. W. Derby, 1855.

Secondary Works

Booth, Bradford A. "A Note on an Index to the American Annuals and Gift Books." *American Literature* 10, no. 3 (1938): 349–350.

Griffits, Thomas E. *The Rudiments of Lithography.* London: Faber and Faber, 1956.

Lovejoy, David S. "American Painting in Early Nineteenth-Century Gift Books." *American Quarterly* 7, no. 4 (1955): 345–361.

McLean, Ruari. *Victorian Book Design and Colour Printing.* New York: Oxford University Press, 1963.

Renier, Anne. *Friendship's Offering: An Essay on the Annuals and Gift Books of the Nineteenth Century.* London: Private Libraries Association, 1964.

Risley, Kristen A. "Christmas in Our Western Home: The Cultural Work of a Norwegian-American Christmas Annual." *American Periodicals* 13 (2003): 50–83.

Tompkins, Jane. *Sensational Designs: The Cultural Work of American Fiction, 1790–1860.* New York: Oxford University Press, 1985.

Thompson, Ralph. "The Liberty Bell and Other Anti-Slavery Gift-Books." *New England Quarterly* 7, no. 1 (1934): 154–168.

Zboray, Ronald J., and Mary Saracino Zboray. "Books, Reading, and the World of Goods in Antebellum New England." *American Quarterly* 48, no. 4 (1996): 587–622.

Lorinda B. Cohoon

GODEY'S LADY'S BOOK

When the Philadelphia entrepreneur Louis Antoine Godey (1804–1878) launched the *Lady's Book* in July 1830, nothing in its initial numbers suggested how important it would become to nineteenth-century American literature. It was neither the first American women's magazine—that honor belongs to the *Lady's Magazine,* founded in 1792—nor was it particularly innovative. Like the other women's magazines of its day, *Godey's Lady's Book* was a miscellany of stories and poems, musical compositions, and fashions. But while other such magazines, like the *Ladies' Literary Portfolio* and the *Intellectual Regale or Ladies' Tea-Tray,* quickly disappeared, Louis Godey's publication lasted until nearly the end of the century and at its peak in the 1850s it enjoyed a readership of more than 150,000, making it the most popular magazine before the Civil War. Influential in both literary and cultural matters, the *Lady's Book* played a key role in nineteenth-century fashion, launched the careers of many of the century's most popular writers, and served as a vehicle for countless middle-class trends, from hairstyles to house designs. Generally published under the title *Godey's Lady's Book*—a title first used in 1840—the magazine was often identified simply as the *Lady's Book* and even more audaciously as "the Book," suggesting not only its size (anywhere from fifty to more than one hundred pages each month) but also its central place in popular nineteenth-century American culture.

A MARRIAGE OF POPULARITY AND RESPECTABILITY: LOUIS GODEY AND SARAH J. HALE

Louis Godey's most important decision as publisher was arguably his hiring of Sarah Josepha Hale (1788–1879) as editor in 1837. Author of the 1827 in January 1837, when the two magazines officially merged. Hale's motives in accepting Godey's offer are not certain, but the *Ladies' Magazine* apparently faced serious financial difficulties, and Godey agreed to let Hale edit the Philadelphia magazine from Boston until 1841, when her youngest of five children graduated from college. The ultimate success of *Godey's Lady's Book* is largely explained by the complementary talents of Godey and Hale. After the merger Godey's fashion plates became even more prominent, but Hale's influence was apparent as well in the growing number of original stories and poetry, in the book reviews, and in the educational and literary essays. Together they created a truly miscellaneous magazine with features on all sorts of topics, from sewing and cooking to history and science and to fashion and music. Although the magazine underwent numerous changes during its long run (before eventually folding in 1898), the editor-publisher duo sustained their vision of the magazine, one based on a marriage of popularity and respectability, throughout most of its existence. Hale and Godey retired together in December 1877, when she was eighty-nine and he was seventy-three.

ILLUSTRATIONS

Engravings and fashion plates played a pivotal part in the overwhelming success of the *Lady's Book*. Described as the magazine's "embellishments," these illustrations were a source of considerable pride, and Louis Godey frequently boasted to readers of their expense, particularly of the relatively new technology of engraving on steel, which allowed much finer detail than the older method of engraving on wood. Landscapes and religious scenes were especially common, as were illustrations created specifically for the magazine's poetry and fiction. John Sartain, William E. Tucker, Joseph Ives Pease, and Archibald L. Dick were some of the engravers.

Although Hale had initially opposed an emphasis on fashion while she was editor of the *Ladies' Magazine*, steel engravings of the latest fashions proved to be a defining feature of the *Lady's Book*. Initially Godey published one fashion plate every few months, but he soon offered at least one per issue and often more, and the 1860s saw the introduction of "extension plates," which were wide enough to necessitate folding. Still sought after by collectors, the fashion plates were hand-colored, and at one point Godey employed more than 150 women to complete the painting each month. Generally depicting small groups of women in often intimate and carefully decorated settings, the fashion plates reinforced the middle-class perspective of the magazine.

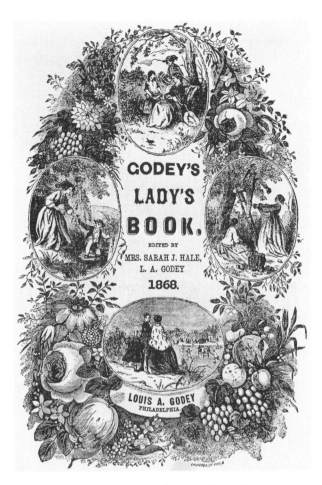

Title page of *Godey's Lady's Book*, 1868. © BETTMANN/ CORBIS

novel *Northwood,* which contrasts domestic life in the American North and South, Hale had been editor of Boston's *Ladies' Magazine* since 1828. Unlike most early American women's magazines—including *Godey's Lady's Book*—which emphasized fashion and "light" literature, often pirated from other magazines, Hale's *Ladies' Magazine* maintained a largely intellectual tone. Designed to be both educational and literary, Hale's *Ladies' Magazine* published original stories and poetry, and the nonfiction featured biographical sketches of famous contemporary women, book reviews, and essays on such topics as women's education and English poetry. In her editorial columns Hale addressed topics such as property rights for married women and increased work opportunities for women. Although Hale did publish fashion plates for part of the *Ladies' Magazine*'s existence, she directly criticized popular interest in fashion.

Although Hale's and Godey's approaches to attracting women readers differed significantly, Godey hired Hale as the editor of the *Lady's Book* beginning

GENDER, POLITICS, AND SEPARATE SPHERES

If Louis Godey shaped the *Lady's Book* primarily through his financial commitment to "embellishments," then Hale's greatest influence on the magazine was in terms of its gender politics and literary offerings. In large part because Hale objected to suffrage for women, the *Lady's Book* has been widely described as antifeminist, and the magazine has been criticized for supposedly ignoring political events. Other scholars have offered a more nuanced view of the magazine's representation of both gender and politics, one that recognizes both its deep conservatism and its commitment to certain kinds of social reform.

At the center of Hale's—and thus the magazine's—ideology of gender was a belief that men and women are essentially different. Though she never endorsed the idea that women were incapable of rational thought—indeed women's education was one of Hale's favorite causes—she repeatedly asserted that women were essentially more moral and more compassionate than men. As she explained in her first essay in the *Lady's Book*, the "strength of man's character is in his physical propensities," while "the strength of woman lies in her moral sentiments" (January 1837, pp. 1–2).

While this popular understanding of sexual difference was used to severely restrict women's roles in the nineteenth century, it was flexible enough to serve other agendas as well. Indeed, in Hale's version popularized in the *Lady's Book*, this notion of an absolute sexual difference proved to be empowering both for Hale and her middle-class white readers. Unlike some of her contemporaries who used this same understanding of sexual difference to argue that women's responsibilities were entirely familial and domestic, Hale argued that because women were more moral than men, women should have increased influence in the world. Thus Hale could argue, for example, as she did repeatedly, that women, such as Elizabeth Blackwell, should be medical doctors. As she explained in one essay, "The study of medicine belongs to woman's department of knowledge; its practice is in harmony with the duties of mother and nurse, which she must fulfill. It is not going out of her sphere to prescribe for the sick; she must do this by the fireside, the bedside, in the 'inner chamber,' where her true place is. It is man who is there out of his sphere" (March 1852, p. 187). In its advocacy of increased opportunities for women based on a conservative notion of women's supposedly natural domestic tendencies, this statement is typical of much of the *Lady's Book*. The notion of women's essential difference from men proved especially appealing to editors and

publishers in the periodical industry, in large part because it supported the existence of a separate women's culture, an idea on which women's magazines are largely based.

But while it empowered middle-class white women—authors, editors, and readers alike—this notion of a separate women's culture proved limiting in other ways. Most notably, the magazine maintained a fairly conflicted stance toward politics. The magazine's official policy was that "polemical, political" topics were forbidden, and the *Lady's Book* has been repeatedly scorned for supposedly ignoring the Civil War. In fact, however, as several other scholars have suggested, the magazine did address political subjects, although generally with a domestic perspective. In the years preceding the Civil War, for instance, Hale occasionally suggested that the solution to the nation's sectional debates could be found domestically—by sharing a national Thanksgiving meal or by sending personal letters to family members in distant regions of the country. Other political subjects that were already explicitly linked to women, private homes, and families—such as women's education—were addressed more frequently and more directly.

LITERARY CONTENTS

Literature—especially fiction (both short stories and serialized novels), poetry, and occasionally drama—was a key feature of the magazine. One sign of the magazine's literary importance is the number of nineteenth-century authors who published in the *Lady's Book*. Edgar Allan Poe, Harriet Beecher Stowe, Lydia Sigourney, William Gilmore Simms, Nathaniel P. Willis, Ralph Waldo Emerson, Washington Irving, Caroline Kirkland, and T. S. Arthur all published in the *Lady's Book*, at least occasionally.

Scholars continue to debate the merits of the magazine's fiction and poetry. Some have dismissed the magazine's contents as little more than sentimental trash, with selections like Poe's "The Literati of New York City" and "The Cask of Amontillado" seen as anomalies. In this view, the magazine's fiction, for example, is seen as relying on intrusive and moralistic narrators, stock characters (especially fainting women and saintly, dying children), and formulaic plots. More severely criticized even than the magazine's fiction, the poetry in the *Lady's Book* has been denounced as nothing more than the morbidly sentimental "light" verse of the poetess.

Other scholars, particularly feminists interested in new interpretations of sentimental and domestic literature, have offered alternative views. The magazine's fiction has been compared to the popular novels of the day, particularly those which, as Nina Baym has described, feature stories of heroines who must make their way in the world, depending primarily on their own efforts and virtues. Similarly Laura McCall's analysis has found that the women characters in the *Lady's Book* tend to be intelligent, independent, and physically strong. The magazine's poetry has also been reinterpreted, with some scholars suggesting that Hale urged women poets to avoid the "light" verse associated with the poetess and instead promoted an idea of the woman poet as having considerable public authority, based on her supposedly innate moral sense.

Though debates about the merits of the magazine's literature continue, scholars are increasingly recognizing the extent to which the *Lady's Book* influenced literary culture, particularly in regard to its support of American authors. Hale was well connected with writers. She published and reviewed their work, and she consistently earned their respect and friendship. Moreover, as she had done previously with the *Ladies' Magazine*, Hale insisted on original submissions. She also avoided anonymous submissions, preferring instead to identify her contributors, and supported the idea that authors should be paid for their work. In 1845 the magazine strengthened its support of professionalization of authorship by becoming the first American magazine to copyright its contents. Also key was the magazine's payment rates, frequently described as some of the most liberal in the periodical industry. These conditions as well as the magazine's strong readership proved appealing for many of the century's authors. Harriet Beecher Stowe, for example, published more in the *Lady's Book* before *Uncle Tom's Cabin* (1852) than in any other periodical. Like many other authors of the time, the *Lady's Book* offered Stowe not only reasonable payment for her work but also access to a large audience.

Overall, then, the reputation of the *Lady's Book* within American literary history continues to evolve. While never part of elite literary culture, the magazine was seen in its own day as a respected literary magazine for women. Throughout much of the twentieth century the *Lady's Book* was largely dismissed as a quaint Victorian artifact, but that reputation too has changed, and *Godey's Lady's Book* is increasingly recognized as an influential part of antebellum literary culture.

See also Book and Periodical Illustration; Domestic Fiction; Editors; Education; Fashion; Female Authorship; Periodicals; Publishers; Reform; Sentimentalism; Suffrage

BIBLIOGRAPHY

Primary Work

Godey's Lady's Book. 1830–1898.

Secondary Works

Baym, Nina. *Woman's Fiction: A Guide to Novels by and about Women in America, 1820–1870.* 2nd ed. Urbana: University of Illinois Press, 1993.

Bulsterbaum, Allison. "*Godey's Lady's Book.*" In *American Literary Magazines: The Eighteenth and Nineteenth Centuries,* edited by Edward E. Chielens, pp. 144–150. New York: Greenwood Press, 1986.

Entrikin, Isabelle Webb. *Sarah Josepha Hale and "Godey's Lady's Book."* Lancaster, Pa.: Lancaster Press, 1946.

Lehuu, Isabelle. "Sentimental Figures: Reading *Godey's Lady's Book* in Antebellum America." In *The Culture of Sentiment: Race, Gender, and Sentimentality in Nineteenth-Century America,* edited by Shirley Samuels, pp. 73–91. New York: Oxford University Press, 1992.

McCall, Laura. "'The Reign of Brute Force Is Now Over': A Content Analysis of *Godey's Lady's Book,* 1830–1860." *Journal of the Early Republic* 9 (1989): 217–236.

Mott, Frank Luther. "*Godey's Lady's Book.*" In his *A History of American Magazines, 1741–1850,* pp. 580–594. New York: D. Appleton, 1930.

Okker, Patricia. *Our Sister Editors: Sarah J. Hale and the Tradition of Nineteenth-Century American Women Editors.* Athens: University of Georgia Press, 1995.

Tonkovich, Nicole. "Rhetorical Power in the Victorian Parlor: *Godey's Lady's Book* and the Gendering of Nineteenth-Century Rhetoric." In *Oratorical Culture in Nineteenth-Century America: Transformations in the Theory and Practice of Rhetoric,* edited by Gregory Clark and S. Michael Halloran, pp. 158–183. Carbondale: Southern Illinois University Press, 1993.

Patricia Okker

GOTHIC FICTION

What does American gothic fiction have to tell about history or, more precisely, about how writers use and transfuse history in their works? For a long time, the answer to this question would have appeared to be largely self-evident: the American gothic, the standard critical line went, reveals little about American history. From its inception in the Englishman Horace Walpole's (1717–1797) *The Castle of Otranto* (1764), gothic fiction registered not only the fissures in Enlightenment humanism and rationalism but also the revolutionary tendencies of the late eighteenth

***The Money Diggers*, 1832.** This painting by John Quidor is representative of the gothic themes—mysterious settings, the macabre—that he often employed. © BROOKLYN MUSEUM OF ART, NEW YORK, USA/THE BRIDGEMAN ART LIBRARY

century. Despite these origins, critics have read the gothic primarily as a mode focused more on psychic than on historical depth and complexity. Thanks in large part, perhaps, to the legacy of Sigmund Freud, who transferred many of the gothic's most cherished conventions (buried secrets, hidden ancestries, repressed desires, imprisoning vaults, mysterious passageways) to the self, the gothic has long been seen as a mode that expresses, above all, the nightmare landscape of the unconscious, the drives of the id, the neurotic, haunted ego.

This reading of the gothic has had particular appeal in the American context, given the long-standing (if increasingly contested) myth of America as a land without the kind of dense historical fabric—the heritable past—that is often viewed as a key ingredient of gothic literature. Many of the characteristic features of what might be called "classic" gothic texts such as Walpole's *Otranto* or the late-eighteenth-century

novels of another British writer, Ann Radcliffe (1764–1823)—haunted (and usually decaying) castles and debased aristocrats, disputes over land title and long-held family estates, corrupt monks and designing prioresses, propertied heiresses under siege—seemed rooted in an ancientness of culture and institution that the "new" nation appeared to lack. In the absence of the intricate social networks and ancient cultures of Old World Europe, critics who read in this vein suggest, American writers cast the gothic into a form that meditates particularly, often obsessively, on the intricacies of the inner self, on that mysterious interior landscape that Nathaniel Hawthorne (1804–1864) calls, in "The Custom-House" introduction to *The Scarlet Letter* (1850), the "inmost Me" (p. 7).

The critic Leslie Fiedler, whose *Love and Death in the American Novel* (1960) functions as one of the most important early explorations of the centrality of the gothic in the American literary tradition, offers a complicated example of this ahistorical reading of the American gothic. Arguing against critical tendencies to devalue the gothic as a sensational, formulaic, and market-driven mode, Fiedler associates what he calls the "serious American novel" with the emergence of the gothic (p. 143). Yet although Fiedler acknowledges that "behind the gothic lies a theory of history, a particular sense of the past" (p. 136), his efforts to elevate the American gothic to the status of "serious" literature relies on a conventional reading of the gothic that in the end empties it of historical import. Above all else, Fiedler declares, the gothic is, finally, a "method for dealing with the night-time impulses of the psyche" (p. 140).

Since roughly the 1980s, critics have taken up Fiedler's invitation to consider the gothic's centrality to the American literary canon. Unlike Fiedler, however, these more recent critics have turned their attention to what, precisely, has so long been excluded from assessments and readings of the gothic: the historical conditions out of which U.S. gothic fiction emerged and on which that fiction meditates. In works by such critics as Cathy Davidson (*Revolution and the Word*, 1986), Lawrence Buell (*New England Literary Culture*, 1986), and Kari Winter (*Subjects of Slavery, Agents of Change*, 1992), critical understanding of the gothic takes a new and notably contextual turn. For these critics the gothic is, for example, a mode by which American writers explore the ideological cracks in the new Republic's social and political foundations, the dangers of individualism, the disfiguring effects of regional provincialism, or the terrifying oppression of women under white male patriarchy. Expanding on these openings, Teresa Goddu turns to a full-scale study of the gothic's historical impulses in *Gothic America: Narrative, History, and Nation* (1997). Insisting that the gothic is a key form by which writers engage the nation's conflicted ideological foundations, Goddu follows traces left by Fiedler, who establishes a relationship between race and the gothic, and especially by Toni Morrison, whose 1992 *Playing in the Dark* argues that the nation's racial history motivates and indeed haunts its early literature. In particular, Goddu demonstrates the gothic's function in responding to the young nation's deepest historical traumas by showing how race and slavery are central to the American gothic imagination.

Given the groundbreaking critical work done by Goddu, Morrison, Buell, Davidson, and others, it has become increasingly difficult to read the early American gothic in ahistorical terms. American gothic fiction of the nineteenth century, as such critics have helped make plain, unveils a history that is present but often unseen or unacknowledged, bearing witness precisely to the historical realities that underlie (and often undercut) American ideals. Whether recounting what the early American gothicist Charles Brockden Brown (1771–1810) called "incidents of Indian hostility, and the perils of the western wilderness" (p. 3) or the brutality of white settlers, telling the story of the violence, both real and figurative, done in the name of slavery or of domestic spaces invaded by sexual cruelty and emotional abuse, recording the realities of patriarchal oppression or the unseen and sordid underbelly of the American industrial machine, American gothic fiction, as is now more widely recognized, tells the story of a nation divided against its own democratic promise.

THE HAUNTED HOUSE OF THE NATION

This reading of the gothic character of the nineteenth-century nation runs counter to the un-gothic image of America purveyed by many cultural commentators in the same period. Writing in 1839 for the *United States Magazine and Democratic Review*, John L. O'Sullivan offers an ebullient paean to the American democratic experiment that might be seen as representative of much of the period's public rhetoric. Celebrating the "magnificent domain" of what he calls the "nation of many nations," O'Sullivan provides a sort of architectural blueprint for the nation (indeed, the globe) that contrasts starkly with the haunting depictions of the American experience offered by a wide array of gothic texts. "Governed" as it is by the "law of equality, the law of brotherhood—of 'peace and good will amongst men,'" the United States, in O'Sullivan's view, is "destined" to be the site of the "noblest temple ever dedicated to the worship of the Most High." The "floor" of this temple, he proclaims, "shall be a hemisphere— its roof the firmament of the star-studded heavens, and its congregation an Union of many Republics, comprising hundreds of happy millions, calling, owning no man master" (p. 427).

The crowing confidence of rhetoric such as O'Sullivan's notwithstanding, many Americans recognized that the democratic ideals so often publicly celebrated could not be reconciled with actual experience. The fifty-year period between 1820 and 1870 witnessed, for example, a number of deeply traumatic events that belied the image of "happy" masterless "millions," including the genocidal removal of Native Americans to undesirable western lands, the expansion and territorial extension of U.S. slavery, the violent convulsions of the Civil War, and the divisive political battles fought in its aftermath. Although less neatly demarcated by dates and years, such "events" as the Industrial Revolution and the often acrimonious debate over the rights of women posed further problems for the national self-image. For many Americans, in short, the paradisal mansion that O'Sullivan celebrates had no earthly counterpart. And it is here, in drawing the distinction between the historical real and the ahistorical ideal, that the gothic becomes instrumental. In the American gothic indeed, the nation looks far more like a haunted house than a utopian "mansion." Deploying the gothic's conventional interest in space (locked rooms, underground vaults, secret passageways), nineteenth-century American writers work to tell the story of a nation that betrays its own ideals. From the burial vaults of Edgar Allan Poe's stories of the 1830s and 1840s to the attic of the Custom House where Nathaniel Hawthorne "finds" Hester Prynne's lost story in *The Scarlet Letter*; from the "haunted" garret of Simon Legree's hellish plantation in Harriet Beecher Stowe's *Uncle Tom's Cabin* (1852) to the "L-shaped chamber" where Harriet Wilson's mixed-race character, "Nig," is quarantined in *Our Nig* (1859); from the crawl space where the fugitive slave Linda Brent hides for seven years in Harriet Jacobs's *Incidents in the Life of a Slave Girl* (1861) to the damp, underground cellar into which the narrator of Rebecca Harding Davis's *Life in the Iron Mills* (1861) commands one to descend as she launches her exposé of the deforming effects of industrial capitalism—American gothic texts draw attention to that which O'Sullivan's glorious vision of the American "temple" denies. These confining spaces function as reminders of the disturbing, sometimes even horrifying truths that the nation as a whole would rather keep buried. Inside this "nation of nations," such texts remind their readers, are prisons and ghosts of the nation's own making. And ultimately American gothic texts remind their readers that the nation will have to confront its troubled past and its blighted present to exorcise its ghosts if it wishes to achieve its democratic possibility.

THE AMERICAN STORY OF BLOOD
Among the many ways in which American gothic fiction in the early to mid-nineteenth century draws attention to the haunting gap between national ideals and national realities is in telling the story of American race relations—a story that is, in many respects, a story of blood. One of the most remarkable and daring features of the democratic experiment as it emerged in the late eighteenth century was the creation of a nation based on ideals rather than on bloodlines. Rejecting inherited monarchy, laws of inheritance that privileged firstborn sons, and other kinship-based vestiges of feudal and monarchial societies, this new, democratic nation would predicate itself not on the legacies of blood but on the natural rights of freestanding individuals. Yet even the founders revealed their own unwillingness or inability to do away with the idea and the importance of blood. Indeed the rhetoric of blood becomes increasingly instrumental in drawing racial lines, marking whites as fundamentally different from blacks, Native Americans, and a host of "others." The effort to enlist blood as a means of creating a privileged space for whiteness can be seen, for example, in *Notes on the State of Virginia* (first English edition, 1787), in which Thomas Jefferson asserts that the "inferiority [of blacks] is not the effect merely of their condition of life" (p. 190) and admits the possibility of natural "distinction[s]" between blacks and whites (p. 191).

The cautious appeal that Jefferson makes to scientifically verifiable differences between whites and other groups became more common at the turn into the nineteenth century, when the need to justify the abrogation of freedom in a republic founded on principles of liberty and autonomy (the existence of racial servitude, for example, or genocidal policies with regard to Native Americans) intensified. As, in short, white Americans found it increasingly necessary to delineate precise and verifiable lines between blacks and whites, Native Americans and whites, immigrants and "Anglo-Saxons," appeals to the biological, blood-based foundations of race to which Jefferson nods become more and more frequent. Enlisting the help of such pseudoscientific tools as cranial measurement, physiognomy, and phrenology, leading race thinkers in the early nineteenth century—Louis Agassiz, Samuel Morton, George Gliddon, and Josiah Nott among them—worked to make racial "differences" innate, something inherited through the blood. The law of hypodescent (also known as the "one-drop rule," which designates that "one drop" of "black blood" classifies a person as black) and the prevalence in popular culture of such terms as "half-breed," "mulatto," "quadroon," and "octoroon" reflect the broad appeal of such notions of race as blood, as does the anxiety about the negative effects of blood "mixing" that one finds in treatises against and laws prohibiting intermarriage. In blood, in short, theorists of race found "evidence" of the existence of "real" race. And in the United States they found an audience widely responsive to their ideas.

BLOOD IN THE GOTHIC
From slave narratives to short stories to novels, many gothic texts between 1820 and 1870 reflect on the newfound significance of racial bloodlines. At times, these texts try to work against the grain of antebellum race theory and to undermine the notion that race is a

real and transmittable essence locked in human veins; at other times, the investigation into the meaning of blood appears to be far more inconclusive. Regardless, gothic fiction's nearly obsessive return to race and blood highlights the nation's unfinished revolution, the enduring questions about bloodlines, ancestries, and racial "essences" that compromise the nation's democratic ideals.

This gothic preoccupation with blood is evident in texts as diverse as James Fenimore Cooper's *The Last of the Mohicans* (1826), Poe's *The Narrative of Arthur Gordon Pym of Nantucket* (1838), and Hannah Crafts's *The Bondwoman's Narrative* (c. 1850s). Although typically read as a historical romance, *The Last of the Mohicans* has a number of features that are characteristic of early gothic novels: a besieged heroine (Cora Munro) whose virtue and life are threatened by a dark, Byronic antihero (Magua); sublime landscapes, at once beautiful and forbidding, that house hidden dangers and that are often, at least for the white characters, perilously difficult to navigate; "silent grave[s] and crumbling ruin[s]" (p. 135) that bear witness to past scenes of violence; "houseless" and unquiet ghosts of dispossessed native people; masquerade and mistaken identities; and perhaps above all, an obsession with bloodlines and secrets of ancestry. At the center of this second novel in the Leatherstocking Tales is Natty Bumppo (here called "Hawkeye"), a white scout who repeatedly stresses his racially pure lineage. He is, as he claims obsessively throughout the text, a "white man without a cross" (p. 59). The novel's interest in racial taxonomies extend to other "unmixed" characters (Hawkeye's boon companion, Chingachgook, and Chingachgook's son, Uncas, the titular "Mohican") as well as to those who are, like Cora (the daughter of a white father and a West Indian woman with slave ancestry). tragically, indeed fatally "mixed." Although some of the bloodshed that takes place in this insistently brutal text happens during conventional warfare, the bloodiest scenes are ones of racial violence; most notable is a massacre scene in which "two thousand raving savages" slaughter thousands of whites retreating from a surrendered fort (p. 181). Cooper (1789–1851) presents the site of the massacre and the nation itself as a land "fattened with human blood" (p. 187), reminding his readers of the violence engendered not only by imperial claims but also by taxonomies of race and race difference. Yet while Cooper seems to want to imagine an alternative and more benevolent "mixed" society that is not based on bloodlines, he is unable, in the end, to do so: the future is vested not in Uncas and Cora, who are allowed to "marry" only in death, but rather in two white characters, Duncan and Alice, who ride off to

embark on a new life in the "settlements of the 'palefaces'" (p. 373). Like many more conventionally gothic novels, from Radcliffe's *The Mysteries of Udolpho* (1794) to Hawthorne's *The House of the Seven Gables* (1851), *The Last of the Mohicans* ends with the promise of order restored, but it is an order that is qualified and compromised: the budding society that Cooper imagines at the end of *Mohicans*—one that must be, like Hawkeye himself, "without a cross"—remains haunted by those whose blood sets them outside its confines.

Like *The Last of the Mohicans*, Poe's *The Narrative of Arthur Gordon Pym of Nantucket* ends with an image of total whiteness, but a whiteness whose meaning is more mysterious and inscrutable. In *Pym*, Poe (1809–1849), perhaps not unexpectedly, works more directly and extensively than does Cooper in the gothic vein, turning in particular to the conventions of what has been called gothic "horror": rotting corpses and decaying flesh, underground vaults, live burial, incipient madness, even cannibalism. Yet as in *Mohicans,* many of the text's most horrifying images and events are those that highlight anxieties about and blood spilled in the name of race. Indeed *Pym* is even more preoccupied than *Mohicans* with racial categories and bloodlines. From Dirk Peters, the "half breed" who functions as a "line manager" (p. 84) on the ship of which Arthur Gordon Pym is part of the crew, to the "jet black" "savages" (p. 189) who inhabit the island of Tsalal, the "perfectly white" animal with "brilliant scarlet claws" (p. 188) that Pym and his shipmates discover on their journey southward to Antarctica, and the mystifying "figure" of "perfect whiteness" (p. 239) in the novel's final scene, Poe's text delineates and "manages" the "lines" of race with excessive care. Indeed *The Narrative of Arthur Gordon Pym* tries to imagine race as being like the water on Tsalal—a miraculous substance "made up of a number of distinct veins, each of a distinct hue," that do not "commingle" (p. 194). Yet even as the narrative works relentlessly to police and stabilize racial categories—appealing, as it does so, to scientific views of racial inheritances and identifiable racial bloodlines—it also, over and over, reveals the ways in which such categories are unreliable and unpredictable. White men become blackened in death, the "hybrid" Peters is rewritten as a "white man" (p. 212), and racial identity itself becomes shifty, changeable.

It is in the context of the novel's challenges to stable racial meanings (the very meanings to which the text itself at the same time appeals) that one must read its notoriously ambiguous and terrifying final episode. The narrative action of *Pym* simply ends by showing

Pym, Peters, and their "jet-black" Tsalalian companion being drawn inexorably toward a chasm, presided over by a "shrouded human figure, very larger in proportions than any dweller among men" and with "perfect" snow-white skin (p. 239). On the one hand, such a gothic figure—flawlessly white, yet monstrous in proportions, unrecognizable, unclassifiable—suggests that the very notion of pure and "perfect" race exists only in the realm of fantasy. Simultaneously, the image serves as a reminder of the destructiveness of that same fantasy: Pym and Peters become increasingly "listless" and "apathetic" as they proceed toward the chasm, and their "perfectly" black companion expires as he moves closer to "perfect" whiteness. In this ending, Poe's novel refuses even the uneasy closure that many gothic novels, including Cooper's *Mohicans,* seem to offer. Cooper's text embraces, albeit with some hesitation, a national future of "unmixed" bloodlines. But Poe's *Pym* cannot even be said to come to an end: in a "Note" that follows the novel's final chapter, one learns that "the few remaining chapters which were to have completed [Pym's] narrative . . . have been irrecoverably lost" through an "accident" that appears to have claimed both Pym and his manuscript (p. 240). Such refusal to bring the story's narrative and its racial implications to an end serves as Poe's reminder that the gothic story of race—excessive and indeterminate, fantastic and destructive, desired and feared—cannot, finally, be told.

Perhaps more than any other text in the antebellum period, Hannah Crafts's gothic novel *The Bondwoman's Narrative* (undiscovered until the late twentieth century and not published until 2002), explores the frightfully ambiguous significance of race as blood. Like many other antebellum narratives of slavery, both fictional and nonfictional—William and Ellen Craft's *Running a Thousand Miles for Freedom* (1860), Frank Webb's *The Garies and Their Friends* (1857), William Wells Brown's *Clotel* (1853), for example, *The Bondwoman's Narrative* exploits the unreliability of skin as a racial marker. Crafts describes numerous light-skinned African American characters who move back and forth across the color line to suggest, as does Poe, that race is a fiction, a story written on (not inherent in) the skin. Because the skin "lies" about race, the slaveholding society depicted in *The Bondwoman's Narrative* requires gothic villains like Mr. Trappe, a lawyer and slave speculator who polices the lines between "blacks" and "whites" by "scenting out the African taint" (p. 239) in the blood of those presumed to be white and then selling those so "tainted" into slavery. Trappe is a hard worker, perpetually digging, traveling, snooping, spying, reading. But while the strenuous labor

involved in his efforts to entrap whites with their "black" blood points to the difficulty of maintaining the fiction of race, the novel cannot seem to put that fiction to rest. Thus Crafts's novel, like both Cooper's and Poe's, makes one look over and over again at blood: the blood of tortured slaves that "manures" the roots of a haunted tree (p. 21); the "clotted gore" oozing from the throat of a white suicide (p. 68); the blood that gushes in a torrent from the mouth of a woman sold into slavery (p. 103). Through these repeated depictions of bloodshed, *The Bondwoman's Narrative* reminds its readers, of course, of slavery's relentless brutality. But Crafts's attention to blood also works on the level of metaphor. Over and over again, Crafts brings blood—that which lurks below the surface, palpable but invisible—to the surface, spilling it as if in an effort to scrutinize it, understand its meaning and implications. In short, although *The Bondwoman's Narrative* tries to work against the notion that race is locatable in human veins, the amount of blood spilled in its course marks the questions about blood and racial "essence" that Crafts herself cannot, finally, resolve.

In writing stories of blood in the antebellum period, Cooper, Poe, and Crafts are not, of course, alone. Stowe's *Uncle Tom's Cabin,* Hawthorne's *The House of the Seven Gables,* and Herman Melville's "Benito Cereno" (1856) are just a sampling of the many texts that explore, in a gothic vein, what blood might mean in a still-new nation that promised, at its inception, to do away with blood as a founding idea. Writing in a period when blood assumed new, "scientific" importance as a means of demarcating, on the basis of biology, privileged whites from "others"—African Americans, Native Americans, Chinese immigrants, Hispanics—these authors remind their readers again and again that, far from rejecting blood, the nation was embracing it anew, in ever more virulent and violent forms.

As the nation moved into the crisis and conflagration of the Civil War and the uneasy period of reconciliation and early Reconstruction, blood would assume an even more terrifying and bewildering significance. Americans witnessed not only the heretofore unimaginable brutality of the war itself—enabled by new technologies of warfare and brought home in the forms of the dead and wounded and in the form of photographic images—but also a stunning increase in racial violence and the emergence of white supremacist discourse in the postwar period. As if in an effort to counter a reality that had become more terrifying than any fiction could be, many war-era writers, from

Elizabeth Stoddard (1823–1902) to Louisa May Alcott (1832–1888) to Rebecca Harding Davis, wrote texts that rejected the gothic's embrace of chaos, violence, and entrapment in favor of romances that strove for reunion and reconciliation. Yet haunting such texts—Stoddard's *Two Men* (1865) or Davis's *Waiting for the Verdict* (1867), for example—are the very questions about the relationship between blood, race, and national identity that circulate throughout gothic fiction in the prewar period.

See also The Bondwoman's Narrative; Democracy; Ethnology; Indian Wars and Dispossession; Leatherstocking Tales; Manifest Destiny; Miscegenation; Slavery

BIBLIOGRAPHY

Primary Works

Brown, Charles Brockden. *Edgar Huntly; or, Memoirs of a Sleep-Walker.* 1799. Edited by Norman S. Grabo. New York: Penguin, 1988.

Cooper, James Fenimore. *The Last of the Mohicans.* 1826. New York: Bantam, 1989.

Crafts, Hannah. *The Bondwoman's Narrative.* c. 1850s. Edited by Henry Louis Gates Jr. New York: Warner, 2002.

Hawthorne, Nathaniel. *The Scarlet Letter: A Romance.* 1850. New York: Penguin, 2003.

Jefferson, Thomas. *Notes on the State of Virginia.* 1787. In *The Portable Thomas Jefferson,* edited by Merrill D. Peterson. New York: Viking, 1975.

O'Sullivan, John. "The Great Nation of Futurity." *United States Magazine and Democratic Review* 6 (1839): 426–430.

Poe, Edgar Allan. *The Narrative of Arthur Gordon Pym of Nantucket.* 1838. Edited by Harold Beaver. New York: Penguin, 1975.

Secondary Works

Botting, Fred. *Gothic.* London and New York: Routledge, 1996.

Buell, Lawrence. *New England Literary Culture from Revolution through Renaissance.* Cambridge, U.K., and New York: Cambridge University Press, 1986.

Davidson, Cathy N. *Revolution and the Word: The Rise of the Novel in America.* New York: Oxford University Press, 1986.

Fiedler, Leslie A. *Love and Death in the American Novel.* 1960. Normal, Ill.: Dalkey Archive Press, 1997.

Goddu, Teresa. *Gothic America: Narrative, History, and Nation.* New York: Columbia University Press, 1997.

Kilgour, Maggie. *The Rise of the Gothic Novel.* London: Routledge, 1995.

Martin, Robert K., and Eric Savoy, eds. *American Gothic: New Interventions in a National Narrative.* Iowa City: University of Iowa Press, 1998.

Morrison, Toni. *Playing in the Dark: Whiteness and the Literary Imagination.* Cambridge, Mass.: Harvard University Press, 1992.

Ringe, Donald. *American Gothic: Imagination and Reason in Nineteenth-Century Fiction.* Lexington: University Press of Kentucky, 1982.

Williams, Anne. *Art of Darkness: A Poetics of Gothic.* Chicago: University of Chicago Press, 1995.

Winter, Kari. *Subjects of Slavery, Agents of Change: Women and Power in Gothic Novels and Slave Narratives, 1790–1865.* Athens: University of Georgia Press, 1992.

Ellen Weinauer